HARRAP'S
FRENCH
and ENGLISH
pocket
DICTIONARY

McGraw·Hill

New York Chicago San Francisco Lisbon London Madrid Mexico City
Milan New Delhi San Juan Seoul Singapore Sydney Toronto

1 2 3 4 5 6 7 8 9 0 BAN/BAN 3 2 1 0 9 8 7 6 5 4

ISBN 0-07-144070-4

McGraw-Hill books are available at special quantity discounts to
use as premiums and sales promotions, or for use in corporate
training programs. For more information, please write to the
Director of Special Sales, Professional Publishing, McGraw-Hill,
Two Penn Plaza, New York, NY 10121-2298. Or contact your local
bookstore.

This book is printed on acid-free paper.

Editors
Isabelle Elkaim
Stuart Fortey

with
Rachel Skeet

Managing Editor
Anna Stevenson

Publishing Manager
Patrick White

Prepress
David Reid
Claire Williamson

Contents

Preface

This new edition of the Harrap's French and English Pocket Dictionary aims to provide all students of French at beginner and intermediate level with a reliable, comprehensive and user-friendly dictionary in a compact form. The clear, systematic layout of information makes the dictionary an easy-to-use tool and its coverage of vocabulary should ensure that it becomes an invaluable resource.

This dictionary covers all essential words and phrases needed and packs a wealth of vocabulary into its pages. Colloquial and idiomatic language is well represented, as are words from a wide range of specialized fields, such as information technology, sports and finance.

Extra help is provided in the form of a supplement comprising information on French irregular verbs, together with a section on numbers, a 29-page conversation guide, a feature on using the telephone and a useful vocabulary builder.

Abbreviations

gloss	=	glose
[introduces an explanation]		[introduit une explication]
cultural equivalent	≃	équivalent culturel
[introduces a translation		[introduit une traduction
which has a roughly		dont les connotations dans
equivalent status		la langue cible sont
in the target language]		comparables]
abbreviation	*abbr, abrév*	abréviation
adjective	*adj*	adjectif
adverb	*adv*	adverbe
agriculture	*Agr*	agriculture
American English	*Am*	anglais américain
anatomy	*Anat*	anatomie
architecture	*Archit*	architecture
slang	*Arg*	argot
astrology	*Astrol*	astrologie
cars	*Aut*	automobile
auxiliary	*aux*	auxiliaire
aviation	*Aviat*	aviation
Belgian French	*Belg*	belgicisme
biology	*Biol*	biologie
botany	*Bot*	botanique
British English	*Br*	anglais britannique
Canadian French	*Can*	canadianisme
chemistry	*Chem, Chim*	chimie
cinema	*Cin*	cinéma
commerce	*Com*	commerce
computing	*Comptr*	informatique
conjunction	*conj*	conjonction
cooking	*Culin*	cuisine
economics	*Econ, Écon*	économie
electricity, electronics	*El, Él*	électricité, électronique
exclamation	*exclam*	exclamation
feminine	*f*	féminin
familiar	*Fam*	familier
figurative	*Fig*	figuré
finance	*Fin*	finance
geography	*Geog, Géog*	géographie
geology	*Geol, Géol*	géologie

grammar	*Gram*	grammaire
gymnastics	*Gym*	gymnastique
history	*Hist*	histoire
humorous	*Hum*	humoristique
invariable	*inv*	invariable
journalism	*Journ*	journalisme
law	*Jur*	droit
linguistics	*Ling*	linguistique
masculine	*m*	masculin
mathematics	*Math*	mathématique
medicine	*Med, Méd*	médecine
military	*Mil*	militaire
music	*Mus*	musique
noun	*n*	nom
shipping	*Naut*	nautisme
feminine noun	*nf*	nom féminin
feminine plural noun	*nfpl*	nom féminin pluriel
masculine noun	*nm*	nom masculin
masculine and feminine noun	*nmf*	nom masculin et féminin
masculine plural noun	*nmpl*	nom masculin pluriel
plural noun	*npl*	nom pluriel
computing	*Ordinat*	ordinateurs, informatique
pejorative	*Pej, Péj*	péjoratif
philosophy	*Phil*	philosophie
photography	*Phot*	photographie
physics	*Phys*	physique
plural	*pl*	pluriel
politics	*Pol*	politique
past participle	*pp*	participe passé
prefix	*pref, préf*	préfixe
preposition	*prep, prép*	préposition
pronoun	*pron*	pronom
past tense	*pt*	prétérit
something	*qch*	quelque chose
registered trademark	®	marque déposée
rail	*Rail*	chemin de fer
religion	*Rel*	religion
somebody	*sb*	quelqu'un
school	*Sch, Scol*	domaine scolaire
Scottish English	*Scot*	anglais d'Écosse
singular	*sing*	singulier
something	*sth*	quelque chose
suffixe	*suff*	suffixe
technology	*Tech*	technologie

telecommunications	*Tel, Tēl*	télécommunications
theatre	*Theat, Théât*	théâtre
television	*TV*	télévision
typography, printing	*Typ*	typographie, imprimerie
university	*Univ*	domaine universitaire
verb	*v*	verbe
intransitive verb	*vi*	verbe intransitif
reflexive verb	*vpr*	verbe pronominal
transitive verb	*vt*	verbe transitif
inseparable transitive verb [eg: he **looks after** the children]	*vt insep*	verbe transitif à particule inséparable
separable transitive verb [eg: she **sent** the present **back** *or* she **sent back** the present]	*vt sep*	verbe transitif à particule séparable

All other labels are written in full.

French Pronunciation

French pronunciation is shown in this dictionary using the symbols of the IPA (International Phonetic Alphabet). In the table below, examples of French words using these sounds are given, followed by English words which have a similar sound. Where there is no equivalent in English, an explanation is given.

IPA symbol	French example	English example
Consonants		
[b]	bébé	but
[d]	donner	door
[f]	forêt	fire
[g]	gare	get
[ʒ]	jour	pleasure
[k]	carte	kitten
[l]	lire	lonely
[m]	maman	mat
[n]	ni	now
[ŋ]	parking	singing
[ɲ]	campagne	canyon
[p]	patte	pat
[r]	rare	Like an English /r/ but pronounced at the back of the throat
[s]	soir	sit
[ʃ]	chose	sham
[t]	table	tap
[v]	valeur	value
[z]	zéro	zero
Vowels		
[a]	chat	cat
[ɑ]	âge	gasp
[e]	été	bay
[ɛ]	père	bed
[ə]	le	amend
[ø]	deux	Does not exist in English: [e] pronounced with the lips rounded
[œ]	seul	curtain

[i]	vite	bee – not quite as long as the English [i:]
[ɔ]	donner	cot – slightly more open than the English /o/
[o]	chaud	daughter – but higher than its English equivalent
[u]	tout	you – but shorter than its English equivalent
[y]	voiture	Does not exist in English: [i] with lips rounded
[ɑ̃]	enfant	Nasal sound pronounced lower and further back in the mouth than [ɔ̃]

Vowels

[ɛ̃]	vin	Nasal sound: /a/ sound pronounced letting air pass through the nose
[ɔ̃]	bonjour	Nasal sound: closed /o/ sound pronounced letting air pass through the nose
[œ̃]	un	Nasal sound: like [ɛ̃] but with lips more rounded

Semi-vowels

[w]	voir	week
[j]	yoyo, paille	yard
[ɥ]	nuit	Does not exist in English: the vowel [y] elided with the following vowel

Aa

A, a¹ [eɪ] *n* (a) A, a *m inv*; **5A** *(in address, street number)* 5 bis; **to go from A to B** aller du point A au point B (b) *Sch (grade)* **to get an A in French** = avoir une très bonne note en français, ≃ avoir entre 16 et 20 en français (c) *(street atlas)* **an A to Z of London** un plan de Londres

A² [ə, *stressed* eɪ]

> **a** devient **an** [ən, *stressed* æn] devant voyelle ou h muet.

indefinite article (a) *(in general)* un, une; **a man** un homme; **an apple** une pomme; **an hour** une heure

(b) *(definite article in French)* **60 pence a kilo** 60 pence le kilo; **50 km an hour** 50 km à l'heure; **I have a broken arm** j'ai le bras cassé

(c) *(article omitted in French)* **he's a doctor/a father** il est médecin/père; **Caen, a town in Normandy** Caen, ville de Normandie; **what a man!** quel homme!; **a hundred** cent

(d) *(a certain)* **a Mr Smith** un certain M. Smith

(e) *(time)* **twice a month** deux fois par mois

aback [ə'bæk] *adv* **taken a. (by)** déconcerté (par)

abandon [ə'bændən] **1** *n* abandon *m* **2** *vt* abandonner; **to a. ship** abandonner le navire

abbey ['æbɪ] *(pl* -**eys***) n* abbaye *f*

abbreviate [ə'briːvɪeɪt] *vt* abréger ▪ **abbreviation** *n* abréviation *f*

abdicate ['æbdɪkeɪt] *vt & vi* abdiquer

abdomen ['æbdəmən] *n* abdomen *m*

abduct [æb'dʌkt] *vt (kidnap)* enlever ▪ **abduction** *n* enlèvement *m*, rapt *m*

ability [ə'bɪlətɪ] *(pl* -**ies***) n* capacité *f* (**to do** de faire); **to the best of my a.** de mon mieux

ablaze [ə'bleɪz] *adj* en feu; *Fig* **a. with** *(light)* resplendissant de

able ['eɪbəl] *adj* capable; **to be a. to do sth** être capable de faire qch, pouvoir faire qch; **to be a. to swim/drive** savoir nager/conduire ▪ **able-bodied** *adj* robuste

abnormal [æb'nɔːməl] *adj* anormal

aboard [ə'bɔːd] **1** *adv (on ship, plane)* à bord; **to go a.** monter à bord **2** *prep* **a. the ship/plane** à bord du navire/de l'avion; **a. the train** dans le train

abolish [ə'bɒlɪʃ] *vt* abolir ▪ **abolition** [æbə'lɪʃən] *n* abolition *f*

abominable [ə'bɒmɪnəbəl] *adj* abominable

Aborigine [æbə'rɪdʒɪnɪ] *n* Aborigène *mf* (d'Australie)

abort [ə'bɔːt] **1** *vt (space flight, computer program)* avorter **2** *vi Med* faire une fausse couche ▪ **abortion** *n* avortement *m*; **to have an a.** se faire avorter

ABOUT [ə'baʊt] **1** *adv* (a) *(approximately)* à peu près, environ; **at a. two o'clock** vers deux heures

(b) *(here and there)* çà et là, ici et là; *Fig* **there's a lot of flu a. at the moment** il y a beaucoup de cas de grippe en ce moment; **there's a rumour a. (that...)** il y a une rumeur qui circule (selon laquelle...); **to look a.** regarder autour de soi; **to follow someone a.** suivre quelqu'un partout

2 *prep* (a) *(around)* **a. the garden** autour du jardin

(b) *(near to)* **a. here** par ici

(c) *(concerning)* au sujet de; **to talk a. sth** parler de qch; **a book a. sth** un livre sur qch; **what's it (all) a.?** de quoi s'agit-il?

(d) *(+ infinitive)* **a. to do** sur le point

de faire; **I was a. to say…** j'étais sur le point de dire…

above [ə'bʌv] **1** *adv* au-dessus; *(in book)* ci-dessus; **from a.** d'en haut; **the floor a.** l'étage *m* du dessus

2 *prep* (**a**) *(in height, hierarchy)* au-dessus de; **he's a. me** *(in rank)* c'est mon supérieur; **she's not a. lying** elle n'est pas incapable de mentir; **he's not a. asking** il n'est pas trop fier pour demander; **a. all** surtout

(**b**) *(with numbers)* plus de ■ **above-board 1** *adj* honnête **2** *adv* sans tricherie ■ **above-mentioned** *adj* susmentionné

abreast [ə'brest] *adv* côte à côte, de front; **four a.** par rangs de quatre; **to keep a. of sth** se tenir au courant de qch

abroad [ə'brɔːd] *adv* à l'étranger; **from a.** de l'étranger

abrupt [ə'brʌpt] *adj* (*sudden*) brusque, soudain; *(rude)* brusque, abrupt; *(slope, style)* abrupt

abscess ['æbses] *n* abcès *m*

absence ['æbsəns] *n* absence *f*; **in the a. of** *(person)* en l'absence de; *(thing)* faute de

absent 1 ['æbsənt] *adj* absent (**from** de) **2** [æb'sent] *vt* **to a. oneself (from)** s'absenter (de) ■ **absent-minded** *adj* distrait

absentee [æbsən'tiː] *n* absent, -e *mf*

absolute ['æbsəluːt] *adj* absolu; *(proof)* indiscutable; **he's an a. fool!** il est complètement idiot!; **it's an a. disgrace!** c'est une honte! ■ **absolutely** *adv* absolument; **you're a. right** tu as tout à fait raison

absorb [əb'zɔːb] *vt* *(liquid)* absorber; *(shock)* amortir; **to be absorbed in sth** être plongé dans qch ■ **absorbent** *adj* absorbant

abstain [əb'steɪn] *vi* Pol s'abstenir; **to a. from sth/from doing sth** s'abstenir de qch/de faire qch

abstract ['æbstrækt] **1** *adj* abstrait **2** *n* (**a**) *(notion)* **the a.** l'abstrait *m* (**b**) *(summary)* résumé *m*

absurd [əb'sɜːd] *adj* absurde, ridicule

abundant [ə'bʌndənt] *adj* abondant ■ **abundantly** *adv* **a. clear** parfaitement clair

abuse 1 [ə'bjuːs] *n* *(of power)* abus *m* (**of** de); *(of child)* mauvais traitements *mpl*; *(insults)* injures *fpl* **2** [ə'bjuːz] *vt* *(misuse)* abuser de; *(ill-treat)* maltraiter; *(insult)* injurier ■ **abusive** [ə'bjuːsɪv] *adj* *(person, language)* grossier, -ère

abysmal [ə'bɪzməl] *adj* Fam *(bad)* exécrable

academic [ækə'demɪk] **1** *adj* (**a**) *(year, diploma)* (*of school*) scolaire; *(of university)* universitaire (**b**) *(scholarly)* intellectuel, -elle (**c**) *(theoretical)* **the issue is of purely a. interest** cette question n'a d'intérêt que d'un point de vue théorique; **this is a. now** cela n'a plus d'importance **2** *n* *(teacher)* universitaire *mf*

academy [ə'kædəmɪ] *(pl* -ies) *n* *(society)* académie *f*; *(military)* école *f*

accelerate [ək'seləreɪt] **1** *vt* accélérer **2** *vi* *(of pace)* s'accélérer; *(of vehicle, driver)* accélérer ■ **accelerator** *n* accélérateur *m*

accent ['æksənt] *n* accent *m*

accept [ək'sept] *vt* accepter ■ **acceptable** *adj* *(worth accepting, tolerable)* acceptable; **to be a. to sb** convenir à qn

access ['ækses] **1** *n* accès *m* (**to sth** à qch; **to sb** auprès de qn); *Comptr* **a. provider** fournisseur *m* d'accès; **a. road** route *f* d'accès **2** *vt* *Comptr* accéder à ■ **accessible** *adj* accessible

accessories [ək'sesərɪz] *npl* *(objects)* accessoires *mpl*

accessory [ək'sesərɪ] *(pl* -ies) *n Law* *(accomplice)* complice *mf* (**to** de)

accident ['æksɪdənt] *n* accident *m*; **by a.** accidentellement; *(by chance)* par hasard ■ **accidental** *adj* accidentel, -elle ■ **accidentally** *adv* accidentellement; *(by chance)* par hasard

acclaim [ə'kleɪm] **1** *n* *(critical)* **a.** éloges *mpl* **2** *vt* *(cheer)* acclamer; *(praise)* faire l'éloge de

acclimatize [ə'klaɪmətaɪz] *(Am* **acclimate** ['ækləmeɪt]) *vi* s'acclimater

accommodate [ə'kɒmədeɪt] *vt* (**a**)

(of house) loger (**b**) *(oblige)* rendre service à ■ **accommodating** *adj* accommodant, obligeant

accommodation [əkɒmə'deɪʃən] *n* (*Am* **accommodations**) *(lodging)* logement *m*; *(rented room(s))* chambre(s) *f(pl)*

accompany [ə'kʌmpənɪ] *(pt & pp* -**ied**) *vt* accompagner

accomplice [ə'kʌmplɪs] *n* complice *mf*

accomplish [ə'kʌmplɪʃ] *vt (task, duty)* accomplir; *(aim)* atteindre ■ **accomplishment** *n (of task, duty)* accomplissement *m*; *(thing achieved)* réalisation *f*

accord [ə'kɔːd] **1** *n* accord *m*; **of my own a.** de mon plein gré **2** *vt (grant)* accorder ■ **accordance** *n* **in a. with** conformément à

according [ə'kɔːdɪŋ] **according to** *prep* selon, d'après ■ **accordingly** *adv* en conséquence

accordion [ə'kɔːdɪən] *n* accordéon *m*

accost [ə'kɒst] *vt* accoster, aborder

account [ə'kaʊnt] **1** *n* (**a**) *(with bank or company)* compte *m* (**b**) *(report)* compte rendu *m*; *(explanation)* explication *f* (**c**) *(expressions)* **by all accounts** au dire de tous; **on a. of** à cause de; **on no a.** en aucun cas; **to take sth into a.** tenir compte de qch **2** *vi* **to a. for** *(explain)* expliquer; *(give reckoning of)* rendre compte de; *(represent)* représenter ■ **accountable** *adj* responsable (**for/to** de/devant)

accountant [ə'kaʊntənt] *n* comptable *mf*

accounting [ə'kaʊntɪŋ] *n* comptabilité *f*

accumulate [ə'kjuːmjʊleɪt] **1** *vt* accumuler **2** *vi* s'accumuler

accuracy ['ækjʊrəsɪ] *n* exactitude *f*, précision *f*

accurate ['ækjʊrət] *adj* exact, précis

accuse [ə'kjuːz] *vt* **to a. sb (of sth/of doing sth)** accuser qn (de qch/de faire qch) ■ **accusation** *n* accusation *f*; **to make an a. against sb** lancer une accusation contre qn ■ **accused** *n Law* **the a.** l'accusé, -e *mf*

accustom [ə'kʌstəm] *vt* habituer, accoutumer ■ **accustomed** *adj* **to be a. to sth/to doing sth** être habitué à qch/à faire qch; **to get a. to sth/to doing sth** s'habituer à qch/à faire qch

ace [eɪs] *n* (**a**) *(card, person)* as *m* (**b**) *(at tennis)* ace *m*

ache [eɪk] **1** *n* douleur *f* **2** *vi* faire mal; **my head aches** j'ai mal à la tête

achieve [ə'tʃiːv] *vt (result)* obtenir; *(aim)* atteindre; *(ambition)* réaliser; *(victory)* remporter; **to a. success** réussir ■ **achievement** *n (success)* réussite *f*; *(of ambition)* réalisation *f*

aching [eɪkɪŋ] *adj* douloureux, -euse

acid ['æsɪd] *adj & n* acide (*m*); **a. rain** pluies *fpl* acides

acknowledge [ək'nɒlɪdʒ] *vt* reconnaître (**as** pour); *(greeting)* répondre à ■ **acknowledg(e)ment** *n (of letter)* accusé *m* de réception; *(receipt)* reçu *m*; *(confession)* aveu *m* (**of** de)

acne ['æknɪ] *n* acné *f*

acoustics [ə'kuːstɪks] *npl* acoustique *f*

acquaint [ə'kweɪnt] *vt* **to be acquainted with** *(person)* connaître; *(fact)* savoir ■ **acquaintance** *n (person, knowledge)* connaissance *f*

acquire [ə'kwaɪə(r)] *vt* acquérir; *(taste)* prendre (**for** à); *(friends)* se faire

acquit [ə'kwɪt] *(pt & pp* -**tt**-) *vt* (**a**) *Law* **to a. sb (of a crime)** acquitter qn (**b**) **to a. oneself badly/well** mal/bien s'en tirer

acre ['eɪkə(r)] *n* ≃ demi-hectare *m*, acre *f*; *Fam* **acres of space** plein de place

acrimonious [ækrɪ'məʊnɪəs] *adj (person, remark)* acrimonieux, -euse, hargneux, -euse; *(attack, dispute)* virulent

acrobat ['ækrəbæt] *n* acrobate *mf* ■ **acrobatics** *npl* acrobaties *fpl*

acronym ['ækrənɪm] *n* sigle *m*

across [ə'krɒs] **1** *prep (from side to side of)* d'un côté à l'autre de; *(on the other side of)* de l'autre côté de; *(crossways)* en travers de; **a bridge a. the river** un pont sur la rivière; **to walk** *or* **go a.** *(street, lawn)* traverser; **to run/swim**

a. traverser en courant/à la nage **2** *adv* **to be a kilometre a.** *(wide)* avoir un kilomètre de large; **to get sth a. to sb** faire comprendre qch à qn

acrylic [ə'krɪlɪk] *adj (paint, fibre)* acrylique; *(garment)* en acrylique

act [ækt] **1** *n* **(a)** *(deed)* acte *m*; **a. (of parliament)** loi *f*; **caught in the a.** pris sur le fait **(b)** *Theatre (part of play)* acte *m*; *(in circus, cabaret)* numéro *m*; *Fig* **to get one's a. together** se secouer; *Fam* **in on the a.** dans le coup **2** *vt (part)* jouer; **to a. the fool** faire l'idiot **3** *vi* **(a)** *(take action, behave)* agir; **it's time to a.** il est temps d'agir; **to a. as secretary/etc** faire office de secrétaire/*etc*; **to a. (up)on** *(affect)* agir sur; *(advice)* suivre; **to a. on behalf of sb** représenter qn; *Fam* **to a. up** *(of person, machine)* faire des siennes **(b)** *(in play, film)* jouer; *(pretend)* jouer la comédie **▪ acting 1** *adj (temporary)* intérimaire **2** *n (of play)* représentation *f*; *(art)* jeu *m*; *(career)* théâtre *m*

action ['ækʃən] *n* action *f*; *(military)* combats *mpl*; *(legal)* procès *m*, action *f*; **to take a.** prendre des mesures; **to put into a.** *(plan)* exécuter; **out of a.** *(machine)* hors service; *(person)* hors de combat

active ['æktɪv] **1** *adj* actif, -ive; *(interest, dislike)* vif *(f* vive); *(volcano)* en activité **2** *n Gram* actif *m* **▪ activity** *(pl* -**ies)** *n* activité *f*; *(in street)* animation *f*

actor ['æktə(r)] *n* acteur *m* **▪ actress** *n* actrice *f*

actual ['æktʃʊəl] *adj* réel *(f* réelle); *(example)* concret, -ète; **the a. book** le livre même; **in a. fact** en réalité **▪ actually** *adv (truly)* réellement; *(in fact)* en réalité, en fait

acupuncture ['ækjʊpʌŋktʃə(r)] *n* acuponcture *f*

acute [ə'kjuːt] *adj (pain, angle)* aigu *(f* aiguë); *(anxiety, emotion)* vif *(f* vive); *(mind, observer)* perspicace; *(shortage)* grave **▪ acutely** *adv (suffer, feel)* profondément; *(painful)* extrêmement

AD [eɪ'diː] *(abbr* **anno Domini)** apr. J.-C.

ad [æd] *n Fam (on radio, TV)* pub *f*; *(private, in newspaper)* annonce *f*; *Br* **small ad**, *Am* **want ad** petite annonce *f*

adapt [ə'dæpt] **1** *vt* adapter **(to** à); **to a. oneself to sth** s'adapter à qch **2** *vi* s'adapter **▪ adaptable** *adj (person)* souple; *(instrument)* adaptable **▪ adapter, adaptor** *n (for use abroad)* adaptateur *m*; *(for several plugs)* prise *f* multiple

add [æd] **1** *vt* ajouter **(to/that** à/que); **to a. (up** *or* **together)** *(numbers)* additionner; **to a. in** inclure **2** *vi* **to a. to** *(increase)* augmenter; **to a. up to** *(total)* s'élever à; *(mean)* signifier; *(represent)* constituer

adder ['ædə(r)] *n* vipère *f*

addict ['ædɪkt] *n* **drug a.** toxicomane *mf*, drogué, -ée *mf*; **TV a.** fana(tique) *mf* de la télé **▪ addicted** *adj* **to be a. to drugs** être toxicomane; **to be a. to alcohol** être alcoolique; **to be a. to cigarettes** ne pas pouvoir se passer de tabac **▪ addictive** *adj (drug, TV)* qui crée une dépendance

addition [ə'dɪʃən] *n* addition *f*; *(increase)* augmentation *f*; **in a.** de plus; **in a. to** en plus de **▪ additional** *adj* supplémentaire

additive ['ædɪtɪv] *n* additif *m*

address 1 [*Br* ə'dres, *Am* 'ædres] *n (on letter, parcel)* adresse *f*; *(speech)* allocution *f* **2** [ə'dres] *vt (person, audience)* s'adresser à; *(words, speech)* adresser **(to** à); *(letter)* mettre l'adresse sur

adept [ə'dept] *adj* expert **(in** *or* **at** à)

adequate ['ædɪkwət] *adj (enough)* suffisant; *(acceptable)* convenable; *(performance)* acceptable **▪ adequately** *adv (sufficiently)* suffisamment; *(acceptably)* convenablement

adhere [əd'hɪə(r)] *vi* **to a. to** adhérer à; *(decision, rule)* s'en tenir à **▪ adhesive** [-'hiːsɪv] *adj & n* adhésif *(m)*

adjacent [ə'dʒeɪsənt] *adj (house, angle)* adjacent **(to** à)

adjective ['ædʒɪktɪv] *n* adjectif *m*

adjoin [ə'dʒɔɪn] *vt* être attenant à

■ **adjoining** *adj* attenant

adjourn [ə'dʒɜːn] **1** *vt (postpone)* ajourner; *(session)* suspendre **2** *vi* suspendre la séance

adjust [ə'dʒʌst] *vt (machine)* régler; *(machine part)* ajuster, régler; *(salaries, prices)* (r)ajuster; *(clothes)* rajuster; **to a. to sth** s'adapter à qch ■ **adjustable** *adj (seat)* réglable

ad-lib [æd'lɪb] *vi (pt & pp -bb-)* improviser

administer [əd'mɪnɪstə(r)] *vt* administrer **(to** à) ■ **administration** *n* administration *f; (government)* gouvernement *m* ■ **administrator** *n* administrateur, -trice *mf*

admiral ['ædmərəl] *n* amiral *m*

admire [əd'maɪə(r)] *vt* admirer **(for** sth pour qch; **for doing sth** de faire qch) ■ **admirable** *adj* admirable

admit [əd'mɪt] *(pt & pp -tt-)* **1** *vt (let in)* laisser entrer; *(to hospital, college)* admettre; *(acknowledge)* reconnaître, admettre **(that** que) **2** *vi* **to a. to sth** avouer qch; *(mistake)* reconnaître qch ■ **admission** *n (to theatre)* entrée *f* **(to** à *ou* de); *(to club, school)* admission *f; (acknowledgement)* aveu *m;* **a. (charge)** (prix *m* d')entrée *f* ■ **admittance** *n* entrée *f;* **'no a.'** 'entrée interdite' ■ **admittedly** [-ɪdlɪ] *adv* de l'aveu général

adolescent [ædə'lesənt] *n* adolescent, -e *mf*

adopt [ə'dɒpt] *vt* adopter; *Pol (candidate)* choisir ■ **adopted** *adj (child)* adopté; *(son, daughter)* adoptif, -ive; *(country)* d'adoption ■ **adoptive** *adj (parent)* adoptif, -ive

adore [ə'dɔː(r)] *vt* adorer **(doing** faire) ■ **adorable** *adj* adorable

Adriatic [eɪdrɪ'ætɪk] *n* **the A.** l'Adriatique *f*

adult ['ædʌlt, ə'dʌlt] **1** *n* adulte *mf* **2** *adj (animal)* adulte; **a. class/film** classe *f*/ film *m* pour adultes

adultery [ə'dʌltərɪ] *n* adultère *m;* **to commit a.** commettre l'adultère

advance [əd'vɑːns] **1** *n (movement, money)* avance *f; (of science)* progrès

mpl; **advances** *(sexual)* avances *fpl;* **in a.** *(book, inform, apply)* à l'avance; *(pay)* d'avance; *(arrive)* en avance **2** *adj (payment)* anticipé; **a. booking** réservation *f* **3** *vt* **(a)** *(put forward)* faire avancer **(b)** *(science, one's work)* faire progresser; *(opinion)* avancer **4** *vi (go forward, progress)* avancer; **to a. towards sb** s'avancer *ou* avancer vers qn ■ **advanced** *adj* avancé; *(studies, level)* supérieur; *(course)* de niveau supérieur; **a. in years** âgé

advantage [əd'vɑːntɪdʒ] *n* avantage *m* **(over** sur); **to take a. of** *(situation)* profiter de; *(person)* exploiter; *(woman)* séduire; **a. Hewitt** *(in tennis)* avantage Hewitt

advent ['ædvent] *n* arrivée *f,* avènement *m; Rel* **A.** l'Avent *m*

adventure [əd'ventʃə(r)] **1** *n* aventure *f* **2** *adj (film, story)* d'aventures ■ **adventurous** *adj* aventureux, -euse

adverb ['ædvɜːb] *n* adverbe *m*

adverse ['ædvɜːs] *adj* défavorable; *(effect)* négatif, -ive

advert ['ædvɜːt] *n Br* pub *f; (private, in newspaper)* annonce *f*

advertise ['ædvətaɪz] **1** *vt (commercially)* faire de la publicité pour; *(privately)* passer une annonce pour vendre **2** *vi* faire de la publicité; *(privately)* passer une annonce **(for** pour trouver) ■ **advertising** *n* publicité *f;* **a. agency** agence *f* de publicité; **a. campaign** campagne *f* de publicité

advertisement [*Br* əd'vɜːtɪsmənt, *Am* ædvər'taɪzmənt] *n* publicité *f; (private or in newspaper)* annonce *f; (poster)* affiche *f; TV* **the advertisements** la publicité

advice [əd'vaɪs] *n* conseil(s) *m(pl); Com (notification)* avis *m;* **a piece of a.** un conseil; **to ask sb's a.** demander conseil à qn; **to take sb's a.** suivre les conseils de qn

advise [əd'vaɪz] *vt* **(a)** *(counsel)* conseiller; *(recommend)* recommander; **to a. sb to do sth** conseiller à qn de faire qch; **to a. sb against doing sth** déconseiller à qn de faire qch **(b)**

(inform) **to a. sb that...** aviser qn que... ■ **advisable** *adj (action)* à conseiller; **it's a. to wait/***etc* il est plus prudent d'attendre/*etc* ■ **adviser, advisor** *n* conseiller, -ère *mf*

advocate 1 ['ædvəkət] *n (of cause)* défenseur *m*; *(lawyer)* avocat, -e *mf* **2** ['ædvəkeɪt] *vt* préconiser

aerial ['eərɪəl] **1** *n Br* antenne *f* **2** *adj (photo)* aérien, -enne

aerobics [eə'rəʊbɪks] *npl* aérobic *m*

aeroplane ['eərəpleɪn] *n Br* avion *m*

aerosol ['eərəsɒl] *n* aérosol *m*

aesthetic [*Br* iːs'θetɪk, *Am* es'θetɪk] *adj* esthétique

affair ['əfeə(r)] *n (matter, concern)* affaire *f*; **(love) a.** liaison *f*; **state of affairs** situation *f*

affect [ə'fekt] *vt (concern)* concerner; *(move, pretend to have)* affecter; *(harm)* nuire à; *(influence)* influer sur; **to be deeply affected by sth** être très affecté par qch ■ **affected** *adj (manner)* affecté

affection [ə'fekʃən] *n* affection *f* **(for** pour) ■ **affectionate** *adj* affectueux, -euse

affinity [ə'fɪnɪtɪ] *(pl* -ies*) n* affinité *f*

affirm [ə'fɜːm] *vt* affirmer ■ **affirmative 1** *adj* affirmatif, -ive **2** *n* affirmative *f*; **to answer in the a.** répondre par l'affirmative

affix [ə'fɪks] *vt (stamp, signature)* apposer

afflict [ə'flɪkt] *vt* affliger **(with** de) ■ **affliction** *n (misery)* affliction *f*; *(disability)* infirmité *f*

affluent ['æflʊənt] *adj* riche; **a. society** société *f* d'abondance

afford [ə'fɔːd] *vt (pay for)* **I can't a. it/ a new car** je n'ai pas les moyens de l'acheter/d'acheter une nouvelle voiture; **he can't a. the time (to read it)** il n'a pas le temps (de le lire); **I can a. to wait** je peux me permettre d'attendre ■ **affordable** *adj (price)* abordable

Afghanistan [æf'gænɪstɑːn] *n* l'Afghanistan *m*

afield [ə'fiːld] *adv* **further a.** plus loin

afloat [ə'fləʊt] *adv (ship, swimmer,*

business) à flot; *(awash)* submergé; **to stay a.** *(of ship)* rester à flot; *(of business)* se maintenir à flot

afraid [ə'freɪd] *adj* **to be a.** avoir peur **(of** de); **to be a. to do** *or* **of doing sth** avoir peur de faire qch; **I'm a. (that) he'll fall** j'ai peur qu'il (ne) tombe; **I'm a. he's out** je regrette, il est sorti

afresh [ə'freʃ] *adv* de nouveau; **to start a.** recommencer

Africa ['æfrɪkə] *n* l'Afrique *f* ■ **African 1** *adj* africain **2** *n* Africain, -e *mf*

after ['ɑːftə(r)] **1** *adv* après; **soon/ long a.** peu/longtemps après; **the month a.** le mois d'après; **the day a.** le lendemain

2 *prep* après; **a. three days** au bout de trois jours; **the day a. the battle** le lendemain de la bataille; **a. eating** après avoir mangé; **day a. day** jour après jour; **a. all** après tout; **it's a. five** il est cinq heures passées; *Am* **ten a. four** quatre heures dix; **to be a. sb/ sth** *(seek)* chercher qn/qch

3 *conj* après que; **a. he saw you** après qu'il t'a vu ■ **after-effects** *npl* suites *fpl*, séquelles *fpl* ■ **afterlife** *n* vie *f* après la mort ■ **aftermath** *n* suites *fpl* ■ **after-sales service** *n* service *m* après-vente ■ **aftershave** *n* (lotion *f*) après-rasage *m*, after-shave *m inv* ■ **afterthought** *n* réflexion *f* après coup; **to add/say sth as an a.** ajouter/dire qch après coup ■ **afterward(s)** *adv* après, plus tard

afternoon [ɑːftə'nuːn] *n* après-midi *m ou f inv*; **in the a.** l'après-midi; **at three in the a.** à trois heures de l'après-midi; **every Monday a.** tous les lundis après-midi; **good a.!** bonjour!

again [ə'gen] *adv* de nouveau, encore une fois; *(furthermore)* en outre; **to go down/up a.** redescendre/remonter; **she won't do it a.** elle ne le fera plus; **never a.** plus jamais; **a. and a.** bien des fois; **what's his name a.?** comment s'appelle-t-il déjà?

against [ə'genst, ə'geɪnst] *prep* contre; **to lean a. sth** s'appuyer contre qch; **to go** *or* **be a. sth** s'opposer à qch; **a. the**

law illégal; *Br* **a. the rules,** *Am* **a. the rule** interdit, contraire aux règlements; **the pound rose a. the dollar** la livre est en hausse par rapport au dollar

age [eɪdʒ] **1** *n* âge *m*; **(old) a.** vieillesse *f*; **what a. are you?, what's your a.?** quel âge as-tu?; **five years of a.** âgé de cinq ans; **under a.** trop jeune, mineur; *Fam* **to wait (for) ages** attendre une éternité; **a. gap** différence *f* d'âge; **a. limit** limite *f* d'âge

2 *vt & vi* (*pres p* **ag(e)ing**) vieillir ▪ **aged** *adj* (a) [eɪdʒd] **a. ten** âgé de dix ans (b) ['eɪdʒɪd] vieux (*f* vieille), âgé; **the a.** les personnes *fpl* âgées

agenda [ə'dʒendə] *n* ordre *m* du jour

agent ['eɪdʒənt] *n* agent *m*; (*car dealer*) concessionnaire *mf* ▪ **agency** *n* agence *f*

aggravate ['ægrəveɪt] *vt* (*make worse*) aggraver; *Fam* (*annoy*) exaspérer

aggregate ['ægrɪgət] **1** *adj* global **2** *n* (*total*) ensemble *m*; **on a.** au total

aggressive [ə'gresɪv] *adj* agressif, -ive

aggrieved [ə'griːvd] *adj* (*offended*) blessé, froissé; (*tone*) peiné

aghast [ə'gɑːst] *adj* horrifié (**at** par)

agile [*Br* 'ædʒaɪl, *Am* 'ædʒəl] *adj* agile

agitated ['ædʒɪteɪtɪd] *adj* agité

agnostic [æg'nɒstɪk] *adj & n* agnostique (*mf*)

ago [ə'gəʊ] *adv* **a year a.** il y a un an; **how long a.?** il y a combien de temps (de cela)?; **long a.** il y a longtemps; **a short time a.** il y a peu de temps

agonizing ['ægənaɪzɪŋ] *adj* (*pain*) atroce; (*situation*) angoissant

agony ['ægənɪ] (*pl* **-ies**) *n* (*pain*) douleur *f* atroce; (*anguish*) angoisse *f*; **to be in a.** être au supplice; **a. column** (*in newspaper*) courrier *m* du cœur

agree [ə'griː] **1** *vi* (*come to an agreement*) se mettre d'accord; (*be in agreement*) être d'accord (**with** avec); (*of facts, dates*) concorder; (*of verb*) s'accorder; **to a. (up)on** (*decide*) convenir de; **to a. to sth/to doing sth** consentir à qch/à faire qch

2 *vt* (*plan*) se mettre d'accord sur; (*date, price*) convenir de; (*approve*) approuver; **to a. to do sth** accepter de faire qch; **to a. that...** admettre que... ▪ **agreed** *adj* (*time, place*) convenu ▪ **agreement** *n* (*contract, assent*) & *Gram* accord *m* (**with** avec); **to be in a. with sb** être d'accord avec qn; **to come to an a.** se mettre d'accord

agreeable [ə'griːəbəl] *adj* (*pleasant*) agréable; **to be a.** (*agree*) être d'accord; **to be a. to sth** consentir à qch

agriculture ['ægrɪkʌltʃə(r)] *n* agriculture *f* ▪ **agricultural** *adj* agricole

aground [ə'graʊnd] *adv* **to run a.** (*of ship*) (s')échouer

ahead [ə'hed] *adv* (*in space*) en avant; (*leading*) en tête; (*in the future*) à l'avenir; **a. of** (*in space*) devant; (*in time*) avant; **one hour/etc a. (of)** une heure/etc d'avance (sur); **to be a. of schedule** être en avance; **to go on a.** partir devant; **to go a.** (*advance*) avancer; (*continue*) continuer; (*start*) commencer; **go a.!** allez-y!; **to think a.** prévoir

aid [eɪd] **1** *n* (*help*) aide *f*; (*device*) accessoire *m*; **with the a. of sb** avec l'aide de qn; **with the a. of sth** à l'aide de qch; **in a. of** (*charity*) au profit de **2** *vt* aider (**sb to do** qn à faire)

aide [eɪd] *n* collaborateur, -trice *mf*

AIDS [eɪdz] (*abbr* **Acquired Immune Deficiency Syndrome**) *n* SIDA *m*

ailing ['eɪlɪŋ] *adj* (*ill*) souffrant; (*company*) en difficulté ▪ **ailment** *n* affection *f*

aim [eɪm] **1** *n* but *m*; **to take a. (at)** viser; **with the a. of** dans le but de **2** *vt* (*gun*) braquer (**at** sur); (*stone*) lancer (**at** à ou vers); (*blow, remark*) décocher (**at** à) **3** *vi* viser; **to a. at sb** viser qn; **to a. to do sth** avoir l'intention de faire qch ▪ **aimless** *adj* (*existence*) sans but

air [eə(r)] **1** *n* (a) (*atmosphère*) air *m*; **in the open a.** en plein air; **by a.** (*travel*) en ou par avion; (*send letter, goods*) par avion; **to be** *or* **go on (the) a.** (*of person*) passer à l'antenne; (*of programme*) être diffusé; **to throw sth in(to) the a.** jeter qch en l'air; *Fig* **there's something in the a.** il se prépare quelque

chose; *Aut* **a. bag** airbag *m*; **a. base** base *f* aérienne; **a. bed** matelas *m* pneumatique; **a. fare** prix *m* du billet d'avion; **a. force** armée *f* de l'air; **a. freshener** désodorisant *m* (*pour la maison*)

(b) (*appearance, tune*) air *m*; **to put on airs** se donner des airs; **with an a. of sadness** d'un air triste

2 *vt* (*room*) aérer; (*views*) exposer ■ **air-conditioning** *n* climatisation *f* ■ **aircraft** *n inv* avion *m*; **a. carrier** porte-avions *m inv* ■ **airfield** *n* terrain *m* d'aviation ■ **airgun** *n* carabine *f* à air comprimé ■ **airlift** *vt* transporter par avion ■ **airline** *n* compagnie *f* aérienne; **a. ticket** billet *m* d'avion ■ **airmail** *n* poste *f* aérienne; **by a.** par avion ■ **airplane** *n Am* avion *m* ■ **airport** *n* aéroport *m* ■ **air-raid shelter** *n* abri *m* antiaérien ■ **airship** *n* dirigeable *m* ■ **airtight** *adj* hermétique ■ **air-traffic controller** *n* contrôleur *m* aérien, aiguilleur *m* du ciel

airy ['eərɪ] (**-ier, -iest**) *adj* (*room*) clair et spacieux, -euse; *Fig* (*manner*) désinvolte

aisle [aɪl] *n* (*in supermarket, cinema*) allée *f*; (*in plane*) couloir *m*; (*in church*) (*on side*) nef *f* latérale; (*central*) allée *f* centrale

ajar [ə'dʒɑ:(r)] *adj & adv* (*door*) entrouvert

alarm [ə'lɑ:m] **1** *n* (*warning, fear, device*) alarme *f*; (*mechanism*) sonnerie *f* (d'alarme); **false a.** fausse alerte *f*; **a. clock** réveil *m* **2** *vt* (*frighten*) alarmer; (*worry*) inquiéter; **they were alarmed at the news** la nouvelle les a beaucoup inquiétés

alas [ə'læs] *exclam* hélas!

Albania [æl'beɪnɪə] *n* l'Albanie *f* ■ **Albanian 1** *adj* albanais **2** *n* Albanais, -e *mf*

album ['ælbəm] *n* (*book, record*) album *m*

alcohol ['ælkəhɒl] *n* alcool *m* ■ **alcoholic 1** *adj* (*person*) alcoolique; **a. drink** boisson *f* alcoolisée **2** *n* (*person*) alcoolique *mf*

alcove ['ælkəʊv] *n* alcôve *f*

ale [eɪl] *n* bière *f*

alert [ə'lɜ:t] **1** *adj* (*watchful*) vigilant; (*lively*) (*mind, baby*) éveillé **2** *n* alerte *f*; **on the a.** sur le qui-vive **3** *vt* alerter

A level ['eɪlevəl] *n Br* (*exam*) ≃ épreuve *f* de baccalauréat

algebra ['ældʒɪbrə] *n* algèbre *f*

Algeria [æl'dʒɪərɪə] *n* l'Algérie *f* ■ **Algerian 1** *adj* algérien, -enne **2** *n* Algérien, -enne *mf*

alias ['eɪlɪəs] **1** *adv* alias **2** (*pl* **aliases**) *n* nom *m* d'emprunt

alibi ['ælɪbaɪ] *n* alibi *m*

alien ['eɪlɪən] **1** *adj* étranger, -ère (**to** à) **2** *n* (*from outer space*) extraterrestre *mf*; *Formal* (*foreigner*) étranger, -ère *mf* ■ **alienate** *vt* (*friend, supporters, readers*) s'aliéner; **to feel alienated** se sentir exclu

alight¹ [ə'laɪt] *adj* (*fire*) allumé; (*building*) en feu; (*face*) éclairé; **to set sth a.** mettre le feu à qch

alight² [ə'laɪt] (*pt & pp* **alighted** *or* **alit**) *vi* (**a**) *Formal* (*from bus, train*) descendre (**from** de) (**b**) (*of bird*) se poser (**on** sur)

align [ə'laɪn] *vt* aligner

alike [ə'laɪk] **1** *adj* (*people, things*) semblables, pareils, -eilles; **to look** *or* **be a.** se ressembler **2** *adv* de la même manière; **summer and winter a.** été comme hiver

alimony [*Br* 'ælɪmənɪ, *Am* 'ælɪməʊnɪ] *n Law* pension *f* alimentaire

alit [ə'lɪt] *pt & pp of* **alight²**

alive [ə'laɪv] *adj* vivant, en vie; **to stay a.** survivre; **a. and well** bien portant; *Fam* **a. and kicking** plein de vie

ALL [ɔ:l] **1** *adj* tout, toute, *pl* tous, toutes; **a. day** toute la journée; **a. men** tous les hommes; **a. the girls** toutes les filles; **a. four of them** tous les quatre; **for a. his wealth** malgré toute sa fortune

2 *pron* (*everyone*) tous *mpl*, toutes *fpl*; (*everything*) tout; **my sisters are a. here** toutes mes sœurs sont ici; **he ate it a., he ate a. of it** il a tout mangé; **take a. of it** prends (le) tout; **a. of us** nous tous; **a. together** tous ensemble;

a. **(that)** he has tout ce qu'il a; a. **in a.** à tout prendre; **anything at a.** quoi que ce soit; **if there's any wind at a.** s'il y a le moindre vent; **nothing at a.** rien du tout; **not at a.** pas du tout; *(after 'thank you')* il n'y a pas de quoi

3 *adv* tout; **a. alone** tout seul; **a. bad** entièrement mauvais; **a. over** *(everywhere)* partout; *(finished)* fini; **a. too soon** bien trop tôt; *Sport* **six a.** six partout; *Fam* **not a. there** un peu fêlé ▪ **all-night** *adj (party)* qui dure toute la nuit; *(shop)* ouvert toute la nuit ▪ **all-out** *adj (effort)* acharné; *(war, strike)* tous azimuts ▪ **all-purpose** *adj (tool)* universel, -elle ▪ **all-round** *adj (knowledge)* approfondi; *(athlete)* complet, -ète ▪ **all-time** *adj (record)* jamais battu; **to reach an a. low/high** arriver à son point le plus bas/le plus haut

allegation [ælɪ'geɪʃən] *n* accusation *f*

allege [ə'ledʒ] *vt* prétendre (**that** que) ▪ **alleged** *adj (so-called) (crime, fact)* prétendu; *(author, culprit)* présumé; **he is a. to be...** on prétend qu'il est...

allegiance [ə'liːdʒəns] *n (to party, cause)* fidélité *f* (**to** à)

allergy ['ælədʒɪ] *(pl* -**ies**) *n* allergie *f* (**to** à) ▪ **allergic** [ə'lɜːdʒɪk] *adj* allergique (**to** à)

alleviate [ə'liːvɪeɪt] *vt (pain, suffering)* soulager; *(burden, task)* alléger; *(problem)* remédier à

alley ['ælɪ] *(pl* -**eys**) *n* ruelle *f; Fam* **that's (right) up my a.** c'est mon rayon

alliance [ə'laɪəns] *n* alliance *f*

allied ['ælaɪd] *adj (country)* allié; *(matters)* lié

alligator ['ælɪgeɪtə(r)] *n* alligator *m*

allocate ['æləkeɪt] *vt (assign)* affecter (**to** à); *(distribute)* répartir

allot [ə'lɒt] *(pt & pp* -**tt**-) *vt (assign)* attribuer (**to** à); *(distribute)* répartir; **in the allotted time** dans le temps imparti ▪ **allotment** *n Br (land)* jardin *m* ouvrier

allow [ə'laʊ] **1** *vt* permettre (**sb sth** qch à qn); *(give, grant)* accorder (**sb sth** qch à qn); *(request)* accéder à; **to a. sb to do** permettre à qn de faire; **to a.**

an hour/a metre/*etc* prévoir une heure/un mètre/*etc;* **it's not allowed** c'est interdit; **you're not allowed to go** on vous interdit de partir **2** *vi* **to a. for sth** tenir compte de qch ▪ **allowable** *adj (acceptable)* admissible; *(expense)* déductible

allowance [ə'laʊəns] *n* allocation *f; (for travel, housing, food)* indemnité *f (tax-free amount)* abattement *m;* **to make allowances for** *(person)* être indulgent envers; *(thing)* tenir compte de

alloy ['ælɔɪ] *n* alliage *m*

all right [ɔːl'raɪt] **1** *adj (satisfactory)* bien *inv; (unharmed)* sain et sauf; *(undamaged)* intact; *(without worries)* tranquille; **it's a.** ça va; **are you a.?** ça va?; **I'm a.** *(healthy)* je vais bien; *(financially)* je m'en sors; **to be a. at maths** se débrouiller en maths; **the TV is a. now** *(fixed)* la télé marche maintenant **2** *adv (well)* bien; **a.!** *(in agreement)* d'accord!; **is it a. if I smoke?** ça ne vous dérange pas si je fume?

allude [ə'luːd] *vi* **to a. to** faire allusion à ▪ **allusion** *n* allusion *f*

ally 1 ['ælaɪ] *(pl* -**ies**) *n* allié, -e *mf* **2** [ə'laɪ] *(pt & pp* -**ied**) *vt* **to a. oneself with** s'allier à *ou* avec

almighty [ɔːl'maɪtɪ] **1** *adj* **(a)** *(powerful)* tout-puissant *(f* toute-puissante) **(b)** *Fam (enormous)* terrible, formidable **2** *n* **the A.** le Tout-Puissant

almond ['ɑːmənd] *n* amande *f*

almost ['ɔːlməʊst] *adv* presque; **he a. fell** il a failli tomber

alone [ə'ləʊn] *adj & adv* seul; **an expert a. can...** seul un expert peut...; **I did it (all) a.** je l'ai fait (tout) seul; **to leave** *or* **let a.** *(person)* laisser tranquille; *(thing)* ne pas toucher à; **I can't afford a bike, let a. a car!** je n'ai pas les moyens de m'acheter un vélo, encore moins une voiture

along [ə'lɒŋ] **1** *prep (all)* **a.** (tout) le long de; **to walk a. the shore** marcher le long du rivage; **to walk a. the street** marcher dans la rue; **a. here** par ici; *Fig* **somewhere a. the way** à un moment donné

2 *adv* **to move a.** avancer; **I'll be** *or*

come a. shortly je viendrai tout à l'heure; **come a.!** venez donc!; **to bring sth a.** apporter qch; **to bring sb a.** amener qn; **all a.** *(all the time)* dès le début; *(all the way)* d'un bout à l'autre; **a. with** ainsi que

alongside [əlɒŋ'saɪd] *prep & adv* à côté (de); **a. the kerb** le long du trottoir

aloof [ə'lu:f] **1** *adj* distant **2** *adv* à distance

aloud [ə'laʊd] *adv* à haute voix

alphabet ['ælfəbet] *n* alphabet *m* ■ **alphabetical** *adj* alphabétique

Alps [ælps] *npl* **the A.** les Alpes *fpl* ■ **Alpine** *adj (club, range)* alpin; *(scenery)* alpestre

already [ɔːl'redɪ] *adv* déjà

alright [ɔːl'raɪt] *adv Fam* = **all right**

Alsatian [æl'seɪʃən] *n (dog)* berger *m* allemand

also ['ɔːlsəʊ] *adv* aussi, également; *(moreover)* de plus

altar ['ɔːltə(r)] *n* autel *m*

alter ['ɔːltə(r)] **1** *vt* changer; *(clothing)* retoucher **2** *vi* changer ■ **alteration** *n* changement *m* **(in** de); *(of clothing)* retouche *f*; **alterations** *(to building)* travaux *mpl*

alternate 1 [ɔːl'tɜːnət] *adj* alterné; **on a. days** tous les deux jours **2** ['ɔːltəneɪt] *vt* faire alterner **3** ['ɔːltəneɪt] *vi* alterner **(with** avec); *El* **alternating current** courant *m* alternatif

alternative [ɔːl'tɜːnətɪv] **1** *adj (other)* de remplacement; **an a. way** une autre façon; **a. medicine** médecine *f* douce **2** *n (choice)* alternative *f*; **she had no a. but to obey** elle n'a pas pu faire autrement que d'obéir ■ **alternatively** *adv* **(or) a.** ou alors, ou bien

although [ɔːl'ðəʊ] *adv* bien que *(+ subjunctive)*

altitude ['æltɪtjuːd] *n* altitude *f*

altogether [ɔːltə'geðə(r)] *adv (completely)* tout à fait; *(on the whole)* somme toute; **how much a.?** combien en tout?

aluminium [*Br* æljʊ'mɪnɪəm] *(Am* **aluminum** [ə'luːmɪnəm]) *n* aluminium *m*

always ['ɔːlweɪz] *adv* toujours; **he's a.**

criticizing il est toujours à critiquer; **as a.** comme toujours

am [æm, *unstressed* əm] *see* **be**

a.m. [eɪ'em] *adv* du matin

amalgamate [ə'mælgəmeɪt] *vt & vi* fusionner

amateur ['æmətə(r)] **1** *n* amateur *m* **2** *adj (interest, sports, performance)* d'amateur; **a. painter/actress** peintre *m*/actrice *f* amateur

amaze [ə'meɪz] *vt* stupéfier ■ **amazed** *adj* stupéfait **(at sth** de qch); *(filled with wonder)* émerveillé; **I was a. by his courage** son courage m'a stupéfié ■ **amazing** *adj (surprising)* stupéfiant; *(incredible)* extraordinaire

ambassador [æm'bæsədə(r)] *n* ambassadeur, -drice *mf*

amber ['æmbə(r)] *n* ambre *m*; **a. (light)** *(of traffic signal)* (feu *m*) orange *m*

ambiguous [æm'bɪgjʊəs] *adj* ambigu *(f* ambiguë)

ambition [æm'bɪʃən] *n* ambition *f* ■ **ambitious** *adj* ambitieux, -euse

ambivalent [æm'bɪvələnt] *adj* ambivalent

ambulance ['æmbjʊləns] *n* ambulance *f*; **a. driver** ambulancier, -ère *mf*

ambush ['æmbʊʃ] **1** *n* embuscade *f* **2** *vt* tendre une embuscade à; **to be ambushed** tomber dans une embuscade

amend [ə'mend] *vt (text)* modifier; *Pol (law)* amender

amends [ə'mendz] *npl* **to make a.** se racheter; **to make a. for sth** réparer qch

amenities [*Br* ə'miːnɪtɪz, *Am* ə'menɪtɪz] *npl (of town)* aménagements *mpl*; *(shops)* commerces *mpl*

America [ə'merɪkə] *n* l'Amérique *f*; **North/South A.** l'Amérique *f* du Nord/du Sud ■ **American 1** *adj* américain **2** *n* Américain, -e *mf*

amiable ['eɪmɪəbəl] *adj* aimable

amicable ['æmɪkəbəl] *adj* amical

amid(st) [ə'mɪd(st)] *prep* au milieu de, parmi

amiss [ə'mɪs] *adv & adj* **something is**

a. *(wrong)* quelque chose ne va pas; **that wouldn't go a.** ça ne ferait pas de mal

ammunition [æmjʊ'nɪʃən] *n* munitions *fpl*

among(st) [ə'mʌŋ(st)] *prep (amidst)* parmi; *(between)* entre; **a. the crowd/books/others/etc** parmi la foule/les livres/les autres/*etc*; **a. friends** entre amis; **a. other things** entre autres (choses)

amoral [eɪ'mɒrəl] *adj* amoral

amount [ə'maʊnt] **1** *n* quantité *f*; *(sum of money)* somme *f*; *(total figure of invoice, debt)* montant *m*; *(scope, size)* importance *f* **2** *vi* **to a. to** *(bill)* s'élever à; *Fig* **it amounts to blackmail** ce n'est rien d'autre que du chantage; **it amounts to the same thing** ça revient au même

amp [æmp] *n (unit of electricity)* ampère *m*; *Br* **3-a. plug** prise *f* avec fusible de 3 ampères

ample ['æmpəl] *adj* **(a)** *(plentiful)* abondant **(b)** *(large) (woman, bosom)* fort **(c)** *(roomy) (garment)* large

amplify ['æmplɪfaɪ] *(pt & pp -ied) vt (essay, remarks)* développer; *(sound)* amplifier ▪ **amplifier** *n* amplificateur *m*

amputate ['æmpjʊteɪt] *vt* amputer; **to a. sb's hand/etc** amputer qn de la main/*etc*

amuse [ə'mjuːz] *vt* amuser; **to keep sb amused** distraire qn ▪ **amusement** *n* amusement *m*, divertissement *m*; *(pastime)* distraction *f*; **amusements** *(at fairground)* attractions *fpl*; *(gambling machines)* machines *fpl* à sous; **a. arcade** salle *f* de jeux; **a. park** parc *m* d'attractions

an [æn, *unstressed* ən] *see* **a**

an(a)emic [ə'niːmɪk] *adj* anémique; **to become a.** faire de l'anémie

an(a)esthetic [ænəs'θetɪk] *n (process)* anesthésie *f*; *(substance)* anesthésique *m*; **under a.** sous anesthésie; **general/local a.** anesthésie *f* générale/locale

analogy [ə'nælədʒɪ] *(pl -ies) n* analogie *f* **(with** avec)

analyse ['ænəlaɪz] *vt* analyser ▪ **analysis** *(pl -yses* [-əsiːz]) *n* analyse *f* ▪ **analyst** *n* analyste *mf*

anarchy ['ænəkɪ] *n* anarchie *f* ▪ **anarchist** *n* anarchiste *mf*

anatomy [ə'nætəmɪ] *n* anatomie *f*

ancestor ['ænsestə(r)] *n* ancêtre *m*

anchor ['æŋkə(r)] **1** *n* ancre *f* **2** *vt (ship)* mettre à l'ancre **3** *vi* jeter l'ancre, mouiller

anchovy [*Br* 'æntʃəvɪ, *Am* æn'tʃəʊvɪ] *(pl -ies) n* anchois *m*

ancient ['eɪnʃənt] *adj* ancien, -enne; *(pre-medieval)* antique

and [ænd, *unstressed* ən(d)] *conj* et; **a knife a. fork** un couteau et une fourchette; **my mother a. father** mon père et ma mère; **two hundred a. two** deux cent deux; **four a. three quarters** quatre trois quarts; **nice a. warm** bien chaud; **better a. better** de mieux en mieux; **she can read a. write** elle sait lire et écrire; **go a. see** va voir; **I knocked a. knocked** j'ai frappé pendant un bon moment

anemic [ə'niːmɪk] *adj* = **anaemic**

anesthetic [ænɪs'θetɪk] *n* = **anaesthetic**

angel ['eɪndʒəl] *n* ange *m* ▪ **angelic** *adj* angélique

anger ['æŋgə(r)] **1** *n* colère *f*; **in a., out of a.** sous le coup de la colère **2** *vt* mettre en colère

angina [æn'dʒaɪnə] *n* angine *f* de poitrine

angle[1] ['æŋgəl] *n* angle *m*; **at an a.** en biais

angle[2] ['æŋgəl] *vi (fish)* pêcher à la ligne; *Fig* **to a. for** *(compliments)* quêter ▪ **angler** *n* pêcheur, -euse *mf* à la ligne

Anglican ['æŋglɪkən] *adj & n* anglican, -e *(mf)*

Anglo- ['æŋgləʊ] *pref* anglo- ▪ **Anglo-Saxon** *adj & n* anglo-saxon, -onne *(mf)*

angry ['æŋgrɪ] *(-ier, -iest) adj (person)* en colère, fâché; *(look)* furieux, -euse; **an a. letter** une lettre indignée; **a. words** des paroles indignées; **to get a. (with)** se fâcher (contre)

anguish ['æŋgwɪʃ] *n* angoisse *f*

animal ['ænɪməl] *n* animal *m*

animated ['ænɪmeɪtɪd] *adj (lively)* animé; **to become a.** s'animer

animation [ænɪ'meɪʃən] *n (liveliness) & Cin* animation *f*

aniseed ['ænɪsiːd] *n (as flavouring)* anis *m*

ankle ['æŋkəl] *n* cheville *f*; **a. sock** socquette *f*

annex¹ [ə'neks] *vt* annexer

annex², *Br* **annexe** ['æneks] *n (building)* annexe *f*

anniversary [ænɪ'vɜːsərɪ] *(pl -ies) n (of event)* anniversaire *m*

announce [ə'naʊns] *vt* annoncer; *(birth, marriage)* faire part de ■ **announcement** *n (statement)* annonce *f*; *(notice of birth, marriage, death) (in newspaper)* avis *m*; *(private letter)* faire-part *m inv* ■ **announcer** *n (on TV)* speaker, -ine *mf*

annoy [ə'nɔɪ] *vt (inconvenience)* ennuyer; *(irritate)* agacer ■ **annoyed** *adj* fâché; **to get a. (with)** se fâcher (contre) ■ **annoying** *adj* ennuyeux, -euse

annual ['ænjʊəl] **1** *adj* annuel, -elle **2** *n (yearbook)* annuaire *m*; *(children's)* album *m*; *(plant)* plante *f* annuelle ■ **annually** *adv (every year)* tous les ans; *(per year)* par an

annul [ə'nʌl] *(pt & pp -ll-) vt (contract, marriage)* annuler

anoint [ə'nɔɪnt] *vt* oindre **(with** de)

anomalous [ə'nɒmələs] *adj* anormal ■ **anomaly** *(pl -ies) n* anomalie *f*

anonymous [ə'nɒnɪməs] *adj* anonyme

anorak ['ænəræk] *n* anorak *m*

anorexia [ænə'reksɪə] *n* anorexie *f* ■ **anorexic** *adj & n* anorexique *(mf)*

another [ə'nʌðə(r)] *adj & pron* un(e) autre; **a. man** *(different)* un autre homme; **a. month** *(additional)* encore un mois; **a. ten** encore dix; **one a.** l'un(e) l'autre, *pl* les un(e)s les autres; **they love one a.** ils s'aiment

answer ['ɑːnsə(r)] **1** *n* réponse *f*; *(to problem, riddle) & Math* solution *f* **(to** de); *(reason)* explication *f*; **in a. to your**

letter en réponse à votre lettre **2** *vt (person, question, letter)* répondre à; *(prayer, wish)* exaucer; **he answered yes** il a répondu oui; **to a. the door** ouvrir la porte; **to a. the phone** répondre au téléphone **3** *vi* répondre ■ **answering machine** *n* répondeur *m*

ant [ænt] *n* fourmi *f*

antagonize [æn'tægənaɪz] *vt* provoquer (l'hostilité de)

Antarctic [æn'tɑːktɪk] **1** *adj* antarctique **2** *n* **the A.** l'Antarctique *m*

antenatal [æntɪ'neɪtəl] *adj Br* prénatal; **a. classes** préparation *f* à l'accouchement

antenna¹ [æn'tenə] *(pl -ae [-iː]) n (of insect)* antenne *f*

antenna² [æn'tenə] *(pl -as) n Am (for TV, radio)* antenne *f*

anthem ['ænθəm] *n* **national a.** hymne *m* national

anthology [æn'θɒlədʒɪ] *(pl -ies) n* anthologie *f*

anti- [*Br* 'æntɪ, *Am* 'æntaɪ] *pref* anti- ■ **antibiotic** *adj & n* antibiotique *(m)* ■ **anticlimax** *n* déception *f* ■ **anticlockwise** *adv Br* dans le sens inverse des aiguilles d'une montre ■ **antidote** *n* antidote *m* ■ **antifreeze** *n (for vehicle)* antigel *m* ■ **antihistamine** *n (drug)* antihistaminique *m* ■ **antiperspirant** *n* déodorant *m* ■ **anti-Semitic** *adj* antisémite ■ **antiseptic** *adj & n* antiseptique *(m)* ■ **antisocial** *adj (unsociable)* peu sociable

anticipate [æn'tɪsɪpeɪt] *vt (foresee)* anticiper; *(expect)* s'attendre à, prévoir; *(forestall)* devancer ■ **anticipation** *n (expectation)* attente *f*; *(foresight)* prévision *f*; **in a. of** en prévision de; **in a.** *(thank, pay)* d'avance

antics ['æntɪks] *npl* singeries *fpl*; **he's up to his a. again** il a encore fait des siennes

antiquated ['æntɪkweɪtɪd] *adj (expression, custom)* vieillot, -otte; *(person)* vieux jeu *inv*; *(object, machine)* antédiluvien, -enne

antique [æn'tiːk] **1** *adj (furniture)*

ancien, -enne; *(of Greek or Roman anti-quity)* antique; **a. dealer** antiquaire *mf*; **a. shop** magasin *m* d'antiquités **2** *n* antiquité *f*, objet *m* d'époque

Antwerp ['æntwɜ:p] *n* Anvers *m* ou *f*

anxiety [æŋ'zaɪətɪ] *(pl -ies)* *n (worry)* inquiétude *f* (**about** au sujet de); *(fear)* anxiété *f*; *(eagerness)* désir *m* (**to do de** faire; **for sth** de qch)

anxious ['æŋkʃəs] *adj (worried)* inquiet, -ète (**about** pour); *(troubled)* anxieux, -euse; *(causing worry)* angoissant; *(eager)* impatient (**to do** de faire)

ANY ['enɪ] **1** *adj* (**a**) *(in questions)* du, de la, des; **have you a. milk/tickets?** avez-vous du lait/des billets? (**b**) *(in negatives)* de; *(the slightest)* aucun; **he hasn't got a. milk/tickets** il n'a pas de lait/de billets; **there isn't a. doubt/problem** il n'y a aucun doute/problème (**c**) *(no matter which)* n'importe quel; **ask a. doctor** demande à n'importe quel médecin (**d**) *(every)* tout; **at a. moment** à tout moment; **in a. case, at a. rate** de toute façon **2** *pron* (**a**) *(no matter which one)* n'importe lequel; *(somebody)* quelqu'un; **if a. of you...** si l'un d'entre vous..., si quelqu'un parmi vous... (**b**) *(quantity)* en; **have you got a.?** en as-tu?; **I don't see a.** je n'en vois pas **3** *adv* **not a. further/happier** pas plus loin/plus heureux, -euse; **I don't see him a. more** je ne le vois plus; **a. more tea?** encore un peu de thé?; **I'm not a. better** je ne vais pas mieux

anybody ['enɪbɒdɪ] *pron* (**a**) *(somebody)* quelqu'un; **do you see a.?** tu vois quelqu'un?; **more than a.** plus que tout autre (**b**) *(in negatives)* personne; **he doesn't know a.** il ne connaît personne (**c**) *(no matter who)* n'importe qui; **a. would think that...** on croirait que...

anyhow ['enɪhaʊ] *adv (at any rate)* de toute façon; *Fam (badly)* n'importe comment

anyone ['enɪwʌn] *pron* = **anybody**

anyplace ['enɪpleɪs] *adv Am* = **anywhere**

anything ['enɪθɪŋ] *pron* (**a**) *(something)* quelque chose; **can you see a.?** tu vois quelque chose? (**b**) *(in negatives)* rien; **he doesn't do a.** il ne fait rien; **without a.** sans rien (**c**) *(everything)* tout; **a. you like** tout ce que tu veux; *Fam* **like a.** *(work)* comme un fou (**d**) *(no matter what)* **a. (at all)** n'importe quoi

anyway ['enɪweɪ] *adv (at any rate)* de toute façon

anywhere ['enɪweə(r)] *adv* (**a**) *(no matter where)* n'importe où (**b**) *(everywhere)* partout; **a. you go** où que vous alliez, partout où vous allez; **a. you like** (là) où tu veux (**c**) *(somewhere)* quelque part; **is he going a.?** va-t-il quelque part? (**d**) *(in negatives)* nulle part; **he doesn't go a.** il ne va nulle part; **without a. to put it** sans un endroit où le/la mettre

apart [ə'pɑːt] *adv* (**a**) *(separated)* **we kept them a.** nous les tenions séparés; **two years a.** à deux ans d'intervalle; **they are a metre a.** ils se trouvent à un mètre l'un de l'autre; **to come a.** *(of two objects)* se séparer; **to tell two things/people a.** distinguer deux choses/personnes (l'une de l'autre) (**b**) *(to pieces)* **to tear a.** mettre en pièces; **to take a.** démonter (**c**) *(to one side)* à part; **joking a.** sans blague; **a. from** *(except for)* à part

apartment [ə'pɑːtmənt] *n* appartement *m*; *Am* **a. building, a. house** immeuble *m* (d'habitation)

apathy ['æpəθɪ] *n* apathie *f*

ape [eɪp] **1** *n* grand singe *m* **2** *vt (imitate)* singer

aperitif [əperɪ'tiːf] *n* apéritif *m*

aperture ['æpətʃʊə(r)] *n* ouverture *f*

apiece [ə'piːs] *adv* chacun; **£2 a.** 2 livres pièce *ou* chacun

apologetic [əpɒlə'dʒetɪk] *adj (letter)* plein d'excuses; *(smile)* d'excuse; **to be a. (about)** s'excuser (de)

apology [əˈpɒlədʒɪ] (*pl* -**ies**) *n* excuses *fpl* ■ **apologize** *vi* s'excuser (**for** de); **he apologized for being late** il s'est excusé de son retard; **to a. to sb (for)** faire ses excuses à qn (pour)

apostle [əˈpɒsəl] *n* apôtre *m*

apostrophe [əˈpɒstrəfɪ] *n* apostrophe *f*

appal [əˈpɔːl] (*Am* **appall**) (*pt & pp* -**ll**-) *vt* consterner; **to be appalled (at)** être horrifié (par) ■ **appalling** *adj* épouvantable

apparatus [æpəˈreɪtəs] *n (equipment, organization)* appareil *m*; *Br (in gym)* agrès *mpl*

apparel [əˈpærəl] *n* vêtements *mpl*

apparent [əˈpærənt] *adj (seeming)* apparent; *(obvious)* évident; **it's a. that...** il est clair que... ■ **apparently** *adv* apparemment; **a. she's going to Venice** il paraît qu'elle va à Venise

appeal [əˈpiːl] **1** *n (charm)* attrait *m*; *(interest)* intérêt *m*; *(call)* appel *m*; *(pleading)* supplication *f*; *(to a court)* appel *m* **2** *vt* (**a**) *(in court)* faire appel (**b**) **to a. to sb** *(attract)* plaire à qn; *(interest)* intéresser qn; *(ask for help)* faire appel à qn; **to a. to sb's generosity** faire appel à la générosité de qn; **to a. to sb for sth** demander qch à qn; **to a. to sb to do sth** supplier qn de faire qch ■ **appealing** *adj (attractive) (offer, idea)* séduisant; *(begging) (look)* suppliant

appear [əˈpɪə(r)] *vi (become visible)* apparaître; *(seem, be published)* paraître; *(on stage, in film)* jouer; *(in court)* comparaître; **it appears that...** *(it seems that)* il semble que... (+ *subjunctive or indicative)*; *(it is rumoured that)* il paraît que... (+ *indicative)* ■ **appearance** *n (act)* apparition *f*; *(look)* apparence *f*; *(of book)* parution *f*; **to put in an a.** faire acte de présence; **to keep up appearances** sauver les apparences

appendix [əˈpendɪks] (*pl* -**ixes** [-ɪksɪz] *or* -**ices** [-ɪsiːz]) *n (in book, body)* appendice *m*; **to have one's a. out** se faire opérer de l'appendicite ■ **appendicitis** *n* appendicite *f*

appetite [ˈæpɪtaɪt] *n* appétit *m* ■ **appetizer** *n (drink)* apéritif *m*; *(food)* amuse-gueule *m inv* ■ **appetizing** *adj* appétissant

applaud [əˈplɔːd] **1** *vt (clap)* applaudir; *(approve of)* approuver, applaudir à **2** *vi* applaudir ■ **applause** *n* applaudissements *mpl*

apple [ˈæpəl] *n* pomme *f*; *Br* **stewed apples** compote *f* de pommes; **cooking a.** pomme *f* à cuire; **eating a.** pomme *f* de dessert; **a. core** trognon *m* de pomme; **a. pie** tarte *f* aux pommes; **a. sauce** compote *f* de pommes; **a. tree** pommier *m*

appliance [əˈplaɪəns] *n* appareil *m*

applicable [əˈplɪkəbəl] *adj (rule)* applicable (**to** à); *(relevant)* pertinent (**to** à)

applicant [ˈæplɪkənt] *n* candidat, -e *mf* (**for** à)

application [æplɪˈkeɪʃən] *n* (**a**) *(request)* demande *f* (**for** de); *(for job)* candidature *f* (**for** de); *(for membership)* demande *f* d'inscription; **a. (form)** *(for job)* formulaire *m* de candidature; *(for club)* formulaire *m* d'inscription (**b**) *(diligence)* application *f*

apply [əˈplaɪ] (*pt & pp* -**ied**) **1** *vt (put on, carry out)* appliquer; *(brake)* appuyer sur; **to a. oneself (to)** s'appliquer (à) **2** *vi (be relevant)* s'appliquer (**to** à); **to a. for** *(job)* poser sa candidature à; **to a. to sb (for)** *(ask)* s'adresser à qn (pour) ■ **applied** *adj (maths, linguistics)* appliqué

appoint [əˈpɔɪnt] *vt (person)* nommer (**to a post** à un poste; **to do** pour faire); *(director, minister)* nommer; *(secretary, clerk)* engager; *(time, place)* fixer; **at the appointed time** à l'heure dite ■ **appointment** *n* nomination *f*; *(meeting)* rendez-vous *m inv*; *(post)* situation *f*; **to make an a. with** prendre rendez-vous avec

appraise [əˈpreɪz] *vt* évaluer ■ **appraisal** *n* évaluation *f*

appreciate [əˈpriːʃɪeɪt] **1** *vt (enjoy, value, assess)* apprécier; *(understand)* comprendre; *(be grateful for)* être reconnaissant de **2** *vi (of goods)* prendre

de la valeur ∎ **appreciation** *n* (**a**) *(gratitude)* reconnaissance *f*; *(judgement)* appréciation *f* (**b**) *(rise in value)* augmentation *f* (de la valeur) ∎ **appreciative** *adj (grateful)* reconnaissant (**of** de); *(favourable)* élogieux, -euse; **to be a. of** *(enjoy)* apprécier

apprehend [æprɪ'hend] *vt (seize, arrest)* appréhender

apprehensive [æprɪ'hensɪv] *adj* inquiet, -ète (**about** de *ou* au sujet de); **to be a. of** appréhender

apprentice [ə'prentɪs] *n* apprenti, -e *mf* ∎ **apprenticeship** *n* apprentissage *m*

approach [ə'prəʊtʃ] **1** *n (method)* façon *f* de s'y prendre; *(path, route)* voie *f* d'accès; *(of winter, vehicle)* approche *f* **2** *vt (draw near to)* s'approcher de; *(go up to, tackle)* aborder; **to a. sb about sth** parler à qn de qch; **he's approaching forty** il va sur ses quarante ans **3** *vi (of person, vehicle)* s'approcher; *(of date)* approcher ∎ **approachable** *adj (person)* d'un abord facile

appropriate 1 [ə'prəʊprɪət] *adj (place, clothes, means)* approprié (**to** à); *(remark, time)* opportun; **a. to** *or* **for** qui convient à **2** [ə'prəʊprɪeɪt] *vt (steal)* s'approprier; *(set aside)* affecter (**for** à)

approve [ə'pruːv] *vt* approuver; **to a. of** *(conduct, decision, idea)* approuver; **I don't a. of him** il ne me plaît pas ∎ **approval** *n* approbation *f*; **on a.** *(goods)* à l'essai

approving [ə'pruːvɪŋ] *adj (look)* approbateur, -trice

approximate 1 [ə'prɒksɪmət] *adj* approximatif, -ive **2** [ə'prɒksɪmeɪt] *vi* **to a. to sth** se rapprocher de qch

apricot ['eɪprɪkɒt] *n* abricot *m*

April ['eɪprəl] *n* avril *m*; **A. fool!** poisson d'avril!

apron ['eɪprən] *n (garment)* tablier *m*

apt [æpt] *adj (remark, reply, means)* qui convient; *(word, name)* bien choisi; **to be a. to do sth** avoir tendance à faire qch ∎ **aptly** *adv (described)* justement; *(chosen)* bien

aptitude ['æptɪtjuːd] *n* aptitude *f* (**for**

pour); *(of student)* don *m* (**for** pour)

aquarium [ə'kweərɪəm] *n* aquarium *m*

Aquarius [ə'kweərɪəs] *n (sign)* le Verseau

aquatic [ə'kwætɪk] *adj (plant)* aquatique; *(sport)* nautique

Arab ['ærəb] **1** *adj* arabe **2** *n* Arabe *mf* ∎ **Arabian** *adj* arabe ∎ **Arabic** *adj & n (language)* arabe *(m)*; **A. numerals** chiffres *mpl* arabes

arbitrary ['ɑːbɪtrərɪ] *adj* arbitraire

arbitration [ɑːbɪ'treɪʃən] *n* arbitrage *m*

arc [ɑːk] *n (of circle)* arc *m*

arcade [ɑː'keɪd] *n (for shops) (small)* passage *m* couvert; *(large)* galerie *f* marchande

arch [ɑːtʃ] **1** *n (of bridge)* arche *f*; *(of building)* voûte *f*, arc *m*; *(of foot)* cambrure *f* **2** *vt* **to a. one's back** *(inwards)* se cambrer; *(outwards)* se voûter

arch- [ɑːtʃ] *pref* **a.-enemy** ennemi *m* juré; **a.-rival** grand rival *m*

archaeology [ɑːkɪ'ɒlədʒɪ] *n* archéologie *f* ∎ **archaeologist** *n* archéologue *mf*

archaic [ɑː'keɪɪk] *adj* archaïque

archbishop [ɑːtʃ'bɪʃəp] *n* archevêque *m*

archeologist [ɑːkɪ'ɒlədʒɪst] *n* = **archaeologist**

archeology [ɑːkɪ'ɒlədʒɪ] *n* = **archaeology**

archer ['ɑːtʃə(r)] *n* archer *m*

archetype ['ɑːkɪtaɪp] *n* archétype *m*

architect ['ɑːkɪtekt] *n* architecte *mf* ∎ **architecture** *n* architecture *f*

archives ['ɑːkaɪvz] *npl* archives *fpl*

archway ['ɑːtʃweɪ] *n* voûte *f*

arctic ['ɑːktɪk] **1** *adj* arctique; *(weather)* polaire, glacial **2** *n* **the A.** l'Arctique *m*

ardent ['ɑːdənt] *adj (supporter)* ardent, chaud

ardour ['ɑːdə(r)] *n* ardeur *f*

arduous ['ɑːdjʊəs] *adj* pénible, ardu

are [ɑː(r)] *see* **be**

area ['eərɪə] *n (of country)* région *f*; *(of*

town) quartier *m*; *Mil* zone *f*; *(surface)* superficie *f*; *Fig (of knowledge)* domaine *m*; **kitchen a.** coin-cuisine *m*; **play a.** aire *f* de jeux; *Am* **a. code** *(in phone number)* indicatif *m*

arena [əˈriːnə] *n (for sports) & Fig* arène *f*

aren't [ɑːnt] = **are not**

Argentina [ɑːdʒənˈtiːnə] *n* l'Argentine *f*

arguable [ˈɑːgjʊəbəl] *adj* discutable

argue [ˈɑːgjuː] **1** *vt (matter)* discuter (de); *(position)* défendre; **to a. that...** soutenir que... **2** *vi (quarrel)* se disputer (**with/about** avec/au sujet de); *(reason)* raisonner (**with/about** avec/sur)

argument [ˈɑːgjʊmənt] *n (quarrel)* dispute *f*; *(debate)* discussion *f*; *(point)* argument *m*; **to have an a. with sb** *(quarrel)* se disputer avec qn ▪ **argumentative** *adj (person)* querelleur, -euse

Aries [ˈeəriːz] *n (sign)* le Bélier; **to be A.** être Bélier

arise [əˈraɪz] *(pt* **arose**, *pp* **arisen** [əˈrɪzən]) *vi (of problem, opportunity)* se présenter; *(of cry, objection)* s'élever; *(result)* provenir (**from** de)

aristocracy [ærɪˈstɒkrəsɪ] *n* aristocratie *f* ▪ **aristocrat** [*Br* ˈærɪstəkræt, *Am* əˈrɪstəkræt] *n* aristocrate *mf*

arithmetic [əˈrɪθmətɪk] *n* arithmétique *f*

ark [ɑːk] *n* **Noah's a.** l'arche *f* de Noé

arm¹ [ɑːm] *n* bras *m*; **a. in a.** bras dessus bras dessous; **with open arms** à bras ouverts ▪ **armband** *n* brassard *m* ▪ **armchair** *n* fauteuil *m* ▪ **armpit** *n* aisselle *f*

arm² [ɑːm] *vt (with weapon)* armer (**with** de) ▪ **armaments** *npl* armements *mpl*

armistice [ˈɑːmɪstɪs] *n* armistice *m*

armour [ˈɑːmə(r)] *n (of knight)* armure *f*; *(of tank)* blindage *m* ▪ **armoured, armour-plated** [ˈɑːməpleɪtɪd] *adj (car)* blindé

arms [ɑːmz] *npl (weapons)* armes *fpl*; **the a. race** la course aux armements

army [ˈɑːmɪ] **1** *(pl* -**ies**) *n* armée *f*; **to join the a.** s'engager **2** *adj (uniform)* militaire

A road [ˈeɪrəʊd] *n Br* ≃ route *f* nationale

aroma [əˈrəʊmə] *n* arôme *m* ▪ **aromatherapy** *n* aromathérapie *f* ▪ **aromatic** [ærəʊˈmætɪk] *adj* aromatique

arose [əˈrəʊz] *pp of* **arise**

around [əˈraʊnd] **1** *prep* autour de; *(approximately)* environ; **to travel a. the world** faire le tour du monde **2** *adv* autour; **all a.** tout autour; **a. here** par ici; **to follow sb a.** suivre qn partout; **to rush a.** courir dans tous les sens; **is Jack a.?** est-ce que Jack est dans le coin?; **he's still a.** il est encore là; **there's a lot of flu a.** beaucoup de gens ont la grippe en ce moment

arouse [əˈraʊz] *vt (suspicion, anger, curiosity)* éveiller

arrange [əˈreɪndʒ] *vt* arranger; *(time, meeting)* fixer; **to a. to do sth** s'arranger pour faire qch ▪ **arrangement** *n (layout, agreement, for music)* arrangement *m*; **arrangements** *(preparations)* préparatifs *mpl*; *(plans)* projets *mpl*; **to make arrangements to do sth** prendre des dispositions pour faire qch

arrears [əˈrɪəz] *npl (payment)* arriéré *m*; **to be in a.** avoir du retard dans ses paiements

arrest [əˈrest] **1** *vt (criminal, progress)* arrêter **2** *n (of criminal)* arrestation *f*; **under a.** en état d'arrestation

arrive [əˈraɪv] *vi* arriver; **to a. at** *(conclusion, decision)* arriver à, parvenir à ▪ **arrival** *n* arrivée *f*; **on my a.** à mon arrivée; **new a.** nouveau venu *m*, nouvelle venue *f*; *(baby)* nouveau-né, -e *mf*

arrogant [ˈærəgənt] *adj* arrogant ▪ **arrogance** *n* arrogance *f*

arrow [ˈærəʊ] *n* flèche *f*

arson [ˈɑːsən] *n* incendie *m* criminel

art [ɑːt] *n* art *m*; **faculty of arts, arts faculty** faculté *f* des lettres; **arts degree** ≃ licence *f* ès lettres; **a. exhibition** exposition *f* d'œuvres d'art; **a. gallery** *(museum)* musée *m* d'art;

(shop) galerie *f* d'art; **a. school** école *f* des beaux-arts

artery ['ɑːtərɪ] *(pl* **-ies)** *n* artère *f*

arthritis [ɑːˈθraɪtɪs] *n* arthrite *f*

artichoke ['ɑːtɪtʃəʊk] *n* **(globe) a.** artichaut *m*; **Jerusalem a.** topinambour *m*

article ['ɑːtɪkəl] *n* article *m*; **a. of clothing** vêtement *m*; *Br* **articles** *(of lawyer)* contrat *m* de stage

articulate 1 [ɑːˈtɪkjʊlət] *adj (person)* qui s'exprime clairement; *(speech)* clair **2** [ɑːˈtɪkjʊleɪt] *vt & vi (speak)* articuler ■ **articulation** [-ˈleɪʃən] *n* articulation *f*

artificial [ɑːtɪˈfɪʃəl] *adj* artificiel, -elle

artillery [ɑːˈtɪlərɪ] *n* artillerie *f*

artist ['ɑːtɪst] *n* artiste *mf* ■ **artiste** *n (singer, dancer)* artiste *mf* ■ **artistic** *adj (pattern, treasure)* artistique; *(person)* artiste

artless ['ɑːtləs] *adj* naturel, -elle

arty ['ɑːtɪ] *adj Pej* du genre artiste

AS [æz, *unstressed* əz] **1** *adv* **(a)** *(with manner)* comme; **as promised/planned** comme promis/prévu; **as you like** comme tu veux; **such as** comme, tel que; **as much as I can** (au)tant que je peux; **as it is** *(this being the case)* les choses étant ainsi; **to leave sth as it is** laisser qch comme ça *ou* tel quel; **it's late as it is** il est déjà tard; **as if, as though** comme si; **you look as if** *or* **as though you're tired** tu as l'air fatigué **(b)** *(comparison)* **as tall as you** aussi grand que vous; **as white as a sheet** blanc *(f* blanche) comme un linge; **as much as you** autant que vous; **as much money as** autant d'argent que; **as many people as** autant de gens que; **twice as big as** deux fois plus grand que; **the same as** le même que **2** *conj* **(a)** *(expressing time)* **as always** comme toujours; **as I was leaving, as I left** comme je partais; **as one grows older** à mesure que l'on vieillit; **as he slept** pendant qu'il dormait; **one day as...** un jour que...; **as from, as of** *(time)* à partir de

(b) *(expressing reason)* puisque, comme; **as it's late...** puisqu'il est tard..., comme il est tard...

(c) *(though)* **(as) clever as he is...** si intelligent qu'il soit...

(d) *(concerning)* **as for that** quant à cela

(e) *(+ infinitive)* **so as to...** de manière à...; **so stupid as to...** assez bête pour...

3 *prep* comme; **she works as a cashier** elle est caissière, elle travaille comme caissière; **dressed up as a clown** déguisé en clown; **as a teacher** en tant que professeur

asap [eɪeseɪˈpiː] *(abbr* **as soon as possible)** dès que possible

ascend [əˈsend] **1** *vt (throne)* accéder à; *(stairs, mountain)* gravir **2** *vi* monter ■ **ascent** *n* ascension *f* **(of** de); *(slope)* côte *f*

ascertain [æsəˈteɪn] *vt (discover)* établir; *(check)* s'assurer de; **to a. that...** s'assurer que...

ash [æʃ] *n* **(a)** *(of cigarette, fire)* cendre *f*. **A. Wednesday** mercredi *m* des Cendres **(b)** *(tree)* frêne *m* ■ **ashtray** *n* cendrier *m*

ashamed [əˈʃeɪmd] *adj* **to be/feel a. (of sb/sth)** avoir honte (de qn/qch); **to be a. of oneself** avoir honte; **to make sb a.** faire honte à qn

ashore [əˈʃɔː(r)] *adv* à terre; **to go a.** débarquer

Asia ['eɪʃə, 'eɪʒə] *n* l'Asie *f* ■ **Asian 1** *adj* asiatique; *Br (from Indian subcontinent)* = du sous-continent indien **2** *n* Asiatique *mf*; *Br (from Indian subcontinent)* = personne originaire du sous-continent indien

aside [əˈsaɪd] **1** *adv* de côté; **to take** *or* **draw sb a.** prendre qn à part; **to step a.** s'écarter; *Am* **a. from** en dehors de **2** *n (in play, film)* aparté *m*

ask [ɑːsk] **1** *vt (request, inquire about)* demander; *(invite)* inviter **(to sth** à qch); **to a. sb sth** demander qch à qn; **to a. sb about sb/sth** interroger qn sur qn/qch; **to a. (sb) a question** poser une question (à qn); **to a. sb the**

time/way demander l'heure/son chemin à qn; **to a. sb for sth** demander qch à qn; **to a. sb to do** *(request)* demander à qn de faire; *(invite)* inviter qn à faire; **to a. to leave/etc** demander à partir/*etc*
2 *vi (inquire)* se renseigner (**about** sur); *(request)* demander; **to a. for sb/sth** demander qn/qch; **to a. after** *or* **about sb** demander des nouvelles de qn; **the asking price** le prix demandé

askew [ə'skju:] *adv* de travers

asleep [ə'sli:p] *adj* endormi; *(arm, leg)* engourdi; **to be a.** dormir; **to fall a.** s'endormir

asparagus [ə'spærəgəs] *n (plant)* asperge *f; (food)* asperges *fpl*

aspect ['æspekt] *n* aspect *m; (of house)* orientation *f*

asphyxiate [æs'fɪksɪeɪt] *vt* asphyxier

aspire [ə'spaɪə(r)] *vi* **to a. to** aspirer à ■ **aspiration** [æspɪ'reɪʃən] *n* aspiration *f*

aspirin ['æsprɪn] *n* aspirine *f*

ass [æs] *n* âne *m*

assailant [ə'seɪlənt] *n* agresseur *m*

assassin [ə'sæsɪn] *n* assassin *m* ■ **assassinate** *vt* assassiner ■ **assassination** *n* assassinat *m*

assault [ə'sɔ:lt] **1** *n (military)* assaut *m; (crime)* agression *f* **2** *vt (attack)* agresser; **to be sexually assaulted** être victime d'une agression sexuelle

assemble [ə'sembəl] **1** *vt (objects, ideas)* assembler; *(people)* rassembler; *(machine)* monter **2** *vi* se rassembler ■ **assembly** *n (meeting)* assemblée *f; (of machine)* montage *m*, assemblage *m; (in school)* rassemblement *m (avant les cours);* **a. line** *(in factory)* chaîne *f* de montage

assent [ə'sent] **1** *n* assentiment *m* **2** *vi* consentir (**to** à)

assert [ə'sɜ:t] *vt* affirmer (**that** que); *(rights)* faire valoir; **to a. oneself** s'affirmer ■ **assertion** *n (statement)* affirmation *f, (of rights)* revendication *f* ■ **assertive** *adj (forceful) (tone, person)* affirmatif, -ive; *(authoritarian)* autoritaire

assess [ə'ses] *vt (value, damage)* évaluer; *(situation)* analyser; *(decide amount of)* fixer le montant de; *(person)* juger ■ **assessment** *n (of value, damage)* évaluation *f, (of situation)* analyse *f; (of person)* jugement *m*

asset ['æset] *n (advantage)* atout *m;* **assets** *(of business)* avoir *m*

assign [ə'saɪn] *vt (give)* attribuer; *(day, time)* fixer; *(appoint)* nommer; *(send, move)* affecter (**to** à) ■ **assignment** *n (task)* mission *f; (for student)* devoir *m*

assimilate [ə'sɪmɪleɪt] **1** *vt (absorb)* assimiler **2** *vi (of immigrants)* s'assimiler

assist [ə'sɪst] *vt & vi* aider (**in doing** *or* **to do** à faire) ■ **assistance** *n* aide *f;* **to be of a. to sb** aider qn ■ **assistant 1** *n* assistant, -e *mf; Br (in shop)* vendeur, -euse *mf* **2** *adj* adjoint

associate 1 [ə'səʊʃɪeɪt] *vt* associer (**with sth** à *ou* avec qch; **with sb** à qn) **2** [ə'səʊʃɪeɪt] *vi* **to a. with sb** *(mix socially)* fréquenter qn **3** [ə'səʊʃɪət] *n & adj* associé, -e *(mf)* ■ **association** [-'eɪʃən] *n* association *f*

assorted [ə'sɔ:tɪd] *adj (different)* variés; *(foods)* assortis ■ **assortment** *n* assortiment *m;* **an a. of people** des gens de toutes sortes

assume [ə'sju:m] *vt (a) (suppose)* supposer (**that** que); **let us a. that...** supposons que... (+ *subjunctive)* **(b)** *(take on) (power, control)* prendre; *(responsibility, role)* assumer; *(attitude, name)* adopter ■ **assumed** *adj (feigned)* faux *(f* fausse); **a. name** nom *m* d'emprunt ■ **assumption** [ə'sʌmpʃən] *n (supposition)* supposition *f;* **on the a. that...** en supposant que... (+ *subjunctive)*

assure [ə'ʃʊə(r)] *vt* assurer ■ **assurance** *n (a) (confidence, promise)* assurance *f* **(b)** *Br (insurance)* assurance *f*

asterisk ['æstərɪsk] *n* astérisque *m*

asthma [*Br* 'æsmə, *Am* 'æzmə] *n* asthme *m*

astonish [ə'stɒnɪʃ] *vt* étonner; **to be astonished (at sth)** s'étonner (de qch) ■ **astonishing** *adj* étonnant ■ **astonishment** *n* étonnement *m*

astound [ə'staʊnd] *vt* stupéfier ▪ **as- tounding** *adj* stupéfiant

astray [ə'streɪ] *adv* **to go a.** s'égarer; **to lead a.** détourner du droit chemin

astride [ə'straɪd] **1** *adv* à califourchon **2** *prep* à cheval sur

astrology [ə'strɒlədʒɪ] *n* astrologie *f*

astronaut ['æstrənɔːt] *n* astronaute *mf*

astronomy [ə'strɒnəmɪ] *n* astrono- mie *f* ▪ **astronomer** *n* astronome *mf*

astute [ə'stjuːt] *adj (crafty)* rusé; *(cle- ver)* astucieux, -euse

asylum [ə'saɪləm] *n* asile *m*

AT [æt, *unstressed* ət] *prep* **(a)** à; **at the end** à la fin; **at school** à l'école; **at work** au travail; **at six (o'clock)** à six heures; **at Easter** à Pâques; **to drive at 10 mph** rouler à ≃ 15 km; **to buy/sell at 10 euros a kilo** acheter/vendre (à) 10 euros le kilo **(b)** chez; **at the doctor's** chez le mé- decin; **at home** chez soi, à la maison **(c)** en; **at sea** en mer; **at war** en guerre; **good at maths** fort en maths **(d)** contre; **angry at** fâché contre **(e)** sur; **to shoot at** tirer sur; **at my request** sur ma demande **(f)** de; **to laugh at sb/sth** rire de qn/ qch; **surprised at sth** surpris de qch **(g)** (au)près de; **at the window** près de la fenêtre **(h)** par; **six at a time** six par six **(i)** *(phrases)* **at night** la nuit; **to look at** regarder; **while you're at it** tant que tu y es

ate [eɪt] *pt of* eat

atheist ['eɪθɪɪst] *n* athée *mf*

Athens ['æθənz] *n* Athènes *m ou f*

athlete ['æθliːt] *n* athlète *mf*; **a.'s foot** *(disease)* mycose *f* ▪ **athletic** *adj* athlé- tique ▪ **athletics** *npl Br* athlétisme *m*; *Am* sport *m*

Atlantic [ət'læntɪk] **1** *adj (coast, ocean)* atlantique **2** *n* **the A.** l'Atlan- tique *m*

atlas ['ætləs] *n* atlas *m*

atmosphere ['ætməsfɪə(r)] *n* atmos- phère *f* ▪ **atmospheric** [-'ferɪk] *adj* at- mosphérique

atom ['ætəm] *n* atome *m*; **a. bomb** bombe *f* atomique ▪ **atomic** *adj* ato- mique

atrocious [ə'trəʊʃəs] *adj* atroce ▪ **atrocity** *n (cruel action)* atrocité *f*

attach [ə'tætʃ] *vt* attacher **(to** à); *(docu- ment)* joindre **(to** à); **attached to sb** *(fond of)* attaché à qn ▪ **attachment** *n* **(a)** *(affection)* attachement *m* **(to sb** à qn) **(b)** *(tool)* accessoire *m* **(c)** *(to e- mail)* fichier *m* joint

attack [ə'tæk] **1** *n (military)* attaque *f* **(on** contre); *(on someone's life)* attentat *m*; *(of illness)* crise *f*; *(of fever)* accès *m* **2** *vt* attaquer; *(problem, plan)* s'attaquer à **3** *vi* attaquer ▪ **attacker** *n* agresseur *m*

attain [ə'teɪn] *vt (aim)* atteindre; *(goal, ambition)* réaliser; *(rank)* parvenir à

attempt [ə'tempt] **1** *n* tentative *f*; **to make an a. to do** tenter de faire **2** *vt* tenter; *(task)* entreprendre; **to a. to do** tenter de faire; **attempted murder** tentative *f* d'assassinat

attend [ə'tend] **1** *vt (meeting)* assister à; *(course)* suivre; *(school, church)* aller à **2** *vi* assister; **to a. to** *(take care of)* s'occuper de

attendance [ə'tendəns] *n* présence *f* **(at** à); *(people)* assistance *f*; **(school) a.** scolarité *f*; **in a.** de service ▪ **atten- dant** *n* employé, -e *mf*; *(in service sta- tion)* pompiste *mf*; *Br (in museum)* gardien, -enne *mf*

attention [ə'tenʃən] *n* attention *f*; **to pay a.** faire *ou* prêter attention **(to** à); **for the a. of** à l'attention de ▪ **atten- tive** *adj (heedful)* attentif, -ive **(to** à); *(thoughtful)* attentionné **(to** pour)

attest [ə'test] **1** *vt (certify, confirm)* confirmer **2** *vi* **to a. to** témoigner de

attic ['ætɪk] *n* grenier *m*

attitude ['ætɪtjuːd] *n* attitude *f*

attorney [ə'tɜːnɪ] *(pl* -eys) *n Am (law- yer)* avocat *m*

attract [ə'trækt] *vt* attirer ▪ **attraction** *n (charm, appeal)* attrait *m*; *(place, per- son)* attraction *f*; *(between people)* atti- rance *f*; *Phys* attraction *f* terrestre

attractive [ə'træktɪv] *adj (house,*

room, person, car) beau (*f* belle); *(price, offer)* intéressant; *(landscape)* attrayant

attribute 1 ['ætrɪbjuːt] *n (quality)* attribut *m* **2** [ə'trɪbjuːt] *vt (ascribe)* attribuer **(to** à)

aubergine ['əʊbəʒiːn] *n Br* aubergine *f*

auburn ['ɔːbən] *adj (hair)* auburn *inv*

auction ['ɔːkʃən] **1** *n* vente *f* aux enchères **2** *vt* **to a. (off)** vendre aux enchères ▪ **auctioneer** *n* commissaire-priseur *m*

audacity [ɔː'dæsɪtɪ] *n* audace *f*

audible ['ɔːdɪbəl] *adj (sound, words)* audible

audience ['ɔːdɪəns] *n* **(a)** *(of speaker, musician, actor)* public *m*; *(of radio broadcast)* auditeurs *mpl*; **TV a.** téléspectateurs *mpl* **(b)** *(interview)* audience *f* **(with sb** avec qn)

audio ['ɔːdɪəʊ] *adj (cassette, system)* audio *inv*; **a. tape** cassette *f* audio ▪ **audiotypist** *n* audiotypiste *mf* ▪ **audiovisual** *adj* audiovisuel, -elle

audit ['ɔːdɪt] **1** *n* audit *m* **2** *vt (accounts)* vérifier

audition [ɔː'dɪʃən] **1** *n* audition *f* **2** *vt & vi* auditionner

auditorium [ɔːdɪ'tɔːrɪəm] *n (of theatre, concert hall)* salle *f*

August ['ɔːgəst] *n* août *m*

aunt [ɑːnt] *n* tante *f* ▪ **auntie, aunty** (*pl* -ies) *n Fam* tata *f*

au pair [əʊ'peə(r)] *n* **a. (girl)** jeune fille *f* au pair

aura ['ɔːrə] *n (of place)* atmosphère *f*; *(of person)* aura *f*

austere [ɔː'stɪə(r)] *adj* austère ▪ **austerity** *n* austérité *f*

Australia [ɒ'streɪlɪə] *n* l'Australie *f* ▪ **Australian 1** *adj* australien, -enne **2** *n* Australien, -enne *mf*

Austria ['ɒstrɪə] *n* l'Autriche *f* ▪ **Austrian 1** *adj* autrichien, -enne **2** *n* Autrichien, -enne *mf*

authentic [ɔː'θentɪk] *adj* authentique ▪ **authenticate** *vt* authentifier

author ['ɔːθə(r)] *n* auteur *m*

authority [ɔː'θɒrɪtɪ] (*pl* -ies) *n* autorité *f*; *(permission)* autorisation *f* **(to do** de faire); **to be in a.** *(in charge)* être responsable ▪ **authoritarian** *adj & n* autoritaire *(mf)* ▪ **authoritative** *adj (report, book)* qui fait autorité; *(tone, person)* autoritaire

authorize ['ɔːθəraɪz] *vt* autoriser **(to do** à faire) ▪ **authorization** [-'zeɪʃən] *n* autorisation *f* **(to do** de faire)

autistic [ɔː'tɪstɪk] *adj* autiste

auto ['ɔːtəʊ] (*pl* -os) *n Am* auto *f*

autobiography [ɔːtəʊbaɪ'ɒgrəfɪ] (*pl* -ies) *n* autobiographie *f*

autograph ['ɔːtəgrɑːf] **1** *n* autographe *m*; **a. book** album *m* d'autographes **2** *vt* dédicacer **(for sb** à qn)

automatic [ɔːtə'mætɪk] *adj* automatique

automobile ['ɔːtəməbiːl] *n Am* automobile *f*

autonomous [ɔː'tɒnəməs] *adj* autonome ▪ **autonomy** *n* autonomie *f*

autopsy ['ɔːtɒpsɪ] (*pl* -ies) *n* autopsie *f*

autumn ['ɔːtəm] *n* automne *m*; **in a.** en automne

auxiliary [ɔːg'zɪljərɪ] (*pl* -ies) *adj & n* auxiliaire *(mf)*; **a. (verb)** (verbe *m*) auxiliaire *m*

avail [ə'veɪl] **1** *n* **to no a.** en vain **2** *vt* **to a. oneself of** profiter de ▪ **availability** *n (of object)* disponibilité *f*; *(of education)* accessibilité *f*

available [ə'veɪləbəl] *adj* disponible; **tickets are still a.** il reste des tickets; **this model is a. in black or green** ce modèle existe en noir et en vert

avalanche ['ævəlɑːnʃ] *n* avalanche *f*

Ave *(abbr* Avenue) av.

avenge [ə'vendʒ] *vt* venger; **to a. oneself (on)** se venger (de)

avenue ['ævənjuː] *n* avenue *f*; *Fig (possibility)* possibilité *f*

average ['ævərɪdʒ] **1** *n* moyenne *f*; **on a.** en moyenne; **above/below a.** au-dessus/au-dessous de la moyenne **2** *adj* moyen, -enne **3** *vt (do)* faire en moyenne; *(reach)* atteindre la moyenne de; *(figures)* faire la moyenne de

averse [ə'vɜːs] *adj* **to be a. to doing** répugner à faire

aversion [ə'vɜːʃən] *n (dislike)* aversion *f*; **to have an a. to sth/to doing sth** avoir de la répugnance pour qch/à faire qch

avert [ə'vɜːt] *vt (prevent)* éviter; **to a. one's eyes (from)** *(turn away)* détourner les yeux (de)

aviation [eɪvɪ'eɪʃən] *n* aviation *f*

avid ['ævɪd] *adj* avide (**for** de)

avocado [ævə'kɑːdəʊ] *(pl* **-os**) *n* avocat *m*

avoid [ə'vɔɪd] *vt* éviter; **to a. doing** éviter de faire ▪ **avoidable** *adj* évitable

await [ə'weɪt] *vt* attendre

awake [ə'weɪk] **1** *adj* réveillé, éveillé; **he's still a.** il ne dort pas encore **2** *(pt* **awoke,** *pp* **awoken)** *vi* se réveiller **3** *vt* réveiller ▪ **awaken 1** *vi* se réveiller **2** *vt* réveiller

award [ə'wɔːd] **1** *n (prize)* prix *m*, récompense *f*; *(scholarship)* bourse *f* **2** *vt (money)* attribuer; *(prize)* décerner; **to a. damages** *(of judge)* accorder des dommages-intérêts

aware [ə'weə(r)] *adj* **to be a. of** *(conscious)* être conscient de; *(informed)* être au courant de; *(realize)* se rendre compte de; **to become a. of/that** se rendre compte de/que ▪ **awareness** *n* conscience *f*

AWAY [ə'weɪ] *adv* (a) *(distant)* loin; **5 km a.** à 5 km (de distance)

(b) *(in time)* **ten days a.** dans dix jours

(c) *(absent, gone)* absent; **to drive a.** partir (en voiture); **to fade/melt a.** disparaître/fondre complètement

(d) *(to one side)* **to look** *or* **turn a.** détourner les yeux

(e) *(continuously)* **to work/talk a.** travailler/parler sans arrêt

(f) *Br* **to play a.** *(of team)* jouer à l'extérieur

awe [ɔː] *n* crainte *f* (mêlée de respect); **to be in a. of sb** éprouver pour qn une crainte mêlée de respect ▪ **awesome** *adj (impressive)* impressionnant; *(frightening)* effrayant; *Am Fam (excellent)* super *inv*

awful ['ɔːfəl] *adj* affreux, -euse; *(terrifying)* effroyable; *Fam* **an a. lot (of)** énormément (de); **I feel a. (about it)** j'ai vraiment honte ▪ **awfully** *adv (suffer)* affreusement; *(very) (good, pretty)* extrêmement; *(bad, late)* affreusement

awkward ['ɔːkwəd] *adj* (a) *(clumsy) (person, gesture)* maladroit (b) *(difficult)* difficile; *(cumbersome)* gênant; *(tool)* peu commode; *(time)* mal choisi; *(silence)* gêné ▪ **awkwardly** *adv (walk)* maladroitement; *(speak)* d'un ton gêné; *(placed, situated)* à un endroit peu pratique

awning ['ɔːnɪŋ] *n (of tent)* auvent *m*; *(over shop, window)* store *m*; *(canvas or glass canopy)* marquise *f*

awoke [ə'wəʊk] *pt of* **awake**

awoken [ə'wəʊkən] *pp of* **awake**

axe [æks] *(Am* **ax**) **1** *n* hache *f*; *Fig (reduction)* coupe *f* sombre; **to get the a.** *(of project)* être abandonné; *(of worker)* être mis à la porte; *Fig* **to have an a. to grind** agir dans un but intéressé **2** *vt (costs)* réduire; *(job)* supprimer; *(project)* abandonner

axis ['æksɪs] *(pl* **axes** ['æksiːz]) *n* axe *m*

axle ['æksəl] *n* essieu *m*

Bb

B, b [biː] *n* B, b *m inv*; **2B** *(number)* 2 ter

BA [biːˈeɪ] *n (abbr* Bachelor of Arts) **to have a BA in history** ≃ avoir une licence en histoire

babble [ˈbæbəl] **1** *vi (mumble)* bredouiller; *(of baby, stream)* gazouiller **2** *n inv (of voices)* rumeur *f*; *(of baby, stream)* gazouillis *m*

baboon [bəˈbuːn] *n* babouin *m*

baby [ˈbeɪbɪ] *(pl* -ies) *n* bébé *m*; **b. boy** petit garçon *m*; **b. girl** petite fille *f*; **b. tiger**/*etc* bébé-tigre/*etc m*; **b. clothes/ toys**/*etc* vêtements *mpl*/jouets *mpl*/*etc* de bébé; *Am* **b. carriage** landau *m*; **b. sling** kangourou *m*, porte-bébé *m* ■ **baby-sit** *(pt & pp* -sat, *pres p* -sitting) *vi* faire du baby-sitting ■ **baby-sitter** *n* baby-sitter *mf*

bachelor [ˈbætʃələ(r)] *n* (a) *(not married)* célibataire *m* (b) *Univ* **B. of Arts/ of Science** *(person)* ≃ licencié, -e *mf* ès lettres/ès sciences; *(qualification)* ≃ licence *f* de lettres/de sciences

back [bæk] **1** *n (of person, animal, hand)* dos *m*; *(of chair)* dossier *m*; *(of house, vehicle, train, head)* arrière *m*; *(of room)* fond *m*; *(of page)* verso *m*; *(of fabric)* envers *m*; *(in sport)* arrière *m*; **at the b. of the book** à la fin du livre; **at the b. of the car** à l'arrière de la voiture; **at the b. of one's mind** derrière la tête; **b. to front** devant derrière, à l'envers; *Fam* **to get off sb's b.** ficher la paix à qn; *Fam* **to get sb's b. up** braquer qn

2 *adj (wheel, seat)* arrière *inv*; **b. door** porte *f* de derrière; **b. room** pièce *f* du fond; **b. street** rue *f* écartée; **b. tooth** molaire *f*

3 *adv (behind)* en arrière; **far b., a long way b.** loin derrière; **a month b.** il y a un mois; **to go b. and forth** aller et venir; **to come b.** revenir; **he's b.** il est de retour, il est revenu; **the journey there and b.** le voyage aller et retour

4 *vt (with money)* financer; *(horse)* parier sur; *(vehicle)* faire reculer; **to be backed with** *(of curtain, picture)* être renforcé de; **to b. sb (up)** *(support)* appuyer qn; *Comptr* **to b. up** sauvegarder

5 *vi (move backwards)* reculer; **to b. down** faire marche arrière; **to b. out** *(withdraw)* se retirer; *(of vehicle)* sortir en marche arrière; **to b. on to** *(of house)* donner par derrière sur; **to b. up** *(of vehicle)* faire marche arrière ■ **backache** *n* mal *m* de dos ■ **backbencher** *n Br Pol* député *m* de base ■ **backbone** *n* colonne *f* vertébrale; *(of fish)* grande arête *f*; *Fig (main support)* pivot *m* ■ **backpack** *n* sac *m* à dos ■ **backside** *n Fam (buttocks)* derrière *m* ■ **backstage** *adv* dans les coulisses ■ **backstroke** *n (in swimming)* dos *m* crawlé ■ **backup** *n* appui *m*; *Am (tailback)* embouteillage *m*; *Comptr* sauvegarde *f* ■ **backyard** *n Br (enclosed area)* arrière-cour *f*; *Am (garden)* jardin *m* de derrière

backer [ˈbækə(r)] *n (supporter)* partisan *m*; *(on horses)* parieur, -euse *mf*; *(financial)* commanditaire *m*

backfire [bækˈfaɪə(r)] *vi* (a) *(of vehicle)* pétarader (b) *Fig* **to b. on sb** *(of plot)* se retourner contre qn

backgammon [ˈbækgæmən] *n* backgammon *m*

background [ˈbækgraʊnd] *n* fond *m*, arrière-plan *m*; *(educational)* formation *f*; *(professional)* expérience *f*; *(environment)* milieu *m*; *(circumstances)* contexte *m*; **b. music/noise** musique *f*/bruit *m* de fond

backlash [ˈbæklæʃ] *n* retour *m* de bâton

backlog ['bæklɒg] *n* a b. of work du travail en retard

backward ['bækwəd] **1** *adj (person, country)* arriéré; *(glance)* en arrière **2** *adv* = **backwards** ▪ **backwards** *adv* en arrière; *(walk)* à reculons; *(fall)* à la renverse; **to go** *or* **move b.** reculer

bacon ['beɪkən] *n* bacon *m*; **b. and eggs** œufs *mpl* au bacon

bacteria [bæk'tɪərɪə] *npl* bactéries *fpl*

bad [bæd] (**worse, worst**) *adj* mauvais; *(wicked)* méchant; *(sad)* triste; *(accident, wound)* grave; *(tooth)* carié; *(arm, leg)* malade; *(pain)* violent; **b. language** gros mots *mpl*; **b. cheque** chèque *m* sans provision; **to feel b.** *(ill)* se sentir mal; **to be b. at maths** être mauvais en maths; **things are b.** ça va mal; **it's not b.** ce n'est pas mal; **to go b.** *(of fruit, meat)* se gâter; *(of milk)* tourner; **too b.!** tant pis! ▪ **bad-mannered** *adj* mal élevé ▪ **bad-tempered** *adj* grincheux, -euse

bade [bæd] *pt of* bid

badge [bædʒ] *n (of plastic, bearing slogan or joke)* badge *m*; *(of metal, bearing logo)* pin's *m*; *(of postman, policeman)* plaque *f*; *(on school uniform)* insigne *m*

badger ['bædʒə(r)] **1** *n (animal)* blaireau *m* **2** *vt* importuner

badly ['bædlɪ] *adv* mal; *(hurt)* grièvement; **to be b. mistaken** se tromper lourdement; **b. off** dans la gêne; **to want sth b.** avoir grande envie de qch

badminton ['bædmɪntən] *n* badminton *m*

baffle ['bæfəl] *vt (person)* laisser perplexe

bag [bæg] *n* sac *m*; **bags** *(luggage)* bagages *mpl*; *(under eyes)* poches *fpl*; *Fam Pej* **an old b.** une vieille taupe; *Fam* **in the b.** dans la poche

baggage ['bægɪdʒ] *n* bagages *mpl*; *Am* **b. car** fourgon *m*; **b. handler** *(in airport)* bagagiste *mf*; *Am* **b. room** consigne *f*

baggy ['bægɪ] (**-ier, -iest**) *adj (garment) (out of shape)* déformé; *(by design)* large

bagpipes ['bægpaɪps] *npl* cornemuse *f*

Bahamas [bə'hɑːməz] *npl* **the B.** les Bahamas *fpl*

bail [beɪl] **1** *n Law* caution *f*; **on b.** sous caution; **to grant sb b.** libérer qn sous caution **2** *vt* **to b. sb out** *Law* se porter garant de qn; *Fig* tirer qn d'affaire **3** *vi* **to b. out** *(from aircraft)* s'éjecter

bailiff ['beɪlɪf] *n (law officer)* huissier *m*; *Br (of landowner)* régisseur *m*

bait [beɪt] **1** *n* appât *m* **2** *vt* (a) *(fishing hook)* amorcer (b) *(annoy)* tourmenter

bake [beɪk] **1** *vt (bread)* cuire au four **2** *vi (of person) (make cakes)* faire de la pâtisserie; *(make bread)* faire du pain; *(of food)* cuire (au four); *Fam* **it's baking (hot)** on crève de chaleur ▪ **baked** *adj (potatoes, apples)* au four; **b. beans** haricots *mpl* blancs à la tomate

baker ['beɪkə(r)] *n* boulanger, -ère *mf* ▪ **bakery** *n* boulangerie *f*

baking ['beɪkɪŋ] *n* cuisson *f*; **b. powder** levure *f* chimique; **b. tin** moule *m* à pâtisserie

balaclava [bælə'klɑːvə] *n Br* passe-montagne *m*

balance ['bæləns] **1** *n (equilibrium)* équilibre *m*; *(of account)* solde *m*; *(remainder)* reste *m*; *(in accounting)* bilan *m*; *(for weighing)* balance *f*; **to lose one's b.** perdre l'équilibre ou **to strike a b.** trouver le juste milieu; **on b.** à tout prendre; **b. of payments** balance *f* des paiements; **b. sheet** bilan *m*

2 *vt* maintenir en équilibre **(on** sur); *(budget, account)* équilibrer; *(compare)* mettre en balance; **to b. (out)** *(compensate for)* compenser

3 *vi (of person)* se tenir en équilibre; *(of accounts)* être en équilibre, s'équilibrer; **to b. (out)** *(even out)* s'équilibrer

balcony ['bælkənɪ] *(pl* **-ies)** *n* balcon *m*

bald [bɔːld] (**-er, -est**) *adj* chauve; *(statement)* brutal; *(tyre)* lisse; **b. patch** *or* **spot** tonsure *f*

balk [bɔːk] *vi* reculer **(at** devant)

Balkans ['bɔːlkənz] *npl* **the B.** les Balkans *fpl*

ball[1] [bɔːl] *n* balle *f*; *(inflated, for football, rugby)* ballon *m*; *(for snooker, pool)* bille *f*; *(of string, wool)* pelote *f*; *(sphere)*

boule f; (of meat, fish) boulette f; Fam **to be on the b.** (alert) avoir de la présence d'esprit; (knowledgeable) connaître son affaire; **b. bearing** roulement m à billes; Am **b. game** match m de base-ball; Fig **it's a whole new b. game** c'est une tout autre affaire ∎ **ballpark** n stade m de base-ball

ball² [bɔːl] n (dance) bal m (pl bals)

ballad ['bæləd] n (poem) ballade f; (song) romance f

ballast ['bæləst] **1** n lest m **2** vt lester

ballet ['bæleɪ] n ballet m ∎ **ballerina** n ballerine f

balloon [bə'luːn] n (toy, airship) ballon m; (in cartoon) bulle f

ballot ['bælət] **1** n (voting) scrutin m; **b. paper** bulletin m de vote; **b. box** urne f **2** vt (members) consulter (par un scrutin)

ballpoint (pen) ['bɔːlpɔɪnt(pen)] n stylo m à bille

ballroom ['bɔːlruːm] n salle f de danse

Baltic ['bɔːltɪk] n **the B.** la Baltique

bamboo [bæm'buː] n bambou m; **b. shoots** pousses fpl de bambou

ban [bæn] **1** n interdiction f; **to impose a b. on sth** interdire qch **2** (pt & pp -nn-) vt interdire; **to b. sb from doing sth** interdire à qn de faire qch; **to b. sb from** (club) exclure qn de

banal [bə'næl] adj banal (mpl -als)

banana [bə'nɑːnə] n banane f

band [bænd] **1** n (a) (strip) bande f; (of hat) ruban m; **rubber** or **elastic b.** élastique m (b) (group of people) bande f; (of musicians) (petit) orchestre m; (pop group) groupe m **2** vi **to b. together** se (re)grouper

bandage ['bændɪdʒ] **1** n (strip) bande f; (dressing) bandage m **2** vt **to b. (up)** (arm, leg) bander; (wound) mettre un bandage sur; **to b. sb's arm** bander le bras à qn

Band-aid® ['bændeɪd] n Am pansement m adhésif

B and B, B & B [biːənd'biː] n (abbr **bed and breakfast**) (service) ≃ chambre f avec petit déjeuner; **to stay at a B and B** ≃ prendre une chambre d'hôte

bandit ['bændɪt] n bandit m

bandwagon ['bændwægən] n Fig **to jump on the b.** prendre le train en marche

bandy¹ ['bændɪ] (-ier, -iest) adj **to have b. legs** avoir les jambes arquées

bandy² ['bændɪ] (pt & pp -ied) vt **to b. about** (story, rumour) faire circuler

bang¹ [bæŋ] **1** n (blow, noise) coup m (violent); (of gun) détonation f; (of door) claquement m

2 vt (hit) cogner, frapper; (door) (faire) claquer; **to b. one's head** se cogner la tête

3 vi cogner, frapper; (of door) claquer; **to b. into sb/sth** heurter qn/qch

4 exclam vlan!, pan!; **to go b.** éclater

bang² [bæŋ] adv Br Fam (exactly) exactement; **b. in the middle** en plein milieu; **b. on six** à six heures tapantes

banger ['bæŋə(r)] n Br (a) Fam (sausage) saucisse f (b) (firecracker) pétard m (c) Fam **old b.** (car) vieille guimbarde f

bangle ['bæŋgəl] n bracelet m

bangs [bæŋz] npl Am (of hair) frange f

banish ['bænɪʃ] vt bannir

banister ['bænɪstə(r)] n banister(s) rampe f (d'escalier)

banjo ['bændʒəʊ] (pl -os or -oes) n banjo m

bank¹ [bæŋk] **1** n (of river) bord m, rive f; (raised) berge f; (of earth) talus m; (of sand) banc m; **the Left B.** (in Paris) la Rive gauche **2** vt **to b. (up)** (earth) amonceler; (fire) couvrir **3** vi (of aircraft) virer

bank² [bæŋk] **1** n (for money) banque f; **b. account** compte m en banque; **b. card** carte f d'identité bancaire; Br **b. holiday** jour m férié; Br **b. note** billet m de banque **2** vt (money) mettre à la banque **3** vi avoir un compte en banque (**with** à) ∎ **banker** n banquier, -ère mf; Br **b.'s card** carte f d'identité bancaire ∎ **banking 1** adj (transaction) bancaire **2** n (activity, profession) la banque

bank³ [bæŋk] vi **to b. on sb/sth** (rely on) compter sur qn/qch

bankrupt ['bæŋkrʌpt] **1** adj **to go b.**

faire faillite **2** *vt* mettre en faillite

banner ['bænə(r)] *n* banderole *f*; *(military flag)* & *Fig* bannière *f*

banns [bænz] *npl* bans *mpl*; **to put up the b.** publier les bans

banquet ['bæŋkwɪt] *n* banquet *m*

banter ['bæntə(r)] **1** *n* plaisanteries *fpl* **2** *vi* plaisanter

baptism ['bæptɪzəm] *n* baptême *m* ▪ **Baptist** *n* & *adj* baptiste *(mf)*

baptize [bæp'taɪz] *vt* baptiser

bar [bɑ:(r)] **1** *n* **(a)** *(of metal)* barre *f*; *(of gold)* lingot *m*; *(of chocolate)* tablette *f*; *(on window)* barreau *m*; **b. of soap** savonnette *f*; **behind bars** *(criminal)* sous les verrous; *Law* **the B.** le barreau; **b. code** *(on product)* code-barres *m* **(b)** *(pub)* bar *m*; *(counter)* bar *m*, comptoir *m* **(c)** *(group of musical notes)* mesure *f* **2** *(pt & pp -rr-) vt* **(a)** **to b. sb's way** barrer le passage à qn; **barred window** fenêtre *f* munie de barreaux **(b)** *(prohibit)* interdire (**sb from doing** à qn de faire); *(exclude)* exclure (**from** à) **3** *prep (except)* sauf; **b. none** sans exception ▪ **barmaid** *n Br* serveuse *f* (de bar) ▪ **barman** *(pl* -men*) n Br* barman *m* ▪ **bartender** *n Am* barman *m*

Barbados [bɑ:'beɪdɒs] *n* la Barbade

barbaric [bɑ:'bærɪk] *adj* barbare

barbecue ['bɑ:bɪkju:] **1** *n* barbecue *m* **2** *vt* cuire au barbecue

barbed wire [bɑ:bd'waɪə(r)] *n* fil *m* de fer barbelé; *(fence)* barbelés *mpl*

barber ['bɑ:bə(r)] *n* coiffeur *m* pour hommes

bare [beə(r)] **1** (-er, -est) *adj* nu; *(tree, hill)* dénudé; *(room, cupboard)* vide; *(mere)* simple; **the b. necessities** le strict nécessaire; **with his b. hands** à mains nues **2** *vt (arm, wire)* dénuder ▪ **barefoot 1** *adv* nu-pieds **2** *adj* aux pieds nus

barely ['beəlɪ] *adv (scarcely)* à peine; **b. enough** tout juste assez

bargain ['bɑ:gɪn] **1** *n (deal)* marché *m*, affaire *f*; **a b.** *(good buy)* une occasion, une bonne affaire; **to make a b. (with sb)** faire un marché (avec qn); **into the**

b. *(in addition)* par-dessus le marché; **b. price** prix *m* exceptionnel **2** *vi (negotiate)* négocier; *(haggle)* marchander; **to b. for** *or* **on sth** *(expect)* s'attendre à qch

barge [bɑ:dʒ] **1** *n* péniche *f* **2** *vi* **to b. in** *(enter room)* faire irruption; *(interrupt)* interrompre

bark¹ [bɑ:k] *n (of tree)* écorce *f*

bark² [bɑ:k] **1** *n* aboiement *m* **2** *vi* aboyer

barley ['bɑ:lɪ] *n* orge *f*; **b. sugar** sucre *m* d'orge

barn [bɑ:n] *n (for crops)* grange *f*; *(for horses)* écurie *f*; *(for cattle)* étable *f* ▪ **barnyard** *n* cour *f* de ferme

barometer [bə'rɒmɪtə(r)] *n* baromètre *m*

baron ['bærən] *n* baron *m*; *Fig (industrialist)* magnat *m*; **press/oil b.** magnat de la presse/du pétrole ▪ **baroness** *n* baronne *f*

barracks ['bærəks] *npl* caserne *f*

barrage [*Br* 'bærɑ:ʒ, *Am* bə'rɑ:ʒ] *n (across river)* barrage *m*; *Fig* **a b. of questions** un feu roulant de questions

barrel ['bærəl] *n* **(a)** *(cask)* tonneau *m*; *(of oil)* baril *m* **(b)** *(of gun)* canon *m* **(c)** **b. organ** orgue *m* de Barbarie

barren ['bærən] *adj (land, woman, ideas)* stérile; *(style)* aride

barricade ['bærɪkeɪd] **1** *n* barricade *f* **2** *vt* barricader; **to b. oneself (in)** se barricader (dans)

barrier ['bærɪə(r)] *n also Fig* barrière *f*; *Br* **(ticket) b.** *(of station)* portillon *m*; **sound b.** mur *m* du son

barring ['bɑ:rɪŋ] *prep* sauf

barrister ['bærɪstə(r)] *n Br* ≃ avocat *m*

barrow ['bærəʊ] *n (wheelbarrow)* brouette *f*; *(cart)* charrette *f* ou voiture *f* à bras

barter ['bɑ:tə(r)] **1** *n* troc *m* **2** *vt* troquer (**for** contre)

base [beɪs] **1** *n* **(a)** *(bottom, main ingredient)* base *f*; *(of tree, lamp)* pied *m*; **b. rate** *(of bank)* taux *m* de base **(b)** *(military)* base *f* **2** *adj (dishonourable)* bas *(f* basse) **3** *vt* baser, fonder (**on** sur);

based in London (person, company) basé à Londres

baseball ['beɪsbɔːl] n base-ball m

basement ['beɪsmənt] n sous-sol m

bash [bæʃ] **1** n (bang) coup m; Br Fam **to have a b.** (try) essayer un coup **2** vt. (hit) cogner; **to b. (about)** (ill-treat) malmener; **to b. in** or **down** (door, fence) défoncer

bashful ['bæʃfəl] adj timide

basic ['beɪsɪk] **1** adj essentiel, -elle, de base; (elementary) élémentaire; (pay, food) de base; (room, house, meal) tout simple **2** n **the basics** l'essentiel m ■ **basically** adv (on the whole) en gros; (in fact) en fait; (fundamentally) au fond

basil [Br 'bæzəl, Am 'beɪzəl] n basilic m

basin [Br 'beɪsən, Am 'beɪzən] n **(a)** (made of plastic) bassine f; (for soup, food) (grand) bol m; (portable washbasin) cuvette f; (sink) lavabo m **(b)** (of river) bassin m

basis ['beɪsɪs] (pl -ses [-siːz]) n (for discussion) base f; (for opinion, accusation) fondement m; (of agreement) bases fpl; **on the b. of** d'après; **on a weekly b.** chaque semaine

basket ['bɑːskɪt] n panier m; (for bread, laundry, litter) corbeille f ■ **basketball** n basket(-ball) m

Basque [bæsk] **1** adj basque **2** n Basque mf

bass¹ [beɪs] **1** n Mus basse f **2** adj (note, voice, instrument) bas (f basse)

bass² [bæs] n (sea fish) bar m; (freshwater fish) perche f

bassoon [bə'suːn] n basson m

bat¹ [bæt] n (animal) chauve-souris f

bat² [bæt] **1** n (for cricket, baseball) batte f; (for table-tennis) raquette f; **off my own b.** de ma propre initiative **2** (pt & pp -tt-) vt **(a)** (ball) frapper **(b) she didn't b. an eyelid** elle n'a pas sourcillé

batch [bætʃ] n (of people) groupe m; (of letters) paquet m; (of books) lot m; (of loaves) fournée f; (of papers) liasse f

bath [bɑːθ] **1** (pl **baths** [bɑːðz]) n bain m; (tub) baignoire f; **to have** or **take a b.** prendre un bain; **b. towel** drap m de bain; Br **swimming baths** piscine f **2** vt

Br baigner ■ **bathrobe** n Br peignoir m de bain; Am robe f de chambre ■ **bathroom** n salle f de bain(s); Am (toilet) toilettes fpl ■ **bathtub** n baignoire f

bathe [beɪð] **1** vt baigner; (wound) laver **2** vi (swim) se baigner; Am (have bath) prendre un bain ■ **bathing** n baignades fpl; **b. suit**, Br **b. costume** maillot m de bain

baton [Br 'bætən, Am bə'tɒn] n (of conductor) baguette f; (of policeman) matraque f; (of soldier, drum majorette) bâton m; (in relay race) témoin m

battalion [bə'tæljən] n bataillon m

batter ['bætə(r)] **1** n pâte f à frire **2** vt (strike) cogner sur; (person) frapper; (town) pilonner; **to b. down** (door) défoncer ■ **battered** adj (car, hat) cabossé; (house) délabré; (face) meurtri; **b. child** enfant m martyr; **b. wife** femme f battue

battery ['bætərɪ] (pl -ies) n (in vehicle, of guns, for hens) batterie f; (in radio, appliance) pile f; **b. hen** poule f de batterie

battle ['bætəl] **1** n bataille f; (struggle) lutte f; Fam **that's half the b.** la partie est à moitié gagnée **2** vi se battre, lutter ■ **battlefield** n champ m de bataille ■ **battleship** n cuirassé m

bawl [bɔːl] vt & vi **to b. (out)** brailler; Fam **to b. sb out** engueuler qn

bay¹ [beɪ] **1** n **(a)** (part of coastline) baie f **(b)** (in room) renfoncement m; **b. window** bow-window m, oriel m **(c)** Br (for loading) aire f de chargement **(d)** **at b.** (animal, criminal) aux abois; **to keep** or **hold at b.** (enemy, wild dog) tenir en respect; (disease) juguler **2** vi aboyer **3** adj (horse) bai

bay² [beɪ] n (tree) laurier m; **b. leaf** feuille f de laurier

bayonet ['beɪənɪt] n baïonnette f

bazaar [bə'zɑː(r)] n (market, shop) bazar m; (charity sale) vente f de charité

BC [biː'siː] (abbr before Christ) av. J.-C.

BE [biː] (present tense **am, are, is**; past tense **was, were**; pp **been**; pres p **being**) **1** vi **(a)** (gen) être; **it is green/ small/etc** c'est vert/petit/etc; **he's a**

doctor il est médecin; **he's an Eng-lishman** c'est un Anglais; **it's him** c'est lui; **it's them** ce sont eux; **it's three (o'clock)** il est trois heures; **it's the sixth of May,** *Am* it's May sixth nous sommes le six mai; **to be hot/right/lucky** avoir chaud/raison/de la chance; **my feet are cold** j'ai froid aux pieds

(b) *(with age, height)* avoir; **to be twenty** *(age)* avoir vingt ans; **to be 2 metres high** avoir 2 m de haut; **to be 6 feet tall** ≃ mesurer 1,80 m

(c) *(with health)* aller; **how are you?** comment vas-tu?; **I'm well/not well** je vais bien/mal

(d) *(with place, situation)* se trouver, être; **she's in York** elle se trouve *ou* elle est à York

(e) *(exist)* être; **the best painter there is** le meilleur peintre qui soit

(f) *(go, come)* **I've been to see her** je suis allé la voir; **he's (already) been** il est (déjà) venu

(g) *(with weather, calculations)* faire; **it's nice** il fait beau; **it's foggy** il y a du brouillard; **2 and 2 are 4** 2 et 2 font 4

(h) *(cost)* coûter, faire; **it's 20 pence** ça coûte 20 pence; **how much is it?** ça fait combien?, c'est combien?

2 *v aux* **(a)** **I am going** je vais; **I was going** j'allais; **I'll be staying** je vais rester; **I'm listening to the radio** je suis en train d'écouter la radio; **what has she been doing?** qu'est-ce qu'elle a fait?; **she's been there some time** elle est là depuis un moment; **he was killed** il a été tué; **I've been waiting (for) two hours** j'attends depuis deux heures; **it is said** on dit

(b) *(in questions and answers)* **isn't it?/aren't you?**/etc n'est-ce pas?, non?; **she's ill, is she?** *(in surprise)* alors, comme ça, elle est malade?; **he isn't English, is he?** il n'est pas anglais, si?

(c) *(+ infinitive)* **he is to come at once** *(must)* il doit venir tout de suite

(d) **there is/are** il y a; *(pointing)* voilà; **here is/are** voici; **there she is** la voilà; **here they are** les voici

beach [biːtʃ] *n* plage *f*

beacon ['biːkən] *n (for ship, aircraft)* balise *f; (lighthouse)* phare *m*

bead [biːd] *n (small sphere)* perle *f, (of rosary)* grain *m; (of sweat)* goutte *f,* gouttelette *f;* **(string of) beads** collier *m*

beak [biːk] *n* bec *m*

beaker ['biːkə(r)] *n* gobelet *m*

beam [biːm] **1** *n* **(a)** *(of wood)* poutre *f* **(b)** *(of light, sunlight)* rayon *m; (of head-light, flashlight)* faisceau *m* (lumineux) **2** *vi (of light)* rayonner; *(of sun, moon)* briller; *(smile broadly)* sourire large-ment; **to b. with pride/joy** rayonner de fierté/joie **3** *vt (signals, programme)* transmettre **(to** à)

bean [biːn] *n* haricot *m; (of coffee)* grain *m; Fam* **to be full of beans** être plein d'énergie

bear¹ [beə(r)] *n (animal)* ours *m;* **b. cub** ourson *m*

bear² [beə(r)] **1** *(pt* bore, *pp* borne) *vt (carry, show)* porter; *(endure)* suppor-ter; *(resemblance)* offrir; **I can't b. him/it** je ne peux pas le supporter/supporter ça; **to b. sth in mind** *(re-member)* se souvenir de qch; *(take into account)* tenir compte de qch **2** *vi* **to b. left/right** *(turn)* tourner à gauche/droite; **to b. up** tenir le coup; **b. up!** courage!

bearable ['beərəbəl] *adj* supportable

beard [bɪəd] *n* barbe *f;* **to have a b.** porter la barbe

bearing ['beərɪŋ] *n (relevance)* rap-port *m* **(on** avec); *(posture, conduct)* port *m; (of ship, aircraft)* position *f;* **to get one's bearings** s'orienter

beast [biːst] *n* bête *f; Fam (person)* brute *f*

beat [biːt] **1** *n (of heart, drum)* batte-ment *m; (of policeman)* ronde *f; (in mu-sic)* rythme *m* **2** *(pt* beat, *pp* beaten [biːtən]) *vt* battre; *Fam* **it beats me** ça me dépasse; *Fam* **b. it!** fiche le camp!; **to b. sb to it** devancer qn; **to b. down** *or* **in** *(door)* défoncer; **to b. sb up** ta-basser qn **3** *vi* battre; *(at door)* frapper **(at** à); *Fam* **to b. about** *or* **around the bush** tourner autour du pot ■ **beating** *n (blows, defeat)* raclée *f; (of heart, drums)* battement *m*

beater ['bi:tə(r)] *n (whisk)* fouet *m*

beautician [bju:'tɪʃən] *n* esthéticienne *f*

beautiful ['bju:tɪfəl] *adj* (très) beau (*f* belle); *(superb)* merveilleux, -euse

beauty ['bju:tɪ] *(pl* -ies) *n (quality, woman)* beauté *f*; **it's a b.!** *(car, house)* c'est une merveille!; **b. parlour** *or* **salon** institut *m* de beauté; **b. spot** *(on skin)* grain *m* de beauté; *Br (in countryside)* endroit *m* pittoresque

beaver ['bi:və(r)] **1** *n* castor *m* **2** *vi* **to b. away (at sth)** travailler dur (à qch)

became [bɪ'keɪm] *pt of* **become**

because [bɪ'kɒz] *conj* parce que; **b. of** à cause de

beckon ['bekən] *vt & vi* **to b. (to) sb (to do sth)** faire signe à qn (de faire qch)

become [bɪ'kʌm] *(pt* became, *pp* become) *vi* devenir; **to b. a painter** devenir peintre; **to b. thin** maigrir; **what has b. of her?** qu'est-elle devenue?

becoming [bɪ'kʌmɪŋ] *adj (clothes)* seyant; *(modesty)* bienséant

bed [bed] *n* lit *m*; *(flowerbed)* parterre *m*; *(of vegetables)* carré *m*; *(of sea)* fond *m*; *(of river)* lit *m*; *(of rock)* couche *f*; **to go to b.** (aller) se coucher; **to put sb to b.** coucher qn; **in b.** couché; **to get out of b.** se lever; **to make the b.** faire le lit; **b. and breakfast** *(in hotel)* chambre *f* avec petit déjeuner; **to stay in a b. and breakfast** ≃ prendre une chambre d'hôte; *Br* **b. settee** (canapé *m*) convertible *m* ■ **bedclothes** *npl*, **bedding** *n* couvertures *fpl* et draps *mpl* ■ **bedridden** *adj* alité ■ **bedroom** *n* chambre *f* à coucher ■ **bedside** *n* chevet *m*; **b. lamp/book/table** lampe *f*/livre *m*/table *f* de chevet ■ **bedsit, bedsitter** ['bedsɪtə(r)] *n Br* chambre *f* meublée ■ **bedspread** *n* dessus-de-lit *m inv* ■ **bedtime** *n* heure *f* du coucher; **b. story** histoire *f* (*pour endormir les enfants*)

bedraggled [bɪ'drægəld] *adj (clothes, person)* débraillé et tout trempé

bee [bi:] *n* abeille *f* ■ **beehive** *n* ruche *f*

beech [bi:tʃ] *n (tree, wood)* hêtre *m*

beef [bi:f] *n* bœuf *m* ■ **beefburger** *n* hamburger *m*

been [bi:n] *pp of* **be**

beeper ['bi:pə(r)] *n* récepteur *m* d'appels, bip *m*

beer [bɪə(r)] *n* bière *f*; **b. glass** chope *f*

beet [bi:t] *n Am* betterave *f*

beetle ['bi:təl] *n* scarabée *m*

beetroot ['bi:tru:t] *n Br* betterave *f*

before [bɪ'fɔ:(r)] **1** *adv* avant; *(already)* déjà; *(in front)* devant; **the month b.** le mois d'avant *ou* précédent; **the day b.** la veille; **I've seen it b.** je l'ai déjà vu; **I've never done it b.** je ne l'ai (encore) jamais fait

2 *prep (time)* avant; *(place)* devant; **the year b. last** il y a deux ans; **b. my very eyes** sous mes yeux

3 *conj* avant que (ne) (*+ subjunctive*), avant de (*+ infinitive*); **b. he goes** avant qu'il (ne) parte; **b. going** avant de partir

befriend [bɪ'frend] *vt* **to b. sb** se prendre d'amitié pour qn

beg [beg] **1** *(pt & pp* -gg-*) vt* **to b. (for)** *(favour, help)* demander; *(bread, money)* mendier; **to b. sb to do sth** supplier qn de faire qch **2** *vi (in street)* mendier; *(ask earnestly)* supplier

began [bɪ'gæn] *pt of* **begin**

beggar ['begə(r)] *n* mendiant, -e *mf*; *Br Fam (person)* type *m*; **lucky b.** veinard, -e *mf*

begin [bɪ'gɪn] **1** *(pt* began, *pp* begun, *pres p* beginning*) vt* commencer; *(fashion, campaign)* lancer; *(bottle, sandwich)* entamer; *(conversation)* engager; **to b. doing** *or* **to do sth** commencer *ou* se mettre à faire qch; **he began laughing** il s'est mis à rire

2 *vi* commencer (**with** par; **by doing** par faire); **beginning from** à partir de; **to b. with** *(first of all)* d'abord ■ **beginner** *n* débutant, -e *mf* ■ **beginning** *n* commencement *m*, début *m*; **in** *or* **at the b.** au début, au commencement

begrudge [bɪ'grʌdʒ] *vt (envy)* envier **(sb sth** qch à qn); *(reproach)* reprocher **(sb sth** qch à qn); *(give unwillingly)* donner à contrecœur; **to b. doing sth** faire qch à contrecœur

begun [bɪ'gʌn] *pp of* begin

behalf [bɪ'hɑːf] *n* on b. of sb, on sb's b. *(representing)* au nom de qn, de la part de qn; *(in the interests of)* en faveur de qn

behave [bɪ'heɪv] *vi* se conduire; to b. (oneself) se tenir bien; *(of child)* être sage ■ **behaviour** *(Am* **behavior)** *n* conduite *f,* comportement *m*; to be on one's best b. se tenir particulièrement bien

behind [bɪ'haɪnd] **1** *prep* derrière; *(in terms of progress)* en retard sur **2** *adv* derrière; *(late)* en retard; to be b. with one's work avoir du travail en retard **3** *n Fam (buttocks)* derrière *m*

beige [beɪʒ] *adj & n* beige *(m)*

Beijing [beɪ'dʒɪŋ] *n* Beijing *m ou f*

being ['biːɪŋ] *n (person, soul)* être *m*; to come into b. naître

belated [bɪ'leɪtɪd] *adj* tardif, -ive

belch [beltʃ] **1** *n* renvoi *m* **2** *vi (of person)* roter **3** *vt* to b. (out) *(smoke)* vomir

Belgium ['beldʒəm] *n* la Belgique ■ **Belgian 1** *adj* belge **2** *n* Belge *mf*

belief [bɪ'liːf] *n (believing, thing believed)* croyance *f* (in sb en qn; in sth à *ou* en qch); *(trust)* confiance *f,* foi *f* (in en); *(religious faith)* foi *f*

believe [bɪ'liːv] **1** *vt* croire; I don't b. it c'est pas possible; I b. I'm right je crois avoir raison, je crois que j'ai raison **2** *vi* croire (in sth à qch); to believe in God croire en Dieu; I b. so/not je crois que oui/que non; to b. in doing sth croire qu'il faut faire qch ■ **believable** *adj* crédible ■ **believer** *n (religious)* croyant, -e *mf*; to be a b. in sth croire à qch

belittle [bɪ'lɪtəl] *vt* dénigrer

bell [bel] *n (large) (of church)* cloche *f*; *(small)* clochette *f*; *(in phone, mechanism, alarm)* sonnerie *f*; *(on door, bicycle)* sonnette *f*; b. tower clocher *m* ■ **bellboy, bellhop** *n Am* groom *m*

bellow ['beləʊ] *vi* beugler, mugir

belly ['belɪ] *(pl* -ies) *n* ventre *m*; *Fam* b. button nombril *m*; b. dancing danse *f* du ventre

belong [bɪ'lɒŋ] *vi* appartenir (to à); to b. to a club être membre d'un club; that book belongs to me ce livre m'appartient *ou* est à moi; the cup belongs here cette tasse se range ici ■ **belongings** *npl* affaires *fpl*

beloved [bɪ'lʌvɪd] *adj & n Literary* bien-aimé, -e *(mf)*

below [bɪ'ləʊ] **1** *prep (lower than)* au-dessous de; *(under)* sous; *(with numbers)* moins de; *Fig (unworthy of)* indigne de **2** *adv* en dessous; *(in text)* ci-dessous; on the floor b. à l'étage du dessous; it's 10 degrees b. il fait moins 10

belt [belt] **1** *n* ceinture *f*; *(in machine)* courroie *f*; *(area)* zone *f,* région *f* **2** *vi* to b. up *(fasten seat belt)* attacher sa ceinture; *Br Fam* b. up! *(shut up)* boucle-la! **3** *vt Fam (hit) (ball)* cogner dans; *(person)* flanquer un gnon à

bemused [bɪ'mjuːzd] *adj* perplexe

bench [bentʃ] *n (seat)* banc *m*; *(work table)* établi *m*; *Law* the B. *(magistrates)* la magistrature (assise); *(court)* le tribunal; *Sport* to be on the b. être remplaçant, -e

bend [bend] **1** *n* courbe *f*; *(in river, pipe)* coude *m*; *(in road)* virage *m*; *Fam* round the b. *(mad)* cinglé **2** *(pt & pp* bent) *vt* courber; *(leg, arm)* plier; to b. one's head baisser la tête; to b. the rules faire une entorse au règlement **3** *vi (of branch)* plier; *(of road)* tourner; *(of river)* faire un coude; to b. (down) *(stoop)* se courber; to b. (over *or* forward) se pencher

beneath [bɪ'niːθ] **1** *prep* sous; *(unworthy of)* indigne de **2** *adv* (au-)dessous

benefactor ['benɪfæktə(r)] *n* bienfaiteur *m* ■ **benefactress** *n* bienfaitrice *f*

beneficial [benɪ'fɪʃəl] *adj* bénéfique

benefit ['benɪfɪt] **1** *n (advantage)* avantage *m*; *(money)* allocation *f*; benefits *(of science, education)* bienfaits *mpl*; to sb's b. dans l'intérêt de qn; for your (own) b. pour vous, pour votre bien; to be of b. (to sb) faire du bien (à qn); b. concert concert *m* de bienfaisance **2** *vt* faire du bien à; *(be useful to)*

profiter à **3** *vi* **to b. from doing sth** gagner à faire qch

Benelux ['benɪlʌks] *n* Benelux *m*

benevolent [bɪ'nevələnt] *adj* bienveillant

benign [bɪ'naɪn] *adj (kind)* bienveillant; *(climate)* doux (*f* douce); **b. tumour** tumeur *f* bénigne

bent [bent] **1** *adj (nail, mind)* tordu; *Fam (dishonest)* pourri; **b. on doing sth** résolu à faire qch **2** *n (talent)* aptitude *f* **(for** pour); *(inclination, liking)* penchant *m*, goût *m* **(for** pour) **3** *pt & pp of* bend

bequeath [bɪ'kwiːð] *vt Formal* léguer **(to** à)

bereaved [bɪ'riːvd] **1** *adj* endeuillé **2** *npl* **the b.** la famille du défunt/de la défunte ■ **bereavement** *n* deuil *m*

beret [*Br* 'bereɪ, *Am* bə'reɪ] *n* béret *m*

Berlin [bɜː'lɪn] *n* Berlin *m ou f*

Bermuda [bə'mjuːdə] *n* les Bermudes *fpl*

berry ['berɪ] *(pl* -**ies)** *n* baie *f*

berserk [bə'zɜːk] *adj* **to go b.** devenir fou furieux (*f* folle furieuse)

berth [bɜːθ] **1** *n* (a) *(in ship, train)* couchette *f* **(b)** *(anchorage)* poste *m* à quai; *Fig* **to give sb a wide b.** éviter qn comme la peste **2** *vi (of ship)* aborder à quai

beset [bɪ'set] *(pt & pp* beset, *pres p* besetting) *vt* assaillir

beside [bɪ'saɪd] *prep* à côté de; **that's b. the point** ça n'a rien à voir

besides [bɪ'saɪdz] **1** *prep (in addition to)* en plus de; *(except)* excepté; **there are ten of us b. Paul** nous sommes dix sans compter Paul; **what else can you do b. singing?** que savez-vous faire à part chanter? **2** *adv (in addition)* en plus; *(moreover)* d'ailleurs

besiege [bɪ'siːdʒ] *vt (of soldiers, crowd)* assiéger; *Fig (annoy)* assaillir **(with** de)

besought [bɪ'sɔːt] *pt & pp of* beseech

best [best] **1** *adj* meilleur; **my b. dress** ma plus belle robe; **the b. part of** *(most)* la plus grande partie de; **the b. thing is to accept** le mieux c'est d'ac-

cepter; **'b. before…'** *(on product)* 'à consommer avant…'; **b. man** *(at wedding)* garçon *m* d'honneur

2 *n* **the b. (one)** le meilleur, la meilleure; **it's for the b.** c'est pour le mieux; **at b.** au mieux; **to do one's b.** faire de son mieux; **to look one's b., to be at one's b.** être à son avantage; **to the b. of my knowledge** autant que je sache; **to make the b. of sth** *(accept)* s'accommoder de qch; **to get the b. out of sth** tirer le meilleur parti de qch; **in one's Sunday b.** endimanché; **all the b.!** *(when leaving)* prends bien soin de toi!; *(good luck)* bonne chance!; *(in letter)* amicalement

3 *adv* **(the) b.** *(play, sing)* le mieux; **to like sb/sth (the) b.** aimer qn/qch le plus; **I think it b. to wait** je juge prudent d'attendre ■ **best-seller** *n (book)* best-seller *m*

bet [bet] **1** *n* pari *m* **2** *(pt & pp* bet *or* betted, *pres p* betting) *vt* parier (**on** sur; **that** que); *Fam* **you b.!** tu parles! ■ **betting** *n* paris *mpl*; *Br* **b. shop** ≃ PMU *m*

betray [bɪ'treɪ] *vt (person, secret)* trahir ■ **betrayal** *n (disloyalty)* trahison *f*; *(disclosure) (of secret)* révélation *f*

better ['betə(r)] **1** *adj* meilleur (**than** que); **I need a b. car** j'ai besoin d'une meilleure voiture; **that's b.** c'est mieux; **she's (much) b.** *(in health)* elle va (beaucoup) mieux; **to get b.** *(recover)* se remettre; *(improve)* s'améliorer; **it's b. to go** il vaut mieux partir; **the b. part of** *(most)* la plus grande partie de

2 *adv* mieux (**than** que); **b. dressed/ known/etc** mieux habillé/connu/etc; **to look b.** *(of ill person)* avoir meilleure mine; **b. and b.** de mieux en mieux; **so much the b., all the b.** tant mieux (**for** pour); **I'd b. go** il vaut mieux que je parte; **to be b. off** *(financially)* être plus à l'aise

3 *n* **to get the b. of sb** l'emporter sur qn; **to change for the b.** *(of person)* changer en bien; *(of situation)* s'améliorer; **one's betters** ses supérieurs *mpl*

4 *vt (improve)* améliorer; *(do better*

than) dépasser; **to b. oneself** améliorer sa condition; **to b. sb's results**/*etc* dépasser les résultats/*etc* de qn

between [bɪ'twiːn] **1** *prep* entre; **in b.** entre **2** *adv* **in b.** *(space)* au milieu; *(time)* dans l'intervalle

beware [bɪ'weə(r)] *vi* se méfier (**of** de); **b.!** attention!; **'b. of the dog!'** 'attention, chien méchant!'

bewilder [bɪ'wɪldə(r)] *vt* dérouter, laisser perplexe

beyond [bɪ'jɒnd] **1** *prep* (a) *(further than)* au-delà de; **b. reach/doubt** hors de portée/de doute; **b. belief** incroyable; **b. my/our/**etc** means** au-dessus de mes/nos/*etc* moyens; **it's b. me** ça me dépasse (b) *(except)* sauf **2** *adv (further)* au-delà

bias ['baɪəs] **1** *n* (a) *(inclination)* penchant *m* (**towards** pour); *(prejudice)* préjugé *m*, parti pris *m* (**towards/against** en faveur de/contre) (b) **cut on the b.** *(fabric)* coupé dans le biais **2** *(pt & pp* **-ss-** *or* **-s-)** *vt* influencer (**towards/against** en faveur de/contre) ▪ **bias(s)ed** *adj* partial; **to be b. against** avoir des préjugés contre

bib [bɪb] *n (for baby)* bavoir *m*

bible ['baɪbəl] *n* bible *f*; **the B.** la Bible ▪ **biblical** *adj* biblique

bibliography [bɪblɪ'ɒɡrəfɪ] *(pl* **-ies)** *n* bibliographie *f*

biceps ['baɪseps] *n inv (muscle)* biceps *m*

bicker ['bɪkə(r)] *vi* se chamailler

bicycle ['baɪsɪkəl] *n* bicyclette *f*; **by b.** à bicyclette

bid¹ [bɪd] **1** *n* (a) *(offer)* offre *f*; *(at auction)* enchère *f* (**for** pour) (b) *(attempt)* tentative *f* **2** *(pt & pp* **bid***, pres p* **bidding)** *vt (sum of money)* offrir; *(at auction)* faire une enchère de **3** *vi* faire une offre (**for** pour); *(at auction)* faire une enchère (**for** sur) ▪ **bidder** *n (at auction)* enchérisseur, -euse *mf*; **to the highest b.** au plus offrant

bid² [bɪd] *(pt* **bade***, pp* **bidden** ['bɪdən] *or* **bid***, pres p* **bidding)** *vt Literary (command)* commander (**sb to do** à qn de faire); *(say, wish)* dire, souhaiter

bide [baɪd] *vt* **to b. one's time** attendre le bon moment

big [bɪɡ] **(bigger, biggest)** *adj (tall, large)* grand; *(fat)* gros (*f* grosse); *(drop, increase)* fort; **to get big(ger)** *(taller)* grandir; *(fatter)* grossir; **my b. brother** mon grand frère; *Fam* **b. mouth** grande gueule *f*; **b. toe** gros orteil *m* ▪ **bighead** *n Fam* crâneur, -euse *mf* ▪ **bigshot, bigwig** *n Fam* gros bonnet *m*

bigot ['bɪɡət] *n* sectaire *mf*; *(religious)* bigot, -e *mf* ▪ **bigoted** *adj* sectaire; *(religious)* bigot

bike [baɪk] *n Fam* vélo *m*; *(motorbike)* moto *f*

bikini [bɪ'kiːnɪ] *n* Bikini® *m*; **b. briefs** mini-slip *m*

bilberry ['bɪlbərɪ] *(pl* **-ies)** *n* myrtille *f*

bilingual [baɪ'lɪŋɡwəl] *adj* bilingue

bill¹ [bɪl] **1** *n* (a) *(invoice)* facture *f*; *(in restaurant)* addition *f*; *(in hotel)* note *f* (b) *Am (banknote)* billet *m*; (c) *(bank draft)* effet *m* (d) *(notice)* affiche *f* (e) *Pol* projet *m* de loi; **B. of Rights** = les dix premiers amendements de la Constitution américaine **2** *vt* (a) **to b. sb** envoyer la facture à qn (b) *(publicize)* annoncer ▪ **billboard** *n* panneau *m* d'affichage

bill² [bɪl] *n (of bird)* bec *m*

billiards ['bɪljədz] *n* billard *m*

billion ['bɪljən] *n* milliard *m* ▪ **billionaire** *n* milliardaire *mf*

billow ['bɪləʊ] **1** *n (of smoke)* volute *f* **2** *vi (of smoke)* tourbillonner; *(of sea)* se soulever; *(of sail)* se gonfler

bimonthly [baɪ'mʌnθlɪ] *adj (every two weeks)* bimensuel, -elle; *(every two months)* bimestriel, -elle

bin [bɪn] **1** *n* boîte *f*; *(for litter)* poubelle *f* **2** *(pt & pp* **-nn-)** *vt Fam* mettre à la poubelle

binary ['baɪnərɪ] *adj* binaire

bind [baɪnd] **1** *(pt & pp* **bound)** *vt (fasten)* attacher; *(book)* relier; *(fabric, hem)* border; *(unite)* lier; **to b. sb hand and foot** ligoter qn; **to be bound by sth** être lié par qch **2** *n Fam (bore)* plaie *f* ▪ **binding 1** *n (of book)* reliure *f* **2** *adj*

(contract) qui lie; **to be b. on sb** *(legally)* lier qn

binder ['baɪndə(r)] *n (for papers)* classeur *m*

binge [bɪndʒ] *n Fam* **to go on a b.** *(drinking)* faire la bringue; *(eating)* se gaver

bingo ['bɪŋgəʊ] *n* ≃ loto *m*

binoculars [bɪ'nɒkjʊləz] *npl* jumelles *fpl*

biochemistry [baɪəʊ'kemɪstrɪ] *n* biochimie *f*

biodegradable [baɪəʊdɪ'greɪdəbəl] *adj* biodégradable

biography [baɪ'ɒgrəfɪ] *(pl* -ies) *n* biographie *f*

biology [baɪ'ɒlədʒɪ] *n* biologie *f* ■ **biological** *adj* biologique; **b. warfare** guerre *f* bactériologique

bird [bɜːd] *n* (a) *(animal)* oiseau *m*; *(fowl)* volaille *f*; **b. of prey** oiseau *m* de proie; **b.'s-eye view** perspective *f* à vol d'oiseau; *Fig* vue *f* d'ensemble (b) *Br Fam (girl)* nana *f* ■ **birdseed** *n* graines *fpl* pour oiseaux

birth [bɜːθ] *n* naissance *f*; **to give b. to** donner naissance à; **from b.** *(blind, deaf)* de naissance; **b. certificate** acte *m* de naissance; **b. control** limitation *f* des naissances; **b. rate** (taux *m* de) natalité *f* ■ **birthday** *n* anniversaire *m*; **happy b.!** joyeux anniversaire!; **b. party** fête *f* d'anniversaire; *Fig* **in one's b. suit** *(man)* en costume d'Adam; *(woman)* en costume d'Ève ■ **birthmark** *n* tache *f* de naissance ■ **birthplace** *n* lieu *m* de naissance; *(house)* maison *f* natale

biscuit ['bɪskɪt] *n Br* biscuit *m*, petit gâteau *m*; *Am* petit pain *m* au lait

bishop ['bɪʃəp] *n* évêque *m*; *(in chess)* fou *m*

bit¹ [bɪt] *n* (a) *(of string, time)* bout *m*; **a b.** *(a little)* un peu; **not a b.** pas du tout; **a b. of luck** une chance; **b. by b.** petit à petit; **in bits (and pieces)** en morceaux (b) *(coin)* pièce *f* (c) *(of horse)* mors *m* (d) *(of drill)* mèche *f* (e) *Comptr* bit *m*

bit² [bɪt] *pt of* **bite**

bitch [bɪtʃ] **1** *n (dog)* chienne *f*; *very Fam Pej (woman)* garce *f* **2** *vi Fam (complain)* râler (**about** après)

bite [baɪt] **1** *n* (a) *(wound)* morsure *f*; *(from insect)* piqûre *f*; *Fishing* touche *f* (b) *(mouthful)* bouchée *f*; **to have a b. to eat** manger un morceau **2** *(pt* **bit,** *pp* **bitten** ['bɪtən]) *vt* mordre; *(of insect)* piquer; **to b. one's nails** se ronger les ongles; **to b. sth off** arracher qch d'un coup de dents **3** *vi* mordre; *(of insect)* piquer; **to b. into sth** mordre dans qch ■ **biting** *adj (cold)* mordant; *(wind)* cinglant

bitter ['bɪtə(r)] **1** *n Br (beer)* = bière anglaise brune **2** *adj (person, taste, irony)* amer, -ère; *(cold, wind)* glacial; *(criticism)* acerbe; *(shock, fate)* cruel *(f* cruelle); *(conflict)* violent; **to feel b. (about sth)** être plein d'amertume (à cause de qch) ■ **bitterly** *adv* **to cry/regret b.** pleurer/regretter amèrement; **b. disappointed** cruellement déçu; **it's b. cold** il fait un froid de canard ■ **bittersweet** *adj* doux-amer *(f* douce-amère); *Am* **b. chocolate** chocolat *m* noir

bizarre [bɪ'zɑː(r)] *adj* bizarre

blab [blæb] *(pt & pp* **-bb-**) *vi* jaser

black [blæk] **1** (-er, -est) *adj* noir; **b. eye** œil *m* au beurre noir; **b. and blue** *(bruised)* couvert de bleus; *Aviat* **b. box** boîte *f* noire; *Br* **b. ice** verglas *m*; *Br* **b. pudding** boudin *m* noir; *Fig* **b. sheep** brebis *f* galeuse **2** *n (colour)* noir *m*; *(person)* Noir, -e *mf* ■ **blackberry** *(pl* -ies) *n* mûre *f* ■ **blackbird** *n* merle *m* (noir) ■ **blackboard** *n* tableau *m* (noir) ■ **blackcurrant** *n* cassis *m* ■ **blacken** *vt & vi* noircir ■ **blacklist 1** *n* liste *f* noire **2** *vt* mettre sur la liste noire ■ **blackmail 1** *n* chantage *m* **2** *vt* faire chanter; **to b. sb into doing sth** faire chanter qn pour qu'il/elle fasse qch ■ **blackout** *n* panne *f* d'électricité; *(during war)* black-out *m inv*; *(fainting fit)* évanouissement *m*; *(news)* **b.** black-out *m inv* ■ **blacksmith** *n* forgeron *m*; *(working with horses)* maréchal-ferrant *m*

► **black out** *vi (faint)* s'évanouir

bladder ['blædə(r)] *n* vessie *f*

blade [bleɪd] *n* lame *f*; **b. of grass** brin *m* d'herbe

blame [bleɪm] **1** *n* responsabilité *f*; *(criticism)* blâme *m*; **to lay the b. (for sth) on sb** faire porter à qn la responsabilité (de qch); **to take the b. for sth** endosser la responsabilité de qch **2** *vt* rendre responsable, faire porter la responsabilité à **(for** de); **to b. sb for doing sth** reprocher à qn d'avoir fait qch; **you're to b.** c'est de ta faute ■ **blameless** *adj* irréprochable

blanch [blɑːntʃ] **1** *vt (vegetables)* blanchir **2** *vi (turn pale)* blêmir

bland [blænd] **(-er, -est)** *adj (person)* terne; *(food)* insipide; *(remark, joke)* quelconque

blank [blæŋk] **1** *adj (paper, page)* blanc *(f* blanche), vierge; *(cheque)* en blanc; *(look, mind)* vide; **b. tape** cassette *f* vierge **2** *n (space)* blanc *m*; *(cartridge)* cartouche *f* à blanc; **to fire blanks** tirer à blanc; **my mind's a b.** j'ai un trou

blanket ['blæŋkɪt] **1** *n (on bed)* couverture *f*; *(of snow, leaves)* couche *f* **2** *adj (term, remark)* général

blankly ['blæŋklɪ] *adv* **to look b. at sb/sth** *(without expression)* regarder qn/qch, le visage inexpressif; *(without understanding)* regarder qn/qch sans comprendre

blare [bleə(r)] **1** *n (noise)* beuglements *mpl*; *(of trumpet)* sonnerie *f* **2** *vi* **to b. (out)** *(of radio)* beugler; *(of music, car horn)* retentir

blasé ['blɑːzeɪ] *adj* blasé

blasphemous ['blæsfəməs] *adj (text)* blasphématoire; *(person)* blasphémateur, -trice

blast [blɑːst] **1** *n* explosion *f*; *(air from explosion)* souffle *m*; *(of wind)* rafale *f*; *(of trumpet)* sonnerie *f*; **(at) full b.** *(loud)* à fond **2** *vt (hole, tunnel)* creuser *(en dynamitant)*; *Fam (criticize)* démolir **3** *exclam Br Fam* zut! ■ **blasted** *adj Br Fam* fichu ■ **blast-off** *n (of spacecraft)* mise *f* à feu

blatant ['bleɪtənt] *adj (obvious)* flagrant; *(shameless)* éhonté

blaze [bleɪz] **1** *n (fire)* feu *m*; *(large)* incendie *m*; *Fig (splendour)* éclat *m*; **a b. of colour** une explosion de couleurs; **b. of light** torrent *m* de lumière **2** *vi (of fire, sun)* flamboyer; *(of light, eyes)* être éclatant **3** *vt Fig* **to b. a trail** ouvrir la voie ■ **blazing** *adj (burning)* en feu; *(sun)* brûlant; *Fig (argument)* violent

blazer ['bleɪzə(r)] *n* blazer *m*

bleach [bliːtʃ] **1** *n (household)* (eau *f* de) Javel *f*; *(for hair)* décolorant *m* **2** *vt (clothes)* passer à l'eau de Javel; *(hair)* décolorer

bleak [bliːk] **(-er, -est)** *adj (appearance, countryside, weather)* morne; *(outlook)* lugubre; *(prospect)* peu encourageant

bleat [bliːt] *vi* bêler

bleed [bliːd] *(pt & pp* **bled** [bled]) **1** *vi* saigner; **to b. to death** saigner à mort; **her nose is bleeding** elle saigne du nez **2** *vt (radiator)* purger

bleep [bliːp] **1** *n* bip *m* **2** *vt* appeler au bip **3** *vi* faire bip ■ **bleeper** *n (pager)* bip *m*

blemish ['blemɪʃ] **1** *n (fault)* défaut *m*; *(mark)* marque *f* **2** *vt Fig (reputation)* entacher

blend [blend] **1** *n* mélange *m* **2** *vt* mélanger **(with** à *ou* avec) **3** *vi* se mélanger; *(of styles, colours)* se marier **(with** avec) ■ **blender** *n* mixer *m*

bless [bles] *vt* bénir; **to be blessed with sth** être doté de qch; **b. you!** *(when sneezing)* à vos souhaits! ■ **blessed** *adj* **(a)** *(holy)* béni **(b)** *Fam (blasted)* fichu ■ **blessing** *n Rel* bénédiction *f*; *(benefit)* bienfait *m*; **it was a b. in disguise** finalement, ça a été une bonne chose

blew [bluː] *pt of* **blow**[2]

blind[1] [blaɪnd] **1** *adj* aveugle; **b. person** aveugle *mf*; **b. in one eye** borgne; *Fig* **to be b. to sth** ne pas voir qch; **b. alley** impasse *f*; **b. date** = rencontre arrangée avec quelqu'un qu'on ne connaît pas **2** *npl* **the b.** les aveugles *mpl* **3** *adv* **b. drunk** ivre mort **4** *vt (dazzle, make blind)* aveugler

blind[2] [blaɪnd] *n Br (on window)* store *m*

blindfold ['blaɪndfəʊld] **1** n bandeau m **2** vt bander les yeux à **3** adv les yeux bandés

blindly ['blaɪndlɪ] adv Fig aveuglément

blink [blɪŋk] **1** n clignement m; Br Fam **on the b.** (machine) détraqué **2** vt **to b. one's eyes** cligner des yeux **3** vi (of person) cligner des yeux; (of eyes) cligner; (of light) clignoter

blissful ['blɪsfʊl] adj (wonderful) merveilleux, -euse; (very happy) (person) aux anges ▪ **blissfully** adv (happy) merveilleusement; **to be b. unaware that...** ne pas se douter le moins du monde que...

blister ['blɪstə(r)] **1** n (on skin) ampoule f **2** vi se couvrir d'ampoules

blitz [blɪts] **1** n (air attack) raid m éclair; (bombing) bombardement m aérien; Fam (onslaught) offensive f **2** vt bombarder

blizzard ['blɪzəd] n tempête f de neige

bloated ['bləʊtɪd] adj (swollen) gonflé

blob [blɒb] n (of ink, colour) tache f

block [blɒk] **1** n (of stone) bloc m; (of buildings) pâté m de maisons; (in pipe) obstruction f; **b. of flats** immeuble m; Am **a b. away** une rue plus loin; **b. booking** réservation f de groupe; **b. capitals** or **letters** majuscules fpl **2** vt (obstruct) bloquer; (pipe) boucher; (view) cacher; **to b. up** (pipe, hole) boucher ▪ **blockage** n obstruction f ▪ **blockbuster** n (film) film m à grand spectacle

bloke [bləʊk] n Br Fam type m

blond [blɒnd] adj & n blond (m) ▪ **blonde** adj & n blonde (f)

blood [blʌd] n sang m; **b. bank** banque f du sang; **b. bath** bain m de sang; **b. donor** donneur, -euse mf de sang; **b. group** groupe m sanguin; **b. poisoning** empoisonnement m du sang; **b. pressure** tension f artérielle; **high b. pressure** hypertension f; **to have high b. pressure** avoir de la tension; Am **b. sausage** boudin m; **b. test** prise f de sang ▪ **bloodshed** n effusion f

de sang ▪ **bloodshot** adj (eye) injecté de sang ▪ **bloodstream** n sang m ▪ **bloodthirsty** adj sanguinaire

bloody ['blʌdɪ] **1** (-ier, -iest) adj (a) (covered in blood) ensanglanté (b) Br very Fam foutu; **a b. liar** un sale menteur; **you b. fool!** espèce de connard! **2** adv Br Fam (very) vachement; **it's b. hot!** il fait une putain de chaleur! ▪ **bloody-minded** adj pas commode

bloom [bluːm] **1** n fleur f; **in b.** (tree) en fleur(s); (flower) éclos **2** vi (of tree, flower) fleurir; Fig (of person) s'épanouir ▪ **blooming** adj (a) (in bloom) en fleur(s); (person) resplendissant; (thriving) florissant (b) Br Fam (for emphasis) sacré; **you b. idiot!** espèce d'idiot!

blossom ['blɒsəm] **1** n fleurs fpl **2** vi fleurir; **to b. (out)** (of person) s'épanouir

blot [blɒt] **1** n tache f **2** (pt & pp -tt-) vt (stain) tacher; (dry) sécher; **to b. sth out** (obliterate) effacer qch ▪ **blotting paper** n (papier m) buvard m

blotch [blɒtʃ] n tache f ▪ **blotchy** (-ier, -iest) adj couvert de taches; (face, skin) marbré

blouse [blaʊz] n chemisier m

blow¹ [bləʊ] n (hit, setback) coup m; **to come to blows** en venir aux mains

blow² [bləʊ] **1** (pt blew, pp blown) vt (of wind) pousser; (of person) (smoke, glass) souffler; (bubbles) faire; (trumpet) souffler dans; (kiss) envoyer (**to** à); Br Fam (money) claquer (**on sth** pour s'acheter qch); **to b. a fuse** faire sauter un plomb; **to b. one's nose** se moucher; **to b. a whistle** donner un coup de sifflet **2** vi (of wind, person) souffler; (of fuse) sauter; (of papers) (in wind) s'éparpiller

▸ **blow away 1** vt sep (of wind) emporter **2** vi (of hat, paper) s'envoler

▸ **blow down 1** vt sep (chimney, fence) faire tomber **2** vi (fall) tomber

▸ **blow off** vt sep (hat) emporter; (arm) arracher

▸ **blow out 1** vt sep (candle) souffler; (cheeks) gonfler **2** vi (of light) s'éteindre

▸ **blow over 1** vt & vi = blow down **2** vi (of quarrel) se tasser

▸**blow up 1** *vt sep (building)* faire sauter; *(pump up)* gonfler; *(photo)* agrandir **2** *vi (explode)* exploser

blow-dry ['bləʊdraɪ] **1** *n* brushing® *m* **2** *vt* **to b. sb's hair** faire un brushing® à qn

blown [bləʊn] *pp of* **blow**

blowout ['bləʊaʊt] *n* (a) *(tyre)* éclatement *m* (b) *Br Fam (meal)* gueuleton *m*

blowtorch ['bləʊtɔːtʃ] *n* chalumeau *m*

bludgeon ['blʌdʒən] **1** *n* gourdin *m* **2** *vt* matraquer

blue [bluː] **1** (-er, -est) *adj* bleu; *Fam* **to feel b.** avoir le cafard; *Fam* **b. movie** film *m* porno **2** *n* bleu *m*; **blues** *(music)* le blues; *Fam* **the blues** *(depression)* le cafard; **out of the b.** *(unexpectedly)* sans crier gare ▪ **bluebell** *n* jacinthe *f* des bois ▪ **blueberry** *(pl* -ies) *n* airelle *f* ▪ **bluebottle** *n* mouche *f* de la viande ▪ **blueprint** *n Fig* plan *m*

bluff [blʌf] **1** *n* bluff *m* **2** *vt & vi* bluffer

blunder ['blʌndə(r)] **1** *n (mistake)* gaffe *f* **2** *vi* faire une gaffe

blunt [blʌnt] **1** (-er, -est) *adj (edge)* émoussé; *(pencil)* mal taillé; *(question, statement)* direct; *(person)* brusque **2** *vt (blade)* émousser; *(pencil)* épointer

blur [blɜː(r)] **1** *n* tache *f* floue **2** *(pt & pp* -rr-) *vt (outline)* brouiller ▪ **blurred** *adj (image, outline)* flou

blurb [blɜːb] *n* notice *f* publicitaire

blurt [blɜːt] *vt* **to b. (out)** *(secret)* laisser échapper; *(excuse)* bredouiller

blush [blʌʃ] **1** *n* rougeur *f* **2** *vi* rougir (**with** de)

blustery ['blʌstərɪ] *adj (weather)* de grand vent; *(wind)* violent

boar [bɔː(r)] *n (wild)* **b.** sanglier *m*

board¹ [bɔːd] **1** *n (piece of wood)* planche *f*; *(for notices)* panneau *m*; *(for games)* tableau *m*; *(cardboard)* carton *m*; **on b. (a ship/plane)** à bord (d'un navire/avion) **2** *vt (ship, plane)* monter à bord de; *(bus, train)* monter dans; **to b. up** *(door)* condamner **3** *vi* **flight Z001 is now boarding** vol Z001, embarquement immédiat ▪ **boarding** *n (of passengers)* embarquement *m*; **b. pass** carte *f* d'embarquement ▪ **board-**

walk *n Am (on beach)* promenade *f*

board² [bɔːd] *n (committee)* conseil *m*; **b. (of directors)** conseil *m* d'administration; **b. (of examiners)** jury *m* (d'examen); **across the b.** *(pay increase)* global; *(apply)* globalement; **b. room** salle *f* du conseil

board³ [bɔːd] **1** *n (food)* pension *f*; **b. and lodging**, *Br* **full b.** pension *f* complète; *Br* **half b.** demi-pension *f* **2** *vi (lodge)* être en pension (**with** chez); **boarding house** pension *f* de famille; **boarding school** pensionnat *m* ▪ **boarder** *n* pensionnaire *mf*

boast [bəʊst] **1** *n* vantardise *f* **2** *vt* se glorifier de **3** *vi* se vanter (**about** *or* **of** de) ▪ **boastful** *adj* vantard

boat [bəʊt] *n* bateau *m*; *(small)* canot *m*; *(liner)* paquebot *m*; **by b.** en bateau; *Fig* **in the same b.** logé à la même enseigne; **b. race** course *f* d'aviron

bode [bəʊd] *vi to* **b. well/ill (for)** être de bon/mauvais augure (pour)

bodily ['bɒdɪlɪ] **1** *adj (need)* physique **2** *adv (lift, seize)* à bras-le-corps; *(carry)* dans ses bras

body ['bɒdɪ] *(pl* -ies) *n* corps *m*; *(of car)* carrosserie *f*; *(quantity)* masse *f*; *(institution)* organisme *m*; *(dead)* **b.** cadavre *m*; **b. building** culturisme *m*; **b. warmer** gilet *m* matelassé ▪ **bodyguard** *n* garde *m* du corps ▪ **bodywork** *n* carrosserie *f*

bog [bɒg] **1** *n (swamp)* marécage *m* **2** *vt* **to get bogged down in** *(mud, work)* s'enliser (dans); *(details)* se perdre (dans)

bogus ['bəʊgəs] *adj* faux *(f* fausse)

boil¹ [bɔɪl] *n (pimple)* furoncle *m*

boil² [bɔɪl] **1** *n* **to come to the b.** bouillir; **to bring sth to the b.** amener qch à ébullition **2** *vt* **to b. (up)** faire bouillir; **to b. the kettle** mettre de l'eau à chauffer **3** *vi* bouillir; *Fig* **to b. down to** *(of situation, question)* revenir à; **to b. over** *(of milk)* déborder; *Fig (of situation)* empirer ▪ **boiled** *adj* bouilli; **b. egg** œuf *m* à la coque ▪ **boiling 1** *n* ébullition *f*; **to be at b. point** *(of liquid)* bouillir **2** *adj* **b. (hot)** bouillant;

it's b. (hot) *(weather)* il fait une chaleur infernale

boiler [ˈbɔɪlə(r)] *n* chaudière *f*; *Br* **b. suit** bleus *mpl* de chauffe

boisterous [ˈbɔɪstərəs] *adj (noisy)* bruyant; *(child)* turbulent; *(meeting)* houleux, -euse

bold [bəʊld] **(-er, -est)** *adj* hardi

bolster [ˈbəʊlstə(r)] **1** *n (pillow)* traversin *m* **2** *vt (confidence, pride)* renforcer, consolider

bolt [bəʊlt] **1** *n* (a) *(on door)* verrou *m*; *(for nut)* boulon *m* (b) *(dash)* **to make a b. for the door** se précipiter vers la porte (c) **b. of lightning** éclair *m* **2** *adv* **b. upright** tout droit **3** *vt* (a) *(door)* verrouiller (b) *(food)* engloutir **4** *vi (dash)* se précipiter; *(run away)* détaler; *(of horse)* s'emballer

bomb [bɒm] **1** *n* bombe *f*; **b. scare** alerte *f* à la bombe **2** *vt (from the air)* bombarder; *(of terrorist)* faire sauter une bombe dans ou à ■ **bombshell** *n* **to come as a b.** faire l'effet d'une bombe ■ **bombsite** *n* zone *f* bombardée

bombard [bɒmˈbɑːd] *vt (with bombs, questions)* bombarder (**with** de)

bona fide [bəʊnəˈfaɪdɪ] *adj* véritable

bond [bɒnd] **1** *n (link)* lien *m*; *(agreement)* engagement *m*; *Fin* obligation *f* **2** *vt (of glue)* coller (**to** à) **3** *vi (form attachment)* créer des liens affectifs (**with** avec)

bone [bəʊn] **1** *n* os *m*; *(of fish)* arête *f*; **b. china** porcelaine *f* tendre **2** *vt (meat)* désosser; *(fish)* ôter les arêtes de **3** *vi Fam* **to b. up on** *(subject)* bûcher ■ **bone-dry** *adj* complètement sec (*f* sèche) ■ **bone-idle** *adj Br* paresseux, -euse

bonfire [ˈbɒnfaɪə(r)] *n (for celebration)* feu *m* de joie; *Br (for dead leaves)* feu *m* (de jardin)

bonkers [ˈbɒŋkəz] *adj Br Fam* dingue

bonnet [ˈbɒnɪt] *n (hat)* bonnet *m*; *Br (of vehicle)* capot *m*

bonus [ˈbəʊnəs] *(pl* **-uses** [-əsɪz]) *n* prime *f*; **no-claims b.** *(in motor insurance)* bonus *m*

boo [buː] **1** *exclam (to frighten)* hou! **2** *n*

boos huées *fpl* **3** *(pt & pp* **booed)** *vt & vi* huer

boob [buːb] *Br Fam* **1** *n* (a) *(mistake)* gaffe *f* (b) **boobs** *(breasts)* nénés *mpl* **2** *vi* gaffer

booby-trap [ˈbuːbɪtræp] **1** *n* engin *m* piégé **2** *(pt & pp* **-pp-)** *vt* piéger

book [bʊk] **1** *n* livre *m*; *(record)* registre *m*; *(of tickets)* carnet *m*; *(for exercises and notes)* cahier *m*; **books** *(accounts)* comptes *mpl*; **b. club** club *m* du livre

2 *vt (seat)* réserver; *Br* **to b. sb** *(for traffic offence)* dresser une contravention à qn; **fully booked** *(hotel)* complet, -ète; *(person)* pris

3 *vi* **to b. (up)** réserver des places; **to b. in** *(to hotel)* signer le registre; **to b. into a hotel** prendre une chambre dans un hôtel ■ **bookcase** *n* bibliothèque *f* ■ **bookend** *n* serre-livres *m inv* ■ **bookie** *n* *Fam* bookmaker *m* ■ **booking** *n* réservation *f*; **b. office** bureau *m* de location ■ **bookkeeping** *n* comptabilité *f* ■ **booklet** *n* brochure *f* ■ **bookmaker** *n* bookmaker *m* ■ **bookmark** *n* marque-page *m* ■ **bookseller** *n* libraire *mf* ■ **bookshelf** *n* étagère *f* ■ **bookshop** (*Am* **bookstore**) *n* librairie *f* ■ **bookstall** *n* kiosque *m* à journaux ■ **bookworm** *n* passionné, -e *mf* de lecture

boom [buːm] **1** *n* (a) *(noise)* grondement *m* (b) *(economic)* boom *m* **2** *vi* (a) *(of thunder, gun)* gronder (b) *(of business, trade)* être florissant

boor [bʊə(r)] *n* rustre *m*

boost [buːst] **1** *n* **to give sb a b.** remonter le moral à qn **2** *vt (increase)* augmenter; *(economy)* stimuler; **to b. sb's morale** remonter le moral à qn ■ **booster** *n* **b. (injection)** rappel *m*

boot¹ [buːt] **1** *n* (a) *(footwear)* botte *f*; **(ankle) b.** bottillon *m*; **(knee) b.** bottine *f*; *Fam* **to get the b.** être mis à la porte (b) *Br (of vehicle)* coffre *m* (c) **to b.** *(in addition)* en plus **2** *vt Fam (kick)* donner un coup/des coups de pied à; **to b. sb out** mettre qn à la porte

boot² [buːt] *Comptr* **1** *vt* amorcer **2** *vi* s'amorcer

booth [bu:θ, bu:ð] *n (for phone, in language lab)* cabine *f; (at fair)* stand *m; (for voting)* isoloir *m*

booze [bu:z] *Fam* 1 *n* alcool *m* 2 *vi* picoler ▪ **boozer** *n Fam (person)* poivrot, -e *mf; Br (pub)* pub *m*

border ['bɔ:də(r)] 1 *n (of country, & Fig* frontière *f; (edge)* bord *m; (of garden)* bordure *f* 2 *adj (town)* frontière *inv* 3 *vt (street)* border; **to b. (on)** *(country)* avoir une frontière commune avec; *(resemble, verge on)* être voisin de

bore¹ [bɔ:(r)] 1 *vt (weary)* ennuyer; **to be bored** s'ennuyer 2 *n (person)* raseur, -euse *mf;* **it's a b.** c'est ennuyeux *ou* rasoir ▪ **boredom** *n* ennui *m* ▪ **boring** *adj* ennuyeux, -euse

bore² [bɔ:(r)] 1 *n (of gun)* calibre *m* 2 *vt (hole)* percer; *(rock, well)* forer, creuser 3 *vi* forer

bore³ [bɔ:(r)] *pt of* **bear²**

born [bɔ:n] *adj* né; **to be b.** naître; **he was b. in Paris/in 1980** il est né à Paris/en 1980

borne [bɔ:n] *pp of* **bear²**

borough ['bʌrə] *n* circonscription *f* électorale urbaine

borrow ['bɒrəʊ] *vt* emprunter (**from** à)

Bosnia ['bɒznɪə] *n* la Bosnie

bosom ['bʊzəm] *n (chest, breasts)* poitrine *f; (breast)* sein *m; Fig (heart, soul)* sein *m*

boss [bɒs] 1 *n* patron, -onne *mf* 2 *vt* **to b. sb around** *or* **about** donner des ordres à qn ▪ **bossy (-ier, -iest)** *adj Fam* autoritaire

botany ['bɒtənɪ] *n* botanique *f*

botch [bɒtʃ] *vt Fam* **to b. (up)** *(spoil)* bâcler; *(repair badly)* rafistoler

both [bəʊθ] 1 *adj* les deux; **b. brothers** les deux frères

2 *pron (at the same time)* tous/toutes (les) deux; **b. of the boys** les deux garçons; **b. of us** tous les deux; **b. of them died** ils sont morts tous les deux

3 *adv (at the same time)* à la fois; **b. in England and in France** en Angleterre comme en France; **b. you and I know that…** vous et moi, nous savons que…

bother ['bɒðə(r)] 1 *n (trouble)* ennui *m; (effort)* peine *f; (inconvenience)* dérangement *m* 2 *vt (annoy, worry)* ennuyer; *(disturb)* déranger; *(pester)* importuner; *(hurt, itch) (of foot, eye)* gêner; **to b. doing** *or* **to do sth** se donner la peine de faire qch; **I can't be bothered** ça ne me dit rien 3 *vi* **to b. about** *(worry about)* se préoccuper de; *(deal with)* s'occuper de; **don't b.!** ce n'est pas la peine!

bottle ['bɒtəl] 1 *n* bouteille *f; (for perfume)* flacon *m; (for baby)* biberon *m;* **b. bank** conteneur *m* pour verre usagé; **b. opener** ouvre-bouteilles *m inv* 2 *vt (milk, wine)* mettre en bouteilles; **to b. up** *(feeling)* refouler ▪ **bottle-feed (pt & pp -fed)** *vt* nourrir au biberon ▪ **bottleneck** *n (in road)* goulot *m* d'étranglement; *(in traffic)* bouchon *m*

bottom ['bɒtəm] 1 *n (of sea, box)* fond *m; (of page, hill)* bas *m; (of table)* bout *m; (buttocks)* derrière *m;* **to be (at the) b. of the class** être le dernier/la dernière de la classe

2 *adj (shelf)* inférieur, du bas; **b. floor** rez-de-chaussée *m;* **b. gear** première vitesse *f;* **b. part** *or* **half** partie *f* inférieure; *Fig* **the b. line is that…** le fait est que… ▪ **bottomless** *adj (funds)* inépuisable; **b. pit** gouffre *m*

bought [bɔ:t] *pt & pp of* **buy**

boulder ['bəʊldə(r)] *n* rocher *m*

bounce [baʊns] 1 *n* rebond *m* 2 *vt (ball)* faire rebondir 3 *vi (of ball)* rebondir (**off** contre); *(of person)* faire des bonds; *Fam (of cheque)* être sans provision

bouncer ['baʊnsə(r)] *n Fam (doorman)* videur *m*

bound¹ [baʊnd] *adj* (a) **b. to do** *(obliged)* obligé de faire; *(certain)* sûr de faire; **it's b. to snow** il va sûrement neiger; **to be b. for** *(of person, ship)* être en route pour; *(of train, plane)* être à destination de (b) **b. up with** *(connected)* lié à

bound² [baʊnd] 1 *n (leap)* bond *m* 2 *vi* bondir

bound³ [baʊnd] *pt & pp of* **bind**

boundary ['baʊndərɪ] (pl -ies) n limite f

bounds [baʊndz] npl limites fpl; **out of b.** (place) interdit

bouquet [bəʊ'keɪ] n (of flowers, wine) bouquet m

bout [baʊt] n (of fever, coughing, violence) accès m; (of asthma, malaria) crise f; (session) séance f; (period) période f; (in boxing) combat m; **a b. of flu** une grippe

boutique [buː'tiːk] n boutique f (de mode)

bow¹ [bəʊ] n (weapon) arc m; (of violin) archet m; (knot) nœud m; **b. tie** nœud m papillon ▪ **bow-legged** adj aux jambes arquées

bow² [baʊ] **1** n (with knees bent) révérence f; (nod) salut m **2** vt **to b. one's head** incliner la tête **3** vi s'incliner (**to** devant); (nod) incliner la tête (**to** devant); **to b. down (to)** (submit) s'incliner (devant)

bow³ [baʊ] n (of ship) proue f

bowels ['baʊəlz] npl intestins mpl

bowl¹ [bəʊl] n (small dish) bol m; (for salad) saladier m; (for soup) assiette f creuse; (of toilet) cuvette f

bowl² [bəʊl] **1** n **bowls** (game) boules fpl **2** vi (in cricket) lancer la balle ▪ **bowling** n (tenpin) b. bowling m; **b. alley** bowling m; **b. ball** boule f de bowling; **b. green** terrain m de boules

▸**bowl over** vt sep (knock down) renverser; Fig (astound) **to be bowled over by sth** être stupéfié par qch

box [bɒks] **1** n **boîte** f; (larger) caisse f; (made of cardboard) carton m; (in theatre) loge f; (for horse, in stable) box m; Br Fam (television) télé f; **b. office** bureau m de location; Br **b. room** (for storage) débarras m; (bedroom) petite chambre f
2 vt (a) **to b. (up)** mettre en boîte/caisse; **to b. in** (enclose) enfermer (**b**) **to b. sb's ears** gifler qn
3 vi boxer ▪ **boxing** n (a) (sport) boxe f; **b. gloves/match** gants mpl/combat m de boxe; **b. ring** ring m (**b**) Br **B. Day** le lendemain de Noël

boxer ['bɒksə(r)] n (fighter) boxeur m; (dog) boxer m

boy [bɔɪ] n garçon m ▪ **boyfriend** n petit ami m

boycott ['bɔɪkɒt] **1** n boycottage m **2** vt boycotter

bra [brɑː] n soutien-gorge m

brace [breɪs] **1** n (dental) appareil m dentaire; (on leg, arm) appareil m orthopédique; (for fastening) attache f; Br **braces** (for trousers) bretelles fpl **2** vt **to b. oneself for sth** (news, shock) se préparer à qch ▪ **bracing** adj (air) vivifiant

bracelet ['breɪslɪt] n bracelet m

bracket ['brækɪt] **1** n (for shelves) équerre f; (in writing) parenthèse f; (group) groupe m; (for tax) tranche f; **in brackets** entre parenthèses **2** vt mettre entre parenthèses

brag [bræg] (pt & pp -gg-) vi se vanter (**about** or **of sth** de qch; **about doing sth** de faire qch)

braid [breɪd] **1** n (of hair) tresse f; (trimming) galon m **2** vt (hair) tresser; (trim) galonner

Braille [breɪl] n braille m; **in B.** en braille

brain [breɪn] **1** n cerveau m; (of animal, bird) cervelle f; Fam **to have brains** être intelligent; Fam **to have sth on the b.** être obsédé par qch; **b. death** mort f cérébrale; **b. drain** fuite f des cerveaux **2** vt Fam (hit) assommer ▪ **brainchild** n trouvaille f ▪ **brainstorm** n Am (brilliant idea) idée f géniale; Br (mental confusion) aberration f ▪ **brainwash** vt faire un lavage de cerveau à ▪ **brainwave** n idée f géniale

brainy ['breɪnɪ] (-ier, -iest) adj Fam intelligent

brake [breɪk] **1** n frein m; **b. light** stop m **2** vi freiner

bran [bræn] n son m

branch [brɑːntʃ] **1** n branche f; (of road) embranchement m; (of river) bras m; (of shop) succursale f; (of bank) agence f; **b. office** succursale f **2** vi **to b. off** (of road) bifurquer; **to b. out** (of company, person) étendre ses activités;

(of family, tree) se ramifier

brand [brænd] **1** *n (on product, on cattle)* marque *f; (type)* type *m*, style *m*; **b. name** marque *f* **2** *vt (mark)* marquer; *Fig* **to be branded as a liar/coward** avoir une réputation de menteur/lâche

brandish ['brændɪʃ] *vt* brandir

brand-new [brænd'njuː] *adj* tout neuf *(f* toute neuve)

brandy ['brændɪ] *(pl* -**ies**) *n* cognac *m; (made with fruit)* eau-de-vie *f*

brash [bræʃ] *adj* exubérant

brass [brɑːs] *n* cuivre *m; (instruments in orchestra)* cuivres *mpl; Fam* **b. band** fanfare *f*

brat [bræt] *n Pej (child)* morveux, -euse *mf; (badly behaved)* sale gosse *mf*

brave [breɪv] **1** (-**er**, -**est**) *adj* courageux, -euse **2** *n (native American)* brave *m* **3** *vt (danger)* braver ▪ **bravery** *n* courage *m*

brawl [brɔːl] **1** *n (fight)* bagarre *f* **2** *vi* se bagarrer

Brazil [brə'zɪl] *n* le Brésil ▪ **Brazilian 1** *adj* brésilien, -enne **2** *n* Brésilien, -enne *mf*

breach [briːtʃ] **1** *n (of rule)* violation *f* **(of** de); **b. of contract** rupture *f* de contrat; **b. of trust** abus *m* de confiance **2** *vt (law, code)* enfreindre à; *(contract)* rompre

bread [bred] *n* pain *m; Fam (money)* blé *m;* **loaf of b.** pain *m;* **brown b.** pain *m* bis; **(slice** *or* **piece of) b. and butter** pain *m* beurré; **b. knife** couteau *m* à pain ▪ **breadbin** *(Am* **breadbox**) *n* boîte *f* à pain ▪ **breadboard** *n* planche *f* à pain ▪ **breadcrumb** *n* miette *f* de pain; **breadcrumbs** *(in cooking)* chapelure *f* ▪ **breaded** *adj* pané ▪ **breadline** *n* **on the b.** indigent ▪ **breadwinner** *n* **to be the b.** faire bouillir la marmite

breadth [bretθ] *n* largeur *f*

break [breɪk] **1** *n* cassure *f; (in bone)* fracture *f; (with person, group)* rupture *f; (in journey)* interruption *f; (rest)* repos *m; (in activity)* pause *f; (at school)* récréation *f; (holidays)* vacances *fpl*

2 *(pt* **broke**, *pp* **broken**) *vt* casser; *(into pieces, with force)* briser; *(silence, spell, vow)* rompre; *(strike, will, ice)* briser; *(agreement, promise)* manquer à; *(law)* violer; *(record)* battre; *(journey)* interrompre; *(news)* annoncer **(to** à); *(habit)* se débarrasser de; **to b. one's arm** se casser le bras; **to b. sb's heart** briser le cœur à qn; *Fam* **to b. the sound barrier** franchir le mur du son; **to b. a fall** amortir une chute

3 *vi* se casser; *(into pieces, of heart, of voice)* se briser; *(of boy's voice)* muer; *(of spell)* se rompre; *(of weather)* changer; *(of news)* éclater; *(of day)* se lever; *(stop work)* faire la pause; **to b. in two** se casser en deux; **to b. free** se libérer; **to b. loose** se détacher ▪ **breakable** *adj* fragile ▪ **breakage** *n* **were there any breakages?** est-ce qu'il y a eu de la casse? ▪ **breakdown** *n (of machine)* panne *f; (of argument, figures)* analyse *f; (of talks, negotiations)* échec *m; (of person)* dépression *f; Br* **b. lorry** *or* **van** dépanneuse *f*

▸**break away 1** *vi* se détacher **2** *vt sep* détacher

▸**break down 1** *vt sep (door)* enfoncer; *(resistance)* briser; *(argument, figures)* analyser **2** *vi (of machine)* tomber en panne; *(of talks, negotiations)* échouer; *(of person) (have nervous breakdown)* craquer; *(start crying)* éclater en sanglots

▸**break in 1** *vi (of burglar)* entrer par effraction; *(interrupt)* interrompre **2** *vt sep (door)* enfoncer; *(horse)* dresser

▸**break into** *vt insep (house)* entrer par effraction; *(safe)* forcer; **to b. into song/a run** se mettre à chanter/courir

▸**break off 1** *vt sep (detach) (twig, handle)* détacher; *(relations)* rompre **2** *vi (become detached)* se casser; *(stop)* s'arrêter; **to b. off with sb** rompre avec qn

▸**break out** *vi (of war, fire)* éclater; *(escape)* s'échapper **(of** de); **to b. out in a rash** se couvrir de boutons

▸**break through 1** *vi (of sun, army)* percer **2** *vt insep (defences)* percer; *(barrier)* forcer; *(wall)* faire une brèche dans

▸**break up 1** *vt sep (reduce to pieces)*

mettre en morceaux; *(marriage)* briser; *(fight)* mettre fin à **2** *vi (end)* prendre fin; *(of group)* se disperser; *(of marriage)* se briser; *(from school)* partir en vacances

breakfast ['brekfəst] *n* petit déjeuner *m*; **to have b.** prendre le petit déjeuner; **b. TV** émissions *fpl* (télévisées) du matin

break-in ['breɪkɪn] *n* cambriolage *m*

breaking-point ['breɪkɪŋpɔɪnt] *n* **at b.** *(person, patience)* à bout; *(marriage)* au bord de la rupture

breakthrough ['breɪkθru:] *n (discovery)* découverte *f* fondamentale

breast [brest] *n (of woman)* sein *m*; *(chest)* poitrine *f*; *(of chicken)* blanc *m* ▪ **breastfeed** *(pt & pp* **-fed)** *vt* allaiter ▪ **breaststroke** *n (in swimming)* brasse *f*

breath [breθ] *n* souffle *m*; **bad b.** mauvaise haleine *f*; **out of b.** à bout de souffle; **to hold one's b.** retenir son souffle; **under one's b.** tout bas ▪ **breathalyser®** *n* Alcotest® *m* ▪ **breathless** *adj* hors d'haleine ▪ **breathtaking** *adj* à couper le souffle

breathe [bri:ð] **1** *vi (of person, animal)* respirer; **to b. in** inhaler; **to b. out** expirer **2** *vt* respirer; **to b. a sigh of relief** pousser un soupir de soulagement ▪ **breathing** *n* respiration *f*; *Fig* **b. space** moment *m* de repos

bred [bred] **1** *pt & pp of* **breed 2** *adj* **well-b.** bien élevé

breed [bri:d] **1** *n* race *f* **2** *(pt & pp* **bred)** *vt (animals)* élever; *Fig (hatred, violence)* engendrer **3** *vi (of animals)* se reproduire ▪ **breeding** *n (of animals)* élevage *m*; *Fig (manners)* éducation *f*

breeze [bri:z] *n* brise *f* ▪ **breezy (-ier, -iest)** *adj* **(a)** *(weather, day)* frais *(f* fraîche), venteux, -euse **(b)** *(cheerful)* jovial; *(relaxed)* décontracté

brew [bru:] **1** *n (drink)* breuvage *m*; *(of tea)* infusion *f* **2** *vt (beer)* brasser; *Fig (trouble, plot)* préparer **3** *vi (of beer)* fermenter; *(of tea)* infuser; *Fig (of storm)* se préparer ▪ **brewery** *(pl* **-ies)** *n* brasserie *f*

bribe [braɪb] **1** *n* pot-de-vin *m* **2** *vt*

acheter, soudoyer; **to b. sb into doing sth** soudoyer qn pour qu'il fasse qch ▪ **bribery** *n* corruption *f*

brick [brɪk] *n* brique *f*; **b. wall** mur en briques ▪ **bricklayer** *n* maçon *m*

bridal ['braɪdəl] *adj (ceremony, bed)* nuptial; **b. suite** *(in hotel)* suite *f* nuptiale

bride [braɪd] *n* mariée *f*; **the b. and groom** les mariés *mpl* ▪ **bridegroom** *n* marié *m* ▪ **bridesmaid** *n* demoiselle *f* d'honneur

bridge¹ [brɪdʒ] **1** *n* pont *m*; *(on ship)* passerelle *f*; *(of nose)* arête *f*; *(on teeth)* bridge *m* **2** *vt* **to b. a gap** combler une lacune

bridge² [brɪdʒ] *n (game)* bridge *m*

brief¹ [bri:f] **(-er, -est)** *adj* bref *(f* brève); **in b.** en résumé ▪ **briefly** *adv (say)* brièvement; *(hesitate, smile)* un court instant

brief² [bri:f] **1** *n (instructions)* instructions *fpl*; *(legal)* dossier *m*; *Fig (task)* tâche *f* **2** *vt* donner des instructions à; *(inform)* mettre au courant **(on** de) ▪ **briefing** *n (information)* instructions *fpl*; *(meeting)* briefing *m*

briefcase ['bri:fkeɪs] *n* serviette *f*

briefs [bri:fs] *npl (underwear)* slip *m*

brigade [brɪ'geɪd] *n* brigade *f*

bright [braɪt] **1** **(-er, -est)** *adj (star, eyes, situation)* brillant; *(light, colour)* vif *(f* vive); *(weather, room)* clair; *(clever)* intelligent; *(happy)* joyeux, -euse; *(future)* prometteur, -euse; *.(idea)* génial **2** *adv* **b. and early** de bon matin ▪ **brightly** *adv (shine)* avec éclat

brighten ['braɪtən] **1** *vt* **to b. (up)** *(room)* égayer **2** *vi* **to b. (up)** *(of weather)* s'éclaircir; *(of face)* s'éclairer; *(of person)* s'égayer

brilliant ['brɪljənt] *adj (light)* éclatant; *(person, idea, career)* brillant; *Br Fam (fantastic)* super *inv*

brim [brɪm] **1** *n (of hat, cup)* bord *m* **2** *(pt & pp* **-mm-)** *vi* **to b. over (with)** déborder (de)

bring [brɪŋ] *(pt & pp* **brought)** *vt (person, animal, car)* amener; *(object)* apporter; *(cause)* provoquer; **it has**

brought me great happiness cela m'a procuré un grand bonheur; **to b. sth to sb's attention** attirer l'attention de qn sur qch; **to b. sth to an end** mettre fin à qch

▸**bring about** *vt sep* provoquer

▸**bring along** *vt sep (object)* apporter; *(person)* amener

▸**bring back** *vt sep (person)* ramener; *(object)* rapporter; *(memories)* rappeler

▸**bring down** *vt sep (object)* descendre; *(overthrow)* faire tomber; *(reduce)* réduire; *(shoot down) (plane)* abattre

▸**bring forward** *vt sep (in time or space)* avancer; *(witness)* produire

▸**bring in** *vt sep (object)* rentrer; *(person)* faire entrer; *(introduce)* introduire; *(income)* rapporter

▸**bring off** *vt sep (task)* mener à bien

▸**bring out** *vt sep (object)* sortir, *(person)* faire sortir; *(meaning)* faire ressortir; *(book)* publier; *(product)* lancer

▸**bring round** *vt sep (revive)* ranimer; *(convert)* convaincre; **she brought him round to her point of view** elle a su le convaincre

▸**bring to** *vt sep* **to b. sb to** ranimer qn

▸**bring together** *vt sep (friends, members)* réunir; *(reconcile)* réconcilier; *(put in touch)* mettre en contact

▸**bring up** *vt sep (object)* monter; *(child)* élever; *(question)* soulever; *(subject)* mentionner; *(food)* rendre

brink [brɪŋk] *n* bord *m*; **on the b. of sth** au bord de qch

brisk [brɪsk] *(-er, -est) adj (lively)* vif (*f* vive); **at a b. pace** vite; **business is b.** les affaires marchent bien

bristle ['brɪsəl] **1** *n* poil *m* **2** *vi* se hérisser

Britain ['brɪtən] *n* la Grande-Bretagne ▪ **British 1** *adj* britannique. **the B. Isles** les îles *fpl* Britanniques; **B. Summer Time** heure *f* d'été *(en Grande-Bretagne)* **2** *npl* **the B.** les Britanniques *mpl* ▪ **Briton** *n* Britannique *mf*

Brittany ['brɪtəni] *n* la Bretagne

brittle ['brɪtəl] *adj* cassant

broad [brɔːd] *(-er, -est) adj (wide)* large; *(accent)* prononcé; **in b. daylight** en plein jour; **the b. outline of** *(plan)* les grandes lignes de; **b. bean** fève *f*; *Am Sport* **b. jump** saut *m* en longueur ▪ **broad-minded** *adj (person)* à l'esprit large; ▪ **broad-shouldered** *adj* large d'épaules ▪ **broaden 1** *vt* élargir **2** *vi* s'élargir ▪ **broadly** *adv* **b. (speaking)** en gros

broadcast ['brɔːdkɑːst] **1** *n* émission *f* **2** *(pt & pp* **broadcast)** *vt* diffuser **3** *vi (of station)* émettre; *(of person)* parler à la radio/à la télévision

broccoli ['brɒkəlɪ] *n inv (plant)* brocoli *m*; *(food)* brocolis *mpl*

brochure ['brəʊʃə(r)] *n* brochure *f*

broil [brɔɪl] *vt & vi Am* griller

broke [brəʊk] **1** *pt of* **break 2** *adj Fam (penniless)* fauché ▪ **broken 1** *pp of* **break 2** *adj (man, voice, line)* brisé; *(ground)* accidenté; *(spirit)* abattu; **in b. English** en mauvais anglais; **b. home** famille *f* désunie

broker ['brəʊkə(r)] *n (for shares, currency)* agent *m* de change; *(for goods, insurance)* courtier, -ère *mf*

bronchitis [brɒŋ'kaɪtɪs] *n* bronchite *f*

bronze [brɒnz] *n* bronze *m*; **b. statue** statue *f* en bronze

brooch [brəʊtʃ] *n (ornament)* broche *f*

brood [bruːd] **1** *n* couvée *f* **2** *vi (of bird)* couver; *Fig* **to b. over sth** *(of person)* ruminer qch ▪ **broody (-ier, -iest)** *adj (person) (sulky)* maussade; *(dreamy)* rêveur, -euse; *Br Fam (woman)* en mal d'enfant

broom [bruːm] *n* (a) *(for sweeping)* balai *m* (b) *(plant)* genêt *m*

broth [brɒθ] *n (thin)* bouillon *m*; *(thick)* potage *m*

brothel ['brɒθəl] *n* maison *f* close

brother ['brʌðə(r)] *n* frère *m* ▪ **brother-in-law** *(pl* **brothers-in-law)** *n* beau-frère *m*

brought [brɔːt] *pt & pp of* **bring**

brow [braʊ] *n* (a) *(forehead)* front *m* (b) *(of hill)* sommet *m*

brown [braʊn] **1** *(-er, -est) adj* marron *inv*; *(hair)* châtain; *(tanned)* bronzé **2** *n* marron *m* **3** *vt (food)* faire dorer **4** *vi (of food)* dorer

Brownie ['braʊnɪ] *n (girl scout)* ≃ jeannette *f*

brownie ['braʊnɪ] *n (cake)* brownie *m*

browse [braʊz] **1** *vt Comptr* **to b. the Web** naviguer sur le Web **2** *vi (in bookshop)* feuilleter des livres; *(in shop, supermarket)* regarder; **to b. through** *(book)* feuilleter

bruise [bruːz] **1** *n* bleu *m*; *(on fruit)* meurtrissure *f* **2** *vt* **to b. one's knee/hand** se faire un bleu au genou/à la main ▪ **bruised** *adj (covered in bruises)* couvert de bleus

brunch [brʌntʃ] *n* brunch *m*

brunette [bruːˈnet] *n* brunette *f*

brunt [brʌnt] *n* **to bear the b. of** *(attack, anger)* subir le plus gros de; *(expense)* assumer la plus grosse part de

brush [brʌʃ] **1** *n (tool)* brosse *f*; *(for shaving)* blaireau *m*; *(for sweeping)* balayette *f*; **to give sth a b.** donner un coup de brosse à qch
2 *vt (teeth, hair)* brosser; *(clothes)* donner un coup de brosse à; **to b. sb/sth aside** écarter qn/qch; **to b. sth away** *or* **off** enlever qch; **to b. up (on) one's French** se remettre au français **3** *vi* **to b. against sb/sth** effleurer qn/qch ▪ **brush-off** *n Fam* **to give sb the b.** envoyer promener qn

brusque [bruːsk] *adj* brusque

Brussels ['brʌsəlz] *n* Bruxelles *m ou f*; **B. sprouts** choux *mpl* de Bruxelles

brutal ['bruːtəl] *adj* brutal; *(attack)* sauvage

brute [bruːt] **1** *n (animal)* bête *f*; *(person)* brute *f* **2** *adj* **by b. force** par la force

BSc [biːesˈsiː] *(Am* **BS** [biːˈes]) *(abbr* **Bachelor of Science)** *(person)* ≃ licencié, -e *mf* ès sciences; *(qualification)* ≃ licence *f* de sciences

BSE [biːesˈiː] *(abbr* **bovine spongiform encephalopathy)** *n* EBS *f*, maladie *f* de la vache folle

bubble ['bʌbəl] **1** *n (of air, soap)* bulle *f*; **b. bath** bain *m* moussant; **b. gum** chewing-gum *m* **2** *vi (of liquid)* bouillonner; **to b. over (with)** déborder (de)

bubbly ['bʌblɪ] **1** *adj (liquid)* plein de

bulles; *(person, personality)* débordant de vitalité **2** *n Fam* champ *m*

buck [bʌk] **1** *n* (a) *Am Fam* dollar *m* (b) *(of rabbit)* mâle *m* **2** *vt Fam* **to b. sb up** remonter le moral à qn **3** *vi Fam* **to b. up** *(become livelier)* reprendre du poil de la bête; *(hurry)* se grouiller

bucket ['bʌkɪt] *n* seau *m*

buckle ['bʌkəl] **1** *n* boucle *f* **2** *vt* (a) *(fasten)* boucler (b) *(deform)* déformer **3** *vi (deform)* se déformer

bud [bʌd] **1** *n (on tree)* bourgeon *m*; *(on flower)* bouton *m* **2** *(pt & pp* **-dd-)** *vi* bourgeonner; *(of flower)* pousser des boutons ▪ **budding** *adj (talent)* naissant; *(doctor)* en herbe

Buddhist ['bʊdɪst] *adj & n* bouddhiste *(mf)*

buddy ['bʌdɪ] *(pl* **-ies)** *n Am Fam* pote *m*

budge [bʌdʒ] **1** *vi* bouger **2** *vt* faire bouger

budgerigar ['bʌdʒərɪgaː(r)] *n Br* perruche *f*

budget ['bʌdʒɪt] **1** *n* budget *m* **2** *vi* dresser un budget; **to b. for sth** inscrire qch au budget

budgie ['bʌdʒɪ] *n Br Fam* perruche *f*

buff [bʌf] **1** *adj* **b.(-coloured)** chamois *inv* **2** *n Fam* **jazz/film b.** fanatique *mf* de jazz/de cinéma

buffalo ['bʌfələʊ] *(pl* **-oes** *or* **-o)** *n* buffle *m*; **(American) b.** bison *m*

buffer ['bʌfə(r)] *n (on train)* tampon *m*; *(at end of track)* butoir *m*; *Fig (safeguard)* protection *f* **(against** contre)

buffet¹ ['bʊfeɪ] *n (meal, café)* buffet *m*; **cold b.** viandes *fpl* froides; *Br* **b. car** *(on train)* wagon-restaurant *m*

buffet² ['bʌfɪt] *vt (of waves)* secouer; *(of wind, rain)* cingler

bug¹ [bʌg] **1** *n* (a) *(insect)* bestiole *f*; *(bedbug)* punaise *f*; *Fam (germ)* microbe *m* (b) *(in machine)* défaut *m*; *Comptr* bogue *m* (c) *(listening device)* micro *m* **2** *(pt & pp* **-gg-)** *vt (room)* installer des micros dans

bug² [bʌg] *(pt & pp* **-gg-)** *vt Fam (nag)* embêter

buggy ['bʌgɪ] *(pl* **-ies)** *n Br* **(baby) b.**

(pushchair) poussette *f; Am (pram)* landau *m*

build [bɪld] **1** *n (of person)* carrure *f* **2** *(pt & pp* **built** [bɪlt]) *vt* construire; **to b. sth up** *(increase)* augmenter qch; *(business)* monter qch **3** *vi* **to b. up** *(of tension, pressure)* augmenter; *(of dust, snow, interest)* s'accumuler; *(of traffic)* devenir dense ▪ **builder** *n (skilled)* maçon *m; (unskilled)* ouvrier *m; (contractor)* entrepreneur *m* ▪ **building** *n* bâtiment *m; (flats, offices)* immeuble *m; (action)* construction *f;* **b. site** chantier *m; Br* **b. society** ≃ société *f* de crédit immobilier ▪ **build-up** *n (increase)* augmentation *f; (of dust)* accumulation *f; (for author, book)* publicité *f*

built-in [bɪlt'ɪn] *adj (cupboard)* encastré; *(part of machine)* incorporé; *Fig (innate)* inné

built-up [bɪltʌp] *adj* urbanisé; **b. area** agglomération *f*

bulb [bʌlb] *n (of plant)* bulbe *m; (of lamp)* ampoule *f*

bulge [bʌldʒ] **1** *n* renflement *m* **2** *vi* **to b. (out)** bomber; *(of eyes)* sortir de la tête ▪ **bulging** *adj* bombé; *(eyes)* protubérant; **to be b. (with)** *(of bag, pocket)* être bourré (de)

bulimia [buˈlɪmɪə] *n* boulimie *f*

bulk [bʌlk] *n inv (of building, parcel)* volume *m; (of person)* grosseur *f;* **the b. of sth** la majeure partie de qch; **in b.** *(buy, sell)* en gros ▪ **bulky (-ier, -iest)** *adj* volumineux, -euse

bull [bʊl] *n* **(a)** *(animal)* taureau *m* **(b)** *very Fam (nonsense)* conneries *fpl* ▪ **bullfight** *n* corrida *f*

bulldozer ['bʊldəʊzə(r)] *n* bulldozer *m*

bullet ['bʊlɪt] *n* balle *f* ▪ **bulletproof** *adj (car)* blindé; **b. glass** vitre *f* blindée; *Br* **b. jacket,** *Am* **b. vest** gilet *m* pare-balles *inv*

bulletin ['bʊlətɪn] *n* bulletin *m; Am* **b. board** panneau *m* d'affichage

bullion ['bʊljən] *n* **gold b.** lingots *mpl* d'or

bull's-eye ['bʊlzaɪ] *n (of target)* centre *m;* **to hit the b.** mettre dans le mille

bully ['bʊlɪ] **1** *(pl* **-ies)** *n* terreur *f* **2** *(pt & pp* **-ied)** *vt (ill-treat)* maltraiter

bum [bʌm] *Fam* **1** *n* **(a)** *(loafer)* clochard, -e *mf; (good-for-nothing)* bon *m* à rien, bonne *f* à rien **(b)** *Br (buttocks)* derrière *m;* **b. bag** banane *f* **2** *(pt & pp* **-mm-)** *vi* **to b. (around)** *(be idle)* glander; *(travel)* vadrouiller **3** *vt* **to b. sth off sb** taxer qch à qn

bump [bʌmp] **1** *n (impact)* choc *m; (jerk)* secousse *f; (on road, body)* bosse *f* **2** *vt (of car)* heurter; **to b. one's head/knee** se cogner la tête/le genou; **to b. into** *(of person)* se cogner contre; *(of car)* rentrer dans; *(meet)* tomber sur ▪ **bumper** **1** *n (of car)* pare-chocs *m inv* **2** *adj (crop, year)* exceptionnel, -elle

bumpy ['bʌmpɪ] **(-ier, -iest)** *adj (road, ride)* cahoteux, -euse

bun [bʌn] *n* **(a)** *(cake)* petit pain *m* au lait **(b)** *(of hair)* chignon *m*

bunch [bʌntʃ] *n (of flowers)* bouquet *m; (of keys)* trousseau *m; (of bananas)* régime *m; (of grapes)* grappe *f; (of people)* bande *f*

bundle ['bʌndəl] **1** *n* paquet *m; (of papers)* liasse *f; (of firewood)* fagot *m* **2** *vt (put)* fourrer **(into** dans); *(push)* pousser **(into** dans); **to b. up** *(newspapers, letters)* mettre en paquet **3** *vi* **to b. (oneself) up** (bien) se couvrir

bungalow ['bʌŋgələʊ] *n* pavillon *m* de plain-pied

bungle ['bʌŋgəl] **1** *vt* gâcher **2** *vi* se tromper

bunk [bʌŋk] *n (in ship, train)* couchette *f;* **b. beds** lits *mpl* superposés

bunker ['bʌŋkə(r)] *n Mil & Golf* bunker *m; (for coal)* coffre *m* à charbon

bunny ['bʌnɪ] *(pl* **-ies)** *n Fam* **b. (rabbit)** petit lapin *m*

buoy [bɔɪ] **1** *n* bouée *f* **2** *vt Fig* **to b. up** *(support)* soutenir

buoyant ['bɔɪənt] *adj (in water)* qui flotte; *Fig (economy, prices)* stable; *Fig (person, mood)* plein d'allant

burden ['bɜːdən] **1** *n* fardeau *m* **2** *vt* charger **(with** de); *Fig* accabler **(with** de)

bureau ['bjʊərəʊ] *(pl* **-eaux** [-əʊz]) *n*

(office) bureau *m*; *Br (desk)* secrétaire *m*; *Am (chest of drawers)* commode *f*

bureaucracy [bjʊə'rɒkrəsɪ] *n* bureaucratie *f* ∎ **bureaucrat** *n* bureaucrate *mf*

burger ['bɜːgə(r)] *n* hamburger *m*

burglar ['bɜːglə(r)] *n* cambrioleur, -euse *mf*; **b. alarm** alarme *f* antivol ∎ **burglarize** *vt Am* cambrioler ∎ **burgle** *vt Br* cambrioler

burial ['berɪəl] **1** *n* enterrement *m* **2** *adj (service)* funèbre; **b. ground** cimetière *m*

burn [bɜːn] **1** *n* brûlure *f* **2** *(pt & pp* **burned** *or* **burnt)** *vt* brûler; **to b. sth down** incendier qch **3** *vi* brûler; **to b. down** *(of house)* être détruit par les flammes; *(of fuse)* sauter ∎ **burning 1** *adj* en feu; *(fire)* allumé; *Fig (fever)* dévorant **2** *n* **a smell of b.** une odeur de brûlé

burner ['bɜːnə(r)] *n (on stove)* brûleur *m*; *Fig* **to put sth on the back b.** remettre qch à plus tard

burp [bɜːp] *Fam* **1** *n* rot *m* **2** *vi* roter

burrow ['bʌrəʊ] **1** *n (hole)* terrier *m* **2** *vt & vi* creuser

burst [bɜːst] **1** *n (of shell)* éclatement *m*, explosion *f*; *(of laughter)* éclat *m*; *(of applause)* salve *f*; *(of thunder)* coup *m*; *(surge)* élan *m*
2 *(pt & pp* **burst)** *vt (bubble, balloon, boil)* crever; *(tyre)* faire éclater; **to b. open** *(door)* ouvrir brusquement
3 *vi (of bubble, balloon, boil, tyre, cloud)* crever; *(with force) (of shell, boiler, tyre)* éclater; **to b. into a room** faire irruption dans une pièce; **to b. into flames** prendre feu; **to b. into tears** fondre en larmes; **to b. out laughing** éclater de rire; **to b. open** *(of door)* s'ouvrir brusquement

bury ['berɪ] *(pt & pp* **-ied)** *vt (body)* enterrer; *(hide)* enfouir; *(plunge)* plonger **(in** dans); **buried in one's work** plongé dans son travail

bus [bʌs] *(pl* **buses** *or* **busses)** *n* autobus *m*, bus *m*; *(long-distance)* autocar *m*, car *m*; **by b.** en bus/en car; **b. driver** chauffeur *m* de bus/car; **b. shelter** Abribus® *m*; **b. station** gare *f* routière; **b. stop** arrêt *m* de bus

bush [bʊʃ] *n* buisson *m*; **the b.** *(land)* la brousse ∎ **bushy (-ier, -iest)** *adj (hair, tail)* touffu

bushed [bʊʃt] *adj Fam (tired)* crevé

business ['bɪznɪs] **1** *n* affaires *fpl*, commerce *m*; *(shop)* commerce *m*; *(company, task, concern, matter)* affaire *f*; **the textile/construction b.** l'industrie *f* du textile/de la construction; **big b.** les grosses entreprises *fpl*; **to go out of b.** *(stop trading)* fermer; **that's none of your b.!, mind your own b.!** ça ne vous regarde pas!
2 *adj* commercial; *(meeting, trip, lunch)* d'affaires; **b. card** carte *f* de visite; **b. hours** *(office)* heures *fpl* de bureau; *(shop)* heures *fpl* d'ouverture; **b. school** école *f* de commerce ∎ **businessman** *(pl* **-men)** *n* homme *m* d'affaires ∎ **businesswoman** *(pl* **-women)** *n* femme *f* d'affaires

bust [bʌst] **1** *n (statue)* buste *m*; *(of woman)* poitrine *f* **2** *adj Fam (broken)* fichu; **to go b.** *(bankrupt)* faire faillite **3** *(pt & pp* **bust** *or* **busted)** *vt Fam (break)* bousiller; *(arrest)* coffrer ∎ **bust-up** *n Fam (quarrel)* engueulade *f*; *(break-up)* rupture *f*

bustle ['bʌsəl] **1** *n* animation *f* **2** *vi* **to b. (about)** s'affairer

busy ['bɪzɪ] **1** **(-ier, -iest)** *adj* occupé; *(active)* actif, -ive; *(day)* chargé; *(street)* animé; *Am (phone, line)* occupé; **to be b. doing** *(in the process of)* être occupé à faire; **to keep oneself b.** s'occuper; **the shops were very b.** il y avait plein de monde dans les magasins; *Am* **b. signal** sonnerie *f* occupé **2** *vt* **to b. oneself** s'occuper **(with sth** à qch; **doing sth** à faire qch) ∎ **busybody** *(pl* **-ies)** *n Fam* fouineur, -euse *mf*

but [bʌt, *unstressed* bət] **1** *conj* mais **2** *prep (except)* sauf; **b. for him** sans lui; **no one b. you** personne d'autre que toi; **the last b. one** l'avant-dernier, -ère *mf*

butcher ['bʊtʃə(r)] **1** *n* boucher *m*; **b.'s (shop)** boucherie *f* **2** *vt (people)* massacrer; *(animal)* abattre

butler ['bʌtlə(r)] *n* maître *m* d'hôtel

butt [bʌt] **1** *n (of cigarette)* mégot *m*; *(of gun)* crosse *f*; *Am Fam (buttocks)* derrière *m* **2** *vt (with head)* donner un coup de tête à **3** *vi* **to b. in** intervenir

butter ['bʌtə(r)] **1** *n* beurre *m*; *Br* **b. bean** = gros haricot blanc; **b. dish** beurrier *m* **2** *vt* beurrer; *Fam* **to b. sb up** passer de la pommade à qn ▪ **butterscotch** *n* caramel *m* dur au beurre

butterfly ['bʌtəflaɪ] (*pl* -ies) *n* papillon *m*; *Fam* **to have butterflies** avoir l'estomac noué; **b. stroke** *(in swimming)* brasse *f* papillon

buttock ['bʌtək] *n* fesse *f*

button ['bʌtən] **1** *n* bouton *m*; *(of phone)* touche *f*; *Am (badge)* badge *m* **2** *vt* **to b. (up)** boutonner **3** *vi* **to b. (up)** *(of garment)* se boutonner ▪ **buttonhole 1** *n* boutonnière *f* **2** *vt Fam (person)* coincer

buy [baɪ] **1** *n* **a good b.** une bonne affaire **2** *(pt & pp* **bought)** *vt* (a) *(purchase)* acheter (**from sb** à qn; **for sb** à *ou* pour qn) (b) *Am Fam (believe)* avaler; **I'll b. that!** je veux bien le croire! ▪ **buyer** *n* acheteur, -euse *mf*

buzz [bʌz] **1** *n* (a) *(noise)* bourdonnement *m* (b) *Fam (phone call)* **to give sb a b.** passer un coup de fil à qn **2** *vt* **to b. sb** *(using buzzer)* appeler qn **3** *vi* bourdonner; *Fam* **to b. off** se tirer ▪ **buzzer** *n* *(internal phone)* Interphone® *m*; *(of bell, clock)* sonnerie *f*

BY [baɪ] **1** *prep* (a) *(agent)* par; de; **hit/chosen by** frappé/choisi par; **surrounded/followed by** entouré/suivi de; **a book/painting by...** un livre/tableau de...

(b) *(manner, means)* par; en; à; de; **by sea** par mer; **by mistake** par erreur; **by car/train** en voiture/train; **by bicycle** à bicyclette; **by moonlight** au clair de lune; **by doing** en faisant; **one by one** un à un; **day by day** de jour en jour; **by sight/day** de vue/jour; **(all) by oneself** tout seul

(c) *(next to)* à côté de; *(near)* près de; **by the lake/sea** au bord du lac/de la mer; **to go** *or* **pass by the bank/school** passer devant la banque/l'école

(d) *(before in time)* avant; **by Monday** avant lundi, d'ici lundi; **by now** à cette heure-ci; **by yesterday** (dès) hier

(e) *(amount, measurement)* à; **by the kilo** au kilo; **taller by a metre** plus grand d'un mètre; **paid by the hour** payé à l'heure

(f) *(according to)* à, d'après; **by my watch** à ma montre; **it's fine** *or* **OK** *or* **all right by me** je n'y vois pas d'objection

2 *adv* **close by** tout près; **to go** *or* **pass by** passer; **by and large** en gros

bye(-bye) ['baɪ('baɪ)] *exclam Fam* salut!, au revoir!

by-law ['baɪlɔː] *n* arrêté *m* (municipal)

bypass ['baɪpɑːs] **1** *n* rocade *f*; **(heart) b. operation** pontage *m* **2** *vt (town)* contourner; *Fig (ignore)* court-circuiter

bystander ['baɪstændə(r)] *n* passant, -e *mf*

byte [baɪt] *n Comptr* octet *m*

Cc

C, c¹ [siː] *n* C, c *m inv*

c² (*abbr* **cent(s)**) ct

cab [kæb] *n* taxi *m*; *(of lorry)* cabine *f*

cabaret ['kæbəreɪ] *n* cabaret *m*

cabbage ['kæbɪdʒ] *n* chou *m* *(pl* choux)

cabin ['kæbɪn] *n* *(on ship)* cabine *f*; *(hut)* cabane *f*; *Aviat* **c. crew** équipage *m*

cabinet¹ ['kæbɪnɪt] *n* *(cupboard)* armoire *f*; *(for display)* vitrine *f*; **(filing) c.** classeur *m* *(meuble)*

cabinet² ['kæbɪnɪt] *n* *(government ministers)* gouvernement *m*; **c. minister** ministre *m*

cable ['keɪbəl] **1** *n* câble *m*; **c. car** *(with overhead cable)* téléphérique *m*; **c. television** la télévision par câble **2** *vt* *(message)* câbler **(to** à)

cactus ['kæktəs] (*pl* **-ti** [-taɪ] *or* **-tuses** [-təsɪz]) *n* cactus *m*

caddie ['kædɪ] *n* *Golf* caddie *m*

cadet [kə'det] *n* élève *m* officier

cadge [kædʒ] *vt* *Fam* **to c. money from** *or* **off sb** taper qn

café ['kæfeɪ] *n* café *m*

caffeine ['kæfiːn] *n* caféine *f*

cage [keɪdʒ] **1** *n* cage *f* **2** *vt* **to c. (up)** mettre en cage

cajole [kə'dʒəʊl] *vt* enjôler

cake [keɪk] *n* gâteau *m*; *(small)* pâtisserie *f*

calamity [kə'læmɪtɪ] (*pl* **-ies**) *n* calamité *f*

calculate ['kælkjʊleɪt] *vti* calculer; **to c. that...** *(estimate)* calculer que... ■ **calculated** *adj* *(deliberate)* délibéré; **a c. risk** un risque calculé ■ **calculation** [-'leɪʃən] *n* calcul *m* ■ **calculator** *n* calculatrice *f*

calendar ['kælɪndə(r)] *n* calendrier *m*; *Am (for engagements)* agenda *m*; **c. month** mois *m* civil

calf [kɑːf] *(pl* **calves**) *n* **(a)** *(animal)* veau *m* **(b)** *(part of leg)* mollet *m*

calibre ['kælɪbə(r)] (*Am* **caliber**) *n* calibre *m*

call [kɔːl] **1** *n* *(shout)* cri *m*; *(visit)* visite *f*; **(telephone) c.** appel *m* (téléphonique); **to make a c.** téléphoner **(to** à); **to give sb a c.** téléphoner à qn; *Br* **c. box** cabine *f* téléphonique; **c. centre** centre *m* d'appels

2 *vt* *(phone)* appeler; **he's called David** il s'appelle David; **to c. sb a liar** traiter qn de menteur

3 *vi* appeler; *(cry out)* crier; *(visit)* passer

▶**call back 1** *vt sep* rappeler **2** *vi* rappeler

▶**call by** *vi* *(visit)* passer

▶**call for** *vt insep* *(require)* demander; *(collect)* passer prendre

▶**call in 1** *vt sep* *(into room)* faire entrer; *(police)* appeler **2** *vi* **to c. in (on sb)** *(visit)* passer (chez qn)

▶**call off** *vt sep* *(cancel)* annuler; *(strike)* mettre fin à

▶**call on** *vt insep* *(visit)* passer voir; **to c. on sb to do** *(urge)* sommer qn de faire

▶**call out 1** *vt sep* *(shout)* crier; *(doctor)* appeler; *(workers)* donner une consigne de grève à **2** *vi* *(shout)* crier; **to c. out to sb** interpeller qn

▶**call round** *vi* *(visit)* passer

▶**call up** *vt sep* *(phone)* appeler; *Mil (recruits)* appeler (sous les drapeaux)

caller ['kɔːlə(r)] *n* visiteur, -euse *mf*; *(on phone)* correspondant, -e *mf*

callous ['kæləs] *adj* *(cruel)* insensible

calm [kɑːm] **1** (**-er, -est**) *adj* calme, tranquille; **keep c.!** restez calme! **2** *n*

calme *m* 3 *vt* **to c. (down)** calmer 4 *vi* **to c. down** se calmer ▪ **calmly** *adv* calmement

calorie ['kælərɪ] *n* calorie *f*

calves [kɑːvz] *pl of* **calf**

camcorder ['kæmkɔːdə(r)] *n* camé-scope® *m*

came [keɪm] *pt of* **come**

camel ['kæməl] *n* chameau *m*

camera ['kæmrə] *n* appareil photo *m*; *(for film, video)* caméra *f*

camouflage ['kæməflɑːʒ] 1 *n* camouflage *m* 2 *vt also Fig* camoufler

camp¹ [kæmp] 1 *n* camp *m*, campement *m*; **c. bed** lit *m* de camp 2 *vi* **to c. (out)** camper ▪ **camper** *n (person)* campeur, -euse *mf*; *(vehicle)* camping-car *m* ▪ **camping** *n* camping *m*; **c. site** *(terrain m de)* camping *m* ▪ **campsite** *n* camping *m*

camp² [kæmp] *adj (effeminate)* efféminé

campaign [kæm'peɪn] 1 *n (political, military)* campagne *f*; **press/publicity c.** campagne *f* de presse/publicité 2 *vi* faire campagne (**for/against** pour/contre) ▪ **campaigner** *n* militant, -e *mf* (**for** pour)

campus ['kæmpəs] *n (of university)* campus *m*

CAN¹ [kæn, *unstressed* kən] *(pt* **could)**

> Le verbe **can** n'a ni infinitif, ni gérondif, ni participe. Pour exprimer l'infinitif ou le participe, on aura recours à la forme correspondante de **be able to** (he wanted to be able to speak English; she has always been able to swim). La forme négative est **can't**, qui s'écrit **cannot** dans la langue soutenue.

v aux (be able to) pouvoir; *(know how to)* savoir; **he couldn't help me** il ne pouvait pas m'aider; **she c. swim** elle sait nager; **he could do it tomorrow** il pourrait le faire demain; **he could have done it** il aurait pu le faire; **you could be wrong** *(possibility)* tu as peut-être tort; **he can't be dead** *(probability)* il ne peut pas être mort; **c. I come in?** *(permission)* puis-je entrer?; **yes, you c.!** oui!

can² [kæn] 1 *n (for food)* boîte *f*; *(for beer)* can(n)ette *f* 2 *(pt & pp* **-nn-)** *vt* mettre en boîte ▪ **canned** *adj* en boîte, en conserve; **c. beer** bière *f* en can(n)ette; **c. food** conserves *fpl* ▪ **can-opener** *n* ouvre-boîtes *m inv*

Canada ['kænədə] *n* le Canada ▪ **Canadian** 1 *adj* canadien, -enne 2 *n* Canadien, -enne *mf*

canal [kə'næl] *n* canal *m*

canary [kə'neərɪ] *(pl* **-ies)** *n* canari *m*

cancel ['kænsəl] 1 *(Br* **-ll-**, *Am* **-l-)** *vt (flight, appointment)* annuler; *(goods, taxi)* décommander; *(train)* supprimer 2 *vi* se décommander ▪ **cancellation** [-'leɪʃən] *n* annulation *f*; *(of train)* suppression *f*

cancer ['kænsə(r)] *n* cancer *m*; **stomach/skin c.** cancer *m* de l'estomac/la peau

candid ['kændɪd] *adj* franc *(f* franche)

candidate ['kændɪdeɪt] *n* candidat, -e *mf* (**for** à)

candle ['kændəl] *n (made of wax)* bougie *f*; *(in church)* cierge *m* ▪ **candlelight** *n* **to have dinner by c.** dîner aux chandelles ▪ **candlestick** *n* bougeoir *m*; *(taller)* chandelier *m*

candy ['kændɪ] *(pl* **-ies)** *n Am* bonbon *m*; *(sweets)* bonbons *mpl*; **c. store** confiserie *f* ▪ **candyfloss** *n Br* barbe *f* à papa

cane [keɪn] 1 *n (stick)* canne *f*; *(for punishment)* baguette *f* 2 *vt (punish)* frapper avec une baguette

canine ['keɪnaɪn] *adj (tooth, race)* canin

canister ['kænɪstə(r)] *n* boîte *f* (en métal)

cannabis ['kænəbɪs] *n (drug)* cannabis *m*

cannon ['kænən] *(pl* **-s** *or* **cannon)** *n* canon *m*

cannot ['kænɒt] = **can not**

canoe [kə'nuː] *n* canoë *m*; *(dugout)* pirogue *f* ▪ **canoeing** *n* **to go c.** faire du canoë-kayak

canola [kə'nəʊlə] *n* colza *m*

canopy ['kænəpɪ] *(pl* **-ies)** *n (awning)* auvent *m*; *(made of glass)* marquise *f*

can't [kɑːnt] = can not

canteen [kæn'tiːn] *n (in school, factory)* cantine *f; Br* **c. of cutlery** ménagère *f*

canvas ['kænvəs] *n* (**a**) *(cloth)* (grosse) toile *f; (for embroidery)* canevas *m* (**b**) *(painting)* toile *f*

canvass ['kænvəs] *vt (opinions)* sonder; **to c. sb** *(seek votes)* solliciter le suffrage de qn; *(seek orders)* solliciter des commandes de qn ▪ **canvassing** *n (for orders)* démarchage *m; (for votes)* démarchage *m* électoral

canyon ['kænjən] *n* cañon *m*, canyon *m*

cap¹ [kæp] *n* (**a**) *(hat)* casquette *f; (for shower, of sailor)* bonnet *m; (of soldier)* képi *m* (**b**) *(of tube, valve)* bouchon *m; (of bottle)* capsule *f; (of pen)* capuchon *m* (**c**) *(of child's gun)* amorce *f*

cap² [kæp] *(pt & pp* **-pp-)** *vt* (**a**) *(outdo)* surpasser (**b**) *Br (spending)* limiter

capable ['keɪpəbəl] *adj (person)* capable (**of sth** de qch; **of doing sth** de faire qch) ▪ **capability** *n* capacité *f*

capacity [kə'pæsɪtɪ] *(pl* **-ies)** *n (of container)* capacité *f; (ability)* aptitude *f,* capacité *f* (**for sth** pour qch; **for doing sth** à faire qch); *(output)* rendement *m;* **in my c. as a doctor** en ma qualité de médecin

cape [keɪp] *n (cloak)* cape *f; (of cyclist)* pèlerine *f*

capital ['kæpɪtəl] **1** *adj (letter, importance)* capital; **c. punishment** peine *f* capitale **2** *n* (**a**) **c. (city)** capitale *f;* **c. (letter)** majuscule *f* (**b**) *(money)* capital *m* ▪ **capitalism** *n* capitalisme *m* ▪ **capitalist** *adj & n* capitaliste *(mf)* ▪ **capitalize** *vi* **to c. on** tirer parti de

capsize [kæp'saɪz] **1** *vt* faire chavirer **2** *vi* chavirer

capsule [*Br* 'kæpsjuːl, *Am* 'kæpsəl] *n (of medicine)* gélule *f;* **(space) c.** capsule *f* spatiale

captain ['kæptɪn] **1** *n* capitaine *m* **2** *vt (ship)* commander; *(team)* être le capitaine de

caption ['kæpʃən] *n (of illustration)* légende *f; (of film, article)* sous-titre *m*

captivate ['kæptɪveɪt] *vt* captiver

captive ['kæptɪv] *n* captif, -ive *mf* ▪ **captivity** *n* **in c.** en captivité

capture ['kæptʃə(r)] **1** *n* capture *f; (of town)* prise *f* **2** *vt (person, animal)* capturer; *(escaped prisoner or animal)* reprendre; *(town)* prendre; *Fig (mood)* rendre

car [kɑː(r)] *n* voiture *f,* automobile *f; (train carriage)* wagon *m,* voiture *f;* **c. insurance/industry** assurance *f*/industrie *f* automobile; **the c. door** la portière de la voiture; **c. crash** accident *m* de voiture; **c. ferry** ferry *m; Br* **c. hire** location *f* de voitures; *Br* **c. park** parking *m;* **c. phone** téléphone *m* de voiture; **c. radio** autoradio *m;* **c. rental** location *f* de voitures; **c. wash** *(machine)* = station de lavage automatique pour voitures ▪ **carport** *n* abri *m* pour voiture

carafe [kə'ræf] *n* carafe *f*

caramel ['kærəməl] *n* caramel *m*

carat ['kærət] *n* carat *m;* **18-c. gold** or *m* (à) 18 carats

caravan ['kærəvæn] *n* caravane *f; (horse-drawn)* roulotte *f;* **c. site** camping *m* pour caravanes

carbohydrates [kɑːbəʊ'haɪdreɪts] *npl* hydrates *mpl* de carbone; *(in food)* glucides *mpl*

carbon ['kɑːbən] *n* carbone *m;* **c. dioxide** dioxyde *m* de carbone, gaz *m* carbonique

card [kɑːd] *n* carte *f; (cardboard)* carton *m;* **(index) c.** fiche *f;* **to play cards** jouer aux cartes ▪ **cardboard** *n* carton *m;* **c. box** boîte *f* en carton, carton *m* ▪ **cardphone** *n* téléphone *m* à carte

cardigan ['kɑːdɪgən] *n* cardigan *m*

cardinal ['kɑːdɪnəl] *n Rel* cardinal *m*

care [keə(r)] **1** *n (attention)* soin *m; (protection)* soins *mpl; (worry)* souci *m;* **to take c. to do** veiller à faire; **to take c. not to do** faire attention à ne pas faire; **to take c. of sb/sth** s'occuper de qn/qch; **to take c. of oneself** *(manage)* savoir se débrouiller tout seul; *(keep healthy)* faire bien attention à soi; **take c.!** *(goodbye)* au revoir!; **'c. of'** *(on envelope)* 'chez' ▪ **caregiver**

n (professional) aide *mf* à domicile; *(relative)* = personne s'occupant d'un parent malade ou âgé

2 *vt* **I don't c. what he says** peu m'importe ce qu'il en dit

3 *vi* **I don't c.** ça m'est égal; **who cares?** qu'est-ce que ça peut faire?; **to c. about** *(feel concern about)* se soucier de; **to c. about** *or* **for sb** *(be fond of)* avoir de la sympathie pour qn; **to c. for sb** *(look after)* soigner qn

career [kə'rɪə(r)] **1** *n* carrière *f* **2** *vi* **to c. along** aller à vive allure

carefree ['keəfriː] *adj* insouciant

careful ['keəfəl] *adj (exact, thorough)* soigneux, -euse **(about** de); *(cautious)* prudent; **to be c. of** *or* **with sth** faire attention à qch; **be c.!** (fais) attention! ■ **carefully** *adv (thoroughly)* avec soin; *(cautiously)* prudemment

careless ['keələs] *adj* négligent; *(work)* peu soigné; **c. mistake** faute *f* d'étourderie ■ **carelessness** *n* négligence *f*

carer ['keərə(r)] *n (relative)* = personne s'occupant d'un parent malade ou âgé

caress [kə'res] **1** *n* caresse *f* **2** *vt* caresser

caretaker ['keəteɪkə(r)] *n* gardien, -enne *mf*, concierge *mf*

cargo ['kɑːgəʊ] *(pl* **-oes** *or* **-os)** *n* cargaison *f*; **c. ship** cargo *m*

Caribbean [*Br* kærɪ'biːən, *Am* kə'rɪbɪən] **1** *adj* caraïbe **2** *n* **the C. (islands)** les Antilles *fpl*

caricature ['kærɪkətʃʊə(r)] **1** *n* caricature *f* **2** *vt* caricaturer

caring ['keərɪŋ] *adj (loving)* aimant; *(understanding)* très humain

carnation [kɑː'neɪʃən] *n* œillet *m*

carnival ['kɑːnɪvəl] *n* carnaval *m (pl* -als)

carol ['kærəl] *n* chant *m* de Noël

carp [kɑːp] **1** *n inv (fish)* carpe *f* **2** *vi* se plaindre **(at** de)

carpenter ['kɑːpɪntə(r)] *n (for house building)* charpentier *m*; *(for light woodwork)* menuisier *m* ■ **carpentry** *n* charpenterie *f*; *(light woodwork)* menuiserie *f*

carpet ['kɑːpɪt] **1** *n (rug)* tapis *m*; *(fitted)* moquette *f* **2** *vt* recouvrir d'un tapis/d'une moquette

carriage ['kærɪdʒ] *n Br (of train)* voiture *f*; *(horse-drawn)* voiture *f*, équipage *m*; *Br (transport of goods)* transport *m*; *(cost)* frais *mpl*; *(of typewriter)* chariot *m* ■ **carriageway** *n Br* chaussée *f*

carrier ['kærɪə(r)] *n (company, airline)* transporteur *m*; *Br* **c. (bag)** sac *m* en plastique

carrot ['kærət] *n* carotte *f*

carry ['kærɪ] *(pt & pp* **-ied)** **1** *vt* porter; *(goods, passengers)* transporter; *(gun, money)* avoir sur soi; *Math (in calculation)* retenir **2** *vi (of sound)* porter

▸ **carry away** *vt sep* emporter; **to be** *or* **get carried away** *(excited)* s'emballer

▸ **carry back** *vt sep (thing)* rapporter; *(person)* ramener

▸ **carry forward** *vt sep (in bookkeeping)* reporter

▸ **carry off** *vt sep (take away)* emporter

▸ **carry on 1** *vt sep (continue)* continuer **(doing** à faire); *(negotiations)* mener; *(conversation)* poursuivre **2** *vi (continue)* continuer; *Pej (behave badly)* se conduire mal; **to c. on with sth** continuer qch

▸ **carry out** *vt sep (plan, promise)* mettre à exécution; *(order)* exécuter; *(repair, reform)* effectuer; *(duty)* accomplir; *Am (meal)* emporter

▸ **carry through** *vt sep (plan)* mener à bien

carrycot ['kærɪkɒt] *n Br* porte-bébé *m inv*

cart [kɑːt] **1** *n (horse-drawn)* charrette *f*; *(handcart)* voiture *f* à bras; *Am (in supermarket)* Caddie® *m* **2** *vt Fam* **to c. (around)** trimbaler

carton ['kɑːtən] *n (box)* carton *m*; *(of milk, fruit juice)* brique *f*; *(of cigarettes)* cartouche *f*; *(of cream)* pot *m*

cartoon [kɑː'tuːn] *n (in newspaper)* dessin *m* humoristique; *(film)* dessin *m* animé; **c. (strip)** bande *f* dessinée

cartridge ['kɑːtrɪdʒ] *n* cartouche *f*

carve [kɑːv] *vt (cut)* tailler (**out of** dans); *(name)* graver; *(sculpt)* sculpter; **to c. (up)** *(meat)* découper ▪ **carving 1** *adj* **c. knife** couteau *m* à découper **2** *n* **(wood) c.** sculpture *f* sur bois

cascade [kæsˈkeɪd] *vi* tomber en cascade

case¹ [keɪs] *n (instance, situation)* & *Med* cas *m*; *Law* affaire *f*; *Fig (arguments)* arguments *mpl*; **in any c.** en tout cas; **in c. it rains** au cas où il pleuvrait; **in c. of** en cas de

case² [keɪs] *n (bag)* valise *f*; *(crate)* caisse *f*; *(for pen, glasses, camera, violin, cigarettes)* étui *m*; *(for jewels)* écrin *m*

cash [kæʃ] **1** *n (coins, banknotes)* liquide *m*; *Fam (money)* sous *mpl*; **to pay (in) c.** payer en liquide; **c. box** caisse *f*; *Br* **c. desk** caisse *f*; **c. dispenser** *or* **machine** distributeur *m* de billets; **c. price** prix *m* (au) comptant; **c. register** caisse *f* enregistreuse **2** *vt* **to c. a cheque** *or Am* **check** *(of person)* encaisser un chèque; *(of bank)* payer un chèque

cashew [ˈkæʃuː] *n* **c. (nut)** noix *f* de cajou

cashier [kæˈʃɪə(r)] *n* caissier, -ère *mf*

casino [kəˈsiːnəʊ] *(pl -os)* *n* casino *m*

casket [ˈkɑːskɪt] *n (box)* coffret *m*; *(coffin)* cercueil *m*

casserole [ˈkæsərəʊl] *n (covered dish)* cocotte *f*; *(stew)* ragoût *m*

cassette [kəˈset] *n (audio, video)* cassette *f*; *(for camera)* cartouche *f*; **c. player** lecteur *m* de cassettes; **c. recorder** magnétophone *m* à cassettes

cast [kɑːst] **1** *n (actors)* acteurs *mpl*; *(list of actors)* distribution *f*; *Med* **in a c.** dans le plâtre **2** *(pt & pp cast) vt (throw)* jeter; *(light, shadow)* projeter; *(glance)* jeter (**at** à *ou* sur); **to c. doubt on sth** jeter le doute sur qch; **c. iron** fonte *f* ▪ **cast-iron** *adj (pan)* en fonte; *Fig (alibi, excuse)* en béton

caster [ˈkɑːstə(r)] *n (wheel)* roulette *f*; *Br* **c. sugar** sucre *m* en poudre

castle [ˈkɑːsəl] *n* château *m*; *(in chess)* tour *f*

castoffs [ˈkɑːstɒfs] *npl* vieux vêtements *mpl*

castrate [kæˈstreɪt] *vt* châtrer

casual [ˈkæʒʊəl] *adj (offhand) (remark, glance)* en passant; *(relaxed, informal)* décontracté; *(conversation)* à bâtons rompus; *(clothes)* sport *inv*; *(careless)* désinvolte; *(employment, worker)* temporaire ▪ **casually** *adv (remark, glance)* en passant; *(informally)* avec décontraction; *(dress)* sport; *(carelessly)* avec désinvolture

casualty [ˈkæʒʊəltɪ] *(pl -ies)* *n* victime *f*; *Br* **c. (department)** *(in hospital)* (service *m* des) urgences *fpl*

cat [kæt] *n* chat *m*; *(female)* chatte *f*

catalogue [ˈkætəlɒg] *(Am* **catalog**) **1** *n* catalogue *m* **2** *vt* cataloguer

catalyst [ˈkætəlɪst] *n Chem & Fig* catalyseur *m*

catapult [ˈkætəpʌlt] **1** *n (toy)* lance-pierres *m inv* **2** *vt* catapulter

catastrophe [kəˈtæstrəfɪ] *n* catastrophe *f*

catch [kætʃ] **1** *n (in fishing)* prise *f*; *(of a whole day)* pêche *f*; *(difficulty)* piège *m*; *(on door)* loquet *m*

2 *(pt & pp caught) vt (ball, thief, illness)* attraper; *(fish, train, bus)* prendre; *(grab)* prendre, saisir; *(surprise)* surprendre; *(understand)* saisir; *(garment)* accrocher (**on** à); **to c. sb's eye** *or* **attention** attirer l'attention de qn; **to c. sight of sb/sth** apercevoir qn/qch; **to c. fire** prendre feu; **to c. sb doing** surprendre qn à faire; **to c. sb out** prendre qn en défaut; **to c. sb up** rattraper qn

3 *vi* **her skirt (got) caught in the door** sa jupe s'est prise dans la porte; **to c. up with sb** rattraper qn ▪ **catching** *adj (illness)* contagieux, -euse

catchy [ˈkætʃɪ] *(-ier, -iest) adj (tune, slogan)* facile à retenir

category [ˈkætɪgərɪ] *(pl -ies)* *n* catégorie *f* ▪ **categorical** *adj* catégorique

cater [ˈkeɪtə(r)] *vi (provide food)* s'occuper des repas (**for** pour); **to c. to,** *Br* **to c. for** *(need, taste)* satisfaire ▪ **caterer** *n* traiteur *m* ▪ **catering** *n* restauration *f*; **to do the c.** s'occuper des repas

caterpillar ['kætəpɪlə(r)] *n* chenille *f*

cathedral [kə'θiːdrəl] *n* cathédrale *f*

Catholic ['kæθlɪk] *adj & n* catholique *(mf)*

cattle ['kætəl] *npl* bétail *m*

caught [kɔːt] *pt & pp of* **catch**

cauliflower ['kɒlɪflaʊə(r)] *n* chou-fleur *m*

cause [kɔːz] **1** *n (origin, ideal) & Law* cause *f; (reason)* raison *f,* motif *m* (**of** de) **2** *vt* causer, occasionner; **to c. trouble for sb** créer *ou* causer des ennuis à qn

caution ['kɔːʃən] **1** *n (care)* prudence *f; (warning)* avertissement *m* **2** *vt (warn)* avertir; *Sport* donner un avertissement à ▪ **cautious** *adj* prudent

cavalry ['kævəlrɪ] *n* cavalerie *f*

cave [keɪv] **1** *n* grotte *f* **2** *vi* **to c. in** *(of ceiling)* s'effondrer; *(of floor)* s'affaisser

cavern ['kævən] *n* caverne *f*

cavity ['kævɪtɪ] *(pl* **-ies)** *n* cavité *f*

CD [siː'diː] *(abbr* **compact disc)** *n* CD *m;* **CD player** lecteur *m* de CD

CD-ROM [siːdiː'rɒm] *(abbr* **compact disc read-only memory)** *n Comptr* CD-ROM *m inv*

cease [siːs] **1** *vt* cesser (**doing** de faire) **2** *vi* cesser ▪ **cease-fire** *n* cessez-le-feu *m inv* ▪ **ceaseless** *adj* incessant

cedar ['siːdə(r)] *n (tree, wood)* cèdre *m*

ceiling ['siːlɪŋ] *n (of room) & Fig (limit)* plafond *m*

celebrate ['selɪbreɪt] **1** *vt (event)* célébrer, fêter; *(mass)* célébrer **2** *vi* faire la fête ▪ **celebration** [-'breɪʃən] *n (event)* fête *f;* **the celebrations** les festivités *fpl*

celebrity [sə'lebrətɪ] *(pl* **-ies)** *n* célébrité *f*

celery ['selərɪ] *n* céleri *m*

celibate ['selɪbət] *adj* **to be c.** ne pas avoir de rapports sexuels; *(by choice)* être chaste

cell [sel] *n* cellule *f; El* élément *m*

cellar ['selə(r)] *n* cave *f*

cello ['tʃeləʊ] *(pl* **-os)** *n* violoncelle *m*

cellophane® ['seləfeɪn] *n* Cellophane® *f*

cellphone ['selfəʊn] *n Am* (téléphone *m*) portable *m*

cellular ['seljʊlə(r)] *adj* cellulaire; **c. phone** téléphone *m* cellulaire

Celsius ['selsɪəs] *adj* Celsius *inv*

cement [sɪ'ment] **1** *n* ciment *m;* **c. mixer** bétonnière *f* **2** *vt also Fig* cimenter

cemetery ['semətrɪ] *(pl* **-ies)** *n* cimetière *m*

censor ['sensə(r)] **1** *n* censeur *m* **2** *vt* censurer ▪ **censorship** *n* censure *f*

census ['sensəs] *n* recensement *m*

cent [sent] *n (coin)* cent *m*

centenary [*Br* sen'tiːnərɪ, *Am* sen'tenərɪ] *(pl* **-ies)** *n* centenaire *m*

center ['sentə(r)] *n Am* = **centre**

centigrade ['sentɪgreɪd] *adj* centigrade

centimetre ['sentɪmiːtə(r)] *n* centimètre *m*

central ['sentrəl] *adj* central; **C. London** le centre de Londres; **c. heating** chauffage *m* central ▪ **centralize** *vt* centraliser

centre ['sentə(r)] *(Am* **center)** **1** *n* centre *m; Football* **c. forward** avant-centre *m* **2** *vt (attention, interest)* concentrer (**on** sur)

century ['sentʃərɪ] *(pl* **-ies)** *n* siècle *m;* **in the twenty-first c.** au vingt et unième siècle

ceramic [sə'ræmɪk] *adj (tile)* en céramique

cereal ['sɪərɪəl] *n* céréale *f;* **(breakfast) c.** céréales *fpl (pour le petit déjeuner)*

ceremony ['serɪmənɪ] *(pl* **-ies)** *n (event)* cérémonie *f*

certain ['sɜːtən] *adj* **(a)** *(sure)* certain **(that** que**); she's c. to come, she'll come for c.** c'est certain qu'elle viendra; **to be c. of sth** être certain *ou* sûr de qch; **for c.** *(say, know)* avec certitude **(b)** *(particular, some)* certain; **c. people** certaines personnes ▪ **certainly** *adv (undoubtedly)* certainement; *(yes)* bien sûr ▪ **certainty** *(pl* **-ies)** *n* certitude *f*

certificate [sə'tɪfɪkɪt] *n* certificat *m*; *(from university)* diplôme *m*

certify ['sɜːtɪfaɪ] *(pt & pp -ied) vt (document, signature)* certifier; *Am* **certified letter** ≃ lettre *f* recommandée; *Am* **certified public accountant** expert-comptable *m*

chain [tʃeɪn] **1** *n (of rings, mountains)* chaîne *f*; *(of events)* suite *f*; *(of lavatory)* chasse *f* d'eau; **c. reaction** réaction *f* en chaîne; **c. saw** tronçonneuse *f*; **c. store** magasin *m* à succursales multiples **2** *vt* **to c. (up)** *(dog)* mettre à l'attache ■ **chain-smoker** *n* **to be a c.** fumer cigarette sur cigarette

chair [tʃeə(r)] **1** *n* chaise *f*; *(armchair)* fauteuil *m*; *Univ (of professor)* chaire *f*; **the c.** *(office of chairperson)* la présidence; **c. lift** télésiège *m* **2** *vt (meeting)* présider ■ **chairman** *(pl -men)*, ■ **chairperson** *n* président, -e *mf*

chalet ['ʃæleɪ] *n* chalet *m*

chalk [tʃɔːk] **1** *n* craie *f* **2** *vt* marquer à la craie

challenge ['tʃælɪndʒ] **1** *n* défi *m*; *(task)* challenge *m*, gageure *f* **2** *vt* défier **(sb to do** qn de faire); *(question, dispute)* contester ■ **challenger** *n Sport* challenger *m*

chamber ['tʃeɪmbə(r)] *n (room, assembly, of gun)* chambre *f*; **c. music/orchestra** musique *f*/orchestre *m* de chambre ■ **chambermaid** *n* femme *f* de chambre

champagne [ʃæm'peɪn] *n* champagne *m*

champion ['tʃæmpɪən] **1** *n* champion, -onne *mf*; **c. skier, skiing c.** champion, -onne *mf* de ski **2** *vt (support)* se faire le champion de ■ **championship** *n* championnat *m*

chance [tʃɑːns] **1** *n (luck)* hasard *m*; *(possibility)* chance *f*; *(opportunity)* occasion *f*; *(risk)* risque *m*; **by c.** par hasard; **to have the c. to do sth** *or* **of doing sth** avoir l'occasion de faire qch; **to give sb a c.** donner une chance à qn; **to take a c.** tenter le coup **2** *adj (remark)* fait au hasard **3** *vt* **to c. it** risquer le coup

chancellor ['tʃɑːnsələ(r)] *n Pol* chancelier *m*

chandelier [ʃændə'lɪə(r)] *n* lustre *m*

change [tʃeɪndʒ] **1** *n* changement *m*; *(money)* monnaie *f*; **for a c.** pour changer; **a c. of clothes** des vêtements de rechange **2** *vt (modify)* changer; *(exchange)* échanger **(for** pour *ou* contre); *(money)* changer **(into** en); *(transform)* changer, transformer **(into** en); **to c. trains/colour/one's skirt** changer de train/de couleur/de jupe; **to c. gear** *(in vehicle)* changer de vitesse; **to c. the subject** changer de sujet; **to get changed** *(put on other clothes)* se changer **3** *vi (alter)* changer; *(change clothes)* se changer; **to c. into sth** *(be transformed)* se changer *ou* se transformer en qch; **she changed into a dress** elle a mis une robe; **to c. over** passer **(from** de; **to** à) ■ **changeable** *adj (weather, mood)* changeant ■ **changeover** *n* passage *m* **(from** de; **to** à)

changing ['tʃeɪndʒɪŋ] *n* **c. room** vestiaire *m*; *(in shop)* cabine *f* d'essayage

channel ['tʃænəl] **1** *n (on television)* chaîne *f*; *(for boats)* chenal *m*; *(groove)* rainure *f*; *(of communication, distribution)* canal *m*; *Geog* **the C.** la Manche; **the C. Islands** les îles Anglo-Normandes; **the C. Tunnel** le tunnel sous la Manche **2** *(Br -ll-, Am -l-) vt (energies, crowd, money)* canaliser **(into** vers)

chant [tʃɑːnt] **1** *vt (slogan)* scander **2** *vi (of demonstrators)* scander des slogans

chaos ['keɪɒs] *n* chaos *m* ■ **chaotic** *adj (situation, scene)* chaotique

chapel ['tʃæpəl] *n* chapelle *f*; *(nonconformist church)* temple *m*

chaplain ['tʃæplɪn] *n* aumônier *m*

chapped ['tʃæpt] *adj (hands, lips)* gercé

chapter ['tʃæptə(r)] *n* chapitre *m*

character ['kærɪktə(r)] *n* **(a)** *(of person, place)* caractère *m*; *(in book, film)* personnage *m*; *(person)* individu *m*; *(unusual person)* personnage *m* **(b)** *(letter)* caractère *m* ■ **characteristic** *adj & n* caractéristique *(f)*

charcoal ['tʃɑːkəʊl] *n Art* fusain *m*

charge¹ [tʃɑːdʒ] **1** *n (in battle)* charge *f*; *Law* chef *m* d'accusation; *(care)* garde *f*; **to take c. of sth** prendre qch en charge; **to be in c. of** être responsable de **2** *vt (battery, soldiers)* charger; *Law (accuse)* inculper (**with** de) **3** *vi (rush)* se précipiter; *(soldiers)* charger ▪ **charger** *n (for battery)* chargeur *m*

charge² [tʃɑːdʒ] **1** *n (cost)* prix *m*; **charges** *(expenses)* frais *mpl* **2** *vt (amount)* demander (**for** pour); **to c. sb** faire payer qn

charity ['tʃærɪtɪ] *(pl -ies) n (kindness, alms)* charité *f*; *(society)* œuvre *f* de charité

charm [tʃɑːm] **1** *n (attractiveness)* charme *m*; *(trinket)* breloque *f* **2** *vt* charmer ▪ **charming** *adj* charmant

chart [tʃɑːt] *n (map)* carte *f*; *(table)* tableau *m*; *(graph)* graphique *m*; **(pop) charts** hit-parade *m*

charter ['tʃɑːtə(r)] *n (aircraft)* charter *m*; **c. flight** vol *m* charter ▪ **chartered accountant** *n Br* expert-comptable *m*

chase [tʃeɪs] **1** *n* poursuite *f* **2** *vt* poursuivre; **to c. sb away** *or* **off** chasser qn **3** *vi* **to c. after sb/sth** courir après qn/qch

chasm ['kæzəm] *n also Fig* abîme *m*, gouffre *m*

chassis ['ʃæsɪ] *n (of vehicle)* châssis *m*

chaste [tʃeɪst] *adj* chaste

chat [tʃæt] **1** *n* petite conversation *f*; *Comptr* bavardage *m*; **to have a c.** causer (**with** avec); *Comptr* **c. room** site *m* de bavardage **2** *(pt & pp -tt-) vi* causer (**with** avec); *Comptr* bavarder **3** *vt Br Fam* **to c. sb up** draguer qn

chatter ['tʃætə(r)] **1** *n* bavardage *m* **2** *vi (of person)* bavarder; **his teeth were chattering** il claquait des dents

chatty ['tʃætɪ] *(-ier, -iest) adj (person)* bavard; *(letter)* plein de détails

chauffeur ['ʃəʊfə(r)] *n* chauffeur *m*

chauvinist ['ʃəʊvɪnɪst] *n Pej* **(male) c.** macho *m*, phallocrate *m*

cheap [tʃiːp] **1** *(-er, -est) adj* bon marché *inv*, pas cher (*f* pas chère); *(rate, fare)* réduit; *(worthless)* sans valeur; *(vulgar)* de mauvais goût; **cheaper** meilleur marché *inv*, moins cher (*f* moins chère) **2** *adv (buy)* (à) bon marché, au rabais ▪ **cheaply** *adv* (à) bon marché

cheat [tʃiːt] **1** *n (at games)* tricheur, -euse *mf*; *(crook)* escroc *m* **2** *vt (deceive)* tromper; *(defraud)* frauder; **to c. sb out of sth** escroquer qch à qn **3** *vi (at games)* tricher

check¹ [tʃek] *n* **c. (pattern)** carreaux *mpl* ▪ **checked** *adj (patterned)* à carreaux

check² [tʃek] **1** *n* vérification *f* (**on** de); *(inspection)* contrôle *m*; *(in chess)* échec *m*; *Am (tick)* ≃ croix *f*; *Am (receipt)* reçu *m*; *Am (restaurant bill)* addition *f*; *Am (cheque)* chèque *m*; **to keep a c. on sth** contrôler qch **2** *vt (examine)* vérifier; *(inspect)* contrôler; *(mark off)* cocher; *Am (baggage)* mettre à la consigne **3** *vi* vérifier; **to c. on sth** vérifier qch; **to c. on sb** surveiller qn ▪ **checkbook** *n Am* carnet *m* de chèques ▪ **check-in** *n (at airport)* enregistrement *m* (des bagages) ▪ **checking account** *n Am* compte *m* courant ▪ **checklist** *n* liste *f* de contrôle; *Aviat* check-list *f* ▪ **checkout** *n (in supermarket)* caisse *f* ▪ **checkpoint** *n* poste *m* de contrôle ▪ **checkroom** *n Am* vestiaire *m*; *Am (left-luggage office)* consigne *f* ▪ **checkup** *n (medical)* bilan *m* de santé; **to have a c.** faire un bilan de santé

▸ **check in 1** *vt sep (luggage)* enregistrer **2** *vi (arrive)* arriver; *(sign in)* signer le registre; *(at airport)* se présenter à l'enregistrement

▸ **check out 1** *vt sep (confirm)* confirmer **2** *vi (at hotel)* régler sa note

▸ **check up** *vi* vérifier

checkers ['tʃekərz] *npl Am* jeu *m* de dames

cheddar ['tʃedə(r)] *n* cheddar *m* *(fromage)*

cheek [tʃiːk] *n* joue *f*; *Br (impudence)* culot *m* ▪ **cheeky** *(-ier, -iest) adj Br (person, reply)* insolent

cheer [tʃɪə(r)] **1** *n* **cheers** *(shouts)* acclamations *fpl*; *Fam* **cheers!** *(when*

drinking) à votre santé!; *(thanks)* merci!
2 *vt (applaud)* acclamer; **to c. sb up**
(comfort) remonter le moral à qn;
(amuse) faire sourire qn **3** *vi* applaudir;
to c. up reprendre courage; **c. up!** (du)
courage! ■ **cheering** *n (shouts)* acclamations *fpl*

cheerful ['tʃɪəfəl] *adj* gai

cheerio [tʃɪərɪ'əʊ] *exclam Br* salut!,
au revoir!

cheese [tʃiːz] *n* fromage *m* ■ **cheese-
burger** *n* cheeseburger *m* ■ **cheese-
cake** *n* cheesecake *m*, tarte *f* au
fromage blanc

chef [ʃef] *n* chef *m* (cuisinier)

chemical 1 *adj* chimique **2** *n* produit
m chimique

chemist ['kemɪst] *n Br (pharmacist)*
pharmacien, -enne *mf*; *(scientist)* chi-
miste *mf*; *Br* **c.'s (shop)** pharmacie *f*
■ **chemistry** *n* chimie *f*

cheque [tʃek] *n Br* chèque *m*; **c. card**
carte *f* d'identité bancaire *(sans laquelle
un chéquier n'est pas valable)* ■ **cheque-
book** *n Br* carnet *m* de chèques

cherry ['tʃerɪ] *(pl* -ies) *n* cerise *f*

chess [tʃes] *n* échecs *mpl* ■ **chess-
board** *n* échiquier *m*

chest [tʃest] *n* (a) *(part of body)* poi-
trine *f*; *Fig* **to get it off one's c.** dire
ce qu'on a sur le cœur (b) *(box)* coffre
m; **c. of drawers** commode *f*

chestnut ['tʃesnʌt] **1** *n (nut)* châtai-
gne *f*; *(cooked)* marron *m* **2** *adj (hair)*
châtain

chew [tʃuː] **1** *vt* **to c. (up)** mâcher **2** *vi*
mastiquer; **chewing gum** chewing-
gum *m*

chewy ['tʃuːɪ] *adj (meat)* caoutchou-
teux, -euse; *(sweet)* mou (*f* molle)

chick [tʃɪk] *n (chicken)* poussin *m*

chicken ['tʃɪkɪn] **1** *n* poulet *m* **2** *vi*
Fam **to c. out** se dégonfler ■ **chicken-
pox** *n* varicelle *f*

chickpea ['tʃɪkpiː] *n* pois *m* chiche

chief [tʃiːf] **1** *n* chef *m*; *Fam (boss)* pa-
tron *m* **2** *adj (most important)* principal;
Com **c. executive** directeur *m* général
■ **chiefly** *adv* principalement, surtout

chilblain ['tʃɪlbleɪn] *n* engelure *f*

child [tʃaɪld] *(pl* **children**) *n* enfant *mf*;
c. abuse mauvais traitements *mpl* à en-
fant, maltraitance *f*; **c. care** *(for work-
ing parents)* crèches *fpl* et garderies
fpl; *Br* **c. minder** assistante *f* mater-
nelle ■ **childhood** *n* enfance *f* ■ **child-
ish** *adj* puéril ■ **childlike** *adj* enfantin
■ **childproof** *adj (lock, bottle)* que les
enfants ne peuvent pas ouvrir

children ['tʃɪldrən] *pl of* **child**

chill [tʃɪl] **1** *n* froid *m*; *(illness)* refroi-
dissement *m*; **to catch a c.** prendre
froid **2** *vt (wine, melon)* mettre au frais;
(meat) réfrigérer

chilli ['tʃɪlɪ] *(pl* -**is** *or* -**ies**) *n (vegetable)*
piment *m*; *(dish)* chili *m* con carne; **c.
powder** ≃ chili *m*

chilly ['tʃɪlɪ] (**-ier, -iest**) *adj* froid; **it's
c.** il fait (un peu) froid

chime [tʃaɪm] *vi (of bell)* carillonner;
(of clock) sonner

chimney ['tʃɪmnɪ] *(pl* -**eys**) *n* chemi-
née *f*

chimpanzee [tʃɪmpæn'ziː] *n* chim-
panzé *m*

chin [tʃɪn] *n* menton *m*

China ['tʃaɪnə] *n* la Chine ■ **Chinese 1**
adj chinois **2** *n inv (person)* Chinois, -e
mf; *(language)* chinois *m*

china ['tʃaɪnə] **1** *n inv* porcelaine *f* **2**
adj en porcelaine

chink [tʃɪŋk] **1** *n (slit)* fente *f* **2** *vt* faire
tinter

chip [tʃɪp] **1** *n (splinter)* éclat *m*;
(break) ébréchure *f*; *(counter)* jeton *m*;
Comptr puce *f*; **chips** *Br (French fries)*
frites *fpl*; *Am (crisps)* chips *fpl*; *Br* **c.
shop** = boutique où l'on vend du pois-
son pané et des frites **2** *(pt & pp* -**pp-**)
vt (cup) ébrécher; *(paint)* écailler

chiropodist [kɪ'rɒpədɪst] *n Br* pédi-
cure *mf*

chirp [tʃɜːp] *vi (of bird)* pépier

chisel ['tʃɪzəl] **1** *n* ciseau *m* **2** *(Br* -**ll-**,
Am -**l-**) *vt* ciseler

chives [tʃaɪvz] *npl* ciboulette *f*

chlorine ['klɔːriːn] *n Chem* chlore *m*

choc-ice ['tʃɒkaɪs] *n Br* = glace indivi-
duelle enrobée de chocolat

chocolate ['tʃɒklɪt] **1** n chocolat m;
hot c. chocolat m chaud; **plain c.** cho-
colat m à croquer **2** adj (made of choco-
late) en chocolat; (chocolate-flavoured)
au chocolat

choice [tʃɔɪs] n choix m; **to make a c.**
choisir

choir ['kwaɪə(r)] n chœur m ▪ **choir-
boy** n jeune choriste m

choke [tʃəʊk] **1** n (of car) starter m **2** vt
(strangle) étrangler; (clog) boucher **3** vi
she choked on a fishbone elle a failli
s'étouffer avec une arête

cholesterol [kə'lestərɒl] n cholestérol
m

choose [tʃuːz] **1** (pt **chose**, pp **chosen**)
vt choisir; **to c. to do sth** choisir de
faire qch **2** vi choisir ▪ **choos(e)y**
(**choosier**, **choosiest**) adj Fam difficile
(**about** sur)

chop [tʃɒp] **1** n (of lamb, pork) côtelette
f **2** (pt & pp **-pp-**) vt (wood) couper (à la
hache); (food) couper en morceaux; (fi-
nely) hacher; **to c. down** (tree) abattre;
to c. off (branch, finger) couper; **to c.
up** couper en morceaux

choppy ['tʃɒpɪ] (**-ier, -iest**) adj (sea)
agité

chopsticks ['tʃɒpstɪks] npl baguettes
fpl (pour manger)

choral ['kɔːrəl] adj choral

chord [kɔːd] n Mus accord m

chore [tʃɔː(r)] n corvée f; (household)
chores travaux mpl du ménage

chorus ['kɔːrəs] n (of song) refrain m;
(singers) chœur m; (dancers) troupe f

chose [tʃəʊz] pt of **choose**

chosen ['tʃəʊzən] pp of **choose**

Christ [kraɪst] n le Christ ▪ **Christian**
adj & n chrétien, -enne (mf); **C. name**
prénom m ▪ **Christianity** n christia-
nisme m

christen ['krɪsən] vt (person, ship)
baptiser ▪ **christening** n baptême m

Christmas ['krɪsməs] **1** n Noël m; **at
C. (time)** à Noël; **Merry** or **Happy C.!**
Joyeux Noël! **2** adj (tree, card, Day,
party) de Noël; **C. Eve** la veille de Noël

chrome [krəʊm], **chromium** ['krəʊm-
ɪəm] n chrome m

chronic ['krɒnɪk] adj (disease, state)
chronique

chronological [krɒnə'lɒdʒɪkəl] adj
chronologique; **in c. order** par ordre
chronologique

chubby ['tʃʌbɪ] (**-ier, -iest**) adj (person,
hands) potelé; (cheeks) rebondi

chuck [tʃʌk] vt Fam (throw) lancer;
(boyfriend, girlfriend) plaquer; Br **to c.
(in** or **up)** (give up) laisser tomber; **to c.
out** (throw away) balancer; (from
house, school, club) vider

chuckle ['tʃʌkəl] vi rire tout bas

chug [tʃʌg] (pt & pp **-gg-**) vi **to c. along**
(of vehicle) avancer lentement; (of train)
haleter

chum [tʃʌm] n Fam copain m, copine
f

chunk [tʃʌŋk] n (gros) morceau m

church [tʃɜːtʃ] n église f; **to go to c.**
aller à l'église; **c. hall** salle f paroissiale
▪ **churchyard** n cimetière m

churn [tʃɜːn] vt Pej **to c. out** (books)
pondre (en série); (goods) produire en
série

chute [ʃuːt] n Br (in pool, playground)
toboggan m; (for rubbish) vide-ordures
m inv

CID [siːaɪ'diː] (abbr **Criminal Investi-
gation Department**) n Br ≃ PJ f

cider ['saɪdə(r)] n cidre m

cigar [sɪ'gɑː(r)] n cigare m

cigarette [sɪgə'ret] n cigarette f; **c.
end** mégot m

cinder ['sɪndə(r)] n cendre f

cinema ['sɪnəmə] n (art) cinéma m; Br
(place) cinéma; Br **to go to the c.** aller
au cinéma ▪ **cinemagoer** n Br ciné-
phile mf

cinnamon ['sɪnəmən] n cannelle f

circle ['sɜːkəl] **1** n (shape, group, range)
cercle m; Theatre balcon m **2** vt (move
round) tourner autour de; (surround)
entourer (**with** de) **3** vi (of aircraft,
bird) décrire des cercles

circuit ['sɜːkɪt] n (electrical path, jour-
ney, for motor racing) circuit m; El **c.
breaker** disjoncteur m

circular ['sɜːkjʊlə(r)] **1** adj circulaire **2**

n (letter) circulaire *f; (advertisement)* prospectus *m*

circulate ['sɜːkjʊleɪt] **1** *vt* faire circuler **2** *vi* circuler ∎ **circulation** [-'leɪʃən] *n (of air, blood, money)* circulation *f; (of newspaper)* tirage *m*

circumcised ['sɜːkəmsaɪzd] *adj* circoncis

circumference [sɜː'kʌmfərəns] *n* circonférence *f*

circumstance ['sɜːkəmstæns] *n* circonstance *f*; **circumstances** *(financial)* situation *f* financière; **in** *or* **under the circumstances** étant donné les circonstances; **in** *or* **under no circumstances** en aucun cas

circus ['sɜːkəs] *n* cirque *m*

citizen ['sɪtɪzən] *n* citoyen, -enne *mf*; *(of city)* habitant, -e *mf*

citrus ['sɪtrəs] *adj* **c. fruit(s)** agrumes *mpl*

city ['sɪtɪ] *(pl* **-ies)** *n* (grande) ville *f*, cité *f*; *Br* **the C.** la City *(quartier des affaires de Londres)*; **c. centre** centre-ville *m*; *Am* **c. hall** hôtel *m* de ville

civil ['sɪvəl] *adj* **(a)** *(rights, war, marriage)* civil; **c. servant** fonctionnaire *mf*; **c. service** fonction *f* publique **(b)** *(polite)* civil

civilian [sɪ'vɪljən] *adj & n* civil, -e *(mf)*

civilize ['sɪvɪlaɪz] *vt* civiliser ∎ **civilization** [-'zeɪʃən] *n* civilisation *f*

claim [kleɪm] **1** *n (demand) (for damages, compensation)* demande *f* d'indemnisation; *(as a right)* revendication *f; (statement)* affirmation *f; (right)* droit *m* (**to** à); **(insurance) c.** demande *f* d'indemnité

2 *vt (as a right)* réclamer, revendiquer; *(payment, benefit, reduction)* demander à bénéficier de; **to c. damages (from sb)** réclamer des dommages et intérêts (à qn); **to c. that...** *(assert)* prétendre que... ∎ **claimant** *n Br (for social benefits, insurance)* demandeur, -euse *mf*

clam [klæm] *n* palourde *f*

clamber ['klæmbə(r)] *vi* **to c. up** grimper

clamour ['klæmə(r)] *(Am* **clamor)** **1**

n clameur *f* **2** *vi* **to c. for sth** demander qch à grands cris

clamp [klæmp] **1** *n (clip-like)* pince *f*; **(wheel) c.** *(for vehicle)* sabot *m* (de Denver) **2** *vt* serrer; *(vehicle)* mettre un sabot à **3** *vi* **to c. down on** sévir contre ∎ **clampdown** *n* coup *m* d'arrêt **(on** à)

clan [klæn] *n also Fig* clan *m*

clang [klæŋ] *n* son *m* métallique

clap [klæp] *(pt & pp* **-pp-)** *vti (applaud)* applaudir; **to c. (one's hands)** applaudir; *(once)* frapper dans ses mains ∎ **clapping** *n* applaudissements *mpl*

claret ['klærət] *n (wine)* bordeaux *m* rouge

clarify ['klærɪfaɪ] *(pt & pp* **-ied)** *vt* clarifier ∎ **clarification** [-ɪ'keɪʃən] *n* clarification *f*

clarinet [klærɪ'net] *n* clarinette *f*

clarity ['klærətɪ] *n (of expression, argument)* clarté *f; (of sound)* pureté *f*

clash [klæʃ] **1** *n (of interests)* conflit *m; (of events)* coïncidence *f* **2** *vi (of objects)* s'entrechoquer; *(of interests, armies)* s'affronter; *(of colours)* jurer (**with** avec); *(coincide)* tomber en même temps (**with** que)

clasp [klɑːsp] **1** *n (fastener)* fermoir *m; (of belt)* boucle *f* **2** *vt (hold)* serrer; **to c. one's hands** joindre les mains

class [klɑːs] **1** *n* classe *f; (lesson)* cours *m* **2** *vt* classer (**as** comme) ∎ **classmate** *n* camarade *mf* de classe ∎ **classroom** *n* (salle *f* de) classe *f*

classic ['klæsɪk] **1** *adj* classique **2** *n (writer, work)* classique *m* ∎ **classical** *adj* classique

classify ['klæsɪfaɪ] *(pt & pp* **-ied)** *vt* classer ∎ **classification** *n* classification *f* ∎ **classified** *adj (information, document)* confidentiel, -elle; **c. advertisement** petite annonce *f*

classy ['klɑːsɪ] **(-ier, -iest)** *adj Fam* chic *inv*

clatter ['klætə(r)] *n* fracas *m*

clause [klɔːz] *n (in sentence)* proposition *f; (in legal document)* clause *f*

claustrophobic [klɔːstrə'fəʊbɪk] *adj (person)* claustrophobe; *(room, atmosphere)* oppressant

claw [klɔ:] **1** n (of lobster) pince f; (of cat, sparrow) griffe f; (of eagle) serre f **2** vt (scratch) griffer

clay [kleɪ] n argile f

clean [kli:n] **1** (-er, -est) adj propre; (clear-cut) net (f nette); (joke) pour toutes les oreilles; (game, fight) dans les règles; **to come c.** tout avouer **2** adv (utterly) complètement **3** n **to give sth a c.** nettoyer qch **4** vt nettoyer; (wash) laver; **to c. one's teeth** se brosser ou se laver les dents; **to c. out** (room) nettoyer à fond; (empty) vider; **to c. up** (room) nettoyer; Fig (reform) épurer **5** vi **to c. (up)** faire le nettoyage ▪ **cleaner** n (in home) femme f de ménage; **(dry) c.** teinturier, -ère mf ▪ **cleaning** n nettoyage m; (housework) ménage m; **c. woman** femme f de ménage ▪ **cleanly** adv (break, cut) net ▪ **clean-shaven** adj (with no beard or moustache) glabre; (closely shaven) rasé de près

cleanse [klenz] vt (wound) nettoyer; **cleansing cream** crème f démaquillante

clear [klɪə(r)] **1** (-er, -est) adj (sky, water, sound, thought) clair; (glass) transparent; (outline, photo, skin, majority) net (f nette); (road) libre; (winner) incontesté; (obvious) évident, clair; (certain) certain; **to make oneself c.** se faire comprendre; **it is c. that...** il est évident ou clair que... **2** adv **to keep** or **steer c. of** se tenir à l'écart de; **to get c. of** (away from) s'éloigner de **3** vt (table) débarrasser; (road, area) dégager; (accused person) disculper; (cheque) compenser; (debts) liquider; (through customs) dédouaner; (for security) autoriser; **to c. one's throat** s'éclaircir la gorge **4** vi (of weather) s'éclaircir; (of fog) se dissiper ▪ **clearing** n (in woods) clairière f ▪ **clearly** adv (explain, write) clairement; (see, understand) bien; (obviously) évidemment

▶ **clear away** vt sep (remove) enlever

▶ **clear off** vi Fam (leave) filer

▶ **clear out** vt sep (empty) vider; (remove) enlever

▶ **clear up 1** vt sep (mystery) éclaircir; (room) ranger **2** vi (of weather) s'éclaircir; (tidy) ranger

clearance ['klɪərəns] n (sale) liquidation f; (space) dégagement m; (permission) autorisation f

clear-cut [klɪə'kʌt] adj net (f nette)

clef [klef] n Mus clef f

clench [klentʃ] vt **to c. one's fist/ teeth** serrer le poing/les dents

clergy ['klɜ:dʒɪ] n clergé m ▪ **clergyman** (pl -men) n ecclésiastique m

clerical ['klerɪkəl] adj (job) d'employé; (work) de bureau

clerk [Br klɑ:k, Am klɜ:k] n employé, -e mf de bureau; Am (in store) vendeur, -euse mf

clever ['klevə(r)] (-er, -est) adj intelligent; (smart, shrewd) astucieux, -euse; (skilful) habile (**at sth** à qch; **at doing** à faire); (ingenious) (machine, plan) ingénieux, -euse; (gifted) doué; **c. with one's hands** adroit de ses mains ▪ **cleverly** adv intelligemment; (ingeniously) astucieusement; (skilfully) habilement

cliché ['kli:ʃeɪ] n cliché m

click [klɪk] **1** n bruit m sec **2** vi faire un bruit sec; Fam **it suddenly clicked** ça a fait tilt

client ['klaɪənt] n client, -e mf ▪ **clientele** n clientèle f

cliff [klɪf] n falaise f

climate ['klaɪmɪt] n (weather) & Fig (conditions) climat m

climax ['klaɪmæks] n point m culminant; (sexual) orgasme m

climb [klaɪm] **1** n montée f **2** vt **to c. (up)** (steps, hill) gravir; (mountain) faire l'ascension de; (tree, ladder) grimper à; **to c. (over)** (wall) escalader; **to c. down (from)** (wall, tree) descendre de; (hill) descendre **3** vi (of plant) grimper; **to c. (up)** (steps, tree, hill) monter; **to c. down** descendre; Fig (back down) revenir sur sa décision ▪ **climber** n (mountaineer) alpiniste mf; (on rocks) varappeur, -euse mf; (plant)

plante *f* grimpante ■ **climbing** *n*
(mountain) c. alpinisme *m*; **(rock-)c.**
varappe *f*

climb-down ['klaɪmdaʊn] *n* reculade
f

clinch [klɪntʃ] *vt (deal)* conclure

cling [klɪŋ] *(pt & pp* **clung)** *vi* s'accro-
cher **(to** à); *(stick)* adhérer **(to** à)

clinic ['klɪnɪk] *n Br (private)* clinique *f*;
(part of hospital) service *m* ■ **clinical**
adj Med clinique

clink [klɪŋk] **1** *vt* faire tinter **2** *vi* tinter

clip [klɪp] **1** *n* **(a)** *(for paper)* trombone
m; *(fastener)* attache *f*; *(of brooch, of
cyclist, for hair)* pince *f* **(b)** *(of film)* ex-
trait *m* **2** *(pt & pp* **-pp-)** *vt (paper)* atta-
cher *(avec un trombone); (cut)* couper;
(hedge) tailler; *(ticket)* poinçonner; **to
c. (on)** *(attach)* attacher **(to** à) **3** *vi* **to
c. together** s'emboîter ■ **clippers** *npl*
(for hair) tondeuse *f*; *(for fingernails)*
coupe-ongles *m inv* ■ **clipping** *n Am
(from newspaper)* coupure *f*

clique [kliːk] *n Pej* clique *f*

cloak [kləʊk] *n* cape *f* ■ **cloakroom** *n*
vestiaire *m*; *Br (lavatory)* toilettes *fpl*

clock [klɒk] *n (large)* horloge *f*, *(small)*
pendule *f*; *Br Fam (mileometer)* comp-
teur *m*; **round the c.** vingt-quatre heu-
res sur vingt-quatre; **to put the clocks
forward/back** *(in spring, autumn)*
avancer/retarder les pendules; **c. radio**
radioréveil *m*; **c. tower** clocher *m*
■ **clockwise** *adv* dans le sens des ai-
guilles d'une montre ■ **clockwork 1**
adj (toy) mécanique **2** *n* **to go like c.**
marcher comme sur des roulettes

clog [klɒg] **1** *n (shoe)* sabot *m* **2** *(pt & pp*
-gg-) *vt* **to c. (up)** *(obstruct)* boucher

cloister ['klɔɪstə(r)] *n* cloître *m*

close¹ [kləʊs] **1 (-er, -est)** *adj (in dis-
tance, time, relationship)* proche; *(colla-
boration, resemblance, connection)*
étroit; *(friend)* intime; *(contest)* serré;
(study) rigoureux, -euse; *Br* **it's c.** *(of
weather)* il fait lourd; **c. to** *(near)* près
de, proche de; **that was a c. shave** *or*
call il s'en est fallu de peu
2 *adv* **c. (by), c. at hand** tout près; **we
stood/sat c. together** nous étions de-

bout/assis serrés les uns contre les au-
tres; **to follow c. behind** suivre de
près ■ **close-fitting** *adj (clothes)* ajusté
■ **closing 1** *n* fermeture *f* **2** *adj (re-
marks)* dernier, -ère; **c. date** *(for appli-
cation)* date *f* limite; **c. time** heure *f* de
fermeture ■ **close-up** *n* gros plan *m*

close² [kləʊz] **1** *n (end)* fin *f* **2** *vt (door,
shop, account, book, eye)* fermer; *(road)*
barrer; *(gap)* réduire; *(deal)* conclure **3**
vi (of door) se fermer; *(of shop)* fermer
■ **closed** *adj (door, shop)* fermé; **c.-
circuit television** télévision *f* en circuit
fermé ■ **closure** *n (of business, factory)*
fermeture *f* (définitive)

▶**close down 1** *vt sep (business, fac-
tory)* fermer (définitivement) **2** *vi (of
TV channel)* terminer les émissions; *(of
business, factory)* fermer (définitive-
ment)

▶**close in** *vi (approach)* approcher; **to
c. in on sb** se rapprocher de qn

▶**close up 1** *vt sep* fermer **2** *vi (of shop-
keeper)* fermer; *(of wound)* se refermer;
(of line of people) se resserrer

closet ['klɒzɪt] *n Am (cupboard)* pla-
card *m*; *(wardrobe)* penderie *f*

clot [klɒt] **1** *n (of blood)* caillot *m* **2** *(pt
& pp* **-tt-)** *vi (of blood)* (se) coaguler

cloth [klɒθ] *n* tissu *m*; *(for dusting)*
chiffon *m*; *(for dishes)* torchon *m*; *(ta-
blecloth)* nappe *f* ■ **clothing** *n (clothes)*
vêtements *mpl*

clothes [kləʊðz] *npl* vêtements *mpl*; **to
put one's c. on** s'habiller; **to take
one's c. off** se déshabiller; **c. line**
corde *f* à linge; *Br* **c. peg,** *Am* **c. pin**
pince *f* à linge; **c. shop** magasin *m* de
vêtements

cloud [klaʊd] **1** *n* nuage *m* **2** *vi* **to c.
over** *(of sky)* se couvrir ■ **cloudy (-ier,
-iest)** *adj (weather, sky)* nuageux, -
-euse; *(liquid)* trouble

clove [kləʊv] *n (spice)* clou *m* de giro-
fle; **c. of garlic** gousse *f* d'ail

clover ['kləʊvə(r)] *n* trèfle *m*

clown [klaʊn] **1** *n* clown *m* **2** *vi* **to c.
around** *or* **about** faire le clown

club [klʌb] **1** *n* **(a)** *(society)* club *m* **(b)**
(nightclub) boîte *f* de nuit **(c)** *(weapon)*
massue *f*; *(in golf)* club *m* **(d) clubs** *(in*

cards) trèfle *m* **2** *(pt & pp* **-bb-**) *vi Br* **to c. together** se cotiser (**to buy** sth pour acheter qch)

clue [klu:] *n* indice *m; (of crossword)* définition *f; Fam* **I don't have a c.** je n'en ai pas la moindre idée

clump [klʌmp] *n (of flowers, trees)* massif *m*

clumsy ['klʌmzɪ] **(-ier, -iest)** *adj* maladroit

clung [klʌŋ] *pt & pp of* **cling**

cluster ['klʌstə(r)] **1** *n* groupe *m* **2** *vi* se grouper

clutch [klʌtʃ] **1** *n (in car)* embrayage *m; (pedal)* pédale *f* d'embrayage **2** *vt* tenir fermement **3** *vi* **to c. at** essayer de saisir

clutter ['klʌtə(r)] **1** *n (objects)* désordre *m* **2** *vt* **to c. (up)** *(room, table)* encombrer (**with** de)

cm *(abbr* **centimetre(s))** cm

Co *(abbr* **company)** Cie

co- [kəʊ] *pref* co-

c/o *(abbr* **care of)** *(on envelope)* chez

coach [kəʊtʃ] **1** *n* (**a**) *Br (train carriage)* voiture *f*, wagon *m; Br (bus)* car *m; (horse-drawn)* carrosse *m* (**b**) *(for sports)* entraîneur, -euse *mf* **2** *vt (sportsman, team)* entraîner

coal [kəʊl] **1** *n* charbon *m* **2** *adj (fire)* de charbon; **c. industry** industrie *f* houillère ▪ **coalmine** *n* mine *f* de charbon

coalition [kəʊə'lɪʃən] *n* coalition *f*

coarse [kɔːs] **(-er, -est)** *adj (person, manners)* grossier, -ère, vulgaire; *(surface, fabric)* grossier, -ère

coast [kəʊst] *n* côte *f*

coaster ['kəʊstə(r)] *n (for glass)* dessous-de-verre *m inv*

coat [kəʊt] **1** *n* manteau *m; (overcoat)* pardessus *m; (jacket)* veste *f; (of animal)* pelage *m; (of paint)* couche *f;* **c. hanger** cintre *m* **2** *vt* couvrir (**with** de); *(with chocolate, sugar)* enrober (**with** de) ▪ **coating** *n* couche *f*

coax [kəʊks] *vt* **to c. sb to do** *or* **into doing sth** amener qn à faire qch par des cajoleries

cob [kɒb] *n (of corn)* épi *m*

cobbled ['kɒbəld] *adj (street)* pavé

cobweb ['kɒbweb] *n* toile *f* d'araignée

Coca-Cola® [kəʊkə'kəʊlə] *n* Coca-Cola® *m*

cocaine [kəʊ'keɪn] *n* cocaïne *f*

cock [kɒk] *n (rooster)* coq *m*

cockerel ['kɒkərəl] *n* jeune coq *m*

cockney ['kɒknɪ] *adj & n* cockney *(mf) (natif des quartiers est de Londres)*

cockpit ['kɒkpɪt] *n (of aircraft)* poste *m* de pilotage

cockroach ['kɒkrəʊtʃ] *n* cafard *m*

cocktail ['kɒkteɪl] *n* cocktail *m;* **fruit c.** macédoine *f* de fruits; **c. party** cocktail *m*

cocky ['kɒkɪ] **(-ier, -iest)** *adj Fam* culotté

cocoa ['kəʊkəʊ] *n* cacao *m*

coconut ['kəʊkənʌt] *n* noix *f* de coco

COD [si:əʊ'di:] *(abbr* **cash on delivery)** *n Br Com* paiement *m* à la livraison

cod [kɒd] *n* morue *f; (as food)* cabillaud *m*

code [kəʊd] *n* code *m;* **in c.** *(letter, message)* codé; **c. word** code

co-educational [kəʊedjʊ'keɪʃənəl] *adj (school, teaching)* mixte

coerce [kəʊ'ɜːs] *vt* contraindre (**sb into doing** qn à faire)

coexist [kəʊɪg'zɪst] *vi* coexister

coffee ['kɒfɪ] *n* café *m;* **c. with milk,** *Br* **white c.** café *m* au lait; **black c.** café *m* noir; *Br* **c. bar, c. house** café *m;* **c. break** pause-café *f;* **c. pot** cafetière *f;* **c. table** table *f* basse

coffin ['kɒfɪn] *n* cercueil *m*

cog [kɒg] *n* dent *f*

cognac ['kɒnjæk] *n* cognac *m*

cohabit [kəʊ'hæbɪt] *vi* vivre en concubinage (**with** avec)

coherent [kəʊ'hɪərənt] *adj (logical)* cohérent; *(way of speaking)* compréhensible, intelligible

coil [kɔɪl] *n (of wire, rope)* rouleau *m; (contraceptive)* stérilet *m*

coin [kɔɪn] *n* pièce *f* (de monnaie)

coincide [kəʊɪn'saɪd] *vi* coïncider (**with** avec) ▪ **coincidence** *n* coïncidence *f*

coke [kəʊk] *n (fuel)* coke *m; (Coca-Cola®)* Coca® *m inv*

colander ['kʌləndə(r)] *n (for vegetables)* passoire *f*

cold [kəʊld] **1** (**-er, -est**) *adj* froid; **to be** *or* **feel c.** *(of person)* avoir froid; **my hands are c.** j'ai froid aux mains; **it's c.** *(of weather)* il fait froid; **to get c.** *(of weather)* se refroidir; *(of food)* refroidir; *Fam* **to get c. feet** se dégonfler; *Br* **c. meats,** *Am* **c. cuts** viandes *fpl* froides

 2 *n* (**a**) *(temperature)* froid *m* (**b**) *(illness)* rhume *m;* **to have a c.** être enrhumé; **to catch a c.** attraper un rhume; **to get a c.** s'enrhumer ▪ **coldness** *n* froideur *f*

coleslaw ['kəʊlslɔː] *n* = salade de chou cru à la mayonnaise

collaborate [kə'læbəreɪt] *vi* collaborer (**on** à) ▪ **collaboration** [-'reɪʃən] *n* collaboration *f*

collage ['kɒlɑːʒ] *n (picture)* collage *m*

collapse [kə'læps] **1** *n* effondrement *m; (of government)* chute *f* **2** *vi (of person, building)* s'effondrer; *(faint)* se trouver mal; *(of government)* tomber

collar ['kɒlə(r)] *n (on garment)* col *m; (of dog)* collier *m*

colleague ['kɒliːg] *n* collègue *mf*

collect [kə'lekt] **1** *vt (pick up)* ramasser; *(gather)* rassembler; *(information)* recueillir; *(stamps)* collectionner; **to c. money** *(in street, church)* quêter; **to c. sb** *(pick up)* passer prendre qn **2** *vi (in street, church)* quêter (**for** pour) **3** *adv Am* **to call** *or* **phone sb c.** téléphoner à qn en PCV

collection [kə'lekʃən] *n (of objects, stamps)* collection *f; (of poems)* recueil *m; (of money for church)* quête *f; (of mail)* levée *f*

collector [kə'lektə(r)] *n (of stamps)* collectionneur, -euse *mf*

college ['kɒlɪdʒ] *n Br (of further education)* établissement *m* d'enseignement supérieur; *Am (university)* université *f;* **to be at c.** être étudiant

collide [kə'laɪd] *vi* entrer en collision (**with** avec) ▪ **collision** *n* collision *f*

colloquial [kə'ləʊkwɪəl] *adj* familier, -ère

colon ['kəʊlən] *n* (**a**) *(punctuation mark)* deux-points *m* (**b**) *Anat* côlon *m*

colonel ['kɜːnəl] *n* colonel *m*

colonial [kə'ləʊnɪəl] *adj* colonial

colony ['kɒlənɪ] (*pl* **-ies**) *n* colonie *f*

colossal [kə'lɒsəl] *adj* colosse

colour ['kʌlə(r)] (*Am* **color**) **1** *n* couleur *f* **2** *adj (photo, television)* en couleurs; *(television set)* couleur *inv* **3** *vt* colorer; **to c. (in)** *(drawing)* colorier ▪ **coloured** *adj (person, pencil)* de couleur; *(glass)* coloré ▪ **colouring** *n (in food)* colorant *m; (shade, effect)* coloris *m;* **c. book** album *m* de coloriages

colour-blind ['kʌləblaɪnd] *adj* daltonien, -enne

colourful ['kʌləfəl] *adj (crowd, story)* coloré; *(person)* pittoresque

column ['kɒləm] *n* colonne *f; (newspaper feature)* rubrique *f*

coma ['kəʊmə] *n* **in a c.** dans le coma

comb [kəʊm] **1** *n* peigne *m* **2** *vt Fig (search)* ratisser, passer au peigne fin; **to c. one's hair** se peigner

combat ['kɒmbæt] *n* combat *m*

combination [kɒmbɪ'neɪʃən] *n* combinaison *f;* **in c. with** en association avec; **c. lock** serrure *f* à combinaison

combine [kəm'baɪn] *vt (activities, qualities, elements, sounds)* combiner; *(efforts)* joindre, unir

combustion [kəm'bʌstʃən] *n* combustion *f*

COME [kʌm] (*pt* **came,** *pp* **come**) *vi* venir (**from** de; **to** à); **to c. home** rentrer (à la maison); **to c. first** *(in race, exam)* se classer premier; **c. and see me** viens me voir; **to c. near** *or* **close to doing sth** faillir faire qch; **in the years to c.** dans les années à venir

▸ **come about** *vi (happen)* arriver

▸ **come across 1** *vi* **to c. across well/badly** bien/mal passer **2** *vt insep (find)* tomber sur

▸ **come along** *vi* venir (**with** avec);

(progress) (of work) avancer; *(of student)* progresser

▶**come away** *vi (leave, come off)* partir **(from** de); **to c. away from sb/sth** *(step or move back from)* s'écarter de qn/qch

▶**come back** *vi* revenir; *(return home)* rentrer

▶**come by** *vt insep (obtain)* obtenir; *(find)* trouver

▶**come down 1** *vi* descendre; *(of rain, temperature, price)* tomber; *(of building)* être démoli **2** *vt insep (stairs, hill)* descendre

▶**come down with** *vt insep (illness)* attraper

▶**come for** *vt insep* venir chercher

▶**come forward** *vi (make oneself known, volunteer)* se présenter

▶**come in** *vi (enter)* entrer; *(of train)* arriver; *(of money)* rentrer; **to c. in useful** être bien utile

▶**come in for** *vt insep* **to c. in for criticism** faire l'objet de critiques

▶**come into** *vt insep (room)* entrer dans; *(money)* hériter de

▶**come off 1** *vi (of button)* se détacher; *(succeed)* réussir **2** *vt insep (fall from)* tomber de; *(get down from)* descendre de

▶**come on** *vi (make progress) (of work)* avancer; *(of student)* progresser; **c. on!** allez!

▶**come out** *vi* sortir; *(of sun, book)* paraître; *(of stain)* s'enlever, partir; *(of photo)* réussir; *(of homosexual)* révéler son homosexualité; **to c. out (on strike)** se mettre en grève

▶**come over** *vi (visit)* passer **(to** chez); **to c. over to** *(approach)* s'approcher de

▶**come round** *vi (visit)* passer **(to** chez); *(regain consciousness)* revenir à soi

▶**come through 1** *vi (survive)* s'en tirer **2** *vt insep (crisis)* sortir indemne de

▶**come to 1** *vi (regain consciousness)* revenir à soi **2** *vt insep (amount to)* revenir à; **to c. to a conclusion** arriver à une conclusion; **to c. to a decision** se décider

▶**come under** *vt insep (heading)* être classé sous

▶**come up 1** *vi (rise)* monter; *(of question, job)* se présenter **2** *vt insep (stairs)* monter

▶**come up against** *vt insep (problem)* se heurter à

▶**come upon** *vt insep (book, reference)* tomber sur

▶**come up to** *vt insep (reach)* arriver jusqu'à; *(approach)* s'approcher de

▶**come up with** *vt insep (idea, money)* trouver

comeback ['kʌmbæk] *n* **to make a c.** *(of actor, athlete)* faire un come-back

comedy ['kɒmɪdɪ] *(pl* **-ies)** *n* comédie *f* ▪ **comedian** *n* comique *mf*

comet ['kɒmɪt] *n* comète *f*

comfort ['kʌmfət] **1** *n (ease)* confort *m; (consolation)* réconfort *m,* consolation *f* **2** *vt* consoler ▪ **comfortable** *adj (chair, house)* confortable; *(rich)* aisé

comfortably ['kʌmftəblɪ] *adv (sit)* confortablement; *(win)* facilement; **c. off** *(rich)* à l'aise financièrement

comic ['kɒmɪk] **1** *adj* comique **2** *n Br (magazine)* bande *f* dessinée, BD *f;* **c. strip** bande *f* dessinée ▪ **comical** *adj* comique

coming ['kʌmɪŋ] **1** *adj (future) (years, election)* à venir; **the c. days** les prochains jours **2** *n* **comings and goings** allées *fpl* et venues *fpl*

comma ['kɒmə] *n* virgule *f*

command [kə'mɑːnd] **1** *n (order)* ordre *m; (authority)* commandement *m; (mastery)* maîtrise *f* **(of** de); *Comptr* commande *f* **2** *vt (order)* commander **(sb to do** à qn de faire) ▪ **commander** *n Mil* commandant *m* ▪ **commanding** *adj (authoritative)* imposant; *(position)* dominant; **c. officer** commandant *m*

commandment [kə'mɑːndmənt] *n Rel* commandement *m*

commemorate [kə'meməreɪt] *vt* commémorer ▪ **commemoration** [-'reɪʃən] *n* commémoration *f*

commence [kə'mens] *vti Formal* commencer **(doing** à faire)

commend [kə'mend] *vt (praise)* louer ▪ **commendable** *adj* louable

comment ['kɒment] **1** *n* commentaire

m (**on** sur) **2** *vi* faire des commentaires (**on** sur); **to c. on** *(text, event, news item)* commenter; **to c. that...** remarquer que... ■ **commentary** *(pl -ies) n* commentaire *m*; **live c.** *(on TV or radio)* reportage *m* en direct ■ **commentator** *n* commentateur, -trice *mf* (**on** de)

commerce ['kɒmɜːs] *n* commerce *m* ■ **commercial** [kə'mɜː:(ʃəl]) **1** *adj* commercial **2** *n (advertisement)* publicité *f*; **the commercials** la publicité

commercialize [kə'mɜːʃəlaɪz] *vt Pej (event)* transformer en une affaire de gros sous

commiserate [kə'mɪzəreɪt] *vi* **to c. with sb** être désolé pour qn

commission [kə'mɪʃən] **1** *n (fee, group)* commission *f*; *(order for work)* commande *f* **2** *vt (artist)* passer une commande à; *(book)* commander; **to c. sb to do sth** charger qn de faire qch ■ **commissioner** *n Br* **(police) c.** commissaire *m* de police

commit [kə'mɪt] *(pt & pp -tt-) vt (crime)* commettre; *(bind)* engager; *(devote)* consacrer; **to c. suicide** se suicider; **to c. oneself** *(make a promise)* s'engager (**to** à) ■ **commitment** *n (duty, responsibility)* obligation *f*; *(promise)* engagement *m*; *(devotion)* dévouement *m* (**to** à)

committee [kə'mɪtɪ] *n* comité *m*

commodity [kə'mɒdɪtɪ] *(pl -ies) n Econ* marchandise *f*, produit *m*

common ['kɒmən] *(-er, -est) adj (shared, vulgar)* commun; *(frequent)* courant, commun; **in c.** *(shared)* en commun (**with** avec); **to have nothing in c.** n'avoir rien de commun (**with** avec); **c. room** *(for students)* salle *f* commune; *(for teachers)* salle *f* des professeurs; **c. sense** sens *m* commun, bon sens *m* ■ **commonly** *adv* communément

commonplace ['kɒmənpleɪs] *adj* courant

Commonwealth ['kɒmənwelθ] *n Br* **the C.** le Commonwealth

commotion [kə'məʊʃən] *n (disruption)* agitation *f*

communal [kə'mjuːnəl] *adj (shared) (bathroom, kitchen)* commun; *(of the community)* communautaire

commune ['kɒmjuːn] *n (district)* commune *f*; *(group)* communauté *f*

communicate [kə'mjuːnɪkeɪt] **1** *vt* communiquer **2** *vi (of person)* communiquer (**with** avec) ■ **communication** [-'keɪʃən] *n* communication *f*; *Br* **c. cord** *(on train)* signal *m* d'alarme

Communion [kə'mjuːnjən] *n* **(Holy) C.** communion; **to take C.** communier

communism ['kɒmjʊnɪzəm] *n* communisme *m* ■ **communist** *adj & n* communiste *(mf)*

community [kə'mjuːnɪtɪ] **1** *(pl -ies) n* communauté *f*; **the student c.** les étudiants *mpl* **2** *adj (life, spirit)* communautaire; **c. centre** centre *m* socioculturel

commute [kə'mjuːt] *vi* **to c. (to work)** faire la navette entre son domicile et son travail ■ **commuter** *n* banlieusard, -e *mf*; **c. train** train *m* de banlieue

compact[1] [kəm'pækt] *adj (car, crowd, substance)* compact; **c. disc** ['kɒmpækt] disque *m* compact

compact[2] ['kɒmpækt] *n (for face powder)* poudrier *m*

companion [kəm'pænjən] *n (person)* compagnon *m*, compagne *f*

company ['kʌmpənɪ] *(pl -ies) n (companionship)* compagnie *f*; *(guests)* invités *mpl*, -es *fpl*; *(business)* société *f*, compagnie *f*; **(theatre) c.** compagnie *f* (théâtrale); **to keep sb c.** tenir compagnie à qn; **c. car** voiture *f* de société

comparable ['kɒmpərəbəl] *adj* comparable (**with** *or* **to** à)

comparative [kəm'pærətɪv] *adj (relative) (costs, comfort)* relatif, -ive ■ **comparatively** *adv* relativement

compare [kəm'peə(r)] **1** *vt* comparer (**with** *or* **to** à); **compared to** *or* **with** en comparaison de **2** *vi* être comparable (**with** à) ■ **comparison** [kəm'pærɪsən] *n* comparaison *f* (**between** entre; **with** avec); **by** *or* **in c.** en comparaison

compartment [kəm'pɑːtmənt] *n* compartiment *m*

compass ['kʌmpəs] *n* (**a**) *(for finding direction)* boussole *f* (**b**) **(pair of) compasses** compas *m*

compassion [kəm'pæʃən] *n* compassion *f*

compatible [kəm'pætɪbəl] *adj* compatible

compatriot [kəm'pætrɪət, kəm'peɪtrɪət] *n* compatriote *mf*

compel [kəm'pel] (*pt & pp* **-ll-**) *vt* forcer, obliger; **to c. sb to do sth** forcer qn à faire qch ■ **compelling** *adj (argument)* convaincant

compensate ['kɒmpənseɪt] **1** *vt* **to c. sb** *(with payment, reward)* dédommager qn (**for** de) **2** *vi* compenser; **to c. for sth** *(make up for)* compenser qch ■ **compensation** [-'seɪʃən] *n (financial)* dédommagement *m; (consolation)* compensation *f*

compère ['kɒmpeə(r)] *n* animateur, -trice *mf*

compete [kəm'piːt] *vi (take part in race)* concourir (**in** à); **to c. (with sb)** rivaliser (avec qn); *(in business)* faire concurrence (à qn); **to c. for sth** se disputer qch

competent ['kɒmpɪtənt] *adj (capable)* compétent (**to do** pour faire) ■ **competently** *adv* avec compétence

competition [kɒmpə'tɪʃən] *n* (**a**) *(rivalry)* rivalité *f; (between companies)* concurrence *f; (contest)* concours *m; (in sport)* compétition *f*

competitive [kəm'petɪtɪv] *adj (price, market)* compétitif, -ive; *(person)* qui a l'esprit de compétition ■ **competitor** *n* concurrent, -e *mf*

compile [kəm'paɪl] *vt (list, catalogue)* dresser; *(documents)* compiler

complacent [kəm'pleɪsənt] *adj* content de soi

complain [kəm'pleɪn] *vi* se plaindre (**to sb** à qn; **of** *or* **about sb/sth** de qn/qch; **that** que) ■ **complaint** *n* plainte *f; (in shop)* réclamation *f; (illness)* maladie *f*

complement ['kɒmplɪment] *vt* compléter

complete [kəm'pliːt] **1** *adj (whole)* complet, -ète; *(utter)* total; *(finished)* achevé **2** *vt (finish)* achever; *(form)* compléter ■ **completely** *adv* complètement

complex ['kɒmpleks] **1** *adj* complexe **2** *n (feeling, buildings)* complexe *m* ■ **complexion** [kəm'plekʃən] *n (of face)* teint *m*

complicate ['kɒmplɪkeɪt] *vt* compliquer ■ **complication** *n* complication *f*

compliment 1 ['kɒmplɪmənt] *n* compliment *m;* **to pay sb a c.** faire un compliment à qn **2** ['kɒmplɪment] *vt* **to c. sb on sth** *(bravery)* féliciter qn de qch; *(dress, haircut)* faire des compliments à qn sur qch ■ **complimentary** [-'mentərɪ] *adj* (**a**) *(praising)* élogieux, -euse (**b**) *(free)* gratuit; **c. ticket** billet *m* de faveur

comply [kəm'plaɪ] (*pt & pp* **-ied**) *vi* **to c. with** *(order)* obéir à; *(request)* accéder à

component [kəm'pəʊnənt] *n (of structure, furniture)* élément *m; (of machine)* pièce *f*

compose [kəm'pəʊz] *vt* composer; **to c. oneself** se calmer ■ **composed** *adj* calme ■ **composer** *n (of music)* compositeur, -trice *mf* ■ **composition** [kɒmpə'zɪʃən] *n (in music, art, chemistry)* composition *f*

compost ['kɒmpɒst] *n* compost *m*

composure [kəm'pəʊʒə(r)] *n* sang-froid *m*

compound ['kɒmpaʊnd] **1** *n (word)* & *Chem (substance)* composé *m; (area)* enclos *m.* **2** *adj (word, substance)* & *Fin (interest)* composé

comprehend [kɒmprɪ'hend] *vt* comprendre

comprehensive [kɒmprɪ'hensɪv] **1** *adj* complet, -ète; *(study)* exhaustif, -ive; *(knowledge)* étendu; *(insurance)* tous risques *inv* **2** *adj & n Br* **c. (school)** ≃ établissement *m* d'enseignement secondaire *(n'opérant pas de sélection à l'entrée)*

compress [kəm'pres] *vt (gas, air)* comprimer

comprise [kəm'praɪz] *vt (consist of)* comprendre; *(make up)* constituer

compromise ['kɒmprəmaɪz] **1** *n* compromis *m* **2** *vt (person, security)* compromettre **3** *vi* transiger (**on** sur)

compulsion [kəm'pʌlʃən] *n (urge)* besoin *m*; *(obligation)* contrainte *f* ▪ **compulsive** *adj (smoker, gambler, liar)* invétéré

compulsory [kəm'pʌlsərɪ] *adj* obligatoire

computer [kəm'pjuːtə(r)] **1** *n* ordinateur *m* **2** *adj (program, system, network)* informatique; *(course, firm)* d'informatique; **c. game** jeu *m* électronique; **c. science** informatique *f* ▪ **computerized** *adj* informatisé

computing [kəm'pjuːtɪŋ] *n* informatique *f*

con [kɒn] *Fam* **1** *n* arnaque *f*; **c. man** arnaqueur *m* **2** *(pt & pp* **-nn-***) vt* arnaquer; **to be conned** se faire arnaquer

conceal [kən'siːl] *vt (hide) (object)* dissimuler (**from sb** à qn); *(plan, news)* cacher (**from sb** à qn)

concede [kən'siːd] **1** *vt* concéder (**to** à; **that** que) **2** *vi* s'incliner

conceited [kən'siːtɪd] *adj* vaniteux, -euse

conceive [kən'siːv] **1** *vt (idea, child)* concevoir **2** *vi (of woman)* concevoir; **to c. of sth** concevoir qch ▪ **conceivable** *adj* concevable; **it's c. that...** il est concevable que... (*+ subjunctive*)

concentrate ['kɒnsəntreɪt] **1** *vt* concentrer (**on** sur) **2** *vi* se concentrer (**on** sur); **to c. on doing sth** s'appliquer à faire qch ▪ **concentration** [-'treɪʃən] *n* concentration *f*; **c. camp** camp *m* de concentration

concept ['kɒnsept] *n* concept *m*

concern [kən'sɜːn] **1** *n (matter)* affaire *f*; *(worry)* inquiétude *f*; **his c. for** son souci de; **(business) c.** entreprise *f* **2** *vt* concerner; **to be concerned about** *(be worried)* s'inquiéter de; **as far as I'm concerned...** en ce qui me concerne... ▪ **concerned** *adj (anxious)* inquiet, -ète (**about/at** au sujet de); **the person c.** *(in question)* la personne

dont il s'agit; *(involved)* la personne concernée ▪ **concerning** *prep* en ce qui concerne

concert ['kɒnsət] *n* concert *m*; **c. hall** salle *f* de concert

concerto [kən'tʃɜːtəʊ] *(pl* **-os***) n* concerto *m*; **piano c.** concerto *m* pour piano

concession [kən'seʃən] *n* concession *f* (**to** à)

conciliatory [kən'sɪlɪətərɪ, *Am* -tɔːrɪ] *adj (tone, person)* conciliant

concise [kən'saɪs] *adj* concis

conclude [kən'kluːd] **1** *vt (end, settle)* conclure; **to c. that...** *(infer)* conclure que... **2** *vi (of event)* se terminer (**with** par); *(of speaker)* conclure ▪ **conclusion** *n* conclusion *f* ▪ **conclusive** *adj* concluant

concoct [kən'kɒkt] *vt (dish, scheme)* concocter ▪ **concoction** *n (dish, drink)* mixture *f*

concourse ['kɒŋkɔːs] *n (in airport, train station)* hall *m*

concrete ['kɒŋkriːt] **1** *n* béton *m*; **c. wall** mur *m* en béton **2** *adj (ideas, example)* concret, -ète

concur [kən'kɜː(r)] *(pt & pp* **-rr-***) vi (agree)* être d'accord (**with** avec)

concurrently [kən'kʌrəntlɪ] *adv* simultanément

concussion [kən'kʌʃən] *n (injury)* commotion *f* cérébrale

condemn [kən'dem] *vt* condamner (**to** à); *(building)* déclarer inhabitable

condense [kən'dens] *vt* condenser ▪ **condensation** [kɒnden'seɪʃən] *n (mist)* buée *f*

condescend [kɒndɪ'send] *vi* condescendre (**to do** à faire)

condition [kən'dɪʃən] *n (stipulation, circumstance)* condition *f*; *(state)* état *m*, condition *f*; *(disease)* maladie *f*; **on the c. that...** à la condition que... (*+ subjunctive*); **in good c.** en bon état; **in/out of c.** en bonne/mauvaise forme ▪ **conditional** *adj* conditionnel, -elle

conditioner [kən'dɪʃənə(r)] *n* **(hair) c.** après-shampooing *m*

condo ['kɒndəʊ] (*pl* -**os**) *n Am* = **condominium**

condolences [kən'dəʊlənsɪz] *npl* condoléances *fpl*

condom ['kɒndɒm] *n* préservatif *m*

condominium [kɒndə'mɪnɪəm] *n Am (building)* immeuble *m* en copropriété; *(apartment)* appartement *m* en copropriété

condone [kən'dəʊn] *vt (overlook)* fermer les yeux sur; *(forgive)* excuser

conducive [kən'djuːsɪv] *adj* **to be c. to** être favorable à

conduct 1 ['kɒndʌkt] *n (behaviour, directing)* conduite *f* **2** [kən'dʌkt] *vt (campaign, inquiry, experiment)* mener; *(orchestra)* diriger; *(electricity, heat)* conduire; **to c. oneself** se conduire; **conducted tour** *(of building, region)* visite *f* guidée

conductor [kən'dʌktə(r)] *n (of orchestra)* chef *m* d'orchestre; *Br (on bus)* receveur *m*; *Am (on train)* chef *m* de train

cone [kəʊn] *n* cône *m*; *(for ice cream)* cornet *m*; **pine** *or* **fir c.** pomme *f* de pin; *Br* **traffic c.** cône de chantier

confectionery [kən'fekʃənərɪ] *n (sweets)* confiserie *f*; *(cakes)* pâtisserie *f*

confederation [kənfedə'reɪʃən] *n* confédération *f*

confer [kən'fɜː(r)] *(pt & pp* -**rr**-*)* **1** *vt (grant)* octroyer **(on** à**) 2** *vi (talk together)* se consulter **(on** *or* **about** sur**); to c. with sb** consulter qn

conference ['kɒnfərəns] *n* conférence *f*; *(scientific, academic)* congrès *m*; **press** *or* **news c.** conférence *f* de presse

confess [kən'fes] **1** *vt* avouer, confesser **(that** que; **to sb** à qn**);** *Rel* confesser **2** *vi* avouer; *Rel* se confesser; **to c. to sth** *(crime)* avouer *ou* confesser qch **▪ confession** *n* aveu *m*, confession *f*; *Rel* confession *f*; **to go to c.** aller à confesse

confetti [kən'fetɪ] *n* confettis *mpl*

confide [kən'faɪd] **1** *vt* confier **(to** à; **that** que**) 2** *vi* **to c. in sb** se confier à qn

confidence ['kɒnfɪdəns] *n (trust)* confiance *f* **(in** en**); (self-)c.** confiance *f* en soi; **in c.** en confidence; **c. trick** escroquerie *f* **▪ confident** *adj (smile, exterior)* confiant; **(self-)c.** sûr de soi **▪ confidently** *adv* avec confiance

confidential [kɒnfɪ'denʃəl] *adj* confidentiel, -elle **▪ confidentially** *adv* en confidence

confine [kən'faɪn] *vt* **(a)** *(limit)* limiter **(to** à**); to c. oneself to doing sth** se limiter à faire qch **(b)** *(keep prisoner)* enfermer **(to/in** dans**) ▪ confined** *adj (space)* réduit; **c. to bed** alité; **c. to one's room** obligé de garder la chambre

confirm [kən'fɜːm] *vt* confirmer **(that** que**) ▪ confirmation** [kɒnfə'meɪʃən] *n also Rel* confirmation *f* **▪ confirmed** *adj (bachelor)* endurci; *(smoker)* invétéré

confiscate ['kɒnfɪskeɪt] *vt* confisquer **(from** à**)**

conflict 1 ['kɒnflɪkt] *n* conflit *m* **2** [kən'flɪkt] *vi (of statement)* être en contradiction **(with** avec**);** *(of dates, events, programmes)* tomber en même temps **(with** que**) ▪ conflicting** *adj (views, theories, evidence)* contradictoire; *(dates)* incompatible

conform [kən'fɔːm] *vi (of person)* se conformer **(to** *or* **with** à**);** *(of ideas, actions)* être en conformité **(to** with**);** *(of product)* être conforme **(to** *or* **with** à**)**

confront [kən'frʌnt] *vt (danger)* affronter; *(problem)* faire face à; **to c. sb** *(be face to face with)* se trouver en face de qn; *(oppose)* s'opposer à qn; **to c. sb with sth** mettre qn en face de qch **▪ confrontation** [kɒnfrʌn'teɪʃən] *n* confrontation *f*

confuse [kən'fjuːz] *vt (make unsure)* embrouiller; **to c. sb/sth with** *(mistake for)* confondre qn/qch avec; **to c. matters** *or* **the issue** embrouiller la question **▪ confused** *adj (situation, noises, idea)* confus; **to get c.** s'embrouiller **▪ confusing** *adj* déroutant **▪ confusion** [-ʒən] *n (bewilderment)* perplexité *f*; *(disorder, lack of clarity)* confusion *f*

congested [kən'dʒestɪd] *adj (street,*

town, lungs) congestionné; *(nose)* bouché ■ **congestion** [-tʃən] *n (traffic)* encombrements *mpl*; *(overcrowding)* surpeuplement *m*

congratulate [kən'grætʃʊleɪt] *vt* féliciter (**sb on sth** qn de qch; **sb on doing sth** qn d'avoir fait qch) ■ **congratulations** [-'leɪʃənz] *npl* félicitations *fpl* (**on** pour)

congregate ['kɒŋgrɪgeɪt] *vi* se rassembler ■ **congregation** [-'geɪʃən] *n (worshippers)* fidèles *mpl*

Congress ['kɒŋgres] *n Am Pol* le Congrès *(assemblée législative américaine)*

conifer ['kɒnɪfə(r)] *n* conifère *m*

conjunction [kən'dʒʌŋkʃən] *n* **in c. with** conjointement avec

connect [kə'nekt] **1** *vt* relier (**with** *or* **to** à); *(telephone, washing machine)* brancher; **to c. sb with sb** *(on phone)* mettre qn en communication avec qn; **to c. sb/sth with sb/sth** établir un lien entre qn/qch et qn/qch
2 *vi* **to c. with** *(of train, bus)* assurer la correspondance avec ■ **connected** *adj (facts, events)* lié; **to be c. with** *(have to do with, relate to)* avoir un lien avec

connection [kə'nekʃən] *n (link)* rapport *m*, lien *m* (**with** avec); *(train, bus)* correspondance *f*; *(phone call)* communication *f*; *(between electrical wires)* contact *m*; **connections** *(contacts)* relations *fpl*; **to have no c. with** n'avoir aucun rapport avec; **in c. with** à propos de

connive [kə'naɪv] *vi* **to c. with sb** être de connivence avec qn

connoisseur [kɒnə'sɜ:(r)] *n* connaisseur *m*

connotation [kɒnə'teɪʃən] *n* connotation *f*

conquer ['kɒŋkə(r)] *vt (country)* conquérir; *(enemy, habit, difficulty)* vaincre ■ **conquest** *n* conquête *f*

cons [kɒnz] *npl* **the pros and (the) c.** le pour et le contre

conscience ['kɒnʃəns] *n* conscience *f*; **to have sth on one's c.** avoir qch sur la conscience

conscientious [kɒnʃɪ'enʃəs] *adj* consciencieux, -euse; **c. objector** objecteur *m* de conscience

conscious ['kɒnʃəs] *adj (awake)* conscient; **to make a c. effort to do sth** faire un effort particulier pour faire qch; **c. of sth** *(aware)* conscient de qch ■ **consciously** *adv (knowingly)* consciemment ■ **consciousness** *n* **to lose/regain c.** perdre/reprendre connaissance

conscript 1 ['kɒnskrɪpt] *n (soldier)* conscrit *m* **2** [kən'skrɪpt] *vt* enrôler ■ **conscription** [kən'skrɪpʃən] *n* conscription *f*

consecutive [kən'sekjʊtɪv] *adj* consécutif, -ive

consensus [kən'sensəs] *n* consensus *m*

consent [kən'sent] **1** *n* consentement *m* **2** *vi* consentir (**to** à)

consequence ['kɒnsɪkwəns] *n (result)* conséquence *f* ■ **consequently** *adv* par conséquent

conservative [kən'sɜːvətɪv] **1** *adj (estimate)* modeste; *(view, attitude)* traditionnel, -elle; *(person)* traditionaliste; *Br Pol* conservateur, -trice **2** *n Br Pol* conservateur, -trice *mf*

conservatory [kən'sɜːvətrɪ] *(pl* -**ies**) *n Br (room)* véranda *f*

conserve [kən'sɜːv] *vt (energy, water, electricity)* faire des économies de ■ **conservation** [kɒnsə'veɪʃən] *n (of energy)* économies *fpl*; *(of nature)* protection *f* de l'environnement

consider [kən'sɪdə(r)] *vt (think over)* considérer; *(take into account)* tenir compte de; *(an offer)* étudier; **to c. doing sth** envisager de faire qch; **to c. that...** considérer que...; **I c. her (as) a friend** je la considère comme une amie; **all things considered** tout bien considéré

considerable [kən'sɪdərəbəl] *adj (large)* considérable; *(much)* beaucoup de ■ **considerably** *adv* considérablement

considerate [kən'sɪdərət] *adj* attentionné (**to** à l'égard de)

consideration [kənsɪdə'reɪʃən] *n* considération *f*; **to take sth into c.** prendre qch en considération

considering [kən'sɪdərɪŋ] **1** *prep* étant donné **2** *conj* **c. (that)** étant donné que

consignment [kən'saɪnmənt] *n* (goods) envoi *m*

consist [kən'sɪst] *vi* consister (**of** en; **in** en; **in doing** à faire)

consistent [kən'sɪstənt] *adj* (unchanging) (quality, results) constant ▪ **consistency** *n* (of substance, liquid) consistance *f* ▪ **consistently** *adv* (always) constamment; (regularly) régulièrement

console¹ [kən'səʊl] *vt* consoler ▪ **consolation** *n* consolation *f*; **c. prize** lot *m* de consolation

console² ['kɒnsəʊl] *n* (control desk) console *f*

consolidate [kən'sɒlɪdeɪt] *vt* consolider

consonant ['kɒnsənənt] *n* consonne *f*

conspicuous [kən'spɪkjʊəs] *adj* (noticeable) bien visible; (striking) manifeste; (showy) voyant

conspiracy [kən'spɪrəsɪ] (*pl* -ies) *n* conspiration *f*

conspire [kən'spaɪə(r)] *vi* conspirer (**against** contre); **to c. to do sth** comploter de faire qch

constable ['kɒnstəbəl] *n Br* (**police**) **c.** agent *m* de police

constant ['kɒnstənt] *adj* (frequent) incessant; (unchanging) constant ▪ **constantly** *adv* constamment, sans cesse

constellation [kɒnstə'leɪʃən] *n* constellation *f*

constipated ['kɒnstɪpeɪtɪd] *adj* constipé

constituent [kən'stɪtjʊənt] *n Pol* (voter) électeur, -trice *mf* ▪ **constituency** (*pl* -ies) *n* circonscription *f* électorale; (voters) électeurs *mpl*

constitute ['kɒnstɪtjuːt] *vt* constituer ▪ **constitution** *n* constitution *f*

constraint [kən'streɪnt] *n* contrainte *f*

construct [kən'strʌkt] *vt* construire

construction *n* (building, structure, in grammar) construction *f*; **under c.** en construction; **c. site** chantier *m* ▪ **constructive** *adj* constructif, -ive

consul ['kɒnsəl] *n* consul *m* ▪ **consulate** [-sjʊlət] *n* consulat *m*

consult [kən'sʌlt] **1** *vt* consulter **2** *vi* **to c. with sb** discuter avec qn; *Br* **consulting room** (of doctor) cabinet *m* de consultation ▪ **consultation** [kɒnsəl'teɪʃən] *n* consultation *f*

consultancy [kən'sʌltənsɪ] (*pl* -ies) *n* **c. (firm)** cabinet-conseil *m* ▪ **consultant** *n Br* (doctor) spécialiste *mf*; (adviser) consultant *m*

consume [kən'sjuːm] *vt* (food, supplies) consommer; (of fire) consumer; (of grief, hate) dévorer ▪ **consumer** *n* consommateur, -trice *mf* ▪ **consumption** [-'sʌmpʃən] *n* consommation *f*

contact ['kɒntækt] **1** *n* (act of touching) contact *m*; (person) relation *f*; **in c. with** en contact avec; **c. lenses** lentilles *fpl* de contact **2** *vt* contacter

contagious [kən'teɪdʒəs] *adj* (disease) contagieux, -euse

contain [kən'teɪn] *vt* (enclose, hold back) contenir ▪ **container** *n* (box, jar) récipient *m*; (for transporting goods) conteneur *m*

contaminate [kən'tæmɪneɪt] *vt* contaminer

contemplate ['kɒntəmpleɪt] *vt* (look at) contempler; (consider) envisager (**doing** de faire)

contemporary [kən'tempərərɪ] **1** *adj* contemporain (**with** de); (style) moderne **2** (*pl* -ies) *n* (person) contemporain, -e *mf*

contempt [kən'tempt] *n* mépris *m*; **to hold sb/sth in c.** mépriser qn/qch ▪ **contemptible** *adj* méprisable ▪ **contemptuous** *adj* méprisant; **to be c. of sth** mépriser qch

contend [kən'tend] *vi* **to c. with** (problem) faire face à ▪ **contender** *n* (in sport) concurrent, -e *mf*; (in election, for job) candidat, -e *mf*

content¹ [kən'tent] *adj* (happy) satisfait (**with** de) ▪ **contented** *adj* satisfait

■ **contentment** n contentement m

content² ['kɒntent] n (of book, text, film) (subject matter) contenu m; **contents** contenu m; (in book) table f des matières; **alcoholic/iron c.** teneur f en alcool/fer

contest 1 ['kɒntest] n (competition) concours m; (fight) lutte f; (in boxing) combat m **2** [kən'test] vt (dispute) contester ■ **contestant** [kən'testənt] n concurrent, -e mf; (in fight) adversaire mf

context ['kɒntekst] n contexte m; **in/out of c.** en/hors contexte

continent ['kɒntɪnənt] n continent m; **the C.** l'Europe f continentale; **on the C.** en Europe ■ **continental** [-'nentəl] adj (of Europe) européen, -enne; **c. breakfast** petit déjeuner m à la française

contingent [kən'tɪndʒənt] n (group) contingent m ■ **contingency** (pl -ies) n éventualité f; **c. plan** plan m d'urgence

continual [kən'tɪnjʊəl] adj continuel, -elle

continue [kən'tɪnjuː] **1** vt continuer (**to do** or **doing** à ou de faire); **to c. (with)** (work, speech) poursuivre; (resume) reprendre **2** vi continuer; (resume) reprendre

continuous [kən'tɪnjʊəs] adj continu; Sch & Univ **c. assessment** contrôle m continu des connaissances ■ **continuously** adv sans interruption

contour ['kɒntʊə(r)] n contour m

contraception [kɒntrə'sepʃən] n contraception f ■ **contraceptive** n contraceptif m

contract¹ ['kɒntrækt] **1** n contrat m; **to be under c.** être sous contrat; **c. work** travail m en sous-traitance **2** vt **to c. work out** sous-traiter du travail ■ **contractor** n entrepreneur m

contract² [kən'trækt] **1** vt (illness) contracter **2** vi (shrink) se contracter

contradict [kɒntrə'dɪkt] vt (person, statement) contredire; (deny) démentir; **to c. oneself** se contredire ■ **contradictory** adj contradictoire

contraption [kən'træpʃən] n Fam machin m

contrary ['kɒntrərɪ] **1** adj (opposite) contraire (**to** à) **2** adv **c. to** contrairement à **3** n contraire m; **on the c.** au contraire; **unless you/I/etc hear to the c.** sauf avis contraire

contrast 1 ['kɒntrɑːst] n contraste m; **in c. to** par opposition à **2** [kən'trɑːst] vt mettre en contraste **3** [kən'trɑːst] vi contraster (**with** avec)

contravention [kɒntrə'venʃən] n **in c. of a treaty** en violation d'un traité

contribute [kən'trɪbjuːt] **1** vt (time, clothes) donner (**to** à); (article) écrire (**to** pour); **to c. money to** verser de l'argent à **2** vi **to c. to** contribuer à; (publication) collaborer à; (discussion) prendre part à; (charity) donner à ■ **contribution** [kɒntrɪ'bjuːʃən] n contribution f ■ **contributor** n (to newspaper) collaborateur, -trice mf; (of money) donateur, -trice mf

contrive [kən'traɪv] vt **to c. to do sth** trouver moyen de faire qch

contrived [kən'traɪvd] adj qui manque de naturel

control [kən'trəʊl] **1** n contrôle m; (authority) autorité f (**over** sur); **(self-)c.** la maîtrise (de soi); **the situation** or **everything is under c.** je/il/etc contrôle la situation; **to lose c. of** (situation, vehicle) perdre le contrôle de; **out of c.** (situation, crowd) difficilement maîtrisable; Comptr **c. key** touche f de contrôle; **c. panel** tableau m de bord

2 (pt & pp **-ll-**) vt (business, organization) diriger; (prices, quality) contrôler; (emotion, reaction) maîtriser; (disease) enrayer; **to c. oneself** se contrôler

controversy ['kɒntrəvɜːsɪ] (pl -ies) n controverse f ■ **controversial** [-'vɜːʃəl] adj controversé

convalesce [kɒnvə'les] vi (rest) être en convalescence

convenience [kən'viːnɪəns] n commodité f; Br **(public) conveniences** toilettes fpl; **c. food(s)** plats mpl tout préparés; **c. store** magasin m de proximité

convenient [kən'viːnɪənt] adj commode, pratique; **to be c. (for)**

(suit) convenir (à) ▪ **conveniently** *adv*
c. situated bien situé

convention [kən'venʃən] *n (custom)*
usage *m*; *(agreement)* convention *f*;
(conference) convention *f*, congrès *m*
▪ **conventional** *adj* conventionnel,
-elle

converge [kən'vɜːdʒ] *vi* converger **(on**
sur)

conversation [kɒnvə'seɪʃən] *n*
conversation *f* **(with** avec)

convert [kən'vɜːt] **1** ['kɒnvɜːt] *n*
converti, -e *mf* **2** *vt (change)* convertir
(into or **to** en); *(building)* aménager
(into, to en); *Rel* **to c. sb** convertir qn
(to à) **3** *vi (change religion)* se convertir
(to à) ▪ **conversion** *n* conversion *f*; *(of
building)* aménagement *m*

convertible [kən'vɜːtəbəl] **1** *adj*
(sofa) convertible **2** *n (car)* décapotable *f*

convey [kən'veɪ] *vt (transport)* trans-
porter; *(communicate)* transmettre
▪ **conveyor belt** *n* tapis *m* roulant

convict 1 ['kɒnvɪkt] *n* détenu *m* **2**
[kən'vɪkt] *vt* déclarer coupable **(of** de)
▪ **conviction** [kən'vɪkʃən] *n (for crime)*
condamnation *f*; *(belief)* conviction *f*
(that que)

convince [kən'vɪns] *vt* convaincre **(of**
sth de qch; **sb to do sth** qn de faire
qch) ▪ **convincing** *adj (argument, per-
son)* convaincant

convoy ['kɒnvɔɪ] *n* convoi *m*

cook [kʊk] **1** *n (person)* cuisinier, -ère
mf **2** *vt (meal)* préparer; *(food)* (faire)
cuire **3** *vi (of food)* cuire; *(of person)*
faire la cuisine ▪ **cookbook** *n* livre *m*
de cuisine ▪ **cooker** *n Br (stove)* cuisi-
nière *f* ▪ **cookery** *n* cuisine *f*; *Br* **c. book**
livre *m* de cuisine ▪ **cooking** *n (activity,
food)* cuisine *f*; *(process)* cuisson *f*; **to
do the c.** faire la cuisine; **c. apple**
pomme *f* à cuire

cookie ['kʊkɪ] *n Am* gâteau *m* sec

cool [kuːl] **1 (-er, -est)** *adj (weather,
place, wind)* frais *(f* fraîche); *(tea, soup)*
tiède; *(calm)* calme; *(unfriendly)* froid;
Fam (good) cool *inv*; *Fam (fashionable)*
branché; **a (nice) c. drink** une boisson
(bien) fraîche; **the weather is c., it's c.**

il fait frais; **to keep sth c.** tenir qch au
frais

2 *n* **to keep/lose one's c.** garder/per-
dre son sang-froid

3 *vt* **to c. (down)** refroidir, rafraîchir

4 *vi* **to c. (down** or **off)** *(of hot liquid)*
refroidir; *(of enthusiasm)* se refroidir; *(of
angry person)* se calmer; **to c. off** *(by
drinking, swimming)* se rafraîchir
▪ **cooler** *n (for food)* glacière *f*

coop [kuːp] *vt* **to c. up** *(person, animal)*
enfermer

co-op ['kəʊɒp] *n* coopérative *f*

cooperate [kəʊ'ɒpəreɪt] *vi* coopérer
(in à; **with** avec) ▪ **cooperation** *n* coo-
pération *f*

coordinate [kəʊ'ɔːdɪneɪt] *vt* coor-
donner ▪ **coordination** [-'neɪʃən] *n*
coordination *f*

cop [kɒp] *n Fam (policeman)* flic *m*

cope [kəʊp] *vi* **to c. with** *(problem, de-
mand)* faire face à

copier ['kɒpɪə(r)] *n (photocopier)* pho-
tocopieuse *f*

copper ['kɒpə(r)] *n (metal)* cuivre *m*;
Br **coppers** *(coins)* petite monnaie *f*

copy ['kɒpɪ] **1** *(pl* **-ies)** *n (of letter,
document)* copie *f*; *(of book, magazine)*
exemplaire *m*; *(of photo)* épreuve *f* **2** *(pt
& pp* **-ied)** *vt* copier; **to c. out** or **down**
(text, letter) copier **3** *vi* copier

coral ['kɒrəl] *n* corail *m*

cord [kɔːd] *n* **(a)** *(of curtain, bell, pyja-
mas)* cordon *m*; *(electrical)* cordon élec-
trique **(b) cords** *(trousers)* pantalon *m*
en velours côtelé

cordial ['kɔːdɪəl] **1** *adj (friendly)* cor-
dial **2** *n Br* **(fruit) c.** sirop *m*

cordless ['kɔːdləs] *adj* **c. phone** télé-
phone *m* sans fil

cordon ['kɔːdən] **1** *n* cordon *m* **2** *vt* **to
c. off** *(road)* barrer; *(area)* boucler

corduroy ['kɔːdərɔɪ] *n* velours *m* cô-
telé

core [kɔː(r)] *n (of apple)* trognon *m*; *(of
problem)* cœur *m*; *(group of people)*
noyau *m*

cork [kɔːk] **1** *n (material)* liège *m*;
(stopper) bouchon *m* **2** *vt (bottle)* bou-
cher ▪ **corkscrew** *n* tire-bouchon *m*

corn¹ [kɔːn] *n Br (wheat)* blé *m*; *Am (maize)* maïs *m*; **c. on the cob** maïs *m* en épi, *Can* blé *m* en Inde

corn² [kɔːn] *n (on foot)* cor *m*

cornbread ['kɔːnbred] *n Am* pain *m* à la farine de maïs

corner ['kɔːnə(r)] **1** *n (of street, room, page, screen)* coin *m*; *(bend in road)* virage *m*; *(in football)* corner *m*; **it's just round the c.** c'est juste au coin; **c. shop** épicerie *f* du coin **2** *vt (person, animal)* acculer

cornet ['kɔːnɪt] *n Br (of ice cream)* cornet *m*

cornflakes ['kɔːnfleɪks] *npl* corn flakes *mpl*

cornstarch ['kɔːnstɑːtʃ] *n* fécule *f* de maïs

corny ['kɔːnɪ] (**-ier, -iest**) *adj Fam (joke)* nul *(f* nulle*)*; *(film)* tarte

coronary ['kɒrənərɪ] *(pl* **-ies**) *n Med* infarctus *m*

coronation [kɒrə'neɪʃən] *n* couronnement *m*

corporal¹ ['kɔːpərəl] *n (in army)* caporal-chef *m*

corporal² ['kɔːpərəl] *adj* **c. punishment** châtiment *m* corporel

corporate ['kɔːpərət] *adj (decision)* collectif, -ive

corporation [kɔːpə'reɪʃən] *n (business)* société *f*

corps [kɔː(r), *pl* kɔːz] *n inv Mil & Pol* corps *m*; **the press c.** les journalistes *mpl*

corpse [kɔːps] *n* cadavre *m*

correct [kə'rekt] **1** *adj (accurate)* exact; *(proper)* correct; **he's c.** il a raison; **the c. time** l'heure exacte **2** *vt* corriger ▪ **correction** *n* correction *f*

correspond [kɒrɪ'spɒnd] *vi* correspondre ▪ **corresponding** *adj (matching)* correspondant; *(similar)* semblable

correspondence [kɒrɪ'spɒndəns] *n* correspondance *f*; **c. course** cours *m* par correspondance

corridor ['kɒrɪdɔː(r)] *n* couloir *m*, corridor *m*

corrosion [kə'rəʊʒən] *n* corrosion *f*

corrugated ['kɒrəgeɪtɪd] *adj* ondulé

corrupt [kə'rʌpt] **1** *adj* corrompu **2** *vt* corrompre ▪ **corruption** *n* corruption *f*

Corsica ['kɔːsɪkə] *n* la Corse

cosmetic [kɒz'metɪk] **1** *adj* **c. surgery** chirurgie *f* esthétique **2** *n* produit *m* de beauté

cosmopolitan [kɒzmə'pɒlɪtən] *adj* cosmopolite

cost [kɒst] **1** *n* coût *m*; **the c. of living** le coût de la vie; **at any c., at all costs** à tout prix

 2 *(pt & pp* cost*)* *vti* coûter; **how much does it c.?** ça coûte combien? ▪ **costly** (**-ier, -iest**) *adj (expensive) (car, trip)* coûteux, -euse

costume ['kɒstjuːm] *n* costume *m*; *Br* **(swimming) c.** maillot *m* de bain

cosy ['kəʊzɪ] **1** (**-ier, -iest**) *adj Br (house)* douillet, -ette; *(atmosphere)* intime **2** *n* **(tea) c.** couvre-théière *m*

cot [kɒt] *n Br (for child)* lit *m* d'enfant; *Am (camp bed)* lit *m* de camp

cottage ['kɒtɪdʒ] *n* petite maison *f* de campagne; **(thatched) c.** chaumière *f*; **c. cheese** fromage *m* blanc (maigre)

cotton ['kɒtən] *n* coton *m*; *(yarn)* fil *m* de coton; *Br* **c. wool,** *Am* **absorbent c.** coton *m* hydrophile, ouate *f*; **c. shirt** chemise *f* en coton; *Am* **c. candy** barbe *f* à papa

couch [kaʊtʃ] *n (sofa)* canapé *m*; *(for doctor's patient)* lit *m*

couchette [kuː'ʃet] *n Br (on train)* couchette *f*

cough [kɒf] **1** *n* toux *f*; **c. syrup** *or* **medicine,** *Br* **c. mixture** sirop *m* pour la toux **2** *vt* **to c. up** *(blood)* cracher **3** *vi* tousser

could [kʊd, *unstressed* kəd] *pt of* **can¹**

couldn't ['kʊdənt] = **could not**

council ['kaʊnsəl] *n* **(town/city) c.** conseil *m* municipal; *Br* **c. flat/house** ≃ HLM *f*; *Br* **c. tax** = impôt regroupant taxe d'habitation et impôts locaux ▪ **councillor** *n* **(town) c.** conseiller *m* municipal

counselling ['kaʊnsəlɪŋ] *(Am* **counseling***)* *n* assistance *f* psychosociale

count¹ [kaʊnt] **1** *n (calculation)* compte *m*; **to keep c. of sth** tenir le compte de qch

 2 *vt (find number of, include)* compter; *(consider)* considérer; **c. me in!** j'en suis!; **c. me out!** ne compte pas sur moi!

 3 *vi* compter; **to c. against sb** jouer contre qn; **to c. on sb/sth** *(rely on)* compter sur qn/qch; **to c. on doing sth** compter faire qch ▪ **countdown** *n* compte *m* à rebours

count² [kaʊnt] *n (title)* comte *m*

counter ['kaʊntə(r)] **1** *n* **(a)** *(in shop, bar)* comptoir *m*; *(in bank)* guichet *m* **(b)** *(in games)* jeton *m* **(c)** *(counting device)* compteur *m* **2** *adv* **c. to** contrairement à **3** *vt (threat)* répondre à; *(effects)* neutraliser **4** *vi* riposter **(with** par)

counter- ['kaʊntə(r)] *pref* contre-

counterattack ['kaʊntərətæk] **1** *n* contre-attaque *f* **2** *vti* contre-attaquer

counterclockwise [kaʊntə'klɒkwaɪz] *adj & adv Am* dans le sens inverse des aiguilles d'une montre

counterfeit ['kaʊntəfɪt] **1** *adj* faux *(f* fausse) **2** *vt* contrefaire

counterpart ['kaʊntəpɑːt] *n (thing)* équivalent *m*; *(person)* homologue *mf*

countless ['kaʊntlɪs] *adj* innombrable

country ['kʌntrɪ] *(pl* -ies) **1** *n* pays *m*; *(opposed to town)* campagne *f*; **in the c.** à la campagne **2** *adj (house, road)* de campagne; **c. and western music** country *f* ▪ **countryman** *(pl* -men) *n* **(fellow) c.** compatricte *m* ▪ **countryside** *n* campagne *f*; **in the c.** à la campagne

county ['kaʊntɪ] *(pl* -ies) *n* comté *m*

coup [kuː, *pl* kuːz] *n Pol* coup *m* d'État

couple ['kʌpəl] **1** *n (of people)* couple *m*; **a c. of** deux ou trois; *(a few)* quelques **2** *vt (connect)* accoupler

coupon ['kuːpɒn] *n (for discount)* bon *m*; *(form)* coupon *m*

courage ['kʌrɪdʒ] *n* courage *m* ▪ **courageous** [kə'reɪdʒəs] *adj* courageux, -euse

courgette [kʊə'ʒet] *n Br* courgette *f*

courier ['kʊrɪə(r)] *n (for tourists)* guide *mf*; *(messenger)* messager *m*

course [kɔːs] **1** *n* **(a)** *(of river, time, events)* cours *m*; *(of ship)* route *f*; **c. of action** ligne *f* de conduite; **in the c. of** au cours de; **in due c.** en temps utile **(b)** *(lessons)* cours *m* **(c)** *Med* **c. of treatment** traitement *m* **(d)** *(of meal)* plat *m*; **first c.** entrée *f* **(e)** *(for race)* parcours *m*; *(for horseracing)* champ *m* de courses; *(for golf)* terrain *m* **2** *adv* **of c.!** bien sûr!; **of c. not!** bien sûr que non!

court¹ [kɔːt] *n (of king)* cour *f*; *(for trials)* cour *f*, tribunal *m*; *(for tennis)* court *m*; **to go to c.** aller en justice; **to take sb to c.** poursuivre qn en justice ▪ **courthouse** *n Am* palais *m* de justice ▪ **courtroom** *n Law* salle *f* d'audience ▪ **courtyard** *n* cour *f*

court² [kɔːt] **1** *vt (woman)* faire la cour à; *(danger)* aller au-devant de **2** *vi* **to be courting** *(of couple)* se fréquenter

courteous ['kɜːtɪəs] *adj* poli, courtois ▪ **courtesy** [-təsɪ] *(pl* -ies) *n* politesse *f*, courtoisie *f*; **c. car** = voiture mise à la disposition d'un client par un hôtel, un garage etc

cousin ['kʌzən] *n* cousin, -e *mf*

cover ['kʌvə(r)] **1** *n (lid)* couvercle *m*; *(of book)* couverture *f*; *(for furniture, typewriter)* housse *f*; **to take c.** se mettre à l'abri; **under c.** *(sheltered)* à l'abri; **c. charge** *(in restaurant)* couvert *m*

 2 *vt* couvrir **(with** *or* **in** de); *(include)* englober; *(treat)* traiter; *(distance)* parcourir; *(event)* *(in newspaper, on TV)* couvrir; *(insure)* assurer **(against** contre); **to c. up** recouvrir; *(truth, tracks)* dissimuler; *(scandal)* étouffer

 3 *vi* **to c. for sb** *(of colleague)* remplacer qn; **to c. up for sb** cacher la vérité pour protéger qn ▪ **cover-up** *n* **there was a c.** on a étouffé l'affaire

coverage ['kʌvərɪdʒ] *n (on TV, in newspaper)* couverture *f* médiatique

coveralls ['kʌvərɔːlz] *n* bleu *m* de travail

covering ['kʌvərɪŋ] *n (wrapping)* enveloppe *f*; *(layer)* couche *f*; **c. letter** lettre *f* jointe

cow [kaʊ] n vache f; very Fam (nasty woman) peau f de vache ■ **cowboy** n cow-boy m; Br Fam Pej (workman) rigolo m

coward ['kaʊəd] n lâche mf

cower ['kaʊə(r)] vi (with fear) trembler

cozy ['kəʊzɪ] adj Am = cosy

crab [kræb] n (crustacean) crabe m

crack¹ [kræk] 1 n (split) fente f; (in glass, china, bone) fêlure f; (noise) craquement m 2 vt (glass, ice) fêler; (nut) casser; (whip) faire claquer; (problem) résoudre; (code) déchiffrer; Fam (joke) raconter 3 vi se fêler; (of branch, wood) craquer; **to c. down on** prendre des mesures énergiques en matière de

crack² [kræk] adj (first-rate) (driver, skier) d'élite; **c. shot** fin tireur m

crack³ [kræk] n (drug) crack m

cracker ['krækə(r)] n (a) (biscuit) biscuit m salé (b) (firework) pétard m; **Christmas c.** diablotin m

crackle ['krækəl] vi (of fire) crépiter; (of frying) grésiller; (of radio) crachoter

cradle ['kreɪdəl] 1 n berceau m 2 vt bercer

craft [krɑːft] 1 n (skill) art m; (job) métier m 2 vt façonner ■ **craftsman** (pl -men) n artisan m ■ **craftsmanship** n (skill) art m

crafty ['krɑːftɪ] (-ier, -iest) adj astucieux, -euse; Pej rusé

cram [kræm] (pt & pp -mm-) 1 vt **to c. sth into** (force) fourrer qch dans; **to c. with** (fill) bourrer de 2 vi **to c. into** (of people) s'entasser dans; **to c. (for an exam)** bûcher

cramp [kræmp] n (pain) crampe f (**in** à)

cramped [kræmpt] adj (surroundings) exigu (f exiguë)

crane [kreɪn] 1 n (machine, bird) grue f 2 vt **to c. one's neck** tendre le cou

crank¹ [kræŋk] n (handle) manivelle f

crank² [kræŋk] n Fam (person) excentrique mf; (fanatic) fanatique mf

crash [kræʃ] 1 n (accident) accident m; (collapse of firm) faillite f; (noise) fracas m; **c. course/diet** cours m/régime m intensif; **c. barrier** (on road) glissière f

de sécurité; **c. helmet** casque m; **c. landing** atterrissage m en catastrophe 2 exclam (of fallen object) patatras! 3 vt (car) avoir un accident avec; **to c. one's car into sth** rentrer dans qch (avec sa voiture) 4 vi (of car, plane) s'écraser; **to c. into** rentrer dans

crate [kreɪt] n (large) caisse f; (small) cageot m; (for bottles) casier m

crater ['kreɪtə(r)] n cratère m; (bomb) **c.** entonnoir m

craving ['kreɪvɪŋ] n envie f (**for** de)

crawl [krɔːl] 1 n (swimming stroke) crawl m 2 vi (of snake, animal) ramper; (of child) marcher à quatre pattes; (of vehicle) avancer au pas; **to be crawling with** grouiller de

crayon ['kreɪən] n (wax) crayon m gras

craze [kreɪz] n engouement m (**for** pour)

crazy ['kreɪzɪ] (-ier, -iest) adj fou (f folle) (**about** de); **to drive sb c.** rendre qn fou; **to run/work like c.** courir/travailler comme un fou

creak [kriːk] vi (of hinge) grincer; (of floor, timber) craquer

cream [kriːm] n (of milk, lotion) crème f; **c. of tomato soup** crème f de tomates; **c. cake** gâteau m à la crème; **c. cheese** fromage m à tartiner

creamy ['kriːmɪ] (-ier, -iest) adj crémeux, -euse

crease [kriːs] 1 n pli m 2 vt froisser 3 vi se froisser

create [kriː'eɪt] vt créer ■ **creation** n création f ■ **creative** adj (person, activity) créatif, -ive ■ **creator** n créateur, -trice mf

creature ['kriːtʃə(r)] n (animal) bête f; (person) créature f

crèche [kreʃ] n Br (nursery) crèche f

credentials [krɪ'denʃəlz] npl (proof of ability) références fpl

credible ['kredɪbəl] adj crédible ■ **credibility** n crédibilité f

credit ['kredɪt] 1 n (financial) crédit m; (merit) mérite m; (from university) unité f de valeur; **credits** (of film) générique m; **to buy sth on c.** acheter qch à

crédit; **to be in c.** *(of account)* être créditeur; *(of person)* avoir un solde positif; **to her c., she refused** c'est tout à son honneur d'avoir refusé; **c. card** carte *f* de crédit **2** *vt (of bank)* créditer **(sb with sth** qn de qch); *(believe)* croire

credulous ['kredjʊləs] *adj* crédule

creek [kri:k] *n (bay)* crique *f*; *Am (stream)* ruisseau *m*

creep [kri:p] **1** *n Fam* **it gives me the creeps** ça me fait froid dans le dos **2** *(pt & pp* **crept)** *vi* ramper; *(silently)* se glisser (furtivement); *(slowly)* avancer lentement ■ **creepy (-ier, -iest)** *adj Fam* sinistre

cremate [krɪ'meɪt] *vt* incinérer ■ **cremation** *n* crémation *f*

crematorium [kremə'tɔ:rɪəm] *(pl* -ia [-ɪə]) *(Am* **crematory** ['kri:mətɔ:rɪ]) *n* crématorium *m*

crept [krept] *pt & pp of* **creep**

crescent ['kresənt] *n (shape)* croissant *m*; *Br Fig (street)* rue *f* en demi-lune

crest [krest] *n (of wave, mountain, bird)* crête *f*; *(of hill)* sommet *m*; *(on seal, letters)* armoiries *fpl*

Crete [kri:t] *n* la Crète

crevice ['krevɪs] *n (crack)* fente *f*

crew [kru:] *n (of ship, plane)* équipage *m*; *Fam (gang)* équipe *f*; **c. cut** coupe *f* en brosse

crib [krɪb] **1** *n Am (cot)* lit *m* d'enfant; *(cradle)* berceau *m* **2** *(pt & pp* -bb-) *vti Fam* pomper

cricket¹ ['krɪkɪt] *n (game)* cricket *m*

cricket² ['krɪkɪt] *n (insect)* grillon *m*

crime [kraɪm] *n* crime *m*; *Law* délit *m*; *(criminal activity)* criminalité *f*

criminal ['krɪmɪnəl] *adj & n* criminel, -elle *(mf)*; **c. offence** *(minor)* délit *m*; *(serious)* crime *m*; **c. record** casier *m* judiciaire

crimson ['krɪmzən] *adj & n* cramoisi *(m)*

cringe [krɪndʒ] *vi (show fear)* avoir un mouvement de recul; *(be embarrassed)* avoir envie de rentrer sous terre

crinkle ['krɪŋkəl] **1** *n (in paper, fabric)* pli *m* **2** *vt (paper, fabric)* froisser

cripple ['krɪpəl] **1** *n (lame)* estropié, -e *mf*; *(disabled)* infirme *mf* **2** *vt (disable)* rendre infirme; *Fig (nation, system)* paralyser

crisis ['kraɪsɪs] *(pl* **crises** ['kraɪsi:z]) *n* crise *f*

crisp [krɪsp] **1** (-er, -est) *adj (biscuit)* croustillant; *(apple, vegetables)* croquant **2** *npl Br* **(potato) crisps** chips *fpl* ■ **crispbread** *n* pain *m* suédois

criterion [kraɪ'tɪərɪən] *(pl* -ia [-ɪə]) *n* critère *m*

critic ['krɪtɪk] *n (reviewer)* critique *mf*; *(opponent)* détracteur, -trice *mf* ■ **critical** *adj* critique ■ **critically** *adv (examine)* en critique; **to be c. ill** être dans un état critique ■ **criticism** [-sɪzəm] *n* critique *f* ■ **criticize** [-saɪz] *vti* critiquer

croak [krəʊk] *vi (of frog)* croasser

Croatia [krəʊ'eɪʃə] *n* la Croatie

crockery ['krɒkərɪ] *n* vaisselle *f*

crocodile ['krɒkədaɪl] *n* crocodile *m*

crocus ['krəʊkəs] *(pl* -uses [-əsɪz]) *n* crocus *m*

crook [krʊk] *n (thief)* escroc *m*

crooked ['krʊkɪd] *adj (hat, picture)* de travers; *(deal, person)* malhonnête

crop [krɒp] **1** *n (harvest)* récolte *f*; *(produce)* culture *f* **2** *(pt & pp* -pp-) *vt (hair)* couper ras **3** *vi* **to c. up** *(of issue)* survenir; *(of opportunity)* se présenter; *(of name)* être mentionné

cross¹ [krɒs] **1** *n* croix *f*; **a c. between** *(animal)* un croisement entre; *Fig* **it's a c. between a car and a van** c'est un compromis entre une voiture et une camionnette **2** *vt (street, room)* traverser; *(barrier, threshold)* franchir; *(legs, animals)* croiser; *(cheque)* barrer; **to c. off or out** *(word, name)* rayer; **to c. over** *(road)* traverser **3** *vi (of paths)* se croiser; **to c. over** traverser

cross² [krɒs] *adj (angry)* fâché **(with** contre); **to get c.** se fâcher **(with** contre) ■ **cross-country** *adj* **c. race** cross *m*; **c. runner** coureur, -euse *mf* de fond ■ **cross-legged** *adj & adv* **to sit c.** être assis en tailleur ■ **crossroads** *n* carrefour *m* ■ **cross-section** *n* coupe *f* transversale; *(sample)* échantillon *m*

représentatif ■ **crossword (puzzle)** *n* mots *mpl* croisés

crossing ['krɒsɪŋ] *n (of sea, river)* traversée *f*; *Br* **(pedestrian) c.** passage *m* clouté

crotch [krɒtʃ] *n (of garment, person)* entrejambe *m*

crouch [kraʊtʃ] *vi* to c. **(down)** *(of person)* s'accroupir; *(of animal)* se tapir

crow [krəʊ] **1** *n* corbeau *m*; **as the c. flies** à vol d'oiseau **2** *vi (of cock)* chanter; *Fig (boast)* se vanter **(about** de)

crowbar ['krəʊbɑː(r)] *n* levier *m*

crowd [kraʊd] **1** *n* foule *f*; *Fam (group of people)* bande *f*; **there was quite a c.** il y avait beaucoup de monde **2** *vt (street)* envahir; **to c. people/objects into** entasser des gens/des objets dans **3** *vi* to c. **into** *(of people)* s'entasser dans; **to c. round sb/sth** se presser autour de qn/qch; **to c. together** se serrer ■ **crowded** *adj* plein **(with** de); *(train, room)* bondé; *(city)* surpeuplé; **it's very c.** il y a beaucoup de monde

crown [kraʊn] **1** *n (of king)* couronne *f*; *(of head, hill)* sommet *m*; **the C.** *(monarchy)* la Couronne **2** *vt* couronner

crucial ['kruːʃəl] *adj* crucial

crucify ['kruːsɪfaɪ] *(pt & pp* **-ied)** *vt* crucifier ■ **crucifix** [-fɪks] *n* crucifix *m*

crude [kruːd] **(-er, -est)** *adj (manners, person, language)* grossier, -ère; *(painting, work)* rudimentaire; **c. oil** pétrole *m* brut

cruel [krʊəl] **(crueller, cruellest)** *adj* cruel, -elle ■ **cruelty** *n* cruauté *f*

cruise [kruːz] **1** *n* croisière *f*; **to go on a c.** partir en croisière; **c. ship** bateau *m* de croisière **2** *vi (of ship)* croiser; *(of vehicle)* rouler; *(of taxi)* marauder; *(of tourists)* faire une croisière

crumb [krʌm] *n* miette *f*

crumble ['krʌmbəl] **1** *vt (bread)* émietter **2** *vi (of bread)* s'émietter; *(collapse) (of resistance)* s'effondrer; **to c. (away)** *(in small pieces)* s'effriter

crumpet ['krʌmpɪt] *n Br* = petite crêpe grillée servie beurrée

crumple ['krʌmpəl] **1** *vt* froisser **2** *vi* se froisser

crunch [krʌntʃ] *vt (food)* croquer

crusade [kruːˈseɪd] *n Hist & Fig* croisade *f*

crush [krʌʃ] **1** *n (crowd)* foule *f*; *(rush)* bousculade *f*; *Fam* **to have a c. on sb** en pincer pour qn **2** *vt* écraser; *(clothes)* froisser; *(cram)* entasser **(into** dans)

crust [krʌst] *n* croûte *f* ■ **crusty (-ier, -iest)** *n (bread)* croustillant

crutch [krʌtʃ] *n* **(a)** *(of invalid)* béquille *f* **(b)** *(crotch)* entrejambe *m*

cry [kraɪ] **1** *(pl* **cries)** *n (shout)* cri *m* **2** *(pt & pp* **cried)** *vt* **to c. (out)** *(shout)* crier **3** *vi (weep)* pleurer; **to c. (out)** pousser un cri; **to c. for help** appeler au secours; **to c. over sb/sth** pleurer qn/qch ■ **crying** *n (weeping)* pleurs *mpl*

crypt [krɪpt] *n* crypte *f*

crystal ['krɪstəl] *n* cristal *m*; **c. vase** vase *m* en cristal

cub [kʌb] *n* **(a)** *(of animal)* petit *m* **(b)** *(scout)* louveteau *m*

Cuba ['kjuːbə] *n* Cuba *f*

cube [kjuːb] *n* cube *m*; *(of meat, vegetables)* dé *m*; *(of sugar)* morceau *m* ■ **cubic** *adj* **c. capacity** volume *m*; *(of engine)* cylindrée *f*; **c. metre** mètre *m* cube

cubicle ['kjuːbɪkəl] *n (for changing clothes)* cabine *f*

cuckoo ['kʊkuː] *(pl* **-oos)** *n (bird)* coucou *m*

cucumber ['kjuːkʌmbə(r)] *n* concombre *m*

cuddle ['kʌdəl] **1** *n* câlin *m*; **to give sb a c.** faire un câlin à qn **2** *vt (hug)* serrer dans ses bras; *(caress)* câliner **3** *vi (of lovers)* se faire des câlins ■ **cuddly (-ier, -iest)** *adj (person)* mignon, -onne à croquer; **c. toy** peluche *f*

cue¹ [kjuː] *n (in theatre)* réplique *f*; *(signal)* signal *m*

cue² [kjuː] *n (billiard)* **c.** queue *f* de billard

cuff [kʌf] *n (of shirt)* poignet *m*; *Am (of trousers)* revers *m*; **off the c.** *(remark)* impromptu; **c. link** bouton *m* de manchette

cul-de-sac ['kʌldəsæk] *n Br* impasse *f*

culinary ['kʌlɪnərɪ] *adj* culinaire

culminate ['kʌlmɪneɪt] *vi* **to c. in** aboutir à

culprit ['kʌlprɪt] *n* coupable *mf*

cult [kʌlt] *n* culte *m*; **c. film** film *m* culte

cultivate ['kʌltɪveɪt] *vt (land, mind)* cultiver ■ **cultivated** *adj* cultivé

culture ['kʌltʃə(r)] *n* culture *f* ■ **cultural** *adj* culturel, -elle ■ **cultured** *adj (person, mind)* cultivé

cumbersome ['kʌmbəsəm] *adj* encombrant

cunning ['kʌnɪŋ] **1** *adj (ingenious)* astucieux, -euse; *(devious)* rusé **2** *n* astuce *f*; *Pej* ruse *f*

cup [kʌp] *n* tasse *f*; *(prize)* coupe *f*; **c. final** *(in football)* finale *f* de la coupe

cupboard ['kʌbəd] *n Br* armoire *f*; *(built into wall)* placard *m*

cupcake ['kʌpkeɪk] *n* petit gâteau *m*

curable ['kjʊərəbəl] *adj* guérissable

curate ['kjʊərɪt] *n* vicaire *m*

curb [kɜːb] **1** *n* (a) *(limit)* **to put a c. on** mettre un frein à (b) *Am (kerb)* bord *m* du trottoir **2** *vt (feelings)* refréner; *(ambitions)* modérer; *(expenses)* réduire

cure ['kjʊə(r)] **1** *n* remède *m* **(for** contre**) 2** *vt* (a) *(person, illness)* guérir; **to c. sb of** guérir qn de (b) *(meat, fish) (smoke)* fumer; *(salt)* saler; *(dry)* sécher

curious ['kjʊərɪəs] *adj* curieux, -euse **(about** de**); to be c. to know/see** être curieux de savoir/voir ■ **curiosity** *(pl* -ies*) n* curiosité *f* **(about** de**)**

curl [kɜːl] **1** *n (in hair)* boucle *f* **2** *vti (hair)* boucler; *(with small, tight curls)* friser **3** *vi* **to c. up** *(shrivel)* se racornir ■ **curler** *n* bigoudi *m* ■ **curly** (-ier, -iest) *adj (hair)* bouclé; *(having many tight curls)* frisé

currant ['kʌrənt] *n (dried grape)* raisin *m* de Corinthe

currency ['kʌrənsɪ] *(pl* -ies*) n (money)* monnaie *f*; **(foreign) c.** devises *fpl* (étrangères)

current ['kʌrənt] **1** *adj (fashion, trend)* actuel, -elle; *(opinion, use)* courant; *(year, month)* en cours; **c. account** *(in bank)* compte *m* courant; **c. affairs**

questions *fpl* d'actualité **2** *n (of river, air, electricity)* courant *m* ■ **currently** *adv* actuellement

curriculum [kə'rɪkjʊləm] *(pl* -la [-lə]*) n* programme *m* scolaire; *Br* **c. vitae** curriculum vitae *m inv*

curry ['kʌrɪ] *(pl* -ies*) n (dish)* curry *m*, cari *m*

curse [kɜːs] **1** *n* malédiction *f*; *(swearword)* juron *m*; *(scourge)* fléau *m* **2** *vt* maudire; **cursed with sth** affligé de qch **3** *vi (swear)* jurer

cursor ['kɜːsə(r)] *n Comptr* curseur *m*

cursory ['kɜːsərɪ] *adj* superficiel, -elle

curt [kɜːt] *adj* brusque

curtail [kɜː'teɪl] *vt (visit)* écourter

curtain ['kɜːtən] *n* rideau *m*; **to draw the curtains** *(close)* tirer les rideaux

curts(e)y ['kɜːtsɪ] **1** *(pl* -ies *or* -eys*) n* révérence *f* **2** *(pt & pp* -ied*) vi* faire une révérence **(to** à**)**

curve [kɜːv] **1** *n* courbe *f*; *(in road)* virage *m* **2** *vt* courber **3** *vi* se courber; *(of road)* faire une courbe ■ **curved** *adj (line)* courbe

cushion ['kʊʃən] **1** *n* coussin *m* **2** *vt (shock)* amortir

cushy ['kʊʃɪ] (-ier, -iest) *adj Fam (job, life)* pépère

custard ['kʌstəd] *n* crème *f* anglaise; *(when set)* crème *f* renversée

custody ['kʌstədɪ] *n (of child, important papers)* garde *f*

custom ['kʌstəm] *n* coutume *f*; *(of individual)* habitude *f*; *(customers)* clientèle *f* ■ **customary** *adj* habituel, -elle; **it is c. to...** il est d'usage de...

customer ['kʌstəmə(r)] *n* client, -e *mf*; *Pej (individual)* individu *m*

customs ['kʌstəmz] *npl* **(the) c.** la douane; **to go through c.** passer la douane; **c. officer** douanier *m*

cut [kʌt] **1** *n (mark)* coupure *f*; *(stroke)* coup *m*; *(of clothes, hair)* coupe *f*; *(in salary, prices)* réduction *f*; *(of meat)* morceau *m*

2 *(pt & pp* cut, *pres p* cutting*) vt* couper; *(meat, chicken)* découper; *(glass, diamond, tree)* tailler; *(salary, prices, profits)* réduire; **to c. sb's hair** couper

les cheveux à qn; **to c. sth open** ouvrir qch avec un couteau/des ciseaux/*etc*; **to c. sth short** *(visit)* écourter qch **3** *vi (of knife, scissors)* couper

▸ **cut back** *vt sep & vi* réduire ▪ **cutback** *n* réduction *f*

▸ **cut down 1** *vt sep* (**a**) *(tree)* abattre (**b**) *(reduce)* réduire **2** *vi* réduire

▸ **cut in** *vi (interrupt)* interrompre; *(in vehicle)* faire une queue de poisson (**on sb** à qn)

▸ **cut off** *vt sep (piece, limb, hair)* couper; *(isolate)* isoler

▸ **cut out 1** *vt sep (article)* découper; *(remove)* enlever; *(eliminate)* supprimer; **to c. out drinking** s'arrêter de boire; *Fam* **c. it out!** ça suffit!; **c. out to be a doctor** fait pour être médecin **2** *vi (of car engine)* caler

▸ **cut up** *vt sep* couper en morceaux; *(meat, chicken)* découper; **to be very c. up about sth** *(upset)* être complètement chamboulé par qch

cute [kjuːt] **(-er, -est)** *adj Fam (pretty)* mignon, -onne

cutlery [ˈkʌtləri] *n* couverts *mpl*

cutlet [ˈkʌtlɪt] *n* côtelette *f*

cut-price [kʌtˈpraɪs] *adj* à prix réduit

cutting [ˈkʌtɪŋ] **1** *n (from newspaper)* coupure *f*; *(plant)* bouture *f* **2** *adj (wind, remark)* cinglant

CV [siːˈviː] *(abbr* **curriculum vitae)** *n Br* CV *m*

cybercafé [saɪbəˈkæfeɪ] *n* cybercafé *m*

cyberspace [ˈsaɪbəspeɪs] *n Comptr* cyberespace *m*

cycle¹ [ˈsaɪkəl] **1** *n (bicycle)* bicyclette *f*; **c. lane** voie *f* réservée aux vélos; **c. path** piste *f* cyclable **2** *vi* aller à bicyclette (**to** à); *(as activity)* faire de la bicyclette ▪ **cycling** *n* cyclisme *m* ▪ **cyclist** *n* cycliste *mf*

cycle² [ˈsaɪkəl] *n (series, period)* cycle *m*

cylinder [ˈsɪlɪndə(r)] *n* cylindre *m*

cymbal [ˈsɪmbəl] *n* cymbale *f*

cynical [ˈsɪnɪkəl] *adj* cynique

Cyprus [ˈsaɪprəs] *n* Chypre *f*

cyst [sɪst] *n Med* kyste *m*

Czech [tʃek] **1** *adj* tchèque; **the C. Republic** la République tchèque **2** *n (person)* Tchèque *mf*; *(language)* tchèque *m*

Dd

D, d [di:] *n* D, d *m inv*

dab [dæb] **1** *n* a d. of un petit peu de **2** (*pt & pp* **-bb-**) *vt (wound, brow)* tamponner; **to d. sth on sth** appliquer qch (à petits coups) sur qch

dabble ['dæbəl] *vi* **to d. in politics/journalism** faire vaguement de la politique/du journalisme

dad [dæd] *n Fam* papa *m* ▪ **daddy** (*pl* **-ies**) *n Fam* papa *m*

daffodil ['dæfədɪl] *n* jonquille *f*

daft [dɑ:ft] (**-er, -est**) *adj Fam* bête

dagger ['dægə(r)] *n* dague *f*

daily ['deɪlɪ] **1** *adj* quotidien, -enne; (*wage*) journalier, -ère **d. paper** quotidien *m* **2** *adv* chaque jour, quotidiennement; **twice a d.** deux fois par jour **3** (*pl* **-ies**) *n (newspaper)* quotidien *m*

dainty ['deɪntɪ] (**-ier, -iest**) *adj* délicat

dairy ['deərɪ] **1** (*pl* **-ies**) *n (factory)* laiterie *f*; (*shop*) crémerie *f* **2** *adj* laitier, -ère; **d. produce** produits *mpl* laitiers

daisy ['deɪzɪ] (*pl* **-ies**) *n* pâquerette *f*; (*bigger*) marguerite *f*

dam [dæm] *n (wall)* barrage *m*

damage ['dæmɪdʒ] **1** *n* dégâts *mpl*; (*harm*) préjudice *m*; **damages** (*in court*) dommages-intérêts *mpl* **2** *vt (object)* endommager, abîmer; (*health*) nuire à; (*eyesight*) abîmer; (*plans, reputation*) compromettre ▪ **damaging** *adj (harmful)* préjudiciable (**to** à)

damn [dæm] **1** *n Fam* **he doesn't care** *or* **give a d.** il s'en fiche pas mal **2** *adj Fam* fichu **3** *adv Fam (very)* vachement **4** *vt (condemn, doom)* condamner; (*curse*) maudire; *Fam* **d. him!** qu'il aille se faire voir! **5** *exclam Fam* **d. (it)!** mince! ▪ **damned** *Fam* **1** *adj (awful)* fichu **2** *adv* vachement

damp [dæmp] **1** (**-er, -est**) *adj* humide; (*skin*) moite **2** *n* humidité *f* ▪ **damp(en)** *vt* humecter; **to d. (down)** (*enthusiasm, zeal*) refroidir

damson ['dæmzən] *n* prune *f* de Damas

dance [dɑ:ns] **1** *n* danse *f*; (*social event*) bal *m* (*pl* bals); **d. hall** dancing *m* **2** *vt (waltz, tango)* danser **3** *vi* danser ▪ **dancing** *n* danse *f*

dandelion ['dændɪlaɪən] *n* pissenlit *m*

dandruff ['dændrʌf] *n* pellicules *fpl*

Dane [deɪn] *n* Danois, -e *mf*

danger ['deɪndʒə(r)] *n* danger *m* (**to** pour); **in d.** en danger; **out of d.** hors de danger; **to be in d. of doing sth** risquer de faire qch ▪ **dangerous** *adj* dangereux, -euse (**to** pour)

dangle ['dæŋgəl] **1** *vt* balancer **2** *vi (hang)* pendre; (*swing*) se balancer

Danish ['deɪnɪʃ] **1** *adj* danois **2** *n (language)* danois *m*

dare [deə(r)] *vt* **to d. (to) do sth** oser faire qch; **I d. say he tried** il a essayé, c'est bien possible; **to d. sb to do sth** défier qn de faire qch ▪ **daring 1** *adj* audacieux, -euse **2** *n* audace *f*

dark [dɑ:k] **1** (**-er, -est**) *adj (room, night)* & *Fig* sombre; (*colour, skin, hair, eyes*) foncé; **it's d. at six** il fait nuit à six heures; **d. glasses** lunettes *fpl* noires **2** *n* obscurité *f*; **after d.** une fois la nuit tombée; *Fig* **to keep sb in the d.** laisser qn dans l'ignorance (**about** de) ▪ **dark-haired** *adj* aux cheveux bruns ▪ **dark-skinned** *adj (person)* à peau brune

darken ['dɑ:kən] **1** *vt* assombrir; (*colour*) foncer **2** *vi* s'assombrir; (*of colour*) foncer

darkness ['dɑ:knəs] *n* obscurité *f*

darkroom ['dɑ:kru:m] *n (for photography)* chambre *f* noire

darling ['dɑːlɪŋ] *n (favourite)* chouchou, -oute *mf*; **(my) d.** (mon) chéri/ (ma) chérie

darn [dɑːn] *vt (mend)* repriser

dart [dɑːt] **1** *n (in game)* fléchette *f*; **darts** *(game)* fléchettes *fpl* **2** *vi (dash)* se précipiter (**for** vers)

dash [dæʃ] **1** *n* (a) *(run, rush)* ruée *f*; **to make a d. for sth** se ruer vers qch (b) **a d. of** sth un petit peu de qch (c) *(handwritten stroke)* trait *m*; *(punctuation sign)* tiret *m* **2** *vt (throw)* jeter; **to d. off** *(letter)* écrire en vitesse **3** *vi (rush)* se précipiter; **to d. in/out** entrer/sortir en vitesse; **to d. off** *or* **away** filer ■ **dashboard** *n (of vehicle)* tableau *m* de bord

data ['deɪtə] *npl* informations *fpl*; *Comptr* données *fpl*; **d. base** base *f* de données; **d. processing** informatique *f*

date¹ [deɪt] **1** *n (day)* date *f*; *Fam (meeting)* rendez-vous *m inv*; *Fam (person)* ami, -e *mf*; **d. of birth** date *f* de naissance; **up to d.** *(in fashion)* à la mode; *(information)* à jour; *(well-informed)* au courant (**on** de); **out of d.** *(old-fashioned)* démodé; *(expired)* périmé **2** *vt (letter)* dater; *Fam (girl, boy)* sortir avec **3** *vi (go out of fashion)* dater; **to d. back to, to d. from** dater de

date² [deɪt] *n (fruit)* datte *f*

dated ['deɪtɪd] *adj* démodé

daughter ['dɔːtə(r)] *n* fille *f* ■ **daughter-in-law** *(pl* **daughters-in-law)** *n* belle-fille *f*

dawdle ['dɔːdəl] *vi* traînasser

dawn [dɔːn] **1** *n* aube *f*; **at d.** à l'aube **2** *vi (of day)* se lever; **it dawned on him that...** il s'est rendu compte que...

day [deɪ] *n (period of daylight, 24 hours)* jour *m*; *(referring to duration)* journée *f*; **all d. (long)** toute la journée; **what d. is it?** quel jour sommes-nous?; **the following** *or* **next d.** le lendemain; **the d. before** la veille; **the d. before yesterday** *or* **before last** avant-hier; **the d. after tomorrow** après-demain; **in those days** en ce temps-là; **these days** de nos jours ■ **daybreak** *n* point *m* du jour ■ **day-**

dream 1 *n* rêverie *f* **2** *vi* rêvasser ■ **daylight** *n* (lumière *f* du) jour *m* ■ **daytime** *n* journée *f*, jour *m*

daze [deɪz] **1** *n* **in a d.** étourdi; *(because of drugs)* hébété; *(astonished)* ahuri **2** *vt (by blow)* étourdir

dazzle ['dæzəl] *vt* éblouir

dead [ded] **1** *adj* mort; *(numb) (limb)* engourdi; **the phone's d.** il n'y a pas de tonalité; **d. end** *(street) & Fig* impasse *f*; **a d. stop** un arrêt complet **2** *npl* **the d.** les morts *mpl* **3** *adv (completely)* totalement; *Fam (very)* très; **to stop d.** s'arrêter net

deaden ['dedən] *vt (shock)* amortir; *(pain)* calmer

deadline ['dedlaɪn] *n* date *f* limite; *(hour)* heure *f* limite

deadlock ['dedlɒk] *n Fig* impasse *f*

deadly ['dedlɪ] **1** (-ier, -iest) *adj (poison, blow, enemy)* mortel, -elle; **d. weapon** arme *f* meurtrière **2** *adv (pale, boring)* mortellement

deaf [def] **1** *adj* sourd; **d. and dumb** sourd-muet *(f* sourde-muette) **2** *npl* **the d.** les sourds *mpl* ■ **deafen** *vt* assourdir

deal¹ [diːl] *n* **a good** *or* **great d. (of)** *(a lot)* beaucoup (de)

deal² [diːl] *n* **1** *(in business)* marché *m*, affaire *f*; *(in card games)* donne *f*; **to make** *or* **do a d. (with sb)** conclure un marché (avec qn); **it's a d.!** d'accord!; *Ironic* **big d.!** la belle affaire! **2** *(pt & pp* **dealt)** *vt* **to d. (out)** *(cards, money)* distribuer **3** *vi (trade)* traiter (**with sb** avec qn); **to d. in** faire le commerce de; **to d. with** *(take care of)* s'occuper de; *(concern) (of book)* traiter de, parler de ■ **dealer** *n* marchand, -e *mf* (**in** de); *(for cars)* concessionnaire *mf*; *(in drugs)* revendeur, -euse *mf*; *(in card games)* donneur, -euse *mf* ■ **dealings** *npl* relations *fpl* (**with** avec); *(in business)* transactions *fpl*

dealt [delt] *pt & pp of* **deal**

dear [dɪə(r)] **1** (-er, -est) *adj (loved, precious, expensive)* cher *(f* chère); **D. Madam** *(in letter)* Madame; **D. Sir** Monsieur; **D. Jane** chère Jane; **oh d.!**

oh là là! **2** *n* **(my) d.** *(darling)* (mon) chéri/(ma) chérie; *(friend)* mon cher/ ma chère **3** *adv (cost, pay)* cher

dearly ['dɪəlɪ] *adv (love)* tendrement; *(very much)* beaucoup; **to pay d. for sth** payer qch cher

death [deθ] *n* mort *f*; **to be bored to d.** s'ennuyer à mourir; **to be scared to d.** être mort de peur; **to be sick to d.** en avoir vraiment marre (**of** de); **d. certificate** acte *m* de décès; **d. penalty** peine *f* de mort; **d. sentence** condamnation *f* à mort ∎ **deathly** *adj (silence, paleness)* de mort

debate [dɪ'beɪt] **1** *n* débat *m* **2** *vti* discuter ∎ **debatable** *adj* **it's d. whether she will succeed** il est difficile de dire si elle réussira

debit ['debɪt] **1** *n* débit *m*; **in d.** *(account)* débiteur **2** *vt* débiter (**sb with sth** qn de qch)

debris ['debriː] *n (of building)* décombres *mpl*; *(of plane, car)* débris *mpl*

debt [det] *n* dette *f*; **to be in d.** avoir des dettes; **to run** or **get into d.** faire des dettes ∎ **debtor** *n* débiteur, -trice *mf*

debut ['debjuː] *n (on stage)* début *m*; **to make one's d.** faire ses débuts

decade ['dekeɪd] *n* décennie *f*

decadent ['dekədənt] *adj* décadent

decaffeinated [diː'kæfɪneɪtɪd] *adj* décaféiné

decanter [dɪ'kæntə(r)] *n* carafe *f*

decay [dɪ'keɪ] **1** *n (rot)* pourriture *f*; *(of tooth)* carie *f*; **to fall into d.** *(of building)* tomber en ruine **2** *vi (go bad)* se gâter; *(rot)* pourrir; *(of tooth)* se carier

deceased [dɪ'siːst] **1** *adj* décédé **2** *n* **the d.** le défunt/la défunte

deceit [dɪ'siːt] *n* tromperie *f* ∎ **deceitful** *adj (person)* fourbe; *(behaviour)* malhonnête

deceive [dɪ'siːv] *vti* tromper; **to d. oneself** se faire des illusions

December [dɪ'sembə(r)] *n* décembre *m*

decent ['diːsənt] *adj (respectable)* convenable; *(good)* bon (*f* bonne); *(kind)* gentil, -ille ∎ **decency** *n* décence

f; *(kindness)* gentillesse *f*

deception [dɪ'sepʃən] *n* tromperie *f* ∎ **deceptive** *adj* trompeur, -euse

decide [dɪ'saɪd] **1** *vt (outcome, future)* décider de; *(question, matter)* régler; **to d. to do sth** décider de faire qch; **to d. that...** décider que... **2** *vi (make decisions)* décider; *(make up one's mind)* se décider (**on doing** à faire); **to d. on sth** décider de qch; *(choose)* choisir qch

decimal ['desɪməl] **1** *adj* décimal; **d. point** virgule *f* **2** *n* décimale *f*

decipher [dɪ'saɪfə(r)] *vt* déchiffrer

decision [dɪ'sɪʒən] *n* décision *f*

decisive [dɪ'saɪsɪv] *adj (action, event, tone)* décisif, -ive; *(person)* résolu

deck [dek] **1** *n* **(a)** *(of ship)* pont *m*; **top d.** *(of bus)* impériale *f* **(b)** **d. of cards** jeu *m* de cartes **(c)** *(of record player)* platine *f* **2** *vt* **to d. (out)** *(adorn)* orner ∎ **deckchair** *n* chaise *f* longue

declare [dɪ'kleə(r)] *vt* déclarer (**that** que); *(result)* proclamer ∎ **declaration** *n* déclaration *f*

decline [dɪ'klaɪn] **1** *n* déclin *m*; *(fall)* baisse *f* **2** *vt (offer)* décliner; **to d. to do sth** refuser de faire qch **3** *vi (become less) (of popularity, birthrate)* être en baisse; *(deteriorate) (of health, strength)* décliner; *(refuse)* refuser

decode [diː'kəʊd] *vt (message)* décoder ∎ **decoder** *n* Comptr & TV décodeur *m*

decompose [diːkəm'pəʊz] *vi (rot)* se décomposer

decor ['deɪkɔː(r)] *n* décor *m*

decorate ['dekəreɪt] *vt (cake, house, soldier)* décorer (**with** de); *(hat, skirt)* orner (**with** de); *(paint)* peindre; *(wallpaper)* tapisser ∎ **decoration** *n* décoration *f* ∎ **decorative** *adj* décoratif, -ive ∎ **decorator** *n Br (house painter)* peintre *m* décorateur; **(interior) d.** décorateur, -trice *mf*

decrease 1 ['diːkriːs] *n* diminution *f* (**in** de) **2** [dɪ'kriːs] *vti* diminuer

decree [dɪ'kriː] **1** *n (by court)* jugement *m*; *(municipal)* arrêté *m* **2** *(pt & pp* **-eed)** *vt* décréter (**that** que)

decrepit [dɪ'krepɪt] *adj (building)* en

ruine; *(person)* décrépit

dedicate ['dedɪkeɪt] *vt (devote)* consacrer (**to** à); *(book)* dédier (**to** à); **to d. oneself to sth** se consacrer à qch ■ **dedicated** *adj (teacher)* consciencieux, -euse ■ **dedication** *n (in book)* dédicace *f*; *(devotion)* dévouement *m*

deduce [dɪ'djuːs] *vt (conclude)* déduire (**from** de; **that** que)

deduct [dɪ'dʌkt] *vt* déduire (**from** de) ■ **deductible** *adj (from income) (expenses)* déductible ■ **deduction** *n (subtraction, conclusion)* déduction *f*

deed [diːd] *n* action *f*, acte *m*; *(feat)* exploit *m*; *(legal document)* acte *m* notarié

deep [diːp] **1** (**-er, -est**) *adj* profond; *(snow)* épais (*f* épaisse); *(voice)* grave; *(musical note)* bas (*f* basse); **to be 6 metres d.** avoir 6 mètres de profondeur; **d. in thought** plongé dans ses pensées; **d. red** rouge foncé **2** *adv* profondément ■ **deeply** *adv* profondément

deepen ['diːpən] **1** *vt (increase)* augmenter; *(canal, knowledge)* approfondir **2** *vi (of river)* devenir plus profond; *(of mystery)* s'épaissir; *(of voice)* devenir plus grave

deep-freeze [diːp'friːz] **1** *n* congélateur *m* **2** *vt* surgeler

deer [dɪə(r)] *n inv* cerf *m*

deface [dɪ'feɪs] *vt (damage)* dégrader; *(daub)* barbouiller

default [dɪ'fɔːlt] *n* **by d.** par défaut; **to win by d.** gagner par forfait

defeat [dɪ'fiːt] **1** *n* défaite *f* **2** *vt (opponent, army)* vaincre; **that defeats the purpose** *or* **object** ça va à l'encontre du but recherché

defect[1] ['diːfekt] *n* défaut *m*

defect[2] [dɪ'fekt] *vi (of party member, soldier)* déserter

defective [dɪ'fektɪv] *adj (machine)* défectueux, -euse

defence [dɪ'fens] (*Am* **defense**) *n* défense *f* (**against** contre); **in his d.** à sa décharge

defend [dɪ'fend] *vti* défendre ■ **defendant** *n (accused)* prévenu, -e *mf*

■ **defender** *n* défenseur *m*; *(of sports title)* tenant, -e *mf*

defense [dɪ'fens] *n Am* = **defence**

defensive [dɪ'fensɪv] **1** *adj* défensif, -ive; **to be d.** être sur la défensive **2** *n* **on the d.** sur la défensive

defer [dɪ'fɜː(r)] (*pt & pp* **-rr-**) *vt (postpone)* différer

defiant [dɪ'faɪənt] *adj (person)* provocant ■ **defiance** *n (resistance)* défi *m* (**of** à)

deficient [dɪ'fɪʃənt] *adj (not adequate)* insuffisant; *(faulty)* défectueux, -euse; **to be d. in** manquer de ■ **deficiency** (*pl* **-ies**) *n (shortage)* manque *m*; *(in vitamins, minerals)* carence *f* (**in** de); *(flaw)* défaut *m*

deficit ['defɪsɪt] *n* déficit *m*

define [dɪ'faɪn] *vt* définir

definite ['defɪnɪt] *adj (exact) (date, plan, answer)* précis; *(clear) (improvement, advantage)* net (*f* nette); *(firm) (offer, order)* ferme; *(certain)* certain; **he was quite d.** il a été tout à fait formel; **d. article** *(in grammar)* article *m* défini ■ **definitely** *adv* certainement; *(improved, superior)* nettement; *(say)* catégoriquement

definition [defɪ'nɪʃən] *n* définition *f*

deflect [dɪ'flekt] *vt (bullet)* faire dévier

deformed [dɪ'fɔːmd] *adj (body)* difforme

defraud [dɪ'frɔːd] *vt (customs, State)* frauder; **to d. sb of sth** escroquer qch à qn

defrost [diː'frɒst] *vt (fridge)* dégivrer; *(food)* décongeler

defuse [diː'fjuːz] *vt (bomb, conflict)* désamorcer

defy [dɪ'faɪ] (*pt & pp* **-ied**) *vt (person, death, logic)* défier; *(efforts)* résister à; **to d. sb to do sth** défier qn de faire qch

degenerate 1 [dɪ'dʒenərət] *adj & n* dégénéré, -e *(mf)* **2** [dɪ'dʒenəreɪt] *vi* dégénérer (**into** en)

degrading [dɪ'greɪdɪŋ] *adj* dégradant

degree [dɪ'griː] *n* (**a**) *(of angle, temperature, extent)* degré *m*; **it's 20 degrees** *(temperature)* il fait 20 degrés;

to some d., to a certain d. jusqu'à un certain point; **to such a d.** à tel point (**that** que) (**b**) *(from university)* diplôme *m*; *(Bachelor's)* ≃ licence *f*; *(Master's)* ≃ maîtrise *f*; *(PhD)* ≃ doctorat *m*

dehydrated [diːhaɪˈdreɪtɪd] *adj* déshydraté; **to get d.** se déshydrater

de-ice [diːˈaɪs] *vt (car window)* dégivrer

dejected [dɪˈdʒektɪd] *adj* abattu

delay [dɪˈleɪ] **1** *n (lateness)* retard *m*; *(waiting period)* délai *m*; **without d.** sans tarder **2** *vt* retarder; *(payment)* différer; **to d. doing sth** tarder à faire qch; **to be delayed** avoir du retard **3** *vi (be slow)* tarder (**in doing** à faire)

delegate 1 [ˈdelɪgət] *n* délégué, -e *mf* **2** [ˈdelɪgeɪt] *vt* déléguer (**to** à) ■ **delegation** *n* délégation *f*

delete [dɪˈliːt] *vt* supprimer

deliberate [dɪˈlɪbərət] *adj (intentional)* délibéré; *(slow)* mesuré ■ **deliberately** *adv (intentionally)* délibérément

delicate [ˈdelɪkət] *adj* délicat ■ **delicacy** *(pl -ies) n (quality)* délicatesse *f*; *(food)* mets *m* délicat

delicatessen [delɪkəˈtesən] *n (shop)* épicerie *f* fine

delicious [dɪˈlɪʃəs] *adj* délicieux, -euse

delight [dɪˈlaɪt] **1** *n (pleasure)* plaisir *m*, joie *f* **2** *vt* ravir **3** *vi* **to d. in doing sth** prendre plaisir à faire qch ■ **delighted** *adj* ravi (**with** de qch; **to do** de faire; **that** que)

delightful [dɪˈlaɪtfəl] *adj* charmant; *(meal, perfume, sensation)* délicieux, -euse

delinquent [dɪˈlɪŋkwənt] *adj & n* délinquant, -e *(mf)*

delirious [dɪˈlɪrɪəs] *adj* délirant; **to be d.** délirer

deliver [dɪˈlɪvə(r)] *vt* (**a**) *(goods)* livrer; *(letters)* distribuer; *(hand over)* remettre (**to** à) (**b**) *(rescue)* délivrer (**from** de) (**c**) **to d. a woman's baby** accoucher une femme (**d**) *(speech)* prononcer; *(warning, ultimatum)* lancer

delivery [dɪˈlɪvərɪ] *(pl -ies) n* (**a**) *(of goods)* livraison *f*; *(of letters)* distribution *f* (**b**) *(birth)* accouchement *m* (**c**) *(speaking)* débit *m*

delude [dɪˈluːd] *vt* tromper; **to d. oneself** se faire des illusions ■ **delusion** *n* illusion *f*; *(in mental illness)* aberration *f* mentale

de luxe [dɪˈlʌks] *adj* de luxe

demand [dɪˈmɑːnd] **1** *n* exigence *f*; *(claim)* revendication *f*; *(for goods)* demande *f* (**for** pour); **to be in (great) d.** être très demandé; **to make demands on sb** exiger beaucoup de qn **2** *vt* exiger (**sth from sb** qch de qn); *(rights, more pay)* revendiquer; **to d. that...** exiger que... ■ **demanding** *adj* exigeant

demeaning [dɪˈmiːnɪŋ] *adj* dégradant

demeanour [dɪˈmiːnə(r)] *(Am* **demeanor)** *n (behaviour)* comportement *m*

demo [ˈdeməʊ] *(pl -os) n Fam (demonstration)* manif *f*

democracy [dɪˈmɒkrəsɪ] *(pl -ies) n* démocratie *f* ■ **democratic** *adj (institution)* démocratique; *(person)* démocrate

demolish [dɪˈmɒlɪʃ] *vt* démolir

demon [ˈdiːmən] *n* démon *m*

demonstrate [ˈdemənstreɪt] **1** *vt* démontrer; *(machine)* faire une démonstration de; **to d. how to do sth** montrer comment faire qch **2** *vi (protest)* manifester ■ **demonstration** [-ˈstreɪʃən] *n* démonstration *f*; *(protest)* manifestation *f* ■ **demonstrator** *n (protester)* manifestant, -e *mf*

demoralize [dɪˈmɒrəlaɪz] *vt* démoraliser

demote [dɪˈməʊt] *vt* rétrograder

den [den] *n (of lion, person)* antre *m*

denial [dɪˈnaɪəl] *n (of rumour, allegation)* démenti *m*

denigrate [ˈdenɪgreɪt] *vt* dénigrer

denim [ˈdenɪm] *n* denim *m*; **denims** *(jeans)* jean *m*

Denmark [ˈdenmɑːk] *n* le Danemark

denomination [dɪnɒmɪˈneɪʃən] *n*

(religion) confession *f*; *(of coin, bank-note)* valeur *f*

denote [dɪ'nəʊt] *vt* dénoter

denounce [dɪ'naʊns] *vt (person, injustice)* dénoncer (**to** à)

dense [dens] (**-er, -est**) *adj* dense; *Fam (stupid)* lourd ■ **densely** *adv* d. populated très peuplé

dent [dent] **1** *n (in car, metal)* bosse *f* **2** *vt* cabosser

dental ['dentəl] *adj* dentaire; **d. appointment** rendez-vous *m inv* chez le dentiste

dentist ['dentɪst] *n* dentiste *mf*; **to go to the d.** aller chez le dentiste

dentures ['dentʃəz] *npl* dentier *m*

deny [dɪ'naɪ] (*pt & pp* **-ied**) *vt* nier (**doing** avoir fait; **that** que); *(rumour)* démentir; **to d. sb sth** refuser qch à qn

deodorant [diː'əʊdərənt] *n* déodorant *m*

depart [dɪ'pɑːt] *vi* partir; *(deviate)* s'écarter (**from** de)

department [dɪ'pɑːtmənt] *n* département *m*; *(in office)* service *m*; *(in shop)* rayon *m*; *(of government)* ministère *m*; **d. store** grand magasin *m*

departure [dɪ'pɑːtʃə(r)] *n* départ *m*; **d. lounge** *(in airport)* salle *f* d'embarquement

depend [dɪ'pend] *vi* dépendre (**on** *or* **upon** de); **to d. (up)on** *(rely on)* compter sur (**for sth** pour qch) ■ **dependant** *n* personne *f* à charge ■ **dependent** *adj (relative, child)* à charge; **to be d. (up)on** dépendre de; **to be d. on sb** *(financially)* être à la charge de qn

depict [dɪ'pɪkt] *vt (describe)* décrire; *(in pictures)* représenter

deplorable [dɪ'plɔːrəbəl] *adj* déplorable

deploy [dɪ'plɔɪ] *vt (troops)* déployer

deport [dɪ'pɔːt] *vt (foreigner, criminal)* expulser

deposit [dɪ'pɒzɪt] **1** *n* **(a)** *(in bank)* dépôt *m*; *(part payment)* acompte *m*; *(returnable)* caution *f* **(b)** *(sediment)* dépôt *m*; *(of gold, oil)* gisement *m* **2** *vt (object, money)* déposer

depot [*Br* 'depəʊ, *Am* 'diːpəʊ] *n (for goods)* dépôt *m*; *Am (railroad station)* gare *f*; *Am* (**bus**) **d.** gare *f* routière

depraved [dɪ'preɪvd] *adj* dépravé

depreciate [dɪ'priːʃɪeɪt] *vi (fall in value)* se déprécier

depress [dɪ'pres] *vt (discourage)* déprimer ■ **depressed** *adj (person, market)* déprimé; **to get d.** se décourager ■ **depression** *n* dépression *f*

deprive [dɪ'praɪv] *vt* priver (**of** de) ■ **deprived** *adj (child)* défavorisé

depth [depθ] *n* profondeur *f*; **in the depths of** *(forest, despair)* au plus profond de; *(winter)* au cœur de; **in d.** en profondeur

deputy ['depjʊtɪ] (*pl* **-ies**) *n (replacement)* remplaçant, -e *mf*; *(assistant)* adjoint, -e *mf*

derailed [dɪ'reɪld] *adj* **to be d.** *(of train)* dérailler

derelict ['derɪlɪkt] *adj (building)* abandonné

derision [dɪ'rɪʒən] *n* dérision *f*

derisory [dɪ'raɪsərɪ] *adj (amount)* dérisoire

derive [dɪ'raɪv] **1** *vt* provenir (**from** de); **to be derived from** provenir de **2** *vi* **to d. from** provenir de ■ **derivation** *n Ling* dérivation *f*

descend [dɪ'send] **1** *vt (stairs, hill)* descendre; **to be descended from** descendre de **2** *vi* descendre (**from** de); **to d. upon** *(of tourists)* envahir; *(attack)* faire une descente sur; **in descending order** en ordre décroissant ■ **descendant** *n* descendant, -e *mf*

descent [dɪ'sent] *n* **(a)** *(of aircraft)* descente *f* **(b)** *(ancestry)* origine *f*; **to be of Norman d.** être d'origine normande

describe [dɪ'skraɪb] *vt* décrire ■ **description** *n* description *f*

desert¹ ['dezət] *n* désert *m*; **d. island** île *f* déserte

desert² [dɪ'zɜːt] **1** *vt (person)* abandonner; *(place, cause)* déserter **2** *vi (of soldier)* déserter ■ **deserted** *adj* désert

deserve [dɪ'zɜːv] *vt* mériter (**to do** de

faire) ■ **deserving** *adj (person)* méritant; *(action, cause)* méritoire

design [dɪ'zaɪn] **1** *n* (**a**) *(pattern)* motif *m*; *(sketch)* plan *m*; *(of dress, car, furniture)* modèle *m* (**b**) *(aim)* dessein *m*; **to have designs on** avoir des vues sur **2** *vt (car, building)* concevoir; *(dress)* créer; **designed to do sth/for sth** conçu pour faire qch/pour qch ■ **designer** *n (artistic)* dessinateur, -trice *mf*; *(industrial)* concepteur-dessinateur *m*; *(of clothes)* styliste *mf*; *(well-known)* couturier *m*; **d. clothes** vêtements *mpl* de marque

designate ['dezɪgneɪt] *vt* désigner

desire [dɪ'zaɪə(r)] **1** *n* désir *m* **2** *vt* désirer (**to do** faire) ■ **desirable** *adj* désirable

desk [desk] *n (in school)* table *f*; *(in office)* bureau *m*; *Br (in shop)* caisse *f*; **(reception)** *(in hotel)* réception *f*; *Am* **d. clerk** *(in hotel)* réceptionniste *mf*

desktop ['desktɒp] *n Comptr* bureau *m*; **d. computer** ordinateur *m* de bureau; **d. publishing** publication *f* assistée par ordinateur

desolate ['desələt] *adj (deserted)* désolé; *(dreary, bleak)* morne, triste

despair [dɪ'speə(r)] **1** *n* désespoir *m*; **to be in d.** être au désespoir **2** *vi* désespérer (**of sb** de qn; **of doing** de faire)

despatch [dɪ'spætʃ] *n & vt* = **dispatch**

desperate ['despərət] *adj* désespéré; **to be d. for** *(money, love)* avoir désespérément besoin de; *(cigarette, baby)* mourir d'envie d'avoir ■ **desperately** *adv (ill)* gravement

despicable [dɪ'spɪkəbəl] *adj* méprisable

despise [dɪ'spaɪz] *vt* mépriser

despite [dɪ'spaɪt] *prep* malgré

despondent [dɪ'spɒndənt] *adj* abattu

dessert [dɪ'zɜːt] *n* dessert *m* ■ **dessertspoon** *n Br* cuillère *f* à dessert

destination [destɪ'neɪʃən] *n* destination *f*

destine ['destɪn] *vt* destiner (**for** à; **to do** à faire)

destiny ['destɪnɪ] *(pl -ies)* *n* destin *m*, destinée *f*

destitute ['destɪtjuːt] *adj (poor)* indigent

destroy [dɪ'strɔɪ] *vt* détruire; *(cat, dog)* faire piquer

destruction [dɪ'strʌkʃən] *n* destruction *f* ■ **destructive** *adj (person, war)* destructeur, -trice

detach [dɪ'tætʃ] *vt* détacher (**from** de) ■ **detached** *adj Br* **d. house** maison *f* individuelle

detachable [dɪ'tætʃəbəl] *adj* amovible

detail ['diːteɪl] *n (item of information)* détail *m*; **in d.** en détail; **to go into d.** entrer dans les détails ■ **detailed** *adj (account)* détaillé

detain [dɪ'teɪn] *vt (delay)* retenir; *(prisoner)* placer en détention; *(in hospital)* garder ■ **detention** *n (at school)* retenue *f*

detect [dɪ'tekt] *vt* détecter

detective [dɪ'tektɪv] *n (police officer)* ≃ inspecteur *m* de police; *(private)* détective *m* privé; **d. film/novel** film *m*/roman *m* policier

detector [dɪ'tektə(r)] *n* détecteur *m*

deter [dɪ'tɜː(r)] *(pt & pp -rr-)* *vt* **to d. sb** dissuader qn (**from doing** de faire)

detergent [dɪ'tɜːdʒənt] *n* détergent *m*

deteriorate [dɪ'tɪərɪəreɪt] *vi* se détériorer

determine [dɪ'tɜːmɪn] *vt (cause, date)* déterminer; **to d. to do sth** décider de faire qch ■ **determined** *adj (look, person)* déterminé; **to be d. to do sth** être décidé à faire qch

deterrent [dɪ'terənt] *n* **to be a d., to act as a d.** être dissuasif, -ive

detest [dɪ'test] *vt* détester (**doing** faire)

detonate ['detəneɪt] **1** *vt* faire exploser **2** *vi* exploser

detour ['diːtʊə(r)] *n* détour *m*; **to make a d.** faire un détour

detract [dɪ'trækt] *vi* **to d. from** *(make less)* diminuer

detriment ['detrɪmənt] *n* **to the d. of** au détriment de ■ **detrimental** *adj* préjudiciable (**to** à)

devaluation [di:væljʊ'eɪʃən] *n (of money)* dévaluation *f*

devastate ['devəsteɪt] *vt (crop, village)* dévaster; *(person)* anéantir ▪ **devastating** *adj (news, results)* accablant

develop [dɪ'veləp] **1** *vt (theory, argument)* développer; *(area, land)* mettre en valeur; *(habit)* contracter; *(photo)* développer **2** *vi (grow)* se développer; *(of event, crisis)* se produire; *(of talent, illness)* se manifester; **to d. into** devenir ▪ **developing** *adj* **d. country** pays *m* en voie de développement

developer [dɪ'veləpə(r)] *n* **(property) d.** promoteur *m*

development [dɪ'veləpmənt] *n (growth, progress)* développement *m*; **(housing) d.** lotissement *m*; *(large)* grand ensemble *m*; **a (new) d.** *(in situation)* un fait nouveau

deviate ['di:vɪeɪt] *vi* dévier (**from** de)

device [dɪ'vaɪs] *n (instrument, gadget)* dispositif *m*; *(scheme)* procédé *m*; **explosive d.** engin *m* explosif; **left to one's own devices** livré à soi-même

devil ['devəl] *n* diable *m*; *Fam* **what/where/why the d....?** que/où/pourquoi diable...?

devious ['di:vɪəs] *adj (mind, behaviour)* tortueux, -euse

devise [dɪ'vaɪz] *vt* imaginer; *(plot)* ourdir

devoid [dɪ'vɔɪd] *adj* **d. of** dénué *ou* dépourvu de

devote [dɪ'vəʊt] *vt* consacrer (**to** à) ▪ **devoted** *adj* dévoué; *(admirer)* fervent

devotion [dɪ'vəʊʃən] *n (to friend, family, cause)* dévouement *m* (**to sb** à qn); *(religious)* dévotion *f*

devour [dɪ'vaʊə(r)] *vt (eat, engulf, read)* dévorer

devout [dɪ'vaʊt] *adj (person)* dévot

dew [dju:] *n* rosée *f*

diabetes [daɪə'bi:ti:z] *n* diabète *m* ▪ **diabetic** [-'betɪk] **1** *adj* diabétique **2** *n* diabétique *mf*

diagnose [daɪəg'nəʊz] *vt* diagnostiquer ▪ **diagnosis** [-'nəʊsɪs] (*pl* **-oses** [-əʊsi:z]) *n* diagnostic *m*

diagonal [daɪ'ægənəl] **1** *adj* diagonal **2** *n* diagonale *f* ▪ **diagonally** *adv* en diagonale

diagram ['daɪəgræm] *n* schéma *m*

dial ['daɪəl] **1** *n* cadran *m*; *Am* **d. tone** tonalité *f* **2** (*Br* **-ll-**, *Am* **-l-**) *vt (phone number)* composer; *(person)* appeler ▪ **dialling** *n Br* **d. code** indicatif *m*; *Br* **d. tone** tonalité *f*

dialect ['daɪəlekt] *n* dialecte *m*

dialogue ['daɪəlɒg] (*Am* **dialog**) *n* dialogue *m*

diameter [daɪ'æmɪtə(r)] *n* diamètre *m*

diamond ['daɪəmənd] *n* **(a)** *(stone)* diamant *m*; *(shape)* losange *m*; **d. necklace** rivière *f* de diamants **(b)** **diamond(s)** *(in card games)* carreau *m*

diaper ['daɪpər] *n Am* couche *f*

diarrh(o)ea [daɪə'ri:ə] *n* diarrhée *f*; **to have d.** avoir la diarrhée

diary ['daɪərɪ] (*pl* **-ies**) *n Br (for appointments)* agenda *m*; *(private)* journal *m* (intime)

dice [daɪs] *n inv* dé *m*

dictate [dɪk'teɪt] **1** *vt (letter, conditions)* dicter (**to** à) **2** *vi* dicter qn ▪ **dictation** *n* dictée *f*

dictator [dɪk'teɪtə(r)] *n* dictateur *m*

dictionary ['dɪkʃənərɪ] (*pl* **-ies**) *n* dictionnaire *m*

did [dɪd] *pt of* **do**

die [daɪ] (*pt & pp* **died**, *pres p* **dying**) *vi* mourir (**of** *or* **from** de); *Fig* **to be dying to do sth** mourir d'envie de faire qch; **to be dying for sth** avoir une envie folle de qch; **to d. away** *(of noise)* mourir; **to d. down** *(of storm)* se calmer; **to d. out** *(of custom)* mourir

diesel ['di:zəl] *adj & n* **(engine)** (moteur *m*) diesel *m*; **d. (oil)** gazole *m*

diet ['daɪət] **1** *n (usual food)* alimentation *f*; *(restricted food)* régime *m*; **to go on a d.** faire un régime **2** *vi* être au régime

differ ['dɪfə(r)] *vi* différer (**from** de); *(disagree)* ne pas être d'accord (**from** avec)

difference ['dɪfərəns] *n* différence *f* (**in** de); **d. of opinion** différend *m*; **it**

makes no d. ça n'a pas d'importance

different ['dɪfərənt] *adj* différent (**from** de); *(another)* autre; *(various)* divers

differentiate [dɪfə'renʃɪeɪt] **1** *vt* différencier (**from** de) **2** *vi* faire la différence (**between** entre) ■ **differently** *adv* différemment (**from** de)

difficult ['dɪfɪkəlt] *adj* difficile (**to do** à faire)

difficulty ['dɪfɪkəltɪ] *(pl* -ies) *n* difficulté *f*; **to have d. doing sth** avoir du mal à faire qch;

dig [dɪg] **1** *n (with elbow)* coup de coude; *Fam (remark)* pique *f* **2** *(pt & pp* **dug,** *pres p* **digging)** *vt (ground, garden)* bêcher; *(hole, grave)* creuser; **to d. sth into sth** *(push)* planter qch dans qch; **to d. out** *(from ground)* déterrer; *Fam (find)* dénicher; **to d. up** *(from ground)* déterrer; *(road)* excaver **3** *vi (dig a hole)* creuser

digest [daɪ'dʒest] *vti* digérer ■ **digestion** *n* digestion *f*

digit ['dɪdʒɪt] *n (number)* chiffre *m* ■ **digital** *adj* numérique; *(tape, recording)* audionumérique

dignified ['dɪgnɪfaɪd] *adj* digne ■ **dignity** *n* dignité *f*

digress [daɪ'gres] *vi* faire une digression

dilapidated [dɪ'læpɪdeɪtɪd] *adj (house)* délabré

dilemma [daɪ'lemə] *n* dilemme *m*

diligent ['dɪlɪdʒənt] *adj* appliqué

dilute [daɪ'luːt] *vt* diluer

dim [dɪm] **1** (**dimmer, dimmest**) *adj (light)* faible; *(room)* sombre; *(memory)* vague; *(person)* stupide **2** *(pt & pp* -**mm**-) *vt (light)* baisser; *Am* **to d. one's headlights** se mettre en code

dime [daɪm] *n Am (pièce f de)* dix cents *mpl*

dimension [daɪ'menʃən] *n* dimension *f*

diminish [dɪ'mɪnɪʃ] *vti* diminuer

dimple ['dɪmpəl] *n* fossette *f*

din [dɪn] *n (noise)* vacarme *m*

dine [daɪn] *vi* dîner (**on** *or* **off** de); **to d.**

out aller dîner au restaurant ■ **diner** *n (person)* dîneur, -euse *mf*; *Am (restaurant)* petit restaurant *m* ■ **dining** *n* d. **car** *(on train)* wagon-restaurant *m*; **d. room** salle *f* à manger

dinghy ['dɪŋgɪ] *(pl* -ies) *n* petit canot *m*; *(rubber)* d. canot *m* pneumatique

dingy ['dɪndʒɪ] (-**ier,** -**iest**) *adj (room)* minable; *(colour)* terne

dinner ['dɪnə(r)] *n (evening meal)* dîner *m*; *(lunch)* déjeuner *m*; **to have d.** dîner; **d. jacket** smoking *m*; **d. party** dîner *m*; **d. plate** grande assiette *f*; **d. service, d. set** service *m* de table

dinosaur ['daɪnəsɔː(r)] *n* dinosaure *m*

dip [dɪp] **1** *n (in road)* petit creux *m*; **to go for a d.** *(swim)* faire trempette **2** *(pt & pp* -**pp**-) *vt* plonger; *Br* **to d. one's headlights** se mettre en code **3** *vi (of road)* plonger; **to d. into** *(pocket, savings)* puiser dans; *(book)* feuilleter

diploma [dɪ'pləʊmə] *n* diplôme *m*

diplomat ['dɪpləmæt] *n* diplomate *mf* ■ **diplomatic** *adj* diplomatique

dire ['daɪə(r)] *adj (situation)* affreux, -euse; *(consequences)* tragique; *(poverty, need)* extrême; **to be in d. straits** être dans une mauvaise passe

direct [daɪ'rekt] **1** *adj (result, flight, person)* direct; *Br* d. **debit** prélèvement *m* automatique
2 *adv* directement
3 *vt (gaze, light, attention)* diriger (**at** sur); *(traffic)* régler; *(letter, remark)* adresser (**to** à); *(film)* réaliser; *(play)* mettre en scène; **to d. sb to** *(place)* indiquer à qn le chemin de; **to d. sb to do sth** charger qn de faire qch

direction [daɪ'rekʃən] *n* direction *f*, sens *m*; **directions** *(orders)* indications *fpl*; **directions (for use)** mode *m* d'emploi

directly [daɪ'rektlɪ] *adv (without detour)* directement; *(exactly)* juste; *(at once)* tout de suite; **d. in front** juste devant

director [daɪ'rektə(r)] *n* directeur, -trice *mf*; *(board member)* administrateur, -trice *mf*; *(of film)* réalisateur, -trice *mf*; *(of play)* metteur *m* en scène

directory [daɪ'rektərɪ] (pl -ies) n (phone book) annuaire m; (of addresses) & Comptr répertoire m; **telephone d.** annuaire m du téléphone; Br **d. enquiries** renseignements mpl téléphoniques

dirt [dɜːt] n saleté f; (mud) boue f; (earth) terre f; Fam **d. cheap** très bon marché

dirty ['dɜːtɪ] **1** (-ier, -iest) adj sale; (job) salissant; (word) grossier, -ère; **to get d.** se salir; **to get sth d.** salir qch; **a d. joke** une histoire cochonne; **a d. trick** un sale tour **2** vt salir

disability [dɪsə'bɪlɪtɪ] (pl -ies) n (injury) infirmité f; (condition) invalidité f; Fig désavantage m

disabled [dɪ'seɪbəld] **1** adj handicapé **2** npl **the d.** les handicapés mpl

disadvantage [dɪsəd'vɑːntɪdʒ] **1** n désavantage m **2** vt désavantager

disagree [dɪsə'griː] vi ne pas être d'accord (**with** avec); **to d. with sb** (of food, climate, medicine) ne pas réussir à qn **■ disagreement** n désaccord m; (quarrel) différend m

disagreeable [dɪsə'griːəbəl] adj désagréable

disappear [dɪsə'pɪə(r)] vi disparaître **■ disappearance** n disparition f

disappoint [dɪsə'pɔɪnt] vt décevoir **■ disappointing** adj décevant **■ disappointment** n déception f

disapproval [dɪsə'pruːvəl] n désapprobation f

disapprove [dɪsə'pruːv] vi **to d. of sb/sth** désapprouver qn/qch

disarray [dɪsə'reɪ] n **in d.** (army, political party) en plein désarroi; (clothes, hair) en désordre

disaster [dɪ'zɑːstə(r)] n désastre m, catastrophe f; **d. area** région f sinistrée **■ disastrous** adj désastreux, -euse

disband [dɪs'bænd] **1** vt dissoudre **2** vi se dissoudre

disbelief [dɪsbə'liːf] n incrédulité f

disc [dɪsk] (Am **disk**) n disque m; **d. jockey** disc-jockey m

discard [dɪs'kɑːd] vt (get rid of) se débarrasser de; (plan) abandonner

discern [dɪ'sɜːn] vt discerner **■ discerning** adj (person) averti

discernible [dɪ'sɜːnəbəl] adj perceptible

discharge 1 ['dɪstʃɑːdʒ] n (of gun, electricity) décharge f; (dismissal) renvoi m; (freeing) libération f **2** [dɪs'tʃɑːdʒ] vt (patient) laisser sortir; (employee) renvoyer; (soldier, prisoner) libérer; (gun) décharger

disciple [dɪ'saɪpəl] n disciple m

discipline ['dɪsɪplɪn] **1** n (behaviour, subject) discipline f **2** vt (control) discipliner; (punish) punir

disclose [dɪs'kləʊz] vt révéler **■ disclosure** [-ʒə(r)] n révélation f

disco ['dɪskəʊ] (pl -os) n discothèque f

discolour [dɪs'kʌlə(r)] (Am **discolor**) vt décolorer; (teeth) jaunir

discomfort [dɪs'kʌmfət] n (physical) petite douleur f; (mental) malaise m

disconcerting [dɪskən'sɜːtɪŋ] adj déconcertant

disconnect [dɪskə'nekt] vt (unfasten) détacher; (unplug) débrancher; (gas, telephone, electricity) couper

discontented [dɪskən'tentɪd] adj mécontent (**with** de)

discord ['dɪskɔːd] n (disagreement) discorde f

discotheque ['dɪskətek] n (club) discothèque f

discount 1 ['dɪskaʊnt] n (on article) réduction f; (on account paid early) escompte m; **d. store** solderie f **2** [dɪs'kaʊnt] vt (story) ne pas tenir compte de

discourage [dɪs'kʌrɪdʒ] vt décourager (**sb from doing** qn de faire)

discover [dɪs'kʌvə(r)] vt découvrir (**that** que) **■ discovery** (pl -ies) n découverte f

discredit [dɪs'kredɪt] vt (cast slur on) discréditer

discreet [dɪ'skriːt] adj discret, -ète

discrepancy [dɪ'skrepənsɪ] (pl -ies) n décalage m (**between** entre)

discretion [dɪ'skreʃən] n (tact) discrétion f

discriminate [dɪ'skrɪmɪneɪt] *vi* **to d. against** faire de la discrimination envers; **to d. between** distinguer entre ■ **discrimination** [-'neɪʃən] *n (bias)* discrimination *f*

discus ['dɪskəs] *n Sport* disque *m*

discuss [dɪ'skʌs] *vt* discuter de ■ **discussion** *n* discussion *f*

disdain [dɪs'deɪn] *n* dédain *m*

disease [dɪ'ziːz] *n* maladie *f*

disembark [dɪsɪm'bɑːk] *vti* débarquer

disenchanted [dɪsɪn'tʃɑːntɪd] *adj* désenchanté

disfigured [dɪs'fɪgə(r)] *adj* défiguré

disgrace [dɪs'greɪs] **1** *n (shame)* honte *f* **(to** à) **2** *vt* déshonorer ■ **disgraceful** *adj* honteux, -euse

disgruntled [dɪs'grʌntəld] *adj* mécontent

disguise [dɪs'gaɪz] **1** *n* déguisement *m*; **in d.** déguisé **2** *vt* déguiser **(as** en)

disgust [dɪs'gʌst] **1** *n* dégoût *m* **(for** *or* **at** *or* **with** de) **2** *vt* dégoûter ■ **disgusted** *adj* dégoûté **(at** *or* **by** *or* **with** de); **to be d. with sb** *(annoyed)* être fâché contre qn ■ **disgusting** *adj* dégoûtant

dish [dɪʃ] **1** *n (container, food)* plat *m*; **to do the dishes** faire la vaisselle **2** *vt* **to d. out** *or* **up** *(food)* servir ■ **dishcloth** *n (for washing)* lavette *f*; *(for drying)* torchon *m* ■ **dishtowel** *n* torchon *m* (à vaisselle) ■ **dishwasher** *n (machine)* lave-vaisselle *m inv*

dishevelled [dɪ'ʃevəld] *(Am* **disheveled)** *adj (person, hair)* ébouriffé

dishonest [dɪs'ɒnɪst] *adj* malhonnête ■ **dishonesty** *n* malhonnêteté *f*

dishonourable [dɪs'ɒnərəbəl] *(Am* **dishonorable)** *adj* déshonorant

disillusion [dɪsɪ'luːʒən] *vt* décevoir; **to be disillusioned** être déçu **(with** de)

disinclined [dɪsɪŋ'klaɪnd] *adj* peu disposé **(to do** à faire)

disinfect [dɪsɪn'fekt] *vt* désinfecter ■ **disinfectant** *n* désinfectant *m*

disinherit [dɪsɪn'herɪt] *vt* déshériter

disintegrate [dɪs'ɪntɪgreɪt] *vi* se désintégrer

disinterested [dɪs'ɪntrɪstɪd] *adj (impartial)* désintéressé

disjointed [dɪs'dʒɔɪntɪd] *adj (words, style)* décousu

disk [dɪsk] *n* **(a)** *Am* = **disc (b)** *Comptr* disque *m*; *(floppy)* disquette *f*; **on d.** sur disque; **d. drive** unité *f* de disques ■ **diskette** *n Comptr* disquette *f*

dislike [dɪs'laɪk] **1** *n* aversion *f* **(for** *or* **of** pour); **to take a d. to sb/sth** prendre qn/qch en grippe **2** *vt* ne pas aimer **(doing** faire)

dislocate ['dɪsləkeɪt] *vt (limb)* démettre; **to d. one's shoulder** se démettre l'épaule

dislodge [dɪs'lɒdʒ] *vt* faire bouger, déplacer; *(enemy)* déloger

disloyal [dɪs'lɔɪəl] *adj* déloyal

dismal ['dɪzməl] *adj* lugubre ■ **dismally** *adv (fail, behave)* lamentablement

dismantle [dɪs'mæntəl] *vt (machine)* démonter; *(organization)* démanteler

dismay [dɪs'meɪ] **1** *n* consternation *f* **2** *vt* consterner

dismiss [dɪs'mɪs] *vt (from job)* renvoyer **(from** de); *(official)* destituer; *(thought, suggestion)* écarter; **to d. a case** *(of judge)* classer une affaire ■ **dismissal** *n* renvoi *m*; *(of official)* destitution *f*

dismount [dɪs'maʊnt] *vi (of person)* descendre **(from** de)

disobedient [dɪsə'biːdɪənt] *adj* désobéissant

disobey [dɪsə'beɪ] **1** *vt* désobéir à **2** *vi* désobéir

disorder [dɪs'ɔːdə(r)] *n (confusion)* désordre *m*; *(illness, riots)* troubles *mpl* ■ **disorderly** *adj (behaviour)* désordonné; *(meeting, crowd)* houleux, -euse

disorganized [dɪs'ɔːgənaɪzd] *adj* désorganisé

disorientate [dɪs'ɔːrɪənteɪt] *(Am* **disorient** [dɪs'ɔːrɪənt]) *vt* désorienter

disown [dɪs'əʊn] *vt* renier

disparaging [dɪsˈpærɪdʒɪŋ] *adj (remark)* désobligeant

dispatch [dɪsˈpætʃ] **1** *n (sending)* expédition *f* (**of** de); *(message)* dépêche *f* **2** *vt (send, finish off)* expédier; *(troops, messenger)* envoyer

dispel [dɪˈspel] *(pt & pp* **-ll-)** *vt* dissiper

dispensary [dɪˈspensərɪ] *(pl* **-ies)** *n (in chemist's shop)* officine *f*

dispense [dɪˈspens] **1** *vt (give out)* distribuer; *(medicine)* préparer **2** *vi* **to d. with** *(do without)* se passer de ▪ **dispenser** *n (device)* distributeur *m*

disperse [dɪˈspɜːs] **1** *vt* disperser **2** *vi* se disperser

displace [dɪsˈpleɪs] *vt (shift)* déplacer; *(replace)* supplanter

display [dɪˈspleɪ] **1** *n (in shop)* étalage *m*; *(of paintings, handicrafts)* exposition *f*; **d. (unit)** *(of computer)* moniteur *m*; **on d.** exposé **2** *vt (goods)* exposer; *(sign, notice)* afficher; *(emotion)* manifester; *(talent, concern, ignorance)* faire preuve de

displeased [dɪsˈpliːzd] *adj* mécontent (**with** de)

disposable [dɪˈspəʊzəbəl] *adj Br (plate, nappy)* jetable; *(income)* disponible

disposal [dɪˈspəʊzəl] *n (of waste)* évacuation *f*; **at sb's d.** à la disposition de qn

dispose¹ [d. spəʊz] *vi* **to d. of** *(get rid of)* se débarrasser de; *(throw away)* jeter; *(matter, problem)* régler

dispose² [dɪˈspəʊz] *vt* **to be disposed to do** être disposé à faire; **well-disposed towards** bien disposé envers

disposition [dɪspəˈzɪʃən] *n (character)* tempérament *m*

dispossess [dɪspəˈzes] *vt* déposséder (**of** de)

disproportionate [dɪsprəˈpɔːʃənət] *adj* disproportionné

disprove [dɪsˈpruːv] *(pp* **disproved,** *Law* **disproven** [-ˈprəʊvən]) *vt* réfuter

dispute [dɪˈspjuːt] **1** *n (quarrel)* dispute *f*; *(legal)* litige *m*; **(industrial) d.** conflit *m* social **2** *vt (claim, will)* contester

disqualify [dɪsˈkwɒlɪfaɪ] *(pt & pp* **-ied)** *vt (make unfit)* rendre inapte (**from** à); *Sport* disqualifier; **to d. sb from driving** retirer son permis à qn ▪ **disqualification** *n Sport* disqualification *f*

disregard [dɪsrɪˈgɑːd] **1** *n* mépris *m* (**for** de) **2** *vt* ne tenir aucun compte de

disrepair [dɪsrɪˈpeə(r)] *n* **in (a state of) d.** délabré

disreputable [dɪsˈrepjʊtəbəl] *adj* peu recommandable; *(behaviour)* honteux, -euse

disrepute [dɪsrɪˈpjuːt] *n* **to bring sb/sth into d.** discréditer qn/qch

disrespectful [dɪsrɪˈspektfʊl] *adj* irrespectueux, -euse (**to** envers)

disrupt [dɪsˈrʌpt] *vt (traffic, class)* perturber; *(communications)* interrompre; *(plan)* déranger ▪ **disruption** *n* perturbation *f*

disruptive [dɪsˈrʌptɪv] *adj* perturbateur, -trice

dissatisfied [dɪˈsætɪsfaɪd] *adj* mécontent (**with** de) ▪ **dissatisfaction** [-ˈfækʃən] *n* mécontentement *m* (**with** devant)

dissent [dɪˈsent] **1** *n* désaccord *m* **2** *vi* être en désaccord (**from** avec)

dissertation [dɪsəˈteɪʃən] *n* mémoire *m*

dissident [ˈdɪsɪdənt] *adj & n* dissident, -e *(mf)*

dissimilar [dɪˈsɪmɪlə(r)] *adj* différent (**to** de)

dissipate [ˈdɪsɪpeɪt] *vt (fog, fears)* dissiper; *(energy, fortune)* gaspiller

dissociate [dɪˈsəʊʃɪeɪt] *vt* dissocier (**from** de)

dissolute [ˈdɪsəluːt] *adj* dissolu

dissolve [dɪˈzɒlv] **1** *vt* dissoudre **2** *vi* se dissoudre

dissuade [dɪˈsweɪd] *vt* dissuader (**from doing** de faire)

distance [ˈdɪstəns] *n* distance *f*; **in the d.** au loin; **from a d.** de loin; **to keep one's d.** garder ses distances

distant [ˈdɪstənt] *adj* lointain; *(relative)* éloigné; *(reserved)* distant

distasteful [dɪs'teɪstfʊl] *adj* déplaisant

distil [dɪ'stɪl] (*pt & pp* **-ll-**) *vt* distiller; **distilled water** eau *f* déminéralisée

distinct [dɪ'stɪŋkt] *adj* **(a)** *(clear)* clair; *(preference, improvement, difference)* net (*f* nette) **(b)** *(different)* distinct **(from** de) ■ **distinctly** *adv* *(see, hear)* distinctement; *(remember)* très bien; *(better, easier)* nettement

distinction [dɪ'stɪŋkʃən] *n* distinction *f*; *(in exam)* mention *f* bien

distinctive [dɪ'stɪŋktɪv] *adj* distinctif, -ive

distinguish [dɪ'stɪŋgwɪʃ] *vti* distinguer **(from** de; **between** entre); **to d. oneself** se distinguer **(as** en tant que)

distinguished [dɪ'stɪŋgwɪʃd] *adj* distingué

distort [dɪ'stɔːt] *vt* déformer ■ **distortion** *n* *(of features, sound)* distorsion *f*; *(of truth)* déformation *f*

distract [dɪ'strækt] *vt* distraire (**from** de) ■ **distracted** *adj* préoccupé

distraction [dɪ'strækʃən] *n* distraction *f*

distraught [dɪ'strɔːt] *adj* éperdu

distress [dɪ'stres] **1** *n* *(mental)* détresse *f*; *(physical)* douleur *f* **2** *vt* bouleverser ■ **distressing** *adj* bouleversant

distribute [dɪ'strɪbjuːt] *vt* *(give out)* & *Com (supply)* distribuer; *(spread evenly)* répartir ■ **distribution** [-'bjuː-ʃən] *n* distribution *f*

distributor [dɪs'trɪbjʊtə(r)] *n* *(in car, of films)* distributeur *m*

district ['dɪstrɪkt] *n* région *f*; *(of town)* quartier *m*; *(administrative)* district *m*

distrust [dɪs'trʌst] **1** *n* méfiance *f* (**of** à l'égard de) **2** *vt* se méfier de

disturb [dɪ'stɜːb] *vt* *(sleep, water)* troubler; *(papers, belongings)* déranger; **to d. sb** *(bother)* déranger qn; *(worry, alarm)* troubler qn ■ **disturbing** *adj* *(worrying)* inquiétant; *(annoying, irksome)* gênant

disturbance [dɪ'stɜːbəns] *n* *(noise)* tapage *m*; **disturbances** *(riots)* troubles *mpl*

disunity [dɪs'juːnɪtɪ] *n* désunion *f*

disuse [dɪs'juːs] *n* **to fall into d.** tomber en désuétude ■ **disused** *adj* *(building)* désaffecté

ditch [dɪtʃ] **1** *n* fossé *m* **2** *vt* Fam *(get rid of)* se débarrasser de; *(plan)* laisser tomber

ditto ['dɪtəʊ] *adv* idem

dive [daɪv] **1** *n* *(of swimmer, goalkeeper)* plongeon *m*; *(of aircraft)* piqué *m* **2** (*pt* **dived**, *Am* **dove**) *vi* plonger; *(of plane)* piquer ■ **diver** *n* plongeur, -euse *mf*; *(deep-sea)* scaphandrier *m*

diverge [daɪ'vɜːdʒ] *vi* diverger (**from** de)

diverse [daɪ'vɜːs] *adj* divers ■ **diversity** *n* diversité *f* ■ **diversify** (*pt & pp* **-ied**) *vi* *(of firm)* se diversifier

diversion [daɪ'vɜːʃən] *n Br (on road)* déviation *f*; *(amusement)* distraction *f*; **to create a d.** faire diversion

divert [daɪ'vɜːt] *vt* *(attention, suspicions, river, plane)* détourner; *Br (traffic)* dévier; *(amuse)* divertir

divide [dɪ'vaɪd] *vt Math* diviser (**into** en; **by** par); *(food, money, time)* partager (**between** *or* **among** entre); **to d. sth (off) (from sth)** séparer qch (de qch); **to d. sth up** *(share out)* partager qch

divine [dɪ'vaɪn] *adj* divin

diving ['daɪvɪŋ] *n* *(underwater)* plongée *f* sous-marine; **d. board** plongeoir *m*

division [dɪ'vɪʒən] *n* division *f*; *(distribution)* partage *m*; *Sport* **first d.** première division

divorce [dɪ'vɔːs] **1** *n* divorce *m* **2** *vt* *(husband, wife)* divorcer de; *Fig (idea)* séparer (**from** de) **3** *vi* divorcer ■ **divorced** *adj* divorcé (**from** de); **to get d.** divorcer ■ **divorcee** [dɪvɔː'siː, *Am* dɪvɔːr'seɪ] *n* divorcé, -e *mf*

divulge [dɪ'vʌldʒ] *vt* divulguer

DIY [diːaɪ'waɪ] *(abbr* **do-it-yourself**) *n Br* bricolage *m*

dizzy ['dɪzɪ] **(-ier, -iest)** *adj* **to be** *or* **feel d.** avoir le vertige; **to make sb (feel) d.** donner le vertige à qn

DJ ['diːdʒeɪ] *(abbr* **disc-jockey**) *n* disc-jockey *m*

DO [duː]

Les formes négatives sont **don't/doesn't** et **didn't**, qui deviennent **do not/does not** et **did not** dans un style plus soutenu.

1 *(3rd person sing present tense* **does**, *pt* **did**, *pp* **done**, *pres p* **doing**) *v aux* **do you know?** savez-vous?, est-ce que vous savez?; **I do not** *or* **don't see** je ne vois pas; **he did say so** *(emphasis)* il l'a bien dit; **do stay** reste donc; **you know him, don't you?** tu le connais, n'est-ce pas?; **better than I do** mieux que je ne le fais; **so do I** moi aussi; **don't!** non!

2 *vt* faire; **what does she do?** *(in general)* qu'est-ce qu'elle fait?, que fait-elle?; **what is she doing?** *(now)* qu'est-ce qu'elle fait?, que fait-elle?; **what have you done (with...)?** qu'as-tu fait (de...)?; **well done** *(congratulations)* bravo!; *(steak)* bien cuit; **it's over and done (with)** c'est fini; **that'll do me** *(suit)* ça m'ira; *Br Fam* **I've been done** *(cheated)* je me suis fait avoir; **to do sb out of sth** escroquer qch à qn; *Fam* **I'm done (in)** *(tired)* je suis claqué; **to do out** *(clean)* nettoyer; **to do over** *(redecorate)* refaire; **to do up** *(coat, buttons)* boutonner; *(zip)* fermer; *(house)* refaire; *(goods)* emballer

3 *vi* **do as you're told** fais ce qu'on te dit; **that will do** *(be OK)* ça ira; *(be enough)* ça suffit; **have you done?** vous avez fini?; **to do well/badly** *(of person)* bien/mal se débrouiller; **business is doing well** les affaires marchent bien; **how are you doing?** *(comment)* ça va?; **how do you do** *(introduction)* enchanté; *(greeting)* bonjour; **to make do** se débrouiller; **to do away with sb/sth** supprimer qn/qch; **I could do with a coffee** *(need, want)* je prendrais bien un café; **it has to do with...** *(relates to)* cela a à voir avec...; *(concerns)* cela concerne...

4 *n* *(pl* **dos**) *Br Fam (party)* fête *f*

docile ['dəʊsaɪl] *adj* docile

dock [dɒk] **1** *n* **(a)** *(for ship)* dock *m* **(b)** *(in court)* banc *m* des accusés **2** *vi* *(of*

ship) *(at quayside)* accoster; *(in port)* relâcher

doctor ['dɒktə(r)] **1** *n (medical)* médecin *m*, docteur *m*; *(having doctor's degree)* docteur *m* **2** *vt (text, food)* altérer; *Br (cat)* châtrer ■ **doctorate** *n* doctorat *m* (**in** ès/en)

document ['dɒkjʊmənt] *n* document *m* ■ **documentary** [-'mentərɪ] *(pl* **-ies)** *n (film)* documentaire *m*

dodge [dɒdʒ] **1** *n (trick)* truc *m* **2** *vt (question)* esquiver; *(person)* éviter; *(pursuer)* échapper à; *(tax)* éviter de payer **3** *vi (to one side)* faire un saut de côté; **to d. through** *(crowd)* se faufiler dans

Dodgems® ['dɒdʒəmz] *npl* autos *fpl* tamponneuses

dodgy ['dɒdʒɪ] **(-ier, -iest)** *adj Fam (suspect)* louche; *(not working properly)* en mauvais état; *(risky)* risqué

does [dʌz] *see* **do**

doesn't ['dʌzənt] = **does not**

dog¹ [dɒg] *n* chien *m*; *(female)* chienne *f*

dog² [dɒg] *(pt & pp* **-gg-)** *vt (follow)* suivre de près

doggedly ['dɒgɪdlɪ] *adv* obstinément

doing ['duːɪŋ] *n* **that's your d.** c'est toi qui as fait ça

do-it-yourself [duːɪtjə'self] *n Br* bricolage *m*; **d. store/book** magasin *m*/livre *m* de bricolage

dole [dəʊl] *n Br* **d. (money)** allocation *f* de chômage; **to go on the d.** s'inscrire au chômage

doll [dɒl] *n* poupée *f*; *Br* **doll's house** maison *f* de poupée

dollar ['dɒlə(r)] *n* dollar *m*

dollhouse ['dɒlhaʊs] *n Am* maison *f* de poupée

dollop ['dɒləp] *n (of cream, purée)* grosse cuillerée *f*

dolphin ['dɒlfɪn] *n* dauphin *m*

domain [dəʊ'meɪn] *n (land, sphere)* domaine *m*

dome [dəʊm] *n* dôme *m*

domestic [də'mestɪk] *adj (appliance, use, tasks)* ménager, -ère; *(animal)*

domestique; *(policy, flight, affairs)* intérieur

dominant ['dɒmɪnənt] *adj* dominant; *(person)* dominateur, -trice

dominate ['dɒmɪneɪt] *vti* dominer

domineering [dɒmɪ'nɪərɪŋ] *adj (person, character)* dominateur, -trice

domino ['dɒmɪnəʊ] *(pl* **-oes)** *n* domino *m*; **dominoes** *(game)* dominos *mpl*

donate [dəʊ'neɪt] **1** *vt* faire don de; *(blood)* donner **2** *vi* donner ▪ **donation** *n* don *m*

done [dʌn] *pp of* **do**

donkey ['dɒŋkɪ] *(pl* **-eys)** *n* âne *m*

donor ['dəʊnə(r)] *n* donneur, -euse *mf*

don't [dəʊnt] = **do not**

donut ['dəʊnʌt] *n Am* beignet *m*

doom [duːm] **1** *n (fate)* destin *m* **2** *vt* condamner **(to** à); **to be doomed (to failure)** *(of project)* être voué à l'échec

door [dɔː(r)] *n* porte *f*; *(of vehicle, train)* portière *f*; **d. handle** poignée *f* de porte ▪ **doorbell** *n* sonnette *f* ▪ **doorknob** *n* bouton *m* de porte ▪ **doorman** *(pl* **-men)** *n (of hotel)* portier *m* ▪ **doormat** *n* paillasson *m* ▪ **doorstep** *n* seuil *m* ▪ **door-to-door** *adj* **d. salesman** démarcheur *m* ▪ **doorway** *n* **in the d.** dans l'embrasure de la porte

dope [dəʊp] *n Fam* **(a)** *(drugs)* drogue *f* **(b)** *(idiot)* andouille *f*

dormitory [Br 'dɔːmɪtrɪ, Am 'dɔːrmɪtɔːrɪ] *(pl* **-ies)** *n* dortoir *m*; *Am (university residence)* résidence *f* universitaire

dosage ['dəʊsɪdʒ] *n (amount)* dose *f*

dose [dəʊs] *n* dose *f*; **a d. of flu** une grippe

dossier ['dɒsɪeɪ] *n (papers)* dossier *m*

dot [dɒt] **1** *n* point *m*; *Fam* **on the d.** à l'heure pile **2** *(pt & pp* **-tt-)** *vt (letter)* mettre un point sur; **dotted with** parsemé de; **dotted line** pointillé *m*

dote [dəʊt] *vt* **to d. on** adorer

dot-matrix [dɒt'meɪtrɪks] *n Comptr* **d. printer** imprimante *f* matricielle

double ['dʌbəl] **1** *adj* double; **a d. bed** un grand lit; **a d. room** une chambre pour deux personnes; **d. 's'** deux 's'; **d. three four two** *(phone number)* trente-trois quarante-deux

2 *adv (twice)* deux fois; *(fold)* en deux; **he earns d. what I do** il gagne le double de moi

3 *n* double *m*; *(person)* double *m*, sosie *m*; *(stand-in in film)* doublure *f*

4 *vt* doubler; **to d. sth back** *or* **over** *(fold)* replier qch; **to be doubled up with pain/laughter** être plié (en deux) de douleur/rire

5 *vi* doubler; **to d. back** *(of person)* revenir en arrière ▪ **double-bass** *n Br (instrument)* contrebasse *f* ▪ **double-check** *vti* revérifier ▪ **double-cross** *vt* doubler ▪ **double-decker** *n* **d. (bus)** autobus *m* à impériale ▪ **double-glazing** *n (window)* double vitrage *m*

doubt [daʊt] **1** *n* doute *m*; **I have no d. about it** je n'en doute pas; **no d.** *(probably)* sans doute; **in d.** *(result, career)* dans la balance **2** *vt* douter de; **to d. whether** *or* **that** *or* **if...** douter que... *(+ subjunctive)*

doubtful ['daʊtfəl] *adj (person, future, success)* incertain; **to be d. (about sth)** avoir des doutes (sur qch); **it's d. whether** *or* **that** *or* **if...** il n'est pas certain que... *(+ subjunctive)* ▪ **doubtless** *adv* sans doute

dough [dəʊ] *n* pâte *f*; *Fam (money)* blé *m*

doughnut ['dəʊnʌt] *n* beignet *m*

dove¹ [dʌv] *n* colombe *f*

dove² [dəʊv] *Am pt of* **dive**

Dover ['dəʊvə(r)] *n* Douvres *m ou f*

dowdy ['daʊdɪ] *(* **-ier, -iest)** *adj* peu élégant

DOWN [daʊn] **1** *adj* **d. payment** acompte *m*

2 *adv* en bas; *(to the ground)* à terre; **d. there** *or* **here** en bas; *Fam* **to feel d.** *(depressed)* avoir le cafard; **d. to** *(in series, numbers, dates)* jusqu'à; **d. under** aux antipodes, en Australie

3 *prep (at bottom of)* en bas de; *(from top to bottom of)* du haut en bas de; *(along)* le long de; **to go d.** *(hill, street, stairs)* descendre; **to live d. the street**

habiter plus loin dans la rue
4 *vt* **to d. a drink** vider un verre ■ **down-and-out 1** *adj* sur le pavé **2** *n* clochard, -e *mf* ■ **downcast** *adj* découragé ■ **downfall** *n* chute *f* ■ **downhearted** *adj* découragé ■ **downhill** *adv* en pente; **to go d.** descendre; *(of sick person, business)* aller de plus en plus mal ■ **down-market** *adj Br (car, furniture)* bas de gamme *inv*; *(neighbourhood)* populaire ■ **downpour** *n* averse *f* ■ **downright 1** *adj (rogue)* véritable; *(refusal)* catégorique **2** *adv (rude, disagreeable)* franchement ■ **downstairs 1** ['daʊnsteəz] *adj (room, neighbours) (below)* d'en bas; *(on the ground floor)* du rez-de-chaussée **2** [daʊn'steəz] *adv* en bas; *(to the ground floor)* au rez-de-chaussée; **to come** *or* **go d.** descendre l'escalier ■ **down-to-earth** *adj* terre-à-terre *inv* ■ **downtown** *adv Am* en ville; **d. Chicago** le centre de Chicago ■ **downward** *adj* vers le bas; *(path)* qui descend; *(trend)* à la baisse ■ **downward(s)** *adv* vers le bas

doze [dəʊz] **1** *n* petit somme *m* **2** *vi* sommeiller; **to d. off** s'assoupir

dozen ['dʌzən] *n* douzaine *f*; **a d. books/eggs** une douzaine de livres/d'œufs; *Fig* **dozens of** des dizaines de

Dr *(abbr* **Doctor)** Docteur

drab [dræb] *adj* terne; *(weather)* gris

draft¹ [drɑːft] **1** *n* (a) *(outline)* ébauche *f*; *(of letter)* brouillon *m* (b) *Am (military)* conscription *f* **2** *vt* (a) **to d. (out)** *(sketch out)* faire le brouillon de; *(write out)* rédiger (b) *Am (conscript)* appeler sous les drapeaux

draft² [drɑːft] *n Am* = **draught**

drafty ['drɑːftɪ] (-**ier**, -**iest**) *adj Am* = **draughty**

drag [dræg] **1** *n Fam* **it's a d.!** *(boring)* c'est la barbe! **2** *(pt & pp* -**gg**-) *vt* traîner; **to d. sb/sth along** (en)traîner qn/qch; **to d. sb away from** arracher qn à; **to d. sb into** entraîner qn dans **3** *vi* traîner; **to d. on** *or* **out** *(of film, day)* traîner en longueur

dragon ['drægən] *n* dragon *m*

dragonfly ['drægənflaɪ] *(pl* -**ies**) *n* libellule *f*

drain [dreɪn] **1** *n (sewer)* égout *m*; *(in street)* bouche *f* d'égout **2** *vt (glass, tank)* vider; *(vegetables)* égoutter; **to d. (off)** *(liquid)* faire écouler; **to feel drained** être épuisé **3** *vi* **to d. (off)** *(of liquid)* s'écouler ■ **draining** *n* **d. board** paillasse *f*

drainpipe ['dreɪnpaɪp] *n* tuyau *m* d'évacuation

drama ['drɑːmə] *n (event)* drame *m*; *(dramatic art)* théâtre *m*

dramatic [drə'mætɪk] *adj* dramatique; *(very great, striking)* spectaculaire

dramatize ['dræmətaɪz] *vt (exaggerate)* dramatiser; *(novel)* adapter pour la scène/l'écran

drank [dræŋk] *pt of* **drink**

drape [dreɪp] *vt (person, shoulders)* draper **(with** de) ■ **drapes** *npl Am (curtains)* rideaux *mpl*

drastic ['dræstɪk] *adj (change, measure)* radical; *(remedy)* puissant

draught [drɑːft] *(Am* **draft**) *n* (a) *(wind)* courant *m* d'air (b) *Br* **draughts** *(game)* dames *fpl* (c) **d. beer** bière *f* (à la) pression

draughty ['drɑːftɪ] *(Am* **drafty**) (-**ier**, -**iest**) *adj (room)* plein de courants d'air

draw¹ [drɔː] **1** *n Sport* match *m* nul; *(lottery)* tirage *m* au sort; *(attraction)* attraction *f*
2 *(pt* **drew**, *pp* **drawn**) *vt* (a) *(pull)* tirer; *(pass, move)* passer **(over** sur; **into** dans); **to d. up** *(chair)* approcher; *(contract, list, plan)* dresser, rédiger
(b) *(extract)* retirer; *(pistol, sword)* dégainer; *Fig (strength, comfort)* retirer, puiser **(from** de)
(c) *(attract)* attirer
3 *vi Sport* faire match nul; **to d. near (to)** s'approcher (de); *(of time)* approcher (de); **to d. back** *(go backwards)* reculer; **to d. up** *(of vehicle)* s'arrêter

draw² [drɔː] **1** *(pt* **drew**, *pp* **drawn**) *vt (picture)* dessiner; *(circle)* tracer; *Fig (parallel, distinction)* faire **(between** entre) **2** *vi (as artist)* dessiner

drawback ['drɔːbæk] *n* inconvénient *m*

drawer [drɔː(r)] *n (in furniture)* tiroir *m*

drawing ['drɔːɪŋ] *n* dessin *m*; *Br* **d. pin** punaise *f*; **d. room** salon *m*

drawl [drɔːl] *n* voix *f* traînante

drawn [drɔːn] 1 *pp of* draw[1,2] 2 *adj* **d. match** *or* **game** match *m* nul

dread [dred] 1 *n* terreur *f* 2 *vt (exam)* appréhender; **to d. doing sth** appréhender de faire qch

dreadful ['dredfəl] *adj* épouvantable; *(child)* insupportable; **I feel d.** *(ill)* je me sens vraiment pas bien; **I feel d. about it** j'ai vraiment honte ■ **dreadfully** *adv* terriblement; **to be d. sorry** regretter infiniment

dream [driːm] 1 *n* rêve *m*; **to have a d.** faire un rêve (**about** de); **a d. world** un monde imaginaire 2 *(pt & pp* **dreamed** *or* **dreamt** [dremt]) *vt* rêver (**that** que); **I never dreamt that...** *(imagined)* je n'aurais jamais songé que...; **to d. sth up** imaginer qch 3 *vi* rêver (**of** *or* **about sb/sth** de qn/qch; **of** *or* **about doing** de faire)

dreary ['drɪərɪ] (**-ier, -iest**) *adj* morne

drench [drentʃ] *vt* tremper; **to get drenched** se faire tremper (jusqu'aux os)

dress [dres] 1 *n (garment)* robe *f*; *(style of dressing)* tenue *f*; *Br* **d. circle** *(in theatre)* premier balcon *m*; **d. rehearsal** *(in theatre)* (répétition *f*) générale *f* 2 *vt (person)* habiller *(wound)* panser; *(salad)* assaisonner; **to get dressed** s'habiller 3 *vi* s'habiller; **to d. up** *(smartly)* bien s'habiller; *(in disguise)* se déguiser (**as** en)

dressing ['dresɪŋ] *n (for wound)* pansement *m*; *(seasoning)* assaisonnement *m*; *Br* **d. gown** robe *f* de chambre; **d. room** *(in theatre)* loge *f*; *(in shop)* cabine *f* d'essayage; **d. table** coiffeuse *f*

drew [druː] *pt of* draw[1,2]

dribble ['drɪbəl] *vi* **(a)** *(of baby)* baver; *(of liquid)* tomber goutte à goutte **(b)** *(of footballer)* dribbler

dribs [drɪbz] *npl* **in d. and drabs** par petites quantités; *(arrive)* par petits groupes

dried [draɪd] *adj* *(fruit)* sec *(f* sèche); *(milk, eggs)* en poudre; *(flowers)* séché

drier ['draɪə(r)] *n* = **dryer**

drift [drɪft] 1 *n (movement)* mouvement *m*; *(of snow)* congère *f*; *(meaning)* sens *m* général 2 *vi (through air)* être emporté par le vent; *(on water)* être emporté par le courant; *(of ship)* dériver; *Fig (of person, nation)* aller à la dérive

drill [drɪl] 1 *n* **(a)** *(tool)* perceuse *f*; *(bit)* mèche *f*; *(pneumatic)* marteau *m* piqueur; *(dentist's)* roulette *f* **(b)** *(exercise)* exercice *m*; *(correct procedure)* marche *f* à suivre 2 *vt (wood)* percer; *(tooth)* fraiser 3 *vi* **to d. for oil** faire de la recherche pétrolière

drily ['draɪlɪ] *adv (remark)* sèchement, d'un ton sec

drink [drɪŋk] 1 *n* boisson *f*; **to have a d.** boire quelque chose; *(alcoholic)* prendre un verre 2 *(pt* **drank,** *pp* **drunk)** *vt* boire 3 *vi* boire (**out of** dans); **to d. up** finir son verre ■ **drink-driving** *n Br* conduite *f* en état d'ivresse ■ **drinking** *n* **d. chocolate** chocolat *m* en poudre; **d. water** eau *f* potable

drinkable ['drɪŋkəbəl] *adj (fit for drinking)* potable; *(not unpleasant)* buvable

drip [drɪp] 1 *n (drop)* goutte *f*; *(sound)* bruit *m* de l'eau qui goutte; *Med* **to be on a d.** être sous perfusion 2 *(pt & pp* **-pp-)** *vt (paint)* laisser tomber goutte à goutte; **you're dripping water everywhere!** tu mets de l'eau partout! 3 *vi (of water, rain)* goutter; *(of tap)* fuir

drive [draɪv] 1 *n (in car)* promenade *f* en voiture; *(road to private house)* allée *f*; *(energy)* énergie *f*; *(campaign)* campagne *f*; *Comptr* lecteur *m*; **an hour's d.** une heure de voiture 2 *(pt* **drove,** *pp* **driven)** *vt (vehicle, train, passenger)* conduire (**to** à); *(machine)* actionner; **to d. sb to do sth** pousser qn à faire qch; **to d. sb mad** *or* **crazy** rendre qn fou/folle; **he drives a Ford** il a une Ford 3 *vi (drive a car)* conduire; *(go by car)*

rouler; **to d. on the left** rouler à gauche; **to d. to Paris** aller en voiture à Paris; **to d. to work** aller au travail en voiture; *Fig* **what are you driving at?** où veux-tu en venir?

▸**drive along** *vi (in car)* rouler

▸**drive away 1** *vt sep (chase away)* chasser **2** *vi (in car)* partir en voiture

▸**drive back 1** *vt sep (passenger)* ramener (en voiture); *(enemy)* repousser **2** *vi (in car)* revenir (en voiture)

▸**drive in** *vt sep (nail)* enfoncer

▸**drive off** *vi (in car)* partir (en voiture)

▸**drive on** *vi (in car)* continuer sa route

▸**drive out** *vt sep (chase away)* chasser

▸**drive up** *vi (in car)* arriver (en voiture)

drive-in ['draɪvɪn] *adj Am* **d. (movie theater)** drive-in *m inv*; **d. (restaurant)** = restaurant où l'on est servi dans sa voiture

drivel ['drɪvəl] *n* idioties *fpl*

driven ['drɪvən] *pp of* **drive**

driver ['draɪvə(r)] *n (of car)* conducteur, -trice *mf*; *(of taxi, truck)* chauffeur *m*; **(train** or **engine) d.** mécanicien *m*; **she's a good d.** elle conduit bien; *Am* **d.'s license** permis *m* de conduire

driveway ['draɪvweɪ] *n (road to house)* allée *f*

driving ['draɪvɪŋ] *n (in car)* conduite *f*; **d. lesson** leçon *f* de conduite; *Br* **d. licence** permis *m* de conduire; **d. school** auto-école *f*; **d. test** examen *m* du permis de conduire

drizzle ['drɪzəl] *vi* bruiner

droop [druːp] *vi (of flower)* se faner; *(of head)* pencher; *(of eyelids, shoulders)* tomber

drop [drɒp] **1** *n* **(a)** *(of liquid)* goutte *f*; **eye/nose drops** gouttes *fpl* pour les yeux/le nez
(b) *(fall)* baisse *f*, chute *f* (**in** de); *(distance of fall)* hauteur *f* de chute; *(slope)* descente *f*
2 *(pt & pp* **-pp-)** *vt* laisser tomber; *(price, voice)* baisser; *(bomb)* larguer; *(passenger, goods from vehicle)* déposer; *(leave out)* faire sauter, omettre; *(get rid of)* supprimer; *(team member)*

écarter; **to d. sb off** *(from vehicle)* déposer qn; **to d. sb a line** écrire un petit mot à qn; **to d. a hint that...** laisser entendre que...
3 *vi (fall)* tomber; *(of person)* se laisser tomber; *(of price)* baisser; **to d. back** or **behind** rester en arrière; **to d. by** or **in** *(visit sb)* passer; **to d. off** *(fall asleep)* s'endormir; *(fall off)* tomber; *(of interest, sales)* diminuer; **to d. out** *(fall out)* tomber; *(withdraw)* se retirer; *(of student)* laisser tomber ses études; **to d. round** *(visit sb)* passer

dropout ['drɒpaʊt] *n* marginal, -e *mf*; *(student)* étudiant, -e *mf* qui abandonne ses études

droppings ['drɒpɪŋz] *npl (of animal)* crottes *fpl*; *(of bird)* fiente *f*

drought [draʊt] *n* sécheresse *f*

drove [drəʊv] *pt of* **drive**

drown [draʊn] **1** *vt* noyer; **to d. oneself, to be drowned** se noyer **2** *vi* se noyer

drowsy ['draʊzɪ] **(-ier, -iest)** *adj* **to be** or **feel d.** avoir sommeil

drudgery ['drʌdʒərɪ] *n* corvée *f*

drug [drʌg] **1** *n (against illness)* médicament *m*; *(narcotic)* drogue *f*; **drugs** *(narcotics in general)* la drogue; **to be on drugs, to take drugs** se droguer; **d. addict** drogué, -e *mf*; **d. dealer** *(large-scale)* trafiquant *m* de drogue; *(small-scale)* petit trafiquant *m* de drogue, dealer *m* **2** *(pt & pp* **-gg-)** *vt* droguer

druggist ['drʌgɪst] *n Am* pharmacien, -enne *mf*

drugstore ['drʌgstɔːr] *n Am* drugstore *m*

drum [drʌm] **1** *n Mus* tambour *m*; *(for oil)* bidon *m*; **the drums** *(of rock group)* la batterie **2** *(pt & pp* **-mm-)** *vt* **to d. sth into sb** enfoncer qch dans la tête de qn; **to d. up** *(support, interest)* rechercher ▪ **drummer** *n* tambour *m*; *(in rock group)* batteur *m* ▪ **drumstick** *n (for drum)* baguette *f* de tambour; *(of chicken)* pilon *m*

drunk [drʌŋk] **1** *pp of* **drink 2** *adj* ivre; **to get d.** s'enivrer **3** *n* ivrogne *mf* ▪ **drunkard** *n* ivrogne *mf* ▪ **drunken**

adj (person) (regularly) ivrogne; *(driver)* ivre; *(quarrel, brawl)* d'ivrogne

dry [draɪ] **1 (drier, driest)** *adj* sec *(f* sèche); *(well, river)* à sec; *(day)* sans pluie; *(subject, book)* aride; **to wipe sth d.** essuyer qch
 2 *vt* sécher; *(by wiping)* essuyer; *(clothes)* faire sécher; **to d. the dishes** essuyer la vaisselle; **to d. sth off** *or* **up** sécher qch
 3 *vi* sécher; **to d. off** sécher; **to d. up** sécher; *(dry the dishes)* essuyer la vaisselle; *(of stream)* se tarir ▪ **dryer** *n (for hair, clothes)* séchoir *m*

dry-clean [draɪ'kliːn] *vt* nettoyer à sec ▪ **dry-cleaner** *n* **the d.'s** *(shop)* le pressing, la teinturerie

dual ['djuːəl] *adj* double; *Br* **d. carriageway** route *f* à deux voies

dub [dʌb] *(pt & pp* **-bb-)** *vt (film)* doubler **(into** en)

dubious ['djuːbɪəs] *adj (offer, person)* douteux, -euse; **I'm d. about going** *or* **about whether to go** je me demande si je dois y aller

duchess ['dʌtʃɪs] *n* duchesse *f*

duck [dʌk] **1** *n* canard *m* **2** *vt (head)* baisser subitement **3** *vi* se baisser ▪ **duckling** *n* caneton *m*

due [djuː] *adj (money, sum)* dû (*f* due) **(to** à); *(rent, bill)* à payer; *(fitting, proper)* qui convient; **he's d. (to arrive)** il doit arriver d'un moment à l'autre; **in d. course** *(when appropriate)* en temps voulu; *(eventually)* le moment venu; **d. to** par suite de, en raison de

duel ['djuːəl] **1** *n* duel *m* **2** *(Br* **-ll-,** *Am* **-l-)** *vi* se battre en duel

duet [djuː'et] *n* duo *m*

duffel, duffle ['dʌfəl] *adj* **d. coat** duffel-coat *m*

dug [dʌg] *pt & pp of* **dig**

duke [djuːk] *n* duc *m*

dull [dʌl] **1 (-er, -est)** *adj (boring)* ennuyeux, -euse; *(colour, character)* terne; *(weather)* maussade; *(sound, ache)* sourd; *(edge, blade)* émoussé **2** *vt (pain)* endormir

duly ['djuːlɪ] *adv (properly)* dûment; *(as expected)* comme prévu

dumb [dʌm] **(-er, -est)** *adj* muet *(f* muette); *Fam (stupid)* bête

dumbfound [dʌm'faʊnd] *vt* sidérer

dummy ['dʌmɪ] **1** *(pl* **-ies)** *n Br (of baby)* tétine *f*; *(for displaying clothes)* mannequin *m*; *(of ventriloquist)* pantin *m* **2** *adj* factice

dump [dʌmp] **1** *n (for refuse)* décharge *f*; *Fam Pej (town)* trou *m*; *Fam Pej (house)* baraque *f* **2** *vt (rubbish)* déposer; *Fam* **to d. sb** plaquer qn

dumpling ['dʌmplɪŋ] *n (in stew)* boulette *f* de pâte

dune [djuːn] *n* **(sand) d.** dune *f*

dung [dʌŋ] *n (of horse)* crottin *m*; *(of cattle)* bouse *f*; *(manure)* fumier *m*

dungarees [dʌŋgə'riːz] *npl (of child, workman)* salopette *f*; *Am (jeans)* jean *m*

dunk [dʌŋk] *vt* tremper

dupe [djuːp] *vt* duper

duplex ['duːpleks] *n Am (apartment)* duplex *m*

duplicate 1 ['djuːplɪkət] *n* double *m*; **in d.** en deux exemplaires **2** ['djuːplɪkeɪt] *vt (key, map)* faire un double de; *(on machine)* photocopier

durable ['djʊərəbəl] *adj (material, shoes)* résistant

duration [djʊə'reɪʃən] *n* durée *f*

duress [djʊ'res] *n* **under d.** sous la contrainte

during ['djʊərɪŋ] *prep* pendant, durant

dusk [dʌsk] *n (twilight)* crépuscule *m*

dust [dʌst] **1** *n* poussière *f*; **d. cover** *or* **sheet** *(for furniture)* housse *f*; **d. cover** *or* **jacket** *(for book)* jaquette *f* **2** *vt (furniture)* dépoussiérer **3** *vi* faire la poussière ▪ **dustbin** *n Br* poubelle *f* ▪ **dustman** *(pl* **-men)** *n Br* éboueur *m* ▪ **dustpan** *n* pelle *f* (à poussière) ▪ **dusty (-ier, -iest)** *adj* poussiéreux, -euse

duster ['dʌstə(r)] *n* chiffon *m*

Dutch [dʌtʃ] **1** *adj* hollandais **2** *n* **(a) the D.** *(people)* les Hollandais *mpl* **(b)** *(language)* hollandais *m*

duty ['djuːtɪ] *(pl* **-ies)** *n* devoir *m*; *(tax)*

droit *m*; **duties** *(responsibilities)* fonctions *fpl*; **to be on/off d.** être/ne pas être de service

duty-free ['djuːtɪ'friː] *adj (goods, shop)* hors taxe *inv*

duvet ['duːveɪ] *n Br* couette *f*

DVD [diːviː'diː] *(abbr Digital Versatile Disk, Digital Video Disk) n Comptr* DVD *m inv*, disque *m* vidéo numérique

dwarf [dwɔːf] *n* nain, -e *mf*

dwell [dwel] *(pt & pp* **dwelt** [dwelt]) *vi* demeurer; **to d. (up)on** *(think about)* penser sans cesse à; *(speak about)* parler sans cesse de

dwindle ['dwɪndəl] *vi* diminuer (peu à peu)

dye [daɪ] **1** *n* teinture *f* **2** *vt* teindre; **to d. sth green** teindre qch en vert

dying ['daɪɪŋ] **1** *pres p of* **die**[1] **2** *adj (person, animal)* mourant; *(wish, words)* dernier, -ère **3** *n (death)* mort *f*

dynamic [daɪ'næmɪk] *adj* dynamique

dynamite ['daɪnəmaɪt] *n* dynamite *f*

dynamo ['daɪnəməʊ] *(pl* **-os**) *n* dynamo *f*

dyslexic [dɪs'leksɪk] *adj & n* dyslexique *(mf)*

Ee

E, e [i:] *n (letter)* E, e *m inv*

each [i:tʃ] **1** *adj* chaque; **e. one** chacun, -e; **e. one of us** chacun d'entre nous

2 *pron* chacun, -e; **e. other** l'un(e) l'autre, *pl* les un(e)s les autres; **to see/greet e. other** se voir/se saluer **e. of us** chacun, -e d'entre nous

eager ['i:gə(r)] *adj (impatient)* impatient (**to do** de faire); *(enthusiastic)* plein d'enthousiasme ▪ **eagerly** *adv (work)* avec enthousiasme; *(await)* avec impatience

eagle ['i:gəl] *n* aigle *m*

ear [ɪə(r)] *n* oreille *f*; **to play it by e.** improviser ▪ **earache** *n* mal *m* d'oreille ▪ **earphones** *npl* écouteurs *mpl* ▪ **earplug** *n* boule *f* Quiès® ▪ **earring** *n* boucle *f* d'oreille ▪ **earshot** *n* **within e.** à portée de voix

early ['ɜːlɪ] **1** (**-ier, -iest**) *adj (first)* premier, -ère; *(death)* prématuré; *(age)* jeune; *(painting, work)* de jeunesse; *(retirement)* anticipé; **it's e.** *(on clock)* il est tôt; *(referring to meeting, appointment)* c'est tôt; **to be e.** *(ahead of time)* être en avance; **in the e. 1990s** au début des années 90; **to be in one's e. fifties** avoir à peine plus de cinquante ans

2 *adv* tôt, de bonne heure; *(ahead of time)* en avance; *(die)* prématurément **earlier (on)** plus tôt; **at the earliest** au plus tôt

earmark ['ɪəmɑːk] *vt (funds)* assigner (**for** à)

earn [ɜːn] *vt* gagner; *(interest)* rapporter; **to e. one's living** gagner sa vie ▪ **earnings** *npl (wages)* salaire *m*; *(profits)* bénéfices *mpl*

earnest ['ɜːnɪst] **1** *adj (serious)* sérieux, -euse **2** *n* **in e.** sérieusement

earth [ɜːθ] *n (ground)* sol *m*; *(soil)* terre *f*; *Br (electrical wire)* terre *f*, masse *f*; **the E.** *(planet)* la Terre; **where/what on e....?** où/que diable...? ▪ **earthquake** *n* tremblement *m* de terre

ease [i:z] **1** *n (facility)* facilité *f*; **with e.** facilement; **to be at e./ill at e.** être à l'aise/mal à l'aise **2** *vt (pain)* soulager; *(mind)* calmer; *(tension)* réduire; *(restrictions)* assouplir **3** *vi* **to e. (off** *or* **up)** *(of pressure)* diminuer; *(of demand)* baisser; *(of pain)* se calmer

easily ['i:zɪlɪ] *adv* facilement; **e. the best** de loin le meilleur/la meilleure

east [i:st] **1** *n* est *m*; **(to the) e. of** à l'est de; **the E.** *(Eastern Europe)* l'Est *m*; *(the Orient)* l'Orient *m*

2 *adj (coast)* est *inv*; *(wind)* d'est; **E. Africa** l'Afrique *f* orientale

3 *adv* à l'est; *(travel)* vers l'est ▪ **eastbound** *adj (traffic)* en direction de l'est; *Br (carriageway)* est *inv* ▪ **easterly** *adj (direction)* de l'est ▪ **eastern** *adj (coast)* est *inv*; **E. France** l'est *m* de la France; **E. Europe** l'Europe *f* de l'Est ▪ **eastward(s)** *adj & adv* vers l'est

Easter ['i:stə(r)] *n* Pâques *fpl*; **Happy E.!** joyeuses Pâques!; **E. egg** œuf *m* de Pâques

easy ['i:zɪ] **1** (**-ier, -iest**) *adj (not difficult)* facile; *(solution)* simple; *(pace)* modéré; **e. chair** fauteuil *m* **2** *adv* doucement; **go e. on the salt** vas-y mollo avec le sel; **go e. on him** ne sois pas trop dur avec lui; **take it e.** *(rest)* repose-toi; *(work less)* ne te fatigue pas; *(calm down)* calme-toi; *(go slow)* ne te presse pas ▪ **easygoing** *adj (carefree)* insouciant; *(easy to get along with)* facile à vivre

eat [i:t] (*pt* **ate** [*Br* et, eɪt, *Am* eɪt], *pp* **eaten** ['i:tən]) **1** *vt* manger; *(meal)* prendre; **to e. sth up** *(finish)* finir qch

2 *vi* manger; **to e. into one's savings** entamer ses économies; **to e. out** manger dehors ▪ **eater** *n* **big e.** gros mangeur *m*, grosse mangeuse *f*

eaves [i:vz] *npl* avant-toit *m* ▪ **eavesdrop** (*pt & pp* **-pp-**) *vti* **to e. (on)** écouter avec indiscrétion

ebb [eb] **1** *n* **the e. and flow** le flux et le reflux; *Fig* **to be at a low e.** *(of patient, spirits)* être déprimé **2** *vi Fig* **to e. (away)** *(of strength)* décliner

EC [i:'si:] *(abbr* **European Community**) *n* CE *f*

eccentric [ɪk'sentrɪk] *adj & n* excentrique *(mf)*

ecclesiastical [ɪkli:zɪ'æstɪkəl] *adj* ecclésiastique

echo ['ekəʊ] **1** *(pl* **-oes**) *n* écho *m* **2** *(pt & pp* **echoed**) *vt Fig (repeat)* répéter **3** *vi* résonner **(with** de)

eclipse [ɪ'klɪps] *n* *(of sun, moon)* éclipse *f*

ecological [i:kə'lɒdʒɪkəl] *adj* écologique

economic [i:kə'nɒmɪk] *adj* économique; *(profitable)* rentable ▪ **economical** *adj* économique ▪ **economics 1** *n* économie *f* **2** *npl (profitability)* aspect *m* financier

economize [ɪ'kɒnəmaɪz] *vti* économiser **(on** sur)

economy [ɪ'kɒnəmɪ] *(pl* **-ies**) *n* économie *f*; *Av* **e. class** classe *f* économique

ecstasy ['ekstəsɪ] *(pl* **-ies**) *n (state)* extase *f*; *(drug)* ecstasy *f* ▪ **ecstatic** [ek'stætɪk] *adj* fou *(f* folle) de joie; **to be e. about** s'extasier sur

edge [edʒ] **1** *n* bord *m*; *(of forest)* lisière *f*; *(of town)* abords *mpl*; *(of page)* marge *f*; *(of knife, blade)* tranchant *m* **2** *vt (clothing)* border **(with** de) **3** *vi* **to e. forward** avancer doucement

edgeways ['edʒweɪz] *(Am* **edgewise** ['edʒwaɪz]) *adv* de côté; *Fam* **I can't get a word in e.** je ne peux pas en placer une

edgy ['edʒɪ] *(***-ier, -iest***) adj* énervé

edible ['edɪbəl] *adj (safe to eat)* comestible; *(fit to eat)* mangeable

edifice ['edɪfɪs] *n (building)* édifice *m*

Edinburgh ['edɪnbərə] *n* Édimbourg *m* ou *f*

edit ['edɪt] *vt (newspaper)* diriger; *(article)* corriger; *(prepare for publication)* préparer pour la publication; *(film)* monter

edition [ɪ'dɪʃən] *n* édition *f*

editor ['edɪtə(r)] *n (of newspaper)* rédacteur, -trice *mf* en chef; *(of film)* monteur, -euse *mf*; *Comptr (software)* éditeur *m*

educate ['edjʊkeɪt] *vt (bring up)* éduquer; *(in school)* instruire ▪ **educated** *adj* **(well-)e.** *(person)* instruit

education [edjʊ'keɪʃən] *n* éducation *f*; *(teaching)* enseignement *m*; *(training)* formation *f*; *(university subject)* pédagogie *f* ▪ **educational** *adj (qualification)* d'enseignement; *(method, theory, content)* pédagogique; *(game, film, system)* éducatif, -ive; *(establishment)* scolaire

eel [i:l] *n* anguille *f*

eerie ['ɪərɪ] *(***-ier, -iest***) adj* sinistre

effect [ɪ'fekt] **1** *n (result, impression)* effet *m* **(on** sur); **in e.** en fait; **to come into e., to take e.** *(of law)* entrer en vigueur **2** *vt (change, rescue)* effectuer

effective [ɪ'fektɪv] *adj (efficient)* efficace; *(actual)* réel *(f* réelle); **to become e.** *(of law)* prendre effet ▪ **effectively** *adv (efficiently)* efficacement; *(in fact)* effectivement

efficient [ɪ'fɪʃənt] *adj* efficace; *(productive)* performant ▪ **efficiently** *adv* efficacement

effort ['efət] *n* effort *m*; **to make an e.** faire un effort **(to** pour) ▪ **effortlessly** *adv* sans effort

e.g. [i:'dʒi:] *(abbr* **exempli gratia**) p. ex.

egg¹ [eg] *n* œuf *m*; **e. timer** sablier *m* ▪ **eggplant** *n Am* aubergine *f*

egg² [eg] *vt* **to e. sb on** encourager qn **(to do** à faire)

ego ['i:gəʊ] *(pl* **-os**) *n* **to have an enormous e.** avoir une très haute opinion de soi-même

egoistic(al) [i:gəʊ'ɪstɪk(əl)] *adj* égoïste

Egypt ['i:dʒɪpt] *n* l'Égypte *f* ■ **Egyptian** [ɪ'dʒɪpʃən] **1** *adj* égyptien, -enne **2** *n* Égyptien, -enne *mf*

eight [eɪt] *adj & n* huit *(m)* ■ **eighth** *adj & n* huitième *(mf)*; **an e.** *(fraction)* un huitième

eighteen [eɪ'tːn] *adj & n* dix-huit *(m)* ■ **eighteenth** *adj & n* dix-huitième *(mf)*

eighty ['eɪtɪ] *adj & n* quatre-vingts *(m)*; **e.-one** quatre-vingt-un; **in the eighties** dans les années 80 ■ **eightieth** *adj & n* quatre-vingtième *(mf)*

Eire ['eərə] *n* l'Eire *f*

either ['aɪðə(r), iːðə(r)] **1** *adj & pron* (one or other) l'un(e) ou l'autre; *(with negative)* ni l'un(e) ni l'autre; *(each)* chaque; **on e. side** des deux côtés **2** *adv* **she can't swim e.** elle ne sait pas nager non plus; **I don't e.** (ni) moi non plus **3** *conj* **e.... or...** ou... ou... soit... soit...; *(with negative)* ni... ni...

eject [ɪ'dʒekt] **1** *vt (troublemaker)* expulser (**from** de); *(from machine)* éjecter **2** *vi (of pilot)* s'éjecter

elaborate[1] [ɪ'læbərət] *adj (meal)* élaboré; *(scheme)* compliqué; *(description)* détaillé; *(style)* recherché

elaborate[2] [ɪ'læbəreɪt] **1** *vt (theory)* élaborer **2** *vi* entrer dans les détails (**on** de)

elapse [ɪ'læps] *vi* s'écouler

elastic [ɪ'læstɪk] **1** *adj* élastique; *Br* **e. band** élastique *m* **2** *n (fabric)* élastique *m*

elated [ɪ'leɪtɪd] *adj* transporté de joie

elbow ['elbəʊ] **1** *n* coude *m* **2** *vt* **to e. one's way** se frayer un chemin en jouant des coudes (**through** à travers)

elder ['eldə(r)] *adj & n (of two people)* aîné, -e *(mf)* ■ **eldest** *adj & n* aîné, -e *(mf)*; **his/her e. brother** l'aîné de ses frères

elderly ['eldəlɪ] **1** *adj* âgé **2** *npl* **the e.** les personnes *fpl* âgées

elect [ɪ'lekt] *vt (by voting)* élire (**to** à)

election [ɪ'lekʃən] **1** *n* élection *f*; **general e.** élections *fpl* législatives **2** *adj (campaign)* électoral; *(day, results)* des élections

electoral [ɪ'lektərəl] *adj* électoral ■ **electorate** *n* électorat *m*

electric [ɪ'lektrɪk] *adj* électrique; **e. blanket** couverture *f* chauffante; *Br* **e. fire** radiateur *m* électrique; **e. shock** décharge *f* électrique ■ **electrical** *adj* électrique

electrician [ɪlek'trɪʃən] *n* électricien *m*

electricity [ɪlek'trɪsɪtɪ] *n* électricité *f*

electrify [ɪ'lektrɪfaɪ] *(pt & pp* -**ied**) *vt (excite)* électriser

electronic [ɪlek'trɒnɪk] *adj* électronique ■ **electronics** *n (subject)* électronique *f*

elegant ['elɪgənt] *adj* élégant ■ **elegantly** *adv* avec élégance

element ['eləmənt] *n (component, chemical, person)* élément *m*; *(of heater, kettle)* résistance *f*; **the elements** *(bad weather)* les éléments *mpl*; **to be in one's e.** être dans son élément

elementary [elɪ'mentərɪ] *adj* élémentaire; *Am (school)* primaire

elephant ['elɪfənt] *n* éléphant *m*

elevate ['elɪveɪt] *vt* élever (**to** à)

elevator ['elɪveɪtə(r)] *n Am* ascenseur *m*

eleven [ɪ'levən] *adj & n* onze *(m)* ■ **eleventh** *adj & n* onzième *(mf)*

elicit [ɪ'lɪsɪt] *vt* tirer (**from** de)

eligible ['elɪdʒəbəl] *adj (for post)* admissible (**for** à); **to be e. for sth** *(entitled to)* avoir droit à qch

eliminate [ɪ'lɪmɪneɪt] *vt* éliminer

elite [eɪ'liːt] *n* élite *f* (**of** de)

elongated ['iːlɒŋgeɪtɪd] *adj* allongé

elope [ɪ'ləʊp] *vi (of lovers)* s'enfuir (**with** avec)

eloquent ['eləkwənt] *adj* éloquent

else [els] *adv* d'autre; **somebody/anybody e.** quelqu'un/n'importe qui d'autre; **everybody e.** tous les autres; **something e.** autre chose; **anything e.?** *(in shop)* est-ce qu'il vous faut autre chose?; **somewhere e.**, *Am* **someplace e.** ailleurs, autre part; **nowhere e.** nulle part ailleurs; **who e.?** qui d'autre?; **or e.** ou bien, sinon ■ **elsewhere** *adv* ailleurs

elude [ɪ'luːd] *vt* échapper à ■ **elusive** *adj (person)* insaisissable

emaciated [ɪ'meɪsɪeɪtɪd] *adj* émacié

e-mail ['iːmeɪl] **1** *n* courrier *m* électronique, mél *m*; **e. address** adresse *f* électronique **2** *vt* envoyer un courrier électronique *ou* un mél à

emanate ['eməneɪt] *vi* émaner (**from** de)

emancipation [ɪmænsɪ'peɪʃən] *n* émancipation *f*

embankment [ɪm'bæŋkmənt] *n (of path)* talus *m*; *(of river)* berge *f*

embargo [ɪm'bɑːgəʊ] *(pl* **-oes)** *n* embargo *m*

embark [ɪm'bɑːk] *vi* (s')embarquer; **to e. on sth** s'embarquer dans qch

embarrass [ɪm'bærəs] *vt* embarrasser ■ **embarrassing** *adj* embarrassant

embassy ['embəsɪ] *(pl* **-ies)** *n* ambassade *f*

embellish [ɪm'belɪʃ] *vt* embellir

embers ['embəz] *npl* braises *fpl*

embezzle [ɪm'bezəl] *vt (money)* détourner

emblem ['embləm] *n* emblème *m*

embody [ɪm'bɒdɪ] *(pt & pp* **-ied)** *vt (express)* exprimer; *(represent)* incarner

embrace [ɪm'breɪs] **1** *n* étreinte *f* **2** *vt (person)* étreindre; *Fig (belief)* embrasser **3** *vi* s'étreindre

embroider [ɪm'brɔɪdə(r)] *vt (cloth)* broder; *Fig (story, facts)* enjoliver ■ **embroidery** *n* broderie *f*

embryo ['embrɪəʊ] *(pl* **-os)** *n* embryon *m*

emerald ['emərəld] *n* émeraude *f*

emerge [ɪ'mɜːdʒ] *vi* apparaître (**from** de); *(from hole)* sortir; *(from water)* émerger

emergency [ɪ'mɜːdʒənsɪ] **1** *(pl* **-ies)** *n (situation, case)* urgence *f*; **in an e.** en cas d'urgence **2** *adj (measure, operation, services)* d'urgence; **e. exit** sortie *f* de secours; **e. landing** atterrissage *m* forcé

emigrant ['emɪgrənt] *n* émigrant, -e *mf* ■ **emigrate** [-greɪt] *vi* émigrer

eminent ['emɪnənt] *adj* éminent

emission [ɪ'mɪʃən] *n (of gas, light)* émission *f*

emit [ɪ'mɪt] *(pt & pp* **-tt-)** *vt (light, heat)* émettre

emotion [ɪ'məʊʃən] *n (strength of feeling)* émotion *f*; *(individual feeling)* sentiment *m*

emotional [ɪ'məʊʃənəl] *adj (person, reaction)* émotif, -ive; *(speech, plea)* émouvant

emotive [ɪ'məʊtɪv] *adj (word)* affectif, -ive

empathy ['empəθɪ] *n* compassion *f*

emperor ['empərə(r)] *n* empereur *m*

emphasis ['emfəsɪs] *(pl* **-ases** [-əsiːz]) *n (in word or phrase)* accent *m*; *(insistence)* insistance *f*

emphasize ['emfəsaɪz] *vt (importance)* souligner; *(word, fact)* insister sur, souligner; *(syllable)* appuyer sur; **to e. that...** souligner que...

emphatic [em'fætɪk] *adj (denial, refusal) (clear)* catégorique; *(forceful)* énergique

empire ['empaɪə(r)] *n* empire *m*

employ [ɪm'plɔɪ] *vt (person, means)* employer ■ **employee** [em'plɔɪiː] *n* employé, -e *mf* ■ **employer** *n* patron, -onne *mf* ■ **employment** *n* emploi *m*; **e. agency** bureau *m* de placement

emptiness ['emptɪnɪs] *n* vide *m*

empty ['emptɪ] **1** (**-ier, -iest**) *adj* vide; *(threat, promise)* vain; **on an e. stomach** à jeun **2** *npl* **empties** *(bottles)* bouteilles *fpl* vides **3** *(pt & pp* **-ied)** *vt* **to e. (out)** *(box, pocket, liquid)* vider; *(objects from box)* sortir (**from** *or* **out of** de) **4** *vi (of building, tank)* se vider ■ **empty-handed** *adv* **to return e.** revenir les mains vides

emulate ['emjʊleɪt] *vt* imiter

enable [ɪ'neɪbəl] *vt* **to e. sb to do sth** permettre à qn de faire qch

enamel [ɪ'næməl] **1** *n* émail *m (pl* émaux) **2** *adj* en émail

enamoured [ɪ'næməd] *(Am* **enamored)** *adj* **e. of** *(thing)* séduit par; *(person)* amoureux, -euse de

encapsulate [ɪnˈkæpsjʊleɪ] vt *(ideas, views)* résumer

encase [ɪnˈkeɪs] vt *(cover)* envelopper **(in** dans)

enchanting [ɪnˈtʃɑːntɪŋ] *adj* enchanteur, -eresse

encircle [ɪnˈsɜːkəl] vt entourer; *(of army, police)* encercler

encl *(abbr* **enclosure(s))** PJ

enclose [ɪnˈkləʊz] vt *(send with letter)* joindre **(in** *or* **with** à); *(fence off)*, clôturer **= enclosed** *adj (receipt, document)* ci-joint; **please find e....** veuillez trouver ci-joint...

enclosure [ɪnˈkləʊʒə(r)] n *(in letter)* pièce f jointe; *(place)* enceinte f

encompass [ɪnˈkʌmpəs] vt *(include)* inclure

encore [ˈɒŋkɔː(r)] *exclam & n* bis *(m)*

encounter [ɪnˈkaʊntə(r)] **1** n rencontre f **2** vt *(person, resistance)* rencontrer

encourage [ɪnˈkʌrɪdʒ] vt encourager **(to do** à faire) **= encouragement** n encouragement m

encroach [ɪnˈkrəʊtʃ] vi empiéter **(on** *or* **upon** sur)

encyclop(a)edia [ɪnsaɪkləˈpiːdɪə] n encyclopédie f

end [end] **1** n *(extremity)* bout m, extrémité f; *(of month, meeting, book)* fin f; *(purpose)* but m; **at an e.** *(discussion, war)* fini; *(period of time)* écoulé; **in the e.** à la fin; **to come to an e.** prendre fin; **for days on e.** pendant des jours et des jours; **to stand sth on e.** mettre qch debout
2 *adj (row, house)* dernier, -ère
3 vt finir, terminer **(with** par); *(rumour, speculation)* mettre fin à
4 vi finir, se terminer; **to e. up doing sth** finir par faire qch; **he ended up in prison/a doctor** il a fini en prison/médecin

endanger [ɪnˈdeɪndʒə(r)] vt mettre en danger; **endangered species** espèce f menacée

endearing [ɪnˈdɪərɪŋ] *adj (quality)* qui inspire la sympathie

endeavour [ɪnˈdevə(r)] *(Am* **endeavor) 1** n effort m **(to do** pour faire) **2** vi

s'efforcer **(to do** de faire)

ending [ˈendɪŋ] n fin f; *(of word)* terminaison f

endless [ˈendləs] *adj (speech, series, list)* interminable; *(countless)* innombrable

endorse [ɪnˈdɔːs] vt *(cheque)* endosser; *(action, plan)* approuver **= endorsement** n *Br (on driving licence)* = contravention inscrite sur le permis de conduire

endow [ɪnˈdaʊ] vt **to be endowed with** *(of person)* être doté de **= endowment** n dotation f

endurance [ɪnˈdjʊərəns] n endurance f

endure [ɪnˈdjʊə(r)] **1** vt *(violence)* endurer; *(person, insult)* supporter **2** vi *(last)* survivre

enemy [ˈenəmɪ] **1** *(pl* **-ies)** n ennemi, -e mf **2** *adj (army, tank)* ennemi

energetic [enəˈdʒetɪk] *adj* énergique

energy [ˈenədʒɪ] **1** *(pl* **-ies)** n énergie f **2** *adj (resources)* énergétique; **e. crisis** crise f de l'énergie

enforce [ɪnˈfɔːs] vt *(law)* faire respecter; *(discipline)* imposer **(on** à)

engage [ɪnˈɡeɪdʒ] vt *(take on)* engager **= engaged** *adj* **(a)** *(occupied) (person, toilet, phone)* occupé **(b) e. (to be married)** fiancé; **to get e.** se fiancer

engagement [ɪnˈɡeɪdʒmənt] n *(to marry)* fiançailles fpl; *(meeting)* rendez-vous m inv; **e. ring** bague f de fiançailles

engine [ˈendʒɪn] n *(of vehicle, aircraft)* moteur m; *(of train)* locomotive f; *(of ship)* machine f

engineer [endʒɪˈnɪə(r)] **1** n ingénieur m; *Br (repairer)* dépanneur m; **civil e.** ingénieur m des travaux publics **2** vt *(arrange secretly)* manigancer **= engineering** n ingénierie f; **(civil) e.** génie m civil

England [ˈɪŋɡlənd] n l'Angleterre f

English [ˈɪŋɡlɪʃ] **1** *adj* anglais; **E. teacher** professeur m d'anglais; **the E. Channel** la Manche **2** n *(language)* anglais m; **the E.** *(people)* les Anglais mpl **= Englishman** *(pl* **-men)** n Anglais m

■ **English-speaking** *adj* anglophone
■ **Englishwoman** (*pl* **-women**) *n* Anglaise *f*

engraving [ɪn'greɪvɪŋ] *n* gravure *f*

engrossed [ɪn'grəʊst] *adj* **e. in one's work/book** absorbé par son travail/ dans sa lecture

engulf [ɪn'gʌlf] *vt* engloutir

enhance [ɪn'hɑːns] *vt (beauty, prestige)* rehausser; *(value)* augmenter

enigma [ɪ'nɪɡmə] *n* énigme *f*

enjoy [ɪn'dʒɔɪ] *vt (like)* aimer (**doing** faire); *(meal)* savourer; *(benefit from)* jouir de; **to e. oneself** s'amuser ■ **enjoyable** *adj* agréable; *(meal)* excellent ■ **enjoyment** *n* plaisir *m*

enlarge [ɪn'lɑːdʒ] 1 *vt* agrandir 2 *vi* **to e. (up)on sth** s'étendre sur qch ■ **enlargement** *n (increase)* & *Phot* agrandissement *m*

enlighten [ɪn'laɪtən] *vt* éclairer (**sb on** *or* **about sth** qn sur qch ■ **enlightening** *adj* instructif, -ive

enlist [ɪn'lɪst] 1 *vt (recruit)* engager; *(supporter)* recruter; *(support)* s'assurer 2 *vi (in the army)* s'engager

enormous [ɪ'nɔːməs] *adj* énorme; *(explosion, blow)* terrible; *(patience, gratitude, success)* immense ■ **enormously** *adv (very much)* énormément; *(very)* extrêmement

enough [ɪ'nʌf] 1 *adj* assez de; **e. time/cups** assez de temps/de tasses 2 *pron* assez; **to have e. to live on** avoir de quoi vivre; **to have had e. of sb/ sth** en avoir assez de qn/qch; **that's e.** ça suffit 3 *adv (work, sleep)* assez; **big/ good e.** assez grand/bon (**to** pour)

enquire [ɪn'kwaɪə(r)] *vti* = **inquire**

enquiry [ɪn'kwaɪərɪ] *n* = **inquiry**

enrage [ɪn'reɪdʒ] *vt* mettre en rage

enrich [ɪn'rɪtʃ] *vt* enrichir; *(soil)* fertiliser

enrol [ɪn'rəʊl] (*Am* **enroll**) (*pt & pp* **-ll-**) 1 *vt* inscrire 2 *vi* s'inscrire (**on** *or* **for** à) ■ **enrolment** (*Am* **enrollment**) *n* inscription *f*

ensemble [ɒn'sɒmbəl] *n (musicians, clothes)* ensemble *m*

ensue [ɪn'sjuː] *vi* s'ensuivre ■ **ensuing**

adj (in the past) qui a suivi; *(in the future)* qui suivra

ensure [ɪn'ʃʊə(r)] *vt* assurer; **to e. that...** s'assurer que...

entail [ɪn'teɪl] *vt (involve)* occasionner; **what does the job e.?** en quoi le travail consiste-t-il?

entangle [ɪn'tæŋɡəl] *vt* **to get entangled in sth** *(of person, animal)* s'empêtrer dans qch

enter ['entə(r)] 1 *vt (room, army)* entrer dans; *(race, competition)* participer à; *(write down) (on list)* inscrire (**in** dans; **on** sur); *(in accounts book)* porter (**in** sur); *Comptr (data)* entrer; **it didn't e. my head** *or* **mind** ça ne m'est pas venu à l'esprit (**that** que) 2 *vi* entrer; **to e. for** *(exam)* se présenter à; *(race)* se faire inscrire à; **to e. into** *(relations)* entrer en; *(negotiations)* entamer; *(agreement)* conclure; *(contract)* passer (**with** avec)

enterprise ['entəpraɪz] *n (undertaking, firm)* entreprise *f*; *(spirit, initiative)* initiative *f* ■ **enterprising** *adj (person)* entreprenant

entertain [entə'teɪn] 1 *vt* amuser, distraire; *(guest)* recevoir; *(idea, possibility)* envisager 2 *vi (receive guests)* recevoir ■ **entertainer** *n (comedian)* comique *mf*; *(singer, dancer)* artiste *mf* de music-hall ■ **entertainment** *n* amusement *m*; *(show)* spectacle *m*

enthusiasm [ɪn'θjuːzɪæzəm] *n* enthousiasme *m* ■ **enthusiast** *n* enthousiaste *mf*; **jazz e.** passionné, -e *mf* de jazz

enthusiastic [ɪnθjuːzɪ'æstɪk] *adj* enthousiaste; *(golfer, photographer)* passionné; **to get e.** s'emballer (**about** pour)

entice [ɪn'taɪs] *vt* attirer (**into** dans); **to e. sb to do sth** inciter qn à faire qch ■ **enticing** *adj* séduisant

entire [ɪn'taɪə(r)] *adj* entier, -ère ■ **entirely** *adv* entièrement

entirety [ɪn'taɪərətɪ] *n* intégralité *f*; **in its e.** dans son intégralité

entitle [ɪn'taɪtəl] *vt* **to e. sb to sth/to do sth** donner à qn le droit à qch/de faire qch ■ **entitled** *adj* **to be e. to do**

sth avoir le droit de faire qch; **to be e. to sth** avoir droit à qch

entrance ['entrəns] n entrée f (**to** de); (to university, school) admission f (**to** à); **e. fee** droit m d'entrée

entrant ['entrənt] n (in race) concurrent, -e mf; (for exam) candidat, -e mf

entrée ['ɒntreɪ] n Culin (course before main dish) entrée f; Am (main dish) plat m principal

entrepreneur [ɒntrəprə'nɜː(r)] n entrepreneur m

entrust [ɪn'trʌst] vt confier (**to** à); **to e. sb with sth** confier qch à qn

entry ['entrɪ] n entrée f; (in race) concurrent, -e mf; (to be judged in competition) objet m/œuvre f/projet m soumis(e) au jury; **e. form** feuille f d'inscription; **'no e.'** (on door) 'entrée interdite'; (road sign) 'sens interdit'

envelope ['envələʊp] n enveloppe f

enviable ['envɪəbəl] adj enviable

envious ['envɪəs] adj envieux, -euse (**of** de); **to be e. of sb** envier qn

environment [ɪn'vaɪərənmənt] n (social, moral) milieu m; **the e.** (natural) l'environnement m ■ **environmental** [-'mentəl] adj (policy) de l'environnement; **e. disaster** catastrophe f écologique ■ **environmentally** adv **e. friendly product** produit m qui ne nuit pas à l'environnement

envisage [ɪn'vɪzɪdʒ] (Am **envision** [ɪn'vɪʒən]) vt (imagine) envisager; (foresee) prévoir; **to e. doing sth** envisager de faire qch

envoy ['envɔɪ] n (messenger) envoyé, -e mf; (diplomat) ministre m plénipotentiaire

envy ['envɪ] 1 n envie f 2 (pt & pp -ied) vt envier; **to e. sb sth** envier qch à qn

ephemeral [ɪ'femərəl] adj éphémère

epic ['epɪk] 1 adj épique 2 n (poem, novel) épopée f; (film) film m à grand spectacle

epidemic [epɪ'demɪk] n épidémie f

epileptic [epɪ'leptɪk] adj & n épileptique (mf)

epilogue ['epɪlɒg] n épilogue m

episode ['epɪsəʊd] n (part of story) épisode m; (incident) incident m

epitaph ['epɪtɑːf] n épitaphe f

epitome [ɪ'pɪtəmɪ] n **to be the e. of sth** être l'exemple même de qch ■ **epitomize** vt incarner

epoch ['iːpɒk] n époque f

equal ['iːkwəl] 1 adj égal (**to** à); **to be e. to sth** (in quantity) égaler qch; (good enough) être à la hauteur de qch 2 n (person) égal, -e mf 3 (Br -ll-, Am -l-) vt égaler (**in** en)

equality [ɪ'kwɒlətɪ] n égalité f

equalize ['iːkwəlaɪz] vi (in sport) égaliser

equally ['iːkwəlɪ] adv (to an equal degree, also) également; (divide) en parts égales

equals ['iːkwəlz] n **e. sign** signe m d'égalité

equation [ɪ'kweɪʒən] n Math équation f

equator [ɪ'kweɪtə(r)] n équateur m; **at** or **on the e.** sous l'équateur

equilibrium [iːkwɪ'lɪbrɪəm] n équilibre m

equip [ɪ'kwɪp] (pt & pp **-pp-**) vt (provide with equipment) équiper (**with** de); (prepare) préparer (**for** pour); **to be (well-)equipped to do sth** être compétent pour faire qch ■ **equipment** n équipement m; (in factory) matériel m

equivalent [ɪ'kwɪvələnt] adj & n équivalent (m)

era [Br 'ɪərə, Am 'erə] n époque f; (historical, geological) ère f

eradicate [ɪ'rædɪkeɪt] vt éradiquer

erase [Br ɪ'reɪz, Am ɪ'reɪs] vt effacer; (with eraser) gommer ■ **eraser** n gomme f

erect [ɪ'rekt] 1 adj (upright) droit 2 vt (building) construire; (statue, monument) ériger; (scaffolding) monter; (tent) dresser

erode [ɪ'rəʊd] vt (of sea) éroder; Fig (confidence) miner ■ **erosion** [-ʒən] n érosion f

erotic [ɪ'rɒtɪk] adj érotique

errand ['erənd] *n* commission *f*, course *f*; **to run errands for sb** faire des courses pour qn

erratic [ɪ'rætɪk] *adj (unpredictable) (behaviour)* imprévisible; *(service, machine)* fantaisiste; *(person)* lunatique; *(irregular) (performance, results)* irrégulier, -ère

error ['erə(r)] *n (mistake)* erreur *f*; **typing/printing e.** faute *f* de frappe/d'impression

erupt [ɪ'rʌpt] *vi (of volcano)* entrer en éruption; *(of war, violence)* éclater ▪ **eruption** *n (of volcano)* éruption *f*; *(of violence)* flambée *f*

escalate ['eskəleɪt] *vi (of war, violence)* s'intensifier; *(of prices)* monter en flèche

escalator ['eskəleɪtə(r)] *n* escalier *m* roulant

escapade ['eskəpeɪd] *n* frasque *f*

escape [ɪ'skeɪp] **1** *n (of gas, liquid)* fuite *f*; *(of person)* évasion *f*; **he had a lucky or narrow e.** il l'a échappé belle **2** *vt (death, punishment)* échapper à **3** *vi (of gas, animal)* s'échapper (**from** de); *(of prisoner)* s'évader (**from** de)

escort 1 ['eskɔːt] *n (for convoy)* escorte *f*; *(of woman)* cavalier *m* **2** [ɪ'skɔːt] *vt* escorter; *(prisoner)* conduire sous escorte

Eskimo ['eskɪməʊ] *(pl* **-os)** *n* Esquimau, -aude *mf*

especially [ɪs'peʃəlɪ] *adv (in particular)* surtout; *(more than normally)* particulièrement; *(for a purpose)* (tout) spécialement; **e. as** d'autant plus que

espresso [e'spresəʊ] *(pl* **-os)** *n* express *m*

Esq *(abbr* **Esquire)** *Br* **John Smith Esq** = Monsieur John Smith

essay ['eseɪ] *n (at school)* rédaction *f*; *(at university)* dissertation *f* (**on** sur)

essence ['esəns] *n (distinctive quality)* essence *f*; *Culin (extract)* extrait *m*; **the e. of sth** *(main point)* l'essentiel *m* de qch; **in e.** essentiellement

essential [ɪ'senʃəl] **1** *adj (principal)* essentiel, -elle; *(necessary)* indispensable, essentiel, -elle; **it's e. that...** il

est indispensable que... *(+ subjunctive)* **2** *npl* **the essentials** l'essentiel *m* (**of** de)

establish [ɪ'stæblɪʃ] *vt* établir; *(state, society, company)* fonder; *(post)* créer ▪ **established** *adj* **(well-)e.** *(company)* solide; *(fact)* reconnu; *(reputation)* établi ▪ **establishment** *n (institution, company)* établissement *m*; **the E.** *(dominant group)* les classes *fpl* dirigeantes

estate [ɪ'steɪt] *n (land)* terres *fpl*, propriété *f*; *(possessions)* biens *mpl*; *(property after death)* succession *f*; *Br* **e. agent** agent *m* immobilier; *Br* **e. car** break *m*

esteem [ɪ'stiːm] **1** *n* estime *f*; **to hold sb in high e.** avoir qn en haute estime **2** *vt* estimer

esthetic [es'θetɪk] *adj Am* esthétique

estimate 1 ['estɪmət] *n* évaluation *f*; *Com* devis *m* **2** ['estɪmeɪt] *vt (value)* estimer, évaluer; *(consider)* estimer (**that** que)

estranged [ɪ'streɪndʒd] *adj* **her e. husband** son mari, dont elle vit séparée

estuary ['estjʊərɪ] *(pl* **-ies)** *n* estuaire *m*

etc [et'setərə] *(abbr* **et cetera)** *adv* etc

etching ['etʃɪŋ] *n (picture)* eau-forte *f*

eternal [ɪ'tɜːnəl] *adj* éternel, -elle ▪ **eternity** *n* éternité *f*

ethical ['eθɪkəl] *adj* moral, éthique

ethics ['eθɪks] *n* éthique *f*, morale *f*; *(of profession)* déontologie *f*

ethnic ['eθnɪk] *adj* ethnique

etiquette ['etɪket] *n* étiquette *f*

etymology [etɪ'mɒlədʒɪ] *n* étymologie *f*

EU [iː'juː] *(abbr* **European Union)** *n* UE *f*

euphemism ['juːfəmɪzəm] *n* euphémisme *m*

euphoria [juː'fɔːrɪə] *n* euphorie *f*

euro ['jʊərəʊ] *(pl* **-os)** *n (currency)* euro *m*

Euro- ['jʊərəʊ] *pref* euro-; **E.-MP** député *m* européen

Europe ['jʊərəp] *n* l'Europe *f* ■ **European** [-'pi:ən] **1** *adj* européen, -enne; **E. Union** Union *f* européenne **2** *n* Européen, -enne *mf*

evacuate [ɪ'vækjʊeɪt] *vt* évacuer

evade [ɪ'veɪd] *vt* éviter, esquiver; *(pursuer)* échapper à; *(law, question)* éluder; **to e. tax** frauder le fisc

evaluate [ɪ'væljʊeɪt] *vt* évaluer (**at** à)

evangelical [i:væn'dʒelɪkəl] *adj* évangélique

evaporate [ɪ'væpəreɪt] *vi (of liquid)* s'évaporer; **evaporated milk** lait *m* condensé

evasion [ɪ'veɪʒən] *n (of pursuer, responsibilities, question)* dérobade *f* (**of** devant); **tax e.** évasion *f* fiscale

evasive [ɪ'veɪsɪv] *adj* évasif, -ive

eve [i:v] *n* **on the e. of** à la veille de

even ['i:vən] **1** *adj (equal, flat)* égal; *(smooth)* uni; *(regular)* régulier, -ère; *(temperature)* constant; *(number)* pair; *Fig* **to get e. with sb** prendre sa revanche sur qn; **to break e.** *(financially)* s'y retrouver
2 *adv* même; **e. better/more** encore mieux/plus; **e. if** *or* **though...** bien que... *(+ subjunctive)*; **e. so** quand même
3 *vt* **to e. sth (out** *or* **up)** égaliser qch ■ **evenly** *adv (equally)* de manière égale; *(regularly)* régulièrement

evening ['i:vnɪŋ] *n* soir *m*; *(referring to duration, event)* soirée *f*; **tomorrow/yesterday e.** demain/hier soir; **in the e.,** *Am* **evenings** le soir; **at seven in the e.** à sept heures du soir; **every Tuesday e.** tous les mardis soir; **e. meal/paper** repas *m*/journal *m* du soir; **e. class** cours *m* du soir; **e. dress** *(of man)* tenue *f* de soirée; *(of woman)* robe *f* du soir

event [ɪ'vent] *n* événement *m*; *(in sport)* épreuve *f* ■ **eventful** *adj (day, journey, life)* mouvementé; *(occasion)* mémorable

eventual [ɪ'ventʃʊəl] *adj (final)* final, définitif, -ive ■ **eventuality** [-tjʊ'ælətɪ] *(pl* **-ies)** *n* éventualité *f* ■ **eventually** *adv* finalement; *(some day)* par la suite

ever ['evə(r)] *adv* jamais; **have you e. been to Spain?** es-tu déjà allé en Espagne?; **the first e.** le tout premier; **e. since (1990)** depuis (1990), **for e.** pour toujours; **e. so sorry** vraiment désolé; **she's e. so nice** elle est tellement gentille; **all she e. does is criticize** elle ne fait que critiquer

evergreen ['evəgri:n] *n* arbre *m* à feuilles persistantes

everlasting [evə'lɑːstɪŋ] *adj* éternel, -elle

every ['evrɪ] *adj* chaque; **e. time** chaque fois (**that** que); **e. one** chacun; **e. second** *or* **other day** tous les deux jours; **e. so often, e. now and then** de temps en temps

everybody ['evrɪbɒdɪ] *pron* tout le monde ■ **everyday** *adj (happening, life)* de tous les jours; *(ordinary)* banal *(mpl* **-als)**; **in e. use** d'usage courant ■ **everyone** *pron* = **everybody** ■ **everyplace** *adv Am* = **everywhere** ■ **everything** *pron* tout; **e. (that) I have** tout ce que j'ai ■ **everywhere** *adv* partout; **e. she goes** où qu'elle aille

evict [ɪ'vɪkt] *vt* expulser (**from** de)

evidence ['evɪdəns] *n (proof)* preuve(s) *f(pl)*; *(testimony)* témoignage *m*; **to give e.** témoigner (**against** contre)

evident ['evɪdənt] *adj* évident (**that** que); **it is e. from...** il apparaît de... (**that** que) ■ **evidently** *adv (clearly)* manifestement; *(apparently)* apparemment

evil ['i:vəl] **1** *adj (spell, influence, person)* malfaisant; *(deed, system)* mauvais **2** *n* mal *m*

evoke [ɪ'vəʊk] *vt (conjure up)* évoquer ■ **evocative** [ɪ'vɒkətɪv] *adj* évocateur, -trice (**of** de)

evolution [i:və'lu:ʃən] *n* évolution *f*

evolve [ɪ'vɒlv] **1** *vt (system)* mettre au point **2** *vi (of society, idea)* évoluer; *(of plan)* se développer

ewe [ju:] *n* brebis *f*

ex [eks] *n Fam (former spouse)* ex *mf*

ex- [eks] *pref* ex-; **ex-minister** ancien ministre *m*

exact [ɪg'zækt] **1** *adj* exact **2** *vt (demand)* exiger (**from** de); *(money, promise)* extorquer (**from** à) ■ **exactly** *adv* exactement

exaggerate [ɪg'zædʒəreɪt] *vti* exagérer

exam [ɪg'zæm] *(abbr* **examination)** *n* examen *m*

examine [ɪg'zæmɪn] *vt (evidence, patient, question)* examiner; *(accounts, luggage)* vérifier; *(passport)* contrôler; *(student)* interroger ■ **examination** *n* examen *m*; *(of accounts)* vérification *f*; *(of passport)* contrôle *m*

example [ɪg'zɑːmpəl] *n* exemple *m*; **for e.** par exemple; **to set an e.** *or* a **good e.** donner l'exemple (**to** à); **to set a bad e.** donner le mauvais exemple (**to** à)

exasperate [ɪg'zɑːspəreɪt] *vt* exaspérer

excavate ['ekskəveɪt] *vt (dig)* creuser; *(archaeological site)* faire des fouilles dans ■ **excavation** [-'veɪʃən] *n (archaeological)* fouilles *fpl*

exceed [ɪk'siːd] *vt* dépasser; *(one's powers)* excéder

exceedingly [ɪk'siːdɪŋlɪ] *adv* extrêmement

excel [ɪk'sel] *(pt & pp* -ll-*)* **1** *vt (be better than)* surpasser **2** *vi* **to e. in** *or* **at sth** exceller en qch

excellent ['eksələnt] *adj* excellent

except [ɪk'sept] **1** *prep* sauf, excepté; **e. for** à part; **e. that...** sauf que... **2** *vt* excepter (**de** from)

exception [ɪk'sepʃən] *n* exception *f*; **with the e. of...** à l'exception de...

exceptional [ɪk'sepʃənəl] *adj* exceptionnel, -elle

excerpt ['eksɜːpt] *n (from film, book)* extrait *m*

excess ['ekses] *n* excès *m*; *(surplus)* excédent *m*; **a sum in e. of...** une somme qui dépasse...; **e. luggage** excédent *m* de bagages

excessive [ɪk'sesɪv] *adj* excessif, -ive ■ **excessively** *adv (too much)* excessivement; *(very)* extrêmement

exchange [ɪks'tʃeɪndʒ] **1** *n* échange *m*; *Fin (of currency)* change *m*; **(telephone) e.** central *m* téléphonique; **in e.** en échange (**for** de); **e. rate** taux *m* de change **2** *vt* échanger (**for** contre)

Exchequer [ɪks'tʃekə(r)] *n Br* **Chancellor of the E.** ≃ ministre *m* des Finances

excitable [ɪk'saɪtəbəl] *adj* nerveux, -euse

excite [ɪk'saɪt] *vt (get worked up)* surexciter; *(enthuse)* passionner; *(provoke, stimulate)* exciter ■ **excited** *adj (happy)* surexcité; *(nervous)* énervé; *(enthusiastic)* enthousiaste; **to get e. (about)** s'exciter (pour); *(angry)* s'énerver (contre) ■ **exciting** *adj (book, adventure)* passionnant

excitement [ɪk'saɪtmənt] *n* agitation *f*; *(enthusiasm)* enthousiasme *m*

exclaim [ɪk'skleɪm] *vti* s'écrier (**that** que) ■ **exclamation** *n* exclamation *f*; *Br* **e. mark,** *Am* **e. point** point *m* d'exclamation

exclude [ɪk'skluːd] *vt* exclure (**from** de); **excluding...** à l'exclusion de...

exclusive [ɪk'skluːsɪv] *adj (right, interview, design)* exclusif, -ive; *(club, group)* fermé ■ **exclusively** *adv* exclusivement

excruciating [ɪk'skruːʃɪeɪtɪŋ] *adj* atroce

excursion [ɪk'skɜːʃən] *n* excursion *f*

excuse 1 [ɪk'skjuːs] *n* excuse *f*; **to make an e., to make excuses** se trouver une excuse **2** [ɪk'skjuːz] *vt (forgive, justify)* excuser; *(exempt)* dispenser (**from** de); **e. me!** excusez-moi!, pardon!

ex-directory [eksdaɪ'rektərɪ] *adj Br* **to be e.** être sur la liste rouge

execute ['eksɪkjuːt] *vt (prisoner, order)* exécuter; *(plan)* mettre à exécution

execution [eksɪ'kjuːʃən] *n* exécution *f*

executive [ɪg'zekjʊtɪv] **1** *adj (job)* de cadre; *(car)* de luxe **2** *n (person)* cadre *m*

exemplary [ɪg'zemplərɪ] *adj* exemplaire

exemplify [ɪg'zemplɪfaɪ] *(pt & pp* -ied*) vt* illustrer

exempt [ɪg'zempt] **1** *adj (person)* dispensé (**from** de) **2** *vt* dispenser (**from** de; **from doing** de faire)

exemption [ɪg'zem(p)ʃən] *n* dispense *f* (**from** de)

exercise ['eksəsaɪz] **1** *n* exercice *m*; **e. book** cahier *m* **2** *vt* exercer; *(dog, horse)* promener; *(caution, restraint)* user de **3** *vi* faire de l'exercice

exert [ɪg'zɜːt] *vt* exercer; *(force)* employer; **to e. oneself** se donner du mal ▪ **exertion** *n* effort *m*

exhale [eks'heɪl] *vi* expirer

exhaust [ɪg'zɔːst] **1** *n* **e. (fumes)** gaz *mpl* d'échappement; **e. (pipe)** tuyau *m* d'échappement **2** *vt (person, resources)* épuiser ▪ **exhausted** *adj (person, resources)* épuisé ▪ **exhausting** *adj* épuisant

exhaustive [ɪg'zɔːstɪv] *adj (list)* exhaustif, -ive; *(analysis)* détaillé; *(inquiry)* approfondi

exhibit [ɪg'zɪbɪt] **1** *n* objet *m* exposé; *(in court)* pièce *f* à conviction **2** *vt (put on display)* exposer ▪ **exhibition** [eksɪ'bɪʃən] *n* exposition *f*

exhilarating [ɪg'zɪləreɪtɪŋ] *adj (experience)* grisant

exile ['egzaɪl] **1** *n (banishment)* exil *m*; *(person)* exilé, -e *mf* **2** *vt* exiler

exist [ɪg'zɪst] *vi* exister; *(live)* survivre (**on** avec) ▪ **existing** *adj (situation, circumstances)* actuel, -elle; *(law)* existant

existence [ɪg'zɪstəns] *n* existence *f*; **to come into e.** être créé; **to be in e.** exister

exit ['eksɪt, 'egzɪt] **1** *n* sortie *f* **2** *vi (leave)* & *Comptr* sortir

exodus ['eksədəs] *n inv* exode *m*

exorbitant [ɪg'zɔːbɪtənt] *adj* exorbitant

exotic [ɪg'zɒtɪk] *adj* exotique

expand [ɪk'spænd] **1** *vt (production, influence)* accroître; *(knowledge)* étendre; *(trade, range, idea)* développer **2** *vi (of knowledge)* s'étendre; *(of trade)* se développer; *(of production)* augmenter; *(of gas)* se dilater; **to e. on** développer

expanse [ɪk'spæns] *n* étendue *f*

expatriate [*Br* eks'pætrɪət, *Am* eks-'peɪtrɪət] *adj & n* expatrié, -e *(mf)*

expect [ɪk'spekt] *vt (anticipate)* s'attendre à; *(think)* penser (**that** que); *(await)* attendre; **to e. to do sth** compter faire qch; **to e. that...** *(anticipate)* s'attendre à ce que... *(+ subjunctive)*; **to be expecting a baby** attendre un enfant; **as expected** comme prévu

expectation [ekspek'teɪʃən] *n* **to come up to expectations** se montrer à la hauteur

expedient [ɪks'piːdɪənt] **1** *adj* opportun **2** *n* expédient *m*

expedition [ekspɪ'dɪʃən] *n* expédition *f*

expel [ɪk'spel] *(pt & pp -ll-)* *vt* expulser (**from** de); *(from school)* renvoyer

expend [ɪk'spend] *vt (energy, money)* dépenser ▪ **expendable** *adj (person)* qui n'est pas irremplaçable

expenditure [ɪk'spendɪtʃə(r)] *n (of money, energy)* dépense *f*

expense [ɪk'spens] *n* frais *mpl*, dépense *f*; *Com* **expenses** frais *mpl*; **at the e. of sb/sth** aux dépens de qn/qch

expensive [ɪk'spensɪv] *adj (goods, hotel, shop)* cher (*f* chère) ▪ **expensively** *adv* **e. dressed/furnished** habillé/meublé luxueusement

experience [ɪk'spɪərɪəns] **1** *n* expérience *f*; **from** or **by e.** par expérience **2** *vt (emotion)* ressentir; *(hunger, success)* connaître; *(difficulty)* éprouver ▪ **experienced** *adj (person)* expérimenté; **to be e. in sth** s'y connaître en qch

experiment 1 [ɪk'sperɪmənt] *n* expérience *f* **2** [ɪk'sperɪment] *vi* expérimenter (**on** sur); **to e. with sth** *(technique, drugs)* essayer qch

expert ['ekspɜːt] **1** *n* expert *m* (**on** or **in** en) **2** *adj* expert (**in sth** en qch; **in** or **at doing** à faire) ▪ **expertise** [-tiːz] *n* compétence *f* (**in** en)

expiration [ekspə'reɪʃən] *n Am* = **expiry**

expire [ɪk'spaɪə(r)] *vi* expirer ▪ **expired** *adj (ticket, passport)* périmé

expiry [ɪk'spaɪərɪ] (*Am* **expiration** [ekspə'reɪʃən]) *n* expiration *f*; **e. date** *(on ticket)* date *f* d'expiration; *(on product)* date *f* limite d'utilisation

explain [ɪk'spleɪn] *vt* expliquer (**to** à; **that** que); *(reasons)* exposer; *(mystery)* éclaircir

explanation [eksplə'neɪʃən] *n* explication *f*

explanatory [ɪk'splænətərɪ] *adj* explicatif, -ive

expletive [ɪk'spliːtɪv] *n* juron *m*

explicit [ɪk'splɪsɪt] *adj* explicite ■ **explicitly** *adv* explicitement

explode [ɪk'spləʊd] **1** *vt (bomb)* faire exploser **2** *vi (of bomb)* exploser

exploit 1 [ɪk'splɔɪt] *n* exploit *m* **2** [ɪk'splɔɪt] *vt (person, land)* exploiter ■ **exploitation** [eksplɔɪ'teɪʃən] *n* exploitation *f*

exploratory [ɪk'splɒrətərɪ] *adj (talks, surgery)* exploratoire

explore [ɪk'splɔː(r)] *vt* explorer; *(causes, possibilities)* examiner

explosion [ɪk'spləʊʒən] *n* explosion *f*

explosive [ɪk'spləʊsɪv] **1** *adj (weapon, situation)* explosif, -ive **2** *n* explosif *m*

export 1 ['ekspɔːt] *n (activity, product)* exportation *f* **2** [ɪk'spɔːt] *vt* exporter (**to** vers; **from** de) ■ **exporter** *n* exportateur, -trice *mf*; *(country)* pays *m* exportateur

expose [ɪk'spəʊz] *vt (to air, cold, danger)* & *Phot* exposer (**to** à); *(plot, scandal)* révéler; *(criminal)* démasquer

exposure [ɪk'spəʊʒə(r)] *n* exposition *f* (**to** à); *Phot* pose *f*; **to get a lot of e.** *(in the media)* faire l'objet d'une importante couverture médiatique

express[1] [ɪk'spres] *vt* exprimer; **to e. oneself** s'exprimer

express[2] [ɪk'spres] **1** *adj (letter, delivery)* exprès *inv*; *(train)* rapide, express *inv* **2** *adv (send)* en exprès **3** *n (train)* rapide *m*, express *m inv*

expression [ɪk'spreʃən] *n* expression *f*

expressive [ɪk'spresɪv] *adj* expressif, -ive

expressly [ɪks'preslɪ] *adv (forbid)* expressément

expressway [ɪk'spresweɪ] *n Am* autoroute *f*

expulsion [ɪk'spʌlʃən] *n* expulsion *f*; *(from school)* renvoi *m*

exquisite [ɪk'skwɪzɪt] *adj* exquis

extend [ɪk'stend] **1** *vt (in space)* étendre; *(in time)* prolonger (**by** de); *(hand)* tendre (**to sb** à qn); *(house)* agrandir; *(knowledge)* accroître; *(thanks)* offrir (**to** à) **2** *vi (in space)* s'étendre (**to** jusqu'à); *(in time)* se prolonger

extension [ɪk'stenʃən] *n (for table)* rallonge *f*; *(to building)* annexe *f*; *(for telephone)* poste *m*; *(for essay)* délai *m* supplémentaire

extensive [ɪk'stensɪv] *adj (powers, forests)* vaste; *(repairs, damage)* important ■ **extensively** *adv (very much)* énormément

extent [ɪk'stent] *n (scope)* étendue *f*; *(size)* importance *f*; **to a large** *or* **great e.** dans une large mesure; **to some e.** *or* **a certain e.** dans une certaine mesure; **to such an e. that...** à tel point que...

exterior [ɪk'stɪərɪə(r)] *adj* & *n* extérieur *(m)*

exterminate [ɪk'stɜːmɪneɪt] *vt* exterminer

external [ɪk'stɜːnəl] *adj (trade, event)* extérieur; *(wall)* externe

extinct [ɪk'stɪŋkt] *adj (volcano)* éteint; *(species, animal)* disparu

extinguish [ɪk'stɪŋgwɪʃ] *vt* éteindre ■ **extinguisher** *n (fire)* **e.** extincteur *m*

extortionate [ɪk'stɔːʃənət] *adj* exorbitant

extra ['ekstrə] **1** *adj (additional)* supplémentaire; **to be e.** *(spare)* être en trop; *(cost more)* être un supplément; **e. charge** supplément *m*; **e. time** *(in sport)* prolongation *f* **2** *adv (more than usual)* extrêmement; **to pay e.** payer un supplément; **wine costs** *or* **is £10 e.** il y a un supplément de 10 livres pour le vin **3** *n (perk)* à-côté *m*; *(actor in film)* figurant, -e *mf*; *(on bill)* supplément *m*

extra- ['ekstrə] *pref* extra-

extract 1 ['ekstrækt] *n* extrait *m* **2** [ɪk'strækt] *vt* extraire (**from** de); *(information, money)* soutirer (**from** à)

extra-curricular [ekstrəkə'rɪkjʊlə(r)] *adj Sch* extrascolaire

extraordinary [ɪk'strɔːdənərɪ] *adj* extraordinaire

extravagant [ɪk'strævəgənt] *adj (behaviour, idea)* extravagant; *(wasteful)* dépensier, -ère; *(tastes)* dispendieux, -euse ▪ **extravagance** *n (of behaviour)* extravagance *f*; *(wastefulness)* gaspillage *m*; *(thing bought)* folie *f*

extreme [ɪk'striːm] **1** *adj* extrême **2** *n* extrême *m*; **to carry** *or* **take sth to extremes** pousser qch à l'extrême ▪ **extremely** *adv* extrêmement

extremist [ɪk'striːmɪst] *adj & n* extrémiste *(mf)*

extremity [ɪk'stremətɪ] *(pl -ies) n* extrémité *f*

extrovert ['ekstrəvɜːt] *n* extraverti, -e *mf*

exuberant [ɪg'zjuːbərənt] *adj* exubérant

exude [ɪg'zjuːd] *vt (health, honesty)* respirer

eye [aɪ] **1** *n* œil *m* (*pl* yeux); **to have one's e. on sth** avoir qch en vue; **to keep an e. on sb/sth** surveiller qn/qch; *Am* **e. doctor** opticien, -enne *mf* **2** *vt* regarder ▪ **eyebrow** *n* sourcil *m* ▪ **eyelash** *n* cil *m* ▪ **eyelid** *n* paupière *f* ▪ **eyeliner** *n* eye-liner *m* ▪ **eyeshadow** *n* fard *m* à paupières ▪ **eyesight** *n* vue *f* ▪ **eyesore** *n* horreur *f* ▪ **eye-witness** *n* témoin *m* oculaire

▸ **eye up** *vt sep* reluquer

Ff

F, f [ef] *n (letter)* F, f *m inv*

fable ['feɪbəl] *n* fable *f*

fabric ['fæbrɪk] *n (cloth)* tissu *m*, étoffe *f*

fabricate ['fæbrɪkeɪt] *vt* fabriquer

fabulous ['fæbjʊləs] *adj (legendary, incredible)* fabuleux, -euse

face [feɪs] **1** *n (of person)* visage *m*, figure *f*; *(expression)* mine *f*; *(of clock)* cadran *m*; *(of building)* façade *f*; *(of cube)* face *f*; *(of cliff)* paroi *f*; **f. down(wards)** *(person)* face contre terre; *(thing)* à l'envers; **f. to f.** face à face; **to save/lose f.** sauver/perdre la face; *Br* **f. cloth** gant *m* de toilette

2 *vt (danger, enemy, problem)* faire face à; **to f., to be facing** *(be opposite)* être en face de; *(of window, door, room)* donner sur; **faced with** *(prospect, problem)* confronté à; *(defeat)* menacé par

3 *vi* **to f. north** *(of building)* être orienté au nord; **to f. up to** *(danger, problem)* faire face à; *(fact)* accepter

faceless ['feɪsləs] *adj* anonyme

face-lift ['feɪslɪft] *n (by surgeon)* lifting *m*; *(of building)* ravalement *m*

facetious [fə'siːʃəs] *adj (person)* facétieux; -euse

facial ['feɪʃəl] **1** *adj (expression)* du visage **2** *n* soin du visage

facilitate [fə'sɪlɪteɪt] *vt* faciliter ■ **facilities** *npl (for sports, cooking)* équipements *mpl*; *(in harbour, airport)* installations *fpl*

fact [fækt] *n* fait *m*; **as a matter of f., in f.** en fait

faction ['fækʃən] *n* faction *f*

factor ['fæktə(r)] *n* facteur *m*

factory ['fæktərɪ] *(pl* **-ies)** *n (large)* usine *f*; *(small)* fabrique *f*

factual ['fæktʃʊəl] *adj* basé sur les faits

faculty ['fækəltɪ] *(pl* **-ies)** *n (of mind, in university)* faculté *f*

fad [fæd] *n (fashion)* mode *f* (**for** de); *(personal habit)* marotte *f*

fade [feɪd] *vi (of flower, material, colour)* se faner; *(of light)* baisser; **to f. (away)** *(of memory, smile)* s'effacer; *(of sound)* s'affaiblir; *(of person)* dépérir

fag [fæg] *n Br Fam (cigarette)* clope *m* ou *f*

fail [feɪl] **1** *n* **without f.** sans faute **2** *vt (exam)* échouer à; *(candidate)* recaler; **to f. to do** *(forget)* manquer de faire; *(not be able)* ne pas arriver à faire **3** *vi (of person, plan)* échouer; *(of business)* faire faillite; *(of health, sight)* baisser; *(of memory, strength)* défaillir; *(of brakes)* lâcher ■ **failed** *adj (attempt, poet)* raté ■ **failing 1** *n (fault)* défaut *m* **2** *prep* à défaut de; **f. this, f. that** à défaut

failure ['feɪljə(r)] *n* échec *m*; *(of business)* faillite *f*; *(person)* raté, -e *mf*

faint [feɪnt] **1** (**-er, -est**) *adj (weak) (voice, trace, breeze, hope)* faible; *(colour)* pâle; **to feel f.** se sentir mal **2** *vi* s'évanouir (**with** *or* **from** de)

fair¹ [feə(r)] *n (trade fair)* foire *f*; *Br (funfair)* fête *f* foraine ■ **fairground** *n* parc *m* d'attractions

fair² [feə(r)] **1** (**-er, -est**) *adj* (a) *(just)* juste; *(game, fight)* loyal; **f. play** fairplay *m inv* (b) *(rather good)* assez bon (*f* bonne); *(price)* raisonnable; **a f. amount (of)** *(a lot)* pas mal (de) (c) *(wind)* favorable; *(weather)* beau (*f* belle) **2** *adv (fight)* loyalement; **to play f.** jouer franc jeu ■ **fairly** *adv* (a) *(treat)* équitablement; *(act, fight, get)* loyalement (b) *(rather)* assez

fair³ [feə(r)] *adj (hair, person)* blond; *(complexion, skin)* clair ■ **fair-haired** *adj* blond

fairy ['feərɪ] *(pl -ies) n* fée *f* ■ **fairytale** *n* conte *m* de fées

faith [feɪθ] *n* foi *f*; **to have f. in sb** avoir foi en qn; **in good/bad f.** *(act)* de bonne/mauvaise foi

faithful ['feɪθfəl] *adj* fidèle ■ **faithfully** *adv* fidèlement; *Br* **yours f.** *(in letter)* veuillez agréer l'expression de mes sentiments distingués

fake [feɪk] **1** *adj* faux (*f* fausse) **2** *n (object)* faux *m*; *(person)* imposteur *m* **3** *vt (signature)* contrefaire **4** *vi (pretend)* faire semblant

fall [fɔːl] **1** *n (of person, snow, city)* chute *f*; *(in price, demand)* baisse *f*; *Am (season)* automne *m* **2** *(pt* fell, *pp* fallen) *vi* tomber; *(of price, temperature)* baisser; **the dollar is falling** le dollar est en baisse; **to f. into** *(hole, trap)* tomber dans; *(habit)* prendre; **to f. off a bicycle/ladder** tomber d'une bicyclette/échelle; **to f. out of a window** tomber d'une fenêtre; **to f. over sth** tomber en butant contre qch; **to f. asleep** s'endormir; **to f. ill** tomber malade

▸ **fall apart** *vi (of book, machine)* tomber en morceaux; *(of person)* s'effondrer

▸ **fall back on** *vt insep (resort to)* se rabattre sur

▸ **fall behind** *vi (in work, payments)* prendre du retard

▸ **fall down** *vi* tomber; *(of building)* s'effondrer

▸ **fall for** *vt insep (person)* tomber amoureux, -euse de; *(trick)* se laisser prendre à

▸ **fall in** *vi (collapse)* s'écrouler

▸ **fall off** *vi (come off)* tomber; *(of numbers)* diminuer

▸ **fall out** *vi (quarrel)* se brouiller (**with** avec)

▸ **fall over** *vi* tomber; *(of table, vase)* se renverser

▸ **fall through** *vi (of plan)* tomber à l'eau, échouer

fallacy ['fæləsɪ] *(pl -ies) n* erreur *f*

fallen ['fɔːlən] **1** *pp of* fall **2** *adj* tombé;

f. leaves feuilles *fpl* mortes

fallible ['fæləbəl] *adj* faillible

false [fɔːls] *adj* faux (*f* fausse); **f. teeth** dentier *m*

falsify ['fɔːlsɪfaɪ] *(pt & pp -ied) vt (forge)* falsifier

falter ['fɔːltə(r)] *vi (of voice, speaker)* hésiter

fame [feɪm] *n* renommée *f* ■ **famed** *adj* renommé (**for** pour)

familiar [fə'mɪljə(r)] *adj (well-known)* familier, -ère (**to** à); **to be f. with sb/sth** bien connaître qn/qch; **he looks f.** je l'ai déjà vu (quelque part)

familiarize [fə'mɪljəraɪz] *vt* **to f. oneself with sth** se familiariser avec qch

family ['fæmɪlɪ] **1** *(pl -ies) n* famille *f* **2** *adj (name, doctor, jewels)* de famille; *(planning, problems, business)* familial; **f. man** homme *m* attaché à sa famille

famine ['fæmɪn] *n* famine *f*

famished ['fæmɪʃt] *adj* affamé

famous ['feɪməs] *adj* célèbre (**for** pour)

fan¹ [fæn] **1** *n (held in hand)* éventail *m* *(pl -ails)*; *(mechanical)* ventilateur *m* **2** *(pt & pp -nn-) vt (person)* éventer

fan² [fæn] *n (of person)* fan *mf*; *(of team)* supporter *m*; **to be a jazz/sports f.** être passionné de jazz/de sport

fanatic [fə'nætɪk] *n* fanatique *mf* ■ **fanatical** *adj* fanatique

fanciful ['fænsɪfəl] *adj* fantaisiste

fancy ['fænsɪ] **1** *n* **I took a f. to it, it took my f.** j'en ai eu envie **2** *adj (jewels, hat, button)* fantaisie *inv*; *(car)* de luxe; *(house, restaurant)* chic *inv*; *Br* **f. dress** déguisement *m*; *Br* **f. dress party** soirée *f* déguisée **3** *(pt & pp -ied) vt* (a) *Br Fam (want)* avoir envie de; **he fancies her** elle lui plaît (b) **to f. that...** *(imagine)* se figurer que...; *(think)* croire que...

fanfare ['fænfeə(r)] *n* fanfare *f*

fantastic [fæn'tæstɪk] *adj* fantastique; *(wealth, size)* prodigieux, -euse; *Fam (excellent)* formidable

fantasy ['fæntəsɪ] *(pl -ies) n (imagination)* fantaisie *f*; *(dream)* chimère *f*;

(fanciful, sexual) fantasme *m* ▪ **fanta-size** *vi* fantasmer (**about** sur)

FAR [fɑ:(r)] **1** (**farther** or **further, farthest** or **furthest**) *adj* **the f. side/ end** l'autre côté/bout; **the F. East** l'Extrême-Orient *m*; *Pol* **the f. left/right** l'extrême gauche *f*/droite *f* **2** *adv* (a) *(in distance)* loin (**from** de); **how f. is it to Toulouse?** combien y a-t-il d'ici à Toulouse?; **is it f. to…?** sommes-nous/suis-je/*etc* loin de…?; **how f. has he got with his work?** où en est-il dans son travail?; **as f. as** jusqu'à; **as f.** or **so f. as I know** autant que je sache; **as f.** or **so f. as I'm concerned** en ce qui me concerne; **f. from doing sth** loin de faire qch; **f. away** or **off** au loin; **to be f. away** être loin (**from** de)

(b) *(in time)* **as f. back as 1820** dès 1820; **so f.** jusqu'ici

(c) *(much)* **f. bigger/more expensive** beaucoup plus grand/plus cher (*f* chère) (**than** que); **f. more/better** beaucoup plus/mieux (**than** que); **by f.** de loin ▪ **far-away** *adj (country)* lointain; *(look)* perdu dans le vague ▪ **far-fetched** *adj* tiré par les cheveux ▪ **far-reaching** *adj* de grande portée ▪ **far-sighted** *adj* clairvoyant

farce [fɑ:s] *n* farce *f* ▪ **farcical** *adj* grotesque

fare [feə(r)] **1** *n (for journey) (in train, bus)* prix *m* du billet; *(in taxi)* prix *m* de la course **2** *vi (manage)* se débrouiller

farewell [feə'wel] **1** *n & exclam* adieu *(m)* **2** *adj (party, speech)* d'adieu

farm [fɑ:m] **1** *n* ferme *f* **2** *adj (worker, produce)* agricole **3** *vt* cultiver **4** *vi* être agriculteur, -trice ▪ **farmer** *n* fermier, -ère *mf*, agriculteur, -trice *mf* ▪ **farmhouse** *n* ferme *f* ▪ **farming** *n* agriculture *f*; *(breeding)* élevage *m* ▪ **farmyard** *n* cour *f* de ferme

fart [fɑ:t] *Fam* **1** *n* pet *m* **2** *vi* péter

farther ['fɑ:ðə(r)] **1** *comparative of* **far 2** *adv* plus loin; **f. forward** plus avancé; **to get f. away** s'éloigner ▪ **farthest 1** *superlative of* **far 2** *adj* le plus éloigné **3** *adv* le plus loin

fascinate ['fæsɪneɪt] *vt* fasciner ▪ **fascinating** *adj* fascinant

fascist ['fæʃɪst] *adj & n* fasciste *(mf)*

fashion ['fæʃən] **1** *n* (a) *(in clothes)* mode *f*; **in f.** à la mode; **out of f.** démodé; **f. show** défilé *m* de mode (b) *(manner)* façon *f*; **after a f.** tant bien que mal **2** *vt (form)* façonner; *(make)* confectionner ▪ **fashionable** *adj* à la mode ▪ **fashionably** *adv (dressed)* à la mode

fast¹ [fɑ:st] **1** (**-er, -est**) *adj* rapide; **to be f.** *(of clock)* avancer (**by** de); **f. food** restauration *f* rapide; **f. food restaurant** fast-food *m* **2** *adv* (a) *(quickly)* vite; **how f.?** à quelle vitesse? (b) **f. asleep** profondément endormi

fast² [fɑ:st] **1** *n* jeûne *m* **2** *vi* jeûner

fasten ['fɑ:sən] **1** *vt* attacher (**to** à); *(door, window)* fermer; **to f. sth down** attacher qch **2** *vi (of dress)* s'attacher; *(of door, window)* se fermer ▪ **fastener, fastening** *n (clip)* attache *f*; *(hook)* agrafe *f*; *(press stud)* bouton-pression *m*; *(of bag)* fermoir *m*

fat [fæt] **1** (**fatter, fattest**) *adj* gras (*f* grasse); *(cheeks, salary, book)* gros (*f* grosse); **to get f.** grossir **2** *n* graisse *f*; *(on meat)* gras *m*

fatal ['feɪtəl] *adj* mortel, -elle ▪ **fatally** *adv* **f. wounded** mortellement blessé

fatality [fə'tælətɪ] *(pl* **-ies***) n (person)* victime *f*

fate [feɪt] *n* destin *m*, sort *m* ▪ **fateful** *adj (words, day)* fatidique

father ['fɑ:ðə(r)] **1** *n* père *m*; **F. Christmas** le père Noël **2** *vt (child)* engendrer ▪ **father-in-law** *(pl* **fathers-in-law***) n* beau-père *m*

fatherhood ['fɑ:ðəhʊd] *n* paternité *f*

fatherly ['fɑ:ðəlɪ] *adj* paternel, -elle

fatigue [fə'ti:g] *n (tiredness)* fatigue *f*

fatten ['fætən] *vt* **to f. (up)** engraisser ▪ **fattening** *adj (food)* qui fait grossir

fatty ['fætɪ] (**-ier, -iest**) *adj (food)* gras (*f* grasse)

faucet ['fɔ:sɪt] *n Am (tap)* robinet *m*

fault [fɔ:lt] **1** *n (blame)* faute *f*; *(defect, failing)* défaut *m*; *Geol* faille *f*; **to find f. (with)** trouver à redire (à); **it's your f.**

c'est (de) ta faute **2** *vt* **to f. sb/sth** trouver des défauts chez qn/à qch

faultless ['fɔ:ltləs] *adj* irréprochable

faulty ['fɔ:ltɪ] **(-ier, -iest)** *adj* défectueux, -euse

favour ['feɪvə(r)] (*Am* **favor**) **1** *n* (*act of kindness*) service *m*; (*approval*) faveur *f*; **to do sb a f.** rendre service à qn; **in f. (with sb)** bien vu (de qn); **to be in f. of sth** être partisan de qch **2** *vt* (*encourage*) favoriser; (*support*) être partisan de ■ **favourable** (*Am* **favorable**) *adj* favorable (**to** à)

favourite ['feɪvərɪt] (*Am* **favorite**) **1** *adj* favori, -ite, préféré **2** *n* favori, -ite *mf* ■ **favouritism** (*Am* **favoritism**) *n* favoritisme *m*

fawn [fɔ:n] **1** *n* (*deer*) faon *m* **2** *adj & n* (*colour*) fauve (*m*)

fax [fæks] **1** *n* (*message*) télécopie *f*, fax *m*; **f. (machine)** télécopieur *m*, fax *m* **2** *vt* (*message*) faxer; **to f. sb** envoyer un fax à qn

fear [fɪə(r)] **1** *n* peur *f*; (*worry*) crainte *f*; **for f. of doing sth** de peur de faire qch; **for f. that...** de peur que... (*+ ne + subjunctive*) **2** *vt* craindre; **I f. that he might leave** je crains qu'il ne parte **3** *vi* **to f. for one's life** craindre pour sa vie ■ **fearful** *adj* (*person*) apeuré; (*noise, pain, consequence*) épouvantable ■ **fearless** *adj* intrépide

feasible ['fi:zəbəl] *adj* faisable

feast [fi:st] **1** *n* festin *m*; (*religious*) fête *f* **2** *vi* **to f. on sth** se régaler de qch

feat [fi:t] *n* exploit *m*

feather ['feðə(r)] *n* plume *f*

feature ['fi:tʃə(r)] **1** *n* (*of face, person*) trait *m*; (*of thing, place, machine*) caractéristique *f*; **f. (article)** article *m* de fond; **f. (film)** long métrage *m* **2** *vt* (*of newspaper, exhibition, film*) (*present*) présenter; (*portray*) représenter; **a film featuring Nicole Kidman** un film ayant pour vedette Nicole Kidman **3** *vi* (*appear*) figurer (**in** dans)

February ['februərɪ] *n* février *m*

fed [fed] **1** *pt & pp of* **feed 2** *adj Fam* **to be f. up** en avoir marre *ou* ras le bol (**with** de)

federal ['fedərəl] *adj* fédéral ■ **federation** [-'reɪʃən] *n* fédération *f*

fee [fi:] *n* **fee(s)** (*of doctor, lawyer*) honoraires *mpl*; (*of artist*) cachet *m*; (*for registration, examination*) droits *mpl*; (*for membership*) cotisation *f*; **school** *or* **tuition fees** frais *mpl* d'inscription

feeble ['fi:bəl] **(-er, -est)** *adj* faible; (*excuse, smile*) pauvre; (*attempt*) peu convaincant

feed [fi:d] **1** *n* (*animal food*) nourriture *f*; (*for baby*) (*from breast*) tétée *f*; (*from bottle*) biberon *m* **2** (*pt & pp* **fed**) *vt* donner à manger à; (*baby*) (*from breast*) donner la tétée à; (*from bottle*) donner son biberon à; **to f. sb sth** faire manger qch à qn **3** *vi* (*eat*) manger; **to f. on sth** se nourrir de qch

feedback ['fi:dbæk] *n* (*response*) réactions *fpl*

feel [fi:l] **1** *n* (*touch*) toucher *m*; **to have a f. for sth** avoir qch dans la peau **2** (*pt & pp* **felt**) *vt* (*be aware of*) sentir; (*experience*) éprouver, ressentir; (*touch*) tâter; **to f. that...** penser que...; **to f. one's way** avancer à tâtons **3** *vi* **to f. (about)** (*grope*) tâtonner; (*in pocket*) fouiller (**for sth** pour trouver qch); **it feels hard** c'est dur au toucher; **to f. tired/old** se sentir fatigué/vieux (*f* vieille); **I f. hot/sleepy/hungry** j'ai chaud/sommeil/faim; **she feels better** elle va mieux; **to f. like sth** (*want*) avoir envie de qch; **it feels like cotton** on dirait du coton; **what do you f. about...?** que pensez-vous de...?; **I f. bad about it** ça m'ennuie

feeling ['fi:lɪŋ] *n* (*emotion, impression*) sentiment *m*; (*physical*) sensation *f*; **to have a f. for** (*music, painting*) être sensible à

feet [fi:t] *pl of* **foot**[1]

feign [feɪn] *vt* feindre

feline ['fi:laɪn] *adj* félin

fell [fel] **1** *pt of* **fall 2** *vt* (*tree*) abattre; (*opponent*) terrasser

fellow ['feləʊ] *n* **(a)** (*man, boy*) gars *m* **(b)** (*companion*) **f. countryman/f. countrywoman** compatriote *mf*; **f. worker** collègue *mf* **(c)** (*of society*) membre *m*

fellowship ['feləʊʃɪp] *n (scholarship)* bourse *f* de recherche

felt¹ [felt] *pt & pp of* **feel**

felt² [felt] *n* feutre *m* ▪ **felt-tip** *n* f. (pen) crayon-feutre *m*

female ['fiːmeɪl] **1** *adj (person, name, voice)* féminin; *(animal)* femelle **2** *n (woman)* femme *f*; *(girl)* fille *f*; *(animal, plant)* femelle *f*

feminine ['femɪnɪn] **1** *adj* féminin **2** *n (in grammar)* féminin *m* ▪ **feminist** *adj & n* féministe *(mf)*

fence [fens] **1** *n (barrier)* clôture *f*; *(more solid)* barrière *f*; *(in race)* obstacle *m* **2** *vt* **to f. (in)** *(land)* clôturer **3** *vi (as sport)* faire de l'escrime ▪ **fencing** *(sport)* escrime *f*

fend [fend] **1** *vi* **to f. for oneself** se débrouiller **2** *vt* **to f. off** *(blow)* parer

fender ['fendə(r)] *n Am (of car)* aile *f*

ferment [fə'ment] *vi* fermenter

ferocious [fə'rəʊʃəs] *adj* féroce

ferret ['ferɪt] **1** *n (animal)* furet *m* **2** *vt* **to f. out** *(object, information)* dénicher

ferry ['ferɪ] **1** *(pl* **-ies)** *n* ferry-boat *m*; *(small, for river)* bac *m* **2** *(pt & pp* **-ied)** *vt* transporter

fertile [*Br* 'fɜːtaɪl, *Am* 'fɜːrtəl] *adj (land, imagination)* fertile; *(person, animal)* fécond ▪ **fertilizer** *n* engrais *m*

fervent ['fɜːvənt] *adj* fervent

festival ['festɪvəl] *n (of music, film)* festival *m (pl* **-als);** *(religious)* fête *f*

festive ['festɪv] *adj* de fête; *(mood)* festif, -ive; **the f. season** les fêtes *fpl* de fin d'année ▪ **festivities** *npl* festivités *fpl*

fetch [fetʃ] *vt* **(a)** *(bring)* aller chercher **(b)** *(be sold for)* rapporter

fête [feɪt] **1** *n Br* fête *f* **2** *vt* fêter

fetus ['fiːtəs] *n Am =* **foetus**

feud [fjuːd] *n* querelle *f*

fever ['fiːvə(r)] *n* fièvre *f*; **to have a f.** *(temperature)* avoir de la fièvre ▪ **feverish** *adj (person, activity)* fiévreux, -euse

FEW [fjuː] **1** *adj* **(a)** *(not many)* peu de; **f. towns** peu de villes; **every f. days** tous les trois ou quatre jours; **one of the f. books** l'un des rares livres; **f.**

and far between rarissime **(b)** *(some)* **a f. towns** quelques villes; **a f. more books** encore quelques livres; **quite a f...., a good f....** bon nombre de... **2** *pron* peu; **f. came** peu sont venus; **f. of them** un petit nombre d'entre eux; **a f.** quelques-un(e)s **(of** de); **a f. of us** quelques-uns d'entre nous

fewer ['fjuːə(r)] **1** *adj* moins de; **f. houses** moins de maisons **(than** que); **to be f. (than)** être moins nombreux (que) **2** *pron* moins ▪ **fewest 1** *adj* le moins de **2** *pron* le moins

fiancé [fɪ'ɒnseɪ] *n* fiancé *m*

fiancée [fɪ'ɒnseɪ] *n* fiancée *f*

fiasco [fɪ'æskəʊ] *(pl* **-os,** *Am* **-oes)** *n* fiasco *m*

fib [fɪb] *Fam* **1** *n* bobard *m* **2** *(pt & pp* **-bb-)** *vi* raconter des bobards

fibre ['faɪbə(r)] *(Am* **fiber)** *n* fibre *f*; *(in diet)* fibres *fpl*

fickle ['fɪkəl] *adj* inconstant

fiction ['fɪkʃən] *n (invention)* fiction *f*; *(works of)* f. livres *mpl* de fiction ▪ **fictional** *adj (character)* fictif, -ive

fictitious [fɪk'tɪʃəs] *adj* fictif, -ive

fiddle ['fɪdəl] **1** *n* **(a)** *(violin)* violon *m* **(b)** *Br Fam (dishonest act)* combine *f* **2** *vt Br Fam (accounts)* truquer **3** *vi* **to f. about** *(waste time)* traînailler; **to f. (about) with sth** tripoter qch

fiddly ['fɪdlɪ] **(-ier, -iest)** *adj Fam (task)* minutieux, -euse

fidget ['fɪdʒɪt] **1** *n* **to be a f.** ne pas tenir en place **2** *vi* **to f. (about)** gigoter ▪ **fidgety** *adj* agité

field [fiːld] *n* champ *m*; *(for sports)* terrain *m*; *(sphere)* domaine *m*

fierce [fɪəs] **(-er, -est)** *adj (animal, warrior, tone)* féroce; *(attack, wind)* violent

fiery ['faɪərɪ] **(-ier, -iest)** *adj (person, speech)* fougueux, -euse

fifteen [fɪf'tiːn] *adj & n* quinze *(m)* ▪ **fifteenth** *adj & n* quinzième *(mf)*

fifth [fɪfθ] *adj & n* cinquième *(mf)*; **a f.** *(fraction)* un cinquième

fifty ['fɪftɪ] *adj & n* cinquante *(m)*

fig 115 **final**

■ **fifty-fifty** *adj & adv* a **f. chance** une chance sur deux; **to split the profits f.** partager les bénéfices moitié-moitié ■ **fiftieth** *adj & n* cinquantième *(mf)*

fig [fɪg] *n* figue *f*

fight [faɪt] **1** *n (between people)* bagarre *f; (between boxers, soldiers)* combat *m; (struggle)* lutte *f* (**against/for** contre/pour); *(quarrel)* dispute *f* **2** *(pt & pp* **fought)** *vt (person)* se battre contre; *(decision, enemy)* combattre; *(fire, temptation)* lutter contre; **to f. a battle** livrer bataille; *Pol* **to f. an election** se présenter à une élection; **to f. off** *(attacker, attack)* repousser **3** *vi* se battre (**against** contre); *(of soldiers)* combattre; *(struggle)* lutter (**against/for** contre/pour); *(quarrel)* se disputer; **to f. back** *(retaliate)* se défendre; **to f. over sth** se disputer qch

fighter ['faɪtə(r)] *n (determined person)* battant, -e *mf; (in brawl, battle)* combattant, -e *mf; (boxer)* boxeur *m; (aircraft)* avion *m* de chasse

fighting ['faɪtɪŋ] *n (brawling)* bagarres *fpl; Mil* combat *m*

figment ['fɪgmənt] *n* **it's a f. of your imagination** c'est le fruit de ton imagination

figurative ['fɪgjʊrətɪv] *adj (meaning)* figuré; *(art)* figuratif, -ive

figure¹ [*Br* 'fɪgə(r), *Am* 'fɪgjə(r)] *n* (**a**) *(numeral)* chiffre *m* (**b**) *(shape)* forme *f; (outline)* silhouette *f;* **she has a nice f.** elle est bien faite (**c**) *(diagram)* figure *f;* **f. skating** patinage *m* artistique (**d**) *(expression, word)* **a f. of speech** une figure de rhétorique (**e**) *(important person)* personnage *m*

figure² [*Br* 'fɪgə(r), *Am* 'fɪgjə(r)] **1** *vt* **to f. that...** *(think)* penser que...; *(estimate)* supposer que...; **to f. out** *(person, motive)* arriver à comprendre; *(answer)* trouver; *(amount)* calculer **2** *vi (appear)* figurer (**on** sur); **to f. on doing sth** compter faire qch

file¹ [faɪl] **1** *n (tool)* lime *f* **2** *vt* **to f. (down)** limer

file² [faɪl] **1** *n (folder)* chemise *f; (documents)* dossier *m* (**on** sur); *Comptr* fichier *m;* **to be on f.** figurer au dossier **2** *vt (document)* classer; *(complaint, claim)* déposer

file³ [faɪl] **1** *n (line)* file *f;* **in single f.** en file indienne **2** *vi* **to f. in/out** entrer/ sortir à la queue leu leu; **to f. past sb/ sth** défiler devant qn/qch ■ **filing** *adj* **f. cabinet** classeur *m (meuble)*

fill [fɪl] **1** *n* **to eat one's f.** manger à sa faim **2** *vt* remplir (**with** de); *(tooth)* plomber; *(time)* occuper; **to f. in** *(form)* remplir; *(hole)* combler; **to f. sb in on sth** mettre qn au courant de qch; **to f. out** *(form)* remplir; **to f. up** *(container)* remplir **3** *vi* **to f. (up)** se remplir (**with** de); **to f. in for sb** remplacer qn; **to f. up** *(with petrol)* faire le plein

fillet [*Br* 'fɪlɪt, *Am* fɪ'leɪ] **1** *r (of fish, meat)* filet *m* **2** *(Am pt & pp* [fɪ'leɪd]) *vt (fish)* découper en filets; *(meat)* désosser

filling ['fɪlɪŋ] **1** *adj (meal)* nourrissant **2** *n (in tooth)* plombage *m; (in food)* garniture *f;* **f. station** station-service *f*

film [fɪlm] **1** *n* film *m; (for camera, layer)* pellicule *f; (for food)* film *m* plastique **2** *adj (studio, technician, critic)* de cinéma; **f. star** vedette *f* de cinéma **3** *vt* filmer **4** *vi (of film maker, actor)* tourner

Filofax® ['faɪləfæks] *n* organiseur *m*

filter ['fɪltə(r)] **1** *n* filtre *m; Br (traffic sign)* flèche *f* de dégagement; **f. coffee** café *m* filtre **2** *vt* filtrer **3** *vi* **to f. through** filtrer ■ **filter-tipped** *adj (cigarette)* bout filtre *inv*

filth [fɪlθ] *n* saleté *f; Fig (obscenities)* saletés *fpl* ■ **filthy** (**-ier, -iest**) *adj (hands, shoes)* sale; *(language)* obscène; *(habit)* dégoûtant

fin [fɪn] *n (of fish)* nageoire *f; (of shark)* aileron *m*

final ['faɪnəl] **1** *adj (last)* dernier, -ère; *(definite)* définitif, -ive **2** *n (in sport)* finale *f; Univ* **finals** examens *mpl* de dernière année ■ **finalist** *n* finaliste *mf* ■ **finalize** *vt (plan)* mettre au point; *(date)* fixer définitivement; *(deal)* conclure ■ **finally** *adv (lastly)* enfin; *(eventually)* finalement; *(irrevocably)* définitivement

finale [fɪ'nɑːlɪ] *n (musical)* finale *m*

finance ['faɪnæns] **1** *n* finance *f*; **finances** *(of person)* finances *fpl*; *(of company)* situation *f* financière **2** *vt* financer

financial [faɪ'nænʃəl] *adj* financier, -ère; *Br* **f. year** exercice *m* comptable

financier [faɪ'nænsɪə(r)] *n* financier *m*

find [faɪnd] **1** *n (discovery)* découverte *f* **2** *(pt & pp* **found)** *vt* trouver; **I f. that…** je trouve que…
▸**find out 1** *vt (secret, information)* découvrir; *(person)* prendre en défaut **2** *vi (inquire)* se renseigner (**about** sur); **to f. out about sth** *(discover)* apprendre qch

findings ['faɪndɪŋz] *npl* conclusions *fpl*

fine¹ [faɪn] **1** *n (money)* amende *f*; *(for driving offence)* contravention *f* **2** *vt* **to f. sb £100** infliger une amende de 100 livres à qn

fine² [faɪn] **1** (**-er, -est**) *adj* (**a**) *(thin, not coarse) (hair, needle)* fin; *(gold, metal)* pur; *(distinction)* subtil (**b**) *(very good)* excellent; *(beautiful) (weather, statue)* beau *(f* belle); **it's f.** *(weather)* il fait beau; **he's f.** *(healthy)* il va bien **2** *adv (very well)* très bien ■ **finely** *adv (dressed)* magnifiquement; *(embroidered, ground)* finement; **f. chopped** haché menu

finger ['fɪŋgə(r)] **1** *n* doigt *m*; **little f.** petit doigt *m*, auriculaire *m* **2** *vt* tâter ■ **fingernail** *n* ongle *m* ■ **fingertip** *n* bout *m* du doigt

finish ['fɪnɪʃ] **1** *n (end)* fin *f*; *(of race)* arrivée *f*; *(of article, car)* finition *f* **2** *vt* **to f. sth** (**off** *or* **up)** finir qch; **to f. doing sth** finir de faire qch **3** *vi (of meeting, event)* finir, se terminer; *(of person)* finir, terminer; **to have finished with** *(object)* ne plus avoir besoin de; *(activity, person)* en avoir fini avec; **to f. off** *(of person)* finir, terminer ■ **finishing** *adj* **f. line** *(of race)* ligne *f* d'arrivée; **to put the f. touches to sth** mettre la dernière main à qch ■ **finished** *adj (ended, complete, ruined)* fini

finite ['faɪnaɪt] *adj* fini

Finland ['fɪnlənd] *n* la Finlande ■ **Finn** *n* Finlandais, -e *mf*, Finnois, -e *mf* ■ **Finnish 1** *adj* finlandais, finnois **2** *n (language)* finnois *m*

fir [fɜː(r)] *n* sapin *m*

fire ['faɪə(r)] **1** *n* feu *m*; *(accidental)* incendie *m*; *Br (electric heater)* radiateur *m*; **to light** *or* **make a f.** faire du feu; **to set f. to sth** mettre le feu à qch; **on f.** en feu; **f.!** *(alarm)* au feu!; **to open f.** ouvrir le feu; **f. alarm** sirène *f* d'incendie; *Br* **f. brigade,** *Am* **f. department** pompiers *mpl*; **f. engine** voiture *f* des pompiers; **f. escape** escalier *m* de secours; **f. station** caserne *f* des pompiers
 2 *vt (cannon)* tirer; *(pottery)* cuire; **to f. a gun** tirer un coup de fusil/de pistolet; **to f. questions at sb** bombarder qn de questions; **to f. sb** *(dismiss)* renvoyer qn
 3 *vi* tirer (**at** sur); **f.!** feu! ■ **firearm** *n* arme *f* à feu ■ **fireguard** *n* garde-feu *m inv* ■ **fireman** (*pl* **-men)** *n* sapeur-pompier *m* ■ **fireplace** *n* cheminée *f* ■ **fireproof** *adj (door)* ignifugé ■ **fireside** *n* **by the f.** au coin du feu ■ **firewood** *n* bois *m* de chauffage ■ **firework** *n* fusée *f*; *(firecracker)* pétard *m*; **fireworks,** *Br* **f. display** feu *m* d'artifice

firm¹ [fɜːm] *n (company)* entreprise *f*, firme *f*

firm² [fɜːm] **1** (**-er, -est**) *adj (earth, decision)* ferme; *(foundations)* solide **2** *adv* **to stand f.** tenir bon *ou* ferme ■ **firmly** *adv (believe)* fermement; *(shut)* bien

first [fɜːst] **1** *adj* premier, -ère; **f. aid** premiers secours *mpl*
 2 *adv* d'abord; *(for the first time)* pour la première fois; **f. of all, f. and foremost** tout d'abord; **at f.** d'abord; **to come f.** *(in race)* arriver premier; *(in exam)* être reçu premier
 3 *n (person, thing)* premier, -ère *mf*; **f. (gear)** *(of vehicle)* première *f* ■ **first-class 1** *adj* excellent; *(ticket)* de première classe; *(mail)* ordinaire **2** *adv (travel)* en première ■ **first-hand** *adj* **to have (had) f. experience of sth** avoir fait l'expérience personnelle de

qch ▪ **first-rate** *adj* excellent

firstly ['fɜːstlɪ] *adv* premièrement

fish [fɪʃ] **1** (*pl inv or* **-es** [-ɪz]) *n* poisson *m*; **f. bone** arête *f*; *Br* **f. fingers**, *Am* **f. sticks** bâtonnets *mpl* de poisson; **f. shop** poissonnerie *f*; **f. tank** aquarium *m*

2 *vt* **to f. sth out** (*from water*) repêcher qch

3 *vi* pêcher ▪ **fish-and-chip** *adj Br* **f. shop** = magasin où on vend du poisson frit et des frites ▪ **fishing** *n* pêche *f*; **to go f.** aller à la pêche; **f. boat** bateau *m* de pêche; **f. net** filet *m* (de pêche); **f. rod** canne à pêche

fisherman ['fɪʃəmən] (*pl* **-men**) *n* pêcheur *m*

fishmonger ['fɪʃmʌŋgə(r)] *n* poissonnier, -ère *mf*

fishy ['fɪʃɪ] (**-ier, -iest**) *adj* (*smell, taste*) de poisson; *Fig* (*suspicious*) louche

fist [fɪst] *n* poing *m* ▪ **fistful** *n* poignée *f* (**of** de)

fit¹ [fɪt] **1** (**fitter, fittest**) *adj* (**a**) (*healthy*) en forme; **to keep f.** se maintenir en forme

(**b**) (*suitable*) propre (**for** à; **to do** à faire); (*worthy*) digne (**for** de; **to do** de faire); (*able*) apte (**for** à, **to do** à faire)

2 *n* **a good f.** (*clothes*) à la bonne taille; **a tight f.** (*clothes*) ajusté

3 (*pt & pp* **-tt-**) *vt* (*be the right size for*) aller bien à; (*match*) correspondre à; (*put in*) poser; (*go in*) aller dans; (*go on*) aller sur; **to f. sth (on) to sth** (*put*) poser qch sur qch; (*adjust*) adapter qch à qch; (*fix*) fixer qch à qch; **to f. sth in** (*install*) poser qch; (*insert*) faire entrer qch

4 *vi* (*of clothes, lid, key, plug*) aller; **this shirt fits** (*fits me*) cette chemise me va; **to f. (in)** (*go in*) aller; (*of facts, plans*) cadrer (**with** avec); **he doesn't f. in** il n'est pas à sa place

fit² [fɪt] *n* (*seizure*) attaque *f*; **a f. of coughing** une quinte de toux; **in fits and starts** par à-coups

fitness ['fɪtnɪs] *n* (*health*) santé *f*; (*for job*) aptitude *f* (**for** à)

fitted ['fɪtɪd] *adj Br* (*cupboard*) en-

castré; (*garment*) ajusté; **f. carpet** moquette *f*; **f. kitchen** cuisine *f* intégrée

fitting ['fɪtɪŋ] **1** *adj* (*suitable*) approprié (**to** à) **2** *n* **f. room** cabine *f* d'essayage; **fittings** (*in house*) installations *fpl*

five [faɪv] *adj & n* cinq (*m*) ▪ **fiver** *n Br Fam* billet *m* de cinq livres

fix [fɪks] **1** *vt* (*make firm, decide*) fixer (**to** à); (*mend*) réparer; (*deal with*) arranger; (*prepare*) préparer; *Fam* (*election*) truquer; **to f. sth on** (*lid*) mettre qch en place; **to f. sth up** (*trip, meeting*) arranger qch **2** *n Fam* **in a f.** dans le pétrin

fixed [fɪkst] *adj* (*price*) fixe; (*idea*) bien arrêté

fixture ['fɪkstʃə(r)] *n* (**a**) (*in sport*) rencontre *f* (**b**) **fixtures** (*in house*) installations *fpl*

fizz [fɪz] *vi* (*of champagne*) pétiller ▪ **fizzy** (**-ier, -iest**) *adj* gazeux, -euse

▶ **fizzle out** ['fɪzəl] *vi* (*of firework*) rater; *Fam* (*of plan*) tomber à l'eau

flabbergasted ['flæbəgɑːstɪd] *adj Fam* sidéré

flabby ['flæbɪ] (**-ier, -iest**) *adj* (*person*) bouffi; (*skin*) mou (*f* molle)

flag [flæg] **1** *n* drapeau *m*; *Naut* pavillon *m*; (*for charity*) insigne *m* **2** (*pt & pp* **-gg-**) *vt* marquer; **to f. down a taxi** héler un taxi **3** *vi* (*of person, conversation*) faiblir ▪ **flagpole** *n* mât *m*

flagrant ['fleɪgrənt] *adj* flagrant

flagstone ['flægstəʊn] *n* dalle *f*

flair [fleə(r)] *n* (*intuition*) don *m* (**for** pour); **to have a f. for business** avoir le sens des affaires

flake [fleɪk] **1** *n* (*of snow*) flocon *m*; (*of paint*) écaille *f*; (*of soap*) paillette *f* **2** *vi* **to f. (off)** (*of paint*) s'écailler ▪ **flaky** *adj Br* **f. pastry** pâte *f* feuilletée

flamboyant [flæm'bɔɪənt] *adj* (*person*) extraverti

flame [fleɪm] *n* flamme *f*; **to go up in flames** prendre feu

flamingo [flə'mɪŋgəʊ] (*pl* **-os** *or* **-oes**) *n* flamant *m*

flammable ['flæməbəl] *adj* inflammable

flan [flæn] *n* tarte *f*

flank [flæŋk] **1** *n* flanc *m* **2** *vt* flanquer (**with** *or* **by** de)

flannel ['flænəl]. *n Br (face cloth)* gant *m* de toilette

flap [flæp] **1** *n (of pocket, envelope)* rabat *m*; *(of table)* abattant *m* **2** *(pt & pp* **-pp-)** *vt* **to f. its wings** *(of bird)* battre des ailes **3** *vi (of wings, sail, shutter)* battre

flare [fleə(r)] **1** *n* (**a**) *(rocket)* fusée *f* éclairante (**b**) **(pair of) flares** *(trousers)* pantalon *m* pattes d'éléphant **2** *vi* **to f. up** *(of fire)* s'embraser; *(of violence, trouble)* éclater

flared [fleəd] *adj (skirt)* évasé; *(trousers)* (à) pattes d'éléphant

flash [flæʃ] **1** *n (of light)* éclair *m*; *(for camera)* flash *m*; **f. of lightning** éclair *m* **2** *vt (light)* projeter; *(aim)* diriger (**on** *or* **at** sur); *(show)* montrer rapidement; **to f. one's headlights** faire un appel de phares **3** *vi (shine)* briller; *(on and off)* clignoter; **to f. past** *or* **by** *(rush)* passer comme un éclair ▪ **flashback** *n* retour *m* en arrière ▪ **flashlight** *n Am (torch)* lampe *f* électrique; *(for camera)* flash *m*

flashy ['flæʃɪ] **(-ier, -iest)** *adj Fam (clothes, car)* tape-à-l'œil *inv*

flask [flɑːsk] *n (Thermos®)* Thermos® *f inv*; *(for alcohol)* flasque *f*

flat¹ [flæt] **1** **(flatter, flattest)** *adj* plat; *(tyre, battery)* à plat; *(drink)* éventé; *(refusal)* net *(f* nette); **f. rate** tarif *m* unique; **to put** *or* **lay sth (down) f.** mettre qch à plat **2** *n (puncture)* crevaison *f*; *(of hand)* plat *m*; *(in music)* bémol *m* **3** *adv* **to sing f.** chanter trop bas; **to fall f. on one's face** tomber à plat ventre; **to fall f.** *(of joke, play)* tomber à plat; **f. out** *(work)* d'arrache-pied; *(run)* à toute vitesse ▪ **flatly** *adv (deny, refuse)* catégoriquement

flat² [flæt] *n Br (in building)* appartement *m*

flatmate ['flætmeɪt] *n Br* colocataire *mf*

flatten ['flætən] *vt* aplatir; *(crops)* coucher; *(town, buildings)* raser

flatter ['flætə(r)] *vt* flatter ▪ **flattering** *adj (remark, words)* flatteur, -euse

flattery ['flætərɪ] *n* flatterie *f*

flaunt [flɔːnt] *vt (show off)* faire étalage de

flavour ['fleɪvə(r)] *(Am* **flavor**) **1** *n (taste)* goût *m*; *(of ice cream)* parfum *m* **2** *vt (food)* relever (**with** de); **lemon-flavoured** (parfumé) au citron ▪ **flavouring** *(Am* **flavoring**) *n (seasoning)* assaisonnement *m*; *(in cake, ice cream)* parfum *m*

flaw [flɔː] *n* défaut *m* ▪ **flawed** *adj* qui a un défaut/des défauts ▪ **flawless** *adj* parfait

flea [fliː] *n* puce *f*; **f. market** marché *m* aux puces

fleck [flek] *n (mark)* petite tache *f*

fled [fled] *pt & pp of* **flee**

flee [fliː] **1** *(pt & pp* **fled)** *vt (place)* s'enfuir de; *(danger)* fuir **2** *vi* s'enfuir, fuir

fleece [fliːs] **1** *n (of sheep)* toison *f*; *(garment)* fourrure *f* polaire **2** *vt Fam (overcharge)* écorcher ▪ **fleecy (-ier, -iest)** *adj (gloves)* molletonné

fleet [fliːt] *n (of ships)* flotte *f*; *(of taxis, buses)* parc *m* ▪ **fleeting** *adj (visit, moment)* bref *(f* brève)

Flemish ['flemɪʃ] **1** *adj* flamand **2** *n (language)* flamand *m*

flesh [fleʃ] *n* chair *f*; **in the f.** en chair et en os

flew [fluː] *pt of* **fly²**

flex [fleks] **1** *n (wire)* fil *m*; *(for telephone)* cordon *m* **2** *vt (limb)* fléchir; *(muscle)* faire jouer

flexible ['fleksɪbəl] *adj* flexible

flexitime ['fleksɪtaɪm] *n* horaires *mpl* flexibles *ou* à la carte

flick [flɪk] **1** *n (with finger)* chiquenaude *f*; *Br* **f. knife** couteau *m* à cran d'arrêt **2** *vt (with finger)* donner une chiquenaude à; **to f. sth off** *(remove)* enlever qch d'une chiquenaude; **to f. a switch** pousser un bouton **3** *vi* **to f. through** *(book, magazine)* feuilleter

flicker ['flɪkə(r)] *vi (of flame, light)* vaciller

flier ['flaɪə(r)] *n (leaflet)* prospectus *m*

flies [flaɪz] *npl (of trousers)* braguette *f*

flight [flaɪt] *n* (a) *(of bird, aircraft)* vol *m*; **f. attendant** *(man)* steward *m*; *(woman)* hôtesse *f* de l'air (b) *(floor)* étage *m*; **f. of stairs** escalier *m* (c) *(escape)* fuite *f* (**from** de); **to take f.** prendre la fuite

flimsy ['flɪmzɪ] (**-ier, -iest**) *adj (cloth, structure) (light)* (trop) léger, -ère; *(thin)* (trop) mince; *(excuse)* piètre

flinch [flɪntʃ] *vi (with pain)* tressaillir

fling [flɪŋ] **1** *n (affair)* aventure *f* **2** *(pt & pp* **flung)** *vt* jeter

flint [flɪnt] *n (of lighter)* pierre *f*

flip [flɪp] **1** *(pt & pp* **-pp-)** *vt: (with finger)* donner une chiquenaude à; **to f. a coin** jouer à pile ou face; **to f. sth over** retourner qch **2** *vi* **to f. through a book** feuilleter un livre

flip-flops ['flɪpflɒps] *npl* tongs *fpl*

flippant ['flɪpənt] *adj* désinvolte

flipper ['flɪpə(r)] *n (of swimmer)* palme *f*; *(of animal)* nageoire *f*

flirt [flɜːt] **1** *n* charmeur, -euse *mf* **2** *vi* flirter (**with** avec)

flit [flɪt] *(pt & pp* **-tt-)** *vi (fly)* voltiger; *Fig* **to f. in and out** *(of person)* entrer et sortir rapidement

float [fləʊt] **1** *n (for fishing line)* bouchon *m*; *(for swimming)* flotteur *m*; *(in procession)* char *m* **2** *vt (idea)* lancer; *(company)* introduire en Bourse **3** *vi* flotter (**on** sur); **to f. down the river** descendre la rivière ▪ **floating** *adj (wood)* flottant; **f. voters** électeurs *mpl* indécis

flock [flɒk] **1** *n (of sheep)* troupeau *m*; *(of birds)* volée *f*; *(of people)* foule *f* **2** *vi* **people are flocking to the exhibition** les gens vont en foule voir l'exposition

flood [flʌd] **1** *n* inondation *f* **2** *vt (land, bathroom, market)* inonder (**with** de); **to f. (out)** *(house)* inonder **3** *vi (of river)* déborder; **to f. in** *(of people, money)* affluer ▪ **flooding** *n* inondation(s) *f(pl)*

floodlight ['flʌdlaɪt] **1** *n* projecteur *m* **2** *(pt & pp* **-lit)** *vt* illuminer

floor [flɔː(r)] **1** *n (of room)* sol *m*; *(wooden)* plancher *m*; *(storey)* étage *m*;

on the f. par terre; **on the first f.** *Br* au premier étage; *Am (ground floor)* au rez-de-chaussée **2** *vt (knock down)* envoyer au tapis; *(puzzle)* stupéfier

floorboard ['flɔːbɔːd] *n* latte *f (de plancher)*

flop [flɒp] *Fam* **1** *n* fiasco *m*; *(play)* four *m* **2** *(pt & pp* **-pp-)** *vi (fail) (of business)* échouer; *(of play, film)* faire un four; **to f. down** s'effondrer

floppy ['flɒpɪ] (**-ier, -iest**) *adj (soft)* mou *(f* molle); *(clothes)* (trop) large; *Comptr* **f. disk** disquette *f*

floral ['flɔːrəl] *adj (material, pattern)* à fleurs

florist ['flɒrɪst] *n* fleuriste *mf*

floss [flɒs] *n* (**dental**) **f.** fil *m* dentaire

flour ['flaʊə(r)] *n* farine *f*

flourish ['flʌrɪʃ] **1** *n (gesture)* grand geste *m*; *(decoration)* fioriture *f* **2** *vt (wave)* brandir **3** *vi (of person, plant)* prospérer; *(of arts, business)* être florissant ▪ **flourishing** *adj (plant)* qui prospère; *(business)* florissant

flow [fləʊ] **1** *n (of river)* courant *m*; *(of tide)* flux *m*; *(of current, information, blood)* circulation *f*; *(of liquid)* écoulement *m*; **f. of traffic** circulation *f*; **f. chart** organigramme *m* **2** *vi* couler; *(of electric current)* circuler; *(of hair, clothes)* flotter; *(of traffic)* s'écouler; **to f. in** *(of money)* affluer ▪ **flowing** *adj (movement, style)* fluide; *(hair, beard)* flottant

flower ['flaʊə(r)] **1** *n* fleur *f*; **in f.** en fleur(s); **f. bed** parterre *m*; **f. pot** pot *m* de fleurs; **f. shop** fleuriste *mf* **2** *vi* fleurir ▪ **flowering** *adj (in bloom)* en fleurs; *(producing flowers) (shrub)* à fleurs

flowery ['flaʊərɪ] *adj (style)* fleuri; *(material)* à fleurs

flown [fləʊn] *pp of* **fly²**

flu [fluː] *n (influenza)* grippe *f*

fluctuate ['flʌktʃʊeɪt] *vi* varier ▪ **fluctuation** [-'eɪʃən] *n* variation *f* (**in** de)

fluent ['fluːənt] *adj* **he's f. in Russian, his Russian is f.** il parle couramment le russe; **to be a f. speaker** s'exprimer

avec facilité ■ **fluently** *adv (write, express oneself)* avec facilité; *(speak language)* couramment

fluff [flʌf] *n* peluche *f* ■ **fluffy (-ier, -iest)** *adj (toy)* en peluche

fluid ['fluːɪd] **1** *adj* fluide; *(plans)* mal défini; **f. ounce** = 0,031 2 *n* fluide *m*, liquide *m*

fluke [fluːk] *n Fam* coup *m* de chance; **by a f.** par hasard

flung [flʌŋ] *pt & pp of* **fling**

flunk [flʌŋk] *Am Fam* **1** *vt (exam)* être collé à; *(pupil)* coller **2** *vi (in exam)* être collé

fluorescent [fluəˈresənt] *adj* fluorescent

fluoride ['fluəraɪd] *n* fluorure *m*; **f. toothpaste** dentifrice *m* au fluor

flurry ['flʌrɪ] *(pl -ies) n (of snow)* bourrasque *f*; **a f. of activity** une soudaine activité

flush [flʌʃ] **1** *adj (level)* de niveau (**with** de) **2** *n* (**a**) *(blush)* rougeur *f* (**b**) *(in toilet)* chasse *f* d'eau **3** *vt* **to f. sth (out)** *(clean)* nettoyer qch à grande eau; **to f. the toilet** tirer la chasse d'eau **4** *vi (blush)* rougir (**with** de)

fluster ['flʌstə(r)] *vt* démonter; **to get flustered** se démonter

flute [fluːt] *n* flûte *f*

flutter ['flʌtə(r)] **1** *vt* **to f. its wings** *(of bird)* battre des ailes **2** *vi (of bird, butterfly)* voleter; *(of flag)* flotter

fly¹ [flaɪ] *(pl -ies) n (insect)* mouche *f*

fly² [flaɪ] **1** *(pt* **flew***, pp* **flown***) vt (aircraft)* piloter; *(passengers)* transporter; *(flag)* arborer; *(kite)* faire voler; **to f. the Atlantic** traverser l'Atlantique en avion

2 *vi (of bird, aircraft)* voler; *(of passenger)* aller en avion; *(of time)* passer vite; *(of flag)* flotter; **to f. away** or **off** s'envoler; **to f. across** or **over** *(country, city)* survoler; **I must f.!** il faut que je file! ■ **flyer** *n* = **flier** ■ **flying 1** *n (as passenger)* voyage *m* en avion **2** *adj* **to pass with f. colours** réussir haut la main; **to get off to a f. start** prendre un très bon départ; **f. saucer** soucoupe *f* volante; **f. visit** visite *f* éclair *inv* ■ **fly-**

over *n Br (bridge)* pont-route *m*

fly³ [flaɪ] *n Br (on trousers)* braguette *f*

foal [fəʊl] *n* poulain *m*

foam [fəʊm] **1** *n (on sea, mouth)* écume *f*; *(on beer)* mousse *f*; **f. bath** bain *m* moussant; **f. rubber** caoutchouc *m* Mousse® **2** *vi (of beer, soap)* mousser

focal ['fəʊkəl] *adj* focal

focus ['fəʊkəs] **1** *(pl* **focuses** ['fəʊkəsəz] *or* **foci** ['fəʊkaɪ]) *n (of attention, interest)* centre *m*; *(optical)* foyer *m*; **the photo is in f./out of f.** la photo est nette/floue

2 *vt (image, camera)* mettre au point; *(attention, efforts)* concentrer (**on** sur)

3 *vi* **to f. on sb/sth** *(with camera)* faire la mise au point sur qn/qch

4 *vti* **to f. (one's) eyes on sb/sth** fixer les yeux sur qn/qch; **to f. (one's attention) on sb/sth** se tourner vers qn/qch

fodder ['fɒdə(r)] *n* fourrage *m*

foe [fəʊ] *n* ennemi, -e *mf*

foetus ['fiːtəs] *(Am* **fetus***) n* fœtus *m*

fog [fɒg] *n* brouillard *m* ■ **foglamp, foglight** *n (on vehicle)* phare *m* antibrouillard

fogey ['fəʊgɪ] *n* = **fogy**

foggy ['fɒgɪ] **(-ier, -iest)** *adj* brumeux, -euse; **it's f.** il y a du brouillard; *Fam* **I haven't got the foggiest (idea)** je n'en ai pas la moindre idée

fogy ['fəʊgɪ] *n* old f. vieux schnock *m*

foil [fɔɪl] **1** *n* (**a**) *(for cooking)* papier *m* alu (**b**) *(sword)* fleuret *m* **2** *vt (plans)* contrecarrer

fold [fəʊld] **1** *n (in paper, cloth)* pli *m* **2** *vt* plier; **to f. away** or **down** or **up** *(chair)* plier; **to f. back** or **over** *(blanket)* replier; **to f. one's arms** croiser les bras **3** *vi Fam (of business)* fermer ses portes; **to f. (away** or **down** or **up)** *(of chair)* se plier ■ **folding** *adj (chair, bed)* pliant

-fold [fəʊld] *suff* **1** *adj* **tenfold** par dix **2** *adv* **tenfold** dix fois

folder ['fəʊldə(r)] *n (file holder)* chemise *f*; *Comptr* répertoire *m*

foliage ['fəʊlɪɪdʒ] *n* feuillage *m*

folk [fəʊk] **1** *(Am* **folks***) npl* gens *mpl*;

Fam **my folks** *(parents)* mes parents *mpl* **2** *adj (dance, costume)* folklorique; **f. music** *(contemporary)* folk *m*

follow ['fɒləʊ] **1** *vt* suivre; *(career)* poursuivre; **to f. through** *(plan, idea)* mener à son terme; **to f. up** *(idea, story)* creuser; *(clue, case)* suivre; *(letter)* donner suite à; *(remark)* faire suivre (**with** de); *(advantage)* exploiter **2** *vi (of person, event)* suivre; **it follows that...** il s'ensuit que...; **to f. on** *(come after)* suivre

follower ['fɒləʊə(r)] *n (of ideas, politician)* partisan *m*

following ['fɒləʊɪŋ] **1** *adj* suivant **2** *n (of politician)* partisans *mpl* **3** *prep* à la suite de

folly ['fɒlɪ] *(pl -ies) n* folie *f*

fond [fɒnd] (*-er, -est*) *adj (loving)* affectueux, -euse; *(memory, thought)* doux *(f* douce); **to be (very) f. of sb/ sth** aimer beaucoup qn/qch ▪ **fondly** *adv* tendrement

fondle ['fɒndəl] *vt* caresser

font [fɒnt] *n* (a) *Rel* fonts *mpl* baptismaux (b) *Typ & Comptr* police *f* de caractères

food [fu:d] **1** *n* nourriture *f; (particular substance)* aliment *m; (cooking)* cuisine *f; (for cats, dogs, pigs)* pâtée *f; (for plants)* engrais *m* **2** *adj (industry)* alimentaire; **f. poisoning** intoxication *f* alimentaire

foodstuffs ['fu:dstʌfs] *npl* denrées *fpl* alimentaires

fool [fu:l] **1** *n* imbécile *mf;* **to make a f. of sb** *(ridicule)* ridiculiser qn; *(trick)* rouler qn; **to make a f. of oneself** se couvrir de ridicule **2** *vt (trick)* duper **3** *vi* **to f. about** *or* **around** faire l'imbécile; *(waste time)* perdre son temps

foolish ['fu:lɪʃ] *adj* bête ▪ **foolishly** *adv* bêtement

foolproof ['fu:lpru:f] *adj (scheme)* infaillible

foot¹ [fʊt] *(pl* feet) *n* pied *m; (of animal)* patte *f; (unit of measurement)* = 30,48 cm, pied *m;* **at the f. of** *(page, stairs)* au bas de; **on f.** à pied ▪ **football** *n (soccer)* football *m; (American* game) football *m* américain; *(ball)* ballon *m* ▪ **footballer** *n Br* joueur, -euse *mf* de football ▪ **footbridge** *n* passerelle *f* ▪ **foothold** *n* prise *f* (de pied); *Fig* position *f;* **to gain a f.** *(of person)* prendre pied (**in** dans) ▪ **footnote** *n* note *f* de bas de page; *Fig (extra comment)* post-scriptum *m inv* ▪ **footpath** *n* sentier *m* ▪ **footstep** *n* pas *m;* **to follow in sb's footsteps** suivre les traces de qn ▪ **footstool** *n* petit tabouret *m* ▪ **footwear** *n* chaussures *fpl*

foot² [fʊt] *vt (bill)* payer

footage ['fʊtɪdʒ] *n Cin* séquences *fpl*

footing ['fʊtɪŋ] *n* (a) *(balance)* **to lose one's f.** perdre l'équilibre (b) *(level)* **to be on an equal f.** être sur un pied d'égalité (**with** avec)

FOR [fɔ:(r), *unstressed* fə(r)] **1** *prep* pour; *(for a distance or period of)* pendant; *(in spite of)* malgré; **what's it f.?** ça sert à quoi?; **I did it f. love/pleasure** je l'ai fait par amour/par plaisir; **to swim/rush f.** *(towards)* nager/se précipiter vers; **a train f.** un train à destination de; **the road f. London** la route de Londres; **it's time f. breakfast** c'est l'heure du petit déjeuner; **to come f. dinner** venir dîner; **to sell sth f. 7 dollars** vendre qch 7 dollars; **what's the French f. 'book'?** comment dit-on 'book' en français?; **she walked f. a kilometre** elle a marché pendant un kilomètre; **he was away f. a month** il a été absent pendant un mois; **he's been here f. a month** il est ici depuis un mois; **I haven't seen him f. ten years** ça fait dix ans que je ne l'ai pas vu, je ne l'ai pas vu depuis dix ans; **it's easy f. her to do it** il lui est facile de le faire; **f. that to be done** pour que ça soit fait **2** *conj (because)* car

forbad [fə'bæd] *pt of* **forbid**

forbade [fə'bæd, fə'beɪd] *pt of* **forbid**

forbid [fə'bɪd] *(pt* **forbad(e)**, *pp* **forbidden** [fə'bɪdən], *pres p* **forbidding**) *vt* interdire, défendre (**sb to do** à qn de faire); **to f. sb sth** interdire qch à qn; **she is f. to leave** il lui est interdit de partir ▪ **forbidden 1** *pp of* **forbid 2**

adj (fruit, region) défendu

force [fɔːs] **1** *n* force *f*; **the (armed) forces** les forces *fpl* armées; **by f.** de force; **in f.** *(rule)* en vigueur; *(in great numbers)* en force **2** *vt* forcer (**to do** à faire); *(impose)* imposer (**on** à); *(door, lock)* forcer; *(confession)* arracher (**from** à); **to f. sth into sth** faire entrer qch de force dans qch ▪ **forced** *adj* **f. to do** obligé *ou* forcé de faire; **a f. smile** un sourire forcé

forceful ['fɔːsfəl] *adj* énergique

ford [fɔːd] **1** *n* gué *m* **2** *vt (river)* passer à gué

fore [fɔː(r)] *n* **to come to the f.** *(of issue)* passer au premier plan

forearm ['fɔːrɑːm] *n* avant-bras *m inv*

foreboding [fɔːˈbəʊdɪŋ] *n (feeling)* pressentiment *m*

forecast ['fɔːkɑːst] **1** *n (of weather)* prévisions *fpl*; *(in racing)* pronostic *m* **2** *(pt & pp* forecast(ed)) *vt* prévoir; *(in racing)* pronostiquer

forecourt ['fɔːkɔːt] *n (of hotel)* avant-cour *f*; *(of petrol station)* devant *m*

forefinger ['fɔːfɪŋɡə(r)] *n* index *m*

forefront ['fɔːfrʌnt] *n* **in the f. of** au premier plan de

forego [fɔːˈɡəʊ] *(pp* -gone) *vt* renoncer à

foreground ['fɔːɡraʊnd] *n* premier plan *m*

forehead ['fɒrɪd, 'fɔːhed] *n* front *m*

foreign ['fɒrɪn] *adj (language, person, country)* étranger, -ère; *(trade)* extérieur; *(travel, correspondent)* à l'étranger; **F. Minister**, *Br* **F. Secretary** *n* ministre *m* des Affaires étrangères; *Br* **F. Office** ministère *m* des Affaires étrangères ▪ **foreigner** *n* étranger, -ère *mf*

foreman ['fɔːmən] *(pl* -men) *n (worker)* contremaître *m*

foremost ['fɔːməʊst] *adj* principal

forerunner ['fɔːrʌnə(r)] *n (person)* précurseur *m*

foresee [fɔːˈsiː] *(pt* -saw, *pp* -seen) *vt* prévoir

foreshadow [fɔːˈʃædəʊ] *vt* annoncer

foresight ['fɔːsaɪt] *n* prévoyance *f*

forest ['fɒrɪst] *n* forêt *f*

forestall [fɔːˈstɔːl] *vt* devancer

foretell [fɔːˈtel] *(pt & pp* -told) *vt* prédire

forever [fəˈrevə(r)] *adv (for always)* pour toujours; *(continually)* sans cesse

foreword ['fɔːwɜːd] *n* avant-propos *m inv*

forfeit ['fɔːfɪt] **1** *n (in game)* gage *m* **2** *vt (lose)* perdre

forge [fɔːdʒ] **1** *vt (signature, money)* contrefaire; **to f. a passport** faire un faux passeport **2** *vi* **to f. ahead** *(progress)* aller de l'avant ▪ **forged** *adj* faux *(f* fausse)

forgery ['fɔːdʒərɪ] *(pl* -ies) *n* contrefaçon *f*

forget [fəˈget] **1** *(pt* forgot, *pp* forgotten, *pres p* forgetting) *vt* oublier (**to do** de faire); *Fam* **f. it!** *(when thanked)* pas de quoi!; *(it doesn't matter)* laisse tomber! **2** *vi* oublier; **to f. about sb/sth** oublier qn/qch ▪ **forgetful** *adj* **to be f.** avoir une mauvaise mémoire

forgive [fəˈgɪv] *(pt* -gave, *pp* -given) *vt* pardonner (**sb sth** qch à qn) ▪ **forgiveness** *n* pardon *m*

forgo [fɔːˈɡəʊ] *(pp* -gone) *vt* renoncer à

forgot [fəˈgɒt] *pt of* **forget**

forgotten [fəˈgɒtən] *pp of* **forget**

fork [fɔːk] **1** *n (for eating)* fourchette *f*; *(for gardening, in road)* fourche *f* **2** *vt Fam* **to f. out** *(money)* allonger **3** *vi (of road)* bifurquer; *Fam* **to f. out** *(pay)* casquer (**for** *or* **on** pour) ▪ **forklift** *n* **f. (truck)** chariot *m* élévateur

forlorn [fəˈlɔːn] *adj (forsaken)* abandonné; *(unhappy)* triste

form [fɔːm] **1** *n (shape, type, style)* forme *f*; *(document)* formulaire *m*; *Br Sch* classe *f*; **in the f. of** sous forme de; **on f., in good** *or* **top f.** en (pleine) forme **2** *vt (group, basis, character)* former; *(clay)* façonner; *(habit)* contracter; *(obstacle)* constituer; **to f. part of sth** faire partie de qch **3** *vi (appear)* se former

formal ['fɔːməl] *adj (person, tone)* cérémonieux, -euse; *(announcement,*

dinner, invitation) officiel, -elle; *(agreement)* en bonne et due forme; *(language)* soutenu; **f. dress** tenue *f* de soirée ▪ **formality** [-'mælɪtɪ] *(pl -ies)* *n (procedure)* formalité *f* ▪ **formally** *adv (declare)* officiellement; **f. dressed** en tenue de soirée

format ['fɔːmæt] **1** *n* format *m* **2** *(pt & pp* -tt-) *vt Comptr* formater

formation [fɔː'meɪʃən] *n* formation *f*

former ['fɔːmə(r)] **1** *adj (previous) (president, teacher, job, house)* ancien, -enne *(before noun)* **2** *pron* **the f.** celui-là, celle-là ▪ **formerly** *adv* autrefois

formidable ['fɔːmɪdəbəl] *adj* effroyable

formula ['fɔːmjʊlə] *n* (a) *(pl -as or -ae* [-iː]) *(rule, symbols)* formule *f* (b) *(pl -as) (baby food)* lait *m* en poudre ▪ **formulate** [-leɪt] *vt* formuler

fort [fɔːt] *n Mil* fort *m*

forth [fɔːθ] *adv* en avant; **and so f.** et ainsi de suite

forthcoming [fɔːθ'kʌmɪŋ] *adj* (a) *(event)* à venir (b) *(available)* disponible (c) *(informative)* expansif, -ive **(about** sur)

forthright ['fɔːθraɪt] *adj* franc *(f* franche)

fortieth ['fɔːtɪəθ] *adj & n* quarantième *(mf)*

fortify ['fɔːtɪfaɪ] *(pt & pp* -ied) *vt (strengthen)* fortifier; **to f. sb** *(of food, drink)* réconforter qn, remonter qn ▪ **fortification** [-fɪ'keɪʃən] *n* fortification *f*

fortnight ['fɔːtnaɪt] *n Br* quinzaine *f* de jours

fortress ['fɔːtrɪs] *n* forteresse *f*

fortunate ['fɔːtʃənət] *adj* heureux, -euse; **to be f.** *(of person)* avoir de la chance; **it's f. (for her) that...** c'est heureux (pour elle) que... *(+ subjunctive)* ▪ **fortunately** *adv* heureusement

fortune ['fɔːtʃuːn] *n (wealth)* fortune *f; (luck)* chance *f* ▪ **fortune-teller** *n* diseur, -euse *mf* de bonne aventure

forty ['fɔːtɪ] *adj & n* quarante *(m)*

forum ['fɔːrəm] *n* forum *m*

forward ['fɔːwəd] **1** *adj (position)*

avant *inv; (movement)* en avant; *Fig (impudent)* effronté **2** *n (in sport)* avant *m* **3** *adv* en avant; **to go f.** avancer **4** *vt (letter)* faire suivre; *(goods)* expédier

forwards ['fɔːwədz] *adv* = **forward**

fossil ['fɒsəl] *n* fossile *m*

foster ['fɒstə(r)] *adj* **f. child** = enfant placé dans une famille d'accueil; **f. parents** parents *mpl* nourriciers

fought [fɔːt] *pt & pp of* **fight**

foul [faʊl] **1** (-er, -est) *adj* (a) *(smell, taste, weather, person)* infect; *(breath)* fétide; *(language)* grossier, -ère; *(place)* immonde (b) **f. play** *(in sport)* jeu *m* irrégulier; *(in law)* acte *m* criminel **2** *n (in sport)* faute *f* **3** *vt Fam* **to f. up** *(ruin)* gâcher

found[1] [faʊnd] *pt & pp of* **find**

found[2] [faʊnd] *vt (town, party)* fonder; *(opinion, suspicions)* fonder, baser **(on** sur) ▪ **founder** *n* fondateur, -trice *mf*

foundation [faʊn'deɪʃən] *n (basis)* fondement *m*; **the foundations** *(of building)* les fondations *fpl*

fountain ['faʊntɪn] *n* fontaine *f*; **f. pen** stylo-plume *m*

four [fɔː(r)] *adj & n* quatre *(m)*; **on all fours** à quatre pattes ▪ **fourth** *adj & n* quatrième *(mf)* ▪ **four-letter** *adj* **f. word** gros mot *m*

foursome ['fɔːsəm] *n* groupe *m* de quatre personnes

fourteen [fɔː'tiːn] *adj & n* quatorze *(m)* ▪ **fourteenth** *adj & n* quatorzième *(mf)*

fowl [faʊl] *n inv* volaille *f*

fox [fɒks] **1** *n* renard *m* **2** *vt (puzzle)* laisser perplexe; *(deceive)* duper

foyer ['fɔɪeɪ] *n (in theatre)* foyer *m*; *(in hotel)* hall *m*

fraction ['frækʃən] *n* fraction *f*

fracture ['fræktʃə(r)] **1** *n* fracture *f* **2** *vt* fracturer; **to f. one's leg** se fracturer la jambe

fragile [*Br* 'frædʒaɪl, *Am* 'frædʒəl] *adj* fragile

fragment ['frægmənt] *n* fragment *m*

fragrant ['freɪɡrənt] *adj* parfumé ▪ **fragrance** *n* parfum *m*

frail [freɪl] **(-er, -est)** *adj (person)* frêle; *(health)* fragile

frame [freɪm] **1** *n (of picture, bicycle)* cadre *m; (of door, window)* encadrement *m; (of spectacles)* monture *f;* **f. of mind** état *m* d'esprit **2** *vt (picture)* encadrer; *Fig (proposals, ideas)* formuler ∎ **framework** *n* structure *f;* **(with)in the f. of** *(context)* dans le cadre de

franc [fræŋk] *n* franc *m*

France [frɑːns] *n* la France

franchise ['fræntʃaɪz] *n (right to vote)* droit *m* de vote; *(right to sell product)* franchise *f*

Franco- ['fræŋkəʊ] *pref* franco-

frank¹ [fræŋk] **(-er, -est)** *adj (honest)* franc *(f* franche) ∎ **frankly** *adv* franchement

frank² [fræŋk] *vt (letter)* affranchir

frantic ['fræntɪk] *adj (activity, shouts, pace)* frénétique; *(attempt, efforts)* désespéré ∎ **frantically** *adv* frénétiquement; *(run, search)* comme un fou/une folle; *(work)* avec frénésie

fraternize ['frætənaɪz] *vi* fraterniser **(with** avec)

fraud [frɔːd] *n* **(a)** *(crime)* fraude *f* **(b)** *(person)* imposteur *m* ∎ **fraudulent** *adj* frauduleux, -euse

fraught [frɔːt] *adj (situation)* tendu; **f. with** plein de

fray [freɪ] *vi (of garment)* s'effilocher; *(of rope)* s'user ∎ **frayed** *adj (garment)* élimé

freak [friːk] **1** *n (person)* monstre *m; Fam* **jazz f.** fana *mf* de jazz **2** *adj (result, weather)* anormal
▸ **freak out** *Fam* **1** *vt sep (shock, scare)* faire flipper **2** *vi (panic)* paniquer; *(get angry)* piquer une crise

freckle ['frekəl] *n* tache *f* de rousseur ∎ **freckled** *adj* couvert de taches de rousseur

free [friː] **1 (freer, freest)** *adj (at liberty, not occupied)* libre; *(without cost)* gratuit; *(lavish)* généreux, -euse **(with** de); **to get f.** se libérer; **to be f. to do sth** être libre de faire qch; **f. of charge** gratuit; **f. gift** cadeau *m;* **f. kick** *(in football)* coup *m* franc; **f. trade** libre-échange *m*

2 *adv* **f. (of charge)** gratuitement **3** *(pt & pp* **freed)** *vt (prisoner, country)* libérer; *(trapped person)* dégager; *(untie)* détacher ∎ **Freefone**® *n Br (phone number)* ≃ numéro *m* vert ∎ **freelance 1** *adj* indépendant **2** *n* travailleur, -euse *mf* indépendant(e) **3** *adv* **to work f.** travailler en indépendant ∎ **Freepost**® *n Br* ≃ correspondance-réponse *f* ∎ **free-range** *adj Br* **f. egg** œuf *m* de ferme ∎ **freestyle** *n (in swimming)* nage *f* libre ∎ **freeway** *n Am* autoroute *f*

freedom ['friːdəm] *n* liberté *f*

freely ['friːlɪ] *adv (speak, act, circulate)* librement; *(give)* sans compter

freeze [friːz] **1** *n (in weather)* gel *m; (of prices, salaries)* blocage *m* **2** *(pt* **froze,** *pp* **frozen)** *vt (food)* congeler; *(credits, river)* geler; *(prices, wages)* bloquer; **frozen food** surgelés *mpl* **3** *vi* geler; **to f. to death** mourir de froid; **to f. up** *or* **over** *(of lake)* geler ∎ **freezer** *n (deep-freeze)* congélateur *m; (ice-box)* freezer *m* ∎ **freezing 1** *adj (weather)* glacial; *(hands, feet)* gelée; **it's f.** il gèle **2** *n* **it's 5 degrees below f.** il fait 5 degrés au-dessous de zéro **3** *adv* **f. cold** très froid

freight [freɪt] *n Com (goods)* cargaison *f;* **f. train** train *m* de marchandises ∎ **freighter** *n (ship)* cargo *m*

French [frentʃ] **1** *adj* français; *(teacher)* de français; *(embassy)* de France; **F. fries** frites *fpl* **2** *n (language)* français *m;* **the F.** *(people)* les Français *mpl* ∎ **Frenchman** *(pl* **-men)** *n* Français *m* ∎ **French-speaking** *adj* francophone ∎ **Frenchwoman** *(pl* **-women)** *n* Française *f*

frenzy ['frenzɪ] *(pl* **-ies)** *n* frénésie *f* ∎ **frenzied** *adj (activity)* frénétique; *(attack)* violent

frequency ['friːkwənsɪ] *(pl* **-ies)** *n* fréquence *f*

frequent 1 ['friːkwənt] *adj* fréquent **2** [frɪ'kwent] *vt* fréquenter ∎ **frequently** *adv* fréquemment

fresh [freʃ] **1 (-er, -est)** *adj* frais *(f* fraîche); *(new)* nouveau *(f* nouvelle); *Am Fam (cheeky)* insolent; **to get some f. air** prendre l'air **2** *adv* **to be f. from**

(school, university) sortir tout juste de ■ **freshly** adv (arrived, picked) fraîchement

▶**freshen up** ['freʃən] **1** vi (have a wash) faire un brin de toilette **2** vt sep (house) retaper

fret [fret] (pt & pp -tt-) vi (worry) se faire du souci

friction ['frɪkʃən] n friction f

Friday ['fraɪdeɪ] n vendredi m ; **Good F.** le vendredi saint

fridge [frɪdʒ] n frigo m

fried [fraɪd] **1** pt & pp of **fry 2** adj frit; **f. egg** œuf m sur le plat

friend [frend] n ami, -e mf ■ **friendly 1** (-ier, -iest) adj amical **2** n (match) match m amical ■ **friendship** z amitié f

fright [fraɪt] n peur f; **to give sb a f.** faire peur à qn

frighten ['fraɪtən] vt effrayer faire peur à; **to f. sb away** or **off** faire fuir qn ■ **frightened** adj effrayé; **to be f.** avoir peur (**of** de) ■ **frightening** adj effrayant

frightful ['fraɪtfəl] adj affreux, -euse

frill [frɪl] n volant m

fringe [frɪndʒ] n (a) (of hair, on clothes) frange f (b) (margin) **on the fringes of society** en marge de la société

frisk [frɪsk] vt (search) fouiller

frisky ['frɪskɪ] (-ier, -iest) adj (lively) vif (f vive)

fritter ['frɪtə(r)] **1** n Culin beignet m **2** vt **to f. away** gaspiller

frivolous ['frɪvələs] adj frivole

frizzy ['frɪzɪ] adj crépu

fro [frəʊ] adv **to go to and f.** aller et venir

frock [frɒk] n (dress) robe f

frog [frɒg] n grenouille f

frolic ['frɒlɪk] (pt & pp -ck-) vi **to f. (about)** gambader

FROM [frɒm, unstressed frəm] prep (a) (expressing origin) de; **a letter f. sb** une lettre de qn; **to suffer f. sth** souffrir de qch; **where are you f.?** d'où êtes-vous?; **a train f. Paris** un train en provenance de Paris; **to be 10 m**

(away) **f. the house** être à 10 m de la maison

(b) (expressing time) à partir de; **f. today (on), as f. today** à partir d'aujourd'hui; **f. the beginning** dès le début

(c) (expressing range) **f.... to...** de... à...; **f. morning till night** du matin au soir; **they take children f. the age of five** ils acceptent les enfants à partir de cinq ans

(d) (expressing source) de; **to take/ borrow sth f. sb** prendre/emprunter qch à qn; **to drink f. a cup** boire dans une tasse

(e) (expressing removal) de; **to take sth f. sb** prendre qch à qn; **to take sth f. a box/f. the table** prendre qch dans une boîte/sur la table

(f) (according to) d'après; **f. what I saw...** d'après ce que j'ai vu...

(g) (on behalf of) de la part de; **tell her f. me** dis-lui de ma part

front [frʌnt] **1** n devant m; (of boat, car) avant m; (of building) façade f; (of crowd) premier rang m; Mil, Pol & Met front m; **in f. of sb/sth** devant qn/qch; **in f.** devant; (further ahead) en avant; (in race) en tête **2** adj (tooth, garden) de devant; (car seat) avant inv. (row, page) premier, -ère; **f. door** porte f d'entrée **3** vt (organization) être à la tête de; (TV programme) présenter ■ **frontrunner** n Fig favori, -ite mf ■ **front-wheel** adj Aut **f. drive** traction f avant

frontier ['frʌntɪə(r)] n frontière f

frost [frɒst] **1** n gel m **2** vi **to f. up** (of window) se couvrir de givre

frostbite ['frɒstbaɪt] n gelure f ■ **frostbitten** adj gelé

frosting ['frɒstɪŋ] n Am (on cake) glaçage m

frosty ['frɒstɪ] (-ier, -iest) adj (air, night) glacé; Fig (welcome) glacial; **it's f.** il gèle

froth [frɒθ] **1** n (on beer) mousse f; (on waves) écume f **2** vi (liquid) mousser ■ **frothy** (-ier, -iest) adj (beer) mousseux, -euse

frown [fraʊn] **1** n froncement m de

sourcils **2** *vi* froncer les sourcils; *Fig* **to f. (up)on** désapprouver

froze [frəʊz] *pt of* **freeze**

frozen ['frəʊzən] *pp of* **freeze**

frugal ['fruːgəl] *adj* frugal

fruit [fruːt] *n* fruit *m*; **some f.** *(one item)* un fruit; *(more than one)* des fruits; **f. juice** jus *m* de fruits; **f. salad** salade *f* de fruits; *Br* **f. machine** *(for gambling)* machine *f* à sous ■ **fruitcake** *n* cake *m*

fruitful ['fruːtfəl] *adj* *(meeting, discussion)* fructueux, -euse ■ **fruitless** *adj* *(attempt, search)* infructueux, -euse

frustrate [frʌ'streɪt] *vt* *(person)* frustrer; *(plans)* contrarier ■ **frustrating** *adj* frustrant ■ **frustration** *n* frustration *f*

fry [fraɪ] *(pt & pp* **fried) 1** *vt* faire frire **2** *vi* frire ■ **frying** *n* **f. pan** poêle *f* (à frire)

ft *(abbr* **foot, feet)** pied(s) *m(pl)*

fudge [fʌdʒ] **1** *n* *(sweet)* caramel *m* mou **2** *vt* **to f. the issue** éluder une question

fuel [fjʊəl] *n* combustible *m*; *(for engine)* carburant *m*; **f. oil** mazout *m*; **f. tank** *(in vehicle)* réservoir *m*

fugitive ['fjuːdʒɪtɪv] *n* fugitif, -ive *mf*

fulfil [fʊl'fɪl] *(Am* **fulfill)** *(pt & pp* -ll-) *vt* *(ambition, dream)* réaliser; *(condition, duty)* remplir; *(desire, need)* satisfaire ■ **fulfilling** *adj* satisfaisant ■ **fulfilment** *(Am* **fulfillment)** *n* *(of ambition)* réalisation *f* (**of** de); *(satisfaction)* épanouissement *m*

full [fʊl] **1** (-er, -est) *adj* plein (**of** de); *(bus, theatre, hotel, examination)* complet, -ète; *(amount)* intégral; *(day, programme)* chargé; *(skirt)* bouffant; **to be f. (up)** *(of person)* n'avoir plus faim; *(of hotel)* être complet; **at f. speed** à toute vitesse; **f. name** nom et prénom; *Br* **f. stop** point *m*

2 *n* **in f.** *(pay)* intégralement; *(write)* en toutes lettres

3 *adv* **to know f. well** savoir fort bien ■ **full-length** *adj* *(portrait)* en pied; *(dress)* long (*f* longue); **f. film** long métrage *m* ■ **full-scale** *adj* *(model)* grandeur nature *inv*; *(operation)* de grande

envergure ■ **full-time** *adj & adv (work)* à plein temps

fully ['fʊlɪ] *adv (completely)* entièrement; *(understand)* parfaitement; *(at least)* au moins ■ **fully-fledged** *(Am* **full-fledged)** *adj (engineer, teacher)* diplômé; *(member)* à part entière ■ **fully-grown** *adj* adulte

fumble ['fʌmbəl] *vi* **to f. (about)** *(grope)* tâtonner; *(search)* fouiller (**for** pour trouver)

fume [fjuːm] *vi* **to be fuming** *(of person)* rager ■ **fumes** *npl* émanations *fpl*; *(from car)* gaz *mpl* d'échappement

fun [fʌn] *n* plaisir *m*; **for f., for the f. of it** pour le plaisir; **to be (good** or **great) f.** être (très) amusant; **to have (some) f.** s'amuser; **to make f. of sb/ sth** se moquer de qn/qch

function ['fʌŋkʃən] **1** *n (role, duty) & Comptr* fonction *f*; *(party)* réception *f* **2** *vi* fonctionner; **to f. as** faire fonction de ■ **functional** *adj* fonctionnel, -elle

fund [fʌnd] **1** *n (of money)* fonds *m*; **funds** fonds *mpl* **2** *vt* financer

fundamental [fʌndə'mentəl] *adj* fondamental

funeral ['fjuːnərəl] *n* enterrement *m*; *(grandiose)* funérailles *fpl*; **f. service** service *m* funèbre; *Br* **f. parlour,** *Am* **f. home** entreprise *f* de pompes funèbres

funfair ['fʌnfeə(r)] *n Br* fête *f* foraine

fungus ['fʌŋgəs] *(pl* -gi [-gaɪ]) *n (plant)* champignon *m*; *(on walls)* moisissure *f*

funnel ['fʌnəl] *n* (a) *(of ship)* cheminée *f* (b) *(for filling)* entonnoir *m*

funny ['fʌnɪ] (-ier, -iest) *adj (amusing)* drôle; *(strange)* bizarre; **a f. idea** une drôle d'idée ■ **funnily** *adv* **f. enough, I was just about to...** bizarrement, j'étais sur le point de...

fur [fɜː(r)] **1** *n (of animal, for wearing)* fourrure *f*; *(of dog, cat)* poil *m*; **f. coat** manteau *m* de fourrure **2** *(pt & pp* -rr-) *vi Br* **to f. (up)** *(of kettle)* s'entartrer

furious ['fjʊərɪəs] *adj (violent, angry)* furieux, -euse (**with** or **at** contre); *(efforts, struggle)* violent

furnace ['fɜːnɪs] *n (forge)* fourneau *m*

furnish ['fɜːnɪʃ] *vt* (**a**) *(room, house)* meubler (**b**) *(supply)* fournir (**sb with sth** qch à qn) ▪ **furnishings** *npl* ameublement *m*

furniture ['fɜːnɪtʃə(r)] *n* meubles *mpl*; **a piece of f.** un meuble

furrow ['fʌrəʊ] *n (in earth, on brow)* sillon *m*

furry ['fɜːrɪ] *adj (animal)* à poil; *(toy)* en peluche

further ['fɜːðə(r)] **1** *adv & adj* = **farther 2** *adj (additional)* supplémentaire; *Br* **f. education** = enseignement supérieur dispensé par un établissement autre qu'une université **3** *adv (more)* davantage **4** *vt (cause, research, career)* promouvoir ▪ **furthermore** *adv* en outre ▪ **furthest** *adj & adv* = **farthest**

furtive ['fɜːtɪv] *adj* sournois

fury ['fjʊərɪ] *n (violence, anger)* fureur *f*

fuse [fjuːz] **1** *n (wire)* fusible *m*; *(of bomb)* amorce *f* **2** *vt (join)* fusionner; *Br* **to f. the lights** faire sauter les plombs **3** *vi Br* **the lights have fused** les plombs ont sauté

fusion ['fjuːʒən] *n* fusion *f*

fuss [fʌs] **1** *n* histoires *fpl*; **to kick up** *or* **make a f.** faire des histoires; **to make a f. of sb** être aux petits soins pour qn **2** *vi* faire des histoires; **to f. over sb** être aux petits soins pour qn ▪ **fussy (-ier, -iest)** *adj* exigeant (**about** sur); **I'm not f.** *(I don't mind)* ça m'est égal

futile [*Br* 'fjuːtaɪl, *Am* 'fjuːtəl] *adj (remark)* futile; *(attempt)* vain

futon ['fuːtɒn] *n* futon *m*

future ['fjuːtʃə(r)] **1** *n* avenir *m*; *(in grammar)* futur *m*; **in (the) f.** à l'avenir **2** *adj* futur; **my f. wife** ma future épouse; **the f. tense** le futur

fuze [fjuːz] *n & vti Am* = **fuse**

fuzzy ['fʌzɪ] **(-ier, -iest)** *adj* (**a**) *(unclear) (picture, idea)* flou (**b**) *(hair)* crépu

Gg

G, g [dʒiː] *n (letter)* G, g *m inv*

gabble ['gæbəl] *vi (chatter)* jacasser; *(indistinctly)* bredouiller

gable ['geɪbəl] *n* pignon *m*

gadget ['gædʒɪt] *n* gadget *m*

gaffe [gæf] *n (blunder)* gaffe *f*

gag [gæg] **1** *n* (a) *(on mouth)* bâillon *m* (b) *Fam (joke)* blague *f* **2** *(pt & pp -gg-)* *vt (person)* bâillonner; *Fig (press)* museler **3** *vi (choke)* s'étouffer (**on** avec)

gaily ['geɪlɪ] *adv* gaiement

gain [geɪn] **1** *n (increase)* augmentation *f* (**in** de); *(profit)* gain *m*; *Fig (advantage)* avantage *m* **2** *vt (obtain, win)* gagner; *(experience, reputation)* acquérir; **to g. speed/weight** prendre de la vitesse/du poids **3** *vi (of clock)* avancer; **to g. on sb** gagner du terrain sur qn; **to g. by sth** bénéficier de qch

gala [*Br* 'gɑːlə, *Am* 'geɪlə] *n* gala *m*; *Br* **swimming g.** concours *m* de natation

galaxy ['gæləksɪ] *(pl -ies)* *n* galaxie *f*

gale [geɪl] *n* grand vent *m*

gallant ['gælənt] *adj (brave)* brave; *(polite)* galant

gallery ['gælərɪ] *(pl -ies)* *n (room)* galerie *f*; *(museum)* musée *m*; *(for public, press)* tribune *f*

Gallic ['gælɪk] *adj (French)* français

gallon ['gælən] *n* gallon *m* (*Br* = 4,5 *l*, *Am* = 3,8 *l*)

gallop ['gæləp] **1** *n* galop *m* **2** *vi* galoper

gamble ['gæmbəl] **1** *n (risk)* coup *m* risqué **2** *vt (bet)* parier, jouer **3** *vi* jouer (**on** sur; **with** avec); **to g. on sth** *(count on)* miser sur qch ▪ **gambler** *n* joueur, -euse *mf* ▪ **gambling** *n* jeu *m*

game¹ [geɪm] *n* (a) *(activity)* jeu *m*; *(of football, cricket)* match *m*; *(of tennis, chess, cards)* partie *f*; **to have a g. of football/tennis** faire un match de football/une partie de tennis; *Br* **games** *(in school)* le sport; **g. show** *(on television)* jeu *m* télévisé; *(on radio)* jeu *m* radiophonique (b) *(animals, birds)* gibier *m*

game² [geɪm] *adj (brave)* courageux, -euse; **to be g. (to do sth)** être partant (pour faire qch)

gammon ['gæmən] *n Br* jambon *m*

gang [gæŋ] **1** *n (of children, friends)* bande *f*; *(of workers)* équipe *f*; *(of criminals)* gang *m* **2** *vi* **to g. up on** *or* **against** se mettre à plusieurs contre

gangster ['gæŋstə(r)] *n* gangster *m*

gangway ['gæŋweɪ] *n Br* passage *m*; *(in train, plane)* couloir *m*; *(on ship)* passerelle *f*; *(in bus, cinema, theatre)* allée *f*

gaol [dʒeɪl] *n & vt Br* = **jail**

gap [gæp] *n (space)* espace *m* (**between** entre); *(in wall, fence)* trou *m*; *(in time)* intervalle *m*; *(in knowledge)* lacune *f*

gape [geɪp] *vi (stare)* rester bouche bée; **to g. at sb/sth** regarder qn/qch bouche bée ▪ **gaping** *adj* béant

garage [*Br* 'gærɑː(d)ʒ, 'gærɪdʒ, *Am* gə'rɑːʒ] *n* garage *m*

garbage ['gɑːbɪdʒ] *n Am* ordures *fpl*; **g. can** poubelle *f*; **g. man** *or* **collector** éboueur *m*

garbanzo [gɑː'bænzəʊ] *n* **g. (bean)** pois *m* chiche

garbled ['gɑːbəld] *adj* confus

garden ['gɑːdən] **1** *n* jardin *m*; **gardens** *(park)* parc *m*; **g. centre** jardinerie *f*; **g. party** garden-party *f* **2** *vi* jardiner, faire du jardinage ▪ **gardener** *n* jardinier, -ère *mf* ▪ **gardening** *n* jardinage *m*

gargle ['gɑːgəl] *vi* se gargariser

garish [*Br* 'geərɪʃ, *Am* 'gærɪʃ] *adj*

(clothes) voyant; *(colour)* criard *(light)* cru

garland ['gɑːlənd] *n* guirlande *f*

garlic ['gɑːlɪk] *n* ail *m*; **g. bread** = pain chaud au beurre d'ail

garment ['gɑːmənt] *n* vêtement *m*

garnish ['gɑːnɪʃ] **1** *n* garniture *f* **2** *vt* garnir (**with** de)

garter ['gɑːtə(r)] *n (round leg)* arretière *f*; *(for socks)* fixe-chaussette *m*; *Am (attached to belt)* jarretelle *f*

gas [gæs] **1** *n* gaz *m inv*; *Am (gasoline)* essence *f*; *Br* **g. cooker** cuisinière *f* à gaz; *Br* **g. heater, g. fire** radiateur *m* à gaz; *Am* **g. station** station-service *f*; **g. stove** *(large)* cuisinière *f* à gaz; *(portable)* réchaud *m* à gaz; *Am* **g. tank** réservoir *m* à essence **2** *(pt & pp -ss-)* *vt (person)* asphyxier; *(deliberately)* gazer

gash [gæʃ] **1** *n* entaille *f* **2** *vt* **to g. one's knee** se faire une blessure profonde au genou

gasoline ['gæsəliːn] *n Am* essence *f*

gasp [gɑːsp] **1** *n* halètement *m*; *(of surprise)* sursaut *m* **2** *vi* avoir le souffle coupé (**with** *or* **in** de); **to g. for breath** haleter

gassy ['gæsɪ] *(-ier, -iest)* *adj* gazeux, -euse

gastric ['gæstrɪk] *adj* gastrique

gate [geɪt] *n (in garden, field)* barrière *f*; *(made of metal)* grille *f*; *(of castle, at airport)* porte *f*; *(at stadium)* entrée *f*

gâteau ['gætəʊ] *(pl -eaux* [-əʊz]*) n Br (cake)* gros gâteau *m* à la crème

gatecrash ['geɪtkræʃ] *vt* **to g. a party** s'inviter à une réception

gateway ['geɪtweɪ] *n* entrée *f*

gather ['gæðə(r)] **1** *vt* (**a**) *(people, objects)* rassembler; *(pick up)* ramasser; *(flowers, fruit)* cueillir; *(information)* recueillir; **to g. speed** prendre de la vitesse; **to g. in** *(crops, harvest)* rentrer **to g. one's strength** rassembler ses forces (**b**) *(understand)* **I g. that...** je crois comprendre que... (**c**) *(sew pleats in)* froncer

2 *vi* *(of people)* se rassembler; *(of clouds)* se former; *(of dust)* s'accumuler; **to g. round** *(come closer)* s'approcher;

to g. round sb entourer qn

gathering ['gæðərɪŋ] *n (group)* rassemblement *m*

gauge [geɪdʒ] **1** *n (instrument)* jauge *f*; *Fig* **to be a g. of sth** permettre de jauger qch **2** *vt* évaluer

gaunt [gɔːnt] *adj* décharné

gauze [gɔːz] *n* gaze *f*

gave [geɪv] *pt of* **give**

gawk [gɔːk], **gawp** [gɔːp] *vi* **to g. at sb/sth** regarder qn/qch bouche bée

gay [geɪ] *(-er, -est)* **1** *adj* (**a**) *(homosexual)* homosexuel, -elle (**b**) *Old-fashioned (cheerful)* gai **2** *n* homosexuel, -elle *mf*

gaze [geɪz] **1** *n* regard *m* **2** *vi* **to g. at sb/sth** regarder fixement qn/qch

GB [dʒiː'biː] *(abbr* **Great Britain**) *n* GB

GCSE [dʒiːsiːes'iː] *(abbr* **General Certificate of Secondary Education**) *n Br* = diplôme de fin de premier cycle de l'enseignement secondaire, sanctionnant une matière déterminée

gear [gɪə(r)] **1** *n* (**a**) *Fam (equipment)* attirail *m*; *(belongings)* affaires *fpl*; *(clothes)* fringues *fpl* (**b**) *(on car, bicycle)* vitesse *f*; **in g.** *(vehicle)* en prise; *Br* **g. lever,** *Am* **g. shift** levier *m* de *(changement de)* vitesse **2** *vt* **to g. sth to sth** adapter qch à qch; **to be geared up to do sth** être prêt à faire qch ▪ **gearbox** *n* boîte *f* de vitesses

geese [giːs] *pl of* **goose**

gel [dʒel] *n* gel *m*

gelatin(e) [*Br* 'dʒelətiːn, *Am* -tən] *n* gélatine *f*

gem [dʒem] *n (stone)* pierre *f* précieuse; *Fig (person)* perle *f*; *Fig (thing)* bijou *m* *(pl* -oux*)*

gen [dʒen] *Br Fam* **1** *n (information)* tuyaux *mpl* **2** *(pt & pp -nn-)* *vi* **to g. up on sb/sth** se rancarder sur qn/qch

gender ['dʒendə(r)] *n (in grammar)* genre *m*; *(of person)* sexe *m*

gene [dʒiːn] *n Biol* gène *m*

general ['dʒenərəl] **1** *adj* général; **in g.** en général; **the g. public** le grand public; *Am* **g. delivery** poste *f* restante **2** *n Mil* général *m*

generalize ['dʒenərəlaɪz] vi générali-
ser ∎ **generalization** [-'zeɪʃən] n géné-
ralisation f

generally ['dʒenərəlɪ] adv générale-
ment; **g. speaking** de manière géné-
rale

generate ['dʒenəreɪt] vt (fear, hope,
unemployment) engendrer; (heat, elec-
tricity) produire; (interest, ideas) faire
naître; (jobs) créer

generation [dʒenə'reɪʃən] n (of peo-
ple, products) génération f; (of electri-
city) production f; **g. gap** conflit m des
générations

generator ['dʒenəreɪtə(r)] n généra-
teur m

generosity [dʒenə'rɒsɪtɪ] n généro-
sité f

generously ['dʒenərəslɪ] adv géné-
reusement

genesis ['dʒenəsɪs] n genèse f

genetic [dʒɪ'netɪk] adj génétique; **g.
engineering** génie m génétique ∎ **ge-
netically** adv **g. modified** génétique-
ment modifié ∎ **genetics** n génétique f

Geneva [dʒɪ'niːvə] n Genève m ou f

genitals ['dʒenɪtəlz] npl organes mpl
génitaux

genius ['dʒiːnɪəs] n (ability, person)
génie m

gent [dʒent] n Br Fam monsieur m;
gents' shoes chaussures fpl pour
hommes; **the gents** (toilet) les toilettes
fpl des hommes

gentle ['dʒentəl] (-er, -est) adj (person,
sound, slope) doux (f douce); (hint) dis-
cret, -ète; (exercise, speed) modéré
∎ **gently** adv doucement; (land) en
douceur

gentleman ['dʒentəlmən] (pl -men) n
monsieur m; (well-bred) gentleman m

genuine ['dʒenjʊɪn] adj (leather, dia-
mond) véritable; (signature, work of
art) authentique; (sincere) sincère
∎ **genuinely** adv (sincerely) sincère-
ment

geography [dʒɪ'ɒgrəfɪ] n géogra-
phie f ∎ **geographical** [dʒɪə'græfɪkəl]
adj géographique

geology [dʒɪ'ɒlədʒɪ] n géologie f

∎ **geological** [dʒɪə'lɒdʒɪkəl] adj géo-
logique

geometry [dʒɪ'ɒmɪtrɪ] n géométrie f
∎ **geometric(al)** [dʒɪə'metrɪk(əl)] adj
géométrique

geriatric [dʒerɪ'ætrɪk] adj (hospital)
gériatrique

germ [dʒɜːm] n (causing disease) mi-
crobe m

German ['dʒɜːmən] **1** adj allemand; **G.
teacher** professeur m d'allemand; **G.
measles** rubéole f **2** n (person) Alle-
mand, -e mf; (language) allemand m

Germany ['dʒɜːmənɪ] n l'Allemagne f

germinate ['dʒɜːmɪneɪt] vi (of seed,
idea) germer

gesticulate [dʒe'stɪkjʊleɪt] vi gesti-
culer

gesture ['dʒestʃə(r)] **1** n geste m **2** vi
to g. to sb to do sth faire signe à qn
de faire qch

GET [get] (pt & Br pp got, Am pp got-
ten, pres p getting) **1** vt (obtain) obte-
nir, avoir; (find) trouver; (buy) acheter;
(receive) recevoir; (catch) attraper;
(bus, train) prendre; (seize) prendre,
saisir; (fetch) aller chercher; (put) met-
tre; (derive) tirer (from de); (prepare)
préparer; (lead) mener; (hit with fist,
stick) atteindre; (reputation) se faire;
Fam (understand) piger; Fam (annoy)
énerver; **to g. sb to do sth** faire faire
qch à qn; **to g. sth done** faire faire qch;
to g. sth clean/dirty nettoyer/salir
qch; **to g. sth to sb** (send) faire parve-
nir qch à qn; **to g. sb to the station**
amener qn à la gare; **can I g. you any-
thing?** je te rapporte quelque chose?
2 vi (go) aller (**to** à); (arrive) arriver (**to**
à); (become) devenir; **to g. old** vieillir;
to g. caught/run over se faire pren-
dre/écraser; **to g. dressed/washed**
s'habiller/se laver; **to g. paid** être payé;
where have you got or Am **gotten
to?** où en es-tu?; **you've got to stay**
(must) tu dois rester; **to g. to do sth**
(succeed in doing) parvenir à faire qch;
to g. going (leave) se mettre en route;
(start working) se mettre au travail
∎ **getaway** n (escape) fuite f ∎ **get-**

together *n Fam* réunion *f* ∎ **get-up** *n Fam (clothes)* accoutrement *m*

▸ **get about** *vi* se déplacer; *(of news)* circuler

▸ **get across 1** *vt sep (message)* faire passer **2** *vi (succeed in crossing)* traverser; **to g. across to sb that...** faire comprendre à qn que...

▸ **get along** *vi (manage)* se débrouiller; *(progress)* avancer; *(be on good terms)* s'entendre (**with** avec); *(leave)* s'en aller

▸ **get around** *vi* = **get about**

▸ **get at** *vt insep (reach)* atteindre; **what is he getting at?** où veut-il en venir?

▸ **get away** *vi (leave)* s'en aller; *(escape)* se sauver; **to g. away with a fine** s'en tirer avec une amende; **he got away with that crime** il n'a pas été inquiété pour ce crime

▸ **get back 1** *vt sep (recover)* récupérer; **to g. one's own back on sb** se venger de qn **2** *vi (return)* revenir; **to g. back at sb** se venger de qn

▸ **get by** *vi (manage)* se débrouiller

▸ **get down 1** *vi (go down)* descendre (**from** de); **to g. down to** *(work)* se mettre à **2** *vt sep (bring down)* descendre (**from** de); *Fam* **to g. sb down** *(depress)* déprimer qn **3** *vt insep* **to g. down the stairs/a ladder** descendre l'escalier/d'une échelle

▸ **get in 1** *vt sep (stock up with)* faire provision de; **to g. sb in** *(call for)* faire venir qn **2** *vi (enter)* entrer; *(come home)* rentrer; *(enter vehicle or train)* monter; *(arrive)* arriver; *(be elected)* être élu

▸ **get into** *vt insep* entrer dans; *(vehicle, train)* monter dans; *(habit)* prendre; **to g. into bed/a rage** se mettre au lit/en colère

▸ **get off 1** *vt sep (remove)* enlever; *(send)* expédier; *(in court)* faire acquitter; *Fam* **to g. off doing sth** se dispenser de faire qch **2** *vt insep* **to g. off a chair** se lever d'une chaise; **to g. off a bus** descendre d'un bus **3** *vi (leave)* partir; *(from vehicle or train)* descendre (**from** de); *(escape punishment)* s'en tirer

▸ **get on 1** *vt sep (shoes, clothes)* mettre

2 *vt insep (bus, train)* monter dans **3** *vi (enter bus or train)* monter; *(manage)* se débrouiller; *(succeed)* réussir; *(be on good terms)* s'entendre (**with** avec); **how are you getting on?** comment ça va?; **how did you g. on?** *(in exam)* comment ça s'est passé?; **to be getting on (in years)** se faire vieux (*f* vieille); **to g. onto sb** *(on phone)* contacter qn; **to g. on with** *(task)* continuer

▸ **get out 1** *vt sep (remove)* enlever; *(bring out)* sortir **2** *vi* sortir; *(from vehicle or train)* descendre (**of** or **from** de); **to g. out of** *(obligation)* échapper à; *(danger)* se tirer de; *(habit)* perdre

▸ **get over 1** *vt sep (ideas)* faire passer; **let's g. it over with** finissons-en **2** *vt insep (illness)* se remettre de; *(shock)* revenir de

▸ **get round 1** *vt insep (obstacle)* contourner **2** *vi (visit)* passer; **to g. round to doing sth** trouver le temps de faire qch

▸ **get through 1** *vt sep (communicate)* **to g. sth through to sb** faire comprendre qch à qn **2** *vt insep (hole)* passer par; *(task)* venir à bout de; *(exam, interview)* survivre à; *(food)* consommer **3** *vi (pass)* passer; *(pass exam)* être reçu; **to g. through to sb** *(communicate with)* se faire comprendre de qn; *(on the phone)* obtenir la communication avec qn

▸ **get together** *vi (of people)* se réunir

▸ **get up 1** *vt sep* **to g. sb up** *(out of bed)* faire lever qn; **to g. sth up** *(bring up)* monter qch **2** *vt insep (ladder, stairs)* monter **3** *vi (rise, stand up)* se lever (**from** de); **to g. up to something** *or* **to mischief** faire des bêtises; **where have you got up to?** *(in book)* où en es-tu?

ghastly ['gɑːstlɪ] (**-ier, -iest**) *adj (horrible)* épouvantable

gherkin ['gɜːkɪn] *n* cornichon *m*

ghetto ['getəʊ] (*pl* **-oes** *or* **-os**) *n* ghetto *m*; *Fam* **g. blaster** radiocassette *f*

ghost [gəʊst] *n* fantôme *m*; **g. story** histoire *f* de fantômes ∎ **ghostly** *adj* spectral

giant ['dʒaɪənt] **1** *adj (tree, packet)* géant **2** *n* géant *m*

gibe [dʒaɪb] **1** *n* moquerie *f* **2** *vi* **to g. at sb** se moquer de qn

giddy ['gɪdɪ] **(-ier, -iest)** *adj* **to be** *or* **feel g.** avoir le vertige; **to make sb g.** donner le vertige à qn

gift [gɪft] *n* cadeau *m*; *(talent, donation)* don *m*; *Br* **g. voucher** *or* **token** chèque-cadeau *m* ▪ **gifted** *adj* doué **(with** de; **for** pour)

gift-wrapped ['gɪftræpt] *adj* sous paquet-cadeau

gig [gɪg] *n Fam (pop concert)* concert *m*

gigantic [dʒaɪ'gæntɪk] *adj* gigantesque

giggle ['gɪgəl] **1** *n* petit rire *m* bête **2** *vi* rire (bêtement)

gilt [gɪlt] **1** *adj* doré **2** *n* dorure *f*

gimmick ['gɪmɪk] *n (trick, object)* truc *m*

gin [dʒɪn] *n (drink)* gin *m*

ginger ['dʒɪndʒə(r)] **1** *adj (hair)* roux *(f* rousse) **2** *n (spice)* gingembre *m*; **g. beer** limonade *f* au gingembre ▪ **gingerbread** *n* pain *m* d'épice

gipsy ['dʒɪpsɪ] *(pl* **-ies)** *n* bohémien, -enne *mf*; *(Eastern European)* tsigane *mf*; *(Spanish)* gitan, -e *mf*

giraffe [dʒɪ'ræf, *Br* dʒɪ'rɑːf] *n* girafe *f*

girl [gɜːl] *n (child)* (petite) fille *f*, fillette *f*; *(young woman)* jeune fille *f*; **English g.** jeune Anglaise *f*; **G. Guide** éclaireuse *f* ▪ **girlfriend** *n (of girl)* amie *f*; *(of boy)* petite amie *f* ▪ **girlish** *adj* de (jeune) fille

giro ['dʒaɪrəʊ] *(pl* **-os)** *n Br* **bank g.** virement *m* bancaire; **g. account** compte *m* courant postal, CCP *m*

gist [dʒɪst] *n* **to get the g. of sth** saisir l'essentiel de qch

GIVE [gɪv] **1** *n (of fabric)* élasticité *f* **2** *(pt* **gave***, pp* **given)** *vt* donner; *(as present)* offrir; *(support)* apporter; *(smile, gesture, pleasure)* faire; *(sigh)* pousser; *(look)* jeter; *(blow)* porter; **to g. sth to sb, to g. sb sth** donner *ou* offrir qch à qn; **to g. way** *(of branch, person)* céder; *(of roof)* s'effondrer; *(in* *vehicle)* céder la priorité **(to** à)

3 *vi* (a) *(donate)* donner **(b)** *(of shoes)* se faire; *(of support)* céder

▸**give away** *vt sep (prize)* distribuer; *(money)* donner; *(betray)* trahir

▸**give back** *vt sep (return)* rendre

▸**give in 1** *vt sep (hand in)* remettre **2** *vi (surrender)* céder **(to** à)

▸**give off** *vt sep (smell, heat)* dégager

▸**give out** *vt sep (hand out)* distribuer; *(make known)* annoncer

▸**give over** *vi Br Fam* **g. over!** arrête!

▸**give up 1** *vt sep (possessions)* abandonner; *(activity)* renoncer à; *(seat)* céder **(to** à); **to g. up smoking** cesser de fumer **2** *vi* abandonner

given ['gɪvən] **1** *pp of* **give 2** *adj (fixed)* donné **3** *conj (considering)* étant donné; **g. that...** étant donné que...

glacier [*Br* 'glæsɪə(r), *Am* 'gleɪʃər] *n* glacier *m*

glad [glæd] *adj (person)* content **(of/about** de; **that** que + *subjunctive)* ▪ **gladly** *adv* volontiers

glamorous ['glæmərəs] *adj (person, dress)* élégant; *(job)* prestigieux, -euse

glance [glɑːns] **1** *n* coup *m* d'œil **2** *vi* **to g. at sb/sth** jeter un coup d'œil à qn/qch

gland [glænd] *n* glande *f*

glare [gleə(r)] **1** *n (look)* regard *m* furieux **2** *vi* **to g. at sb** foudroyer qn (du regard) ▪ **glaring** *adj (light)* éblouissant; *(eyes)* furieux, -euse; **a g. mistake** une faute grossière

glass [glɑːs] **1** *n* verre *m* **2** *adj (bottle)* de verre; **g. door** porte *f* vitrée ▪ **glassful** *n* (plein) verre *m*

glasses ['glɑːsɪz] *npl (spectacles)* lunettes *fpl*

glaze [gleɪz] **1** *n (on pottery)* vernis *m* **2** *vt (window)* vitrer; *(pottery)* vernisser

gleam [gliːm] **1** *n* lueur *f* **2** *vi* luire

glean [gliːn] *vt (information)* glaner

glee [gliː] *n* joie *f*

glen [glen] *n Scot* vallon *m*

glide [glaɪd] *vi* glisser; *(of aircraft, bird)* planer ▪ **glider** *n (aircraft)* planeur *m* ▪ **gliding** *n (sport)* vol *m* à voile

glimmer ['glɪmə(r)] **1** n (light, of hope) faible lueur f **2** vi luire (faiblement)

glimpse [glɪmps] **1** n aperçu m; **to catch** or **get a g. of sth** entrevoir qch **2** vt entrevoir

glint [glɪnt] vi (of light, eye) briller

glisten ['glɪsən] vi (of wet surface) briller; (of water) miroiter

glitter ['glɪtə(r)] vi scintiller

gloat [gləʊt] vi jubiler (**over** à l'idée de)

global ['gləʊbəl] adj (universal) mondial; (comprehensive) global; **g. warming** réchauffement m de la planète ▪ **globalization** n Econ mondialisation f

globe [gləʊb] n globe m

gloom [glu:m] n (sadness) morosité f; (darkness) obscurité f ▪ **gloomy** (-ier, -iest) adj (sad) morose; (dark, dismal) sombre

glorious ['glɔ:rɪəs] adj (splendid) magnifique; (full of glory) glorieux, -euse

glory ['glɔ:rɪ] **1** n gloire f; (great beauty) splendeur f **2** vi **to g. in sth** se glorifier de qch

gloss [glɒs] **1** n (shine) lustre m; **g. paint** peinture f brillante **2** vt **to g. over sth** glisser sur qch ▪ **glossy** (-ier, -iest) adj brillant; (photo) glacé; (magazine) de luxe

glossary ['glɒsərɪ] (pl -ies) n glossaire m

glove [glʌv] n gant m; **g. compartment** (in car) boîte f à gants

glow [gləʊ] **1** n (light) lueur f **2** vi (of sky, fire) rougeoyer; Fig (of eyes, person) rayonner (**with** de) ▪ **glowing** adj (account, terms, reference) enthousiaste

glue [glu:] **1** n colle f **2** vt coller (**to/on** à)

glum [glʌm] (**glummer, glummest**) adj triste

glutton ['glʌtən] n goinfre mf

GM [dʒi:'em] (abbr **genetically modified**) adj génétiquement modifié

GMT [dʒi:em'ti:] (abbr **Greenwich Mean Time**) n GMT m

gnat [næt] n moucheron m

gnaw [nɔ:] vti **to g. (at) sth** ronger qch

gnome [nəʊm] n gnome m

GO [gəʊ] **1** (pl **goes**) n (turn) tour m; (energy) dynamisme m; **to have a go at (doing) sth** essayer (de faire) qch; **at** or **in one go** d'un seul coup; **on the go** en mouvement; **to make a go of sth** réussir qch

2 (3rd person sing present tense **goes**; pt **went**; pp **gone**; pres p **going**) vt (make sound) faire; **to go it alone** se lancer en solo

3 vi aller (**to** à; **from** de); (depart) partir, s'en aller; (disappear) disparaître; (be sold) se vendre; (function) marcher; (progress) aller; (become) devenir; (of time) passer; (of hearing, strength) baisser; (of fuse) sauter; (of light bulb) griller; **to go well/badly** (of event) se passer bien/mal; **she's going to do sth** (is about to, intends to) elle va faire qch; **it's going to rain** il va pleuvoir; **it's all gone** (finished) il n'y en a plus; **to go and get sb/sth** (fetch) aller chercher qn/qch; **to go and see** aller voir; **to go riding/on a trip** faire du cheval/un voyage; **to go to a doctor/lawyer** aller voir un médecin/un avocat; **is there any beer going?** y a-t-il de la bière?; **two hours to go** encore deux heures

▸ **go about 1** vi (of person) se promener; (of rumour) circuler **2** (get on with) s'occuper de; (set about) se mettre à; **how do you go about it?** comment est-ce qu'on procède?

▸ **go across 1** vt insep traverser **2** vi (cross) traverser; (go) aller (**to** à); **to go across to sb('s)** faire un saut chez qn

▸ **go after** vt insep (chase) poursuivre; (job) essayer d'obtenir

▸ **go against** vt insep (contradict) aller à l'encontre de; (be unfavourable to) être défavorable à

▸ **go ahead** vi (take place) avoir lieu; (go in front) passer devant; **to go ahead with sth** entreprendre qch; **go ahead!** allez-y!

▸ **go along** vi (proceed) se dérouler; **to go along with sb/sth** être d'accord avec qn/qch; **we'll see as we go**

along nous verrons au fur et à mesure

▸**go around** *vi* = go about

▸**go away** *vi* partir, s'en aller

▸**go back** *vi (return)* revenir; *(step back, retreat)* reculer; **to go back to sleep** se rendormir; **to go back to doing sth** se remettre à faire qch; **to go back to** *(in time)* remonter à; **to go back on one's promise** *or* **word** revenir sur sa promesse

▸**go by 1** *vt insep (act according to)* se fonder sur; *(judge from)* juger d'après; **to go by the name of...** être connu sous le nom de... **2** *vi* passer

▸**go down 1** *vt insep (stairs, street)* descendre **2** *vi* descendre; *(fall down)* tomber; *(of ship)* sombrer; *(of sun)* se coucher; *(of temperature, price)* baisser; *(of tyre, balloon)* se dégonfler; **to go down well/badly** être bien/mal reçu

▸**go for** *vt insep (fetch)* aller chercher; *(attack)* attaquer; **the same goes for you** ça vaut aussi pour toi

▸**go forward(s)** *vi* avancer

▸**go in** *vi* (r)entrer; *(of sun)* se cacher; *Br* **to go in for** *(exam)* s'inscrire à; **she doesn't go in for cooking** elle n'est pas très portée sur la cuisine

▸**go into** *vt insep (enter)* entrer dans; *(examine)* examiner

▸**go off 1** *vt insep (lose liking for)* se lasser de **2** *vi (leave)* partir; *(go bad)* se gâter; *(of alarm)* se déclencher; *(of bomb)* exploser

▸**go on** *vi* continuer (**doing** à faire); *(travel)* poursuivre sa route; *(happen)* se passer; *(last)* durer; **to go on to sth** passer à qch; *Fam* **to go on at sb** *(nag)* s'en prendre à qn; *Fam* **to go on about sb/sth** parler sans cesse de qn/qch

▸**go out** *vi* sortir; *(of light, fire)* s'éteindre; *(of tide)* descendre; *(depart)* partir; *(date)* sortir ensemble; **to go out for a meal** aller au restaurant; **to go out with sb** sortir avec qn; **to go out to work** travailler (hors de chez soi)

▸**go over 1** *vt insep* (**a**) *(cross over)* traverser; **the ball went over the wall** la balle est passée par-dessus le mur (**b**) *(examine)* passer en revue; *(speech)* revoir **2** *vi (go)* aller (**to** à); *(to enemy)* passer (**to** à); **to go over to sb** aller vers qn; **to go over to sb's** *(visit)* faire un saut chez qn

▸**go round 1** *vt insep* **to go round a corner** tourner au coin; **to go round the shops** faire les magasins; **to go round the world** faire le tour du monde **2** *vi (turn)* tourner; *(make a detour)* faire le tour; *(of rumour)* circuler; **to go round to sb's** faire un saut chez qn; **there is enough to go round** il y en a assez pour tout le monde

▸**go through 1** *vt insep (suffer, undergo)* subir; *(examine)* passer en revue; *(search)* fouiller; *(spend)* dépenser; *(wear out)* user; *(perform)* accomplir; **to go through with sth** aller jusqu'au bout de qch **2** *vi* passer; *(of deal)* être conclu

▸**go under** *vi (of ship)* couler; *Fig (of firm)* faire faillite

▸**go up 1** *vt insep* monter **2** *vi* monter; *(explode)* sauter; **to go up to sth** *(approach)* se diriger vers qch; *(reach)* aller jusqu'à qch

▸**go with** *vt insep* aller de pair avec; **the company car goes with the job** le poste donne droit à une voiture de fonction

▸**go without** *vt insep* se passer de

goad [gəʊd] *vt* **to g. sb (on)** aiguillonner qn

go-ahead ['gəʊəhed] **1** *adj* dynamique **2** *n* **to get the g.** avoir le feu vert; **to give sb the g.** donner le feu vert à qn

goal [gəʊl] *n* but *m* ▪ **goalkeeper** *n* gardien *m* de but, goal *m* ▪ **goalpost** *n* poteau *m* de but

goat [gəʊt] *n* chèvre *f*

gobble ['gɒbəl] *vt* **to g. (up** *or* **down)** *(food)* engloutir

go-between ['gəʊbɪtwiːn] *n* intermédiaire *mf*

goblet ['gɒblɪt] *n* verre *m* à pied

god [gɒd] *n* dieu *m*; **G.** Dieu; *Fam* **oh G.!, my G.!** mon Dieu! ▪ **goddaughter** *n* filleule *f* ▪ **godfather** *n* parrain *m* ▪ **godforsaken** *adj (place)* perdu ▪ **godmother** *n* marraine *f* ▪ **godson** *n* filleul *m*

goddam(n) ['gɒdæm] *adj Am Fam* foutu

goddess ['gɒdɪs] *n* déesse *f*

godsend ['gɒdsend] *n* **to be a g.** être un don du ciel

goes [gəʊz] *3rd person sing present tense & npl of* **go**

goggles ['gɒgəlz] *npl* lunettes *fpl (de protection, de plongée)*

going ['gəʊɪŋ] **1** *n* **it's hard** *or* **heavy g.** c'est difficile **2** *adj* **the g. rate** le tarif en vigueur; **a g. concern** une affaire qui tourne ▪ **goings-on** *npl Pej* activités *fpl*

go-kart ['gəʊkɑːt] *n (for racing)* kart *m*

gold [gəʊld] **1** *n* or *m* **2** *adj (watch)* en or; *(coin, dust)* d'or; **g. medal** *(in sport)* médaille *f* d'or ▪ **golden** *adj (of gold colour)* doré; **g. rule** règle *f* d'or ▪ **goldmine** *n* mine *f* d'or ▪ **gold-plated** *adj* plaqué or ▪ **goldsmith** *n* orfèvre *m*

goldfish ['gəʊldfɪʃ] *n* poisson *m* rouge

golf [gɒlf] *n* golf *m*; **g. club** *(stick, association)* club *m* de golf; **g. course** parcours *m* de golf ▪ **golfer** *n* golfeur, -euse *mf*

gone [gɒn] **1** *pp of* **go 2** *adj Br Fam* **it's g. two** il est plus de deux heures

gong [gɒŋ] *n* gong *m*

GOOD [gʊd] **1** **(better, best)** *adj* bon (*f* bonne); *(kind)* gentil, -ille; *(well-behaved)* sage; **my g. friend** mon cher ami; **g.!** bon!, bien!; **very g.!** *(all right)* très bien!; **that isn't g. enough** *(bad)* ça ne va pas; *(not sufficient)* ça ne suffit pas; **that's g. of you** c'est gentil de ta part; **to taste g.** avoir bon goût; **to feel g.** se sentir bien; **to have g. weather** avoir beau temps; **to be g. at French** être bon en français; **to be g. at swimming/telling jokes** savoir bien nager/raconter des blagues; **to be g. with children** savoir s'y prendre avec les enfants; **a g. many, a g. deal (of)** beaucoup (de); **as g. as** *(almost)* pratiquement; **g. afternoon, g. morning** bonjour; *(on leaving someone)* au revoir; **g. evening** bonsoir; **g. night**

bonsoir; *(before going to bed)* bonne nuit

2 *n (advantage, virtue)* bien *m*; **for her (own) g.** pour son bien; **for the g. of your family/career** pour ta famille/carrière; **it will do you (some) g.** ça te fera du bien; **it's no g. crying/shouting** ça ne sert à rien de pleurer/crier; **that's no g.** *(worthless)* ça ne vaut rien; *(bad)* ça ne va pas; **for g.** *(leave, give up)* pour de bon ▪ **good-for-nothing** *n* propre-à-rien *mf* ▪ **good-looking** *adj* beau (*f* belle)

goodbye [gʊd'baɪ] *exclam & n* au revoir *(m inv)*

goodness ['gʊdnɪs] *n* bonté *f*; **my g.!** mon Dieu!

goods [gʊdz] *npl* marchandises *fpl*; **g. train** train *m* de marchandises

goodwill [gʊd'wɪl] *n (willingness)* bonne volonté *f*; *(benevolence)* bienveillance *f*

goose [guːs] *(pl* **geese**) *n* oie *f*; **g. Br pimples** *or Am* **bumps** chair *f* de poule ▪ **gooseflesh** *n* chair *f* de poule

gooseberry ['gʊzbərɪ] *(pl* **-ies**) *n* groseille *f* à maquereau

gorge [gɔːdʒ] **1** *n (ravine)* gorge *f* **2** *vt* **to g. oneself** se gaver (**on** de)

gorgeous ['gɔːdʒəs] *adj* magnifique

gorilla [gə'rɪlə] *n* gorille *m*

gormless ['gɔːmləs] *adj Br Fam* balourd

gory ['gɔːrɪ] **(-ier, -iest)** *adj (bloody)* sanglant

gosh [gɒʃ] *exclam Fam* mince (alors)!

go-slow [gəʊ'sləʊ] *n Br (strike)* grève *f* du zèle

gospel ['gɒspəl] *n* évangile *m*

gossip ['gɒsɪp] **1** *n (talk)* bavardages *mpl*; *(malicious)* cancans *mpl*; *(person)* commère *f*; **g. column** *(in newspaper)* échos *mpl* **2** *vi* bavarder; *(maliciously)* colporter des commérages

got [gɒt] *pt & Br pp of* **get**

Gothic ['gɒθɪk] *adj & n* gothique *(m)*

gotten ['gɒtən] *Am pp of* **get**

gourmet ['gʊəmeɪ] *n* gourmet *m*

govern ['gʌvən] **1** *vt (rule)* gouverner;

(city, province) administrer; *(influence)* déterminer **2** *vi (rule)* gouverner

government ['gʌvənmənt] **1** *n* gouvernement *m*; **local g.** administration *f* locale **2** *adj (decision, policy)* gouvernemental

governor ['gʌvənə(r)] *n* gouverneur *m*; *(of school)* administrateur, -trice *mf*; *(of prison)* directeur, -trice *mf*

gown [gaʊn] *n (of woman)* robe *f*; *Br (of judge, lecturer)* toge *f*

GP [dʒiː'piː] *(abbr* **general practitioner)** *n Br* généraliste *mf*

grab [græb] *(pt & pp* **-bb-)** *vt* **to g. (hold of) sb/sth** saisir qn/qch; **to g. sth from sb** arracher qch à qn

grace [greɪs] **1** *n (charm, goodwill, religious mercy)* grâce *f*; *Rel* **to say g.** dire le bénédicité; **ten days' g.** dix jours de grâce **2** *vt (adorn)* orner; *(honour)* honorer **(with** de**)** ■ **graceful** *adj (movement, person)* gracieux, -euse

gracious ['greɪʃəs] *adj (kind)* aimable **(to** envers**)**; *Fam* **good g.!** bonté divine!

grade [greɪd] **1** *n* **(a)** *(rank)* grade *m*; *(in profession)* échelon *m*; *(quality)* qualité *f*; *Am* **g. crossing** passage *m* à niveau **(b)** *Am Sch (mark)* note *f*; *(year)* classe *f*; **g. school** école *f* primaire **2** *vt (classify)* classer; *Am (exam)* noter

gradient ['greɪdɪənt] *n (slope)* dénivellation *f*

gradual ['grædʒʊəl] *adj* progressif, -ive; *(slope)* doux *(f* douce**)** ■ **gradually** *adv* progressivement

graduate 1 ['grædʒʊət] *n Br (from university)* ≃ licencié, -e *mf*; *Am (from high school)* ≃ bachelier, -ère *mf* **2** ['grædʒʊeɪt] *vi Br (from university)* ≃ obtenir sa licence; *Am (from high school)* ≃ obtenir son baccalauréat; **to g. from sth to sth** passer de qch à qch ■ **graduation** *n Univ* remise *f* des diplômes

graffiti [grə'fiːtɪ] *npl* graffiti *mpl*

grain [greɪn] *n* **(a)** *(seed, particle)* grain *m*; *(cereals)* céréales *fpl* **(b)** *(in wood, leather)* grain *m*

gram [græm] *n* gramme *m*

grammar ['græmə(r)] *n* grammaire *f*; *Br* **g. school** ≃ lycée *m* ■ **grammatical** *adj* grammatical

gramme [græm] *n* gramme *m*

grand [grænd] **1** **(-er, -est)** *adj (splendid)* grandiose; *Fam (excellent)* excellent; **g. piano** piano *m* à queue; **g. total** somme *f* totale **2** *n inv Br Fam* mille livres *fpl*; *Am Fam* mille dollars *mpl* ■ **grandchild** *(pl* **-children)** *n* petit-fils *m*, petite-fille *f*; **grandchildren** petits-enfants *mpl* ■ **grand(d)ad** *n Fam* papi *m* ■ **granddaughter** *n* petite-fille *f* ■ **grandfather** *n* grand-père *m* ■ **grandma** *n Fam* mamie *f* ■ **grandmother** *n* grand-mère *f* ■ **grandpa** *n Fam* papi *m* ■ **grandparents** *npl* grands-parents *mpl* ■ **grandson** *n* petit-fils *m*

grandstand ['grændstænd] *n* tribune *f*

granite ['grænɪt] *n* granit *m*

granny ['grænɪ] *(pl* **-ies)** *n Fam* mamie *f*

grant [grɑːnt] **1** *n* subvention *f*; *(for student)* bourse *f* **2** *vt* accorder **(to** à**)**; *(request)* accéder à; *(prayer, wish)* exaucer; *(admit)* admettre **(that** que**)**; **to take sth for granted** considérer qch comme allant de soi; **to take sb for granted** ne pas avoir d'égard pour qn

granule ['grænjuːl] *n* granule *m*

grape [greɪp] *n* grain *m* de raisin; **some grapes** du raisin; **g. juice** jus *m* de raisin

grapefruit ['greɪpfruːt] *n* pamplemousse *m*

graph [græf, grɑːf] *n* graphique *m*; **g. paper** papier *m* millimétré

graphic ['græfɪk] *adj (description)* très détaillé; **g. artist** graphiste *mf* ■ **graphics** *npl* **(computer)** g. graphiques *mpl*

grapple ['græpəl] *vi* **to g. with** *(problem)* se débattre avec

grasp [grɑːsp] **1** *n (hold)* prise *f*; *(understanding)* compréhension *f*; **within sb's g.** à la portée de qn **2** *vt (seize, understand)* saisir ■ **grasping** *adj (mean)* avide

grass [grɑːs] *n* herbe *f*; *(lawn)* gazon *m* ■ **grasshopper** *n* sauterelle *f* ■ **grassy** *adj* herbeux, -euse

grate [greɪt] **1** *n (for fireplace)* grille *f* **2** *vt (cheese, carrot)* râper **3** *vi (of sound)* grincer ■ **grater** *n* râpe *f* ■ **grating 1** *adj (sound)* grinçant **2** *n (bars)* grille *f*

grateful ['greɪtfəl] *adj* reconnaissant (**to** à; **for** de); *(words, letter)* de remerciement ■ **gratefully** *adv* avec reconnaissance

gratified ['grætɪfaɪd] *adj (pleased)* satisfait (**by** *or* **with** de; **to do** de faire) ■ **gratifying** *adj* très satisfaisant

gratis ['grætɪs, 'greɪtɪs] *adv* gratis

gratitude ['grætɪtjuːd] *n* gratitude *f* (**for** de)

gratuitous [grə'tjuːɪtəs] *adj (act)* gratuit

grave¹ [greɪv] *n* tombe *f* ■ **gravestone** *n* pierre *f* tombale ■ **graveyard** *n* cimetière *m*

grave² [greɪv] **(-er, -est)** *adj (serious)* grave; *(manner, voice)* solennel, -elle

gravel ['grævəl] *n* gravier *m*; **g. path** allée *f* de gravier

gravitate ['grævɪteɪt] *vi* **to g. towards sth** *(be drawn to)* être attiré par qch; *(move towards)* se diriger vers qch

gravity ['grævɪtɪ] *n* **(a)** *Phys (force)* pesanteur *f* **(b)** *(seriousness)* gravité *f*

gravy ['greɪvɪ] *n* = sauce à base de jus de viande

gray [greɪ] *adj, n & vi Am* = **grey**

graze¹ [greɪz] **1** *n (wound)* écorchure *f* **2** *vt (scrape)* écorcher

graze² [greɪz] *vi (of cattle)* paître

grease [griːs] **1** *n* graisse *f* **2** *vt* graisser ■ **greasy (-ier, -iest)** *adj* graisseux, -euse; *(hair, skin, food)* gras *(f* grasse)

great [greɪt] **(-er, -est)** *adj* grand; *(effort, heat)* gros *(f* grosse), grand; *Fam (very good)* génial; *Fam* **to be g. at tennis** être très doué pour le tennis; **a g. deal** *or* **number (of), a g. many** beaucoup (de); **G. Britain** la Grande-Bretagne; **Greater London** le grand Londres ■ **great-grandfather** *n* arrière-grand-père *m* ■ **great-grandmother** *n* arrière-grand-mère *f*

greatly ['greɪtlɪ] *adv* très; *(much)* beaucoup

Greece [griːs] *n* la Grèce

greed [griːd] *n* avidité *f* (**for** de); *(for food)* gourmandise *f* ■ **greedy (-ier, -iest)** *adj* avide (**for** de); *(for food)* gourmand

Greek [griːk] **1** *adj* grec *(f* grecque) **2** *n (person)* Grec *m*, Grecque *f*; *(language)* grec *m*

green [griːn] **1 (-er, -est)** *adj* vert; *Fig (immature)* inexpérimenté; *Pol* écologiste; **to turn** *or* **go g.** *(of traffic lights)* passer au vert; *(of person, garden, tree)* verdir; *Am* **g. card** ≃ permis *m* de travail **2** *n (colour)* vert *m*; *(grassy area)* pelouse *f*; **greens** *(vegetables)* légumes *mpl* verts; *Pol* **the Greens** les Verts *mpl* ■ **greenery** *n* verdure *f* ■ **greengrocer** *n Br* marchand, -e *mf* de fruits et légumes ■ **greenhouse** *n* serre *f*; **the g. effect** l'effet *m* de serre

greet [griːt] *vt (say hello to)* saluer; *(welcome)* accueillir ■ **greeting** *n* accueil *m*; **greetings** *(for birthday, festival)* vœux *mpl*

gregarious [grɪ'geərɪəs] *adj* sociable

grenade [grə'neɪd] *n (bomb)* grenade *f*

grew [gruː] *pt of* **grow**

grey [greɪ] **1** *adj* **(-er, -est)** gris; **to be going g.** grisonner **2** *n* gris *m* **3** *vi (of hair)* grisonner ■ **grey-haired** *adj* aux cheveux gris ■ **greyhound** *n* lévrier *m*

grid [grɪd] *n (bars)* grille *f*; *(on map)* quadrillage *m*

griddle ['grɪdəl] *n (for cooking)* tôle *f*

gridlock ['grɪdlɒk] *n (traffic jam)* embouteillage *m*

grief [griːf] *n* chagrin *m*; **to come to g.** échouer

grievance ['griːvəns] *n* grief *m*; **grievances** *(complaints)* doléances *fpl*

grieve [griːv] *vt* affliger **2** *vi* **to g. for sb/over sth** pleurer qn/qch

grill [grɪl] **1** *n (utensil)* gril *m*; *(dish)* grillade *f* **2** *vt* griller

grille [grɪl] *n (bars)* grille *f*

grim [grɪm] **(grimmer, grimmest)** *adj (stern)* sinistre; *Fam (bad)* lamentable

grimace ['grɪməs] **1** *n* grimace *f* **2** *vi* grimacer

grime [graɪm] *n* crasse *f* ■ **grimy** (**-ier, -iest**) *adj* crasseux, -euse

grin [grɪn] **1** *n* large sourire *m* **2** (*pt & pp* **-nn-**) *vi* avoir un large sourire

grind [graɪnd] **1** *n Fam* (*work*) corvée *f* **2** (*pt & pp* **ground**) *vt* (*coffee, pepper*) moudre; *Am* (*meat*) hacher **3** *vi* **to g. to a halt** s'immobiliser ■ **grinder** *n* **coffee g.** moulin *m* à café

grip [grɪp] **1** *n* (*hold*) prise *f*; (*handle*) poignée *f*; *Fig* **to get to grips with sth** s'attaquer à qch **2** (*pt & pp* **-pp-**) *vt* (*seize*) saisir; (*hold*) empoigner; **the audience was gripped by the play** la pièce a captivé les spectateurs ■ **gripping** *adj* passionnant

grisly ['grɪzlɪ] *adj* (*gruesome*) horrible

gristle ['grɪsəl] *n* (*in meat*) nerfs *mpl*

grit [grɪt] **1** *n* (*sand*) sable *m*; (*gravel*) gravillons *mpl* **2** (*pt & pp* **-tt-**) *vt* (a) (*road*) sabler (b) **to g. one's teeth** serrer les dents

groan [grəʊn] **1** *n* (*of pain*) gémissement *m*; (*of dissatisfaction*) grognement *m* **2** *vi* (*with pain*) gémir; (*complain*) grogner

grocer ['grəʊsə(r)] *n* épicier, -ère *mf*; **g.'s (shop)** épicerie *f* ■ **groceries** *npl* (*food*) provisions *fpl* ■ **grocery** (*pl* **-ies**) *n Am* (*shop*) épicerie *f*

groin [grɔɪn] *n* aine *f*

groom [gruːm] **1** *n* (a) (*bridegroom*) marié *m* (b) (*for horses*) lad *m* **2** *vt* (*horse*) panser; **to g. sb for sth** préparer qn pour qch

groove [gruːv] *n* (*in wood, metal*) rainure *f*; (*in record*) sillon *m*

grope [grəʊp] *vi* **to g. (about) for sth** chercher qch à tâtons

gross [grəʊs] **1** *adj* (a) (*total*) (*weight, income, profit*) brut (b) (**-er, -est**) (*coarse*) grossier, -ère; (*injustice*) flagrant **2** *n inv* grosse *f* **3** *vt* gagner brut ■ **grossly** *adv* (*negligent*) extrêmement; (*exaggerated*) grossièrement; (*unfair*) vraiment

grotesque [grəʊ'tesk] *adj* grotesque

grotto ['grɒtəʊ] (*pl* **-oes** *or* **-os**) *n* grotte *f*

grotty ['grɒtɪ] (**-ier, -iest**) *adj Br Fam* minable

ground¹ [graʊnd] **1** *n* (*earth*) terre *f*, sol *m*; (*land*) terrain *m*; (*estate*) terres *fpl*; **grounds** (*gardens*) parc *m*; *Fig* (*reasons*) motifs *mpl*; **on the g.** (*lying, sitting*) par terre; **to gain/lose g.** gagner/perdre du terrain; *Br* **g. floor** rez-de-chaussée *m* inv **2** *vt* (*aircraft*) interdire de vol ■ **grounding** *n* (*basic knowledge*) bases *fpl* (**in** de) ■ **groundless** *adj* sans fondement ■ **groundsheet** *n* tapis *m* de sol ■ **groundwork** *n* travail *m* préparatoire

ground² [graʊnd] **1** *pt & pp of* **grind 2** *adj* (*coffee*) moulu; *Am* **g. meat** viande *f* hachée **3** *npl* (**coffee**) **grounds** marc *m* (de café)

group [gruːp] **1** *n* groupe *m* **2** *vt* **to g. (together)** grouper **3** *vi* se grouper ■ **grouping** *n* (*group*) groupe *m*

grovel ['grɒvəl] (*Br* **-ll-**, *Am* **-l-**) *vi* (*be humble*) ramper, s'aplatir (**to** devant)

grow [grəʊ] **1** (*pt* **grew**, *pp* **grown**) *vt* (*vegetables*) cultiver; **to g. a beard** se laisser pousser la barbe **2** *vi* (*of person*) grandir; (*of plant, hair*) pousser; (*of economy, feeling*) croître; (*of firm, town*) se développer; (*of gap, family*) s'agrandir; **to g. to like sth** finir par aimer qch; **when I g. up** quand je serai grand; **it'll g. on you** (*of music, book*) tu finiras par t'y intéresser ■ **grower** *n* (*person*) cultivateur, -trice *mf* (**of** de) ■ **growing** *adj* (*child*) en pleine croissance; (*number, discontent*) grandissant

growl [graʊl] **1** *n* grognement *m* **2** *vi* grogner (**at** contre)

grown [grəʊn] **1** *pp of* **grow 2** *adj* (*man, woman*) adulte

grown-up ['grəʊnʌp] **1** *n* grande personne *f* **2** *adj* (*ideas, behaviour*) d'adulte

growth [grəʊθ] *n* croissance *f*; (*increase*) augmentation *f* (**in** de); (*lump*) grosseur *f* (**on** à)

grub [grʌb] *n* (a) *Fam* (*food*) bouffe *f* (b) (*insect*) larve *f*

grubby ['grʌbɪ] (**-ier, -iest**) *adj* sale

grudge [grʌdʒ] **1** *n* rancune *f*; **to have**

a g. against sb garder rancune à qn **2** *vt* **to g. sb sth** *(give)* donner qch à qn à contrecœur ▪ **grudgingly** *adv* à contrecœur

gruelling ['gruəlɪŋ] *(Am* **grueling)** *adj (journey, experience)* épuisant

gruesome ['gru:səm] *adj* horrible

gruff [grʌf] **(-er, -est)** *adj* bourru

grumble ['grʌmbəl] *vi (complain)* grommeler; **to g. about sth** rouspéter contre qch

grumpy ['grʌmpɪ] **(-ier, -iest)** *adj* grincheux, -euse

grunt [grʌnt] **1** *n* grognement *m* **2** *vti* grogner

guarantee [gærən'tiː] **1** *n* garantie *f* **2** *vt* garantir **(against** contre); *(vouch for)* se porter garant de; **to g. sb that...** garantir à qn que...

guard [gɑːd] **1** *n (supervision)* garde *f*; *(sentry)* garde *m*; *(on train)* chef *m* de train; **under g.** sous surveillance; **on one's g.** sur ses gardes; **on g. (duty)** de garde; **to catch sb off (his/her) g.** prendre qn au dépourvu **2** *vt (protect)* garder **3** *vt insep* **to g. against** *(protect oneself)* se prémunir contre; *(prevent)* empêcher; **to g. against doing sth** se garder de faire qch

guardian ['gɑːdɪən] *n (of child)* tuteur, -trice *mf*; *(protector)* gardien, -enne *mf*

guerilla, guerrilla [gə'rɪlə] *n (person)* guérillero *m*

guess [ges] **1** *n (estimate)* estimation *f*; **to make** *or* **take a g.** deviner; **at a g.** à vue de nez **2** *vt* deviner **(that** que); *(suppose)* supposer, croire **3** *vi* deviner; **I g. (so)** je crois ▪ **guesswork** *n* conjecture *f*; **by g.** au jugé

guest [gest] *n* invité, -e *mf*; *(in hotel)* client, -e *mf*; *(at meal)* convive *mf*; **g. room** chambre *f* d'amis; **g. speaker** conférencier, -ère *mf* ▪ **guesthouse** *n* pension *f* de famille

guidance ['gaɪdəns] *n (advice)* conseils *mpl*

guide [gaɪd] **1** *n (person)* guide *m*; *(indication)* indication *f*; **g. (book)** guide *m*; *Br* **(Girl) G.** éclaireuse *f*; **g. dog** chien *m* d'aveugle **2** *vt (lead)* guider

▪ **guided** *adj (missile)* guidé; **g. tour** visite *f* guidée ▪ **guidelines** *npl* directives *fpl*

guild [gɪld] *n* association *f*

guilt [gɪlt] *n* culpabilité *f* ▪ **guilty (-ier, -iest)** *adj* coupable; **to find sb g./not g.** déclarer qn coupable/non coupable

guinea ['gɪnɪ] *n* **g. pig** *(animal)* & *Fig* cobaye *m*

guise [gaɪz] *n* **under the g. of** sous l'apparence de

guitar [gɪ'tɑː(r)] *n* guitare *f* ▪ **guitarist** *n* guitariste *mf*

gulf [gʌlf] *n (in sea)* golfe *m*; *(chasm)* gouffre *m* **(between** entre)

gull [gʌl] *n* mouette *f*

gullible ['gʌlɪbəl] *adj* crédule

gulp [gʌlp] **1** *n (of drink)* gorgée *f*; **in** *or* **at one g.** d'un coup **2** *vt* **to g. (down)** engloutir **3** *vi (with surprise)* avoir la gorge serrée

gum¹ [gʌm] *n (in mouth)* gencive *f*

gum² [gʌm] **1** *n* (a) *(glue)* colle *f* (b) *(for chewing)* chewing-gum *m* **2** *(pt & pp* **-mm-)** *vt* coller

gun [gʌn] **1** *n* pistolet *m*; *(rifle)* fusil *m*; *(firing shells)* canon *m* **2** *(pt & pp* **-nn-)** *vt sep* **to g. down** abattre ▪ **gunfire** *n* coups *mpl* de feu; *(in battle)* tir *m* d'artillerie ▪ **gunpowder** *n* poudre *f* à canon ▪ **gunshot** *n* coup *m* de feu

gurgle ['gɜːgəl] *vi (of water)* gargouiller; *(of baby)* gazouiller

gush [gʌʃ] *vi* **to g. (out)** jaillir **(of** de)

gust [gʌst] **1** *n (of wind)* rafale *f* **2** *vi (of wind)* souffler par rafales

gusto ['gʌstəʊ] *n* **with g.** avec entrain

gut [gʌt] **1** *n (inside body)* intestin *m*; *Fam* **guts** *(insides)* entrailles *fpl*; *(courage)* cran *m* **2** *(pt & pp* **-tt-)** *vt (of fire)* ravager

gutter ['gʌtə(r)] *n (on roof)* gouttière *f*; *(in street)* caniveau *m* ▪ **guttering** *n* gouttières *fpl*

guy [gaɪ] *n Fam (man)* type *m*

guzzle ['gʌzəl] *vt (eat)* engloutir; *(drink)* siffler

gym [dʒɪm] *n (activity)* gym *f*; *(gymnasium)* gymnase *m*; **g. shoes** chaussures

fpl de gym ■ **gymnasium** [-'neɪzɪəm] *n* gymnase *m* ■ **gymnastics** *n* gymnastique *f*

gynaecologist [gaɪnɪ'kɒlədʒɪst]

(*Am* **gynecologist**) *n* gynécologue *mf*

gypsy ['dʒɪpsɪ] *n* = **gipsy**

gyrate [dʒaɪ'reɪt] *vi* tournoyer

Hh

H, h [eɪtʃ] *n (letter)* H, h *m inv*; **H bomb** bombe *f* H

habit ['hæbɪt] *n* **(a)** *(custom, practice)* habitude *f*; **to be in/get into the h. of doing sth** avoir/prendre l'habitude de faire qch; **to make a h. of doing sth** avoir pour habitude de faire qch **(b)** *Fam (addiction)* accoutumance *f* **(c)** *(of monk, nun)* habit *m*

habitat ['hæbɪtæt] *n (of animal, plant)* habitat *m*

habitual [hə'bɪtʃʊəl] *adj* habituel, -elle; *(smoker, drunk)* invétéré

hack [hæk] *vt (cut)* tailler

hacker ['hækə(r)] *n Comptr* pirate *m* informatique

hackneyed ['hæknɪd] *adj (saying)* rebattu

had [hæd] *pt & pp of* **have**

haemorrhage ['hemərɪdʒ] *(Am* **hemorrhage)** *n* hémorragie *f*

haemorrhoids ['hemərɔɪdz] *(Am* **hemorrhoids)** *npl Med* hémorroïdes *fpl*

hag [hæg] *n Pej* **(old) h.** vieille taupe *f*

haggard ['hægəd] *adj* hâve

haggle ['hægəl] *vi* marchander; **to h. over the price of sth** chicaner sur le prix de qch ▪ **haggling** *n* marchandage *m*

Hague [heɪg] *n* **The H.** La Haye

hail[1] [heɪl] **1** *n* grêle *f* **2** *vi* **it's hailing** il grêle

hail[2] [heɪl] **1** *vt (greet)* saluer **(as** comme); *(taxi)* héler **2** *vt insep* **to h. from** *(of person)* être originaire de

hair [heə(r)] *n (on head)* cheveux *mpl*; *(on body, of animal)* poils *mpl*; **a h.** *(on head)* un cheveu; *(on body, of animal)* un poil; **by a h.'s breadth** de justesse ▪ **hairbrush** *n* brosse *f* à cheveux ▪ **haircut** *n* coupe *f* de cheveux; **to have a h.** se faire couper les cheveux ▪ **hairdo** *(pl* **-dos)** *n Fam* coiffure *f* ▪ **hairdresser** *n* coiffeur, -euse *mf* ▪ **hairdryer** *n* sèche-cheveux *m inv* ▪ **hairgrip** *n* pince *f* à cheveux ▪ **hairnet** *n* résille *f* ▪ **hairpin** *n* épingle *f* à cheveux; **h. bend** *(in road)* virage *m* en épingle à cheveux ▪ **hairspray** *n* laque *f* ▪ **hairstyle** *n* coiffure *f*

-haired [heəd] *suff* **long-/red-h.** aux cheveux longs/roux

hairy ['heərɪ] *(-ier, -iest) adj (person, animal, body)* poilu

half [hɑːf] **1** *(pl* **halves)** *n* moitié *f*; *(part of match)* mi-temps *f*; *Br (half fare)* demi-tarif *m*; *Br (beer)* demi *m*; **h. (of) the apple** la moitié de la pomme; **h. past one** une heure et demie; **ten and a h.** dix et demi; **h. a dozen** une demi-douzaine; **to cut in h.** couper en deux

2 *adj* demi; **h. board** demi-pension *f*; **h. fare** demi-tarif *m*; **at h. price** à moitié prix

3 *adv (dressed, full, asleep)* à moitié; **h. as much as** moitié moins que ▪ **half-caste** *n* métis, -isse *mf* ▪ **half-day** *n* demi-journée *f* ▪ **half-hearted** *adj (person, manner)* peu enthousiaste ▪ **half-hour** *n* demi-heure *f* ▪ **half-light** *n* demi-jour *m* ▪ **half-open** *adj* entrouvert ▪ **half-price** *adj & adv* à moitié prix ▪ **half-term** *n Br Sch* congé *m* de milieu de trimestre ▪ **half-time** *n (in game)* mi-temps *f* ▪ **halfway** *adv (between places)* à mi-chemin **(between** entre)

hall [hɔːl] *n (room)* salle *f*; *(entrance room)* entrée *f*; *(of hotel)* hall *m*; *(mansion)* manoir *m*; *Br Univ* **h. of residence** résidence *f* universitaire

hallelujah [hælɪ'luːjə] *n & exclam* alléluia *(m)*

hallo [hə'ləʊ] *exclam* = **hello**

Hallowe'en [hæləʊ'iːn] *n* = veille de la Toussaint durant laquelle les enfants se déguisent en fantôme ou en sorcière

hallucination [həluːsɪ'neɪʃən] *n* hallucination *f*

hallway ['hɔːlweɪ] *n* entrée *f*

halo ['heɪləʊ] (*pl* -oes *or* -os) *n* auréole *f*

halt [hɔːlt] **1** *n* halte *f*; **to come to a h.** s'arrêter **2** *exclam* halte! **3** *vt* arrêter **4** *vi* (*of soldiers*) faire halte; (*of production*) s'arrêter

halve [hɑːv] *vt* (*reduce by half*) réduire de moitié; (*divide in two*) diviser en deux

ham [hæm] *n* (*meat*) jambon *m*; **h. and eggs** œufs *mpl* au jambon

hamburger ['hæmbɜːgə(r)] *n* hamburger *m*

hammer ['hæmə(r)] **1** *n* marteau *m* **2** *vt* (*nail*) enfoncer (**into** dans); (*metal*) marteler; *Fam* (*defeat*) écraser; **to h. sth out** (*agreement, plan*) mettre au point qch

hammock ['hæmək] *n* hamac *m*

hamper ['hæmpə(r)] **1** *n Br* (*for food*) panier *m*; *Am* (*laundry basket*) panier *m* à linge **2** *vt* (*hinder*) gêner

hamster ['hæmstə(r)] *n* hamster *m*

hand¹ [hænd] **1** *n* (**a**) (*part of the body*) main *f*; **to hold sth in one's h.** tenir qch à la main; **to hold hands** se tenir par la main; **by h.** (*make, sew*) à la main; **on the one h....** d'une part...; **on the other h....** d'autre part...; **to lend sb a (helping) h.** donner un coup de main à qn; **to get out of h.** (*of child*) devenir impossible; (*of situation*) devenir incontrôlable; **h. in h.** la main dans la main (**b**) (*of clock*) aiguille *f*; (*in card game*) jeu *m*; (*style of writing*) écriture *f* **2** *adj* (*luggage, grenade*) à main; (*cream, lotion*) pour les mains ▪ **handbag** *n* sac *m* à main ▪ **handball** *n* handball *m* ▪ **handbook** *n* (*manual*) manuel *m*; (*guide*) guide *m* ▪ **handbrake** *n* frein *m* à main ▪ **handmade** *adj* fait à la main ▪ **handshake** *n* poignée *f* de main

▪ **hands-on** *adj* (*experience*) pratique ▪ **handwriting** *n* écriture *f* ▪ **handwritten** *adj* écrit à la main

hand² [hænd] *vt* (*give*) donner (**to** à); **to h. sth in** remettre qch; **to h. sth out** distribuer qch; **to h. sth over** remettre qch; **to h. sth round** faire circuler qch

handful ['hændfʊl] *n* (*bunch, group*) poignée *f*

handicap ['hændɪkæp] **1** *n* (*disadvantage, in sport*) handicap *m* **2** (*pt & pp* -pp-) *vt* handicaper ▪ **handicapped** *adj* (*disabled*) handicapé

handicraft ['hændɪkrɑːft] *n* (*skill*) artisanat *m*

handkerchief ['hæŋkətʃɪf] (*pl* -chiefs) *n* mouchoir *m*

handle ['hændəl] **1** *n* (*of door*) poignée *f*; (*of knife*) manche *m*; (*of cup*) anse *f*; (*of saucepan*) queue *f* **2** *vt* (*manipulate*) manier; (*touch*) toucher à; (*deal with*) s'occuper de; (*vehicle*) manœuvrer; (*difficult child*) s'y prendre avec

handout ['hændaʊt] *n* (*leaflet*) prospectus *m*; (*money*) aumône *f*

handsome ['hænsəm] *adj* (*person, building*) beau (*f* belle); (*profit, sum*) considérable ▪ **handsomely** *adv* (*generously*) généreusement

handy ['hændɪ] (-ier, -iest) *adj* (*convenient*) commode; (*useful*) pratique; (*skilful*) habile (**at doing** à faire); **to come in h.** être utile; **the flat is h. for the shops** l'appartement est près des commerces ▪ **handyman** (*pl* -men) *n* homme *m* à tout faire

hang¹ [hæŋ] **1** *n Fam* **to get the h. of sth** piger qch **2** (*pt & pp* **hung**) *vt* suspendre (**on/from** à); (*on hook*) accrocher (**on** *or* **from** à); (*wallpaper*) poser **3** *vi* (*dangle*) pendre ▪ **hanging** *adj* suspendu (**from** à); **h. on the wall** accroché au mur ▪ **hang-up** *n Fam* complexe *m*

▸ **hang about, hang around** *vi* (*loiter*) traîner; *Fam* (*wait*) poireauter

▸ **hang down** *vi* (*dangle*) pendre

▸ **hang on** *vi* (*hold out*) tenir le coup; *Fam* (*wait*) patienter; **to h. on to sth** garder qch

▸**hang out 1** vt sep (washing) étendre **2** vi (from pocket, box) dépasser; Fam (spend time) traîner

▸**hang together** vi (of facts) se tenir

▸**hang up 1** vt sep (picture) accrocher **2** vi (on phone) raccrocher

hang² [hæŋ] (pt & pp hanged) vt (criminal) pendre (**for** pour)

hanger ['hæŋə(r)] n (**coat**) h. cintre m

hang-glider ['hæŋglaɪdə(r)] n Deltaplane m ■ **hang-gliding** n vol m libre

hangover ['hæŋəʊvə(r)] n Fam gueule f de bois

hankie, hanky ['hæŋkɪ] (pl -ies) n Fam mouchoir m

haphazard [hæp'hæzəd] adj (choice, decision) pris au hasard

happen ['hæpən] vi arriver, se produire; **to h. to sb** arriver à qn **do you h. to have...?** est-ce que par hasard vous avez...?

happily ['hæpɪlɪ] adv joyeusement; (contentedly) tranquillement; (fortunately) heureusement

happiness ['hæpɪnəs] n bonheur m

happy ['hæpɪ] (-ier, -iest) adj heureux, -euse (**to do** de faire; **about** de); **H. New Year!** bonne année!; **H. Christmas!** joyeux Noël!; **h. birthday!** joyeux anniversaire! ■ **happy-go-lucky** adj insouciant

harass [Br 'hærəs, Am hə'ræs] vt harceler ■ **harassment** n harcèlement m

harbour ['hɑːbə(r)] (Am **harbor**) **1** n port m **2** vt (fugitive) cacher; (hope, suspicion) nourrir

hard [hɑːd] (-er, -est) **1** adj (not soft, severe) dur; (difficult) difficile, dur; (water) calcaire; **to be h. on sb** être dur avec qn; **to be h. of hearing** être dur d'oreille; Fam **h. up** (broke) fauché; Comptr **h. disk** disque m dur; **h. drugs** drogues fpl dures; **h. shoulder** (on motorway) bande f d'arrêt d'urgence **2** adv (work) dur; (pull, push, hit) fort; (study) assidûment; (rain) à verse; **to think h.** réfléchir bien; **to try h.** faire de son mieux; **h. at work** en plein travail ■ **hardback** n livre m relié ■ **hardball** n (game) base-ball m; (ball) balle f

de base-ball ■ **hardboard** n aggloméré m ■ **hard-boiled** adj (egg) dur ■ **hardearned** adj (money) durement gagné; (rest) bien mérité ■ **hard-wearing** adj résistant ■ **hard-working** adj travailleur, -euse

harden ['hɑːdən] **1** vt endurcir; **to become hardened to sth** s'endurcir à qch **2** vi (of substance, attitude) durcir

hardly ['hɑːdlɪ] adv à peine; **I had h. arrived when...** j'étais à peine arrivé que...; **h. anyone/anything** presque personne/rien; **h. ever** presque jamais

hardware ['hɑːdweə(r)] n inv quincaillerie f; Comptr & Mil matériel m

hardy ['hɑːdɪ] (-ier, -iest) adj résistant

hare [heə(r)] n lièvre m

harm [hɑːm] **1** n (hurt) mal m; (wrong) tort m; **to do sb h.** faire du mal à qn **2** vt (physically) faire du mal à; (health, interests, cause) nuire à; (object) abîmer ■ **harmful** adj (influence) néfaste; (substance) nocif, -ive ■ **harmless** adj (person) inoffensif, -ive; (hobby, joke) innocent

harmonica [hɑː'mɒnɪkə] n harmonica m

harmonious [hɑː'məʊnɪəs] adj harmonieux, -euse

harmonize ['hɑːmənaɪz] **1** vt harmoniser **2** vi s'harmoniser

harmony ['hɑːmənɪ] (pl -ies) n harmonie f

harness ['hɑːnɪs] **1** n (for horse, baby) harnais m **2** vt (horse) harnacher; Fig (resources) exploiter

harp [hɑːp] **1** n harpe f **2** vi Fam **to h. on about sth** revenir sans arrêt sur qch

harrowing ['hærəʊɪŋ] adj (story) poignant; (experience) très éprouvant

harsh [hɑːʃ] (-er, -est) adj (person, treatment) dur; (winter, climate) rude; (sound, voice) strident; (light) cru; **to be h. with sb** être dur envers qn

harvest ['hɑːvɪst] **1** n moisson f; (of fruit) récolte f **2** vt moissonner; (fruit) récolter

has [hæz] see **have**

has-been ['hæzbiːn] n Fam Pej has been mf inv

hashish ['hæʃiːʃ] *n* haschisch *m*

hassle ['hæsəl] *n Fam* embêtements *mpl*

haste [heɪst] *n* hâte *f*; **in h.** à la hâte; **to make h.** se hâter

hasten ['heɪsən] **1** *vt* hâter **2** *vi* se hâter (**to do** de faire)

hasty ['heɪstɪ] (**-ier, -iest**) *adj (departure)* précipité; *(visit)* rapide; *(decision)* hâtif, -ive ■ **hastily** *adv (write, prepare)* hâtivement; *(say)* précipitamment

hat [hæt] *n* chapeau *m*; *(of child)* bonnet *m*

hatch [hætʃ] **1** *n Br (in kitchen)* passe-plat *m* **2** *vt* faire éclore; *Fig (plot)* tramer **3** *vi (of chick, egg)* éclore

hatchback ['hætʃbæk] *n (car) (three-door)* trois-portes *f inv*; *(five-door)* cinq-portes *f inv*

hate [heɪt] **1** *n* haine *f* **2** *vt* haïr, détester; **to h. doing** *or* **to do sth** détester faire qch ■ **hateful** *adj* odieux, -euse

hatred ['heɪtrɪd] *n* haine *f*

haughty ['hɔːtɪ] (**-ier, -iest**) *adj* hautain

haul [hɔːl] **1** *n (fish caught)* prise *f*; *(of thief)* butin *m*; **a long h.** *(trip)* un long voyage **2** *vt (pull)* tirer

haunt [hɔːnt] **1** *n (place)* lieu *m* de rendez-vous; *(of criminal)* repaire *m* **2** *vt* hanter ■ **haunted** *adj (house)* hanté

HAVE [hæv] **1** *(3rd person sing present tense* **has,** *pt & pp* **had,** *pres p* **having)** *vt* avoir; *(meal, bath, lesson)* prendre; **he has (got) a big house** il a une grande maison; **she doesn't h.** *or* **hasn't got a car** elle n'a pas de voiture; **to h. a drink** prendre un verre; **to h. a walk/dream** faire une promenade/un rêve; **to h. a wash** se laver; **to h. a pleasant holiday** passer d'agréables vacances; **to h. flu** avoir la grippe; **will you h. some tea?** est-ce que tu veux du thé?; **to let sb h. sth** donner qch à qn; *Fam* **you've had it!** tu es fichu!; *Fam* **I've been had** *(cheated)* je me suis fait avoir; **to h. gloves/a dress on** porter des gants/une robe; **to h. sb over** *or* **round** inviter qn chez soi

2 *v aux* avoir; *(with entrer, monter, sor-tir etc & pronominal verbs)* être; **to h. decided** avoir décidé; **to h. gone** être allé; **to h. cut oneself** s'être coupé; **she has been punished** elle a été punie, on l'a punie; **I've got to go, I h. to go** je dois partir, il faut que je parte; **I don't h. to go** je ne suis pas obligé de partir; **to h. sb do sth** faire faire qch à qn; **to h. one's hair cut** se faire couper les cheveux; **he's had his suitcase brought up** il a fait monter sa valise; **I've had my car stolen** on m'a volé mon auto; **I've been doing it for months** je le fais depuis des mois; **you h. told him, haven't you?** tu le lui as dit, n'est-ce pas?; **you've seen this film before no I haven't!** tu as déjà vu ce film mais non!; **you haven't done the dishes yes I h.!** tu n'as pas fait la vaisselle mais si, je l'ai faite!; **after he had eaten** *or* **after having eaten, he left** après avoir mangé, il partit

▶ **have on** *vt sep* **(a)** *(be wearing)* porter **(b)** *Br Fam (fool)* **to h. sb on** faire marcher qn **(c)** *(have arranged)* **to h. a lot on** avoir beaucoup à faire; **to h. nothing on** n'avoir rien de prévu

▶ **have out** *vt sep* **(a)** *(have removed)* **to h. a tooth out** se faire arracher une dent **(b)** *(resolve)* **to h. it out with sb** s'expliquer avec qn

haven ['heɪvən] *n* refuge *m*

haven't ['hævənt] = **have not**

havoc ['hævək] *n* ravages *mpl*; **to wreak** *or* **cause h.** faire des ravages

hawk [hɔːk] *n* faucon *m*

hay [heɪ] *n* foin *m* ■ **hayfever** *n* rhume *m* des foins ■ **haystack** *n* meule *f* de foin

haywire ['heɪwaɪə(r)] *adj* **to go h.** *(of machine)* se détraquer; *(of plan)* mal tourner

hazard ['hæzəd] **1** *n* risque *m*; *Br Aut* **h. (warning) lights** feux *mpl* de détresse **2** *vt (remark)* risquer ■ **hazardous** *adj* dangereux, -euse

haze [heɪz] *n* brume *f*

hazelnut ['heɪzəlnʌt] *n* noisette *f*

hazy ['heɪzɪ] (**-ier, -iest**) *adj (weather)*

brumeux, -euse; *(photo, idea,* flou

he [hi:] **1** *pron* il; *(stressed)* lui; **he's a happy man** c'est un homme heureux; **he and I** lui et moi **2** *n Fam* **it's a he** *(baby)* c'est un garçon

head [hed] **1** *n (of person, hammer)* tête *f*; *(leader)* chef *m*; *Br (of school)* directeur, -trice *mf*; *(of bed)* chevet *m*, tête *f*; **h. of hair** chevelure *f*; **h. of state** chef *m* d'État; **h. first** la tête la première; **at the h. of** *(in charge of)* à la tête de; **it didn't enter my h.** ça ne m'es pas venu à l'esprit **(that** que); **heads or tails?** pile ou face?; **per h., a h.** *(each)* par personne

2 *adj* **h. office** siège *m* social; **h. waiter** maître *m* d'hôtel

3 *vt (group, firm)* être à la tête de; *(list, poll)* être en tête de; **to h. sb off** détourner qn de son chemin; **to h. sth off** éviter qch

4 *vi* **to h. for, to be heading for** *(place)* se diriger vers ▪ **headache** *n* mal *m* de tête; *Fig (problem)* casse-tête *m inv*; **to have a h.** avoir mal à la tête ▪ **headlamp, headlight** *n (of vehicle)* phare *m* ▪ **headline** *n (of newspaper, TV news)* titre *m* ▪ **headlong** *adv (fall)* la tête la première; *(rush)* tête baissée ▪ **headmaster** *n Br (of school)* directeur *m* ▪ **headmistress** *n Br (of school)* directrice *f* ▪ **head-on** *adv & adj* de front ▪ **headphones** *npl* écouteurs *mpl* ▪ **headquarters** *npl (of company, political party)* siège *m* (social) *(of army, police)* quartier *m* général, QG *m* ▪ **headrest** *n* appuie-tête *m inv* ▪ **head-scarf** *(pl* **-scarves)** *n* foulard *m* ▪ **head-strong** *adj* têtu

headed ['hedɪd] *adj Br* **h. (note)paper** papier *m* à en-tête

header ['hedə(r)] *n (in football)* (coup *m* de) tête *f*

heading ['hedɪŋ] *n (of chapter, page)* titre *m*; *(of subject)* rubrique *f*; *(printed on letter)* en-tête *m*

heady ['hedɪ] **(-ier, -iest)** *adj (wine, perfume)* capiteux, -euse; *(atmosphere)* enivrant

heal [hi:l] **1** *vt (wound)* cicatriser **2** *vi* **to h. (up)** *(of wound)* cicatriser

health [helθ] *n* santé *f*; **in good/bad h.** en bonne/mauvaise santé; **h. food shop** *or Am* **store** magasin *m* de produits biologiques; **h. resort** station *f* climatique; *Br* **the (National) H. Service** ≃ la Sécurité sociale

healthy ['helθɪ] **(-ier, -iest)** *adj (person)* en bonne santé; *(food, attitude)* sain; *(appetite)* robuste

heap [hi:p] **1** *n* tas *m*; *Fam* **heaps of** *(money, people)* des tas de **2** *vt* entasser; **to h. sth on sb** *(praise, gifts)* couvrir qn de qch; *(insults, work)* accabler qn de qch

hear [hɪə(r)] *(pt & pp* **heard** [hɜ:d]) **1** *vt* entendre; *(listen to)* écouter; *(learn)* apprendre **(that** que); **I heard him come** or **coming** je l'ai entendu venir; **have you heard the news?** connais-tu la nouvelle?; **h., h.!** bravo!

2 *vi* entendre; **to h. from sb** avoir des nouvelles de qn; **I've heard of him** j'ai entendu parler de lui

hearing ['hɪərɪŋ] *n* **(a)** *(sense)* ouïe *f*; **h. aid** audiophone *m* **(b)** *(of committee)* séance *f*; *(inquiry)* audition *f*

hearse [hɜ:s] *n* corbillard *m*

heart [hɑ:t] *n* cœur *m*; **hearts** *(in card games)* cœur *m*; **(off) by h.** *(know)* par cœur; **at h.** au fond; **h. attack** crise *f* cardiaque ▪ **heartache** *n* chagrin *m* ▪ **heartbeat** *n* battement *m* de cœur ▪ **heartbreaking** *adj* navrant ▪ **heart-broken** *adj* inconsolable

heartening ['hɑːtənɪŋ] *adj* encourageant

hearth [hɑ:θ] *n* foyer *m*

hearty ['hɑːtɪ] **(-ier, -iest)** *adj (appetite, meal)* gros *(f* grosse)

heat [hi:t] **1** *n* **(a)** chaleur *f*; *(heating)* chauffage *m*; *(of oven)* température *f*; **on a low h.** *(cook)* à feu doux; **h. wave** vague *f* de chaleur **(b)** *(in competition)* éliminatoire *f* **2** *vti* **to h. (up)** chauffer ▪ **heated** *adj (swimming pool)* chauffé; *(argument)* animé ▪ **heating** *n* chauffage *m*

heater ['hiːtə(r)] *n* radiateur *m*

heath [hi:θ] *n (land)* lande *f*

heather ['heðə(r)] *n* bruyère *f*

heave [hi:v] *vt (lift)* soulever avec effort; *(pull)* tirer fort; *Fam (throw)* balancer

heaven ['hevən] *n* paradis *m*, ciel *m*; *Fam* **good heavens!** mon Dieu!

heavily ['hevɪlɪ] *adv (walk, tax)* lourdement; *(breathe)* bruyamment; *(smoke, drink)* beaucoup; **h. in debt** lourdement endetté; **to rain h.** pleuvoir à verse; **to be h. defeated** subir une lourde défaite

heavy ['hevɪ] (**-ier, -iest**) *adj* lourd; *(work, cold)* gros (*f* grosse); *(blow)* violent; *(rain)* fort; *(traffic)* dense; *(timetable, schedule)* chargé; **to be a h. drinker/smoker** boire/fumer beaucoup ▪ **heavyweight** *n (in boxing)* poids *m* lourd; *Fig* personnage *m* important

Hebrew ['hi:bru:] *n (language)* hébreu *m*

heck [hek] *n Fam* zut!; **a h. of a lot** des masses (**of** de)

heckle ['hekəl] *vt* interpeller ▪ **heckling** *n* chahut *m*

hectic ['hektɪk] *adj (busy)* agité; *(eventful)* mouvementé

he'd [hi:d] = **he had, he would**

hedge [hedʒ] **1** *n (in garden, field)* haie *f* **2** *vi (answer evasively)* ne pas se mouiller

hedgehog ['hedʒhɒg] *n* hérisson *m*

hedgerow ['hedʒrəʊ] *n Br* haie *f*

heed [hi:d] **1** *n* **to pay h. to sth, to take h. of sth** tenir compte de qch **2** *vt* tenir compte de

heel [hi:l] *n (of foot, shoe)* talon *m*

hefty ['heftɪ] (**-ier, -iest**) *adj (large, heavy)* gros (*f* grosse); *(person)* costaud

height [haɪt] *n* hauteur *f*; *(of person)* taille *f*; *(of mountain, aircraft)* altitude *f*; **the h. of** *(success, fame, glory)* l'apogée *m* de; *(folly)* le comble de; **at the h. of** *(summer, storm)* au cœur de

heighten ['haɪtən] *vt (tension, interest)* augmenter

heir [eə(r)] *n* héritier *m*; **to be h. to sth** être l'héritier de qch ▪ **heiress** *n* héritière *f* ▪ **heirloom** *n* **a family h.** un objet de famille

held [held] *pt & pp of* **hold**

helicopter ['helɪkɒptə(r)] *n* hélicoptère *m* ▪ **heliport** *n* héliport *m*

hell [hel] *n* enfer *m*; *Fam* **a h. of a lot (of)** énormément (de); *Fam* **what the h. are you doing?** qu'est-ce que tu fous?

he'll [hi:l] = **he will**

hello [hə'ləʊ] *exclam* bonjour!; *(answering phone)* allô!

helm [helm] *n (of ship)* barre *f*

helmet ['helmɪt] *n* casque *m*

help [help] **1** *n* aide *f*; *Br (cleaning woman)* femme *f* de ménage; *(office or shop workers)* employés, -es *mfpl*; **with the h. of sth** à l'aide de qch; **h.!** au secours! **2** *vt* aider; **to h. sb do** *or* **to do sth** aider qn à faire qch; **to h. oneself (to sth)** se servir (de qch); **to h. sb out** aider qn; **I can't h. laughing** je ne peux pas m'empêcher de rire **3** *vt* aider ▪ **helper** *n* assistant, -e *mf* ▪ **helping** *n (serving)* portion *f*

helpful ['helpfəl] *adj (person)* serviable; *(useful)* utile

helpless ['helpləs] *adj (powerless)* impuissant

helpline ['helplaɪn] *n* service *m* d'assistance téléphonique

hem [hem] **1** *n* ourlet *m* **2** *(pt & pp* **-mm-**) *vt (garment)* ourler; **to be hemmed in** *(surrounded)* être cerné (**by** de)

hemisphere ['hemɪsfɪə(r)] *n* hémisphère *m*

hemorrhage ['hemərɪdʒ] *n Am* = **haemorrhage**

hemorrhoids ['hemərɔɪdz] *npl Am* = **haemorrhoids**

hen [hen] *n* poule *f*

hence [hens] *adv* (**a**) *(thus)* d'où (**b**) *(from now)* **ten years h.** d'ici dix ans

her [hɜ:(r)] **1** *pron* la, l'; *(after prep, 'than', 'it is')* elle; **(to) h.** *(indirect)* lui; **I saw h.** je l'ai vue; **I gave it (to) h.** je le lui ai donné **2** *possessive adj* son, sa, *pl* ses

herb [*Br* hɜ:b, *Am* ɜ:b] *n* herbe *f* aromatique ▪ **herbal** *adj* **h. tea** tisane *f*

herd [hɜːd] **1** n troupeau m **2** vt (cattle, people) rassembler

here [hɪə(r)] **1** adv ici; **h. it/he is** le voici; **h. she comes!** la voilà!; **h. is a good example** voici un bon exemple; **I won't be h. tomorrow** je ne serai pas là demain; **h. and there** ça et là; **h. you are!** (take this) tenez! **2** exclam **h.!** (giving sb sth) tenez! ■ **hereabouts** adv par ici

hereditary [hɪˈredɪtərɪ] adj héréditaire

heritage [ˈherɪtɪdʒ] n patrimoine m

hero [ˈhɪərəʊ] (pl -oes) n héros m ■ **heroic** adj héroïque ■ **heroine** n héroïne f

heroin [ˈherəʊɪn] n (drug) héroïne f

heron [ˈherən] n héron m

herring [ˈherɪŋ] n hareng m

hers [hɜːz] possessive pron le sien, la sienne, pl les sien(ne)s; **this hat is h.** ce chapeau est à elle ou est le sien; **a friend of h.** un ami à elle

herself [hɜːˈself] pron elle-même; (reflexive) se, s'; (after prep) elle; **she cut h.** elle s'est coupée

hesitant [ˈhezɪtənt] adj hésitant

hesitate [ˈhezɪteɪt] **1** vt **to h. to do sth** hésiter à faire qch **2** vi hésiter (**over** or **about** sur) ■ **hesitation** n hésitation f

heterosexual [hetərəˈseksʃʊəl] adj & n hétérosexuel, -elle (mf)

hexagon [ˈheksəgən] n hexagone m

hey [heɪ] exclam (calling sb) hé!, ohé!; (expressing surprise, annoyance) hé!

hi [haɪ] exclam Fam salut!

hibernate [ˈhaɪbəneɪt] vi hiberner

hiccup, hiccough [ˈhɪkʌp] **1** n hoquet m; Fig (in plan) accroc m; **to have (the) hiccups** or **(the) hiccoughs** avoir le hoquet **2** vi hoqueter

hide¹ [haɪd] (pt hid [hɪd], pp hidden [ˈhɪdən]) **1** vt cacher (**from** à) **2** vi **to h. (away** or **out)** se cacher (**from** de)

hide² [haɪd] n (skin) peau f ■ **hide-and-seek** n **to play h.** jouer à cache-cache

hideaway [ˈhaɪdəweɪ] n cachette f

hideous [ˈhɪdɪəs] adj (ugly) hideux, -euse; (horrific) horrible

hide-out [ˈhaɪdaʊt] n cachette f

hiding¹ [ˈhaɪdɪŋ] n **to go into h.** se cacher; **h. place** cachette f

hiding² [ˈhaɪdɪŋ] n Fam **a good h.** (thrashing) une bonne raclée

hierarchy [ˈhaɪərɑːkɪ] (pl -ies) n hiérarchie f

hi-fi [ˈhaɪfaɪ] **1** n (system, equipment) chaîne f hi-fi **2** adj hi-fi inv

high [haɪ] **1** (-er, -est) adj haut; (speed) grand; (price, standards) élevé; (number, ideal) grand, élevé; (voice, tone) aigu (f aiguë); Fam (on drugs) défoncé; **to be 5 metres h.** avoir 5 mètres de haut; **it is h. time that you went** il est grand temps que tu y ailles; **h. jump** (sporting event) saut m en hauteur; **h. school** ≃ lycée m; Br **h. street** grand-rue f; **h. tide** marée f haute

2 adv **h. (up)** (fly, throw, aim) haut

3 n **a new h., an all-time h.** (peak) un nouveau record ■ **highchair** n chaise f haute ■ **high-class** adj (service) de premier ordre; (person) raffiné ■ **high-powered** adj (engine, car) très puissant; (job) à hautes responsabilités ■ **high-profile** adj (person) très en vue; (campaign) de grande envergure ■ **high-rise** adj Br **h. building** tour f ■ **high-speed** adj ultrarapide; **h. train** train m à grande vitesse ■ **high-tech** adj (appliance) perfectionné; (industry) de pointe

highbrow [ˈhaɪbraʊ] adj & n intellectuel, -elle (mf)

higher [ˈhaɪə(r)] **1** adj (number, speed, quality) supérieur (**than** à); **h. education** enseignement m supérieur **2** adv (fly, aim) plus haut (**than** que)

highlands [ˈhaɪləndz] npl régions fpl montagneuses

highlight [ˈhaɪlaɪt] **1** n (of visit, day) point m culminant; (of show) clou m; (in hair) reflet m **2** vt souligner; (with marker) surligner

highly [ˈhaɪlɪ] adv (very) très; (recommend) chaudement; **h. paid** très bien payé; **to speak h. of sb** dire beaucoup

de bien de qn; *Br* **h. strung** hypersensible

Highness ['haɪnɪs] *n* His/Her Royal H. Son Altesse *f*

highway ['haɪweɪ] *n Am (motorway)* autoroute *f*; *Br* **H. Code** code *m* de la route

hijack ['haɪdʒæk] **1** *n* détournement *m* **2** *vt (plane)* détourner ■ **hijacker** *n (of plane)* pirate *m* de l'air

hike [haɪk] **1** *n (walk)* randonnée *f* **2** *vi* faire de la randonnée ■ **hiker** *n* randonneur, -euse *mf*

hilarious [hɪ'leərɪəs] *adj* hilarant

hill [hɪl] *n* colline *f*; *(slope)* pente *f* ■ **hillside** *n* **on the h.** à flanc de coteau ■ **hilly** (-ier, -iest) *adj* vallonné

him [hɪm] *pron* le, l'; *(after prep, 'than', 'it is')* lui; **(to) h.** *(indirect)* lui; **I saw h.** je l'ai vu; **I gave it (to) h.** je le lui ai donné

himself [hɪm'self] *pron* lui-même; *(reflexive)* se, s'; *(after prep)* lui; **he cut h.** il s'est coupé

hind [haɪnd] *adj* **h. legs** pattes *fpl* de derrière

hinder ['hɪndə(r)] *vt (obstruct)* gêner; *(delay)* retarder; **to h. sb from doing sth** empêcher qn de faire qch ■ **hindrance** *n* obstacle *m*

hindsight ['haɪndsaɪt] *n* **with h.** avec le recul

Hindu ['hɪnduː] **1** *adj* hindou **2** *n* Hindou, -e *mf*

hinge [hɪndʒ] **1** *n* gond *m*, charnière *f* **2** *vt insep* **to h. on** *(depend on)* dépendre de

hint [hɪnt] **1** *n (insinuation)* allusion *f*; *(sign)* signe *m*; *(clue)* indice *m* **2** *vt* laisser entendre **(that** que) **3** *vt insep* **to h. at sb/sth** faire allusion à qn/qch

hip [hɪp] *n* hanche *f*

hippie ['hɪpɪ] *n* hippie *mf*

hippopotamus [hɪpə'pɒtəməs] *n* hippopotame *m*

hire ['haɪə(r)] **1** *n* location *f*; **for h.** à louer; *Br (sign on taxi)* 'libre'; **on h.** en location; *Br* **on h. purchase** à crédit **2** *vt (vehicle)* louer; *(worker)* engager; **to h. sth out** louer qch

his [hɪz] **1** *possessive pron* le sien, la sienne, *pl* les sien(ne)s; **this hat is h.** ce chapeau est à lui *ou* est le sien; **a friend of h.** un ami à lui **2** *possessive adj* son, sa, *pl* ses

Hispanic [hɪ'spænɪk] *Am* **1** *adj* hispano-américain **2** *n* Hispano-Américain, -e *mf*

hiss [hɪs] **1** *n* sifflement *m*; **hisses** *(booing)* sifflets *mpl* **2** *vti* siffler

history ['hɪstərɪ] *(pl* -ies) *n (study, events)* histoire *f*; **medical h.** antécédents *mpl* médicaux ■ **historian** *n* historien, -enne *mf* ■ **historic(al)** [hɪ'stɒrɪk(əl)] *adj* historique

hit [hɪt] **1** *n (blow)* coup *m*; *(in shooting)* tir *m* réussi; *(success)* succès *m*; *Comptr (visit to website)* hit *m*, contact *m*; **h. (song)** hit *m*
 2 *(pt & pp* hit, *pres p* hitting) *vt (beat)* frapper; *(bump into)* heurter; *(reach)* atteindre; *(affect)* toucher; *(problem, difficulty)* rencontrer; *Fam* **to h. it off** s'entendre bien **(with sb** avec qn)
 3 *vi* frapper; **to h. back** riposter **(at** à); **to h. out at sb** *(physically)* frapper qn; *(verbally)* s'en prendre à qn; **to h. (up)on sth** *(solution, idea)* trouver qch ■ **hit-and-run** *n* **h. driver** chauffard *m* (qui prend la fuite) ■ **hit-or-miss** *adj (chancy, random)* aléatoire

hitch [hɪtʃ] **1** *n (difficulty)* problème *m* **2** *vt (fasten)* accrocher **(to** à) **3** *vti* **to h. (a ride)**, *Br* **to h. a lift** faire du stop **(to** jusqu'à) ■ **hitchhike** *vi* faire du stop **(to** jusqu'à) ■ **hitchhiker** *n* auto-stoppeur, -euse *mf* ■ **hitchhiking** *n* auto-stop *m*

HIV [eɪtʃaɪ'viː] *(abbr* **human immuno-deficiency virus)** *n (virus)* VIH *m*; **HIV positive** séropositif, -ive; **HIV negative** séronégatif, -ive

hive [haɪv] **1** *n* ruche *f* **2** *vt* **to h. off** *(separate)* séparer

hoard [hɔːd] **1** *n* réserve *f*; *(of money)* trésor *m* **2** *vt* amasser

hoarding ['hɔːdɪŋ] *n Br (for advertising)* panneau *m* d'affichage

hoarse [hɔːs] (-er, -est) *adj* enroué

hoax [həʊks] *n* canular *m*

hob [hɒb] *n (on stove)* plaque *f* chauffante

hobby ['hɒbɪ] *(pl -ies) n* passe-temps *m inv*

hockey ['hɒkɪ] *n* hockey *m*; *Br (field hockey)* hockey *m* sur gazon; *Am (ice hockey)* hockey *m* sur glace; **h. stick** crosse *f* de hockey

hog [hɒg] **1** *n (pig)* porc *m* châtré **2** *(pt & pp -gg-) vt Fam* monopoliser

hoist [hɔɪst] **1** *n (machine)* palan *m* **2** *vt* hisser

HOLD [həʊld] **1** *n (grip)* prise *f*; *(of ship)* cale *f*; *(of plane)* soute *f*; **to get h. of** *(grab)* saisir; *(contact)* joindre; *(find)* trouver; **to be on h.** *(of project)* être en suspens; **to put sb on h.** *(on phone)* mettre qn en attente

2 *(pt & pp held) vt* tenir; *(heat, attention)* retenir; *(post)* occuper; *(record)* détenir; *(title, opinion)* avoir; *(party, exhibition)* organiser; *(ceremony)* célébrer; *(contain)* contenir; *(keep)* garder; **to h. sb prisoner** retenir qn prisonnier; **to h. one's breath** retenir son souffle; **h. the line!** *(on phone)* ne quittez pas!; **h. it!** *(stay still)* ne bouge pas!; **to be held** *(of event)* avoir lieu

3 *vi (of nail, rope)* tenir; *(of weather)* se maintenir ▪ **hold-up** *n (attack)* hold-up *m inv*; *Br (traffic jam)* ralentissement *m*; *(delay)* retard *m*

▸**hold back** *vt sep (restrain)* retenir; *(hide)* cacher **(from sb** à qn)

▸**hold down** *vt sep (person on ground)* maintenir au sol; **to h. down a job** *(keep)* garder un emploi; *(occupy)* avoir un emploi

▸**hold forth** *vi Pej (talk)* disserter

▸**hold off 1** *vt sep (enemy)* tenir à distance **2** *vi* **if the rain holds off** s'il ne pleut pas

▸**hold on 1** *vt sep (keep in place)* tenir en place **2** *vi (wait)* patienter; *(stand firm)* tenir bon; **h. on!** *(on phone)* ne quittez pas!; **h. on (tight)!** tenez bon!

▸**hold on to** *vt insep (cling to)* tenir bien; *(keep)* garder

▸**hold out 1** *vt sep (offer)* offrir; *(hand)* tendre **2** *vi (resist)* résister; *(last)* durer

▸**hold over** *vt sep (postpone)* remettre

▸**hold together** *vt sep (nation, group)* assurer l'union de

▸**hold up** *vt sep (raise)* lever; *(support)* soutenir; *(delay)* retarder; *(rob)* attaquer

holdall ['həʊldɔːl] *n Br* fourre-tout *m inv*

holder ['həʊldə(r)] *n* **(a)** *(of passport, degree, post)* titulaire *mf*; *(of record, card, ticket)* détenteur, -trice *mf* **(b)** *(container)* support *m*

hole [həʊl] *n* trou *m*

holiday ['hɒlɪdeɪ] **1** *n Br* **holiday(s)** *(from work, school)* vacances *fpl*; **a h.** *(day off)* un congé; **a (public** *or* **bank) h.**, *Am* **a legal h.** un jour férié; **to be/ go on h.** être/partir en vacances **2** *adj (camp, clothes)* de vacances ▪ **holiday-maker** *n Br* vacancier, -ère *mf*

Holland ['hɒlənd] *n* la Hollande

hollow ['hɒləʊ] **1** *adj* creux *(f* creuse); *(promise)* vain **2** *n* creux *m* **3** *vt* **to h. sth out** évider qch

holly ['hɒlɪ] *n* houx *m*

holy ['həʊlɪ] *(-ier, -iest) adj* saint; *(bread, water)* bénit; *(ground)* sacré

homage ['hɒmɪdʒ] *n* hommage *m*; **to pay h. to sb** rendre hommage à qn

home¹ [həʊm] **1** *n* maison *f*; *(country)* patrie *f*; **at h.** à la maison, chez soi; **to feel at h.** se sentir chez soi; **make yourself at h.** faites comme chez vous **2** *adv* à la maison, chez soi; **to go** *or* **come (back) h.** rentrer chez soi **3** *adj (cooking)* familial; *(visit, match)* à domicile; **h. address** adresse *f* personnelle; *Br* **h. help** aide *f* ménagère; *Br* **H. Office** ≃ ministère *m* de l'Intérieur; **h. owner** propriétaire *mf*; *Comptr* **h. page** page *f* d'accueil; *Br* **H. Secretary** ≃ ministre *m* de l'Intérieur; **h. team** équipe *f* qui reçoit; **h. town** ville *f* natale ▪ **homegrown** *adj (fruit, vegetables)* du jardin; *(not grown abroad)* du pays ▪ **homeland** *n* patrie *f* ▪ **homemade** *adj* (fait) maison *inv* ▪ **homesick** *adj* **to be h.** avoir le mal du pays

home² [həʊm] *vi* **to h. in on sth** se diriger automatiquement sur qch

homeless ['həʊmlɪs] **1** *adj* sans abri **2**

npl **the h.** les sans-abri *mpl*

homely ['həʊmlɪ] (**-ier, -iest**) *adj (comfortable)* agréable et sans prétention; *Am (ugly)* sans charme

homeward ['həʊmwəd] **1** *adj (trip)* de retour **2** *adv* **h. bound** sur le chemin de retour

homework ['həʊmwɜːk] *n Sch* devoirs *mpl*

homicide ['hɒmɪsaɪd] *n* homicide *m*

homosexual [həʊmə'sekʃʊəl] *adj & n* homosexuel, -elle *(mf)*

honest ['ɒnɪst] *adj* honnête (**with** avec) ■ **honestly** *adv* honnêtement ■ **honesty** *n* honnêteté *f*

honey ['hʌnɪ] *n* miel *m* ■ **honeymoon** *n* voyage *m* de noces

honk [hɒŋk] *vi (of driver)* klaxonner

honorary ['ɒnərərɪ] *adj (member)* honoraire; *(title)* honorifique

honour ['ɒnə(r)] *(Am* **honor**) **1** *n* honneur *m*; **in h. of** en l'honneur de; *Br Univ* **honours degree** diplôme *m* universitaire **2** *vt* honorer (**with** de)

honourable ['ɒnərəbəl] *(Am* **honorable**) *adj* honorable

hood [hʊd] *n (of coat)* capuche *f*; *(with eye-holes)* cagoule *f*; *Br (of car, pram)* capote *f*; *Am (car bonnet)* capot *m*

hoof [huːf] *(pl* **hoofs** [huːfs] *or* **hooves** [huːvz]) *n* sabot *m*

hook [hʊk] **1** *n* crochet *m*; *(on clothes)* agrafe *f*; *(for fishing)* hameçon *m*; **off the h.** *(phone)* décroché **2** *vt* **to h. (on** *or* **up)** accrocher (**to** à) ■ **hooked** *adj (nose)* crochu; *Fam* **to be h. on sth** être accro à qch

hook(e)y ['hʊkɪ] *n Am Fam* **to play h.** sécher (les cours)

hooligan ['huːlɪgən] *n* hooligan *m*

hoot [huːt] *vi Br (of vehicle)* klaxonner; *(of owl)* hululer ■ **hooter** *n Br (of vehicle)* Klaxon® *m*

hoover® ['huːvə(r)] *Br* **1** *n* aspirateur *m* **2** *vt (room)* passer l'aspirateur dans; *(carpet)* passer l'aspirateur sur; **to h. sth up** *(dust, crumbs)* enlever qch à l'aspirateur

hop [hɒp] **1** *n (leap)* saut *m* **2** *(pt & pp*

-pp-) *vi (jump)* sautiller; *(on one leg)* sauter à cloche-pied **3** *vt Fam* **h. it!** fiche le camp!

hope [həʊp] **1** *n* espoir *m* **2** *vt* **to h. to do sth** espérer faire qch; **to h. that...** espérer que... **3** *vi* espérer; **to h. for sth** espérer qch; **I h. so/not** j'espère que oui/non ■ **hopeful** *adj (person)* optimiste; *(situation)* encourageant; **to be h. that...** avoir bon espoir que... ■ **hopefully** *adv (with luck)* avec un peu de chance ■ **hopeless** ['həʊplɪs] *adj* désespéré; *Fam (useless, bad)* nul *(f* nulle) ■ **hopelessly** *adv (lost)* complètement; *(in love)* éperdument

horde [hɔːd] *n* horde *f*

horizon [hə'raɪzən] *n* horizon *m*; **on the h.** à l'horizon ■ **horizontal** *adj* horizontal

hormone ['hɔːməʊn] *n* hormone *f*

horn [hɔːn] *n (of animal)* corne *f*; *(on vehicle)* Klaxon® *m*; *(musical instrument)* cor *m*

hornet ['hɔːnɪt] *n* frelon *m*

horoscope ['hɒrəskəʊp] *n* horoscope *m*

horrendous [hɒ'rendəs] *adj* horrible

horrible ['hɒrəbəl] *adj* horrible

horrid ['hɒrɪd] *adj (unpleasant)* affreux, -euse; *(unkind)* méchant

horrific [hə'rɪfɪk] *adj* horrible

horrify ['hɒrɪfaɪ] *(pt & pp* **-ied**) *vt* horrifier

horror ['hɒrə(r)] *n* horreur *f*; **h. film** film *m* d'horreur; **h. story** histoire *f* épouvantable

hors d'œuvre [ɔː'dɜːv] *(pl inv or* **hors d'œuvres**) *n* hors-d'œuvre *m inv*

horse [hɔːs] *n* (**a**) *(animal)* cheval *m*; **to go h. riding** faire du cheval; **h. racing** courses *fpl* (**b**) **h. chestnut** *(fruit)* marron *m* ■ **horseback** *n* **on h.** à cheval; *Am* **to go h. riding** faire du cheval ■ **horsepower** *n (unit)* cheval-vapeur *m* ■ **horseradish** *n* raifort *m*

horticulture ['hɔːtɪkʌltʃə(r)] *n* horticulture *f*

hose [həʊz] **1** *n (pipe)* tuyau *m* **2** *vt* arroser (au jet d'eau); **to h. sth down**

(car) laver qch au jet ■ **hosepipe** *n Br* tuyau *m* d'arrosage

hospitable [hɒˈspɪtəbəl] *adj* hospitalier, -ère (**to** envers) ■ **hospitality** [-ˈtælɪtɪ] *n* hospitalité *f*

hospital [ˈhɒspɪtəl] *n* hôpital *m*; **in h.,** *Am* **in the h.** à l'hôpital; **h. bed** lit *m* d'hôpital; **h. staff** personnel *m* hospitalier ■ **hospitalize** *vt* hospitaliser

host¹ [həʊst] **1** *n (of guests)* hôte *m*; *(on TV or radio show)* présentateur, -trice *mf*; **h. country** pays *m* d'accueil **2** *vt (programme)* présenter

host² [həʊst] *n* **a h. of** *(many)* une foule de

host³ [həʊst] *n Rel* hostie *f*

hostage [ˈhɒstɪdʒ] *n* otage *m*; **to take sb h.** prendre qn en otage; **to be held h.** être retenu en otage

hostel [ˈhɒstəl] *n* foyer *m*; **(youth) h.** auberge *f* de jeunesse

hostess [ˈhəʊstɪs] *n (in house, nightclub)* hôtesse *f*; **(air) h.** hôtesse *f* (de l'air)

hostile [*Br* ˈhɒstaɪl, *Am* ˈhɒstəl] *adj* hostile (**to** *or* **towards** à)

hostility [hɒsˈtɪlɪtɪ] *n* hostilité *f* (**to** *or* **towards** envers); **hostilities** *(in battle)* hostilités *fpl*

hot¹ [hɒt] (**hotter, hottest**) *adj* chaud; *(spice)* fort; **to be** *or* **feel h.** avoir chaud; **it's h.** il fait chaud ■ **hotcake** *n* crêpe *f* ■ **hotdog** *n* hot dog *m* ■ **hotheaded** *adj* exalté ■ **hotly** *adv* passionnément ■ **hotplate** *n* chauffe-plat *m*; *(on stove)* plaque *f* chauffante ■ **hotwater** *n* **h. bottle** bouillotte *f*

hot² [hɒt] *(pt & pp* -tt-*) vi Fam* **to h. up** *(increase)* s'intensifier; *(become dangerous or excited)* s'envenimer

hotchpotch [ˈhɒtʃpɒtʃ] *n Fam* fatras *m*

hotel [həʊˈtel] *n* hôtel *m*; **h. room/bed** chambre *f*/lit *m* d'hôtel

hound [haʊnd] **1** *n (dog)* chien *m* de chasse **2** *vt (pursue)* traquer; *(bother, worry)* harceler

hour [ˈaʊə(r)] *n* heure *f*; **half an h.** une demi-heure; **a quarter of an h.** un quart d'heure; **paid £10 an h.** payé 10 livres (de) l'heure; **10 miles an h.** 10 miles à l'heure; **h. hand** *(of watch, clock)* petite aiguille *f*

hourly [ˈaʊəlɪ] **1** *adj (rate, pay)* horaire **2** *adv* toutes les heures; **h. paid, paid h.** payé à l'heure

house 1 [haʊs] *(pl -ses* [-zɪz]*) n* maison *f*; *Pol* **the H. of Commons/Lords** la Chambre des communes/lords; **the Houses of Parliament** le Parlement; **the H. of Representatives** la Chambre des représentants; **at/to my h.** chez moi; **on the h.** *(free of charge)* aux frais de la maison; **h. plant** plante *f* d'intérieur; **h. prices** prix *mpl* de l'immobilier; **h. wine** vin *m* maison

2 [haʊz] *vt* loger; *(of building)* abriter ■ **houseboat** *n* péniche *f* aménagée ■ **housebound** *adj* confiné chez soi ■ **household** *n* ménage *m*; **h. chores** tâches *fpl* ménagères ■ **householder** *n (owner)* propriétaire *mf* ■ **housekeeper** *n (employee)* gouvernante *f* ■ **housekeeping** *n* ménage *m* ■ **houseproud** *adj* qui s'occupe méticuleusement de sa maison ■ **housetrained** *adj Br (dog)* propre ■ **housewarming** *n & adj* **to have a h. (party)** pendre la crémaillère ■ **housewife** *(pl -wives) n* ménagère *f* ■ **housework** *n* ménage *m*

housing [ˈhaʊzɪŋ] *n* logement *m*; *(houses)* logements *mpl*; *Br* **h. estate** lotissement *m*; *(council-owned)* cité *f*

hovel [ˈhɒvəl] *n* taudis *m*

hover [ˈhɒvə(r)] *vi (of bird, aircraft)* planer; **to h. (around)** *(of person)* rôder

hovercraft [ˈhɒvəkrɑːft] *n* aéroglisseur *m*

how [haʊ] *adv* comment; **h. kind!** comme c'est gentil!; **h. long/high is...?** quelle est la longueur/hauteur de...?; **h. much?, h. many?** combien?; **h. much time?** combien de temps?; **h. many apples?** combien de pommes?; **h. about some coffee?** (si on prenait) du café?; **h. do you do?** *(greeting)* enchanté; *Fam* **h.'s that?, h. so?, h. come?** comment ça?

however [haʊˈevə(r)] **1** *adv* **h. big he**

may be si grand soit-il; **h. she may do it, h. she does it** de quelque manière qu'elle le fasse; **h. did she find out?** comment a-t-elle bien pu l'apprendre? **2** *conj* cependant

howl [haʊl] **1** *n* hurlement *m*; **h. of laughter** éclat *m* de rire **2** *vi* hurler; *(of wind)* mugir

HP [eɪtʃ'piː] *(abbr* **hire purchase)** *n Br* achat *m* à crédit

hp *(abbr* **horsepower)** CV

HQ [eɪtʃ'kjuː] *(abbr* **headquarters)** *n* QG *m*

hub [hʌb] *n (of wheel)* moyeu *m; Fig* centre *m* ▪ **hubcap** *n (of wheel)* enjoliveur *m*

huddle ['hʌdəl] *vi* **to h. (together)** se blottir (les uns contre les autres)

huff [hʌf] *n Fam* **in a h.** *(offended)* fâché

hug [hʌg] **1** *n* **to give sb a h.** serrer qn (dans ses bras) **2** *(pt & pp* **-gg-)** *vt (person)* serrer dans ses bras

huge [hjuːdʒ] *adj* énorme

hull [hʌl] *n (of ship)* coque *f*

hullo [hʌ'ləʊ] *exclam Br* bonjour!; *(answering phone)* allô!

hum [hʌm] **1** *n (of insect)* bourdonnement *m* **2** *(pt & pp* **-mm-)** *vt (tune)* fredonner **3** *vi (of insect)* bourdonner; *(of person)* fredonner; *(of engine)* ronronner

human ['hjuːmən] **1** *adj* humain; **h. being** être *m* humain; **h. rights** droits *mpl* de l'homme **2** *n* être *m* humain

humane [hjuː'meɪn] *adj (kind)* humain

humanity [hjuː'mænətɪ] *n (human beings, kindness)* humanité *f*

humble ['hʌmbəl] **1** *adj* humble **2** *vt* humilier

humid ['hjuːmɪd] *adj* humide ▪ **humidity** *n* humidité *f*

humiliate [hjuː'mɪlɪeɪt] *vt* humilier ▪ **humiliation** [-'eɪʃən] *n* humiliation *f*

humility [hjuː'mɪlɪtɪ] *n* humilité *f*

humorous ['hjuːmərəs] *adj (book, writer)* humoristique; *(person, situation)* drôle

humour ['hjuːmə(r)] *(Am* **humor)** **1** *n (fun)* humour *m* **2** *vt* **to h. sb** faire plaisir à qn

hump [hʌmp] *n (lump, mound in road)* bosse *f*

hunch [hʌntʃ] **1** *n Fam (intuition)* intuition *f* **2** *vt* **to h. one's shoulders** rentrer les épaules ▪ **hunchback** *n* bossu, -e *mf*

hundred ['hʌndrəd] *adj & n* cent *(m)*; **a h. pages** cent pages; **two h. pages** deux cents pages; **hundreds of** des centaines de ▪ **hundredth** *adj & n* centième *(mf)* ▪ **hundredweight** *n Br* = 50,8 kg, 112 livres; *Am* = 45,3 kg, 100 livres

hung [hʌŋ] *pt & pp of* **hang**[1]

Hungary ['hʌŋgərɪ] *n* la Hongrie ▪ **Hungarian** [-'geərɪən] **1** *adj* hongrois **2** *n (person)* Hongrois, -e *mf; (language)* hongrois *m*

hunger ['hʌŋgə(r)] *n* faim *f* ▪ **hungry** **(-ier, -iest)** *adj* **to be** *or* **feel h.** avoir faim; **h. for sth** avide de qch

hunk [hʌŋk] *n (piece)* gros morceau *m*

hunt [hʌnt] **1** *n (search)* recherche *f* **(for** de); *(for animals)* chasse *f* **2** *vt (animals)* chasser; *(pursue)* poursuivre; **to h. down** *(animal, fugitive)* traquer **3** *vi (kill animals)* chasser; **to h. for sth** rechercher qch ▪ **hunter** *n* chasseur *m* ▪ **hunting** *n* chasse *f*

hurdle ['hɜːdəl] *n (fence in race)* haie *f; Fig (problem)* obstacle *m*

hurl [hɜːl] *vt (throw)* jeter, lancer **(at** à); **to h. insults** *or* **abuse at sb** lancer des insultes à qn

hurray [hʊ'reɪ] *exclam* hourra!

hurricane [*Br* 'hʌrɪkən, *Am* 'hʌrɪkeɪn] *n* ouragan *m*

hurried ['hʌrɪd] *adj (decision)* précipité; *(work)* fait à la hâte; *(visit)* éclair *inv*

hurry ['hʌrɪ] **1** *n* hâte *f*; **in a h.** à la hâte; **to be in a h.** être pressé; **to be in a h. to do sth** avoir hâte de faire qch; **there's no h.** rien ne presse **2** *(pt & pp* **-ied)** *vt (person)* presser; *(work)* hâter **3** *vi* se dépêcher, se presser **(to do** de faire); **to h. up** se dépêcher; **to h. out** sortir à la hâte; **to h. towards**

sb/sth se précipiter vers qn/qch

hurt [hɜːt] **1** *adj (wounded, offended)* blessé **2** *n (emotional)* blessure *f* **3** *(pt & pp* **hurt)** *vt (physically)* faire du mal à; *(causing a wound)* blesser; *(emotionally)* faire de la peine à; *(reputation, chances)* nuire à; **to h. sb's feelings** blesser qn **4** *vi* faire mal; **his arm hurts** son bras lui fait mal ▪ **hurtful** *adj (remark)* blessant

hurtle ['hɜːtəl] *vi* **to h. along** aller à toute vitesse

husband ['hʌzbənd] *n* mari *m*

hush [hʌʃ] **1** *n* silence *m* **2** *exclam* chut! **3** *vt (person)* faire taire; *(baby)* calmer; **to h. up** *(scandal)* étouffer ▪ **hushed** *adj (voice)* étouffé; *(silence)* profond

husky ['hʌskɪ] **(-ier, -iest)** *adj (voice)* rauque

hustle ['hʌsəl] **1** *n* **h. and bustle** effervescence *f* **2** *vt (shove, push)* **to h. sb away** emmener qn de force

hut [hʌt] *n* cabane *f*; *(dwelling)* hutte *f*

hybrid ['haɪbrɪd] *adj & n* hybride *(m)*

hydrogen ['haɪdrədʒən] *n Chem* hydrogène *m*

hygiene ['haɪdʒiːn] *n* hygiène *f* ▪ **hy-**gienic *adj* hygiénique

hymn [hɪm] *n* cantique *m*

hype [haɪp] *n Fam (publicity)* battage *m* publicitaire

hyper- ['haɪpə(r)] *pref* hyper-

hypermarket ['haɪpəmɑːkɪt] *n* hypermarché *m*

hyphen ['haɪfən] *n* trait *m* d'union ▪ **hyphenated** *adj (word)* à trait d'union

hypnotize ['hɪpnətaɪz] *vt* hypnotiser

hypochondriac [haɪpə'kɒndrɪæk] *n* hypocondriaque *mf*

hypocrisy [hɪ'pɒkrɪsɪ] *n* hypocrisie *f* ▪ **hypocrite** ['hɪpəkrɪt] *n* hypocrite *mf* ▪ **hypocritical** [hɪpə'krɪtɪkəl] *adj* hypocrite

hypothesis [haɪ'pɒθɪsɪs] *(pl* **-theses** [-θɪsiːz]) *n* hypothèse *f* ▪ **hypothetical** [haɪpə'θetɪkəl] *adj* hypothétique

hysterical [hɪs'terɪkəl] *adj (very upset)* qui a une crise de nerfs; *Fam (funny)* tordant ▪ **hysterics** *npl (tears)* crise *f* de nerfs; **to be in h.** avoir une crise de nerfs; *(with laughter)* être écroulé de rire

Ii

I¹, i [aɪ] *n (letter)* I, i *m inv*

I² [aɪ] *pron* je, j'; *(stressed)* moi

ice¹ [aɪs] **1** *n* glace *f; (on road)* verglas *m;* **i. cream** glace *f;* **i. cube** glaçon *m;* **i. hockey** hockey *m* sur glace **2** *vi* **to i. over** *or* **up** *(of lake)* geler; *(of window)* se givrer ▪ **iceberg** *n* iceberg *m* ▪ **icebox** *n Am (fridge)* réfrigérateur *m; Br (in fridge)* freezer *m* ▪ **iced** *adj (tea, coffee)* glacé ▪ **ice-skating** *n* patinage *m* (sur glace)

ice² [aɪs] *vt Br (cake)* glacer ▪ **icing** *n Br (on cake)* glaçage *m*

Iceland ['aɪslənd] *n* l'Islande *f* ▪ **Icelandic** [-'lændɪk] *adj* islandais

icicle ['aɪsɪkəl] *n* glaçon *m (de gouttière etc)*

icon ['aɪkɒn] *n* icône *f*

icy ['aɪsɪ] (**-ier, -iest**) *adj (road)* verglacé; *(water, hands)* glacé

ID [aɪ'di:] *n* pièce *f* d'identité

I'd [aɪd] = I had, I would

idea [aɪ'dɪə] *n* idée *f;* **I have an i. that...** j'ai l'impression que...

ideal [aɪ'dɪəl] *adj & n* idéal *(m)*

idealistic [aɪdɪə'lɪstɪk] *adj* idéaliste

ideally [aɪ'dɪəlɪ] *adv* idéalement; **i., we should stay** l'idéal, ce serait que nous restions

identical [aɪ'dentɪkəl] *adj* identique (**to** *or* **with** à)

identify [aɪ'dentɪfaɪ] (*pt & pp* **-ied**) *vt* identifier; **to i. (oneself) with** s'identifier avec ▪ **identification** [-fɪ'keɪʃən] *n* identification *f;* **to have (some) i.** *(document)* avoir une pièce d'identité

identity [aɪ'dentɪtɪ] (*pl* **-ies**) *n* identité *f;* **i. card** carte *f* d'identité

ideology [aɪdɪ'ɒlədʒɪ] (*pl* **-ies**) *n* idéologie *f*

idiom ['ɪdɪəm] *n (phrase)* expression *f* idiomatique

idiosyncrasy [ɪdɪə'sɪŋkrəsɪ] (*pl* **-ies**) *n* particularité *f*

idiot ['ɪdɪət] *n* idiot, -e *mf* ▪ **idiotic** [-'ɒtɪk] *adj* idiot, bête

idle ['aɪdəl] **1** *adj (unoccupied)* désœuvré; *(lazy)* oisif, -ive; *(rumour)* sans fondement; **to lie i.** *(of machine)* être au repos **2** *vt* **to i. away the** *or* **one's time** passer son temps à ne rien faire **3** *vi (of engine, machine)* tourner au ralenti

idol ['aɪdəl] *n* idole *f* ▪ **idolize** *vt (adore)* idolâtrer

idyllic [aɪ'dɪlɪk] *adj* idyllique

i.e. [aɪ'i:] *(abbr* id est*)* c'est-à-dire

if [ɪf] *conj* si; **if he comes** s'il vient; **if so** si c'est le cas; **if not** sinon; **as if** comme si; **if necessary** s'il le faut

ignite [ɪg'naɪt] **1** *vt* mettre le feu à **2** *vi* prendre feu ▪ **ignition** [-'nɪʃən] *n (in vehicle)* allumage *m;* **to switch on/off the i.** mettre/couper le contact; **i. key** clef *f* de contact

ignorance ['ɪgnərəns] *n* ignorance *f* (**of** de) ▪ **ignorant** *adj* ignorant (**of** de)

ignore [ɪg'nɔ:(r)] *vt* ignorer

I'll [aɪl] = I will, I shall

ill [ɪl] **1** *adj (sick)* malade; *(bad)* mauvais; **i. will** malveillance *f* **2** *npl* **ills** maux *mpl* **3** *adv* mal ▪ **ill-advised** *adj (person)* malavisé ▪ **ill-informed** *adj* mal renseigné ▪ **ill-mannered** *adj* mal élevé

illegal [ɪ'li:gəl] *adj* illégal

illegible [ɪ'ledʒəbəl] *adj* illisible

illegitimate [ɪlɪ'dʒɪtɪmət] *adj* illégitime

illicit [ɪ'lɪsɪt] *adj* illicite

illiterate [ɪ'lɪtərət] *adj & n* analphabète *(mf)*

illness ['ɪlnɪs] *n* maladie *f*

illogical [ɪ'lɒdʒɪkəl] *adj* illogique

illuminate [ɪ'luːmɪneɪt] *vt (monument)* illuminer; *(street, question)* éclairer

illusion [ɪ'luːʒən] *n* illusion *f* (**about** sur)

illustrate ['ɪləstreɪt] *vt (with pictures, examples)* illustrer (**with** de) ▪ **illustration** *n* illustration *f*

image ['ɪmɪdʒ] *n* image *f*; (public) i. *(of company)* image *f* de marque; **he's the (living** *or* **spitting** *or* **very) i. of his brother** c'est tout le portrait de son frère ▪ **imagery** *n* imagerie *f*

imaginary [ɪ'mædʒɪnərɪ] *adj* imaginaire

imagination [ɪmædʒɪ'neɪʃən] *n* imagination *f*

imaginative [ɪ'mædʒɪnətɪv] *adj (plan, novel)* original; *(person)* imaginatif, -ive

imagine [ɪ'mædʒɪn] *vt* imaginer (**that** que) ▪ **imaginable** *adj* imaginable

imitate ['ɪmɪteɪt] *vt* imiter ▪ **imitation** *n* imitation *f*; *Br* **i. jewellery,** *Am* **i. jewelry** faux bijoux *mpl*

immaculate [ɪ'mækjʊlət] *adj* impeccable

immaterial [ɪmə'tɪərɪəl] *adj* sans importance (**to** pour)

immature [ɪmə'tʃʊə(r)] *adj (person)* immature

immediate [ɪ'miːdɪət] *adj* immédiat ▪ **immediately 1** *adv (at once)* tout de suite, immédiatement; **it's i. above/below** c'est juste au-dessus/ en dessous **2** *conj Br (as soon as)* dès que

immense [ɪ'mens] *adj* immense ▪ **immensely** *adv (rich)* immensément; **to enjoy oneself i.** s'amuser énormément

immerse [ɪ'mɜːs] *vt (in liquid)* plonger; *Fig* **to i. oneself in sth** se plonger dans qch ▪ **immersion** *n Br* **i. heater** chauffe-eau *m inv* électrique

immigrate ['ɪmɪgreɪt] *vi* immigrer ▪ **immigrant** *adj & n* immigré, -e *(mf)* ▪ **immigration** *n* immigration *f*

imminent ['ɪmɪnənt] *adj* imminent

immobile [*Br* ɪ'məʊbaɪl, *Am* ɪ'məʊbəl] *adj* immobile ▪ **immobilize** *vt* immobiliser

immoral [ɪ'mɒrəl] *adj* immoral

immortal [ɪ'mɔːtəl] *adj* immortel, -elle

immune [ɪ'mjuːn] *adj Med (to disease)* immunisé (**to** contre); *Fig* **i. to criticism** imperméable à la critique ▪ **immunize** ['ɪmjʊnaɪz] *vt* immuniser (**against** contre)

impact ['ɪmpækt] *n* impact *m*; **to make an i. on sb/sth** avoir un impact sur qn/qch

impair [ɪm'peə(r)] *vt (sight, hearing)* diminuer, affaiblir

impartial [ɪm'pɑːʃəl] *adj* impartial

impassable [ɪm'pɑːsəbəl] *adj (road)* impraticable; *(river)* infranchissable

impasse [*Br* æm'pɑːs, *Am* 'ɪmpæs] *n (situation)* impasse *f*

impassive [ɪm'pæsɪv] *adj* impassible

impatient [ɪm'peɪʃənt] *adj* impatient (**to do** de faire); **to get i. (with sb)** s'impatienter (contre qn)

impeccable [ɪm'pekəbəl] *adj (manners, person)* impeccable

impede [ɪm'piːd] *vt* gêner; **to i. sb from doing** *(prevent)* empêcher qn de faire

impediment [ɪm'pedɪmənt] *n* obstacle *m*; **speech i.** défaut *m* d'élocution

impending [ɪm'pendɪŋ] *adj* imminent

impenetrable [ɪm'penɪtrəbəl] *adj (forest, mystery)* impénétrable

imperative [ɪm'perətɪv] **1** *adj* **it is i. that he should come** il faut impérativement qu'il vienne **2** *n (in grammar)* impératif *m*

imperceptible [ɪmpə'septəbəl] *adj* imperceptible (**to** à)

imperfect [ɪm'pɜːfɪkt] **1** *adj* imparfait; *(goods)* défectueux, -euse **2** *adj & n* **i. (tense)** *(in grammar)* imparfait *(m)* ▪ **imperfection** [-pə'fekʃən] *n* imperfection *f*

imperial [ɪm'pɪərɪəl] *adj* impérial; *Br* **i. measure** = système de mesure anglo-saxon utilisant les miles, les pints etc

impersonal [ɪm'pɜːsənəl] *adj* impersonnel, -elle

impersonate [ɪm'pɜːsəneɪt] *vt (pretend to be)* se faire passer pour; *(imitate)* imiter

impertinent [ɪm'pɜːtɪnənt] *adj* impertinent (**to** envers)

impervious [ɪm'pɜːvɪəs] *adj also Fig* imperméable (**to** à)

impetuous [ɪm'petjʊəs] *adj* impétueux, -euse

impetus ['ɪmpɪtəs] *n* impulsion *f*

impinge [ɪm'pɪndʒ] *vi* **to i. on sth** *(affect)* affecter qch; *(encroach on)* empiéter sur qch

implant 1 ['ɪmplɑːnt] *n Med* implant *m* **2** [ɪm'plɑːnt] *vt Med* implanter (**in** dans); *(ideas)* inculquer (**in** à)

implement[1] ['ɪmplɪmənt] *n (tool)* instrument *m*; *(utensil)* ustensile *m*

implement[2] ['ɪmplɪment] *vt (carry out)* mettre en œuvre

implicate ['ɪmplɪkeɪt] *vt* impliquer (**in** dans) ▪ **implication** *n (consequence)* conséquence *f*; *(innuendo)* insinuation *f*; *(impact)* portée *f*; **by i.** implicitement

implicit [ɪm'plɪsɪt] *adj (implied)* implicite; *(absolute)* absolu

implore [ɪm'plɔː(r)] *vt* implorer (**sb to do** qn de faire)

imply [ɪm'plaɪ] *(pt & pp -ied) vt (insinuate)* insinuer (**that** que); *(presuppose)* supposer (**that** que); *(involve)* impliquer (**that** que) ▪ **implied** *adj* implicite

impolite [ɪmpə'laɪt] *adj* impoli

import 1 ['ɪmpɔːt] *n (item, activity)* importation *f* **2** [ɪm'pɔːt] *vt (goods) & Comptr* importer (**from** de) ▪ **importer** *n* importateur, -trice *mf*

importance [ɪm'pɔːtəns] *n* importance *f*; **to be of i.** avoir de l'importance

important [ɪm'pɔːtənt] *adj* important (**to/for** pour); **it's i. that...** il est important que... (+ *subjunctive*)

impose [ɪm'pəʊz] *vt (conditions, silence)* imposer (**on** à); *(fine, punishment)* infliger (**on sb** à qn) **2** *vi (take advantage)* s'imposer; **to i. on sb** abu-

ser de la gentillesse de qn ▪ **imposition** [-pə'zɪʃən] *n (inconvenience)* dérangement *m*

imposing [ɪm'pəʊzɪŋ] *adj* imposant

impossible [ɪm'pɒsəbəl] **1** *adj* impossible (**to do** à faire); **it is i. (for us) to do it** il (nous) est impossible de le faire **2** *n* **to do the i.** faire l'impossible ▪ **impossibility** *(pl -ies) n* impossibilité *f*

impostor [ɪm'pɒstə(r)] *n* imposteur *m*

impotent ['ɪmpətənt] *adj* impuissant

impound [ɪm'paʊnd] *vt (of police)* saisir; *(vehicle)* mettre à la fourrière

impoverished [ɪm'pɒvərɪʃd] *adj* appauvri

impractical [ɪm'præktɪkəl] *adj* peu réaliste

imprecise [ɪmprɪ'saɪs] *adj* imprécis

impregnate ['ɪmpregneɪt] *vt (soak)* imprégner (**with** de)

impress [ɪm'pres] *vt (person)* impressionner; **to be impressed with** *or* **by sb/sth** être impressionné par qn/qch

impression [ɪm'preʃən] *n* impression *f*; **to be under** *or* **have the i. that...** avoir l'impression que...; **to make a good/bad i. on sb** faire une bonne/mauvaise impression à qn ▪ **impressionable** *adj (person)* impressionnable

impressionist [ɪm'preʃənɪst] *n (mimic)* imitateur, -trice *mf*

impressive [ɪm'presɪv] *adj* impressionnant

imprint 1 ['ɪmprɪnt] *n* empreinte *f* **2** [ɪm'prɪnt] *vt* imprimer

imprison [ɪm'prɪzən] *vt* emprisonner ▪ **imprisonment** *n* emprisonnement *m*; **life i.** la prison à vie

improbable [ɪm'prɒbəbəl] *adj (unlikely)* improbable; *(unbelievable)* invraisemblable

impromptu [ɪm'prɒmptjuː] *adj (speech, party)* improvisé

improper [ɪm'prɒpə(r)] *adj* (**a**) *(indecent)* indécent (**b**) *(use, purpose)* mauvais; *(behaviour)* déplacé

improve [ɪm'pruːv] **1** *vt* améliorer; *(technique, invention)* perfectionner;

to i. one's English se perfectionner en anglais **2** *vi* s'améliorer; *(of business)* reprendre ▪ **improvement** *n* amélioration *f* (**in** de); *(progress)* progrès *mpl*; **to be an i. on sth** *(be better than)* être meilleur que qch

improvise ['ɪmprəvaɪz] *vti* improviser ▪ **improvisation** *n* improvisation *f*

impudent ['ɪmpjʊdənt] *adj* impudent

impulse ['ɪmpʌls] *n* impulsion *f*; **on i.** sur un coup de tête ▪ **impulsive** *adj* *(person)* impulsif, -ive

impunity [ɪm'pju:nɪtɪ] *n* **with i.** impunément

impurity [ɪm'pjʊərɪtɪ] *(pl* -ies*)* *n* impureté *f*

IN [ɪn] **1** *prep* **(a)** dans; **in the box/ the school** dans la boîte/l'école **in an hour('s time)** dans une heure; **in so far as** dans la mesure où
(b) à; **in school** à l'école; **in Paris** à Paris; **in the USA** aux USA; **in pencil** au crayon; **in spring** au printemps; **the woman in the red dress** la femme à la robe rouge
(c) en; **in summer/French** en été/ français; **in Spain** en Espagne; **in May** en mai; **in 2001** en 2001; **in an hour** *(during an hour)* en une heure; **in doing sth** en faisant qch; **dressed in black** habillé en noir
(d) de; **in a soft voice** d'une voix douce; **the best in the class** le meilleur/la meilleure de la classe; **an increase in salary** une augmentation de salaire; **at six in the evening** à six heures du soir
(e) chez; **in children/animals** chez les enfants/les animaux; **in Shakespeare** chez Shakespeare
(f) **in the morning** le matin; **he hasn't done it in months** ça fait des mois qu'il ne l'a pas fait; **one in ten** un sur dix; **in tens** dix par dix; **in hundreds/thousands** par centaines/milliers; **in here** ici; **in there** là-dedans
2 *adv* **to be in** *(home)* être là; *(of train)* être arrivé; *(in fashion)* être en vogue; *(in power)* être au pouvoir; **day in, day out** jour après jour; **in on a secret** au courant d'un secret; **we're in for some**

rain/trouble on va avoir de la pluie/ des ennuis
3 *npl* **the ins and outs of** les moindres détails de

in- [ɪn] *pref* in-

inability [ɪnə'bɪlɪtɪ] *(pl* -ies*)* *n* incapacité *f* (**to do** de faire)

inaccessible [ɪnək'sesəbəl] *adj* inaccessible

inaccurate [ɪn'ækjʊrət] *adj* inexact

inadequate [ɪn'ædɪkwət] *adj* *(quantity)* insuffisant; *(person)* pas à la hauteur; *(work)* médiocre

inadmissible [ɪnəd'mɪsəbəl] *adj* inadmissible

inadvertently [ɪnəd'vɜːtəntlɪ] *adv* par inadvertance

inadvisable [ɪnəd'vaɪzəbəl] *adj* **it is i. to go out alone** il est déconseillé de sortir seul

inanimate [ɪn'ænɪmət] *adj* inanimé

inappropriate [ɪnə'prəʊprɪət] *adj* *(unsuitable) (place, clothes)* peu approprié; *(remark, moment)* inopportun

inarticulate [ɪnɑː'tɪkjʊlət] *adj* *(person)* incapable de s'exprimer

inasmuch as [ɪnəz'mʌtʃəz] *conj* *(because)* dans la mesure où; *(to the extent that)* en ce sens que

inattentive [ɪnə'tentɪv] *adj* inattentif, -ive (**to** à)

inaudible [ɪn'ɔːdɪbəl] *adj* inaudible

inauguration [ɪnɔː'gjʊreɪʃən] *n* inauguration *f*; *(of official)* investiture *f*

inborn [ɪn'bɔːn] *adj* inné

Inc *(abbr* **Incorporated)** *Am Com* ≃ SARL

incalculable [ɪn'kælkjʊləbəl] *adj* incalculable

incapable [ɪn'keɪpəbəl] *adj* incapable (**of doing** de faire)

incapacitate [ɪnkə'pæsɪteɪt] *vt* rendre infirme

incense¹ ['ɪnsens] *n* *(substance)* encens *m*

incense² [ɪn'sens] *vt* rendre furieux, -euse

incentive [ɪn'sentɪv] *n* motivation *f*; *(payment)* prime *f*; **to give sb an i. to**

work encourager qn à travailler

incessant [ɪn'sesənt] *adj* incessant

incestuous [ɪn'sestjʊəs] *adj* incestueux, -euse

inch [ɪntʃ] **1** *n* pouce *m (2,54 cm)*; **i. by i.** petit à petit **2** *vti* **to i. (one's way) forward** avancer tout doucement

incident ['ɪnsɪdənt] *n* incident *m*; *(in book, film)* épisode *m*

incidental [ɪnsɪ'dentəl] *adj (additional)* accessoire; **i. music** *(in film)* musique *f* ■ **incidentally** *adv (by the way)* au fait

incinerator [ɪn'sɪnəreɪtə(r)] *n* incinérateur *m*

incision [ɪn'sɪʒən] *n* incision *f*

incisive [ɪn'saɪsɪv] *adj* incisif, -ive

incite [ɪn'saɪt] *vt* inciter (**to do** à faire)

inclination [ɪnklɪ'neɪʃən] *n (liking)* inclination *f*; *(desire)* envie *f* (**to do** de faire)

incline 1 ['ɪnklaɪn] *n (slope)* pente *f* **2** [ɪn'klaɪn] *vt (bend, tilt)* incliner; **to be inclined to do sth** *(feel desire to)* avoir bien envie de faire qch; *(tend to)* avoir tendance à faire qch **3** [ɪn'klaɪn] *vi* **to i. to** *or* **towards sth** pencher pour qch

include [ɪn'kluːd] *vt (contain)* comprendre, inclure; *(in letter)* joindre; **to be included** être compris; *(on list)* être inclus ■ **including** *prep* y compris; **not i.** sans compter; **i. service** service compris

inclusive [ɪn'kluːsɪv] *adj* inclus; **from the fourth to the tenth of May i.** du quatre au dix mai inclus; **to be i. of** comprendre; **i. of tax** toutes taxes comprises

incoherent [ɪnkəʊ'hɪərənt] *adj* incohérent

income ['ɪŋkʌm] *n* revenu *m* (**from** de); **private i.** rentes *fpl*; **i. tax** impôt *m* sur le revenu

incoming ['ɪnkʌmɪŋ] *adj (president)* nouveau (*f* nouvelle); **i. calls** *(on telephone)* appels *mpl* de l'extérieur; **i. tide** marée *f* montante

incomparable [ɪn'kɒmpərəbəl] *adj* incomparable

incompatible [ɪnkəm'pætəbəl] *adj* incompatible (**with** avec)

incompetent [ɪn'kɒmpɪtənt] *adj* incompétent

incomplete [ɪnkəm'pliːt] *adj* incomplet, -ète

incomprehensible [ɪnkɒmprɪ'hensəbəl] *adj* incompréhensible

inconceivable [ɪnkən'siːvəbəl] *adj* inconcevable

inconclusive [ɪnkən'kluːsɪv] *adj* peu concluant

inconsiderate [ɪnkən'sɪdərət] *adj (action, remark)* inconsidéré; *(person)* sans égards pour les autres

inconsistent [ɪnkən'sɪstənt] *adj (person)* incohérent; *(uneven)* irrégulier, -ère

inconspicuous [ɪnkən'spɪkjʊəs] *adj* qui passe inaperçu

inconvenient [ɪnkən'viːnɪənt] *adj (moment)* mauvais; *(arrangement)* peu commode; **it's i. (for me) to...** ça me dérange de... ■ **inconvenience 1** *n (bother)* dérangement *m*; *(disadvantage)* inconvénient *m* **2** *vt* déranger

incorporate [ɪn'kɔːpəreɪt] *vt (contain)* contenir; *(introduce)* incorporer (**into** dans)

incorrect [ɪnkə'rekt] *adj* incorrect

increase [ɪn'kriːs] **1** ['ɪnkriːs] *n* augmentation *f* (**in** *or* **of** de); **on the i.** en hausse **2** *vt* augmenter **3** *vi* augmenter; **to i. in price** augmenter ■ **increasing** *adj* croissant ■ **increasingly** *adv* de plus en plus

incredible [ɪn'kredəbəl] *adj* incroyable

incredulous [ɪn'kredjʊləs] *adj* incrédule

increment ['ɪŋkrəmənt] *n* augmentation *f*

incriminate [ɪn'krɪmɪneɪt] *vt* incriminer ■ **incriminating** *adj* compromettant

incubate ['ɪŋkjʊbeɪt] *vt (eggs)* couver ■ **incubator** *n (for baby)* couveuse *f*

incur [ɪn'kɜː(r)] *(pt & pp* **-rr-)** *vt (expenses)* encourir; *(debt)* contracter; *(criticism, anger)* s'attirer

incurable [ɪn'kjʊərəbəl] *adj* incurable

indebted [ɪn'detɪd] *adj* **i. to sb for sth/for doing sth** redevable à qn de qch/d'avoir fait qch

indecent [ɪn'diːsənt] *adj (obscene)* indécent

indecisive [ɪndɪ'saɪsɪv] *adj (person)* indécis

indeed [ɪn'diːd] *adv* en effet; **very good i.** vraiment très bon; **thank you very much i.!** merci infiniment!

indefensible [ɪndɪ'fensəbəl] *adj* indéfendable

indefinite [ɪn'defɪnət] *adj (duration, number)* indéterminé; *(plan)* mal défini ■ **indefinitely** *adv* indéfiniment

indented [ɪn'dentɪd] *adj (edge, coastline)* découpé

independence [ɪndɪ'pendəns] *n* indépendance *f*

independent [ɪndɪ'pendənt] *adj* indépendant (**of** de); *(opinions, reports)* de sources différentes ■ **independently** *adv* de façon indépendante; **i. of** indépendamment de

indescribable [ɪndɪ'skraɪbəbəl] *adj* indescriptible

indestructible [ɪndɪ'strʌktəbəl] *adj* indestructible

indeterminate [ɪndɪ'tɜːmɪnət] *adj* indéterminé

index ['ɪndeks] **1** *n (in book)* index *m*; *(in library)* fichier *m*; *(number, sign)* indice *m*; **i. card** fiche *f*; **i. finger** index *m* **2** *vt (classify)* classer

India ['ɪndɪə] *n* l'Inde *f* ■ **Indian 1** *adj* indien, -enne **2** *n* Indien, -enne *mf*

indicate ['ɪndɪkeɪt] *vt* indiquer (**that** que); **I was indicating right** *(in vehicle)* j'avais mis mon clignotant droit ■ **indication** *n (sign)* signe *m*; *(information)* indication *f*

indicative [ɪn'dɪkətɪv] *adj* **to be i. of** *(symptomatic)* être symptomatique de

indicator ['ɪndɪkeɪtə(r)] *n (sign)* indication *f* (**of** de); *Br (in vehicle)* clignotant *m*

indifferent [ɪn'dɪfərənt] *adj* indifférent (**to** à); *(mediocre)* médiocre

indigestion [ɪndɪ'dʒestʃən] *n* troubles *mpl* digestifs; **(an attack of) i.** une indigestion

indignant [ɪn'dɪgnənt] *adj* indigné (**at** *or* **about** de)

indirect [ɪndaɪ'rekt] *adj* indirect

indiscreet [ɪndɪ'skriːt] *adj* indiscret, -ète

indiscriminately [ɪndɪ'skrɪmɪnətlɪ] *adv (at random)* au hasard; *(without discrimination)* sans discernement

indispensable [ɪndɪ'spensəbəl] *adj* indispensable (**to** à)

indisputable [ɪndɪ'spjuːtəbəl] *adj* incontestable

indistinct [ɪndɪ'stɪŋkt] *adj* indistinct

indistinguishable [ɪndɪ'stɪŋgwɪʃəbəl] *adj* indifférenciable (**from** de)

individual [ɪndɪ'vɪdʒʊəl] **1** *adj (separate, personal)* individuel, -elle; *(specific)* particulier, -ère **2** *n (person)* individu *m* ■ **individually** *adv (separately)* individuellement

indivisible [ɪndɪ'vɪzəbəl] *adj* indivisible

indoctrinate [ɪn'dɒktrɪneɪt] *vt* endoctriner

Indonesia [ɪndəʊ'niːzɪə] *n* l'Indonésie *f*

indoor ['ɪndɔː(r)] *adj (games, shoes)* d'intérieur; *(swimming pool)* couvert ■ **indoors** *adv* à l'intérieur; **to go/come i.** rentrer

induce [ɪn'djuːs] *vt (persuade)* persuader (**to do** de faire); *(cause)* provoquer

indulge [ɪn'dʌldʒ] **1** *vt (sb's wishes)* satisfaire; *(child)* gâter **2** *vi* **to i. in sth** *(ice cream, cigar)* s'offrir qch; *(hobby, vice)* s'adonner à qch ■ **indulgent** *adj* indulgent (**to** envers)

industrial [ɪn'dʌstrɪəl] *adj* industriel, -elle; *Br* **to take i. action** se mettre en grève; *Br* **i. estate,** *Am* **i. park** zone *f* industrielle ■ **industrialist** *n* industriel *m* ■ **industrialized** *adj* industrialisé

industrious [ɪn'dʌstrɪəs] *adj* travailleur, -euse

industry ['ɪndəstrɪ] *(pl* **-ies)** *n (economic sector)* industrie *f*; *(hard work)* application *f*

inedible [ɪn'edəbəl] *adj* immangeable

ineffective [ɪnɪ'fektɪv] *adj (measure)* inefficace; *(person)* incapable

ineffectual [ɪnɪ'fektʃʊəl] *adj (measure)* inefficace; *(person)* incompétent

inefficient [ɪnɪ'fɪʃənt] *adj (person, measure)* inefficace; *(machine)* peu performant

ineligible [ɪn'elɪdʒəbəl] *adj (candidate)* inéligible; **to be i. for sth** *(scholarship)* ne pas avoir droit à qch

inept [ɪ'nept] *adj (incompetent)* incompétent; *(foolish)* inepte

inequality [ɪnɪ'kwɒlətɪ] *(pl* -ies) *n* inégalité *f*

inert [ɪ'nɜːt] *adj* inerte

inescapable [ɪnɪ'skeɪpəbəl] *adj (outcome)* inéluctable; *(conclusion)* incontournable

inevitable [ɪn'evɪtəbəl] *adj* inévitable

inexcusable [ɪnɪk'skjuːzəbəl] *adj* inexcusable

inexpensive [ɪnɪk'spensɪv] *adj* bon marché *inv*

inexperienced [ɪnɪks'pɪərɪənst] *adj* inexpérimenté

inexplicable [ɪnɪk'splɪkəbəl] *adj* inexplicable

infallible [ɪn'fæləbəl] *adj* infaillible

infamous ['ɪnfəməs] *adj (well-known)* tristement célèbre; *(crime)* infâme

infant ['ɪnfənt] *n* bébé *m*; *Br* **i. school** = école primaire pour enfants de cinq à sept ans

infantry ['ɪnfəntrɪ] *n* infanterie *f*

infatuated [ɪn'fætʃʊeɪtɪd] *adj* entiché **(with** de)

infect [ɪn'fekt] *vt (wound, person)* infecter; *(water, food)* contaminer; **to get** *or* **become infected** s'infecter ■ **infection** *n* infection *f* ■ **infectious** [-ʃəs] *adj (disease)* infectieux, -euse

infer [ɪn'fɜː(r)] *(pt & pp* -rr-) *vt* déduire **(from** de; **that** que)

inferior [ɪn'fɪərɪə(r)] **1** *adj* inférieur **(to** à); *(goods, work)* de qualité inférieure **2** *n (person)* inférieur, -e *mf* ■ **in-**

feriority [-rɪ'ɒrɪtɪ] *n* infériorité *f*

infernal [ɪn'fɜːnəl] *adj* infernal

inferno [ɪn'fɜːnəʊ] *(pl* -os) *n (blaze)* brasier *m*

infertile [*Br* ɪn'fɜːtaɪl, *Am* ɪn'fɜːrtəl] *adj (person, land)* stérile

infest [ɪn'fest] *vt* infester **(with** de)

infidelity [ɪnfɪ'delɪtɪ] *(pl* -ies) *n* infidélité *f*

infiltrate ['ɪnfɪltreɪt] **1** *vt* infiltrer **2** *vi* s'infiltrer **(into** dans)

infinite ['ɪnfɪnɪt] *adj* infini ■ **infinitely** *adv* infiniment

infinitive [ɪn'fɪnɪtɪv] *n (in grammar)* infinitif *m*

infinity [ɪn'fɪnɪtɪ] *n Math & Phot* infini *m*

infirmary [ɪn'fɜːmərɪ] *(pl* -ies) *n (hospital)* hôpital *m*

inflamed [ɪn'fleɪmd] *adj (throat, wound)* enflammé; **to become i.** s'enflammer

inflammable [ɪn'flæməbəl] *adj* inflammable ■ **inflammation** [-flə'meɪʃən] *n* inflammation *f*

inflate [ɪn'fleɪt] *vt (balloon, prices)* gonfler ■ **inflatable** *adj* gonflable

inflation [ɪn'fleɪʃən] *n Econ* inflation *f*

inflexible [ɪn'fleksəbəl] *adj* inflexible

inflict [ɪn'flɪkt] *vt (punishment, defeat)* infliger **(on** à); *(wound, damage)* occasionner **(on** à)

influence ['ɪnflʊəns] **1** *n* influence *f* **(on** sur) **2** *vt* influencer ■ **influential** [-'enʃəl] *adj* influent

influenza [ɪnflʊ'enzə] *n* grippe *f*

influx ['ɪnflʌks] *n* afflux *m* **(of** de)

info ['ɪnfəʊ] *n Fam* renseignements *mpl* **(on** sur)

inform [ɪn'fɔːm] **1** *vt* informer **(of** *or* **about** de; **that** que) **2** *vi* **to i. on sb** dénoncer qn ■ **informed** *adj* **to keep sb i. of sth** tenir qn au courant de qch

informal [ɪn'fɔːməl] *adj (unaffected)* simple; *(casual)* décontracté; *(tone, language)* familier, -ère; *(unofficial)* officieux, -euse ■ **informally** *adv (unaffectedly)* avec simplicité; *(casually)*

avec décontraction; *(meet, discuss)* officieusement

information [ɪnfə'meɪʃən] *n (facts, news)* renseignements *mpl* (about *or* on *sur*); *Comptr* information *f*; **a piece of i.** un renseignement, une information; **to get some i.** se renseigner; **i. technology** informatique *f*

informative [ɪn'fɔːmətɪv] *adj* instructif, -ive

infrequent [ɪn'friːkwənt] *adj* peu fréquent

infringe [ɪn'frɪndʒ] **1** *vt (rule, law)* enfreindre à **2** *vt insep* **to i. upon sth** empiéter sur qch

infuriating [ɪn'fjuːrɪeɪtɪŋ] *adj* exaspérant

infusion [ɪn'fjuːʒən] *n (drink)* infusion *f*

ingenious [ɪn'dʒiːnɪəs] *adj* ingénieux, -euse

ingrained [ɪn'greɪnd] *adj (prejudice, attitude)* enraciné; **i. dirt** crasse *f*

ingredient [ɪn'griːdɪənt] *n* ingrédient *m*

inhabit [ɪn'hæbɪt] *vt* habiter ■ **inhabitant** *n* habitant, -e *mf*

inhale [ɪn'heɪl] *vt (gas, fumes)* inhaler; *(cigarette smoke)* avaler

inherent [ɪn'hɪərənt] *adj* inhérent (in à)

inherit [ɪn'herɪt] *vt* hériter (**from** de); *(title)* accéder à ■ **inheritance** *n (legacy)* héritage *m*

inhibit [ɪn'hɪbɪt] *vt (progress, growth)* entraver; *(of person)* inhiber; **to i. sb from doing sth** empêcher qn de faire qch ■ **inhibited** *adj (person)* inhibé ■ **inhibition** *n* inhibition *f*

inhospitable [ɪnhɒ'spɪtəbəl] *adj* inhospitalier, -ère

inhuman [ɪn'hjuːmən] *adj* inhumain ■ **inhumane** [-'meɪn] *adj* inhumain

initial [ɪ'nɪʃəl] **1** *adj* initial **2** *npl* **initials** *(letters)* initiales *fpl*; *(signature)* paraphe *m* **3** *(Br* **-ll-,** *Am* **-l-)** *vt* parapher ■ **initially** *adv* au début, initialement

initiate [ɪ'nɪʃɪeɪt] *vt (reform, negotiations)* amorcer; *(attack, rumour, project)* lancer

initiative [ɪ'nɪʃətɪv] *n* initiative *f*

inject [ɪn'dʒekt] *vt* injecter (**into** dans); **to i. sth into sb, to i. sb with sth** faire une piqûre de qch à qn ■ **injection** *n* injection *f*, piqûre *f*; **to give sb an i.** faire une piqûre à qn

injure ['ɪndʒə(r)] *vt (physically)* blesser; *(reputation)* nuire à; **to i. one's foot** se blesser au pied ■ **injured 1** *adj* blessé **2** *npl* **the i.** les blessés *mpl*

injury ['ɪndʒərɪ] *(pl* **-ies)** *n (physical)* blessure *f*; **i. time** *(in sport)* arrêts *mpl* de jeu

injustice [ɪn'dʒʌstɪs] *n* injustice *f*

ink [ɪŋk] *n* encre *f*

inlaid [ɪn'leɪd] *adj (with jewels)* incrusté (**with** de); *(with wood)* marqueté

inland 1 ['ɪnlənd, 'ɪnlænd] *adj* intérieur; *Br* **the I. Revenue** ≃ le fisc **2** [ɪn'lænd] *adv (travel)* vers l'intérieur

in-laws ['ɪnlɔːz] *npl* belle-famille *f*

inlet ['ɪnlet] *n (of sea)* crique *f*

inmate ['ɪnmeɪt] *n (of prison)* détenu, -e *mf*; *(of asylum)* interné, -e *mf*

inn [ɪn] *n* auberge *f*

innate [ɪ'neɪt] *adj* inné

inner ['ɪnə(r)] *adj* intérieur; *(feelings)* intime; **i. circle** *(of society)* initiés *mpl*; **i. city** quartiers *mpl* déshérités du centre-ville; **i. tube** chambre *f* à air ■ **innermost** *adj* le plus profond *(f* la plus profonde); *(thoughts)* le plus secret *(f* la plus secrète)

inning ['ɪnɪŋ] *n (in baseball)* tour *m* de batte ■ **innings** *n inv (in cricket)* tour *m* de batte

innocent ['ɪnəsənt] *adj* innocent

innovation [ɪnə'veɪʃən] *n* innovation *f*

innumerable [ɪ'njuːmərəbəl] *adj* innombrable

inoculate [ɪ'nɒkjʊleɪt] *vt* vacciner (**against** contre) ■ **inoculation** *n* inoculation *f*

inoffensive [ɪnə'fensɪv] *adj* inoffensif, -ive

inopportune [ɪn'ɒpətjuːn] *adj* inopportun

in-patient ['ɪnpeɪʃənt] *n Br* malade *mf* hospitalisé(e)

input ['ɪnpʊt] **1** *n (contribution)* contribution *f*; *Comptr (operation)* entrée *f*; *(data)* données *fpl* **2** *(pt & pp* **-put)** *vt Comptr (data)* entrer

inquest ['ɪnkwest] *n (legal investigation)* enquête *f*

inquire [ɪn'kwaɪə(r)] **1** *vt* demander; **to i. how to get to...** demander le chemin de... **2** *vi* se renseigner (**about** sur); **to i. after sb** demander des nouvelles de qn; **to i. into sth** faire des recherches sur qch

inquiry [ɪn'kwaɪrɪ] *(pl* **-ies)** *n (request for information)* demande *f* de renseignements; *(official investigation)* enquête *f*; **to make inquiries** demander des renseignements; *(of police)* enquêter

inquisitive [ɪn'kwɪzɪtɪv] *adj* curieux, -euse

insane [ɪn'seɪn] *adj* dément, fou *(f* folle); **to go i.** perdre la raison

insatiable [ɪn'seɪʃəbəl] *adj* insatiable

inscribe [ɪn'skraɪb] *vt* inscrire; *(book)* dédicacer (**to** à) ■ **inscription** [-'skrɪpʃən] *n* inscription *f*; *(in book)* dédicace *f*

insect ['ɪnsekt] *n* insecte *m*; **i. repellent** anti-moustiques *m inv*

insecure [ɪnsɪ'kjʊə(r)] *adj (unsafe)* peu sûr; *(job, future)* précaire; *(person)* angoissé

insemination [ɪnsemɪ'neɪʃən] *n* **artificial i.** insémination *f* artificielle

insensitive [ɪn'sensɪtɪv] *adj (person)* insensible (**to** à); *(remark)* indélicat

inseparable [ɪn'sepərəbəl] *adj* inséparable (**from** de)

insert [ɪn'sɜːt] *vt* insérer (**in** or **into** dans) ■ **insertion** *n* insertion *f*

inside 1 ['ɪnsaɪd] *adj* intérieur; *(information)* obtenu à la source; *Aut* **the i. lane** *(in Britain)* la voie de gauche; *(in Europe, US)* la voie de droite
2 ['ɪn'saɪd] *n* intérieur *m*; *Fam* **insides** *(stomach)* entrailles *fpl*; **on the i.** à l'intérieur (**of** de); **i. out** *(clothes)* à l'envers; *(know, study)* à fond
3 [ɪn'saɪd] *adv* à l'intérieur
4 [ɪn'saɪd] *prep* à l'intérieur de, dans; *(time)* en moins de

insider [ɪn'saɪdə(r)] *n* initié, -e *mf*

insidious [ɪn'sɪdɪəs] *adj* insidieux, -euse

insight ['ɪnsaɪt] *n* perspicacité *f*; *(into question)* aperçu *m*

insignificant [ɪnsɪg'nɪfɪkənt] *adj* insignifiant

insincere [ɪnsɪn'sɪə(r)] *adj* peu sincère

insinuate [ɪn'sɪnjʊeɪt] *vt (suggest)* insinuer (**that** que)

insipid [ɪn'sɪpɪd] *adj* insipide

insist [ɪn'sɪst] **1** *vt (maintain)* soutenir (**that** que); **I i. that you come** or **on your coming** *(I demand it)* j'insiste pour que tu viennes **2** *vi* insister; **to i. on sth** *(demand)* exiger qch; *(assert)* affirmer qch; **to i. on doing sth** tenir à faire qch

insistence [ɪn'sɪstəns] *n* insistance *f*
■ **insistent** *adj (person)* pressant; **to be i. (that)** insister (pour que + *subjunctive*)

insolent ['ɪnsələnt] *adj* insolent

insoluble [ɪn'sɒljʊbəl] *adj* insoluble

insolvent [ɪn'sɒlvənt] *adj (financially)* insolvable

insomnia [ɪn'sɒmnɪə] *n* insomnie *f*

insomuch as [ɪnsəʊ'mʌtʃəz] *adv* = inasmuch as

inspect [ɪn'spekt] *vt* inspecter; *(tickets)* contrôler; *(troops)* passer en revue
■ **inspector** *n* inspecteur, -trice *mf*; *(on train)* contrôleur, -euse *mf*

inspire [ɪn'spaɪə(r)] *vt* inspirer; **to i. sb to do sth** pousser qn à faire qch ■ **inspiration** [-spə'reɪʃən] *n* inspiration *f*; *(person)* source *f* d'inspiration

instability [ɪnstə'bɪlɪtɪ] *n* instabilité *f*

install [ɪn'stɔːl] *(Am* **instal)** *vt* installer

instalment [ɪn'stɔːlmənt] *(Am* **installment)** *n (part payment)* versement *m*; *(of serial, story)* épisode *m*; *(of publication)* fascicule *m*; **to pay by instalments** payer par versements échelonnés; *Am* **to buy on the i. plan** acheter à crédit

instance ['ɪnstəns] *n (example)* exemple *m; (case)* cas *m;* **for i.** par exemple; **in this i.** dans le cas présent

instant ['ɪnstənt] **1** *adj* immédiat; **i. coffee** café *m* instantané **2** *n (moment)* instant *m;* **this (very) i.** *(at once)* à l'instant; **the i. that I saw her** dès que je l'ai vue ▪ **instantly** *adv* immédiatement

instantaneous [ɪnstən'teɪnɪəs] *adj* instantané

instead [ɪn'sted] *adv (in place of sth)* à la place; *(in place of sb)* à ma/ta/*etc* place; **i. of sth** au lieu de qch; **i. of doing sth** au lieu de faire qch; **i. of him/her** à sa place

instigate ['ɪnstɪgeɪt] *vt* provoquer ▪ **instigator** *n* instigateur, -trice *mf*

instil [ɪn'stɪl] *(Am* **instill)** *(pt & pp -ll-) vt (idea)* inculquer **(into** à); *(doubt)* instiller **(in** à)

instinct ['ɪnstɪŋkt] *n* instinct *m;* **by i.** d'instinct ▪ **instinctive** *adj* instinctif, -ive

institute ['ɪnstɪtjuːt] **1** *n* institut *m* **2** *vt (rule, practice)* instituer; *(legal inquiry)* ordonner

institution [ɪnstɪ'tjuːʃən] *n (organization, custom)* institution *f; (public, financial, religious, psychiatric)* établissement *m*

instruct [ɪn'strʌkt] *vt (teach)* enseigner **(sb in sth** qch à qn); **to i. sb about sth** *(inform)* instruire qn de qch; **to i. sb to do** *(order)* charger qn de faire ▪ **instruction** [-ʃən] *n (teaching, order)* instruction *f;* **instructions (for use)** mode *m* d'emploi ▪ **instructor** *n (for judo, dance)* professeur *m; (for skiing, swimming)* moniteur, -trice *mf;* **driving i.** moniteur, -trice *mf* d'auto-école

instrument ['ɪnstrəmənt] *n* instrument *m*

instrumental [ɪnstrə'mentəl] *adj (music)* instrumental; **to be i. in sth/in doing sth** contribuer à qch/à faire qch

insubordinate [ɪnsə'bɔːdɪnət] *adj* insubordonné

insufferable [ɪn'sʌfərəbəl] *adj* intolérable

insufficient [ɪnsə'fɪʃənt] *adj* insuffisant ▪ **insufficiently** *adv* insuffisamment

insulate ['ɪnsjʊleɪt] *vt (against cold) & El* isoler; *(against sound)* insonoriser ▪ **insulation** *n* isolation *f; (against sound)* insonorisation *f; (material)* isolant *m*

insulin ['ɪnsjʊlɪn] *n* insuline *f*

insult 1 ['ɪnsʌlt] *n* insulte *f* **(to** à) **2** [ɪn'sʌlt] *vt* insulter

insure [ɪn'ʃʊə(r)] *vt* **(a)** *(house, car, goods)* assurer **(against** contre) **(b)** *Am =* **ensure** ▪ **insurance** *n* assurance *f;* **i. policy** police *f* d'assurance

insurmountable [ɪnsə'maʊntəbəl] *adj* insurmontable

intact [ɪn'tækt] *adj* intact

intake ['ɪnteɪk] *n (of food)* consommation *f; (of students, schoolchildren)* admissions *fpl*

intangible [ɪn'tændʒəbəl] *adj* intangible

integral ['ɪntɪgrəl] *adj* intégral; **to be an i. part of sth** faire partie intégrante de qch

integrate ['ɪntɪgreɪt] **1** *vt* intégrer **(into** dans) **2** *vi* s'intégrer **(into** dans) ▪ **integration** *n* intégration *f;* **(racial) i.** déségrégation *f* raciale

integrity [ɪn'tegrətɪ] *n* intégrité *f*

intellect ['ɪntɪlekt] *n* intelligence *f,* intellect *m* ▪ **intellectual** *adj & n* intellectuel, -elle *(mf)*

intelligence [ɪn'telɪdʒəns] *n* intelligence *f*

intelligent [ɪn'telɪdʒənt] *adj* intelligent

intelligible [ɪn'telɪdʒəbəl] *adj* intelligible

intend [ɪn'tend] *vt (gift, remark)* destiner **(for** à); **to be intended to do sth** être destiné à faire qch; **to i. to do sth** avoir l'intention de faire qch ▪ **intended** *adj (deliberate)* voulu; *(planned)* prévu

intense [ɪn'tens] *adj* intense; *(interest)* vif *(f* vive); *(person)* passionné ▪ **intensely** *adv (look at)* intensément; *Fig (very)* extrêmement

intensify [ɪn'tensɪfaɪ] *(pt & pp* -**ied**) **1**
vt intensifier **2** *vi* s'intensifier

intensity [ɪn'tensətɪ] *n* intensité *f*

intensive [ɪn'tensɪv] *adj* intensif, -ive;
in i. care en réanimation

intent [ɪn'tent] **1** *adj (look)* intense; **to
be i. on doing** être résolu à faire **2** *n* in-
tention *f*; **to all intents and purposes**
quasiment

intention [ɪn'tenʃən] *n* intention *f* (**of
doing** de faire)

intentional [ɪn'tenʃənəl] *adj* inten-
tionnel, -elle; **it wasn't i.** ce n'était pas
fait exprès ▪ **intentionally** *adv* inten-
tionnellement, exprès

inter [ɪn'tɜ:(r)] *(pt & pp* -**rr-**) *vt* enterrer

inter- ['ɪntə(r)] *pref* inter-

interact [ɪntər'ækt] *vi (of person)*
communiquer (**with** avec); *(of several
people)* communiquer entre eux/elles;
(of chemicals) réagir (**with** avec)

interactive [ɪntə'ræktɪv] *adj Comptr*
interactif, -ive

intercept [ɪntə'sept] *vt* intercepter

interchange ['ɪntətʃeɪndʒ] *n Br (on
road)* échangeur *m*

interchangeable [ɪntə'tʃeɪndʒəbəl]
adj interchangeable

inter-city [ɪntə'sɪtɪ] *adj Br* **i. train**
train *m* de grandes lignes

intercom ['ɪntəkɒm] *n* Interphone®
m

interconnected [ɪntəkə'nektɪd] *adj
(facts)* lié(e)s

intercourse ['ɪntəkɔ:s] *n (sexual)*
rapports *mpl* sexuels

interdependent [ɪntədɪ'pendənt]
adj interdépendant; *(parts of machine)*
solidaire

interest ['ɪntərest, 'ɪntrɪst] **1** *n* intérêt
m; *(hobby)* centre *m* d'intérêt; *(money)*
intérêts *mpl*; **to take an i. in sb/sth**
s'intéresser à qn/qch; **to lose i. in sb/
sth** se désintéresser de qn/qch; **to be
of i. to sb** intéresser qn **2** *vt* intéresser
▪ **interested** *adj* intéressé; **to be i. in
sb/sth** s'intéresser à qn/qch; **are you
i.?** ça vous intéresse? ▪ **interest-free**
adj (loan) sans intérêts; *(credit)* gratuit
▪ **interesting** *adj* intéressant

interfere [ɪntə'fɪə(r)] *vi (meddle)* se
mêler (**in** de); **to i. with sth** *(hinder)*
gêner qch; *(touch)* toucher à qch

interference [ɪntə'fɪərəns] *n* ingé-
rence *f*; *(on television, radio)* parasites
mpl

interim ['ɪntərɪm] **1** *n* **in the i.** entre-
temps **2** *adj (measure)* provisoire

interior [ɪn'tɪərɪə(r)] *adj & n* intérieur
(m)

interlock [ɪntə'lɒk] *vi (of machine
parts)* s'emboîter

interlude ['ɪntəlu:d] *n (on TV)* inter-
lude *m*; *(in theatre)* intermède *m*; *(per-
iod of time)* intervalle *m*

intermediary [ɪntə'mi:dɪərɪ] *(pl
-ies)* *n* intermédiaire *mf*

intermediate [ɪntə'mi:dɪət] *adj* in-
termédiaire; *(course, student)* de niveau
moyen

intermission [ɪntə'mɪʃən] *n* entracte
m

intermittent [ɪntə'mɪtənt] *adj* inter-
mittent

intern 1 ['ɪntɜ:n] *n Am Med* interne *mf*
2 [ɪn'tɜ:n] *vt (imprison)* interner

internal [ɪn'tɜ:nəl] *adj* interne; *(flight,
policy)* intérieur; *Am* **the I. Revenue
Service** ≃ le fisc ▪ **internally** *adv* in-
térieurement

international [ɪntə'næʃənəl] **1** *adj*
international **2** *n (match)* rencontre *f*
internationale; *(player)* international *m*

Internet ['ɪntənet] *n Comptr* **the I.**
l'Internet *m*; **I. access** accès *m* (à l')In-
ternet; **I. service provider** fournisseur
m d'accès Internet

interpret [ɪn'tɜ:prɪt] **1** *vt* interpréter
2 *vi (translate for people)* faire l'inter-
prète ▪ **interpretation** *n* interprétation
f ▪ **interpreter** *n* interprète *mf*

interrelated [ɪntərɪ'leɪtɪd] *adj* lié

interrogate [ɪn'terəgeɪt] *vt* interro-
ger ▪ **interrogation** [-'geɪʃən] *n* inter-
rogation *f*; *(by police)* interrogatoire *m*

interrupt [ɪntə'rʌpt] **1** *vt* interrompre
2 *vi* **I'm sorry to i.** je suis désolé de
vous interrompre ▪ **interruption** *n* in-
terruption *f*

intersect [ɪntə'sekt] **1** *vt* couper **2** *vi*

se couper ■ **intersection** *r.* intersection *f; (of roads)* croisement *m*

interstate ['ɪntəsteɪt] *n* autoroute *f*

interval ['ɪntəvəl] *n* intervalle *m; Br (in theatre, cinema)* entracte *m;* **at intervals** *(in time)* de temps à autre; *(in space)* par intervalles; **at five-minute intervals** toutes les cinq minutes

intervene [ɪntə'viːn] *vi (of person)* intervenir **(in** dans); *(of event)* survenir ■ **intervention** [-'venʃən] *n* intervention *f*

interview ['ɪntəvjuː] **1** *n* entretien *m* **(with** avec); *TV & Journ* interview *m ou f* **2** *vt (for job)* faire passer un entretien à; *TV & Journ* interviewer ■ **interviewer** *n TV* intervieweur, -euse *mf; (for research, in canvassing)* enquêteur, -euse *mf*

intestine [ɪn'testɪn] *n* intestin *m*

intimate ['ɪntɪmət] *adj* intime; *(friendship)* profond; *(knowledge)* approfondi ■ **intimately** *adv* intimement

intimidate [ɪn'tɪmɪdeɪt] *vt* intimider

into ['ɪntuː, *unstressed* 'ɪntə] *prep* **(a)** dans; **to put sth i. sth** mettre qch dans qch; **to go i. a room** entrer dans une pièce

(b) en; **to translate i. French** traduire en français; **to change sb i. sth** changer qn en qch; **to break sth i. pieces** briser qch en morceaux; **to go i. town** aller en ville

(c) *Math* **three i. six goes two** six divisé par trois fait deux

(d) *Fam* **to be i. jazz** être branché jazz

intolerable [ɪn'tɒlərəbəl] *adj* intolérable **(that** que + *subjunctive)*

intolerance [ɪn'tɒlərəns] *n* intolérance *f* ■ **intolerant** *adj* intolérant

intonation [ɪntə'neɪʃən] *n* intonation *f*

intoxicated [ɪn'tɒksɪkeɪtɪd] *adj* ivre

intransigent [ɪn'trænsɪdʒənt] *adj* intransigeant

intransitive [ɪn'trænsɪtɪv] *adj (in grammar)* intransitif, -ive

intricate ['ɪntrɪkət] *adj* compliqué

intrigue 1 ['ɪntriːg] *n (plot)* intrigue *f* **2** [ɪn'triːg] *vt (interest)* intriguer ■ **intri-**

guing *adj (news, attitude)* curieux, -euse

introduce [ɪntrə'djuːs] *vt (bring in, insert)* introduire **(into** dans); *(programme, subject)* présenter; **to i. sb (to sb)** présenter qn (à qn)

introduction [ɪntrə'dʌkʃən] *n* introduction *f; (of person to person)* présentation *f* ■ **introductory** *adj (words, speech)* d'introduction; *(course)* d'initiation

introvert ['ɪntrəvɜːt] *n* introverti, -e *mf*

intrude [ɪn'truːd] *vi (of person)* déranger **(on sb** qn) ■ **intruder** *n* intrus, -e *mf* ■ **intrusion** *n (bother)* dérangement *m; (interference)* intrusion *f* **(into** dans)

intuition [ɪntjuː'ɪʃən] *n* intuition *f*

inundate ['ɪnʌndeɪt] *vt* inonder **(with** de); **inundated with work/letters** submergé de travail/lettres

invade [ɪn'veɪd] *vt* envahir ■ **invader** *n* envahisseur, -euse *mf*

invalid[1] ['ɪnvəlɪd] *adj & n* malade *(mf); (disabled person)* infirme *(mf)*

invalid[2] [ɪn'vælɪd] *adj (ticket, passport)* non valable ■ **invalidate** *vt (ticket)* annuler; *(election, law)* invalider; *(theory)* infirmer

invaluable [ɪn'væljʊəbəl] *adj* inestimable

invariably [ɪn'veərɪəblɪ] *adv* invariablement

invasion [ɪn'veɪʒən] *n* invasion *f*

invent [ɪn'vent] *vt* inventer ■ **invention** *n* invention *f* ■ **inventor** *n* inventeur, -trice *mf*

inventory ['ɪnvəntərɪ] *(pl* **-ies)** *n* inventaire *m*

invert [ɪn'vɜːt] *vt (order)* intervertir; *(turn upside down)* renverser; *Br* **inverted commas** guillemets *mpl*

invest [ɪn'vest] **1** *vt (money)* investir **(in** dans); *(time, effort)* consacrer **(in** à) **2** *vi* **to i. in** *(company)* investir dans; *Fig (car)* se payer ■ **investment** *n* investissement *m* ■ **investor** *n (in shares)* investisseur *m*

investigate [ɪn'vestɪgeɪt] *vt (examine)* examiner; *(crime)* enquêter sur

■ **investigation** *n* examen *m*, étude *f*; *(inquiry by journalist, police)* enquête *f* **(of** *or* **into** sur) ■ **investigator** *n (detective)* enquêteur, -euse *mf*; *(private)* détective *m*

invigilator [ɪn'vɪdʒɪleɪtə(r)] *n Br* surveillant, -e *mf (à un examen)*

invigorating [ɪn'vɪɡəreɪtɪŋ] *adj* vivifiant

invincible [ɪn'vɪnsəbəl] *adj* invincible

invisible [ɪn'vɪzəbəl] *adj* invisible

invite 1 [ɪn'vaɪt] *vt* inviter (**to do** à faire); *(ask for)* demander; **to i. sb out** inviter qn (à sortir) **2** ['ɪnvaɪt] *n Fam* invit' *f* ■ **invitation** [-vɪ'teɪʃən] *n* invitation *f*

invoice ['ɪnvɔɪs] **1** *n* facture *f* **2** *vt (goods)* facturer; *(person)* envoyer la facture à

invoke [ɪn'vəʊk] *vt* invoquer

involuntary [ɪn'vɒləntəri] *adj* involontaire

involve [ɪn'vɒlv] *vt (entail)* entraîner; **to i. sb in sth** impliquer qn dans qch; *(in project)* associer qn à qch; **the job involves going abroad** le poste nécessite des déplacements à l'étranger

involved [ɪn'vɒlvd] *adj* **(a) to be i. in an accident** avoir un accident; **fifty people were i. in the project** cinquante personnes ont pris part au projet; **to be i. with sb** *(emotionally)* avoir une liaison avec qn; **the factors i.** *(at stake)* les facteurs en jeu; **the person i.** *(concerned)* la personne en question **(b)** *(complicated)* compliqué

involvement [ɪn'vɒlvmənt] *n* participation *f* (**in** à); *(commitment)* engagement *m* (**in** dans)

invulnerable [ɪn'vʌlnərəbəl] *adj* invulnérable

inward ['ɪnwəd] **1** *adj & adv (movement, move)* vers l'intérieur **2** *adj (inner) (happiness)* intérieur; *(thoughts)* intime ■ **inwardly** *adv (laugh, curse)* intérieurement ■ **inwards** *adv* vers l'intérieur

iodine [*Br* 'aɪədiːn, *Am* 'aɪədaɪn] *n (antiseptic)* teinture *f* d'iode

IOU [aɪəʊ'juː] *(abbr* **I owe you)** *n* reconnaissance *f* de dette

IQ [aɪ'kjuː] *(abbr* **intelligence quotient)** *n* QI *m inv*

Iran [ɪ'rɑːn, ɪ'ræn] *n* l'Iran *m* ■ **Iranian** [ɪ'reɪnɪən, *Am* ɪ'rɑːnɪən] **1** *adj* iranien, -enne **2** *n* Iranien, -enne *mf*

Iraq [ɪ'rɑːk] *n* l'Irak *m* ■ **Iraqi 1** *adj* irakien, -enne **2** *n* Irakien, -enne *mf*

irate [aɪ'reɪt] *adj* furieux, -euse

Ireland ['aɪələnd] *n* l'Irlande *f* ■ **Irish** ['aɪrɪʃ] **1** *adj* irlandais **2** *n (language)* irlandais *m*; **the I.** *(people)* les Irlandais *mpl* ■ **Irishman** *(pl* -**men)** *n* Irlandais *m* ■ **Irishwoman** *(pl* -**women)** *n* Irlandaise *f*

iris ['aɪrɪs] *n (plant, of eye)* iris *m*

iron ['aɪən] **1** *n* fer *m*; *(for clothes)* fer *m* à repasser **2** *vt (clothes)* repasser; *Fig* **to i. out difficulties** aplanir les difficultés ■ **ironing** *n* repassage *m*; **i. board** planche *f* à repasser

ironmonger ['aɪənmʌŋɡə(r)] *n* quincaillier, -ère *mf*; **i.'s (shop)** quincaillerie *f*

irony ['aɪərəni] *n* ironie *f* ■ **ironic(al)** [aɪ'rɒnɪk(əl)] *adj* ironique

irrational [ɪ'ræʃənəl] *adj* irrationnel, -elle

irrefutable [ɪrɪ'fjuːtəbəl] *adj (evidence)* irréfutable

irregular [ɪ'reɡjʊlə(r)] *adj* irrégulier, -ère ■ **irregularity** [-'lærɪtɪ] *(pl* -**ies)** *n* irrégularité *f*

irrelevant [ɪ'reləvənt] *adj* sans rapport (**to** avec); *(remark)* hors de propos; **that's i.** ça n'a rien à voir (avec la question)

irreparable [ɪ'repərəbəl] *adj (harm, loss)* irréparable

irreplaceable [ɪrɪ'pleɪsəbəl] *adj* irremplaçable

irresistible [ɪrɪ'zɪstəbəl] *adj (person, charm)* irrésistible

irrespective [ɪrɪ'spektɪv] *prep* **i. of** indépendamment de

irresponsible [ɪrɪ'spɒnsəbəl] *adj (act)* irréfléchi; *(person)* irresponsable

irreverent [ɪ'revərənt] *adj* irrévérencieux, -euse

irreversible [ɪrɪ'vɜːsəbəl] *adj (process)* irréversible; *(decision)* irrévocable

irrigate ['ɪrɪgeɪt] *vt* irriguer

irritable ['ɪrɪtəbəl] *adj (easily annoyed)* irritable

irritant ['ɪrɪtənt] *n (to eyes, skin)* irritant *m*

irritate ['ɪrɪteɪt] *vt (annoy, inflame)* irriter ■ **irritating** *adj* irritant

is [ɪz] *see* be

Islam ['ɪzlɑːm] *n* l'Islam *m* ■ **Islamic** [ɪz'læmɪk] *adj* islamique

island ['aɪlənd] *n* île *f*; **(traffic) i.** refuge *m* (pour piétons) ■ **islander** *n* insulaire *mf*

isle [aɪl] *n* île *f*

isn't ['ɪzənt] = **is not**

isolate ['aɪsəleɪt] *vt* isoler **(from** de) ■ **isolated** *adj (remote, unique)* isolé ■ **isolation** *n* isolement *m*; **in i.** isolement

ISP [aɪes'piː] *(abbr* **Internet Service Provider)** *n Comptr* fournisseur *m* d'accès Internet

Israel ['ɪzreɪl] *n* Israël *m* ■ **Israeli 1** *adj* israélien, -enne **2** *n* Israélien, -enne *mf*

issue ['ɪʃuː] **1** *n (of newspaper, magazine)* numéro *m*; *(matter)* question *f*; **at i.** *(at stake)* en cause; **to make an i.** *or* **a big i. of sth** faire toute une affaire de qch **2** *vt (book)* publier; *(tickets)* distribuer; *(passport)* délivrer; *(order)* donner; *(warning)* lancer; *(stamps, banknotes)* émettre; *(supply)* fournir **(with** de; **to** à); **to i. a statement** faire une déclaration

IT [ɪt] *pron* **(a)** *(subject)* il, elle; *(object)* le, la, l'; **(to) it** *(indirect object)* lui; **it** bites *(dog)* il mord; **I've done it** je l'ai fait

(b) *(impersonal)* il; **it's snowing** il neige; **it's hot** il fait chaud

(c) *(non-specific)* ce, cela, ça; **it's good** c'est bon; **who is it?** qui est-ce?; **to consider it wise to do sth** juger prudent de faire qch; **it was Paul who...** c'est Paul qui... **to have it in for sb** en vouloir à qn

(d) **of it, from it, about it** en; **in it, to it, at it** y; **on it** dessus; **under it** dessous

italics [ɪ'tælɪks] *npl* italique *m*; **in i.** en italique

Italy ['ɪtəlɪ] *n* l'Italie *f* ■ **Italian** [ɪ'tælɪən] **1** *adj* italien, -enne **2** *n (person)* Italien, -enne *mf*; *(language)* italien *m*

itch [ɪtʃ] **1** *n* démangeaison *f* **2** *vi (of person)* avoir des démangeaisons; **his arm itches** son bras le *ou* lui démange; *Fig* **to be itching to do sth** brûler d'envie de faire qch

item ['aɪtəm] *n (in collection, on list, in newspaper)* article *m*; *(matter)* question *f*; **i. of clothing** vêtement *m*; **news i.** information *f* ■ **itemize** *vt (invoice)* détailler

itinerary [aɪ'tɪnərərɪ] *(pl* **-ies)** *n* itinéraire *m*

its [ɪts] *possessive adj* son, sa, *pl* ses ■ **itself** *pron* lui-même, elle-même; *(reflexive)* se, s'; **by i.** tout seul

I've [aɪv] = **I have**

ivory ['aɪvərɪ] *n* ivoire *m*

ivy ['aɪvɪ] *n* lierre *m*

Jj

J, j [dʒeɪ] *n (letter)* J, j *m inv*

jab [dʒæb] **1** *n* coup *m*; *Br Fam (injection)* piqûre *f* **2** *(pt & pp* **-bb-)** *vt (knife, stick)* enfoncer **(into** dans); *(prick)* piquer **(with** du bout de)

jack [dʒæk] **1** *n* **(a)** *(for vehicle)* cric *m* **(b)** *(card)* valet *m* **2** *vt* **to j. up** *(vehicle)* soulever *(avec un cric)*

jacket ['dʒækɪt] *n (coat)* veste *f*; *(of book)* jaquette *f*; *Br* **j. potato** pomme *f* de terre en robe des champs

jackknife ['dʒæknaɪf] **1** *(pl* **-knives)** *n* couteau *m* de poche **2** *vi Br (of truck)* se mettre en travers de la route

jackpot ['dʒækpɒt] *n* gros lot *m*

Jacuzzi® [dʒə'kuːzɪ] *n* Jacuzzi® *m*

jagged ['dʒægɪd] *adj* déchiqueté

jail [dʒeɪl] **1** *n* prison *f* **2** *vt* emprisonner **(for** pour)

jam¹ [dʒæm] *n (preserve)* confiture *f*; **strawberry j.** confiture *f* de fraises ▪ **jamjar** *n* pot *m* à confiture

jam² [dʒæm] **1** *n* **(traffic) j.** embouteillage *m* **2** *(pt & pp* **-mm-)** *vt (squeeze, make stuck)* coincer; *(street, corridor)* encombrer; **to j. sth into sth** entasser qch dans qch; **to j. on the brakes** écraser la pédale de frein **3** *vi (get stuck)* se coincer ▪ **jammed** *adj (machine)* coincé; *(street)* encombré ▪ **jam-packed** *adj (hall, train)* bourré

Jamaica [dʒə'meɪkə] *n* la Jamaïque

jangle ['dʒæŋɡəl] *vi* cliqueter

janitor ['dʒænɪtə(r)] *n Am & Scot (caretaker)* concierge *m*

January ['dʒænjʊərɪ] *n* janvier *m*

Japan [dʒə'pæn] *n* le Japon ▪ **Japanese** [dʒæpə'niːz] **1** *adj* japonais **2** *n (person)* Japonais, -e *mf*; *(language)* japonais *m*

jar¹ [dʒɑː(r)] *n (container)* pot *m*; *(large, glass)* bocal *m*

jar² [dʒɑː(r)] **1** *n (jolt)* choc *m* **2** *(pt & pp* **-rr-)** *vt (shake)* ébranler **3** *vi (of noise)* grincer; *(of colours, words)* jurer **(with** avec) ▪ **jarring** *adj (noise, voice)* discordant

jargon ['dʒɑːɡən] *n* jargon *m*

jaunt [dʒɔːnt] *n (journey)* balade *f*

javelin ['dʒævlɪn] *n* javelot *m*

jaw [dʒɔː] *n Anat* mâchoire *f*

jaywalking ['dʒeɪwɔːkɪŋ] *n* = délit mineur qui consiste à traverser une rue en dehors des clous ou au feu vert

jazz [dʒæz] **1** *n* jazz *m* **2** *vt Fam* **to j. up** *(clothes, room, style)* égayer qch; *(music)* jazzifier qch

jealous ['dʒeləs] *adj* jaloux, -ouse **(of** de) ▪ **jealousy** *n* jalousie *f*

jeans [dʒiːnz] *npl* **(pair of) j.** jean *m*

Jeep® [dʒiːp] *n* Jeep® *f*

jeer [dʒɪə(r)] **1** *n* **jeers** *(boos)* huées *fpl*. **2** *vt (boo)* huer; *(mock)* se moquer de **3** *vi* **to j. at sb/sth** *(boo)* huer qn/qch; *(mock)* se moquer de qn/qch ▪ **jeering 1** *adj* railleur, -euse **2** *n (mocking)* railleries *fpl*; *(of crowd)* huées *fpl*

jell [dʒel] *vi Fam (of ideas)* prendre tournure

jello® ['dʒeləʊ] *n Am (dessert)* gelée *f*

jelly ['dʒelɪ] *(pl* **-ies)** *n (preserve, dessert)* gelée *f* ▪ **jellyfish** *n* méduse *f*

jeopardy ['dʒepədɪ] *n* **in j.** en péril ▪ **jeopardize** *vt* mettre en danger

jerk [dʒɜːk] **1** *n* secousse *f* **2** *vt (pull)* tirer brusquement

jerky ['dʒɜːkɪ] **(-ier, -iest)** *adj (movement, voice)* saccadé

Jersey ['dʒɜːzɪ] *n* Jersey *m ou f*

jersey ['dʒɜːzɪ] *(pl* **-eys)** *n (garment)* tricot *m*; *(of footballer)* maillot *m*

jest [dʒest] **1** *n* plaisanterie *f*; **in j.** pour rire **2** *vi* plaisanter

Jesus ['dʒi:zəs] *n* Jésus *m*; **J. Christ** Jésus-Christ *m*

jet [dʒet] **1** *n* (a) *(plane)* avion *m* à réaction; **j. engine** réacteur *m*, moteur *m* à réaction; **j. lag** fatigue *f* due au décalage horaire (b) *(steam, liquid)* jet *m* **2** *vi Fam* **to j. off** s'envoler (**to** pour)

jet-black [dʒet'blæk] *adj* (noir) de jais

jetfoil ['dʒetfɔil] *n* hydroglisseur *m*

jet-lagged ['dʒetlægd] *adj* qui souffre du décalage horaire

jetty ['dʒeti] *(pl* -ies) *n* jetée *f*; *(landing place)* embarcadère *m*

Jew [dʒu:] *n (man)* Juif *m*; *(woman)* Juive *f* ▪ **Jewish** *adj* juif *(f* juive)

jewel ['dʒu:əl] *n* bijou *m (pl* -oux); *(in watch)* rubis *m* ▪ **jeweller** *(Am* **jeweler)** *n* bijoutier, -ère *mf* ▪ **jewellery** *(Am* **jewelry)** *n* bijoux *mpl*

jibe [dʒaɪb] *n & vi* = **gibe**

Jiffy ['dʒɪfɪ] *n* **J. bag**® enveloppe *f* matelassée

jiffy ['dʒɪfɪ] *n Fam* instant *m*

jig [dʒɪg] *n (dance, music)* gigue *f*

jigsaw ['dʒɪgsɔ:] *n* **j. (puzzle)** puzzle *m*

jilt [dʒɪlt] *vt (lover)* laisser tomber

jingle ['dʒɪŋgəl] **1** *vt* faire tinter **2** *vi (of keys, bell)* tinter

jinx [dʒɪŋks] *n (spell, curse)* mauvais sort *m*

jittery ['dʒɪtərɪ] *adj Fam* **to be j.** être à cran

job [dʒɒb] *n (employment, post)* travail *m*, emploi *m*; *(task)* tâche *f*; **to have a (hard) j. doing** *or* **to do sth** avoir du mal à faire qch; **j. offer** offre *f* d'emploi

Jobcentre ['dʒɒbsentə(r)] *n Br* ≃ agence *f* nationale pour l'emploi

jobless ['dʒɒbləs] *adj* au chômage

jockey ['dʒɒkɪ] *(pl* -eys) *n* jockey *m*

jocular ['dʒɒkjʊlə(r)] *adj* jovial

jog [dʒɒg] *(pt & pp* -gg-) **1** *vt (shake)* secouer; *(push)* pousser; *Fig (memory)* rafraîchir **2** *vi (for fitness)* faire du jogging ▪ **jogging** *n (for fitness)* jogging *m*; **to go jogging** aller faire un jogging

john [dʒɒn] *n Am Fam* **the j.** *(lavatory)* le petit coin

join [dʒɔɪn] **1** *n* raccord *m*

2 *vt* (a) *(put together)* joindre; *(wires, pipes)* raccorder; *(words, towns)* relier; **to j. two things together** relier une chose à une autre; **to j. sb** *(catch up with, meet)* rejoindre qn; *(associate oneself with, go with)* se joindre à qn (**in doing** pour faire)

(b) *(become a member of)* s'inscrire à; *(army, police, company)* entrer dans; **to j. the queue** *or Am* **line** prendre la queue

3 *vi* (a) *(of roads, rivers)* se rejoindre; **to j. (together** *or* **up)** *(of objects)* se joindre (**with** à); **to j. in sth** prendre part à qch

(b) *(become a member)* devenir membre; *Mil* **to j. up** s'engager

joiner ['dʒɔɪnə(r)] *n Br* menuisier *m*

joint [dʒɔɪnt] **1** *n* (a) *(in body)* articulation *f*; *Br (meat)* rôti *m*; *Tech* joint *m*; *(in carpentry)* assemblage *m* (b) *Fam (nightclub)* boîte *f* (c) *Fam (cannabis cigarette)* joint *m* **2** *adj (decision)* commun; **j. account** compte *m* joint; **j. efforts** efforts *mpl* conjugués ▪ **jointly** *adv* conjointement

joke [dʒəʊk] **1** *n* plaisanterie *f*; *(trick)* tour *m* **2** *vi* plaisanter (**about** sur) ▪ **joker** *n* plaisantin *m*; *(card)* joker *m* ▪ **jokingly** *adv (say)* en plaisantant

jolly ['dʒɒlɪ] *(-ier, -iest) adj (happy)* gai

jolt [dʒɒlt] **1** *n* secousse *f* **2** *vt (shake)* secouer

jostle ['dʒɒsəl] **1** *vt (push)* bousculer **2** *vi (push each other)* se bousculer (**for sth** pour obtenir qch)

jot [dʒɒt] *(pt & pp* -tt-) *vt* **to j. sth down** noter qch ▪ **jotter** *n (notepad)* bloc-notes *m*

journal ['dʒɜ:nəl] *n (periodical)* revue *f*; *(diary)* journal *m*; **to keep a j.** tenir un journal

journalism ['dʒɜ:nəlɪzəm] *n* journalisme *m* ▪ **journalist** *n* journaliste *mf*

journey ['dʒɜ:nɪ] **1** *(pl* -eys) *n (trip)* voyage *m*; *(distance)* trajet *m*; **to go on**

a j. partir en voyage **2** *vi* voyager

jovial ['dʒəʊvɪəl] *adj* jovial

joy [dʒɔɪ] *n* joie *f*; **the joys of** *(country-side, motherhood)* les plaisirs *mpl* de ▪ **joyful** *adj* joyeux, -euse

joyrider ['dʒɔɪraɪdə(r)] *n* = chauffard qui conduit une voiture volée

joystick ['dʒɔɪstɪk] *n* *(of aircraft, computer)* manche *m* à balai

jubilant ['dʒuːbɪlənt] *adj* **to be j.** jubiler

jubilee ['dʒuːbɪliː] *n* **(golden) j.** jubilé *m*

judder ['dʒʌdə(r)] **1** *n* vibration *f* **2** *vi* *(shake)* vibrer

judge [dʒʌdʒ] **1** *n* juge *m* **2** *vti* juger; **to j. sb by** *or* **on sth** juger qn sur *ou* d'après qch; **judging by...** à en juger par... ▪ **judg(e)ment** *n* jugement *m*

judicial [dʒuː'dɪʃəl] *adj* judiciaire

judo ['dʒuːdəʊ] *n* judo *m*

jug [dʒʌg] *n* cruche *f*; *(for milk)* pot *m*

juggle ['dʒʌgəl] **1** *vt* jongler avec **2** *vi* jongler **(with** avec) ▪ **juggler** *n* jongleur, -euse *mf*

juice [dʒuːs] *n* jus *m* ▪ **juicy (-ier, -iest)** *adj* *(fruit)* juteux, -euse; *(meat)* succulent; *Fig (story)* savoureux, -euse

jukebox ['dʒuːkbɒks] *n* juke-box *m*

July [dʒuː'laɪ] *n* juillet *m*

jumble ['dʒʌmbəl] **1** *n* *(disorder)* fouillis *m*; *Br (unwanted articles)* bric-à-brac *m inv*; *Br* **j. sale** vente *f* de charité *(articles d'occasion uniquement)* **2** *vt* **to j. (up)** *(objects, facts)* mélanger

jumbo ['dʒʌmbəʊ] **1** *adj* *(packet)* géant **2** *(pl* **-os)** *adj & n* **j. (jet)** jumbo-jet *(m)*

jump [dʒʌmp] **1** *n* *(leap)* saut *m*; *(start)* sursaut *m*; *(increase)* hausse *f* soudaine; *Am* **j. rope** corde *f* à sauter

2 *vt* *(ditch)* sauter; *Br* **to j. the queue** passer avant son tour, resquiller

3 *vi* sauter **(at** sur); *(start)* sursauter; *(of price)* faire un bond; **to j. across sth** traverser qch d'un bond; **to j. in** *or* **on** *(train, vehicle, bus)* sauter dans; **to j. off** *or* **out** sauter; *(from bus)* descendre; **to j. off sth, to j. out of sth** sauter de qch; **to j. out of the window** sauter par la fenêtre; **to j. up** se lever d'un bond ▪ **jumpy** ['dʒʌmpɪ] **(-ier, -iest)** *adj* nerveux, -euse

jumper ['dʒʌmpə(r)] *n Br* pull(-over) *m*; *Am (dress)* robe *f* chasuble

junction ['dʒʌŋkʃən] *n* *(crossroads)* carrefour *m*; *Br* **j. 23** *(on motorway)* *(exit)* la sortie 23; *(entrance)* l'entrée *f* 23

June [dʒuːn] *n* juin *m*

jungle ['dʒʌŋgəl] *n* jungle *f*

junior ['dʒuːnɪə(r)] **1** *adj* *(younger)* plus jeune; *(in rank, status)* subalterne; *(teacher, doctor)* jeune; **to be sb's j.** être plus jeune que qn; *(in rank, status)* être au-dessous de qn; *Br* **j. school** école *f* primaire *(entre 7 et 11 ans)*; *Am* **j. high school** ≃ collège *m* d'enseignement secondaire

2 *n* cadet, -ette *mf*; *(in school)* petit, -e *mf*; *(in sports)* junior *mf*, cadet, -ette *mf*

junk [dʒʌŋk] **1** *n* *(unwanted objects)* bric-à-brac *m inv*; *(inferior goods)* camelote *f*; *(bad film, book)* navet *m*; **j. food** cochonneries *fpl*; **j. mail** prospectus *mpl*; **j. shop** boutique *f* de brocanteur **2** *vt Fam (get rid of)* balancer

junkie ['dʒʌŋkɪ] *n Fam* drogué, -e *mf*

jury ['dʒʊərɪ] *(pl* **-ies)** *n* *(in competition, court)* jury *m*

just [dʒʌst] **1** *adv* *(exactly, slightly)* juste; *(only)* juste, seulement; *(simply)* (tout) simplement; **it's j. as I thought** c'est bien ce que je pensais; **she has/had j. left** elle vient/venait de partir; **he j. missed it** il l'a manqué de peu; **j. as big/light** tout aussi grand/léger **(as** que); **j. a moment!** un instant!; **j. one** un(e) seul(e) **(of** de); **j. about** *(approximately)* à peu près; *(almost)* presque; **to be j. about to do sth** être sur le point de faire qch **2** *adj (fair)* juste **(to** envers)

justice ['dʒʌstɪs] *n* justice *f*; **it doesn't do you j.** *(photo)* cela ne vous avantage pas

justify ['dʒʌstɪfaɪ] *(pt & pp* **-ied)** *vt* justifier; **to be justified in doing sth** *(have reason)* être fondé à faire qch

■ **justifiable** *adj* justifiable ■ **justification** [-fɪˈkeɪʃən] *n* justification *f*
jut [dʒʌt] (*pt & pp* **-tt-**) *vi* **to j. out** faire saillie
juvenile [ˈdʒuːvənaɪl, *Am* -ənəl] **1** *n (in law)* mineur, -e *mf* **2** *adj (court)* pour enfants; *Pej (behaviour)* puéril; **j. delinquent** jeune délinquant, -e *mf*
juxtapose [dʒʌkstəˈpəʊz] *vt* juxtaposer

Kk

K, k [keɪ] *n (letter)* K, k *m inv*

kangaroo [kæŋɡə'ru:] *n* kangourou *m*

karate [kə'rɑːtɪ] *n* karaté *m*

kebab [kə'bæb] *n* brochette *f*

keel [kiːl] **1** *n (of boat)* quille *f* **2** *vi* **to k. over** *(of boat)* chavirer

keen [kiːn] *adj* **(a)** *Br (eager, enthusiastic)* plein d'enthousiasme; **to be k. on sth** *(music, sport)* être passionné de qch; **he is k. on her/the idea** elle/l'idée lui plaît beaucoup **(b)** *(edge, appetite)* aiguisé; *(interest)* vif (*f* vive); *(mind)* pénétrant; *(wind)* glacial

KEEP [kiːp] **1** *(pt & pp* **kept)** *vt* garder; *(shop, car)* avoir; *(diary, promise)* tenir; *(family)* entretenir; *(rule)* respecter; *(delay, detain)* retenir; *(put)* mettre; **to k. doing sth** continuer à faire qch; **to k. sth clean** garder qch propre; **to k. sth from sb** dissimuler qch à qn; **to k. sb from doing sth** empêcher qn de faire qch; **to k. sb waiting/working** faire attendre/travailler qn; **to k. an appointment** se rendre à un rendez-vous

2 *vi (remain)* rester; *(continue)* continuer; *(of food)* se conserver; **how is he keeping?** comment va-t-il?; **to k. still** rester immobile; **to k. left** tenir sa gauche; **to k. going** continuer; **to k. at it** *(keep doing it)* persévérer

3 *n (food)* subsistance *f*; *Fam* **for keeps** pour toujours

▸ **keep away 1** *vt (person)* éloigner **(from** de) **2** *vi* ne pas s'approcher **(from** de)

▸ **keep back 1** *vt sep (crowd)* contenir; *(delay, withhold)* retarder; *(hide)* cacher **(from** à) **2** *vi* ne pas s'approcher **(from** de)

▸ **keep down** *vt sep (restrict)* limiter; *(price, costs)* maintenir bas

▸ **keep in** *vt sep (not allow out)* empêcher de sortir; *(as punishment in school)* garder en retenue

▸ **keep off 1** *vt sep (person)* éloigner; **k. your hands off!** n'y touche pas! **2** *vt insep* **'k. off the grass'** 'défense de marcher sur les pelouses' **3** *vi (not go near)* ne pas s'approcher

▸ **keep on 1** *vt sep (hat, employee)* garder; **to k. on doing sth** continuer à faire qch **2** *vi* **to k. on at sb** harceler qn

▸ **keep out 1** *vt sep* empêcher d'entrer **2** *vi* rester en dehors **(of** de)

▸ **keep to 1** *vt insep (subject, path)* ne pas s'écarter de; *(room)* garder **2** *vi* **to k. to the left** tenir sa gauche; **to k. to oneself** rester à l'écart

▸ **keep up 1** *vt sep (continue, maintain)* continuer; *(keep awake)* empêcher de dormir; **to k. up appearances** sauver les apparences **2** *vi (continue)* continuer; *(follow)* suivre; **to k. up with sb** *(follow)* aller à la même allure que qn; *(in quality of work)* se maintenir à la hauteur de qn

keeper ['kiːpə(r)] *n (in park, in zoo, goalkeeper)* gardien, -enne *mf*

keeping ['kiːpɪŋ] *n* **in k. with** conformément à

kennel ['kenəl] *n Br* niche *f*

Kenya ['kiːnjə, 'kenjə] *n* le Kenya

kept [kept] **1** *pt & pp of* **keep 2** *adj* **well or nicely k.** *(house)* bien tenu

kerb [kɜːb] *n Br* bord *m* du trottoir

kernel ['kɜːnəl] *n (of nut)* amande *f*

kerosene ['kerəsiːn] *n (aircraft fuel)* kérosène *m*; *Am (paraffin)* pétrole *m* (lampant)

ketchup ['ketʃəp] *n* ketchup *m*

kettle ['ketəl] *n* bouilloire *f*; **the k. is boiling** l'eau bout; **to put the k. on**

mettre l'eau à chauffer

key [ki:] **1** *n* clef *f*, clé *f*; *(of piano, typewriter, computer)* touche *f*; *Fig* **the k. to happiness/success** la clé du bonheur/ de la réussite **2** *adj (industry, post)* clef, clé **3** *vt* **to k. in** *(data)* saisir ■ **keyboard** *n (of piano, computer)* clavier *m* ■ **keyhole** *n* trou *m* de serrure ■ **keynote** *n (of speech)* point *m* essentiel ■ **keyring** *n* porte-clefs *m inv*

keyed [ki:d] *adj* **to be k. up** être surexcité

khaki ['kɑːkɪ] *adj & n* kaki *(m) inv*

kick [kɪk] **1** *n* coup *m* de pied; *(of horse)* ruade *f* **2** *vt* donner un coup de pied/ des coups de pied à; *(of horse)* lancer une ruade à **3** *vi* donner des coups de pied; *(of horse)* ruer ■ **kickoff** *n (in football)* coup *m* d'envoi

▸**kick down, kick in** *vt sep (door)* démolir à coups de pied

▸**kick off** *vi (of footballer)* donner le coup d'envoi; *Fam (start)* démarrer

▸**kick out** *vt sep Fam (throw out)* flanquer dehors

▸**kick up** *vt sep Br Fam* **to k. up a fuss** faire des histoires

kid [kɪd] **1** *n* **(a)** *Fam (child)* gosse *mf*; *Fam* **my k. brother** mon petit frère **(b)** *(goat)* chevreau *m* **2** *(pt & pp* **-cd-***) vti Fam (joke, tease)* faire marcher; **to be kidding** plaisanter; **no kidding!** sans blague!

kidnap ['kɪdnæp] *(pt & pp* **-pp-***, Am* **-p-***) vt* kidnapper ■ **kidnapper** *n* ravisseur, -euse *mf* ■ **kidnapping** *n* enlèvement *m*

kidney ['kɪdnɪ] *(pl* **-eys***) n* rein *m*; *(as food)* rognon *m*; **k. bean** haricot *m* rouge

kill [kɪl] **1** *vt (person, animal, plant)* tuer; **to k. oneself** se tuer; *Fam* **my feet are killing me** j'ai les pieds en compote; **to k. time** tuer le temps **2** *vt* tuer ■ **killer** *n* tueur, -euse *mf* ■ **killing** *n (of person)* meurtre *m*; *(of group)* massacre *m*; *(of animal)* mise *f* à mort

killjoy ['kɪldʒɔɪ] *n* rabat-joie *mf inv*

kilo ['kiːləʊ] *(pl* **-os***) n* kilo *m* ■ **kilogram(me)** ['kɪləgræm] *n* kilogramme *m*

kilobyte ['kɪləbaɪt] *n Comptr* kilooctet *m*

kilometre [kɪ'lɒmɪtə(r)] *(Am* **kilometer***) n* kilomètre *m*

kilt [kɪlt] *n* kilt *m*

kin [kɪn] *n* **one's next of k.** son plus proche parent

kind¹ [kaɪnd] *n (sort, type)* genre *m*, espèce *f* **(of** de); **what k. of drink is it?** qu'est-ce que c'est comme boisson?; *Fam* **k. of worried/sad** plutôt inquiet/triste

kind² [kaɪnd] **(-er, -est)** *adj (helpful, pleasant)* gentil, -ille **(to** avec); **that's k. of you** c'est gentil de votre part

kindergarten ['kɪndəgɑːtən] *n* jardin *m* d'enfants

kindly ['kaɪndlɪ] **1** *adv* gentiment; **k. wait** ayez la bonté d'attendre **2** *adj (person)* bienveillant

kindness ['kaɪndnɪs] *n* gentillesse *f*

king [kɪŋ] *n* roi *m* ■ **kingdom** *n* royaume *m*; **animal/plant k.** règne *m* animal/végétal ■ **king-size(d)** *adj* géant

kiosk ['kiːɒsk] *n* kiosque *m*; *Br* **(telephone) k.** cabine *f* téléphonique

kip [kɪp] *(pt & pp* **-pp-***) vi Br Fam (sleep)* roupiller

kipper ['kɪpə(r)] *n* hareng *m* salé et fumé

kiss [kɪs] **1** *n* baiser *m*; **the k. of life** *(in first aid)* le bouche-à-bouche **2** *vt (person)* embrasser **3** *vi* s'embrasser

kit [kɪt] **1** *n* équipement *m*, matériel *m*; *(set of articles)* trousse *f*; *Br (belongings)* affaires *fpl*; *Br (sports clothes)* tenue *f*; **first-aid k.** trousse *f* de pharmacie; **(do-it-yourself) k.** kit *m* **2** *(pt & pp* **-tt-***) vt Br* **to k. sb out** équiper qn **(with** de)

kitchen ['kɪtʃɪn] *n* cuisine *f*; **k. sink** évier *m*; **k. units** éléments *mpl* de cuisine ■ **kitchenette** *n* coin-cuisine *m*

kite [kaɪt] *n (toy)* cerf-volant *m*

kitten ['kɪtən] *n* chaton *m*

kitty ['kɪtɪ] *(pl* **-ies***) n (fund)* cagnotte *f*

kiwi ['kiːwiː] *n (bird, fruit)* kiwi *m*

klutz [klʌts] *n Am Fam* balourd, -ourde *mf*

km (*abbr* **kilometre(s)**) km

knack [næk] *n (skill)* talent *m*; **to have the k. of doing sth** avoir le don de faire qch

knackered ['nækəd] *adj Br Fam (tired)* vanné

knapsack ['næpsæk] *n* sac *m* à dos

knead [niːd] *vt (dough)* pétrir

knee [niː] *n* genou *m*; **to go down on one's knees** s'agenouiller ▪ **kneecap** *n* rotule *f*

kneel [niːl] (*pt & pp* **knelt** *or* **kneeled**) *vi* **to k. (down)** s'agenouiller (**before** devant); **to be kneeling (down)** être à genoux

knelt [nelt] *pt & pp of* **kneel**

knew [njuː] *pt of* **know**

knickers ['nɪkəz] *npl Br (underwear)* culotte *f*

knick-knack ['nɪknæk] *n Fam* babiole *f*

knife [naɪf] **1** (*pl* **knives**) *n* couteau *m*; *(penknife)* canif *m* **2** *vt* poignarder

knight [naɪt] **1** *n* chevalier *m*; *(chess piece)* cavalier *m* **2** *vt Br* **to be knighted** être fait chevalier ▪ **knighthood** *n Br* titre *m* de chevalier

knit [nɪt] (*pt & pp* **-tt-**) **1** *vt* tricoter **2** *vi* tricoter; **to k. (together)** *(of bones)* se ressouder ▪ **knitting** *n (activity, material)* tricot *m*; **k. needle** aiguille *f* à tricoter

knob [nɒb] *n (on door)* poignée *f*; *(on radio)* bouton *m*; **a k. of butter** une noix de beurre

knock [nɒk] **1** *n (blow)* coup *m*; **there's a k. at the door** on frappe à la porte **2** *vt (strike)* frapper; *(collide with)* heurter; **to k. one's head on sth** se cogner la tête contre qch **3** *vi (strike)* frapper; **to k. against** *or* **into sth** heurter qch ▪ **knocker** *n (for door)* marteau *m* ▪ **knockout** *n (in boxing)* knock-out *m inv*

▸**knock about** *vt sep (ill-treat)* malmener

▸**knock back** *vt sep Br Fam (drink, glass)* s'envoyer (derrière la cravate)

▸**knock down** *vt sep (object, pedestrian)* renverser; *(house, tree, wall)* abattre; *(price)* baisser

▸**knock in** *vt sep (nail)* enfoncer

▸**knock off 1** *vt sep (person, object)* faire tomber (**from** de); *Fam (do quickly)* expédier; **to k. $50 off (the price)** baisser le prix de 50 dollars **2** *vi Fam (stop work)* s'arrêter de travailler

▸**knock out** *vt sep (make unconscious)* assommer; *(boxer)* mettre K.-O.; *(beat in competition)* éliminer

▸**knock over** *vt sep (pedestrian, object)* renverser

knot [nɒt] **1** *n* (a) *(in rope)* nœud *m*; *Fig* **to tie the k.** se marier (b) *Naut (unit of speed)* nœud *m* **2** (*pt & pp* **-tt-**) *vt* nouer

KNOW [nəʊ] **1** *n Fam* **to be in the k.** être au courant
2 (*pt* **knew**, *pp* **known**) *vt (facts, language)* savoir; *(person, place)* connaître; *(recognize)* reconnaître (**by** à); **to k. that...** savoir que...; **to k. how to do sth** savoir faire qch; **for all I k.** que je sache; **I'll let you k.** je vous le ferai savoir; **to k. (a lot) about cars/sewing** s'y connaître en voitures/couture; **to get to k. sb** apprendre à connaître qn **3** *vi* savoir; **I k.** je (le) sais; **I wouldn't k., I k. nothing about it** je n'en sais rien; **to k. about sth** être au courant de qch; **do you k. of a good dentist?** connais-tu un bon dentiste? ▪ **know-how** *n Fam* savoir-faire *m inv* ▪ **know-it-all** *n Fam Pej* je-sais-tout *mf* ▪ **knowingly** *adv (consciously)* sciemment

knowledge ['nɒlɪdʒ] *n (of fact)* connaissance *f*; *(learning)* connaissances *fpl*, savoir *m*; **(not) to my k. (pas)** à ma connaissance; **general k.** culture *f* générale ▪ **knowledgeable** *adj* savant; **to be k. about sth** bien s'y connaître en qch

known [nəʊn] **1** *pp of* **know 2** *adj* connu; **she is k. to be...** on sait qu'elle est...

knuckle ['nʌkəl] *n* articulation *f* (du doigt)

▶**knuckle down** *vi Fam* se mettre au boulot; **to k. down to sth** se mettre à qch

Koran [kə'rɑːn] *n* **the K.** le Coran

Korea [kə'rɪə] *n* la Corée

kosher ['kəʊʃə(r)] *adj Rel (food)* kasher *inv*

kudos ['kjuːdɒs] *n (glory)* gloire *f*; *(prestige)* prestige *m*

Kuwait [kʊ'weɪt] *n* le Koweït

Ll

L, l [el] *n (letter)* L, l *m inv*

lab [læb] *n Fam* labo *m* ▪ **laboratory** [ləˈbɒrətrɪ, *Am* ˈlæbrətɔːrɪ] *n* laboratoire *m*

label [ˈleɪbəl] **1** *n* étiquette *f*; *(of record company)* label *m* **2** *(Br* **-ll-**, *Am* **-l-)** *vt* étiqueter qn de menteur *Fig* **to l. sb (as) a liar** qualifier qn de menteur

laborious [ləˈbɔːrɪəs] *adj* laborieux, -euse

labour [ˈleɪbə(r)] *(Am* **labor)** **1** *n (work)* travail *m*; *(workers)* main-d'œuvre *f*; *Br* **L.** *(political party)* le parti travailliste; **in l.** *(woman)* en train d'accoucher; *Am* **L. Day** fête *f* de travail **2** *adj (market)* du travail; **l. force** effectifs *mpl*; *Am* **l. union** syndicat *m* **3** *vi (toil)* peiner **(over** sur**)** ▪ **labourer** *(Am* **laborer)** *n (on roads)* manœuvre *m*; *(on farm)* ouvrier *m* agricole

labyrinth [ˈlæbərɪnθ] *n* labyrinthe *m*

lace [leɪs] **1** *n (a) (cloth)* dentelle *f* **(b)** *(of shoe)* lacet *m* **2** *vt* **to l. (up)** *(tie up)* lacer

lack [læk] **1** *n* manque *m* **(of** de**)**; **for l. of sth** à défaut de qch **2** *vt* manquer de **3** *vi* **to be lacking** manquer **(in** de**)**

lad [læd] *n Fam (young man)* jeune gars *m*; *(child)* garçon *m*

ladder [ˈlædə(r)] **1** *n* échelle *f*; *Br (in tights)* maille *f* filée **2** *vti Br* filer

laden [ˈleɪdən] *adj* chargé **(with** de**)**

lady [ˈleɪdɪ] *(pl* **-ies)** *n* dame *f*; **a young l.** une jeune fille; *(married)* une jeune dame; **Ladies and Gentlemen!** Mesdames, Mesdemoiselles, Messieurs!; **the ladies' room**, *Br* **the ladies** les toilettes *fpl* pour dames

ladybird [ˈleɪdɪbɜːd] *(Am* **ladybug** [ˈleɪdɪbʌg]**)** *n* coccinelle *f*

lag [læg] **1** *n* **time l.** *(between events)* décalage *m*; *(between countries)* déca-

lage *m* horaire **2** *(pt & pp* **-gg-)** *vt (pipe)* isoler **3** *vi* **to l. behind** *(in progress, work)* avoir du retard; *(dawdle)* être à la traîne

lager [ˈlɑːgə(r)] *n Br* bière *f* blonde

lagoon [ləˈguːn] *n* lagune *f*; *(of atoll)* lagon *m*

laid [leɪd] *pt & pp of* **lay³** ▪ **laid-back** *adj Fam* cool *inv*

lain [leɪn] *pp of* **lie²**

lair [leə(r)] *n* tanière *f*

lake [leɪk] *n* lac *m*

lamb [læm] *n* agneau *m*

lame [leɪm] **(-er, -est)** *adj (person, argument)* boiteux, -euse; *(excuse)* piètre; **to be l.** *(of person)* boiter

lament [ləˈment] *vt* **to l. (over)** se lamenter sur

laminated [ˈlæmɪneɪtɪd] *adj (glass)* feuilleté; *(wood, plastic)* stratifié

lamp [læmp] *n* lampe *f* ▪ **lamppost** *n* réverbère *m* ▪ **lampshade** *n* abat-jour *m inv*

lance [lɑːns] **1** *n (weapon)* lance *f* **2** *vt (abscess)* inciser

land [lænd] **1** *n* terre *f*; *(country)* pays *m*; **(plot of) l.** terrain *m*
 2 *adj (reform)* agraire
 3 *vt (passengers, cargo)* débarquer; *(aircraft)* poser; *(blow)* flanquer **(on** à**)**; *Fam (job, prize)* décrocher
 4 *vi (of aircraft)* atterrir; *(of passengers)* débarquer; *(of bomb, missile)* tomber; **to l. up in a ditch/in jail** se retrouver dans un fossé/en prison ▪ **landing** *n* **(a)** *(of aircraft)* atterrissage *m*; *(of cargo, troops)* débarquement *m* **(b)** *(of staircase)* palier *m* ▪ **landlady** *(pl* **-ies)** *n* propriétaire *f*; *(of pub)* patronne *f* ▪ **landlord** *n* propriétaire *m*; *(of pub)* patron *m* ▪ **landmark** *n* point *m* de repère ▪ **landowner** *n*

propriétaire *m* foncier ■ **lardslide** *n* *(falling rocks)* glissement *m* de terrain; *(election victory)* raz de marée *m inv* électoral

landscape ['lændskeɪp] *n* paysage *m*

lane [leɪn] *n (in country)* chemin *m; (in town)* ruelle *f; (division of road)* voie *f; (line of traffic)* file *f; (for shipping, swimming)* couloir *m*

language ['læŋgwɪdʒ] **1** *n (of a people)* langue *f; (faculty, style)* langage *m* **2** *adj (laboratory)* de langues; *(teacher, studies)* de langue(s)

languish ['læŋgwɪʃ] *vi* languir **(for** *or* **after** après)

lanky ['læŋkɪ] **(-ier, -iest)** *adj* dégingandé

lantern ['læntən] *n* lanterne *f*

lap [læp] **1** *n* (a) *(of person)* genoux *mpl* (b) *(in race)* tour *m* de piste **2** *(pt & pp* **-pp-)** *vt* **to l. up** *(drink)* laper **3** *vi (of waves)* clapoter

lapel [lə'pel] *n* revers *m*

lapse [læps] **1** *n* (a) *(in concentration, standards)* baisse *f;* **a l. of memory** un trou de mémoire (b) *(interval)* laps *m* de temps; **a l. of time** un intervalle **(between** entre) **2** *vi* (a) *(of concentration, standards)* baisser (b) *(expire, of subscription)* expirer

laptop ['læptɒp] *adj & n* **l. (computer)** ordinateur *m* portable

larceny ['lɑːsənɪ] *n Am* vol *m* simple

lard [lɑːd] *n* saindoux *m*

larder ['lɑːdə(r)] *n* garde-manger *m inv*

large [lɑːdʒ] **(-er, -est)** *adj (big)* grand; *(fat, bulky)* gros *(f* grosse); *(quantity)* grand, important; **to become** *or* **grow** *or* **get l.** s'agrandir; *(of person)* grossir; **at l.** *(of prisoner, animal)* en liberté; *(as a whole)* en général ■ **large-scale** *adj (operation, reform)* de grande envergure

largely ['lɑːdʒlɪ] *adv* en grande partie

lark¹ [lɑːk] *n (bird)* alouette *f*

lark² [lɑːk] *Fam* **1** *n (joke)* rigolade *f* **2** *vi Br* **to l. about** faire le fou/la folle

larva ['lɑːvə] *(pl* **-vae** [-viː]*)* *n* larve *f*

laryngitis [lærɪn'dʒaɪtɪs] *n Med* laryngite *f*

lasagne, lasagna [lə'zænjə] *n* lasagnes *fpl*

laser ['leɪzə(r)] *n* laser *m;* **l. beam/ printer** rayon *m*/imprimante *f* laser

lash¹ [læʃ] **1** *n (with whip)* coup *m* de fouet **2** *vt (strike)* fouetter; *(tie)* attacher **(to** à) **3** *vi* **to l. out at sb** *(hit)* donner des coups à qn; *(criticize)* fustiger qn

lash² [læʃ] *n (eyelash)* cil *m*

lass [læs] *n Br* jeune fille *f*

last¹ [lɑːst] **1** *adj* dernier, -ère; **the l. ten lines** les dix dernières lignes; **l. night** *(evening)* hier soir; *(night)* la nuit dernière; **l. name** nom *m* de famille **2** *adv (lastly)* en dernier lieu; *(on the last occasion)* (pour) la dernière fois; **to leave l.** sortir le dernier **3** *n (person, object)* dernier, -ère *mf;* **l. but one** avant-dernier *m (f* avant-dernière); **at (long) l.** enfin ■ **last-minute** *adj (decision)* de dernière minute

last² [lɑːst] *vi* durer; **to l. (out)** *(endure, resist)* tenir (le coup); *(of money, supplies)* suffire; **it lasted me ten years** ça m'a fait dix ans

lasting ['lɑːstɪŋ] *adj (impression, peace)* durable

lastly ['lɑːstlɪ] *adv* en dernier lieu

latch [lætʃ] **1** *n* loquet *m;* **the door is on the l.** la porte n'est pas fermée à clef **2** *vt insep Fam* **l. onto** *(understand)* piger; *(adopt)* adopter

late¹ [leɪt] **1** **(-er, -est)** *adj (meal, season, hour)* tardif, -ive; *(stage)* avancé; *(edition)* dernier, -ère; **to be l. (for sth)** être en retard (pour qch); **he's an hour l.** il a une heure de retard; **it's l.** il est tard; **in the l. nineties** à la fin des années 90; **to be in one's l. forties** approcher de la cinquantaine; **at a later date** à une date ultérieure; **at the latest** au plus tard **2** *adv (in the day, season)* tard; *(not on time)* en retard; **it's getting l.** il se fait tard; **later (on)** plus tard; **of l.** récemment

late² [leɪt] *adj* **the l. Mr Smith** feu Monsieur Smith

latecomer ['leɪtkʌmə(r)] ■ *n* retardataire *mf*

lately ['leɪtlɪ] *adv* dernièrement

latent ['leɪtənt] *adj (disease, tendency)* latent

lateral ['lætərəl] *adj* latéral

lather ['lɑːðə(r)] **1** *n* mousse *f* **2** *vt* savonner

Latin ['lætɪn] **1** *adj* latin; **L. America** l'Amérique *f* latine ∎ **L. American 1** *adj* d'Amérique latine **2** *n* Latino-Américain, -e *mf* **2** *n (language)* latin *m*

latitude ['lætɪtjuːd] *n (on map, freedom)* latitude *f*

latter ['lætə(r)] **1** *adj (later, last-named)* dernier, -ère; *(second)* deuxième **2** *n* **the l.** le dernier *(f* la dernière); *(of two)* le second *(f* la seconde)

lattice ['lætɪs] *n* treillis *m*

laudable ['lɔːdəbəl] *adj* louable

laugh [lɑːf] **1** *n* rire *m*; **to have a good l.** bien rire **2** *vt* **to l. sth off** tourner qch en plaisanterie **3** *vi* rire **(at/about** de) ∎ **laughing** *adj* riant; **it's no l. matter** il n'y a pas de quoi rire; **to be the l. stock** of être la risée de

laughable ['lɑːfəbəl] *adj* ridicule

laughter ['lɑːftə(r)] *n* rire(s) *m(pl)*

launch [lɔːntʃ] **1** *n* (a) *(motorboat)* vedette *f; (pleasure boat)* bateau *m* de plaisance (b) *(of ship, rocket, product)* lancement *m* **2** *vt (ship, rocket, product)* lancer **3** *vi* **to l. (out) into** *(begin)* se lancer dans

launder ['lɔːndə(r)] *vt (clothes, money)* blanchir

launderette [lɔːndə'ret] *(Am* **Laundromat®** ['lɔːndrəmæt]) *n* laverie *f* automatique

laundry ['lɔːndrɪ] *n (place)* blanchisserie *f; (clothes)* linge *m*; **to do the l.** faire la lessive

lava ['lɑːvə] *n* lave *f*

lavatory ['lævətərɪ] *(pl* -ies) *n* toilettes *fpl*

lavender ['lævɪndə(r)] *n* lavande *f*

lavish ['lævɪʃ] **1** *adj* prodigue **(with** de); *(meal, décor, gift)* somptueux, -euse; *(expenditure)* excessif, -ive **2** *vt* **to l. sth on sb** couvrir qn de qch

law [lɔː] *n (rule, rules)* loi *f; (study,*

profession, system) droit *m*; **against the l.** illégal; **court of l., l. court** cour *f* de justice; **l. and order** l'ordre *m* public

lawful ['lɔːfəl] *adj (action)* légal; *(claim)* légitime

lawless ['lɔːləs] *adj (country)* anarchique

lawn [lɔːn] *n* pelouse *f*, gazon *m*; **l. mower** tondeuse *f* à gazon

lawsuit ['lɔːsuːt] *n* procès *m*

lawyer ['lɔːjə(r)] *n (in court)* avocat, -e *mf; (for wills, sales)* notaire *m; (legal expert)* juriste *mf*

lax [læks] *adj (person)* laxiste; *(discipline, behaviour)* relâché

laxative ['læksətɪv] *n* laxatif *m*

lay¹ [leɪ] *pt of* **lie²**

lay² [leɪ] *adj (non-religious)* laïque; **l. person** profane *mf* ∎ **layman** *(pl* -men) *n (nonspecialist)* profane *mf*

lay³ [leɪ] *(pt & pp* **laid)** **1** *vt (put down, place)* poser; *(blanket)* étendre **(over** sur); *(trap)* tendre; *(egg)* pondre; *Br* **to l. the table** mettre la table **2** *vi (of bird)* pondre ∎ **layabout** *n Fam* fainéant, -e *mf* ∎ **lay-by** *(pl* -bys) *n Br (for vehicles)* aire *f* de stationnement ∎ **layout** *n* disposition *f; (of text)* mise *f* en page

▸ **lay down** *vt sep (put down)* poser; *(arms)* déposer; *(principle, condition)* établir; **to l. down the law** dicter sa loi **(to** à)

▸ **lay into** *vt insep Fam (physically)* rosser; *(verbally)* voler dans les plumes à

▸ **lay off** *vt sep* **to l. sb off** *(worker)* licencier qn

▸ **lay on** *vt sep Br (install)* installer; *(supply)* fournir

▸ **lay out** *vt sep (garden)* dessiner; *(house)* concevoir; *(display)* disposer; *Fam (money)* mettre **(on** dans)

layer ['leɪə(r)] *n* couche *f*

laze [leɪz] *vi* **to l. (about** *or* **around)** paresser

lazy ['leɪzɪ] **(-ier, -iest)** *adj (person)* paresseux, -euse ∎ **lazybones** *n Fam* flemmard, -e *mf*

lb *(abbr* **libra)** **3lb** 3 livres *(unité de poids)*

lead¹ [led] *n (metal)* plomb *m*; *(of pencil)* mine *f* ▪ **leaded** *adj (petrol)* au plomb ▪ **lead-free** *adj (paint)* sans plomb

lead² [li:d] **1** *n (distance or time ahead)* avance *f* (**over** sur); *(example)* exemple *m*; *(clue)* indice *m*; *(in film)* rôle *m* principal; *Br (for dog)* laisse *f*; *(electric wire)* fil *m* électrique; **to take the l.** *(in race)* prendre la tête; **to be in the l.** *(in race)* être en tête; *(in match)* mener (à la marque)

2 *(pt & pp* **led)** *vt (guide, conduct, take)* mener, conduire (**to** à); *(team, government)* diriger; *(expedition, attack)* commander; *(procession)* être en tête de; **to l. a happy life** mener une vie heureuse; **to l. sb in/out** faire entrer/sortir qn; **to l. sb to do sth** *(cause, induce)* amener qn à faire qch

3 *vi (of street, door)* mener, conduire (**to** à); *(in race)* être en tête; *(in match)* mener (à la marque); *(go ahead)* aller devant; **to l. to sth** *(result in)* aboutir à qch; *(cause)* mener à qch; **to l. up to** *(precede)* précéder

▸ **lead away** *vt sep* emmener
▸ **lead off** *vt sep* emmener
▸ **lead on** *vt sep (deceive)* tromper, duper

leader ['li:də(r)] *n* (**a**) *(person)* chef *m*; *(of country, party)* dirigeant, -e *mf*; *(of strike, riot)* meneur, -euse *mf*; *(guide)* guide *m*; **to be the l.** *(in race)* être en tête (**b**) *Br (newspaper article)* éditorial *m* ▪ **leadership** *n* direction *f*; *(qualities)* qualités *fpl* de chef; *(leaders) (of country, party)* dirigeants *mpl*

leading ['li:dɪŋ] *adj (best, most important)* principal; **a l. figure, a l. light** un personnage marquant

leaf [li:f] **1** *(pl* **leaves)** *n* feuille *f*; *(of book)* feuillet *m*; *(of table)* rallonge *f* **2** *vi* **to l. through** *(book)* feuilleter

leaflet ['li:flɪt] *n* prospectus *m*; *(containing instructions)* notice *f*

league [li:g] *n (alliance)* ligue *f*; *(in sport)* championnat *m*; *Pej* **in l. with** de connivence avec

leak [li:k] **1** *n (in pipe, information)* fuite *f*; *(in boat)* voie *f* d'eau **2** *vt Fig (information)* divulguer; **the pipe was leaking gas** du gaz fuyait du tuyau **3** *vi (of liquid, pipe, tap)* fuir; *(of ship)* faire eau; *Fig* **to l. out** *(of information)* être divulgué

leaky ['li:kɪ] **(-ier, -iest)** *adj (kettle, pipe, tap)* qui fuit; *(roof)* qui a une fuite

lean¹ [li:n] **(-er, -est)** *adj (meat)* maigre; *(person)* mince

lean² [li:n] *(pt & pp* **leaned** *or* **leant** [lent]) **1** *vt* **to l. sth on/against sth** appuyer qch sur/contre qch **2** *vi (of object)* pencher; *(of person)* se pencher; **to l. against/on sth** *(of person)* s'appuyer contre/sur qch; **to l. forward** *(of person)* se pencher (en avant); **to l. over** *(of person)* se pencher; *(of object)* pencher ▪ **leaning** *adj* penché; **l. against** *(resting)* appuyé contre ▪ **leanings** *npl* tendances *fpl* (**towards** à)

leap [li:p] **1** *n (jump)* bond *m*, saut *m*; *Fig (change, increase)* bond *m*; **l. year** année *f* bissextile **2** *(pt & pp* **leaped** *or* **leapt)** *vi* bondir, sauter; **to l. to one's feet, to l. up** se lever d'un bond

leapt [lept] *pt & pp of* **leap**

learn [lɜ:n] *(pt & pp* **learned** *or* **learnt** [lɜ:nt]) **1** *vt* apprendre (**that** que); **to l. (how) to do sth** apprendre à faire qch **2** *vi* apprendre; **to l. about sth** *(study)* étudier qch; *(hear about)* apprendre qch ▪ **learned** [-ɪd] *adj* savant ▪ **learner** *n (beginner)* débutant, -e *mf*; *(student)* étudiant, -e *mf* ▪ **learning** *n (of language)* apprentissage *m* (**of** de); *(knowledge)* savoir *m*

lease [li:s] **1** *n* bail *m* (*pl* baux) **2** *vt (house)* louer à bail (**from/to** à)

leash [li:ʃ] *n (of dog)* laisse *f*; **on a l.** en laisse

least [li:st] **1** *adj* **the l.** *(smallest amount of)* le moins de; **he has (the) l. talent** il a le moins de talent (**of all** de tous); **the l. effort/noise** le moindre effort/bruit **2** *n* **the l.** le moins; **at l.** du moins; *(with quantity)* au moins; **not in the l.** pas du tout **3** *adv (work, eat)* le moins; **the l. difficult** le moins difficile; **l. of all** *(especially not)* surtout pas

leather ['leðə(r)] *n* cuir *m*

leave [liːv] **1** n (holiday) congé m; (of soldier, permission) permission f; **to be on l.** être en congé; (of soldier) être en permission; **to take (one's) l. of sb** prendre congé de qn **2** (pt & pp **left**) vt (allow to remain, forget) laisser; (depart from) quitter; **to l. sth with sb** (entrust, give) laisser qch à qn; **to be left (over)** rester; **there's no bread left** il ne reste plus de pain; **I'll l. it (up) to you** je m'en remets à toi **3** vi (go away) partir (**from** de; **for** pour)

▶ **leave behind** vt sep **to l. sth behind** (on purpose) laisser qch; (accidentally) oublier qch; **to l. sb behind** (not take) partir sans qn; (surpass) dépasser qn; (in race, at school) distancer qn

▶ **leave off** vt sep (lid) ne pas remettre; Fam **to l. off doing sth** (stop) arrêter de faire qch

▶ **leave on** vt sep (clothes) garder

▶ **leave out** vt sep (forget to put) oublier de mettre; (deliberately omit) décider de ne pas inclure; (when reading) (word, line) sauter; (exclude) exclure

Lebanon ['lebənən] n le Liban

lecherous ['letʃərəs] adj lubrique

lecture ['lektʃə(r)] **1** n (public speech) conférence f; (as part of series at university) cours m magistral; (scolding) sermon m; **l. hall** amphithéâtre m **2** vt Fam (scold) faire la morale à **3** vi faire une conférence/un cours ▪ **lecturer** n conférencier, -ère mf; (at university) enseignant, -e mf

led [led] pt & pp of **lead²**

ledge [ledʒ] n (on wall, window) rebord m

ledger ['ledʒə(r)] n grand livre m

leek [liːk] n poireau m

leer [lɪə(r)] vi **to l. at sb** (lustfully) regarder qn d'un air lubrique

leeway ['liːweɪ] n marge f (de manœuvre)

left¹ [left] pt & pp of **leave** ▪ **left-luggage** n Br **l. office** consigne f

left² [left] **1** adj (side, hand) gauche **2** n gauche f; **on** or **to the l.** à gauche (**of** de) **3** adv à gauche ▪ **left-hand** adj de

gauche; **on the l. side** à gauche (**of** de); **l. drive** conduite f à gauche ▪ **left-handed** adj (person) gaucher, -ère ▪ **left-wing** adj (views, government) de gauche

leftovers ['leftəʊvəz] npl restes mpl

leg [leg] n jambe f; (of dog, bird) patte f; (of table) pied m; (of journey) étape f; **l. of chicken, chicken l.** cuisse f de poulet; **to pull sb's l.** (make fun of) mettre qn en boîte

legacy ['legəsɪ] (pl -ies) n (in a will) & Fig legs m

legal ['liːgəl] adj (lawful) légal; (affairs, adviser) juridique ▪ **legalize** vt légaliser ▪ **legally** adv légalement

legend ['ledʒənd] n (story, inscription) légende f ▪ **legendary** adj légendaire

leggings ['legɪŋz] npl (of woman) caleçon m

legible ['ledʒɪbəl] adj lisible

legislation [ledʒɪs'leɪʃən] n (laws) législation f; (piece of) **l.** loi f

legislative ['ledʒɪslətɪv] adj législatif, -ive

legislature ['ledʒɪslətjə(r)] n (corps m) législatif m

legitimate [lɪ'dʒɪtɪmət] adj légitime

legroom ['legruːm] n place f pour les jambes

leisure [Br 'leʒə(r), Am 'liːʒər] n **l. (time)** loisirs mpl; **l. centre** or **complex** centre m de loisirs; **at (one's) l.** à tête reposée ▪ **leisurely** [Br 'leʒəlɪ, Am 'liːʒərlɪ] adj (walk, occupation) peu fatigant; (meal, life) tranquille; **at a l. pace, in a l. way** sans se presser

lemon ['lemən] n citron m; Br **l. drink, l. squash** citronnade f; **l. tea** thé m au citron ▪ **lemonade** n (still) citronnade f; Br (fizzy) limonade f

lend [lend] (pt & pp **lent**) vt prêter (**to** à); (support) apporter (**to** à); Fig (charm, colour) donner (**to** à) ▪ **lender** n prêteur, -euse mf

length [leŋθ] n (in space) longueur f; (section of road, string) tronçon m; (of cloth) métrage m; (duration) durée f; **at l.** (at last) enfin; **at (great) l.** (in detail) dans le détail; **to go to great lengths**

se donner beaucoup de mal (**to do** pour faire)

lengthen ['leŋθən] *vt (garment)* allonger; *(holiday, visit)* prolonger ■ **lengthwise** *adv* dans le sens de la longueur ■ **lengthy** (**-ier, -iest**) *adj* long (*f* longue)

lenient ['li:nɪənt] *adj* indulgent (**to** envers) ■ **leniently** *adv* avec indulgence

lens [lenz] (*pl* **lenses** [-zəz]) *n* lentille *f*; *(in spectacles)* verre *m*; *(of camera)* objectif *m*

Lent [lent] *n Rel* carême *m*

lent [lent] *pt & pp of* **lend**

lentil ['lentəl] *n* lentille *f*

leopard ['lepəd] *n* léopard *m*

leotard ['li:əta:d] *n* justaucorps *m*

lesbian ['lezbɪən] **1** *adj* lesbien, -enne **2** *n* lesbienne *f*

less [les] **1** *adj & pron* moins (də) (**than** que); **l. time** moins de temps; **she has l. (than you)** elle en a moins (que toi); **l. than a kilo** moins d'un kilo **2** *adv* moins (**than** que); **l. (often)** moins souvent; **one l.** un(e) de moins **3** *prep* moins

-less [ləs] *suff* sans; **childless** sans enfants

lessen ['lesən] *vti* diminuer

lesser ['lesə(r)] **1** *adj* moindre **2** *n* **the l. of** le/la moindre de

lesson ['lesən] *n* leçon *f*; **an English l.** une leçon d'anglais; *Fig* **he has learnt his l.** ça lui a servi de leçon

lest [lest] *conj* de peur que... (+ *ne* – subjunctive)

LET¹ [let] **1** (*pt & pp* **let**, *pres p* **letting**) *vt (allow)* **to l. sb do sth** laisser qn faire qch; **to l. sb have sth** donner qch à qn; **to l. go of sb/sth** lâcher qn/qch **2** *v aux* **l.'s eat/go** mangeons/partons; **l.'s go for a stroll** allons nous promener; **l. him come** qu'il vienne ■ **letdown** *n* déception *f*

▸ **let down** *vt sep (lower)* baisser; *(hair)* dénouer; *(tyre)* dégonfler; **to l. sb down** *(disappoint)* décevoir qn; **don't l. me down** je compte sur toi

▸ **let in** *vt sep (person, dog)* faire entrer; *(light)* laisser entrer; **to l. sb in on sth** mettre qn au courant de qch; **to l. oneself in for trouble** s'attirer des ennuis

▸ **let off** *vt sep (firework)* tirer; *(bomb)* faire exploser; *(gun)* faire partir; **to l. sb off** *(allow to leave)* laisser partir qn; *(not punish)* ne pas punir qn; **to be l. off with a fine** s'en tirer avec une amende; **to l. sb off doing sth** dispenser qn de faire qch

▸ **let on** *vi Fam* **to l. on that...** *(reveal)* dire que...

▸ **let out** *vt sep (allow to leave)* laisser sortir; *(prisoner)* relâcher; *(cry, secret)* laisser échapper; *(skirt)* élargir

▸ **let up** *vi (of rain, person)* s'arrêter

let² [let] (*pt & pp* **let**, *pres p* **letting**) *vt* **to l. (out)** *(house, room)* louer

lethal ['li:θəl] *adj (blow, dose)* mortel, -elle; *(weapon)* meurtrier, -ère

lethargic [lɪ'θɑ:dʒɪk] *adj* léthargique

letter ['letə(r)] *n (message, part of word)* lettre *f*; **l. opener** coupe-papier *m inv* ■ **letterbox** *n Br* boîte *f* aux lettres ■ **letterheaded** *adj* **l. paper** papier *m* à en-tête ■ **lettering** *n (letters)* lettres *fpl*

lettuce ['letɪs] *n* laitue *f*

letup ['letʌp] *n* répit *m*

level ['levəl] **1** *n* niveau *m*; **at eye l.** à hauteur des yeux **2** *adj (surface)* plat; *(equal in score)* à égalité (**with** avec); *(in height)* à la même hauteur (**with** que); *Br* **l. crossing** *(for train)* passage *m* à niveau **3** (*Br* **-ll-**, *Am* **-l-**) *vt (surface, differences)* aplanir; *(building)* raser; *(gun)* braquer (**at** sur); *(accusation)* lancer (**at** contre) **4** *vi* **to l. off** *or* **out** *(of prices)* se stabiliser ■ **level-headed** *adj* équilibré

lever [*Br* 'li:və(r), *Am* 'levər] *n* levier *m*

levy ['levɪ] **1** (*pl* **-ies**) *n (tax)* impôt *m* (**on** sur) **2** (*pt & pp* **-ied**) *vt (tax)* lever

lewd [lu:d] (**-er, -est**) *adj* obscène

liability [laɪə'bɪlɪtɪ] *n (legal responsibility)* responsabilité *f* (**for** de); *(disadvantage)* handicap *m*; *Fin* **liabilities** *(debts)* passif *m*

liable ['laɪəbəl] *adj* **l. to** *(dizziness)* sujet, -ette à; *(fine, tax)* passible de; **to be**

l. to do sth risquer de faire qch; **l. for sth** *(responsible)* responsable de qch

liaise [liːˈeɪz] *vi* travailler en liaison **(with** avec**)** ▪ **liaison** [liːˈeɪzɒn] *n (contact, love affair)* liaison *f*

liar [ˈlaɪə(r)] *n* menteur, -euse *mf*

libel [ˈlaɪbəl] **1** *n (in law)* diffamation *f* **2** *(Br -ll-, Am -l-) vt* diffamer (par écrit)

liberal [ˈlɪbərəl] **1** *adj (open-minded)* & *Pol* libéral; *(generous)* généreux, -euse **(with** de**) 2** *n Pol* libéral, -e *mf*

liberate [ˈlɪbəreɪt] *vt* libérer ▪ **liberation** *n* libération *f*

liberty [ˈlɪbətɪ] *(pl -ies) n* liberté *f*; **to be at l. to do sth** être libre de faire qch; **to take liberties with sb/sth** prendre des libertés avec qn/qch

library [ˈlaɪbrərɪ] *(pl -ies) n* bibliothèque *f* ▪ **librarian** [-ˈbreərɪən] *n* bibliothécaire *mf*

libretto [lɪˈbretəʊ] *(pl -os) n Mus* livret *m*

Libya [ˈlɪbɪə] *n* la Libye

lice [laɪs] *pl of* **louse**

licence [ˈlaɪsəns] *(Am* **license***) n (permit)* permis *m*; *(for trading)* licence *f*; **(TV) l.** redevance *f*; **l. plate/number** *(of vehicle)* plaque *f*/numéro *m* d'immatriculation

license [ˈlaɪsəns] **1** *n Am =* **licence 2** *vt* accorder un permis/une licence à

lick [lɪk] *vt* lécher

licorice [ˈlɪkərɪʃ, ˈlɪkərɪs] *n* réglisse *f*

lid [lɪd] *n (of box, pan)* couvercle *m*

lie¹ [laɪ] **1** *n* mensonge *m* **2** *(pt & pp* **lied**, *pres p* **lying***) vi (tell lies)* mentir

lie² [laɪ] *(pt* **lay**, *pp* **lain**, *pres p* **lying***) vi* **(a)** *(of person, animal) (be in a flat position)* être allongé; *(get down)* s'allonger; **to be lying on the grass** être allongé sur l'herbe; **he lay asleep** il dormait; **here lies...** *(on tomb)* ci-gît... **(b)** *(of object)* être, se trouver; **the problem lies in the fact that...** le problème réside dans le fait que... ▪ **lie-down** *n Br* **to have a l.** faire une sieste ▪ **lie-in** *n Br* **to have a l.** faire la grasse matinée

▸ **lie about, lie around** *vi (of objects, person)* traîner

▸ **lie down** *vi* s'allonger; **to be lying down** être allongé

▸ **lie in** *vi Br* faire la grasse matinée

lieu [luː] *n* **in l. of sth** au lieu de qch

lieutenant [luːˈtenənt, *Br* lefˈtenənt] *n* lieutenant *m*

life [laɪf] *(pl* **lives***) n* vie *f*; *(of battery, machine)* durée *f* de vie; **to come to l.** *(of party, street)* s'animer; **to take one's (own) l.** se donner la mort; **l. expectancy** espérance *f* de vie; **l. insurance** assurance-vie *f*; **l. jacket** gilet *m* de sauvetage ▪ **lifebelt** *n* ceinture *f* de sauvetage ▪ **lifeboat** *n* canot *m* de sauvetage ▪ **lifebuoy** *n* bouée *f* de sauvetage ▪ **lifeguard** *n* maître nageur *m* ▪ **lifeless** *adj* sans vie ▪ **lifelike** *adj* très ressemblant ▪ **lifelong** *adj* de toute sa vie; *(friend)* de toujours ▪ **lifesize(d)** *adj* grandeur nature *inv* ▪ **lifestyle** *n* style *m* de vie ▪ **lifetime** *n* vie *f*; *Fig* éternité *f*

lift [lɪft] **1** *n Br (elevator)* ascenseur *m*; **to give sb a l.** emmener qn en voiture **(to** à**) 2** *vt* lever; *(heavy object)* soulever; *Fig (ban)* lever; *Fig (steal)* piquer **(from** à**) 3** *vi (of fog)* se lever ▪ **lift-off** *n (of space vehicle)* décollage *m*

▸ **lift down** *vt sep (take down)* descendre **(from** de**)**

▸ **lift off 1** *vt sep (take down)* descendre **(from** de**) 2** *vi (of spacecraft)* décoller

▸ **lift out** *vt sep (take out)* sortir

▸ **lift up** *vt sep (arm, object, eyes)* lever; *(heavy object)* soulever

ligament [ˈlɪgəmənt] *n* ligament *m*

light¹ [laɪt] **1** *n* lumière *f*; *(on vehicle)* feu *m*; *(vehicle headlight)* phare *m*; **by the l. of sth** à la clarté de qch; **in the l. of...** *(considering)* à la lumière de...; **to bring sth to l.** mettre qch en lumière; **to come to l.** être découvert; **do you have a l.?** *(for cigarette)* est-ce que vous avez du feu?; **to set l. to sth** mettre le feu à qch; **turn right at the lights** tournez à droite après les feux; **l. bulb** ampoule *f*; **l. switch** interrupteur *m*

2 *adj* **it will soon be l.** il fera bientôt jour

3 *(pt & pp* **lit** *or* **lighted***) vt (fire, candle, gas)* allumer; *(match)* allumer,

gratter; **to l. (up)** *(room)* éclairer; *(cigarette)* allumer

4 *vi* to l. up *(of smoker)* allumer une cigarette/un cigare/sa pipe ■ **lighting** *n (act, system)* éclairage *m*

light² [laɪt] *adj (bright, not dark)* clair; **a l. green jacket** une veste vert clair

light³ [laɪt] *adj (in weight, quantity, strength)* léger, -ère; *(task)* facile; **l. rain** pluie *f* fine; **to travel l.** voyager avec peu de bagages ■ **light-hearted** *adj* enjoué

lighten ['laɪtən] *vt (make less heavy)* alléger

lighter ['laɪtə(r)] *n* briquet *m*; *(for cooker)* allume-gaz *m inv*

lighthouse ['laɪthaʊs] *n* phare *m*

lightly ['laɪtlɪ] *adv* légèrement; **to get off l.** s'en tirer à bon compte

lightning ['laɪtnɪŋ] **1** *n* éclairs *mpl*; **(flash of) l.** éclair *m* **2** *adj (speed)* foudroyant; *(visit)* éclair *inv*

lightweight ['laɪtweɪt] **1** *adj (shoes, fabric)* léger, -ère; *Fig & Pej (person)* pas sérieux, -euse **2** *n (in boxing)* poids *m* léger

like¹ [laɪk] **1** *prep* comme; **l. this** comme ça; **what's he l.?** comment est-il?; **to be** *or* **look l. sb/sth** ressembler à qn/qch; **what was the book l.?** comment as-tu trouvé le livre?

2 *adv* **nothing l. as big** loin d'être aussi grand

3 *conj Fam (as)* comme; **do l. I do** fais comme moi

4 *n* **...and the l.** ...et ainsi de suite; **the likes of you** des gens de ton acabit

like² [laɪk] **1** *vt* aimer (bien) **(to do** *or* **doing** faire); **I l. him** je l'aime bien; **I'd l. to come** j'aimerais bien venir; **I'd l. a kilo of apples** je voudrais un kilo de pommes; **would you l. an apple?** voulez-vous une pomme?; **if you l.** si vous voulez

2 *npl* **one's likes and dislikes** nos préférences *fpl* ■ **liking** *n* **a l. for** *(person)* de la sympathie pour; *(thing)* du goût pour; **to my l.** à mon goût

likeable ['laɪkəbəl] *adj* sympathique

likely ['laɪklɪ] **1 (-ier, -iest)** *adj (result,* event)* probable; *(excuse)* vraisemblable; **it's l. (that) she'll come** il est probable qu'elle viendra **2** *adv* **very l.** très probablement ■ **likelihood** *n* probabilité *f*; **there isn't much l. that...** il y a peu de chances que... (+ *subjunctive)*

liken ['laɪkən] *vt* comparer **(to** à)

likeness ['laɪknɪs] *n (similarity)* ressemblance *f*; **it's a good l.** c'est très ressemblant

likewise ['laɪkwaɪz] *adv (similarly)* de même

lilac ['laɪlək] **1** *n* lilas *m* **2** *adj (colour)* lilas *inv*

Lilo® ['laɪləʊ] *(pl* **-os)** *n Br* matelas *m* pneumatique

lily ['lɪlɪ] *(pl* **-ies)** *n* lis *m*

limb [lɪm] *n (of body)* membre *m*

limber ['lɪmbə(r)] *vi* **to l. up** se chauffer

lime [laɪm] *n (fruit)* citron *m* vert

limelight ['laɪmlaɪt] *n* **to be in the l.** occuper le devant de la scène

limit ['lɪmɪt] **1** *n* limite *f*; *(restriction)* limitation *f* **(on** de); *Fam* **that's the l.!** c'est le comble!; **within limits** jusqu'à un certain point **2** *vt* limiter **(to** à); **to l. oneself to sth/doing sth** se borner à qch/faire qch ■ **limitation** *n* limitation *f*

limited ['lɪmɪtɪd] *adj (restricted)* limité; *(edition)* à tirage limité; *Br* **l. company** société *f* à responsabilité limitée; *Br* **(public) l. company** *(with shareholders)* société *f* anonyme

limousine [lɪmə'ziːn] *n (car)* limousine *f*

limp¹ [lɪmp] **1** *n* **to have a l.** boiter **2** *vi (of person)* boiter

limp² [lɪmp] **(-er, -est)** *adj (soft)* mou *(f* molle); *(flabby) (skin)* flasque; *(person, hat)* avachi

line¹ [laɪn] **1** *n* ligne *f*; *(stroke)* trait *m*; *(of poem)* vers *m*; *(wrinkle)* ride *f*; *(track)* voie *f*; *(rope)* corde *f*; *(row)* rangée *f*; *(of vehicles)* file *f*; *(queue of people)* file *f*, queue *f*; *(of goods)* ligne *f* (de produits); **to learn one's lines** *(of actor)* apprendre son texte; **to be on the l.** *(at other end of phone line)* être au bout du fil; *(at risk) (of job)* être menacé; *Am*

to stand in l. faire la queue; **in l. with sth** conforme à qch; **along the same lines** *(work, think, act)* de la même façon; *Fam* **to drop sb a l.** *(send a letter)* envoyer un mot à qn; **l. dancing** = danse de style country effectuée en rangs

2 *vt* **to l. the street** *(of trees)* border la rue; *(of people)* s'aligner le long du trottoir; **to l. up** *(children, objects)* aligner; *(arrange)* organiser; **lined paper** papier *m* réglé

3 *vi* **to l. up** s'aligner; *Am (queue up)* faire la queue ▪ **line-up** *n (row of people)* file *f*; *TV (of guests)* plateau *m*

line² [laɪn] *vt (clothes)* doubler

linen ['lɪnɪn] *n (sheets)* linge *m*; *(material)* (toile *f* de) lin *m*

liner ['laɪnə(r)] *n* (a) *(ocean)* l. paquebot *m* (b) *Br* **(dust)bin l.,** *Am* **garbage can l.** sac-poubelle *m*

linesman ['laɪnzmən] *(pl* **-men)** *n (in football)* juge *m* de touche

linger ['lɪŋgə(r)] *vi* **to l. (on)** *(of person)* s'attarder; *(of smell, memory)* persister; *(of doubt)* subsister

linguist ['lɪŋgwɪst] *n (specialist)* linguiste *mf* ▪ **linguistic** *adj* linguistique ▪ **linguistics** *n* linguistique *f*

lining ['laɪnɪŋ] *n (of clothes)* doublure *f*

link [lɪŋk] **1** *n (connection)* & *Comptr* lien *m*; *(of chain)* maillon *m*; *(by road, rail)* liaison *f* **2** *vt (connect)* relier **(to** à); *(relate, associate)* lier **(to** à); **to l. up** relier; *(computer)* connecter **3** *vi* **to l. up** *(of companies, countries)* s'associer; *(of roads)* se rejoindre

lino ['laɪnəʊ] *(pl* **-os)** *n Br* lino *m*

lint [lɪnt] *n (bandage)* tissu *m* ouaté; *(fluff)* peluches *fpl*

lion ['laɪən] *n* lion *m*; **l. cub** lionceau *m*

lip [lɪp] *n (of person)* lèvre *f*; *(of cup)* bord *m* ▪ **lip-read** *(pt & pp* **-read** [-red]) *vi* lire sur les lèvres ▪ **lipstick** *n* rouge *m* à lèvres

liqueur *[Br* lɪ'kjʊə(r), *Am* lɪ'kɜːr] *n* liqueur *f*

liquid ['lɪkwɪd] *n & adj* liquide *(m)*

liquidate ['lɪkwɪdeɪt] *vt (debt)* & *Fam (kill)* liquider

liquidizer ['lɪkwɪdaɪzə(r)] *n Br (for fruit juices, purées)* mixeur *m* ▪ **liquidize** *vt Br* passer au mixeur

liquor ['lɪkə(r)] *n Am* alcool *m*; **l. store** magasin *m* de vins et de spiritueux

liquorice ['lɪkərɪʃ, 'lɪkərɪs] *n Br* réglisse *f*

lira ['lɪərə] *(pl* **lire** ['lɪəreɪ]) *n* lire *f*

lisp [lɪsp] **1** *n* **to have a l.** zézayer **2** *vi* zézayer

list [lɪst] **1** *n* liste *f* **2** *vt (things)* faire la liste de; *(names)* mettre sur la liste; *(name one by one)* énumérer; *Br* **listed building** monument *m* classé

listen ['lɪsən] *vi* écouter; **to l. to sb/sth** écouter qn/qch; **to l. (out) for** *(telephone, person)* guetter ▪ **listener** *n (to radio)* auditeur, -trice *mf*

listless ['lɪstləs] *adj* apathique

lit [lɪt] *pt & pp of* **light¹**

liter ['liːtə(r)] *n Am* litre *m*

literal ['lɪtərəl] *adj* littéral; *(not exaggerated)* réel *(f* réelle)

literally ['lɪtərəlɪ] *adv* littéralement; *(really)* réellement ▪ **literary** *adj* littéraire

literate ['lɪtərət] *adj* qui sait lire et écrire

literature ['lɪtərətʃə(r)] *n* littérature *f*; *(pamphlets)* documentation *f*

lithe [laɪð] *adj* agile

litigation [lɪtɪ'geɪʃən] *n* litige *m*

litre ['liːtə(r)] *(Am* **liter)** *n* litre *m*

litter ['lɪtə(r)] **1** *n* (a) *(rubbish)* détritus *mpl*; *(papers)* papiers *mpl* (b) *Br* **l. bin** boîte *f* à ordures; *(young animals)* portée *f*; *(for cat)* litière *f* **2** *vt Br* **to be littered with sth** être jonché de qch

LITTLE ['lɪtəl] **1** *n* peu *m*; **I've l. left** il m'en reste peu; **she eats l.** elle mange peu; **I have a l.** j'en ai un peu

2 *adj* (a) *(small)* petit; **a l. bit** un (petit) peu (b) *(not much)* peu de; **l. time/money** peu de temps/d'argent; **a l. time/money** un peu de temps/d'argent

3 *adv (somewhat, rather)* peu; **l. by l.** peu à peu; **as l. as possible** le moins possible; **a l. heavy/better** un peu

lourd/mieux; **to work a l.** travailler un peu

live¹ [laɪv] **1** adj (**a**) (electric wire) sous tension; (plugged in) (appliance) branché; (ammunition) réel (f réelle), de combat (**b**) (alive) vivant **2** adj & adv (on radio, television) en direct; **a l. broadcast** une émission en direct; **a l. recording** un enregistrement public

live² [lɪv] **1** vt (life) mener, vivre **2** vi vivre; **where do you l.?** où habitez-vous?; **to l. in Paris** habiter (à) Paris
▸ **live down** vt sep faire oublier
▸ **live off** vt insep (eat) vivre de; (sponge off) vivre aux crochets de
▸ **live on 1** vt sep = **live off 2** vi (of memory) survivre
▸ **live through** vt insep (experience) vivre
▸ **live up to** vt insep (sb's expectations) se montrer à la hauteur de

livelihood ['laɪvlɪhʊd] n **my l.** mon gagne-pain; **to earn one's** or **a l.** gagner sa vie

lively ['laɪvlɪ] (**-ier, -iest**) adj (person, style) plein de vie; (story) vivant; (mind) vif (f vive); (discussion, conversation) animé
▸ **liven up** ['laɪvən] **1** vt sep (person) égayer; (party) animer **2** vi (of person, party) s'animer

liver ['lɪvə(r)] n foie m

livestock ['laɪvstɒk] n bétail m

livid ['lɪvɪd] adj (angry) furieux, -euse

living ['lɪvɪŋ] **1** adj (alive) vivant; **within l. memory** de mémoire d'homme; **the l.** les vivants mpl **2** n (livelihood) vie f; **to make** or **earn a** or **one's l.** gagner sa vie; **l. room** salle f de séjour

lizard ['lɪzəd] n lézard m

load [ləʊd] **1** n (object carried, burden) charge f; (freight) chargement m; (strain, weight) poids m; Fam **a l. of**, **loads of** (people, money) un tas de **2** vt (truck, gun) charger (**with** de); **to l. up** (car, ship) charger (**with** de) **3** vi **to l. (up)** prendre un chargement

loaded ['ləʊdɪd] adj (gun, vehicle) chargé; Fam (rich) plein aux as

loaf [ləʊf] **1** (pl **loaves**) n pain m **2** vi **to l. (about)** fainéanter

loan [ləʊn] **1** n (money lent) prêt m; (money borrowed) emprunt m; **on l. from** prêté par **2** vt (lend) prêter (**to** à)

loathe [ləʊð] vt détester (**doing** faire)

lobby ['lɒbɪ] **1** (pl **-ies**) n (**a**) (of hotel) hall m; (of theatre) foyer m (**b**) (in politics) groupe m de pression **2** (pt & pp **-ied**) vt faire pression sur **3** vi **to l. for sth** faire pression pour obtenir qch

lobster ['lɒbstə(r)] n homard m; (spiny) langouste f

local ['ləʊkəl] **1** adj local; (regional) régional; (of the neighbourhood) du quartier; **a l. phone call** (within town) une communication urbaine **2** n Br Fam (pub) bistrot m du coin; **the locals** (people) les gens mpl du coin

locality [ləʊ'kælətɪ] (pl **-ies**) n (neighbourhood) environs mpl

locally ['ləʊkəlɪ] adv dans le quartier

locate [ləʊ'keɪt] vt (find) repérer; (pain, noise, leak) localiser; (situate) situer; **to be located in Paris** être situé à Paris ▪ **location** n (site) emplacement m; **on l.** (shoot a film) en extérieur

lock¹ [lɒk] n (of hair) mèche f

lock² [lɒk] **1** n (**a**) (on door, chest) serrure f; (anti-theft) **l.** (on vehicle) antivol m (**b**) (on canal) écluse f **2** vt (door, car) fermer à clef **3** vi fermer à clef
▸ **lock away** vt sep (prisoner) enfermer; (jewels) mettre sous clef
▸ **lock in** vt sep (person) enfermer, **to l. sb in sth** enfermer qn dans qch
▸ **lock out** vt sep (person) enfermer dehors
▸ **lock up 1** vt sep (house, car) fermer à clef; (prisoner) enfermer; (jewels) mettre sous clef, enfermer **2** vi fermer à clef

locker ['lɒkə(r)] n (in school) casier m; (for luggage) (at station, airport) casier m de consigne automatique; (for clothes) vestiaire m (métallique); Am Sport **l. room** vestiaire m

locket ['lɒkɪt] n médaillon m

locksmith ['lɒksmɪθ] n serrurier m

locomotive [ləʊkə'məʊtɪv] n locomotive f

locust ['ləʊkəst] n sauterelle f

lodge [lɒdʒ] **1** n (house) pavillon m; (of porter) loge f **2** vt (person) loger **3** vi (of bullet) se loger (**in** dans)

lodger ['lɒdʒə(r)] n (room and meals) pensionnaire mf; (room only) locataire mf

lodgings ['lɒdʒɪŋz] n (flat) logement m; (room) chambre f; **in l.** en meublé

loft [lɒft] n grenier m

lofty ['lɒftɪ] (**-ier, -iest**) adj (high, noble) élevé

log [lɒg] **1** n (tree trunk) tronc m d'arbre; (for fire) bûche f; **l. cabin** hutte f en rondin; **l. fire** feu m de bois **2** (pt & pp **-gg-**) vt (facts) noter **3** vi Comptr **to l. in/out** entrer/sortir ■ **logbook** n (on ship) journal m de bord; (on plane) carnet m de vol

logic ['lɒdʒɪk] n logique f ■ **logical** adj logique ■ **logically** adv logiquement

logistics [lə'dʒɪstɪks] n logistique f

logo ['ləʊgəʊ] (pl **-os**) n logo m

loiter ['lɔɪtə(r)] vi traîner

loll [lɒl] vi (in armchair) se prélasser

lollipop ['lɒlɪpɒp] n sucette f; Br **l. man/lady** = contractuel ou contractuelle qui aide les écoliers à traverser la rue ■ **lolly** (pl **-ies**) n Fam (lollipop) sucette f; (ice) **l.** glace f à l'eau

London ['lʌndən] **1** n Londres m ou f **2** adj londonien, -enne

lone [ləʊn] adj solitaire

loneliness ['ləʊnlɪnəs] n solitude f ■ **lonely** (**-ier, -iest**) adj (road, house, life) solitaire; (person) seul

loner ['ləʊnə(r)] n solitaire mf

LONG¹ [lɒŋ] **1** (**-er, -est**) adj long (f longue); **to be 10 metres l.** avoir 10 mètres de long; **to be six weeks l.** durer six semaines; **how l. is…?** quelle est la longueur de…?; (time) quelle est la durée de…?; **a l. time** longtemps; **l. jump** (sport) saut m en longueur

2 adv (a long time) longtemps; **has he been here l.?** il y a longtemps qu'il est ici?; **how l.?** (in time) combien de temps?; **not l.** peu de temps; **before l.** sous peu; **no longer** ne… plus; **a bit**

longer (wait) encore un peu; **I won't be l.** je n'en ai pas pour longtemps; **don't be l.** dépêche-toi; **all summer/winter l.** tout l'été/l'hiver; **l. live the queen!** vive la reine!; **as l. as, so l. as** (provided that) pourvu que (+ subjunctive); **as l. as I live** tant que je vivrai ■ **long-distance** adj (race) de fond; (phone call) interurbain ■ **long-haired** adj aux cheveux longs ■ **long-life** adj (battery) longue durée inv; (milk) longue conservation inv ■ **long-range** adj (forecast) à long terme ■ **longsighted** adj (person) presbyte ■ **longstanding** adj de longue date ■ **long-term** adj à long terme ■ **long-winded** adj (speech, speaker) verbeux, -euse

long² [lɒŋ] vi **to l. for sth** avoir très envie de qch; **to l. to do sth** avoir très envie de faire qch ■ **longing** n désir m

longitude ['lɒndʒɪtjuːd] n longitude f

loo [luː] (pl **loos**) n Br Fam **the l.** le petit coin

look [lʊk] **1** n (glance) regard m; (appearance) air m, allure f; **to have a l. (at sth)** jeter un coup d'œil (à qch); **to have a l. (for sth)** chercher (qch); **to have a l. (a)round** regarder; (walk) faire un tour; **let me have a l.** fais voir **2** vt **to l. sb in the face** regarder qn dans les yeux

3 vi regarder; **to l. tired/happy** (seem) avoir l'air fatigué/heureux; **to l. pretty/ugly** être joli/laid; **you l. like** or **as if** or **as though you're tired** tu as l'air fatigué; **to l. like an apple** avoir l'air d'une pomme; **you l. like my brother** tu ressembles à mon frère; **it looks like rain** on dirait qu'il va pleuvoir; **what does he l. like?** comment est-il?; **to l. well** or **good** (of person) avoir bonne mine; **you l. good in that hat** ce chapeau te va très bien; **that looks bad** (action) ça fait mauvais effet

► **look after** vt insep (take care of) s'occuper de; (keep safely) garder (**for sb** pour qn); **to l. after oneself** (keep healthy) faire bien attention à soi; (manage, cope) se débrouiller

► **look around 1** vt insep (town, shops) faire un tour dans **2** vi (have a look)

regarder; *(walk round)* faire un tour

▶**look at** *vt insep* regarder; *(consider)* considérer

▶**look away** *vi* détourner les yeux

▶**look back** *vi* regarder derrière soi; *(in time)* regarder en arrière

▶**look down** *vi* baisser les yeux; *(from a height)* regarder en bas; **to l. down on** *(consider scornfully)* regarder de haut

▶**look for** *vt insep (seek)* chercher

▶**look forward to** *vt insep (event)* attendre avec impatience; **to l. forward to doing sth** avoir hâte de faire qch

▶**look in** *vi* regarder à l'intérieur; **to l. in on sb** passer voir qn

▶**look into** *vt insep (examine)* examiner; *(find out about)* se renseigner sur

▶**look on 1** *vt insep (consider)* considérer **(as** comme**) 2** *vi (watch)* regarder; **to l. on to** *(of window, house)* donner sur

▶**look out** *vi (be careful)* faire attention; **to l. out for sb/sth** *(seek)* chercher qn/qch; *(watch)* guetter qn/qch; **to l. out on to** *(of window, house)* donner sur

▶**look over** *vt insep (examine fully)* examiner; *(briefly)* parcourir; *(region, town)* parcourir, visiter

▶**look round 1** *vt insep (visit)* visiter **2** *vi (have a look)* regarder; *(walk round)* faire un tour; *(look back)* se retourner; **to l. round for sb/sth** *(seek)* chercher qn/qch

▶**look through** *vt insep (inspect)* passer en revue

▶**look up 1** *vt sep (word)* chercher; **to l. sb up** *(visit)* passer voir qn **2** *vi (of person)* lever les yeux; *(into the air or sky)* regarder en l'air; *(improve) (of situation)* s'améliorer; *Fig* **to l. up to sb** respecter qn

-looking ['lʊkɪŋ] *suff* **pleasant-/tired-l.** à l'air agréable/fatigué

lookout ['lʊkaʊt] *n (soldier)* guetteur *m*; **l. (post)** observatoire *m*; **to be on the l. for sb/sth** guetter qn/qch

loom [luːm] **1** *n (weaving machine)* métier *m* à tisser **2** *vi* **to l. (up)** *(of mountain)* apparaître indistinctement;

(of event) paraître imminent

loony ['luːnɪ] *(pl* **-ies)** *n & adj Fam* dingue *(mf)*

loop [luːp] *n* boucle *f*

loophole ['luːphəʊl] *n (in law)* vide *m* juridique

loose [luːs] **1** (**-er, -est**) *adj (screw, belt, knot)* desserré; *(tooth, stone)* qui bouge; *(page)* détaché; *(clothes)* flottant; *(hair)* dénoué; *(translation)* vague; *(articles for sale)* en vrac; *Br (cheese, tea)* au poids; **there's an animal/prisoner l.** *(having escaped)* il y a un animal échappé/un prisonnier évadé; **l. change** petite monnaie *f*; **to come l.** *(of knot, screw)* se desserrer; *(of page)* se détacher; *(of tooth)* se mettre à bouger; **to get l.** *(of dog)* se détacher; **to set** *or* **turn l.** *(dog)* lâcher **2** *n* **on the l.** *(prisoner)* en cavale; *(animal)* en liberté

loosely ['luːslɪ] *adv (hang)* lâchement; *(hold, tie)* sans serrer; *(translate)* de façon approximative

loosen ['luːsən] *vt (knot, belt, screw)* desserrer; *(rope)* détendre; **to l. one's grip** relâcher son étreinte

loot [luːt] **1** *n* butin *m*; *Fam (money)* fric *m* **2** *vt* piller ▪ **looting** *n* pillage *m*

lop [lɒp] *(pt & pp* **-pp-)** *vt* **to l. (off)** couper

lop-sided [lɒp'saɪdɪd] *adj (crooked)* de travers

lord [lɔːd] *n* seigneur *m*; *(British title)* lord *m*; **the L.** *(God)* le Seigneur; *Fam* **good L.!** bon sang!

lorry ['lɒrɪ] *(pl* **-ies)** *n Br* camion *m*; *(heavy)* poids *m* lourd; **l. driver** camionneur *m*; **(long-distance) l. driver** routier *m*

lose [luːz] *(pt & pp* **lost) 1** *vt* perdre; **to l. one's life** trouver la mort **(in** dans**); to l. one's way, to get lost** *(of person)* se perdre; *Fam* **get lost!** fous le camp!; **that lost us the war/our jobs** cela nous a coûté la guerre/notre travail; **the clock loses six minutes a day** la pendule retarde de six minutes par jour **2** *vi* perdre; **to l. out** être perdant; **to l. to sb** *(in contest)* être battu par qn

■ **loser** n (in contest) perdant, -e mf; Fam (failure in life) minable mf ■ **losing** adj (number, team, horse) perdant

loss [lɒs] n perte f; **to sell sth at a l.** vendre qch à perte; **to make a l.** (financially) perdre de l'argent

lost [lɒst] 1 pt & pp of **lose** 2 adj perdu; Br **l. property**, Am **l. and found** objets mpl trouvés

lot¹ [lɒt] n (destiny) sort m; (batch) lot m; **to draw lots** tirer au sort

lot² [lɒt] n **the l.** (everything) (le) tout; **the l. of you** vous tous; **a l. of, lots of** beaucoup de; **a l.** beaucoup; **quite a l.** pas mal (**of** de)

lotion ['ləʊʃən] n lotion f

lottery ['lɒtərɪ] (pl -ies) n loterie f; **l. ticket** billet m de loterie

loud [laʊd] 1 (-er, -est) adj (voice, music) fort; (noise, cry) grand; (laugh) gros (f grosse); (gaudy) voyant 2 adv (shout) fort; **out l.** tout haut ■ **loudly** adv (speak, laugh, shout) fort ■ **loudspeaker** n haut-parleur m; (for speaking to crowd) porte-voix m inv; (of stereo system) enceinte f

lounge [laʊndʒ] 1 n (in house, hotel) salon m; **airport l.** salle f d'aéroport 2 vi (loll in armchair) se prélasser; **to l. about** (idle) paresser

louse [laʊs] (pl **lice**) n (insect) pou m

lousy ['laʊzɪ] (-ier, -iest) adj Fam (bad) nul (f nulle); (food, weather) dégueulasse; **to feel l.** être mal fichu

lout [laʊt] n voyou m

love [lʌv] 1 n (a) (feeling) amour m; **in l.** amoureux, -euse (**with** de); **they're in l.** ils s'aiment; **give him/her my l.** (greeting) dis-lui bien des choses de ma part; **l. affair** liaison f (**b**) (in tennis) rien m; **15 l.** 15 à rien 2 vt (person) aimer; (thing, activity) adorer (**to do** or **doing** faire) ■ **loving** adj affectueux, -euse

lovely ['lʌvlɪ] (-ier, -iest) adj (idea, smell) très bon (f bonne); (pretty) joli; (charming) charmant; (kind) gentil, -ille; **the weather's l.**, **it's l.** il fait beau; (**it's**) **l. to see you!** je suis ravi de te voir!

lover ['lʌvə(r)] n (man) amant m; (woman) maîtresse f; **a l. of music/art** un amateur de musique/d'art

low¹ [ləʊ] 1 (-er, -est) adj bas (f basse); (speed, income, intelligence) faible; (opinion, quality) mauvais; **she's l. on** (money) elle n'a plus beaucoup de; **to feel l.** (depressed) être déprimé; **lower** inférieur; Am **l. beams** (of vehicle) codes mpl
2 (-er, -est) adv bas; **to turn (down) l.** mettre plus bas; **to run l.** (of supplies) s'épuiser
3 n **to reach a new l.** or **an all-time l.** (of prices) atteindre leur niveau le plus bas ■ **low-cut** adj décolleté ■ **low-down** n Fam (facts) tuyaux mpl ■ **low-fat** adj (milk) écrémé; (cheese) allégé ■ **low-key** adj (discreet) discret, -ète ■ **low-paid** adj mal payé

low² [ləʊ] vi (of cattle) meugler

lower ['ləʊə(r)] vt baisser; **to l. sb/sth** (by rope) descendre qn/qch; Fig **to l. oneself** s'abaisser

lowly ['ləʊlɪ] (-ier, -iest) adj humble

loyal ['lɔɪəl] adj loyal (**to** envers) ■ **loyalty** n loyauté f

lozenge ['lɒzɪndʒ] n (tablet) pastille f; (shape) losange m

LP [el'piː] (abbr **long-playing record**) n 33 tours m inv

L-plate ['elpleɪt] n Br = plaque apposée sur une voiture pour signaler que le conducteur est en conduite accompagnée

Ltd (abbr **Limited**) Br Com ≃ SARL

lubricate ['luːbrɪkeɪt] vt lubrifier; (machine, car wheels) graisser

lucid ['luːsɪd] adj lucide

luck [lʌk] n (chance) chance f; (good fortune) (bonne) chance f, bonheur m; **to be in l.** avoir de la chance; **to be out of l.** ne pas avoir de chance; **to wish sb l.** souhaiter bonne chance à qn; **bad l.** malchance f; **hard l.!, tough l.!** pas de chance!

luckily ['lʌkɪlɪ] adv heureusement

lucky ['lʌkɪ] (-ier, -iest) adj (person) chanceux, -euse; **to be l.** (of person) avoir de la chance; **it's l. that...** c'est

une chance que... *(+ subjunctive)*; **l. number** chiffre *m* porte-bonheur

lucrative ['lu:krətɪv] *adj* lucratif, -ive

ludicrous ['lu:dɪkrəs] *adj* ridicule

luggage ['lʌgɪdʒ] *n* bagages *mpl*; **a piece of l.** un bagage; **hand l.** bagages *mpl* à main; **l. compartment** compartiment *m* à bagages

lukewarm ['lu:kwɔ:m] *adj* (water, soup) tiède

lull [lʌl] **1** *n* arrêt *m*; *(in storm)* accalmie *f* **2** *vt* **to l. sb to sleep** endormir qn en le/la berçant

lullaby ['lʌləbaɪ] *(pl* -ies) *n* berceuse *f*

lumber[1] ['lʌmbə(r)] *n (timber)* bois *m* de charpente; *Br (junk)* bric-à-brac *m inv* ■ **lumberyard** *n Am* dépôt *m* de bois

lumber[2] ['lʌmbə(r)] *vt Br Fam* **to l. sb with sb/sth** coller qn/qch à qn

luminous ['lu:mɪnəs] *adj (colour paper, ink)* fluorescent; *(dial, clock)* lumineux, -euse

lump [lʌmp] **1** *n* morceau *m*; *(in soup)* grumeau *m*; *(bump)* bosse *f*; *(swelling)* grosseur *f*; **l. sum** somme *f* forfaitaire **2** *vt* **to l. together** réunir; *Fig & Pej* mettre dans le même sac ■ **lumpy** (-ier, -iest) *adj (soup)* grumeleux, -euse; *(surface)* bosselé

lunar ['lu:nə(r)] *adj* lunaire; **l. eclipse** éclipse *f* de lune

lunatic ['lu:nətɪk] *n* fou *m*, folle *f*

lunch [lʌntʃ] **1** *n* déjeuner *m*; **to have l.** déjeuner; **l. break, l. hour, l. time** heure *f* du déjeuner **2** *vi* déjeuner (**on** or **off** de) ■ **lunchbox** *n* = boîte dans laquelle on transporte son déjeuner

luncheon ['lʌnʃən] *n* déjeuner *m*; *Br* **l. voucher** Chèque-Restaurant *m*

lung [lʌŋ] *n* poumon *m*

lunge [lʌndʒ] *vi* **to l. at sb** se ruer sur qn

lurch [lɜ:tʃ] **1** *n Fam* **to leave sb in the l.** laisser qn dans le pétrin **2** *vi (of person)* tituber

lure [lʊə(r)] **1** *n (attraction)* attrait *m* **2** *vt* attirer (par la ruse) (**into** dans)

lurid ['lʊərɪd] *adj (story, description)* cru; *(gaudy)* voyant

lurk [lɜ:k] *vi (hide)* être tapi (**in** dans); *(prowl)* rôder

luscious ['lʌʃəs] *adj (food)* appétissant

lush [lʌʃ] *adj (vegetation)* luxuriant; *(wealthy) (surroundings)* luxueux, -euse

lust [lʌst] **1** *n (for person)* désir *m*; *(for object)* convoitise *f* (**for** de); *(for power, knowledge)* soif *f* (**for** de) **2** *vi* **to l. after** *(object, person)* convoiter; *(power, knowledge)* avoir soif de

lustre ['lʌstə(r)] *(Am* **luster**) *n (gloss)* lustre *m*

Luxembourg ['lʌksəmbɜ:g] *n* le Luxembourg

luxury ['lʌkʃərɪ] **1** *n* luxe *m* **2** *adj (goods, car, home)* de luxe ■ **luxurious** [lʌg'ʒʊərɪəs] *adj* luxueux, -euse

lying ['laɪɪŋ] **1** *pres p of* lie[1,2] **2** *n* mensonges *mpl* **3** *adj (person)* menteur, -euse

lynch [lɪntʃ] *vt* lyncher

lyric ['lɪrɪk] *adj* lyrique ■ **lyrics** *npl (of song)* paroles *fpl*

Mm

M, m [em] *n (letter)* M, m *m inv*

m (a) *(abbr* **metre**) mètre *m* (b) *(abbr* **mile**) mile *m*

MA *(abbr* **Master of Arts**) *n Univ* to have an MA in French ≃ avoir une maîtrise de français

mac [mæk] *n Br Fam (raincoat)* imper *m*

macabre [mə'kɑːbrə] *adj* macabre

machine [mə'ʃiːn] *n (apparatus, car, system)* machine *f*; **m. gun** mitrailleuse *f*

machinery [mə'ʃiːnəri] *n (machines)* machines *fpl*; *(works)* mécanisme *m*

mackerel ['mækrəl] *n* maquereau *m*

mackintosh ['mækɪntɒʃ] *n Br* imperméable *m*

macro ['mækrəʊ] *(pl* **-os**) *n Comptr* macrocommande *f*

mad [mæd] **(madder, maddest)** *adj* fou *(f* folle); **to be m. at sb** être furieux, -euse contre qn ▪ **madly** *adv (insanely, desperately)* comme un fou/une folle ▪ **madman** *(pl* **-men**) *n* fou *m* ▪ **madness** *n* folie *f*

madam ['mædəm] *n* yes, m. oui, madame

made [meɪd] *pt & pp of* make ▪ **made-to-measure** *adj Br (garment)* (fait) sur mesure

magazine [mægə'ziːn] *n* (a) *(periodical, TV or radio broadcast)* magazine *m* (b) *(of gun, slide projector)* magasin *m*

magic ['mædʒɪk] **1** *adj* magique **2** *n* magie *f* ▪ **magician** [mə'dʒɪʃən] *n* magicien, -enne *mf*

magistrate ['mædʒɪstreɪt] *n* magistrat *m*

magnet ['mægnɪt] *n* aimant *m* ▪ **magnetic** [-'netɪk] *adj* magnétique

magnificent [mæg'nɪfɪsənt] *adj* magnifique

magnify ['mægnɪfaɪ] *(pt & pp* **-ied**) *vt (image)* grossir; **magnifying glass** loupe *f*

mahogany [mə'hɒgəni] *n* acajou *m*

maid [meɪd] *n (servant)* bonne *f*

maiden ['meɪdən] *adj (flight, voyage)* inaugural; **m. name** nom *m* de jeune fille

mail [meɪl] **1** *n (system)* poste *f*; *(letters)* courrier *m*; *(e-mails)* méls *mpl*, courrier *m* électronique **2** *adj (bag, train)* postal; **m. order** vente *f* par correspondance **3** *vt* poster; **mailing list** liste *f* d'adresses ▪ **mailbox** *n Am & Comptr* boîte *f* aux lettres

maim [meɪm] *vt* mutiler

main¹ [meɪn] *adj* principal; **m. course** plat *m* de résistance; **m. road** grande route *f*

main² [meɪn] *n* **water/gas m.** conduite *f* d'eau/de gaz; **the mains** *(electricity)* le secteur ▪ **mainland** *n* continent *m* ▪ **mainly** *adv* principalement; **they were m. Spanish** la plupart étaient espagnols

mainstay ['meɪnsteɪ] *n (of organization, policy)* pilier *m*

maintain [meɪn'teɪn] *vt (continue)* maintenir; *(machine, road)* entretenir; **to m. that...** affirmer que... ▪ **maintenance** ['meɪntənəns] *n (of vehicle, road)* entretien *m*; *(alimony)* pension *f* alimentaire

maize [meɪz] *n Br* maïs *m*

majesty ['mædʒəstɪ] *n* majesté *f*; **Your M.** Votre Majesté ▪ **majestic** [mə'dʒestɪk] *adj* majestueux, -euse

major ['meɪdʒə(r)] **1** *adj (main, great) & Mus* majeur **2** *n* (a) *(officer)* commandant *m* (b) *Am Univ (subject)* dominante *f* **3** *vi Am Univ* **to m. in** se spécialiser en

Majorca [mə'jɔːkə] n Majorque f
majority [mə'dʒɒrətɪ] (pl -ies) n majorité f (of de); **the m. of people** la plupart des gens

MAKE [meɪk] **1** (pt & pp made) vt faire; (tool, vehicle) fabriquer; **to m. a decision** prendre une décision; **to m. sb happy/sad** rendre qn heureux/triste; **to m. sb do sth** faire faire qch à qn; Fam **to m. it** (succeed) réussir; **sorry I can't m. it to the meeting** désolé, je ne pourrai pas assister à la réunion; **what time do you m. it?** quelle heure avez-vous?; **what do you m. of it?** qu'en penses-tu?; **he made 10 pounds on it** ça lui a rapporté 10 livres; **to be made of wood** être en bois; **made in France** fabriqué en France
2 vi **to m. do** (manage) se débrouiller (**with** avec); **to m. do with sb/sth** (be satisfied with) se contenter de qn/qch; **to m. believe that one is...** faire semblant d'être...
3 n (brand) marque f; **of French m.** de fabrication française ■ **make-up** n (for face) maquillage m; (of team, group) constitution f
▸ **make for** vt insep (go towards) aller vers
▸ **make off** vi Fam (leave) filer
▸ **make out 1** vt sep (see, hear) distinguer; (understand) comprendre; (decipher) déchiffrer; (cheque, list) faire; Fam **to m. out that...** (claim) prétendre que... **2** vi Fam (manage) se débrouiller
▸ **make over** vt sep (transfer) céder (**to** à); (change, convert) transformer (**into** en)
▸ **make up 1** vt sep (story) inventer; (put together) (list, collection, bed) faire; (prepare) préparer; (form) former, composer; (loss) compenser; (quantity) compléter; (quarrel) régler; **to m. oneself up** se maquiller
2 vi (of friends) se réconcilier; **to m. up for** (loss, damage, fault) compenser; (lost time, mistake) rattraper

makeshift ['meɪkʃɪft] adj (arrangement, building) de fortune
malaria [mə'leərɪə] n Med paludisme m

male [meɪl] **1** adj (child, animal) mâle; (sex) masculin; **m. nurse** infirmier m **2** n (person) homme m; (animal) mâle m
malfunction [mæl'fʌŋkʃən] vi fonctionner mal
malice ['mælɪs] n méchanceté f ■ **malicious** [mə'lɪʃəs] adj malveillant
malignant [mə'lɪgnənt] adj **m. tumour** or **growth** tumeur f maligne
mall [mɔːl] n Am (shopping) **m.** centre m commercial
malnutrition [mælnjuː'trɪʃən] n malnutrition f
malt [mɔːlt] n malt m
Malta ['mɔːltə] n Malte f
mammal ['mæməl] n mammifère m
man [mæn] **1** (pl men) n (adult male) homme m; (player in sports team) joueur m; (humanity) l'homme m; (chess piece) pièce f; Fam **my old m.** (father) mon père; (husband) mon homme
2 (pt & pp -nn-) vt (be on duty at) être de service à; (machine) assurer le fonctionnement de; (plane, ship) être membre de l'équipage de
manage ['mænɪdʒ] **1** vt (company, project) diriger; (shop, hotel) être le gérant de; (economy, money, time, situation) gérer; **to m. to do sth** (succeed) réussir ou arriver à faire qch; (by being smart) se débrouiller pour faire qch
2 vi (succeed) y arriver; (make do) se débrouiller (**with** avec); **to m. without sb/sth** se passer de qn/qch; **managing director** directeur, -trice mf général, -e ■ **management** n (running, managers) direction f; (of property, economy) gestion f; (executive staff) cadres mpl
manager ['mænɪdʒə(r)] n (of company) directeur, -trice mf; (of shop, café) gérant, -e mf; (business) **m.** (of singer, boxer) manager m ■ **manageress** n directrice f; (of shop, café) gérante f
mandate ['mændeɪt] n mandat m
mane [meɪn] n crinière f
maneuver [mə'nuːvər] n & vti Am = **manoeuvre**
mangle ['mæŋgəl] vt (body) mutiler
mango ['mæŋgəʊ] (pl -oes or -os) n mangue f

manhunt ['mænhʌnt] *n* chasse *f* à l'homme

mania ['meɪnɪə] *n (liking)* passion *f; (psychological)* manie *f*

maniac ['meɪnɪæk] *n* fou *m*, folle *f*

manicure ['mænɪkjʊə(r)] *n* manucure *f*

manifesto [mænɪ'festəʊ] *(pl* **-os** *or* **-oes)** *n Pol* manifeste *m*

manipulate [mə'nɪpjʊleɪt] *vt* manipuler

mankind [mæn'kaɪnd] *n* l'humanité *f*

man-made ['mænmeɪd] *adj (lake)* artificiel, -elle; *(fibre)* synthétique

manner ['mænə(r)] *n (way)* manière *f; (behaviour)* comportement *m;* **manners** *(social habits)* manières *fpl;* **in this m.** *(like this)* de cette manière; **to have good/bad manners** être bien/mal élevé

mannerism ['mænərɪzəm] *n Pej* tic *m*

manoeuvre [mə'nu:və(r)] *(Am* **maneuver)** **1** *n* manœuvre *f* **2** *vti* manœuvrer

manpower ['mænpaʊə(r)] *n (labour)* main-d'œuvre *f*

mansion ['mænʃən] *n (in town)* hôtel *m* particulier; *(in country)* manoir *m*

manslaughter ['mænslɔ:tə(r)] *n (in law)* homicide *m* involontaire

mantelpiece ['mæntəlpi:s] *n* dessus *m* de cheminée; **on the m.** sur la cheminée

manual ['mænjʊəl] **1** *adj (work, worker)* manuel, -elle **2** *n (book)* manuel *m*

manufacture [mænjʊ'fæktʃə(r)] **1** *n* fabrication *f; (of cars)* construction *f* **2** *vt* fabriquer; *(cars)* construire ■ **manufacturer** *n* fabricant, -e *mf; (of cars)* constructeur *m*

manure [mə'njʊə(r)] *n* fumier *m*

manuscript ['mænjʊskrɪpt] *n* manuscrit *m*

many ['menɪ] **1** *adj* beaucoup de; **(a good** *or* **great) m. of** un (très) grand nombre de; **how m.?** combien (de)?; **too m.** trop de **2** *pron* beaucoup; **too m.** trop; **m. of them** beaucoup d'entre eux; **as m. as fifty** *(up to)* jusqu'à cinquante

map [mæp] **1** *n* carte *f; (plan of town, underground)* plan *m* **2** *(pt & pp* **-pp-)** *vt* **to m. out** *(plan, programme)* élaborer

maple ['meɪpəl] *n (tree, wood)* érable *m;* **m. syrup** sirop *m* d'érable

marathon ['mærəθən] *n* marathon *m*

marble ['mɑ:bəl] *n (substance)* marbre *m; (toy ball)* bille *f*

March [mɑ:tʃ] *n* mars *m*

march [mɑ:tʃ] **1** *n* marche *f* **2** *vi (of soldiers, demonstrators)* défiler; *(walk in step)* marcher au pas

mare [meə(r)] *n* jument *f*

margarine [mɑ:dʒə'ri:n] *n* margarine *f*

margin ['mɑ:dʒɪn] *n (on page)* marge *f;* **to win by a narrow m.** gagner de justesse ■ **marginally** *adv* très légèrement

marijuana [mærɪ'wɑ:nə] *n* marijuana *f*

marinate ['mærɪneɪt] *vti Culin* (faire) mariner

marine [mə'ri:n] **1** *adj (life, flora)* marin **2** *n (soldier)* fusilier *m* marin; *Am* marine *m*

marital ['mærɪtəl] *adj* conjugal; **m. status** situation *f* de famille

maritime ['mærɪtaɪm] *adj* maritime

mark [mɑ:k] **1** *n (symbol)* marque *f; (stain, trace)* tache *f*, marque *f; (token, sign)* signe *m; (in test, exam)* note *f* **2** *vt* marquer; *(exam)* noter; **to m. sth off** *(separate)* délimiter qch; *(on list)* cocher qch; **to m. sb out** distinguer qn

marked [mɑ:kt] *adj (noticeable)* marqué

market ['mɑ:kɪt] **1** *n* marché *m;* **to put sth on the m.** mettre qch en vente; **on the black m.** au marché noir; **m. price** prix *m* courant **2** *vt* commercialiser ■ **marketing** *n* marketing *m*, mercatique *f* ■ **marketplace** *n (in village, town)* place *f* du marché

markings ['mɑ:kɪŋz] *npl (on animal)* taches *fpl; (on road)* signalisation *f* horizontale

marmalade ['mɑːməleɪc] *n* confiture *f* d'oranges

marooned [mə'ruːnd] *adj* abandonné

marriage ['mærɪdʒ] *n* ma:iage *m*; **m. certificate** extrait *m* d'acte de mariage

marrow ['mærəʊ] *n Br (vegetable)* courge *f*

marry ['mærɪ] **1** *(pt & pp -ied) vt* épouser, se marier avec; *(of priest)* marier **2** *vi* se marier ▪ **married** *adj* marié; **m. life** vie *f* maritale; **m. name** nom *m* de femme mariée; **to get m.** se marier

marsh [mɑːʃ] *n* marais *m*, marécage *m*

marshal ['mɑːʃəl] *n (in army)* maréchal *m*; *(district police officer)* commissaire *m*; *(police chief)* commissaire *m* de police; *(fire chief)* capitaine *m* des pompiers

martial ['mɑːʃəl] *adj* martial

martyr ['mɑːtə(r)] *n* martyr, -e *mf*

marvel ['mɑːvəl] **1** *n (wonder)* merveille *f* **2** *(Br -ll-, Am -l-) vi* s'émerveiller **(at** de)

marvellous ['mɑːvələs] *(Am **marvelous**) adj* merveilleux, -euse

Marxist ['mɑːksɪst] *adj & n* marxiste *(mf)*

marzipan ['mɑːzɪpæn] *n* pâte *f* d'amandes

mascara [mæ'skɑːrə] *n* mascara *m*

masculine ['mæskjʊlɪn] *adj* masculin

mash [mæʃ] **1** *n Br (potatoes)* purée *f* (de pommes de terre) **2** *vt* **to m. (up)** *(vegetables)* écraser (en purée); **mashed potatoes** purée *f* de pommes de terre

mask [mɑːsk] **1** *n* masque *m* **2** *vt (cover, hide)* masquer **(from** à)

masochist ['mæsəkɪst] *n* masochiste *mf*

mason ['meɪsən] *n (stonemason, Freemason)* maçon *m* ▪ **masonry** *n* maçonnerie *f*

mass¹ [mæs] **1** *n Phys & (shapeless substance)* masse *f*; **a m. of** *(many)* une multitude de; *Pol* **the masses** le peuple **2** *adj (demonstration, culture)* de masse; *(protests)* en masse; *(unemployment, destruction)* massif, -ive; **m.**

media mass media *mpl*; **m. production** production *f* en série

3 *vi (of troops, people)* se masser ▪ **mass-produce** *vt* fabriquer en série

mass² [mæs] *n (church service)* messe *f*

massacre ['mæsəkə(r)] **1** *n* massacre *m* **2** *vt* massacrer

massage ['mæsɑːʒ] **1** *n* massage *m* **2** *vt* masser

massive ['mæsɪv] *adj (increase, dose, vote)* massif, -ive; *(amount, building)* énorme

mast [mɑːst] *n (of ship)* mât *m*; *(for TV, radio)* pylône *m*

master ['mɑːstə(r)] **1** *n* maître *m*; *Br (teacher)* professeur *m*; **M. of Arts/Science** *(qualification)* ≃ maîtrise *f* ès lettres/sciences; *(person)* ≃ maître *mf* ès lettres/sciences; **m. of ceremonies** *(presenter)* animateur, -trice *mf*; **m. copy** original *m*; **m. key** passe-partout *m inv*; **m. plan** plan *m* d'action **2** *vt* maîtriser; *(subject, situation)* dominer

mastermind ['mɑːstəmaɪnd] **1** *n (person)* cerveau *m* **2** *vt* organiser

masterpiece ['mɑːstəpiːs] *n* chef-d'œuvre *m*

mastery ['mɑːstərɪ] *n* maîtrise *f* **(of** de)

masturbate ['mæstəbeɪt] *vi* se masturber

mat [mæt] *n* tapis *m*; *(of straw)* natte *f*; *(at door)* paillasson *m*; **(table) m.** *(for plates)* set *m* de table; *(for dishes)* dessous-de-plat *m inv*

match¹ [mætʃ] *n (for lighting fire, cigarette)* allumette *f* ▪ **matchbox** *n* boîte *f* d'allumettes ▪ **matchstick** *n* allumette *f*

match² [mætʃ] *n (in sport)* match *m*

match³ [mætʃ] **1** *n (equal)* égal, -e *mf*; *(marriage)* mariage *m*; **to be a good m.** *(of colours, people)* aller bien ensemble; **to meet one's m.** trouver son maître

2 *vt (of clothes, colour)* être assorti à; *(coordinate)* assortir; *(equal)* égaler; **to m. up** *(colours, clothes, plates)* assortir

3 *vi (of colours, clothes)* être assortis, -es ▪ **matching** *adj* assorti

mate¹ [meɪt] **1** n *(of animal) (male)* mâle m; *(female)* femelle f; *Br (friend)* copain m, copine f **2** vi *(of animals)* s'accoupler (**with** avec)

mate² [meɪt] **1** n *(in chess)* mat m **2** vt mettre mat

material [mə'tɪərɪəl] **1** adj *(needs, world)* matériel, -elle; *(important)* essentiel, -elle **2** n *(substance)* matière f; *(cloth)* tissu m; *(for book)* matériaux mpl; **material(s)** *(equipment)* matériel m ▪ **materialistic** adj matérialiste

materialize [mə'tɪərɪəlaɪz] vi se matérialiser; *(of hope, threat)* se réaliser

maternal [mə'tɜːnəl] adj maternel, -elle

maternity [mə'tɜːnətɪ] n **m. dress** robe f de grossesse; **m. hospital, m. unit** maternité f; **m. leave** congé m de maternité

mathematical [mæθə'mætɪkəl] adj mathématique

mathematics [mæθə'mætɪks] n *(subject)* mathématiques fpl ▪ **maths** *(Am* **math**) n Fam maths fpl

matinée ['mætɪneɪ] n *(of play, film)* matinée f

matrimony ['mætrɪmənɪ] n mariage m

matt [mæt] adj *(paint, paper)* mat

matter ['mætə(r)] **1** n *(substance)* matière f; *(issue, affair)* question f; **as a m. of fact** en fait; **no m. what she does** quoi qu'elle fasse; **no m. who you are** qui que vous soyez; **what's the m.?** qu'est-ce qu'il y a?; **there's something the m. with my leg** j'ai quelque chose à la jambe

2 vi *(be important)* importer (**to** à); **it doesn't m. if/when/who...** peu importe si/quand/qui...; **it doesn't m.** ça ne fait rien

matter-of-fact [mætərəv'fækt] adj *(person, manner)* terre à terre inv

mattress ['mætrəs] n matelas m

mature [mə'tʃʊə(r)] **1** adj *(person)* mûr; *(cheese)* fort **2** vi *(person)* mûrir

maul [mɔːl] vt *(of animal)* mutiler

maximize ['mæksɪmaɪz] vt maximaliser

maximum ['mæksɪməm] **1** *(pl* **-ima** [-ɪmə] *or* **-imums**) n maximum m **2** adj maximal

May [meɪ] n mai m

MAY [meɪ] *(pt* **might** [maɪt])

May et **might** peuvent s'utiliser indifféremment ou presque dans les expressions de la catégorie (a).

v aux **(a)** *(expressing possibility)* **he m. come** il se peut qu'il vienne; **I m.** or **might be wrong** je me trompe peut-être; **he m.** or **might have lost it** il se peut qu'il l'ait perdu; **we m.** or **might as well go** autant y aller; **she's afraid I m.** or **might get lost** elle a peur que je ne me perde

(b) Formal *(for asking permission)* **m. I stay?** puis-je rester?; **you m. go** tu peux partir

(c) Formal *(expressing wish)* **m. you be happy** sois heureux; **m. the best man win!** que le meilleur gagne!

maybe ['meɪbiː] adv peut-être

mayhem ['meɪhem] n *(chaos)* pagaille f

mayonnaise [meɪə'neɪz] n mayonnaise f

mayor [meə(r)] n maire m

maze [meɪz] n labyrinthe m

MBA *(abbr* **Master of Business Administration)** n MBA m, maîtrise f de gestion

me [miː] pron me, m'; *(after prep, 'than', 'it is')* moi; **(to) me** *(indirect)* me, m'; **he helps me** il m'aide; **he gave it to me** il me l'a donné

meadow ['medəʊ] n pré m, prairie f

meagre ['miːgə(r)] *(Am* **meager)** adj maigre

meal [miːl] n *(food)* repas m

mean¹ [miːn] *(pt & pp* **meant)** vt *(of word, event)* signifier; *(of person)* vouloir dire; *(result in)* entraîner; *(represent)* représenter; **to m. to do sth** avoir l'intention de faire qch; **it means a lot to me** c'est très important pour moi; **I didn't m. to!** je ne l'ai pas fait exprès!

mean² [miːn] **(-er, -est)** adj *(miserly)*

avare; *(nasty)* méchant

mean³ [miːn] **1** *adj (average)* moyen, -enne **2** *n Math (average mid-point)* moyenne *f*

meaning ['miːnɪŋ] *n* sens *m*, signification *f* ■ **meaningful** *adj* significatif, -ive ■ **meaningless** *adj* vide de sens

means [miːnz] **1** *n (method)* moyen *m* **(to do** *or* **of doing** de faire**); by m. of...** au moyen de...**; by no m.** nullement **2** *npl (wealth)* moyens *mpl*

meant [ment] *pt & pp of* **mean**

meantime ['miːntaɪm] *adv & n* **(in the) m.** *(at the same time)* pendant ce temps; *(between two events)* entre-temps

meanwhile ['miːnwaɪl] *adv (at the same time)* pendant ce temps; *(between two events)* entre-temps

measles ['miːzəlz] *n Med* rougeole *f*

measure ['meʒə(r)] **1** *n* mesure *f; (ruler)* règle *f* **2** *vt* mesurer; **to m. sth out** *(ingredient)* mesurer qch **3** *vi* **to m. up to** *(task)* être à la hauteur de

measurement ['meʒəmənt] *n* mesure *f*; **hip/waist measurement(s)** tour *m* de hanches/de taille

meat [miːt] *n* viande *f; (of crab, lobster)* chair *f; Fig* substance *f*

mechanic [mɪ'kænɪk] *n* mécanicien, -enne *mf* ■ **mechanical** *adj* mécanique ■ **mechanics** *n (science)* mécanique *f*; **the m.** *(working parts)* le mécanisme

mechanism ['mekənɪzəm] *n* mécanisme *m*

medal ['medəl] *n* médaille *f*

medallion [mə'dæljən] *n* médaillon *m*

meddle ['medəl] *vi (interfere)* se mêler **(in** de**); *(tamper)* toucher **(with** à**)**

media ['miːdɪə] *npl* **1 the m.** les médias *mpl* **2** *pl of* **medium**

mediaeval [medɪ'iːvəl] *adj* médiéval

mediate ['miːdɪeɪt] *vi* servir d'intermédiaire **(between** entre**)** ■ **mediator** *n* médiateur, -trice *mf*

medical ['medɪkəl] **1** *adj* médical; *(school, studies)* de médecine; *(student)* en médecine; **m. insurance** assurance *f* maladie

2 *n (in school, army)* visite *f* médicale; *(private)* examen *m* médical

medication [medɪ'keɪʃən] *n* médicaments *mpl*; **to be on m.** être en traitement

medicine ['medəsən] *n (substance)* médicament *m; (science)* médecine *f*; **m. cabinet, m. chest** (armoire *f* à) pharmacie *f*

medieval [medɪ'iːvəl] *adj* médiéval

mediocre [miːdɪ'əʊkə(r)] *adj* médiocre

meditate ['medɪteɪt] *vi* méditer **(on** sur**)** ■ **meditation** *n* méditation *f*

Mediterranean [medɪtə'reɪnɪən] **1** *adj* méditerranéen, -enne **2** *n* **the M.** la Méditerranée

medium ['miːdɪəm] **1** *adj (average, middle)* moyen, -enne **2** *n* **(a)** *(pl* **media** ['miːdɪə]**)** *(for conveying data or publicity)* support *m* **(b)** *(pl* **mediums)** *(person)* médium *m* ■ **medium-sized** *adj* de taille moyenne

medley ['medlɪ] *(pl* **-eys)** *n* mélange *m; (of songs, tunes)* pot-pourri *m*

meet [miːt] **1** *vt (pt & pp* **met)** *(person, team)* rencontrer; *(by arrangement)* retrouver; *(pass in street, road)* croiser; *(fetch)* aller chercher; *(wait for)* attendre; *(debt, enemy, danger)* faire face à; *(need)* combler; **have you met my husband?** connaissez-vous mon mari?

2 *vi (of people, teams)* se rencontrer; *(by arrangement)* se retrouver; *(of club, society)* se réunir; *(of rivers)* se rejoindre

3 *n Am Sport* réunion *f*

▸ **meet up** *vi (by arrangement)* se retrouver; **to m. up with sb** retrouver qn

▸ **meet with** *vt insep (problem, refusal)* se heurter à; *(accident)* avoir; *Am* **to m. with sb** rencontrer qn; *(as arranged)* retrouver qn

meeting ['miːtɪŋ] *n (for business)* réunion *f; (large)* assemblée *f; (by accident)* rencontre *f; (by arrangement)* rendez-vous *m inv*; **to be in a m.** être en réunion; **m. place** lieu *m* de rendez-vous

megaphone ['megǝfǝʊn] *n* porte-voix *m inv*

mellow ['melǝʊ] (-er, -est) *adj (wine)* moelleux, -euse; *(flavour)* suave; *(colour, voice)* chaud

melodic [mɪ'lɒdɪk] *adj* mélodique

melodrama ['melǝdrɑːmǝ] *n* mélodrame *m* ▪ **melodramatic** [-drǝ'mætɪk] *adj* mélodramatique

melody ['melǝdɪ] *(pl* -ies) *n* mélodie *f*

melon ['melǝn] *n* melon *m*

melt [melt] **1** *vt* faire fondre; **to m. down** *(metal object)* fondre **2** *vi* fondre

member ['membǝ(r)] *n* membre *m*; *Br* **M. of Parliament,** *Am* **M. of Congress** ≃ député *m* ▪ **membership** *n (state)* adhésion *f* (**of** à); *(members)* membres *mpl*; **m. card** carte *f* de membre; **m. fee** cotisation *f*

memento [mǝ'mentǝʊ] *(pl* -os *or* -oes) *n* souvenir *m*

memo ['memǝʊ] *(pl* -os) *n* note *f* de service

memoirs ['memwɑːz] *npl (autobiography)* mémoires *mpl*

memorable ['memǝrǝbǝl] *adj* mémorable

memorial [mǝ'mɔːrɪǝl] **1** *adj* commémoratif, -ive; **m. service** commémoration *f* **2** *n* mémorial *m*

memorize ['memǝraɪz] *vt* mémoriser

memory ['memǝrɪ] *(pl* -ies) *n (faculty)* & *Comptr* mémoire *f*; *(recollection)* souvenir *m*; **to the** *or* **in m. of...** à la mémoire de...

men [men] *npl see* **man**; **the men's room** les toilettes *fpl* pour hommes

menace ['menɪs] **1** *n (danger)* danger *m*; *(threat)* menace *f* **2** *vt* menacer

mend [mend] *vt (repair)* réparer; *(clothes)* raccommoder

menial ['miːnɪǝl] *adj (work)* subalterne

meningitis [menɪn'dʒaɪtɪs] *n Med* méningite *f*

menopause ['menǝpɔːz] *n* ménopause *f*

menstruation [menstrʊ'eɪʃǝn] *n* menstruation *f*

menswear ['menzweǝ(r)] *n* vêtements *mpl* pour hommes

mental ['mentǝl] *adj* mental; **m. block** blocage *m*

mentality [men'tælǝtɪ] *(pl* -ies) *n* mentalité *f* ▪ **mentally** *adv* mentalement; **he's m. handicapped** c'est un handicapé mental; **she's m. ill** c'est une malade mentale

mention ['menʃǝn] **1** *n* mention *f* **2** *vt* mentionner; **not to m....** sans parler de...; **don't m. it!** il n'y a pas de quoi!

menu ['menjuː] *n (in restaurant) (for set meal)* menu *m*; *(list)* carte *f*; *Comptr* menu

MEP [emiː'piː] *(abbr* **Member of the European Parliament)** *n* député *m* du Parlement européen

merchandise ['mɜːtʃǝndaɪz] *n* marchandises *fpl*

merchant ['mɜːtʃǝnt] *n (trader)* négociant, -e *mf*; *(retailer)* commerçant, -e *mf*

merciless ['mɜːsɪlǝs] *adj* impitoyable

mercury ['mɜːkjʊrɪ] *n (metal)* mercure *m*

mercy ['mɜːsɪ] *(pl* -ies) *n* pitié *f*; *(of God)* miséricorde *f*; **at the m. of** à la merci de

mere [mɪǝ(r)] *adj* simple; **she's a m. child** ce n'est qu'une enfant ▪ **merely** *adv* simplement

merge [mɜːdʒ] **1** *vt (companies)* & *Comptr* fusionner **2** *vi (blend)* se mêler (**with** à); *(of roads)* se rejoindre; *(of companies, banks)* fusionner ▪ **merger** *n Com* fusion *f*

merit ['merɪt] **1** *n* mérite *m* **2** *vt* mériter

merry ['merɪ] (-ier, -iest) *adj (happy, drunk)* gai ▪ **merry-go-round** *n* manège *m*

mesh [meʃ] *n (of net, sieve)* mailles *fpl*

mesmerize ['mezmǝraɪz] *vt* hypnotiser

mess [mes] **1** *n (confusion)* désordre *m*; *(muddle)* gâchis *m*; *(dirt)* saletés *fpl*; **in a m.** en désordre; *(in trouble)* dans le pétrin; **to make a m. of sth** *(do badly, get dirty)* saloper qch

2 *vt Br Fam* **to m. sb about** *(bother,*

treat badly) embêter qn; **to m. sth up** *(plans)* ficher qch en l'air; *(hair, room, papers)* mettre qch en désordre

3 *vi* **to m. about** *or* **around** *(waste time)* traîner; *(play the fool)* faire l'imbécile; **to m. about** *or* **around with sth** *(fiddle with)* tripoter avec qch

message ['mesɪdʒ] *n* message *m*

messenger ['mesɪndʒə(r)] *n* messager, -ère *mf*; *(in office, hotel)* coursier, -ère *mf*

messy ['mesɪ] **(-ier, -iest)** *adj (untidy)* en désordre; *(dirty)* sale; *(job)* salissant

met [met] *pt & pp of* **meet**

metal ['metəl] *n* métal *m*; **m. ladder** échelle *f* métallique ■ **metallic** [mɪ'tælɪk] *adj (sound)* métallique; *(paint)* métallisé ■ **metalwork** *n (study, craft)* travail *m* des métaux; *(objects)* ferronnerie *f*

metaphor ['metəfə(r)] *n* métaphore *f* ■ **metaphorical** [-'fɒrɪkəl] *adj* métaphorique

meteor ['miːtɪə(r)] *n* météore *m*

meteorological [miːtɪərə'lɒdʒɪkəl] *adj* météorologique

meter[1] ['miːtə(r)] *n (device)* compteur *m*; **(parking) m.** parcmètre *m*

meter[2] ['miːtə(r)] *n Am (measurement)* mètre *m*

method ['meθəd] *n* méthode *f* ■ **methodical** [mɪ'θɒdɪkəl] *adj* méthodique

meticulous [mɪ'tɪkjʊləs] *adj* méticuleux, -euse

metre ['miːtə(r)] *(Am* **meter)** *n* mètre *m* ■ **metric** ['metrɪk] *adj* métrique

metropolitan [metrə'pɒlɪtən] *adj* métropolitain

Mexico ['meksɪkəʊ] *n* le Mexique ■ **Mexican 1** *adj* mexicain **2** *n* Mexicain, -e *mf*

miaow [miː'aʊ] **1** *exclam* miaou! **2** *vi* miauler

mice [maɪs] *pl of* **mouse**

mickey ['mɪkɪ] *n Br Fam* **to take the m. out of sb** charrier qn

microchip ['maɪkrəʊtʃɪp] *n Comptr* microprocesseur *m*

microfilm ['maɪkrəʊfɪlm] *n* microfilm *m*

microphone ['maɪkrəfəʊn] *n* micro *m*

microscope ['maɪkrəskəʊp] *n* microscope *m*

microwave ['maɪkrəʊweɪv] *n* **m. (oven)** (four *m* à) micro-ondes *m inv*

mid [mɪd] *adj* **(in) m. June** (à) la mi-juin; **in m. air** en plein ciel; **to be in one's m.-twenties** avoir environ vingt-cinq ans

midday [mɪd'deɪ] **1** *n* **at m.** à midi **2** *adj (sun, meal)* de midi

middle ['mɪdəl] **1** *n* milieu *m*; *Fam (waist)* taille *f*; **(right) in the m. of sth** au (beau) milieu de qch

2 *adj (central)* du milieu; **the M. Ages** le Moyen Âge; **the M. East** le Moyen-Orient; **the m. class(es)** les classes moyennes; **m. name** deuxième prénom *m* ■ **middle-aged** *adj* d'âge mûr ■ **middle-class** *adj* bourgeois ■ **middle-of-the-road** *adj (politics, views)* modéré; *(music)* grand public *inv*

midge [mɪdʒ] *n* moucheron *m*

midget ['mɪdʒɪt] *n (small person)* nain, -e *mf*

midnight ['mɪdnaɪt] *n* minuit *m*

midst [mɪdst] *n* **in the m. of** *(middle)* au milieu de

midway [mɪd'weɪ] *adj & adv* à mi-chemin

midweek [mɪd'wiːk] *adv* en milieu de semaine

midwife ['mɪdwaɪf] **(pl -wives)** *n* sage-femme *f*

might[1] [maɪt] *v aux see* **may** La forme **mightn't** s'écrit **might not** dans un style plus soutenu.

might[2] [maɪt] *n (strength)* force *f* ■ **mighty (-ier, -iest) 1** *adj* puissant; *Fam (very great)* sacré **2** *adv Am Fam (very)* rudement

migraine ['miːɡreɪn, 'maɪɡreɪn] *n* migraine *f*

migrate [maɪ'ɡreɪt] *vi (of people)* émigrer; *(of birds)* migrer ■ **migrant** ['maɪɡrənt] *adj & n m.* **(worker)** (travailleur, -euse *mf*) immigré, -e

mike [maɪk] (abbr **microphone**) n Fam micro m

mild [maɪld] (-er, -est) adj (weather, cheese, soap, person) doux (f douce); (punishment) léger, -ère; (curry) peu épicé

mile [maɪl] n mile m; **he lives miles away** il habite très loin d'ici ■ **mileage** n (distance) ≃ kilométrage m; (rate of fuel consumption) consommation f ■ **mileometer** n Br ≃ compteur m kilométrique ■ **milestone** n (in history, career) étape f importante

militant ['mɪlɪtənt] adj & n militant, -e (mf)

military ['mɪlɪtərɪ] 1 adj militaire 2 n **the m.** les militaires mpl

milk [mɪlk] 1 n lait m; **m. chocolate** chocolat m au lait; **m. shake** milkshake m 2 vt (cow) traire; Fig (exploit) exploiter ■ **milky** (-ier, -iest) adj (coffee, tea) au lait

mill [mɪl] 1 n (for flour) moulin m; (textile factory) filature f 2 vi **to m. around** (of crowd) grouiller

millennium [mɪ'lenɪəm] (pl -nia [-nɪə]) n millénaire m

milligram(me) ['mɪlɪgræm] n milligramme m

millimetre ['mɪlɪmiːtə(r)] (Am **millimeter**) n millimètre m

million ['mɪljən] n million m; **a m. men** un million d'hommes; **two m.** deux millions ■ **millionaire** n millionnaire mf

milometer [maɪ'lɒmɪtə(r)] n Br ≃ compteur m kilométrique

mime [maɪm] 1 n (art) mime m 2 vti mimer; (of singer) chanter en play-back

mimic ['mɪmɪk] 1 n imitateur, -trice mf 2 (pt & pp -ck-) vt imiter

mince [mɪns] 1 n (meat) viande f hachée; **m. pie** (containing fruit) = tartelette fourrée aux fruits secs et aux épices 2 vt hacher ■ **mincemeat** n (dried fruit) = mélange de fruits secs et d'épices utilisé en pâtisserie ■ **mincer** n (machine) hachoir m

MIND¹ [maɪnd] n esprit m; (sanity) raison f; Br **to my m.** à mon avis; **to**

change one's m. changer d'avis; **to speak one's m.** dire ce que l'on pense; Br **to be in two minds** (undecided) hésiter; **to bear** or **keep sth in m.** garder qch à l'esprit; **to have sb/sth in m.** avoir qn/qch en vue; **to make up one's m.** se décider; Fam **to be out of one's m.** avoir perdu la tête; **it's on my m.** cela me préoccupe; Br **to have a good m. to do sth** avoir bien envie de faire qch

MIND² [maɪnd] 1 vt Br (pay attention to) faire attention à; (look after) garder; Br **m. you don't fall** fais attention à ne pas tomber; **I don't m. the cold/noise** le froid/bruit ne me gêne pas; **if you don't m. my asking...** si je peux me permettre...; **never m. the car** peu importe la voiture; Br **m. you...** remarquez...; **m. your own business!** occupe-toi de tes affaires!

2 vi **I don't m.** ça m'est égal; **do you m. if I smoke?** ça vous gêne si je fume?; **never m.!** ça ne fait rien!, tant pis!; Br **m. (out)!** (watch out) attention!

mind-boggling ['maɪndbɒglɪŋ] adj stupéfiant

minder ['maɪndə(r)] n Fam (bodyguard) gorille m

mindless ['maɪndləs] adj (job, destruction) stupide

mine¹ [maɪn] possessive pron le mien, la mienne, pl les mien(ne)s; **this hat is m.** ce chapeau est à moi ou est le mien; **a friend of m.** un ami à moi, un de mes amis

mine² [maɪn] 1 n (a) (for coal, gold) & Fig mine f (b) (explosive) mine f 2 vt (coal, gold) extraire ■ **mining** n exploitation f minière

mineral ['mɪnərəl] adj & n minéral (m); **m. water** eau f minérale

mingle ['mɪŋgəl] vi (of things) se mêler (with à); (of people) parler un peu à tout le monde

miniature ['mɪnɪtʃə(r)] 1 adj (train, model) miniature inv 2 n miniature f; **in m.** en miniature

minicab ['mɪnɪkæb] n Br radio-taxi m

minimal ['mɪnɪməl] adj minimal

minimize ['mɪnɪmaɪz] *vt* minimiser
minimum ['mɪnɪməm] **1** (*pl* -ima *or* -imums) *n* minimum *m* **2** *adj* minimal; **m. wage** salaire *m* minimum
miniskirt ['mɪnɪskɜːt] *n* minijupe *f*
minister ['mɪnɪstə(r)] *n Br (politician)* ministre *m*; *(of religion)* pasteur *m* ▪ **ministry** (*pl* -ies) *n Br Pol* ministère *m*
minor ['maɪnə(r)] **1** *adj (unimportant)* & *Mus* mineur; *Med (operation)* bénin, -igne; *(road)* secondaire **2** *n (in age)* mineur, -e *mf*
minority [maɪ'nɒrətɪ] **1** (*pl* -ies) *n* minorité *f*; **to be in the** *or* **a m.** être minoritaire **2** *adj* minoritaire
mint¹ [mɪnt] **1** *n* **the (Royal) M.** ≃ l'hôtel *m* de la Monnaie **2** *vt (coins)* frapper
mint² [mɪnt] *n (herb)* menthe *f*; *(sweet)* bonbon *m* à la menthe
minus ['maɪnəs] **1** *adj* & *n* **m. (sign)** (signe *m*) moins *m* **2** *prep (with numbers)* moins; *Fam (without)* sans; **it's m. 10 (degrees)** il fait moins 10
minute¹ ['mɪnɪt] *n (of time)* minute *f*; **this (very) m.** *(now)* tout de suite; **any m. (now)** d'une minute à l'autre ▪ **minutes** *npl (of meeting)* procès-verbal *m*
minute² [maɪ'njuːt] *adj (tiny)* minuscule
miracle ['mɪrəkəl] *n* miracle *m* ▪ **miraculous** [mɪ'rækjʊləs] *adj* miraculeux, -euse
mirror ['mɪrə(r)] *n* miroir *m*, glace *f*; **(rearview) m.** *(of vehicle)* rétroviseur *m*
misbehave [mɪsbɪ'heɪv] *vi* se conduire mal
miscalculate [mɪs'kælkjʊleɪt] *vt* faire une erreur de calcul; *Fig* faire un mauvais calcul
miscarriage [mɪs'kærɪdʒ] *n Med* **to have a m.** faire une fausse couche. **m. of justice** erreur *f* judiciaire
miscellaneous [mɪsə'leɪnɪəs] *adj* divers
mischief ['mɪstʃɪf] *n* espièglerie *f*; **to get into m.** faire des bêtises ▪ **mischievous** *adj (naughty)* espiègle; *(malicious)* méchant

misconduct [mɪs'kɒndʌkt] *n (bad behaviour)* inconduite *f*
misdemeanor [mɪsdɪ'miːnə(r)] *n Am (crime)* délit *m*
miser ['maɪzə(r)] *n* avare *mf* ▪ **miserly** *adj* avare
miserable ['mɪzərəbəl] *adj (wretched)* misérable; *(unhappy)* malheureux, -euse; *(awful)* affreux, -euse
misery ['mɪzərɪ] (*pl* -ies) *n (suffering)* malheur *m*; *(sadness)* détresse *f*
misfire [mɪs'faɪə(r)] *vi (of plan)* rater
misfit ['mɪsfɪt] *n Pej* inadapté, -e *mf*
misfortune [mɪs'fɔːtʃuːn] *n* malheur *m*
misgivings [mɪs'gɪvɪŋz] *npl (doubts)* doutes *mpl* (**about** sur); *(fears)* craintes *fpl* (**about** à propos de)
misguided [mɪs'gaɪdɪd] *adj (attempt)* malencontreux, -euse
mishandle [mɪs'hændəl] *vt (situation)* mal gérer; *(person)* malmener
mishap ['mɪshæp] *n* incident *m*
misinform [mɪsɪn'fɔːm] *vt* mal renseigner
misinterpret [mɪsɪn'tɜːprɪt] *vt* mal interpréter
mislay [mɪs'leɪ] (*pt* & *pp* -laid) *vt* égarer
mislead [mɪs'liːd] (*pt* & *pp* -led) *vt* tromper ▪ **misleading** *adj* trompeur, -euse
mismanage [mɪs'mænɪdʒ] *vt* mal gérer
misplace [mɪs'pleɪs] *vt (lose)* égarer
misprint ['mɪsprɪnt] *n* faute *f* d'impression, coquille *f*
mispronounce [mɪsprə'naʊns] *vt* mal prononcer
misrepresent [mɪsreprɪ'zent] *vt (theory)* dénaturer; *(person)* présenter sous un faux jour
Miss [mɪs] *n* Mademoiselle *f*
miss [mɪs] **1** *n* coup *m* raté; **that was** *or* **we had a near m.** on l'a échappé belle; *Fam* **I'll give it a m.** *(not go)* je n'y irai pas
2 *vt (train, target, opportunity)* manquer, rater; *(not see)* ne pas voir; *(not*

understand) ne pas comprendre; *(feel the lack of)* regretter; **to m. sth out** *(accidentally)* oublier qch; *(intentionally)* omettre qch

3 *vi* manquer *ou* rater son coup; **to m. out on sth** rater qch

missile [*Br* 'mɪsaɪl, *Am* 'mɪsəl] *n (rocket)* missile *m*; *(object thrown)* projectile *m*

missing ['mɪsɪŋ] *adj (absent)* absent; *(in war, after disaster)* disparu; *(object)* manquant; **there are two cups/students m.** il manque deux tasses/étudiants; **to go m.** disparaître

mission ['mɪʃən] *n* mission *f*

missionary ['mɪʃənərɪ] *(pl* **-ies)** *n Rel* missionnaire *m*

misspell [mɪs'spel] *(pt & pp* **-ed** *or* **-spelt)** *vt* mal écrire

mist [mɪst] **1** *n (fog)* brume *f*; *(on glass)* buée *f* **2** *vi* **to m. over** *or* **up** s'embuer

mistake [mɪ'steɪk] **1** *n* erreur *f*, faute *f*; **to make a m.** faire une erreur; **by m.** par erreur **2** *(pt* **-took,** *pp* **-taken)** *vt (meaning, intention)* se tromper sur; **to m. sb for** prendre qn pour ■ **mistaken** *adj (belief, impression)* erroné; **to be m.** *(of person)* se tromper **(about** sur) ■ **mistakenly** *adv* par erreur

Mister ['mɪstə(r)] *n* Monsieur *m*

mistreat [mɪs'triːt] *vt* maltraiter

mistress ['mɪstrɪs] *n* maîtresse *f*; *Br (in secondary school)* professeur *m*

mistrust [mɪs'trʌst] **1** *n* méfiance *f* **2** *vt* se méfier de

misty ['mɪstɪ] *(-ier, -iest) adj (foggy)* brumeux, -euse

misunderstand [mɪsʌndə'stænd] *(pt & pp* **-stood)** *vti* mal comprendre ■ **misunderstanding** *n (disagreement)* mésentente *f*; *(misconception)* malentendu *m*

misuse 1 [mɪs'juːs] *n (of equipment, resources)* mauvais emploi *m*; *(of power)* abus *m* **2** [mɪs'juːz] *vt (equipment, resources)* mal employer; *(power)* abuser de

mitt(en) [mɪt, 'mɪtən] *n (glove)* moufle *f*

mix [mɪks] **1** *n (mixture)* mélange *m* **2**

vt mélanger; *(cement, drink, cake)* préparer; **to m. up** *(papers)* mélanger; *(mistake)* confondre **(with** avec); **to be mixed up in sth** être mêlé à qch **3** *vi (blend)* se mélanger; **to m. with sb** *(socially)* fréquenter qn

mixed [mɪkst] *adj (school, marriage)* mixte; *(nuts, chocolates)* assortis; **to be (all) m. up** *(of person)* être désorienté; *(of facts, account)* être confus

mixer ['mɪksə(r)] *n (for cooking)* mixeur *m*

mixture ['mɪkstʃə(r)] *n* mélange *m*

mix-up ['mɪksʌp] *n* confusion *f*

mm *(abbr* **millimetre(s))** mm

moan [məʊn] **1** *n (sound)* gémissement *m* **2** *vi (make sound)* gémir; *(complain)* se plaindre **(to** à; **about** de; **that** que)

mob [mɒb] **1** *n (crowd)* foule *f* **2** *(pt & pp* **-bb-)** *vt* prendre d'assaut

mobile [*Br* 'məʊbaɪl, *Am* 'məʊbəl] **1** *adj* mobile; **m. home** mobile home *m*; *Br* **m. phone** téléphone *m* portable **2** *n Br (phone)* portable *m*

mobilize ['məʊbɪlaɪz] *vti* mobiliser

mock [mɒk] **1** *adj (false)* simulé; *Br Sch* **m. exam** examen *m* blanc **2** *vt* se moquer de; *(mimic)* singer ■ **mockery** *n (act)* moqueries *fpl*; *(farce, parody)* parodie *f*; **to make a m. of sth** tourner qch en ridicule

mode [məʊd] *n (manner, way) & Comptr* mode *m*

model ['mɒdəl] **1** *n (example, person)* modèle *m*; *(small version)* maquette *f*; *(in fashion show, magazine* mannequin *m*; **(scale) m.** modèle *m* réduit

2 *adj (behaviour, student)* modèle; *(car, plane)* modèle réduit *inv*

3 *(Br* **-ll-,** *Am* **-l-)** *vt (clay)* modeler; *(hats, dresses)* présenter; **to m. sth on** modeler qch sur

4 *vi (for fashion)* être mannequin; *(pose for artist)* poser

modem ['məʊdəm] *n Comptr* modem *m*

moderate ['mɒdərət] **1** *adj* modéré **2** *n Pol* modéré, -e *mf* ■ **moderately** *adv (in moderation)* modérément; *(averagely)* moyennement

moderation [mɒdəˈreɪʃən] *n* modération *f*; **in m.** avec modération

modern [ˈmɒdən] *adj* moderne; **m. languages** langues *fpl* vivantes

modernize [ˈmɒdənaɪz] *vt* moderniser

modest [ˈmɒdɪst] *adj (unassuming, moderate)* modeste

modify [ˈmɒdɪfaɪ] *(pt & pp -ied) vt* modifier ■ **modification** *n* modification *f* (**to** à)

module [ˈmɒdjuːl] *n* module *m*

moist [mɔɪst] *(-er, -est) adj* humide; *(skin, hand)* moite ■ **moisten** [ˈmɔɪsən] *vt* humecter

moisture [ˈmɔɪstʃə(r)] *n* humidité *f*; *(on glass)* buée *f* ■ **moisturizer** *n* crème *f* hydratante

mold [məʊld] *n & vt Am* = **mould**

mole [məʊl] *n* (a) *(on skin)* grain *m* de beauté (b) *(animal, spy)* taupe *f*

molecule [ˈmɒlɪkjuːl] *n* molécule *f*

molest [məˈlest] *vt (child, woman)* agresser (sexuellement)

molt [məʊlt] *vi Am* = **moult**

mom [mɒm] *n Am Fam* maman *f*

moment [ˈməʊmənt] *n* moment *m*, instant *m*; **at the m.** en ce moment; **for the m.** pour le moment; **in a m.** dans un instant; **any m. (now)** d'un instant à l'autre

momentary [ˈməʊməntərɪ] *adj* momentané ■ **momentarily** [*Br* ˈməʊməntərɪlɪ, *Am* məʊmənˈterɪlɪ] *adv (temporarily)* momentanément; *Am (soon)* tout de suite

momentum [məʊˈmentəm] *n (speed)* élan *m*; **to gather** *or* **gain m.** *(of campaign)* prendre de l'ampleur

mommy [ˈmɒmɪ] *n Am Fam* maman *f*

monarch [ˈmɒnək] *n* monarque *m* ■ **monarchy** *(pl -ies) n* monarchie *f*

monastery [ˈmɒnəstərɪ] *(pl -ies) n* monastère *m*

Monday [ˈmʌndeɪ] *n* lundi *m*

monetary [ˈmʌnɪtərɪ] *adj* monétaire

money [ˈmʌnɪ] *n* argent *m*; **to make m.** *(of person)* gagner de l'argent; *(of business)* rapporter de l'argent ■ **moneybox** *n* tirelire *f* ■ **moneylender** *n* prêteur, -euse *mf*

mongrel [ˈmʌŋɡrəl] *n* bâtard *m*

monitor [ˈmɒnɪtə(r)] **1** *n Comptr, TV & Tech (screen, device)* moniteur *m* **2** *vt (check)* surveiller

monk [mʌŋk] *n* moine *m*

monkey [ˈmʌŋkɪ] *(pl -eys) n* singe *m*

monologue [ˈmɒnəlɒɡ] *n* monologue *m*

monopoly [məˈnɒpəlɪ] *n* monopole *m* ■ **monopolize** *vt* monopoliser

monotonous [məˈnɒtənəs] *adj* monotone

monster [ˈmɒnstə(r)] *n* monstre *m*

monstrosity [mɒnˈstrɒsətɪ] *(pl -ies) n* monstruosité *f*

monstrous [ˈmɒnstrəs] *adj* monstrueux, -euse

month [mʌnθ] *n* mois *m* ■ **monthly 1** *adj* mensuel, -elle; **m. payment** mensualité *f* **2** *(pl -ies) n (periodical)* mensuel *m* **3** *adv* tous les mois

Montreal [mɒntrɪˈɔːl] *n* Montréal *m ou f*

monument [ˈmɒnjʊmənt] *n* monument *m*

moo [muː] *(pt & pp mooed) vi* meugler

mood [muːd] *n (of person)* humeur *f*; *(in grammar)* mode *m*; **in a good/bad m.** de bonne/mauvaise humeur; **to be in the m. to do** *or* **for doing sth** être d'humeur à faire qch

moody [ˈmuːdɪ] *(-ier, -iest) adj (bad-tempered)* maussade; *(changeable)* lunatique

moon [muːn] *n* lune *f* ■ **moonlight** *n* **by m.** au clair de lune

moor [mʊə(r)] **1** *n (heath)* lande *f* **2** *vt (ship)* amarrer **3** *vi (of ship)* mouiller

moose [muːs] *n inv (animal)* élan *m*

mop [mɒp] **1** *n (for floor)* balai *m* à franges; *(with sponge)* balai-éponge *m* **2** *(pt & pp -pp-) vt* **to m. sth up** *(liquid)* éponger qch

mope [məʊp] *vi* **to m. about** broyer du noir

moped [ˈməʊped] *n* Mobylette® *f*

moral [ˈmɒrəl] **1** *adj* moral **2** *n (of*

story) morale *f*; **morals** *(principles)* moralité *f* ▪ **morale** [mɒ'rɑːl] *n* moral *m* ▪ **morality** [mə'rælətɪ] *n* moralité *f*

morbid ['mɔːbɪd] *adj* morbide

MORE [mɔː(r)] **1** *adj* plus de; **m. cars** plus de voitures; **he has m. books than you** il a plus de livres que toi; **a few m. months** quelques mois de plus; **(some) m. tea** encore du thé; **(some) m. details** d'autres détails; **m. than a kilo/ten** plus d'un kilo/de dix **2** *adv (to form comparative of adjectives and adverbs)* plus (**than** que); **m. and m.** de plus en plus; **m. or less** plus ou moins **3** *pron* plus; **have some m.** reprenez-en; **she doesn't have any m.** elle n'en a plus; **the m. he shouts, the m. hoarse he gets** plus il crie, plus il s'enroue; **what's m.** qui plus est

moreover [mɔː'rəʊvə(r)] *adv* de plus

morning ['mɔːnɪŋ] **1** *n* matin *m*; *(referring to duration)* matinée *f*; **in the m.** le matin; *(during the course of the morning)* pendant la matinée; *(tomorrow)* demain matin; **every Tuesday m.** tous les mardis matin **2** *adj (newspaper)* du matin ▪ **mornings** *adv Am* le matin

Morocco [mə'rɒkəʊ] *n* le Maroc ▪ **Moroccan 1** *adj* marocain **2** *n* Marocain, -e *mf*

moron ['mɔːrɒn] *n* crétin, -e *mf*

mortal ['mɔːtəl] *adj & n* mortel, -elle *(mf)*

mortgage ['mɔːgɪdʒ] *n (money lent)* prêt *m* immobilier; *(money borrowed)* emprunt *m* immobilier

mortuary ['mɔːtʃʊərɪ] *(pl -ies)* *n* morgue *f*

mosaic [məʊ'zeɪɪk] *n* mosaïque *f*

Moscow [*Br* 'mɒskəʊ, *Am* 'mɒskaʊ] *n* Moscou *m ou f*

Moslem ['mɒzlɪm] *adj & n* musulman, -e *(mf)*

mosque [mɒsk] *n* mosquée *f*

mosquito [mɒ'skiːtəʊ] *(pl -oes or -os)* *n* moustique *m*

moss [mɒs] *n* mousse *f*

MOST [məʊst] **1** *adj* (a) *(the majority of)* la plupart de; **m. women** la plupart des femmes (b) *(greatest amount of)* **the m.** le plus de; **I have the m. books** j'ai le plus de livres **2** *adv* (a) *(to form superlative of adjectives and adverbs)* plus; **the m. beautiful** le plus beau (*f* la plus belle) (**in/of** de); **to talk (the) m.** parler le plus; **m. of all** *(especially)* surtout (b) *(very)* extrêmement **3** *pron* (a) *(the majority)* la plupart; **m. of the people/the time** la plupart des gens/du temps; **m. of the cake** la plus grande partie du gâteau; **m. of them** la plupart d'entre eux (b) *(greatest amount)* le plus; **he earns the m.** c'est lui qui gagne le plus; **to make the m. of sth** *(situation, talent)* tirer le meilleur parti de qch; *(holiday)* profiter au maximum de qch; **at (the very) m.** tout au plus ▪ **mostly** *adv (in the main)* surtout; *(most often)* le plus souvent

MOT [eməʊ'tiː] *(abbr Ministry of Transport)* *n Br* = contrôle obligatoire des véhicules de plus de trois ans

motel [məʊ'tel] *n* motel *m*

moth [mɒθ] *n* papillon *m* de nuit; *(in clothes)* mite *f*

mother ['mʌðə(r)] *n* mère *f*; **M.'s Day** la fête des Mères ▪ **motherhood** *n* maternité *f* ▪ **mother-in-law** *(pl* **mothers-in-law)** *n* belle-mère *f* ▪ **mother-to-be** *(pl* **mothers-to-be)** *n* future mère *f*

motion ['məʊʃən] **1** *n (of arm)* mouvement *m*; *(in meeting)* motion *f*; **to set sth in m.** mettre qch en mouvement; **m. picture** film *m* **2** *vti* **to m. (to) sb to do sth** faire signe à qn de faire qch ▪ **motionless** *adj* immobile

motivate ['məʊtɪveɪt] *vt (person, decision)* motiver ▪ **motivation** *n* motivation *f*

motive ['məʊtɪv] *n* motif *m* (**for** de)

motor ['məʊtə(r)] **1** *n (engine)* moteur

m; *Br Fam (car)* auto *f* **2** *adj (industry, insurance)* automobile; **m. racing** courses *fpl* automobiles ■ **motorbike** *n* moto *f* ■ **motorboat** *n* canot *m* à moteur ■ **motorcycle** *n* moto *f*, motocyclette *f* ■ **motorcyclist** *n* motocycliste *mf* ■ **motorist** *n Br* automobiliste *mf* ■ **motorway** *n Br* autoroute *f*

motto ['mɒtəʊ] *(pl -oes or -os) n* devise *f*

mould¹ [məʊld] *(Am* **mold) 1** *n (shape)* moule *m* **2** *vt (clay, person's character)* modeler

mould² [məʊld] *(Am* **mold)** *n (fungus)* moisissure *f*

mouldy ['məʊldɪ] *(Am* **moldy)** **(-ier, -iest)** *adj* moisi; **to go m.** moisir

moult [məʊlt] *(Am* **molt)** *vi* muer

mound [maʊnd] *n (of earth)* tertre *m*; *Fig (untidy pile)* tas *m*

mount [maʊnt] **1** *n (frame for photo or slide)* cadre *m* **2** *vt (horse, jewel, photo, demonstration)* monter; *(ladder)* monter à **3** *vi* **(a)** *(on horse)* se mettre en selle **(b)** *(increase, rise)* monter; **to m. up** *(add up)* monter, augmenter; *(accumulate) (of debts, bills)* s'accumuler

mountain ['maʊntɪn] *n* montagne *f*; **m. bike** vélo *m* tout-terrain, VTT *m* ■ **mountaineer** *n* alpiniste *mf* ■ **mountaineering** *n* alpinisme *m* ■ **mountainous** *adj* montagneux, -euse

mourn [mɔːn] *vti* **to m. (for) sb** pleurer qn ■ **mourner** *n* = personne assistant aux obsèques ■ **mourning** *n* deuil *m*; **in m.** en deuil

mouse [maʊs] *(pl* **mice** [maɪs]) *n (animal) & Comptr* souris *f*

mousse [muːs] *n* mousse *f*

moustache [*Br* məˈstɑː.ʃ, *Am* ˈmʌstæʃ] *n* moustache *f*

mouth [maʊθ] *(pl -s* [maʊðz]) *n (of person, horse)* bouche *f*; *(of other animals)* gueule *f*; *(of river)* embouchure *f*; *(of cave, harbour)* entrée *f* ■ **mouthful** ['maʊθfʊl] *n (of food)* bouchée *f*; *(of liquid)* gorgée *f* ■ **mouth-organ** *n* harmonica *m* ■ **mouthpiece** *n (of musical instrument)* embouchure *f*; *(spokesperson)* porte-parole *m inv* ■ **mouthwash**

n bain *m* de bouche ■ **mouth-watering** *adj* appétissant

movable ['muːvəbəl] *adj* mobile

move [muːv] **1** *n* mouvement *m*; *(change of house)* déménagement *m*; *(change of job)* changement *m* d'emploi; *(in game)* coup *m*; **to make a m.** *(leave)* se préparer à partir; *(act)* passer à l'action; **it's your m.** *(turn)* c'est à toi de jouer; *Fam* **to get a m. on** se grouiller **2** *vt* déplacer; *(arm, leg)* remuer; *(employee)* muter; *(piece in game)* jouer; **to m. sb** *(emotionally)* émouvoir qn; **to m. house** déménager

3 *vi* bouger; *(change position)* se déplacer **(to** à); *(leave)* partir; *(act)* agir; *(play)* jouer; *(change house)* déménager; **to m. to Paris** aller habiter Paris

▸ **move about** *vi* se déplacer; *(fidget)* remuer

▸ **move along** *vi* avancer

▸ **move around** *vi* = **move about**

▸ **move away** *vi (go away)* s'éloigner; *(move house)* déménager

▸ **move back 1** *vt sep (chair)* reculer; *(to its original position)* remettre en place **2** *vi (withdraw)* reculer; *(return)* retourner **(to** à)

▸ **move down** *vt sep (take down)* descendre

▸ **move forward** *vt sep & vi* avancer

▸ **move in** *vi (into house)* emménager

▸ **move off** *vi (go away)* s'éloigner; *(of vehicle)* démarrer

▸ **move out** *vi (out of house)* déménager

▸ **move over 1** *vt sep* pousser **2** *vi (make room)* se pousser

▸ **move up** *vi (on seats)* se pousser

movement ['muːvmənt] *n* mouvement *m*

movie ['muːvɪ] *n* film *m*; **the movies** *(cinema)* le cinéma; **m. star** vedette *f* de cinéma; *Am* **m. theater** cinéma *m*

moving ['muːvɪŋ] *adj* en mouvement; *(vehicle)* en marche; *(touching)* émouvant

mow [məʊ] *(pp* **mown** [məʊn] *or* **mowed)** *vt* **to m. the lawn** tondre le gazon ■ **mower** *n* **(lawn) m.** tondeuse *f* (à gazon)

MP [em'pi:] (*abbr* **Member of Parliament**) *n* député *m*

mph [empi:'eɪtʃ] (*abbr* **miles per hour**) ≃ km/h

Mr ['mɪstə(r)] *n* **Mr Brown** M. Brown

Mrs ['mɪsɪz] *n* **Mrs Brown** Mme Brown

MS [em'es] (*abbr* **Master of Science**) *n Am Univ* **to have an MS in chemistry** avoir une maîtrise de chimie

Ms [mɪz] *n* **Ms Brown** ≃ Mme Brown (*ne renseigne pas sur le statut de famille*)

MSc [emes'si:] (*abbr* **Master of Science**) *n Univ* **to have an M. in chemistry** avoir une maîtrise de chimie

MUCH [mʌtʃ] **1** *adj*

> Hormis dans la langue soutenue et dans certaines expressions, ne s'utilise que dans des structures négatives ou interrogatives.

beaucoup de; **not m. time/money** pas beaucoup de temps/d'argent; **how m. sugar do you want?** combien de sucre voulez-vous?; **twice as m. traffic** deux fois plus de circulation; **too m. work** trop de travail

 2 *adv* beaucoup; **very m.** beaucoup; **m. better** bien meilleur; **I love him so m.** je l'aime tellement; **she doesn't say very m.** elle ne dit pas grand-chose

 3 *pron* beaucoup; **there isn't m. left** il n'en reste pas beaucoup; **it's not m. of a garden** ce n'est pas terrible comme jardin; **twice as m.** deux fois plus; **as m. as you like** autant que tu veux; *Fam* **that's a bit m.!** c'est un peu fort!

muck [mʌk] **1** *n* (*manure*) fumier *m*; *Fig* (*filth*) saleté *f* **2** *vt Br Fam* **to m. sth up** (*task*) bâcler qch; (*plans*) chambouler qch **3** *vi Br Fam* **to m. about** *or* **around** (*waste time*) traîner; (*play the fool*) faire l'imbécile ▪ **mucky** (**-ier, -iest**) *adj Fam* sale

mud [mʌd] *n* boue *f* ▪ **muddy** (**-ier, -iest**) *adj* (*water, road*) boueux, -euse; (*hands*) couvert de boue ▪ **mudguard** *n* garde-boue *m inv*

muddle ['mʌdəl] **1** *n* confusion *f*; **to be in a m.** (*person*) ne plus s'y retrou-

ver; (*of things*) être en désordre **2** *vt* (*facts*) mélanger; **to get muddled** (*of person*) s'embrouiller

muesli ['mju:zlɪ, 'mu:zlɪ] *n* muesli *m*

muffin ['mʌfɪn] *n* (*cake*) muffin *m*

muffled ['mʌfəld] *adj* (*noise*) sourd

muffler ['mʌflə(r)] *n Am* (*on vehicle*) silencieux *m*

mug[1] [mʌg] *n* (**a**) (*for tea, coffee*) grande tasse *f*; (**beer**) **m.** chope *f* (**b**) *Br Fam* (*fool*) poire *f*

mug[2] [mʌg] (*pt & pp* **-gg-**) *vt* (*attack in street*) agresser ▪ **mugger** *n* agresseur *m*

mule [mju:l] *n* (*male*) mulet *m*; (*female*) mule *f*

multicoloured ['mʌltɪkʌləd] *adj* multicolore

multimedia [mʌltɪ'mi:dɪə] *adj* multimédia

multimillionaire [mʌltɪmɪljə'neə(r)] *n* multimillionnaire *mf*

multiple ['mʌltɪpəl] **1** *adj* multiple **2** *n Math* multiple *m*

multiple-choice [mʌltɪpəl'tʃɔɪs] *adj* à choix multiple

multiplication [mʌltɪplɪ'keɪʃən] *n* multiplication *f*

multiply ['mʌltɪplaɪ] (*pt & pp* **-ied**) **1** *vt* multiplier **2** *vi* (*of animals, insects*) se multiplier

multiracial [mʌltɪ'reɪʃəl] *adj* multiracial

multistorey [mʌltɪ'stɔːrɪ] (*Am* **multistoried**) *adj* (*car park*) à plusieurs niveaux

multitude ['mʌltɪtju:d] *n* multitude *f*

mum [mʌm] *n Br Fam* maman *f*

mumble ['mʌmbəl] *vti* marmotter

mummy[1] ['mʌmɪ] (*pl* **-ies**) *n Br Fam* (*mother*) maman *f*

mummy[2] ['mʌmɪ] (*pl* **-ies**) *n* (*embalmed body*) momie *f*

mumps [mʌmps] *n Med* oreillons *mpl*

munch [mʌntʃ] *vti* (*chew*) mâcher

municipal [mju:'nɪsɪpəl] *adj* municipal

mural ['mjʊərəl] *n* peinture *f* murale

murder ['mɜːdə(r)] **1** *n* meurtre *m* **2** *vt* *(kill)* assassiner ∎ **murderer** *n* meurtrier, -ère *mf*, assassin *m*

murky ['mɜːkɪ] (**-ier, -iest**) *adj (water, business, past)* trouble

murmur ['mɜːmə(r)] **1** *n* murmure *m* **2** *vti* murmurer

muscle ['mʌsəl] *n* muscle *m* ∎ **muscular** ['mʌskjʊlə(r)] *adj (person, arm)* musclé

museum [mjuːˈzɪəm] *n* musée *m*

mush [mʌʃ] *n (pulp)* bouillie *f* ∎ **mushy** (**-ier, -iest**) *adj (food)* en bouillie

mushroom ['mʌʃrʊm] *n* champignon *m*

music ['mjuːzɪk] *n* musique *f* ∎ **musical 1** *adj* musical; **m. instrument** instrument *m* de musique **2** *n (film, play)* comédie *f* musicale ∎ **musician** [-ˈzɪʃən] *n* musicien, -enne *mf*

Muslim ['mʊzlɪm] *adj & n* musulman, -e *(mf)*

mussel ['mʌsəl] *n* moule *f*

MUST [mʌst] **1** *n* **this is a m.** c'est indispensable; **this film is a m.** il faut absolument voir ce film
2 *v aux* (**a**) *(expressing necessity)* **you m. obey** tu dois obéir, il faut que tu obéisses (**b**) *(expressing probability)* **she m. be clever** elle doit être intelligente; **I m. have seen it** j'ai dû le voir

mustache ['mʌstæʃ] *n Am* moustache *f*

mustard ['mʌstəd] *n* moutarde *f*

muster ['mʌstə(r)] *vt (gather)* rassembler

mustn't ['mʌsənt] = **must not**

musty ['mʌstɪ] (**-ier, -iest**) *adj (smell, taste)* de moisi

mute [mjuːt] *adj (silent) & Ling* muet *(f* muette)

mutiny ['mjuːtɪnɪ] **1** *(pl* **-ies**) *n* mutinerie *f* **2** *(pt & pp* **-ied**) *vi* se mutiner

mutter ['mʌtə(r)] *vti* marmonner

mutton ['mʌtən] *n (meat)* mouton *m*

mutual ['mjuːtʃʊəl] *adj (help, love)* mutuel, -elle; *(friend)* commun ∎ **mutually** *adv* mutuellement

muzzle ['mʌzəl] **1** *n (device for dog)* muselière *f*; *(snout)* museau *m* **2** *vt (animal, the press)* museler

my [maɪ] *possessive adj* mon, ma, *pl* mes

myself [maɪˈself] *pron* moi-même; *(reflexive)* me, m'; *(after prep)* moi; **I wash m.** je me lave

mystery ['mɪstərɪ] *(pl* **-ies**) *n* mystère *m* ∎ **mysterious** [mɪsˈtɪərɪəs] *adj* mystérieux, -euse

mystical ['mɪstɪkəl] *adj* mystique

mystify ['mɪstɪfaɪ] *(pt & pp* **-ied**) *vt (bewilder)* déconcerter

myth [mɪθ] *n* mythe *m* ∎ **mythology** *(pl* **-ies**) *n* mythologie *f*

Nn

N, n [en] *n (letter)* N, n *m inv*

nab [næb] *(pt & pp* **-bb-)** *vt Fam (catch, arrest)* coffrer

nag [næg] *(pt & pp* **-gg-)** *vti* **to n. (at) sb** *(of person)* être sur le dos de qn

nail [neɪl] **1** *n* (a) *(of finger, toe)* ongle *m*; **n. file** lime *f* à ongles; **n. polish,** *Br* **n. varnish** vernis *m* à ongles (b) *(metal)* clou *m* **2** *vt* clouer; **to n. sth down** *(lid)* clouer qch

naïve [naɪˈiːv] *adj* naïf (*f* naïve)

naked [ˈneɪkɪd] *adj (person, flame)* nu

name [neɪm] **1** *n* nom *m*; *(reputation)* réputation *f*; **my n. is...** je m'appelle...; **in the n. of** au nom de; **first n., given n.** prénom *m* **2** *vt* nommer; *(ship, street)* baptiser; *(date, price)* fixer

namely [ˈneɪmlɪ] *adv* à savoir

nanny [ˈnænɪ] *(pl* **-ies)** *n* nurse *f*; *Fam (grandmother)* mamie *f*

nap [næp] **1** *n (sleep)* **to have** *or* **take a n.** faire un petit somme **2** *(pt & pp* **-pp-)** *vi* faire un somme

napkin [ˈnæpkɪn] *n (at table)* serviette *f*

nappy [ˈnæpɪ] *(pl* **-ies)** *n Br (for baby)* couche *f*

narcotic [nɑːˈkɒtɪk] *adj & n* narcotique *(m)*

narrate [nəˈreɪt] *vt* raconter ■ **narrative** [ˈnærətɪv] *n* récit *m* ■ **narrator** *n* narrateur, -trice *mf*

narrow [ˈnærəʊ] **1** *(-er, -est) adj* étroit **2** *vt* **to n. (down)** *(choice, meaning)* limiter **3** *vi (of path)* se rétrécir ■ **narrowly** *adv (only just)* de peu; **he n. escaped being killed** il a bien failli être tué

narrow-minded [nærəʊˈmaɪndɪd] *adj* borné

nasty [ˈnɑːstɪ] *(-ier, -iest) adj (bad)* mauvais; *(spiteful)* méchant (**to** *or* **towards** avec)

nation [ˈneɪʃən] *n* nation *f*

national [ˈnæʃənəl] **1** *adj* national; **n. anthem** hymne *m* national; *Br* **N. Health Service** ≃ Sécurité *f* sociale; *Br* **n. insurance** contributions *fpl* sociales **2** *n (citizen)* ressortissant, -e *mf*

nationalist [ˈnæʃənəlɪst] *n* nationaliste *mf*

nationality [næʃəˈnælətɪ] *(pl* **-ies)** *n* nationalité *f*

nationalize [ˈnæʃənəlaɪz] *vt* nationaliser

nationwide [ˈneɪʃənwaɪd] *adj & adv* dans tout le pays

native [ˈneɪtɪv] **1** *adj (country)* natal *(mpl* **-als);** *(tribe, plant)* indigène; **to be an English n. speaker** avoir l'anglais comme langue maternelle **2** *n (person)* indigène *mf*; **to be a n. of** être originaire de

NATO [ˈneɪtəʊ] *(abbr* North Atlantic Treaty Organization) *n Mil* OTAN *f*

natter [ˈnætə(r)] *vi Br Fam* bavarder

natural [ˈnætʃərəl] *adj* naturel, -elle; *(talent)* inné ■ **naturally** *adv (unaffectedly, of course)* naturellement; *(by nature)* de nature

nature [ˈneɪtʃə(r)] *n (world, character)* nature *f*; **by n.** de nature; **n. reserve** réserve *f* naturelle

naughty [ˈnɔːtɪ] *(-ier, -iest) adj (child)* vilain

nausea [ˈnɔːzɪə] *n* nausée *f* ■ **nauseate** [ˈnɔːzɪeɪt] *vt* écœurer ■ **nauseous** [ˈnɔːʃəs] *adj Am* **to feel n.** *(sick)* avoir envie de vomir

nautical [ˈnɔːtɪkəl] *adj* nautique

naval [ˈneɪvəl] *adj* naval *(mpl* **-als);**

nave ... (officer) de marine
maritime; (of church) nef f

nave [neɪv] n (of wheel) nombril m

navel [...] ...

navigate ['næ...] 1 vt (boat) piloter; (river) na... sur 2 vi naviguer

... **l -ies**) n marine f 2 ... marine inv

navy ['ne... (bl... n Pol & Hist nazi, -e
adj n. ...

Nazi [...] (ta bene) NB
(mf) ..., -est) prep n. (to)

NB ... end vers la fin
ne... n. to st... près de
...ore or less) plus ou

... roche; **in the n. fu**-
... nir proche; **to the**
...calculate) à un euro
...Br côté m gauche, Am

... .ch) approcher de
... [nɪə'baɪ] adv tout près 2
... adj proche

... ['nɪəlɪ] adv presque she
...) n. fell elle a failli tomber

...t [niːt] (-er, -est) adj (clothes, work)
...igné; (room) bien rangé; Am Fam
(good) super inv ■ **neatly** adv (carefully) avec soin; (skilfully) habilement

necessary ['nesɪsərɪ] adj nécessaire ■ **necessarily** [-'serəlɪ] adv **not n.** pas forcément

necessity [nɪ'sesətɪ] (pl **-ies**) n (obligation, need) nécessité f; **to be a n.** être indispensable ■ **necessitate** vt nécessiter

neck [nek] n cou m; (of dress) encolure f; (of bottle) goulot m

necklace ['neklɪs] n collier m ■ **necktie** n cravate f

nectarine ['nektəriːn] n (fruit) nectarine f, brugnon m

need [niːd] 1 n besoin m; **to be in n. of sth** avoir besoin de qch; **there's no n. (for you) to do that** tu n'as pas besoin de faire cela

2 vt avoir besoin de; **you n. it** tu en as besoin; **her hair needs cutting** il faut qu'elle se fasse couper les cheveux

3 v aux **I needn't have rushed** ce

n'était pas la peine de me presser; **you needn't worry** inutile de t'inquiéter

needle ['niːdəl] n aiguille f; (of record player) saphir m ■ **needlework** n couture f; (object) ouvrage m

needlessly ['niːdlɪslɪ] adv inutilement

needy ['niːdɪ] (**-ier, -iest**) adj nécessiteux, -euse

negative ['negətɪv] 1 adj négatif, -ive 2 n (of photo) négatif m

neglect [nɪ'glekt] 1 n (of person) négligence f 2 vt (person, health, work) négliger; (garden, car) ne pas s'occuper de; (duty) manquer à; **to n. to do sth** négliger de faire qch ■ **neglected** adj (appearance) négligé; (garden, house) mal tenu; **to feel n.** se sentir abandonné

negligent ['neglɪdʒənt] adj négligent

negligible ['neglɪdʒəbəl] adj négligeable

negotiate [nɪ'gəʊʃɪeɪt] vti (discuss) négocier ■ **negotiation** n négociation f

neigh [neɪ] vi hennir

neighbour ['neɪbə(r)] (Am **neighbor**) n voisin, -e mf

neighbourhood ['neɪbəhʊd] (Am **neighborhood**) n (district) quartier m, voisinage m; (neighbours) voisinage m; **in the n. of $10/10 kilos** dans les 10 dollars/10 kilos

neighbouring ['neɪbərɪŋ] (Am **neighboring**) adj voisin

neither [Br 'naɪðə(r), Am 'niːðə(r)] 1 conj **n.... nor...** ni... ni...; **he n. sings nor dances** il ne chante ni ne danse 2 adv **n. do I/n. can I** (ni) moi non plus 3 adj **n. boy came** aucun des deux garçons n'est venu 4 pron **n. (of them)** aucun(e) (des deux)

neon ['niːɒn] adj **n. sign** enseigne f au néon

nephew ['nefjuː] n neveu m

nerve [nɜːv] n nerf m; (courage) courage m; Fam (impudence) culot m; Fam **he gets on my nerves** il me tape sur les nerfs ■ **nerve-racking** adj éprouvant

nervous ['nɜːvəs] *adj (apprehensive)* nerveux, -euse; **to be n. about sth/ doing sth** être nerveux à l'idée de qch/de faire qch

nest [nest] **1** *n* nid *m*; *Fig* **n. egg** pécule *m* **2** *vi (of bird)* nicher

nestle ['nesəl] *vi* se pelotonner (**up to** contre)

Net [net] *n Comptr* **the N.** le Net

net¹ [net] *n* filet *m*

net² [net] **1** *adj (profit, weight)* net (*f* nette) **2** *(pt & pp* **-tt-)** *vt (of person, company)* gagner net

Netherlands ['neðələndz] *npl* **the N.** les Pays-Bas *mpl*

nettle ['netəl] *n* ortie *f*

network ['netwɜːk] *n* réseau *m*

neurotic [njʊ'rɒtɪk] *adj & n* névrosé, -e *(mf)*

neuter ['njuːtə(r)] **1** *adj & n Gram* neutre *(m)* **2** *vt (cat)* châtrer

neutral ['njuːtrəl] **1** *adj* neutre; *(policy)* de neutralité **2** *n* **in n. (gear)** *(vehicle)* au point mort ▪ **neutralize** *vt* neutraliser

never ['nevə(r)] *adv (not ever)* (ne...) jamais; **she n. lies** elle ne ment jamais; **n. again** plus jamais ▪ **never-ending** *adj* interminable

nevertheless [nevəðə'les] *adv* néanmoins

new [njuː] *adj* (**a**) (**-er, -est**) nouveau (*f* nouvelle); *(brand-new)* neuf (*f* neuve); **to be n. to** *(job)* être nouveau dans; *(city)* être un nouveau-venu (*f* une nouvelle-venue) dans (**b**) *(different)* **a n. glass/pen** un autre verre/stylo ▪ **newborn** *adj* **a n. baby** un nouveau-né, une nouveau-née ▪ **newcomer** [-kʌmə(r)] *n* nouveau-venu *m*, nouvelle-venue *f* (**to** dans) ▪ **newly** *adv* nouvellement ▪ **newlyweds** *n* jeunes mariés *mpl*

news [njuːz] *n* nouvelles *fpl*; *(in the media)* informations *fpl*; **a piece of n.** une nouvelle; **sports n.** *(newspaper column)* rubrique *f* sportive ▪ **newsagent** *n Br* marchand, -e *mf* de journaux ▪ **newsdealer** *n Am* marchand, -e *mf* de journaux ▪ **newsflash** *n* flash *m*

d'informations ▪ n̲e̲w̲s̲l̲e̲t̲t̲e̲r̲ *n (of club, group)* bulletin *m* ▪ n̲e̲w̲s̲p̲a̲p̲e̲r̲ *n* journal *m* ▪ **newsreade**... *Br* présentateur, -trice *mf* de journal

New Zealand [njuː'...] ... la Nouvelle-Zélande

next [nekst] **1** *adj* pr... *house)* d'à côté; *(followi...* **month** *(in the future)* le n... **the n. day** le lendemain; v̲?̲ **ten days** d'ici dix jours; yc̲ ton tour; **the n. size up** l... dessus; **to live n. door** hab... (**to** de)
 2 *n (in series)* suivant, -e *mf*
 3 *adv (afterwards)* ensuite *(now)* maintenant; **when you** c̲... la prochaine fois que tu viendras *(beside)* à côté de

next-door ['nekstdɔː(r)] *adj* **n. ne** **bour/room** voisin *m*/pièce *f* d'à côt...

NHS [eneɪtʃ'es] *(abbr* **National Hea** **Service)** *n Br* ≃ Sécurité *f* sociale

nibble ['nɪbəl] *vti* grignoter

nice [naɪs] (**-er, -est**) *adj (pleasant)* agréable; *(tasty)* bon (*f* bonne); *(physically attractive)* beau (*f* belle); *(kind)* gentil, -ille (**to** avec); **n. and warm** bien chaud; **have a n. day!** bonne journée! ▪ **nicely** *adv (well)* bien

niche [niːʃ, nɪtʃ] *n (recess)* niche *f*; **(market) n.** créneau *m*

nick [nɪk] **1** *n (on skin, wood)* entaille *f*; *(in blade, crockery)* brèche *f*; **in the n. of time** juste à temps **2** *vt Br Fam (steal)* piquer

nickel ['nɪkəl] *n Am (coin)* pièce *f* de cinq cents ▪ *Am* **nickel-and-dime store** *n* ≃ magasin *m* à prix unique

nickname ['nɪkneɪm] **1** *n (informal)* surnom *m* **2** *vt* surnommer

niece [niːs] *n* nièce *f*

night [naɪt] **1** *n* nuit *f*; *(evening)* soir *m*; **at n.** la nuit; **last n.** *(evening)* hier soir; *(night)* cette nuit; **to have an early/a late n.** se coucher tôt/tard
 2 *adj (work, flight)* de nuit; **n. shift** *(job)* poste *m* de nuit; *(workers)* équipe *f* de nuit ▪ **nightcap** *n (drink)* = boisson alcoolisée ou chaude prise avant de se

coucher ▪ **nightclub** n boîte f de nuit ▪ **nightdress** ['naɪtdres], **nightgown** ['naɪtgəʊn], Fam **nightie** ['naɪtɪ] n chemise f de nuit ▪ **nightfall** n at n. à la tombée de la nuit ▪ **nightlife** n vie f nocturne ▪ **night-time** n nuit f

nightingale ['naɪtɪŋgeɪl] n rossignol m

nightly ['naɪtlɪ] **1** adv chaque nuit; (every evening) chaque soir **2** adj de chaque nuit/soir

nightmare ['naɪtmeə(r)] n cauchemar m

nil [nɪl] n (nothing) & Br (score) zéro m; **two n.** deux à zéro

Nile [naɪl] n the N. le Nil

nimble ['nɪmbəl] (-er, -est) adj (person) souple

nine [naɪn] adj & n neuf (m)

nineteen [naɪn'tiːn] adj & n dix-neuf (m)

ninety ['naɪntɪ] adj & n quatre-vingt-dix (m)

ninth ['naɪnθ] adj & n neuvième (mf); **a n.** (fraction) un neuvième

nip [nɪp] **1** (pt & pp -pp-) vt (pinch) pincer **2** vi Br Fam **to n. round to sb's house** faire un saut chez qn; **to n. out** sortir un instant

nipple ['nɪpəl] n mamelon m; Am (on baby's bottle) tétine f

nitrogen ['naɪtrədʒən] n azote m

NO [nəʊ] **1** (pl noes or nos) n non m inv
2 adj (not any) pas de; **there's no bread** il n'y a pas de pain; **I have no idea** je n'ai aucune idée; **no child came** aucun enfant n'est venu; **of no importance** sans importance
3 adv (interjection) non; **no more time** plus de temps; **no more/fewer than ten** pas plus/moins de dix

noble ['nəʊbəl] (-er, -est) adj noble ▪ **nobility** n noblesse f

nobody ['nəʊbɒdɪ] **1** pron (ne...) personne; **n. came** personne n'est venu; **he knows n.** il ne connaît personne **2** n **a n.** une nullité

nod [nɒd] **1** n signe m de tête **2** (pt & pp

-dd-) vti **to n. (one's head)** faire un signe de tête **3** vi Fam **to n. off** s'assoupir

noise [nɔɪz] n bruit m; **to make a n.** faire du bruit

noisy ['nɔɪzɪ] (-ier, -iest) adj (person, street) bruyant ▪ **noisily** adv bruyamment

nominal ['nɒmɪnəl] adj nominal; (rent, salary) symbolique

nominate ['nɒmɪneɪt] vt (appoint) nommer; (propose) proposer (**for** comme candidat à) ▪ **nomination** n (appointment) nomination f; (proposal) candidature f

nondescript ['nɒndɪskrɪpt] adj très ordinaire

NONE [nʌn] **1** pron aucun, -e mf; (in filling out a form) néant; **n. of them** aucun d'eux; **she has n. (at all)** elle n'en a pas (du tout); **n. came** pas un(e) seul(e) n'est venu(e)
2 adv **n. too hot** pas très chaud; **he's n. the wiser (for it)** il n'est pas plus avancé ▪ **nonetheless** adv néanmoins

nonentity [nɒ'nentətɪ] (pl -ies) n (person) nullité f

nonexistent [nɒnɪg'zɪstənt] adj inexistant

non-fiction [nɒn'fɪkʃən] n ouvrages mpl généraux

nonsense ['nɒnsəns] n bêtises fpl; **that's n.** c'est absurde

non-smoker [nɒn'sməʊkə(r)] n (person) non-fumeur, -euse mf; (compartment on train) compartiment m non-fumeurs

non-stop [nɒn'stɒp] **1** adj sans arrêt; (train, flight) sans escale **2** adv (work) sans arrêt; (fly) sans escale

noodles ['nuːdəlz] npl nouilles fpl; (in soup) vermicelles mpl

noon [nuːn] n midi m

no-one ['nəʊwʌn] pron = nobody

noose [nuːs] n nœud m coulant

nor [nɔː(r)] conj ni; **neither you n. me** ni toi ni moi; **she neither drinks n. smokes** elle ne fume ni ne boit; **n. do I/can I/etc** (ni) moi non plus

norm [nɔːm] n norme f

normal ['nɔːməl] **1** *adj* normal **2** *n* **above/below n.** au-dessus/au-dessous de la normale ■ **normally** *adv* normalement

north [nɔːθ] **1** *n* nord *m*; **(to the) n. of** au nord de

2 *adj (coast)* nord *inv*; *(wind)* du nord; **N. America/Africa** Amérique *f*/ Afrique *f* du Nord; **N. American** *adj* nord-américain; *n* Nord-Américain, -e *mf*

3 *adv* au nord; *(travel)* vers le nord ■ **northbound** *adj (traffic)* en direction du nord; *Br (carriageway)* nord *inv* ■ **north-east** *n & adj* nord-est *(m)* ■ **northerly** ['nɔːðəlɪ] *adj (direction)* du nord ■ **northern** ['nɔːðən] *adj (coast)* nord *inv*; *(town)* du nord; **N. France** le nord de la France; **N. Ireland** l'Irlande *f* du Nord ■ **northerner** ['nɔːðənə(r)] *n* habitant, -e *mf* du Nord ■ **northward(s)** *adj & adv* vers le nord ■ **north-west** *n & adj* nord-ouest *(m)*

Norway ['nɔːweɪ] *n* la Norvège ■ **Norwegian 1** *adj* norvégien, -enne **2** *n (person)* Norvégien, -enne *mf*; *(language)* norvégien *m*

nose [nəʊz] *n* nez *m*; **her n. is bleeding** elle saigne du nez ■ **nosebleed** *n* saignement *m* de nez

nosey ['nəʊzɪ] **(-ier, -iest)** *adj Fam* indiscret, -ète

no-smoking [nəʊ'sməʊkɪŋ] *adj (carriage, area)* non-fumeurs

nostalgic [nɒs'tældʒɪk] *adj* nostalgique

nostril ['nɒstrəl] *n (of person)* narine *f*

nosy ['nəʊzɪ] *adj* = **nosey**

NOT [nɒt]

À l'oral, et à l'écrit dans un style familier, on utilise généralement **not** à la forme contractée lors qu'il suit un modal ou un auxiliaire (**don't go!; she wasn't there; he couldn't see me**).

adv **(a)** (ne...) pas; **he's n. there, he isn't there** il n'est pas là; **n. yet** pas encore; **n. at all** pas du tout; *(after 'thank you')* je vous en prie

(b) non; **I think/hope n.** je pense/ j'espère que non; **n. guilty** non coupable; **isn't she?/don't you?/**etc* non?

notable ['nəʊtəbəl] *adj* notable ■ **notably** *adv (noticeably)* notablement; *(particularly)* notamment

notch [nɒtʃ] **1** *n (in wood)* encoche *f*; *(in belt, wheel)* cran *m* **2** *vt* **to n. up** *(points)* marquer; *(victory)* remporter

note [nəʊt] **1** *n (information, reminder) & Mus* note *f*; *Br (banknote)* billet *m*; *(letter)* mot *m*; **to take (a) n. of sth, to make a n. of sth** prendre note de qch **2** *vt (notice)* remarquer, noter; **to n. sth down** *(word, remark)* noter qch ■ **notebook** *n* carnet *m*; *(for school)* cahier *m* ■ **notepad** *n* bloc-notes *m* ■ **notepaper** *n* papier *m* à lettres

noted ['nəʊtɪd] *adj* éminent

nothing ['nʌθɪŋ] **1** *pron* (ne...) rien; **he knows n.** il ne sait rien; **n. at all** rien du tout; **n. much** pas grand-chose; **I've got n. to do with it** je n'y suis pour rien; **for n.** *(in vain, free of charge)* pour rien

2 *adv* **to look n. like sb** ne ressembler nullement à qn

3 *n* **to come to n.** être anéanti

notice ['nəʊtɪs] **1** *n (notification)* avis *m*; *(sign)* pancarte *f*, écriteau *m*; *(poster)* affiche *f*; **to give sb (advance) n.** *(inform)* avertir qn (of de); **n. (to quit), n. of dismissal** congé *m*; **to give in** *or* **hand in one's n.** *(resign)* donner sa démission; **to take n.** faire attention (**of** à); **until further n.** jusqu'à nouvel ordre; **at short n.** au dernier moment

2 *vt* remarquer (**that** que) ■ **noticeboard** *n Br* tableau *m* d'affichage

noticeable ['nəʊtɪsəbəl] *adj* perceptible

notify ['nəʊtɪfaɪ] **(***pt & pp* **-ied)** *vt (inform)* avertir (**sb of sth** qn de qch); *(announce)* notifier (**to** à) ■ **notification** [-fɪ'keɪʃən] *n* avis *m*

notion ['nəʊʃən] *n* notion *f*

notorious [nəʊ'tɔːrɪəs] *adj* tristement célèbre; *(criminal)* notoire

nought [nɔːt] *n Br Math* zéro *m*

noun [naʊn] *n* nom *m*

nourish ['nʌrɪʃ] *vt* nourrir ■ **nourishment** *n* nourriture *f*

novel ['nɒvəl] **1** n roman m **2** adj (new) nouveau (f nouvelle), original ■ **novelist** n romancier, -ère mf ■ **novelty** n nouveauté f

November [nəʊ'vembə(r)] n novembre m

novice ['nɒvɪs] n (beginner) débutant, -e mf (at en)

now [naʊ] **1** adv maintenant; **for n.** pour le moment; **from n. on** désormais; **until n., up to n.** jusqu'ici, jusqu'à maintenant; **n. and then** de temps à autre; **she ought to be here by n.** elle devrait déjà être ici **2** conj **n. (that)…** maintenant que…

nowadays ['naʊədeɪz] adv de nos jours

nowhere ['nəʊweə(r)] adv nulle part; **n. else** nulle part ailleurs; **n. near enough** loin d'être assez

nozzle ['nɒzəl] n embout m; (of hose) jet m

nuance ['nju:ɑ:ns] n nuance f

nuclear ['nju:klɪə(r)] adj nucléaire

nucleus ['nju:klɪəs] (pl -clei [-klɪaɪ]) n noyau m (pl -aux)

nude [nju:d] **1** adj nu **2** n nu m; **in the n.** tout nu (f toute nue)

nudge [nʌdʒ] **1** n coup m de coude **2** vt pousser du coude

nudist ['nju:dɪst] **1** n nudiste mf **2** adj (camp) de nudistes

nuisance ['nju:səns] n **to be a n.** être embêtant

null [nʌl] adj **n. (and void)** nul (et non avenu) (f nulle (et non avenue))

numb [nʌm] adj (stiff) (hand) engourdi

number ['nʌmbə(r)] **1** n nombre m; (of page, house, telephone) numéro m; (song) chanson f; **a/any n. of** un certain/grand nombre de **2** vt (assign number to) numéroter ■ **numberplate** n Br plaque f d'immatriculation

numeral ['nju:mərəl] n chiffre m

numerical [nju:'merɪkəl] adj numérique

numerous ['nju:mərəs] adj nombreux, -euse

nun [nʌn] n religieuse f

nurse [nɜːs] **1** n infirmière f; (for children) nurse f **2** vt (look after) soigner; (suckle) allaiter ■ **nursing** n (care) soins mpl; (job) profession f d'infirmière; Br **n. home** (for old people) maison f de retraite

nursery ['nɜːsərɪ] (pl -ies) n (children's room) chambre f d'enfants; (for plants, trees) pépinière f; **(day) n.** (school) garderie f; **n. rhyme** comptine f; **n. school** école f maternelle

nut¹ [nʌt] n (fruit) = noix, noisette ou autre fruit sec de cette nature; **Brazil n.** noix f du Brésil ■ **nutcrackers** npl casse-noix m inv ■ **nutshell** n Fig **in a n.** en un mot

nut² [nʌt] n (for bolt) écrou m

nut³ [nʌt] n Fam (crazy person) cinglé, -e mf ■ **nutcase** n Fam cinglé, -e mf

nutmeg ['nʌtmeg] n muscade f

nutritious [nju:'trɪʃəs] adj nutritif, -ive ■ **nutrition** [-ʃən] n nutrition f

nuts [nʌts] adj Fam (crazy) cinglé

nylon ['naɪlɒn] n Nylon® m; **n. shirt** chemise f en Nylon®

Oo

O, o [əʊ] *n (letter)* O, o *m inv*

oaf [əʊf] *n* balourd *m*

oak [əʊk] *n (tree, wood)* chêne *m*

OAP [əʊeɪ'piː] *(abbr* **old-age pensioner)** *n Br* retraité, -e *mf*

oar [ɔː(r)] *n* aviron *m*, rame *f*

oasis [əʊ'eɪsɪs] *(pl* **oases** [əʊ'eɪsiːz]) *n* oasis *f*

oath [əʊθ] *(pl* **-s** [əʊðz]) *n (promise)* serment *m; (profanity)* juron *m*

oats [əʊts] *npl* avoine *f;* **(porridge) o.** flocons *mpl* d'avoine

obedient [ə'biːdɪənt] *adj* obéissant ■ **obedience** *n* obéissance *f* (**to** à)

obese [əʊ'biːs] *adj* obèse

obey [ə'beɪ] **1** *vt* obéir à **2** *vi* obéir

obituary [ə'bɪtʃʊərɪ] *(pl* **-ies**) *n* nécrologie *f*

object¹ ['ɒbdʒɪkt] *n (thing)* objet *m; (aim)* but *m*, objet; *(in grammar)* complément *m* d'objet

object² [əb'dʒekt] **1** *vt* **to o. that...** objecter que... **2** *vi* émettre une objection; **to o. to sth/to doing sth** ne pas être d'accord avec qch/pour faire qch

objection [əb'dʒekʃən] *n* objection *f*

objective [əb'dʒektɪv] **1** *adj (impartial)* objectif, -ive **2** *n (aim, target)* objectif *m*

obligation [ɒblɪ'geɪʃən] *n* obligation *f;* **to be under an o. to do sth** être dans l'obligation de faire qch

obligatory [ə'blɪgətərɪ] *adj* obligatoire

oblige [ə'blaɪdʒ] *vt* **(a)** *(compel)* **to o. sb to do sth** obliger qn à faire qch **(b)** *(help)* rendre service à; **to be obliged to sb** être reconnaissant à qn (**for** de) ■ **obliging** *adj* serviable

oblique [ə'bliːk] *adj (line, angle)* oblique; *(reference)* indirect

oblivion [ə'blɪvɪən] *n* oubli *m* ■ **oblivious** *adj* inconscient (**to** *or* **of** de)

oblong ['ɒblɒŋ] **1** *adj (rectangular)* rectangulaire **2** *n* rectangle *m*

obnoxious [əb'nɒkʃəs] *adj (person, behaviour)* odieux, -euse

oboe ['əʊbəʊ] *n* hautbois *m*

obscene [əb'siːn] *adj* obscène ■ **obscenity** [əb'senətɪ] *(pl* **-ies**) *n* obscénité *f*

obscure [əb'skjʊə(r)] **1** *adj* obscur **2** *vt (hide)* cacher; *(confuse)* obscurcir

observant [əb'zɜːvənt] *adj* observateur, -trice

observation [ɒbzə'veɪʃən] *n (observing, remark)* observation *f;* **under o.** *(hospital patient)* en observation

observe [əb'zɜːv] *vt* observer; **to o. the speed limit** respecter la limitation de vitesse ■ **observer** *n* observateur, -trice *mf*

obsess [əb'ses] *vt* obséder ■ **obsession** *n* obsession *f* ■ **obsessive** *adj (idea)* obsédant; *(person)* obsessionnel, -elle; **to be o. about sth** être obsédé par qch

obsolete ['ɒbsəliːt] *adj* obsolète; *(design, model)* dépassé

obstacle ['ɒbstəkəl] *n* obstacle *m*

obstinate ['ɒbstɪnət] *adj* obstiné

obstruct [əb'strʌkt] *vt (block) (road, pipe)* obstruer; *(view)* cacher; *(hinder)* gêner ■ **obstruction** *n (action, in sport)*, *Med & Pol* obstruction *f; (obstacle)* obstacle *m; (in pipe)* bouchon *m*

obtain [əb'teɪn] *vt* obtenir

obvious ['ɒbvɪəs] *adj* évident (**that** que) ■ **obviously** *adv (of course)* évidemment; *(conspicuously)* manifestement

occasion [ə'keɪʒən] *n (time, opportunity)* occasion *f*; *(event)* événement *m*; **on the o. of...** à l'occasion de...; **on several occasions** à plusieurs reprises

occasional [ə'keɪʒənəl] *adj* occasionnel, -elle; **she drinks the o. whisky** elle boit un whisky de temps en temps ■ **occasionally** *adv* de temps en temps

occupant ['ɒkjʊpənt] *n (of house, car)* occupant, -e *mf*

occupation [ɒkjʊ'peɪʃən] *n* (**a**) *(pastime)* occupation *f*; *(profession)* métier *m* (**b**) *(of house, land)* occupation *f*

occupier ['ɒkjʊpaɪə(r)] *n (of house)* occupant, -e *mf*; *(of country)* occupant *m*

occupy ['ɒkjʊpaɪ] *(pt & pp -ied)* *vt (space, time, attention)* occuper; **to keep oneself occupied** s'occuper (**doing** à faire)

occur [ə'kɜː(r)] *(pt & pp -rr-)* *vi (happen)* avoir lieu; *(of opportunity)* se présenter; *(be found)* se trouver; **it occurs to me that...** il me vient à l'esprit que...

occurrence [ə'kʌrəns] *n (event)* événement *m*

ocean ['əʊʃən] *n* océan *m*

o'clock [ə'klɒk] *adv* **(it's) three o.** (il est) trois heures

octagonal [ɒk'tægənəl] *adj* octogonal

October [ɒk'təʊbə(r)] *n* octobre *m*

octopus ['ɒktəpəs] *n* pieuvre *f*

odd [ɒd] *adj* (**a**) *(strange)* bizarre, curieux, -euse
(**b**) *(number)* impair
(**c**) *(left over)* **sixty o.** soixante et quelques; **an o. glove/sock** un gant/une chaussette dépareillé(e)
(**d**) *(occasional)* **I smoke the o. cigarette** je fume une cigarette de temps en temps; **o. jobs** petits travaux *mpl* ■ **oddly** *adv* bizarrement; **o. enough, he was elected** chose curieuse, il a été élu

odds [ɒdz] *npl* (**a**) *(in betting)* cote *f*; *(chances)* chances *fpl*; *Fam* **it makes no o.** ça n'a pas d'importance (**b**) *(expressions)* **to be at o. (with sb)** être en désaccord (avec qn); *Fam* **o. and ends** des bricoles *fpl*

odious ['əʊdɪəs] *adj* odieux, -euse

odometer [əʊ'dɒmɪtə(r)] *n Am* compteur *m* kilométrique

odour ['əʊdə(r)] *(Am* **odor**) *n* odeur *f*

OF [əv, *stressed* ɒv] *prep* de, d'; **of the boy** du garçon; **of the boys** des garçons; **of wood/paper** de *ou* en bois/papier; **she has a lot of it/of them** elle en a beaucoup; **there are ten of us** nous sommes dix; **a friend of his** un ami à lui, un de ses amis; **that's nice of you** c'est gentil de ta part; **of no value/interest** sans valeur/intérêt; *Br* **the fifth of June** le cinq juin

OFF [ɒf] **1** *adj (light, gas, radio)* éteint; *(tap)* fermé; *(switched off at mains)* coupé; *(removed)* enlevé; *(cancelled)* annulé; *(not fit to eat or drink)* mauvais; *(milk, meat)* tourné; **I'm o. today** j'ai congé aujourd'hui
2 *adv* **to be o.** *(leave)* partir; **a day o.** *(holiday)* un jour de congé; **I have today o.** j'ai congé aujourd'hui; **five percent o.** une réduction de cinq pour cent; **on and o., o. and on** *(sometimes)* de temps à autre
3 *prep (from)* de; *(distant)* éloigné de; **to fall o. the wall/ladder** tomber du mur/de l'échelle; **to take sth o. the table** prendre qch sur la table; **she's o. her food** elle ne mange plus rien ■ **off-chance** *n* **on the o.** à tout hasard ■ **off-colour** *(Am* **off-color**) *adj Br (ill)* patraque; *(indecent)* d'un goût douteux ■ **offhand 1** *adj* désinvolte **2** *adv (immediately)* au pied levé ■ **off-licence** *n Br* ≃ magasin *m* de vins et de spiritueux ■ **off-line** *adj (computer)* autonome ■ **off-peak** *adj (rate, price)* **heures creuses** *inv* ■ **off-putting** *adj Br Fam* peu engageant ■ **offside** *adj* **to be o.** *(of footballer)* être hors jeu ■ **offspring** *n* progéniture *f* ■ **off-the-peg** *(Am* **off-the-rack**) *adj (clothes)* de confection

offence [ə'fens] *(Am* **offense**) *n (against the law)* infraction *f*; *(more serious)* délit *m*; **to take o.** s'offenser (**at** de); **to give o.** offenser

offend [ə'fend] *vt* offenser; **to be of-fended** s'offenser (**at** de) ▪ **offender** *n (criminal)* délinquant, -e *mf*

offense [ə'fens] *n Am* = **offence**

offensive [ə'fensɪv] **1** *adj* choquant **2** *n* offensive *f*; **to be on the o.** être passé à l'offensive

offer ['ɒfə(r)] **1** *n* offre *f*; **to make sb an o.** faire une offre à qn; **on (special) o.** en promotion **2** *vt* offrir; *(explanation)* donner; *(apologies)* présenter; **to o. sb sth, to o. sth to sb** offrir qch à qn; **to o. to do sth** proposer *ou* offrir de faire qch ▪ **offering** *n (gift)* offrande *f*

office ['ɒfɪs] *n* **(a)** *(room)* bureau *m*; *Am (of doctor)* cabinet *m*; **o. hours** heures *fpl* de bureau; **o. worker** employé, -e *mf* de bureau **(b)** *(position)* fonctions *fpl*; **to be in o.** être au pouvoir

officer ['ɒfɪsə(r)] *n (in the army, navy)* officier *m*; **(police) o.** agent *m* de police

official [ə'fɪʃəl] **1** *adj* officiel, -elle **2** *n* responsable *mf*; *(civil servant)* fonctionnaire *mf* ▪ **officially** *adv* officiellement

offset ['ɒfset, ɒf'set] *(pt & pp* **offset**, *pres p* **offsetting)** *vt (compensate for)* compenser

often ['ɒf(t)ən] *adv* souvent; **how o.?** combien de fois?; **every so o.** de temps en temps

oh [əʊ] *exclam* oh!, ah!; *(in pain)* aïe!; **oh yes!** mais oui!

oil [ɔɪl] **1** *n (for machine, cooking)* huile *f*; *(petroleum)* pétrole *m*; *(fuel)* mazout *m* **2** *adj (industry)* pétrolier, -ère; *(painting, paint)* à l'huile; **o. lamp** lampe *f* à pétrole **3** *vt (machine)* huiler ▪ **oilcan** *n* burette *f* ▪ **oilfield** *n* gisement *m* de pétrole ▪ **oily (-ier, -iest)** *adj (hands, rag)* graisseux, -euse; *(skin, hair)* gras *(f* grasse)

ointment ['ɔɪntmənt] *n* pommade *f*

OK, okay ['əʊ'keɪ] **1** *adj & adv see* **all right 2** *(pt & pp* **OKed, okayed**, *pres p* **OKing, okaying)** *vt* donner le feu vert à

old [əʊld] **1** (**-er, -est**) *adj* vieux *(f* vieille); *(former)* ancien, -enne; **how o. is he?** quel âge a-t-il?; **he's ten years**

o. il a dix ans; **he's older than me** il est plus âgé que moi; **the oldest son** le fils aîné; **to get** *or* **grow old(er)** vieillir; **o. age** vieillesse *f*; **o. man** vieillard *m*, vieil homme *m*; **o. people** les personnes *fpl* âgées; **o. people's home** maison *f* de retraite; *Fam* **any o. how** n'importe comment

2 *npl* **the o.** les personnes *fpl* âgées

old-fashioned [əʊld'fæʃənd] *adj (out-of-date)* démodé; *(person)* vieux jeu *inv*; *(traditional)* d'autrefois

olive ['ɒlɪv] *n (fruit)* olive *f*; **o. oil** huile *f* d'olive

Olympic [ə'lɪmpɪk] *adj* **the O. Games** les jeux *mpl* Olympiques

omelet(te) ['ɒmlɪt] *n* omelette *f*; **cheese o.** omelette *f* au fromage

omen ['əʊmən] *n* augure *m*

ominous ['ɒmɪnəs] *adj* inquiétant; *(event)* de mauvais augure

omit [əʊ'mɪt] *(pt & pp* **-tt-)** *vt* omettre **(to do** de faire) ▪ **omission** *n* omission *f*

ON [ɒn] **1** *prep* **(a)** *(expressing position)* sur; **on page 4** à la page 4; **on the right/left** à droite/gauche **(b)** *(about)* sur **(c)** *(expressing manner or means)* **on the train/plane** dans le train/l'avion; **to be on** *(a course)* suivre; *(project)* travailler à; *(salary)* toucher; *(team, committee)* faire partie de; *Fam* **it's on me!** *(I'll pay)* c'est pour moi! **(d)** *(with time)* **on Monday** lundi; **on Mondays** le lundi; **on (the evening of) May 3rd** le 3 mai (au soir); **on my arrival** à mon arrivée **(e)** *(+ present participle)* en; **on learning that...** en apprenant que...

2 *adv (ahead)* en avant; *(in progress)* en cours; *(lid, brake)* mis; *(light, radio)* allumé; *(gas, tap)* ouvert; *(machine)* en marche; **she has her hat on** elle a mis son chapeau; **I've got something on** *(I'm busy)* je suis pris; **the strike is on** la grève aura lieu; **what's on?** *(on TV)* qu'est-ce qu'il y a à la télé?; *(in theatre, cinema)* qu'est-ce qu'on joue?; **he went on and on about it** il n'en finissait pas; *Fam* **that's just not on!** c'est inadmissible!; **I've been on to him** *(on*

phone) je l'ai eu au bout du fil ■ **on-going** *adj (project, discussion)* en cours ■ **on-line** *adj (computer)* en ligne

once [wʌns] **1** *adv (on one occasion)* une fois; *(formerly)* autrefois; **o. a month** une fois par mois; **o. again, o. more** encore une fois; **at o.** *(immediately)* tout de suite; **all at o.** *(suddenly)* tout à coup; *(at the same time)* à la fois **2** *conj* une fois que

ONE [wʌn] **1** *adj* (a) un, une; **page o.** la page un; **twenty-o.** vingt et un
(b) *(only)* seul
(c) *(same)* le même (*f* la même); **in the o. bus** dans le même bus
2 *pron* (a) un, une; **do you want o.?** en veux-tu (un)?; **o. of them** l'un d'eux, l'une d'elles; **a big/small o.** un grand/ petit; **this o.** celui-ci, celle-ci; **that o.** celui-là, celle-là; **the o. who/which...** celui/celle qui...; **another o.** un(e) autre; **I for o.** pour ma part
(b) *(impersonal)* on; **o. knows** on sait; **it helps o.** ça vous aide; **o.'s family** sa famille ■ **one-off, one-of-a-kind** *adj Fam* unique ■ **one-sided** *adj (biased)* partial; *(contest)* inégal ■ **one-time** *adj (former)* ancien, -enne ■ **one-to-one** *adj (discussion)* en tête à tête ■ **one-way** *adj (street)* à sens unique; **o. ticket** billet *m* simple

oneself [wʌn'self] *pron* soi-même; *(reflexive)* se, s'; **to cut o.** se couper

onion ['ʌnjən] *n* oignon *m*

onlooker ['ɒnlʊkə(r)] *n* spectateur, -trice *mf*

only ['əʊnlɪ] **1** *adj* seul; **the o. one** le seul, la seule; **an o. son** un fils unique **2** *adv* seulement, ne... que; **I o. have ten** je n'en ai que dix, j'en ai dix seulement; **if o.** si seulement; **I have o. just seen it** je viens tout juste de le voir; **o. he knows** lui seul le sait **3** *conj Fam (but)* mais

onset ['ɒnset] *n (of disease, winter)* début *m*

onto ['ɒntuː, *unstressed* 'ɒntə] *prep* = **on to**

onward(s) ['ɒnwəd(z)] *adv* en avant; **from that day o.** à partir de ce jour-là

opaque [əʊ'peɪk] *adj* opaque

open ['əʊpən] **1** *adj* ouvert; *(view, road)* dégagé; *(post, job)* vacant; *(airline ticket)* open *inv*; **in the o. air** au grand air; **o. to** *(criticism, attack)* exposé à; *(ideas, suggestions)* ouvert à; **to leave sth o.** *(date)* ne pas préciser qch
2 *n* **(out) in the o.** *(outside)* dehors; **to sleep (out) in the o.** dormir à la belle étoile
3 *vt* ouvrir; *(arms, legs)* écarter; **to o. sth out** *(paper, map)* ouvrir qch; **to o. sth up** *(bag, shop)* ouvrir qch
4 *vi (of flower, door, eyes)* s'ouvrir; *(of shop, office)* ouvrir; *(of play)* débuter; **to o. on to sth** *(of window)* donner sur qch; **to o. out** *(widen)* s'élargir; **to o. up** *(of flower, person)* s'ouvrir; *(of shopkeeper)* ouvrir ■ **open-air** *adj (pool)* en plein air ■ **open-minded** *adj* à l'esprit ouvert ■ **open-plan** *adj (office)* paysager, -ère

opening ['əʊpənɪŋ] **1** *n* ouverture *f*; *(job, trade outlet)* débouché *m*; *(opportunity)* occasion *f* favorable; **late-night o.** *(of shops)* nocturne *f*
2 *adj (time, hours, speech)* d'ouverture; **o. night** *(of play, musical)* première *f*

openly ['əʊpənlɪ] *adv* ouvertement

opera ['ɒprə] *n* opéra *m*

operate ['ɒpəreɪt] **1** *vt (machine)* faire fonctionner; *(service)* assurer **2** *vi* (a) **to o. on sb (for sth)** *(of surgeon)* opérer qn (de qch) (b) *(of machine)* fonctionner; *(of company)* opérer ■ **operating** *adj Br* **o. theatre**, *Am* **o. room** salle *f* d'opération; *Comptr* **o. system** système *m* d'exploitation

operation [ɒpə'reɪʃən] *n Med, Mil & Math* opération *f*; *(of machine)* fonctionnement *m*; **in o.** *(machine)* en service; *(plan)* en vigueur; **to have an o.** se faire opérer

operator ['ɒpəreɪtə(r)] *n (on phone, machine)* opérateur, -trice *mf*

opinion [ə'pɪnjən] *n* opinion *f*; **in my o.** à mon avis

opponent [ə'pəʊnənt] *n* adversaire *mf*

opportune ['ɒpətjuːn] *adj* opportun

opportunity [ɒpə'tjuːnətɪ] (pl -ies) n occasion f (**to do** or **of doing** de faire); **opportunities** (prospects) perspectives fpl; **to take the o. to do sth** profiter de l'occasion pour faire qch

oppose [ə'pəʊz] vt s'opposer à ■ **opposed** adj opposé (**to** à); **as o. to...** par opposition à... ■ **opposing** adj (viewpoints) opposé; (team) adverse

opposite ['ɒpəzɪt] **1** adj (side) opposé; (house, page) d'en face; **in the o. direction** en sens inverse **2** adv en face; **the house o.** la maison d'en face **3** prep o. (**to**) en face de **4** n **the o.** le contraire

opposition [ɒpə'zɪʃən] n opposition f (**to** à); **the o.** (rival camp) l'adversaire m; (in business) la concurrence

oppress [ə'pres] vt (treat cruelly) opprimer ■ **oppression** n oppression f ■ **oppressive** adj (heat) accablant, étouffant; (ruler, regime) oppressif, -ive

opt [ɒpt] vi **to o. for sth** opter pour qch; **to o. to do sth** choisir de faire qch; **to o. out** se désengager (**of** de)

optical ['ɒptɪkəl] adj optique; (instrument, illusion) d'optique

optician [ɒp'tɪʃən] n (dispensing) opticien, -enne mf

optimism ['ɒptɪmɪzəm] n optimisme m ■ **optimistic** adj optimiste (**about** quant à)

optimum ['ɒptɪməm] adj & n optimum (m)

option ['ɒpʃən] n (choice) choix m; (school subject) matière f à option; **she has no o.** elle n'a pas le choix ■ **optional** adj facultatif, -ive

or [ɔː(r)] conj ou; **he doesn't drink or smoke** il ne boit ni ne fume; **ten or so** environ dix

oral ['ɔːrəl] **1** adj oral **2** n (exam) oral m

orange ['ɒrɪndʒ] **1** n (fruit) orange f; **o. juice** jus m d'orange **2** adj & n (colour) orange (m) inv

orbit ['ɔːbɪt] **1** n (of planet) orbite f **2** vt être en orbite autour de

orchard ['ɔːtʃəd] n verger m

orchestra ['ɔːkɪstrə] n orchestre m; Am **the o.** (in theatre) l'orchestre m

orchid ['ɔːkɪd] n orchidée f

ordeal [ɔː'diːl] n épreuve f

order ['ɔːdə(r)] **1** n (instruction, arrangement) & Rel ordre m; (purchase) commande f; **in o.** (passport) en règle; **in o. of age** par ordre d'âge; **in o. to do sth** afin de faire qch; **in o. that...** afin que... (+ subjunctive); **out of o.** (machine) en panne; (telephone) en dérangement; **o. form** bon m de commande **2** vt (meal, goods) commander; (taxi) appeler; **to o. sb to do sth** ordonner à qn de faire qch **3** vi (in café) commander

orderly ['ɔːdəlɪ] adj (room, life) ordonné; (crowd) discipliné

ordinary ['ɔːdɪnrɪ] adj ordinaire; **it's out of the o.** ça sort de l'ordinaire; **she was just an o. tourist** c'était une touriste comme une autre

organ ['ɔːgən] n (**a**) (part of body) organe m (**b**) (musical instrument) orgue m

organic [ɔː'gænɪk] adj organique; (vegetables, farming) biologique

organism ['ɔːgənɪzəm] n organisme m

organization [ɔːgənaɪ'zeɪʃən] n organisation f

organize ['ɔːgənaɪz] vt organiser ■ **organizer** n (person) organisateur, -trice mf; (personal) **o.** (diary) agenda m

orgasm ['ɔːgæzəm] n orgasme m

oriental [ɔːrɪ'entəl] adj oriental

orientate ['ɔːrɪənteɪt] (Am **orient** ['ɔːrɪənt]) vt orienter

origin ['ɒrɪdʒɪn] n origine f

original [ə'rɪdʒɪnəl] **1** adj (novel, innovative) original; (first) d'origine **2** n (document, painting) original m ■ **originally** adv (at first) à l'origine

originate [ə'rɪdʒɪneɪt] **1** vt être à l'origine de **2** vi (begin) prendre naissance (**in** dans); **to o. from** (of idea) émaner de

ornament ['ɔːnəmənt] n ornement m ■ **ornamental** [-'mentəl] adj ornemental

ornate [ɔː'neɪt] adj très orné

orphan ['ɔ:fən] *n* orphelin, -e *mf*

orthodox ['ɔ:θədɒks] *adj* orthodoxe

Oscar ['ɒskə(r)] *n Cin* oscar *m*

ostentatious [ɒsten'teɪʃəs] *adj* prétentieux, -euse

ostrich ['ɒstrɪtʃ] *n* autruche *f*

other ['ʌðə(r)] **1** *adj* autre; **o. doctors** d'autres médecins; **the o. one** l'autre *mf*

2 *pron* **the o.** l'autre *mf*; **(some) others** d'autres; **none o. than, no o. than** nul autre que

3 *adv* **o. than** autrement que ▪ **otherwise** *adv & conj* autrement que

ouch [aʊtʃ] *exclam* aïe!

ought [ɔ:t]

> La forme négative **ought not** s'écrit **oughtn't** en forme contractée.

v aux (**a**) *(expressing obligation, desirability)* **you o. to leave** tu devrais partir; **I o. to have done it** j'aurais dû le faire (**b**) *(expressing probability)* **it o. to be ready** ça devrait être prêt

ounce [aʊns] *n (unit of weight)* = 28,35 g, once *f*

our [aʊə(r)] *possessive adj* notre, *pl* nos

ours [aʊəz] *possessive pron* le nôtre, la nôtre, *pl* les nôtres; **this book is o.** ce livre est à nous *ou* est le nôtre; **a friend of o.** un de nos amis

ourselves [aʊə'selvz] *pron* nous-mêmes; *(reflexive and after prep)* nous; **we wash o.** nous nous lavons

oust [aʊst] *vt* évincer (**from** de)

OUT [aʊt] **1** *adv (outside)* dehors; *(not at home)* sorti; *(light, fire)* éteint; *(flower)* ouvert; *(book)* publié; **to have a day o.** sortir pour la journée; **the sun's o.** il fait soleil; **the tide's o.** la marée est basse; **you're o.** *(wrong)* tu t'es trompé; *(in game)* tu es éliminé (**of** de); **I was $10 o.** *(under)* il me manquait 10 dollars; **before the week is o.** avant la fin de la semaine; **the journey o.** l'aller *m*; **o. here** ici; **o. there** là-bas

2 *prep* **o. of** *(outside)* hors de; **to be o. of the country** être à l'étranger; **she's o. of town** elle n'est pas en ville; **to look/jump o. of the window** regarder/sauter par la fenêtre; **to drink/take/copy sth o. of sth** boire/prendre/copier qch dans qch; **made o. of wood** fait en bois; **o. of pity/love** par pitié/amour; **four o. of five** quatre sur cinq ▪ **out-of-date** *adj (expired)* périmé; *(old-fashioned)* démodé ▪ **out-of-doors** *adv* dehors ▪ **out-of-the-way** *adj (place)* isolé

outbreak ['aʊtbreɪk] *n (of war, epidemic)* début *m*; *(of violence)* flambée *f*; *(of hostilities)* déclenchement *m*

outburst ['aʊtbɜ:st] *n (of anger, joy)* explosion *f*; *(of violence)* flambée *f*

outcast ['aʊtkɑ:st] *n (social)* **o.** paria *m*

outcome ['aʊtkʌm] *n* résultat *m*, issue *f*

outcry ['aʊtkraɪ] *(pl* -ies) *n* tollé *m*

outdated [aʊt'deɪtɪd] *adj* démodé

outdo [aʊt'du:] *(pt* -did, *pp* -done) *vt* surpasser (**in** en)

outdoor ['aʊtdɔ:(r)] *adj (pool, market)* découvert ▪ **outdoors** *adv* dehors

outer ['aʊtə(r)] *adj* extérieur; **o. space** l'espace *m* intersidéral

outfit ['aʊtfɪt] *n (clothes)* ensemble *m*; **sports/ski o.** tenue *f* de sport/de ski

outgoing ['aʊtgəʊɪŋ] *adj* (**a**) *(minister)* sortant; *(mail)* en partance; **o. calls** *(on phone)* appels *mpl* vers l'extérieur (**b**) *(sociable)* liant ▪ **outgoings** *npl (expenses)* dépenses *fpl*

outgrow [aʊt'grəʊ] *(pt* -grew, *pp* -grown) *vt (habit)* passer l'âge de; **she's outgrown her jacket** sa veste est devenue trop petite pour elle

outing ['aʊtɪŋ] *n (excursion)* sortie *f*

outlast [aʊt'lɑ:st] *vt (object)* durer plus longtemps que; *(person)* survivre à

outlaw ['aʊtlɔ:] **1** *n* hors-la-loi *m inv* **2** *vt (ban)* proscrire

outlay ['aʊtleɪ] *n (expense)* dépenses *fpl*

outlet ['aʊtlet] *n (shop)* point *m* de vente; *(market for goods)* débouché *m*; *(for liquid)* sortie *f*; *(for feelings, energy)* exutoire *m*

outline ['aʊtlaɪn] **1** *n (shape)* contour

m; (of play, novel) résumé *m;* **rough o.** *(of article, plan)* esquisse *f;* **the broad** *or* **general** *or* **main o.** *(of plan, policy)* les grandes lignes **2** *vt (plan, situation)* esquisser

outlive [aʊt'lɪv] *vt* survivre à

outlook ['aʊtlʊk] *n (for future)* perspectives *fpl; (point of view)* façon *f* de voir les choses; *(of weather)* prévisions *fpl*

outmoded [aʊt'məʊdɪd] *adj* démodé

outnumber [aʊt'nʌmbə(r)] *vt* l'emporter en nombre sur

outpatient ['aʊtpeɪʃənt] *n Br* malade *mf* en consultation externe

output ['aʊtpʊt] *n (of goods)* production *f; (computer data)* données *fpl* de sortie

outrage ['aʊtreɪdʒ] **1** *n (scandal)* scandale *m; (anger)* indignation *f* (**at** face à); *(crime)* atrocité *f* **2** *vt (make indignant)* scandaliser

outrageous [aʊt'reɪdʒəs] *adj (shocking)* scandaleux, -euse; *(atrocious)* atroce

outright 1 [aʊt'raɪt] *adv (refuse)* catégoriquement; *(be killed)* sur le coup **2** ['aʊtraɪt] *adj (failure)* total; *(refusal)* catégorique; *(winner)* incontesté

outset ['aʊtset] *n* **at the o.** au début; **from the o.** dès le départ

outside 1 [aʊt'saɪd] *adv* dehors, à l'extérieur; **to go o.** sortir

2 [aʊt'saɪd] *prep* à l'extérieur de, en dehors de; *(in front of)* devant; *(apart from)* en dehors de

3 [aʊt'saɪd] *n* extérieur *m*

4 ['aʊtsaɪd] *adj* extérieur; **the o. lane** *(on road) Br* la voie de droite, *Am* la voie de gauche; **an o. chance** une petite chance

outsider [aʊt'saɪdə(r)] *n (stranger)* étranger, -ère *mf; (horse in race)* outsider *m*

outskirts ['aʊtskɜːts] *npl* banlieue *f*

outspoken [aʊt'spəʊkən] *adj (frank)* franc *(f* franche)

outstanding [aʊt'stændɪŋ] *adj* exceptionnel, -elle; *(problem, business)* en suspens; *(debt)* impayé

outstay [aʊt'steɪ] *vt* **to o. one's welcome** abuser de l'hospitalité de son hôte

outstretched [aʊt'stretʃt] *adj (arm)* tendu

outward ['aʊtwəd] *adj (sign, appearance)* extérieur; **o. journey** *or* **trip** aller *m* ▪ **outward(s)** *adv* vers l'extérieur

oval ['əʊvəl] *adj & n* ovale *(m)*

ovary ['əʊvərɪ] *(pl* -ies) *n Anat* ovaire *m*

ovation [əʊ'veɪʃən] *n* ovation *f;* **to give sb a standing o.** se lever pour applaudir qn

oven ['ʌvən] *n* four *m*

OVER ['əʊvə(r)] **1** *prep (on)* sur; *(above)* au-dessus de; *(on the other side of)* par-dessus; **the bridge o. the river** le pont qui traverse le fleuve; **to jump/ look o. sth** sauter/regarder par-dessus qch; **o. it** *(on)* dessus; *(above)* audessus; **to fight o. sth** se battre pour qch; **o. the phone** au téléphone; *Br* **o. the holidays** pendant les vacances; **o. ten days** *(more than)* plus de dix jours; **men o. sixty** les hommes de plus de soixante ans; **o. and above** en plus de; **he's o. his flu** il est remis de sa grippe

2 *adv (above)* par-dessus; **o. here** ici; **o. there** là-bas; **he's o. in Italy** il est en Italie; **she's o. from Paris** elle est venue de Paris; **to ask sb o.** inviter qn; **to be (all) o.** être terminé; **to start all o. (again)** recommencer à zéro; **a kilo or o.** *(more)* un kilo ou plus; **I have ten o.** *(left)* il m'en reste dix; **o. and o. (again)** *(often)* à plusieurs reprises; **children of five and o.** les enfants de cinq ans et plus

overall 1 ['əʊvərɔːl] *adj (measurement, length)* total; *(result)* global

2 [əʊvər'ɔːl] *adv* dans l'ensemble

3 ['əʊvərɔːl] *n (protective coat)* blouse *f; Am (boiler suit)* bleu *m* de travail ▪ **overalls** *npl Br (boiler suit)* bleu *m* de travail; *Am (dungarees)* salopette *f*

overbearing [əʊvə'beərɪŋ] *adj* autoritaire

overboard ['əʊvəbɔːd] *adv* pardessus bord

overcast [əʊvə'kɑːst] *adj* nuageux, -euse

overcharge [əʊvə'tʃɑːdʒ] *vt* to o. sb for sth faire payer qch trop cher à qn

overcoat ['əʊvəkəʊt] *n* pardessus *m*

overcome [əʊvə'kʌm] (*pt* **-came**, *pp* **-come**) *vt* (*problem, disgust*) surmonter; (*shyness, fear, enemy*) vaincre; **to be o. by grief** être accablé de chagrin

overcook [əʊvə'kʊk] *vt* faire cuire trop

overcrowded [əʊvə'kraʊdɪd] *adj* (*house, country*) surpeuplé; (*bus, train*) bondé

overdo [əʊvə'duː] (*pt* **-did**, *pp* **-done**) *vt* exagérer; (*overcook*) faire cuire trop; **to o. it** se surmener

overdose ['əʊvədəʊs] *n* overdose *f*

overdraft ['əʊvədrɑːft] *n* Fin découvert *m*

overdrawn [əʊvə'drɔːn] *adj* Fin (*account*) à découvert

overdue [əʊvə'djuː] *adj* (*train, bus*) en retard; (*bill*) impayé; (*book*) qui n'a pas été rendu

overestimate [əʊvər'estɪmeɪt] *vt* surestimer

overexcited [əʊvərɪk'saɪtɪd] *adj* surexcité

overflow 1 ['əʊvəfləʊ] *n* (*outlet*) tropplein *m* **2** [əʊvə'fləʊ] *vi* (*of river, bath*) déborder; **to be overflowing with sth** (*of town, shop, house*) regorger de qch

overgrown [əʊvə'grəʊn] *adj* (*garden, path*) envahi par la végétation

overhaul 1 ['əʊvəhɔːl] *n* révision *f* **2** [əʊvə'hɔːl] *vt* (*vehicle, schedule, text*) réviser

overhead 1 [əʊvə'hed] *adv* au-dessus **2** ['əʊvəhed] *adj* (*cable*) aérien, -enne **3** ['əʊvəhed] *n Am* = **overheads** ■ **overheads** *npl Br* (*expenses*) frais *mpl* généraux

overhear [əʊvə'hɪə(r)] (*pt & pp* **-heard**) *vt* (*conversation*) surprendre; (*person*) entendre

overheat [əʊvə'hiːt] *vi* (*of engine*) chauffer

overjoyed [əʊvə'dʒɔɪd] *adj* fou (*f* folle) de joie

overland ['əʊvəlænd] *adj & adv* par voie de terre

overlap [əʊvə'læp] **1** (*pt & pp* **-pp-**) *vt* chevaucher **2** *vi* se chevaucher

overleaf [əʊvə'liːf] *adv* au verso

overload [əʊvə'ləʊd] *vt* surcharger

overlook [əʊvə'lʊk] *vt* (**a**) (*not notice*) ne pas remarquer; (*forget*) oublier; (*disregard*) fermer les yeux sur (**b**) (*of window, house*) donner sur

overnight 1 [əʊvə'naɪt] *adv* (*during the night*) pendant la nuit; Fig (*suddenly*) du jour au lendemain; **to stay o.** passer la nuit **2** ['əʊvənaɪt] *adj* (*train, flight*) de nuit; (*stay*) d'une nuit; **o. bag** (petit) sac *m* de voyage

overpopulated [əʊvə'pɒpjʊleɪtɪd] *adj* surpeuplé

overpower [əʊvə'paʊə(r)] *vt* maîtriser ■ **overpowering** *adj* (*heat, smell*) suffocant

overpriced [əʊvə'praɪst] *adj* trop cher (*f* trop chère)

overrated [əʊvə'reɪtɪd] *adj* surfait

overreach [əʊvə'riːtʃ] *vt* **to o. one-self** trop présumer de ses forces

overreact [əʊvərɪ'ækt] *vi* réagir excessivement

override [əʊvə'raɪd] (*pt* **-rode**, *pp* **-ridden**) *vt* (*be more important than*) l'emporter sur; (*invalidate*) annuler; (*take no notice of*) passer outre à ■ **overriding** *adj* (*importance*) capital; (*factor*) prédominant

overrule [əʊvə'ruːl] *vt* (*decision*) annuler; (*objection*) rejeter

overrun [əʊvə'rʌn] (*pt* **-ran**, *pp* **-run**, *pres p* **-running**) *vt* (*invade*) envahir; (*go beyond*) dépasser

overseas 1 ['əʊvəsiːz] *adj* d'outremer; (*trade*) extérieur **2** [əʊvə'siːz] *adv* à l'étranger

oversee [əʊvə'siː] (*pt* **-saw**, *pp* **-seen**) *vt* (*work*) superviser

overshadow [əʊvə'ʃædəʊ] *vt* (*make less important*) éclipser; (*make gloomy*) assombrir

oversight ['əʊvəsaɪt] *n* oubli *m*, omission *f*

oversleep [əʊvə'sliːp] (*pt & pp* -**slept**) *vi* ne pas se réveiller à temps

overspend [əʊvə'spend] (*pt & pp* -**spent**) *vi* dépenser trop

overstate [əʊvə'steɪt] *vt* exagérer

overstay [əʊvə'steɪ] *vt* **to o. one's welcome** abuser de l'hospitalité de son hôte

overstep [əʊvə'step] (*pt & pp* -**pp**-) *vt* outrepasser; *Fig* **to o. the mark** dépasser les bornes

overt ['əʊvɜːt] *adj* manifeste

overtake [əʊvə'teɪk] (*pt* -**took**, *pp* -**taken**) **1** *vt* dépasser **2** *vi (in vehicle)* doubler, dépasser

overthrow [əʊvə'θrəʊ] (*pt* -**threw**, *pp* -**thrown**) *vt* renverser

overtime ['əʊvətaɪm] **1** *n* heures *fpl* supplémentaires **2** *adv* **to work o.** faire des heures supplémentaires

overturn [əʊvə'tɜːn] **1** *vt (chair, table, car)* renverser; *(boat)* faire chavirer; *Fig (decision)* annuler **2** *vi (of car)* capoter; *(of boat)* chavirer

overweight [əʊvə'weɪt] *adj* trop gros (*f* trop grosse)

overwhelm [əʊvə'welm] *vt (of feelings, heat)* accabler; *(enemy, opponent)* écraser; *(amaze)* bouleverser ■ **overwhelmed** *adj* **o. with** *(work, offers)*

submergé de; **o. by** *(kindness, gift)* vivement touché par ■ **overwhelming** *adj (heat, grief)* accablant; *(majority, defeat)* écrasant; *(desire)* irrésistible

overwork [əʊvə'wɜːk] **1** *n* surmenage *m* **2** *vt (person)* surcharger de travail **3** *vi* se surmener

owe [əʊ] *vt* devoir; **to o. sb sth, to o. sth to sb** devoir qch à qn ■ **owing 1** *adj* **the money o. to me** l'argent que l'on me doit **2** *prep* **o. to** à cause de

owl [aʊl] *n* hibou *m* (*pl* -**oux**)

own [əʊn] **1** *adj* propre
2 *pron* **my o.** le mien, la mienne; **a house of his o.** sa propre maison, sa maison à lui; **to do sth on one's o.** faire qch tout seul; **to be (all) on one's o.** être tout seul; **to get one's o. back (on sb)** se venger (de qn)
3 *vt (possess)* posséder; **who owns this ball?** à qui appartient cette balle?
4 *vi* **to o. up (to sth)** *(confess)* avouer (qch)

owner ['əʊnə(r)] *n* propriétaire *mf* ■ **ownership** *n* possession *f*

ox [ɒks] (*pl* **oxen** ['ɒksən]) *n* bœuf *m*

oxygen ['ɒksɪdʒən] *n* oxygène *m*; **o. mask** masque *m* à oxygène

oyster ['ɔɪstə(r)] *n* huître *f*

oz (*abbr* **ounce**) once *f*

ozone ['əʊzəʊn] *n Chem* ozone *m*; **o. layer** couche *f* d'ozone

Pp

P, p¹ [pi:] *n (letter)* P, p *m inv*

p² [pi:] *(abbr* **penny, pence**) *Br* penny *m*/pence *mpl*

pa [pɑ:] *n Fam (father)* papa *m*

pace [peɪs] **1** *n (speed)* allure *f; (step, measure)* pas *m;* **to keep p. with sb** *(follow)* suivre qn; *(in quality of work)* se maintenir à la hauteur de qn **2** *vi* **to p. up and down** faire les cent pas

pacemaker ['peɪsmeɪkə(r)] *n (for heart)* stimulateur *m* cardiaque

Pacific [pə'sɪfɪk] *adj* **the P. (Ocean)** le Pacifique, l'océan *m* Pacifique

pacifier ['pæsɪfaɪə(r)] *n Am (of baby)* tétine *f*

pacifist ['pæsɪfɪst] *n* pacifiste *mf*

pacify ['pæsɪfaɪ] *(pt & pp* **-ied**) *vt (crowd, person)* calmer

pack [pæk] **1** *n* **(a)** *(of cigarettes, washing powder)* paquet *m; (of beer)* pack *m; (of cards)* jeu *m; (of hounds, wolves)* meute *f;* **a p. of lies** un tissu de mensonges
(b) *(rucksack)* sac *m* à dos
2 *vt (fill)* remplir **(with** de); *(object into box, suitcase)* mettre; *(make into package)* empaqueter; *(crush, compress)* tasser; **to p. one's bags** faire ses valises
3 *vi (fill one's bags)* faire sa valise/ses valises

▸ **pack in** *vt sep Br Fam (stop)* arrêter; *(give up)* laisser tomber

▸ **pack into 1** *vt sep (cram)* entasser dans; *(put)* mettre dans **2** *vt insep (crowd into)* s'entasser dans

▸ **pack off** *vt sep Fam (person)* expédier

▸ **pack up 1** *vt sep (put into box)* emballer; *Fam (give up)* laisser tomber **2** *vi Fam (of machine, vehicle)* tomber en panne

package ['pækɪdʒ] **1** *n* paquet *m; (contract)* contrat *m* global; *Br* **p. deal** *or* **holiday** forfait *m (comprenant au moins transport et logement)* **2** *vt* emballer ▪ **packaging** *n (material, action)* emballage *m*

packed [pækt] *adj (bus, room)* bondé

packet ['pækɪt] *n* paquet *m; Fam* **to cost a p.** coûter les yeux de la tête

packing ['pækɪŋ] *n (material, action)* emballage *m;* **to do one's p.** faire sa valise/ses valises

pact [pækt] *n* pacte *m*

pad [pæd] **1** *n (of cotton wool)* tampon *m; (for writing)* bloc *m;* **ink(ing) p.** tampon encreur **2** *(pt & pp* **-dd-**) *vt* **to p. out** *(speech, essay)* étoffer ▪ **padded** *adj (jacket)* matelassé ▪ **padding** *n (material)* rembourrage *m; (in speech, essay)* remplissage *m*

paddle ['pædəl] **1** *n (for canoe)* pagaie *f;* **to have a p.** patauger **2** *vt* **to p. a canoe** pagayer **3** *vi (walk in water)* patauger

paddling ['pædlɪŋ] *n Br* **p. pool** *(inflatable)* piscine *f* gonflable; *(in park)* pataugeoire *f*

padlock ['pædlɒk] **1** *n* cadenas *m* **2** *vt* cadenasser

paediatrician [pi:dɪə'trɪʃən] *(Am* **pediatrician**) *n* pédiatre *mf*

page¹ [peɪdʒ] *n (of book)* page *f;* **on p. 6** à la page 6

page² [peɪdʒ] **1** *n* **p. (boy)** *(in hotel)* groom *m* **2** *vt* **to p. sb** faire appeler qn; *(by electronic device)* biper qn ▪ **pager** *n* récepteur *m* d'appel

paid [peɪd] **1** *pt & pp of* **pay** **2** *adj (person, work)* rémunéré

pain [peɪn] *n (physical)* douleur *f; (emotional)* peine *f;* **to have a p. in one's arm** avoir une douleur au bras;

to go to *or* **take (great) pains to do sth** se donner du mal pour faire qch; *Fam* **to be a p. (in the neck)** être casse-pieds ■ **painful** *adj (physically)* douloureux, -euse; *(emotionally)* pénible ■ **painless** *adj (not painful)* indolore

painkiller ['peɪnkɪlə(r)] *n* calmant *m*

painstaking ['peɪnzteɪkɪŋ] *adj* minutieux, -euse

paint [peɪnt] **1** *n* peinture *f* **2** *vt* peindre; **to p. sth blue** peindre qch en bleu **3** *vi* peindre ■ **painter** *n* peintre *m; Br* **p. and decorator,** *Am* **(house) p.** peintre-tapissier *m* ■ **painting** *n (activity)* la peinture; *(picture)* tableau *m*, peinture *f*

paintbrush ['peɪntbrʌʃ] *n* pinceau *m*

paintwork ['peɪntwɜːk] *n (of building, vehicle)* peinture *f*

pair [peə(r)] *n* paire *f*; **a p. of shorts/ trousers** un short/pantalon

pajamas [pə'dʒɑːməz] *npl Am* = **pyjamas**

Pakistan [pɑːkɪ'stɑːn] *n* le Pakistan ■ **Pakistani 1** *adj* pakistanais **2** *n* Pakistanais, -e *mf*

pal [pæl] *n Fam* copain *m*, copine *f*

palace ['pælɪs] *n* palais *m*

pale [peɪl] **1** (**-er, -est**) *adj* pâle **2** *vi* pâlir

Palestine ['pæləstaɪn] *n* la Palestine ■ **Palestinian** [-'stɪnɪən] **1** *adj* palestinien, -enne **2** *n* Palestinien, -enne *mf*

palette ['pælɪt] *n (of artist)* palette *f*

palm¹ [pɑːm] *n (of hand)* paume *f*

palm² [pɑːm] *n* **p. (tree)** palmier *m*

pamper ['pæmpə(r)] *vt* dorloter

pamphlet ['pæmflɪt] *n* brochure *f*

pan [pæn] *n (saucepan)* casserole *f*; *(for frying)* poêle *f*

Panama ['pænəmɑː] *n* **the P. Canal** le canal de Panama

pancake ['pænkeɪk] *n* crêpe *f*; **P. Day** mardi *m* gras

panda ['pændə] *n* panda *m*

pandemonium [pændɪ'məʊnɪəm] *n (confusion)* chaos *m; (uproar)* vacarme *m*

pander ['pændə(r)] *vi* **to p. to sb/sth** flatter qn/qch

pane [peɪn] *n* vitre *f*

panel ['pænəl] *n* (**a**) *(of door)* panneau *m;* **(instrument) p.** *(in aircraft, vehicle)* tableau *m* de bord (**b**) *(of judges)* jury *m; (of experts)* comité *m; (of TV or radio guests)* invités *mpl*

panic ['pænɪk] **1** *n* panique *f* **2** *(pt & pp* **-ck-)** *vi* paniquer

panorama [pænə'rɑːmə] *n* panorama *m*

pansy ['pænzɪ] *(pl* **-ies**) *n (flower)* pensée *f*

pant [pænt] *vi* haleter

pantomime ['pæntəmaɪm] *n Br (show)* = spectacle de Noël

pantry ['pæntrɪ] *(pl* **-ies**) *n (larder)* garde-manger *m inv*

pants [pænts] *npl (underwear)* slip *m; Am (trousers)* pantalon *m*

pantyhose ['pæntɪhəʊz] *n Am (tights)* collant *m*

paper ['peɪpə(r)] **1** *n* papier *m; (newspaper)* journal *m; (wallpaper)* papier *m* peint; *(exam)* épreuve *f* écrite; *(student's exercise)* copie *f; (scholarly study, report)* article *m;* **a piece of p.** un bout de papier; **to put sth down on p.** mettre qch par écrit; **papers** *(documents)* papiers **2** *adj (bag)* en papier; *(cup, plate)* en carton; *Br* **p. shop** marchand *m* de journaux; **p. towel** essuie-tout *m inv* **3** *vt (room, wall)* tapisser ■ **paperback** *n* livre *m* de poche ■ **paperclip** *n* trombone *m* ■ **paperweight** *n* presse-papiers *m inv* ■ **paperwork** *n (in office)* écritures *fpl; Pej (red tape)* paperasserie *f*

par [pɑː(r)] *n (in golf)* par *m;* **on a p.** au même niveau (**with** que)

paracetamol [pærə'siːtəmɒl] *n* paracétamol *m*

parachute ['pærəʃuːt] *n* parachute *m;* **p. jump** saut *m* en parachute

parade [pə'reɪd] **1** *n* (**a**) *(procession)* défilé *m* (**b**) *Br (street)* avenue *f* **2** *vt Fig (wealth, knowledge)* faire étalage de **3**

vi (of troops) défiler; **to p. about** *(of person)* se pavaner

paradise ['pærədaɪs] *n* paradis *m*

paradoxically [pærə'dɒksɪklɪ] *adv* paradoxalement

paraffin ['pærəfɪn] *n Br* pétrole *m* lampant; *Br* **p. lamp** lampe *f* à pétrole

paragliding ['pærəglaɪdɪŋ] *n* parapente *m*; **to go p.** faire du parapente

paragraph ['pærəgrɑːf] *n* paragraphe *m*

paralegal ['pærəliːgəl] *n* assistant, -e *mf (d'un avocat)*

parallel ['pærələl] **1** *adj Math* parallèle (**with** *or* **to** à); *Fig (comparable)* semblable (**with** *or* **to** à) **2** *n Math (line)* parallèle *f*; *Fig (comparison)* & *Geog* parallèle *m*

paralysis [pə'ræləsɪs] *(pl* **-yses** [-əsiːz]*)* *n* paralysie *f* ■ **paralyse** ['pærəlaɪz] *(Am* **paralyze***)* *vt* paralyser

paramedic [pærə'medɪk] *n* auxiliaire *mf* médical(e)

paranoid ['pærənɔɪd] *adj* paranoïaque

paraphrase ['pærəfreɪz] *vt* paraphraser

parasite ['pærəsaɪt] *n (person, organism)* parasite *m*

parasol ['pærəsɒl] *n (over table, on beach)* parasol *m*; *(lady's)* ombrelle *f*

parcel ['pɑːsəl] **1** *n* colis *m*, paquet *m* **2** *(Br* **-ll-**, *Am* **-l-***)* *vt* **to p. sth up** empaqueter

parched [pɑːtʃt] *adj* **to be p.** *(of person)* être assoiffé

pardon ['pɑːdən] **1** *n (forgiveness)* pardon *m*; *(in law)* grâce *f*; **I beg your p.** *(apologizing)* je vous prie de m'excuser; **I beg your p.?** *(not hearing)* pardon? **2** *vt (in law)* gracier; **to p. sb (for sth)** pardonner (qch) à qn; **p. (me)!** *(sorry)* pardon!

parent ['peərənt] *n (father)* père *m*; *(mother)* mère *f*; **parents** parents *mpl*

Paris ['pærɪs] *n* Paris *m ou f* ■ **Parisian** [pə'rɪzɪən, *Am* pə'riːʒən] **1** *adj* parisien, -enne **2** *n* Parisien, -enne *mf*

parish ['pærɪʃ] *n (religious)* paroisse *f*; *(civil)* ≃ commune *f*

park¹ [pɑːk] *n (garden)* parc *m*

park² [pɑːk] **1** *vt (vehicle)* garer **2** *vi (of vehicle)* se garer; *(remain parked)* stationner ■ **parking** *n* stationnement *m*; **'no p.'** 'défense de stationner'; *Am* **p. lot** parking *m*; **p. meter** parcmètre *m*; **p. place** *or* **space** place *f* de parking; **p. ticket** contravention *f*

parliament ['pɑːləmənt] *n* parlement *m*

parody ['pærədɪ] **1** *(pl* **-ies***)* *n* parodie *f* **2** *(pt & pp* **-ied***)* *vt* parodier

parole [pə'rəʊl] *n* **to be (out) on p.** être en liberté conditionnelle

parrot ['pærət] *n* perroquet *m*

parsley ['pɑːslɪ] *n* persil *m*

parsnip ['pɑːsnɪp] *n* panais *m*

parson ['pɑːsən] *n* pasteur *m*

part¹ [pɑːt] **1** *n* partie *f*; *(quantity in mixture)* mesure *f*; *(of machine)* pièce *f*; *(of serial)* épisode *m*; *(role in play, film)* rôle *m*; *Am (in hair)* raie *f*; **to take p.** participer (**in** à); **to be a p. of sth** faire partie de qch; **for the most p.** dans l'ensemble; **on the p. of...** de la part de...; **for my p.** pour ma part **2** *adv (partly)* en partie; **p. silk, p. cotton** soie et coton

part² [pɑːt] **1** *vt (separate)* séparer; **to p. one's hair** se faire une raie **2** *vi (of friends)* se quitter; *(of married couple)* se séparer; **to p. with sth** se défaire de qch

partial ['pɑːʃəl] *adj (not total)* partiel, -elle; *(biased)* partial (**towards** envers); **to be p. to sth** avoir un faible pour qch

participate [pɑː'tɪsɪpeɪt] *vi* participer (**in** à) ■ **participant** *n* participant, -e *mf* ■ **participation** *n* participation *f*

particular [pə'tɪkjʊlə(r)] **1** *adj (specific, special)* particulier, -ère; *(exacting)* méticuleux, -euse; **this p. book** ce livre en particulier; **to be p. about sth** faire très attention à qch **2** *n* **in p.** en particulier ■ **particularly** *adv* particulièrement ■ **particulars** *npl (details)* détails *mpl*; **to take down sb's p.** noter les coordonnées de qn

parting ['pɑːtɪŋ] *n Br (in hair)* raie *f*

partition [pɑː'tɪʃən] **1** *(of room)*

cloison *f* 2 *vt* **to p. sth off** cloisonner qch

partly ['pɑːtlɪ] *adv* en partie; **p. English, p. French** moitié anglais, moitié français

partner ['pɑːtnə(r)] *n (in game)* partenaire *mf*; *(in business)* associé, -e *mf*; *(in relationship)* compagnon *m*, compagne *f*; *(dancing)* **p.** cavalier, -ère *mf* ■ **partnership** *n* association *f*; **in p. with** en association avec

partridge ['pɑːtrɪdʒ] *n* perdrix *f*

part-time ['pɑːt'taɪm] *adj & adv* à temps partiel

party ['pɑːtɪ] *(pl* -ies*) n* (a) *(gathering)* fête *f*; **to have** *or* **throw a p.** donner une fête (b) *(group)* groupe *m*; *(political)* parti *m*; *(in contract, lawsuit)* partie *f*

pass¹ [pɑːs] *n (over mountains)* col *m*

pass² [pɑːs] *n (entry permit)* laissez-passer *m inv*; *(for travel)* carte *f* d'abonnement; *(in sport)* passe *f*; **p. mark** *(in exam)* moyenne *f*

pass³ [pɑːs] **1** *vt (move, give)* passer (**to** à); *(go past)* passer devant; *(vehicle, runner)* dépasser; *(exam)* être reçu à; *(law)* voter; **to p. sb** *(in street)* croiser qn; **to p. the time** passer le temps; **to p. sentence** *(of judge)* prononcer le verdict
2 *vi (go past, go away)* passer (**to** à; **through** par); *(in exam)* avoir la moyenne; *(of time)* passer
▸ **pass away** *vi* décéder
▸ **pass by 1** *vt insep (building)* passer devant; **to p. by sb** *(in street)* croiser qn **2** *vi* passer à côté
▸ **pass off** *vt sep* **to p. oneself off as sb** se faire passer pour qn
▸ **pass on** *vt sep (message, illness)* transmettre (**to** à)
▸ **pass out 1** *vt sep (hand out)* distribuer **2** *vi (faint)* s'évanouir
▸ **pass over** *vt insep (ignore)* passer sur
▸ **pass round** *vt sep (cakes, document)* faire passer; *(hand out)* distribuer
▸ **pass through** *vi* passer
▸ **pass up** *vt sep (opportunity)* laisser passer

passable ['pɑːsəbəl] *adj (not bad)* passable

passage ['pæsɪdʒ] *n* (a) *(way through)* passage *m*; *(corridor)* couloir *m*; **with the p. of time** avec le temps (b) *(of text)* passage *m*

passbook ['pɑːsbʊk] *n* livret *m* de caisse d'épargne

passenger ['pæsɪndʒə(r)] *n* passager, -ère *mf*; *(on train)* voyageur, -euse *mf*

passer-by [pɑːsə'baɪ] *(pl* **passers-by***) n* passant, -e *mf*

passing ['pɑːsɪŋ] **1** *adj (vehicle)* qui passe **2** *n (of time)* écoulement *m*; **in p.** en passant

passion ['pæʃən] *n* passion *f*; **to have a p. for sth** adorer qch ■ **passionate** *adj* passionné

passive ['pæsɪv] **1** *adj* passif, -ive **2** *n (in grammar)* passif *m*; **in the p.** au passif

passport ['pɑːspɔːt] *n* passeport *m*; **p. photo** photo *f* d'identité

password ['pɑːswɜːd] *n* mot *m* de passe

past [pɑːst] **1** *n* passé *m*; **in the p.** autrefois
2 *adj (gone by)* passé; *(former)* ancien, -enne; **these p. months** ces derniers mois; **in the p. tense** au passé
3 *prep (in front of)* devant; *(after)* après; *(beyond)* au-delà de; **it's p. four o'clock** il est quatre heures passées
4 *adv* devant; **to go p.** passer

pasta ['pæstə] *n* pâtes *fpl*

paste [peɪst] **1** *n* (a) *(mixture)* pâte *f*; *(of meat)* pâté *m* (b) *(glue)* colle *f* **2** *vt* coller; **to p. sth up** coller qch

pastel [*Br* 'pæstəl, *Am* pæ'stel] *n* pastel *m*

pasteurized ['pæstʃəraɪzd] *adj* **p. milk** lait *m* pasteurisé

pastille [*Br* 'pæstɪl, *Am* pæ'stiːl] *n* pastille *f*

pastime ['pɑːstaɪm] *n* passe-temps *m inv*

pastor ['pɑːstə(r)] *n Rel* pasteur *m*

pastry ['peɪstrɪ] *(pl* -ies*) n (dough)* pâte *f*; *(cake)* pâtisserie *f*

pasture ['pɑːstʃə(r)] n pré m, pâture f

pasty ['pæstɪ] (pl -ies) n (pie) feuilleté m

pat [pæt] (pt & pp -tt-) vt (tap) tapoter; (animal) caresser

patch [pætʃ] 1 n (for clothes) pièce f, (over eye) bandeau m; (of colour) tache f; (of ice) plaque f; Fig **to be going through a bad p.** traverser une mauvaise passe 2 vt **to p. (up)** (clothing) rapiécer; **to p. things up** (after argument) se raccommoder

patchwork ['pætʃwɜːk] n patchwork m

patchy ['pætʃɪ] (-ier, -iest) adj inégal

patent ['peɪtənt, 'pætənt] 1 n brevet m d'invention 2 vt (faire) breveter ■ **patently** adv manifestement

paternal [pə'tɜːnəl] adj paternel, -elle

path [pɑːθ] (pl -s [pɑːðz]) n chemin m; (narrow) sentier m; (in park) allée f; (of river) cours m; (of bullet) trajectoire f

pathetic [pə'θetɪk] adj pitoyable

pathway ['pɑːθweɪ] n sentier m

patience ['peɪʃəns] n (a) (quality) patience f; **to lose p.** perdre patience (**with sb** avec qn) (b) Br (card game) **to play p.** faire une réussite

patient ['peɪʃənt] 1 adj patient 2 n patient, -e mf ■ **patiently** adv patiemment

patio ['pætɪəʊ] (pl -os) n patio m

patriot ['pætrɪət, 'peɪtrɪət] n patriote mf ■ **patriotic** [-rɪ'ɒtɪk, peɪtrɪ'ɒtɪk] adj (views, speech) patriotique; (person) patriote

patrol [pə'trəʊl] 1 n patrouille f; **to be on p.** être de patrouille; **p. car** voiture f de police 2 (pt & pp -ll-) vt patrouiller dans 3 vi patrouiller ■ **patrolman** (pl -men) n Am (policeman) agent m de police

patron ['peɪtrən] n (of arts) protecteur, -trice mf; (of charity) patron, -onne mf; (customer) client, -e mf; Rel **p. saint** patron, -onne mf

patronize [Br 'pætrənaɪz, Am 'peɪtrənaɪz] vt (be condescending towards) traiter avec condescendance ■ **patronizing** adj condescendant

patter ['pætə(r)] n (of footsteps) petit bruit m; (of rain) crépitement m

pattern ['pætən] n (design) dessin m, motif m; (in sewing) patron m; (in knitting) & Fig (norm) modèle m; (tendency) tendance f

paunch [pɔːntʃ] n ventre m

pause [pɔːz] 1 n pause f; (in conversation) silence m 2 vi (stop) faire une pause; (hesitate) hésiter

pave [peɪv] vt (road) paver (**with** de); Fig **to p. the way for sth** ouvrir la voie à qch ■ **paving** n **p. stone** pavé m

pavement ['peɪvmənt] n Br (beside road) trottoir m; Am (roadway) chaussée f

pavilion [pə'vɪljən] n pavillon m

paw [pɔː] n patte f

pawn¹ [pɔːn] n (chess piece) pion m

pawn² [pɔːn] vt mettre en gage ■ **pawnbroker** n prêteur, -euse mf sur gages ■ **pawnshop** n mont-de-piété m

pay [peɪ] 1 n paie f, salaire m; (of soldier) solde f; **p. rise** augmentation f de salaire; Br **p. slip,** Am **p. stub** fiche f de paie

2 (pt & pp **paid**) vt (person, money, bill) payer; (sum, deposit) verser; (yield) (of investment) rapporter; **I paid £5 for it** je l'ai payé 5 livres; **to p. sb to do sth** or **for doing sth** payer qn pour qu'il fasse qch; **to p. sb for sth** payer qch à qn

3 vi payer ■ **payable** adj (due) payable; **to make a cheque p. to sb** libeller un chèque à l'ordre de qn ■ **payment** n paiement m; (of deposit) versement m; **on p. of 20 euros** moyennant 20 euros ■ **payphone** n téléphone m public

▸ **pay back** vt sep (person, loan) rembourser; Fig **I'll p. you back for this!** tu me le paieras!

▸ **pay for** vt insep payer

▸ **pay in** vt sep (cheque, money) verser sur un compte

▸ **pay off 1** vt sep (debt) rembourser; (in instalments) rembourser par acomptes 2 vi (of work, effort) porter ses fruits

▸ **pay out** vt sep (spend) dépenser

▸ **pay up** vi payer

PC [pi:'si:] (**a**) (*abbr* **personal compu-ter**) PC *m*, micro *m* (**b**) (*abbr* **politically correct**) politiquement correct

PE [pi:'i:] (*abbr* **physical education**) *n* EPS *f*

pea [pi:] *n* pois *m*; **peas,** *Br* **garden** *or* **green peas** petits pois *mpl*

peace [pi:s] *n* paix *f*; **p. of mind** tran-quillité *f* d'esprit; **at p.** en paix (**with** avec); **I'd like some p. and quiet** j'ai-merais un peu de silence

peaceful ['pi:sfəl] *adj* (*calm*) paisible; (*non-violent*) pacifique

peach [pi:tʃ] *n* (*fruit*) pêche *f*

peacock ['pi:kɒk] *n* paon *m*

peak [pi:k] **1** *n* (*mountain top*) sommet *m*; (*mountain*) pic *m*; (*of cap*) visière *f*; *Fig* (*of fame, success*) apogée *m* **2** *adj* (*hours, period*) de pointe

peal [pi:l] **1** *n* (*of bells*) sonnerie *f*; **peals of laughter** éclats *mpl* de rire **2** *vi* **to p. (out)** (*of bells*) sonner à toute volée

peanut ['pi:nʌt] *n* cacah(o)uète *f*; **p. butter** beurre *m* de cacah(o)uètes

pear [peə(r)] *n* poire *f*

pearl [pɜ:l] *n* perle *f*; **p. necklace** col-lier *m* de perles

peasant ['pezənt] *n* & *adj* paysan, -anne (*mf*)

peat [pi:t] *n* tourbe *f*

pebble ['pebəl] *n* (*stone*) caillou *m* (*pl* -oux); (*on beach*) galet *m*

pecan ['pi:kən] *n* (*nut*) noix *f* de pécan

peck [pek] *vti* **to p. (at)** (*grain*) picorer; (*person*) donner un coup de bec à

peckish ['pekiʃ] *adj Br* **to be p.** avoir un petit creux

peculiar [pɪ'kju:lɪə(r)] *adj* (*strange*) bizarre; (*special, characteristic*) parti-culier, -ère (**to** à)

pedal ['pedəl] **1** *n* pédale *f*; **p. bin** pou-belle *f* à pédale **2** (*Br* -**ll**-, *Am* -**l**-) *vt* **to p. a bicycle** être à bicyclette **3** *vi* pédaler

pedantic [pɪ'dæntɪk] *adj* pédant

peddle ['pedəl] *vt* (*goods, ideas*) col-porter; (*drugs*) faire du trafic de ▪ **ped-dler** *n* (*door-to-door*) colporteur, -euse *mf*; (*in street*) camelot *m*; (**drug**) **p.** tra-

fiquant, -e *mf* de drogue

pedestal ['pedɪstəl] *n* piédestal *m*

pedestrian [pə'destrɪən] *n* piéton *m*; *Br* **p. crossing** passage *m* pour piétons; *Br* **p. precinct** zone *f* piétonnière

pediatrician [pi:dɪə'trɪʃən] *n Am* = **paediatrician**

pedigree ['pedɪgri:] **1** *n* (*of animal*) pedigree *m*; (*of person*) ascendance *f* **2** *adj* (*animal*) de race

pedlar ['pedlə(r)] *n* (*door-to-door*) col-porteur, -euse *mf*; (*in street*) camelot *m*

pee [pi:] *Fam* **1** *n* **to go for a p.** faire pipi **2** *vi* faire pipi

peek [pi:k] *vi* jeter un coup d'œil furtif (**at** à)

peel [pi:l] **1** *n* (*of vegetable, fruit*) peau *f*; (*of orange, lemon*) écorce *f* **2** *vt* (*vegeta-ble*) éplucher; (*fruit*) peler; **to p. sth off** (*label*) décoller qch **3** *vi* (*of skin, person*) peler; (*of paint*) s'écailler ▪ **peeler** *n* (**potato**) **p.** épluche-légumes *m inv* ▪ **peelings** *npl* épluchures *fpl*

peep [pi:p] *vi* jeter un coup d'œil furtif (**at** à); **to p. out** se montrer

peer [pɪə(r)] **1** *n* (*equal*) & *Br* (*noble-man*) pair *m* **2** *vi* **to p. at sb/sth** scru-ter qn/qch du regard

peeved [pi:vd] *adj* en rogne

peevish ['pi:vɪʃ] *adj* irritable

peg [peg] *n* (*for coat, hat*) patère *f*; (*for drying clothes*) pince *f* à linge; (*for tent*) piquet *m*; (*wooden pin*) cheville *f*; *Br* **to buy sth off the p.** acheter qch en prêt-à-porter

pejorative [pɪ'dʒɒrətɪv] *adj* péjoratif, -ive

pelican ['pelɪkən] *n* pélican *m*; *Br* **p. crossing** feux *mpl* à commande ma-nuelle

pelt [pelt] **1** *vt* bombarder (**with** de) **2** *vi Fam* **it's pelting down** il pleut à verse

pelvis ['pelvɪs] *n Anat* pelvis *m*

pen¹ [pen] *n* (*for writing*) stylo *m*; **p. friend** *or* **pal** correspondant, -e *mf*

pen² [pen] *n* (*for sheep, cattle*) parc *m*

penal ['pi:nəl] *adj* (*code, law*) pénal ▪ **penalize** *vt* pénaliser

penalty ['penəltɪ] (*pl* -ies) *n (prison sentence)* peine *f; (fine)* amende *f; (in football)* penalty *m; (in rugby)* pénalité *f*

pence [pens] *pl of* **penny**

pencil ['pensəl] **1** *n* crayon *m;* **in p.** au crayon; **p. sharpener** taille-crayon *m* **2** (*Br* -ll-, *Am* -l-) *vt Fig* **to p. sth in** fixer qch provisoirement

pendant ['pendənt] *n (around neck)* pendentif *m*

pending ['pendɪŋ] **1** *adj (matter, business)* en attente **2** *prep (until)* en attendant

pendulum ['pendjʊləm] *n* pendule *m*

penetrate ['penɪtreɪt] **1** *vt (substance)* pénétrer; *(mystery)* percer **2** *vti* **to p. (into)** *(forest)* pénétrer dans; *(group)* s'infiltrer dans ▪ **penetrating** *adj (mind, cold)* pénétrant

penguin ['peŋgwɪn] *n* manchot *m*

penicillin [penɪ'sɪlɪn] *n* pénicilline *f*

peninsula [pə'nɪnsjʊlə] *n* presqu'île *f; (larger)* péninsule *f*

penis ['piːnɪs] *n* pénis *m*

penitentiary [penɪ'tenʃərɪ] (*pl* -ies) *n Am* prison *f* centrale

penknife ['pennaɪf] (*pl* -knives) *n* canif *m*

penniless ['penɪləs] *adj* sans le sou

penny ['penɪ] *n* (a) (*pl* -ies) *Br (coin)* penny *m; Am & Can (cent)* cent *m; Fig* **I don't have a p.** je n'ai pas un sou (b) (*pl* pence) *Br (value, currency)* penny *m*

pension ['penʃən] **1** *n* pension *f;* **(retirement) p.** retraite *f; Br* **old age p.** pension *f* de vieillesse **2** *vt* **to p. sb off** mettre qn à la retraite ▪ **pensioner** *n* retraité, -e *mf; Br* **old age p.** retraité, -e *mf*

pent-up ['pentʌp] *adj (feelings)* refoulé

penultimate [pɪ'nʌltɪmət] *adj* avant-dernier, -ère

people ['piːpəl] **1** *n (nation)* peuple *m* **2** *npl (as group)* gens *mpl; (as individuals)* personnes *fpl;* **the p.** *(citizens)* le peuple; **two p.** deux personnes; **English p.** les Anglais *mpl;* **p. think that...** les gens pensent que...

pepper ['pepə(r)] *n* poivre *m; (vegetable)* poivron *m;* **p. mill** moulin *m* à poivre

peppermint ['pepəmɪnt] *n (flavour)* menthe *f; (sweet)* bonbon *m* à la menthe

per [pɜː(r)] *prep* par; **p. annum** par an; **50 pence p. kilo** 50 pence le kilo; **40 km p. hour** 40 km à l'heure

perceive [pə'siːv] *vt (see, hear)* percevoir; *(notice)* remarquer (**that** que)

percentage [pə'sentɪdʒ] *n* pourcentage *m* ▪ **percent** *adv* pour cent

perception [pə'sepʃən] *n* perception *f* (**of** de)

perceptive [pə'septɪv] *adj (person)* perspicace; *(study, remark)* pertinent

perch [pɜːtʃ] **1** *n (for bird)* perchoir *m* **2** *vi* se percher

percolator ['pɜːkəleɪtə(r)] *n* cafetière *f* à pression; *(in café, restaurant)* percolateur *m*

perennial [pə'renɪəl] **1** *adj (plant)* vivace; *(worry)* perpétuel, -elle **2** *n* plante *f* vivace

perfect 1 ['pɜːfɪkt] *adj* parfait; *Gram* **p. tense** parfait *m* **2** ['pɜːfɪkt] *n Gram* parfait *m* **3** [pə'fekt] *vt* parfaire; **to p. one's French** parfaire ses connaissances en français

perfection [pə'fekʃən] *n (quality)* perfection *f* ▪ **perfectly** *adv* parfaitement

perforate ['pɜːfəreɪt] *vt* perforer ▪ **perforation** *n* perforation *f*

perform [pə'fɔːm] **1** *vt (task, miracle)* accomplir; *(duty, function)* remplir; *(play, piece of music)* jouer **2** *vi (act, play)* jouer; *(sing)* chanter; *(dance)* danser; **to p. well/badly** *(in job)* bien/mal s'en tirer ▪ **performance** *n* (a) *(of play)* représentation *f* (b) *(of actor, musician)* interprétation *f; (of athlete)* performance *f; (of company)* résultats *mpl*

performer [pə'fɔːmə(r)] *n (entertainer)* artiste *mf; (in play, of music)* interprète *mf* (**of** de)

perfume ['pɜːfjuːm] *n* parfum *m*

perhaps [pə'hæps] *adv* peut-être; **p. not/so** peut-être que non/que oui; **p. she'll come** peut-être qu'elle viendra, elle viendra peut-être

peril ['perɪl] *n* péril *m*, danger *m*
period ['pɪərɪəd] **1** *n* (a) *(stretch of time)* période *f; (historical)* époque *f; (school lesson)* heure *f* de cours; **(monthly) period(s)** *(of woman)* règles *fpl* (b) *Am (full stop)* point *m;* **I refuse, p.!** je refuse, un point c'est tout! **2** *adj (furniture, costume)* d'époque ▪ **periodical** [-rɪ'ɒdɪkəl] *n (magazine)* périodique *m* ▪ **periodically** [-rɪ'ɒdɪklɪ] *adv* périodiquement
peripheral [pə'rɪfərəl] *n Comptr* périphérique *m*
perish ['perɪʃ] *vi (of person)* périr
perishable ['perɪʃəbəl] *adj (food)* périssable
perjury ['pɜːdʒərɪ] *n* faux témoignage *m*
perk [pɜːk] **1** *n Br Fam (in job)* avantage *m* **2** *vt* **to p. sb up** *(revive)* ragaillardir qn; *(cheer up)* remonter le moral à qn **3** *vi* **to p. up** reprendre du poil de la bête
perm [pɜːm] **1** *n* permanente *f* **2** *vt* **to have one's hair permed** se faire faire une permanente
permanent ['pɜːmənənt] *adj* permanent; *(address)* fixe ▪ **permanently** *adv* à titre permanent
permissible [pə'mɪsəbəl] *adj* permis
permission [pə'mɪʃən] *n* permission *f*, autorisation *f* **(to do** de faire); **to give sb p. (to do sth)** donner la permission à qn (de faire qch)
permissive [pə'mɪsɪv] *adj* permissif, -ive
permit 1 ['pɜːmɪt] *n* permis *m* **2** [pə'mɪt] *(pt & pp* **-tt-)** *vt* permettre **(sb to do** à qn de faire)
perpendicular [pɜːpən'dɪkjʊlə(r)] *adj & n* perpendiculaire *(f)*
perpetrate ['pɜːpɪtreɪt] *vt (crime)* perpétrer ▪ **perpetrator** *n* auteur *m*
perpetual [pə'petʃʊəl] *adj* perpétuel, -elle ▪ **perpetuate** [-ʊeɪt] *vt* perpétuer
perplexed [pə'plekst] *adj* perplexe
persecute ['pɜːsɪkjuːt] *vt* persécuter ▪ **persecution** *n* persécution *f*
persevere [pɜːsɪ'vɪə(r)] *vi* persévérer **(with** dans) ▪ **perseverance** *n* persévérance *f*
Persian ['pɜːʃən, 'pɜːʒən] **1** *adj (carpet, cat)* persan; **the P. Gulf** le golfe Persique **2** *n (language)* persan *m*
persist [pə'sɪst] *vi* persister **(in doing** à faire; **in sth** dans qch) ▪ **persistent** *adj (person)* tenace; *(smell, rumours)* persistant; *(attempts)* continuel, -elle
person ['pɜːsən] *n* personne *f;* **in p.** en personne
personal ['pɜːsənəl] *adj* personnel, -elle; *(friend)* intime; *(life)* privé; *(indiscreet)* indiscret, -ète; **p. computer** ordinateur *m* individuel; **p. organizer** agenda *m* électronique; **p. stereo** baladeur *m*
personality [pɜːsə'nælɪtɪ] *(pl* **-ies)** *n (character, famous person)* personnalité *f*
personally ['pɜːsənəlɪ] *adv* personnellement; *(in person)* en personne
personify [pə'sɒnɪfaɪ] *(pt & pp* **-ied)** *vt* personnifier
personnel [pɜːsə'nel] *n (staff)* personnel *m*
perspective [pə'spektɪv] *n* perspective *f; Fig* **in p.** sous son vrai jour
perspire [pə'spaɪə(r)] *vi* transpirer
persuade [pə'sweɪd] *vt* persuader **(sb to do** qn de faire) ▪ **persuasion** *n* persuasion *f; (creed)* religion *f* ▪ **persuasive** *adj (person, argument)* persuasif, -ive
pertain [pə'teɪn] *vi Formal* **to p. to** *(relate)* se rapporter à
pertinent ['pɜːtɪnənt] *adj* pertinent
perturb [pə'tɜːb] *vt* troubler
Peru [pə'ruː] *n* le Pérou
peruse [pə'ruːz] *vt Formal (read carefully)* lire attentivement; *(skim through)* parcourir
pervade [pə'veɪd] *vt* imprégner ▪ **pervasive** *adj (feeling)* général; *(influence)* omniprésent
perverse [pə'vɜːs] *adj (awkward)* contrariant ▪ **perversion** [-ʃən, *Am* -ʒən] *n (sexual)* perversion *f*
pervert 1 ['pɜːvɜːt] *n (sexual deviant)*

pervers, -e *mf* 2 [pə'vɜːt] *vt* pervertir; *(mind)* corrompre

pessimism ['pesɪmɪzəm] *n* pessimisme *m* ▪ **pessimistic** *adj* pessimiste

pest [pest] *n (animal)* animal *m* nuisible; *(insect)* insecte *m* nuisible; *Fam (person)* plaie *f*

pester ['pestə(r)] *vt* tourmenter; **to p. sb to do sth** harceler qn pour qu'il fasse qch

pesticide ['pestɪsaɪd] *n* pesticide *m*

pet [pet] 1 *n* animal *m* domestique; *(favourite person)* chouchou, -oute *mf*; *(term of address)* petit chou *m* 2 *adj (dog, cat)* domestique; *(favourite)* favori, -ite; **p. shop** animalerie *f* 3 *(pt & pp -tt-) vt (fondle)* caresser 4 *vi Fam* se peloter

petal ['petəl] *n* pétale *m*

peter ['piːtə(r)] *vi* **to p. out** *(of conversation)* tarir; *(of scheme)* n'aboutir à rien; *(of path, stream)* disparaître

petition [pə'tɪʃən] *n (signatures)* pétition *f*; *(request to court of law)* requête *f*

petrify ['petrɪfaɪ] *(pt & pp -ied) vt* pétrifier

petrol ['petrəl] *n Br* essence *f*; **p. station** station-service *f*; **p. tank** réservoir *m* d'essence

petticoat ['petɪkəʊt] *n* jupon *m*

petty ['petɪ] *(-ier, -iest) adj (trivial)* insignifiant; *(mean)* mesquin; **p. cash** petite caisse *f*

pew [pjuː] *n* banc *m* d'église

phantom ['fæntəm] *n* fantôme *m*

pharmacy ['fɑːməsɪ] *(pl -ies) n* pharmacie *f* ▪ **pharmacist** *n* pharmacien, -enne *mf*

phase [feɪz] 1 *n* phase *f* 2 *vt* **to p. sth in/out** introduire/supprimer qch progressivement

PhD [piːeɪtʃ'diː] *(abbr* Doctor of Philosophy) *n (degree)* doctorat *m* (in de); *(person)* docteur *m*

phenomenon [fɪ'nɒmɪnən] *(pl -ena [-ɪnə]) n* phénomène *m* ▪ **phenomenal** *adj* phénoménal

Philippines ['fɪlɪpiːnz] *npl* **the P.** les Philippines *fpl*

philistine ['fɪlɪstaɪn] *n* béotien, -enne *mf*, philistin *m*

philosopher [fɪ'lɒsəfə(r)] *n* philosophe *mf*

philosophical [fɪlə'sɒfɪkəl] *adj* philosophique; *Fig (stoical, resigned)* philosophe

philosophy [fɪ'lɒsəfɪ] *(pl -ies) n* philosophie *f*

phlegm [flem] *n (in throat)* glaires *fpl*

phobia ['fəʊbɪə] *n* phobie *f*

phone [fəʊn] 1 *n* téléphone *m*; **to be on the p.** *(be talking)* être au téléphone; *(have a telephone)* avoir le téléphone; **p. call** coup *m* de téléphone; **to make a p. call** téléphoner (**to** à); **p. book** annuaire *m*; **p. box**, *Br* **p. booth** cabine *f* téléphonique; **p. number** numéro *m* de téléphone
2 *vt* téléphoner (**to** à); **to p. sb (up)** téléphoner à qn; **to p. sb back** rappeler qn
3 *vi* **to p. (up)** téléphoner; **to p. back** rappeler ▪ **phonecard** *n Br* carte *f* de téléphone

phonetic [fə'netɪk] *adj* phonétique

phoney ['fəʊnɪ] *Fam* 1 *(-ier, -iest) adj (company, excuse)* bidon *inv* 2 *n (impostor)* imposteur *m*; *(insincere person)* faux jeton *m*

photo ['fəʊtəʊ] *(pl -os) n* photo *f*; **to take sb's p.** prendre qn en photo; **to have one's p. taken** se faire prendre en photo; **p. album** album *m* de photos

photocopy ['fəʊtəʊkɒpɪ] 1 *(pl -ies) n* photocopie *f* 2 *(pt & pp -ied) vt* photocopier ▪ **photocopier** *n* photocopieuse *f*

photograph ['fəʊtəgrɑːf] 1 *n* photographie *f* 2 *vt* photographier ▪ **photographer** [fə'tɒgrəfə(r)] *n* photographe *mf* ▪ **photography** [fə'tɒgrəfɪ] *n (activity)* photographie *f*

phrase [freɪz] 1 *n (saying)* expression *f*; *(idiom, in grammar)* locution *f*; **p. book** manuel *m* de conversation 2 *vt (verbally)* exprimer; *(in writing)* rédiger

physical ['fɪzɪkəl] *adj* physique; **p. education** éducation *f* physique; **p.**

examination visite *f* médicale

physician [fɪ'zɪʃən] *n* médecin *m*

physics ['fɪzɪks] *n (science)* physique *f*

physiology [fɪzɪ'ɒlədʒɪ] *n* physiologie *f*

physiotherapy [fɪzɪəʊ'θerəpɪ] *n* kinésithérapie *f*

physique [fɪ'ziːk] *n* physique *m*

piano [pɪ'ænəʊ] *(pl* -os*) n* piano *m*
 ▪ **pianist** ['pɪənɪst] *n* pianiste *mf*

pick¹ [pɪk] **1** *n (choice)* choix *m*; **to take one's p.** choisir **2** *vt (choose)* choisir; *(flower, fruit)* cueillir; *(hole)* faire (**in** dans); *(lock)* crocheter; **to p. a fight** chercher la bagarre (**with** avec)
 ▸ **pick at** *vt insep* **to p. at one's food** picorer
 ▸ **pick off** *vt sep (remove)* enlever
 ▸ **pick on** *vt insep (nag, blame)* s'en prendre à
 ▸ **pick out** *vt sep (choose)* choisir; *(identify)* repérer
 ▸ **pick up 1** *vt sep (lift up)* ramasser; *(person into air, weight)* soulever; *(baby)* prendre dans ses bras; *(cold)* attraper; *(habit, accent, speed)* prendre; *(fetch, collect)* passer prendre; *(radio programme)* capter; *(arrest)* arrêter; *(learn)* apprendre; **to p. up the phone** décrocher le téléphone
 2 *vi (improve)* s'améliorer; *(of business)* reprendre; **let's p. up where we left off** reprenons (là où nous en étions restés)

pick² [pɪk] *n (tool)* pic *m*; **ice p.** pic *m* à glace

pickaxe ['pɪkæks] *(Am* **pickax***) n* pioche *f*

picket ['pɪkɪt] *n (in strike)* **p. (line)** piquet *m* de grève

pickle ['pɪkəl] **1** *n* **pickles** *(vegetables) Br* conserves *fpl* (au vinaigre); *Am* concombres *mpl*, cornichons *mpl*; **Fam to be in a p.** être dans le pétrin **2** *vt* conserver dans du vinaigre; **pickled onion** oignon *m* au vinaigre

pickpocket ['pɪkpɒkɪt] *n* pickpocket *m*

pick-up ['pɪkʌp] *n* **p. (truck)** pick-up *m inv (petite camionnette à plateau)*; **p.**

point *(for goods, passengers)* point *m* de ramassage

picky ['pɪkɪ] *(*-ier, -iest*) adj Fam (choosy)* difficile (**about** sur)

picnic ['pɪknɪk] **1** *n* pique-nique *m* **2** *(pt & pp* -ck-*) vi* pique-niquer

picture ['pɪktʃə(r)] **1** *n* image *f*; *(painting)* tableau *m*; *(drawing)* dessin *m*; *(photo)* photo *f*; *Fig (situation)* situation *f*; *Br Fam (film)* film *m*; *Br Fam* **the pictures** le cinéma; **p. frame** cadre *m* **2** *vt* **to p. sth (to oneself)** s'imaginer qch

picturesque [pɪktʃə'resk] *adj* pittoresque

pie [paɪ] *n (open)* tarte *f*; *(with pastry on top)* tourte *f*; **p. chart** camembert *m*

piece [piːs] **1** *n* morceau *m*; *(smaller)* bout *m*; *(in chess, puzzle)* pièce *f*; **to take sth to pieces** démonter qch; **a p. of news/advice/luck** une nouvelle/un conseil/une chance; **in one p.** *(object)* intact **2** *vt* **to p. together** *(facts)* reconstituer

pier [pɪə(r)] *n (for walking, with entertainments)* jetée *f*

pierce [pɪəs] *vt* percer; *(of cold, bullet, sword)* transpercer; **to have one's ears pierced** se faire percer les oreilles
 ▪ **piercing** *adj (voice, look)* perçant; *(wind)* vif *(f* vive*)*

pig [pɪg] *n (animal)* cochon *m*, porc *m*; *Fam (greedy person)* goinfre *m*

pigeon ['pɪdʒɪn] *n* pigeon *m*

pigeonhole ['pɪdʒɪnhəʊl] **1** *n* casier *m* **2** *vt (classify, label)* classer; *(person)* étiqueter

piggy ['pɪgɪ] *n* **p. bank** tirelire *f (en forme de cochon)*

piggyback ['pɪgɪbæk] *n* **to give sb a p.** porter qn sur son dos

pigment ['pɪgmənt] *n* pigment *m*

pigtail ['pɪgteɪl] *n (hair)* natte *f*

pilchard ['pɪltʃəd] *n* pilchard *m*

pile [paɪl] **1** *n (heap)* tas *m*; *(neat stack)* pile *f*; *Fam* **to have piles of** *or* **a p. of things to do** avoir un tas de choses à faire **2** *vt* entasser; *(stack)* empiler
 ▸ **pile up 1** *vt sep* entasser; *(stack)* empiler **2** *vi (accumulate)* s'accumuler

piles [paɪlz] *npl (illness)* hémorroïdes *fpl*

pile-up ['paɪlʌp] *n Fam (on road)* carambolage *m*

pilgrim ['pɪlgrɪm] *n* pèlerin *m* ▪ **pilgrimage** *n* pèlerinage *m*

pill [pɪl] *n* pilule *f*; **to be on the p.** *(of woman)* prendre la pilule

pillage ['pɪlɪdʒ] **1** *n* pillage *m* **2** *vti* piller

pillar ['pɪlə(r)] *n* pilier *m*; *Br* **p. box** boîte *f* aux lettres

pillow ['pɪləʊ] *n* oreiller *m* ▪ **pillowcase** *n* taie *f* d'oreiller

pilot ['paɪlət] **1** *n (of plane, ship)* pilote *m* **2** *adj* **p. light** veilleuse *f*; **p. scheme** projet *m* pilote **3** *vt (plane, ship)* piloter

pimple ['pɪmpəl] *n* bouton *m*

PIN [pɪn] *(abbr* **personal identification number)** *n Br* **P. (number)** code *m* confidentiel

pin [pɪn] **1** *n* épingle *f*; *Br (drawing pin)* punaise *f*; *(in machine)* goupille *f* **2** *(pt & pp* **-nn-)** *vt (attach)* épingler **(to** à); *(to wall)* punaiser **(to** *or* **on** à); **to p. down** *(immobilize)* immobiliser; *(fix)* fixer; **to p. sth up** *(notice)* fixer qch au mur

pinball ['pɪnbɔːl] *n* flipper *m*; **p. machine** flipper *m*

pincers ['pɪnsəz] *npl (tool)* tenailles *fpl*

pinch [pɪntʃ] **1** *n (of salt)* pincée *f*; **to give sb a p.** pincer qn; *Br* **at a p.,** *Am* **in a p.** à la rigueur **2** *vt* pincer; *Br Fam (steal)* piquer **(from** à) **3** *vi (of shoes)* serrer

pine [paɪn] **1** *n (tree, wood)* pin *m*; **p. forest** pinède *f* **2** *vi* **to p. for sb/sth** se languir de qn/qch

pineapple ['paɪnæpəl] *n* ananas *m*

pink [pɪŋk] *adj & n (colour)* rose *(m)*

pinnacle ['pɪnəkəl] *n Fig (of fame, career)* apogée *m*

pinpoint ['pɪnpɔɪnt] *vt (locate)* repérer; *(identify)* identifier

pint [paɪnt] *n* pinte *f (Br = 0,57 l, Am = 0,47 l)*; **a p. of beer** ≃ un demi-litre

pioneer [paɪə'nɪə(r)] **1** *n* pionnier, -ère *mf* **2** *vt* **to p. sth** être le premier/la

première à mettre au point qch

pious ['paɪəs] *adj (person, deed)* pieux *(f* pieuse)

pip [pɪp] *n Br (of fruit)* pépin *m*

pipe [paɪp] **1** *n* tuyau *m*; *(for smoking)* pipe *f*; *(musical instrument)* pipeau *m*; **to smoke a p.** fumer la pipe **2** *vi Fam* **to p. down** *(shut up)* se taire ▪ **piping** *adv* **p. hot** très chaud

pipeline ['paɪplaɪn] *n (for oil)* pipeline *m*; *Fig* **to be in the p.** être en préparation

pirate ['paɪərət] *n* pirate *m* ▪ **pirated** *adj (book, record, CD)* pirate

pissed [pɪst] *adj very Fam (drunk)* bourré; *Am (angry)* en rogne

pistachio [pɪ'stæʃɪəʊ] *(pl* **-os)** *n (nut, flavour)* pistache *f*

pistol ['pɪstəl] *n* pistolet *m*

pit¹ [pɪt] *n (hole)* fosse *f*; *(mine)* mine *f*

pit² [pɪt] *n Am (stone of fruit)* noyau *m* *(pl* -aux); *(smaller)* pépin *m*

pit³ [pɪt] *(pt & pp* **-tt-)** *vt* **to p. oneself against sb** se mesurer à qn

pitch [pɪtʃ] **1** *n* (a) *(for football)* terrain *m* (b) *(of voice)* hauteur *f*; *(musical)* ton *m* **2** *vt (tent)* dresser; *(ball)* lancer **3** *vi Fam* **to p. in** *(cooperate)* mettre du sien ▪ **pitch-black, pitch-dark** *adj* noir comme dans un four

pitcher ['pɪtʃə(r)] *n* cruche *f*

pitfall ['pɪtfɔːl] *n (trap)* piège *m*

pith [pɪθ] *n (of orange)* peau *f* blanche

pitiful ['pɪtɪfəl] *adj* pitoyable ▪ **pitiless** *adj* impitoyable

pittance ['pɪtəns] *n (income)* salaire *m* de misère

pity ['pɪtɪ] **1** *n* pitié *f*; **to take** *or* **have p. on sb** avoir pitié de qn; **what a p.!** quel dommage!; **it's a p. that...** c'est dommage que... *(+ subjunctive)* **2** *(pt & pp* **-ied)** *vt* plaindre

pivot ['pɪvət] **1** *n* pivot *m* **2** *vi* pivoter **(on** sur)

pizza ['piːtsə] *n* pizza *f*

placard ['plækɑːd] *n (on wall)* affiche *f*; *(hand-held)* pancarte *f*

place [pleɪs] **1** *n* endroit *m*, lieu *m*; *(seat, position, rank)* place *f*; *Fam* **my**

p. chez moi; **to lose one's p.** *(in queue)* perdre sa place; *(in book)* perdre sa page; **to take the p. of sb/sth** remplacer qn/qch; **to take p.** *(happen)* avoir lieu; *Br* **to set** *or* **lay three places** *(at the table)* mettre trois couverts; *Am* **some p.** *(somewhere)* quelque part; *Am* **no p.** *(nowhere)* nulle part; **all over the p.** un peu partout; **in the first p.** *(firstly)* en premier lieu; **in p. of** à la place de; **out of p.** *(remark)* déplacé; *(object)* pas à sa place; **p. of work** lieu *m* de travail

2 *vt (put, situate, invest, in sport)* placer; **to be placed third** se classer troisième; **to p. an order with sb** passer une commande à qn

placement ['pleɪsmənt] *n* stage *m*

placid ['plæsɪd] *adj* placide

plague [pleɪg] **1** *n (disease)* peste *f* **2** *vt (of person)* harceler (**with** de)

plaice [pleɪs] *n (fish)* carrelet *m*

plain¹ [pleɪn] **1** (**-er, -est**) *adj (clear, obvious)* clair; *(simple)* simple; *(without a pattern)* uni; *(not beautiful)* quelconque; **in p. clothes** en civil; **to make it p. to sb that...** faire comprendre à qn que...; **p. chocolate** chocolat *m* noir; **p. flour** farine *f (sans levure)* **2** *adv Fam (utterly)* complètement ■ **plainly** *adv (clearly)* clairement; *(frankly)* franchement

plain² [pleɪn] *n (land)* plaine *f*

plait [plæt] **1** *n* tresse *f*, natte *f* **2** *vt* tresser, natter

plan [plæn] **1** *n (proposal, intention)* projet *m*; *(of building, town, essay)* plan *m*; **to go according to p.** se passer comme prévu **2** *(pt & pp -nn-) vt (arrange)* projeter; *(crime)* comploter; *(building, town)* faire le plan de; **to p. to do** *or* **on doing sth** *(intend)* projeter de faire qch; **as planned** comme prévu **3** *vi* faire des projets

plane¹ [pleɪn] *n (aircraft)* avion *m*

plane² [pleɪn] **1** *n (tool)* rabot *m* **2** *vt* raboter

plane³ [pleɪn] *n (level, surface) & Fig* plan *m*

planet ['plænɪt] *n* planète *f*

plank [plæŋk] *n* planche *f*

planning ['plænɪŋ] *n* conception *f*; **family p.** planning *m* familial

plant [plɑːnt] **1** *n* (**a**) *(living thing)* plante *f* (**b**) *(factory)* usine *f*; *(machinery)* matériel *m* **2** *vt (tree, flower)* planter; *(crops, seeds)* semer; *(field)* ensemencer (**with** en); *Fig (bomb)* poser

plantation [plæn'teɪʃən] *n (trees, land)* plantation *f*

plaque [plæk] *n (sign)* plaque *f*; *(on teeth)* plaque *f* dentaire

plaster ['plɑːstə(r)] **1** *n* (**a**) *(on wall)* plâtre *m*; **to put sb's leg in p.** mettre la jambe de qn dans le plâtre; **p. cast** *(for broken bone)* plâtre *m* (**b**) *Br* **(sticking) p.** pansement *m* adhésif **2** *vt (wall)* plâtrer; **to p. sth with** *(cover)* couvrir qch de

plastic ['plæstɪk] **1** *adj (object)* en plastique; **p. bag** sac *m* en plastique; **p. surgery** *(cosmetic)* chirurgie *f* esthétique **2** *n* plastique *m*

plate [pleɪt] *n (dish)* assiette *f*; *(metal sheet)* plaque *f*; *(book illustration)* gravure *f*

plateau ['plætəʊ] *(pl* **-eaus** [-əʊz] *or* **-eaux**) *n (flat land)* plateau *m*

platform ['plætfɔːm] *n (raised surface)* plate-forme *f*; *(in train station)* quai *m*; *(for speaker)* estrade *f*

platinum ['plætɪnəm] *n (metal)* platine *m*

plausible ['plɔːzəbəl] *adj (argument, excuse)* plausible

play [pleɪ] **1** *n (drama)* pièce *f* (de théâtre); *(amusement)* jeu *m*; **to come into p.** entrer en jeu; **a p. on words** un jeu de mots

2 *vt (part, tune, card)* jouer; *(game)* jouer à; *(instrument)* jouer de; *(match)* disputer (**with** avec); *(team, opponent)* jouer contre; *(record, compact disc)* passer; *(radio, tape recorder)* faire marcher; *Fig* **to p. a part in doing/in sth** contribuer à faire/à qch

3 *vi* jouer (**with** avec; **at** à); *(of record player, tape recorder)* marcher; *Fam* **what are you playing at?** à quoi tu

joues? ▪ **playboy** n play-boy m ▪ **playground** n Br (in school) cour f de récréation; (in park) terrain m de jeux ▪ **playgroup** n garderie f ▪ **playmate** n camarade mf de jeu ▪ **playschool** n garderie f ▪ **playtime** n (in school) récréation f ▪ **playwright** n dramaturge mf

▸ **play about, play around** vi jouer, s'amuser

▸ **play back** vt sep (tape) réécouter

▸ **play down** vt sep minimiser

▸ **play on** vt insep (feelings, fears) jouer sur

▸ **play out** vt sep (scene, fantasy) jouer

▸ **play up** vi Fam (of child, machine) faire des siennes

player ['pleɪə(r)] n (in game, of instrument) joueur m, joueuse f; **clarinet p.** joueur m/joueuse f de clarinette

playful ['pleɪfəl] adj (mood, tone) enjoué; (child, animal) joueur (f joueuse)

playing ['pleɪɪŋ] n jeu m; **p. card** carte f à jouer; **p. field** terrain m de jeux

plc [piːel'siː] (abbr **public limited company**) n Br Com ≃ SA f

plea [pliː] n (request) appel m

plead [pliːd] 1 vt (argue) plaider; (as excuse) alléguer 2 vi **to p. with sb (to do sth)** implorer qn (de faire qch); **to p. guilty** plaider coupable

pleasant ['plezənt] adj agréable (**to** avec)

please [pliːz] 1 adv s'il te/vous plaît; **p. sit down** asseyez-vous, je vous prie; **p. do!** bien sûr!, je vous en prie!
2 vt **to p. sb** faire plaisir à qn; (satisfy) contenter qn
3 vi plaire; **do as you p.** fais comme tu veux ▪ **pleased** adj content (**with** de); **p. to meet you!** enchanté! ▪ **pleasing** adj agréable, plaisant

pleasure ['pleʒə(r)] n plaisir m

pleat [pliːt] n pli m ▪ **pleated** adj plissé

pledge [pledʒ] 1 n (promise) promesse f (**to do** de faire) 2 vt promettre (**to do** de faire)

plenty ['plentɪ] n **p. of** beaucoup de; **that's p.** (of food) merci, j'en ai assez ▪ **plentiful** adj abondant

pliers ['plaɪəz] npl pince f

plight [plaɪt] n (crisis) situation f critique

plimsolls ['plɪmsəʊlz] npl Br tennis mpl

plod [plɒd] (pt & pp -dd-) vi **to p. (along)** (walk) avancer laborieusement; (work) travailler laborieusement

plonk¹ [plɒŋk] vt Fam **to p. sth (down)** (drop) poser qch

plonk² [plɒŋk] n Br Fam (wine) pinard m

plot [plɒt] 1 n (conspiracy) complot m; (of novel, film) intrigue f; **p. (of land)** parcelle f de terrain 2 (pt & pp -tt-) vti comploter (**to do** de faire) 3 vt **to p. (out)** (route) déterminer; (graph) tracer

plough [plaʊ] (Am **plow**) 1 n charrue f 2 vt (field) labourer 3 vi labourer ▪ **ploughman** (pl -men) n Br **p.'s lunch** = assiette de fromage ou jambon avec de la salade et des condiments

pluck [plʌk] 1 n courage m 2 vt (hair, feathers) arracher; (flower) cueillir; (fowl) plumer; (eyebrows) épiler; (string of guitar) pincer; **to p. up the courage to do sth** trouver le courage de faire qch ▪ **plucky** (-ier, -iest) adj courageux, -euse

plug [plʌg] 1 n (a) (of cotton wool, wood) tampon m; (for sink, bath) bonde f (b) (electrical) (on device) fiche f; (socket) prise f (de courant) Aut (spark) **p.** bougie f 2 (pt & pp -gg-) vt (a) **to p. (up)** (gap, hole) boucher; **to p. sth in** (appliance) brancher qch (b) Fam (promote) faire de la pub pour ▪ **plughole** n trou m d'écoulement

plum [plʌm] n prune f

plumb [plʌm] adv Am Fam (crazy) complètement

▸ **plumb in** vt sep (washing machine) brancher

plumber ['plʌmə(r)] n plombier m ▪ **plumbing** n (job, system) plomberie f

plummet ['plʌmɪt] vi (of prices) s'effondrer; (of aircraft) plonger

plump [plʌmp] 1 (-er, -est) adj (person, arm) potelé; (chicken) dodu; (cheek) rebondi 2 vi Fam **to p. for sth** se décider pour qch

plunder ['plʌndə(r)] **1** *n (goods)* butin *m* **2** *vt* piller

plunge [plʌndʒ] **1** *n (dive)* plongeon *m*; *Fig (decrease)* chute *f*; *Fam* **to take the p.** *(take on difficult task)* se jeter à l'eau; *(get married)* se marier **2** *vt (thrust)* plonger (**into** dans) **3** *vi (dive)* plonger (**into** dans); *Fig (decrease)* chuter

plural ['plʊərəl] **1** *adj (noun)* au pluriel **2** *n* pluriel *m*; **in the p.** au pluriel

plus [plʌs] **1** *prep* plus; *(as well as)* en plus de **2** *adj (factor) & El* positif, -ive; **twenty p.** plus de vingt **3** *(pl* **plusses** ['plʌsɪz]) *n* **p. (sign)** (signe *m*) plus *m*; **that's a p.** c'est un plus

ply [plaɪ] *(pt & pp* **plied) 1** *vt (trade)* exercer; **to p. sb with questions** bombarder qn de questions **2** *vi* **to p. between** *(travel)* faire la navette entre

p.m. [piː'em] *adv (afternoon)* de l'après-midi; *(evening)* du soir

pneumonia [njuː'məʊnɪə] *n* pneumonie *f*

poach [pəʊtʃ] **1** *vt (egg)* pocher; *(employee)* débaucher **2** *vi (hunt)* braconner

PO Box [piː'əʊbɒks] *(abbr* **Post Office Box)** *n* boîte *f* postale, BP *f*

pocket ['pɒkɪt] **1** *n* poche *f*; **to be out of p.** en être de sa poche; **p. calculator** calculette *f*; **p. money** argent *m* de poche **2** *vt (put in pocket)* empocher; *Fam (steal)* rafler ▪ **pocketbook** *n Am (handbag)* sac *m* à main ▪ **pocketful** *n* **a p. of** une pleine poche de

podium ['pəʊdɪəm] *n* podium *m*

poem ['pəʊɪm] *n* poème *m* ▪ **poet** *n* poète *m* ▪ **poetic** [pəʊ'etɪk] *adj* poétique ▪ **poetry** *n* poésie *f*

poignant ['pɔɪnjənt] *adj* poignant

point [pɔɪnt] **1** *n* **(a)** *(of knife, needle)* pointe *f*; *Br* **points** *(for train)* aiguillage *m*
(b) *(dot, score, degree, argument)* point *m*; *(location)* endroit *m*; *(importance)* intérêt *m*; **to make a p. of doing sth** mettre un point d'honneur à faire qch; **you have a p.** tu as raison; **there's no p. (in) staying** ça ne sert à rien de rester; **to get to the p.** en arriver au fait;

at this p. in time en ce moment; **to be on the p. of doing sth** être sur le point de faire qch; **his good points** ses qualités *fpl*; **p. of view** point *m* de vue
(c) *Math* **three p. five** trois virgule cinq
2 *vt (aim)* diriger; *(camera, gun)* braquer (**at** sur); **to p. one's finger at sb** montrer qn du doigt; **to p. sth out** *(show)* montrer qch; *(error, fact)* signaler qch
3 *vi* **to p. at** *or* **to sb/sth** *(with finger)* montrer qn/qch du doigt; **to p. north** *(of arrow, compass)* indiquer le nord

point-blank [pɔɪnt'blæŋk] **1** *adj (refusal)* catégorique; **at p. range** à bout portant **2** *adv (refuse)* (tout) net

pointed ['pɔɪntɪd] *adj* pointu; *(beard)* en pointe; *Fig (remark, criticism)* pertinent

pointer ['pɔɪntə(r)] *n (on dial)* aiguille *f*; *(stick)* baguette *f*; *(clue)* indice *m*

pointless ['pɔɪntləs] *adj* inutile

poise [pɔɪz] *n (composure)* assurance *f*; *(grace)* grâce *f* ▪ **poised** *adj (composed)* calme; *(hanging)* suspendu; *(balanced)* en équilibre; **to be p. to do sth** *(ready)* être prêt à faire qch

poison ['pɔɪzən] **1** *n* poison *m*; *(of snake)* venin *m* **2** *vt* empoisonner ▪ **poisonous** *adj (fumes, substance)* toxique; *(snake)* venimeux, -euse; *(plant)* vénéneux, -euse

poke [pəʊk] **1** *vt (person)* donner un coup à; *(object)* tâter; *(fire)* attiser; **to p. sth into sth** enfoncer qch dans qch; **to p. one's finger at sb** pointer son doigt vers qn; *Fig* **to p. one's nose into sth** mettre son nez dans qch **2** *vi* **to p. at sth** *(with finger, stick)* tâter qch

poker¹ ['pəʊkə(r)] *n (for fire)* tisonnier *m*

poker² ['pəʊkə(r)] *n (card game)* poker *m*

Poland ['pəʊlənd] *n* la Pologne ▪ **Pole** *n* Polonais, -e *mf* ▪ **Polish** ['pəʊlɪʃ] **1** *adj* polonais **2** *n (language)* polonais *m*

polar ['pəʊlə(r)] *adj* polaire; **p. bear** ours *m* blanc

Polaroid® ['pəʊlərɔɪd] *n (camera, photo)* Polaroid® *m*

pole¹ [pəʊl] *n (rod)* perche *f; (fixed)* poteau *m; (for flag)* hampe *f;* **p. vault** *or* **vaulting** saut *m* à la perche

pole² [pəʊl] *n Geog* pôle *m;* **North/South P.** pôle *m* Nord/Sud

police [pə'liːs] **1** *n* police *f* **2** *adj (inquiry, dog)* policier, -ère; **p. car** voiture *f* de police; **p. station** poste *m* de police **3** *vt (city, area)* maintenir l'ordre dans ▪ **policeman** *(pl* -men) *n* agent *m* de police ▪ **policewoman** *(pl* -women) *n* agent *m* de police

policy ['pɒlɪsɪ] *(pl* -ies) *n* (a) *(of government, organization)* politique *f* (b) **(insurance) p.** police *f* (d'assurance)

polio ['pəʊlɪəʊ] *n* polio *f*

polish ['pɒlɪʃ] **1** *n (for shoes)* cirage *m; (for floor, furniture)* cire *f; (for nails)* vernis *m; Fig* raffinement *m;* **to give sth a p.** faire briller qch **2** *vt (floor, table, shoes)* cirer; *(metal)* astiquer; *Fig (style)* polir; *Fam* **to p. off** *(food)* avaler; *(drink)* descendre; *(work)* expédier; **to p. up one's French** travailler son français

polite [pə'laɪt] *(-er, -est) adj* poli **(to** *or* **with** avec) ▪ **politely** *adv* poliment

political [pə'lɪtɪkəl] *adj.* politique ▪ **politically** *adv* **p. correct** politiquement correct

politician [pɒlɪ'tɪʃən] *n* homme *m/* femme *f* politique

politics ['pɒlɪtɪks] *n* politique *f*

poll [pəʊl] **1** *n (voting)* scrutin *m;* **to go to the polls** aller aux urnes; **(opinion) p.** sondage *m* (d'opinion) **2** *vt (votes)* obtenir; *(people)* sonder

pollen ['pɒlən] *n* pollen *m*

polling ['pəʊlɪŋ] *n (election)* élections *fpl; Br* **p. station,** *Am* **p. place** bureau *m* de vote

pollute [pə'luːt] *vt* polluer ▪ **pollution** *n* pollution *f*

polo ['pəʊləʊ] *n (sport)* polo *m;* **p. neck** *(sweater, neckline)* col *m* roulé

polyester [pɒlɪ'estə(r)] *n* polyester *m;* **p. shirt** chemise *f* en polyester

polythene ['pɒlɪθiːn] *n Br* polyéthy-

lène *m;* **p. bag** sac *m* en plastique

pompous ['pɒmpəs] *adj* pompeux, -euse

pond [pɒnd] *n* étang *m; (smaller)* mare *f; (artificial)* bassin *m*

ponder ['pɒndə(r)] **1** *vt* réfléchir à **2** *vi* **to p. (over sth)** réfléchir (à qch)

pong [pɒŋ] *Br Fam* **1** *n (smell)* puanteur *f* **2** *vi* puer

pony ['pəʊnɪ] *(pl* -ies) *n* poney *m* ▪ **ponytail** *n* queue *f* de cheval

poodle ['puːdəl] *n* caniche *m*

pool¹ [puːl] *n (puddle)* flaque *f; (of blood)* mare *f; (for swimming)* piscine *f*

pool² [puːl] **1** *n (of money, helpers)* réserve *f; (of typists)* pool *m; Br* **the (football) pools** = concours de pronostics des matchs de football **2** *vt (share)* mettre en commun

pool³ [puːl] *n (game)* billard *m* américain

poor [pʊə(r)] **1** *(-er, -est) adj (not rich)* pauvre; *(bad)* mauvais; *(chances)* maigre; *(harvest, reward)* faible; **to be in p. health** ne pas bien se porter **2** *npl* **the p.** les pauvres *mpl* ▪ **poorly 1** *adv* mal; *(clothed, furnished)* pauvrement **2** *adj Br Fam* malade

pop¹ [pɒp] **1** *exclam* pan! **2** *n (noise)* bruit *m* sec; **to go p.** faire pan **3** *(pt & pp* -pp-) *vt* (a) *(balloon)* crever; *(cork)* faire sauter (b) *Fam (put)* mettre **4** *vi* (a) *(burst)* éclater; *(of cork)* sauter (b) *Br Fam* **to p. in** passer; **to p. out** sortir (un instant); **to p. up** surgir

pop² [pɒp] **1** *n (music)* pop *f* **2** *adj (concert, singer, group)* pop *inv*

pop³ [pɒp] *n Am Fam (father)* papa *m*

pop⁴ [pɒp] *n Am* **(soda) p.** *(drink)* soda *m*

popcorn ['pɒpkɔːn] *n* pop-corn *m inv*

pope [pəʊp] *n* pape *m*

poplar ['pɒplə(r)] *n (tree, wood)* peuplier *m*

poppy ['pɒpɪ] *(pl* -ies) *n (red, wild)* coquelicot *m; (cultivated)* pavot *m*

Popsicle® ['pɒpsɪkəl] *n Am (ice lolly)* ≃ Esquimau® *m*

popular ['pɒpjʊlə(r)] *adj* populaire;

(fashionable) à la mode; *(restaurant)* qui a beaucoup de succès ∎ **popularity** [-'lærətɪ] *n* popularité *f* (**with** auprès de)

populated ['pɒpjʊleɪtɪd] *adj* **densely/sparsely populated** très/ peu peuplé

population [pɒpjʊ'leɪʃən] *n* population *f*

porcelain ['pɔːsəlɪn] *n* porcelaine *f*

porch [pɔːtʃ] *n* porche *m*; *Am (veranda)* véranda *f*

pore [pɔː(r)] **1** *n (of skin)* pore *m* **2** *vi* to **p. over sth** *(book, question)* étudier qch de près

pork [pɔːk] *n (meat)* porc *m*; **p. pie** ≃ pâté *m* en croûte

pornography [pɔː'nɒɡrəfɪ] *n* pornographie *f*

porridge ['pɒrɪdʒ] *n* porridge *m*

port¹ [pɔːt] *n (harbour)* port *m*; **p. of call** escale *f*

port² [pɔːt] *n Naut (left-hand side)* bâbord *m*

port³ [pɔːt] *n (wine)* porto *m*

portable ['pɔːtəbəl] *adj* portable

porter ['pɔːtə(r)] *n (for luggage)* porteur *m*; *(door attendant)* chasseur *m*

portfolio [pɔːt'fəʊlɪəʊ] *(pl -os) n (for documents)* porte-documents *m inv*; *(of shares, government minister)* portefeuille *m*; *(of model, artist)* book *m*

porthole ['pɔːthəʊl] *n* hublot *m*

portion ['pɔːʃən] *n* partie *f*; *(share, helping)* portion *f*

portrait ['pɔːtreɪt, 'pɔːtrɪt] *n* portrait *m*

portray [pɔː'treɪ] *vt (describe)* dépeindre ∎ **portrayal** *n (description)* tableau *m*

Portugal ['pɔːtjʊɡəl] *n* le Portugal ∎ **Portuguese** [-'ɡiːz] **1** *adj* portugais **2** *n (person)* Portugais, -e *mf*; *(language)* portugais *m*; **the P.** *(people)* les Portugais

pose [pəʊz] **1** *n (position)* pose *f* **2** *vt (question)* poser; *(threat)* représenter **3** *vi* poser (**for** pour); to **p. as a lawyer** se faire passer pour un avocat

posh [pɒʃ] *adj Fam (smart)* chic *inv*

position [pə'zɪʃən] **1** *n (place, posture, opinion)* position *f*; *(of building, town)* emplacement *m*; *(job, circumstances)* situation *f*; **in a p. to do sth** en mesure de faire qch; **in p.** en place **2** *vt (put)* placer; *(troops)* poster

positive ['pɒzɪtɪv] *adj (person, answer, test)* positif, -ive; *(progress, change)* réel *(f* réelle); *(certain)* sûr, certain (**of** de; **that** que) ∎ **positively** *adv (identify)* formellement; *(think, react)* de façon positive; *(for emphasis)* véritablement

possess [pə'zes] *vt* posséder ∎ **possession** *n (ownership)* possession *f*; *(thing possessed)* bien *m*; **to be in p. of sth** être en possession de qch

possessive [pə'zesɪv] **1** *adj* possessif, -ive **2** *adj & n (in grammar)* possessif *(m)*

possibility [pɒsə'bɪlətɪ] *(pl -ies) n* possibilité *f*

possible ['pɒsəbəl] *adj* possible; **it is p. (for us) to do it** il (nous) est possible de le faire; **it is p. that...** il est possible que... *(+ subjunctive)*; **as soon as p.** dès que possible

possibly ['pɒsəblɪ] *adv* (**a**) *(perhaps)* peut-être (**b**) *(for emphasis)* **to do all one p. can** faire tout son possible (**to do** pour faire); **he cannot p. stay** il ne peut absolument pas rester

post- [pəʊst] *pref* post-; **post-1800** après 1800

post¹ [pəʊst] **1** *n Br (postal system)* poste *f*; *(letters)* courrier *m*; **by p.** par la poste; **p. office** (bureau *m* de) poste *f* **2** *vt (letter)* poster; **to keep sb posted** tenir qn au courant ∎ **postbox** *n Br* boîte *f* aux lettres ∎ **postcard** *n* carte *f* postale ∎ **postcode** *n Br* code *m* postal ∎ **postdate** *vt* postdater ∎ **postman** *(pl -men) n Br* facteur *m* ∎ **postmark** *n* cachet *m* de la poste

post² [pəʊst] **1** *n (job, place)* poste *m* **2** *vt (sentry, guard)* poster; *Br (employee)* affecter (**to** à)

post³ [pəʊst] *n (pole)* poteau *m*; *(of door, bed)* montant *m*; **finishing or**

winning p. *(in race)* poteau *m* d'arrivée

postage ['pəʊstɪdʒ] *n* affranchissement *m* (**to** pour); **p. paid** port *m* payé; **p. stamp** timbre-poste *m*

postal ['pəʊstəl] *adj (services)* postal; *(vote)* par correspondance; *Br* **p. order** mandat *m* postal

poster ['pəʊstə(r)] *n* affiche *f*; *(for decoration)* poster *m*

postgraduate [pəʊst'grædjʊət] **1** *adj* de troisième cycle **2** *n* étudiant, -e *mf* de troisième cycle

posthumous ['pɒstjʊməs] *adj* posthume

postmortem [pəʊst'mɔːtəm] *adj & n* **p. (examination)** autopsie *f* (**on** de)

postpone [pəʊs'pəʊn] *vt* reporter

posture ['pɒstʃə(r)] *n (of body)* posture *f*; *Fig* attitude *f*

postwar ['pəʊstwɔː(r)] *adj* d'après-guerre

posy ['pəʊzɪ] *(pl* **-ies**) *n* petit bouquet *m*

pot¹ [pɒt] *n* pot *m*; *(for cooking)* casserole *f*; *Fam* **to go to p.** aller à la ruine

pot² [pɒt] *n Fam (drug)* hasch *m*

potato [pə'teɪtəʊ] *(pl* **-oes**) *n* pomme *f* de terre; *Br* **p. crisps,** *Am* **p. chips** chips *fpl*

potent ['pəʊtənt] *adj* puissant; *(drink)* fort

potential [pə'tenʃəl] **1** *adj* potentiel, -elle **2** *n* potentiel *m*; **to have p.** avoir du potentiel

pothole ['pɒthəʊl] *n (in road)* nid-de-poule *m*; *(cave)* caverne *f*

potion ['pəʊʃən] *n* potion *f*

potter ['pɒtə(r)] **1** *n (person)* potier, -ère *mf* **2** *vi Br* **to p. about** *(do odd jobs)* bricoler ■ **pottery** *n (art)* poterie *f*; *(objects)* poteries *fpl*; **a piece of p.** une poterie

potty¹ ['pɒtɪ] *n (for baby)* pot *m*

potty² ['pɒtɪ] **(-ier, -iest)** *adj Br Fam (mad)* dingue

pouch [paʊtʃ] *n* bourse *f*; *(for tobacco)* blague *f*

poultry ['pəʊltrɪ] *n* volaille *f*

pounce [paʊns] *vi (of animal)* bondir

(on sur); *(of person)* se précipiter **(on** sur)

pound¹ [paʊnd] *n* (**a**) *(weight)* livre *f* (= 453,6 g) (**b**) **p. (sterling)** livre *f* (sterling)

pound² [paʊnd] *n (for cars, dogs)* fourrière *f*

pound³ [paʊnd] **1** *vt Mil (town)* pilonner **2** *vi (of heart)* battre à tout rompre

pour [pɔː(r)] **1** *vt* verser; **to p. sb a drink** verser à boire à qn **2** *vi* **it's pouring** il pleut à verse

▸ **pour down** *vi* **it's pouring down** il pleut à verse

▸ **pour in 1** *vt sep (liquid)* verser **2** *vi (of water, sunshine)* entrer à flots; *Fig (of people, money)* affluer

▸ **pour off** *vt sep (liquid)* vider

▸ **pour out 1** *vt sep (liquid)* verser; *Fig (anger, grief)* déverser **2** *vi (of liquid)* se déverser; *Fig (of people)* sortir en masse (**from** de)

pout [paʊt] *vi* faire la moue

poverty ['pɒvətɪ] *n* pauvreté *f*

powder ['paʊdə(r)] **1** *n* poudre *f*; **p. puff** houppette *f*; **p. room** toilettes *fpl* pour dames **2** *vt (body, skin)* poudrer; **to p. one's face** *or* **nose** se poudrer ■ **powdered** *adj (milk, eggs)* en poudre

power ['paʊə(r)] **1** *n (ability, authority)* pouvoir *m*; *(strength, nation)* puissance *f*; *(energy)* énergie *f*; *(electric current)* courant *m*; **to be in p.** être au pouvoir; **to have sb in one's p.** tenir qn à sa merci; *Br* **p. failure** *or* **cut** coupure *f* de courant; *Br* **p. station,** *Am* **p. plant** centrale *f* électrique; *Aut* **p. steering** direction *f* assistée

 2 *vt (provide with power)* actionner

powerful ['paʊəfəl] *adj* puissant; *(drug)* fort ■ **powerless** *adj* impuissant (**to do** à faire)

PR [piː'ɑː(r)] *(abbr* **public relations**) *n* RP *fpl*

practical ['præktɪkəl] *adj (tool, knowledge, solution)* pratique; **to be p.** *(of person)* avoir l'esprit pratique; **p. joke** farce *f*

practically ['præktɪkəlɪ] *adv (almost)* pratiquement

practice ['præktɪs] **1** *n (action, exercise, custom)* pratique *f; (in sport)* entraînement *m; (surgery)* centre *m* médical; **in p.** *(in reality)* dans la *ou* en pratique; **to put sth into p.** mettre qch en pratique; **to be out of p.** avoir perdu l'habitude **2** *vti Am* = **practise**

practise ['præktɪs] *(Am* **practice)** **1** *vt (sport, language, art, religion)* pratiquer; *(medicine, law)* exercer; *(musical instrument)* travailler

2 *vi (of musician)* s'exercer; *(of sportsperson)* s'entraîner; *(of doctor, lawyer)* exercer ▪ **practising** *adj (doctor, lawyer)* en exercice; *Rel* pratiquant

practitioner [præk'tɪʃənə(r)] *n* **general p.** (médecin *m*) généraliste *m*

pragmatic [præg'mætɪk] *adj* pragmatique

Prairie ['preərɪ] *n* **the P.** *(in USA)* la (Grande) Prairie; *(in Canada)* les Prairies *fpl*

praise [preɪz] **1** *n* éloges *mpl* **2** *vt* faire l'éloge de; *(God)* louer; **to p. sb for doing** *or* **having done sth** louer qn d'avoir fait qch

pram [præm] *n Br* landau *m (pl* -aus)

prank [præŋk] *n* farce *f*

prawn [prɔːn] *n* crevette *f* rose

pray [preɪ] **1** *vt* **to p. that…** prier pour que… *(+ subjunctive)* **2** *vi* prier; *Fig* **to p. for good weather** prier pour qu'il fasse beau

prayer [preə(r)] *n* prière *f*

pre- [priː] *pref* **pre-1800** avant 1800

preach [priːtʃ] *vti* prêcher; **to p. to sb** prêcher qn; *Fig* faire la morale à qn ▪ **preacher** *n* prédicateur, -trice *mf*

prearrange [priːə'reɪndʒ] *vt* arranger à l'avance

precarious [prɪ'keərɪəs] *adj* précaire

precaution [prɪ'kɔːʃən] *n* précaution *f;* **as a p.** par précaution

precede [prɪ'siːd] *vti* précéder

precedence ['presɪdəns] *n* **to take p. over sb** avoir la préséance sur qn; **to take p. over sth** passer avant qch

precedent ['presɪdənt] *n* précédent *m*

precinct ['priːsɪŋkt] *n Br (for shopping)* zone *f* commerçante piétonnière; *Am (electoral district)* circonscription *f; Am (police district)* secteur *m*

precious ['preʃəs] **1** *adj* précieux, -euse **2** *adv* **p. little** très peu (de)

precipice ['presɪpɪs] *n* précipice *m*

precipitate [prɪ'sɪpɪteɪt] *vt (hasten, throw)* & *Chem* précipiter

precise [prɪ'saɪs] *adj (exact)* précis; *(meticulous)* méticuleux, -euse ▪ **precisely** *adv* précisément; **at three o'clock p.** à trois heures précises ▪ **precision** [-'sɪʒən] *n* précision *f*

preclude [prɪ'kluːd] *vt (prevent)* empêcher *(from doing* de faire); *(possibility)* exclure

precocious [prɪ'kəʊʃəs] *adj* précoce

preconception [priːkən'sepʃən] *n* idée *f* préconçue

precondition [priːkən'dɪʃən] *n* condition *f* préalable

predator ['predətə(r)] *n* prédateur *m*

predecessor ['priːdɪsesə(r)] *n* prédécesseur *m*

predicament [prɪ'dɪkəmənt] *n* situation *f* difficile

predict [prɪ'dɪkt] *vt* prédire ▪ **predictable** *adj* prévisible ▪ **prediction** *n* prédiction *f*

predispose [priːdɪs'pəʊz] *vt* prédisposer *(to do* à faire)

predominant [prɪ'dɒmɪnənt] *adj* prédominant ▪ **predominate** *vi* prédominer *(over* sur)

pre-empt [priː'empt] *vt* devancer

preface ['prefɪs] *n (of book)* préface *f*

prefect ['priːfekt] *n Br Sch* = élève chargé de la surveillance

prefer [prɪ'fɜː(r)] *(pt & pp* -rr-*) vt* préférer *(to* à); **to p. to do sth** préférer faire qch

preferable ['prefərəbəl] *adj* préférable *(to* à)

preference ['prefərəns] *n* préférence *f (for* pour); **in p. to** plutôt que

prefix ['priːfɪks] *n (before word)* préfixe *m*

pregnant ['pregnənt] *adj (woman)* enceinte; *(animal)* pleine; **five months**

p. enceinte de cinq mois ▪ **pregnancy** (*pl* **-ies**) *n* grossesse *f*; **p. test** test *m* de grossesse

prehistoric [pri:hɪ'stɒrɪk] *adj* préhistorique

prejudge [pri:'dʒʌdʒ] *vt* (*question*) préjuger de; (*person*) juger sans connaître

prejudice ['predʒədɪs] **1** *n* (*bias*) préjugé *m* **2** *vt* (*bias*) prévenir (**against/in favour of** contre/en faveur de); (*harm*) nuire à ▪ **prejudiced** *adj* **to be p.** avoir des préjugés (**against/in favour of** contre/en faveur de)

preliminary [prɪ'lɪmɪnərɪ] *adj* préliminaire ▪ **preliminaries** *npl* préliminaires *mpl*

prelude ['prelju:d] *n* prélude *m* (**to** à)

premature [*Br* 'premətʃʊə(r), *Am* pri:mə'tʃʊər] *adj* prématuré

premeditate [pri:'medɪteɪt] *vt* préméditer

premier [*Br* 'premɪə(r), *Am* prɪ'mɪər] *n* Premier ministre *m*

première [*Br* 'premɪeə(r), *Am* prɪ'mɪər] *n* (*of play, film*) première *f*

premises ['premɪsɪz] *npl* locaux *mpl*; **on the p.** sur place

premium ['pri:mɪəm] *n Fin* (*for insurance*) prime *f*; (*additional sum*) supplément *m*

premonition [*Br* premə'nɪʃən, *Am* pri:mə'nɪʃən] *n* prémonition *f*

prenatal [pri:'neɪtəl] *adj Am* prénatal

preoccupy [pri:'ɒkjʊpaɪ] (*pt & pp* **-ied**) *vt* préoccuper au plus haut point; **to be preoccupied** être préoccupé (**with** par) ▪ **preoccupation** *n* préoccupation *f* (**with** pour)

prep [prep] *adj* **p. school** *Br* école *f* primaire privée; *Am* école *f* secondaire privée

pre-packed [pri:'pækt] *adj* (*meat, vegetables*) préemballé

prepaid [pri:'peɪd] *adj* prépayé

preparation [prepə'reɪʃən] *n* préparation *f*; **preparations** préparatifs *mpl* (**for** de)

preparatory [prə'pærətərɪ] *adj* pré-

paratoire; **p. school** *Br* école *f* primaire privée; *Am* école *f* secondaire privée

prepare [prɪ'peə(r)] **1** *vt* préparer (**sth for** qch pour; **sb for** qn à) **2** *vi* se préparer pour; **to p. to do sth** se préparer à faire qch ▪ **prepared** *adj* (*ready*) prêt (**to do** à faire); **to be p. for sth** s'attendre à qch

preposition [prepə'zɪʃən] *n* préposition *f*

preposterous [prɪ'pɒstərəs] *adj* ridicule

prerecorded [pri:rɪ'kɔ:dɪd] *adj* préenregistré

prerequisite [pri:'rekwɪzɪt] *n* (*condition f*) préalable *m*

prerogative [prɪ'rɒgətɪv] *n* prérogative *f*

preschool ['pri:sku:l] *adj* préscolaire

prescribe [prɪ'skraɪb] *vt* (*of doctor*) prescrire ▪ **prescribed** *adj* (*textbook*) (inscrit) au programme ▪ **prescription** *n* (*for medicine*) ordonnance *f*; **on p.** sur ordonnance

presence ['prezəns] *n* présence *f*; **in the p. of** en présence de; **p. of mind** présence *f* d'esprit

present¹ ['prezənt] **1** *adj* (a) (*in attendance*) présent (**at** à; **in** dans) (b) (*current*) actuel, -elle; **the p. tense** le présent **2** *n* **the p.** (*time, tense*) le présent; **for the p.** pour l'instant; **at p.** en ce moment ▪ **present-day** *adj* actuel, -elle ▪ **presently** *adv* (*soon*) bientôt; *Am* (*now*) actuellement

present² **1** ['prezənt] *n* (*gift*) cadeau *m* **2** [prɪ'zent] *vt* (*show, introduce*) présenter (**to** à); (*concert, film*) donner; **to p. sb with** (*gift*) offrir à qn; (*prize*) remettre à qn ▪ **presentable** [prɪ'zentəbəl] *adj* (*person, appearance*) présentable ▪ **presenter** [prɪ'zentə(r)] *n* présentateur, -trice *mf*

presentation [prezən'teɪʃən] *n* présentation *f*; (*of prize*) remise *f*

preservation [prezə'veɪʃən] *n* (*of building*) conservation *f*; (*of species*) protection *f*

preservative [prɪ'zɜ:vətɪv] *n* conservateur *m*

preserve [prɪ'zɜːv] **1** *n (jam)* confiture *f* **2** *vt (keep, maintain)* conserver; *(fruit)* mettre en conserve

preside [prɪ'zaɪd] *vi* présider; **to p. over** *or* **at a meeting** présider une réunion

presidency ['prezɪdənsɪ] *(pl* **-ies)** *n* présidence *f*

president ['prezɪdənt] *n (of country)* président, -e *mf* ▪ **presidential** [-'den-ʃəl] *adj* présidentiel, -elle

press¹ [pres] *n* **(a)** **the p.** *(newspapers)* la presse; **p. conference** conférence *f* de presse; **p. release** communiqué *m* de presse **(b)** *(machine)* presse *f; (for making wine)* pressoir *m*; **(printing) p.** presse *f*

press² [pres] **1** *n* **to give sth a p.** *(clothes)* repasser qch; **p. stud** bouton-pression *m* **2** *vt (button, doorbell)* appuyer sur; *(hand)* serrer; *(clothes)* repasser; **to p. sb to do sth** presser qn de faire qch **3** *vi (push)* appuyer **(on** sur); *(of weight)* faire pression **(on** sur) ▪ **press-up** *n (exercise)* pompe *f*

▸**press down** *vt insep (button)* appuyer sur

▸**press for** *vt sep (demand)* exiger

▸**press on** *vi (carry on)* continuer

pressed [prest] *adj* **to be hard p.** *(in difficulties)* être en difficulté; **to be p. for time** être pressé par le temps

pressing ['presɪŋ] *adj (urgent)* pressant

pressure ['preʃə(r)] **1** *n* pression *f;* **to be under p.** être stressé; **to put p. on sb (to do sth)** faire pression sur qn (pour qu'il fasse qch) **2** *vt* **to p. sb to do sth** *or* **into doing sth** faire pression sur qn pour qu'il fasse qch

pressurize ['preʃəraɪz] *vt* **to p. sb (into doing sth)** faire pression sur qn (pour qu'il fasse qch)

prestige [pre'stiːʒ] *n* prestige *m* ▪ **prestigious** [pres'tɪdʒəs, *Am* pre-'stiːdʒəs] *adj* prestigieux, -euse

presume [prɪ'zjuːm] *vt (suppose)* présumer **(that** que) ▪ **presumably** *adv* sans doute ▪ **presumption** [-'zʌmpʃən] *n* présomption *f*

presumptuous [prɪ'zʌmptʃʊəs] *adj* présomptueux, -euse

pretence [prɪ'tens] *(Am* **pretense)** *n (sham)* simulation *f; (claim, affectation)* prétention *f;* **to make a p. of doing sth** feindre de faire qch; **under false pretences** sous des prétextes fallacieux

pretend [prɪ'tend] **1** *vt (make believe)* faire semblant **(to do** de faire); *(claim, maintain)* prétendre **(to do** faire; **that** que) **2** *vi* faire semblant

pretense [prɪ'tens] *n Am* = **pretence**

pretentious [prɪ'tenʃəs] *adj* prétentieux, -euse

pretext ['priːtekst] *n* prétexte *m;* **on the p. of/that** sous prétexte de/que

pretty ['prɪtɪ] **1** **(-ier, -iest)** *adj* joli **2** *adv Fam (rather, quite)* assez; **p. well, p. much** *(almost)* pratiquement

prevail [prɪ'veɪl] *vi (predominate)* prédominer; *(be successful)* l'emporter **(over** sur); **to p. (up)on sb to do sth** persuader qn de faire qch ▪ **prevailing** *adj* prédominant; *(wind)* dominant

prevalent ['prevələnt] *adj* très répandu

prevent [prɪ'vent] *vt* empêcher **(from doing** de faire) ▪ **prevention** *n* prévention *f*

preview ['priːvjuː] *n (of film, play)* avant-première *f*

previous ['priːvɪəs] **1** *adj* précédent; **to have p. experience** avoir une expérience préalable **2** *adv* **p. to** avant ▪ **previously** *adv* auparavant

prewar ['priː'wɔː(r)] *adj* d'avant-guerre

prey [preɪ] **1** *n* proie *f; Fig* **to be (a) p. to** être en proie à **2** *vi* **to p. on** *(person)* prendre pour cible; *(fears, doubts)* exploiter; **to p. on sb's mind** tourmenter qn

price [praɪs] **1** *n* prix *m;* **he wouldn't do it at any p.** il ne le ferait à aucun prix **2** *adj (control, rise)* des prix; **p. list** tarif *m* **3** *vt* **it's priced at £5** ça coûte 5 livres ▪ **priceless** *adj (invaluable)* qui n'a pas de prix

pricey ['praɪsɪ] **(-ier, -iest)** *adj Fam* cher *(f* chère)

prick [prɪk] **1** n (of needle) piqûre f **2** vt (jab) piquer (**with** avec); (burst) crever ▪ **prickly** (-ier, -iest) adj (plant) à épines; (animal) couvert de piquants; (beard) piquant

pride [praɪd] **1** n (satisfaction) fierté f; (self-esteem) amour-propre m; Pej (vanity) orgueil m; **to take p. in sth** mettre toute sa fierté dans qch **2** vt **to p. oneself on sth/on doing sth** s'enorgueillir de qch/de faire qch

priest [priːst] n prêtre m

prim [prɪm] (**primmer, primmest**) adj **p. (and proper)** (person) collet monté inv; (manner) guindé

primarily [Br 'praɪmərəlɪ, Am praɪ'merəlɪ] adv essentiellement

primary ['praɪmərɪ] **1** adj (main) principal; Br **p. school** école f primaire **2** (pl -ies) n Am (election) primaire f

prime [praɪm] **1** adj (principal) principal; (importance) capital; (excellent) excellent; **P. Minister** Premier ministre m; Math **p. number** nombre m premier **2** n **in the p. of life** dans la fleur de l'âge **3** vt (surface) apprêter ▪ **primer** n (a) (book) manuel m élémentaire (b) (paint) apprêt m

primitive ['prɪmɪtɪv] adj (original) primitif, -ive; (basic) de base

prince [prɪns] n prince m ▪ **princess** n princesse f

principal ['prɪnsɪpəl] **1** adj (main) principal **2** n (of school) proviseur m; (of university) ≃ président, -e mf

principle ['prɪnsɪpəl] n principe m; **in p.** en principe; **on p.** par principe

print [prɪnt] **1** n (of finger, foot) empreinte f; (letters) caractères mpl; (engraving) estampe f; (photo) épreuve f; (fabric) imprimé m; **out of p.** (book) épuisé **2** vt (book, newspaper) imprimer; (photo) tirer; (write) écrire en script; Comptr **to p. out** imprimer ▪ **printed** adj imprimé; **p. matter** imprimés mpl ▪ **printing** n (technique, industry) imprimerie f; (action) tirage m; **p. error** faute f d'impression ▪ **printout** n Comptr sortie f papier

printer ['prɪntə(r)] n (machine) imprimante f

prior ['praɪə(r)] **1** adj antérieur; (experience) préalable **2** adv **p. to sth** avant qch

priority [praɪ'ɒrɪtɪ] (pl -ies) n priorité f (**over** sur)

prison ['prɪzən] **1** n prison f; **in p.** en prison **2** adj (life, system) pénitentiaire; (camp) de prisonniers; **p. officer** gardien, -enne mf de prison ▪ **prisoner** n prisonnier, -ère mf; **to take sb p.** faire qn prisonnier; **p. of war** prisonnier m de guerre

privacy ['praɪvəsɪ, Br 'prɪvəsɪ] n intimité f

private ['praɪvɪt] **1** adj privé; (lesson) particulier, -ère; (letter) confidentiel, -elle; (personal) personnel, -elle; (dinner, wedding) intime; **p. detective, p. investigator,** Fam **p. eye** détective m privé **2** n (a) **in p.** (not publicly) en privé; (have dinner, get married) dans l'intimité (b) (soldier) simple soldat m

privately ['praɪvɪtlɪ] adv (in private) en privé; (in one's heart of hearts) en son for intérieur; (personally) à titre personnel; **p. owned** (company) privé

privatize ['praɪvətaɪz] vt privatiser

privilege ['prɪvɪlɪdʒ] n privilège m ▪ **privileged** adj privilégié; **to be p. to do sth** avoir le privilège de faire qch

prize¹ [praɪz] n prix m; (in lottery) lot m ▪ **prizegiving** n distribution f des prix ▪ **prizewinner** n (in contest) lauréat, -e mf; (in lottery) gagnant, -e mf

prize² [praɪz] vt (value) attacher de la valeur à

prize³ [praɪz] vt Br = **prise**

pro [prəʊ] (pl pros) n Fam (professional) pro mf

probable ['prɒbəbəl] adj probable (**that** que) ▪ **probability** (pl -ies) n probabilité f; **in all p.** selon toute probabilité ▪ **probably** adv probablement

probation [prə'beɪʃən] n **on p.** (criminal) en liberté surveillée; (in job) en période d'essai

probe [prəʊb] **1** *n (device)* sonde *f*; *(inquiry)* enquête *f* (**into** dans) **2** *vt (prod)* sonder; *(inquire into)* enquêter sur **3** *vi* **to p. into sth** *(past, private life)* fouiller dans qch ▪ **probing** *adj (question)* perspicace

problem ['prɒbləm] *n* problème *m*; *Fam* **no p.!** pas de problème! ▪ **problematic** *adj* problématique

procedure [prə'siːdʒə(r)] *n* procédure *f*

proceed [prə'siːd] *vi (go on)* se poursuivre; **to p. with sth** poursuivre qch; **to p. to do sth** se mettre à faire qch

proceedings [prə'siːdɪŋz] *npl (events)* opérations *fpl*; **to take (legal) p.** intenter un procès (**against** contre)

proceeds ['prəʊsiːdz] *npl* recette *f*

process ['prəʊses] **1** *n* processus *m*; *(method)* procédé *m*; **in the p. of doing sth** en train de faire qch **2** *vt (food, data)* traiter; *(film)* développer; **processed food** aliments *mpl* conditionnés

procession [prə'seʃən] *n* défilé *m*

processor ['prəʊsesə(r)] *n Comptr* processeur *m*; **food p.** robot *m* de cuisine

proclaim [prə'kleɪm] *vt* proclamer (**that** que); **to p. sb king** proclamer qn roi

prod [prɒd] *(pt & pp* **-dd-)** *vt (poke)* donner un petit coup dans

prodigy ['prɒdɪdʒɪ] *(pl* **-ies)** *n* prodige *m*; **child p.** enfant *mf* prodige

produce[1] [prə'djuːs] *vt (create)* produire; *(machine)* fabriquer; *(passport, ticket)* présenter; *(documents)* fournir; *(from bag, pocket)* sortir; *(film, play, programme)* produire ▪ **producer** *n* producteur, -trice *mf*

produce[2] ['prɒdjuːs] *n (products)* produits *mpl*

product ['prɒdʌkt] *n (article, creation)* & *Math* produit *m*

production [prə'dʌkʃən] *n* production *f*; *(of play)* mise *f* en scène; **to work on a p. line** travailler à la chaîne

productive [prə'dʌktɪv] *adj* productif, -ive ▪ **productivity** [prɒdʌk'tɪvətɪ] *n* productivité *f*

profession [prə'feʃən] *n* profession *f*; **by p.** de profession ▪ **professional 1** *adj* professionnel, -elle; *(man, woman)* qui exerce une profession libérale; *(army)* de métier; *(piece of work)* de professionnel **2** *n* professionnel, -elle *mf*

professor [prə'fesə(r)] *n Br* ≃ professeur *m* d'université; *Am* = enseignant d'université

proficient [prə'fɪʃənt] *adj* compétent (**in** en)

profile ['prəʊfaɪl] *n (of person, object)* profil *m*; *(description)* portrait *m*; **in p.** de profil; *Fig* **to keep a low p.** garder un profil bas

profit ['prɒfɪt] **1** *n* profit *m*, bénéfice *m*; **to sell at a p.** vendre à profit **2** *vi* **to p. by** *or* **from sth** tirer profit de qch ▪ **profit-making** *adj (aiming to make profit)* à but lucratif; *(profitable)* rentable

profitable ['prɒfɪtəbəl] *adj (commercially)* rentable; *Fig (worthwhile)* profitable

profound [prə'faʊnd] *adj* profond ▪ **profoundly** *adv* profondément

profusely [prə'fjuːslɪ] *adv (bleed)* abondamment; *(thank)* avec effusion; **to apologize p.** se confondre en excuses

programme ['prəʊɡræm] *(Am* **program)** **1** *n (for play, political party, computer)* programme *m*; *(on TV, radio)* émission *f* **2** *(pt & pp* **-mm-)** *vt (machine)* programmer ▪ **programmer** *n* **(computer) p.** programmeur, -euse *mf* ▪ **programming** *n* **(computer) p.** programmation *f*

progress 1 ['prəʊɡres] *n* progrès *m*; **to make (good) p.** faire des progrès; **in p.** en cours **2** [prə'ɡres] *vi (advance, improve)* progresser; *(of story, meeting)* se dérouler

progressive [prə'ɡresɪv] *adj (gradual)* progressif, -ive; *(company, ideas, political party)* progressiste

prohibit [prə'hɪbɪt] *vt* interdire (**sb**

from doing à qn de faire)

prohibitive [prə'hɪbɪtɪv] *adj* prohibitif, -ive

project 1 ['prɒdʒekt] *n (plan, undertaking)* projet *m*; *(at school)* dossier *m*; *Am* **(housing) p.** cité *f* HLM **2** [prə'dʒekt] *vt (propel, show)* projeter **3** [prə'dʒekt] *vi (protrude)* dépasser

projector [prə'dʒektə(r)] *n* projecteur *m*

proliferate [prə'lɪfəreɪt] *vi* proliférer

prolific [prə'lɪfɪk] *adj* prolifique

prologue ['prəʊlɒg] *n* prologue *m* (**to** de)

prolong [prə'lɒŋ] *vt* prolonger

prom [prɒm] *(abbr* **promenade***) n* (a) *Br (at seaside)* front *m* de mer (**b** *Am (dance)* bal *m* d'étudiants

promenade [prɒmə'nɑːd] *n Br (at seaside)* front *m* de mer

prominent ['prɒmɪnənt] *adj (important)* important; *(nose, chin)* proéminent ■ **prominently** *adv* bien en vue

promiscuous [prə'mɪskjʊəs] *adj (person)* qui a de multiples partenaires

promise ['prɒmɪs] **1** *n* promesse *f*; **to show p.** promettre **2** *vt* promettre (**to do** de faire); **to p. sth to sb, to p. sb sth** promettre qch à qn **3** *vi* **I p.!** je te le promets! ■ **promising** *adj* prometteur, -euse

promote [prə'məʊt] *vt (raise in rank, encourage)* promouvoir; *(advertise)* faire la promotion de ■ **promotion** *n* promotion *f*

prompt¹ [prɒmpt] **1** *adj (speedy)* rapide; *(punctual)* ponctuel, -elle **2** *adv* **at eight o'clock p.** à huit heures précises ■ **promptly** *adv (rapidly)* rapidement; *(punctually)* ponctuellement; *(immediately)* immédiatement

prompt² [prɒmpt] *vt* (a) *(cause)* provoquer; **to p. sb to do sth** pousser qn à faire qch (b) *(actor)* souffler à

prone [prəʊn] *adj* **to be p. to sth** être sujet, -ette à qch; **to be p. to do sth** avoir tendance à faire qch

pronoun ['prəʊnaʊn] *n* pronom *m*

pronounce [prə'naʊns] *vt (say, articulate)* prononcer ■ **pronunciation** [-nʌnsɪ'eɪʃən] *n* prononciation *f*

proof [pruːf] *n (evidence)* preuve *f*; *(of book, photo)* épreuve *f*; **p. of identity** pièce *f* d'identité ■ **proofreader** *n* correcteur, -trice *mf*

prop [prɒp] **1** *n (physical support)* support *m*; *(in a play)* accessoire *m* **2** *(pt & pp* **-pp-***) vt* **to p. sth (up) against sth** appuyer qch contre qch; **to p. sth up** *(building, tunnel)* étayer qch; *Fig (economy, regime)* soutenir qch

propaganda [prɒpə'gændə] *n* propagande *f*

propel [prə'pel] *(pt & pp* **-ll-***) vt* propulser ■ **propeller** *n* hélice *f*

proper ['prɒpə(r)] *adj* (a) *(correct)* vrai; *(word)* correct; **the village p.** le village proprement dit (b) *(appropriate)* bon *(f* bonne) *(equipment)* adéquat; *(behaviour)* convenable (c) *Br (downright)* véritable ■ **properly** *adv (suitably)* convenablement; *(correctly)* correctement

property ['prɒpətɪ] **1** *(pl* **-ies***) n* (a) *(land, house)* propriété *f*; *(possessions)* biens *mpl* (b) *(quality)* propriété *f* **2** *adj (market)* immobilier, -ère; **p. developer** promoteur *m* immobilier

prophecy ['prɒfɪsɪ] *(pl* **-ies***) n* prophétie *f*

prophet ['prɒfɪt] *n* prophète *m*

proportion [prə'pɔːʃən] *n (ratio, part)* proportion *f*; **proportions** *(size)* proportions *fpl*; **in p.** proportionné (**to** avec); **out of p.** disproportionné (**to** par rapport à) ■ **proportional, proportionate** *adj* proportionnel, -elle (**to** à)

proposal [prə'pəʊzəl] *n* proposition *f*; *(plan)* projet *m*; *(for marriage)* demande *f* en mariage ■ **proposition** [prɒpə'zɪʃən] *n* proposition *f*

propose [prə'pəʊz] **1** *vt* proposer; **to p. to do sth, to p. doing sth** *(suggest)* proposer de faire qch; *(intend)* se proposer de faire qch **2** *vi* **to p. to sb** demander qn en mariage

proprietor [prə'praɪətə(r)] *n* propriétaire *mf*

pros [prəʊz] *npl* **the p. and cons** le pour et le contre

prose [prəʊz] n prose f; Br (translation) thème m

prosecute ['prɒsɪkjuːt] vt (in law court) poursuivre (en justice) ■ **prosecution** n (in law court) poursuites fpl judiciaires; **the p.** (lawyers) ≃ le ministère public

prospect¹ ['prɒspekt] n (expectation, thought) perspective f; (chance, likelihood) perspectives fpl; **(future) prospects** perspectives fpl d'avenir ■ **prospective** [prə'spektɪv] adj (potential) potentiel, -elle; (future) futur

prospect² [prə'spekt] vi to p. for gold chercher de l'or

prospectus [prə'spektəs] n (publicity leaflet) prospectus m; Br (for university) guide m (de l'étudiant)

prosper ['prɒspə(r)] vi prospérer ■ **prosperity** [-'sperətɪ] n prospérité f ■ **prosperous** adj prospère

prostitute ['prɒstɪtjuːt] n (woman) prostituée f; **male p.** prostitué m ■ **prostitution** n prostitution f

prostrate ['prɒstreɪt] adj (lying flat) sur le ventre

protagonist [prəʊ'tægənɪst] n protagoniste mf

protect [prə'tekt] vt protéger (**from** or **against** de) ■ **protection** n protection f ■ **protective** adj (clothes, screen) de protection; (person, attitude) protecteur, -trice (**to** or **towards** envers)

protein ['prəʊtiːn] n protéine f

protest [prə'test] 1 ['prəʊtest] n protestation f (**against** contre); **in p.** en signe de protestation (**at** contre) 2 vt protester contre; (one's innocence) protester de; **to p. that...** protester en disant que... 3 vi protester (**against** contre) ■ **protester** n contestataire mf

Protestant ['prɒtɪstənt] adj & n protestant, -e (mf)

protracted [prə'træktɪd] adj prolongé

protrude [prə'truːd] vi dépasser (**from** de); (of tooth) avancer ■ **protruding** adj (chin, veins, eyes) saillant

proud [praʊd] (**-er, -est**) adj (person) fier (f fière) (**of** de) ■ **proudly** adv fièrement

prove [pruːv] 1 vt prouver (**that** que); **to p. sb wrong** prouver que qn a tort 2 vi to p. (**to be**) difficile s'avérer difficile ■ **proven** adj (method) éprouvé

proverb ['prɒvɜːb] n proverbe m

provide [prə'vaɪd] 1 vt (supply) fournir; (service) offrir (**to** à); **to p. sb with sth** fournir qch à qn 2 vi to p. for sb (sb's needs) pourvoir aux besoins de qn; (sb's future) assurer l'avenir de qn; **to p. for sth** (make allowance for) prévoir qch ■ **provided, providing** conj **p. (that)...** pourvu que... (+ subjunctive)

province ['prɒvɪns] n province f; **in the provinces** en province ■ **provincial** [prə'vɪnʃəl] adj & n provincial, -e (mf)

provision [prə'vɪʒən] n (clause) disposition f; **provisions** (supplies) provisions fpl

provisional [prə'vɪʒənəl] adj provisoire

provocation [prɒvə'keɪʃən] n provocation f

provocative [prə'vɒkətɪv] adj provocateur, -trice

provoke [prə'vəʊk] vt provoquer; **to p. sb into doing sth** pousser qn à faire qch

prowl [praʊl] 1 n to be on the p. rôder 2 vi to p. (**around**) rôder

proxy ['prɒksɪ] (pl **-ies**) n by p. par procuration

prudent ['pruːdənt] adj prudent

prudish ['pruːdɪʃ] adj pudibond

prune¹ [pruːn] n (dried plum) pruneau m

prune² [pruːn] vt (tree, bush) tailler

pry [praɪ] 1 (pt & pp pried) vt Am to p. open forcer (avec un levier) 2 vi être indiscret, -ète; **to p. into sth** (meddle) mettre son nez dans qch; (sb's reasons) chercher à découvrir qch

PS [piː'es] (abbr postscript) n PS m

psalm [sɑːm] n psaume m

pseudonym ['sjuːdənɪm] n pseudonyme m

psychiatry [saɪ'kaɪətrɪ] n psychiatrie f ■ **psychiatric** [-kɪ'ætrɪk] adj psychia-

trique ▪ **psychiatrist** *n* psychiatre *mf*

psychic ['saɪkɪk] *adj (paranormal)* paranormal

psycho- ['saɪkəʊ] *pref* psycho- ▪ **psychoanalyst** *n* psychanalyste *mf*

psychology [saɪ'kɒlədʒɪ] *n* psychologie *f* ▪ **psychological** [-kə'lɒdʒɪkəl] *adj* psychologique ▪ **psychologist** *n* psychologue *mf*

psychopath ['saɪkəʊpæθ] *n* psychopathe *mf*

PTO *(abbr* **please turn over)** TSVP

pub [pʌb] *n Br* pub *m*

puberty ['pjuːbətɪ] *n* puberté *f*

public ['pʌblɪk] **1** *adj* public, -ique; *(library, swimming pool)* municipal; **p. holiday** jour *m* férié; **p. school** *Br* école *f* privée; *Am* école *f* publique; **p. transport** transports *mpl* en commun **2** *n* public *m*; **in p.** en public

publication [pʌblɪ'keɪʃən] *n* publication *f*

publicity [pʌ'blɪsətɪ] *n* publicité *f*

publicize ['pʌblɪsaɪz] *vt* faire connaître au public

publicly ['pʌblɪklɪ] *adv* publiquement; **p. owned** à capitaux publics

publish ['pʌblɪʃ] *vt* publier ▪ **publisher** *n (person)* éditeur, -trice *mf*; *(company)* maison *f* d'édition

pudding ['pʊdɪŋ] *n (dish)* pudding *m*; *Br (dessert)* dessert *m*

puddle ['pʌdəl] *n* flaque *f* (d'eau)

puff [pʌf] **1** *n (of smoke)* bouffée *f*; *(of wind, air)* souffle *m*; **p. pastry,** *Am* **p. paste** pâte *f* feuilletée **2** *vt* **to p. sth out** *(cheeks, chest)* gonfler qch **3** *vi (of person)* souffler; **to p. at a cigar** tirer sur un cigare

puke [pjuːk] *vi Fam* dégueuler

pull [pʊl] **1** *n (attraction)* attraction *f*; **to give sth a p.** tirer qch **2** *vt (draw, tug)* tirer; *(tooth)* arracher; *(trigger)* appuyer sur; *(muscle)* se froisser; *Fig* **to p. sth apart** *or* **to bits** *or* **to pieces** démolir qch **3** *vi (tug)* tirer **(on** sur)

▸ **pull along** *vt sep (drag)* traîner **(to** jusqu'à)

▸ **pull away 1** *vt sep (move)* éloigner; *(snatch)* arracher **(from** à) **2** *vi (in vehicle)* démarrer

▸ **pull back 1** *vt sep* retirer; *(curtains)* ouvrir **2** *vi (withdraw)* se retirer

▸ **pull down** *vt sep (lower)* baisser; *(knock down)* faire tomber; *(demolish)* démolir

▸ **pull in 1** *vt sep (drag into room)* faire entrer (de force); *(rope)* ramener; *(stomach)* rentrer **2** *vi (arrive)* arriver; *(stop in vehicle)* s'arrêter

▸ **pull off** *vt sep (remove)* enlever; *Fig (plan, deal)* réaliser

▸ **pull on** *vt sep (boots, clothes)* mettre

▸ **pull out 1** *vt sep (tooth, hair)* arracher; *(cork, pin)* enlever **(from** de); *(from pocket, bag)* sortir **(from** de) **2** *vi (of car)* déboîter; *(of train)* partir; *(withdraw)* se retirer **(of** de)

▸ **pull over 1** *vt sep (drag)* traîner **(to** jusqu'à); *(knock down)* faire tomber **2** *vi (in vehicle)* s'arrêter

▸ **pull through** *vi (recover)* s'en tirer

▸ **pull together** *vt sep* **to p. oneself together** se ressaisir

▸ **pull up 1** *vt sep (socks, blinds)* remonter; *(haul up)* hisser; *(plant, tree)* arracher; *(stop)* arrêter **2** *vi (of car)* s'arrêter

pullover ['pʊləʊvə(r)] *n* pull-over *m*

pulp [pʌlp] *n (of fruit)* pulpe *f*

pulse [pʌls] *n Med* pouls *m*

pump¹ [pʌmp] **1** *n (machine)* pompe *f*; *Br* **petrol p.,** *Am* **gas p.** pompe *f* à essence **2** *vt* pomper; **to p. sth up** *(mattress)* gonfler qch

pump² [pʌmp] *n (flat shoe)* escarpin *m*; *(for sports)* tennis *f*

pumpkin ['pʌmpkɪn] *n* potiron *m*

pun [pʌn] *n* jeu *m* de mots

punch¹ [pʌntʃ] **1** *n (blow)* coup *m* de poing; **p. line** *(of joke, story)* chute *f* **2** *vt (person)* donner un coup de poing à; *(sb's nose)* donner un coup de poing sur ▪ **punch-up** *n Br Fam* bagarre *f*

punch² [pʌntʃ] **1** *n (for paper)* perforeuse *f*; *(for tickets)* poinçonneuse *f* **2** *vt (ticket)* poinçonner; *(with date)* composter; *(paper, card)* perforer; **to p. a hole in sth** faire un trou dans qch

punch³ [pʌntʃ] *n (drink)* punch *m*

punctual ['pʌŋktʃʊəl] *adj* ponctuel, -elle ■ **punctually** *adv* à l'heure

punctuation [pʌŋktjʊ'eɪʃən] *n* ponctuation *f*; **p. mark** signe *m* de ponctuation

puncture ['pʌŋktʃə(r)] **1** *n (in tyre)* crevaison *f*; **to have a p.** crever **2** *vt (tyre)* crever **3** *vi (of tyre)* crever

pungent ['pʌndʒənt] *adj* âcre

punish ['pʌnɪʃ] *vt* punir (**for** de); **to p. sb for doing sth** punir qn pour avoir fait qch

punishment ['pʌnɪʃmənt] *n* punition *f*; *(in law)* peine *f*

punk [pʌŋk] *n* punk *mf*; **p. (rock)** le punk

punter ['pʌntə(r)] *n Br (gambler)* parieur, -euse *mf*; *Fam (customer)* client, -e *m*

puny ['pjuːnɪ] (**-ier, -iest**) *adj* chétif, -ive

pupil¹ ['pjuːpəl] *n (student)* élève *mf*

pupil² ['pjuːpəl] *n (of eye)* pupille *f*

puppet ['pʌpɪt] *n* marionnette *f*; **p. show** spectacle *m* de marionnettes

puppy ['pʌpɪ] (*pl* **-ies**) *n (dog)* chiot *m*

purchase ['pɜːtʃɪs] **1** *n (action, thing bought)* achat *m* **2** *vt* acheter (**from** à) ■ **purchaser** *n* acheteur, -euse *mf*

pure [pjʊə(r)] (**-er, -est**) *adj* pur

purée ['pjʊəreɪ] *n* purée *f*

purely ['pjʊəlɪ] *adv* purement

purge [pɜːdʒ] **1** *n* purge *f* **2** *vt* purger (**of** de)

purify ['pjʊərɪfaɪ] (*pt & pp* **-ied**) *vt* purifier

puritanical [pjʊərɪ'tænɪkəl] *adj* puritain

purity ['pjʊərətɪ] *n* pureté *f*

purple ['pɜːpəl] **1** *adj* violet, -ette **2** *n* violet *m*

purpose ['pɜːpəs] *n* (a) *(aim)* but *m*; **on p.** exprès; **for the purposes of** pour les besoins de (b) *(determination)* résolution *f*

purposely ['pɜːpəslɪ] *adv* exprès

purr [pɜː(r)] *vi* ronronner

purse [pɜːs] **1** *n (for coins)* portemonnaie *m inv*; *Am (handbag)* sac *m* à main **2** *vt* **to p. one's lips** pincer les lèvres

pursue [pə'sjuː] *vt* poursuivre; *(fame, pleasure)* rechercher ■ **pursuit** *n (of person)* poursuite *f*; *(of pleasure, glory)* quête *f*; *(activity)* occupation *f*

push [pʊʃ] **1** *n (act of pushing, attack)* poussée *f*; **to give sb/sth a p.** pousser qn/qch; **at a p.** à la rigueur

2 *vt* pousser (**to** *or* **as far as** jusqu'à); *(button)* appuyer sur; *(lever)* abaisser; *(product)* faire la promotion de; *Fam (drugs)* vendre; **to p. sth into/between** enfoncer qch dans/entre; *Fig* **to p. sb into doing sth** pousser qn à faire qch; **to p. sth off the table** faire tomber qch de la table (en le poussant)

3 *vi* pousser; *(on button)* appuyer (**on** sur)

▸ **push about, push around** *vt sep Fam* **to p. sb about** *or* **around** faire de qn ce que l'on veut

▸ **push aside** *vt sep* écarter

▸ **push down** *vt sep (button)* appuyer sur; *(lever)* abaisser

▸ **push in** *vi Br (in queue)* resquiller

▸ **push off** *vi Fam* ficher le camp

▸ **push on** *vi (go on)* continuer; **to p. on with sth** continuer qch

▸ **push over** *vt sep* faire tomber

▸ **push up** *vt sep (lever, collar)* relever; *(sleeves)* remonter; *(increase)* augmenter ■ **push-button** *n* bouton *m*; *(of phone)* touche *f*; **p. phone** téléphone *m* à touches ■ **pushchair** *n Br* poussette *f* ■ **push-up** *n Am (exercise)* pompe *f*

pushed [pʊʃt] *adj* **to be p. for time** être très pressé

pushy ['pʊʃɪ] (**-ier, -iest**) *adj Fam* batailleur, -euse

puss, pussy ['pʊs, 'pʊsɪ] (*pl* **-ies**) *n Fam (cat)* minou *m*

PUT [pʊt] (*pt & pp* **put**, *pres p* **putting**) *vt* mettre; *(on flat surface)* poser; *(problem, argument)* présenter (**to** à); *(question)* poser (**to** à); *(say)* dire; *(estimate)* évaluer (**at** à); **to p. money on a horse** parier sur un cheval; **to p. a lot of work into sth** beaucoup travailler à qch; **to p. it bluntly** pour parler franc

▸ **put across** *vt sep (message, idea)*

faire comprendre (**to** à)

▶**put aside** *vt sep (money, object)* mettre de côté

▶**put away** *vt sep (tidy away)* ranger; **to p. sb away** *(criminal)* mettre qn en prison

▶**put back** *vt sep (replace, postpone)* remettre; *(telephone receiver)* raccrocher; *(clock)* retarder

▶**put by** *vt sep (money)* mettre de côté

▶**put down** *vt sep (on floor, table)* poser; *(a deposit)* verser; *(revolt)* réprimer; *(write down)* inscrire; *(attribute)* attribuer (**to** à); *(kill)* faire piquer; **to p. oneself down** se rabaisser

▶**put forward** *vt sep (clock, meeting, argument)* avancer; *(candidate)* proposer (**for** à)

▶**put in** 1 *vt sep (into box)* mettre dedans; *(insert)* introduire; *(add)* ajouter; *(install)* installer; *(claim, application)* soumettre; *(time)* passer (**doing** à faire) 2 *vi* **to p. in for sth** *(new job, transfer)* faire une demande de qch

▶**put off** *vt sep (postpone)* remettre (à plus tard); *(dismay)* déconcerter; **to p. off doing sth** retarder le moment de faire qch; **to p. sb off sth** dégoûter qn de qch

▶**put on** *vt sep (clothes, shoe, record)* mettre; *(accent)* prendre; *(play, show)* monter; *(gas, radio)* allumer; *(clock)* avancer; **to p. on weight** prendre du poids; **she p. me on to you** elle m'a donné votre adresse; **p. me on to him!** *(on phone)* passez-le-moi!

▶**put out** *vt sep (take outside)* sortir; *(arm, leg, hand)* tendre; *(gas, light)* éteindre; *(inconvenience)* déranger; *(upset)* vexer; *(report, statement)* publier; **to p. one's shoulder out** se démettre l'épaule

▶**put through** *vt sep* **to p. sb through (to sb)** *(on phone)* passer qn (à qn)

▶**put together** *vt sep (assemble)* assembler; *(meal, team)* composer; *(file, report)* préparer; *(collection)* rassembler

▶**put up** *vt sep (lift)* lever; *(tent, fence)* monter; *(statue, ladder)* dresser; *(flag)* hisser; *(building)* construire; *(umbrella)* ouvrir; *(picture, poster)* mettre; *(price, numbers)* augmenter; *(resistance)* offrir; *(candidate)* présenter (**for** à); *(guest)* loger; **to p. sth up for sale** mettre qch en vente

▶**put up with** *vt insep* supporter

putting ['pʌtɪŋ] *n (in golf)* putting *m*; **p. green** green *m*

puzzle ['pʌzəl] **1** *n (jigsaw)* puzzle *m*; *(game)* casse-tête *m inv*; *(mystery)* mystère *m* **2** *vt* laisser perplexe **3** *vi* **to p. over sth** essayer de comprendre qch ▪ **puzzled** *adj* perplexe

PVC [piːviːˈsiː] *n* PVC *m*

pyjamas [pəˈdʒɑːməz] *npl Br* pyjama *m*; **a pair of p.** un pyjama

pylon ['paɪlən] *n* pylône *m*

pyramid ['pɪrəmɪd] *n* pyramide *f*

Pyrex® ['paɪreks] *n* Pyrex® *m*; **P. dish** plat *m* en Pyrex®

Qq

Q, q [kju:] *n (letter)* Q, q *m inv*

quack [kwæk] *n (of duck)* coin-coin *m inv*

quadruple [kwɒˈdru:pəl] *vti* quadrupler

quaint [kweɪnt] **(-er, -est)** *adj (picturesque)* pittoresque; *(old-fashioned)* vieillot, -otte; *(odd)* bizarre

quake [kweɪk] **1** *n Fam* tremblement *m* de terre **2** *vi* trembler (**with** de)

Quaker [ˈkweɪkə(r)] *n Rel* quaker, -eresse *mf*

qualification [kwɒlɪfɪˈkeɪʃən] *n (diploma)* diplôme *m*; *(skill)* compétence *f*; *(modification)* précision *f*

qualify [ˈkwɒlɪfaɪ] *(pt & pp -ied)* **1** *vt* **(a)** *(make competent, in sport)* qualifier **(for sth** pour qch) **(b)** *(modify)* nuancer **2** *vi (of sportsperson)* se qualifier **(for** pour); **to q. as a doctor** obtenir son diplôme de médecin; **to q. for sth** *(be eligible)* avoir droit à qch ▪ **qualified** *adj (competent)* compétent; *(having diploma)* diplômé; *(support)* mitigé

quality [ˈkwɒlətɪ] *(pl -ies) n* qualité *f*

quantity [ˈkwɒntətɪ] *(pl -ies) n* quantité *f*

quarantine [ˈkwɒrəntiːn] *n* quarantaine *f*

quarrel [ˈkwɒrəl] **1** *n* dispute *f*, querelle *f* **2** *(Br -ll-, Am -l-) vi* se disputer **(with** avec); **to q. with sth** ne pas être d'accord avec qch

quarry [ˈkwɒrɪ] *(pl -ies) n (for stone)* carrière *f*

quart [kwɔːt] *n (liquid measurement)* *Br* = 1,14 l, *Am* = 0,95 l

quarter¹ [ˈkwɔːtə(r)] *n* quart *m*; *(of fruit, moon)* quartier *m*; *(division of year)* trimestre *m*; *Am & Can (money)* pièce *f* de 25 cents; **q. (of a) pound** quart *m* de livre; *Br* **a q. past nine**, *Am* **a q. after nine** neuf heures et quart; **a q. to nine** neuf heures moins le quart

quarter² [ˈkwɔːtə(r)] *n (district)* quartier *m*; **(living) quarters** logements *mpl*; *(of soldier)* quartiers *mpl*

quarterback [ˈkwɔːtəbæk] *n* quarterback *m*

quarterfinal [kwɔːtəˈfaɪnəl] *n* quart *m* de finale

quarterly [ˈkwɔːtəlɪ] **1** *adj (magazine, payment)* trimestriel, -elle **2** *adv* tous les trimestres

quartet(te) [kwɔːˈtet] *n (music, players)* quatuor *m*; **(jazz) q.** quartette *m*

quartz [kwɔːts] **1** *n* quartz *m* **2** *adj (watch)* à quartz

quash [kwɒʃ] *vt (rebellion)* réprimer; *(sentence)* annuler

quasi- [ˈkweɪzaɪ] *pref* quasi-

quay [kiː] *n* quai *m*

queasy [ˈkwiːzɪ] **(-ier, -iest)** *adj* **to feel** *or* **be q.** avoir mal au cœur

Quebec [kwɪˈbek] *n* le Québec

queen [kwiːn] *n* reine *f*

queer [ˈkwɪə(r)] **(-er, -est)** *adj (strange)* bizarre

quench [kwentʃ] *vt (thirst)* étancher

query [ˈkwɪərɪ] **1** *(pl -ies) n* question *f* **2** *(pt & pp -ied) vt* mettre en question

quest [kwest] *n* quête *f* **(for** de)

question [ˈkwestʃən] **1** *n* question *f*; **there's no q. of it, it's out of the q.** c'est hors de question; **the matter/person in q.** l'affaire/la personne en question; **q. mark** point *m* d'interrogation **2** *vt* interroger **(about** sur); *(doubt)* mettre en question

questionable ['kwestʃənəbəl] *adj* discutable

questionnaire [kwestʃəneə(r)] *n* questionnaire *m*

queue [kju:] *Br* 1 *n (of people)* queue *f; (of cars)* file *f;* **to form a q., to stand in a q.** faire la queue 2 *vi* **to q. (up)** faire la queue

quiche [ki:ʃ] *n* quiche *f*

quick [kwɪk] 1 (-er, -est) *adj (rapid)* rapide; *(clever)* vif *(f* vive); **be q.!** fais vite!; **to have a q. shower/meal** se doucher/manger en vitesse 2 (-er, -est) *adv Fam* vite

quicken ['kwɪkən] 1 *vt* accélérer 2 *vi* s'accélérer

quickly ['kwɪklɪ] *adv* vite

quid [kwɪd] *n inv Br Fam (pound)* livre *f*

quiet ['kwaɪət] 1 (-er, -est) *adj (silent, still, peaceful)* tranquille, calme; *(machine, vehicle)* silencieux, -euse; *(person, voice, music)* doux *(f* douce); **to be** or **keep q.** *(say nothing)* se taire; *(make no noise)* ne pas faire de bruit; **to keep q. about sth, to keep sth q.** ne rien dire au sujet de qch; **q.!** silence! 2 *n Fam* **on the q.** *(secretly)* en cachette

quieten ['kwaɪətən] *Br* 1 *vt* **to q. (down)** calmer 2 *vi* **to q. down** se calmer

quietly ['kwaɪətlɪ] *adv* tranquillement; *(gently, not loudly)* doucement; *(silently)* silencieusement; *(secretly)* en cachette; *(discreetly)* discrètement

quilt [kwɪlt] *n* édredon *m; Br* **(conti-** nental) q.** *(duvet)* couette *f*

quip [kwɪp] 1 *n* boutade *f* 2 *(pt & pp* **-pp-)** *vti* plaisanter

quirk [kwɜ:k] *n (of character)* particularité *f* ◼ **quirky** (-ier, -iest) *adj* bizarre

quit [kwɪt] *(pt & pp* **quit** or **quitted,** *pres p* **quitting)** 1 *vt (leave)* quitter; *Comptr* sortir de; **to q. doing sth** arrêter de faire qch 2 *vi (give up)* abandonner; *(resign)* démissionner; *Comptr* sortir

quite [kwaɪt] *adv (entirely)* tout à fait; *(really)* vraiment; *(fairly)* assez; **q. good** *(not bad)* pas mal du tout; **q. (so)!** exactement!; **q. a lot** pas mal (**of** de)

quits [kwɪts] *adj* quitte (**with** envers); **to call it q.** en rester là

quiver ['kwɪvə(r)] *vi (of voice)* trembler

quiz [kwɪz] 1 *(pl* **-zz-)** *n (on radio)* jeu *m* radiophonique; *(on TV)* jeu *m* télévisé; *(in magazine)* questionnaire *m* 2 *(pt & pp* **-zz-)** *vt* interroger

quota ['kwəʊtə] *n* quota *m*

quotation [kwəʊ'teɪʃən] *n (from author)* citation *f; (estimate)* devis *m;* **in q. marks** entre guillemets

quote [kwəʊt] 1 *n (from author)* citation *f. (estimate)* devis *m;* **in quotes** entre guillemets 2 *vt (author, passage)* citer; *(reference number)* rappeler; *(price)* indiquer 3 *vi* **to q. from** *(author, book)* citer

Rr

R, r [ɑː(r)] *n (lettre)* R, r *m inv*

rabbi ['ræbaɪ] *n* rabbin *m*

rabbit ['ræbɪt] *n* lapin *m*

rabies ['reɪbiːz] *n* rage *f*

raccoon [rə'kuːn] *n* raton *m* laveur

race¹ [reɪs] **1** *n (contest)* course *f*
2 *vt* **to r. (against** *or* **with) sb** faire une course avec qn
3 *vi (run)* courir ■ **racecourse** *n* champ *m* de courses ■ **racehorse** *n* cheval *m* de course ■ **racetrack** *n Am (for horses)* champ *m* de courses; *Br (for cars, bicycles)* piste *f* ■ **racing** *n* courses *fpl*; **r. car** voiture *f* de course; **r. driver** coureur *m* automobile

race² [reɪs] *n (group)* race *f*; **r. relations** relations *fpl* interraciales ■ **racial** ['reɪʃəl] *adj* racial ■ **racism** *n* racisme *m* ■ **racist** *adj & n* raciste *(mf)*

rack [ræk] **1** *n (for bottles, letters, records)* casier *m*; *(for plates)* égouttoir *m*; **(luggage) r.** porte-bagages *m inv*; **(roof) r.** *(of car)* galerie *f* **2** *vt* **to r. one's brains** se creuser la cervelle

racket¹ ['rækɪt] *n (for tennis)* raquette *f*

racket² ['rækɪt] *n Fam* **(a)** *(din)* vacarme *m* **(b)** *(criminal activity)* racket *m*

radar ['reɪdɑː(r)] *n* radar *m*

radiant ['reɪdɪənt] *adj (person, face)* resplendissant **(with** de)

radiate ['reɪdɪeɪt] **1** *vt (heat, light)* dégager; *Fig (joy, health)* être rayonnant de **2** *vi* rayonner **(from** de) ■ **radiation** *n (radioactivity)* radiation *f*

radiator ['reɪdɪeɪtə(r)] *n (heater)* radiateur *m*

radical ['rædɪkəl] *adj & n* radical, -e *(mf)*

radio ['reɪdɪəʊ] **1** *(pl* **-os)** *n* radio *f*; **on the r.** à la radio; **r. cassette (player)** radiocassette *f* **2** *(pt & pp* **-oed)** *vt (message)* transmettre par radio **(to** à); **to r. sb** contacter qn par radio ■ **radio-controlled** *adj* radioguidé

radioactivity [reɪdɪəʊæk'tɪvɪtɪ] *n* radioactivité *f*

radish ['rædɪʃ] *n* radis *m*

radius ['reɪdɪəs] *(pl* **-dii)** *n* rayon *m*; **within a r. of 10 km** dans un rayon de 10 km

RAF [ɑːreɪ'ef] *(abbr* **Royal Air Force)** *n* = armée de l'air britannique

raffle ['ræfəl] *n* tombola *f*

raft [rɑːft] *n* radeau *m*

rag [ræg] *n* **(a)** *(piece of old clothing)* chiffon *m*; **in rags** *(clothes)* en loques; *(person)* en haillons **(b)** *Fam Pej (newspaper)* torchon *m*

rage [reɪdʒ] **1** *n (of person)* rage *f*; **to fly into a r.** entrer dans une rage folle; *Fam* **to be all the r.** *(of fashion)* faire fureur **2** *vi (be angry)* être furieux, -euse; *(of storm, battle)* faire rage ■ **raging** *adj (storm, fever, fire)* violent

ragged ['rægɪd] *adj (clothes)* en loques; *(person)* en haillons; *(edge)* irrégulier, -ère

raid [reɪd] **1** *n (military)* raid *m*; *(by police)* descente *f*; *(by thieves)* hold-up *m inv*; **air r.** raid *m* aérien **2** *vt* faire un raid/une descente/un hold-up dans

rail [reɪl] **1** *n* **(a)** *(for train)* rail *m*; **by r.** par le train **(b)** *(rod on balcony)* balustrade *f*; *(on stairs)* rampe *f*; *(curtain rod)* tringle *f* **2** *adj (ticket)* de chemin de fer; *(strike)* des cheminots ■ **railcard** *n* carte *f* d'abonnement de train

railings ['reɪlɪŋz] *npl* grille *f*

railroad ['reɪlrəʊd] *n Am (system)* chemin *m* de fer; *(track)* voie *f* ferrée

railway ['reɪlweɪ] *Br* **1** *n (system)* chemin *m* de fer; *(track)* voie *f* ferrée **2** *adj*

(ticket) de chemin de fer; *(timetable)* des chemins de fer; *(network, company)* ferroviaire; **r. line** ligne *f* de chemin de fer; **r. station** gare *f*

rain [reɪn] **1** *n* pluie *f*; **in the r.** sous la pluie **2** *vi* pleuvoir; **it's raining** il pleut ■ **rainbow** *n* arc-en-ciel *m* ■ **raincoat** *n* imperméable *m* ■ **rainfall** *n (amount)* précipitations *fpl* ■ **rainforest** *n* forêt *f* tropicale humide ■ **rainwater** *n* eau *f* de pluie ■ **rainy (-ier, -iest)** *adj* pluvieux, -euse; *(day)* de pluie; **the r. season** la saison des pluies

raise [reɪz] **1** *vt (lift)* lever; *(child, family, voice)* élever; *(salary, price)* augmenter; *(temperature)* faire monter; *(question, protest)* soulever; *(taxes)* lever; **to r. money** réunir des fonds; **to r. the alarm** donner l'alarme **2** *n Am (pay rise)* augmentation *f* (de salaire)

raisin ['reɪzən] *n* raisin *m* sec

rake [reɪk] **1** *n* râteau *m* **2** *vt (soil)* ratisser; **to r. (up)** *(leaves)* ratisser

rally ['rælɪ] **1** *(pl -ies)* *n (political)* rassemblement *m*; *(car race)* rallye *m* **2** *(pt & pp -ied)* *vt (unite, win over)* rallier ̄**to** à) **3** *vi* se rallier **(to** à); *(recover)* reprendre ses forces; **to r. round sb** venir en aide à qn

RAM [ræm] *(abbr* **random access memory)** *n Comptr* mémoire *f* vive

ram [ræm] **1** *n (animal)* bélier *m* **2** *(pt & pp -mm-)* *vt (vehicle)* emboutir; *(ship)* aborder; **to r. sth into sth** enfoncer qch dans qch

ramble ['ræmbəl] **1** *n (hike)* randonnée *f* **2** *vi (hike)* faire une randonnée; **to r. on** *(talk)* divaguer ■ **rambler** *n* randonneur, -euse *mf*

rambling ['ræmblɪŋ] *adj* **(a)** *(house)* plein de coins et de recoins; *(spread out)* vaste **(b)** *(speech)* décousu

ramp [ræmp] *n (for wheelchair)* rampe *f* d'accès; *(in garage)* pont *m* (de graissage); *(on road)* petit dos *m* d'âne

rampant ['ræmpənt] *adj* endémique

ran [ræn] *pt of* **run**

ranch [rɑːntʃ] *n* ranch *m*

rancid ['rænsɪd] *adj* rance

random ['rændəm] **1** *n* **at r.** au hasard

2 *adj (choice)* (fait) au hasard; *(sample)* prélevé au hasard

rang [ræŋ] *pt of* **ring**[2]

range [reɪndʒ] **1** *n* **(a)** *(of gun, voice)* portée *f*; *(of singer's voice)* registre *m*; *(of aircraft, ship)* rayon *m* d'action; *(of colours, prices, products)* gamme *f*; *(of sizes)* choix *m* **(b)** *(of mountains)* chaîne *f* **(c)** *(stove)* fourneau *m* **(d)** **(shooting) r.** champ *m* de tir **2** *vi (vary)* varier **(from** de **to** à); *(extend)* s'étendre

ranger ['reɪndʒə(r)] *n* **(forest) r.** garde *m* forestier

rank[1] [ræŋk] **1** *n (position, class)* rang *m*; *(military grade)* grade *m*; *(row)* rangée *f*; *(for taxis)* station *f* **2** *vt* placer **(among** parmi) **3** *vi* compter **(among** parmi)

rank[2] [ræŋk] **(-er, -est)** *adj (smell)* fétide

ransack ['rænsæk] *vt (house)* mettre sens dessus dessous; *(shop, town)* piller

ransom ['rænsəm] **1** *n* rançon *f*; **to hold sb to r.** rançonner qn **2** *vt* rançonner

rant [rænt] *vi Fam* **to r. and rave** tempêter **(at** contre)

rap [ræp] **1** *n* **(a)** *(blow)* coup *m* sec **(b)** **r. (music)** rap *m* **2** *vi (hit)* frapper **(on** à)

rape [reɪp] **1** *n* viol *m* **2** *vt* violer ■ **rapist** *n* violeur *m*

rapid ['ræpɪd] *adj* rapide ■ **rapidly** *adv* rapidement

rapids ['ræpɪdz] *npl (of river)* rapides *mpl*

rare [reə(r)] *adj* **(a)** **(-er, -est)** *(uncommon)* rare **(b)** *(meat)* saignant ■ **rarely** *adv* rarement ■ **rarity** *(pl -ies)* *n (quality, object)* rareté *f*

raring ['reərɪŋ] *adj* **r. to do sth** impatient de faire qch

rascal ['rɑːskəl] *n* coquin, -e *mf*

rash[1] [ræʃ] *n (on skin) (red patches)* rougeurs *fpl*; *(spots)* (éruption *f* de) boutons *mpl*

rash[2] [ræʃ] **(-er, -est)** *adj (imprudent)* irréfléchi ■ **rashly** *adv* sans réfléchir

rasher ['ræʃə(r)] *n Br* tranche *f* (de bacon)

raspberry ['rɑːzbərɪ] (*pl* **-ies**) *n* (*fruit*) framboise *f*

rat [ræt] *n* rat *m*; *Fig* **r. race** foire *f* d'empoigne

rate [reɪt] **1** *n* (*level, percentage*) taux *m*; (*speed*) rythme *m*; (*price*) tarif *m*; **interest r.** taux *m* d'intérêt; **at the r. of** au rythme de; (*amount*) à raison de; **at this r.** (*slow speed*) à ce train-là; **at any r.** en tout cas **2** *vt* (*regard*) considérer (**as** comme); (*deserve*) mériter; **to r. sb/sth highly** tenir qn/qch en haute estime

rather ['rɑːðə(r)] *adv* (*preferably, quite*) plutôt; **I'd r. stay** j'aimerais mieux rester (**than** que); **I r. liked it** j'ai bien aimé

ratify ['rætɪfaɪ] (*pt & pp* **-ied**) *vt* ratifier

rating ['reɪtɪŋ] *n* (*classification*) classement *m*

ratio ['reɪʃɪəʊ] (*pl* **-os**) *n* rapport *m*

ration ['ræʃən] **1** *n* ration *f*; **rations** (*food*) vivres *mpl* **2** *vt* rationner ▪ **rationing** *n* rationnement *m*

rational ['ræʃənəl] *adj* (*sensible*) raisonnable; (*sane*) rationnel, -elle ▪ **rationalize** *vt* (*organize*) rationaliser; (*explain*) justifier ▪ **rationally** *adv* (*behave*) raisonnablement

rattle ['rætəl] **1** *n* (*for baby*) hochet *m* **2** *vt* (*window*) faire vibrer; (*keys, chains*) faire cliqueter; *Fam* **to r. sth off** (*speech, list*) débiter qch **3** *vi* (*of window*) vibrer

raucous ['rɔːkəs] *adj* (*noisy, rowdy*) bruyant

rave [reɪv] **1** *n* (*party*) rave *f* **2** *vi* (*talk nonsense*) délirer; **to r. about sb/sth** (*enthuse*) ne pas tarir d'éloges sur qn/qch ▪ **raving** *adj* **to be r. mad** être complètement fou (*f* folle)

raven ['reɪvən] *n* corbeau *m*

ravenous ['rævənəs] *adj* **I'm r.** j'ai une faim de loup

ravine [rə'viːn] *n* ravin *m*

ravioli [rævɪ'əʊlɪ] *n* ravioli(s) *mpl*

raw [rɔː] (**-er, -est**) *adj* (*vegetable*) cru; (*data*) brut; **r. material** matière *f* première

ray [reɪ] *n* (*of light, sun*) rayon *m*; *Fig* (*of hope*) lueur *f*

rayon ['reɪɒn] *n* rayonne *f*

razor ['reɪzə(r)] *n* rasoir *m*; **r. blade** lame *f* de rasoir

Rd (*abbr* **road**) rue

re [riː] *prep Com* en référence à; **re your letter** suite à votre lettre

reach [riːtʃ] **1** *n* portée *f*; **within r. of** à portée de; (*near*) à proximité de; **within (easy) r.** (*object*) à portée de main; (*shops*) tout proche **2** *vt* (*place, aim, distant object*) atteindre, arriver à; (*decision*) prendre; (*agreement*) aboutir à; (*contact*) joindre; **to r. a conclusion** arriver à une conclusion; **to r. out one's arm** tendre le bras **3** *vi* (*extend*) s'étendre (**to** jusqu'à); **to r. (out) for sth** tendre le bras pour prendre qch

react [rɪ'ækt] *vi* réagir (**against** contre; **to** à) ▪ **reaction** *n* réaction *f*

reactionary [rɪ'ækʃənərɪ] (*pl* **-ies**) *adj & n* réactionnaire (*mf*)

reactor [rɪ'æktə(r)] *n* réacteur *m*

read [riːd] **1** (*pt & pp* **read** [red]) *vt* lire; (*meter*) relever; (*of instrument*) indiquer; *Br Univ* (*study*) étudier **2** *vi* (*of person*) lire (**about** sur); **to r. to sb** faire la lecture à qn **3** *n* **to be a good r.** être agréable à lire ▪ **readable** *adj* (*handwriting*) lisible; (*book*) facile à lire

▸ **read back** *vt sep* relire
▸ **read out** *vt sep* lire (à haute voix)
▸ **read over** *vt sep* relire
▸ **read through** *vt sep* (*skim*) parcourir
▸ **read up (on)** *vt insep* (*study*) étudier

reader ['riːdə(r)] *n* lecteur, -trice *mf*; (*book*) livre *m* de lecture

readily ['redɪlɪ] *adv* (*willingly*) volontiers; (*easily*) facilement

reading ['riːdɪŋ] *n* lecture *f*; (*of meter*) relevé *m*; **r. glasses** lunettes *fpl* de lecture; **r. lamp** (*on desk*) lampe *f* de bureau; (*at bedside*) lampe *f* de chevet; **r. matter** de quoi lire

readjust [riːə'dʒʌst] **1** *vt* (*instrument*)

régler **2** *vi (of person)* se réadapter (**to** à)

ready ['redɪ] **1** (**-ier, -iest**) *adj* prêt (**to do** à faire; **for sth** pour qch); **to get sb/ sth r.** préparer qn/qch; **to get r.** se préparer (**for sth** pour qch; **to do** à faire); **r. cash, r. money** argent *m* liquide

2 *n* **to be at the r.** être tout prêt (*f* toute prête) ▪ **ready-made** *adj (food)* tout prêt (*f* toute prête); **r. clothes** le prêt-à-porter ▪ **ready-to-wear** *adj* **r. clothes** le prêt-à-porter

real [rɪəl] **1** *adj* vrai; *(leather)* véritable; *(world, danger)* réel (*f* réelle); **in r. life** dans la réalité; *Am* **r. estate** immobilier *m* **2** *adv Fam* vraiment **3** *n Fam* **for r.** pour de vrai

realistic [rɪə'lɪstɪk] *adj* réaliste

reality [rɪ'ælətɪ] (*pl* **-ies**) *n* réalité *f*; **in r.** en réalité

realization [rɪəlaɪ'zeɪʃən] *n (awareness)* prise *f* de conscience

realize ['rɪəlaɪz] *vt* (**a**) *(become aware of)* se rendre compte de; **to r. that...** se rendre compte que... (**b**) *(carry out)* réaliser

really ['rɪəlɪ] *adv* vraiment

Realtor® ['rɪəltɔː(r)] *n Am* agent *m* immobilier

ream [riːm] *n (of paper)* rame *f*

reap [riːp] *vt (crop)* moissonner; *Fig (profits)* récolter

reappear [riːə'pɪə(r)] *vi* réapparaître

rear¹ [rɪə(r)] **1** *n (back part)* arrière *m*; **in** *or* **at the r.** à l'arrière (**of** de) **2** *adj (entrance, legs)* de derrière; *(lights, window)* arrière *inv*

rear² [rɪə(r)] **1** *vt (child, animals)* élever; *(one's head)* relever **2** *vi* **to r. (up)** *(of horse)* se cabrer

rearrange [riːə'reɪndʒ] *vt (hair, room)* réarranger; *(plans)* changer

rearview ['rɪəvjuː] *n* **r. mirror** rétroviseur *m*

reason ['riːzən] **1** *n (cause, sense)* raison *f*; **the r. for/why** la raison de/pour laquelle; **for no r.** sans raison; **it stands to r.** cela va de soi; **within r.** dans des limites raisonnables

2 *vt* **to r. that...** estimer que...

3 *vi* raisonner (**about** sur); **to r. with sb** raisonner qn ▪ **reasoning** *n* raisonnement *m*

reasonable ['riːzənəbəl] *adj (fair)* raisonnable; *(quite good)* passable ▪ **reasonably** *adv (behave, act)* raisonnablement; *(quite)* plutôt

reassure [riːə'ʃʊə(r)] *vt* rassurer ▪ **reassuring** *adj* rassurant

rebate ['riːbeɪt] *n (discount)* rabais *m*; *(refund)* remboursement *m*

rebel 1 ['rebəl] *n* rebelle *mf* **2** ['rebəl] *adj (camp, chief, attack)* des rebelles **3** [rɪ'bel] (*pt & pp* **-ll-**) *vi* se rebeller (**against** contre) ▪ **rebellion** [rɪ'beljən] *n* rébellion *f*

rebound 1 ['riːbaʊnd] *n (of ball)* rebond *m* **2** [rɪ'baʊnd] *vi (of ball)* rebondir; *Fig (of lies, action)* se retourner (**on** contre)

rebuild [riː'bɪld] (*pt & pp* **-built**) *vt* reconstruire

rebuke [rɪ'bjuːk] **1** *n* réprimande *f* **2** *vt* réprimander

recall [rɪ'kɔːl] **1** *n (calling back)* rappel *m* **2** *vt (remember)* se rappeler (**that** que; **doing** avoir fait); *(call back)* rappeler; **to r. sth to sb** rappeler qch à qn

recap ['riːkæp] **1** *n* récapitulation *f* **2** (*pt & pp* **-pp-**) *vi* récapituler

recapitulate [riːkə'pɪtjʊleɪt] *vti* récapituler

recede [rɪ'siːd] *vi (into the distance)* s'éloigner; *(of floods)* baisser ▪ **receding** *adj* **his hairline is r., he has a r. hairline** son front se dégarnit

receipt [rɪ'siːt] *n (for payment, object)* reçu *m* (**for** de); *(for letter, parcel)* récépissé *m*; **receipts** *(at box office)* recette *f*; **on r. of sth** dès réception de qch

receive [rɪ'siːv] *vt* recevoir; *(stolen goods)* receler

receiver [rɪ'siːvə(r)] *n (of phone)* combiné *m*; *(radio)* récepteur *m*; **to pick up** *or* **lift the r.** *(of phone)* décrocher

recent ['riːsənt] *adj* récent; *(development)* dernier, -ère; **in r. months** au cours des derniers mois ▪ **recently** *adv* récemment

reception [rɪ'sepʃən] *n (party, of radio)* réception *f*; *(welcome)* accueil *m*; **r. (desk)** réception *f* ■ **receptionist** *n* réceptionniste *mf*

receptive [rɪ'septɪv] *adj* réceptif, -ive **(to** à)

recess [*Br* rɪ'ses, *Am* 'riːses] *n* (**a**) *(holiday)* vacances *fpl*; *Am (between classes)* récréation *f* (**b**) *(in wall)* renfoncement *m*; *(smaller)* recoin *m*

recession [rɪ'seʃən] *n Econ* récession *f*

recharge [riː'tʃɑːdʒ] *vt (battery, mobile phone)* recharger ■ **rechargeable** *adj (battery)* rechargeable

recipe ['resɪpɪ] *n (for food) & Fig* recette *f* (**for sth** de qch)

recipient [rɪ'sɪpɪənt] *n (of gift, letter)* destinataire *mf*; *(of award)* lauréat, -e *mf*

reciprocal [rɪ'sɪprəkəl] *adj* réciproque ■ **reciprocate 1** *vt* retourner **2** *vi* rendre la pareille

recital [rɪ'saɪtəl] *n (of music)* récital *m* (*pl* -als)

recite [rɪ'saɪt] *vt (poem)* réciter; *(list)* énumérer

reckless ['rekləs] *adj (rash)* imprudent

reckon ['rekən] **1** *vt (calculate)* calculer; *(consider)* considérer; *Fam (think)* penser (**that** que) **2** *vi* calculer, compter; **to r. with** *(take into account)* compter avec; *(deal with)* avoir affaire à; **to r. on sb/sth** *(rely on)* compter sur qn/qch ■ **reckoning** *n (calculation)* calcul *m*

reclaim [rɪ'kleɪm] *vt (lost property, luggage)* récupérer; *(expenses)* se faire rembourser

recline [rɪ'klaɪn] *vi (be stretched out)* être allongé ■ **reclining** *adj* **r. seat** siège *m* à dossier inclinable

recluse [rɪ'kluːs] *n* reclus, -e *mf*

recognition [rekəg'nɪʃən] *n* reconnaissance *f*; **to gain r.** être reconnu

recognize ['rekəgnaɪz] *vt* reconnaître ■ **recognizable** *adj* reconnaissable

recoil [rɪ'kɔɪl] *vi (of person)* avoir un mouvement de recul

recollect [rekə'lekt] *vt* se souvenir de

■ **recollection** *n* souvenir *m*

recommend [rekə'mend] *vt (praise, support, advise)* recommander (**to** à; **for** pour); **to r. sb to do sth** recommander à qn de faire qch ■ **recommendation** *n* recommandation *f*

recompense ['rekəmpens] **1** *n* récompense *f* **2** *vt (reward)* récompenser

reconcile ['rekənsaɪl] *vt (person)* réconcilier (**with** *or* **to** avec); *(opinions, facts)* concilier; **to r. oneself to sth** se résigner à qch

reconditioned [riːkən'dɪʃənd] *adj (engine, machine)* remis à neuf

reconsider [riːkən'sɪdə(r)] **1** *vt* réexaminer **2** *vi* réfléchir

reconstruct [riːkən'strʌkt] *vt (crime)* reconstituer

record 1 ['rekɔːd] *n* (**a**) *(disc)* disque *m*; **r. player** électrophone *m*
(**b**) *(best sporting performance)* record *m*
(**c**) *(report)* rapport *m*; *(background)* antécédents *mpl*; *(file)* dossier *m*; **to make** *or* **keep a r. of sth** garder une trace écrite de qch; **on r.** *(fact, event)* attesté; **(police) r.** casier *m* judiciaire; **(public) records** archives *fpl*
2 ['rekɔːd] *adj* record *inv*; **to be at a r. high/low** être à son taux le plus haut/bas
3 [rɪ'kɔːd] *vt (on tape, in register)* enregistrer; *(in diary)* noter
4 [rɪ'kɔːd] *vi (on tape, of tape recorder)* enregistrer

recorded [rɪ'kɔːdɪd] *adj* enregistré; *(fact)* attesté; *(TV broadcast)* en différé; *Br* **to send sth (by) r. delivery** ≃ envoyer qch en recommandé avec accusé de réception

recorder [rɪ'kɔːdə(r)] *n (musical instrument)* flûte *f* à bec

recording [rɪ'kɔːdɪŋ] *n* enregistrement *m*

recount [rɪ'kaʊnt] *vt (relate)* raconter

recoup [rɪ'kuːp] *vt* récupérer

recourse [rɪ'kɔːs] *n* recours *m*; **to have r. to** avoir recours à

recover [rɪ'kʌvə(r)] **1** *vt (get back)* récupérer; *(one's appetite, balance)* re-

trouver **2** *vi (from illness, shock, surprise)* se remettre (**from** de); *(of economy, country)* se redresser; *(cf sales)* reprendre ■ **recovery** *(pl -ies) n* (**a**) *(from illness)* rétablissement *m*; *(cf economy)* redressement *m* (**b**) *Br* **r. vehicle** dépanneuse *f*

re-create [riːkrɪˈeɪt] *vt* recréer

recreation [rekrɪˈeɪʃən] *n Sch (break)* récréation *f*

recrimination [rɪkrɪmɪˈneɪʃən] *n* récrimination *f*

recruit [rɪˈkruːt] **1** *n* recrue *f* **2** *vt* recruter

rectangle [ˈrektæŋgəl] *n* rectangle *m* ■ **rectangular** *adj* rectangulaire

rectify [ˈrektɪfaɪ] *(pt & pp -ied) vt* rectifier

rector [ˈrektə(r)] *n (priest)* pasteur *m* anglican

recuperate [rɪˈkuːpəreɪt] *vi (from illness)* récupérer

recur [rɪˈkɜː(r)] *(pt & pp -rr-) vi (of event, problem)* se reproduire; *(of illness)* réapparaître; *(of theme)* revenir

recycle [riːˈsaɪkəl] *vt* recycler

red [red] **1** (**redder, reddest**) *adj* rouge; *(hair)* roux *(f* rousse*)*; **to turn** or **go r.** rougir; **the R. Cross** la Croix-Rouge; **r. light** *(traffic light)* feu *m* rouge; *Fig* **r. tape** paperasserie *f* **2** *n (colour)* rouge *m*; **in the r.** *(in debt)* dans le rouge ■ **red-handed** *adv* **to be caught r.** être pris la main dans le sac ■ **redhead** *n* roux *m*, rousse *f* ■ **red-hot** *adj* brûlant

redcurrant [redˈkʌrənt] *n* groseille *f*

redecorate [riːˈdekəreɪt] *vt (repaint)* refaire la peinture de

redeem [rɪˈdiːm] *vt (restore to favour, buy back, free)* racheter; *(gift token, coupon)* échanger; **his one redeeming feature is...** la seule chose qui le rachète, c'est...

redirect [riːdaɪˈrekt] *vt (mail)* faire suivre

redo [riːˈduː] *(pt -did, pp -done) vt* refaire

reduce [rɪˈdjuːs] *vt* réduire (**to** à; **by** de); *(temperature, price)* baisser; **at a**

reduced price à prix réduit; **to be reduced to doing sth** en être réduit à faire qch ■ **reduction** [-ˈdʌkʃən] *n (of temperature, price)* baisse *f*; *(discount)* réduction *f* (**in/on** de/sur)

redundant [rɪˈdʌndənt] *adj (not needed)* superflu; *Br* **to make sb r.** licencier qn ■ **redundancy** *(pl -ies) n Br (of worker)* licenciement *m*; **r. pay** or **payment** or **money** prime *f* de licenciement

reed [riːd] *n (plant)* roseau *m*

reef [riːf] *n* récif *m*

reek [riːk] *vi* **to r.** *(of sth)* puer (qch)

reel [riːl] **1** *n (of thread, film)* bobine *f*; *(for fishing line)* moulinet *m* **2** *vt sep* **to r. off** *(names, statistics)* débiter

re-elect [riːɪˈlekt] *vt* réélire

re-establish [riːɪˈstæblɪʃ] *vt* rétablir

ref [ref] *(abbr referee) n Fam* arbitre *m*

refectory [rɪˈfektərɪ] *(pl -ies) n* réfectoire *m*

refer [rɪˈfɜː(r)] *(pt & pp -rr-)* **1** *vt* **to r. sth to sb** *(submit)* soumettre qch à qn; **to r. sb to a specialist** envoyer qn voir un spécialiste **2** *vt insep* **to r. to** *(allude to)* faire allusion à; *(mention)* parler de; *(apply to)* s'appliquer à; *(consult)* consulter

referee [refəˈriː] **1** *n (in sport)* arbitre *m*; **to give the names of two referees** *(for job)* fournir deux références **2** *vti* arbitrer

reference [ˈrefərəns] *n (source, consultation)* référence *f*; *(allusion)* allusion *f* (**to** à); *(mention)* mention *f* (**to** de); *(for employer)* lettre *f* de référence; **with** or **in r. to** concernant; **r. book** ouvrage *m* de référence

referendum [refəˈrendəm] *n* référendum *m*

refill 1 [ˈriːfɪl] *n (for pen)* cartouche *f*; *(for lighter)* recharge *f*; **would you like a r.?** *(of drink)* je te ressers? **2** [riːˈfɪl] *vt (glass)* remplir à nouveau; *(lighter, pen)* recharger

refine [rɪˈfaɪn] *vt (oil, sugar, manners)* raffiner; *(technique, machine)* perfectionner ■ **refined** *adj (person, manners)* raffiné ■ **refinement** *n (of*

person, manners) raffinement *m*; **refinements** *(technical improvements)* améliorations *fpl*

reflect [rɪ'flekt] **1** *vt* (**a**) *(light, image)* refléter, réfléchir; *Fig (portray)* refléter; **to be reflected (in)** *(of light)* se refléter (dans) (**b**) **to r. that...** se dire que... **2** *vi* (**a**) **to r. on sb** *(of prestige, honour)* rejaillir sur qn; **to r. badly on sb** faire du tort à qn (**b**) *(think)* réfléchir (**on** à)

reflection [rɪ'flekʃən] *n* (**a**) *(image)* & *Fig* reflet *m* (**b**) *(thought, criticism)* réflexion (**on** sur); **on r.** tout bien réfléchi

reflector [rɪ'flektə(r)] *n (on bicycle, vehicle)* cataddioptre *m*

reflex ['riːfleks] *n & adj* réflexe (*m*); **r. action** réflexe *m*

reflexive [rɪ'fleksɪv] *adj (verb)* réfléchi

reform [rɪ'fɔːm] **1** *n* réforme *f* **2** *vt* réformer; *(person, conduct)* corriger **3** *vi (of person)* se réformer

refrain [rɪ'freɪn] **1** *n (of song)* & *Fig* refrain *m* **2** *vi* s'abstenir (**from sth** de qch; **from doing** de faire)

refresh [rɪ'freʃ] *vt (of drink)* rafraîchir; *(of bath)* revigorer; *(of sleep, rest)* reposer; **to r. one's memory** se rafraîchir la mémoire ▪ **refreshing** *adj (drink)* rafraîchissant; *(bath)* revigorant; *(original)* nouveau (*f* nouvelle)

refreshments [rɪ'freʃmənts] *npl* rafraîchissements *mpl*

refrigerate [rɪ'frɪdʒəreɪt] *vt* réfrigérer ▪ **refrigerator** *n (domestic)* réfrigérateur *m*

refuel [riː'fjʊəl] **1** *(Br -ll-, Am -l-) vt (aircraft)* ravitailler en carburant **2** *vi (of aircraft)* se ravitailler en carburant

refuge ['refjuːdʒ] *n* refuge *m*; **to take r.** se réfugier (**in** dans)

refugee [refjʊ'dʒiː] *n* réfugié, -e *mf*

refund 1 ['riːfʌnd] *n* remboursement *m* **2** [rɪ'fʌnd] *vt* rembourser

refurbish [riː'fɜːbɪʃ] *vt* rénover

refusal [rɪ'fjuːzəl] *n* refus *m*

refuse¹ [rɪ'fjuːz] **1** *vt* refuser; **to r. to do sth** refuser de faire qch; **to r. sb sth** refuser qch à qn **2** *vi* refuser

refuse² ['refjuːs] *n Br (rubbish)* ordu-

res *fpl*; **r. collection** ramassage *m* des ordures

refute [rɪ'fjuːt] *vt* réfuter

regain [rɪ'geɪn] *vt (lost ground, favour)* regagner; *(health, sight)* retrouver; **to r. consciousness** reprendre connaissance

regal ['riːgəl] *adj* royal

regard [rɪ'gɑːd] **1** *n (admiration)* respect *m*; *(consideration)* égard *m*; **to hold sb in high r.** tenir qn en haute estime; **with r. to** en ce qui concerne; **to give** *or* **send one's regards to sb** transmettre son meilleur souvenir à qn **2** *vt (admire, respect)* estimer; **to r. sb/ sth as...** considérer qn/qch comme... ▪ **regarding** *prep* en ce qui concerne

regardless [rɪ'gɑːdləs] **1** *adj* **r. of...** *(without considering)* sans tenir compte de... **2** *adv (all the same)* quand même

regenerate [rɪ'dʒenəreɪt] *vt* régénérer

reggae ['regeɪ] *n (music)* reggae *m*

régime [reɪ'ʒiːm] *n* régime *m*

regiment ['redʒɪmənt] *n* régiment *m*

region ['riːdʒən] *n* région *f*; *Fig* **in the r. of** *(about)* environ ▪ **regional** *adj* régional

register ['redʒɪstə(r)] **1** *n* registre *m*; *(in school)* cahier *m* d'appel; **electoral r.** liste *f* électorale; **to take the r.** *(of teacher)* faire l'appel **2** *vt (birth, death)* déclarer; *(record, note)* enregistrer; *(vehicle)* immatriculer; *(complaint)* déposer **3** *vi (enrol)* s'inscrire (**for** à); *(at hotel)* signer le registre; *(of voter)* s'inscrire sur les listes électorales ▪ **registered** *adj (member)* inscrit; *(letter, package)* recommandé; **to send sth by r. post** *or Am* **mail** envoyer qch en recommandé

registration [redʒɪ'streɪʃən] *n (enrolment)* inscription *f*; *Br* **r. (number)** *(of vehicle)* numéro *m* d'immatriculation; *Br* **r. document** *(of vehicle)* ≃ carte *f* grise

registry ['redʒɪstrɪ] *adj & n Br* **r. (office)** bureau *m* de l'état civil; **to get married in a r. office** se marier à la mairie

regret [rɪ'gret] **1** *n* regret *m* **2** *(pt & pp* **-tt-)** *vt* regretter (**to do** de faire; **that** que + *subjunctive*); **to r. doing sth** regretter d'avoir fait qch

regrettable [rɪ'gretəbəl] *adj* regrettable (**that** que + *subjunctive*)

regroup [riː'gruːp] *vi* se regrouper

regular ['regjʊlə(r)] **1** *adj (steady, even, in grammar)* régulier, -ère; *(usual)* habituel, -elle; *(price)* normal; *(size)* moyen, -enne; *(listener, reader)* fidèle; *Am Fam* **a r. guy** un chic type **2** *n (in bar)* habitué, -e *mf* ■ **regularly** *adv* régulièrement

regulate ['regjʊleɪt] *vt (adjust)* régler; *(control)* réglementer ■ **regulations** *npl (rules)* règlement *m*

rehabilitate [riːhə'bɪlɪteɪt] *vt* réhabiliter

rehearse [rɪ'hɜːs] *vti* répéter ■ **rehearsal** *n* répétition *f*

reign [reɪn] **1** *n* règne *m*; **in** or **during the r. of** sous le règne de **2** *vi* régner (**over** sur)

reimburse [riːɪm'bɜːs] *vt* rembourser (**for** de)

reindeer ['reɪndɪə(r)] *n inv* renne *m*

reinforce [riːɪn'fɔːs] *vt* renforcer (**with** de); **reinforced concrete** béton *m* armé ■ **reinforcements** *npl (troops)* renforts *mpl*

reinstate [riːɪn'steɪt] *vt* réintégrer

reiterate [riː'ɪtəreɪt] *vt* réitérer

reject 1 ['riːdʒekt] *n (object)* rebus *m* **2** [rɪ'dʒekt] *vt* rejeter; *(candidate, goods, offer)* refuser ■ **rejection** [rɪ'dʒekʃən] *n* rejet *m*; *(of candidate, goods, offer)* refus *m*

rejoice [rɪ'dʒɔɪs] *vi* se réjouir (**over** or **at** de) ■ **rejoicing** *n* réjouissance *f*

rejoin [rɪ'dʒɔɪn] *vt (join up with)* rejoindre

rejuvenate [rɪ'dʒuːvəneɪt] *vt* rajeunir

relapse ['riːlæps] *n* rechute *f*

relate [rɪ'leɪt] **1** *vt* **(a)** *(narrate)* raconter (**that** que); *(report)* rapporter (**that** que) **(b)** *(connect)* mettre en rapport (**to** avec)
2 *vi* **to r. to** *(apply to)* avoir rapport à; *(person)* avoir des affinités avec ■ **related** *adj (linked)* lié (**to** à); *(languages, styles)* apparenté; **to be r. to sb** *(by family)* être parent de qn

relation [rɪ'leɪʃən] *n* **(a)** *(relative)* parent, -e *mf* **(b)** *(relationship)* rapport *m*; **international relations** relations *fpl* internationales

relationship [rɪ'leɪʃənʃɪp] *n (within family)* lien *m* de parenté; *(between people)* relation *f*; *(between countries)* relations *fpl*; *(connection)* rapport *m*

relative ['relətɪv] **1** *n* parent, -e *mf* **2** *adj (comparative)* relatif, -ive; *(respective)* respectif, -ive; **r. to** *(compared to)* relativement à ■ **relatively** *adv* relativement

relax [rɪ'læks] **1** *vt (person, mind)* détendre; *(grip, pressure)* relâcher; *(law, control)* assouplir **2** *vi (of person)* se détendre; **r.!** *(calm down)* du calme! ■ **relaxed** *adj (person, atmosphere)* détendu ■ **relaxing** *adj* délassant

relaxation [riːlæk'seɪʃən] *n (of person)* détente *f*

relay 1 ['riːleɪ] *n* **r.** *(race)* (course *f* de) relais *m* **2** [riː'leɪ] *vt (information)* transmettre (**to** à)

release [rɪ'liːs] **1** *n (of prisoner)* libération *f*; *(of film)* sortie *f* (**of** de); *(film)* nouveau film *m*; *(record)* nouveau disque *m* **2** *vt (person)* libérer (**from** de); *(brake)* desserrer; *(film, record)* sortir; *(news)* communiquer; **to r. sb's hand** lâcher la main de qn

relegate ['relɪgeɪt] *vt* reléguer (**to** à); *Br* **to be relegated** *(of team)* descendre en division inférieure

relent [rɪ'lent] *vi (of person)* céder

relentless [rɪ'lentləs] *adj* implacable

relevant ['reləvənt] *adj* **(a)** *(apt)* pertinent; **to be r. to sth** avoir rapport à qch; **that's not r.** ça n'a rien à voir **(b)** *(appropriate) (chapter)* correspondant; *(authorities)* compétent; *(qualifications)* requis **(c)** *(topical)* d'actualité ■ **relevance** *n* pertinence *f* (**to** à); *(connection)* rapport *m* (**to** avec)

reliable [rɪ'laɪəbəl] *adj (person, machine)* fiable; *(information)* sûr ■ **reliability** *n (of person)* sérieux *m*; *(of machine)* fiabilité *f*

relic ['relɪk] *n* relique *f*; *Fig* **relics** vestiges *mpl*

relief [rɪ'liːf] **1** *n (comfort)* soulagement *m*; *(help)* secours *m*; *(in art)* relief *m* **2** *adj (train, bus)* supplémentaire; *(work)* de secours; **r. map** carte *f* en relief; *Br* **r. road** route *f* de délestage

relieve [rɪ'liːv] *vt (alleviate)* soulager; *(boredom)* tromper; *(replace)* remplacer; *(free)* libérer; **to r. sb of sth** débarrasser qn de qch; *Hum* **to r. oneself** se soulager

religion [rɪ'lɪdʒən] *n* religion *f* ■ **religious** *adj* religieux, -euse

relinquish [rɪ'lɪŋkwɪʃ] *vt (hope, habit, thought)* abandonner; *(share, claim)* renoncer à

relish ['relɪʃ] **1** *n (pickle)* condiments *mpl*; *(pleasure)* goût *m* (**for** pour); **to do sth with r.** faire qch avec délectation **2** *vt* savourer

reload [riː'ləʊd] *vt (gun, camera)* recharger

relocate [*Br* riː'ləʊ'keɪt, *Am* riː'ləʊkeɪt] *vi (of company)* être transféré; *(of person)* se déplacer

reluctant [rɪ'lʌktənt] *adj (greeting, promise)* accordé à contrecœur; **to be r. (to do sth)** être réticent (à faire qch) ■ **reluctantly** *adv* à contrecœur

rely [rɪ'laɪ] (*pt & pp* -ied) *vi* **to r. (up)on** *(count on)* compter sur; *(be dependent on)* dépendre de

remain [rɪ'meɪn] *vi (stay behind, continue to be)* rester; *(be left)* subsister ■ **remaining** *adj* restant ■ **remains** *npl* restes *mpl*

remainder [rɪ'meɪndə(r)] *n* reste *m*; *(book)* invendu *m* soldé

remark [rɪ'mɑːk] **1** *n* remarque *f* **2** *vt* faire remarquer **3** *vi* **to r. on sth** *(comment)* faire un commentaire sur qch ■ **remarkable** *adj* remarquable ■ **remarkably** *adv* remarquablement

remarry [riː'mærɪ] (*pt & pp* -ied) *vi* se remarier

remedy ['remɪdɪ] **1** (*pl* -ies) *n* remède *m* **2** (*pt & pp* -ied) *vt* remédier à

remember [rɪ'membə(r)] **1** *vt* se souvenir de, se rappeler; *(commemorate)*

commémorer; **to r. that /doing** se rappeler que/d'avoir fait; **to r. to do sth** penser à faire qch; **to r. sb to sb** rappeler qn au bon souvenir de qn **2** *vi* se souvenir, se rappeler

remind [rɪ'maɪnd] *vt* **to r. sb of sth** rappeler qch à qn; **to r. sb to do sth** rappeler à qn de faire qch ■ **reminder** *n (letter, of event)* rappel *m*

reminisce [remɪ'nɪs] *vi* évoquer des souvenirs; **to r. about sth** évoquer qch ■ **reminiscence** *n* souvenir *m*

reminiscent [remɪ'nɪsənt] *adj* **r. of** qui rappelle

remittance [rɪ'mɪtəns] *n (sum)* paiement *m*

remorse [rɪ'mɔːs] *n* remords *m*; **to feel r.** avoir du *ou* des remords ■ **remorseless** *adj* impitoyable

remote [rɪ'məʊt] (-er, -est) *adj* (a) *(far-off)* éloigné (**from** de); **r. control** télécommande *f* (b) *(slight)* vague ■ **remotely** *adv (slightly)* vaguement

removable [rɪ'muːvəbəl] *adj (lining)* amovible

removal [rɪ'muːvəl] *n* (a) *(of control, threat)* suppression *f*; *(of politician)* renvoi *m* (b) *Br* **r. van** camion *m* de déménagement

remove [rɪ'muːv] *vt (clothes, stain, object)* enlever (**from sb** à qn; **from sth** de qch); *(obstacle, threat, word)* supprimer; *(fear, doubt)* dissiper; *(politician)* renvoyer

remover [rɪ'muːvə(r)] *n (for nail polish)* dissolvant *m*; *(for paint)* décapant *m*; *(for stains)* détachant *m*

remunerate [rɪ'mjuːnəreɪt] *vt* rémunérer

rename [riː'neɪm] *vt* rebaptiser; *Comptr (file)* renommer

rendezvous ['rɒndɪvuː, *pl* -vuːz] *n inv* rendez-vous *m inv*

renew [rɪ'njuː] *vt* renouveler; *(resume)* reprendre; *(library book)* renouveler le prêt de ■ **renewed** *adj (efforts)* renouvelé; *(attempt)* nouveau (*f* nouvelle)

renounce [rɪ'naʊns] *vt (give up)* renoncer à; *(disown)* renier

renovate ['renəveɪt] *vt (house)* rénover; *(painting)* restaurer

renowned [rɪ'naʊnd] *adj* renommé (**for** pour)

rent [rent] **1** *n (for house, flat)* loyer *m* **2** *vt* louer; **to r. out** louer; **rented car** voiture *f* de location

rental ['rentəl] *n (of television, car)* location *f; (of telephone)* abonnement *m*

reopen [riː'əʊpən] *vti* rouvrir

reorganize [riː'ɔːgənaɪz] *vt* réorganiser

rep [rep] *(abbr* **representative)** *n Fam* VRP *m*

repair [rɪ'peə(r)] **1** *n* réparation *f;* **under r.** en travaux **2** *vt* réparer

repay [riː'peɪ] *(pt & pp* **-paid)** *vt (pay back)* rembourser; *(reward)* remercier (**for** de) ▪ **repayment** *n* remboursement *m*

repeal [rɪ'piːl] *vt* abroger

repeat [rɪ'piːt] **1** *n (of event)* répétition *f; (on TV, radio)* rediffusion *f*
2 *vt* répéter (**that** que); *(promise, threat)* réitérer; *(class)* redoubler *(TV programme)* rediffuser; **to r. oneself** se répéter
3 *vi* répéter ▪ **repeated** *adj (attempts)* répété; *(efforts)* renouvelé ▪ **repeatedly** *adv* à maintes reprises

repel [rɪ'pel] *(pt & pp* **-ll-)** *vt* repousser ▪ **repellent 1** *adj (disgusting)* repoussant **2** *n* **insect r.** anti-moustiques *minv*

repent [rɪ'pent] *vi* se repentir (**of** de) ▪ **repentant** *adj* repentant

repercussions [riːpə'kʌʃənz] *npl* répercussions *fpl* (**on** sur)

repertoire ['repətwɑː(r)] *n Theatre &* *Fig* répertoire *m* ▪ **repertory** [-tərɪ] *(pl* **-ies)** *n Theatre & Fig* répertoire *m;* **r. theatre** théâtre *m* de répertoire

repetition [repɪ'tɪʃən] *n* répétition ▪ **repetitious, repetitive** [repə'tɪʃəs, rɪ'petɪtɪv] *adj* répétitif, -ive

rephrase [riː'freɪz] *vt* reformuler

replace [rɪ'pleɪs] *vt (take the place of)* remplacer (**by** *or* **with** par); *(put back)* remettre (à sa place); **to r. the receiver** *(on phone)* raccrocher ▪ **replacement** *n (substitution)* remplacement *m* (**of** de);

(person) remplaçant, -e *mf; (machine part)* pièce *f* de rechange

replay 1 ['riːpleɪ] *n (match)* nouvelle rencontre *f; (instant or action)* **r.** *(on TV)* = répétition d'une séquence précédente **2** [riː'pleɪ] *vt (match)* rejouer

replica ['replɪkə] *n* réplique *f*

reply [rɪ'plaɪ] **1** *(pl* **-ies)** *n* réponse *f;* **in r.** en réponse (**to** à) **2** *(pt & pp* **-ied)** *vti* répondre (**to** à; **that** que)

report [rɪ'pɔːt] **1** *n (analysis)* rapport *m; (account)* compte rendu *m; (in media)* reportage *m; Br* **(school) r.,** *Am* **r. card** bulletin *m* scolaire
2 *vt (information)* rapporter; *(accident, theft)* signaler (**to** à); **to r. sb to the police** dénoncer qn à la police
3 *vi (give account)* faire un rapport (**on** sur); *(of journalist)* faire un reportage (**on** sur); *(go)* se présenter (**to** à) ▪ **reported** *adj* **r. speech** *(in grammar)* discours *m* indirect; **it is r. that...** on dit que...; **to be r. missing** être porté disparu ▪ **reporter** *n* reporter *m*

repossess [riːpə'zes] *vt* saisir

represent [reprɪ'zent] *vt* représenter ▪ **representation** *n* représentation *f*

representative [reprɪ'zentətɪv] **1** *adj* représentatif, -ive (**of** de) **2** *n* représentant, -e *mf; Am Pol* ≃ député *m*

repress [rɪ'pres] *vt* réprimer; *(memory, feeling)* refouler; **to be repressed** *(of person)* être un(e) refoulé(e) ▪ **repressive** *adj (régime)* répressif, -ive; *(measures)* de répression

reprieve [rɪ'priːv] *n (cancellation of sentence)* commutation *f* de la peine capitale; *(temporary) & Fig* sursis *m*

reprimand ['reprɪmɑːnd] **1** *n* réprimande *f* **2** *vt* réprimander

reprint ['riːprɪnt] *n* réimpression *f* **2** [riː'prɪnt] *vt* réimprimer

reprisal [rɪ'praɪzəl] *n* représailles *fpl;* **as a r. for, in r. for** en représailles de

reproach [rɪ'prəʊtʃ] **1** *n (blame)* reproche *m* **2** *vt* faire des reproches à; **to r. sb with sth** reprocher qch à qn

reproduce [riːprə'djuːs] **1** *vt* reproduire **2** *vi* se reproduire ▪ **reproduction** [-'dʌkʃən] *n* reproduction *f*

reptile ['reptaɪl] *n* reptile *m*

republic [rɪ'pʌblɪk] *n* république *f*
■ **republican** *adj & n* républicain, -e *(mf)*

repugnant [rɪ'pʌgnənt] *adj* répugnant

repulsive [rɪ'pʌlsɪv] *adj* repoussant

reputable ['repjʊtəbəl] *adj* de bonne réputation ■ **reputed** *adj* **she's r. to be wealthy** on la dit riche

reputation [repjʊ'teɪʃən] *n* réputation *f*

request [rɪ'kwest] **1** *n* demande *f* (**for** de); **on r.** sur demande; **at sb's r.** à la demande de qn; *Br* **r. stop** *(for bus)* arrêt *m* facultatif **2** *vt* demander; **to r. sb to do sth** prier qn de faire qch

require [rɪ'kwaɪə(r)] *vt (of task, problem, situation)* requérir; *(of person)* avoir besoin de; **to be required to do sth** être tenu de faire qch; **the required qualities** les qualités *fpl* requises ■ **requirement** *n (need)* exigence *f*; *(condition)* condition *f* (requise)

requisite ['rekwɪzɪt] *adj* requis

reschedule [*Br* riː'ʃedjuːl, *Am* riː'skedʒʊəl] *vt* changer la date/l'heure de

rescue ['reskjuː] **1** *n (action)* sauvetage *m* (**of** de); **to go/come to sb's r.** aller/venir au secours de qn **2** *adj (team, operation, attempt)* de sauvetage **3** *vt (save)* sauver; *(set free)* délivrer (**from** de)

research [rɪ'sɜːtʃ] **1** *n* recherches *fpl* (**on** *or* **into** sur) **2** *vi* faire des recherches (**on** *or* **into** sur) ■ **researcher** *n* chercheur, -euse *mf*

resemble [rɪ'zembəl] *vt* ressembler à ■ **resemblance** *n* ressemblance *f* (**to** avec)

resent [rɪ'zent] *vt* ne pas aimer ■ **resentment** *n* ressentiment *m*

reservation [rezə'veɪʃən] *n* (a) *(booking)* réservation *f*; **to make a r.** réserver (b) *(doubt)* réserve *f* (c) *(land for Indians, animals)* réserve *f*

reserve [rɪ'zɜːv] **1** *n* (a) *(reticence)* réserve *f* (b) *(stock, land)* réserve *f*; **r. (player)** *(in team)* remplaçant, -e *mf*; *Mil* **the reserves** les réservistes *mpl*; **in r.** en réserve; **r. tank** *(of vehicle, aircraft)* réservoir *m* de secours **2** *vt (room, decision)* réserver; *(right)* se réserver ■ **reserved** *adj (person, room)* réservé

reservoir ['rezəvwɑː(r)] *n (of water)* réservoir *m*

reset [riː'set] *vt (counter)* remettre à zéro

reshuffle [riː'ʃʌfəl] *n* **(cabinet) r.** remaniement *m* (ministériel)

reside [rɪ'zaɪd] *vi* résider

residence ['rezɪdəns] *n (home)* résidence *f*; *(of students)* foyer *m*; *Br* **r. permit** permis *m* de séjour

resident ['rezɪdənt] **1** *n (of country, street)* habitant, -e *mf*; *(of hotel)* pensionnaire *mf*; *(foreigner)* résident, -e *mf* **2** *adj* **to be r. in London** résider à Londres

residential [rezɪ'denʃəl] *adj (neighbourhood)* résidentiel, -elle

resign [rɪ'zaɪn] **1** *vt (job)* démissionner de; **to r. oneself to sth/to doing sth** se résigner à qch/à faire qch **2** *vi* démissionner (**from** de) ■ **resigned** *adj* résigné

resignation [rezɪg'neɪʃən] *n (from job)* démission *f*; *(attitude)* résignation *f*

resilient [rɪ'zɪlɪənt] *adj* élastique; *Fig (person)* résistant

resist [rɪ'zɪst] **1** *vt* résister à; **to r. doing sth** s'empêcher de faire qch **2** *vi* résister ■ **resistance** *n* résistance *f* (**to** à) ■ **resistant** *adj* résistant (**to** à)

resit [riː'sɪt] *(pt & pp* -**sat***, pres p* -**sitting**) *vt Br (exam)* repasser

resolute ['rezəluːt] *adj* résolu ■ **resolution** *n* résolution *f*

resolve [rɪ'zɒlv] **1** *n* résolution *f* **2** *vt (problem)* résoudre; **to r. to do sth** *(of person)* se résoudre à faire qch

resort [rɪ'zɔːt] **1** *n* (a) *(holiday place)* lieu *m* de villégiature; *Br* **seaside r.**, *Am* **beach r.** station *f* balnéaire (b) *(recourse)* **as a last r.**, **in the last r.** en dernier ressort **2** *vi* **to r. to sth** avoir recours à qch; **to r. to doing sth** finir par faire qch

resounding [rɪ'zaʊndɪŋ] *adj (failure)*

retentissant; *(success)* éclatant

resource [rɪ'sɔːs, rɪ'zɔːs] *n* ressource *f*
■ **resourceful** *adj* ingénieux, -euse

respect [rɪ'spekt] **1** *n* respect *m* (**for**
pour); *(aspect)* égard *m*; **in many re-**
spects à bien des égards; **with r. to,**
in r. of en ce qui concerne **2** *vt* respec-
ter

respectable [rɪ'spektəbəl] *adj (de-*
cent, fairly large) respectable; *(fairly*
good) honorable

respective [rɪ'spektɪv] *adj* respectif,
-ive ■ **respectively** *adv* respectivement

respond [rɪ'spɒnd] *vi (answer)* répon-
dre (**to** à); *(react)* réagir (**to** à); **to r. to**
treatment bien réagir (au traitement)
■ **response** *n (answer)* réponse *f*; *(re-*
action) réaction *f*; **in r. to** en réponse à

responsible [rɪ'spɒnsəbəl] *adj* res-
ponsable (**for** de); *(job)* à responsabili-
tés ■ **responsibility** (*pl* **-ies**) *n* res-
ponsabilité *f* (**for** de) ■ **responsibly**
adv de façon responsable

responsive [rɪ'spɒnsɪv] *adj (react-*
ing) qui réagit bien; *(alert)* éveillé; **r. to**
(suggestion) réceptif, -ive à

rest¹ [rest] **1** *n (relaxation)* repos *m*;
(support) support *m*; **to have** *or* **take**
a r. se reposer; **to set** *or* **put sb's mind**
at r. tranquilliser qn; *Am* **r. room** toi-
lettes *fpl*
 2 *vt (lean)* poser (**on** sur); *(horse)* lais-
ser reposer
 3 *vi (relax)* se reposer; *(lean)* être posé
(**on** sur); **to r. on** *(of argument, roof)* re-
poser sur; **a resting place** un lieu de
repos

rest² [rest] **1** *n (remainder)* reste *m* (**of**
de); **the r.** *(others)* les autres *mfpl* **2** *vi*
to r. with sb *(of decision, responsibil-*
ity) incomber à qn

restaurant ['restərɒnt] *n* restaurant
m; *Br* **r. car** *(on train)* wagon-restaurant
m

restful ['restfəl] *adj* reposant

restless ['restləs] *adj* agité

restore [rɪ'stɔː(r)] *vt (give back)* ren-
dre (**to** à); *(order, peace, rights)* rétablir;
(building, painting, monarchy) restau-
rer

restrain [rɪ'streɪn] *vt (person, dog)*
maîtriser; *(crowd, anger)* contenir; **to**
r. sb from doing sth retenir qn pour
qu'il ne fasse pas qch ■ **restrained** *adj*
(manner) réservé ■ **restraint** *n (mod-*
eration) mesure *f*; *(restriction)* restric-
tion *f*

restrict [rɪ'strɪkt] *vt* restreindre; **to r.**
oneself to sth/doing sth se limiter à
qch/à faire qch ■ **restricted** *adj* res-
treint ■ **restriction** *n* restriction *f* (**on** à)

result [rɪ'zʌlt] **1** *n (outcome, success)*
résultat *m*; **as a r.** en conséquence; **as**
a r. of à la suite de **2** *vi* résulter (**from**
de); **to r. in sth** aboutir à qch

resume [rɪ'zjuːm] *vti* reprendre; **to r.**
doing sth se remettre à faire qch ■ **re-**
sumption [-'zʌmpʃən] *n* reprise *f*

résumé ['rezjʊmeɪ] *n (summary)* ré-
sumé *m*; *Am (CV)* curriculum vitae *m*
inv

resurgence [rɪ'sɜːdʒəns] *n* réappari-
tion *f*

resurrect [rezə'rekt] *vt Fig (fashion)*
remettre au goût du jour ■ **resurrec-**
tion *n Rel* résurrection *f*

resuscitate [rɪ'sʌsɪteɪt] *vt Med* rani-
mer

retail ['riːteɪl] **1** *n (vente f au)* détail *m*
2 *adj (price)* de détail **3** *vi* se vendre (au
détail) (**at** à) ■ **retailer** *n* détaillant *m*

retain [rɪ'teɪn] *vt (keep)* conserver;
(hold in place) retenir

retaliate [rɪ'tælɪeɪt] *vi* riposter ■ **re-**
taliation *n* représailles *fpl*; **in r. for** en
représailles à

retch [retʃ] *vi* avoir des haut-le-cœur

rethink [riː'θɪŋk] *(pt & pp* **-thought***)*
vt repenser

reticent ['retɪsənt] *adj* peu communi-
catif, -ive

retire [rɪ'taɪə(r)] *vi* (**a**) *(from work)*
prendre sa retraite (**b**) *(withdraw)* se re-
tirer (**from** de; **to** à); *(go to bed)* aller se
coucher ■ **retired** *adj (no longer work-*
ing) retraité

retirement [rɪ'taɪəmənt] *n* retraite *f*;
r. age l'âge *m* de la retraite

retrace [riː'treɪs] *vt* **to r. one's steps**
revenir sur ses pas

retract [rɪ'trækt] **1** vt (a) (statement) revenir sur (b) (claws) rentrer **2** vi (of person) se rétracter

retrain [ri:'treɪn] **1** vt recycler **2** vi se recycler ▪ **retraining** n recyclage m

retreat [rɪ'tri:t] **1** n (withdrawal) retraite f; (place) refuge m **2** vi se réfugier; (of troops) battre en retraite

retribution [retrɪ'bju:ʃən] n châtiment m

retrieve [rɪ'tri:v] vt (recover) récupérer

retrospect ['retrəspekt] n in r. rétrospectivement

retrospective [retrə'spektɪv] adj rétrospectif, -ive; (law) à effet rétroactif

return [rɪ'tɜ:n] **1** n retour m; Fin (on investment) rapport m; **returns** (profits) bénéfices mpl; Br **r. (ticket)** (billet m) aller et retour m; **many happy returns!** bon anniversaire!; **in r.** en échange (**for** de); **by r. of post** par retour du courrier
2 adj (trip, flight) (de) retour; **r. match** match m retour
3 vt (give back) rendre; (put back) remettre; (bring back) rapporter; (send back) renvoyer; **to r. sb's call** (on phone) rappeler qn
4 vi (come back) revenir; (go back) retourner; (go back home) rentrer; **to r. to** (subject) revenir à

reunion [ri:'ju:njən] n réunion f ▪ **reunite** vt réconcilier; **to be reunited with sb** retrouver qn

reuse [ri:'ju:z] vt réutiliser

reveal [rɪ'vi:l] vt (make known) révéler (**that** que); (make visible) laisser voir ▪ **revealing** adj (sign, comment) révélateur, -trice

revel ['revəl] (Br -ll-, Am -l-) vi faire la fête; **to r. in sth** savourer qch

revelation [revə'leɪʃən] n révélation f

revenge [rɪ'vendʒ] **1** n vengeance f; **to have** or **get one's r. (on sb)** se venger (de qn); **in r.** pour se venger **2** vt venger

revenue ['revənju:] n (income) revenu m; (from sales) recettes fpl

reverence ['revərəns] n révérence f

reversal [rɪ'vɜ:səl] n (of situation, roles) renversement m; (of policy, opinion) revirement m; **r. (of fortune)** revers m (de fortune)

reverse [rɪ'vɜ:s] **1** adj (opposite) contraire; (image) inverse; **in r. order** dans l'ordre inverse
2 n contraire m; (of coin) revers m; (of fabric) envers m; (of paper) verso m; **in r. (gear)** (when driving) en marche arrière
3 vt (situation) renverser; (order, policy) inverser; (decision) revenir sur; **to r. the car** faire marche arrière; Br **to r. the charges** (when phoning) téléphoner en PCV
4 vi Br (in car) faire marche arrière; **to r. in/out** rentrer/sortir en marche arrière

revert [rɪ'vɜ:t] vi **to r. to** revenir à

review [rɪ'vju:] **1** n (a) (of book, film) critique f; **to be under r.** faire l'objet d'une révision (b) (magazine) revue f **2** vt (book, film) faire la critique de; (troops) passer en revue; (situation) faire le point sur; (salary) réviser ▪ **reviewer** n critique m

revise [rɪ'vaɪz] **1** vt (opinion, notes, text) réviser **2** vi (for exam) réviser (**for** pour) ▪ **revision** n révision f

revival [rɪ'vaɪvəl] n (of custom, business, play) reprise f; (of fashion) renouveau m

revive [rɪ'vaɪv] **1** vt (person) ranimer; (custom, industry) faire renaître; (fashion) relancer **2** vi (of person) reprendre connaissance; (of industry) connaître un renouveau; (of interest) renaître

revolt [rɪ'vəʊlt] **1** n révolte f **2** vt (disgust) révolter **3** vi (rebel) se révolter (**against** contre) ▪ **revolting** adj dégoûtant

revolution [revə'lu:ʃən] n révolution f ▪ **revolutionary** (pl -ies) adj & n révolutionnaire (mf)

revolve [rɪ'vɒlv] vi tourner (**around** autour de) ▪ **revolving** adj **r. door(s)** porte f à tambour

revolver [rɪ'vɒlvə(r)] n revolver m

revulsion [rɪ'vʌlʃən] n (disgust) dégoût m

reward [rɪ'wɔːd] **1** *n* récompense *f* (**for** de) **2** *vt* récompenser (**for** de *ou* pour) ▪ **rewarding** *adj* intéressant

rewind [riː'waɪnd] (*pt & pp* **-wound**) *vt* (*tape, film*) rembobiner

rewrite [riː'raɪt] (*pt* **-wrote**, *pp* **-written**) *vt* réécrire

rhetoric ['retərɪk] *n* rhétorique *f* ▪ **rhetorical** [rɪ'tɒrɪkəl] *adj* **r. question** question *f* de pure forme

rheumatism ['ruːmətɪzəm] *n* rhumatisme *m*; **to have r.** avoir des rhumatismes

rhinoceros [raɪ'nɒsərəs] *n* rhinocéros *m*

rhubarb ['ruːbɑːb] *n* rhubarbe *f*

rhyme [raɪm] **1** *n* rime *f*; (*poem*) vers *mpl* **2** *vi* rimer (**with** avec)

rhythm ['rɪðəm] *n* rythme *m* ▪ **rhythmic(al)** ['rɪðmɪk(əl)] *adj* rythmé

rib [rɪb] *n* (*bone*) côte *f*

ribbon ['rɪbən] *n* ruban *m*

rice [raɪs] *n* riz *m*; **r. pudding** riz *m* au lait

rich [rɪtʃ] **1** (**-er, -est**) *adj* (*person, food*) riche; **to be r. in sth** être riche en qch **2** *npl* **the r.** les riches *mpl* ▪ **riches** *npl* richesses *fpl*

rid [rɪd] (*pt & pp* **rid**, *pres p* **ridding**) *vt* débarrasser (**of** de); **to get r. of, to r. oneself of** se débarrasser de ▪ **riddance** ['rɪdəns] *n* Fam **good r.!** bon débarras!

ridden ['rɪdən] *pp of* **ride**

riddle ['rɪdəl] **1** *n* (*puzzle*) devinette *f*; (*mystery*) énigme *f* **2** *vt* cribler (**with** de); **riddled with mistakes** truffé de fautes

ride [raɪd] **1** *n* (*on horse*) promenade *f*; (*on bicycle, in car*) tour *m*; (*in taxi*) course *f*; **to go for a r.** aller faire un tour; **to give sb a r.** (*in car*) emmener qn en voiture; Fam **to take sb for a r.** mener qn en bateau
2 (*pt* **rode**, *pp* **ridden**) *vt* (*horse, bicycle*) monter à; (*a particular horse*) monter; **to know how to r. a bicycle** savoir faire de la bicyclette
3 *vi* (*on horse*) faire du cheval; (*on bicycle*) faire de la bicyclette; **to go rid-**

-ing (*on horse*) faire du cheval; **I ride to work** (*on bicycle*) je vais travailler à bicyclette

rider ['raɪdə(r)] *n* (*on horse*) cavalier, -ère *mf*; (*cyclist*) cycliste *mf*

ridge [rɪdʒ] *n* (*of mountain*) crête *f*

ridicule ['rɪdɪkjuːl] **1** *n* ridicule *m*; **to hold sb/sth up to r.** tourner qn/qch en ridicule **2** *vt* tourner en ridicule, ridiculiser

ridiculous [rɪ'dɪkjʊləs] *adj* ridicule

riding ['raɪdɪŋ] *n* (*horse*) **r.** équitation *f*

rife [raɪf] *adj* (*widespread*) répandu

riffraff ['rɪfræf] *n* racaille *f*

rifle ['raɪfəl] *n* fusil *m*

rift [rɪft] *n* (*in political party*) scission *f*; (*disagreement*) désaccord *m*

rig [rɪg] **1** *n* (*oil*) **r.** derrick *m*; (*at sea*) plate-forme *f* pétrolière **2** (*pt & pp* **-gg-**) *vt* Fam (*result, election*) truquer; **to r. up** (*equipment*) installer

right¹ [raɪt] **1** *adj* (a) (*correct*) bon (*f* bonne), exact; (*word*) juste; **to be r.** (*of person*) avoir raison (**to do** de faire); **it's the r. time** c'est l'heure exacte; **that's r.** c'est ça; **r.!** bon!
(b) (*appropriate*) bon (*f* bonne); **he's the r. man** c'est l'homme qu'il faut
(c) (*morally good*) bien *inv*; **to do the r. thing** faire ce qu'il faut
(d) Fam (*for emphasis*) véritable; **I felt a r. fool** je me suis vraiment senti stupide
(e) Math **r. angle** angle *m* droit
2 *adv* (*straight*) (tout) droit; (*completely*) tout à fait; (*correctly*) correctement; **to put sth r.** (*rectify*) corriger qch; (*fix*) arranger qch; **to put sb r.** détromper qn; **r. round** tout autour (**sth** de qch); **r. behind** juste derrière; **r. here** ici même; **r. away, r. now** tout de suite
3 *n* **to be in the r.** avoir raison; **r. and wrong** le bien et le mal
4 *vt* (*error, wrong, boat, car*) redresser

right² [raɪt] **1** *adj* (*not left*) (*hand, side*) droit **2** *adv* à droite **3** *n* droite *f*; **on** *or* **to the r.** à droite (**of** de) ▪ **right-hand** *adj* de droite; **on the r. side** à droite (**of** de)

right-handed *adj (person)* droitier, -ère ■ **right-wing** *adj Pol* de droite

right³ [raɪt] *n (entitlement)* droit *m* (**to do** de faire); **to have a r. to sth** avoir droit à qch; **to have (the) r. of way** *(on road)* avoir la priorité

rightful ['raɪtfəl] *adj* légitime

rightly ['raɪtlɪ] *adv (correctly)* bien; *(justifiably)* à juste titre

rigid ['rɪdʒɪd] *adj* rigide

rigorous ['rɪgərəs] *adj* rigoureux, -euse

rim [rɪm] *n (of cup)* bord *m; (of wheel)* jante *f*

rind [raɪnd] *n (of cheese)* croûte *f; (of bacon)* couenne *f*

ring¹ [rɪŋ] *n (for finger, curtain)* anneau *m; (for finger, with stone)* bague *f; (on stove)* brûleur *m; (of people, chairs)* cercle *m; (of criminals)* bande *f; (at circus)* piste *f; (for boxing)* ring *m;* **to have rings under one's eyes** avoir les yeux cernés; *Br* **r. road** périphérique *m*

ring² [rɪŋ] **1** *n (sound)* there's a r. at the door on sonne à la porte; *Fam* **to give sb a r.** passer un coup de fil à qn **2** *(pt* **rang***, pp* **rung***) vt (bell)* sonner; *(alarm)* déclencher; **to r. sb** *(on phone)* téléphoner à qn; **to r. the doorbell** sonner à la porte; *Fam* **that rings a bell** ça me dit quelque chose **3** *vi (of bell, phone, person)* sonner; *(of sound, words)* retentir; *(of ears)* bourdonner; *(make a phone call)* téléphoner ■ **ringing** *adj Br* **r. tone** *(on phone)* sonnerie *f*

▸ **ring back 1** *vt sep* **to r. sb back** rappeler qn **2** *vi* rappeler

▸ **ring off** *vi (on phone)* raccrocher

▸ **ring out** *vi (of bell)* sonner; *(of voice, shout)* retentir

▸ **ring up 1** *vt sep* **to r. sb up** téléphoner à qn **2** *vi* téléphoner

ringleader ['rɪŋliːdə(r)] *n Pej (of rebellion, strike)* meneur, -euse *mf*

rink [rɪŋk] *n (for ice-skating)* patinoire *f; (for roller-skating)* piste *f*

rinse [rɪns] **1** *n* rinçage *m;* **to give sth a r.** rincer qch **2** *vt* rincer; **to r. one's hands** se rincer les mains; **to r. out** rincer

riot ['raɪət] **1** *n (uprising)* émeute *f;* **to run r.** se déchaîner **2** *vi (rise up)* faire une émeute; *(of prisoners)* se mutiner ■ **rioter** *n* émeutier, -ère *mf; (vandal)* casseur *m* ■ **rioting** *n* émeutes *fpl*

rip [rɪp] **1** *n* déchirure *f* **2** *(pt & pp* **-pp-***) vt* déchirer; **to r. sth off** arracher qch **(from** de); *Fam (steal)* faucher qch; *Fam* **to r. sb off** *(deceive)* rouler qn; **to r. sth up** déchirer qch **3** *vi (of fabric)* se déchirer ■ **rip-off** *n Fam* arnaque *f*

ripe [raɪp] **(-er, -est)** *adj (fruit)* mûr; *(cheese)* fait ■ **ripen** *vti* mûrir

rise [raɪz] **1** *n (in price, pressure)* hausse *f* (**in** de); *(slope in ground)* montée *f; (of leader, party)* ascension *f; Br* **(pay) r.** augmentation *f* (de salaire); **to give r. to sth** donner lieu à qch

2 *(pt* **rose***, pp* **risen** ['rɪzən]*) vi (of temperature, balloon, price)* monter; *(in society)* s'élever; *(of sun, theatre curtain)* se lever; *(of dough)* lever; *(get up from chair or bed)* se lever; **to r. (up)** *(rebel)* se soulever **(against** contre)

rising ['raɪzɪŋ] *adj (sun)* levant; *(number)* croissant; *(prices)* en hausse

risk [rɪsk] **1** *n* risque *m;* **at r.** *(person)* en danger; *(job)* menacé; **to run the r. of doing sth** courir le risque de faire qch **2** *vt (life, reputation)* risquer; **I can't r. going** je ne peux pas prendre le risque d'y aller ■ **risky (-ier, -iest)** *adj* risqué

rite [raɪt] *n* rite *m; Rel* **the last rites** les derniers sacrements *mpl* ■ **ritual** ['rɪtjʊəl] **1** *adj* rituel, -elle **2** *n* rituel *m*

rival ['raɪvəl] **1** *adj* rival **2** *n* rival, -e *mf* **3** *(Br* **-ll-***, Am* **-l-***) vt (equal)* égaler **(in** en) ■ **rivalry** *(pl* **-ies***) n* rivalité *f* (**between** entre)

river ['rɪvə(r)] **1** *n (small)* rivière *f; (flowing into sea)* fleuve *m* **2** *adj* **r. bank** rive *f* ■ **riverside 1** *n* bord *m* de l'eau **2** *adj* au bord de l'eau

riveting ['rɪvɪtɪŋ] *adj Fig* fascinant

Riviera [rɪvɪ'eərə] *n* **the (French) R.** la Côte d'Azur

road [rəʊd] **1** *n* route *f; (small)* chemin *m; (in town)* rue *f; (roadway)* chaussée *f;* **the Paris r.** la route de Paris; **by r.** par

la route; **to live across** or **over the r.** habiter en face

2 adj (map, safety) routier, -ère; (accident) de la route; **r. sign** panneau m de signalisation; Br **r. works**, Am **r. work** travaux mpl de voirie ■ **roadblock** n barrage m routier ■ **roadside** n bord m de la route

roam [rəʊm] **1** vt parcourir; **to r. the streets** traîner dans les rues **2** vi errer

roar [rɔː(r)] **1** n (of lion) rugissement m; (of person) hurlement m **2** vt **to r. sth (out)** hurler qch **3** vi (of lion, wind, engine) rugir; (of person, crowd) hurler; **to r. with laughter** hurler de rire ■ **roaring** adj **a r. fire** une belle flambée; **to do a r. trade** faire des affaires en or

roast [rəʊst] **1** n (meat) rôti m **2** adj rôti; **r. beef** rosbif m **3** vt (meat, potatoes) faire rôtir **4** vi (of meat) rôtir

rob [rɒb] (pt & pp **-bb-**) vt (person) voler; (shop, bank) dévaliser; **to r. sb of sth** voler qch à qn; Fig (deprive) priver qn de qch ■ **robber** n voleur, -euse mf ■ **robbery** (pl **-ies**) n vol m; **it's daylight r.!** c'est du vol pur et simple!

robe [rəʊb] n (of priest, judge) robe f

robin ['rɒbɪn] n (bird) rouge-gorge m

robot ['rəʊbɒt] n robot m

robust [rəʊ'bʌst] adj robuste

rock¹ [rɒk] **1** n (music) rock m **2** vt (boat) balancer; (building) secouer **3** vi (sway) se balancer; (of building, ground) trembler ■ **rocking** adj **r. chair** fauteuil m à bascule

rock² [rɒk] **1** n (substance) roche f; (boulder, rock face) rocher m; Am (stone) pierre f; Br (sweet) = sucrerie en forme de bâton parfumée à la menthe; **on the rocks** (whisky) avec des glaçons; (marriage) en pleine débâcle; **r. climbing** varappe f; **r. face** paroi f rocheuse

rocket ['rɒkɪt] **1** n fusée f **2** vi (of prices, unemployment) monter en flèche

rocky ['rɒkɪ] (**-ier, -iest**) adj (road) rocailleux, -euse; Fig (relationship) instable

rod [rɒd] n (wooden) baguette f; (metal) tige f; (of curtain) tringle f; (for fishing) canne f à pêche

rode [rəʊd] pt of **ride**

rodent ['rəʊdənt] n rongeur m

rodeo [Br 'rəʊdɪəʊ, Am rəʊ'deɪəʊ] (pl **-os**) n Am rodéo m

rogue [rəʊg] n (dishonest) crapule f; (mischievous) coquin, -e mf

role [rəʊl] n rôle m; **r. model** modèle m

roll [rəʊl] **1** n (of paper) rouleau m; (of drum, thunder) roulement m; (bread) petit pain m; (list) liste f; **r. of film** pellicule f; **to have a r. call** faire l'appel; **r. neck** col m roulé

2 vt (cigarette) rouler; (ball) faire rouler

3 vi (of ball) rouler; (of camera) tourner ■ **rolling** adj (hills) ondulant; **r. pin** rouleau m à pâtisserie

▸ **roll down** vt sep (car window) baisser; (sleeves) redescendre

▸ **roll in** vi Fam (flow in) affluer; (of person) s'amener

▸ **roll on** vi Fam **r. on tonight!** vivement ce soir!

▸ **roll out** vt sep (dough) étaler

▸ **roll over 1** vt sep retourner **2** vi (many times) se rouler; (once) se retourner

▸ **roll up 1** vt sep (map, cloth) rouler; (sleeve) retrousser **2** vi Fam (arrive) s'amener

roller ['rəʊlə(r)] n (for hair, painting) rouleau m; **r. coaster** montagnes fpl russes; **r. skate** patin m à roulettes ■ **roller-skate** vi faire du patin à roulettes

rollerblades ['rəʊləbleɪdz] npl patins mpl en ligne

ROM [rɒm] (abbr **read only memory**) n Comptr mémoire f morte

Roman ['rəʊmən] **1** adj romain **2** n Romain, -e mf **3** adj & n **R. Catholic** catholique (mf)

romance [rəʊ'mæns] n (love) amour m; (affair) aventure f amoureuse; (story) histoire f d'amour; (charm) poésie f

Romania [rəʊ'meɪnɪə] n la Roumanie

■ **Romanian 1** *adj* roumain **2** *n (person)* Roumain, -e *mf*; *(language)* roumain *m*

romantic [rəʊ'mæntɪk] **1** *adj (of love, tenderness)* romantique; *(fanciful, imaginary)* romanesque **2** *n* romantique *mf*

romp [rɒmp] *vi* s'ébattre

rompers ['rɒmpəz] *npl (for baby)* barboteuse *f*

roof [ru:f] *n (of building, vehicle)* toit *m*; *(of tunnel, cave)* plafond *m*; **r. rack** *(of car)* galerie *f* ■ **rooftop** *n* toit *m*

room [ru:m, rʊm] *n* (a) *(in house)* pièce *f*; *(bedroom)* chambre *f*; *(large, public)* salle *f* (b) *(space)* place *f*; **to make r.** faire de la place **(for** pour) ■ **roommate** *n* camarade *mf* de chambre ■ **roomy** (**-ier, -iest**) *adj* spacieux, -euse

roost [ru:st] *vi* se percher

rooster ['ru:stə(r)] *n* coq *m*

root [ru:t] **1** *n (of plant, tooth, hair)* & *Math* racine *f*; *Fig (origin)* origine *f*; *(cause)* cause *f*; **to take r.** *(of plant, person)* prendre racine **2** *vt* **to r. sth out** supprimer qch

rooted ['ru:tɪd] *adj* **deeply r.** bien enraciné **(in** dans); **r. to the spot** *(immobile)* cloué sur place

rope [rəʊp] **1** *n* corde *f*; *(on ship)* cordage *m*; *Fam* **to know the ropes** connaître son affaire **2** *vt Fam* **to r. sb in** recruter qn

rop(e)y ['rəʊpɪ] (**-ier, -iest**) *adj Br Fam (thing)* minable; *(person)* patraque

rosary ['rəʊzərɪ] *(pl* **-ies)** *n Rel* chapelet *m*

rose¹ [rəʊz] *n (flower)* rose *f*

rose² [rəʊz] *pt of* **rise**

rosette [rəʊ'zet] *n* rosette *f*

roster ['rɒstə(r)] *n* **(duty) r.** liste *f* de service

rostrum ['rɒstrəm] *n* tribune *f*; *(for prizewinner)* podium *m*

rosy ['rəʊzɪ] (**-ier, -iest**) *adj (pink)* rose; *Fig (future)* prometteur, -euse

rot [rɒt] **1** *n* pourriture *f*; *Br Fam (nonsense)* inepties *fpl* **2** *(pt & pp* **-tt-)** *vti* pourrir

rota ['rəʊtə] *n* roulement *m*

rotary ['rəʊtərɪ] **1** *adj* rotatif, -ive **2** *(pl* **-ies)** *n Am (for traffic)* rond-point *m*

rotate [rəʊ'teɪt] **1** *vt* faire tourner **2** *vi* tourner

rotation [rəʊ'teɪʃən] *n* **in r.** à tour de rôle

rotten ['rɒtən] *adj (fruit, egg, wood)* pourri; *Fam (bad)* nul (*f* nulle); *Fam (weather)* pourri; *Fam* **to feel r.** *(ill)* être mal fichu

rough¹ [rʌf] **1** (**-er, -est**) *adj (surface)* rugueux, -euse; *(ground)* accidenté; *(life)* rude; *(wine)* âpre; *(neighbourhood)* dur; *(sea)* agité; *(brutal)* brutal **2** *adv Br* **to sleep/live r.** coucher/vivre à la dure **3** *vt Fam* **to r. it** vivre à la dure

rough² [rʌf] **1** (**-er, -est**) *adj (approximate)* approximatif, -ive; **r. guess, r. estimate** approximation *f*; **r. copy, r. draft** brouillon *m*; **r. paper** papier *m* brouillon **2** *vt* **to r. sth out** *(plan)* ébaucher

rough-and-ready [rʌfən'redɪ] *adj (solution)* rudimentaire; *(accommodation)* sommaire

roughen ['rʌfən] *vt* rendre rugueux, -euse

roughly¹ ['rʌflɪ] *adv (brutally)* brutalement

roughly² ['rʌflɪ] *adv (approximately)* à peu près

round [raʊnd] **1** (**-er, -est**) *adj* rond; *Am* **r. trip** aller et retour *m* **2** *adv* autour; **all r., right r.** tout autour; **all year r.** toute l'année; **the wrong way r.** à l'envers **3** *prep* autour de; **r. here** par ici; **r. about** *(approximately)* environ **4** *n Br (slice)* tranche *f*; *(in competition)* manche *f*; *(of golf)* partie *f*; *(in boxing)* round *m*; *(of talks)* série *f*; *(of drinks)* tournée *f* **5** *vt* **to r. sth off** *(meal, speech)* terminer qch *(with* par); **to r. up** *(gather)* rassembler; *(price)* arrondir au chiffre supérieur

roundabout ['raʊndəbaʊt] **1** *adj*

(method, route) indirect **2** *n Br (at funfair)* manège *m*; *(road junction)* rond-point *m*

rounders ['raʊndəz] *npl* = jeu similaire au base-ball

rouse [raʊz] *vt (awaken)* éveiller; **roused (to anger)** en colère

rousing ['raʊzɪŋ] *adj (speech)* vibrant

route [ru:t] *n* itinéraire *m*; *(of aircraft, ship)* route *f*; **bus r.** ligne *f* d'autobus

routine [ru:'ti:n] **1** *n (habit)* routine *f*; **the daily r.** le train-train quotidien **2** *adj (inquiry, work)* de routine; *Pej* routinier, -ère

row¹ [rəʊ] *n (line)* rangée *f*; **two days in a r.** deux jours d'affilée

row² [rəʊ] **1** *n Am* **r. boat** bateau *m* à rames **2** *vt (boat)* faire aller à la rame; *(person)* transporter en canot **3** *vi (in boat)* ramer

row³ [raʊ] **1** *n (noise)* vacarme *m*; *(quarrel)* dispute *f* **2** *vi* se disputer **(with** avec)

rowdy ['raʊdɪ] **(-ier, -iest)** *adj* chahuteur, -euse

rowing ['rəʊɪŋ] *n (as sport)* aviron *m*; *Br* **r. boat** bateau *m* à rames

royal ['rɔɪəl] *adj* royal; **the R. Air Force** = l'armée de l'air britannique

royalty ['rɔɪəltɪ] **1** *n (rank, position)* royauté *f* **2** *npl* **royalties** *(from book)* droits *mpl* d'auteur

rub [rʌb] **1** *n (massage)* friction *f*; **to give sth a r.** frotter qch **2** *(pt & pp* **-bb-)** *vti* frotter

▸ **rub down** *vt sep (person)* frictionner; *(wood, with sandpaper)* poncer

▸ **rub in** *vt sep (cream)* faire pénétrer (en massant); *Fam* **to r. it in** retourner le couteau dans la plaie

▸ **rub off** *vt sep (mark)* effacer

▸ **rub out** *vt sep (mark, writing)* effacer

rubber ['rʌbə(r)] *n (substance)* caoutchouc *m*; *Br (eraser)* gomme *f*; *Am Fam (contraceptive)* capote *f*; **r. band** élastique *m*; **r. stamp** tampon *m*

rubbish ['rʌbɪʃ] *n Br (waste)* ordures *fpl*; *Fig (nonsense)* idioties *fpl*; **Fam that's r.** c'est absurde; *(worthless)* ça ne vaut rien; **r. bin** poubelle *f*

rubbishy ['rʌbɪʃɪ] *adj (book, film)* nul *(f* nulle); *(goods)* de mauvaise qualité

rubble ['rʌbəl] *n* décombres *mpl*

ruby ['ru:bɪ] *(pl* **-ies)** *n (gem)* rubis *m*

rucksack ['rʌksæk] *n* sac *m* à dos

rudder ['rʌdə(r)] *n* gouvernail *m*

ruddy ['rʌdɪ] **(-ier, -iest)** *adj (complexion)* rose; *Br Fam (bloody)* fichu

rude [ru:d] **(-er, -est)** *adj (impolite)* impoli **(to** envers); *(indecent)* obscène

rudiments ['ru:dɪmənts] *npl* rudiments *mpl*

ruffian ['rʌfɪən] *n* voyou *m (pl* -ous)

rug [rʌg] *n* tapis *m*; *(over knees)* plaid *m*

rugby ['rʌgbɪ] *n* **r. (football)** rugby *m*

rugged ['rʌgɪd] *adj (terrain, coast)* accidenté; *(features)* rude

ruin ['ru:ɪn] **1** *n (destruction, rubble, building)* ruine *f*; **in ruins** *(building)* en ruine **2** *vt (health, country, person)* ruiner; *(clothes)* abîmer; *(effect, meal, party)* gâcher ■ **ruined** *adj (person, country)* ruiné; *(building)* en ruine

rule [ru:l] **1** *n* **(a)** *(principle)* règle *f*; *(regulation)* règlement *m*; *(government)* autorité *f*; *Br* **against the rules** or *Am* **r.** contraire au règlement; **as a r.** en règle générale **(b)** *(for measuring)* règle *f* **2** *vt (country)* gouverner; *(decide) (of judge, referee)* décider **(that** que); **to r. sth out** *(exclude)* exclure qch **3** *vi (of king)* régner **(over** sur); *(of judge)* statuer **(against** contre; **on** sur) ■ **ruling 1** *adj Pol* **the r. party** le parti au pouvoir **2** *n (of judge, referee)* décision *f*

ruler ['ru:lə(r)] *n* **(a)** *(for measuring)* règle *f* **(b)** *(king, queen)* souverain, -e *mf*; *(political leader)* dirigeant, -e *mf*

rum [rʌm] *n* rhum *m*

Rumania [ru:'meɪnɪə] *see* **Romania**

rumble ['rʌmbəl] *vi (of train, thunder)* gronder; *(of stomach)* gargouiller

rummage ['rʌmɪdʒ] *vi* **to r. (about)** farfouiller; *Am* **r. sale** vente *f* de charité *(articles d'occasion uniquement)*

rumour ['ru:mə(r)] *(Am* **rumor)** *n* rumeur *f* ■ **rumoured** *(Am* **rumored)** *adj*

it is r. that... on dit que...

rump [rʌmp] *n (of horse)* croupe *f*; **r. steak** romsteck *m*

RUN [rʌn] **1** *n (series)* série *f*; *(running)* course *f*; *(outing)* tour *m*; *(for skiing)* piste *f*; *(in cricket, baseball)* point *m*; *(in stocking)* maille *f* filée; **to go for a r.** aller courir; **on the r.** *(prisoner)* en fuite; **in the long/short r.** à long/court terme

 2 *(pt* **ran**, *pp* **run**, *pres p* **running**) *vt (distance, race)* courir; *(machine)* faire fonctionner; *(business, country)* diriger; *(courses, events)* organiser; *Comptr (program)* exécuter; *(bath)* faire couler; **to r. one's hand over** passer la main sur; **to r. sb to the airport** conduire qn à l'aéroport

 3 *vi* courir; *(flee)* fuir; *(of river, nose, tap)* couler; *(of colour in washing)* déteindre; *(of ink)* baver; *(function) (of machine)* marcher; *(idle) (of engine)* tourner; **to r. down/in/out** descendre/entrer/sortir en courant; **to go running** faire du jogging; **to r. for president** être candidat à la présidence; **it runs in the family** c'est de famille

▸**run about** *vi* courir çà et là
▸**run across** *vt insep (meet)* tomber sur
▸**run along** *vi* **r. along!** filez!
▸**run around** *vi* = **run about**
▸**run away** *vi (flee)* s'enfuir (**from** de)
▸**run down** *vt sep (pedestrian)* renverser; *(knock over and kill)* écraser; *Fig (belittle)* dénigrer; *(restrict)* limiter peu à peu
▸**run into** *vt insep (meet)* tomber sur; *(crash into) (of vehicle)* percuter
▸**run off 1** *vt sep (print)* tirer **2** *vi (flee)* s'enfuir (**with** avec)
▸**run out** *vi (of stocks)* s'épuiser; *(of lease)* expirer; *(of time)* manquer; **to r. out of time/money** manquer de temps/d'argent; **we've r. out of coffee** on n'a plus de café; **I ran out of petrol** *or Am* **gas** je suis tombé en panne d'essence
▸**run over 1** *vt sep (kill)* écraser; *(knock down)* renverser **2** *vt insep*

(notes, text) revoir **3** *vi (of liquid)* déborder
▸**run round** *vt insep (surround)* entourer
▸**run through** *vt insep (recap)* revoir
▸**run up** *vt sep (debts, bill)* laisser s'accumuler

runaway ['rʌnəweɪ] **1** *n* fugitif, -ive *mf* **2** *adj (car, horse)* fou (*f* folle); *(inflation)* galopant

run-down [rʌn'daʊn] *adj (weak, tired)* fatigué; *(district)* délabré

rung[1] [rʌŋ] *n (of ladder)* barreau *m*

rung[2] [rʌŋ] *pp of* **ring**[2]

runner ['rʌnə(r)] *n (athlete)* coureur *m*; *Br* **r. bean** haricot *m* d'Espagne

runner-up [rʌnər'ʌp] *n (in race)* second, -e *mf*

running ['rʌnɪŋ] **1** *n* course *f*; *(of business, country)* gestion *f*; **to be in/out of the r.** être/ne plus être dans la course **2** *adj* **six days r.** six jours de suite; **r. water** eau *f* courante; **r. costs** *(of factory)* frais *mpl* d'exploitation; *(of car)* dépenses *fpl* courantes

runny ['rʌnɪ] (**-ier**, **-iest**) *adj (cream, sauce)* liquide; *(nose)* qui coule

run-up ['rʌnʌp] *n* **in the r. to** *(elections, Christmas)* dans la période qui précède

runway ['rʌnweɪ] *n (for aircraft)* piste *f* (d'envol)

rupture ['rʌptʃə(r)] **1** *n (hernia)* hernie *f* **2** *vt* rompre

rural ['rʊərəl] *adj* rural

ruse [ruːz] *n* ruse *f*

rush[1] [rʌʃ] **1** *n (demand)* ruée *f* (**for** vers; **on** sur); *(confusion)* bousculade *f*; **to be in a r.** être pressé (**to do** de faire); **r. hour** heures *fpl* de pointe

 2 *vt* **to r. sb** *(hurry)* bousculer qn; **to r. sb to hospital** *or Am* **the hospital** transporter qn d'urgence à l'hôpital; **to r. sth** *(job)* faire qch en vitesse; *(decision)* prendre qch à la hâte

 3 *vi (move fast, throw oneself)* se ruer (**at** sur; **towards** vers); *(hurry)* se dépêcher (**to do** de faire); *(of vehicle)* foncer; **to r. out** sortir précipitamment

rush[2] [rʌʃ] *n (plant)* jonc *m*

rusk [rʌsk] *n Br* biscotte *f*

Russia ['rʌʃə] *n* la Russie ■ **Russian 1** *adj* russe **2** *n (person)* Russe *mf; (language)* russe *m*

rust [rʌst] **1** *n* rouille *f* **2** *vi* rouiller

rustic ['rʌstɪk] *adj* rustique

rustle ['rʌsəl] **1** *vt Fam* to r. sth up *(meal, snack)* improviser qch **2** *vi (of leaves)* bruire

rustproof ['rʌstpruːf] *adj* inoxydable

rusty ['rʌstɪ] **(-ier, -iest)** *adj* rouillé

rut [rʌt] *n* ornière *f; Fig* to be in a r. être encroûté

ruthless ['ruːθləs] *adj* impitoyable

RV [ɑːˈviː] *(abbr* recreational vehicle) *n Am* camping-car *m*

rye [raɪ] *n* seigle *m*; r. bread pain *m* de seigle

Ss

S, s [es] *n (letter)* S, s *m inv*

sabotage ['sæbətɑːʒ] **1** *n* sabotage *m*
2 *vt* saboter

sachet ['sæʃeɪ] *n* sachet *m*

sack [sæk] **1** *n (bag)* sac *m*; *Fam* **to get the s.** se faire virer **2** *vt Fam (dismiss)* virer

sacred ['seɪkrɪd] *adj* sacré

sacrifice ['sækrɪfaɪs] **1** *n* sacrifice *m* **2** *vt* sacrifier **(to** à)

sad [sæd] **(sadder, saddest)** *adj* triste **■ sadden** *vt* attrister **■ sadly** *adv (unhappily)* tristement; *(unfortunately)* malheureusement **■ sadness** *n* tristesse *f*

saddle ['sædəl] **1** *n* selle *f* **2** *vt (horse)* seller

sadistic [sə'dɪstɪk] *adj* sadique

sae [eseɪ'iː] *(abbr Br* **stamped addressed envelope**, *Am* **self-addressed envelope)** *n* envelope *f* timbrée

safari [sə'fɑːrɪ] *n* safari *m*

safe [seɪf] **1 (-er, -est)** *adj (person)* en sécurité; *(equipment, animal)* sans danger; *(place, investment, method)* sûr; **s. (and sound)** sain et sauf *(f* saine et sauve*)* **2** *n (for money)* coffre-fort *m* **■ safely** *adv (without risk)* en toute sécurité; *(drive)* prudemment; *(with certainty)* avec certitude

safeguard ['seɪfgɑːd] **1** *n* garantie *f* **(against** contre) **2** *vt* sauvegarder

safety ['seɪftɪ] **1** *n* sécurité *f* **2** *adj (belt, device, margin)* de sécurité; *(pin, chain, valve)* de sûreté

sag [sæg] *(pt & pp* **-gg-)** *vi (of roof, bed)* s'affaisser

saga ['sɑːgə] *n* saga *f*

Sahara [sə'hɑːrə] *n* **the S. (desert)** le Sahara

said [sed] *pt & pp of* **say**

sail [seɪl] **1** *n (on boat)* voile *f*; **to set s.** prendre la mer **2** *vt (boat)* commander **3** *vi (of person, ship)* naviguer; *(leave)* prendre la mer **■ sailing** *n (sport)* voile *f*; **to go s.** faire de la voile; *Br* **s. boat** voilier *m* **■ sailboat** *n Am* voilier *m*

sailor ['seɪlə(r)] *n* marin *m*

saint [seɪnt] *n* saint *m*, sainte *f*

sake [seɪk] *n* **for my/your/his s.** pour moi/toi/lui; **for heaven's** *or* **God's s.!** pour l'amour de Dieu!; **(just) for the s. of eating** simplement pour manger

salad ['sæləd] *n* salade *f*; *Br* **s. cream** = sorte de mayonnaise; **s. dressing** = sauce pour salade

salami [sə'lɑːmɪ] *n* salami *m*

salary ['sælərɪ] *(pl* **-ies)** *n* salaire *m*

sale [seɪl] *n (action, event)* vente *f*; *(at reduced price)* solde *m*; **on s.** en vente; **in the sales** en solde; **(up) for s.** à vendre; *Am* **sales check** *or* **slip** reçu *m*; *Am* **sales tax** ≃ TVA *f* **■ salesclerk** *n Am* vendeur, -euse *mf* **■ salesman** *(pl* **-men)** *n (in shop)* vendeur *m*; *(for company)* représentant *m* **■ saleswoman** *(pl* **-women)** *n (in shop)* vendeuse *f*; *(for company)* représentante *f*

salmon ['sæmən] *n inv* saumon *m*

salon ['sælɒn] *n* **beauty s.** institut *m* de beauté; **hairdressing s.** salon *m* de coiffure

saloon [sə'luːn] *n Am (bar)* bar *m*; *Br* **s. car** berline *f*

salt [sɔːlt] **1** *n* sel *m* **2** *vt* saler **■ saltcellar** *n Br* salière *f* **■ salt-shaker** *n Am* salière *f* **■ saltwater** *adj (lake)* salé; *(fish)* de mer **■ salty (-ier, -iest)** *adj* salé

salute [sə'luːt] **1** *n* salut *m* **2** *vt (greet) & Mil* saluer **3** *vi* faire un salut

salvage ['sælvɪdʒ] *vt (ship)* sauver;

(waste material) récupérer
salvation [sæl'veɪʃən] *n* salut *m*

SAME [seɪm] **1** *adj* même; **the (very) s. house as...** (exactement) la même maison que...
 2 *pron* **the s.** le même, la même, *pl* les mêmes; **I would have done the s.** j'aurais fait la même chose; **it's all the s. to me** ça m'est égal
 3 *adv* **to look the s.** *(of two things)* sembler pareils; **all the s.** *(nevertheless)* tout de même

sample ['sɑːmpəl] **1** *n* échantillon *m*; *(of blood)* prélèvement *m* **2** *vt (wine, cheese)* goûter

sanction ['sæŋkʃən] *n (penalty)* sanction *f*

sanctuary [*Br* 'sæŋktʃʊərɪ, *Am* -erɪ] *(pl* -ies) *n (for fugitive, refugee)* refuge *m*; *(for wildlife)* réserve *f*

sand [sænd] **1** *n* sable *m*; **s. castle** château *m* de sable **2** *vt* **to s. (down)** *(wood)* poncer

sandal ['sændəl] *n* sandale *f*

sandwich ['sænwɪdʒ] **1** *n* sandwich *m*; **cheese s.** sandwich *m* au fromage **2** *vt* **to be sandwiched between** *(of person, building)* être coincé entre

sandy ['sændɪ] *(-ier, -iest) adj* (a) *(beach)* de sable; *(ground)* sablonneux, -euse (b) *(hair)* blond roux *inv*

sane [seɪn] *(-er, -est) adj (person)* sain d'esprit

sang [sæŋ] *pt of* sing

sanitary [*Br* 'sænɪtərɪ, *Am* -erɪ] *adj (fittings)* sanitaire; *Br* **s. towel,** *Am* **s. napkin** serviette *f* hygiénique

sanitation [sænɪ'teɪʃən] *n* hygiène *f* publique; *(plumbing)* installations *fpl* sanitaires

sanity ['sænɪtɪ] *n* santé *f* mentale

sank [sæŋk] *pt of* sink²

Santa Claus ['sæntəklɔːz] *n* le Père Noël

sap [sæp] **1** *n (of tree, plant)* sève *f* **2** *(pt & pp* -pp-) *vt (weaken)* saper

sapphire ['sæfaɪə(r)] *n* saphir *m*

sarcastic [sɑːˈkæstɪk] *adj* sarcastique

sardine [sɑːˈdiːn] *n* sardine *f*

Sardinia [sɑːˈdɪnɪə] *n* la Sardaigne

sat [sæt] *pt & pp of* sit

Satan ['seɪtən] *n* Satan *m*

satchel ['sætʃəl] *n* cartable *m*

satellite ['sætəlaɪt] *n* satellite *m*; **s. dish** antenne *f* parabolique; **s. television** télévision *f* par satellite

satin ['sætɪn] *n* satin *m*

satire ['sætaɪə(r)] *n* satire *f* (**on** contre)
 ■ **satirical** *adj* satirique

satisfaction [sætɪsˈfækʃən] *n* satisfaction *f* ■ **satisfactory** *adj* satisfaisant

satisfy ['sætɪsfaɪ] *(pt & pp* -ied) *vt* satisfaire; *(convince)* persuader (**that** que); *(condition)* remplir; **to be satisfied (with)** être satisfait (de) ■ **satisfying** *adj* satisfaisant; *(meal, food)* substantiel, -elle

satsuma [sæt'suːmə] *n Br* mandarine *f*

saturate ['sætʃəreɪt] *vt* saturer (**with** de)

Saturday ['sætədeɪ] *n* samedi *m*

sauce [sɔːs] *n* sauce *f*; **mint s.** sauce à la menthe

saucepan ['sɔːspən] *n* casserole *f*

saucer ['sɔːsə(r)] *n* soucoupe *f*

Saudi Arabia [saʊdɪəˈreɪbɪə] *n* l'Arabie *f* saoudite

sauna ['sɔːnə] *n* sauna *m*

saunter ['sɔːntə(r)] *vi* flâner

sausage ['sɒsɪdʒ] *n* saucisse *f*; *Br* **s. roll** feuilleté *m* à la viande

savage ['sævɪdʒ] **1** *adj (animal, person)* féroce; *(attack, criticism)* violent **2** *vt (physically)* attaquer

save¹ [seɪv] **1** *vt (rescue)* sauver (**from** de); *(keep)* garder; *(money)* économiser; *(time)* gagner; *Comptr* sauvegarder; **to s. sb's life** sauver la vie de qn; **to s. sb from doing sth** empêcher qn de faire qch **2** *vi* **to s. (up)** faire des économies (**for/on** pour/sur) **3** *n (by goalkeeper)* arrêt *m*

save² [seɪv] *prep Formal (except)* hormis

saving ['seɪvɪŋ] *n (of time, money)* économie *f*; **savings** *(money saved)* économies *fpl*; **savings account** compte *m* d'épargne

saviour ['seɪvjə(r)] (*Am* **savior**) *n* sauveur *m*

savour ['seɪvə(r)] (*Am* **savor**) *vt* savourer ▪ **savoury** (*Am* **savory**) *adj (not sweet)* salé

saw¹ [sɔː] **1** *n* scie *f* **2** (*pt* **sawed**, *pp* **sawn** *or* **sawed**) *vt* scier; **to s. sth off** scier qch ▪ **sawdust** *n* sciure *f*

saw² [sɔː] *pt of* **see¹**

sawn [sɔːn] *pp of* **saw¹**

saxophone ['sæksəfəʊn] *n* saxophone *m*

say [seɪ] **1** (*pt & pp* **said**) *vt* dire (**to** à; **that** que); *(of dial, watch)* indiquer; **to s. again** répéter; **that is to s.** c'est-à-dire

2 *vi* dire; *Am Fam* **s.!** dis donc!; **that goes without saying** ça va sans dire

3 *n* **to have one's s.** avoir son mot à dire; **to have no s.** ne pas avoir voix au chapitre (**in** concernant)

saying ['seɪɪŋ] *n* maxime *f*

scab [skæb] *n (of wound)* croûte *f*

scaffolding ['skæfəldɪŋ] *n* échafaudage *m*

scald [skɔːld] *vt* ébouillanter

scale¹ [skeɪl] **1** *n (of instrument, map)* échelle *f*; *(of salaries)* barème *m*; *Fig (of problem)* étendue *f*; **on a small/large s.** sur une petite/grande échelle **2** *vt* **to s. down** revoir qch à la baisse

scale² [skeɪl] *n (on fish)* écaille *f*; *(in kettle)* dépôt *m* calcaire

scales [skeɪlz] *npl (for weighing)* balance *f*; **(bathroom) s.** pèse-personne *m*

scalp [skælp] *n* cuir *m* chevelu

scamper ['skæmpə(r)] *vi* **to s. off** *or* **away** détaler

scampi ['skæmpɪ] *n* scampi *mpl*

scan [skæn] **1** *n* **to have a s.** passer une échographie **2** (*pt & pp* **-nn-**) *vt (look at briefly)* parcourir; *(scrutinize)* scruter; *Comptr* passer au scanner

scandal ['skændəl] *n (outrage)* scandale *m*; *(gossip)* ragots *mpl* ▪ **scandalous** *adj* scandaleux, -euse

Scandinavia [skændɪ'neɪvɪə] *n* la Scandinavie ▪ **Scandinavian 1** *adj*

scandinave **2** *n* Scandinave *mf*

scanner ['skænə(r)] *n Med & Comptr* scanner *m*

scant [skænt] *adj* insuffisant ▪ **scanty** (**-ier, -iest**) *adj* insuffisant; *(bikini)* minuscule

scapegoat ['skeɪpgəʊt] *n* bouc *m* émissaire

scar [skɑː(r)] **1** *n* cicatrice *f* **2** (*pt & pp* **-rr-**) *vt* marquer d'une cicatrice; *Fig (of experience)* marquer

scarce [skeəs] (**-er, -est**) *adj* rare ▪ **scarcely** *adv* à peine; **s. anything** presque rien

scare [skeə(r)] **1** *n* **to give sb a s.** faire peur à qn **2** *vt* faire peur à; **to s. sb off** faire fuir qn ▪ **scared** *adj* effrayé; **to be s. of sb/sth** avoir peur de qn/qch

scarf [skɑːf] (*pl* **scarves**) *n (long)* écharpe *f*; *(square)* foulard *m*

scarlet ['skɑːlət] *adj* écarlate; **s. fever** scarlatine *f*

scary ['skeərɪ] (**-ier, -iest**) *adj Fam* effrayant

scathing ['skeɪðɪŋ] *adj (remark)* acerbe; **to be s. about sb/sth** faire des remarques acerbes sur qn/qch

scatter ['skætə(r)] **1** *vt (demonstrators)* disperser; *(corn, seed)* jeter à la volée; *(papers)* laisser traîner **2** *vi (of crowd)* se disperser

scavenge ['skævɪndʒ] *vi* **to s. for sth** fouiller pour trouver qch

scenario [sɪ'nɑːrɪəʊ] (*pl* **-os**) *n (of film)* scénario *m*

scene [siːn] *n (in book, film, play)* scène *f*; *(of event, crime, accident)* lieu *m*; *also Fig* **behind the scenes** dans les coulisses; **on the s.** sur les lieux; **to make a s.** faire un scandale

scenery ['siːnərɪ] (*pl* **-ies**) *n (landscape)* paysage *m*; *(in play, film)* décors *mpl*

scenic ['siːnɪk] *adj* pittoresque; **s. route** route *f* touristique

scent [sent] *n (smell)* odeur *f*; *(perfume)* parfum *m*; *(in hunting)* fumet *m*

sceptical ['skeptɪkəl] (*Am* **skeptical**) *adj* sceptique

schedule [Br 'ʃedjuːl, Am 'skedʒʊl] 1 n (plan) programme m; (for trains, buses) horaire m; (list) liste f; **according to s.** comme prévu 2 vt prévoir; (event) fixer la date/l'heure de ■ **scheduled** [Br 'ʃedjuːld, Am 'skedjuːld] adj (planned) prévu; (service, flight, train) régulier, -ère

scheme [skiːm] 1 n (plan) plan m (to do pour faire); (plot) complot m; (arrangement) arrangement m 2 vi Pej comploter ■ **scheming** Pej 1 adj intrigant 2 n machinations fpl

schizophrenic [skɪtsəʊ'frenɪk] adj & n schizophrène (mf)

schmuck [ʃmʌk] n Am Fam andouille f

scholar ['skɒlə(r)] n érudit, -e mf ■ **scholarly** adj érudit ■ **scholarship** n (learning) érudition f; (grant) bourse f d'études

school [skuːl] 1 n école f; (within university) département m; Am Fam (college) université f; Br **secondary s.**, Am **high s.** établissement m d'enseignement secondaire
2 adj (year, book, equipment) scolaire; **s. bag** cartable m; **s. fees** frais mpl de scolarité; Am **s. yard** cour f de récréation ■ **schoolboy** n écolier m ■ **schoolchildren** npl écoliers mpl ■ **schoolfriend** n camarade mf de classe ■ **schoolgirl** n écolière f ■ **schoolteacher** n (primary) instituteur, -trice mf; (secondary) professeur m

science ['saɪəns] n science f; **to study s.** étudier les sciences; **s. fiction** science-fiction f ■ **scientific** adj scientifique ■ **scientist** n scientifique mf

scissors ['sɪzəz] npl ciseaux mpl

scoff [skɒf] 1 vt **to s. at sb/sth** se moquer de qn/qch 2 vti Br Fam (eat) bouffer

scold [skəʊld] vt gronder (**for doing** pour avoir fait)

scone [skəʊn, skɒn] n Br scone m

scoop [skuːp] 1 n (for flour, sugar) pelle f; (for ice cream) cuillère f; (amount) (of ice cream) boule f 2 vt **to s. sth out** (hollow out) évider qch; **to s. sth up** ramasser qch

scooter ['skuːtə(r)] n (for child) trottinette f; (motorcycle) scooter m

scope [skəʊp] n (range) étendue f; (of action) possibilité f

scorch [skɔːtʃ] 1 n **s. (mark)** brûlure f 2 vt roussir ■ **scorching** adj (day) torride; (sun, sand) brûlant

score¹ [skɔː(r)] 1 n (in sport) score m; (in music) partition f; (of film) musique f 2 vt (point, goal) marquer; (exam mark) avoir; (piece of music) adapter (**for** pour) 3 vi (score a goal) marquer; (count points) marquer les points ■ **scoreboard** n tableau m d'affichage ■ **scorer** n marqueur m

score² [skɔː(r)] n **a s. (twenty)** vingt; Fam **scores of** des tas de

scorn [skɔːn] 1 n mépris m 2 vt mépriser ■ **scornful** adj méprisant

scorpion ['skɔːpɪən] n scorpion m

Scot [skɒt] n Écossais, -e mf ■ **Scotland** n l'Écosse f ■ **Scotsman** (pl -men) n Écossais m ■ **Scotswoman** (pl -women) n Écossaise f ■ **Scottish** adj écossais

Scotch [skɒtʃ] 1 n (whisky) scotch m 2 adj Am **S. tape®** Scotch® m

scoundrel ['skaʊndrəl] n crapule f

scour ['skaʊə(r)] vt (pan) récurer; Fig (streets, house) ratisser (**for** à la recherche de) ■ **scourer** n tampon m à récurer

scout [skaʊt] n (boy) **s.** scout m, éclaireur m; Am (girl) **s.** éclaireuse f

scowl [skaʊl] vi lancer des regards noirs (**at** à)

scram [skræm] (pt & pp -mm-) vi Fam se tirer

scramble ['skræmbəl] 1 vt **scrambled eggs** œufs mpl brouillés 2 vi **to s. up a hill** gravir une colline en s'aidant des mains

scrap [skræp] 1 n (a) (piece) bout m (**of** de); (of information) bribe f; **scraps** (food) restes mpl; **s. paper** papier m brouillon
(b) **s. (metal)** ferraille f; **s. heap** tas m de ferraille; **s. dealer, s. merchant** ferrailleur m; **s. yard** casse f
2 (pt & pp -pp-) vt (get rid of) se débarrasser de; (car) envoyer à la casse; Fig

(plan, idea) abandonner ▪ **scrapbook** *n* album *m (de coupures de presse etc)*

scrape [skreɪp] **1** *vt* gratter; *(skin)* érafler; **to s. a living** arriver tout juste à vivre **2** *vi* **to s. against sth** frotter contre qch

▸**scrape away, scrape off** *vt sep* racler

▸**scrape through** *vt insep & vi* **to s. through (an exam)** passer de justesse (à un examen)

▸**scrape together** *vt sep (money, people)* parvenir à rassembler

scratch [skrætʃ] **1** *n (mark, injury)* éraflure *f; (on glass, wood)* rayure *f; Fam* **to start from s.** repartir de zéro; **it isn't up to s.** ce n'est pas au niveau

2 *vt (to relieve itching)* gratter; *(by accident)* érafler; *(glass)* rayer; *(with claw)* griffer; *(write, draw)* griffonner (**on** sur)

3 *vi (of person)* se gratter; *(of pen, new clothes)* gratter ▪ **scratchcard** *n (lottery card)* carte *f* à gratter

scrawl [skrɔːl] **1** *n* gribouillis *m* **2** *vt* gribouiller

scream [skriːm] **1** *n* hurlement *m* **2** *vt* hurler **3** *vi* hurler; **to s. at sb** crier après qn

screech [skriːtʃ] *vti* hurler

screen [skriːn] **1** *n (of TV set, computer, cinema)* écran *m; Comptr* **s. saver** économiseur *m* d'écran

2 *vt (hide)* cacher (**from sb** à qn); *(protect)* protéger (**from** de); *(film)* projeter; *(visitors, calls)* filtrer; *(for disease)* faire subir un test de dépistage à ▪ **screening** *n (of film)* projection *f; (selection)* tri *m; (for disease)* dépistage *m* ▪ **screenplay** *n (of film)* scénario *m*

screw [skruː] **1** *n* vis *f* **2** *vt* visser (**to** à); **to s. sth down or on** visser qch; **to s. sth off** dévisser qch; **to s. sth up** *(paper)* chiffonner qch ▪ **screwdriver** *n* tournevis *m*

scribble ['skrɪbəl] **1** *n* griffonnage *m* **2** *vti* griffonner

script [skrɪpt] *n* (a) *(of film)* script *m; (of play)* texte *m; (in exam)* copie *f* (b) *(handwriting)* script *m*

Scripture(s) ['skrɪptʃə(z)] *n(pl) Rel* les saintes Écritures *fpl*

scroll [skrəʊl] **1** *n* rouleau *m; (manuscript)* manuscrit *m* **2** *vi Comptr* défiler; **to s. down/up** défiler vers le bas/haut

scrounge [skraʊndʒ] *vt Fam (meal)* se faire payer (**off** *or* **from sb** par qn); *(steal)* taper (**off** *or* **from sb** à qn); **to s. money off** *or* **from sb** taper qn ▪ **scrounger** *n Fam* parasite *m*

scrub [skrʌb] **1** *n* (a) **to give sth a s.** bien frotter qch; *Am* **s. brush** brosse *f* dure (b) *(land)* broussailles *fpl* **2** *(pt & pp* **-bb-***) vt (surface)* frotter; *(pan)* récurer; **to s. sth off** *(remove)* enlever qch (à la brosse *ou* en frottant)

scrubbing ['skrʌbɪŋ] *n* **s. brush** brosse *f* dure

scruff [skrʌf] *n* **by the s. of the neck** par la peau du cou

scruffy ['skrʌfɪ] *(*-ier, -iest*) adj (person)* peu soigné

scrum [skrʌm] *n (in rugby)* mêlée *f*

scrupulous ['skruːpjʊləs] *adj* scrupuleux, -euse

scrutinize ['skruːtɪnaɪz] *vt (document)* éplucher

scuba ['skuːbə] *n* **s. diving** la plongée sous-marine

scuff [skʌf] *vt* **to s. sth (up)** *(shoe)* érafler qch

scuffle ['skʌfəl] *n* bagarre *f*

sculpt [skʌlpt] *vti* sculpter ▪ **sculptor** *n* sculpteur *m* ▪ **sculpture** *n (art, object)* sculpture *f*

scum [skʌm] *n* (a) *(froth)* écume *f* (b) *Fam Pej (people)* racaille *f; (person)* ordure *f*

scurry ['skʌrɪ] *vi (rush)* courir; **to s. off** se sauver

sea [siː] **1** *n* mer *f;* **(out) at s.** en mer; **by s.** par mer; **by** *or* **beside the s.** au bord de la mer

2 *adj (level, breeze)* de la mer; *(water, fish, salt)* de mer; *(air)* marin; *(battle)* naval (*mpl* -als); *(route)* maritime; **s. bed, s. floor** fond *m* de la mer ▪ **seafood** *n* fruits *mpl* de mer ▪ **seafront** *n Br* front *m* de mer ▪ **seagull** *n* mouette *f* ▪ **seashell** *n* coquillage *m* ▪ **seaside** *n Br* bord *m* de la mer; **s. resort** station *f*

balnéaire ■ **seashore** *n* rivage *m* ■ **sea-sick** *adj* **to be s.** avoir le mal de mer ■ **seaweed** *n* algues *fpl*

seal¹ [si:l] *n (animal)* phoque *m*

seal² [si:l] **1** *n (stamp)* sceau *m*; *(device for sealing)* joint *m* d'étanchéité **2** *vt (document, container)* sceller; *(stick down)* cacheter; *(make airtight)* fermer hermétiquement; **to s. off an area** boucler un quartier

seam [si:m] *n (in cloth)* couture *f*

search [sɜ:tʃ] **1** *n* recherches *fpl* **(for** de); *(of place)* fouille *f*; **in s. of** à la recherche de; *Comptr* **to do a s. for sth** rechercher qch; *Comptr* **s. engine** moteur *m* de recherche **2** *vt (person, place)* fouiller **(for** pour trouver) **3** *vi* chercher; **to s. for sth** chercher qch ■ **searchlight** *n* projecteur *m*

season¹ ['si:zən] *n* saison *f*; *(of films)* cycle *m*; **in the peak s., in (the) high s.** en haute saison; **in the low** *or* **off s.** en basse saison; **s. ticket** abonnement *m*

season² ['si:zən] *vt (food)* assaisonner ■ **seasoning** *n Culin* assaisonnement *m*

seasonal ['si:zənəl] *adj (work, change)* saisonnier, -ère

seat [si:t] **1** *n* siège *m*; *(of trousers)* fond *m*; **to take** *or* **have a s.** s'asseoir; **s. belt** ceinture *f* de sécurité **2** *vt (at table)* placer; *(on one's lap)* asseoir ■ **seated** *adj (sitting)* assis ■ **seating** *n (seats)* places *fpl* assises

-seater ['si:tə(r)] *suff* **two-s. (car)** voiture *f* à deux places

secluded [sɪ'klu:dɪd] *adj (remote)* isolé ■ **seclusion** *n* solitude *f*

second¹ ['sekənd] **1** *adj* deuxième, second; **every s. week** une semaine sur deux; *Aut* **in s. (gear)** en seconde **2** *adv (say)* deuxièmement; **to come s.** *(in competition)* se classer deuxième; **the s. biggest** le deuxième en ordre de grandeur

3 *n (in series)* deuxième *mf*, second, -e *mf*; *(in month)* deux *m*; **Louis the S.** Louis Deux; **seconds** *(goods)* articles *mpl* défectueux

4 *vt (motion, proposal)* appuyer ■ **second-class** *adj (ticket on train)* de seconde (classe); *(mail)* non urgent; *(product)* de qualité inférieure ■ **secondly** *adv* deuxièmement ■ **second-rate** *adj* médiocre

second² ['sekənd] *n (part of minute)* seconde *f*; **s. hand** *(of clock, watch)* trotteuse *f*

secondary ['sekəndərɪ] *adj* secondaire; *Br* **s. school** établissement *m* secondaire

second-hand [sekənd'hænd] **1** *adj & adv (not new)* d'occasion **2** *adj (report, news)* de seconde main

secrecy ['si:krəsɪ] *n (discretion, silence)* secret *m*

secret ['si:krɪt] **1** *adj* secret, -ète **2** *n* secret *m*; **in s.** en secret ■ **secretly** *adv* secrètement

secretary [*Br* 'sekrətərɪ, *Am* -erɪ] *(pl* **-ies)** *n* secrétaire *mf*; *Br* **Foreign S.,** *Am* **S. of State** ≃ ministre *m* des Affaires étrangères ■ **secretarial** [-'teərɪəl] *adj (work)* administratif, -ive; *(job, course)* de secrétariat

secretive ['si:krətɪv] *adj (person)* secret, -ète; **to be s. about sth** faire des cachotteries à propos de qch

sect [sekt] *n* secte *f*

section ['sekʃən] *n* partie *f*; *(of road)* tronçon *m*; *(of machine)* élément *m*; *(of organization)* département *m*; **the sports s.** *(of newspaper)* la page des sports

sector ['sektə(r)] *n* secteur *m*

secular ['sekjʊlə(r)] *adj (music, art)* profane

secure [sɪ'kjʊə(r)] **1** *adj (person)* en sécurité; *(investment, place)* sûr; *(door, window)* bien fermé **2** *vt (fasten)* attacher; *(window, door)* bien fermer; *(position, future)* assurer; *(support, promise)* procurer; **to s. sth (for oneself)** se procurer qch ■ **securely** *adv (firmly)* solidement; *(safely)* en sûreté

security [sɪ'kjʊərətɪ] *(pl* **-ies)** *n* sécurité *f*; *Fin (for loan, bail)* garantie *f*; **securities** *(stocks, bonds)* titres *mpl*

sedan [sɪ'dæn] *n Am (saloon)* berline *f*

sedate [sɪˈdeɪt] **1** *adj* calme **2** *vt* mettre sous calmants

sedative [ˈsedətɪv] *n* calmant *m*

seduce [sɪˈdjuːs] *vt* séduire ▪ **seductive** [-ˈdʌktɪv] *adj (person, offer)* séduisant

SEE [siː] *(pt* **saw,** *pp* **seen)** *vti* voir; **we'll s.** on verra; **I can s. a hill** je vois une colline; **I saw him run(ning)** je l'ai vu courir; **to s. reason** entendre raison; **s. you (later)!** à tout à l'heure!; **to s. that...** *(make sure that)* faire en sorte que... *(+ subjunctive); (check)* s'assurer que... *(+ indicative);* **to s. sb to the door** accompagner qn jusqu'à la porte

▸ **see about** *vt insep (deal with)* s'occuper de; *(consider)* songer à

▸ **see off** *vt sep (say goodbye to)* dire au revoir à

▸ **see out** *vt sep* accompagner jusqu'à la porte

▸ **see through 1** *vt sep (task)* mener à bien **2** *vt insep* **to s. through sb** percer qn à jour

▸ **see to** *vt insep (deal with)* s'occuper de; *(mend)* réparer; **to s. to it that...** *(make sure that)* faire en sorte que... *(+ subjunctive); (check)* s'assurer que... *(+ indicative)*

seed [siːd] *n* graine *f*; *(of fruit)* pépin *m*; *Fig (source)* germe *m*

seedy [ˈsiːdɪ] **(-ier, -iest)** *adj* miteux, -euse

seeing [ˈsiːɪŋ] *conj* **s. (that)** vu que

seek [siːk] *(pt & pp* **sought)** *vt* chercher **(to do** à faire); *(ask for)* demander **(from** à); **to s. sb out** dénicher qn

seem [siːm] *vi* sembler **(to do** faire); **it seems that...** *(impression)* il semble que... *(+ subjunctive);* **it seems to me that...** il me semble que... *(+ indicative)*

seemingly [ˈsiːmɪŋlɪ] *adv* apparemment

seemly [ˈsiːmlɪ] *adj Formal* bienséant

seen [siːn] *pp of* **see**

seep [siːp] *vi* suinter; **to s. into sth** s'infiltrer dans qch

seesaw [ˈsiːsɔː] *n* balançoire *f* à bascule

see-through [ˈsiːθruː] *adj* transparent

segment [ˈsegmənt] *n* segment *m*; *(of orange)* quartier *m*

segregate [ˈsegrɪgeɪt] *vt* séparer **(from** de) ▪ **segregation** *n* ségrégation *f*

seize [siːz] **1** *vt* saisir; *(power, land)* s'emparer de **2** *vi* **to s. (up)on** *(offer)* sauter sur; **to s. up** *(of engine)* se bloquer

seizure [ˈsiːʒə(r)] *n (of goods, property)* saisie *f*; *Med* crise *f*

seldom [ˈseldəm] *adv* rarement

select [sɪˈlekt] **1** *vt* sélectionner **2** *adj (exclusive)* sélect ▪ **selection** *n* sélection *f*

selective [sɪˈlektɪv] *adj* sélectif, -ive

self [self] *(pl* **selves** [selvz]) *n* **he's back to his old s.** il est redevenu comme avant ▪ **self-addressed** *n* **s. envelope** enveloppe *f* libellée à ses nom et adresse ▪ **self-assured** *adj* sûr de soi ▪ **self-catering** *adj Br (holiday)* en appartement meublé; *(accommodation)* meublé ▪ **self-centred** *(Am* **-centered)** *adj* égocentrique ▪ **self-confidence** *n* confiance *f* en soi ▪ **self-confident** *adj* sûr de soi ▪ **self-conscious** *adj* gêné ▪ **self-contained** *adj (flat)* indépendant ▪ **self-control** *n* maîtrise *f* de soi ▪ **self-defence** *(Am* **-defense)** *n (in law)* légitime défense *f*; **in s.** en état de légitime défense ▪ **self-discipline** *n* autodiscipline *f* ▪ **self-employed** *adj* indépendant ▪ **self-esteem** *n* confiance *f* en soi ▪ **self-evident** *adj* évident ▪ **self-important** *adj* suffisant ▪ **self-indulgent** *adj* complaisant ▪ **self-interest** *n* intérêt *m* personnel ▪ **self-pity** *n* **to be full of s.** s'apitoyer sur son propre sort ▪ **self-portrait** *n* autoportrait *m* ▪ **self-raising** *(Am* **-rising)** *n* **s. flour** = farine contenant de la levure chimique ▪ **self-respect** *n* amour-propre *m* ▪ **self-righteous** *adj* suffisant ▪ **self-sacrifice** *n* abnégation *f* ▪ **self-satisfied** *adj* content de soi ▪ **self-service** *n & adj* libre-service *(m inv)* ▪ **self-sufficient** *adj* indépendant ▪ **self-taught** *adj* autodidacte

selfish ['selfɪʃ] *adj* égoïste; *(motive)* intéressé ■ **selfishness** *n* égoïsme *m* ■ **selfless** *adj* désintéressé

sell [sel] **1** *(pt & pp* **sold)** *vt* vendre; *Fig (idea)* faire accepter; **to s. sb sth, to s. sth to sb** vendre qch à qn; **she sold it to me for $100** elle me l'a vendu 100 dollars **2** *vi (of product)* se vendre; *(of person)* vendre ■ **sell-by** *adj* **s. date** date *f* limite de vente

▸ **sell off** *vt sep* liquider

▸ **sell out** *vt insep* **to have** *or* **be sold out of sth** n'avoir plus de qch; **to be sold out** *(of book, item)* être épuisé; *(of show, concert)* afficher complet

▸ **sell up** *vi (sell home, business)* tout vendre

seller ['selə(r)] *n* vendeur, -euse *mf*

Sellotape® ['seləteɪp] *n Br* Scotch® *m*

semblance ['sembləns] *n* semblant *m*

semen ['siːmən] *n* sperme *m*

semester [sɪ'mestə(r)] *n* semestre *m*

semi- ['semɪ] *pref* semi-, demi- ■ **semicircle** *n* demi-cercle *m* ■ **semicolon** *n* point-virgule *m* ■ **semi-detached** *adj Br* **s. house** maison *f* jumelée ■ **semifinal** *n* demi-finale *f* ■ **semi-skimmed** *adj (milk)* demi-écrémé

seminar ['semɪnɑː(r)] *n* séminaire *m*

semolina [semə'liːnə] *n* semoule *f*

senate ['senɪt] *n* **the S.** le Sénat ■ **senator** [-nətə(r)] *n* sénateur *m*

send [send] *(pt & pp* **sent)** *vt* envoyer **(to** à); **to s. sth to sb, to s. sb sth** envoyer qch à qn; **to s. sb home** renvoyer qn chez soi; *Fam* **to s. sb packing** envoyer promener qn ■ **sender** *n* expéditeur, -trice *mf*

▸ **send away 1** *vt sep (person)* renvoyer **2** *vi* **to s. away for sth** se faire envoyer qch

▸ **send back** *vt sep* renvoyer

▸ **send for** *vt insep* envoyer chercher; *(doctor)* faire venir; *(send away for)* se faire envoyer

▸ **send in** *vt sep (form, invoice, troops)* envoyer; *(person)* faire entrer

▸ **send off 1** *vt sep (letter)* envoyer **(to** à); *(player)* expulser **2** *vi* **to s. off for** sth se faire envoyer qch

▸ **send on** *vt sep (letter)* faire suivre

▸ **send out 1** *vt sep* envoyer **2** *vi* **to s. out for sth** envoyer chercher qch

▸ **send up** *vt sep Br Fam (parody)* se moquer de

senile ['siːnaɪl] *adj* sénile

senior ['siːnɪə(r)] **1** *adj (in age)* aîné; *(in position, rank)* supérieur; **to be sb's s., to be s. to sb** être l'aîné de qn; *(in rank, status)* être le supérieur de qn; **Brown s.** Brown père; **s. citizen** personne *f* âgée; *Am* **s. year** *(in school, college)* dernière année *f* **2** *n* aîné, -e *mf*; *Am (in last year of school or college)* étudiant, -e *mf* de dernière année; *(in sport)* senior *mf*

sensation [sen'seɪʃən] *n* sensation *f* ■ **sensational** *adj* sensationnel, -elle

sense [sens] **1** *n (faculty, awareness, meaning)* sens *m*; **s. of smell** odorat *m*; **a s. of shame** un sentiment de honte; **s. of direction** sens de l'orientation; **to have a s. of humour** avoir le sens de l'humour; **to have the s. to do sth** avoir l'intelligence de faire qch; **to bring sb to his/her senses** ramener qn à la raison; **to make s.** être logique; **to make s. of sth** comprendre qch **2** *vt* sentir (**that** que)

senseless ['sensləs] *adj (pointless)* absurde

sensibility [sensɪ'bɪlətɪ] *n* sensibilité *f*

sensible ['sensəbəl] *adj (wise)* sensé; *(clothes, shoes)* pratique

sensitive ['sensɪtɪv] *adj (person)* sensible **(to** à); *(skin, question)* délicat; *(information)* confidentiel, -elle ■ **sensitivity** *n* sensibilité *f*; *(touchiness)* susceptibilité *f*

sensor ['sensə(r)] *n* détecteur *m*

sensual ['senʃʊəl] *adj* sensuel, -elle ■ **sensuous** *adj* sensuel, -elle

sent [sent] *pt & pp of* **send**

sentence ['sentəns] **1** *n* **(a)** *(words)* phrase *f* **(b)** *(in prison)* peine *f* **2** *vt (criminal)* condamner; **to s. sb to three years (in prison)/to death**

condamner qn à trois ans de prison/à mort

sentiment ['sentɪmənt] *n* sentiment *m* ■ **sentimental** [-'mentəl] *adj* sentimental

separate 1 ['sepərət] *adj (distinct)* séparé; *(organization)* indépendant; *(occasion, entrance)* différent; *(room)* à part **2** ['sepəreɪt] *vt* séparer (**from** de) **3** ['sepəreɪt] *vi* se séparer (**from** de) ■ **separately** ['sepərətlɪ] *adv* séparément ■ **separation** *n* séparation *f*

September [sep'tembə(r)] *n* septembre *m*

septic ['septɪk] *adj (wound)* infecté; **to go** *or* **turn s.** s'infecter

sequel ['si:kwəl] *n (book, film)* suite *f*

sequence ['si:kwəns] *n (order)* ordre *m*; *(series)* succession *f*; *(in film)* & *Comptr, Mus & Cards* séquence *f*; **in s.** dans l'ordre

sequin ['si:kwɪn] *n* paillette *f*

Serbia ['sɜːbɪə] *n* la Serbie

serenade [serə'neɪd] **1** *n* sérénade *f* **2** *vt* chanter la sérénade à

serene [sə'riːn] *adj* serein

sergeant ['sɑːdʒənt] *n Mil* sergent *m*; *(in police)* brigadier *m*

serial ['sɪərɪəl] *n (story, film)* feuilleton *m*; **s. killer** tueur *m* en série; **s. number** numéro *m* de série ■ **serialize** *vt (in newspaper)* publier en feuilleton; *(on television or radio)* adapter en feuilleton

series ['sɪərɪːz] *n inv* série *f*

serious ['sɪərɪəs] *adj (person)* sérieux, -euse; *(illness, mistake, tone)* grave; *(damage)* important; **to be s. about doing sth** envisager sérieusement de faire qch ■ **seriously** *adv* sérieusement; *(ill, damaged)* gravement; **to take sb/sth s.** prendre qn/qch au sérieux

sermon ['sɜːmən] *n* sermon *m*

servant ['sɜːvənt] *n* domestique *mf*

serve [sɜːv] **1** *n (in tennis)* service *m* **2** *vt (country, cause, meal, customer)* servir; *(prison sentence)* purger; *(apprenticeship)* faire; *Fam* **(it) serves you right!** ça t'apprendra! **3** *vi* servir (**as** de); **to s. on** *(committee,*

jury) être membre de ■ **server** *n (in tennis)* serveur, -euse *mf*; *Comptr* serveur *m*

service ['sɜːvɪs] **1** *n (with army, firm, in restaurant, in tennis)* & *Rel* service *m*; *(of machine)* entretien *m*; *(of car)* révision *f*; **to be at sb's s.** être au service de qn; **the (armed) services** les forces *fpl* armées; **s. charge** service *m*; *Br* **s. area** *(on motorway)* aire *f* de service; *Comptr* **s. provider** fournisseur *m* d'accès Internet; **s. station** station-service *f* **2** *vt (machine)* entretenir; *(car)* réviser

serviceman ['sɜːvɪsmən] *(pl* **-men**) *n* militaire *m*

serviette [sɜːvɪ'et] *n Br* serviette *f* de table

servile ['sɜːvaɪl] *adj* servile

serving ['sɜːvɪŋ] *n (of food)* portion *f*; **s. dish** plat *m*

session ['seʃən] *n (meeting, period)* séance *f*; *(university term)* trimestre *m*; *(university year)* année *f* universitaire

set [set] **1** *n (of keys, tools)* jeu *m*; *(of stamps, numbers)* série *f*; *(of people)* groupe *m*; *(of facts, laws)* & *Math* ensemble *m*; *(of books)* collection *f*; *(of dishes)* service *m*; *(kit)* trousse *f*; *(in theatre)* décor *m*; *(for film)* plateau *m*; *(in tennis)* set *m*; **chess s.** jeu *m* d'échecs; **tea s.** service *m* à thé; **television s., TV s.** téléviseur *m* **2** *adj (time, price)* fixe; *(lunch)* à prix fixe; *(school book)* au programme; *(ideas, purpose)* déterminé; **to be s. on doing sth** être résolu à faire qch; **to be dead s. against sth** être formellement opposé à qch; **to be all s.** être prêt (**to do** pour faire); **s. menu** menu *m*; **s. phrase** expression *f* figée **3** *(pt & pp* **set,** *pres p* **setting)** *vt (put)* mettre, poser; *(date, limit, task)* fixer; *(homework)* donner (**for sb** à qn); *(jewel)* sertir; *(watch)* régler; *(alarm clock)* mettre (**for** pour); *(bone fracture)* réduire; *(trap)* tendre (**for** à); **to s. a record** établir un record; **to s. a precedent** créer un précédent; **to s. sb free** libérer qn **4** *vi (of sun)* se coucher; *(of jelly)* prendre; *(of bone)* se ressouder

▸**set about** vt insep (begin) se mettre à; **to s. about doing sth** se mettre à faire qch

▸**set back** vt sep (in time) retarder; Fam (cost) coûter à

▸**set down** vt sep (object) poser

▸**set off 1** vt sep (bomb) faire exploser; (mechanism) déclencher; Fig (beauty) rehausser; **to s. sb off (crying)** faire pleurer qn **2** vi (leave) partir

▸**set out 1** vt sep (display, explain) exposer; (arrange) disposer **2** vi (leave) partir; **to s. out to do sth** avoir l'intention de faire qch

▸**set up 1** vt sep (tent, statue) dresser; (roadblock) mettre en place; (company) créer; (meeting) organiser; (inquiry) ouvrir **2** vi **to s. up in business** s'installer (**as** comme)

setback ['setbæk] n revers m

settee [se'tiː] n canapé m

setting ['setɪŋ] n (surroundings) cadre m; (of sun) coucher m; (on machine) réglage m

settle ['setəl] **1** vt (put in place) installer; (decide, arrange, pay) régler; (date) fixer; (nerves) calmer; (land) coloniser; **that settles it!** c'est décidé! **2** vi (of person, family) s'installer; (of dust) se déposer; (of bird) se poser ▪ **settled** adj (weather, period) stable; (life) rangé

▸**settle down** vi (in chair, house) s'installer; (become quieter) s'assagir; (of situation) se calmer; **to s. down with sb** mener une vie stable avec qn; **to s. down to work** se mettre au travail

▸**settle for** vt insep se contenter de

▸**settle in** vi (in new home) s'installer

▸**settle up** vi (pay) régler; **to s. up with sb** régler qn

settlement ['setəlmənt] n (agreement) accord m; (payment) règlement m; (colony) colonie f

settler ['setlə(r)] n colon m

setup ['setʌp] n Fam (arrangement) système m

seven ['sevən] adj & n sept (m) ▪ **seventh** adj & n septième (mf)

seventeen [sevən'tiːn] adj & n dix-sept (m) ▪ **seventeenth** adj & n dix-septième (mf)

seventy ['sevəntɪ] adj & n soixante-dix (m); **s.-one** soixante et onze ▪ **seventieth** adj & n soixante-dixième (mf)

sever ['sevə(r)] vt couper; Fig (relations) rompre

several ['sevərəl] adj & pron plusieurs (**of** d'entre)

severe [sə'vɪə(r)] adj (person, punishment, tone) sévère; (winter) rigoureux, -euse; (illness, injury) grave; (blow, pain) violent; (cold, frost) intense ▪ **severely** adv (criticize, punish) sévèrement; (damaged, wounded) gravement

sew [səʊ] (pt sewed, pp sewn or sewed) vt coudre; **to s. a button on a shirt** coudre un bouton à une chemise; **to s. sth up** recoudre qch ▪ **sewing** n couture f; **s. machine** machine f à coudre

sewage ['suːɪdʒ] n eaux fpl d'égout ▪ **sewer** n égout m

sewn [səʊn] pp of **sew**

sex [seks] **1** n sexe m; **to have s. with sb** coucher avec qn **2** adj (education, life, act) sexuel, -elle ▪ **sexist** adj & n sexiste (mf)

sexual ['sekʃʊəl] adj sexuel, -elle ▪ **sexuality** [seksjʊ'ælətɪ] n sexualité f ▪ **sexy** ['seksɪ] (-ier, -iest) adj Fam sexy inv

sh [ʃ] exclam chut!

shabby ['ʃæbɪ] (-ier, -iest) adj miteux, -euse; (behaviour, treatment) mesquin

shack [ʃæk] n cabane f

shade [ʃeɪd] **1** n ombre f; (of colour, meaning, opinion) nuance f; (for lamp) abat-jour m inv; **in the s.** à l'ombre; **a s. faster/taller** un rien plus vite/plus grand **2** vt (of tree) ombrager ▪ **shady** (-ier, -iest) adj (place) ombragé; Fig (person, business) louche

shadow ['ʃædəʊ] n ombre f **2** adj Br Pol **s. cabinet** cabinet m fantôme **3** vt **to s. sb** (follow) filer qn

shaft [ʃɑːft] n (a) (of tool) manche m; **s. of light** rayon m de lumière (b) (of mine) puits m; (of lift) cage f

shaggy ['ʃægɪ] (-ier, -iest) adj (hairy) hirsute

shake [ʃeɪk] **1** *n* secousse *f*; **to give sth a s.** secouer qch

2 (*pt* **shook,** *pp* **shaken**) *vt* (*move up and down*) secouer; (*bottle, fist*) agiter; (*building*) faire trembler; *Fig* (*belief, resolution*) ébranler; **to s. one's head** faire non de la tête; **to s. hands with sb** serrer la main à qn; **to s. off** (*dust*) secouer; *Fig* (*illness, pursuer*) se débarrasser de; **to s. up** (*reorganize*) réorganiser de fond en comble

3 *vi* (*of person, windows, voice*) trembler (**with** de)

shaken [ʃeɪkən] *pp of* **shake**

shaky [ʃeɪkɪ] (**-ier, -iest**) *adj* (*voice*) tremblant; (*table, chair*) branlant; (*handwriting*) tremblé; (*health*) précaire

SHALL [ʃæl, *unstressed* ʃəl]

On trouve généralement **I/you/he/**etc **shall** sous leurs formes contractées **I'll/you'll/he'll/**etc. La forme négative correspondante est **shan't,** que l'on écrira **shall not** dans des contextes formels.

v aux (**a**) (*expressing future tense*) **I s. come, I'll come** je viendrai; **we s. not come, we shan't come** nous ne viendrons pas

(**b**) (*making suggestion*) **s. I leave?** veux-tu que je parte?; **let's go in, s. we?** entrons, tu veux bien?

(**c**) *Formal* (*expressing order*) **he s. do it if I order it** il le fera si je l'ordonne

shallow [ʃæləʊ] (**-er, -est**) *adj* (*water, river*) peu profond; *Fig & Pej* (*argument, person*) superficiel, -elle

sham [ʃæm] **1** *n* (*pretence*) comédie *f* **2** *adj* (*false*) faux (*f* fausse); (*illness, emotion*) feint **3** (*pt & pp* **-mm-**) *vt* feindre **4** *vi* faire semblant

shambles [ʃæmbəlz] *n* pagaille *f*

shame [ʃeɪm] **1** *n* (*guilt, disgrace*) honte *f*; **it's a s.** c'est dommage (**to do** de faire); **it's a s. (that)...** c'est dommage que... (*+ subjunctive*); **what a s.!** quel dommage! **2** *vt* (*make ashamed*) faire honte à

shameful [ʃeɪmfəl] *adj* honteux, -euse

shameless [ʃeɪmləs] *adj* impudique

shampoo [ʃæmˈpuː] **1** *n* shampooing *m* **2** *vt* (*carpet*) shampouiner

shandy [ʃændɪ] *n Br* panaché *m*

shan't [ʃɑːnt] = **shall not**

shape [ʃeɪp] **1** *n* forme *f*; **what s. is it?** quelle forme cela a-t-il?; **to take s.** (*of plan*) prendre forme; **to be in good/bad s.** (*of person*) être en bonne/mauvaise forme; (*of business*) marcher bien/mal; **to keep in s.** garder la forme **2** *vt* (*clay*) modeler; (*wood*) façonner (**into** en); *Fig* (*events, future*) influencer **3** *vi* **to s. up** (*of person*) progresser; (*of teams, plans*) prendre forme ▪ **-shaped** *suff* **pear-s.** en forme de poire ▪ **shapeless** *adj* informe ▪ **shapely** (**-ier, -iest**) *adj* bien fait

share [ʃeə(r)] **1** *n* part *f* (**of** *or* **in** de); *Fin* (*in company*) action *f*; **to do one's (fair) s.** mettre la main à la pâte **2** *vt* partager; (*characteristic*) avoir en commun; **to s. sth out** partager qch **3** *vi* partager; **to s. in sth** avoir sa part de qch ▪ **shareholder** *n Fin* actionnaire *mf*

shark [ʃɑːk] *n* (*fish, crook*) requin *m*

sharp [ʃɑːp] **1** (**-er, -est**) *adj* (*knife*) bien aiguisé; (*pencil*) bien taillé; (*point*) aigu (*f* aiguë); (*claws*) acéré; (*rise, fall*) brusque; (*focus*) net (*f* nette); (*contrast*) marqué; (*eyesight*) perçant; (*taste*) acide; (*intelligent*) vif (*f* vive)

2 *adv* **five o'clock s.** cinq heures pile; **to turn s. right/left** tourner tout de suite à droite/à gauche

3 *n Mus* dièse *m*

sharpen [ʃɑːpən] *vt* (*knife*) aiguiser; (*pencil*) tailler

sharply [ʃɑːplɪ] *adv* (*rise, fall*) brusquement; (*contrast*) nettement

shatter [ʃætə(r)] **1** *vt* (*glass*) faire voler en éclats; (*health, hopes*) briser **2** *vi* (*of glass*) voler en éclats ▪ **shattered** *adj Fam* (*exhausted*) crevé ▪ **shattering** *adj* (*news, experience*) bouleversant

shave [ʃeɪv] **1** *n* **to have a s.** se raser **2** *vt* (*person, head*) raser **3** *vi* se raser ▪ **shaver** *n* rasoir *m* électrique ▪ **shaving** *n* (*strip of wood*) copeau *m*; **s. cream, s. foam** mousse *f* à raser

shawl [ʃɔ:l] *n* châle *m*

she [ʃi:] **1** *pron* elle; **she's a happy woman** c'est une femme heureuse **2** *n Fam* **it's a s.** *(of baby)* c'est une fille

sheaf [ʃi:f] *(pl* **sheaves** [ʃi:vz]) *n (of corn)* gerbe *f; (of paper)* liasse *f*

shear [ʃɪə(r)] **1** *vt* tondre **2** *npl* **shears** cisaille *f*

sheath [ʃi:θ] *(pl* **-s** [ʃi:ðz]) *n (for sword)* fourreau *m; (contraceptive)* préservatif *m*

she'd [ʃi:d] = **she had, she would**

shed¹ [ʃed] *n (in garden)* abri *m*

shed² [ʃed] *(pt & pp* **shed,** *pres p* **shedding)** *vt (leaves)* perdre; *(tears, blood)* verser; *Fig* **to s. light on sth** éclairer qch

sheep [ʃi:p] *n inv* mouton *m* ▪ **sheepdog** *n* chien *m* de berger ▪ **sheepskin** *n* peau *f* de mouton

sheepish [ʃi:pɪʃ] *adj* penaud

sheer [ʃɪə(r)] *adj (pure)* pur; *(stockings)* très fin; *(cliff)* à pic; **by s. chance** tout à fait par hasard

sheet [ʃi:t] *n (on bed)* drap *m; (of paper)* feuille *f; (of glass, ice)* plaque *f*

shelf [ʃelf] *(pl* **shelves** [ʃelvz]) *n* étagère *f; (in shop)* rayon *m*

shell [ʃel] **1** *n* **(a)** *(of egg, snail, nut)* coquille *f; (of tortoise, lobster)* carapace *f; (on beach)* coquillage *m; (of peas)* cosse *f* **(b)** *(explosive)* obus *m* **2** *vt* **(a)** *(peas)* écosser; *(nut)* décortiquer **(b)** *(town)* bombarder

she'll [ʃi:l] = **she will, she shall**

shellfish [ʃelfɪʃ] *npl* fruits *mpl* de mer

shelter [ʃeltə(r)] **1** *n (place, protection)* abri *m;* **to take s.** se mettre à l'abri **(from** de) **2** *vt* abriter **(from** de); *(criminal)* accueillir **3** *vi* s'abriter **(from** de) ▪ **sheltered** *adj (place)* abrité

shelve [ʃelv] *vt (postpone)* mettre au placard

shelving [ʃelvɪŋ] *n* rayonnages *mpl*

shepherd [ʃepəd] *n* berger *m; Br* **s.'s pie** ≃ hachis *m* Parmentier

sherbet [ʃɜ:bət] *n Br (powder)* poudre *f* acidulée; *Am (sorbet)* sorbet *m*

sheriff [ʃerɪf] *n Am* shérif *m*

sherry [ʃerɪ] *n* sherry *m*, xérès *m*

shield [ʃi:ld] **1** *n (of warrior)* bouclier *m* **2** *vt* protéger **(from** de)

shift [ʃɪft] **1** *n (change)* changement *m* **(of** *or* **in** de); *(period of work)* poste *m; (workers)* équipe *f;* **s. key** *(on computer, typewriter)* touche *f* des majuscules **2** *vt (move)* déplacer; *(stain)* enlever; *Am* **to s. gear(s)** *(in vehicle)* changer de vitesse **3** *vi (move)* bouger ▪ **shiftwork** *n* travail *m* posté

shifty [ʃɪftɪ] **(-ier, -iest)** *adj (person)* louche

shimmer [ʃɪmə(r)] *vi (of silk)* chatoyer; *(of water)* miroiter

shin [ʃɪn] *n* tibia *m;* **s. pad** *(of hockey player)* jambière *f*

shine [ʃaɪn] **1** *n* brillant *m; (on metal)* éclat *m* **2** *(pt & pp* **shone)** *vt (polish)* faire briller; *(light, torch)* braquer **3** *vi* briller

shiny [ʃaɪnɪ] **(-ier, -iest)** *adj* brillant

ship [ʃɪp] **1** *n* navire *m* **2** *(pt & pp* **-pp-)** *vt (send)* expédier; *(transport)* transporter ▪ **shipment** *n* cargaison *f* ▪ **shipping** *n (traffic)* navigation *f; (ships)* navires *mpl* ▪ **shipwreck** *n* naufrage *m* ▪ **shipwrecked** *adj* naufragé; **to be s.** faire naufrage ▪ **shipyard** *n* chantier *m* naval

shirk [ʃɜ:k] **1** *vt (duty)* se dérober à; *(work)* éviter de faire **2** *vi* tirer au flanc

shirt [ʃɜ:t] *n* chemise *f; (of woman)* chemisier *m; (of sportsman)* maillot *m*

shiver [ʃɪvə(r)] **1** *n* frisson *m* **2** *vi* frissonner **(with** de)

shoal [ʃəʊl] *n (of fish)* banc *m*

shock [ʃɒk] **1** *n (impact, emotional blow)* choc *m;* **(electric) s.** décharge *f* (électrique) **2** *adj (wave, tactics, troops)* de choc; *Aut* **s. absorber** amortisseur *m* **3** *vt (offend)* choquer; *(surprise)* stupéfier ▪ **shocking** *adj (outrageous)* choquant; *(very bad)* atroce

shoddy [ʃɒdɪ] **(-ier, -iest)** *adj (goods)* de mauvaise qualité

shoe [ʃu:] *n* chaussure *f; (for horse)* fer

m à cheval; **s. polish** cirage *m*; **s. shop** magasin *m* de chaussures ▪ **shoelace** *n* lacet *m*

shone [*Br* ʃɒn, *Am* ʃəʊn] *pt & pp of* **shine**

shoo [ʃuː] **1** (*pt & pp* **shooed**) *vt* **to s. (away)** chasser **2** *exclam* ouste!

shook [ʃʊk] *pt of* **shake¹**

shoot [ʃuːt] **1** *n* (*of plant*) pousse *f* **2** (*pt & pp* **shot**) *vt* (*bullet*) tirer; (*arrow*) lancer; (*film, scene*) tourner; **to s. sb** (*kill*) tuer qn par balle; (*wound*) blesser qn par balle; (*execute*) fusiller qn **3** *vi* (*with gun*) tirer (**at** sur); (*of footballer*) shooter ▪ **shooting** *n* (*shots*) coups *mpl* de feu; (*incident*) fusillade *f*; (*of film, scene*) tournage *m*

▸**shoot down** *vt sep* (*plane*) abattre
▸**shoot off** *vi* (*leave quickly*) filer
▸**shoot up** *vi* (*of price*) monter en flèche; (*of plant, child*) pousser vite; (*of rocket*) s'élever

shop [ʃɒp] **1** *n* magasin *m*; (*small*) boutique *f*; (*workshop*) atelier *m*; **at the baker's s.** à la boulangerie, chez le boulanger; *Br* **s. assistant** vendeur, -euse *mf*; **s. window** vitrine *f* **2** (*pt & pp* **-pp-**) *vi* faire ses courses (**at** chez); **to s. around** comparer les prix ▪ **shopkeeper** *n* commerçant, -e *mf* ▪ **shoplifter** *n* voleur, -euse *mf* à l'étalage ▪ **shopper** *n* (*customer*) client, -e *mf* ▪ **shopping 1** *n* (*goods*) achats *mpl*; **to go s.** faire des courses; **to do one's s.** faire ses courses **2** *adj* (*street, district*) commerçant; **s. bag** sac *m* à provisions; **s. centre** centre *m* commercial; **s. list** liste *f* des commissions

shore [ʃɔː(r)] *n* (*of sea*) rivage *m*; (*of lake*) bord *m*; **on s.** à terre

short [ʃɔːt] **1** (**-er, -est**) *adj* court; (*person, distance*) petit; (*impatient, curt*) brusque; **to be s. of sth** être à court de qch; **money/time is s.** l'argent/le temps manque; **a s. time** *or* **while ago** il y a peu de temps; **Tony is s. for Anthony** Tony est le diminutif d'Anthony; **in s.** bref; **s. cut** raccourci *m*; **s. story** nouvelle *f* **2** *adv* **to cut s.** (*hair*) couper court;

(*visit*) abréger; (*person*) couper la parole à; **to stop s. of doing sth** se retenir tout juste de faire qch; **to be running s. of sth** n'avoir presque plus de qch ▪ **shortbread** *n* sablé *m* ▪ **short-circuit 1** *n* court-circuit *m* **2** *vt* court-circuiter **3** *vi* se mettre en court-circuit ▪ **shortcoming** *n* défaut *m* ▪ **shorthand** *n* sténo *f*; **s. typist** sténodactylo *m* ▪ **short-lived** *adj* de courte durée ▪ **short-sighted** *adj* myope; *Fig* (*in one's judgements*) imprévoyant ▪ **short-sleeved** *adj* à manches courtes ▪ **short-staffed** *adj* à court de personnel ▪ **short-term** *adj* à court terme

shortage [ˈʃɔːtɪdʒ] *n* pénurie *f*

shorten [ˈʃɔːtən] *vt* raccourcir

shortly [ˈʃɔːtlɪ] *adv* (*soon*) bientôt; **s. before/after** peu avant/après

shorts [ʃɔːts] *npl* (**pair of**) **s.** short *m*; **boxer s.** caleçon *m*

shot [ʃɒt] **1** *pt & pp of* **shoot 2** *n* (*from gun*) coup *m*; (*with camera*) prise *f* de vue; (*in football*) coup *m* de pied; *Fam* (*injection*) piqûre *f*; **to fire a s.** tirer; **to be a good s.** (*of person*) être bon tireur; **to have a s. at sth/doing sth** essayer qch/de faire qch ▪ **shotgun** *n* fusil *m* de chasse

SHOULD [ʃʊd, *unstressed* ʃəd]

La forme négative **should not** s'écrit **shouldn't** en forme contractée.

v aux (**a**) (*expressing obligation*) **you s. do it** vous devriez le faire; **I s. have stayed** j'aurais dû rester

(**b**) (*expressing possibility*) **the weather s. improve** le temps devrait s'améliorer; **she s. have arrived by now** elle devrait être arrivée à l'heure qu'il est

(**c**) (*expressing preferences*) **I s. like to stay** j'aimerais bien rester; **I s. like to** j'aimerais bien; **I s. hope so** j'espère bien

(**d**) (*in subordinate clauses*) **it's strange (that) she s. say no** il est étrange qu'elle dise non; **he insisted that she s. meet her parents** il a insisté pour qu'elle rencontre ses parents

(**e**) (*in conditional clauses*) **if he s.**

come, s. he come s'il vient
 (f) *(in rhetorical questions)* why s. you suspect me? pourquoi me soupçonnez-vous?; who s. I meet but Martin! et qui a-t-il fallu que je rencontre? Martin!

shoulder ['ʃəʊldə(r)] **1** *n* épaule *f*; **s. bag** sac *m* besace; **s. pad** épaulette *f*; **s. strap** *(of garment)* bretelle *f* **2** *vt (responsibility)* endosser

shout [ʃaʊt] **1** *n* cri *m*; **to give sb a s.** appeler qn **2** *vt* **to s. sth (out)** crier qch **3** *vi* **to s. (out)** crier; **to s. to sb to do sth** crier à qn de faire qch; **to s. at sb** crier après qn ▪ **shouting** *n (shouts)* cris *mpl*

shove [ʃʌv] **1** *n* poussée *f*; **to give sb/sth a s.** pousser qn/qch **2** *vt* pousser; *Fam* **to s. sth into sth** fourrer qch dans qch **3** *vi* pousser; *Fam* **to s. over** *(move over)* se pousser

shovel ['ʃʌvəl] **1** *n* pelle *f* **2** *(Br* **-ll-,** *Am* **-l-)** *vt* pelleter; **to s. leaves up** ramasser des feuilles à la pelle

show [ʃəʊ] **1** *n (concert, play)* spectacle *m*; *(on TV)* émission *f*; *(exhibition)* exposition *f*; *(of force, friendship)* démonstration *f*; *(pretence)* semblant *m* **(of** de); **to be on s.** être exposé; **to put sth on s.** exposer qch; **s. business** le monde du spectacle; **s. jumping** jumping *m*
 2 *(pt* **showed,** *pp* **shown)** *vt* montrer **(to** à; **that** que); *(in exhibition)* exposer; *(film)* passer; *(indicate)* indiquer; **to s. sb sth, to s. sth to sb** montrer qch à qn; **to s. sb to the door** reconduire qn à la porte
 3 *vi (be visible)* se voir; *(of film)* passer ▪ **showdown** *n* confrontation *f* ▪ **show-off** *n Pej* crâneur, -euse *mf* ▪ **showroom** *n* magasin *m* d'exposition
 ▸ **show around** *vt sep* **to s. sb around the town/the house** faire visiter la ville/la maison à qn
 ▸ **show in** *vt sep (visitor)* faire entrer
 ▸ **show off 1** *vt sep Pej (display)* étaler; *(highlight)* faire valoir **2** *vi Pej* crâner
 ▸ **show out** *vt sep (visitor)* reconduire
 ▸ **show round** *vt sep* = **show around**
 ▸ **show up 1** *vt sep (embarrass)* faire

honte à; *(reveal)* faire ressortir **2** *vi (stand out)* ressortir **(against** contre); *Fam (of person)* se présenter

shower ['ʃaʊə(r)] **1** *n (bathing, device)* douche *f*; *(of rain)* averse *f*; **to have** *or* **take a s.** prendre une douche; **s. gel** gel *m* de douche **2** *vt* **to s. sb with** *(gifts, abuse)* couvrir qn de ▪ **showery** *adj* pluvieux, -euse

shown [ʃəʊn] *pp of* **show**

showy ['ʃəʊɪ] **(-ier, -iest)** *adj* voyant

shrank [ʃræŋk] *pt of* **shrink**

shred [ʃred] **1** *n* lambeau *m*; **to tear sth to shreds** mettre qch en lambeaux; *Fig* **not a s. of truth** pas une once de vérité **2** *(pt & pp* **-dd-)** *vt* mettre en lambeaux; *(documents)* déchiqueter; *(food)* couper grossièrement

shrewd [ʃruːd] **(-er, -est)** *adj (person, plan)* astucieux, -euse

shriek [ʃriːk] **1** *n* cri *m* strident **2** *vi* pousser un cri strident; **to s. with pain/laughter** hurler de douleur/de rire

shrill [ʃrɪl] **(-er, -est)** *adj* aigu *(f* aiguë)

shrimp [ʃrɪmp] *n* crevette *f*

shrine [ʃraɪn] *n (place of worship)* lieu *m* saint; *(tomb)* tombeau *m*

shrink [ʃrɪŋk] **1** *(pt* **shrank** *or Am* **shrunk,** *pp* **shrunk** *or* **shrunken)** *vt (of clothes)* faire rétrécir **2** *vi* rétrécir

shrivel ['ʃrɪvəl] *(Br* **-ll-,** *Am* **-l-)** **1** *vt* **to s. (up)** dessécher **2** *vi* **to s. (up)** se dessécher

shroud [ʃraʊd] **1** *n* linceul *m* **2** *vt* **to be shrouded in sth** être enveloppé de qch

Shrove [ʃrəʊv] *adj* **S. Tuesday** mardi *m* gras

shrub [ʃrʌb] *n* arbuste *m*

shrug [ʃrʌg] **1** *n* haussement *m* d'épaules **2** *(pt & pp* **-gg-)** *vt* **to s. one's shoulders** hausser les épaules; **to s. sth off** dédaigner qch

shrunk(en) ['ʃrʌŋk(ən)] *pp of* **shrink**

shudder ['ʃʌdə(r)] *vi (of person)* frémir **(with** de); *(of machine)* vibrer

shuffle ['ʃʌfəl] **1** *vt (cards)* battre **2** *vti* **to s. (one's feet)** traîner les pieds

shun [ʃʌn] *(pt & pp* **-nn-)** *vt* fuir, éviter

shush [ʃʊʃ] *exclam* chut!

shut [ʃʌt] **1** *(pt & pp* shut, *pres p* **shutting)** *vt* fermer **2** *vi (of door)* se fermer; *(of shop, museum)* fermer
▸**shut away** *vt sep (lock away)* enfermer
▸**shut down 1** *vt sep* fermer (définitivement) **2** *vi* fermer (définitivement)
▸**shut in** *vt sep (lock in)* enfermer
▸**shut off** *vt sep (gas, electricity)* couper; *(engine)* arrêter; *(road)* fermer; *(isolate)* isoler
▸**shut out** *vt sep (keep outside)* empêcher d'entrer; *(exclude)* exclure **(of** or **from** de); **to s. sb out** enfermer qn dehors
▸**shut up 1** *vt sep (close)* fermer; *(confine)* enfermer; *Fam (silence)* faire taire **2** *vi Fam (be quiet)* se taire

shutter ['ʃʌtə(r)] *n (on window)* volet *m; (of shop)* store *m; (of camera)* obturateur *m*

shuttle ['ʃʌtəl] **1** *n (bus, train, plane)* navette *f;* **s. service** navette *f* **2** *vi* faire la navette

shy [ʃaɪ] **1** (**-er, -est**) *adj* timide **2** *vi* **to s. away from doing sth** éviter de faire qch

sibling ['sɪblɪŋ] *n (brother)* frère *m; (sister)* sœur *f*

Sicily ['sɪsɪlɪ] *n* la Sicile

sick [sɪk] **1** (**-er, -est**) *adj (ill)* malade; **to be s.** *(be ill)* être malade; *(vomit)* vomir; **to feel s.** avoir mal au cœur; **to be off s., to be on s. leave** être en congé de maladie; **to be s. of sb/sth** en avoir assez de qn/qch; *Fig* **he makes me s.** il m'écœure **2** *n Br Fam (vomit)* vomi *m* **3** *npl* **the s.** *(sick people)* les malades *mpl*

sicken ['sɪkən] **1** *vt* écœurer **2** *vi Br* **to be sickening for something** couver quelque chose ■ **sickening** *adj* écœurant

sickly ['sɪklɪ] (**-ier, -iest**) *adj* maladif, -ive; *(pale, faint)* pâle; *(taste)* écœurant

sickness ['sɪknɪs] *n (illness)* maladie *f*

side [saɪd] **1** *n* côté *m; (of hill, animal)* flanc *m; (of road, river)* bord *m; (of question, character)* aspect *m; (team)* équipe *f;* **at** or **by the s. of** *(nearby)* à

côté de; **at** or **by my s.** à côté de moi, à mes côtés; **s. by s.** l'un à côté de l'autre; **to move to one s.** s'écarter; **on this s.** de ce côté; **to take sides with sb** se ranger du côté de qn; **she's on our s.** elle est de notre côté
2 *adj (lateral)* latéral; *(view, glance)* de côté; *(street)* transversal; *(effect, issue)* secondaire
3 *vi* **to s. with sb** se ranger du côté de qn ■ **sideboard** *n* buffet *m* ■ **sideburns** *npl (hair)* pattes *fpl* ■ **-sided** *suff* **tensided** à dix côtés ■ **sidelight** *n Br (on vehicle)* feu *m* de position ■ **sideline** *n (activity)* activité *f* secondaire; *(around playing field)* ligne *f* de touche ■ **sidestep** *(pt & pp* -**pp**-*) vt* éviter ■ **sidetrack** *vt* distraire; **to get sidetracked** s'écarter du sujet ■ **sidewalk** *n Am* trottoir *m* ■ **sideways** *adv (look, walk)* de côté

siege [siːdʒ] *n (by soldiers, police)* siège *m;* **under s.** assiégé

siesta [sɪ'estə] *n* sieste *f;* **to take** or **have a s.** faire la sieste

sieve [sɪv] *n* tamis *m; (for liquids)* passoire *f*

sift [sɪft] **1** *vt (flour)* tamiser **2** *vi* **to s. through** *(papers)* examiner (à la loupe)

sigh [saɪ] **1** *n* soupir *m* **2** *vti* soupirer

sight [saɪt] **1** *n (faculty)* vue *f; (thing seen)* spectacle *m; (on gun)* viseur *m;* **to lose s. of sb/sth** perdre qn/qch de vue; **to catch s. of sb/sth** apercevoir qn/qch; **at first s.** à première vue; **by s.** de vue; **in s.** *(target, end, date)* en vue; **out of s.** *(hidden)* caché; *(no longer visible)* disparu; **he hates the s. of me** il ne peut pas me voir; **the (tourist) sights** les attractions *fpl* touristiques; **to set one's sights on** *(job)* viser **2** *vt (land)* apercevoir

sightseer ['saɪtsiːə(r)] *n* touriste *mf* ■ **sightseeing** *n* **to go s., to do some s.** faire du tourisme

sign [saɪn] **1** *n* signe *m; (notice)* panneau *m; (over shop, pub)* enseigne *f;* **no s. of** aucune trace de **2** *vt (put signature to)* signer; **to s. on** or **up** *(worker, soldier)* engager **3** *vi* signer; **to s. for** *(letter)* signer le reçu de; *Br* **to s. on** *(on the*

dole) s'inscrire au chômage; **to s. on** *or* **up** *(of soldier, worker)* s'engager; *(for course)* s'inscrire

signal ['sɪgnəl] **1** *n* signal *m*; *Rail Br* **s. box,** *Am* **s. tower** poste *m* d'aiguillage **2** *(Br* **-ll-,** *Am* **-l-)** *vt (be a sign of)* indiquer; *(make gesture to)* faire signe à **3** *vi (make gesture)* faire signe **(to** à); *(of driver)* mettre son clignotant; **to s. (to) sb to do sth** faire signe à qn de faire qch

signature ['sɪgnətʃə(r)] *n* signature *f*; **s. tune** indicatif *m*

significance [sɪg'nɪfɪkəns] *n (meaning)* signification *f*; *(importance)* importance *f*

significant [sɪg'nɪfɪkənt] *cdj (important, large)* important; *(meaningful)* significatif, -ive **■ significantly** *adv (appreciably)* sensiblement

signify ['sɪgnɪfaɪ] *(pt & pp* **-ied)** *vt (mean, make known)* signifier **(that** que)

signpost ['saɪnpəʊst] **1** *n* poteau *m* indicateur **2** *vt* signaliser

silence ['saɪləns] **1** *n* silence *m*; **in s.** en silence **2** *vt* faire taire

silent ['saɪlənt] *adj* silencieux, -euse; *(film, anger)* muet (*f* muette); **to keep** *or* **be s.** garder le silence **(about** sur) **■ silently** *adv* silencieusement

silhouette [sɪluː'et] *n* silhouette *f*

silicon ['sɪlɪkən] *n* silicium *m*; **s. chip** puce *f* électronique

silk [sɪlk] *n* soie *f* **■ silky (-ier, -iest)** *adj* soyeux, -euse

sill [sɪl] *n (of window)* rebord *m*

silly ['sɪlɪ] **(-ier, -iest)** *adj* bête, idiot; **to do something s.** faire une bêtise; **to look s.** avoir l'air ridicule

silver ['sɪlvə(r)] **1** *n* argent *m*; *(plates)* argenterie *f* **2** *adj (spoon)* en argent, d'argent; *(colour)* argenté; **s. jubilee** vingt-cinquième anniversaire *m*; *Br* **s. paper** papier *m* d'argent **■ silver-plated** *adj* plaqué argent

similar ['sɪmɪlə(r)] *adj* semblable **(to** à) **■ similarity** [-'lærɪtɪ] *(pl* **-ies)** *n* ressemblance *f* **(between** entre; **to** avec) **■ similarly** *adv* de la même façon; *(likewise)* de même

simile ['sɪmɪlɪ] *n* comparaison *f*

simmer ['sɪmə(r)] **1** *vt (vegetables)* mijoter **2** *vi (of vegetables)* mijoter; *(of water)* frémir; *Fig (of revolt, hatred)* couver

simple ['sɪmpəl] **(-er, -est)** *adj (easy)* simple **■ simple-minded** *adj* simple d'esprit **■ simplicity** *n* simplicité *f*

simplify ['sɪmplɪfaɪ] *(pt & pp* **-ied)** *vt* simplifier

simply ['sɪmplɪ] *adv (plainly, merely)* simplement; *(absolutely)* absolument

simulate ['sɪmjʊleɪt] *vt* simuler

simultaneous [*Br* sɪməl'teɪnɪəs, *Am* saɪməl'teɪnɪəs] *adj* simultané **■ simultaneously** [*Br* sɪməl'teɪnɪəslɪ, *Am* saɪməl'teɪnɪəslɪ] *adv* simultanément

sin [sɪn] **1** *n* péché *m* **2** *(pt & pp* **-nn-)** *vi* pécher

since [sɪns] **1** *prep (in time)* depuis; **s. then** depuis **2** *conj (in time)* depuis que; *(because)* puisque; **it's a year s. I saw him** ça fait un an que je ne l'ai pas vu **3** *adv (ever)* **s.** depuis

sincere [sɪn'sɪə(r)] *adj* sincère **■ sincerely** *adv* sincèrement; *Br* **yours s.,** *Am* **s.** *(in letter)* veuillez agréer, Madame/Monsieur, mes salutations distinguées **■ sincerity** [-'serətɪ] *n* sincérité *f*

sinful ['sɪnfəl] *adj (act)* coupable; *(waste)* scandaleux, -euse

sing [sɪŋ] *(pt* **sang,** *pp* **sung)** *vti* chanter **■ singer** *n* chanteur, -euse *mf* **■ singing 1** *n (of bird, musical technique)* chant *m* **2** *adj* **s. lesson/teacher** leçon *f*/professeur *m* de chant

singe [sɪndʒ] *vt (cloth)* roussir; *(hair)* brûler

single ['sɪŋgəl] **1** *adj (only one)* seul; *(room, bed)* pour une personne; *(unmarried)* célibataire; **not a s. book** pas un seul livre; **every s. day** tous les jours sans exception; *Br* **s. ticket** aller *m* simple; **s. parent** père *m*/mère *f* célibataire **2** *n Br (ticket)* aller *m* simple; *(record)* single *m*; **singles** *(in tennis)* simples *mpl* **3** *vt* **to s. sb out** sélectionner qn

■ **single-handedly** *adv* tout seul (*f* toute seule) ■ **single-minded** *adj (person)* résolu; *(determination)* farouche ■ **single-sex** *adj Br* s. **school** école *f* non mixte

singly ['sɪŋglɪ] *adv (one by one)* un à un

singular ['sɪŋgjʊlə(r)] **1** *adj (in grammar)* singulier, -ère; *(remarkable)* remarquable **2** *n* singulier *m*; **in the s.** au singulier

sinister ['sɪnɪstə(r)] *adj* sinistre

sink¹ [sɪŋk] *n (in kitchen)* évier *m*; *(in bathroom)* lavabo *m*

sink² [sɪŋk] *(pt* **sank**, *pp* **sunk) 1** *vt (ship)* couler **2** *vi (of ship, person)* couler; *(of water level, sun, price)* baisser; *(collapse)* s'affaisser; **my heart sank** j'ai eu un pincement de cœur; **to s. (down) into** *(mud)* s'enfoncer dans; *(armchair)* s'affaler dans; *Fam* **it hasn't sunk in yet** je n'ai/il n'a/*etc* pas encore digéré la nouvelle

sinner ['sɪnə(r)] *n* pécheur(eresse) *mf*

sinus ['saɪnəs] *n Anat* sinus *m*

sip [sɪp] **1** *n* petite gorgée *f* **2** *(pt & pp* -**pp-**) *vt* siroter

siphon ['saɪfən] **1** *n* siphon *m* **2** *vt* **to s. sth off** *(liquid)* siphonner qch; *(money)* détourner qch

sir [sɜː(r)] *n* monsieur *m*; **S. Walter Raleigh** *(title)* sir Walter Raleigh

siren ['saɪərən] *n* sirène *f*

sister ['sɪstə(r)] *n* sœur *f*; *(nurse)* infirmière-chef *f* ■ **sister-in-law** *(pl* **sisters-in-law)** *n* belle-sœur *f*

sit [sɪt] *(pt & pp* **sat**, *pres p* **sitting) 1** *vt (child on chair)* asseoir; *Br (exam)* se présenter à **2** *vi (of person)* s'asseoir; *(for artist)* poser (**for** pour); *(of assembly)* siéger; **to be sitting** *(of person, cat)* être assis; **she was sitting reading, she sat reading** elle était assise à lire

▸ **sit around** *vi* rester assis à ne rien faire

▸ **sit back** *vi (in chair)* se caler; *(rest)* se détendre; *(do nothing)* ne rien faire

▸ **sit down 1** *vt* **to s. sb down** asseoir qn **2** *vi* s'asseoir; **to be sitting down** être assis

▸ **sit for** *vt insep Br (exam)* se présenter à

▸ **sit in on** *vt insep (lecture)* assister à

▸ **sit on** *vt insep (jury)* être membre de

▸ **sit out** *vt sep (dance)* ne pas prendre part à

▸ **sit through** *vt insep (film)* rester jusqu'au bout de

▸ **sit up** *vi* **to s. up (straight)** s'asseoir (bien droit); **to s. up waiting for sb** veiller jusqu'au retour de qn

sitcom ['sɪtkɒm] *n* sitcom *m*

site [saɪt] *n (position)* emplacement *m*; *(archaeological, on Internet)* site *m*; **(building) s.** chantier *m* (de construction)

sitting ['sɪtɪŋ] *n* séance *f*; *(in restaurant)* service *m*; **s. room** salon *m*

situate ['sɪtʃʊeɪt] *vt* situer; **to be situated** être situé ■ **situation** *n* situation *f*

six [sɪks] *adj & n* six *(m)* ■ **sixth** *adj & n* sixième *(mf)*; **a s.** *(fraction)* un sixième; *Br Sch* **(lower) s. form** ≃ classe *f* de première; *Br Sch* **(upper) s. form** ≃ classe *f* terminale

sixteen [sɪk'stiːn] *adj & n* seize *(m)* ■ **sixteenth** *adj & n* seizième *(mf)*

sixty ['sɪkstɪ] *adj & n* soixante *(m)* ■ **sixtieth** *adj & n* soixantième *(mf)*

size [saɪz] **1** *n (of person, animal, clothes)* taille *f*; *(of shoes, gloves)* pointure *f*; *(of shirt)* encolure *f*; *(measurements)* dimensions *fpl*; *(of packet)* grosseur *f*; *(of town, damage, problem)* étendue *f*; *(of sum)* montant *m*; **hip/chest s.** tour *m* de hanches/de poitrine **2** *vt* **to s. up** *(person)* jauger; *(situation)* évaluer ■ **sizeable** *adj* non négligeable

sizzle ['sɪzəl] *vi* grésiller

skate [skeɪt] **1** *n (on foot)* patin *m* **2** *vi (on ice-skates)* faire du patin à glace; *(on roller-skates)* faire du roller ■ **skateboard** *n* planche *f* à roulettes ■ **skater** *n* patineur, -euse *mf* ■ **skating** *n* patinage *m*; **to go s.** faire du patinage

skeleton ['skelɪtən] *n* squelette *m*; **s. staff** personnel *m* minimum

skeptical ['skeptɪkəl] *adj Am* sceptique

sketch [sketʃ] **1** *n (drawing)* croquis *m*;

(comic play) sketch *m* **2** *vt* **to s. (out)** *(idea, view)* exposer brièvement **3** *vi* faire un/des croquis ■ **sketchy (-ier, -iest)** *adj* vague

skewer ['skjuːə(r)] *n (for meat)* broche *f*; *(for kebab)* brochette *f*

ski [skiː] **1** *(pl skis) n* ski *m*; **s. boot** chaussure *f* de ski; **s. lift** remonte-pente *m*; **s. mask** cagoule *f*, passe-montagne *m*; **s. pants** fuseau *m*; **s. resort** station *f* de ski; **s. run** *or* **slope** piste *f* de ski **2** *(pt* **skied** [skiːd], *pres p* **skiing)** *vi* skier, faire du ski ■ **skier** *n* skieur, -euse *mf* ■ **skiing 1** *n (sport)* ski *m* **2** *adj (clothes)* de ski

skid [skɪd] **1** *n* dérapage *m* **2** *(pt & pp* **-dd-)** *vi* déraper; **to s. into sth** déraper et heurter qch

skill [skɪl] *n (ability)* qualités *fpl*; *(technique)* compétence *f* ■ **skilful** *(Am* **skillful)** *adj* habile **(at doing** à faire; **at sth** en qch) ■ **skilled** *adj* habile **(at doing** à faire; **at sth** en qch); *(worker)* qualifié; *(work)* de spécialiste

skim [skɪm] *(pt & pp* **-mm-)* **1** *vt (milk)* écrémer; *(soup)* écumer; **to s. (over)** **sth** *(surface)* effleurer qch; **skimmed milk** lait *m* écrémé **2** *vt insep* **to s. through** *(book)* parcourir

skimp [skɪmp] *vi (on food, fabric)* lésiner **(on** sur) ■ **skimpy (-ier, -iest)** *adj (clothes)* étriqué; *(meal)* maigre

skin [skɪn] **1** *n* peau *f*; **s. diving** plongée *f* sous-marine **2** *(pt & pp* **-nn-)** *vt (fruit)* peler; *(animal)* écorcher ■ **skin-tight** *adj* moulant

skinflint ['skɪnflɪnt] *n* avare *mf*

skinhead ['skɪnhed] *n Br* skinhead *mf*

skinny ['skɪnɪ] **(-ier, -iest)** *adj* maigre

skint [skɪnt] *adj Br Fam (penniless)* fauché

skip¹ [skɪp] **1** *(pt & pp* **-pp-)** *vt (miss, omit)* sauter; **to s. classes** sécher les cours **2** *vi (hop about)* sautiller; *Br (with rope)* sauter à la corde; *Br* **skipping rope** corde *f* à sauter

skip² [skɪp] *n Br (for rubbish)* benne *f*

skipper ['skɪpə(r)] *n (of ship, team)* capitaine *m*

skirt [skɜːt] *n* jupe *f*

skittle ['skɪtəl] *n Br* quille *f*; **to play skittles** jouer aux quilles

skulk [skʌlk] *vi* rôder

skull [skʌl] *n* crâne *m*

skunk [skʌŋk] *n (animal)* mouffette *f*

sky [skaɪ] *n* ciel *m* ■ **skydiving** *n* parachutisme *m* en chute libre ■ **skylight** *n* lucarne *f* ■ **skyline** *n (horizon)* horizon *m* ■ **skyscraper** *n* gratte-ciel *m inv*

slack [slæk] **1** **(-er, -est)** *adj (not tight)* mou *(f* molle); *(careless)* négligent; **to be s.** *(of rope)* avoir du mou; **business is s.** les affaires vont mal **2** *vi* **to s. off** *(in effort)* se relâcher

slacken ['slækən] **1** *vt* **to s. (off)** *(rope)* relâcher; *(pace, effort)* ralentir **2** *vi* **to s. (off)** *(in effort)* se relâcher; *(of production, demand, speed, enthusiasm)* diminuer

slam [slæm] **1** *(pt & pp* **-mm-)** *vt (door, lid)* claquer; *(hit)* frapper violemment; **to s. sth (down)** *(put down)* poser qch violemment; **to s. on the brakes** écraser la pédale de frein **2** *vi (of door)* claquer

slander ['slɑːndə(r)] **1** *n* calomnie *f* **2** *vt* calomnier

slang [slæŋ] **1** *n* argot *m* **2** *adj (word)* d'argot, argotique

slant [slɑːnt] **1** *n* pente *f*; *Fig (point of view)* perspective *f*; *Fig (bias)* parti *m* pris **2** *vi (of roof, handwriting)* être incliné ■ **slanted, slanting** *adj* penché; *(roof)* en pente

slap [slæp] **1** *n (with hand)* claque *f*; **a s. in the face** une gifle **2** *(pt & pp* **-pp-)** *vt (person)* donner une claque à; **to s. sb's face** gifler qn; **to s. sb's bottom** donner une fessée à qn

slapdash ['slæpdæʃ] *adj (person)* négligent; *(work)* fait à la va-vite

slapstick ['slæpstɪk] *adj & n* **s. (comedy)** grosse farce *f*

slash [slæʃ] **1** *n* entaille *f* **2** *vt (cut)* taillader; *(reduce)* réduire considérablement

slat [slæt] *n* latte *f*

slate [sleɪt] *n* ardoise *f*

slaughter ['slɔːtə(r)] **1** *n (of people)*

massacre m; (of animal) abattage m **2** vt (people) massacrer; (animal) abattre; Fam (defeat) massacrer

slave [sleɪv] **1** n esclave mf **2** vi to s. (away) trimer ▪ **slavery** n esclavage m

sleazy ['sliːzɪ] (-ier, -iest) adj Fam sordide

sledge [sledʒ] (Am **sled** [sled]) n Br luge f

sledgehammer ['sledʒhæmə(r)] n masse f

sleek [sliːk] (-er, -est) adj (smooth) lisse et brillant; Pej (manner) mielleux, -euse

sleep [sliːp] **1** n sommeil m; to have a s., to get some s. dormir; to go to s. (of person) s'endormir; to put an animal to s. (kill) faire piquer un animal **2** (pt & pp slept) vi dormir; Euph to s. with sb coucher avec qn **3** vt this flat sleeps six on peut dormir à six dans cet appartement ▪ **sleeping** adj (asleep) endormi; s. bag sac m de couchage; s. car wagon-lit m; s. pill somnifère m

sleeper ['sliːpə(r)] n (a) to be a light/ sound s. avoir le sommeil léger/lourd (b) Br Rail (on track) traverse f; (bed in train) couchette f; (train) train-couchettes m ▪ **sleepless** adj (night) d'insomnie

sleepy ['sliːpɪ] (-ier, -iest) adj (town, voice) endormi; to be s. (of person) avoir sommeil

sleet [sliːt] **1** n neige f fondue **2** vi it's sleeting il tombe de la neige fondue

sleeve [sliːv] n (of shirt, jacket) manche f; (of record) pochette f; long-/short-sleeved à manches longues/courtes

sleigh [sleɪ] n traîneau m

slender ['slendə(r)] adj (person) svelte; (neck, hand, waist) fin; Fig (small, feeble) faible

slept [slept] pt & pp of sleep

slice [slaɪs] **1** n tranche f; Fig (portion) part f **2** vt to s. sth (up) couper qch en tranches; to s. sth off couper qch

slick [slɪk] **1** (-er, -est) adj (campaign) bien mené; (reply, person) habile **2** n (on beach) marée f noire

slide [slaɪd] **1** n (in playground) toboggan m; (for hair) barrette f; Phot diapositive f; (in prices, popularity) baisse f **2** (pt & pp slid [slɪd]) vt glisser (into dans); (table, chair) faire glisser **3** vi glisser ▪ **sliding** adj (door, panel) coulissant

slight [slaɪt] **1** (-er, -est) adj (small, unimportant) léger, -ère; (chance) faible; the slightest thing la moindre chose; not in the slightest pas le moins du monde **2** n affront m (on à) **3** vt (offend) offenser; (ignore) bouder

slightly ['slaɪtlɪ] adv légèrement

slim [slɪm] **1** (slimmer, slimmest) adj mince **2** (pt & pp -mm-) vi Br suivre un régime

slime [slaɪm] n vase f; (of snail) bave f ▪ **slimy** (-ier, -iest) adj (muddy) boueux (f boueuse); Fig (sticky, smarmy) visqueux, -euse

sling [slɪŋ] **1** n (weapon) fronde f; (for injured arm) écharpe f; in a s. en écharpe **2** (pt & pp slung) vt (throw) lancer

slip [slɪp] **1** n (mistake) erreur f; (garment) combinaison f; (fall) chute f; a s. of paper un bout de papier; (printed) un bordereau; a s. of the tongue un lapsus; Br s. road bretelle f **2** (pt & pp -pp-) vt (slide) glisser (to à; into dans); it slipped my mind ça m'est sorti de l'esprit **3** vi glisser; Fam (of popularity, ratings) baisser; to let sth s. (chance, secret) laisser échapper qch
▸ **slip away** vi (escape) s'éclipser
▸ **slip into** vt insep (room) se glisser dans; (bathrobe) passer
▸ **slip off** vt sep (coat) enlever
▸ **slip on** vt sep (coat) mettre
▸ **slip out** vi (leave) sortir furtivement; (for a moment) sortir (un instant); (of secret) s'éventer
▸ **slip up** vi Fam se planter

slipper ['slɪpə(r)] n pantoufle f

slippery ['slɪpərɪ] adj glissant

slit [slɪt] **1** n fente f **2** (pt & pp slit, pres p slitting) vt (cut) couper; to s. open (sack) éventrer

slither ['slɪðə(r)] vi glisser; (of snake) se couler

slob [slɒb] *n Fam (lazy person)* gros fainéant *m*; *(dirty person)* porc *m*

slobber ['slɒbə(r)] *vi (of dog, baby)* baver

slog [slɒg] *Br Fam* **1** *n* **a (hard) s.** *(effort)* un gros effort **2** *(pt & pp* **-gg-**) *vi* **to s. (away)** trimer

slogan ['sləʊgən] *n* slogan *m*

slop [slɒp] **1** *(pt & pp* **-pp-**) *vt* renverser **2** *vi* **to s. (over)** se renverser

slope [sləʊp] **1** *n* pente *f*; *(of mountain)* versant *m*; *(for skiing)* piste *f* **2** *vi (of ground, roof)* être en pente ▪ **sloping** *adj (roof)* en pente

sloppy ['slɒpɪ] **(-ier, -iest)** *adj (work, appearance)* négligé; *(person)* négligent; *(sentimental)* sentimental

slot [slɒt] **1** *n (slit)* fente *f*; *(in schedule, list)* créneau *m*; **s. machine** *(for vending)* distributeur *m* automatique; *(for gambling)* machine *f* à sous **2** *(pt & pp* **-tt-**) *vt (insert)* insérer (**into** dans) **3** *vi* s'insérer (**into** dans)

slouch [slaʊtʃ] *vi* ne pas se tenir droit; *(in chair)* être avachi

slovenly ['slʌvənlɪ] *adj* négligé

slow [sləʊ] **1 (-er, -est)** *adj* lent; **in s. motion** au ralenti; **to be s.** *(of clock, watch)* retarder; **business is s.** les affaires tournent au ralenti **2** *adv* lentement **3** *vt* **to s. sth down** *or* **up** ralentir qch; *(delay)* retarder qch **4** *vi* **to s. down** *or* **up** ralentir ▪ **slowcoach** *n Br Fam* lambin, -e *mf* ▪ **slowly** *adv* lentement; *(bit by bit)* peu à peu

sludge [slʌdʒ] *n* gadoue *f*

slug [slʌg] **1** *n* **(a)** *(mollusc)* limace *f* **(b)** *Am Fam (bullet)* pruneau *m* **2** *(pt & pp* **-gg-**) *vt Am Fam (hit)* frapper

sluggish ['slʌgɪʃ] *adj (person)* amorphe; **business is s.** les affaires ne marchent pas très bien

slum [slʌm] *n (house)* taudis *m*; **the slums** les quartiers *mpl* délabrés

slump [slʌmp] **1** *n* baisse *f* soudaine (**in** de); *(in prices)* effondrement *m*; *(economic depression)* crise *f* **2** *vi (of person, prices)* s'effondrer

slung [slʌŋ] *pt & pp of* **sling**

slur [slɜː(r)] **1** *n (insult)* insulte *f* **2** *(pt &*

pp **-rr-**) *vt* mal articuler ▪ **slurred** *adj (speech)* indistinct

slush [slʌʃ] *n (snow)* neige *f* fondue

slut [slʌt] *n Pej (promiscuous woman)* salope *f*; *(untidy woman)* souillon *f*

sly [slaɪ] **1 (-er, -est)** *adj (deceitful)* sournois; *(cunning, crafty)* rusé **2** *n* **on the s.** en douce

smack [smæk] **1** *n (blow)* claque *f*; *(on bottom)* fessée *f* **2** *vt (person)* donner une claque à; **to s. sb's face** gifler qn; **to s. sb('s bottom)** donner une fessée à qn **3** *vi* **to s. of** *(be suggestive of)* avoir des relents de

small [smɔːl] **1 (-er, -est)** *adj* petit; **s. change** petite monnaie *f*; **s. talk** banalités *fpl* **2** *adv (cut, chop)* menu; *(write)* petit **3** *n* **the s. of the back** la chute des reins ▪ **small-minded** *adj* à l'esprit étroit ▪ **small-scale** *adj (model)* réduit; *(research)* à petite échelle

smallpox ['smɔːlpɒks] *n* variole *f*

smarmy ['smɑːmɪ] **(-ier, -iest)** *adj Fam Pej* obséquieux, -euse

smart¹ [smɑːt] **(-er, -est)** *adj (in appearance)* élégant; *(clever)* intelligent; *(astute)* astucieux, -euse; *(quick)* rapide; **s. card** carte *f* à puce

smart² [smɑːt] *vi (sting)* brûler

smarten ['smɑːtən] **1** *vt* **to s. sth up** égayer qch **2** *vti* **to s. (oneself) up** se faire beau (*f* belle)

smartly ['smɑːtlɪ] *adv (dressed)* avec élégance

smash [smæʃ] **1** *n (accident)* collision *f*; *(in tennis)* smash *m* **2** *vt (break)* briser; *(shatter)* fracasser; *(record)* pulvériser **3** *vi* **to s. into sth** *(of vehicle)* entrer dans qch; **to s. into pieces** éclater en mille morceaux ▪ **smash-up** *n* collision *f*
▸ **smash down, smash in** *vt sep (door)* enfoncer
▸ **smash up** *vt sep (vehicle)* esquinter

smashing ['smæʃɪŋ] *adj Br Fam (wonderful)* génial

smattering ['smætərɪŋ] *n* **a s. of French** quelques notions *fpl* de français

smear [smɪə(r)] **1** *n (mark)* trace *f* **2** *vt (coat)* enduire (**with** de); *(stain)* tacher

(with de); *(smudge)* faire une trace sur; **to s. sb** calomnier qn

smell [smel] **1** *n* odeur *f*; **(sense of) s.** odorat *m* **2** *(pt & pp* **smelled** *or* **smelt)** *vt* sentir; *(of animal)* flairer **3** *vi (stink)* sentir mauvais; *(have a smell)* sentir; **to s. of smoke** sentir la fumée ▪ **smelly (-ier, -iest)** *adj* **to be s.** sentir mauvais

smelt [smelt] *pt & pp of* **smell**

smile [smaɪl] **1** *n* sourire *m* **2** *vi* sourire **(at sb** à qn; **at sth** de qch)

smirk [smɜːk] *n (smug)* sourire *m* suffisant; *(scornful)* sourire *m* goguenard

smog [smɒg] *n* smog *m*

smoke [sməʊk] **1** *n* fumée *f*; **to have a s.** fumer; **s. detector** *or* **alarm** détecteur *m* de fumée **2** *vt (cigarette)* fumer; **smoked salmon** saumon *m* fumé **3** *vi* fumer; **'no smoking'** 'défense de fumer'; **smoking compartment** *(on train)* compartiment *m* fumeurs ▪ **smoker** *n* fumeur, -euse *mf* ▪ **smoky (-ier, -iest)** *adj (room, air)* enfumé

smooth [smuːð] **1 (-er, -est)** *adj (surface, skin)* lisse; *(cream, sauce)* onctueux, -euse; *(sea, flight)* calme; *Pej (person, manners)* doucereux, -euse; **the s. running of** *(machine, service, business)* la bonne marche de **2** *vt* **to s. sth down** *(hair, sheet, paper)* lisser qch; **to s. sth out** *(paper, sheet, dress)* lisser qch; *(crease)* faire disparaître qch ▪ **smoothly** *adv (without problems)* sans problèmes

smother ['smʌðə(r)] *vt (stifle)* étouffer; **to s. sth in sth** recouvrir qch de qch

smoulder ['sməʊldə(r)] *(Am* **smolder)** *vi (of fire, passion)* couver

smudge [smʌdʒ] **1** *n* tache *f* **2** *vt (paper)* faire des taches sur; *(ink)* étaler

smug [smʌg] **(smugger, smuggest)** *adj (person)* content de soi

smuggle ['smʌgəl] *vt* passer en fraude; **smuggled goods** contrebande *f* ▪ **smuggler** *n* contrebandier, -ère *mf*; *(of drugs)* trafiquant, -e *mf* ▪ **smuggling** *n* contrebande *f*

smut [smʌt] *n inv (obscenity)* cochon-

neries *fpl* ▪ **smutty (-ier, -iest)** *adj (joke)* cochon, -onne

snack [snæk] *n (meal)* casse-croûte *m* inv; **s. bar** snack-bar *m*

snag [snæg] *n (hitch)* problème *m*

snail [sneɪl] *n* escargot *m*

snake [sneɪk] *n* serpent *m*

snap [snæp] **1** *n Fam (photo)* photo *f*; **s. fastener** pression *f*; **cold s.** coup *m* de froid **2** *adj (judgement, decision)* hâtif, -ive **3** *(pt & pp* **-pp-)** *vt (break)* casser net; *(fingers)* faire claquer; **to s. up a bargain** sauter sur une occasion **4** *vi* se casser net; *Fig (of person)* parler sèchement **(at** à); **to s. off** se casser net; *Fam* **s. out of it!** secoue-toi!

snare [sneə(r)] *n* piège *m*

snarl [snɑːl] *vi* grogner (en montrant les dents)

snatch [snætʃ] *vt (grab)* saisir; *(steal)* arracher; **to s. sth from sb** arracher qch à qn

sneak [sniːk] **1** *n Br Fam (telltale)* mouchard, -e *mf* **2** *(pt & pp* **sneaked** *or Am* **snuck)** *vi Br Fam (tell tales)* rapporter; **to s. in/out** entrer/sortir furtivement; **to s. off** s'esquiver

sneaker ['sniːkə(r)] *n Am (shoe)* chaussure *f* de sport

sneer [snɪə(r)] *vi* ricaner; **to s. at sb/ sth** se moquer de qn/qch

sneeze [sniːz] *vi* éternuer

snicker ['snɪkə(r)] *vi Am* = **snigger**

snide [snaɪd] *adj* méprisant

sniff [snɪf] **1** *vt* renifler; **to s. glue** sniffer de la colle **2** *vi* renifler

sniffle ['snɪfəl] **1** *n Fam* **to have the sniffles** avoir un petit rhume **2** *vi* renifler

snigger ['snɪgə(r)] *vi* ricaner

snip [snɪp] **1** *n (cut)* petite entaille *f*; *Br Fam (bargain)* bonne affaire *f* **2** *(pt & pp* **-pp-)** *vt* **to s. sth (off)** couper qch

snivel ['snɪvəl] *(Br* **-ll-,** *Am* **-l-)** *vi* pleurnicher

snob [snɒb] *n* snob *mf* ▪ **snobbish** *adj* snob inv

snooker ['snuːkə(r)] *n (game)* = billard qui se joue avec vingt-deux billes

snoop [snu:p] *vi* fouiner; **to s. on sb** espionner qn

snooze [snu:z] **1** *n* petit somme *m*; **to have a s.** faire un petit somme **2** *vi* faire un petit somme

snore [snɔ:(r)] *vi* ronfler ■ **snoring** *n* ronflements *mpl*

snorkel ['snɔ:kəl] **1** *n* tuba *m* **2** (*Br* -ll-, *Am* -l-) *vi* nager sous l'eau avec un tuba

snort [snɔ:t] *vi (of person)* grogner; *(of horse)* s'ébrouer

snot [snɒt] *n Fam* morve *f*

snout [snaʊt] *n* museau *m*

snow [snəʊ] **1** *n* neige *f* **2** *vi* **it's snowing** il neige **3** *vt* **to be snowed in** être bloqué par la neige; *Fig* **to be snowed under with work** être submergé de travail ■ **snowball 1** *n* boule *f* de neige **2** *vi (increase)* faire boule de neige ■ **snowdrop** *n (flower)* perce-neige *m ou f inv* ■ **snowflake** *n* flocon *m* de neige ■ **snowman** (*pl* **-men**) *n* bonhomme *m* de neige ■ **snowplough** (*Am* **snowplow**) *n* chasse-neige *m inv* ■ **snowshoe** *n* raquette *f* ■ **snowstorm** *n* tempête *f* de neige

snub [snʌb] **1** *n* rebuffade *f* **2** (*pt & pp* **-bb-**) *vt (offer)* rejeter; **to s. sb** snober qn **3** *adj* **s. nose** nez *m* retroussé

snuck [snʌk] *Am pt & pp of* **sneak**

snuff [snʌf] **1** *n* tabac *m* à priser **2** *vt* **to s. (out)** *(candle)* moucher

snug [snʌg] (**snugger, snuggest**) *adj (house)* douillet, -ette; *(garment)* bien ajusté

snuggle ['snʌgəl] *vi* **to s. up to sb** se blottir contre qn

so [səʊ] **1** *adv (to such a degree)* si, tellement (**that** que); *(thus)* ainsi, comme ça; **to work/drink so much that...** travailler/boire tellement que...; **so much courage** tellement de courage (**that** que); **so many books** tant de livres (**that** que); **and so on** et ainsi de suite; **I think so** je crois que oui; **is that so?** c'est vrai?; **so am I** moi aussi; **I told you so** je vous l'avais bien dit; *Fam* **so long!** au revoir!

2 *conj (therefore)* donc; *(in that case)* alors; **so what?** et alors?; **so that...**

pour que... (+ *subjunctive*); **so as to do sth** pour faire qch ■ **So-and-so** *n* **Mr S.** Monsieur Untel ■ **so-called** *adj* soi-disant *inv* ■ **so-so** *adj & adv Fam* comme ci comme ça

soak [səʊk] **1** *vt (drench)* tremper; *(washing, food)* faire tremper; **to be soaked (through** *or* **to the skin)** être trempé (jusqu'aux os); **to s. sth up** absorber qch **2** *vi (of washing)* tremper ■ **soaking** *adj & adv* **s. (wet)** trempé

soap [səʊp] *n* savon *m*; **s. opera** feuilleton *m* populaire; **s. powder** lessive *f* ■ **soapsuds** *npl* mousse *f* de savon

soar [sɔ:(r)] *vi (of bird)* s'élever; *(of price)* monter en flèche

sob [sɒb] **1** *n* sanglot *m* **2** (*pt & pp* **-bb-**) *vi* sangloter

sober ['səʊbə(r)] **1** *adj (sensible)* sobre; **he's s.** *(not drunk)* il n'est pas ivre **2** *vti* **to s. up** dessoûler

soccer ['sɒkə(r)] *n* football *m*

sociable ['səʊʃəbəl] *adj (person)* sociable; *(evening)* amical

social ['səʊʃəl] *adj* social; **to have a good s. life** sortir beaucoup; **S. Security** ≃ la Sécurité sociale; **s. security** *(aid)* aide *f* sociale; *Am (retirement pension)* pension *f* de retraite; **the s. services** les services *mpl* sociaux; **s. worker** assistant, -e *mf* social(e)

socialist ['səʊʃəlɪst] *adj & n* socialiste (*mf*)

socialize ['səʊʃəlaɪz] *vi* fréquenter des gens; **to s. with sb** fréquenter qn

socially ['səʊʃəlɪ] *adv* socialement; *(meet)* en société

society [sə'saɪətɪ] (*pl* **-ies**) *n (community, club, companionship)* société *f*; *(school/university club)* club *m*; **(high) s.** haute société *f*

sociology [səʊsɪ'ɒlədʒɪ] *n* sociologie *f*

sock [sɒk] *n* chaussette *f*

socket ['sɒkɪt] *n Br (of electric plug)* prise *f* de courant; *Br (of lamp)* douille *f*

soda ['səʊdə] *n Am* **s. (pop)** boisson *f* gazeuse; **s. (water)** eau *f* de Seltz

sofa ['səʊfə] *n* canapé *m*; **s. bed** canapé-lit *m*

soft [sɒft] (**-er, -est**) *adj (gentle, not stiff)* doux (*f* douce); *(butter, ground, paste, snow)* mou (*f* molle); *(wood, heart, colour)* tendre; *(indulgent)* indulgent; **s. drink** boisson *f* non alcoolisée; **s. drugs** drogues *fpl* douces; **s. toy** peluche *f* ▪ **soft-boiled** *adj (egg)* à la coque

softball ['sɒftbɔːl] *n* = sorte de base-ball

soften ['sɒfən] **1** *vt (object)* ramollir; *(colour, light, voice, skin)* adoucir **2** *vi* ramollir ▪ **softener** *n* adoucissant *m*

softly ['sɒftlɪ] *adv* doucement

software ['sɒftweə(r)] *n inv Comptr* logiciel *m*; **s. package** progiciel *m*

soggy ['sɒgɪ] (**-ier, -iest**) *adj* trempé

soil [sɔɪl] **1** *n (earth)* terre *f* **2** *vt (dirty)* salir

solar ['səʊlə(r)] *adj* solaire

sold [səʊld] *pt & pp of* **sell**

soldier ['səʊldʒə(r)] *n* soldat *m*

sole[1] [səʊl] **1** *n (of shoe)* semelle *f*; *(of foot)* plante *f* **2** *vt (shoe)* ressemeler

sole[2] [səʊl] *adj (only)* unique; *(rights, representative, responsibility)* exclusif, -ive ▪ **solely** *adv* uniquement

solemn ['sɒləm] *adj* solennel, -elle

solicit [sə'lɪsɪt] **1** *vt (seek)* solliciter **2** *vi (of prostitute)* racoler

solicitor [sə'lɪsɪtə(r)] *n Br (for wills)* notaire *m*

solid ['sɒlɪd] **1** *adj (not liquid)* solide; *(not hollow)* plein; *(gold, silver)* massif, -ive **2** *adv* **frozen s.** complètement gelé; **ten days s.** dix jours d'affilée **3** *n* solide *m*; **solids** *(food)* aliments *mpl* solides ▪ **solidly** *adv (built)* solidement; *(work)* sans interruption

solidarity [sɒlɪ'dærətɪ] *n* solidarité *f* (**with** avec)

solitary ['sɒlɪtərɪ] *adj (lonely, alone)* solitaire; *(only)* seul ▪ **solitude** *n* solitude *f*

solo ['səʊləʊ] **1** (*pl* **-os**) *n Mus* solo *m* **2** *adj (guitar, violin)* solo *inv* **3** *adv (play, sing)* en solo; *(fly)* en solitaire ▪ **soloist** *n Mus* soliste *mf*

soluble ['sɒljʊbəl] *adj (substance, problem)* soluble

solution [sə'luːʃən] *n* (**a**) *(to problem)* solution *f* (**to** de) (**b**) *(liquid)* solution *f*

solve [sɒlv] *vt (problem)* résoudre

solvent ['sɒlvənt] **1** *adj (financially)* solvable **2** *n Chem* solvant *m*

sombre ['sɒmbə(r)] (*Am* **somber**) *adj* sombre

SOME [sʌm] **1** *adj* (**a**) *(a quantity of)* du, de la, des; **s. wine** du vin; **s. water** de l'eau; **s. dogs** des chiens; **s. pretty flowers** de jolies fleurs
(**b**) *(unspecified)* un, une; **s. man (or other)** un homme (quelconque); **for s. reason or other** pour une raison ou pour une autre; **I have been waiting s. time** ça fait un moment que j'attends
(**c**) *(a few)* quelques; *(in contrast to others)* certains; **s. days ago** il y a quelques jours; **s. people think that...** certains pensent que...
2 *pron* (**a**) *(a certain quantity)* en; **I want s.** j'en veux; **s. of my wine** un peu de mon vin; **s. of the time** une partie du temps
(**b**) *(as opposed to others)* certain(e)s; **some say...** certains disent...; **s. of the guests** certains invités
3 *adv (about)* environ; **s. ten years** environ dix ans ▪ **somebody** *pron* quelqu'un; **s. small** quelqu'un de petit ▪ **someday** *adv* un jour ▪ **somehow** *adv (in some way)* d'une manière ou d'une autre; *(for some reason)* on ne sait pourquoi ▪ **someone** *pron* quelqu'un; **s. small** quelqu'un de petit ▪ **someplace** *adv Am* quelque part ▪ **something 1** *pron* quelque chose; **s. awful** quelque chose d'affreux **2** *adv* **she plays s. like...** elle joue un peu comme... ▪ **sometime** *adv* un jour; **s. in May** au mois de mai ▪ **sometimes** *adv* quelquefois, parfois ▪ **somewhat** *adv* quelque peu, assez ▪ **somewhere** *adv* quelque part; **s. about fifteen** *(approximately)* environ quinze

somersault ['sʌməsɔːlt] *n (on ground)* roulade *f*; *(in air)* saut *m* périlleux

son [sʌn] *n* fils *m* ▪ **son-in-law** (*pl*

sons-in-law) n gendre m

sonata [sə'nɑːtə] n sonate f

song [sɒŋ] n chanson f; (of bird) chant m

soon [suːn] (-er, -est) adv (in a short time) bientôt; (quickly) vite; (early) tôt; **s. after** peu après; **as s. as...** aussitôt que...; **no sooner had he spoken than...** à peine avait-il parlé que...; **I'd sooner leave** je préférerais partir; **sooner or later** tôt ou tard

soot [sʊt] n suie f

soothe [suːð] vt calmer

sophisticated [sə'fɪstɪkeɪtɪd] adj (person, taste) raffiné; (machine, method) sophistiqué

sophomore ['sɒfəmɔː(r)] n Am étudiant, -e mf de deuxième année

sopping ['sɒpɪŋ] adj & adv **s. (wet)** trempé

soppy ['sɒpɪ] (-ier, -iest) adj Br Fam (sentimental) sentimental

soprano [sə'prɑːnəʊ] (pl -os) n (singer) soprano mf

sordid ['sɔːdɪd] adj sordide

sore [sɔː(r)] **1** (-er, -est) adj (painful) douloureux, -euse; Am (angry) fâché (at contre); **to have a s. throat** avoir mal à la gorge **2** n (wound) plaie f

sorrow ['sɒrəʊ] n chagrin m

sorry ['sɒrɪ] (-ier, -iest) adj (sight, state) triste; **to be s. (about sth)** (regret) être désolé (de qch); **to feel** or **be s. for sb** plaindre qn; **I'm s. she can't come** je regrette qu'elle ne puisse pas venir; **s.!** pardon!; **to say s.** demander pardon (**to** à)

sort¹ [sɔːt] n sorte f; **a s. of** une sorte de; **all sorts of** toutes sortes de; **what s. of drink is it?** qu'est-ce que c'est comme boisson?; **s. of sad** (somewhat) plutôt triste

sort² [sɔːt] **1** vt (papers) trier; **to s. out** (classify, select) trier; (separate) séparer (**from** de); (organize) ranger; (problem) régler **2** vi **to s. through letters/magazines** trier des lettres/magazines

sought [sɔːt] pt & pp of **seek**

soul [səʊl] n âme f

sound¹ [saʊnd] **1** n son m; (noise) bruit m; **s. effects** bruitage m **2** vt (bell, alarm) sonner; (bugle) sonner de; **to s. one's horn** (in vehicle) klaxonner **3** vi (seem) sembler; **to s. like** sembler être; (resemble) ressembler à; **it sounds like** or **as if...** il semble que... (+ subjunctive or indicative)

sound² [saʊnd] **1** (-er, -est) adj (healthy) sain; (in good condition) en bon état; (basis) solide; (argument) valable; (advice) bon (f bonne); (investment) sûr

2 adv **s. asleep** profondément endormi ■ **soundly** adv (asleep, sleep) profondément

sound³ [saʊnd] vt (test, measure) sonder; **to s. sb out** sonder qn (**about** sur)

soundproof ['saʊndpruːf] **1** adj insonorisé **2** vt insonoriser

soundtrack ['saʊndtræk] n (of film) bande f sonore

soup [suːp] n soupe f; **s. dish** or **plate** assiette f creuse

sour ['saʊə(r)] (-er, -est) adj aigre; (milk) tourné; **to turn s.** (of milk) tourner; (of friendship) se détériorer

source [sɔːs] n (origin) source f

south [saʊθ] **1** n sud m; **(to the) s. of** au sud de

2 adj (coast) sud inv; (wind) du sud; **S. America/Africa** l'Amérique f/l'Afrique f du Sud; **S. American** adj sud-américain; n Sud-Américain, -e mf; **S. African** adj sudafricain; n Sud-Africain, -e mf

3 adv au sud; (travel) vers le sud ■ **southbound** adj (traffic) en direction du sud; Br (carriageway) sud inv ■ **south-east** n & adj sud-est (m) ■ **southerly** adj (direction) du sud ■ **southern** ['sʌðən] adj (town) du sud; (coast) sud inv; **S. Italy** le sud de l'Italie ■ **southerner** ['sʌðənə(r)] n habitant, -e mf du sud ■ **southward(s)** adj & adv vers le sud ■ **south-west** n & adj sud-ouest (m)

souvenir [suːvə'nɪə(r)] n souvenir m

sovereign ['sɒvrɪn] n (monarch) souverain, -e mf ■ **sovereignty** [-rəntɪ] n souveraineté f

sow¹ [saʊ] *n (pig)* truie *f*

sow² [səʊ] *(pt* **sowed,** *pp* **sowed** *or* **sown** [səʊn]) *vt (seeds, doubt)* semer; *(land)* ensemencer (**with** de)

soya ['sɔɪə] *n Br* soja *m*; **s. bean** graine *f* de soja ▪ **soybean** *n Am* graine *f* de soja

spa [spɑː] *n (town)* station *f* thermale

space [speɪs] **1** *n (gap, emptiness, atmosphere)* espace *m*; *(for parking)* place *f*; **to take up s.** prendre de la place; **blank s.** espace *m*, blanc *m*; **s. bar** *(on keyboard)* barre *f* d'espacement **2** *adj (voyage, capsule)* spatial **3** *vt* **to s. out** espacer ▪ **spaceship** *n* vaisseau *m* spatial ▪ **spacing** *n Typ* **in double/single s.** à double/simple interligne

spacious ['speɪʃəs] *adj* spacieux, -euse

spade [speɪd] *n* (a) *(for garden)* bêche *f* (b) *Cards* **spade(s)** pique *m*

spaghetti [spə'getɪ] *n* spaghettis *mpl*

Spain [speɪn] *n* l'Espagne *f*

span [spæn] *(pt & pp* **-nn-)** *vt (of bridge)* enjamber; *Fig (in time)* couvrir

Spaniard ['spænjəd] *n* Espagnol, -e *mf* ▪ **Spanish 1** *adj* espagnol **2** *n (language)* espagnol *m*

spank [spæŋk] *vt* donner une tape sur les fesses à ▪ **spanking** *n* fessée *f*

spanner ['spænə(r)] *n Br (tool)* clef *f*

spare [speə(r)] **1** *adj (extra, surplus)* de *ou* en trop; *(reserve)* de rechange; *(wheel)* de secours; *(available)* disponible; **s. room** chambre *f* d'ami; **s. time** loisirs *mpl*
 2 *n* **s. (part)** *(for vehicle, machine)* pièce *f* détachée
 3 *vt (do without)* se passer de; *(efforts, sb's feelings)* ménager; **to s. sb sth** *(grief, details)* épargner qch à qn; **I can't s. the time** je n'ai pas le temps; **with five minutes to s.** avec cinq minutes d'avance

sparingly ['speərɪŋlɪ] *adv* en petite quantité

spark [spɑːk] **1** *n* étincelle *f*; *Aut* **s. plug** bougie *f* **2** *vt* **to s. off** *(cause)* provoquer

sparkle ['spɑːkəl] *vi* briller; *(of diamond, star)* scintiller ▪ **sparkling** *adj (wine, water)* pétillant

sparrow ['spærəʊ] *n* moineau *m*

sparse [spɑːs] *adj* clairsemé ▪ **sparsely** *adv (populated)* peu; **s. furnished** à peine meublé

spasm ['spæzəm] *n (of muscle)* spasme *m*

spat [spæt] *pt & pp of* **spit**

spate [speɪt] *n* **a s. of sth** *(of letters, calls)* une avalanche de qch; *(of crimes)* une vague de qch

spatter ['spætə(r)] *vt (clothes, person)* éclabousser (**with** de)

speak [spiːk] **1** *(pt* **spoke,** *pp* **spoken)** *vt (language)* parler; *(say)* dire; **to s. one's mind** dire ce que l'on pense
 2 *vi* parler (**about** *or* **of** de); *(formally, in assembly)* prendre la parole; **so to s.** pour ainsi dire; **that speaks for itself** c'est évident; **Jayne speaking!** *(on the telephone)* Jayne à l'appareil!; **to s. out** *or* **up** *(boldly)* parler (franchement); **to s. up** *(more loudly)* parler plus fort

speaker ['spiːkə(r)] *n (at meeting)* intervenant, -e *mf*; *(at conference)* conférencier, -ère *mf*; *(loudspeaker)* enceinte *f*; **to be a Spanish s.** parler espagnol

spear [spɪə(r)] *n* lance *f*

spearmint ['spɪəmɪnt] *adj (sweet)* à la menthe; *(chewing gum)* mentholé

spec [spek] *n Br Fam* **on s.** à tout hasard

special ['speʃəl] **1** *adj* spécial; *(care, attention)* particulier, -ère; *Br* **by s. delivery** en exprès; **s. effects** effets *mpl* spéciaux **2** *n* **today's s.** *(in restaurant)* le plat du jour

specialist ['speʃəlɪst] **1** *n* spécialiste *mf* (**in** de) **2** *adj (dictionary, knowledge)* spécialisé; *(equipment)* de spécialiste ▪ **speciality** [-ʃɪ'ælɪtɪ] *(pl* **-ies)** *n Br* spécialité *f*

specialize ['speʃəlaɪz] *vi* se spécialiser (**in** dans)

specially ['speʃəlɪ] *adv (specifically)* spécialement; *(particularly)* particulièrement

specialty ['speʃəltɪ] *(pl* **-ies)** *n Am* spécialité *f*

species ['spiːʃiːz] *n inv* espèce *f*

specific [spə'sɪfɪk] *adj* précis ∎ **specifically** *adv (explicitly)* expressément; *(exactly)* précisément; *(specially)* spécialement

specify ['spesɪfaɪ] *(pt & pp -ied) vt (state exactly)* préciser; *(stipulate)* stipuler ∎ **specification** [-fɪ'keɪʃən] *n* spécification *f*

specimen ['spesɪmɪn] *n (individual example)* spécimen *m*; *(of urine, blood)* échantillon *m*

speck [spek] *n (stain)* petite tache *f*; *(of dust)* grain *m*; *(dot)* point *m*

speckled ['spekəld] *adj* tacheté

specs [speks] *npl Fam* lunettes *fpl*

spectacle ['spektəkəl] *n (sight)* spectacle *m* ∎ **spectacles** *npl (glasses)* lunettes *fpl*

spectacular [spek'tækjʊlə(r)] *adj* spectaculaire

spectator [spek'teɪtə(r)] *n* spectateur, -trice *mf*

spectre ['spektə(r)] *n* spectre *m (of* de)

spectrum ['spektrəm] *(pl -tra* [-trə]*) n* spectre *m*; *Fig (range)* gamme *f*

speculate ['spekjʊleɪt] **1** *vt* **to s. that...** *(guess)* conjecturer que... **2** *vi Fin* spéculer; **to s. about** *(make guesses)* faire des suppositions sur ∎ **speculation** *n* suppositions *fpl*; *Fin* spéculation *f*

sped [sped] *pt & pp of* **speed**

speech [spiːtʃ] *n (talk, lecture)* discours *m (on or* about sur); *(faculty)* parole *f*; *(diction)* élocution *f*; **to make a s.** faire un discours ∎ **speechless** *adj* muet *(f* muette) **(with** de)

speed [spiːd] **1** *n (rapidity, gear)* vitesse *f*; **at top** *or* **full s.** à toute vitesse; **s. limit** *(on road)* limitation *f* de vitesse

2 *(pt & pp* **sped**) *vt* **to s. sth up** accélérer qch

3 *vi* (a) **to s. up** *(of person)* aller plus vite; **to s. past sth** passer à toute vitesse devant qch

(b) *(pt & pp* **speeded**) *(exceed speed limit)* faire un excès de vitesse ∎ **speedboat** *n* vedette *f* ∎ **speeding** *n (in vehicle)* excès *m* de vitesse ∎ **speedometer** *n Br (in vehicle)* compteur *m* de vitesse

speedy ['spiːdɪ] **(-ier, -iest)** *adj* rapide

spell¹ [spel] *n (magic words)* formule *f* magique; **to cast a s. on sb** jeter un sort à qn ∎ **spellbound** *adj* fasciné

spell² [spel] *n (period)* période *f*; **cold s.** vague *f* de froid

spell³ [spel] *(pt & pp* **spelled** *or* **spelt** [spelt]*) vt (write)* écrire; *(say aloud)* épeler; *(of letters)* former; *Fig (mean)* signifier; **how do you s. it?** comment ça s'écrit?; **to s. sth out** *(word)* épeler qch; *Fig (explain)* expliquer clairement qch ∎ **spell-checker** *n Comptr* correcteur *m* d'orthographe ∎ **spelling** *n* orthographe *f*; **s. mistake** faute *f* d'orthographe

spend [spend] *(pt & pp* **spent**) *vt (money)* dépenser **(on** sur); *(time)* passer **(on sth** sur qch; **doing** à faire); *(energy)* consacrer **(on sth** à qch; **doing** à faire) ∎ **spending** *n* dépenses *fpl*; **s. money** argent *m* de poche ∎ **spendthrift** *n* **to be a s.** être dépensier, -ère

spent [spent] *pt & pp of* **spend**

sperm [spɜːm] *n* sperme *m*

spew [spjuː] *vt* vomir

sphere [sfɪə(r)] *n (of influence, action)*, *Math & Pol* sphère *f* ∎ **spherical** ['sferɪkəl] *adj* sphérique

spice [spaɪs] **1** *n* épice *f*; *Fig (interest)* piquant *m* **2** *vt (food)* épicer; **to s. sth (up)** *(add interest to)* ajouter du piquant à qch ∎ **spicy (-ier, -iest)** *adj* épicé

spider ['spaɪdə(r)] *n* araignée *f*

spike [spaɪk] *n (of metal)* pointe *f* ∎ **spiky (-ier, -iest)** *adj (hair)* tout hérissé

spill [spɪl] *(pt & pp* **spilled** *or* **spilt** [spɪlt]*) 1 vt (liquid)* renverser **2** *vi* se répandre

▸ **spill out** *vt sep (empty)* vider

▸ **spill over** *vi (of liquid)* déborder

spin [spɪn] **1** *n (motion)* tournoiement *m*; *(on ball)* effet *m*; *Fam* **to go for a s.** *(in car)* aller faire un tour

2 *(pt & pp* **spun***, pres p* **spinning**) *vt (wool, cotton)* filer; *(wheel, top)* faire tourner; *(spin-dry)* essorer; **to s. sth out** *(speech)* faire durer qch

3 *vi* tourner; **to s. round** *(of dancer,*

wheel; top, planet) tourner; **my head's spinning** j'ai la tête qui tourne

spinach ['spɪnɪdʒ] *n* épinards *mpl*

spin-dry ['spɪndraɪ] *vt* essorer ▪ **spin-dryer** *n* essoreuse *f*

spine [spaɪn] *n (backbone)* colonne *f* vertébrale; *(of book)* dos *m*

spinster ['spɪnstə(r)] *n* vieille fille *f*

spiral ['spaɪərəl] **1** *n* spirale *f* **2** *adj* en spirale; *(staircase)* en colimaçon **3** *(Br* -ll-, *Am* -l-) *vi (of prices)* s'envoler

spire ['spaɪə(r)] *n (of church)* flèche *f*

spirit ['spɪrɪt] **1** *n (soul, ghost, mood)* esprit *m*; *Fig (determination)* courage *m*; **spirits** *(drink)* spiritueux *mpl*; **in good spirits** de bonne humeur **2** *adj (lamp)* à alcool; **s. level** niveau *m* (à bulle) ▪ **spirited** *adj (campaign, attack)* vigoureux, -euse; *(person, remark)* énergique

spiritual ['spɪrɪtʃʊəl] *adj* spirituel, -elle

spit¹ [spɪt] **1** *n (on ground)* crachat *m*; *(in mouth)* salive *f* **2** *(pt & pp* spat *or* spit, *pres p* spitting) *vt* cracher; **to s. sth out** cracher qch; **to be the spitting image of sb** être le portrait (tout craché) de qn **3** *vi* cracher

spit² [spɪt] *n (for meat)* broche *f*

spite [spaɪt] **1** *n (dislike)* dépit *m*; **in s. of sb/sth** malgré qn/qch; **in s. of the fact that…** bien que… (+ *subjunctive)* **2** *vt* vexer ▪ **spiteful** *adj* vexant

splash [splæʃ] **1** *n (of liquid)* éclaboussure *f*; *Fig (of colour)* tache *f* **2** *vt (spatter)* éclabousser (**with** de) **3** *vi (of mud)* faire des éclaboussures; *(of waves)* clapoter; **to s. (about)** *(in river, mud)* patauger; *(in bath)* barboter; *Fam* **to s. out** *(spend money)* claquer des ronds

splendid ['splendɪd] *adj* splendide ▪ **splendour** *(Am* **splendor)** *n* splendeur *f*

splint [splɪnt] *n* attelle *f*

splinter ['splɪntə(r)] *n (of wood, glass)* éclat *m*; *(in finger)* écharde *f*

split [splɪt] **1** *n* fente *f*; *(tear)* déchirure *f*; *(in political party)* scission *f* **2** *adj* **in a s. second** en une fraction de seconde **3** *(pt & pp* split, *pres p* splitting) *vt (break*

apart) fendre; *(tear)* déchirer; **to s. (up)** *(group)* diviser; *(money, work)* partager (**between** entre) **4** *vi* se fendre; *(tear)* se déchirer; **to s. (up)** *(of group)* se diviser (**into** en); **to s. up** *(because of disagreement)* (of couple, friends) se séparer; *(of crowd)* se disperser; **to s. up with sb** rompre avec qn

spoil [spɔɪl] *(pt & pp* spoilt *or* spoiled) *vt (ruin)* gâcher; *(indulge)* gâter ▪ **spoilsport** *n* rabat-joie *mf inv*

spoilt [spɔɪlt] *pt & pp of* spoil

spoke¹ [spəʊk] *n (of wheel)* rayon *m*

spoke² [spəʊk] *pt of* speak ▪ **spoken 1** *pp of* speak **2** *adj (language)* parlé ▪ **spokesman** *(pl* -men) *n* ▪ **spokesperson, spokeswoman** *(pl* -women) *n* porte-parole *mf inv* (**for** *or* **of** de)

sponge [spʌndʒ] **1** *n* éponge *f*; *Br* **s. bag** trousse *f* de toilette; **s. cake** génoise *f* **2** *vt* **to s. sth down/off** laver/enlever qch avec une éponge **3** *vi Fam* **to s. off** *or* **on sb** vivre aux crochets de qn ▪ **sponger** *n Fam* parasite *m*

sponsor ['spɒnsə(r)] **1** *n* sponsor *m* **2** *vt* sponsoriser ▪ **sponsorship** *n* sponsoring *m*

spontaneous [spɒn'teɪnɪəs] *adj* spontané

spooky ['spuːkɪ] (-ier, -iest) *adj Fam* qui donne le frisson

spoon [spuːn] *n* cuillère *f* ▪ **spoonful** *n* cuillerée *f*

sporadic [spə'rædɪk] *adj* sporadique

sport¹ [spɔːt] *n* sport *m*; **to play** *Br* **s.** *or Am* **sports** faire du sport; **sports club** club *m* de sport; **sports car/ground** voiture *f*/terrain *m* de sport ▪ **sporting** *adj (attitude, person)* sportif, -ive ▪ **sportsman** *(pl* -men) *n* sportif *m* ▪ **sportswoman** *(pl* -women) *n* sportive *f* ▪ **sporty** (-ier, -iest) *adj* sportif, -ive

sport² [spɔːt] *vt (wear)* arborer

spot¹ [spɒt] *n (stain, mark)* tache *f*; *(dot)* point *m*; *(polka dot)* pois *m*; *(drop)* goutte *f*; *(pimple)* bouton *m*; *(place)* endroit *m*; **on the s.** sur place; *(at once)* sur le coup; **to be in a tight s.** *(difficulty)* être dans le pétrin

spot² [spɒt] (*pt & pp* **-tt-**) *vt (notice)* apercevoir

spotless ['spɒtləs] *adj (clean)* impeccable

spotlight ['spɒtlaɪt] *n* projecteur *m*; *(for photography)* spot *m*

spotty ['spɒtɪ] (**-ier, -iest**) *adj (face, person)* boutonneux, -euse

spouse [spaʊs, spaʊz] *n* époux *m*, épouse *f*

spout [spaʊt] **1** *n (of teapot, jug)* bec *m* **2** *vt Pej (say)* débiter

sprain [spreɪn] **1** *n* entorse *f* **2** *vt* **to s. one's ankle/wrist** se fouler la cheville/le poignet

sprang [spræŋ] *pt of* **spring¹**

spray [spreɪ] **1** *n (can, device)* vaporisateur *m*; *(water drops)* gouttelettes *fpl*; *(from sea)* embruns *mpl* **2** *vt (liquid, surface)* vaporiser; *(plant, crops)* pulvériser; *(car)* peindre à la bombe

spread [spred] **1** *n (of idea, religion, language)* diffusion *f*; *(of disease)* propagation *f*; *Fam (meal)* festin *m*; **cheese s.** fromage *m* à tartiner **2** (*pt & pp* **spread**) *vt (stretch, open out)* étendre; *(legs, fingers)* écarter; *(paint, payment, visits, cards)* étaler; *(sand, fear)* répandre; *(news, illness)* propager; **to s. out** *(map, payments, visits)* étaler; *(fingers)* écarter **3** *vi (of fog)* s'étendre; *(of fire, epidemic)* se propager; *(of news, fear)* se répandre; **to s. out** *(of people)* se disperser ■ **spreadsheet** *n Comptr* tableur *m*

spree [spriː] *n* **to go on a spending s.** faire des folies dans les magasins

sprightly ['spraɪtlɪ] (**-ier, -iest**) *adj* alerte

spring¹ [sprɪŋ] **1** *n (device)* ressort *m*; *(leap)* bond *m* **2** (*pt* **sprang**, *pp* **sprung**) *vi (surprise)* faire (**on** à) **3** *vi (leap)* bondir; **to s. to mind** venir à l'esprit; **to s. from** *(stem from)* provenir de; **to s. up** *(appear)* surgir ■ **springboard** *n* tremplin *m*

spring² [sprɪŋ] *n (season)* printemps *m*; **in (the) s.** au printemps; *Br* **s. onion** petit oignon *m* ■ **spring-cleaning** *n*

nettoyage *m* de printemps ■ **springtime** *n* printemps *m*

spring³ [sprɪŋ] *n (of water)* source *f*; **s. water** eau *f* de source

sprinkle ['sprɪŋkəl] *vt (sand)* répandre (**on** *or* **over** sur); **to s. sth with water, to s. water on sth** arroser qch; **to s. sth with sth** *(sugar, salt, flour)* saupoudrer qch de qch

sprint [sprɪnt] *vi (run)* sprinter

sprout [spraʊt] **1** *n* (**Brussels) s.** chou *m* de Bruxelles **2** *vt (leaves)* pousser **3** *vi (of seed, bulb)* pousser

spruce [spruːs] **1** (**-er, -est**) *adj (neat)* impeccable **2** *vt* **to s. oneself up** se faire beau (*f* belle)

sprung [sprʌŋ] *pp of* **spring¹**

spud [spʌd] *n Fam (potato)* patate *f*

spun [spʌn] *pt & pp of* **spin**

spur [spɜː(r)] **1** *n (of horse rider)* éperon *m*; *Fig (stimulus)* aiguillon *m*; **to do sth on the s. of the moment** faire qch sur un coup de tête **2** (*pt & pp* **-rr-**) *vt* **to s. sb on** *(urge on)* aiguillonner qn

spurn [spɜːn] *vt* rejeter

spurt [spɜːt] **1** *n (of energy)* regain *m*; **to put on a s.** foncer **2** *vi* **to s. (out)** *(of liquid)* gicler

spy [spaɪ] **1** (*pl* **-ies**) *n* espion, -onne *mf* **2** *adj (story, film)* d'espionnage **3** (*pt & pp* **-ied**) *vt (notice)* repérer **4** *vi* espionner; **to s. on sb** espionner qn ■ **spying** *n* espionnage *m*

squabble ['skwɒbəl] **1** *n* querelle *f* **2** *vi* se quereller (**over** à propos de)

squad [skwɒd] *n (of workmen, footballers)* équipe *f*; *(of soldiers)* section *f*; *(of police)* brigade *f*

squalid ['skwɒlɪd] *adj* sordide ■ **squalor** *n (poverty)* misère *f*

squander ['skwɒndə(r)] *vt (money, resources)* gaspiller; *(time)* perdre

square ['skweə(r)] **1** *n* carré *m*; *(on chessboard, map)* case *f*; *(in town)* place *f* **2** *adj* carré; *Math* **s. root** racine *f* carrée **3** *vt (settle)* régler; *Math (number)* élever au carré **4** *vi (tally)* cadrer (**with** avec)

squash [skwɒʃ] **1** *n (game)* squash *m*; *(vegetable)* courge *f*; *Br* **lemon/orange**

s. ≃ sirop *m* de citron/d'orange **2** *vt* écraser

squat [skwɒt] **1** *adj (person, object, building)* trapu **2** *(pt & pp* **-tt-)** *vi* squatter; **to s. (down)** s'accroupir; **to be squatting (down)** être accroupi

squawk [skwɔːk] *vi* pousser un cri rauque

squeak [skwiːk] *vi (of person)* pousser un cri aigu; *(of door)* grincer

squeal [skwiːl] *vi* pousser un cri perçant

squeamish ['skwiːmɪʃ] *adj* de nature délicate

squeeze [skwiːz] **1** *n* to give sth a s. presser qch; **to give sb's hand/arm a s.** serrer la main/le bras à qn **2** *vt (press)* presser; **to s. sb's hand** serrer la main à qn; **to s. sth into sth** faire rentrer qch dans qch; **to s. the juice (out)** faire sortir le jus **(of** de) **3** *vi* **to s. through/into sth** *(force oneself)* se glisser par/dans qch; **to s. in** trouver de la place; **to s. up** se serrer **(against** contre)

squelch [skweltʃ] *vi* patauger

squid [skwɪd] *n inv* calmar *m*

squint [skwɪnt] **1** *n* to have a s. loucher **2** *vi* loucher; *(in the sunlight)* plisser les yeux

squirm [skwɜːm] *vi (wriggle)* se tortiller

squirrel [*Br* 'skwɪrəl, *Am* 'skwɜːrəl] *n* écureuil *m*

squirt [skwɜːt] **1** *vt (liquid)* faire gicler **2** *vi (of liquid)* gicler

St (a) *(abbr* **Street)** rue (b) *(abbr* **Saint)** St, Ste

stab [stæb] **1** *n* **s. (wound)** coup *m* de couteau **2** *(pt & pp* **-bb-)** *vt (with knife)* poignarder

stability [stə'bɪlɪtɪ] *n* stabilité *f*

stabilize ['steɪbəlaɪz] **1** *vt* stabiliser **2** *vi* se stabiliser

stable¹ ['steɪbəl] **(-er, -est)** *adj* stable

stable² ['steɪbəl] *n* écurie *f*

stack [stæk] **1** *n (heap)* tas *m*; *Fam* **stacks of** *(lots of)* des tas de **2** *vt* **to s. (up)** entasser

stadium ['steɪdɪəm] *n* stade *m*

staff [stɑːf] *n* personnel *m*; *(of school, university)* professeurs *mpl*; *Br* **s. room** *(in school)* salle *f* des professeurs

stag [stæg] *n* cerf *m*; **s. night** *or* **party** enterrement *m* de la vie de garçon

stage¹ [steɪdʒ] **1** *n (platform)* scène *f*; **on s.** sur scène **2** *vt (play)* monter; *Fig* organiser

stage² [steɪdʒ] *n (phase)* stade *m*

stagger ['stægə(r)] **1** *vt (holidays)* échelonner; *(astound)* stupéfier **2** *vi (reel)* chanceler ■ **staggering** *adj* stupéfiant

stagnant ['stægnənt] *adj* stagnant ■ **stagnate** *vi* stagner

staid [steɪd] *adj* collet monté *inv*

stain [steɪn] **1** *n (mark)* tache *f* **2** *vt (mark)* tacher **(with** de); *(dye)* teinter ■ **stained-glass** *adj* **s. window** vitrail *m* *(pl* -aux) ■ **stainless** *adj* **s. steel** acier *m* inoxydable, Inox®*m*

stair [steə(r)] *n* **a s.** *(step)* une marche; **the stairs** *(staircase)* l'escalier *m* ■ **staircase, stairway** *n* escalier *m*

stake [steɪk] **1** *n* (a) *(post)* pieu *m*; *(for plant)* tuteur *m* (b) *(in betting)* enjeu *m*; **to have a s. in sth** *(share)* avoir des intérêts dans qch; **at s.** en jeu **2** *vt (bet)* jouer **(on** sur)

stale [steɪl] **(-er, -est)** *adj (bread)* rassis; *(air)* vicié; *(joke)* éculé

stalemate ['steɪlmeɪt] *n (in chess)* pat *m*; *Fig* impasse *f*

stalk [stɔːk] **1** *n (of plant)* tige *f*; *(of fruit)* queue *f* **2** *vt (animal, criminal)* traquer; *(celebrity)* harceler **3** *vi* **to s. out** *(walk angrily)* sortir d'un air furieux mais digne

stall [stɔːl] **1** *n (in market)* étal *m*; *Br (for newspapers, flowers)* kiosque *m*; *(in stable)* stalle *f*; *Br* **the stalls** *(in cinema, theatre)* l'orchestre *m* **2** *vt (engine, car)* caler **3** *vi (of car)* caler; **to s. (for time)** chercher à gagner du temps

stamina ['stæmɪnə] *n* résistance *f* physique

stammer ['stæmə(r)] **1** *n* to have a s. être bègue **2** *vi* bégayer

stamp [stæmp] **1** *n (for letter)* timbre *m*;

(mark) cachet *m*; *(device)* tampon *m*; **s. collector** philatéliste *mf* **2** *vt (document)* tamponner; *(letter)* timbrer; *(metal)* estamper; **to s. one's foot** taper du pied; *Br* **stamped addressed envelope**, *Am* **stamped self-addressed envelope** enveloppe *f* timbrée libellée à ses noms et adresse **3** *vi* **to s. on sth** écraser qch

stampede [stæm'piːd] **1** *n* débandade *f* **2** *vi* se ruer

stance [staːns] *n* position *f*

STAND [stænd] **1** *n (opinion)* position *f*; *(support)* support *m*; *(stall)* étal *m*; *(at exhibition)* stand *m*; *(at sports ground)* tribune *f*; **to take a s.** prendre position **2** *(pt & pp* **stood**) *vt (pain, journey)* supporter; *(put straight)* mettre debout; **to s. a chance** avoir des chances; **I can't s. him** je ne peux pas le supporter **3** *vi (be upright)* se tenir debout; *(get up)* se mettre debout; *(remain)* rester debout; *(of building)* se trouver; *(of object)* être
- **stand about, stand around** *vi (in street)* traîner
- **stand aside** *vi* s'écarter
- **stand back** *vi* reculer
- **stand by 1** *vt insep (opinion)* s'en tenir à; *(person)* soutenir **2** *vi (do nothing)* rester sans rien faire; *(be ready)* être prêt
- **stand down** *vi (withdraw)* se retirer
- **stand for** *vt insep (mean)* signifier; *(represent)* représenter; *Br (be candidate for)* être candidat à; *(tolerate)* supporter
- **stand in for** *vt insep (replace)* remplacer
- **stand out** *vi (be visible)* ressortir **(against** sur)
- **stand over** *vt insep (watch closely)* surveiller
- **stand up 1** *vt sep* mettre debout; *Fam* **to s. sb up** poser un lapin à qn **2** *vi (get up)* se lever
- **stand up for** *vt insep (defend)* défendre
- **stand up to** *vt insep (resist)* résister à; *(defend oneself against)* tenir tête à

standard ['stændəd] **1** *n (norm)* norme

f; *(level)* niveau *m*; **standards** *(principles)* principes *mpl* moraux; **s. of living, living standards** niveau *m* de vie **2** *adj (average)* ordinaire; *(model, size)* standard *inv* ■ **standardize** *vt* standardiser

stand-by ['stændbaɪ] **1** *(pl* **-bys)** *n* **on s.** *(troops, emergency services)* prêt à intervenir **2** *adj (plane ticket)* en standby

stand-in ['stændɪn] *n.* remplaçant, -e *mf* **(for** de); *(actor)* doublure *f* **(for** de)

standing ['stændɪŋ] **1** *adj (upright)* debout; *(permanent)* permanent; *Br* **s. order** virement *m* automatique **2** *n (reputation)* réputation *f*; *(social, professional)* rang *m*; **of long s.** de longue date

stand-offish [stænd'ɒfɪʃ] *adj* distant

standpoint ['stændpɔɪnt] *n.* point *m* de vue

standstill ['stændstɪl] *n* **to bring sth to a s.** immobiliser qch; **to come to a s.** s'immobiliser; **at a s.** immobile; *(negotiations, industry)* paralysé

stank [stæŋk] *pt of* **stink**

stanza ['stænzə] *n* strophe *f*

staple¹ ['steɪpəl] *adj (basic)* de base; **s. food** *or* **diet** nourriture *f* de base

staple² ['steɪpəl] **1** *n (for paper)* agrafe *f* **2** *vt* agrafer ■ **stapler** *n (for paper)* agrafeuse *f*

star [staː(r)] **1** *n* étoile *f*; *(famous person)* star *f*; *Br* **four-s. (petrol)** du super **2** *(pt & pp* **-rr-)** *vt (of film)* avoir pour vedette **3** *vi (of actor, actress)* être la vedette **(in** de)

starboard ['staːbəd] *n. Naut* tribord *m*

starch [staːtʃ] *n* amidon *m*

stare [steə(r)] **1** *n* regard *m* fixe **2** *vi* **to s. at sb/sth** fixer qn/qch (du regard)

stark [staːk] **1** **(-er, -est)** *adj; (place)* désolé; *(fact, reality)* brutal; **to be in s. contrast to** contraster nettement avec **2** *adv* **s. naked** complètement nu

start¹ [staːt] **1** *n* début *m*; *(of race)* départ *m*; **for a s.** pour commencer; **from the s.** dès le début; **to make a s.** commencer

2 *vt* commencer; *(packet, conversation)* entamer; *(fashion, campaign, offensive)* lancer; *(engine, vehicle)* mettre en marche; *(business, family)* fonder; **to s. doing** *or* **to do sth** commencer à faire qch

3 *vi* commencer (**with sth** par qch; **by doing** par faire); *(of vehicle)* démarrer; *(leave)* partir (**for** pour); *(in job)* débuter; **to s. with** *(firstly)* pour commencer; **starting from now/10 euros** à partir de maintenant/10 euros ▪ **starting** *adj (point, line, salary)* de départ; **s. post** *(in race)* ligne *f* de départ

▸**start off** *vi (leave)* partir (**for** pour); *(in job)* débuter

▸**start out** *vi (begin)* débuter; *(on journey)* se mettre en route

▸**start up 1** *vt sep (engine, vehicle)* mettre en marche; *(business)* fonder **2** *vi (of engine, vehicle)* démarrer

start² [stɑːt] **1** *n (movement)* sursaut *m*; **to give sb a s.** faire sursauter qn **2** *vi* sursauter

starter ['stɑːtə(r)] *n (in vehicle)* démarreur *m*; *(in meal)* entrée *f*; *(runner)* partant, -e *mf*; *Fam* **for starters** *(firstly)* pour commencer

startle ['stɑːtəl] *vt* faire sursauter

starvation [stɑːˈveɪʃən] **1** *n* faim *f* **2** *adj (wage, ration)* de misère

starve [stɑːv] **1** *vt (make suffer)* faire souffrir de la faim; *Fig (deprive)* priver (**of** de) **2** *vi (suffer)* souffrir de la faim; **to s. to death** mourir de faim; *Fam* **I'm starving!** je meurs de faim!

state¹ [steɪt] **1** *n* (a) *(condition)* état *m*; *(situation)* situation *f*; **not in a (fit) s. to...**, **in no (fit) s. to...** hors d'état de... (b) **S.** *(nation)* État *m*; *Fam* **the States** les États-Unis *mpl* **2** *adj (secret)* d'État; *Br (school, education)* public, -ique; **s. visit** voyage *m* officiel ▪ **state-owned** *adj* étatisé

state² [steɪt] *vt* déclarer (**that** que); *(opinion)* formuler; *(problem)* exposer

statement ['steɪtmənt] *n* déclaration *f*; *(in court)* déposition *f*; **(bank) s.** relevé *m* de compte

statesman ['steɪtsmən] *(pl* **-men)** *n* homme *m* d'État

static ['stætɪk] *adj* statique

station ['steɪʃən] **1** *n (for trains)* gare *f*; *(underground)* station *f*; *(social)* rang *m*; **bus s.** gare *f* routière; **radio s.** station *f* de radio; *Am* **s. wagon** break *m* **2** *vt (position)* placer; **to be stationed at/in** *(of troops)* être en garnison à/en

stationary ['steɪʃənərɪ] *adj (vehicle)* à l'arrêt

stationer ['steɪʃənə(r)] *n* papetier, -ère *mf*; **s.'s (shop)** papeterie *f* ▪ **stationery** *n (articles)* articles *mpl* de bureau; *(paper)* papier *m*

statistic [stəˈtɪstɪk] *n (fact)* statistique *f*; **statistics** *(science)* la statistique

statue ['stætʃuː] *n* statue *f*

stature ['stætʃə(r)] *n (importance)* envergure *f*

status ['steɪtəs] *n (position)* situation *f*; *(legal, official)* statut *m*; *(prestige)* prestige *m*; **s. symbol** marque *f* de prestige

staunch [stɔːntʃ] **(-er, -est)** *adj (resolute)* convaincu; *(supporter)* ardent

stave [steɪv] *vt* **to s. sth off** *(disaster, danger)* conjurer qch; **to s. off hunger** tromper la faim

stay [steɪ] **1** *n (visit)* séjour *m* **2** *vi (remain)* rester; *(reside)* loger; *(visit)* séjourner; **to s. put** ne pas bouger

▸**stay away** *vi* ne pas s'approcher (**from** de); **to s. away from school** ne pas aller à l'école

▸**stay behind** *vi* rester en arrière

▸**stay in** *vi (at home)* rester à la maison; *(of nail, screw, tooth)* tenir

▸**stay out** *vi (outside)* rester dehors; *(not come home)* ne pas rentrer; **to s. out of sth** *(not interfere in)* ne pas se mêler de qch; *(avoid)* éviter qch

▸**stay up** *vi (at night)* ne pas se coucher; *(of fence)* tenir; **to s. up late** se coucher tard

stead [sted] *n* **to stand sb in good s.** être bien utile à qn; **in sb's s.** à la place de qn

steadfast ['stedfɑːst] *adj* dévoué; *(opponent)* constant

steady ['stedɪ] **1 (-ier, -iest)** *adj (firm, stable)* stable; *(hand, voice)* assuré; *(progress, speed, demand)* constant; **to**

be s. on one's feet être solide sur ses jambes **2** *vt* faire tenir; **to s. one's nerves** se calmer; **to s. oneself** retrouver son équilibre ▪ **steadily** *adv (gradually)* progressivement; *(regularly)* régulièrement; *(continuously)* sans arrêt; *(walk)* d'un pas assuré

steak [steɪk] *n (beef)* steak *m*

steal¹ [stiːl] *(pt* **stole,** *pp* **stolen)** *vti* voler **(from sb** à qn)

steal² [stiːl] *(pt* **stole,** *pp* **stolen)** *vi* **to s. in/out** entrer/sortir furtivement

stealthy ['stelθɪ] **(-ier, -iest)** *adj* furtif, -ive

steam [stiːm] **1** *n* vapeur *f; (on glass)* buée *f; Fam* **to let off s.** se défouler; **s. engine/iron** locomotive *f*/fer *m* à vapeur **2** *vt (food)* cuire à la vapeur; **to get steamed up** *(of glass)* se couvrir de buée **3** *vi* **to s. up** *(of glass)* s'embuer ▪ **steamer** *n* bateau *m* à vapeur; *(for food)* panier *m* pour cuisson à la vapeur

steel [stiːl] **1** *n* acier *m* **2** *vt* **to s. oneself** s'armer de courage

steep [stiːp] **1 (-er, -est)** *adj (stairs, slope)* raide; *(hill, path)* escarpé; *Fig (price)* excessif, -ive **2** *vt (soak)* tremper **(in** dans) ▪ **steeply** *adv (rise)* en pente raide; *Fig (of prices)* excessivement

steeple ['stiːpəl] *n* clocher *m*

steer [stɪə(r)] **1** *vt* diriger **2** *vi (of person)* conduire; *(of ship)* se diriger **(for** vers); **to s. clear of sb/sth** éviter qn/qch ▪ **steering** *n (in vehicle)* direction *f;* **s. wheel** volant *m*

stem [stem] **1** *n (of plant)* tige *f; (of glass)* pied *m* **2** *(pt & pp* **-mm-)** *vt (stop)* arrêter **3** *vi* **to s. from sth** provenir de qch

stench [stentʃ] *n* puanteur *f*

step [step] **1** *n (movement, sound)* pas *m; (of stairs)* marche *f; (on train, bus)* marchepied *m; (doorstep)* pas de la porte; *Fig (action)* mesure *f;* **(flight of) steps** *(indoors)* escalier *m; (outdoors)* perron *m; Br* **(pair of) steps** *(ladder)* escabeau *m;* **s. by s.** pas à pas **2** *(pt & pp* **-pp-)** *vi (walk)* marcher **(on** sur) ▪ **stepdaughter** *n* belle-fille *f* ▪ **stepfather** *n* beau-père *m* ▪ **stepladder** *n*

escabeau *m* ▪ **stepmother** *n* belle-mère *f* ▪ **stepson** *n* beau-fils *m*

▸**step aside** *vi* s'écarter
▸**step back** *vi* reculer
▸**step down** *vi* descendre **(from** de); *Fig (withdraw)* se retirer
▸**step forward** *vi* faire un pas en avant
▸**step in** *vi (intervene)* intervenir
▸**step off** *vt insep (chair)* descendre de
▸**step over** *vt insep (obstacle)* enjamber
▸**step up** *vt sep (increase)* augmenter; *(speed up)* accélérer

stereo ['sterɪəʊ] **1** *(pl* **-os)** *n (hi-fi, record player)* chaîne *f* stéréo; **in s.** en stéréo **2** *adj (record)* stéréo *inv; (broadcast)* en stéréo

stereotype ['sterɪətaɪp] *n* stéréotype *m*

sterile [*Br* 'steraɪl, *Am* 'sterəl] *adj* stérile

sterilize ['sterəlaɪz] *vt* stériliser

sterling ['stɜːlɪŋ] *n Br (currency)* livre *f* sterling

stern¹ [stɜːn] **(-er, -est)** *adj* sévère

stern² [stɜːn] *n (of ship)* arrière *m*

steroid ['stɪərɔɪd] *n* stéroïde *m*

stethoscope ['steθəskəʊp] *n* stéthoscope *m*

stew [stjuː] **1** *n* ragoût *m* **2** *vt (meat)* faire cuire en ragoût; *(fruit)* faire de la compote de; **stewed fruit** compote *f* **3** *vi* cuire

steward ['stjuːəd] *n (on plane, ship)* steward *m* ▪ **stewardess** *n (on plane)* hôtesse *f*

stick¹ [stɪk] *n (piece of wood, chalk, dynamite)* bâton *m; (for walking)* canne *f*

stick² [stɪk] **1** *(pt & pp* **stuck)** *vt (glue)* coller; *Fam (put)* fourrer; *Fam (tolerate)* supporter; **to s. sth into sth** fourrer qch dans qch **2** *vi (cling)* coller **(to** à); *(of food in pan)* attacher **(to** dans); *(of drawer)* se coincer
▸**stick by** *vt insep* rester fidèle à
▸**stick down** *vt sep (envelope, stamp)* coller
▸**stick on** *vt sep (stamp, label)* coller
▸**stick out 1** *vt sep (tongue)* tirer; *Fam*

(head or arm from window) sortir **2** *vi (of shirt)* dépasser; *(of tooth)* avancer
▸**stick up** *vt sep (notice)* coller; *Fam (hand)* lever
▸**stick up for** *vt insep* défendre
sticker ['stɪkə(r)] *n* autocollant *m*
sticky ['stɪkɪ] **(-ier, -iest)** *adj* collant; *(label)* adhésif, -ive
stiff [stɪf] **(-er, -est)** *adj* raide; *(joint)* ankylosé; *(brush, paste)* dur; *Fig (person)* guindé; **to have a s. neck** avoir un torticolis; *Fam* **to be bored s.** s'ennuyer à mourir; *Fam* **frozen s.** complètement gelé
stiffen ['stɪfən] **1** *vt* raidir **2** *vi* se raidir
stifle ['staɪfəl] **1** *vt (feeling, person)* étouffer **2** *vi* **it's stifling** on étouffe
stigma ['stɪgmə] *n (moral stain)* flétrissure *f*
stiletto [stɪ'letəʊ] *adj Br* **s. heels** talons *mpl* aiguille
still¹ [stɪl] *adv* encore, toujours; *(even)* encore; *(nevertheless)* tout de même; **better s., s. better** encore mieux
still² [stɪl] **(-er, -est)** *adj (not moving)* immobile; *(calm)* calme; *Br (drink)* non gazeux, -euse; **to stand s.** rester immobile; **s. life** nature *f* morte
stilted ['stɪltɪd] *adj (speech, person)* guindé
stimulate ['stɪmjʊleɪt] *vt* stimuler ▪ **stimulant** *n* stimulant *m* ▪ **stimulus** *(pl* **-li** [-laɪ]) *n (encouragement)* stimulant *m; (physiological)* stimulus *m inv*
sting [stɪŋ] **1** *n* piqûre *f* **2** *(pt & pp* **stung)** *vt (of insect, ointment, wind)* piquer **3** *vi* piquer
stingy ['stɪndʒɪ] **(-ier, -iest)** *adj* avare
stink [stɪŋk] **1** *n* puanteur *f* **2** *(pt & pp* **stank** *or* **stunk,** *pp* **stunk)** *vi* puer; *Fam (of book, film)* être infect **3** *vt* **to s. out** *(room)* empester
stint [stɪnt] **1** *n (period)* période *f* de travail; *(share)* part *f* de travail **2** *vi* **to s. on sth** lésiner sur qch
stipulate ['stɪpjʊleɪt] *vt* stipuler **(that** que) ▪ **stipulation** *n* stipulation *f*
stir [stɜ:(r)] **1** *n* **to give sth a s.** remuer qch; *Fig* **to cause a s.** faire du bruit **2** *(pt & pp* **-rr-)** *vt (coffee, leaves)* remuer;

Fig (excite) exciter; *(incite)* inciter **(sb to do** qn à faire); **to s. up trouble** semer la zizanie; **to s. things up** envenimer les choses **3** *vi (move)* remuer, bouger ▪ **stirring** *adj (speech)* émouvant
stirrup ['stɪrəp] *n* étrier *m*
stitch [stɪtʃ] **1** *n* point *m; (in knitting)* maille *f; (in wound)* point *m* de suture; *(sharp pain)* point *m* de côté; *Fam* **to be in stitches** être plié (de rire) **2** *vt* **to s. (up)** *(sew up)* coudre; *Med* recoudre
stock [stɒk] **1** *n (supply)* provisions *fpl; Com* stock *m; Fin* valeurs *fpl; (soup)* bouillon *m; Fin* **stocks and shares** valeurs *fpl* mobilières; **in s.** *(goods)* en stock; **out of s.** *(goods)* épuisé; *Fig* **to take s.** faire le point **(of** de); **the S. Exchange** *or* **Market** la Bourse
2 *vt (sell)* vendre; *(keep in store)* stocker; **to s. (up)** *(shop)* approvisionner; *(fridge, cupboard)* remplir
3 *vi* **to s. up** s'approvisionner **(with** en) ▪ **stockbroker** *n* agent *m* de change ▪ **stockpile** *vt* faire des réserves de ▪ **stocktaking** *n Br Com* inventaire *m*
stocky ['stɒkɪ] **(-ier, -iest)** *adj* trapu
stodgy ['stɒdʒɪ] **(-ier, -iest)** *adj Fam (food)* bourratif, -ive; *Fig (book)* indigeste
stole¹ [stəʊl] *n (shawl)* étole *f*
stole² [stəʊl] *pt of* **steal**¹,²
stolen ['stəʊlən] *pp of* **steal**¹,²
stomach ['stʌmək] **1** *n* ventre *m; (organ)* estomac *m* **2** *vt (put up with)* supporter ▪ **stomachache** *n* mal *m* de ventre; **to have (a) s.** avoir mal au ventre
stone [stəʊn] *n* pierre *f; (pebble)* caillou *m; (in fruit)* noyau *m; Br (unit of weight)* = 6,348 kg ▪ **stone-cold** *adj* glacé ▪ **stone-deaf** *adj* sourd comme un pot
stoned [stəʊnd] *adj Fam (on drugs)* défoncé **(on** à)
stony ['stəʊnɪ] **(-ier, -iest)** *adj (path)* caillouteux, -euse; *Br Fam* **s. broke** *(penniless)* fauché
stood [stʊd] *pt & pp of* **stand**
stool [stu:l] *n* tabouret *m*
stoop [stu:p] *vi* se baisser; *Fig* **to s. to**

doing sth s'abaisser à faire qch

stop [stɒp] **1** *n (place, halt)* arrêt *m*; *(for plane, ship)* escale *f*; **to put a s. to sth** mettre fin à qch; **to come to a s.** s'arrêter; **s. sign** *(on road)* stop

2 *(pt & pp -pp-) vt* arrêter; *(end)* mettre fin à; *(cheque)* faire opposition à; **to s. sb/sth from doing sth** empêcher qn/qch de faire qch

3 *vi* s'arrêter; *(of pain, bleeding)* cesser; *(stay)* rester; **to s. snowing** cesser de neiger ■ **stopgap** *n* bouche-trou *m* ■ **stopoff** *n* halte *f*; *(in plane journey)* escale *f* ■ **stopover** *n* arrêt *m*; *(in plane journey)* escale *f* ■ **stopwatch** *n* chronomètre *m*

▶ **stop by** *vi (visit)* passer (**sb's** chez qn)

▶ **stop off, stop over** *vi (on journey)* s'arrêter

▶ **stop up** *vt sep (sink, pipe, leak)* boucher

stoppage [ˈstɒpɪdʒ] *n (strike)* débrayage *m*; *Br (in pay)* retenue *f*; **s. time** *(in sport)* arrêts *mpl* de jeu

stopper [ˈstɒpə(r)] *n* bouchon *m*

store [stɔː(r)] **1** *n (supply)* provision *f*; *Fig (of knowledge)* fonds *m*; *(warehouse)* entrepôt *m*; *(shop) Br* grand magasin *m*, *Am* magasin *m*; **to have sth in s. for sb** réserver qch à qn

2 *vt (in warehouse)* stocker; *(furniture)* entreposer; *(food)* ranger; *Comptr (in memory)* mettre en mémoire ■ **storage** *n* emmagasinage *m*; **s. space** espace *m* de rangement; *Comptr* **s. capacity** capacité *f* de mémoire

▶ **store away** *vt sep (put away, file away)* ranger; *(furniture)* entreposer

▶ **store up** *vt sep* accumuler

storekeeper [ˈstɔːkiːpə(r)] *n Am (shopkeeper)* commerçant, -e *mf*

storeroom [ˈstɔːruːm] *n (in house)* débarras *m*; *(in office, shop)* réserve *f*

storey [ˈstɔːrɪ] *(pl -eys) n Br (of building)* étage *m*

stork [stɔːk] *n* cigogne *f*

storm [stɔːm] **1** *n (bad weather)* tempête *f*; *(thunderstorm)* orage *m* **2** *vt (of soldiers, police)* prendre d'assaut **3** *vi* **to s. out** *(angrily)* sortir comme une fu-

rie ■ **stormy** (**-ier, -iest**) *adj (weather, meeting)* orageux, -euse

story[1] [ˈstɔːrɪ] *(pl -ies) n* histoire *f*; *(newspaper article)* article *m*

story[2] [ˈstɔːrɪ] *(pl -ies) n Am (of building)* étage *m*

stout [staʊt] **1** (**-er, -est**) *adj (person)* corpulent; *(shoes)* solide **2** *n Br (beer)* bière *f* brune

stove [stəʊv] *n (for cooking)* cuisinière *f*; *(for heating)* poêle *m*

stow [stəʊ] **1** *vt (cargo)* arrimer; **to s. sth away** *(put away)* ranger qch **2** *vi* **to s. away** *(on ship)* voyager clandestinement ■ **stowaway** *n (on ship,* passager, -ère *mf* clandestin(e)

straddle [ˈstrædəl] *vt (chair, fence)* se mettre à califourchon sur; *(step over, span)* enjamber

straggle [ˈstrægəl] *vi (lag behind)* être à la traîne ■ **straggler** *n* retardataire *mf*

straight [streɪt] **1** (**-er, -est**) *adj* droit; *(hair)* raide; *(honest)* honnête; *(answer)* clair; *(consecutive)* consécutif, -ive; *(conventional)* conformiste; *Fam (heterosexual)* hétéro

2 *adv (in straight line)* droit; *(directly)* directement; *(immediately)* tout de suite; **s. away** *(at once)* tout de suite; *Br* **s. ahead** *or* **on** *(walk)* tout droit; **to look s. ahead** regarder droit devant soi

straightaway [streɪtəˈweɪ] *adv* tout de suite

straighten [ˈstreɪtən] *vt* **to s. (out)** *(wire)* redresser; **to s. (up)** *(tie, hair, room)* arranger

straightforward [streɪtˈfɔːwəd] *adj (easy, clear)* simple; *(frank)* franc (*f* franche)

strain [streɪn] **1** *n* tension *f*; *(mental stress)* stress *m*

2 *vt* (**a**) *(rope, wire)* tendre excessivement; *(muscle)* se froisser; *(ankle, wrist)* se fouler; *(eyes)* fatiguer; *(voice)* forcer; *Fig (patience, friendship)* mettre à l'épreuve; **to s. oneself** *(hurt oneself)* se faire mal; *(tire oneself)* se fatiguer (**b**) *(soup)* passer; *(vegetables)* égoutter **3** *vi* faire un effort (**to do** pour faire)

strained [streɪnd] *adj (muscle)* froissé;

(ankle, wrist) foulé; *(relations)* tendu

strainer ['streɪnə(r)] *n* passoire *f*

strait [streɪt] *n Geog* **strait(s)** détroit *m*; **in financial straits** dans l'embarras

strand [strænd] *n (of wool)* brin *m*; *(of hair)* mèche *f*; *Fig (of story)* fil *m*

stranded ['strændɪd] *adj (person, vehicle)* en rade

strange [streɪndʒ] **(-er, -est)** *adj (odd)* bizarre; *(unknown)* inconnu ■ **strangely** *adv* étrangement; **s. (enough), she...** chose étrange, elle...

stranger ['streɪndʒə(r)] *n (unknown)* inconnu, -e *mf*; *(outsider)* étranger, -ère *mf*

strangle ['stræŋgəl] *vt* étrangler

strap [stræp] **1** *n* sangle *f*; *(on dress)* bretelle *f*; *(on watch)* bracelet *m*; *(on sandal)* lanière *f* **2** *(pt & pp* **-pp-)** *vt* **to s. (down** or **in)** attacher *(avec une sangle)*; **to s. sb in** attacher qn avec une ceinture de sécurité

strapping ['stræpɪŋ] *adj* robuste

strategy ['strætədʒɪ] *(pl* **-ies)** *n* stratégie *f* ■ **strategic** [strə'tiːdʒɪk] *adj* stratégique

straw [strɔː] *n (from wheat, for drinking)* paille *f*

strawberry ['strɔːbərɪ] **1** *(pl* **-ies)** *n* fraise *f* **2** *adj (flavour, ice cream)* à la fraise; *(jam)* de fraises; *(tart)* aux fraises

stray [streɪ] **1** *adj (animal, bullet)* perdu; **a few s. cars** quelques rares voitures **2** *n (dog)* chien *m* errant; *(cat)* chat *m* égaré **3** *vi* s'égarer; **to s. from** *(subject, path)* s'écarter de

streak [striːk] *n (of paint, dirt)* traînée *f*; *(of light)* raie *m*; *(in hair)* mèche *f* ■ **streaked** *adj (marked)* strié; *(stained)* taché **(with** de)

stream [striːm] **1** *n (brook)* ruisseau *m*; *(of light, blood)* jet *m*; *(of people)* flot *m* **2** *vi* ruisseler **(with** de); **to s. in** *(of sunlight, people)* entrer à flots

streamer ['striːmə(r)] *n (banner)* banderole *f*

streamline ['striːmlaɪn] *vt (work, method)* rationaliser ■ **streamlined** *adj (shape)* aérodynamique; *(industry, production)* rationalisé

street [striːt] *n* rue *f*; **s. lamp, s. light** lampadaire *m*; **s. map** plan *m* des rues ■ **streetcar** *n Am (tram)* tramway *m*

strength [streŋθ] *n* force *f*; *(of wood, fabric)* solidité *f* ■ **strengthen** *vt (building, position)* renforcer; *(body, limb)* fortifier

strenuous ['strenjʊəs] *adj (effort)* vigoureux, -euse; *(work)* fatigant

stress [stres] **1** *n (physical)* tension *f*; *(mental)* stress *m*; *(emphasis, in grammar)* accent *m*; **under s.** *(person)* stressé, sous pression; *(relationship)* tendu **2** *vt* insister sur; *(word)* accentuer; **to s. that...** souligner que... ■ **stressful** *adj* stressant

stretch [stretʃ] **1** *n (area)* étendue *f*; *(period of time)* période *f*; *(of road)* tronçon *m*

2 *vt (rope, neck)* tendre; *(shoe, rubber)* étirer; *Fig (income, supplies)* faire durer; **to s. (out)** *(arm, leg)* tendre; *Fig* **to s. one's legs** se dégourdir les jambes; *Fig* **to s. sb** pousser qn à son maximum **3** *vi (of person, elastic)* s'étirer; *(of influence)* s'étendre; **to s. (out)** *(of rope, plain)* s'étendre

stretcher ['stretʃə(r)] *n* brancard *m*

strew [struː] *(pt* **strewed,** *pp* **strewed** or **strewn** [struːn]) *vt (scatter)* éparpiller; **strewn with** *(covered)* jonché de

stricken ['strɪkən] *adj (town, region)* sinistré

strict [strɪkt] **(-er, -est)** *adj (severe, absolute)* strict ■ **strictly** *adv* strictement; **s. forbidden** formellement interdit

stride [straɪd] **1** *n* pas *m*; *Fig* **to make great strides** faire de grands progrès **2** *(pt* **strode)** *vi* **to s. across** or **over** *(fields)* traverser à grandes enjambées; **to s. along/out** avancer/sortir à grands pas

strike [straɪk] **1** *n (of workers)* grève *f*; *Mil* raid *m*; **to go on s.** se mettre en grève **2** *(pt & pp* **struck)** *vt (hit, impress)* frapper; *(collide with)* heurter; *(gold, oil)* trouver; *(match)* craquer; **it strikes me that...** il me semble que... *(+ indicative)* **3** *vi (of workers)* faire grève; *(attack)* attaquer

▸**strike at** vt insep (attack) attaquer

▸**strike back** vi (retaliate) riposter

▸**strike down** vt sep (of illness) terrasser

▸**strike off** vt sep (from list) rayer (from de); **to be struck off** (of doctor) être radié

▸**strike out** vi **to s. out at sb** essayer de frapper qn

▸**strike up** vt sep **to s. up a friendship** se lier amitié (**with sb** avec qn)

striker ['straɪkə(r)] n (worker) gréviste mf; (footballer) buteur m

striking ['straɪkɪŋ] adj (impressive) frappant

string [strɪŋ] **1** n ficelle f; (of apron) cordon m; (of violin, racket) corde f; (of questions) série f; Fig **to pull strings** faire jouer ses relations **2** adj (instrument, quartet) à cordes **3** (pt & pp **strung**) vt (beads) enfiler ▪ **stringed** adj (instrument) à cordes

stringent ['strɪndʒənt] adj rigoureux, -euse

strip [strɪp] **1** n (piece) bande f; (of metal) lame f; (of sports team) tenue f; **s. cartoon** bande f dessinée; Am **s. mall** = centre commercial qui longe une route **2** (pt & pp **-pp-**) vt (undress) déshabiller; (deprive) dépouiller (**of** de); **to s. off** (remove) enlever **3** vi **to s. (off)** (get undressed) se déshabiller ▪ **stripper** n (woman) strip-teaseuse f; (paint) (substance) décapant m ▪ **striptease** n strip-tease m

stripe [straɪp] n rayure f; (indicating rank) galon m ▪ **striped** adj rayé (**with** de)

strive [straɪv] (pt **strove**, pp **striven** ['strɪvən]) vi s'efforcer (**to do** de faire; **for** d'obtenir)

strode [strəʊd] pt of **stride**

stroke [strəʊk] **1** n (movement) coup m; (of pen) trait m; (of brush) touche f; (caress) caresse f; Med (illness) attaque f; **at a s.** d'un coup; **s. of luck** coup m de chance **2** vt (caress) caresser

stroll [strəʊl] **1** n promenade f **2** vi se promener; **to s. in** entrer sans se presser

stroller ['strəʊlə(r)] n Am (for baby) poussette f

strong [strɒŋ] **1** (-**er**, -**est**) adj fort; (shoes, chair, nerves) solide; (interest) vif (f vive); (measures) énergique; (supporter) ardent **2** adv **to be going s.** aller toujours bien ▪ **strong-box** n coffre-fort m ▪ **stronghold** n bastion m ▪ **strongly** adv (protest, defend) énergiquement; (advise, remind, desire) fortement

strove [strəʊv] pt of **strive**

struck [strʌk] pt & pp of **strike**

structure ['strʌktʃə(r)] n structure f; (building) édifice m ▪ **structural** adj structural; (building defect) de construction

struggle ['strʌgəl] **1** n (fight) lutte f (**to do** pour faire); **to have a s. doing** or **to do sth** avoir du mal à faire qch **2** vi (fight) lutter (**with** avec); **to be struggling** (financially) avoir du mal; **to s. to do sth** s'efforcer de faire qch

strung [strʌŋ] pt & pp of **string**

strut¹ [strʌt] (pt & pp **-tt-**) vi **to s. (about** or **around)** se pavaner

strut² [strʌt] n (for frame) étai m

stub [stʌb] **1** n (of pencil, cigarette) bout m; (of cheque) talon m **2** (pt & pp **-bb-**) vt **to s. one's toe** se cogner l'orteil (**on** or **against** contre); **to s. out** (cigarette) écraser

stubble ['stʌbəl] n (on face) barbe f de plusieurs jours

stubborn ['stʌbən] adj (person) têtu

stuck [stʌk] **1** pt & pp of **stick²** **2** adj (caught, jammed) coincé; **s. in bed/indoors** cloué au lit/chez soi; **to get s.** être coincé; **to be s. with sb/sth** se farcir qn/qch

stuck-up [stʌ'kʌp] adj Fam snob

stud¹ [stʌd] n (on football boot) crampon m; (earring) clou m d'oreille ▪ **studded** adj **s. with** (covered) constellé de

stud² [stʌd] n (farm) haras m; (stallion) étalon m

student ['stjuːdənt] **1** n (at university) étudiant, -e mf; (at school) élève mf; **music s.** étudiant, -e mf en musique **2**

adj (life, protest) étudiant; *(restaurant, residence, grant)* universitaire

studio ['stjuːdɪəʊ] *(pl -os) n* studio *m*; *(of artist)* atelier *m*; *Br* **s. flat**, *Am* **s. apartment** studio *m*

studious ['stjuːdɪəs] *adj (person)* studieux, -euse

study ['stʌdɪ] **1** *(pl -ies) n* étude *f*; *(office)* bureau *m* **2** *(pp & pp -ied) vt (learn, observe)* étudier **3** *vi* étudier; **to s. to be a doctor** faire des études de médecine; **to s. for an exam** préparer un examen

stuff [stʌf] **1** *n (possessions)* affaires *fpl*; *Fam* **some s.** *(substance)* un truc; *(things)* des trucs; *Fam* **this s.'s good, it's good s.** c'est bien
2 *vt (pocket)* remplir (**with** de); *(cushion)* rembourrer (**with** avec); *(animal)* empailler; *(chicken, tomatoes)* farcir; **to s. sth into sth** fourrer qch dans qch ■ **stuffing** *n (padding)* bourre *f*; *(for chicken, tomatoes)* farce *f*

stuffy ['stʌfɪ] *(-ier, -iest) adj (room)* qui sent le renfermé; *(person)* vieux jeu *inv*

stumble ['stʌmbəl] *vi* trébucher; **to s. across** *or* **on** *(find)* tomber sur

stump [stʌmp] *n (of tree)* souche *f*; *(of limb)* moignon *m*; *(in cricket)* piquet *m*

stun [stʌn] *(pt & pp -nn-) vt (make unconscious)* assommer; *Fig (amaze)* stupéfier ■ **stunned** *adj (amazed)* stupéfait (**by** par) ■ **stunning** *adj Fam (excellent)* excellent; *Fam (beautiful)* superbe

stung [stʌŋ] *pt & pp of* **sting**

stunk [stʌŋk] *pt & pp of* **stink**

stunt¹ [stʌnt] *n (in film)* cascade *f*; *(for publicity)* coup *m* de pub; **s. man** cascadeur *m*

stunt² [stʌnt] *vt (growth)* retarder ■ **stunted** *adj (person)* rabougri

stupid ['stjuːpɪd] *adj* stupide; **to do/ say a s. thing** faire/dire une stupidité ■ **stupidity** *n* stupidité *f* ■ **stupidly** *adv* bêtement

sturdy ['stɜːdɪ] *(-ier, -iest) adj (person, shoe)* robuste

stutter ['stʌtə(r)] **1** *n* **to have a s.** être bègue **2** *vi* bégayer

sty¹ [staɪ] *n (for pigs)* porcherie *f*

sty², **stye** [staɪ] *n (on eye)* orgelet *m*

style [staɪl] **1** *n* style *m*; *(sophistication)* classe *f* **2** *vt (design)* créer; **to s. sb's hair** coiffer qn

stylish ['staɪlɪʃ] *adj* chic *inv*

stylist ['staɪlɪst] *n* **(hair) s.** coiffeur, -euse *mf*

sub- [sʌb] *pref* sous-, sub-

subconscious [sʌb'kɒnʃəs] *adj & n* subconscient *(m)* ■ **subconsciously** *adv* inconsciemment

subcontract [sʌbkən'trækt] *vt* soustraiter

subdivide [sʌbdɪ'vaɪd] *vt* subdiviser (**into** en)

subdue [səb'djuː] *vt (country, people)* soumettre; *(feelings)* maîtriser ■ **subdued** *adj (light)* tamisé; *(voice, tone)* bas (*f* basse); *(person)* inhabituellement calme

subject¹ ['sʌbdʒɪkt] *n* **(a)** *(matter, in grammar)* sujet *m*; *(at school, university)* matière *f*; **s. matter** *(topic)* sujet *m*; *(content)* contenu *m* **(b)** *(of monarch)* sujet, -ette *mf*

subject² **1** ['sʌbdʒekt] *adj* **to be s. to depression/jealousy** avoir tendance à la dépression/à la jalousie; **it's s. to my agreement** c'est sous réserve de mon accord **2** [səb'dʒekt] *vt* soumettre (**to** à)

subjective [səb'dʒektɪv] *adj* subjectif, -ive ■ **subjectively** *adv* subjectivement

subjunctive [səb'dʒʌŋktɪv] *n* subjonctif *m*

sublet [sʌb'let] *(pt & pp -let, pres p -letting) vt* sous-louer

sublime [sə'blaɪm] *adj* sublime; *(utter)* suprême

submarine ['sʌbməriːn] *n* sous-marin *m*

submerge [səb'mɜːdʒ] *vt (flood, overwhelm)* submerger; *(immerse)* immerger (**in** dans)

submit [səb'mɪt] **1** *(pt & pp -tt-) vt* soumettre (**to** à) **2** *vi* se soumettre (**to** à) ■ **submissive** *adj (person)* soumis;

(attitude) de soumission

subordinate [sə'bɔːdɪnət] **1** *adj* subalterne; **s. to** subordonné à **2** *n* subordonné, -e *mf*

subscribe [səb'skraɪb] *vi (pay money)* cotiser (**to** à); **to s. to a newspaper** s'abonner à un journal ▪ **subscriber** *n (to newspaper, telephone)* abonné, -e *mf* ▪ **subscription** [sʌb'skrɪpʃən] *n (to newspaper)* abonnement *m*; *(to club)* cotisation *f*

subsequent ['sʌbsɪkwənt] *adj* ultérieur (**to** à); **our s. problems** les problèmes que nous avons eus par la suite ▪ **subsequently** *adv* par la suite

subside [səb'saɪd] *vi (of ground, building)* s'affaisser; *(of wind, flood, fever)* baisser ▪ **subsidence** *n (of ground)* affaissement *m*

subsidiary [Brsəb'sɪdɪərɪ, Am-dɪerɪ] **1** *adj* subsidiaire **2** *(pl -ies) n (company)* filiale *f*

subsidize ['sʌbsɪdaɪz] *vt* subventionner ▪ **subsidy** *(pl -ies) n* subvention *f*

substance ['sʌbstəns] *n* substance *f*; *(solidity, worth)* fondement *m*

substantial [səb'stænʃəl] *adj* important; *(meal)* substantiel, -elle ▪ **substantially** *adv* considérablement

substitute ['sʌbstɪtjuːt] **1** *n (thing)* produit *m* de remplacement; *(person)* remplaçant, -e *mf* (**for** de) **2** *vt* **to s. sb/sth for** substituer qn/qch à **3** *vi* **to s. for sb** remplacer qn ▪ **substitution** *n* substitution *f*

subtitle ['sʌbtaɪtəl] **1** *n (of film)* sous-titre *m* **2** *vt (film)* sous-titrer

subtle ['sʌtəl] **(-er, -est)** *adj* subtil

subtotal [sʌb'təʊtəl] *n* sous-total *m*

subtract [səb'trækt] *vt* soustraire (**from** de) ▪ **subtraction** *n* soustraction *f*

suburb ['sʌbɜːb] *n* banlieue *f*; **the suburbs** la banlieue ▪ **suburban** [sə'bɜːbən] *adj (train, house)* de banlieue ▪ **suburbia** [sə'bɜːbɪə] *n* la banlieue; **in s.** en banlieue

subversive [səb'vɜːsɪv] *adj* subversif, -ive

subway ['sʌbweɪ] *n Br (under road)*

passage *m* souterrain; *Am (railroad)* métro *m*

succeed [sək'siːd] **1** *vt* **to s. sb** succéder à qn **2** *vi* réussir (**in doing** à faire; **in sth** dans qch); **to s. to the throne** monter sur le trône ▪ **succeeding** *adj (in past)* suivant; *(in future)* futur; *(consecutive)* consécutif, -ive

success [sək'ses] *n* succès *m*, réussite *f*; **he was a s.** il a eu du succès; **it was a s.** c'était réussi

successful [sək'sesfəl] *adj (effort, venture)* couronné de succès; *(outcome)* heureux, -euse; *(company, businessman)* prospère; *(candidate in exam)* admis, reçu; *(candidate in election)* élu; *(writer, film)* à succès; **to be s.** réussir; **to be s. in doing sth** réussir à faire qch ▪ **successfully** *adv* avec succès

succession [sək'seʃən] *n* succession *f*; **ten days in s.** dix jours consécutifs ▪ **successive** *adj* successif, -ive; **ten s. days** dix jours consécutifs ▪ **successor** *n* successeur *m* (**to** de)

succinct [sək'sɪŋkt] *adj* succinct

succumb [sə'kʌm] *vi* succomber (**to** à)

such [sʌtʃ] **1** *adj (of this or that kind)* tel *(f* telle); **s. a car** une telle voiture; **s. happiness/noise** tant de bonheur/ bruit; **there's no s. thing** ça n'existe pas; **s. as** comme, tel que **2** *adv (so very)* si; *(in comparisons)* aussi; **s. long trips or s. long voyages 3** *pron* happiness **as s.** le bonheur en tant que tel ▪ **suchlike** *pron & adj* **...and s.** ...et autres

suck [sʌk] **1** *vt* sucer; *(of baby)* téter; **to s. (up)** *(with straw, pump)* aspirer; **to s. up or in** *(absorb)* absorber **2** *vi (of baby)* téter

suckle ['sʌkəl] **1** *vt (of woman)* allaiter **2** *vi (of baby)* téter

suction ['sʌkʃən] *n* succion *f*

sudden ['sʌdən] *adj* soudain; **all of a s.** tout à coup ▪ **suddenly** *adv* tout à coup, soudain; *(die)* subitement

suds [sʌdz] *npl* mousse *f* de savon

sue [suː] **1** *vt* poursuivre (en justice) **2** *vi* engager des poursuites judiciaires

suede [sweɪd] *n* daim *m*

suffer ['sʌfə(r)] **1** *vt (loss, damage, defeat)* subir; *(pain)* ressentir; *(tolerate)* supporter **2** *vi* souffrir (**from** de); **your work will s.** ton travail s'en ressentira ▪ **sufferer** *n (from misfortune)* victime *f*; **AIDS s.** malade *mf* du SIDA ▪ **suffering** *n* souffrance *f*

suffice [sə'faɪs] *vi* suffire

sufficient [sə'fɪʃənt] *adj* suffisant; **s. money** *(enough)* suffisamment d'argent; **to be s.** suffire ▪ **sufficiently** *adv* suffisamment

suffix ['sʌfɪks] *n* suffixe *m*

suffocate ['sʌfəkeɪt] **1** *vt* étouffer **2** *vi* suffoquer

sugar ['ʃʊgə(r)] **1** *n* sucre *m*; **s. bowl** sucrier *m*; **s. lump** morceau *m* de sucre **2** *vt (tea)* sucrer

suggest [sə'dʒest] *vt (propose)* suggérer; *(imply)* indiquer ▪ **suggestion** *n* suggestion *f* ▪ **suggestive** *adj* suggestif, -ive; **to be s. of** évoquer

suicide ['su:ɪsaɪd] *n* suicide *m*; **to commit s.** se suicider

suit[1] [su:t] *n* **(a)** *(man's)* costume *m*; *(woman's)* tailleur *m*; **flying/diving/ski s.** combinaison *f* de vol/plongée/ski **(b)** *(in card games)* couleur *f*; *Fig* **to follow s.** faire de même **(c)** *(lawsuit)* procès *m*

suit[2] [su:t] *vt (please, be acceptable to)* convenir à; *(of dress, colour)* aller (bien) à; *(adapt)* adapter (**to** à); **suited to** *(job, activity)* fait pour; *(appropriate to)* qui convient à; **to be well suited** *(of couple)* être bien assorti

suitable ['su:təbəl] *adj* convenable (**for** à); *(candidate, date)* adéquat; *(example)* approprié; **this film is not s. for children** ce film n'est pas pour les enfants

suitcase ['su:tkeɪs] *n* valise *f*

suite [swi:t] *n (rooms)* suite *f*

sulk [sʌlk] *vi* bouder

sullen ['sʌlən] *adj* maussade

sultana [sʌl'tɑ:nə] *n (raisin)* raisin *m* de Smyrne

sum [sʌm] **1** *n (amount of money)* somme *f*; *(mathematical problem)* pro-

blème *m*; **s. total** somme *f* totale **2** *(pt & pp* -mm-*)* *vt* **to s. up** *(summarize)* résumer; *(assess)* évaluer **3** *vi* **to s. up** résumer

summarize ['sʌməraɪz] *vt* résumer ▪ **summary** *(pl* -ies*)* *n* résumé *m*

summer ['sʌmə(r)] **1** *n* été *m*; **in (the) s.** en été **2** *adj* d'été; *Am* **s. camp** colonie *f* de vacances; *Br* **s. holidays**, *Am* **s. vacation** grandes vacances *fpl* ▪ **summertime** *n* été *m*; **in (the) s.** en été

summit ['sʌmɪt] *n* sommet *m*

summon ['sʌmən] *vt (call)* appeler; *(meeting, person)* convoquer (**to** à); **to s. up one's courage/strength** rassembler son courage/ses forces

summons ['sʌmənz] **1** *n (in law)* assignation *f* à comparaître **2** *vt* assigner à comparaître

sumptuous ['sʌmptʃʊəs] *adj* somptueux, -euse

sun [sʌn] **1** *n* soleil *m*; **in the s.** au soleil; **the s. is shining** il fait soleil **2** *(pt & pp* -nn-*)* *vt* **to s. oneself** prendre le soleil ▪ **sunbathe** *vi* prendre un bain de soleil ▪ **sunbed** *n* lit *m* à ultraviolets ▪ **sunblock** *n (cream)* écran *m* total ▪ **sunburn** *n* coup *m* de soleil ▪ **sunburnt** *adj* brûlé par le soleil ▪ **sundial** *n* cadran *m* solaire ▪ **sunflower** *n* tournesol *m* ▪ **sunglasses** *npl* lunettes *fpl* de soleil ▪ **sunhat** *n* chapeau *m* de soleil ▪ **sunlamp** *n* lampe *f* à bronzer ▪ **sunlight** *n* lumière *f* du soleil ▪ **sunrise** *n* lever *m* du soleil ▪ **sunroof** *n (in car)* toit *m* ouvrant ▪ **sunset** *n* coucher *m* du soleil ▪ **sunshade** *n (on table)* parasol *m*; *(portable)* ombrelle *f* ▪ **sunshine** *n* soleil *m* ▪ **sunstroke** *n* insolation *f* ▪ **suntan** *n* bronzage *m*; **s. lotion/oil** crème *f*/huile *f* solaire ▪ **suntanned** *adj* bronzé

Sunday ['sʌndeɪ] *n* dimanche *m*; **S. school** ≃ catéchisme *m*

sundry ['sʌndrɪ] **1** *adj* divers **2** *n* **all and s.** tout le monde

sung [sʌŋ] *pp of* **sing**

sunk [sʌŋk] *pp of* **sink**[2] ▪ **sunken** *adj (rock, treasure)* submergé

sunny ['sʌnɪ] (**-ier, -iest**) *adj (day)* ensoleillé; **it's s.** il fait soleil; **s. periods** *or* **intervals** éclaircies *fpl*

super ['su:pə(r)] *adj Fam* super *inv*

super- ['su:pə(r)] *pref* super-

superb [su:'pɜ:b] *adj* superbe

superficial [su:pə'fɪʃəl] *adj* superficiel, -elle

superfluous [su:'pɜ:flʊəs] *adj* superflu

superglue ['su:pəglu:] *n* colle *f* extraforte

superintendent [su:pərɪn'tendənt] *n Am (of apartment building)* gardien, -enne *mf*; **(police) s.** ≃ commissaire *mf* de police

superior [su:'pɪərɪə(r)] **1** *adj* supérieur (**to** à) **2** *n (person)* supérieur, -eure *mf* ▪ **superiority** [-rɪ'ɒrətɪ] *n* supériorité *f*

superlative [su:'pɜ:lətɪv] **1** *adj* sans pareil **2** *adj & n Gram* superlatif *(m)*

supermarket ['su:pəmɑ:kɪt] *n* supermarché *m*

supernatural [su:pə'nætʃərəl] *adj & n* surnaturel, -elle *(m)*

superpower ['su:pəpaʊə(r)] *n Pol* superpuissance *f*

supersede [su:pə'si:d] *vt* supplanter

supersonic [su:pə'sɒnɪk] *adj* supersonique

superstition [su:pə'stɪʃən] *n* superstition *f* ▪ **superstitious** *adj* superstitieux, -euse

superstore ['su:pəstɔ:r] *n* hypermarché *m*

supervise ['su:pəvaɪz] *vt (person, work)* surveiller; *(research)* superviser ▪ **supervisor** *n* surveillant, -e *mf*; *(in office)* chef *m* de service; *(in store)* chef *m* de rayon

supper ['sʌpə(r)] *n (meal)* dîner *m*; *(snack)* = casse-croûte pris avant d'aller se coucher

supple ['sʌpəl] *adj* souple

supplement 1 ['sʌplɪmənt] *n* supplément *m* (**to** à) **2** ['sʌplɪment] *vt* compléter; **to s. one's income** arrondir ses fins de mois ▪ **supplementary** [-'mentərɪ] *adj* supplémentaire

supplier [sə'plaɪə(r)] *n Com* fournisseur *m*

supply [sə'plaɪ] **1** (*pl* -**ies**) *n (stock)* provision *f*; **s. and demand** l'offre *f* et la demande; *Br* **s. teacher** suppléant, -e *mf* **2** *(pt & pp* -**ied**) *vt (provide)* fournir; *(with gas, electricity, water)* alimenter (**with** en); *(equip)* équiper (**with** de); **to s. sb with sth, to s. sth to sb** fournir qch à qn

support [sə'pɔ:t] **1** *n (backing, person supporting)* soutien *m*; *(thing supporting)* support *m*; **in s. of** *(person)* en faveur de; *(evidence, theory)* à l'appui de **2** *vt (bear weight of)* supporter; *(help, encourage)* soutenir; *(theory, idea)* appuyer; *(family, wife, husband)* subvenir aux besoins de

supporter [sə'pɔ:tə(r)] *n* partisan *m*; *(of football team)* supporter *m*

supportive [sə'pɔ:tɪv] *adj* **to be s. of sb** être d'un grand soutien à qn

suppose [sə'pəʊz] *vti* supposer (**that** que); **I'm supposed to be working** je suis censé travailler; **he's supposed to be rich** on le dit riche; **I s. (so)** je pense; **s.** *or* **supposing (that) you're right** supposons que tu aies raison

suppress [sə'pres] *vt (revolt, feelings, smile)* réprimer; *(fact, evidence)* faire disparaître

supreme [su:'pri:m] *adj* suprême

surcharge ['sɜ:tʃɑ:dʒ] *n (extra charge)* supplément *m*

sure [ʃʊə(r)] (**-er, -est**) *adj* sûr (**of** de; **that** que); **she's s. to accept** c'est sûr qu'elle acceptera; **to make s. of sth** s'assurer de qch; **for s.** à coup sûr; *Fam* **s.!, s. thing!** bien sûr ▪ **surely** *adv (certainly)* sûrement; **s. he didn't refuse?** il n'a quand même pas refusé?

surf [sɜ:f] **1** *n (waves)* ressac *m* **2** *vt Comptr* **to s. the Net** naviguer sur l'Internet ▪ **surfboard** *n* planche *f* de surf ▪ **surfing** *n (sport)* surf *m*; **to go s.** faire du surf

surface ['sɜ:fɪs] **1** *n* surface *f*; **s. area** superficie *f*; **on the s.** *(of water)* à la surface; *Fig (to all appearances)* en apparence **2** *vi (of swimmer)* remonter à la

surface; *Fam (of person, thing)* réapparaître

surge ['sɜːdʒ] **1** *n (of enthusiasm)* vague *f*; *(of anger, pride)* accès *m* **2** *vi (of crowd)* déferler; *(of prices)* monter (soudainement); **to s. forward** *(of person)* se lancer en avant

surgeon ['sɜːdʒən] *n* chirurgien, -enne *mf* ▪ **surgery** ['sɜːdʒərɪ] *n Br (doctor's office)* cabinet *m*; *(period, sitting)* consultation *f*; *(science)* chirurgie *f*; **to have heart s.** se faire opérer du cœur ▪ **surgical** *adj* chirurgical

surly ['sɜːlɪ] **(-ier, -iest)** *adj* revêche

surmount [sə'maʊnt] *vt* surmonter

surname ['sɜːneɪm] *n* nom *m* de famille

surpass [sə'pɑːs] *vt* surpasser **(in** en)

surplus ['sɜːpləs] **1** *n* surplus *m* **2** *adj (goods)* en surplus

surprise [sə'praɪz] **1** *n* surprise *f*; **to give sb a s.** faire une surprise à qn; **s. visit/result** visite *f*/résultat *m* inattendu(e)
2 *vt* étonner, surprendre ▪ **surprised** *adj* surpris **(that** que + *subjunctive*; **at sth** de qch; **at seeing** de voir) ▪ **surprising** *adj* surprenant

surrender [sə'rendə(r)] **1** *n (of soldiers)* reddition *f* **2** *vt (town)* livrer; *(right, claim)* renoncer à **3** *vi (give oneself up)* se rendre **(to** à)

surrogate ['sʌrəgət] *n* substitut *m*; **s. mother** mère *f* porteuse

surround [sə'raʊnd] *vt* entourer **(with** de); *(of army, police)* cerner; **surrounded by** entouré de ▪ **surrounding** *adj* environnant ▪ **surroundings** *npl (of town)* environs *mpl*; *(setting)* cadre *m*

surveillance [sɜː'veɪləns] *n* surveillance *f*

survey 1 ['sɜːveɪ] *n (investigation)* enquête *f*; *(of opinion)* sondage *m*; *(of house)* inspection *f*
2 [sə'veɪ] *vt (look at)* regarder; *(review)* passer en revue; *(house)* inspecter; *(land)* faire un relevé de ▪ **surveyor** *n (of land)* géomètre *m*; *(of house)* expert *m*

survive [sə'vaɪv] **1** *vt* survivre à **2** *vi* survivre ▪ **survival** *n (act)* survie *f*; *(relic)* vestige *m* ▪ **survivor** *n* survivant, -e *mf*

susceptible [sə'septəbəl] *adj (sensitive)* sensible **(to** à)

suspect 1 ['sʌspekt] *n & adj* suspect, -ecte *(mf)* **2** [sə'spekt] *vt* soupçonner **(sb of sth** qn de qch; **sb of doing** qn d'avoir fait); *(have intuition of)* se douter de

suspend [sə'spend] *vt* **(a)** *(hang)* suspendre **(from** à) **(b)** *(service, employee, player)* suspendre; *(pupil)* renvoyer temporairement

suspense [sə'spens] *n (uncertainty)* incertitude *f*; *(in film, book)* suspense *m*; **to keep sb in s.** tenir qn en haleine

suspicion [sə'spɪʃən] *n* soupçon *m*; **to be under s.** être soupçonné

suspicious [sə'spɪʃəs] *adj (person)* soupçonneux, -euse; *(behaviour)* suspect; **to be s. of** *or* **about sth** se méfier de qch

sustain [sə'steɪn] *vt (effort, theory)* soutenir; *(weight)* supporter; *(life)* maintenir; *(damage, loss, attack)* subir; **to s. an injury** être blessé

swagger ['swægə(r)] *vi (walk)* se pavaner

swallow¹ ['swɒləʊ] **1** *vt* avaler; **to s. sth down** avaler qch **2** *vi* avaler

swallow² ['swɒləʊ] *n (bird)* hirondelle *f*

swam [swæm] *pt of* **swim**

swamp [swɒmp] **1** *n* marais *m* **2** *vt (flood, overwhelm)* submerger **(with** de)

swan [swɒn] *n* cygne *m*

swap [swɒp] **1** *n* échange *m* **2** *(pt & pp* **-pp-)** *vt* échanger **(for** contre); **to s. seats** *or* **places** changer de place **3** *vi* échanger

swarm [swɔːm] **1** *n (of bees, people)* essaim *m* **2** *vi (of streets, insects, people)* fourmiller **(with** de)

swat [swɒt] *(pt & pp* **-tt-)** *vt* écraser

sway [sweɪ] **1** *vt* balancer; *Fig (person, public opinion)* influencer **2** *vi* se balancer

swear

swear [sweə(r)] **1** (*pt* **swore**, *pp* **sworn**) *vt (promise)* jurer (**to do** de faire; **that** que); **to s. an oath** prêter serment **2** *vi (take an oath)* jurer (**to sth** de qch); **to s. at sb** injurier qn ▪ **swearword** *n* juron *m*

sweat [swet] **1** *n* sueur *f* **2** *vi* suer ▪ **sweatshirt** *n* sweat-shirt *m*

sweater ['swetə(r)] *n* pull *m*

sweaty ['swetɪ] (**-ier, -iest**) *adj (shirt)* plein de sueur; *(hand)* moite; *(person)* en sueur

Swede [swi:d] *n* Suédois, -e *mf* ▪ **Sweden** *n* la Suède ▪ **Swedish 1** *adj* suédois **2** *n (language)* suédois *m*

sweep [swi:p] **1** (*pt & pp* **swept**) *vt (with broom)* balayer; *(chimney)* ramoner **2** *vi* balayer

▸**sweep aside** *vt sep (opposition, criticism)* écarter

▸**sweep away** *vt sep (leaves)* balayer; *(carry off)* emporter

▸**sweep out** *vt sep (room)* balayer

▸**sweep through** *vt insep (of fear)* saisir; *(of disease)* ravager

▸**sweep up** *vt sep & vi* balayer

sweeping ['swi:pɪŋ] *adj (gesture)* large; *(change)* radical; *(statement)* trop général

sweet [swi:t] **1** (**-er, -est**) *adj* doux (*f* douce); *(tea, coffee, cake)* sucré; *(pretty, kind)* adorable; **to have a s. tooth** aimer les sucreries

2 *n Br (piece of confectionery)* bonbon *m*; *Br (dessert)* dessert *m*; *Br* **s. shop** confiserie *f* ▪ **sweetcorn** *n Br* maïs *m*

sweeten ['swi:tən] *vt (food)* sucrer; *Fig (person)* amadouer

sweetheart ['swi:thɑ:t] *n* petit, -e ami, -e *mf*

swell¹ [swel] **1** (*pt* **swelled**, *pp* **swollen** *or* **swelled**) *vt (river, numbers)* grossir **2** *vi (of hand, leg)* enfler; *(of wood)* gonfler; *(of river, numbers)* grossir; **to s. up** *(of body part)* enfler ▪ **swelling** *n (on body)* enflure *f*

swell² [swel] *adj Am Fam (excellent)* super *inv*

swelter ['sweltə(r)] *vi* étouffer ▪ **sweltering** *adj* étouffant; **it's s.** on étouffe

swept [swept] *pt & pp of* **sweep**

swerve [swɜ:v] *vi (of vehicle)* faire une embardée; *(of player)* faire un écart

swift [swɪft] **1** (**-er, -est**) *adj* rapide **2** *n (bird)* martinet *m* ▪ **swiftly** *adv* rapidement

swill [swɪl] *vt Fam (drink)* écluser; **to s. (out** *or* **down)** rincer à grande eau

swim [swɪm] **1** *n* **to go for a s.** aller nager

2 (*pt* **swam**, *pp* **swum**, *pres p* **swimming**) *vt (river)* traverser à la nage; *(length, crawl)* nager

3 *vi* nager; *(as sport)* faire de la natation; **to go swimming** aller nager; **to s. away** s'éloigner à la nage ▪ **swimmer** *n* nageur, -euse *mf* ▪ **swimming** *n* natation *f*; **s. cap** bonnet *m* de bain; *Br* **s. costume** maillot *m* de bain; *Br* **s. pool** piscine *f*; **s. trunks** slip *m* de bain

swindle ['swɪndəl] **1** *n* escroquerie *f* **2** *vt* escroquer ▪ **swindler** *n* escroc *m*

swine [swaɪn] *n inv Pej (person)* salaud *m*

swing [swɪŋ] **1** *n (in playground)* balançoire *f*; *(movement)* balancement *m*; *(in opinion)* revirement *m*; *(of golfer)* swing *m*

2 (*pt & pp* **swung**) *vt (arms, legs)* balancer; *(axe)* brandir

3 *vi (sway)* se balancer; *(turn)* virer; **to s. round** *(turn suddenly)* se retourner

swipe [swaɪp] *vt (card)* passer dans un lecteur de cartes; *Fam* **to s. sth** *(steal)* faucher qch (**from sb** à qn)

swirl [swɜ:l] *vi* tourbillonner

Swiss [swɪs] **1** *adj* suisse; *Br* **S. roll** roulé *m* **2** *n inv* Suisse *m*, Suissesse *f*; **the S.** les Suisses *mpl*

switch [swɪtʃ] **1** *n (electrical)* interrupteur *m*; *(change)* changement *m* (**in** de); *(reversal)* revirement *m* (**in** de) **2** *vt (money, employee)* transférer (**to** à); *(support, affection)* reporter (**to** sur); *(exchange)* échanger (**for** contre) **3** *vi* **to s. to** *(change to)* passer à ▪ **switchboard** *n Tel* standard *m*; **s. operator** standardiste *mf*

▸**switch off 1** *vt sep (lamp, gas, radio)* éteindre; *(engine)* arrêter; *(electricity)*

couper 2 *vi (of appliance)* s'éteindre
▸**switch on 1** *vt sep (lamp, gas, radio)*
allumer; *(engine)* mettre en marche **2** *vi*
(of appliance) s'allumer
▸**switch over** *vi (changeTV channels)*
changer de chaîne; **to s. over to**
(change to) passer à
Switzerland ['swɪtsələnd] *n* la Suisse
swivel ['swɪvəl] **1** *(Br* -ll-, *Am* -l-) *vi* **to**
s. (round) *(of chair)* pivoter **2** *adj* **s.**
chair chaise *f* pivotante
swollen ['swəʊlən] **1** *pp of* swell[1] **2**
adj (leg) enflé; *(stomach)* gonflé
swoop [swuːp] *vi* faire une descente
(on dans); **to s. (down) on** *(of bird)*
fondre sur
swop [swɒp] *n & vti* = swap
sword [sɔːd] *n* épée *f*
swore [swɔː(r)] *pt of* swear
sworn [swɔːn] *pp of* swear
swot [swɒt] *Br Fam Pej* **1** *n* bûcheur,
-euse *mf* **2** *(pt & pp* -tt-) *vti* **to s.**
(up) bûcher; **to s. up on sth** bûcher
qch
swum [swʌm] *pp of* swim
swung [swʌŋ] *pt & pp of* swing
sycamore ['sɪkəmɔː(r)] *n (maple)* sy-
comore *m*; *Am (plane tree)* platane *m*
syllable ['sɪləbəl] *n* syllabe *f*
syllabus ['sɪləbəs] *n* programme *m*
symbol ['sɪmbəl] *n* symbole *m* ▪ **sym-**
bolic [-'bɒlɪk] *adj* symbolique ▪ **sym-**
bolize *vt* symboliser
symmetrical [sɪ'metrɪkəl] *adj* symé-
trique
sympathetic [sɪmpə'θetɪk] *adj*
(showing pity) compatissant; *(under-*
standing) compréhensif, -ive; **s. to sb/**

sth *(favourable)* bien disposé à l'égard
de qn/qch
sympathize ['sɪmpəθaɪz] *vi* **I s. with**
you *(pity)* je suis désolé (pour vous);
(understanding) je vous comprends
sympathy ['sɪmpəθɪ] *n (pity)* com-
passion *f*; *(understanding)* compréhen-
sion *f*; **to have s. for sb** éprouver de la
compassion pour qn
symphony ['sɪmfənɪ] **1** *(pl* -ies) *n*
symphonie *f* **2** *adj (orchestra, concert)*
symphonique
symptom ['sɪmptəm] *n Med & Fig*
symptôme *m*
synagogue ['sɪnəgɒg] *n* synagogue *f*
synchronize ['sɪŋkrənaɪz] *vt* syn-
chroniser
syndicate ['sɪndɪkət] *n* syndicat *m*
syndrome ['sɪndrəʊm] *n Med & Fig*
syndrome *m*
synonym ['sɪnənɪm] *n* synonyme *m*
▪ **synonymous** [-'nɒnɪməs] *adj* syno-
nyme (**with** de)
synopsis [sɪ'nɒpsɪs] *(pl* -opses [-ɒp-
siːz]) *n* résumé *m*; *(of film)* synopsis *m*
synthetic [sɪn'θetɪk] *adj* synthétique
syphon ['saɪfən] *n & vt* = siphon
syringe [sə'rɪndʒ] *n* seringue *f*
syrup ['sɪrəp] *n* sirop *m*; *Br* **(golden) s.**
mélasse *f* raffinée
system ['sɪstəm] *n (structure) &*
Comptr système *m*; *(human body)* orga-
nisme *m*; *(method)* méthode *f*; **the di-**
gestive s. l'appareil *m* digestif; *Comptr*
systems analyst analyste *m* program-
meur
systematic [sɪstə'mætɪk] *adj* systé-
matique

Tt

T, t [tiː] *n (letter)* T, t *m inv*

ta [tɑː] *exclam Br Fam* merci!

tab [tæb] *n* (**a**) *(label)* étiquette *f* (**b**) *Am Fam (bill)* addition *f* (**c**) *(on computer, typewriter)* tabulateur *m*; **t. key** touche *f* de tabulation

table¹ ['teɪbəl] *n* (**a**) *(furniture)* table *f*; *Br* **to set** *or* **lay/clear the t.** mettre/ débarrasser la table; **(sitting) at the t.** à table; **t. tennis** tennis *m* de table; **t. wine** vin *m* de table (**b**) *(list)* table *f*; **t. of contents** table *f* des matières ▪ **tablecloth** *n* nappe *f* ▪ **tablespoon** *n* ≃ cuillère *f* à soupe ▪ **tablespoonful** *n* ≃ cuillerée *f* à soupe

table² ['teɪbəl] *vt Br (motion)* présenter; *Am (postpone)* ajourner

tablet ['tæblɪt] *n (pill)* comprimé *m*

tabloid ['tæblɔɪd] *n (newspaper)* tabloïd *m*

taboo [tə'buː] *(pl -oos) adj & n* tabou *(m)*

tack [tæk] **1** *n (nail)* clou *m*; *Am (thumbtack)* punaise *f* **2** *vt* **to t. (down)** clouer

tackle ['tækəl] **1** *n (gear)* matériel *m*; *(in rugby)* placage *m*; *(in football)* tacle *m* **2** *vt (task, problem)* s'attaquer à; *(subject)* aborder; *(rugby player)* plaquer; *(football player)* tacler

tacky ['tækɪ] *(-ier, -iest) adj (sticky)* collant; *Fam (shoddy)* minable, moche

tact [tækt] *n* tact *m* ▪ **tactful** *adj (remark)* diplomatique; **to be t.** *(of person)* avoir du tact ▪ **tactless** *adj (person, remark)* qui manque de tact

tactic ['tæktɪk] *n* **a t.** une tactique; **tactics** la tactique ▪ **tactical** *adj* tactique

tag [tæg] **1** *n (label)* étiquette *f* **2** *vi* **to t. along with sb** venir avec qn

tail [teɪl] **1** *n (of animal)* queue *f*; **tails, t. coat** queue-de-pie *f*; **the t. end** la fin

(of de) **2** *vt Fam (follow)* filer **3** *vi* **to t. off** *(lessen)* diminuer ▪ **tailback** *n Br (of traffic)* bouchon *m* ▪ **taillight** *n Am (of vehicle)* feu *m* arrière *inv*

tailor ['teɪlə(r)] **1** *n (person)* tailleur *m* **2** *vt (garment)* faire; *Fig (adjust)* adapter **(to** à)

tainted ['teɪntɪd] *adj (air)* pollué; *(food)* gâté; *Fig (reputation, system)* souillé

TAKE [teɪk] *(pt* took, *pp* taken) *vt* prendre; *(bring)* amener **(to** à); *(by car)* conduire **(to** à); *(escort)* accompagner **(to** à); *(lead away)* emmener **(to** à); *(exam)* passer; *(credit card)* accepter; *(contain)* avoir une capacité de; *(tolerate)* supporter; *Math (subtract)* soustraire **(from** de); **to t. sth to sb** apporter qch à qn; **to t. sth with one** emporter qch; **it takes an army/courage** il faut une armée/du courage **(to do** pour faire); **I took an hour to do it** j'ai mis une heure à le faire; **I t. it that...** je présume que... ▪ **takeaway** *Br* **1** *adj (meal)* à emporter **2** *n (shop)* restaurant *m* qui fait des plats à emporter; *(meal)* plat *m* à emporter ▪ **takeoff** *n (of plane)* décollage *m* ▪ **take-out** *adj & n Am* = **takeaway** ▪ **takeover** *n (of company)* rachat *m*

▸ **take after** *vt insep* **to t. after sb** ressembler à qn

▸ **take along** *vt sep (object)* emporter; *(person)* emmener

▸ **take apart** *vt sep (machine)* démonter

▸ **take away** *vt sep (thing)* emporter; *(person)* emmener; *(remove)* enlever **(from** à); *Math (subtract)* soustraire **(from** de)

▸ **take back** *vt sep* reprendre; *(return)* rapporter; *(statement)* retirer; *(accompany)* ramener **(to** à)

▶**take down** vt sep (object) descendre; (notes) prendre

▶**take in** vt sep (chair, car) rentrer; (skirt) reprendre; (include) inclure; (understand) saisir; Fam (deceive) rouler

▶**take off 1** vt sep (remove) enlever; (lead away) emmener; (mimic) imiter; Math (deduct) déduire (**from** de) **2** vi (of aircraft) décoller

▶**take on** vt sep (work, staff, passenger, shape) prendre

▶**take out** vt sep (from pocket) sortir; (tooth) arracher; (insurance policy, patent) prendre; Fam **to t. it out on sb** passer sa colère sur qn

▶**take over 1** vt sep (become responsible for) reprendre; (buy out) racheter; (overrun) envahir; **to t. over sb's job** remplacer qn **2** vi (relieve) prendre la relève (**from** de); (succeed) prendre la succession (**from** de)

▶**take round** vt sep (bring) apporter (**to** à); (distribute) distribuer; (visitor) faire visiter

▶**take to** vt insep **to t. to doing sth** se mettre à faire qch; **I didn't t. to him/it** il/ça ne m'a pas plu

▶**take up 1** vt sep (carry up) monter; (continue) reprendre; (space, time) prendre; (offer) accepter; (hobby) se mettre à **2** vi **to t. up with sb** se lier avec qn

taken ['teɪkən] adj (seat) pris; (impressed) impressionné (**with** or **by** par); **to be t. ill** tomber malade

takings ['teɪkɪŋz] n (money) recette f

talc [tælk], **talcum powder** ['tælkəmpaʊdə(r)] n talc m

tale [teɪl] n (story) histoire f; (lie) salades fpl; **to tell tales** rapporter (**on sb** sur qn)

talent ['tælənt] n talent m ▪ **talented** adj talentueux, -euse

talk [tɔːk] **1** n (conversation) conversation f (**about** à propos de); (lecture) exposé m (**on** sur); **talks** (negotiations) pourparlers mpl; **to have a t. with sb** parler avec qn

2 vt (nonsense) dire; **to t. politics** parler politique; **to t. sb into doing/out of doing sth** persuader qn de faire/de

ne pas faire qch; **to t. sth over** discuter (de) qch

3 vi parler (**to/about** à/de); (gossip) jaser

talkative ['tɔːkətɪv] adj bavard

tall [tɔːl] (-er, -est) adj (person) grand; (tree, house) haut; Fig **a t. story** une histoire invraisemblable

tally ['tælɪ] (pt & pp -ied) vi correspondre (**with** à)

tambourine [tæmbə'riːn] n tambourin m

tame [teɪm] **1** (-er, -est) adj (animal) apprivoisé; Fig (book, play) fade **2** vt (animal) apprivoiser

tamper ['tæmpə(r)] vt insep **to t. with** (lock, car) essayer de forcer; (machine) toucher à; (documents) trafiquer

tampon ['tæmpɒn] n tampon m (hygiénique)

tan [tæn] **1** n (suntan) bronzage m **2** adj (colour) marron clair inv **3** (pt & pp -nn-) vt (skin) hâler; (leather) tanner **4** vi (of person, skin) bronzer

tangerine [tændʒə'riːn] n mandarine f

tangible ['tændʒəbəl] adj tangible

tangle ['tæŋgəl] n **to get into a t.** (of rope) s'enchevêtrer; (of hair) s'emmêler; Fig (of person) s'embrouiller ▪ **tangled** adj enchevêtré; (hair) emmêlé

tango ['tæŋgəʊ] (pl -os) n tango m

tangy ['tæŋɪ] (-ier, -iest) adj acidulé

tank [tæŋk] n (container) réservoir m; (military vehicle) tank m; (fish) t. aquarium m

tanker ['tæŋkə(r)] n (lorry) camion-citerne m; (oil) t. (ship) pétrolier m

Tannoy® ['tænɔɪ] n Br **over the T.** au haut-parleur

tantalizing ['tæntəlaɪzɪŋ] adj alléchant

tantrum ['tæntrəm] n caprice m

tap¹ [tæp] **1** n Br (for water) robinet m; **t. water** eau f du robinet **2** (pt & pp -pp-) vt (resources) puiser dans; (phone) placer sur écoute

tap² [tæp] **1** n (blow) petit coup m; **t. dancing** claquettes fpl **2** (pt & pp -pp-) vt (hit) tapoter

tape [teɪp] **1** n (**a**) *(ribbon)* ruban m; (**sticky** *or* **adhesive**) **t.** ruban m adhésif; **t. measure** mètre m (à) ruban (**b**) *(for recording)* bande f; *(cassette)* cassette f; **t. deck** platine f cassette; **t. recorder** magnétophone m
2 vt (**a**) *(stick)* scotcher (**b**) *(record)* enregistrer

taper ['teɪpə(r)] **1** n *(candle)* bougie f filée **2** vi s'effiler; *Fig* **to t. off** diminuer

tapestry ['tæpəstrɪ] n tapisserie f

tar [tɑː(r)] n goudron m

target ['tɑːgɪt] **1** n cible f; *(objective)* objectif m **2** vt *(campaign, product)* destiner (**at** à); *(age group)* viser

tariff ['tærɪf] n *(tax)* tarif m douanier; *Br (price list)* tarif m

tarmac ['tɑːmæk] n *Br (on road)* macadam m; *(runway)* piste f

tarnish ['tɑːnɪʃ] vt ternir

tart [tɑːt] **1** (-**er**, -**est**) adj *(sour)* aigre **2** n *(pie)* (large) tarte f; *(small)* tartelette f

tartan ['tɑːtən] **1** n tartan m **2** adj *(skirt, tie)* écossais

task [tɑːsk] n tâche f

tassel ['tæsəl] n gland m

taste [teɪst] **1** n goût m; **in good/bad t.** de bon/mauvais goût; **to have a t. of sth** goûter à qch **2** vt *(detect flavour of)* sentir; *(sample)* goûter; *Fig (experience)* goûter à **3** vi **to t. of** *or* **like sth** avoir un goût de qch; **to t. good** être bon (f bonne)

tasteful ['teɪstfəl] adj de bon goût ■ **tasteless** adj *(food)* insipide; *Fig (joke)* de mauvais goût ■ **tasty** (-**ier**, -**iest**) adj savoureux, -euse

tatters ['tætəz] npl **in t.** *(clothes)* en lambeaux

tattoo [tæ'tuː] **1** *(pl* -**oos**) n *(design)* tatouage m **2** *(pt & pp* -**ooed**) vt tatouer

tatty ['tætɪ] (-**ier**, -**iest**) adj *Br Fam* minable

taught [tɔːt] pt & pp of **teach**

taunt [tɔːnt] **1** n raillerie f **2** vt railler

taut [tɔːt] adj tendu

tax[1] [tæks] **1** n *(on goods)* taxe f, impôt m; *(on income)* impôts mpl; *Br* **road t.** ≃ vignette f automobile

2 adj fiscal; **t. collector** percepteur m; *Br* **(road) t. disc** ≃ vignette f automobile
3 vt *(person)* imposer; *(goods)* taxer ■ **taxable** adj imposable ■ **taxation** n *(taxes)* impôts mpl; *(act)* imposition f ■ **tax-free** adj exempt d'impôts ■ **taxpayer** n contribuable mf

tax[2] [tæks] vt *(put under strain)* mettre à l'épreuve

taxi ['tæksɪ] n taxi m; *Br* **t. rank,** *Am* **t. stand** station f de taxis

tea [tiː] n *(plant, drink)* thé m; *Br (snack)* goûter m; *Br* **high t.** dîner m *(pris tôt dans la soirée)*; *Br* **t. break** ≃ pause-café f; **t. leaves** feuilles fpl de thé; **t. set** service m à thé; *Br* **t. towel** torchon m ■ **teabag** n sachet m de thé ■ **teacup** n tasse f à thé ■ **teapot** n théière f ■ **tearoom** n salon m de thé ■ **teaspoon** n petite cuillère f ■ **teaspoonful** n cuillerée f à café ■ **teatime** n l'heure f du thé

teach [tiːtʃ] **1** *(pt & pp* **taught**) vt apprendre (**sb sth** qch à qn; **that** cue); *(in school, at university)* enseigner (**sb sth** qch à qn); **to t. sb (how) to do sth** apprendre à qn à faire qch **2** vi enseigner ■ **teaching 1** n enseignement m **2** adj *(staff)* enseignant; *(method, material)* pédagogique

teacher ['tiːtʃə(r)] n professeur m; *(in primary school)* instituteur, -trice mf

team [tiːm] **1** n équipe f; *(of horses, oxen)* attelage m; **t. mate** coéquipier, -ère mf **2** vi **to t. up** faire équipe (**with sb** avec qn) ■ **teamwork** n travail m d'équipe

tear[1] [teə(r)] **1** n déchirure f **2** *(pt* **tore**, *pp* **torn**) vt *(rip)* déchirer; *(snatch)* arracher (**from** à); **to t. off** *or* **out** arracher; **to t. up** déchirer **3** vi **to t. along/past** aller/passer à toute vitesse

tear[2] [tɪə(r)] n larme f; **in tears** en larmes

tease [tiːz] **1** n *(person)* taquin, -e mf **2** vt taquiner

technical ['teknɪkəl] adj technique

technician [tek'nɪʃən] n technicien, -enne mf

technique [tek'ni:k] n technique f

technology [tek'nɒlədʒɪ] (pl -ies) n technologie f ■ **technological** [-nə'lɒdʒɪkəl] adj technologique

tedious ['ti:dɪəs] adj fastidieux, -euse

teem [ti:m] vi (swarm) grouiller (**with** de); **to t. (with rain)** pleuvoir à torrents

teenage ['ti:neɪdʒ] adj (boy, girl, behaviour) adolescent; (fashion, magazine) pour adolescents ■ **teenager** n adolescent, -e mf ■ **teens** npl **to be in one's t.** être adolescent

tee-shirt ['ti:ʃɜ:t] n tee-shirt m

teeth [ti:θ] pl of tooth

teethe [ti:ð] vi faire ses dents

teetotaller [ti:'təʊtələ(r)] (Am **teetotaler**) n = personne qui ne boit jamais d'alcool

telecommunications [telɪkəmju:nɪ'keɪʃənz] npl télécommunications fpl

telegram ['telɪgræm] n télégramme m

telegraph ['telɪgrɑːf] adj **t. pole/wire** poteau m/fil m télégraphique

telephone ['telɪfəʊn] 1 n téléphone m; **to be on the t.** (speaking) être au téléphone
 2 adj (call, line, message) téléphonique; Br **t. booth, t. box** cabine f téléphonique; **t. directory** annuaire m du téléphone; **t. number** numéro m de téléphone
 3 vt (message) téléphoner (**to** à); **to t. sb** téléphoner à qn
 4 vi téléphoner ■ **telephonist** n Br téléphoniste mf

telescope ['telɪskəʊp] n télescope m

teletext ['telɪtekst] n télétexte m

televise ['telɪvaɪz] vt téléviser

television [telɪ'vɪʒən] 1 n télévision f; **on (the) t.** à la télévision 2 adj (programme, screen) de télévision; (interview, report) télévisé

telex ['teleks] 1 n (service, message) télex m 2 vt (message) télexer

tell [tel] 1 (pt & pp told) vt dire (**sb sth** qch à qn; **that** que); (story) raconter; (distinguish) distinguer (**from** de); **to t. sb to do sth** dire à qn de faire qch; **to t. the difference** voir la différence (**between** entre); **I could t. she was lying** je savais qu'elle mentait; Fam **to t. sb off** disputer qn
 2 vi dire; (have an effect) se faire sentir; **to t. of** or **about sb/sth** parler de qn/qch; **you can never t.** on ne sait jamais; Fam **to t. on sb** dénoncer qn

telltale ['telteɪl] 1 adj révélateur, -trice 2 n rapporteur, -euse mf

telly ['telɪ] n Br Fam télé f; **on the t.** à la télé

temp [temp] Br Fam 1 n intérimaire mf 2 vi faire de l'intérim

temper ['tempə(r)] 1 n (mood, nature) humeur f; (bad mood) mauvaise humeur f; **in a bad t.** de mauvaise humeur; **to lose one's t.** se mettre en colère 2 vt (moderate) tempérer

temperament ['tempərəmənt] n tempérament m ■ **temperamental** [-'mentəl] adj (person, machine) capricieux, -euse

temperate ['tempərət] adj (climate) tempéré

temperature ['tempərətʃə(r)] n température f

template ['templət, -pleɪt] n gabarit m; Comptr modèle m

temple¹ ['tempəl] n (religious building) temple m

temple² ['tempəl] n Anat tempe f

tempo ['tempəʊ] (pl -os) n (of life, work) rythme m; Mus tempo m

temporary [Br 'tempərərɪ, Am -erɪ] adj temporaire; (secretary) intérimaire ■ **temporarily** [Br tempə'reərəlɪ, Am tempə'reərəlɪ] adv temporairement

tempt [tempt] vt tenter; **tempted to do sth** tenté de faire qch ■ **temptation** n tentation f ■ **tempting** adj tentant

ten [ten] adj & n dix (m)

tenable ['tenəbəl] adj (argument, position) défendable

tenacious [tə'neɪʃəs] adj tenace

tenant ['tenənt] n locataire mf ■ **tenancy** n (lease) location f; (period) occupation f

tend¹ [tend] vi **to t. to do sth** avoir tendance à faire qch; **to t. towards** incliner vers ■ **tendency** (pl -ies) n tendance f (**to do** à faire)

tend² [tend] *vt (look after)* s'occuper de

tender¹ ['tendə(r)] *adj (soft, delicate, loving)* tendre; *(painful)* sensible

tender² ['tendə(r)] **1** *n* to be legal t. *(of money)* avoir cours **2** *vt (offer)* offrir

tenement ['tenəmənt] *n* immeuble *m*

tenner ['tenə(r)] *n Br Fam* billet *m* de 10 livres

tennis ['tenɪs] *n* tennis *m*; **t. court** court *m* de tennis

tenor ['tenə(r)] *n Mus* ténor *m*

tenpin ['tenpɪn] *adj Br* **t. bowling** bowling *m*

tense¹ [tens] **1** (-er, -est) *adj (person, muscle, situation)* tendu **2** *vt* tendre; *(muscle)* contracter **3** *vi* to **t. (up)** *(of person, face)* se crisper ▪ **tension** *n* tension *f*

tense² [tens] *n (in grammar)* temps *m*

tent [tent] *n* tente *f*; *Br* **t. peg** piquet *m* de tente; *Br* **t. pole**, *Am* **t. stake** mât *m* de tente

tentative ['tentətɪv] *adj (not definite)* provisoire; *(hesitant)* timide

tenth [tenθ] *adj & n* dixième *(mf)*; **a t.** *(fraction)* un dixième

tenuous ['tenjʊəs] *adj (link)* ténu

tepid ['tepɪd] *adj (liquid) & Fig* tiède

term [tɜːm] **1** *n (word)* terme *m*; *(period)* période *f*; *Br (of school or university year)* trimestre *m*; *Am (semester)* semestre *m*; **terms** *(conditions)* conditions *fpl*; *(of contract)* termes *mpl*; **to be on good/bad terms** être en bons/mauvais termes (**with sb** avec qn); **in terms of** *(speaking of)* sur le plan de; **to come to terms with sth** se résigner à qch; **in the long/short/medium t.** à long/court/moyen terme **2** *vt* appeler

terminal ['tɜːmɪnəl] **1** *n (electronic) & Comptr* terminal *m*; *(of battery)* borne *f*; **(air) t.** aérogare *f* **2** *adj (patient, illness)* en phase terminale

terminate ['tɜːmɪneɪt] **1** *vt* mettre fin à; *(contract)* résilier; *(pregnancy)* interrompre **2** *vi* se terminer

terminus ['tɜːmɪnəs] *n* terminus *m*

terrace ['terɪs] *n (next to house, on hill)*

terrasse *f*; *Br (houses)* = rangée de maisons attenantes; *Br* **the terraces** *(at football ground)* les gradins *mpl* ▪ **terraced** *n Br* **t. house** = maison située dans une rangée d'habitations attenantes

terrain [təˈreɪn] *n Mil & Geol* terrain *m*

terrestrial [təˈrestrɪəl] *adj* terrestre

terrible ['terəbəl] *adj* terrible ▪ **terribly** *adv Fam (extremely)* terriblement; *(badly)* affreusement mal

terrier ['terɪə(r)] *n (dog)* terrier *m*

terrific [təˈrɪfɪk] *adj Fam (excellent)* super *inv* ▪ **terrifically** *adv Fam (extremely)* terriblement; *(extremely well)* terriblement bien

terrify ['terɪfaɪ] *(pt & pp -ied) vt* terrifier; **to be terrified of sb/sth** avoir une peur bleue de qn/qch ▪ **terrifying** *adj* terrifiant

territory ['terɪtərɪ] *(pl -ies) n* territoire *m*

terror ['terə(r)] *n* terreur *f* ▪ **terrorism** *n* terrorisme *m* ▪ **terrorist** *n & adj* terroriste *(mf)* ▪ **terrorize** *vt* terroriser

test [test] **1** *n (trial)* essai *m*; *(of product)* test *m*; *Sch & Univ* interrogation *f*; *(by doctor)* examen *m*; *(of blood)* analyse *f*.

2 *adj* **t. drive** essai *m* sur route; **t. tube** éprouvette *f*; **t. tube baby** bébé-éprouvette *m*

3 *vt (try)* essayer; *(product, machine)* tester; *(pupil)* interroger; *(of doctor)* examiner; *(blood)* analyser; *Fig (try out)* mettre à l'épreuve; **to t. sb for AIDS** faire subir à qn un test de dépistage du SIDA

4 *vi* to **t. positive** *(for drugs)* être positif, -ive

testament ['testəmənt] *n (will)* testament *m*; *(tribute)* preuve *f*; *Rel* **the Old/New T.** l'Ancien/le Nouveau Testament

testicle ['testɪkəl] *n Anat* testicule *m*

testify ['testɪfaɪ] *(pt & pp -ied)* **1** *vt* to **t. that...** témoigner que... **2** *vi (in law)* témoigner (**against** contre); **to t. to sth** *(be proof of)* témoigner de qch ▪ **testimony** ['testɪmənɪ] *(pl -ies) n* témoignage *m*

tetanus ['tetənəs] *n Med* tétanos *m*

tether ['teðə(r)] *n* **at the end of one's t.** à bout

text [tekst] *n* texte *m*; **t. message** message *m* texte, mini-message *m* ▪ **textbook** *n* manuel *m*

textile ['tekstaɪl] *adj & n* textile *(m)*

texture ['tekstʃə(r)] *n (of fabric, cake)* texture *f; (of paper, wood)* grain *m*

Thames [temz] *n* **the (River) T.** la Tamise

than [ðən, *stressed* ðæn] *conj* que; **happier t. me** plus heureux que moi; **he has more/less t. you** il en a plus/moins que toi; **more t. six** plus de six

thank [θæŋk] *vt* remercier (**for sth** de qch; **for doing** d'avoir fait); **t. you** merci; **no, t. you** (non) merci; **t. God!, t. heavens!, t. goodness!** Dieu merci! ▪ **thanks** *npl* remerciements *mpl*; **(many) t.!** merci (beaucoup)!; **t. to** *(because of)* grâce à

thankful ['θæŋkfəl] *adj* reconnaissant (**for** de); **to be t. that…** être heureux, -euse que… *(+ subjunctive)* ▪ **thankless** *adj* ingrat

Thanksgiving [θæŋks'gɪvɪŋ] *n Am* **T. (Day)** = quatrième jeudi de novembre, commémorant la première action de grâce des colons anglais

THAT [ðət, *stressed* ðæt] **1** *conj (souvent omise)* que; **she said t. she would come** elle a dit qu'elle viendrait

2 *relative pron*

> On peut omettre le pronom relatif **that** sauf s'il est en position sujet.

(subject) qui; *(object)* que; *(with preposition)* lequel, laquelle, *pl* lesquel(le)s; **the boy t. left** le garçon qui est parti; **the book t. I read** le livre que j'ai lu; **the house t. she told me about** la maison dont elle m'a parlé; **the day/morning t. she arrived** le jour/matin où elle est arrivée

3 *(pl* **those***) demonstrative adj* ce, cet *(before vowel or mute h),* cette; *(opposed to 'this')* ce…-là *(f* cette…-là); **t. woman** cette femme(-là); **t. day** ce jour-là; **t. one** celui-là *m,* celle-là *f*

4 *(pl* **those***) demonstrative pron* cela,

Fam ça; **give me t.** donne-moi ça; **t.'s right** c'est exact; **who's t.?** qui est-ce?; **t.'s the house** voilà la maison; **what do you mean by t.?** qu'entends-tu par là?; **t. is (to say)…** c'est-à-dire…

5 *adv Fam (so)* si; **not t. good** pas si bon que ça; **it cost t. much** ça a coûté tant que ça

thatched [θætʃt] *adj (roof)* de chaume; **t. cottage** chaumière *f*

thaw [θɔ:] **1** *n* dégel *m* **2** *vt (snow, ice)* faire fondre; **to t. (out)** *(food)* se décongeler **3** *vi* dégeler; *(of snow, ice)* fondre; *(of food)* décongeler

the [ðə, *before vowel* ðɪ, *stressed* ði:] *definite article* le, l', la, *pl* les; **of t., from t.** du, de l', de la, *pl* des; **to t., at t.** au, à l', à la, *pl* aux; **Elizabeth t. Second** Élisabeth Deux

theatre ['θɪətə(r)] *(Am* **theater***) n (place, art)* théâtre *m; Br* **(operating) t.** *(in hospital)* salle *f* d'opération ▪ **theatrical** [θɪ'ætrɪkəl] *adj also Fig* théâtral

theft [θeft] *n* vol *m*

their [ðeə(r)] *possessive adj* leur, *pl* leurs ▪ **theirs** *possessive pron* le leur, la leur, *pl* les leurs; **this book is t.** ce livre est à eux *ou* est le leur; **a friend of t.** un ami à eux

them [ðəm, *stressed* ðem] *pron* les; *(after prep, 'than', 'it is')* eux *mpl,* elles *fpl;* **(to) t.** *(indirect)* leur; **I see t.** je les vois; **I gave it (to) t.** je le leur ai donné; **ten of t.** dix d'entre eux/elles; **all of t. came** tous sont venus, toutes sont venues; **I like all of t.** je les aime tous/toutes

theme [θi:m] *n* thème *m;* **t. tune** *(of TV, radio programme)* indicatif *m;* **t. park** parc *m* à thème

themselves [ðəm'selvz, *stressed* ðem-'selvz] *pron* eux-mêmes *mpl,* elles-mêmes *fpl; (reflexive)* se, s'; *(after prep)* eux *mpl,* elles *fpl;* **they cut t.** ils/elles se sont coupé(e)s

then [ðen] **1** *adv (at that time)* à cette époque-là, alors; *(just a moment ago)* à ce moment-là; *(next)* ensuite, puis;

(therefore) donc. alors; **from t. on** dès lors; **before t.** avant cela; **until t.** jusque-là, jusqu'alors **2** *adj* **the t. mayor** le maire d'alors

theory ['θɪərɪ] *(pl* -ies) *n* théorie *f*; **in t.** en théorie ▪ **theoretical** *adj* théorique

therapy ['θerəpɪ] *(pl* -ies) *n* thérapeutique *f* ▪ **therapeutic** [-'pjuːtɪk] *adj* thérapeutique

there [ðeə(r)] *adv* là; **(down/over) t.** là-bas; **on t.** là-dessus; **she'll be t.** elle y sera; **t. is, t. are** il y a; *(pointing)* voilà; **t. he is** le voilà; **that man t.** cet homme-là; **t. (you are)!** *(take this)* tenez! ▪ **thereabouts** *adv* dans les environs; *(in amount)* à peu près ▪ **thereby** *adv Formal* ainsi ▪ **therefore** *adv* donc

thermometer [θə'mɒmɪtə(r)] *n* thermomètre *m*

Thermos® ['θɜːməs] *(pl* -moses [-məsəz]) *n***T. (flask)** Thermos® *f*

thermostat ['θɜːməstæt] *n* thermostat *m*

these [ðiːz] *(sing* this) **1** *demonstrative adj* ces; *(opposed to 'those')* ces...-ci; **t. men** ces hommes(-ci); **t. ones** ceux-ci *mpl*, celles-ci *fpl* **2** *demonstrative pron* ceux-ci *mpl*, celles-ci *fpl*; **t. are my friends** ce sont mes amis

thesis ['θiːsɪs] *(pl* theses ['θiːsiːz]) *n* thèse *f*

they [ðeɪ] *pron* **(a)** *(subject)* ils *mpl*, elles *fpl*; *(stressed)* eux *mpl*, elles *fpl*; **t. are doctors** ce sont des médecins **(b)** *(people in general)* on ▪ **they'd** = they had, they would ▪ **they'll** = they will

thick [θɪk] **1** (-er, -est) *adj* épais *(f* épaisse); *Fam (stupid)* lourd **2** *adv (spread)* en couche épaisse ▪ **thickly** *adv (spread)* en couche épaisse

thicken ['θɪkən] **1** *vt* épaissir **2** *vi (of fog)* s'épaissir; *(of cream, sauce)* épaissir ▪ **thickness** *n* épaisseur *f*

thick-skinned [θɪk'skɪnd] *adj (person)* peu susceptible

thief [θiːf] *(pl* thieves) *n* voleur, -euse *mf* ▪ **thieving 1** *adj* voleur, -euse **2** *n* vol *m*

thigh [θaɪ] *n* cuisse *f*

thimble ['θɪmbəl] *n* dé *m* à coudre

thin [θɪn] **1** (thinner, thinnest) *adj (person, slice, paper)* mince; *(soup)* peu épais *(f* peu épaisse); *(crowd, hair)* clairsemé

 2 *adv (spread)* en couche mince; *(cut)* en tranches minces

 3 *(pt & pp* -nn-) *vt* **to t. (down)** *(paint)* diluer

 4 *vi* **to t. out** *(of crowd, mist)* s'éclaircir ▪ **thinly** *adv (spread)* en couche mince; *(cut)* en tranches minces

thing [θɪŋ] *n* chose *f*; **things** *(belongings, clothes)* affaires *fpl*; **poor little t.!** pauvre petit!; **how are things?**, *Fam* **how's things?** comment ça va?; **for one t.... and for another t....** d'abord... et ensuite...

think [θɪŋk] **1** *(pt & pp* thought) *vt* penser *(that* que); **I t. so** je pense *ou* crois que oui; **what do you t. of him?** que penses-tu de lui?; **to t. out** *(plan, method)* élaborer; *(reply)* réfléchir sérieusement à; **to t. sth over** réfléchir à qch; **to t. sth up** *(invent)* inventer qch

 2 *vi* penser *(about/of* à); **to t. (carefully)** réfléchir *(about/of* à); **to t. of doing sth** penser à faire qch; **to t. highly of sb** penser beaucoup de bien de qn

 3 *n Fam* **to have a t.** réfléchir **(about** à)

third [θɜːd] **1** *adj* troisième; **the T. World** le tiers-monde **2** *n* troisième *mf*; **a t.** *(fraction)* un tiers **3** *adv* **to come t.** *(in race)* se classer troisième ▪ **thirdly** *adv* troisièmement

third-party [θɜːd'pɑːtɪ] *adj* **t. insurance** assurance *f* au tiers

third-rate [θɜːd'reɪt] *adj* très inférieur

thirst [θɜːst] *n* soif *f* **(for** de) ▪ **thirsty** (-ier, -iest) *adj* **to be** *ou* **feel t.** avoir soif; **to make sb t.** donner soif à qn

thirteen [θɜː'tiːn] *adj & n* treize *(m)* ▪ **thirteenth** *adj & n* treizième *(mf)*

thirty ['θɜːtɪ] *adj & n* trente *(m)* ▪ **thirtieth** *adj & n* trentième *(mf)*

this [ðɪs] **1** *(pl* these) *demonstrative adj* ce, cet *(before vowel or mute h)*, cette; *(opposed to 'that')* ce...-ci; **t.**

man cet homme(-ci); **t. one** celui-ci *m*, celle-ci *f*

2 (*pl* **these**) *demonstrative pron (subject)* ce, ceci; *(object)* ceci; **I prefer t.** je préfère celui-ci; **who's t.?** qui est-ce?; **t. is Paul** c'est Paul; *(pointing)* voici Paul

3 *adv (so)* **t. high** *(pointing)* haut comme ceci; **t. far** *(until now)* jusqu'ici

thistle ['θɪsəl] *n* chardon *m*

thorn [θɔ:n] *n* épine *f*

thorough ['θʌrə] *adj (search, cleaning, preparation)* minutieux, -euse; *(knowledge, examination)* approfondi ▪ **thoroughly** *adv (completely)* tout à fait; *(carefully)* avec minutie; *(know, clean, wash)* à fond

thoroughfare ['θʌrəfeə(r)] *n Br* 'no t.' 'passage interdit'

those [ðəʊz] **1** (*sing* **that**) *demonstrative adj* ces; *(opposed to 'these')* ces... -là; **t. men** ces hommes(-là); **t. ones** ceux-là *mpl*, celles-là *fpl*

2 (*sing* **that**) *demonstrative pron* ceux-là *mpl*, celles-là *fpl*; **t. are my friends** ce sont mes amis

though [ðəʊ] **1** *conj* bien que (*+ subjunctive*); **(even) t.** même si; **as t.** comme si; **strange t. it may seem** si étrange que cela puisse paraître **2** *adv (however)* pourtant

thought [θɔ:t] **1** *pt & pp of* **think 2** *n* pensée *f*; **(careful) t.** réflexion *f*; **to have second thoughts** changer d'avis; *Br* **on second thoughts**, *Am* **on second t.** à la réflexion

thoughtful ['θɔ:tfəl] *adj (considerate, kind)* attentionné; *(pensive)* pensif, -ive

thoughtless ['θɔ:tləs] *adj* irréfléchi

thousand ['θaʊzənd] *adj & n* mille *(m) inv*; **a t. pages** mille pages; **two t. pages** deux mille pages; **thousands of** des milliers de

thrash [θræʃ] **1** *vt* **to t. sb** donner une correction à qn; *(defeat)* écraser qn **2** *vi* **to t. around** *or* **about** *(struggle)* se débattre ▪ **thrashing** *n (beating)* correction *f*

thread [θred] **1** *n (yarn) & Fig* fil *m*; *(of*

screw) filetage *m* **2** *vt (needle, beads)* enfiler

threat [θret] *n* menace *f* ▪ **threaten 1** *vt* menacer (**to do** de faire; **with sth** de qch) **2** *vi* menacer ▪ **threatening** *adj* menaçant

three [θri:] *adj & n* trois *(m)* ▪ **three-dimensional** *adj* à trois dimensions ▪ **threefold 1** *adj* triple **2** *adv* **to increase t.** tripler ▪ **three-piece** *adj Br* **t. suite** canapé *m* et deux fauteuils assortis ▪ **three-quarters 1** *n* **t. (of)** les trois quarts *mpl* (de) **2** *adv* **it's t. full** c'est aux trois quarts plein

threshold ['θreʃhəʊld] *n* seuil *m*

threw [θru:] *pt of* **throw**

thrifty ['θrɪftɪ] (**-ier, -iest**) *adj* économe

thrill [θrɪl] **1** *n* frisson *m*; **to get a t. out of doing sth** prendre plaisir à faire qch **2** *vt (delight)* réjouir; *(excite)* faire frissonner ▪ **thrilled** *adj* ravi (**with sth** de qch; **to do** de faire) ▪ **thriller** *n* thriller *m* ▪ **thrilling** *adj* passionnant

thrive [θraɪv] *vi (of business, person, plant)* prospérer; **to t. on sth** avoir besoin de qch pour s'épanouir ▪ **thriving** *adj (business)* prospère

throat [θrəʊt] *n* gorge *f*

throb [θrɒb] *(pt & pp* **-bb-)** *vi (of heart)* palpiter; **my head is throbbing** j'ai une douleur lancinante dans la tête

throes [θrəʊz] *npl* **in the t. of** au milieu de; *(illness, crisis)* en proie à; **in the t. of doing sth** en train de faire qch

throne [θrəʊn] *n* trône *m*

throttle ['θrɒtəl] **1** *n (accelerator)* manette *f* des gaz **2** *vt (strangle)* étrangler

through [θru:] **1** *prep (place)* à travers; *(by means of)* par; *(because of)* à cause de; **t. the window/door** par la fenêtre/porte; **t. ignorance** par ignorance; *Am* **Tuesday t. Saturday** de mardi à samedi

2 *adv* à travers; **to go t.** *(of bullet, nail)* traverser; **to let sb t.** laisser passer qn; **to be t. with sb/sth** *(finished)* en avoir fini avec qn/qch; **t. to** *or* **till** jusqu'à; **I'll put you t. (to him)** *(on telephone)* je vous le passe

3 *adj (train, ticket)* direct; *Br* **'no t. road'** *(no exit)* 'voie sans issue'

throughout [θruː'aʊt] **1** *prep* **t. the neighbourhood** dans tout le quartier; **t. the day** pendant toute la journée **2** *adv (everywhere)* partout; *(all the time)* tout le temps

throw [θrəʊ] **1** *n (in sport)* lancer *m*; *(of dice)* coup *m* **2** *(pt* **threw**, *pp* **thrown**) *vt* jeter (**to/at** à); *(javelin, discus)* lancer; *(image, shadow)* projeter; *(of horse)* désarçonner; *(party)* donner; *Fam (baffle)* déconcerter

▸ **throw away** *vt sep (discard)* jeter; *Fig (life, chance)* gâcher

▸ **throw back** *vt sep (ball)* renvoyer (**to** à); *(one's head)* rejeter en arrière

▸ **throw in** *vt sep Fam (include as extra)* donner en prime

▸ **throw out** *vt sep (unwanted object)* jeter; *(suggestion)* repousser; *(expel)* mettre à la porte

▸ **throw up** *vi Fam (vomit)* vomir

thrown [θrəʊn] *pp of* **throw**

thrush [θrʌʃ] *n (bird)* grive *f*

thrust [θrʌst] **1** *n (movement)* mouvement *m* en avant; *(of argument)* idée *f* principale **2** *(pt & pp* **thrust**) *vt* **to t. sth into sth** enfoncer qch dans qch; **to t. sb/sth aside** écarter qn/qch

thud [θʌd] *n* bruit *m* sourd

thug [θʌg] *n* voyou *m* (*pl* -ous)

thumb [θʌm] **1** *n* pouce *m* **2** *vt Fam* **to t. a lift** *or* **a ride** faire du stop **3** *vt* **to t. through a book** feuilleter un livre

thump [θʌmp] **1** *n (blow)* coup *m*; *(noise)* bruit *m* sourd **2** *vt (hit)* frapper; **to t. one's head** se cogner la tête (**on** contre) **3** *vi* frapper, cogner (**on** sur); *(of heart)* battre la chamade

thunder ['θʌndə(r)] **1** *n* tonnerre *m* **2** *vi* tonner; **to t. past** *(of train, truck)* passer dans un bruit de tonnerre ▪ **thunderstorm** *n* orage *m*

Thursday ['θɜːzdeɪ] *n* jeudi *m*

thus [ðʌs] *adv* ainsi

thyme [taɪm] *n* thym *m*

tic [tɪk] *n* tic *m*

tick [tɪk] **1** *n (of clock)* tic-tac *m inv*; *(mark)* ≃ croix *f*; *Fam (moment)* instant

m 2 *vt* **to t. sth (off)** *(on list)* cocher qch **3** *vi* faire tic-tac; *Br* **to t. over** *(of engine, factory)* tourner au ralenti ▪ **ticking** *n (of clock)* tic-tac *m inv*

tickle ['tɪkəl] *vt* chatouiller; *Fig (amuse)* amuser ▪ **ticklish** *adj (person)* chatouilleux, -euse

ticket ['tɪkɪt] *n* billet *m*; *(for bus, metro)* ticket *m*; *Fam (for parking, speeding)* contravention *f*; **(price) t.** étiquette *f*; **t. collector** contrôleur, -euse *mf*; **t. office** guichet *m*

tic-tac-toe [tɪktæk'təʊ] *n Am* morpion *m (jeu)*

tidbit ['tɪdbɪt] *n Am (food)* bon morceau *m*

tide [taɪd] **1** *n* marée *f* **2** *vt* **to t. sb over** dépanner qn

tidy ['taɪdɪ] **1** (**-ier, -iest**) *adj (place, toys)* bien rangé; *(clothes, hair)* soigné; *(person) (methodical)* ordonné; *(in appearance)* soigné **2** *vt* **to t. sth (up** or **away)** ranger qch; **to t. sth out** mettre de l'ordre dans qch; **to t. oneself up** s'arranger **3** *vi* **to t. up** ranger ▪ **tidily** *adv (put away)* soigneusement, avec soin

tie [taɪ] **1** *n (garment)* cravate *f*; *(link)* lien *m*; *(draw)* égalité *f*; *(drawn match)* match *m* nul **2** *vt (fasten)* attacher (**to** à); *(knot)* faire (**in** à); *(shoe)* lacer **3** *vi (draw)* être à égalité; *(at end of match)* faire match nul; *(in race)* être ex aequo

▸ **tie down** *vt sep* attacher

▸ **tie in** *vi (of facts)* concorder

▸ **tie up** *vt sep (animal)* attacher; *(parcel)* ficeler; *(money)* immobiliser; *Fig* **to be tied up** *(busy)* être occupé

tier [tɪə(r)] *n (of seats)* gradin *m*; *(of cake)* étage *m*

tiger ['taɪgə(r)] *n* tigre *m*

tight [taɪt] **1** (**-er, -est**) *adj (clothes, knot, race, bend)* serré; *(control)* strict; *Fam (mean)* radin **2** *adv (hold, shut)* bien; *(squeeze)* fort; **to sit t.** ne pas bouger ▪ **tight-fitting** *adj (garment)* ajusté ▪ **tightly** *adv (hold)* bien; *(squeeze)* fort ▪ **tightrope** *n* corde *f* raide

tighten ['taɪtən] *vt* **to t. (up)** *(bolt)*

serrer; *(rope)* tendre; *Fig (security)* renforcer

tights [taɪts] *npl Br (garment)* collant *m*

tile [taɪl] **1** *n (on roof)* tuile *f; (on wall, floor)* carreau **2** *vt (wall, floor)* carreler ▪ **tiled** *adj (roof)* de tuiles; *(wall, floor)* carrelé

till¹ [tɪl] *prep & conj* = **until**

till² [tɪl] *n Br (for money)* caisse *f* enregistreuse

tilt [tɪlt] **1** *n* inclinaison *f* **2** *vti* pencher

timber ['tɪmbə(r)] *n Br (wood)* bois *m* (de construction)

time [taɪm] **1** *n* temps *m; (period, moment)* moment *m; (age)* époque *f; (on clock)* heure *f; (occasion)* fois *f; Mus* mesure *f;* **in t., with t.** avec le temps; **it's t. to do sth** il est temps de faire qch; **some of the t.** *(not always)* une partie du temps; **most of the t.** la plupart du temps; **all (of) the t.** tout le temps; **in a year's t.** dans un an; **a long t.** longtemps; **a short t.** peu de temps; **to have a good** *or* **a nice t.** s'amuser (bien); **to have t. off** avoir du temps libre; **in no t. (at all)** en un rien de temps; **(just) in t.** *(arrive)* à temps **(for sth** pour qch; **to do** pour faire); **from t. to t.** de temps en temps; **what t. is it?** quelle heure est-il?; **the right** *or* **exact t.** l'heure *f* exacte; **on t.** à l'heure; **at the same t.** en même temps **(as** que); *(simultaneously)* à la fois; **for the t. being** pour le moment; **at the** *or* **that t.** à ce moment-là; **at times** parfois; **(the) next t. you come** la prochaine fois que tu viendras; **(the) last t.** la dernière fois; **one at a t.** un à un; **ten times ten** dix fois dix; **t. difference** décalage *m* horaire; **t. limit** délai *m;* **t. zone** fuseau *m* horaire

2 *vt (sportsman, worker)* chronométrer; *(activity, programme)* minuter; *(choose the time of)* choisir le moment de; *(plan)* prévoir ▪ **time-consuming** *adj* qui prend du temps

timely ['taɪmlɪ] *adj* à propos

timer ['taɪmə(r)] *n (device)* minuteur *m; (sand-filled)* sablier *m; (built into appliance)* programmateur *m; (plugged into socket)* prise *f* programmable

timetable ['taɪmteɪbəl] *n* horaire *m; (in school)* emploi *m* du temps

timid ['tɪmɪd] *adj* timide

timing ['taɪmɪŋ] *n (of election)* moment *m* choisi; *(of musician)* sens *m* du rythme

tin [tɪn] *n (metal)* étain *m; Br (can)* boîte *f;* **cake t.** moule *m* à gâteaux; **t. opener** ouvre-boîtes *m inv* ▪ **tinfoil** *n* papier *m* aluminium

tinge [tɪndʒ] *n* pointe *f* ▪ **tinged** *adj* **t. with sth** teinté de qch

tingle ['tɪŋgəl] *vi* picoter

tinker ['tɪŋkə(r)] *vi* **to t. (about** *or* **around) with sth** bricoler qch

tinkle ['tɪŋkəl] *vi* tinter

tinned [tɪnd] *adj Br* **t. pears/salmon** poires *fpl*/saumon *m* en boîte; **t. food** conserves *fpl*

tinsel ['tɪnsəl] *n* guirlandes *fpl* de Noël

tint [tɪnt] *n* teinte *f; (for hair)* rinçage *m* ▪ **tinted** *adj (paper, glass)* teinté

tiny ['taɪnɪ] (**-ier, -iest**) *adj* minuscule

tip¹ [tɪp] *n (end)* bout *m; (pointed)* pointe *f*

tip² [tɪp] **1** *n Br (rubbish dump)* décharge *f* **2** *(pt & pp* **-pp-)** *vt (pour)* déverser; **to t. sth up** *or* **over** renverser qch; **to t. sth out** *(liquid, load)* déverser qch **(into** dans) **3** *vi* **to t. (up** *or* **over)** *(tilt)* se renverser; *(overturn)* basculer

tip³ [tɪp] **1** *n (money)* pourboire *m; (advice)* conseil *m; (information)* tuyau *m* **2** *(pt & pp* **-pp-)** *vt (waiter)* donner un pourboire à; **to t. off** *(police)* prévenir

tipsy ['tɪpsɪ] (**-ier, -iest**) *adj (drunk)* éméché, gai

tiptoe ['tɪptəʊ] **1** *n* **on t.** sur la pointe des pieds **2** *vi* marcher sur la pointe des pieds; **to t. into/out of a room** entrer dans une pièce/sortir d'une pièce sur la pointe des pieds

tire¹ ['taɪə(r)] **1** *vt* fatiguer; **to t. sb out** épuiser qn **2** *vi* se fatiguer ▪ **tired** *adj* fatigué; **to be t. of sth/doing sth** en avoir assez de qch/de faire qch ▪ **tiredness** *n* fatigue *f* ▪ **tireless** *adj* infatigable ▪ **tiresome** *adj* ennuyeux, -euse ▪ **tiring** *adj* fatigant

tire² ['taɪə(r)] n Am pneu m (pl pneus)

tissue ['tɪʃuː] n (handkerchief) mouchoir m en papier; Biol tissu m; **t. paper** papier m de soie

titbit ['tɪtbɪt] n Br (food) bon morceau m

titillate ['tɪtɪleɪt] vt exciter

title ['taɪtəl] **1** n (name, claim, in sport) titre m; **t. role** (in film, play) rôle-titre m **2** vt intituler

titter ['tɪtə(r)] vi rire bêtement

TO [tə, stressed tuː] **1** prep (a) (towards) à; (until) jusqu'à; **give it to him/her** donne-le-lui; **to go to town** aller en ville; **to go to France/Portugal** aller en France/au Portugal; **to go to the butcher's** aller chez le boucher; **the road to London** la route de Londres; **the train to Paris** le train pour Paris; **kind/cruel to sb** gentil/cruel envers qn; **to my surprise** à ma grande surprise; **it's ten (minutes) to one** il est une heure moins dix; **ten to one** (proportion) dix contre un; **one person to a room** une personne par chambre (b) (with infinitive) **to say/jump** dire/sauter; **(in order) to do sth** pour faire qch; **she tried to** elle a essayé (c) (with adjective) **I'd be happy to do it** je serais heureux de le faire; **it's easy to do** c'est facile à faire **2** adv **to push the door to** fermer la porte; **to go** or **walk to and fro** aller et venir

toad [təʊd] n crapaud m

toadstool ['təʊdstuːl] n champignon m vénéneux

toast¹ [təʊst] **1** n (bread) pain m grillé **2** vt (bread) faire griller ∎ **toaster** n grille-pain m inv

toast² [təʊst] **1** n (drink) toast m **2** vt (person) porter un toast à; (success, event) arroser

tobacco [tə'bækəʊ] (pl -os) n tabac m; Am **t. store** (bureau m de) tabac ∎ **tobacconist** [-kənɪst] n buraliste mf; Br **t.'s (shop)** (bureau m de) tabac m

toboggan [tə'bɒgən] n luge f

today [tə'deɪ] adv aujourd'hui

toddler ['tɒdlə(r)] n enfant mf (en bas âge)

toe [təʊ] **1** n orteil m **2** vt **to t. the line** bien se tenir

toffee ['tɒfɪ] n Br caramel m (dur); **t. apple** pomme f d'amour

together [tə'geðə(r)] adv ensemble; (at the same time) en même temps

toil [tɔɪl] **1** n labeur m **2** vi travailler dur

toilet ['tɔɪlɪt] n Br (room) toilettes fpl; (bowl, seat) cuvette f des toilettes; Br **to go to the t.** aller aux toilettes; **t. paper** papier m hygiénique; **t. roll** rouleau m de papier hygiénique; (paper) papier m hygiénique ∎ **toiletries** npl articles mpl de toilette

token ['təʊkən] **1** n (for vending machine) jeton m (symbol) signe m; Br **book t.** chèque-livre m **2** adj symbolique

told [təʊld] **1** pt & pp of **tell 2** adv **all t.** (taken together) en tout

tolerable ['tɒlərəbəl] adj (bearable) tolérable; (fairly good) acceptable

tolerant ['tɒlərənt] adj tolérant (of à l'égard de) ∎ **tolerance** n tolérance f

tolerate ['tɒləreɪt] vt tolérer

toll [təʊl] **1** n (a) (fee) péage m; **t. road/bridge** route f/pont m à péage (b) **the death t.** le nombre de morts; Fig **to take its t.** faire des dégâts **2** vi (of bell) sonner ∎ **toll-free** Am **1** adj **t. number** ≃ numéro m vert **2** adv (call) gratuitement

tomato [Br tə'mɑːtəʊ, Am tə'meɪtəʊ] (pl -oes) n tomate f; **t. sauce** sauce f tomate

tomb [tuːm] n tombeau m ∎ **tombstone** n pierre f tombale

tomorrow [tə'mɒrəʊ] adv & n demain (m); **t. morning/evening** demain matin/soir; **the day after t.** après-demain

ton [tʌn] n tonne f; Fam **tons of** (lots of) des tonnes de

tone [təʊn] **1** n ton m; (of telephone, radio) tonalité f; (of answering machine) signal m sonore; Br **the engaged t.** (on telephone) la sonnerie occupé **2** vt **to t. sth down** atténuer qch; **to t. up** (muscles, skin) tonifier

tongs [tɒŋz] npl pinces fpl; **sugar t.**

pince *f* à sucre; **curling t.** fer *m* à friser

tongue [tʌŋ] *n (in mouth, language)* langue *f*

tonic ['tɒnɪk] *n (medicine)* fortifiant *m*; **t. (water)** Schweppes® *m*; **gin and t.** gin-tonic *m*

tonight [tə'naɪt] *adv & n (this evening)* ce soir *(m)*; *(during the night)* cette nuit *(f)*

tonne [tʌn] *n (metric)* tonne *f* ▪

tonsil ['tɒnsəl] *n* amygdale *f* ▪ **tonsillitis** [-'laɪtɪs] *n* **to have t.** avoir une angine

too [tu:] *adv* **(a)** *(excessively)* trop; **t. tired to play** trop fatigué pour jouer; **t. much, t. many** trop; **t. much salt** trop de sel; **t. many people** trop de gens; **one t. many** un de trop **(b)** *(also)* aussi; *(moreover)* en plus

took [tʊk] *pt of* **take**

tool [tu:l] *n* outil *m*; **t. bag, t. kit** trousse *f* à outils

tooth [tu:θ] *(pl* **teeth)** *n* dent *f*; **t. decay** carie *f* dentaire ▪ **toothache** *n* mal *m* de dents; **to have t.** avoir mal aux dents ▪ **toothbrush** *n* brosse *f* à dents ▪ **toothpaste** *n* dentifrice *m*

top¹ [tɒp] **1** *n (of mountain, tower, tree)* sommet *m*; *(of wall, ladder, page)* haut *m*; *(of table, box, surface)* dessus *m*; *(of list)* tête *f*; *(of bottle, tube)* bouchon *m*; *(crown cap)* capsule *f*; *(of pen)* capuchon *m*; *(garment)* haut *m*; **(at the) t. of the class** le premier/la première de la classe; **on t.** dessus; *(in bus)* en haut; **on t. of** sur; *Fig (in addition to)* en plus de; **from t. to bottom** de fond en comble; *Fam* **over the t.** *(excessive)* exagéré

2 *adj (drawer, shelf)* du haut; *(step, layer)* dernier, -ère; *(upper)* supérieur; *(in rank, exam)* premier, -ère; *(chief)* principal; *(best)* meilleur; **on the t. floor** au dernier étage; **at t. speed** à toute vitesse; **t. hat** haut-de-forme *m* ▪ **top-secret** *adj* top secret *inv* ▪ **topsy-turvy** *adj & adv* sens dessus dessous [sɑ̃dsydsy]

top² [tɒp] *(pt & pp* **-pp-)** *vt (exceed)* dépasser; *Br* **to t. up** *(glass)* remplir (de

nouveau); **topped with cream** nappé de crème ▪ **topping** *n (of pizza)* garniture *f*

top³ [tɒp] *n* **(spinning) t.** toupie *f*

topic ['tɒpɪk] *n* sujet *m* ▪ **topical** *adj* d'actualité

topple ['tɒpəl] *vi* **to t. (over)** tomber

torch [tɔ:tʃ] *n Br (electric)* lampe *f* de poche; *(flame)* torche *f*

tore [tɔ:(r)] *pt of* **tear¹**

torment 1 ['tɔ:ment] *n* supplice *m* **2** [tɔ:'ment] *vt* tourmenter

torn [tɔ:n] *pp of* **tear¹**

tornado [tɔ:'neɪdəʊ] *(pl* **-oes)** *n* tornade *f*

torpedo [tɔ:'pi:dəʊ] **1** *(pl* **-oes)** *n* torpille *f* **2** *vt* torpiller

torrent ['tɒrənt] *n* torrent *m* ▪ **torrential** [tɒ'renʃəl] *adj* **t. rain** pluie *f* torrentielle

tortoise ['tɔ:təs] *n* tortue *f*

tortuous ['tɔ:tʃʊəs] *adj* tortueux, -euse

torture ['tɔ:tʃə(r)] **1** *n* torture *f*; *Fig* **it's (sheer) t.!** quel supplice! **2** *vt* torturer

Tory ['tɔ:rɪ] *Pol* **1** *n* tory *m* **2** *adj* tory *inv*

toss [tɒs] **1** *vt (throw)* lancer **(to** à); *(pancake)* faire sauter; **to t. sb (about)** *(of boat, vehicle)* ballotter qn; **to t. a coin** jouer à pile ou face **2** *vi* **to t. (about), to t. and turn** *(in bed)* se tourner et se retourner; **let's t. up, let's t. (up) for it** jouons-le à pile ou face

tot [tɒt] **1** *n* **(tiny) t.** tout-petit *m* **2** *(pt & pp* **-tt-)** *vt Fam* **to t. up** *(total)* additionner

total ['təʊtəl] **1** *adj* total; **the t. sales** le total des ventes **2** *n* total *m*; **in t.** au total **3** *(Br* **-ll-,** *Am* **-l-)** *vt (of sum)* s'élever à; **to t. (up)** *(find the total of)* totaliser; **that totals $9** ça fait 9 dollars en tout ▪ **totally** *adv* totalement

totter ['tɒtə(r)] *vi* chanceler

touch [tʌtʃ] **1** *n (contact)* contact *m*; *(sense)* toucher *m*; *(of painter)* touche *f*; **a t. of** *(small amount)* une pointe de; **to have a t. of flu** être un peu grippé; **to be/get in t. with sb** être/se mettre en contact avec qn

2 *vt* toucher; *(interfere with, eat)* toucher à

3 *vi (of lines, hands, ends)* se toucher; **don't t.!** ne touche pas! ■ **touchdown** *n (of aircraft)* atterrissage *m; (in American football)* essai *m* ■ **touched** *adj (emotionally)* touché (**by** de) ■ **touching** *adj (moving)* touchant ■ **touchline** *n* ligne *f* de touche

▸**touch down** *vi (of plane)* atterrir
▸**touch on** *vt insep* aborder
▸**touch up** *vt sep (photo)* retoucher

touchy ['tʌtʃɪ] (**-ier, -iest**) *adj (sensitive)* susceptible (**about** à propos de)

tough [tʌf] (**-er, -est**) *adj (strict, hard)* dur; *(sturdy)* solide ■ **toughen** *vt (body, person)* endurcir

toupee ['tu:peɪ] *n* postiche *m*

tour [tʊə(r)] **1** *n (journey)* voyage *m; (visit)* visite *f; (by artiste, team)* tournée *f; (on bicycle, on foot)* randonnée *f;* **to go on t.** *(of artiste, team)* être en tournée; **(package) t.** voyage *m* organisé; **t. guide** guide *mf;* **t. operator** voyagiste *m* **2** *vt* visiter; *(of artiste, team)* être en tournée en/dans

tourism ['tʊərɪzəm] *n* tourisme *m* ■ **tourist 1** *n* touriste *mf* **2** *adj (region)* touristique; **t. office** syndicat *m* d'initiative

tournament ['tʊənəmənt] *n (in sport) & Hist* tournoi *m*

tout [taʊt] **1** *n* racoleur, -euse *mf* **2** *vi* **to t. for trade** racoler des clients

tow [təʊ] *vt* remorquer; **to t. a car away** *(of police)* mettre une voiture à la fourrière

toward(s) [tə'wɔːd(z)] *prep* vers; *(of feelings)* envers; **cruel t. sb** cruel envers qn

towel ['taʊəl] *n* serviette *f* (de toilette); **(kitchen) t.** *(paper)* essuie-tout *m inv*

tower ['taʊə(r)] **1** *n* tour *f; Br* **t. block** tour **2** *vi* **to t. over sb/sth** dominer qn/qch

town [taʊn] *n* ville *f;* **to go into t.** aller en ville; **t. centre** centre-ville *m; Br* **t. council** conseil *m* municipal; *Br* **t. hall** mairie *f; Br* **t. planning** urbanisme *m*

toxic ['tɒksɪk] *adj* toxique

toy [tɔɪ] **1** *n* jouet *m;* **t. shop** magasin *m* de jouets **2** *adj (gun)* d'enfant; *(car, train)* miniature **3** *vi* **to t. with an idea** caresser une idée

trace [treɪs] **1** *n* trace *f;* **without t.** sans laisser de traces **2** *vt (diagram, picture)* tracer; *(person)* retrouver la trace de; **to t. sth back to...** faire remonter qch à... ■ **tracing** *n (drawing)* calque *m;* **t. paper** papier-calque *m*

track [træk] **1** *n (mark)* trace *f, (trail)* piste *f, (path)* chemin *m,* piste *f; (for trains)* voie *f; (of record, CD, tape)* morceau *m; Am (racetrack)* champ *m* de courses; **to keep t. of sth** surveiller qch; **to lose t. of** *(friend)* perdre de vue; **to be on the right t.** être sur la bonne voie; **t. event** *(in athletics)* épreuve *f* sur piste; *Fig* **t. record** passé *m*

2 *vt* **to t. (down)** *(find)* retrouver ■ **tracksuit** *n* survêtement *m*

tractor ['træktə(r)] *n* tracteur *m*

trade [treɪd] **1** *n* commerce *m; (job)* métier *m; (exchange)* échange *m*

2 *adj (fair, balance, route)* commercial; *(price)* de (demi-)gros; *(secret)* de fabrication; *(barrier)* douanier, -ère; *Br* **t. union** syndicat *m*

3 *vt (exchange)* échanger (**for** contre); **to t. sth in** *(old article)* faire reprendre qch

4 *vi* faire du commerce (**with** avec); **to t. in** *(sugar)* faire le commerce de ■ **trademark** *n* marque *f* de fabrique ■ **trader** *n Br (shopkeeper)* commerçant, -e *mf; (on Stock Exchange)* opérateur, -trice *mf; Br* **street t.** vendeur, -euse *mf* de rue ■ **tradesman** *(pl -men)* *n Br* commerçant *m*

trading ['treɪdɪŋ] **1** *n* commerce *m* **2** *adj (port, debts, activity)* commercial

tradition [trə'dɪʃən] *n* tradition *f* ■ **traditional** *adj* traditionnel, -elle

traffic ['træfɪk] **1** *n* (a) *(on road)* circulation *f; (air, sea, rail)* trafic *m; Am* **t. circle** rond-point *m;* **t. island** refuge *m* (pour piétons); **t. jam** embouteillage *m;* **t. lights** feux *mpl* (de signalisation); **t. warden** contractuel, -elle *mf* (b) *Pej (trade)* trafic *m* (**in** de) **2** *(pt & pp -ck-)*

vi trafiquer (**in** de) ■ **trafficker** *n Pej* trafiquant, -e *mf*

tragedy ['trædʒədɪ] (*pl* -ies) *n* tragédie *f* ■ **tragic** *adj* tragique

trail [treɪl] **1** *n (of smoke, blood, powder)* traînée *f*; *(path)* piste *f*, sentier *m*

2 *vt (drag)* traîner; *(follow)* suivre

3 *vi (drag)* traîner; *(of plant)* ramper; *(move slowly)* se traîner; **to be trailing (behind)** *(in sporting contest)* être mené ■ **trailer** *n* (**a**) *(for car)* remorque *f*; *Am (caravan)* caravane *f*; *Am (camper)* camping-car *m* (**b**) *(advertisement for film)* bande-annonce *f*

train [treɪn] **1** *n* (**a**) *(engine, transport)* train *m*; *(underground)* rame *f*; **t. set** *(toy)* petit train *m* (**b**) *(procession)* file *f*; *(of events)* suite *f*; *(of dress)* traîne *f*; **my t. of thought** le fil de ma pensée

2 *vt (person)* former (**to do** à faire); *(sportsman)* entraîner; *(animal)* dresser (**to do** à faire); **to t. oneself to do sth** s'entraîner à faire qch; **to t. sth on sb/sth** *(aim)* braquer qch sur qn/qch

3 *vi (of sportsman)* s'entraîner; **to t. as a nurse** faire une formation d'infirmière ■ **trained** *adj (skilled)* qualifié; *(nurse, engineer)* diplômé ■ **training** *n* formation *f*; *(in sport)* entraînement *m*; *(of animal)* dressage *m*; **to be in t.** *(of sportsman)* s'entraîner

trainee [treɪ'niː] *n & adj* stagiaire *(mf)*

trainer ['treɪnə(r)] *n (of athlete, racehorse)* entraîneur *m*; *(of animals)* dresseur *m*; *Br* **trainers** *(shoes)* chaussures *fpl* de sport

traipse [treɪps] *vi Fam* **to t. around** *(tiredly)* traîner les pieds; *(wander)* se balader

trait [treɪt] *n* trait *m* (de caractère)

traitor ['treɪtə(r)] *n* traître *m*, traîtresse *f*

tram [træm] *n* tram(way) *m*

tramp [træmp] **1** *n Br (vagrant)* clochard, -e *mf* **2** *vi* marcher d'un pas lourd

trample ['træmpəl] *vti* **to t. sth (underfoot), to t. on sth** piétiner qch

trampoline ['træmpə'liːn] *n* trampoline *m*

trance [trɑːns] *n* **to be in a t.** être en transe

tranquillizer ['træŋkwɪlaɪzə(r)] (*Am* **tranquilizer**) *n* tranquillisant *m*

transaction [træn'zækʃən] *n* opération *f*, transaction *f*

transatlantic [trænzət'læntɪk] *adj* transatlantique

transcend [træn'send] *vt* transcender

transfer 1 ['trænsfɜː(r)] *n* transfert *m* (**to** à); *(of political power)* passation *f*; *Br (picture, design)* décalcomanie *f*; **credit t.** virement *m* bancaire

2 [træns'fɜː(r)] (*pt & pp* -**rr**-) *vt* transférer (**to** à); *(political power)* faire passer (**to** à)

3 [træns'fɜː(r)] *vi* être transféré (**to** à)

transform [træns'fɔːm] *vt* transformer (**into** en) ■ **transformation** [-fə-'meɪʃən] *n* transformation *f* ■ **transformer** *n El* transformateur *m*

transfusion [træns'fjuːʒən] *n* (**blood**) **t.** transfusion *f* (sanguine)

transit ['trænzɪt] *n* **in t.** en transit

transition [træn'zɪʃən] *n* transition *f*

transitional [træn'zɪʃənəl] *adj* de transition

transitive ['trænsɪtɪv] *adj (verb)* transitif

translate [trænz'leɪt] *vt* traduire (**from** de; **into** en) ■ **translation** *n* traduction *f* ■ **translator** *n* traducteur, -trice *mf*

transmit [trænz'mɪt] **1** (*pt & pp* -**tt**-) *vt* transmettre **2** *vti (broadcast)* émettre ■ **transmission** *n* transmission *f*; *(broadcast)* émission *f* ■ **transmitter** *n* *(for radio, TV)* émetteur *m*

transparent [træn'spærənt] *adj* transparent

transpire [træn'spaɪə(r)] *vi Fam (happen)* arriver; **it transpired that...** il s'est avéré que...

transplant 1 ['trænsplɑːnt] *n (surgical)* greffe *f*, transplantation *f* **2** [træns'plɑːnt] *vt* transplanter

transport 1 ['trænspɔːt] *n* transport *m* (**of** de); *Br* **t. café** routier *m (restaurant)* **2** [træn'spɔːt] *vt* transporter

transpose [træn'spəʊz] *vt* transposer

transvestite [trænz'vestaɪt] *n* travesti *m*

trap [træp] **1** *n* piège *m* **2** (*pt & pp* -**pp**-) *vt* prendre au piège; **to t. one's finger** se coincer le doigt (**in** dans) ▪ **trapdoor** *n* trappe *f*

trappings ['træpɪŋz] *npl* signes *mpl* extérieurs

trash [træʃ] *n* (*nonsense*) bêtises *fpl*; (*junk*) bric-à-brac *m inv*; *Am* (*waste*) ordures *fpl*; (*riffraff*) racaille *f*; *Am* **t. can** poubelle *f* ▪ **trashy** (**-ier, -iest**) *adj Fam* à la noix

trauma ['trɔːmə] *n* traumatisme *m* ▪ **traumatic** [-'mætɪk] *adj* traumatisant ▪ **traumatize** *vt* traumatiser

travel ['trævəl] **1** *n* voyage *m*; **t. agent** agent *m* de voyages; **t. insurance** assurance *f* voyage; **t. sickness** (*in car*) mal *m* de la route; (*in aircraft*) mal *m* de l'air
2 (*Br* -**ll**-, *Am* -**l**-) *vt* (*country, distance, road*) parcourir
3 *vi* (*of person*) voyager; (*of vehicle, light, sound*) se déplacer ▪ **travelling** (*Am* **traveling**) **1** *n* voyages *mpl* **2** *adj* (*bag, clothes*) de voyage; (*expenses*) de déplacement; (*musician, circus*) ambulant

traveller ['trævələ(r)] (*Am* **traveler**) *n* voyageur, -euse *mf*; **t.'s cheque** chèque *m* de voyage

travesty ['trævəstɪ] (*pl* -**ies**) *n* parodie *f*; **a t. of justice** un simulacre de justice

tray [treɪ] *n* plateau *m*; (*in office*) corbeille *f*; **baking t.** plaque *f* de four

treacherous ['tretʃərəs] *adj* (*road, conditions*) très dangereux, -euse; (*person, action*) traître ▪ **treachery** (*pl* -**ies**) *n* traîtrise *f*

treacle ['triːkəl] *n Br* mélasse *f*

tread [tred] **1** *n* (*footstep*) pas *m*; (*step of stairs*) marche *f*; (*of tyre*) chape *f* **2** (*pt* **trod**, *pp* **trodden**) *vt* **to t. sth into a carpet** étaler qch sur un tapis (avec ses chaussures) **3** *vi* (*walk*) marcher (**on** sur)

treason ['triːzən] *n* trahison *f*

treasure ['treʒə(r)] **1** *n* trésor *m*; **t. hunt** chasse *f* au trésor **2** *vt* (*value*) te-nir beaucoup à ▪ **treasurer** *n* trésorier, -ère *mf*

treat [triːt] **1** *n* (*pleasure*) plaisir *m*; (*gift*) cadeau *m*; **it's my t.** c'est moi qui régale **2** *vt* (*person, illness, product*) traiter; **to t. sb to sth** offrir qch à qn

treatment ['triːtmənt] *n* traitement *m*

treaty ['triːtɪ] (*pl* -**ies**) *n* (*international*) traité *m*

treble ['trebəl] **1** *adj* triple **2** *n* le triple; **it's t. the price** c'est le triple du prix **3** *vti* tripler

tree [triː] *n* arbre *m*; **t. trunk** tronc *m* d'arbre

trek [trek] **1** *n* (*long walk*) randonnée *f* **2** (*pt & pp* -**kk**-) *vi* faire de la randonnée

tremble ['trembəl] *vi* trembler (**with** de)

tremendous [trə'mendəs] *adj* (*huge*) énorme; (*dreadful*) terrible; (*wonderful*) formidable

trench [trentʃ] *n* tranchée *f*

trend [trend] *n* tendance *f* (**towards** à); (*fashion*) mode *f* ▪ **trendy** (**-ier, -iest**) *adj Br Fam* branché

trespass ['trespəs] *vi* = s'introduire illégalement dans une propriété privée; **'no trespassing'** 'entrée interdite'

trial ['traɪəl] **1** *n* (*in law*) procès *m*; (*test*) essai *m*; (*ordeal*) épreuve *f*; **to go** *or* **be on t., to stand t.** passer en jugement; **by t. and error** par tâtonnements **2** *adj* (*period, flight, offer*) d'essai

triangle ['traɪæŋgəl] *n* triangle *m* ▪ **triangular** [-'æŋgjʊlə(r)] *adj* triangulaire

tribe [traɪb] *n* tribu *f*

tribunal [traɪ'bjuːnəl] *n* tribunal *m*

tribute ['trɪbjuːt] *n* hommage *m*; **to pay t. to** rendre hommage à

trick [trɪk] **1** *n* (*joke, deception, of conjurer*) tour *m*; (*clever method*) astuce *f*; (*in card game*) pli *m*; **to play a t. on sb** jouer un tour à qn **2** *vt* (*deceive*) duper; **to t. sb into doing sth** amener qn à faire qch par la ruse ▪ **trickery** *n* ruse *f*

trickle ['trɪkəl] **1** *n* (*of liquid*) filet *m* **2** *vi* (*of liquid*) couler goutte à goutte; *Fig*

to t. in *(of letters, people)* arriver en petit nombre

tricky ['trɪkɪ] **(-ier, -iest)** *adj (problem)* délicat

tricycle ['traɪsɪkəl] *n* tricycle *m*

trifle ['traɪfəl] **1** *n (insignificant thing)* bagatelle *f*; *Br (dessert)* = dessert où alternent génoise, fruits en gelée et crème anglaise **2** *adv* **a t. wide** un tantinet trop large **3** *vi* **to t. with** plaisanter avec ▪ **trifling** *adj* insignifiant

trigger ['trɪgə(r)] **1** *n (of gun)* détente *f* **2** *vt* **to t. sth (off)** déclencher qch

trilogy ['trɪlədʒɪ] *(pl -ies)* *n* trilogie *f*

trim [trɪm] **1 (trimmer, trimmest)** *adj (neat)* soigné; *(slim)* svelte **2** *n* **to give sb's hair a t.** faire une coupe d'entretien à qn **3** *(pt & pp -mm-)* *vt* couper (un peu); **to t. sth with sth** orner qch de qch ▪ **trimmings** *npl (on clothes)* garniture *f*; *(of meal)* accompagnements *mpl* traditionnels

trinket ['trɪŋkɪt] *n* babiole *f*

trio ['triːəʊ] *(pl -os)* *n* trio *m*

trip [trɪp] **1** *n (journey)* voyage *m*; *(outing)* excursion *f* **2** *(pt & pp -pp-)* *vt* **to t. sb up** faire trébucher qn **3** *vi* **to t. (over** *or* **up)** trébucher; **to t. over sth** trébucher sur qch

triple ['trɪpəl] **1** *adj* triple **2** *vti* tripler ▪ **triplets** *npl (children)* triplés, -es *mfpl*

triplicate ['trɪplɪkət] *n* **in t.** en trois exemplaires

tripod ['traɪpɒd] *n* trépied *m*

triumph ['traɪəmf] **1** *n* triomphe *m* **(over** sur) **2** *vi* triompher **(over** de) ▪ **triumphant** [traɪˈʌmfənt] *adj* triomphant; *(success, welcome, return)* triomphal

trivial ['trɪvɪəl] *adj (unimportant)* insignifiant; *(trite)* banal *(mpl -als)*

trod [trɒd] *pt of* **tread**

trodden ['trɒdən] *pp of* **tread**

trolley ['trɒlɪ] *(pl -eys)* *n Br* chariot *m*; *Br* **(tea) t.** table *f* roulante; *Am* **t. (car)** tramway *m*

trombone [trɒmˈbəʊn] *n* trombone *m*

troop [truːp] **1** *n* bande *f*; *(of soldiers)* troupe *f*; **the troops** *(soldiers)* les trou-

pes *fpl* **2** *vi* **to t. in/out** entrer/sortir en groupe

trophy ['trəʊfɪ] *(pl -ies)* *n* trophée *m*

tropics ['trɒpɪks] *n* **in the tropics** sous les tropiques ▪ **tropical** *adj* tropical

trot [trɒt] **1** *n* trot *m*; *Fam* **on the t.** *(consecutively)* de suite **2** *(pt & pp -tt-)* *vt* **to t. sth out** débiter qch **3** *vi (of horse)* trotter

trouble ['trʌbəl] **1** *n (difficulty)* ennui *m*; *(inconvenience)* problème *m*; *(social unrest, illness)* trouble *m*; **to be in t.** avoir des ennuis; **to get into t.** s'attirer des ennuis; **to have t. doing sth** avoir du mal à faire qch; **to go to the t. of doing sth** se donner la peine de faire qch; **it's no t.** pas de problème **2** *vt (inconvenience)* déranger; *(worry)* inquiéter

troublemaker ['trʌbəlmeɪkə(r)] *n (in school)* élément *m* perturbateur; *(political)* fauteur *m* de troubles

troublesome ['trʌbəlsəm] *adj* pénible

trough [trɒf] *n (for drinking)* abreuvoir *m*; *(for feeding)* auge *f*

troupe [truːp] *n (of actors)* troupe *f*

trousers ['traʊzəz] *npl Br* pantalon *m*; **a pair of t., some t.** un pantalon; **short t.** culottes *fpl* courtes

trout [traʊt] *n inv* truite *f*

trowel ['traʊəl] *n (for cement or plaster)* truelle *f*; *(for plants)* déplantoir *m*

truant ['truːənt] *n* **to play t.** faire l'école buissonnière

truce [truːs] *n Mil* trêve *f*

truck [trʌk] *n (lorry)* camion *m*; **t. driver** camionneur *m*; *Am* **t. stop** *(restaurant)* routier *m* ▪ **trucker** *n Am* camionneur *m*

trudge [trʌdʒ] *vi* marcher péniblement

true [truː] **(-er, -est)** *adj* vrai; *(genuine)* véritable; *(accurate)* exact; *(faithful)* fidèle **(to** à) ▪ **truly** *adv* vraiment; **well and t.** bel et bien

trump [trʌmp] *n* atout *m*

trumpet ['trʌmpɪt] *n* trompette *f*

truncheon ['trʌntʃən] *n Br* matraque *f*

trundle ['trʌndəl] *vti* **to t. along** rouler bruyamment

trunk [trʌŋk] *n (of tree, body)* tronc *m; (of elephant)* trompe *f; (case)* malle *f; Am (of vehicle)* coffre *m;* **trunks** *(for swimming)* slip *m* de bain

trust [trʌst] **1** *n (faith)* confiance *f* (**in** en) **2** *vt (believe in)* faire confiance à; **to t. sb with sth, to t. sth to sb** confier qch à qn; **I t. that...** j'espère que... **3** *vi* **to t. in sb** faire confiance à qn ■ **trusted** *adj (method)* éprouvé

trustworthy ['trʌstwɜːðɪ] *adj* digne de confiance

truth [truːθ] *(pl* **-s** [truːðz]) *n* vérité *f;* **there's some t. in...** il y a du vrai dans... ■ **truthful** *adj (story)* véridique; *(person)* sincère

try [traɪ] **1** *(pl* **-ies)** *n (attempt, in rugby)* essai *m;* **to have a t. at doing sth** essayer de faire qch; **it's worth a t.** ça vaut la peine d'essayer

2 *(pt & pp* **-ied)** *vt (attempt, sample)* essayer; *(food, drink)* goûter à; *(in law court)* juger (**for** pour); **to t. doing** *or* **to do sth** essayer de faire qch

3 *vi* essayer ■ **trying** *adj* difficile

▸**try on** *vt sep (clothes, shoes)* essayer

▸**try out** *vt sep (car, method, recipe)* essayer; *(person)* mettre à l'essai

T-shirt ['tiːʃɜːt] *n* tee-shirt *m*

tub [tʌb] *n (basin)* baquet *m; (bath)* baignoire *f; Br (for ice cream)* pot *m; Br (for flower, bush)* bac *m*

tuba ['tjuːbə] *n Mus* tuba *m*

tube [tjuːb] *n* tube *m; (of tyre)* chambre *f* à air; *Br Fam* **the t.** *(underground railway)* le métro

tuberculosis [tjuːbɜːkjʊˈləʊsɪs] *n Med* tuberculose *f*

tuck [tʌk] **1** *vt (put)* mettre; **to t. sth away** *(put)* ranger qch; *(hide)* cacher qch; **to t. in** *(shirt, blanket)* rentrer; *(child)* border **2** *vi Br Fam* **to t. in** *(start eating)* attaquer

Tuesday ['tjuːzdeɪ] *n* mardi *m*

tuft [tʌft] *n* touffe *f*

tug [tʌg] **1** *n* **to give sth a t.** tirer sur

qch **2** *(pt & pp* **-gg-)** *vt (pull)* tirer sur **3** *vi* tirer (**at** *or* **on** sur)

tuition [tjuːˈɪʃən] *n (lessons)* cours *mpl; (fee)* frais *mpl* de scolarité

tulip ['tjuːlɪp] *n* tulipe *f*

tumble ['tʌmbəl] **1** *n (fall)* chute *f; Br* **t. dryer** *or* **drier** sèche-linge *m inv* **2** *vi (of person)* faire une chute; *Fig (of prices)* chuter

tumbler ['tʌmblə(r)] *n (glass)* verre *m* droit

tummy ['tʌmɪ] *n Fam* ventre *m*

tumour ['tjuːmə(r)] *(Am* **tumor**) *n* tumeur *f*

tuna ['tjuːnə] *n* **t. (fish)** thon *m*

tune [tjuːn] **1** *n (melody)* air *m;* **in t.** *(instrument)* accordé; **out of t.** *(instrument)* désaccordé; **to be** *or* **sing in t./ out of t.** chanter juste/faux; *Fig* **to be in t. with sb/sth** être en harmonie avec qn/qch

2 *vt* **to t. (up)** *(instrument)* accorder; *(engine)* régler

3 *vi* **to t. in** brancher son poste (**to** sur)

tuner ['tjuːnə(r)] *n (on TV, radio)* tuner *m*

tunic ['tjuːnɪk] *n* tunique *f*

Tunisia [tjuːˈnɪzɪə] *n* la Tunisie

tunnel ['tʌnəl] **1** *n* tunnel *m* **2** *(Br* **-ll-,** *Am* **-l-)** *vi* creuser un tunnel (**into** dans)

turban ['tɜːbən] *n* turban *m*

turbulence ['tɜːbjʊləns] *n* turbulence *f*

turf [tɜːf] *n (grass)* gazon *m*

Turkey ['tɜːkɪ] *n* la Turquie ■ **Turk** *n* Turc *m,* Turque *f* ■ **Turkish** **1** *adj* turc *(f* turque); **T. delight** des loukoums *mpl* **2** *n (language)* turc *m*

turkey ['tɜːkɪ] *(pl* **-eys)** *n (bird)* dinde *f*

turmoil ['tɜːmɔɪl] *n* **to be in t.** *(of person)* être dans tous ses états; *(of country)* être en ébullition

turn [tɜːn] **1** *n (of wheel, in game, queue)* tour *m; (in road)* tournant *m; (of events)* tournure *f; Br Fam (fit)* crise *f;* **to take turns** se relayer; **in t.** à tour de rôle; **it's your t. (to play)** c'est à toi (de jouer); **the t. of the century** le tournant du siècle; **t. of phrase** tournure de phrase

2 *vt* tourner; *(mechanically)* faire tourner; *(mattress, pancake)* retourner; **to t. sb/sth into sb/sth** changer qn/qch en qn/qch; **to t. sth red/black** rougir/noircir qch; **to t. sth on sb** *(aim)* braquer qch sur qn; **she has turned twenty** elle a vingt ans passés

3 *vi (of wheel, driver)* tourner; *(of person)* se retourner; **to t. red/black** rougir/noircir; **to t. nasty** *(of person)* devenir méchant; *(of situation)* mal tourner; **to t. to sb** se tourner vers qn; **to t. into sb/sth** devenir qn/qch; **to t. against sb** se retourner contre qn ■ **turn-off** *n (on road)* sortie *f* ■ **turn-out** *n (people)* assistance *f; (at polls)* participation *f* ■ **turnover** *n Com (sales)* chiffre *m* d'affaires; *(of stock)* rotation *f; (of staff)* renouvellement *m* ■ **turnup** *n Br (on trousers)* revers *m*

▸**turn around** *vi (of person)* se retourner

▸**turn away 1** *vt sep (eyes)* détourner **(from** de); *(person)* refuser **2** *vi* se détourner

▸**turn back 1** *vt sep (sheets)* rabattre; *(clock)* retarder **2** *vi (return)* faire demi-tour

▸**turn down** *vt sep (gas, radio)* baisser; *(fold down)* rabattre; *(refuse)* rejeter

▸**turn in 1** *vt sep (person)* livrer à la police **2** *vi Fam (go to bed)* aller au pieu

▸**turn off 1** *vt sep (light, radio)* éteindre; *(tap)* fermer; *(machine)* arrêter; *Fam* **to t. sb off** dégoûter qn **2** *vi (leave road)* sortir

▸**turn on 1** *vt sep (light, radio)* allumer; *(tap)* ouvrir; *(machine)* mettre en marche; *Fam* **to t. sb on** *(sexually)* exciter qn **2** *vi* **to t. on sb** *(attack)* attaquer qn

▸**turn out 1** *vt sep (light)* éteindre; *(pocket, box)* vider; *(produce)* produire **2** *vi (appear, attend)* se déplacer; **it turns out that...** il s'avère que...; **she turned out to be...** elle s'est révélée être...

▸**turn over 1** *vt sep (page)* tourner **2** *vi (of person)* se retourner; *(of car)* faire un tonneau

▸**turn round 1** *vt sep (head)* tourner;

(object) retourner; *(situation)* renverser **2** *vi (of person)* se retourner; *(in vehicle)* faire demi-tour

▸**turn up 1** *vt sep (radio, heat)* mettre plus fort; *(collar)* remonter **2** *vi (arrive)* arriver; *(be found)* être retrouvé

turning ['tɜːnɪŋ] *n Br (street)* petite rue *f; (bend in road)* tournant *m; Fig* **t. point** tournant *m*

turnip ['tɜːnɪp] *n* navet *m*

turnpike ['tɜːnpaɪk] *n Am* autoroute *f* à péage

turnstile ['tɜːnstaɪl] *n* tourniquet *m*

turntable ['tɜːnteɪbəl] *n* platine *f*

turquoise ['tɜːkwɔɪz] *adj* turquoise *inv*

turret ['tʌrɪt] *n* tourelle *f*

turtle ['tɜːtəl] *n Br* tortue *f* de mer; *Am* tortue *f*

tusk [tʌsk] *n* défense *f (dent)*

tussle ['tʌsəl] *n* bagarre *f*

tutor ['tjuːtə(r)] **1** *n* professeur *m* particulier; *(in British university)* directeur, -trice *mf* d'études **2** *vt* donner des cours particuliers à ■ **tutorial** [-'tɔːrɪəl] *n Univ* ≃ travaux *mpl* dirigés

tuxedo [tʌk'siːdəʊ] *(pl* **-os)** *n Am* smoking *m*

TV [tiː'viː] *n* télé *f;* **on TV** à la télé

tweed [twiːd] *n* tweed *m;* **t. jacket** veste *f* en tweed

tweezers ['twiːzəz] *npl* pince *f* à épiler

twelve [twelv] *adj & n* douze *(m)* ■ **twelfth** *adj & n* douzième *(mf)*

twenty ['twentɪ] *adj & n* vingt *(m)* ■ **twentieth** *adj & n* vingtième *(mf)*

twice [twaɪs] *adv* deux fois; **t. as heavy (as)** deux fois plus lourd (que); **t. a month, t. monthly** deux fois par mois

twiddle ['twɪdəl] *vti* **to t. (with) sth** tripoter qch; **to t. one's thumbs** se tourner les pouces

twig[1] [twɪg] *n (of branch)* brindille *f*

twig[2] [twɪg] *(pt & pp* **-gg-)** *vti Br Fam* piger

twilight ['twaɪlaɪt] *n* crépuscule *m*

twin [twɪn] **1** *n* jumeau *m,* jumelle *f;* **t. brother** frère *m* jumeau; **t. sister** sœur *f* jumelle; **t. beds** lits *mpl* jumeaux; **t.**

town ville *f* jumelée **2** (*pt & pp* **-nn-**) *vt* (*town*) jumeler

twine [twaɪn] **1** *n (string)* ficelle *f* **2** *vi (twist)* s'enrouler (**round** autour de)

twinge [twɪndʒ] *n* **a t. (of pain)** un élancement; **a t. of remorse** un peu de remords

twinkle ['twɪŋkəl] *vi (of star)* scintiller; *(of eye)* pétiller

twirl [twɜːl] **1** *vt* faire tournoyer; *(moustache)* tortiller **2** *vi* tournoyer

twist [twɪst] **1** *n (action)* tour *m*; *(bend)* tortillement *m*; *Fig (in story)* tour *m* inattendu

2 *vt (wire, arm)* tordre; *(roll)* enrouler (**round** autour de); **to t. one's ankle** se tordre la cheville; *Fig* **to t. sb's arm** forcer la main à qn; **to t. sth off** *(lid)* dévisser qch

3 *vi (wind)* s'entortiller (**round sth** autour de qch); *(of road, river)* serpenter ■ **twisted** *adj (person, mind, logic)* tordu

twit [twɪt] *n Br Fam* andouille *f*

twitch [twɪtʃ] **1** *n (nervous)* tic *m* **2** *vi (of person)* avoir un tic; *(of muscle)* se contracter nerveusement

twitter ['twɪtə(r)] *vi (of bird)* pépier

two [tuː] *adj & n* deux *(m)* ■ **two-dimensional** *adj* à deux dimensions ■ **two-faced** *adj Fig* hypocrite ■ **two-piece** *adj (suit, swimsuit)* deux-pièces ■ **two-seater** *n (car)* voiture *f* à deux places

twofold ['tuːfəʊld] **1** *adj* double **2** *adv* **to increase t.** doubler

twosome ['tuːsəm] *n* couple *m*

tycoon [taɪ'kuːn] *n* magnat *m*

type¹ [taɪp] *n* (a) *(sort)* genre *m*, type *m* (b) *(print)* caractères *mpl*; **in large t.** en gros caractères

type² [taɪp] **1** *vti (write)* taper (à la machine) **2** *vt* **to t. sth in** *(on computer)* entrer qch au clavier; **to t. sth out** *(letter)* taper qch ■ **typewriter** *n* machine *f* à écrire ■ **typewritten** *adj* dactylographié ■ **typing** *n* dactylographie *f*; **t. error** faute *f* de frappe ■ **typist** *n* dactylo *mf*

typhoid ['taɪfɔɪd] *n Med* typhoïde *f*

typhoon [taɪ'fuːn] *n* typhon *m*

typical ['tɪpɪkəl] *adj* typique (**of** de)

tyrant ['taɪrənt] *n* tyran *m*

tyre ['taɪə(r)] *n Br* pneu *m* (*pl* pneus)

Uu

U, u [juː] *n (letter)* U, u *m inv*
ugh [ʌχ] *exclam* berk!
ugly [ˈʌglɪ] (**-ier, -iest**) *adj* laid
UK [juːˈkeɪ] (*abbr* **United Kingdom**) *n*
the UK le Royaume-Uni
ulcer [ˈʌlsə(r)] *n* ulcère *m*
ulterior [ʌlˈtɪərɪə(r)] *adj* u. motive
arrière-pensée *f*
ultimate [ˈʌltɪmət] *adj (last)* final;
(supreme, best) absolu ■ **ultimately**
adv (finally) finalement; *(basically)* en
fin de compte
ultimatum [ʌltɪˈmeɪtəm] *n* ultima-
tum *m*
ultra- [ˈʌltrə] *pref* ultra-
ultraviolet [ʌltrəˈvaɪələt] *adj* ultra-
violet, -ette
umbrella [ʌmˈbrelə] *n* parapluie *m*
umpire [ˈʌmpaɪə(r)] *n* arbitre *m*
umpteen [ʌmpˈtiːn] *adj Fam* u. times
je ne sais combien de fois ■ **umpteenth**
adj Fam énième
UN [juːˈen] (*abbr* **United Nations**) *n*
the UN les Nations *fpl* unies
unable [ʌnˈeɪbəl] *adj* to be u. to do
sth être incapable de faire qch
unabridged [ʌnəˈbrɪdʒd] *adj* intégral
unacceptable [ʌnəkˈseptəbəl] *adj* in-
acceptable
unaccompanied [ʌnəˈkʌmpənɪd]
adj (person) non accompagné; *(sing-
ing)* sans accompagnement
unaccustomed [ʌnəˈkʌstəmd] *adj*
inaccoutumé; **to be u. to sth/to
doing sth** ne pas être habitué à qch/à
faire qch
unaided [ʌnˈeɪdɪd] *adv* sans aide
unanimous [juːˈnænɪməs] *adj* una-
nime ■ **unanimously** *adv* à l'unanimité
unappetizing [ʌnˈæpɪtaɪzɪŋ] *adj*
peu appétissant

unarmed [ʌnˈɑːmd] *adj* non armé
unashamedly [ʌnəˈʃeɪmədlɪ] *adv*
sans aucune honte
unassuming [ʌnəˈsjuːmɪŋ] *adj* sans
prétention
unattached [ʌnəˈtætʃt] *adj (without
partner)* sans attaches
unattainable [ʌnəˈteɪnəbəl] *adj* in-
accessible
unattended [ʌnəˈtendɪd] *adj* to
leave sb/sth u. laisser qn/qch sans
surveillance
unattractive [ʌnəˈtræktɪv] *adj* peu
attrayant
unauthorized [ʌnˈɔːθəraɪzd] *adj* non
autorisé
unavailable [ʌnəˈveɪləbəl] *adj* to be
u. ne pas être disponible
unavoidable [ʌnəˈvɔɪdəbəl] *adj* iné-
vitable
unaware [ʌnəˈweə(r)] *adj* to be u. of
sth ignorer qch; to be u. that... igno-
rer que... ■ **unawares** *adv* to catch sb
u. prendre qn au dépourvu
unbalanced [ʌnˈbælənst] *adj (mind,
person)* instable
unbearable [ʌnˈbeərəbəl] *adj* insup-
portable
unbeatable [ʌnˈbiːtəbəl] *adj* imbat-
table
unbeaten [ʌnˈbiːtən] *adj (player)* in-
vaincu; *(record)* jamais battu
unbelievable [ʌnbɪˈliːvəbəl] *adj* in-
croyable
unbias(s)ed [ʌnˈbaɪəst] *adj* impartial
unblock [ʌnˈblɒk] *vt (sink, pipe)* dé-
boucher
unbolt [ʌnˈbəʊlt] *vt (door)* déverrouil-
ler
unborn [ʌnˈbɔːn] *adj* u. child enfant
mf à naître

unbreakable [ʌn'breɪkəbəl] *adj* incassable ■ **unbroken** *adj (intact)* intact; *(continuous)* continu; *(record)* jamais battu

unbutton [ʌn'bʌtən] *vt* déboutonner

uncalled-for [ʌn'kɔːldfɔː(r)] *adj* déplacé

uncanny [ʌn'kænɪ] (**-ier, -iest**) *adj* étrange

uncertain [ʌn'sɜːtən] *adj* incertain; **to be u. about sth** ne pas être certain de qch; **it's u. whether** *or* **that...** il n'est pas certain que... *(+ subjunctive)* ■ **uncertainty** (*pl* **-ies**) *n* incertitude *f*

unchanged [ʌn'tʃeɪndʒd] *adj* inchangé ■ **unchanging** *adj* immuable

unclaimed [ʌn'kleɪmd] *adj (luggage)* non réclamé

uncle ['ʌŋkəl] *n* oncle *m*

unclear [ʌn'klɪə(r)] *adj* vague; *(result)* incertain; **it's u. whether...** on ne sait pas très bien si...

uncomfortable [ʌn'kʌmftəbəl] *adj* inconfortable; *(heat, experience)* désagréable; **to feel u.** *(physically)* ne pas être à l'aise; *(ill at ease)* être mal à l'aise

uncommon [ʌn'kɒmən] *adj* peu commun

uncompromising
[ʌn'kɒmprəmaɪzɪŋ] *adj* intransigeant

unconditional [ʌnkən'dɪʃənəl] *adj* sans condition

unconfirmed [ʌnkən'fɜːmd] *adj* non confirmé

unconnected [ʌnkə'nektɪd] *adj* sans lien

unconscious [ʌn'kɒnʃəs] **1** *adj (person)* sans connaissance; *(desire)* inconscient; **to be u. of sth** ne pas avoir conscience de qch **2** *n* **the u.** l'inconscient *m* ■ **unconsciously** *adv* inconsciemment

uncontrollable [ʌnkən'trəʊləbəl] *adj* incontrôlable

unconventional [ʌnkən'venʃənəl] *adj* non conformiste

unconvinced [ʌnkən'vɪnst] *adj* **to be** *or* **remain u.** ne pas être convaincu **(of** de) ■ **unconvincing** *adj* peu convaincant

uncooked [ʌn'kʊkt] *adj* cru

uncooperative [ʌnkəʊ'ɒpərətɪv] *adj* peu coopératif, -ive

uncouth [ʌn'kuːθ] *adj* fruste

uncover [ʌn'kʌvə(r)] *vt* découvrir

undaunted [ʌn'dɔːntɪd] *adj* nullement impressionné

undecided [ʌndɪ'saɪdɪd] *adj (person)* indécis **(about** sur); **I'm u. whether to do it or not** je n'ai pas décidé si je le ferai ou non

undeniable [ʌndɪ'naɪəbəl] *adj* indéniable

under ['ʌndə(r)] **1** *prep* sous; *(less than)* moins de; **children u. nine** les enfants de moins de neuf ans; **u. it** dessous; **u. (the command of) sb** sous les ordres de qn; **u. the circumstances** dans ces circonstances; **to be u. discussion/repair** être en discussion/réparation; **to be u. way** *(in progress)* être en cours; *(on the way)* être en route; **to get u. way** *(of campaign)* démarrer **2** *adv* au-dessous

undercharge [ʌndə'tʃɑːdʒ] *vt* **I undercharged him (for it)** je ne (le) lui ai pas fait payer assez

underclothes ['ʌndəkləʊðz] *npl* sous-vêtements *mpl*

undercooked [ʌndə'kʊkt] *adj* pas assez cuit

undercover ['ʌndəkʌvə(r)] *adj* secret, -ète

undercut [ʌndə'kʌt] *(pt & pp* **-cut,** *pres p* **-cutting)** *vt* vendre moins cher que

underdeveloped [ʌndədɪ'veləpt] *adj (country, region)* sous-développé

underdog ['ʌndədɒg] *n (politically, socially)* opprimé, -e *mf; (likely loser)* outsider *m*

underdone [ʌndə'dʌn] *adj (food)* pas assez cuit; *(steak)* saignant

underestimate [ʌndər'estɪmeɪt] *vt* sous-estimer

underfoot [ʌndə'fʊt] *adv* sous les pieds

undergo [ʌndə'gəʊ] *(pt* **-went,** *pp* **-gone)** *vt* subir; **to u. surgery** être opéré

undergraduate [ʌndə'grædʒʊət] *n* étudiant, -e *mf* de licence

underground 1 ['ʌndəgraʊnd] *adj (subterranean)* souterrain **2** ['ʌndəgraʊnd] *n Br (railway)* métro *m* **3** [ʌndə'graʊnd] *adv* sous terre; *Fig* **to go u.** *(of fugitive)* passer dans la clandestinité

undergrowth ['ʌndəgrəʊθ] *n* broussailles *fpl*

underhand [ʌndə'hænd] *adj* sournois

underline [ʌndə'laɪn] *vt* souligner

underlying [ʌndə'laɪɪŋ] *adj* sousjacent

undermine [ʌndə'maɪn] *vt (weaken)* saper

underneath [ʌndə'niːθ] **1** *prep* sous **2** *adv* (en) dessous; **the book u.** le livre d'en dessous **3** *n* **the u. (of)** le dessous (de)

underpaid [ʌndə'peɪd] *adj* sous-payé

underpants ['ʌndəpænts] *npl (male underwear)* slip *m*

underpass ['ʌndəpɑːs] *n (for pedestrians)* passage *m* souterrain; *(for vehicles)* passage *m* inférieur

underprivileged [ʌndə'prɪvɪlɪdʒd] *adj* défavorisé

underrate [ʌndə'reɪt] *vt* sous-estimer

underside ['ʌndəsaɪd] *n* **the u. (of)** le dessous (de)

understaffed [ʌndə'stɑːft] *adj* **to be u.** manquer de personnel

understand [ʌndə'stænd] *(pt & pp* **-stood)** *vti* comprendre; **I u. that...** je crois comprendre que... ▪ **understanding 1** *n (act, faculty)* compréhension *f*; *(agreement)* accord *m*, entente *f*; *(sympathy)* entente *f*; **on the u. that...** à condition que... *(+ subjunctive)* **2** *adj (person)* compréhensif, -ive ▪ **understood** *adj (agreed)* entendu; *(implied)* sous-entendu

understandable [ʌndə'stændəbəl] *adj* compréhensible

understatement ['ʌndəsteɪtmənt] *n* euphémisme *m*

undertake [ʌndə'teɪk] *(pt* **-took,** *pp* **-taken)** *vt (task)* entreprendre; **to u. to do sth** entreprendre de faire qch

undertaker ['ʌndəteɪkə(r)] *n* entrepreneur *m* de pompes funèbres

undertaking [ʌndə'teɪkɪŋ] *n (task)* entreprise *f*; *(promise)* promesse *f*

undertone ['ʌndətəʊn] *n* **in an u.** à mi-voix

underwater [ʌndə'wɔːtə(r)] *adv* sous l'eau

underwear ['ʌndəweə(r)] *n* sousvêtements *mpl*

undesirable [ʌndɪ'zaɪərəbəl] *adj & n* indésirable *(mf)*

undignified [ʌn'dɪgnɪfaɪd] *adj* indigne

undisciplined [ʌn'dɪsɪplɪnd] *adj* indiscipliné

undiscovered [ʌndɪ'skʌvəd] *adj* **to remain u.** *(of crime, body)* ne pas être découvert

undisputed [ʌndɪ'spjuːtɪd] *adj* incontesté

undistinguished [ʌndɪ'stɪŋgwɪʃt] *adj* médiocre

undo [ʌn'duː] *(pt* **-did,** *pp* **-done)** *vt* défaire; *(bound person)* détacher; *(parcel)* ouvrir; *(mistake, damage)* réparer; *Comptr (command)* annuler ▪ **undoing** *n* ruine *f* ▪ **undone** *adj* **to come u.** *(of knot)* se défaire; **to leave sth u.** *(work)* ne pas faire qch

undoubtedly [ʌn'daʊtɪdlɪ] *adv* indubitablement

undress [ʌn'dres] **1** *vt* déshabiller; **to get undressed** se déshabiller **2** *vi* se déshabiller

undrinkable [ʌn'drɪnkəbəl] *adj* imbuvable

undue [ʌn'djuː] *adj* excessif, -ive ▪ **unduly** *adv* excessivement

unearth [ʌn'ɜːθ] *vt (from ground)* déterrer; *Fig (discover)* mettre à jour

unearthly [ʌn'ɜːθlɪ] *adj Fam* **at an u. hour** à une heure impossible

uneasy [ʌn'iːzɪ] *adj (person)* mal à l'aise; *(silence)* gêné

uneconomic(al) [ʌniːkə'nɒmɪk(əl)] *adj* peu économique

uneducated [ʌn'edjʊkeɪtɪd] *adj*

(person) sans éducation

unemployed [ʌnɪmˈplɔɪd] **1** *adj* au chômage **2** *npl* **the u.** les chômeurs *mpl* ▪ **unemployment** *n* chômage *m*; *Br* **u. benefit** allocation *f* chômage

unenthusiastic [ʌnɪnθjuːzɪˈæstɪk] *adj* peu enthousiaste

unenviable [ʌnˈenvɪəbəl] *adj* peu enviable

unequal [ʌnˈiːkwəl] *adj* inégal

unequivocal [ʌnɪˈkwɪvəkəl] *adj* sans équivoque

uneven [ʌnˈiːvən] *adj* inégal

uneventful [ʌnɪˈventfəl] *adj* sans histoires

unexpected [ʌnɪkˈspektɪd] *adj* inattendu ▪ **unexpectedly** *adv (arrive)* à l'improviste; *(fail, succeed)* contre toute attente

unexplained [ʌnɪkˈspleɪnd] *adj* inexpliqué

unfailing [ʌnˈfeɪlɪŋ] *adj (optimism, courage)* à toute épreuve

unfair [ʌnˈfeə(r)] *adj* injuste **(to sb** envers qn); *(competition)* déloyal ▪ **unfairly** *adv* injustement

unfaithful [ʌnˈfeɪθfəl] *adj* infidèle **(to** à)

unfamiliar [ʌnfəˈmɪlɪə(r)] *adj* inconnu; **to be u. with sth** ne pas connaître qch

unfashionable [ʌnˈfæʃənəbəl] *adj* démodé

unfasten [ʌnˈfɑːsən] *vt* défaire

unfavourable [ʌnˈfeɪvərəbəl] *(Am* **unfavorable)** *adj* défavorable

unfinished [ʌnˈfɪnɪʃt] *adj* inachevé

unfit [ʌnˈfɪt] *adj (unsuitable)* inapte; *(in bad shape)* pas en forme; **to be u. to do sth** être incapable de faire qch

unflattering [ʌnˈflætərɪŋ] *adj* peu flatteur, -euse

unfold [ʌnˈfəʊld] **1** *vt* déplier; *(wings)* déployer **2** *vi (of story)* se dérouler

unforeseeable [ʌnfɔːˈsiːəbəl] *adj* imprévisible ▪ **unforeseen** *adj* imprévu

unforgettable [ʌnfəˈgetəbəl] *adj* inoubliable

unforgivable [ʌnfəˈgɪvəbəl] *adj* impardonnable

unfortunate [ʌnˈfɔːtʃənət] *adj* malchanceux, -euse; *(event)* fâcheux, -euse; **you were u.** tu n'as pas eu de chance ▪ **unfortunately** *adv* malheureusement

unfounded [ʌnˈfaʊndɪd] *adj (rumour)* sans fondement

unfriendly [ʌnˈfrendlɪ] *adj* peu aimable **(to** avec)

unfulfilled [ʌnfʊlˈfɪld] *adj (plan, dream)* non réalisé

unfurnished [ʌnˈfɜːnɪʃt] *adj* non meublé

ungainly [ʌnˈgeɪnlɪ] *adj (clumsy)* gauche

ungrateful [ʌnˈgreɪtfəl] *adj* ingrat

unhappy [ʌnˈhæpɪ] **(-ier, -iest)** *adj (sad, unfortunate)* malheureux, -euse; *(not pleased)* mécontent; **to be u. about doing sth** ne pas vouloir faire qch

unharmed [ʌnˈhɑːmd] *adj* indemne

unhealthy [ʌnˈhelθɪ] **(-ier, -iest)** *adj (person)* maladif, -ive; *(climate, place, job)* malsain

unheard-of [ʌnˈhɜːdɒv] *adj (unprecedented)* inouï

unhelpful [ʌnˈhelpfəl] *adj (person)* peu serviable; *(advice)* peu utile

unhurt [ʌnˈhɜːt] *adj* indemne

unhygienic [ʌnhaɪˈdʒiːnɪk, *Am* -ˈdʒenɪk] *adj* contraire à l'hygiène

uniform [ˈjuːnɪfɔːm] **1** *n* uniforme *m* **2** *adj (regular)* uniforme; *(temperature)* constant

unify [ˈjuːnɪfaɪ] **(pt & pp -ied)** *vt* unifier

unilateral [juːnɪˈlætərəl] *adj* unilatéral

unimaginable [ʌnɪˈmædʒɪnəbəl] *adj* inimaginable ▪ **unimaginative** *adj (person, plan)* qui manque d'imagination

unimportant [ʌnɪmˈpɔːtənt] *adj* sans importance

uninhabitable [ʌnɪnˈhæbɪtəbəl] *adj* inhabitable ▪ **uninhabited** *adj* inhabité

uninhibited [ʌnɪn'hɪbɪtɪd] *adj (person)* sans complexes

uninjured [ʌn'ɪndʒəd] *adj* indemne

uninspiring [ʌnɪn'spaɪərɪŋ] *adj (subject)* pas très inspirant

unintelligible [ʌnɪn'telɪdʒəbəl] *adj* inintelligible

unintentional [ʌnɪn'tenʃənəl] *adj* involontaire

uninterested [ʌn'ɪntrɪstɪd] *adj* indifférent **(in** à) ▪ **uninteresting** *adj* inintéressant

uninterrupted [ʌnɪntə'rʌptɪd] *adj* ininterrompu

uninvited [ʌnɪn'vaɪtɪd] *adv (arrive)* sans invitation ▪ **uninviting** *adj* peu attrayant

union ['ju:nɪən] **1** *n* union *f; (trade union)* syndicat *m* **2** *adj* syndical; **the U. Jack** = le drapeau britannique

unique [ju:'ni:k] *adj* unique

unisex ['ju:nɪseks] *adj (clothes)* unisexe

unison ['ju:nɪsən] *n* **in u.** à l'unisson **(with** de)

unit ['ju:nɪt] *n* unité *f; (of furniture)* élément *m; (system)* bloc *m; (group, team)* groupe *m;* **psychiatric/heart u.** *(of hospital)* service *m* de psychiatrie/cardiologie

unite [ju:'naɪt] **1** *vt* unir; *(country, party)* unifier; **the United Kingdom** le Royaume-Uni; **the United Nations** les Nations *fpl* unies; **the United States (of America)** les États-Unis *mpl* (d'Amérique) **2** *vi* s'unir

unity ['ju:nɪtɪ] *n (cohesion)* unité *f; Fig (harmony)* harmonie *f*

universal [ju:nɪ'vɜ:səl] *adj* universel, -elle

universe ['ju:nɪvɜ:s] *n* univers *m*

university [ju:nɪ'vɜ:sɪtɪ] **1** *(pl* **-ies)** *n* université *f;* **to go to u.** aller à l'université; *Br* **at u.** à l'université **2** *adj (teaching, town, restaurant)* universitaire; *(student, teacher)* d'université

unjust [ʌn'dʒʌst] *adj* injuste

unjustified [ʌn'dʒʌstɪfaɪd] *adj* injustifié

unkind [ʌn'kaɪnd] *adj* pas gentil *(f* pas gentille) **(to sb** avec qn)

unknowingly [ʌn'nəʊɪŋlɪ] *adv* inconsciemment

unknown [ʌn'nəʊn] **1** *adj* inconnu **2** *n (person)* inconnu, -e *mf; Math & Fig* **u. (quantity)** inconnue *f*

unlawful [ʌn'lɔ:fəl] *adj* illégal

unleaded [ʌn'ledɪd] *adj* sans plomb

unleash [ʌn'li:ʃ] *vt (emotion)* susciter

unless [ʌn'les] *conj* à moins que *(+ subjunctive);* **u. she comes** à moins qu'elle ne vienne; **u. you work harder, you'll fail** à moins de travailler plus dur, vous échouerez

unlike [ʌn'laɪk] *prep* **to be u. sb/sth** ne pas être comme qn/qch; **u. her brother, she...** à la différence de son frère, elle...; **it's very u. him to...** ça ne lui ressemble pas du tout de...

unlikely [ʌn'laɪklɪ] *adj* improbable; *(unbelievable)* invraisemblable; **she's u. to win** il est peu probable qu'elle gagne

unlimited [ʌn'lɪmɪtɪd] *adj* illimité

unlisted [ʌn'lɪstɪd] *adj Am (phone number)* sur liste rouge

unload [ʌn'ləʊd] *vti* décharger

unlock [ʌn'lɒk] *vt* ouvrir

unlucky [ʌn'lʌkɪ] **(-ier, -iest)** *adj (person)* malchanceux, -euse; *(number, colour)* qui porte malheur ▪ **unluckily** *adv* malheureusement

unmade [ʌn'meɪd] *adj (bed)* défait

unmanageable [ʌn'mænɪdʒəbəl] *adj (child)* difficile; *(hair)* difficile à coiffer

unmarried [ʌn'mærɪd] *adj* non marié

unmistakable [ʌnmɪ'steɪkəbəl] *adj (obvious)* indubitable; *(face, voice)* caractéristique

unmoved [ʌn'mu:vd] *adj* **to be u. by sth** rester insensible à qch

unnatural [ʌn'nætʃərəl] *adj (abnormal)* anormal; *(affected)* affecté

unnecessary [ʌn'nesəsərɪ] *adj* inutile; *(superfluous)* superflu

unnerve [ʌn'nɜ:v] *vt* troubler

unnoticed [ʌn'nəʊtɪst] *adv* **to go u.** passer inaperçu

unobtainable [ʌnəb'teɪnəbəl] *adj* impossible à obtenir

unoccupied [ʌn'ɒkjʊpaɪd] *adj (house)* inoccupé; *(seat)* libre

unofficial [ʌnə'fɪʃəl] *adj* officieux, -euse; *(visit)* privé; *(strike)* sauvage

unorthodox [ʌn'ɔ:θədɒks] *adj* peu orthodoxe

unpack [ʌn'pæk] **1** *vt (suitcase)* défaire; *(contents)* déballer **2** *vi* défaire sa valise

unpaid [ʌn'peɪd] *adj (bill, sum)* impayé; *(work, worker)* bénévole; *(leave)* non payé

unparalleled [ʌn'pærəleld] *adj* sans égal

unplanned [ʌn'plænd] *adj* imprévu

unpleasant [ʌn'plezənt] *adj* désagréable (**to sb** avec qn)

unplug [ʌn'plʌg] *(pt & pp* -**gg**-*) vt (appliance)* débrancher

unpopular [ʌn'pɒpjʊlə(r)] *adj* impopulaire; **to be u. with sb** ne pas plaire à qn

unprecedented [ʌn'presɪdentɪd] *adj* sans précédent

unpredictable [ʌnprɪ'dɪktəbəl] *adj* imprévisible; *(weather)* indécis

unprepared [ʌnprɪ'peəd] *adj* **to be u. for sth** *(not expect)* ne pas s'attendre à qch

unprofessional [ʌnprə'feʃənəl] *adj (person, behaviour)* pas très professionnel, -elle

unprovoked [ʌnprə'vəʊkt] *adj* gratuit

unpublished [ʌn'pʌblɪʃt] *adj (text, writer)* inédit

unqualified [ʌn'kwɒlɪfaɪd] *adj (teacher)* non diplômé; *(support)* sans réserve; *(success)* parfait; **to be u. to do sth** ne pas être qualifié pour faire qch

unquestionable [ʌn'kwestʃənəbəl] *adj* incontestable

unravel [ʌn'rævəl] *(Br* -**ll**-*, Am* -**l**-*) vt (threads)* démêler; *Fig (mystery)* éclaircir

unreal [ʌn'rɪəl] *adj* irréel, -elle

unrealistic [ʌn'rɪəlɪstɪk] *adj* irréaliste

unreasonable [ʌn'ri:zənəbəl] *adj (person, attitude)* déraisonnable

unrecognizable [ʌn'rekəgnaɪzəbəl] *adj* méconnaissable

unrelated [ʌnrɪ'leɪtɪd] *adj (facts)* sans rapport (**to** avec); **we're u.** il n'y a aucun lien de parenté entre nous

unrelenting [ʌnrɪ'lentɪŋ] *adj* incessant; *(person)* tenace

unreliable [ʌnrɪ'laɪəbəl] *adj* peu fiable

unremarkable [ʌnrɪ'mɑːkəbəl] *adj* quelconque

unrepentant [ʌnrɪ'pentənt] *adj* impénitent

unreservedly [ʌnrɪ'zɜːvɪdlɪ] *adv* sans réserve

unrest [ʌn'rest] *n* agitation *f*, troubles *mpl*

unrestricted [ʌnrɪ'strɪktɪd] *adj* illimité

unrewarding [ʌnrɪ'wɔːdɪŋ] *adj* ingrat; *(financially,* peu rémunérateur, -trice

unrivalled [ʌn'raɪvəld] *(Am* **unrivaled**) *adj* hors pair *inv*

unroll [ʌn'rəʊl] **1** *vt* dérouler **2** *vi* se dérouler

unruly [ʌn'ruːlɪ] *(*-**ier**, -**iest**) *adj* indiscipliné

unsafe [ʌn'seɪf] *adj (place, machine)* dangereux, -euse

unsaid [ʌn'sed] *adj* **to leave sth u.** passer qch sous silence

unsatisfactory [ʌnsætɪs'fæktərɪ] *adj* peu satisfaisant ◾ **unsatisfied** *adj* insatisfait; **u. with sb/sth** peu satisfait de qn/qch

unscheduled [*Br* ʌn'ʃeduːld, *Am* ʌn'skedjʊld] *adj* imprévu

unscrew [ʌn'skruː] *vt* dévisser

unscrupulous [ʌn'skruːpjʊləs] *adj (person)* peu scrupuleux, -euse

unseemly [ʌn'siːmlɪ] *adj* inconvenant

unseen [ʌn'siːn] *adv* **to do sth u.** faire qch sans qu'on vous voie

unselfish [ʌn'selfɪʃ] *adj (person, motive)* désintéressé

unsettle [ʌn'setəl] *vt (person)* troubler

■ **unsettled** *adj (weather, situation)* instable

unshak(e)able [ʌnˈʃeɪkəbəl] *adj* inébranlable

unshaven [ʌnˈʃeɪvən] *adj* pas rasé

unsightly [ʌnˈsaɪtlɪ] *adj* laid

unskilled [ʌnˈskɪld] *adj* non qualifié

unsociable [ʌnˈsəʊʃəbəl] *adj* peu sociable

unsolved [ʌnˈsɒlvd] *adj (mystery)* inexpliqué; *(crime)* dont l'auteur n'est pas connu

unsophisticated [ʌnsəˈfɪstɪkeɪtɪd] *adj* simple

unsound [ʌnˈsaʊnd] *adj (construction)* peu solide; *(method)* peu sûr; *(decision)* peu judicieux, -euse

unspeakable [ʌnˈspiːkəbəl] *adj* indescriptible

unspecified [ʌnˈspesɪfaɪd] *adj* non spécifié

unsporting [ʌnˈspɔːtɪŋ] *adj* qui n'est pas fair-play

unstable [ʌnˈsteɪbəl] *adj* instable

unsteady [ʌnˈstedɪ] *adj (hand, voice, step)* mal assuré; *(table, ladder)* bancal *(mpl* -als) ■ **unsteadily** *adv (walk)* d'un pas mal assuré

unstuck [ʌnˈstʌk] *adj* **to come u.** *(of stamp)* se décoller; *Br Fam (of person, plan)* se casser la figure

unsuccessful [ʌnsəkˈsesfəl] *adj (attempt)* infructueux, -euse; *(outcome, candidate)* malheureux, -euse; *(application)* non retenu; **to be u.** ne pas réussir **(in doing** à faire); *(of book, film, artist)* ne pas avoir de succès ■ **unsuccessfully** *adv* en vain, sans succès

unsuitable [ʌnˈsuːtəbəl] *adj* qui ne convient pas **(for** à); *(manners, clothes)* peu convenable; **to be u. for sth** ne pas convenir à qch ■ **unsuited** *adj* **to be u. to sth** ne pas être fait pour qch; **they're u. (to each other)** ils ne sont pas compatibles

unsupervised [ʌnˈsuːpəvaɪzd] *adv (play)* sans surveillance

unsure [ʌnˈʃʊə(r)] *adj* incertain **(of** *or* **about** de)

unsympathetic [ʌnsɪmpəˈθetɪk] *adj* peu compatissant **(to** à); **u. to a cause/ request** insensible à une cause/requête

untangle [ʌnˈtæŋgəl] *vt (rope, hair)* démêler

unthinkable [ʌnˈθɪŋkəbəl] *adj* impensable, inconcevable

untidy [ʌnˈtaɪdɪ] **(-ier, -iest)** *adj (clothes, hair)* peu soigné; *(room)* en désordre; *(person)* désordonné

untie [ʌnˈtaɪ] *vt (person, hands)* détacher; *(knot, parcel)* défaire

until [ʌnˈtɪl] **1** *prep* jusqu'à; **u. now** jusqu'à présent; **u. then** jusque-là; **not u. tomorrow** pas avant demain; **I didn't see her u. Monday** c'est seulement lundi que je l'ai vue
2 *conj* jusqu'à ce que *(+ subjunctive)*; **u. she comes** jusqu'à ce qu'elle vienne; **do nothing u. I come** ne fais rien avant que j'arrive

untimely [ʌnˈtaɪmlɪ] *adj (remark, question)* inopportun; *(death)* prématuré

untold [ʌnˈtəʊld] *adj (wealth, quantity)* incalculable

untoward [ʌntəˈwɔːd] *adj* fâcheux, -euse

untrue [ʌnˈtruː] *adj* faux *(f* fausse) ■ **untruthful** *adj (person)* menteur, -euse; *(statement)* mensonger, -ère

unusable [ʌnˈjuːzəbəl] *adj* inutilisable

unused¹ [ʌnˈjuːzd] *adj (new)* neuf *(f* neuve); *(not in use)* inutilisé

unused² [ʌnˈjuːst] *adj* **u. to sth/to doing sth** peu habitué à qch/à faire qch

unusual [ʌnˈjuːʒʊəl] *adj (not common)* inhabituel, -elle; *(strange)* étrange ■ **unusually** *adv* exceptionnellement

unveil [ʌnˈveɪl] *vt* dévoiler

unwanted [ʌnˈwɒntɪd] *adj* non désiré

unwarranted [ʌnˈwɒrəntɪd] *adj* injustifié

unwelcome [ʌnˈwelkəm] *adj (news)* fâcheux, -euse; *(gift, visit)* inopportun; *(person)* importun

unwell [ʌnˈwel] *adj* souffrant

unwieldy [ʌnˈwiːldɪ] *adj (package)*

encombrant; *(system)* lourd

unwilling [ʌnˈwɪlɪŋ] *adj* **to be u. to do sth** être réticent à faire qch ▪ **unwillingly** *adv* à contrecœur

unwind [ʌnˈwaɪnd] *(pt & pp* -wound) **1** *vt (thread)* dérouler **2** *vi* se dérouler; *Fam (relax)* décompresser

unwise [ʌnˈwaɪz] *adj* imprudent

unwittingly [ʌnˈwɪtɪŋlɪ] *adv* involontairement

unworthy [ʌnˈwɜːðɪ] *adj* indigne (**of** de)

unwrap [ʌnˈræp] *(pt & pp* -pp-) *vt* déballer

unwritten [ʌnˈrɪtən] *adj (agreement)* verbal

unzip [ʌnˈzɪp] *(pt & pp* -pp-) *vt* ouvrir (la fermeture Éclair® de)

UP [ʌp] **1** *adv* en haut; **to come/go up** monter; **to walk up and down** marcher de long en large; **up there** là-haut; **up above** au-dessus; **further** *or* **higher up** plus haut; **up to** *(as far as)* jusqu'à; **to be up to doing sth** *(capable of)* être de taille à faire qch; **to feel up to doing sth** *(well enough)* être assez bien pour faire qch; **it's up to you to do it** c'est à toi de le faire; **it's up to you** *(you decide)* c'est à toi de décider; **where are you up to?** *(in book)* où en es-tu?; *Fam* **what are you up to?** que fais-tu?; *Fam* **to be well up in** *(versed in)* s'y connaître en

2 *prep* **up a hill** en haut d'une colline; **up a tree** dans un arbre; **up a ladder** sur une échelle; **to live up the street** habiter plus loin dans la rue

3 *adj (out of bed)* levé; **we were up all night** nous sommes restés debout toute la nuit; **the two weeks were up** les deux semaines étaient terminées; *Fam* **what's up?** qu'est-ce qu'il y a?

4 *npl* **ups and downs** des hauts et des bas *mpl*

5 *(pt & pp* -pp-) *vt Fam (price, offer)* augmenter ▪ **up-and-coming** *adj* qui monte ▪ **upbeat** *adj Fam* optimiste ▪ **upbringing** *n* éducation *f* ▪ **update** *vt* mettre à jour ▪ **upgrade** *vt (job)* revaloriser; *(person)* promouvoir;

Comptr (hardware) augmenter la puissance de ▪ **uphill 1** [ʌpˈhɪl] *adv* **to go u.** monter **2** [ˈʌphɪl] *adj Fig (struggle, task)* pénible ▪ **uphold** *(pt & pp* -held) *vt (decision)* maintenir ▪ **upkeep** *n* entretien *m* ▪ **up-market** *adj Br (car, product)* haut de gamme *inv; (area, place)* chic *inv* ▪ **upright 1** *adv (straight)* droit **2** *adj (vertical, honest)* droit ▪ **uprising** *n* insurrection *f* ▪ **uproot** *vt (plant, person)* déraciner ▪ **upside** *adv* **u. down** à l'envers; **to turn sth u. down** retourner qch; *Fig* mettre qch sens dessus dessous ▪ **upstairs 1** [ʌpˈsteəz] *adv* en haut; **to go u.** monter **2** [ˈʌpsteəz] *adj (people, room)* du dessus ▪ **upstream** *adv* en amont ▪ **uptight** *adj Fam (tense)* crispé; *(inhibited)* coincé ▪ **up-to-date** *adj* moderne; *(information)* à jour; *(well-informed)* au courant (**on** de) ▪ **uptown** *n Am* les quartiers *mpl* résidentiels ▪ **upturn** *n (improvement)* amélioration *f* (**in** de) ▪ **upward** *adj (movement)* ascendant; *(path)* qui monte; *(trend)* à la hausse ▪ **upwards** *adv* vers le haut; **from 5 euros u.** à partir de 5 euros; **u. of fifty** cinquante et plus

upheaval [ʌpˈhiːvəl] *n* bouleversement *m*

upholstery [ʌpˈhəʊlstərɪ] *n (padding)* rembourrage *m*; *(covering)* revêtement *m*; *(in car)* sièges *mpl*

upon [əˈpɒn] *prep* sur

upper [ˈʌpə(r)] **1** *adj* supérieur; **u. class** aristocratie *f*; **to have/get the u. hand** avoir/prendre le dessus **2** *n (of shoe)* empeigne *f* ▪ **upper-class** *adj* aristocratique ▪ **uppermost** *adj* le plus haut *(f* la plus haute)

uproar [ˈʌprɔː(r)] *n* tumulte *m*

upset 1 [ʌpˈset] *(pt & pp* -set, *pres p* -setting) *vt (knock over, spill)* renverser; *(person, plans, schedule)* bouleverser

2 [ʌpˈset] *adj (unhappy)* bouleversé (**about** par); **to have an u. stomach** avoir l'estomac dérangé

3 [ˈʌpset] *n (disturbance)* bouleversement *m*; *(surprise)* défaite *f*; **to have a stomach u.** avoir l'estomac dérangé ▪ **upsetting** *adj* bouleversant

upshot ['ʌpʃɒt] n résultat m

urban ['ɜːbən] adj urbain

urge [ɜːdʒ] **1** n forte envie f; **to have an u. to do sth** avoir très envie de faire qch **2** vt **to u. sb to do sth** presser qn de faire qch

urgency ['ɜːdʒənsɪ] n urgence f; **it's a matter of u.** il y a urgence

urgent ['ɜːdʒənt] adj urgent ■ **urgently** adv d'urgence

urine ['jʊərɪn] n urine f ■ **urinate** vi uriner

urn [ɜːn] n urne f; (for coffee or tea) fontaine f

US [juː'es] (abbr United States) n the US les USA mpl

us [əs, stressed ʌs] pron nous; **(to) us** (indirect) nous; **she saw us** elle nous a vus; **he gave it (to) us** il nous l'a donné

USA [juːes'eɪ] (abbr United States of America) n the U. les USA mpl

usage ['juːsɪdʒ] n usage m

use 1 [juːs] n (utilization) emploi m, usage m; (ability, permission to use) emploi m; **to have the u. of sth** avoir l'usage de qch; **to make (good) u. of sth** faire (bon) usage de qch; **to be of u. to sb** être utile à qn; **in u.** en usage; **not in u., out of u.** hors d'usage; **it's no u. crying** ça ne sert à rien de pleurer; **what's the u. of worrying?** à quoi bon s'inquiéter?
2 [juːz] vt (utilize) utiliser, se servir de; (force, diplomacy) avoir recours à; (electricity) consommer; **it's used to do** or **for doing sth** ça sert à faire qch; **it's used as...** ça sert de...; **to u. sth up** (food, fuel) finir; (money) dépenser ■ **use-by** ['juːzbaɪ] adj **u. date** date f limite de consommation

used 1 adj **(a)** [juːzd] (second-hand) d'occasion; (stamp) oblitéré **(b)** [juːst] **to be u. to sth/to doing sth** être habitué à qch/à faire qch; **to get u. to sb/ sth** s'habituer à qn/qch
2 [juːst] v aux **I u. to sing** avant, je chantais; **she u. to jog every Sunday** elle faisait du jogging tous les dimanches

useful ['juːsfəl] adj utile (**to** à); **to come in u.** être utile; **to make oneself u.** se rendre utile ■ **useless** adj inutile; (person) nul (f nulle) (**at** en)

user ['juːzə(r)] n (of train, telephone) usager m; (of road, machine) utilisateur, -trice mf ■ **user-friendly** adj convivial

usher ['ʌʃə(r)] **1** n (in church, theatre) ouvreur m **2** vt **to u. sb in** faire entrer qn ■ **usherette** n ouvreuse f

usual ['juːʒʊəl] **1** adj habituel, -elle; **as u.** comme d'habitude **2** n Fam **the u.** (food, excuse) la même chose que d'habitude ■ **usually** adv d'habitude

usurp [juː'zɜːp] vt usurper

utensil [juː'tensəl] n ustensile m

utility [juː'tɪlətɪ] n (**public**) **u.** service m public

utilize ['juːtɪlaɪz] vt utiliser

utmost ['ʌtməʊst] **1** adj **the u. ease** (greatest) la plus grande facilité; **it is of the u. importance that...** il est de la plus haute importance que... (+ subjunctive)
2 n **to do one's u.** faire de son mieux (**to do** pour faire)

utter¹ ['ʌtə(r)] adj total; (folly, lie) pur; **it's u. nonsense** c'est complètement absurde ■ **utterly** adv complètement

utter² ['ʌtə(r)] vt (cry, sigh) pousser; (word) prononcer; (threat) proférer

U-turn ['juːtɜːn] n (in vehicle) demitour m; Fig (change of policy) virage m à 180°

Vv

V, v [viː] n (letter) V, v m inv

vacant ['veɪkənt] adj (room, seat) libre; (post) vacant ■ **vacancy** (pl -ies) n (post) poste m vacant; (room) chambre f libre

vacate [Br və'keɪt, Am 'veɪkeɪt] vt quitter

vacation [veɪ'keɪʃən] n Am vacances fpl; **to take a v.** prendre des vacances

vaccinate ['væksɪneɪt] vt vacciner ■ **vaccination** n vaccination f ■ **vaccine** [-'siːn] n vaccin m

vacuum ['vækjʊəm] **1** n vide m; **v. cleaner** aspirateur m; Br **v. flask** Thermos® f **2** vt (room) passer l'aspirateur dans; (carpet) passer l'aspirateur sur

vagabond ['vægəbɒnd] n vagabond, -e mf

vagina [və'dʒaɪnə] n Anat vagin m

vague [veɪg] (-er, -est) adj vague; (outline) flou; **he was v. (about it)** il est resté vague ■ **vaguely** adv vaguement

vain [veɪn] (-er, -est) adj (a) (attempt, hope) vain; **in v.** en vain; **her efforts were in v.** ses efforts ont été inutiles (b) (conceited) vaniteux, -euse

valentine ['væləntaɪn] n (card) carte f de la Saint-Valentin; **(Saint) V.'s Day** la Saint-Valentin

valid ['vælɪd] adj valable ■ **validate** vt valider

valley ['vælɪ] (pl -eys) n vallée f

valuable ['væljʊəbəl] **1** adj (object) de valeur; Fig (help, time) précieux, -euse **2** npl **valuables** objets mpl de valeur

value ['væljuː] **1** n valeur f; **to be of v.** avoir de la valeur; **to be good v. (for money)** être d'un bon rapport qualité-prix **2** vt (appreciate) apprécier; (assess) évaluer ■ **valuation** [-jʊ'eɪʃən] n

(by expert) expertise f

valve [vælv] n (of machine, car) soupape f; (of pipe, tube) valve f

van [væn] n (vehicle) camionnette f, fourgonnette f

vandal ['vændəl] n vandale mf ■ **vandalism** n vandalisme m ■ **vandalize** vt saccager

vanilla [və'nɪlə] **1** n vanille f **2** adj (ice cream) à la vanille

vanish ['vænɪʃ] vi disparaître

vanity ['vænɪtɪ] n vanité f

vapour ['veɪpə(r)] (Am **vapor**) n vapeur f

variable ['veərɪəbəl] adj & n variable (f)

variant ['veərɪənt] n variante f

variation [veərɪ'eɪʃən] n variation f

varicose ['værɪkəʊs] adj **v. veins** varices fpl

varied ['veərɪd] adj varié

variety [və'raɪətɪ] n (a) (diversity) variété f; **a v. of** toutes sortes de (b) **v. show** spectacle m de variétés

various ['veərɪəs] adj divers

varnish ['vɑːnɪʃ] **1** n vernis m **2** vt vernir

vary ['veərɪ] (pt & pp -ied) vti varier (in/with en/selon) ■ **varying** adj variable

vase [Br vɑːz, Am veɪs] n vase m

vast [vɑːst] adj immense

VAT [viːeɪ'tiː, væt] (abbr **value added tax**) n Br TVA f

vat [væt] n cuve f

Vatican ['vætɪkən] n **the V.** le Vatican

vault¹ [vɔːlt] n (roof) voûte f; (tomb) caveau m; (cellar) cave f; (in bank) salle f des coffres

vault² [vɔːlt] vti (jump) sauter

VCR [viːsiːˈɑː(r)] (*abbr* **video cassette recorder**) *n* magnétoscope *m*

VDU [viːdiːˈjuː] (*abbr* **visual display unit**) *n* Comptr moniteur *m*

veal [viːl] *n* veau *m*

veer [vɪə(r)] *vi* (*of car*) virer; **to v. off the road** quitter la route

vegan [ˈviːgən] *n* végétalien, -enne *mf*

vegetable [ˈvedʒtəbəl] *n* légume *m* ▪ **vegetarian** [vedʒɪˈteərɪən] *adj & n* végétarien, -enne *(mf)* ▪ **vegetation** [vedʒɪˈteɪʃən] *n* végétation *f*

vehicle [ˈviːɪkəl] *n* véhicule *m*

veil [veɪl] *n* (*covering*) & Fig voile *m* ▪ **veiled** *adj* voilé

vein [veɪn] *n* (*in body*) veine *f*

Velcro® [ˈvelkrəʊ] *n* Velcro® *m*

velvet [ˈvelvɪt] **1** *n* velours *m* **2** *adj* de velours

vending [ˈvendɪŋ] *n* **v. machine** distributeur *m* automatique

vendor [ˈvendə(r)] *n* vendeur, -euse *mf*

veneer [vəˈnɪə(r)] *n* (*wood*) placage *m*; Fig (*appearance*) vernis *m*

vengeance [ˈvendʒəns] *n* vengeance *f*; **to take v. on sb** se venger de qn; Fig **with a v.** de plus belle

venison [ˈvenɪsən] *n* venaison *f*

venom [ˈvenəm] *n* (*poison*) & Fig venin *m*

vent [vent] *n* conduit *m*

ventilate [ˈventɪleɪt] *vt* ventiler, aérer ▪ **ventilation** *n* ventilation *f*, aération *f*

ventriloquist [venˈtrɪləkwɪst] *n* ventriloque *mf*

venture [ˈventʃə(r)] **1** *n* entreprise *f* (hasardeuse) **2** *vt* risquer; **to v. to do sth** se risquer à faire qch **3** *vi* s'aventurer (**into** dans)

venue [ˈvenjuː] *n* (*for meeting, concert*) salle *f*; (*for football match*) stade *m*

veranda(h) [vəˈrændə] *n* véranda *f*

verb [vɜːb] *n* verbe *m* ▪ **verbal** *adj* verbal

verdict [ˈvɜːdɪkt] *n* verdict *m*

verge [vɜːdʒ] **1** *n* Br (*of road*) bord *m*; **on the v. of ruin/tears** au bord de la ruine/des larmes; **to be on the v. of doing sth** être sur le point de faire qch

2 *vi* **to v. on** friser; (*of colour*) tirer sur

verify [ˈverɪfaɪ] (*pt & pp* **-ied**) *vt* vérifier

vermin [ˈvɜːmɪn] *n* (*animals*) animaux *mpl* nuisibles; (*insects, people*) vermine *f*

versatile [Br ˈvɜːsətaɪl, Am ˈvɜːrsətəl] *adj* polyvalent

verse [vɜːs] *n* (*poetry*) vers *mpl*; (*stanza*) strophe *f*; (*of Bible*) verset *m*

versed [vɜːst] *adj* (**well**) **v. in sth** versé dans qch

version [Br ˈvɜːʃən, Am ˈvɜːʒən] *n* version *f*

versus [ˈvɜːsəs] *prep* (*in sport, law*) contre; (*compared to*) comparé à

vertical [ˈvɜːtɪkəl] *adj* vertical

very [ˈverɪ] **1** *adv* très; **v. much** beaucoup; **the v. first** le tout premier (*f* la toute première); **the v. next day** le lendemain même; **at the v. least/most** tout au moins/plus; **at the v. latest** au plus tard

2 *adj* (*emphatic use*) **this v. house** cette maison même; **at the v. end** tout à la fin

vessel [ˈvesəl] *n* (*ship*) vaisseau *m*; (*container*) récipient *m*

vest [vest] *n* maillot *m* de corps; Am (*waistcoat*) gilet *m*

vested [ˈvestɪd] *adj* **to have a v. interest in sth** avoir un intérêt personnel dans qch

vestige [ˈvestɪdʒ] *n* vestige *m*

vet¹ [vet] *n* vétérinaire *mf*

vet² [vet] (*pt & pp* **-tt-**) *vt* Br faire une enquête sur

veteran [ˈvetərən] *n* Mil ancien combattant *m*; Fig vétéran *m*

veto [ˈviːtəʊ] **1** (*pl* **-oes**) *n* veto *m inv* **2** (*pt & pp* **-oed**) *vt* mettre son veto à

via [ˈvaɪə, ˈvɪə] *prep* via, par

viable [ˈvaɪəbəl] *adj* viable

viaduct [ˈvaɪədʌkt] *n* viaduc *m*

vibrant [ˈvaɪbrənt] *adj* (*colour*) vif (*f* vive)

vibrate [vaɪˈbreɪt] *vi* vibrer ▪ **vibration** *n* vibration *f*

vicar [ˈvɪkə(r)] *n* (*in Church of England*)

pasteur *m* ▪ **vicarage** [-rɪdʒ] *n* presby-
tère *m*

vice [vaɪs] *n (depravity, fault)* vice *m*;
Br (tool) étau *m*

vice- [vaɪs] *pref* vice-

vice versa [vaɪs(ɪ)'vɜːsə] *adv* vice
versa

vicinity [və'sɪnətɪ] *n* environs *mpl*; **in
the v. of** aux environs de

vicious ['vɪʃəs] *adj (malicious)* mé-
chant; *(violent)* brutal; **v. circle** cercle
m vicieux

victim ['vɪktɪm] *n* victime *f*; **to be the
v. of** être victime de

victimize ['vɪktɪmaɪz] *vt* persécuter

Victorian [vɪk'tɔːrɪən] **1** *adj* victo-
rien, -enne **2** *n* Victorien, -enne *mf*

victory ['vɪktərɪ] *(pl* -ies) *n* victoire *f*
▪ **victorious** [-'tɔːrɪəs] *adj* victorieux,
-euse

video ['vɪdɪəʊ] **1** *(pl* -os) *n (medium)*
vidéo *f*; *(cassette)* cassette *f* vidéo; *(re-
corder)* magnétoscope *m*; **on v.** sur cas-
sette vidéo
 2 *adj (camera, cassette, game)* vidéo
inv; **v. recorder** magnétoscope *m*
 3 *(pt & pp* -oed) *vt (on camcorder)* fil-
mer en vidéo; *(on video recorder)* enre-
gistrer (sur magnétoscope) ▪ **video-
tape** *n* bande *f* vidéo

vie [vaɪ] *(pres p* vying) *vi* **to v. with sb
(for sth/to do sth)** rivaliser avec qn
(pour qch/pour faire qch)

Vietnam [*Br* vjet'næm, *Am* -'nɑːm] *n* le
Viêt Nam

view [vjuː] **1** *n* vue *f*; *(opinion)* opinion
f; **in my v.** *(opinion)* à mon avis; **in v. of**
(considering) étant donné; **on v.** *(exhi-
bit)* exposé; **with a v. to doing sth**
dans l'intention de faire qch
 2 *vt (regard)* considérer; *(look at)* voir;
(house) visiter ▪ **viewer** *n* **(a)** *TV* télé-
spectateur, -trice *mf* **(b)** *(for slides)* vi-
sionneuse *f* ▪ **viewfinder** *n (in
camera)* viseur *m* ▪ **viewpoint** *n* point
m de vue

vigilant ['vɪdʒɪlənt] *adj* vigilant

vigorous ['vɪgərəs] *adj* vigoureux,
-euse

vile [vaɪl] *(-er, -est) adj (unpleasant)*

abominable; *(food, drink)* infect

villa ['vɪlə] *n* villa *f*

village ['vɪlɪdʒ] *n* village *m* ▪ **villager**
n villageois, -e *mf*

villain ['vɪlən] *n (scoundrel)* scélérat
m; *(in story, play)* méchant *m*

vindicate ['vɪndɪkeɪt] *vt* justifier

vindictive [vɪn'dɪktɪv] *adj* vindicatif,
-ive

vine [vaɪn] *n* vigne *f* ▪ **vineyard**
['vɪnjəd] *n* vigne *f*

vinegar ['vɪnɪgə(r)] *n* vinaigre *m*

vintage ['vɪntɪdʒ] **1** *n (year)* année *f*;
(wine) cru *m* **2** *adj (wine)* de cru; *(car)*
de collection *(datant généralement des
années 1920)*

vinyl ['vaɪnəl] *n* vinyle *m*

viola [vɪ'əʊlə] *n Mus* alto *m*

violate ['vaɪəleɪt] *vt (agreement)* vio-
ler

violence ['vaɪələns] *n* violence *f* ▪ **vio-
lent** *adj* violent ▪ **violently** *adv* vio-
lemment

violet ['vaɪələt] **1** *adj (colour)* violet,
-ette **2** *n (colour)* violet *m*; *(plant)* vio-
lette *f*

violin [vaɪə'lɪn] *n* violon *m* ▪ **violinist**
n violoniste *mf*

VIP [viːaɪ'piː] *(abbr* very important
person) *n* VIP *mf*

viper ['vaɪpə(r)] *n* vipère *f*

virgin ['vɜːdʒɪn] *n* vierge *f*

virile [*Br* 'vɪraɪl, *Am* 'vɪrəl] *adj* viril

virtual ['vɜːtʃʊəl] *adj* quasi; *Comptr*
virtuel, -elle ▪ **virtually** *adv (almost)*
quasiment

virtue ['vɜːtʃuː] *n (goodness, chastity)*
vertu *f*; *(advantage)* mérite *m* ▪ **virtu-
ous** [-tjʊəs] *adj* vertueux, -euse

virus ['vaɪərəs] *n Med & Comptr* virus *m*

Visa® ['viːzə] *n* **V. (card)** carte *f* Visa®

visa ['viːzə] *n* visa *m*

visible ['vɪzəbəl] *adj* visible ▪ **visibi-
lity** *n* visibilité *f*

vision ['vɪʒən] *n (eyesight)* vue *f*; *(fore-
sight)* clairvoyance *f*; *(apparition)* vi-
sion *f*

visit ['vɪzɪt] **1** *n* visite *f*; **to pay sb a v.**
rendre visite à qn

2 *vt (place)* visiter; *(person)* rendre visite à

3 *vi* **to be visiting** être de passage; *Br* **v. hours/card** heures *fpl*/carte *f* de visite ■ **visitor** *n* visiteur, -euse *mf*; *(guest)* invité, -e *mf*

visor ['vaɪzə(r)] *n* visière *f*

visual ['vɪʒʊəl] *adj* visuel, -elle; **v. aid** support *m* visuel; **v. arts** arts *mpl* plastiques ■ **visualize** *vt (imagine)* visualiser; *(foresee)* envisager

vital ['vaɪtəl] *adj* vital; **it's v. that...** il est vital que... *(+ subjunctive)*

vitality [vaɪ'tælɪtɪ] *n* vitalité *f*

vitamin [*Br* 'vɪtəmɪn, *Am* 'vaɪtəmɪn] *n* vitamine *f*

vivacious [vɪ'veɪʃəs] *adj* enjoué

vivid ['vɪvɪd] *adj* vif *(f* vive); *(description)* vivant; *(memory)* clair

V-neck ['viːnek] *adj* à col en V

vocabulary [*Br* və'kæbjʊlərɪ, *Am* -erɪ] *n* vocabulaire *m*

vocal ['vəʊkəl] *adj (cords, music)* vocal; *(noisy, critical)* qui se fait entendre

vocation [vəʊ'keɪʃən] *n* vocation *f* ■ **vocational** *adj* professionnel, -elle

vociferous [və'sɪfərəs] *adj* bruyant

vodka ['vɒdkə] *n* vodka *f*

vogue [vəʊg] *n* vogue *f*; **in v.** en vogue

voice [vɔɪs] **1** *n* voix *f*; **at the top of one's v.** à tue-tête **2** *vt (opinion, feelings)* exprimer

void [vɔɪd] **1** *n* vide *m* **2** *adj (deed, contract)* nul *(f* nulle)

volatile [*Br* 'vɒlətaɪl, *Am* 'vɒlətəl] *adj (person)* inconstant; *(situation)* explosif, -ive

volcano [vɒl'keɪnəʊ] *(pl* -oes) *n* volcan *m*

volley ['vɒlɪ] *n (in tennis)* volée ■ **volleyball** *n* volley(-ball) *m*

volt [vəʊlt] *n* volt *m* ■ **voltage** [-tɪdʒ] *n* voltage *m*

volume ['vɒljuːm] *n (book, capacity, loudness)* volume *m*

voluntary [*Br* 'vɒləntərɪ, *Am* -erɪ] *adj* volontaire; *(unpaid)* bénévole ■ **voluntarily** *adv* volontairement; *(on an unpaid basis)* bénévolement

volunteer [vɒlən'tɪə(r)] **1** *n* volontaire *mf*; *(for charity)* bénévole *mf* **2** *vt (information)* donner spontanément **3** *vi* se porter volontaire **(for sth** pour qch; **to do** pour faire)

vomit ['vɒmɪt] **1** *n* vomi *m* **2** *vti* vomir

vote [vəʊt] **1** *n (choice)* vote *m*; *(election)* scrutin *m*; *(paper)* voix *f*; **to take a v. on sth** voter sur qch; **to have the v.** avoir le droit de vote **2** *vt (funds, bill)* voter **3** *vi* voter; **to v. Labour** voter travailliste ■ **voter** *n (elector)* électeur, -trice *mf* ■ **voting** *n (polling)* scrutin *m*

vouch [vaʊtʃ] *vi* **to v. for sb/sth** répondre de qn/qch

voucher ['vaʊtʃə(r)] *n* coupon *m*, bon *m*; **(gift-)v.** chèque-cadeau *m*

vow [vaʊ] **1** *n* vœu *m* **2** *vt* jurer **(to** à); **to v. to do sth** jurer de faire qch

vowel ['vaʊəl] *n* voyelle *f*

voyage ['vɔɪɪdʒ] *n* voyage *m*

vulgar ['vʌlgə(r)] *adj* vulgaire

vulnerable ['vʌlnərəbəl] *adj* vulnérable

vulture ['vʌltʃə(r)] *n* vautour *m*

Ww

W, w ['dʌbəlju:] n (letter) W, w m inv

wacky ['wækɪ] (**-ier, -iest**) adj Fam farfelu

wad [wɒd] n (of papers, banknotes) liasse f; (of cotton wool) morceau m

waddle ['wɒdəl] vi Fig (of duck, person) se dandiner

wade [weɪd] vi to w. through (mud, water) patauger dans; Fig (book) venir péniblement à bout de

wafer ['weɪfə(r)] n (biscuit) gaufrette f; Rel hostie f

waffle¹ ['wɒfəl] n (cake) gaufre f

waffle² ['wɒfəl] Br Fam 1 n remplissage m 2 vi faire du remplissage

waft [wɒft] vi (of smell, sound) parvenir

wag [wæg] (pt & pp **-gg-**) vt remuer, agiter; to w. one's finger at sb menacer qn du doigt

wage [weɪdʒ] 1 n wage(s) salaire m, paie f; w. earner salarié, -e; mf; Br w. packet (money) paie 2 vt to w. war faire la guerre (on à)

wager ['weɪdʒə(r)] 1 n pari m 2 vt parier (that que)

waggle ['wægəl] vti remuer

wag(g)on ['wægən] n Br (of train) wagon m (découvert); (horse-drawn) charrette f

wail [weɪl] vi (of person) gémir; (of siren) hurler

waist [weɪst] n taille f ▪ **waistcoat** n Br gilet m ▪ **waistline** n taille f

wait [weɪt] 1 n attente f; to lie in w. for sb guetter qn
2 vt to w. one's turn attendre son tour
3 vi (a) attendre; to w. for sb/sth attendre qn/qch; to keep sb waiting faire attendre qn; w. till or until I've gone, w. for me to go attends que je sois parti; I can't w. to see her j'ai

vraiment hâte de la voir (b) to w. on sb servir qn ▪ **waiting 1** n attente f; Br 'no w.' 'arrêt interdit' 2 adj w. list/room liste f/salle f d'attente

▸**wait about, wait around** vi attendre

▸**wait behind** vi rester

▸**wait up** vi veiller; to w. up for sb attendre le retour de qn pour aller se coucher

waiter ['weɪtə(r)] n serveur m ▪ **waitress** n serveuse f

wake¹ [weɪk] (pt woke, pp woken) 1 vt to w. sb (up) réveiller qn 2 vi to w. (up) se réveiller; to w. up to sth prendre conscience de qch

wake² [weɪk] n (of ship) sillage m; Fig in the w. of sth à la suite de qch

Wales [weɪlz] n le pays de Galles

walk [wɔːk] 1 n (short) promenade f; (long) marche f; (gait) démarche f; (path) avenue f; to go for a w., to take a w. aller se promener; to take the dog for a w. promener le chien; five minutes' w. (away) à cinq minutes à pied
2 vt to w. the dog promener le chien; to w. sb home raccompagner qn; I walked 3 miles ≃ j'ai fait presque 5 km à pied
3 vi marcher; (as opposed to cycling, driving) aller à pied; (for exercise, pleasure) se promener; to w. home rentrer à pied ▪ **walker** n marcheur, -euse mf; (for pleasure) promeneur, -euse mf ▪ **walking** n marche f (à pied); w. stick canne f ▪ **walkway** n passage m couvert; **moving w.** trottoir m roulant

▸**walk away** vi s'en aller (**from** de)

▸**walk in** vi entrer

▸**walk off** vi s'en aller; to w. off with sth (steal) partir avec qch

▶**walk out** vi (leave) sortir; Br (of workers) se mettre en grève; **to w. out on sb** quitter qn

▶**walk over** vi to w. over to (go up to) s'approcher de

Walkman® ['wɔːkmən] (pl -mans) n baladeur m, Walkman® m

wall [wɔːl] **1** n mur m; (of cabin, tunnel, stomach) paroi f **2** adj (map, hanging) mural ■ **wallpaper 1** n papier m peint **2** vt tapisser ■ **wall-to-wall** adj w. **carpet(ing)** moquette f

wallet ['wɒlɪt] n portefeuille m

wallow ['wɒləʊ] vi se vautrer

walnut ['wɔːlnʌt] n (nut) noix f; (tree, wood) noyer m

walrus ['wɔːlrəs] (pl -ruses [-rəsəz]) n morse m

waltz [Br wɔːls, Am wɒlts] **1** n valse f **2** vi valser

wand [wɒnd] n (magic) w. baguette f magique

wander ['wɒndə(r)] **1** vt to w. the streets errer dans les rues **2** vi (of thoughts) vagabonder; (of person) errer, vagabonder; **to w. from** (path, subject) s'écarter de

▶**wander about, wander around** vi (roam) errer, vagabonder; (stroll) flâner

▶**wander off** vi (go away) s'éloigner

wangle ['wæŋgəl] vt Br Fam (obtain) se débrouiller pour avoir

want [wɒnt] **1** n (lack) manque m (of de); **for w. of** par manque de; **for w. of money/time** faute d'argent/de temps **2** vt vouloir (to do faire); **I w. him to go** je veux qu'il parte; **the lawn wants cutting** la pelouse a besoin d'être tondue; **you're wanted on the phone** on vous demande au téléphone ■ **wanted** adj (criminal) recherché par la police

wanton ['wɒntən] adj (gratuitous) gratuit

war [wɔː(r)] **1** n guerre f; **at w.** en guerre (**with** avec); **to declare w.** déclarer la guerre (**on** à) **2** adj (wound, crime) de guerre; **w. memorial** monument m aux morts

ward¹ [wɔːd] n (in hospital) salle f

ward² [wɔːd] vt to w. off (blow) éviter; (danger) chasser

warden ['wɔːdən] n (of institution, hostel) directeur, -trice mf

warder ['wɔːdə(r)] n Br gardien m (de prison)

wardrobe ['wɔːdrəʊb] n (cupboard) penderie f; (clothes) garde-robe f

warehouse ['weəhaʊs] (pl -ses [-zɪz]) n entrepôt m

wares [weəz] npl marchandises fpl

warfare ['wɔːfeə(r)] n guerre f

warm [wɔːm] **1** (-er, -est) adj chaud; Fig (welcome) chaleureux, -euse; **to be** or **feel w.** avoir chaud; **to get w.** (of person, room) se réchauffer; **it's w.** (of weather) il fait chaud

2 vt to w. (up) (person, food) réchauffer

3 vi to w. up (of person, room) se réchauffer; (of athlete) s'échauffer ■ **warmly** adv (dress) chaudement; Fig (welcome, thank) chaleureusement ■ **warmth** n chaleur f

warn [wɔːn] vt avertir, prévenir (**that** que); **to w. sb against** or **of sth** mettre qn en garde contre qch ■ **warning** n (caution) avertissement m; (advance notice) avis m; **without w.** sans prévenir; **w. light** (on appliance) voyant m lumineux; Br (hazard) **w. lights** feux mpl de détresse

warp [wɔːp] **1** vt (wood) gauchir; Fig (judgement, person) pervertir **2** vi (of door) gauchir

warrant ['wɒrənt] n (in law) mandat m ■ **warranty** (pl -ies) n Com garantie f

warren ['wɒrən] n (rabbit) w. garenne f

warrior ['wɒrɪə(r)] n guerrier, -ère mf

wart [wɔːt] n verrue f

wartime ['wɔːtaɪm] n in w. en temps de guerre

wary ['weərɪ] (-ier, -iest) adj prudent; **to be w. of sb/sth** se méfier de qn/qch; **to be w. of doing sth** hésiter beaucoup à faire qch

was [wəz, stressed wɒz] pt of **be**

wash [wɒʃ] **1** n to have a w. se laver;

to give sth a w. laver qch

2 *vt* laver; **to w. one's hands** se laver les mains (**of sth** de qch)

3 *vi (have a wash)* se laver ■ **washbasin** *n Br* lavabo *m* ■ **washcloth** *n Am* gant *m* de toilette ■ **washing-up** *n Br* vaisselle *f*; **to do the w.** faire la vaisselle; **w. liquid** liquide *m* vaisselle ■ **washroom** *n Am* toilettes *fpl*

▶**wash down** *vt sep (car, deck)* laver à grande eau; *(food)* arroser (**with** de)

▶**wash off 1** *vt sep* enlever **2** *vi* partir

▶**wash out 1** *vt sep (bowl, cup)* rincer; *(stain)* faire partir (en lavant) **2** *vi (of stain)* partir (au lavage)

▶**wash up 1** *vt sep Br (dishes, forks)* laver **2** *vi Br (do the dishes)* faire la vaisselle; *Am (have a wash)* se débarbouiller

washable ['wɒʃəbəl] *adj* lavable

washer ['wɒʃə(r)] *n (ring)* joint *m*

washing ['wɒʃɪŋ] *n (action)* lavage *m*; *(clothes)* linge *m*; **to do the w.** faire la lessive; **w. machine** machine *f* à laver; *Br* **w. powder** lessive *f*

wasp [wɒsp] *n* guêpe *f*

waste [weɪst] **1** *n* gaspillage *m*; *(of time)* perte *f*; *(rubbish)* déchets *mpl*; **w. material** *or* **products** déchets *mpl*; *Br* **w. ground** *(in town)* terrain *m* vague; **w. land** *(uncultivated)* terres *fpl* incultes; *(in town)* terrain *m* vague; **w. pipe** tuyau *m* d'évacuation

2 *vt (money, food)* gaspiller; *(time)* perdre; *(opportunity)* gâcher; **to w. no time doing sth** ne pas perdre de temps pour faire qch

3 *vi* **to w. away** dépérir ■ **wasted** *adj (effort)* inutile

wastebin ['weɪstbɪn] *n (in kitchen)* poubelle *f*

wasteful ['weɪstfəl] *adj (person)* gaspilleur, -euse; *(process)* peu économique

watch [wɒtʃ] **1** *n* (a) *(timepiece)* montre *f* (b) **to keep a close w. on sb/sth** surveiller qn/qch de près

2 *vt* regarder; *(observe)* observer; *(suspect, baby, luggage)* surveiller; *(be careful of)* faire attention à; **w. it!** attention!

3 *vi* regarder; **to w. out for sb/sth**

guetter qn/qch; **to w. out** *(take care)* faire attention (**for** à); **w. out!** attention!; **to w. over** surveiller ■ **watchdog** *n* chien *m* de garde ■ **watchstrap** *n* bracelet *m* de montre

watchful ['wɒtʃfəl] *adj* vigilant

water ['wɔːtə(r)] **1** *n* eau *f*; **under w.** *(road, field)* inondé; *(swim)* sous l'eau; **w. heater** chauffe-eau *m inv*; **w. pistol** pistolet *m* à eau; **w. polo** water-polo *m*; **w. skiing** ski *m* nautique; **w. wings** brassards *mpl* de natation

2 *vt (plant)* arroser; **to w. sth down** *(wine)* diluer qch; *(text)* édulcorer qch

3 *vi (of eyes)* larmoyer; **it makes my mouth w.** ça me met l'eau à la bouche ■ **watercolour** *(Am* **-color)** *n* aquarelle *f* ■ **watercress** *n* cresson *m* (de fontaine) ■ **waterfall** *n* cascade *f* ■ **watering** *n* **w. can** arrosoir *m* ■ **watermark** *n* filigrane *m* ■ **watermelon** *n* pastèque *f* ■ **waterproof** *adj* imperméable; *(watch)* étanche ■ **watertight** *adj (container)* étanche

watery ['wɔːtərɪ] *adj (soup)* trop liquide; *(coffee, tea)* insipide; *(colour)* délavé

watt [wɒt] *n* watt *m*

wave [weɪv] **1** *n* *(of water, crime)* vague *f*; *(in hair)* ondulation *f*; *Phys* onde *f* **2** *vt (arm, flag)* agiter; *(stick)* brandir **3** *vi (of person)* faire signe (de la main); **to w. to sb** *(signal)* faire signe de la main à qn; *(greet)* saluer qn de la main ■ **waveband** *n* bande *f* de fréquences ■ **wavelength** *n* longueur *f* d'onde; *Fig* **on the same w.** sur la même longueur d'onde

waver ['weɪvə(r)] *vi (of person, flame)* vaciller

wavy ['weɪvɪ] (**-ier, -iest**) *adj (line)* qui ondule; *(hair)* ondulé

wax [wæks] **1** *n* cire *f*; *(for ski)* fart *m* **2** *adj (candle, doll)* de cire; *Am* **w. paper** *(for wrapping)* papier *m* paraffiné **3** *vt* cirer; *(ski)* farter; *(car)* lustrer

WAY [weɪ] **1** *n* (a) *(path, road)* chemin *m* (**to** de); *(direction)* sens *m*, direction *f*; **the w. in** l'entrée *f*; **the w. out** la sortie; **the w. to the station** le chemin pour aller à la gare; **to ask sb**

the w. demander son chemin à qn; **to show sb the w.** montrer le chemin à qn; **to lose one's w.** se perdre; **I'm on my w.** *(coming)* j'arrive; *(going)* je pars; **to make w. for sb** faire de la place à qn; **out of the w.** *(isolated)* isolé; **to get out of the w.** s'écarter; **to go all the w.** aller jusqu'au bout; **to give w.** céder; *Br (in vehicle)* céder le passage **(to** à); **it's a long w. away** *or* **off** c'est très loin; **it's the wrong w. up** c'est dans le mauvais sens; **this w.** par ici; **that w.** par là; **which w.?** par où?

(b) *(manner)* manière *f*; **in this w.** de cette manière; **by w. of** *(via)* par; *Fig (as)* comme; *Fig* **by the w.** à propos; *Fam* **no w.!** *(certainly not)* pas question!; **w. of life** mode *m* de vie

2 *adv Fam* **w. behind** très en arrière; **w. ahead** très en avance **(of** sur)

wayward ['weɪwəd] *adj* difficile

WC [dʌbəlju:'si:] *n* W.-C. *mpl*

we [wi:] *pron* nous; *(indefinite)* on; **we teachers** nous autres professeurs; **we all make mistakes** tout le monde peut se tromper

weak [wi:k] (-er, -est) *adj* faible; *(tea, coffee)* léger, -ère; **to have a w. heart** avoir le cœur fragile ▪ **weakling** *n (in body)* mauviette *f*; *(in character)* faible *mf* ▪ **weakness** *n* faiblesse *f*; *(fault)* point *m* faible; **to have a w. for sb/ sth** avoir un faible pour qn/qch

weaken ['wi:kən] **1** *vt* affaiblir **2** *vi* s'affaiblir

wealth [welθ] *n* richesse *f*; *Fig* **a w. of sth** une abondance de qch ▪ **wealthy 1** (-ier, -iest) *adj* riche **2** *npl* **the w.** les riches *mpl*

weapon ['wepən] *n* arme *f*

wear [weə(r)] **1** *n* (a) **men's w.** vêtements *mpl* pour hommes; **evening w.** tenue *f* de soirée (b) *(use)* **w. and tear** usure *f* naturelle **2** *(pt* **wore,** *pp* **worn)** *vt (garment, glasses)* porter; **to w. black** porter du noir **3** *vi* **to w. thin** *(of clothing)* s'user; **to w. well** *(of clothing)* bien vieillir

▸ **wear down 1** *vt sep* user; **to w. sb down** avoir qn à l'usure **2** *vi* s'user

▸ **wear off** *vi (of colour, pain)* disparaître

▸ **wear out 1** *vt sep (clothes)* user; **to w. sb out** épuiser qn **2** *vi (of clothes)* s'user; *Fig (of patience)* s'épuiser

weary ['wɪərɪ] **1** (-ier, -iest) *adj* las *(f* lasse) **(of doing** de faire) **2** *vi* se lasser **(of** de)

weather ['weðə(r)] **1** *n* temps *m*; **what's the w. like?** quel temps fait-il?; **in hot w.** par temps chaud; **under the w.** *(ill)* patraque **2** *adj* **w. forecast** prévisions *fpl* météorologiques; **w. report** (bulletin *m*) météo *f* **3** *vt (storm)* essuyer; *Fig (crisis)* surmonter ▪ **weatherman** *(pl* -men) *n (on TV, radio)* présentateur *m* météo

weave [wi:v] **1** *(pt* **wove,** *pp* **woven)** *vt (cloth, plot)* tisser; *(basket, garland)* tresser **2** *vi* tisser; *Fig* **to w. in and out of** *(crowd, cars)* se faufiler entre

web [web] *n (of spider)* toile *f*; *Fig (of lies)* tissu *m*; *Comptr* **the W.** le Web; **w. page** page *f* Web; **w. site** site *m* Web

wed [wed] *(pt & pp* -dd-) **1** *vt (marry)* épouser **2** *vi* se marier

we'd [wi:d] = **we had, we would**

wedding ['wedɪŋ] **1** *n* mariage *m*; **golden/silver w.** noces *fpl* d'or/d'argent **2** *adj (anniversary, present, cake)* de mariage; *(dress)* de mariée; **his/her w. day** le jour de son mariage; *Br* **w. ring,** *Am* **w. band** alliance *f*

wedge [wedʒ] **1** *n (of wheel, table)* cale *f* **2** *vt (wheel, table)* caler; *(push)* enfoncer **(into** dans); **to w. a door open** maintenir une porte ouverte avec une cale; **wedged (in) between** coincé entre

Wednesday ['wenzdeɪ] *n* mercredi *m*

wee¹ [wi:] *adj Scot Fam (tiny)* tout petit *(f* toute petite)

wee² [wi:] *vi Br Fam* faire pipi

weed [wi:d] **1** *n (plant)* mauvaise herbe *f* **2** *vti* désherber; *Fig* **to w. sth out** éliminer qch **(from** de) ▪ **weedkiller** *n* désherbant *m* ▪ **weedy** (-ier, -iest) *adj Fam (person)* malingre

week [wi:k] *n* semaine *f*; **tomorrow w., a w. tomorrow** demain en huit

- **weekday** n jour m de semaine

weekend [wiːkˈend] n week-end m; **at** or **on** or **over the w.** ce week-end; *(every weekend)* le week-end

weekly [ˈwiːklɪ] **1** adj hebdomadaire **2** adv toutes les semaines **3** n *(magazine)* hebdomadaire m

weep [wiːp] *(pt & pp* **wept)** vi pleurer

weigh [weɪ] **1** vt peser; **to w. sb/sth down** *(with load)* surcharger qn/qch (with de); **to w. up** *(chances)* peser **2** vi peser; **it's weighing on my mind** ça me tracasse ■ **weighing-machine** n balance f

weight [weɪt] **1** n poids m; **to put on w.** grossir; **to lose w.** maigrir; *Fig* **to carry w.** *(of argument)* avoir du poids **2** vt **to w. sth (down)** *(hold down)* faire tenir qch avec un poids ■ **weightlifter** n haltérophile mf ■ **weightlifting** n haltérophilie f

weighty [ˈweɪtɪ] (-ier, -iest) adj *(serious, important)* grave

weir [wɪə(r)] n barrage m

weird [wɪəd] (-er, -est) adj bizarre

welcome [ˈwelkəm] **1** adj *(person, news, change)* bienvenu; **to make sb w.** faire un bon accueil à qn; **w.!** bienvenue!; **you're w.!** *(after 'thank you')* il n'y a pas de quoi!; **you're w. to use my bike** mon vélo est à ta disposition **2** n accueil m; **to give sb a warm w.** faire un accueil chaleureux à qn **3** vt *(person)* souhaiter la bienvenue à; *(news, change)* accueillir favorablement ■ **welcoming** adj accueillant; *(speech, words)* de bienvenue

welfare [ˈwelfeə(r)] n *(wellbeing)* bien-être m; *Am Fam* **to be on w.** recevoir l'aide sociale; *Br* **the W. State** l'État m providence

we'll [wiːl] = we will, we shall

well¹ [wel] n *(for water, oil)* puits m

well² [wel] **1** (better, best) adj bien; **to be w.** aller bien; **to get w.** se remettre; **it's just as w....** heureusement que... **2** adv bien; **you'd do w. to refuse** tu ferais bien de refuser; **she might (just) as w. have stayed at home** elle aurait

mieux fait de rester chez elle; **as w.** *(also)* aussi; **as w. as** aussi bien que; **as w. as two cats, he has...** en plus de deux chats, il a... **3** exclam eh bien!; **w., w.!** *(surprise)* tiens, tiens!; **huge, w. quite big** énorme, enfin, assez grand ■ **well-behaved** adj sage ■ **well-being** n bien-être m ■ **well-built** adj *(person, car)* solide ■ **well-dressed** adj bien habillé ■ **well-informed** adj bien informé ■ **well-known** adj (bien) connu ■ **well-meaning** adj bien intentionné ■ **well-off** adj riche ■ **well-paid** adj bien payé ■ **well-read** adj instruit ■ **well-timed** adj opportun ■ **well-to-do** adj aisé ■ **wellwisher** n sympathisant, -e mf ■ **well-worn** adj *(clothes, carpet)* très usé

wellington [ˈwelɪŋtən] *(Fam* **welly** [ˈwelɪ], pl -ies) n Br **w. (boot)** botte f de caoutchouc

Welsh [welʃ] **1** adj gallois **2** n *(language)* gallois m; **the W.** *(people)* les Gallois mpl ■ **Welshman** (pl -men) n Gallois m ■ **Welshwoman** (pl -women) n Galloise f

went [went] pt of **go**

wept [wept] pt & pp of **weep**

were [wə(r), stressed wɜː(r)] pt of **be**

we're [wɪə(r)] = we are

west [west] **1** n ouest m; **(to the) w. of** à l'ouest de; *Pol* **the W.** l'Occident m **2** adj *(coast)* ouest inv; *(wind)* d'ouest; **W. Africa** l'Afrique f occidentale; **W. Indian** adj antillais; n Antillais, -e mf; **the W. Indies** les Antilles fpl **3** adv à l'ouest; *(travel)* vers l'ouest ■ **westbound** adj *(traffic)* en direction de l'ouest; *Br (carriageway)* ouest inv ■ **westerly** adj *(direction)* de l'ouest ■ **western 1** adj *(coast)* ouest inv; *Pol (culture)* occidental; **W. Europe** l'Europe f de l'Ouest **2** n *(film)* western m ■ **westerner** n Pol occidental, -e mf ■ **westward** adj & adv vers l'ouest ■ **westwards** adv vers l'ouest

wet [wet] **1** (wetter, wettest) adj mouillé; *(weather)* pluvieux -euse; *(day)* de pluie; **to get w.** se mouiller; **to be w. through** être trempé; **it's w.**

(raining) il pleut; **'w. paint'** 'peinture fraîche'; **w. suit** combinaison *f* de plongée **2** *n* **the w.** *(rain)* la pluie; *(damp)* l'humidité *f* **3** *(pt & pp* **-tt-***)* *vt* mouiller

we've [wiːv] = **we have**

whack [wæk] *vt Fam* donner un grand coup à

whale [weɪl] *n* baleine *f*

WHAT [wɒt] **1** *adj* quel, quelle, *pl* quel(le)s; **w. book?** quel livre?; **w. a fool!** quel idiot!; **w. little she has** le peu qu'elle a
2 *pron* **(a)** *(in questions) (subject)* qu'est-ce qui; *(object)* (qu'est-ce) que; *(after prep)* quoi; **w.'s happening?** qu'est-ce qui se passe?; **w. does he do?** qu'est-ce qu'il fait?, que fait-il?; **w. is it?** qu'est-ce que c'est?; **w.'s that book?** c'est quoi, ce livre?; **w.!** *(surprise)* quoi!, comment!; **w.'s it called?** comment ça s'appelle?; **w. for?** pourquoi?; **w. about going out for lunch?** si on allait déjeuner?
(b) *(in relative construction) (subject)* ce qui; *(object)* ce que; **I know w. will happen/w. she'll do** je sais ce qui arrivera/ce qu'elle fera; **w. I need...** ce dont j'ai besoin...

whatever [wɒt'evə(r)] **1** *adj* **w. (the) mistake** quelle que soit l'erreur; **of w. size** de n'importe quelle taille; **no chance w.** pas la moindre chance; **nothing w.** rien du tout **2** *pron (no matter what)* quoi que *(+ subjunctive)*; **w. you do** quoi que tu fasses; **do w. you want** fais tout ce que tu veux

whatsit ['wɒtsɪt] *n Fam* machin *m*

whatsoever [wɒtsəʊ'evə(r)] *adj* **for no reason w.** sans aucune raison; **none w.** aucun

wheat [wiːt] *n* blé *m*

wheedle ['wiːdəl] *vt* **to w. sb** enjôler qn (**into doing** pour qu'il/elle fasse); **to w. sth out of sb** obtenir qch de qn par la flatterie

wheel [wiːl] **1** *n* roue *f*; **to be at the w.** être au volant **2** *vt (push)* pousser ■ **wheelbarrow** *n* brouette *f* ■ **wheelchair** *n* fauteuil *m* roulant ■ **wheelclamp** *n* sabot *m* de Denver

wheeze [wiːz] *vi* respirer bruyamment ■ **wheezy** (**-ier, -iest**) *adj* poussif, -ive

when [wen] **1** *adv* quand **2** *conj (with time)* quand, lorsque; **w. I finish, w. I've finished** quand j'aurai fini; **the day/moment w.** le jour/moment où

whenever [wen'evə(r)] *conj (at whatever time)* quand; *(each time that)* chaque fois que

where [weə(r)] **1** *adv* où; **w. are you from?** d'où êtes-vous?
2 *conj* où; **I found it w. she'd left it** je l'ai trouvé là où elle l'avait laissé; **the place/house w. I live** l'endroit/la maison où j'habite; ■ **whereabouts 1** *adv* où **2** ['weərəbaʊts] *n* **his w.** l'endroit *m* où il est ■ **whereas** *conj* alors que ■ **whereby** *adv Formal* par quoi

wherever [weər'evə(r)] *conj* **w. you go** *(everywhere)* partout où tu iras, où que tu ailles; **I'll go w. you like** j'irai (là) où vous voudrez

whet [wet] *(pt & pp* **-tt-***)* *vt (appetite, desire)* aiguiser

whether ['weðə(r)] *conj* si; **I don't know w. to leave** je ne sais pas si je dois partir; **w. she does it or not** qu'elle le fasse ou non; **it's doubtful w....** il est douteux que... *(+ subjunctive)*

WHICH [wɪtʃ] **1** *adj (in questions)* quel, quelle, *pl* quel(le)s; **w. book?** quel livre?; **w. one?** lequel/laquelle?; **in w. case** auquel cas
2 *relative pron (subject)* qui; *(object)* que; *(after prep)* lequel, laquelle, *pl* lesquel(le)s; *(referring to a whole clause) (subject)* ce qui; *(object)* ce que; **the house, w. is old...** la maison, qui est vieille...; **the book w. I like...** le livre que j'aime...; **the table w. I put it on...** la table sur laquelle je l'ai mis...; **the film of w. she was speaking** le film dont *ou* duquel elle parlait; **she's ill, w. is sad** elle est malade, ce qui est triste; **he lies, w. I don't like** il ment, ce que je n'aime pas; **after w.** *(whereupon)* après quoi
3 *interrogative pron (in questions)* lequel, laquelle, *pl* lesquel(le)s; **w. of us?** lequel/laquelle d'entre nous?; **w. are**

the best of the books? quels sont les meilleurs de ces livres?

 4 *pron* **w. (one)** *(the one that) (subject)* celui qui, celle qui, *pl* ceux qui, celles qui; *(object)* celui que, celle que, *pl* ceux que, celles que; **I know w. (ones) you want** je sais ceux/celles que vous désirez

whichever [wɪtʃ'evə(r)] **1** *adj (no matter which)* **take w. books interest you** prenez les livres qui vous intéressent; **take w. one you like** prends celui/celle que tu veux **2** *pron (no matter which)* quel que soit celui qui *(f* quelle que soit celle qui); **w. you choose... quel que soit celui que tu choisiras...; **take w. you want** prends celui/celle que tu veux

while [waɪl] **1** *conj (when)* pendant que; *(although)* bien que *(+ subjunctive)*; *(as long as)* tant que; *(whereas)* tandis que; **w. eating** en mangeant **2** *n* **a w.** un moment; **all the w.** tout le temps **3** *vt* **to w. away the time** passer le temps **(doing sth** à faire qch) ▪ **whilst** *conj Br* = **while**

whim [wɪm] *n* caprice *m*; **on a w.** sur un coup de tête

whimper ['wɪmpə(r)] *vi* gémir

whine [waɪn] *vi* gémir

whip [wɪp] **1** *n* fouet *m* **2** *(pt & pp* -**pp-**) *vt* fouetter; **whipped cream** crème *f* fouettée

▶ **whip off** *vt sep Fam (clothes)* enlever rapidement

▶ **whip out** *vt sep Fam* sortir brusquement **(from** de)

▶ **whip up** *vt sep (interest)* susciter; *Fam (meal)* préparer rapidement

whirl [wɜ:l] **1** *vt* **to w. sb/sth (round)** faire tourbillonner qn/qch **2** *vi* **to w. (round)** tourbillonner ▪ **whirlpool** *n* tourbillon *m* ▪ **whirlwind** *n* tourbillon *m*

whirr [wɜ:(r)] *vi* ronfler

whisk [wɪsk] **1** *n (for eggs)* fouet *m* **2** *vt* battre; **to w. away** *or* **off** *(object)* enlever rapidement; *(person)* emmener rapidement

whiskers ['wɪskəz] *npl (of cat)* mous-

taches *fpl*; *(of man)* favoris *mpl*

whisky ['wɪskɪ] *(Am* **whiskey**) *n* whisky *m*

whisper ['wɪspə(r)] **1** *n* chuchotement *m* **2** *vti* chuchoter; **to w. sth to sb** chuchoter qch à l'oreille de qn

whistle ['wɪsəl] **1** *n* sifflement *m*; *(object)* sifflet *m* **2** *vti* siffler

white [waɪt] **1** (**-er, -est**) *adj* blanc *(f* blanche); **to go** *or* **turn w.** blanchir; *Br* **w. coffee** café *m* au lait; **w. lie** pieux mensonge *m*; **w. man** Blanc *m* ▪ **w. woman** Blanche *f* **2** *n (colour, of egg, eye)* blanc *m* ▪ **whitewash 1** *n (paint)* badigeon *m* à la chaux **2** *vt (paint)* badigeonner à la chaux; *Fig (person)* blanchir

Whitsun ['wɪtsən] *n Br* la Pentecôte

whizz [wɪz] **1** *vi (rush)* aller à toute vitesse; **to w. past** *or* **by** passer à toute vitesse **2** *adj Fam* **w. kid** petit prodige *m*

who [hu:] *pron* qui; **w. did it?** qui (est-ce qui) a fait ça?; **the woman w. came** la femme qui est venue; **w. were you talking to?** à qui est-ce que tu parlais?

whodun(n)it [hu:'dʌnɪt] *n Fam* polar *m*

whoever [hu:'evə(r)] *pron (no matter who) (subject)* qui que ce soit qui; *(object)* qui que ce soit que; **w. has seen this** *(anyone who)* quiconque a vu cela; **w. you are** qui que vous soyez; **this man, w. he is** cet homme, quel qu'il soit

whole [həʊl] **1** *adj* entier, -ère; **the w. time** tout le temps; **the w. apple** toute la pomme, la pomme tout entière; **the w. world** le monde entier **2** *n* totalité *f*; **the w. of the village** le village tout entier, tout le village; **on the w., as a w.** dans l'ensemble ▪ **wholefood** *n* aliment *m* complet ▪ **whole-hearted** *adj* sans réserve ▪ **wholemeal** *(Am* **wholewheat**) *adj (bread)* complet, -ète ▪ **wholesome** *adj (food, climate)* sain

wholesale ['həʊlseɪl] **1** *adj (price)* de gros; **w. business** *or* **trade** commerce *m* de gros **2** *adv (buy, sell)* au prix de gros

wholly ['həʊlɪ] *adv* entièrement

whom [hu:m] *pron Formal (object)* que; *(in questions and after prep)* qui; **w. did she see?** qui a-t-elle vu?; **the man w. you know** l'homme que tu connais; **the man of w. we were speaking** l'homme dont nous parlions

whooping ['hu:pɪŋ] *adj* **w. cough** coqueluche *f*

whoops [wʊps] *exclam* houp-là!

whopping ['wɒpɪŋ] *adj Fam (big)* énorme

whore [hɔː(r)] *n Fam* putain *f*

whose [hu:z] *possessive pron & adj* à qui, de qui; **w. book is this?, w. is this book?** à qui est ce livre?; **w. daughter are you?** de qui es-tu la fille?; **the woman w. book I have** la femme dont j'ai le livre; **the man w. mother I spoke to** l'homme à la mère de qui j'ai parlé

why [waɪ] **1** *adv* pourquoi; **w. not?** pourquoi pas? **2** *conj* **the reason w. they...** la raison pour laquelle ils... **3** *exclam (surprise)* tiens!

wick [wɪk] *n (of candle, lighter, oil lamp)* mèche *f*

wicked ['wɪkɪd] *adj (evil)* méchant

wicker ['wɪkə(r)] *n* osier *m*

wicket ['wɪkɪt] *n (cricket stumps)* guichet *m*

wide [waɪd] **1** (-er, -est) *adj* large; *(choice, variety, knowledge)* grand; **to be 3 metres w.** avoir 3 mètres de large **2** *adv (fall, shoot)* loin du but; **w. open** *(eyes, mouth, door)* grand ouvert; **w. awake** complètement réveillé ▪ **widely** *adv (travel)* beaucoup; *(spread)* largement; **it's w. thought that...** on pense généralement que... ▪ **widen 1** *vt* élargir **2** *vi* s'élargir

widespread ['waɪdspred] *adj* répandu

widow ['wɪdəʊ] *n* veuve *f* ▪ **widower** *n* veuf *m*

width [wɪdθ] *n* largeur *f*

wield [wi:ld] *vt (brandish)* brandir; *Fig* **to w. power** exercer le pouvoir

wife [waɪf] *(pl wives) n* femme *f*, épouse *f*

wig [wɪg] *n* perruque *f*

wiggle ['wɪgəl] **1** *vt* remuer **2** *vi (of worm)* se tortiller; *(of tail)* remuer

wild [waɪld] **1** (-er, -est) *adj (animal, flower, region)* sauvage; *(idea)* fou *(f* folle); **w. with joy/anger** fou de joie/colère; **to be w.** *(of person)* mener une vie agitée; *Fam* **I'm not w. about it** ça ne m'emballe pas; **the W. West** le Far West
 2 *adv* **to grow w.** *(of plant)* pousser à l'état sauvage; **to run w.** *(of animals)* courir en liberté; *(of crowd)* se déchaîner
 3 *n* **in the w.** à l'état sauvage; **in the wilds** en pleine brousse ▪ **wildlife** *n* nature *f*

wilderness ['wɪldənəs] *n* région *f* sauvage

wildly ['waɪldlɪ] *adv (cheer)* frénétiquement; *(guess)* au hasard

wilful ['wɪlfəl] *(Am* **willful**) *adj (intentional, obstinate)* volontaire

WILL¹ [wɪl]

On trouve généralement **I/you/he**/etc **will** sous leurs formes contractées **I'll/you'll/he'll**/etc. La forme négative correspondante est **won't**, que l'on écrira **will not** dans des contextes formels.

v aux (expressing future tense) **he w. come, he'll come** il viendra; **you w. not come, you won't come** tu ne viendras pas; **w. you have some tea?** veux-tu du thé?; **w. you be quiet!** veux-tu te taire!; **it won't open** ça ne s'ouvre pas

will² [wɪl] *n (resolve, determination)* volonté *f*; *(legal document)* testament *m*; **free w.** libre arbitre *m*; **against one's w.** à contrecœur; **at w.** à volonté; *(cry)* à la demande

willing ['wɪlɪŋ] *adj (helper, worker)* plein de bonne volonté; **to be w. to do sth** bien vouloir faire qch ▪ **willingly** *adv (with pleasure)* volontiers; *(voluntarily)* de son plein gré ▪ **willingness** *n* bonne volonté *f*; **her w. to do sth** *(enthusiasm)* son empressement à faire qch

willpower ['wɪlpaʊə(r)] *n* volonté *f*

wilt [wɪlt] *vi (of plant)* dépérir

wily ['waɪlɪ] (**-ier, -iest**) *adj* rusé

wimp [wɪmp] *n Fam (weakling)* mauviette *f*

win [wɪn] **1** *n (victory)* victoire *f* **2** (*pt & pp* **won,** *pres p* **winning**) *vt (money, race, prize)* gagner; *(victory)* remporter; *(fame)* acquérir; *(friends)* se faire; *Br* **to w. sb over** *or* **round** gagner qn (**to** à) **3** *vi* gagner ■ **winning 1** *adj (number, horse)* gagnant; *(team)* victorieux, -euse; *(goal)* décisif, -ive **2** *npl* **winnings** gains *mpl*

wince [wɪns] *vi* faire une grimace

winch [wɪntʃ] **1** *n* treuil *m* **2** *vt* **to w. (up)** hisser

wind¹ [wɪnd] **1** *n* vent *m*; *(breath)* souffle *m*; **to have w.** *(in stomach)* avoir des gaz; **to get w. of sth** avoir vent de qch; *Mus* **w. instrument** instrument *m* à vent

2 *vt* **to w. sb** *(of blow)* couper le souffle à qn ■ **windcheater** (*Am* **windbreaker**) *n* coupe-vent *m inv* ■ **windfall** *n (unexpected money)* aubaine *f* ■ **windmill** *n* moulin *m* à vent ■ **windscreen** (*Am* **windshield**) *n (of vehicle)* pare-brise *m inv*; **w. wiper** essuie-glace *m* ■ **windsurfer** *n (person)* véliplanchiste *mf* ■ **windsurfing** *n* **to go w.** faire de la planche à voile ■ **windy** (**-ier, -iest**) *adj* **it's w.** *(of weather)* il y a du vent; **w. day** jour *m* de grand vent

wind² [waɪnd] **1** (*pt & pp* **wound**) *vt (roll)* enrouler (**round** autour de); *(clock)* remonter; **to w. a cassette back** rembobiner une cassette **2** *vi (of river, road)* serpenter ■ **winding** *adj (road)* sinueux, -euse; *(staircase)* en colimaçon

▸ **wind down 1** *vt sep (car window)* baisser **2** *vi Fam (relax)* se détendre

▸ **wind up 1** *vt sep (clock)* remonter; *(meeting, speech)* terminer; *Br Fam* **to w. sb up** faire marcher qn **2** *vi (end up)* finir (**doing sth** par faire qch); **to w. up with sb/sth** se retrouver avec qn/qch

window ['wɪndəʊ] *n* fenêtre *f*; *(pane)* vitre *f*; *(of shop)* vitrine *f*; *(counter)* guichet *m*; *Br* **French w.** porte-fenêtre *f*;

w. box jardinière *f*; *Br* **w. cleaner,** *Am* **w. washer** laveur, -euse *mf* de vitres; *Br* **w. ledge** rebord *m* de fenêtre ■ **windowpane** *n* vitre *f*, carreau *m* ■ **window-shopping** *n* **to go w.** faire du lèche-vitrines ■ **windowsill** *n* rebord *m* de fenêtre

wine [waɪn] *n* vin *m*; **w. bar/bottle** bar *m*/bouteille *f* à vin; **w. cellar** cave *f* à vin; **w. list** carte *f* des vins; **w. tasting** dégustation *f*; **w. waiter** sommelier *m* ■ **wineglass** *n* verre *m* à vin

wing [wɪŋ] *n* aile *f*; **the wings** *(in theatre)* les coulisses *fpl*

wink [wɪŋk] *vi* faire un clin d'œil (**at** à)

winner ['wɪnə(r)] *n* gagnant, -e *mf*

winter ['wɪntə(r)] **1** *n* hiver *m*; **in (the) w.** en hiver **2** *adj* d'hiver ■ **wintertime** *n* hiver *m* ■ **wintry** *adj* hivernal; **w. day** jour *m* d'hiver

wipe [waɪp] **1** *n* **to give sth a w.** essuyer qch **2** *vt* essuyer; **to w. one's feet/hands** s'essuyer les pieds/les mains; **to w. sth away** *or* **off** *or* **up** *(liquid)* essuyer qch; **to w. sth out** *(clean)* essuyer qch; *(destroy)* anéantir qch ■ **wiper** *n* essuie-glace *m*

wire ['waɪə(r)] **1** *n* fil *m*; **w. mesh** *or* **netting** toile *f* métallique **2** *vt* **to w. (up)** *(house)* faire l'installation électrique de; **to w. sth (up) to sth** *(connect electrically)* relier qch à qch ■ **wiring** *n (system)* installation *f* électrique

wisdom ['wɪzdəm] *n* sagesse *f*

wise [waɪz] (**-er, -est**) *adj (in knowledge)* sage; *(advisable)* prudent; **to be none the wiser** ne pas être plus avancé ■ **wisely** *adv* sagement

-wise [waɪz] *suff (with regard to)* **money-w.** question argent

wish [wɪʃ] **1** *n (specific)* souhait *m*, vœu *m*; *(general)* désir *m*; **to do sth against sb's wishes** faire qch contre le souhait de qn; **best wishes, all good wishes** *(in letter)* amitiés *fpl*; **send him my best wishes** fais-lui mes amitiés

2 *vt* souhaiter (**to do** faire); **I w. (that) you could help me** je voudrais que

vous m'aidiez; **I w. she could come** j'aurais bien aimé qu'elle vienne; **I w. you (a) happy birthday/(good) luck** je vous souhaite bon anniversaire/ bonne chance; **I w. I could** si seulement je pouvais

3 *vi* **to w. for sth** souhaiter qch; **as you w.** comme vous voudrez ▪ **wishful** *adj* **it's w. thinking (on your part)** tu prends tes désirs pour des réalités

wisp [wɪsp] *n (of smoke)* traînée *f*; *(of hair)* mèche *f*

wistful ['wɪstfəl] *adj* nostalgique

wit [wɪt] *n (humour)* esprit *m*; *(person)* homme *m*/femme *f* d'esprit; **wits** *(intelligence)* intelligence *f*; **to be at one's wits' or w.'s end** ne plus savoir que faire

witch [wɪtʃ] *n* sorcière *f*

WITH [wɪð] *prep* (a) *(expressing accompaniment)* avec; **come w. me** viens avec moi; **w. no hat/gloves** sans chapeau/gants; **I'll be right w. you** je suis à vous dans une seconde; *Fam* **I'm w. you** *(I understand)* je te suis; *Fam* **to be w. it** *(up-to-date)* être dans le vent

(b) *(at the house, flat of)* chez; **she's staying w. me** elle loge chez moi

(c) *(expressing cause)* de; **to tremble w. fear** trembler de peur; **to be ill w. measles** être malade de la rougeole

(d) *(expressing instrument, means)* **to write w. a pen** écrire avec un stylo; **to fill w. sth** remplir de qch; **satisfied w. sb/sth** satisfait de qn/qch; **w. my own eyes** de mes propres yeux

(e) *(in description)* à; **a woman w. blue eyes** une femme aux yeux bleus

(f) *(despite)* malgré; **w. all his faults** malgré tous ses défauts

withdraw [wɪð'drɔ:] **1** *(pt* **-drew,** *pp* **-drawn)** *vt* retirer **(from** de) **2** *vi* se retirer **(from** de) ▪ **withdrawal** *n* retrait *m* ▪ **withdrawn** *adj (person)* renfermé

withhold [wɪð'həʊld] *(pt & pp* **-held)** *vt (permission, help)* refuser **(from** à); *(decision)* différer; *(money)* retenir **(from** de); *(information)* cacher **(from** à)

within [wɪð'ɪn] **1** *prep (inside)* à l'in-

térieur de; **w. 10 km (of)** *(less than)* à moins de 10 km (de); *(inside an area of)* dans un rayon de 10 km (de); **w. a month** *(return)* avant un mois; *(finish)* en moins d'un mois; **w. sight** en vue **2** *adv* à l'intérieur

without [wɪð'aʊt] **1** *prep* sans; **w. a tie** sans cravate; **w. doing sth** sans faire qch; **to do w. sb/sth** se passer de qn/qch **2** *adv* **to do w.** se priver

withstand [wɪð'stænd] *(pt & pp* **-stood)** *vt* résister à

witness ['wɪtnɪs] **1** *n (person)* témoin *m* **2** *vt (accident)* être témoin de; *(document)* signer (pour attester l'authenticité de)

witty ['wɪtɪ] **(-ier, -iest)** *adj* spirituel, -elle

wives [waɪvz] *pl of* **wife**

wizard ['wɪzəd] *n* magicien *m*; *Fig (genius)* as *m*

wobble ['wɒbəl] *vi (of chair)* branler; *(of jelly, leg)* trembler; *(of wheel)* tourner de façon irrégulière; *(of person)* chanceler ▪ **wobbly** *adj (table, chair)* branlant

woe [wəʊ] *n* malheur *m*

wok [wɒk] *n* poêle *f* chinoise

woke [wəʊk] *pt of* **wake**[1]

woken ['wəʊkən] *pp of* **wake**[1]

wolf [wʊlf] **1** *(pl* **wolves)** *n* loup *m* **2** *vt* **to w. (down)** *(food)* engloutir

woman ['wʊmən] *(pl* **women)** *n* femme *f*; **women's** *(clothes, attitudes, magazine)* féminin; **women's rights** droits *mpl* des femmes

womb [wu:m] *n Anat* utérus *m*

women ['wɪmɪn] *pl of* **woman**

won [wʌn] *pt & pp of* **win**

wonder ['wʌndə(r)] **1** *n (marvel)* merveille *f*; *(feeling)* émerveillement *m*; **it's no w.** ce n'est pas étonnant **(that** que + *subjunctive)*; **it's a w. she wasn't killed** c'est un miracle qu'elle n'ait pas été tuée

2 *vt (ask oneself)* se demander **(if** si; **why** pourquoi)

3 *vi (ask oneself questions)* s'interroger **(about** au sujet de *ou* sur); **I was just wondering** je réfléchissais

wonderful [ˈwʌndəfəl] *adj* merveilleux, -euse

wonky [ˈwɒŋkɪ] (**-ier, -iest**) *adj Br Fam* (table) déglingué; (hat, picture) de travers

won't [wəʊnt] = will not

woo [wuː] (*pt & pp* **wooed**) *vt* (voters) chercher à plaire à

wood [wʊd] *n* (material, forest) bois *m* ▪ **wooded** *adj* boisé ▪ **wooden** *adj* en bois; *Fig* (manner, dancer, actor) raide ▪ **woodland** *n* région *f* boisée ▪ **woodwind** *n* the w. (musical instruments) les bois *mpl* ▪ **woodwork** *n* (school subject) menuiserie *f* ▪ **woodworm** *n* it has w. c'est vermoulu

wool [wʊl] *n* laine *f* ▪ **woollen** (*Am* **woolen**) **1** *adj* (dress) en laine **2** *npl* **woollens** (*Am* **woolens**) (garments) lainages *mpl* ▪ **woolly** (**-ier, -iest**) **1** *adj* en laine; *Fig* (unclear) nébuleux, -euse **2** *n Br Fam* (garment) lainage *m*

word [wɜːd] **1** *n* mot *m*; (promise) parole *f*; **words** (of song) paroles *fpl*; **to have a w. with sb** parler à qn; **to keep one's w.** tenir sa promesse; **in other words** autrement dit; **w. for w.** (report) mot pour mot; (translate) mot à mot; **w. processing** traitement *m* de texte; **w. processor** machine *f* à traitement de texte

2 *vt* (express) formuler ▪ **wording** *n* termes *mpl* ▪ **wordy** (**-ier, -iest**) *adj* prolixe

wore [wɔː(r)] *pt of* wear

work [wɜːk] **1** *n* travail *m*; (literary, artistic) œuvre *f*; **works** (construction) travaux *mpl*; **to be at w.** travailler; **it's hard w. (doing that)** ça demande beaucoup de travail (de faire ça); **to be out of w.** être sans travail; **a day off w.** un jour de congé; **w. permit** permis *m* de travail; **w. station** poste *m* de travail; **w. of art** œuvre *f* d'art

2 *vt* (person) faire travailler; (machine) faire marcher; (metal, wood) travailler

3 *vi* (of person) travailler; (of machine) marcher, fonctionner; (of drug) agir; **to w. loose** (of knot, screw) se desserrer; **to w. towards** (result, agreement, aim) travailler à ▪ **workaholic** [-əˈhɒlɪk] *n*

Fam bourreau *m* de travail ▪ **workforce** *n* main-d'œuvre *f* ▪ **workload** *n* charge *f* de travail ▪ **workman** (*pl* **-men**) *n* ouvrier *m* ▪ **workmanship** *n* travail *m* ▪ **workmate** *n Br* camarade *mf* de travail ▪ **workout** *n* (sports training) séance *f* d'entraînement ▪ **workshop** *n* (place, study course) atelier *m*

▸ **work at** *vt insep* (improve) travailler

▸ **work off** *vt sep* (debt) payer en travaillant; (excess fat) se débarrasser de (par l'exercice)

▸ **work on** *vt insep* (book, problem) travailler à; (French) travailler

▸ **work out 1** *vt sep* (calculate) calculer; (problem) résoudre; (plan) préparer; (understand) comprendre **2** *vi* (succeed) marcher; (do exercises) s'entraîner; **it works out at 50 euros** ça fait 50 euros

▸ **work up 1** *vt sep* **to w. up enthusiasm** s'enthousiasmer (**for** pour); **I worked up an appetite** ça m'a ouvert l'appétit; **to get worked up** s'énerver **2** *vi* **to w. up to sth** se préparer à qch

worker [ˈwɜːkə(r)] *n* travailleur, -euse *mf*; (manual) ouvrier, -ère *mf*; **(office) w.** employé, -e *mf* (de bureau)

working [ˈwɜːkɪŋ] **1** *adj* (day, clothes) de travail; **in w. order** en état de marche; **w. class** classe *f* ouvrière; **w. conditions** conditions *fpl* de travail **2** *npl* **the workings of** (clock) le mécanisme de ▪ **working-class** *adj* ouvrier, -ère

world [wɜːld] **1** *n* monde *m*; **all over the w.** dans le monde entier **2** *adj* (war, production) mondial; (champion, record) du monde; **the W. Cup** (in football) la Coupe du Monde ▪ **worldly** *adj* (person) qui a l'expérience du monde ▪ **worldwide 1** *adj* mondial **2** *adv* dans le monde entier

worm [wɜːm] **1** *n* ver *m* **2** *vt* **to w. one's way into** s'insinuer dans; **to w. sth out of sb** soutirer qch à qn

worn [wɔːn] **1** *pp of* wear **2** *adj* (clothes, tyre) usé ▪ **worn-out** *adj* (object) complètement usé; (person) épuisé

worry [ˈwʌrɪ] **1** (*pl* **-ies**) *n* souci *m*; **it's a w.** ça me cause du souci

2 (*pt & pp* **-ied**) *vt* inquiéter
3 *vi* s'inquiéter (**about sth** de qch; **about sb** pour qn) ■ **worried** *adj* inquiet, -ète (**about** au sujet de) ■ **worrying** *adj* inquiétant

worse [wɜːs] **1** *adj* pire (**than** que); **to get w.** se détériorer; **he's getting w.** *(in health)* il va de plus en plus mal; *(in behaviour)* il se conduit de plus en plus mal
2 *adv* plus mal (**than** que); **I could do w.** j'aurais pu tomber plus mal; **she's w. off (than before)** sa situation est pire (qu'avant); *(financially)* elle est encore plus pauvre (qu'avant)
3 *n* **there's w. to come** le pire reste à venir; **a change for the w.** une détérioration

worsen ['wɜːsən] **1** *vt* aggraver **2** *vi* empirer

worship ['wɜːʃɪp] **1** *n* culte *m* **2** (*pt & pp* **-pp-**) *vt (person, god)* adorer; *Pej (money)* avoir le culte de

worst [wɜːst] **1** *adj* pire; **the w. book I've ever read** le plus mauvais livre que j'aie jamais lu **2** *adv* **(the) w.** le plus mal **3** *n* **the w. (one)** *(object, person)* le/la pire, le/la plus mauvais(e); **the w. (thing) is that…** le pire, c'est que…; **at (the) w.** au pire

worth [wɜːθ] **1** *adj* **to be w. sth** valoir qch; **how much** *or* **what is it w.?** ça vaut combien?; **the film's (well) w. seeing** le film vaut la peine d'être vu **2** *n* valeur *f*; **to buy 50 pence w. of chocolates** acheter pour 50 pence de chocolats; **to get one's money's w.** en avoir pour son argent ■ **worthless** *adj* qui ne vaut rien

worthwhile ['wɜːθ'waɪl] *adj (book, film)* qui vaut la peine d'être lu/vu; *(activity)* qui vaut la peine; *(plan, contribution)* valable; *(cause)* louable; *(satisfying)* qui donne des satisfactions

worthy ['wɜːðɪ] (**-ier, -iest**) *adj (person)* digne; *(cause, act)* louable; **to be w. of sb/sth** être digne de qn/qch

WOULD [wʊd, *unstressed* wəd]

On trouve généralement **I/you/he** etc **would** sous leurs formes contractées

I'd/you'd/he'd etc. La forme négative correspondante est **wouldn't**, que l'on écrira **would not** dans des contextes formels.

v aux (**a**) *(expressing conditional tense)* **I w. stay if I could** je resterais si je le pouvais; **he w. have done it** il l'aurait fait; **I said she'd come** j'ai dit qu'elle viendrait
(**b**) *(willingness, ability)* **w. you help me, please?** veux-tu bien m'aider?; **she wouldn't help me** elle n'a pas voulu m'aider; **w. you like some tea?** prendrez-vous du thé?; **the car wouldn't start** la voiture ne démarrait pas
(**c**) *(expressing past habit)* **I w. see her every day** je la voyais chaque jour

wound¹ [wuːnd] **1** *n* blessure *f* **2** *vt (hurt)* blesser; **the wounded** les blessés *mpl*

wound² [waʊnd] *pt & pp of* **wind²**

wove [wəʊv] *pt of* **weave**

woven ['wəʊvən] *pp of* **weave**

wow [waʊ] *exclam Fam* oh là là!

wrap [ræp] **1** *n Am* **plastic w.** film *m* plastique
2 (*pt & pp* **-pp-**) *vt* **to w. (up)** envelopper; *(parcel)* emballer; *Fig* **wrapped up in** *(engrossed)* absorbé par
3 *vti* **to w. (oneself) up** *(dress warmly)* s'emmitoufler ■ **wrapper** *n (of sweet)* papier *m* ■ **wrapping** *n (action, material)* emballage *m*; **w. paper** papier *m* d'emballage

wreath [riːθ] (*pl* **-s** [riːðz]) *n* couronne *f*

wreck [rek] **1** *n (ship)* épave *f*; *(train)* train *m* accidenté; *(person)* épave *f* (humaine); **to be a nervous w.** être à bout de nerfs **2** *vt (break, destroy)* détruire; *Fig (spoil)* gâcher; *(career, hopes)* briser ■ **wreckage** [-ɪdʒ] *n (of plane, train)* débris *mpl*

wrench [rentʃ] **1** *n Am (tool)* clef *f* (à écrous) **2** *vt* **to w. sth from sb** arracher qch à qn

wrestle ['resəl] *vi* lutter (**with sb** avec qn); *Fig* **to w. with a problem** se débattre avec un problème ■ **wrestler** *n* lutteur, -euse *mf*; *(in all-in wrestling)*

catcheur, -euse *mf* ■ **wrestling** *n* lutte *f*; **(all-in) w.** *(with relaxed rules)* catch *m*

wretch [retʃ] *n (unfortunate person)* malheureux, -euse *mf*; *(rascal)* misérable *mf* ■ **wretched** [-ɪd] *adj (poor, pitiful)* misérable; *(dreadful)* affreux, -euse; *Fam (annoying)* maudit

wriggle ['rɪgəl] **1** *vt (toes, fingers)* tortiller **2** *vi* **to w. (about)** se tortiller; *(of fish)* frétiller; **to w. out of sth** couper à qch

wring [rɪŋ] *(pt & pp wrung) vt* **to w. (out)** *(clothes)* essorer; **to w. one's hands** se tordre les mains

wrinkle ['rɪŋkəl] **1** *n (on skin)* ride *f*; *(in cloth, paper)* pli *m* **2** *vi (of skin)* se rider; *(of cloth)* faire des plis ■ **wrinkled** *adj (skin)* ridé; *(cloth)* froissé

wrist [rɪst] *n* poignet *m* ■ **wristwatch** *n* montre-bracelet *f*

write [raɪt] *(pt wrote, pp written) vti* écrire; **to w. to sb** écrire à qn ■ **write-off** *n Br* **to be a (complete) w.** *(of vehicle)* être bon pour la casse

▸**write away for** *vt insep (details)* écrire pour demander

▸**write back** *vi* répondre

▸**write down** *vt sep* noter

▸**write in 1** *vt sep (insert)* inscrire **2** *vi (send letter)* écrire

▸**write off** *vt sep (debt)* annuler

▸**write out** *vt sep (list, recipe)* noter; *(cheque)* faire

▸**write up** *vt sep (notes)* rédiger

writer ['raɪtə(r)] *n* auteur *m* **(of** de); *(literary)* écrivain *m*

writing ['raɪtɪŋ] *n (handwriting, action, profession)* écriture *f*; **to put sth (down) in w.** mettre qch par écrit; **w. pad** bloc-notes *m*; **w. paper** papier *m* à lettres

written ['rɪtən] *pp of* **write**

wrong [rɒŋ] **1** *adj (sum, idea)* faux *(f* fausse); *(direction, time)* mauvais; *(unfair)* injuste; **to be w.** *(of person)* avoir tort **(to do** de faire); **it's the w. road** ce n'est pas la bonne route; **the clock's w.** la pendule n'est pas à l'heure; **to get the w. number** *(on phone)* se tromper de numéro; **something's w. with the phone** le téléphone ne marche pas bien; **something's w. with her leg** elle a quelque chose à la jambe; **what's w. with you?** qu'est-ce que tu as?; **the w. way round** *or* **up** à l'envers

2 *adv* mal; **to go w.** *(of plan)* mal tourner; *(of vehicle, machine)* tomber en panne; *(of person)* se tromper

3 *n (injustice)* injustice *f*; **to be in the w.** être dans son tort; **right and w.** le bien et le mal

4 *vt* faire du tort à ■ **wrongful** *adj* **w. arrest** arrestation *f* arbitraire ■ **wrongly** *adv (inform, translate)* mal; *(accuse, condemn, claim)* à tort

wrote [rəʊt] *pt of* **write**

wrung [rʌŋ] *pt & pp of* **wring**

wry [raɪ] **(wryer, wryest)** *adj* ironique

Xx

X, x [eks] *n (letter)* X, x *m inv*

xenophobia [*Br* zenəˈfəʊbɪə, *Am* ziːnəʊ-] *n* xénophobie *f*

Xerox® [ˈzɪərɒks] **1** *n (copy)* photocopie *f* **2** *vt* photocopier

Xmas [ˈkrɪsməs] *n Fam* Noël *m*

X-ray [ˈeksreɪ] **1** *n (picture)* radio *f*; **to have an X.** passer une radio **2** *vt* radiographier

xylophone [ˈzaɪləfəʊn] *n* xylophone *m*

Yy

Y, y [waɪ] *n (letter)* Y, y *m inv*

yacht [jɒt] *n (sailing boat)* voilier *m*; *(large private boat)* yacht *m* ▪ **yachting** *n* voile *f*

yap [jæp] *(pt & pp -pp-) vi (of dog)* japper

yard¹ [jɑːd] *n (of house, farm, school, prison)* cour *f*; *(for working)* chantier *m*; *(for storage)* dépôt *m* de marchandises; *Am (garden)* jardin *m*

yard² [jɑːd] *n (measure)* yard *m (= 91,44 cm)*

yarn [jɑːn] *n (thread)* fil *m*; *Fam (tale)* histoire *f* à dormir debout

yawn [jɔːn] *vi* bâiller

year [jɪə(r)] *n* an *m*, année *f*; *(of wine)* année *f*; **school/tax y.** année *f* scolaire/fiscale; **in the y. 2004** en (l'an) 2004; **he's ten years old** il a dix ans; **New Y.** Nouvel An *m*; **New Y.'s Day** le jour de l'An; **New Y.'s Eve** la Saint-Sylvestre ▪ **yearly 1** *adj* annuel, -elle **2** *adv* annuellement; **twice y.** deux fois par an

yearn [jɜːn] *vi* **to y. for sb** languir après qn; **to y. for sth** désirer ardemment qch; **to y. to do sth** brûler de faire qch

yeast [jiːst] *n* levure *f*

yell [jel] *vti* **to y. (out)** hurler; **to y. at sb** *(scold)* crier après qn

yellow ['jeləʊ] **1** *adj (in colour)* jaune; **y. card** *(in football)* carton *m* jaune **2** *n* jaune *m*

yes [jes] **1** *adv* oui; *(after negative question)* si **2** *n* oui *m inv*

yesterday ['jestədeɪ] **1** *adv* hier **2** *n* hier *m*; **y. morning/evening** hier matin/soir; **the day before y.** avant-hier

yet [jet] **1** *adv* (a) *(still)* encore; *(already)* déjà; **she hasn't arrived (as) y.** elle n'est pas encore arrivée; **the best y.** le meilleur jusqu'ici; **y. another mistake** encore une erreur; **not (just) y.** pas pour l'instant (b) *(in questions)* **has he come y.?** est-il arrivé? **2** *conj (nevertheless)* pourtant

yew [juː] *n (tree, wood)* if *m*

yield [jiːld] **1** *n (of field, shares)* rendement *m* **2** *vt (result)* donner; *(interest)* rapporter; *(territory, right)* céder; **to y. a profit** rapporter **3** *vi (surrender)* se rendre; *Am* **'y.'** *(road sign)* 'cédez le passage'

yob [jɒb], **yobbo** ['jɒbəʊ] *(pl yob-(bo)s) n Br Fam* loubard *m*

yoga ['jəʊgə] *n* yoga *m*

yog(h)urt [*Br* 'jɒgət, *Am* 'jəʊgərt] *n* yaourt *m*

yolk [jəʊk] *n* jaune *m* (d'œuf)

you [juː] *pron* (a) *(subject) (pl, polite form sing)* vous; *(familiar form sing)* tu; *(object)* vous, te, t', *pl* vous; *(after prep, 'than', 'it is')* vous, to, *pl* vous; **(to) y.** *(indirect)* vous, te, t', *pl* vous; **I gave it (to) y.** je vous/te l'ai donné; **y. teachers** vous autres professeurs; **y. idiot!** espèce d'imbécile!

(b) *(indefinite)* on; *(object)* vous, te, t', *pl* vous; **y. never know** on ne sait jamais ▪ **you'd** = you had, you would ▪ **you'll** = you will

young [jʌŋ] **1** *(-er, -est) adj* jeune; **she's two years younger than me** elle a deux ans de moins que moi; **my young(er) brother** mon (frère) cadet; **my youngest sister** la cadette de mes sœurs; **y. people** les jeunes *mpl*
2 *n (of animals)* petits *mpl*; **the y.** *(people)* les jeunes *mpl*; **she's my youngest** *(daughter)* c'est ma petite dernière ▪ **youngster** *n* jeune *mf*

your [jɔː(r)] *possessive adj (polite form*

sing, polite and familiar form pl) votre, *pl* vos; *(familiar form sing)* ton, ta, *pl* tes; *(one's)* son, sa, *pl* ses

yours [jɔːz] *possessive pron* le vôtre, la vôtre, *pl* les vôtres; *(familiar form sing)* le tien, la tienne, *pl* les tien(ne)s; **this book is y.** ce livre est à vous *ou* est le vôtre/ce livre est à toi *ou* est le tien; **a friend of y.** un ami à vous/toi

yourself [jɔːˈself] *pron (polite form)* vous-même; *(familiar form)* toi-même; *(reflexive)* vous, te, t'; *(after prep)* vous, toi; **you wash y.** vous vous lavez/tu te laves ▪ **yourselves** *pron pl* vous-mêmes; *(reflexive and after prep)* vous; **did you cut y.?** est-ce que vous vous êtes coupés?

youth [juːθ] *(pl* **-s** [juːðz]*) n (age)* jeunesse *f; (young man)* jeune *m;* **y. club** centre *m* de loisirs pour les jeunes; **y. hostel** auberge *f* de jeunesse ▪ **youthful** *adj (person)* jeune

you've [juːv] = **you have**

yo-yo [ˈjəʊjəʊ] *(pl* **yo-yos**) *n* Yo-Yo® *m inv*

yuppie [ˈyʌpɪ] *n* yuppie *mf*

Zz

Z, z [*Br* zed, *Am* zi:] *n (letter)* Z, z *m inv*

zany ['zeɪnɪ] (**-ier, -iest**) *adj* loufoque

zap [zæp] (*pt & pp* **-pp-**) *vt Fam Comptr* effacer

zeal [zi:l] *n* zèle *m* ■ **zealous** ['zeləs] *adj* zélé

zebra ['zi:brə, *Br* 'zebrə] *n* zèbre *m*; *Br* **z. crossing** passage *m* pour piétons

zero ['zɪərəʊ] (*pl* **-os**) *n* zéro *m*

zest [zest] *n (enthusiasm)* enthousiasme *m*; *(of lemon, orange)* zeste *m*

zigzag ['zɪgzæg] **1** *n* zigzag *m* **2** *adj & adv* en zigzag **3** (*pt & pp* **-gg-**) *vi* zigzaguer

zinc [zɪŋk] *n* zinc *m*

zip [zɪp] **1** *n Br* **z. (fastener)** fermeture *f* Éclair® **2** *adj Am* **z. code** code *m* postal **3** (*pt & pp* **-pp-**) *vt* **to z. sth (up)** remonter la fermeture Éclair® de qch **4** *vi* **to z. past** *(of car)* passer en trombe ■ **zipper** *n Am* fermeture *f* Éclair®

zit [zɪt] *n Fam (pimple)* bouton *m*

zodiac ['zəʊdɪæk] *n* zodiaque *m*

zone [zəʊn] *n* zone *f*

zoo [zu:] (*pl* **zoos**) *n* zoo *m*

zoom [zu:m] **1** *n* **z. lens** zoom *m* **2** *vi* **to z. in** *(of camera)* faire un zoom avant **(on** sur); *Fam* **to z. past** passer comme une flèche

zucchini [zu:'ki:nɪ] (*pl* **-ni** *or* **-nis**) *n Am* courgette *f*

Supplement

French Verb Conjugations
Regular Verbs

	-ER verbs	**-IR verbs**	**-RE verbs**
Infinitive	*donn/er*	*fin/ir*	*vend/re*
1 Present	je donne	je finis	je vends
	tu donnes	tu finis	tu vends
	il donne	il finit	il vend
	nous donnons	nous finissons	nous vendons
	vous donnez	vous finissez	vous vendez
	ils donnent	ils finissent	ils vendent
2 Imperfect	je donnais	je finissais	je vendais
	tu donnais	tu finissais	tu vendais
	il donnait	il finissait	il vendait
	nous donnions	nous finissions	nous vendions
	vous donniez	vous finissiez	vous vendiez
	ils donnaient	ils finissaient	ils vendaient
3 Past historic	je donnai	je finis	je vendis
	tu donnas	tu finis	tu vendis
	il donna	il finit	il vendit
	nous donnâmes	nous finîmes	nous vendîmes
	vous donnâtes	vous finîtes	vous vendîtes
	ils donnèrent	ils finirent	ils vendirent
4 Future	je donnerai	je finirai	je vendrai
	tu donneras	tu finiras	tu vendras
	il donnera	il finira	il vendra
	nous donnerons	nous finirons	nous vendrons
	vous donnerez	vous finirez	vous vendrez
	ils donneront	ils finiront	ils vendront
5 Subjunctive	je donne	je finisse	je vende
	tu donnes	tu finisses	tu vendes
	il donne	il finisse	il vende
	nous donnions	nous finissions	nous vendions
	vous donniez	vous finissiez	vous vendiez
	ils donnent	ils finissent	ils vendent
6 Imperative	donne	finis	vends
	donnons	finissons	vendons
	donnez	finissez	vendez
7 Present participle	donnant	finissant	vendant
8 Past participle	donné	fini	vendu

Note The conditional is formed by adding the following endings to the infinitive: **-ais, -ais, -ait, -ions, -iez, -aient**. The final **e** is dropped in infinitives ending **-re**.

Irregular French Verbs

Listed below are those verbs considered to be the most useful. Forms and tenses not given are fully derivable, such as the third person singular of the **present tense** which is normally formed by substituting 't' for the final 's' of the first person singular, eg 'crois' becomes 'croit', 'dis' becomes 'dit'. Note that the endings of the **past historic** fall into three categories, the 'a' and 'i' categories shown at *donner*, and at *finir* and *vendre*, and the 'u' category which has the following endings: -us, -ut, -ûmes, -ûtes, -urent. Most of the verbs listed below form their past historic with 'u'.

The **imperfect** may usually be formed by adding -ais, -ait, -ions, -iez, -aient to the stem of the first person plural of the present tense, eg 'je buvais' etc may be derived from 'nous buvons' (stem 'buv-' and ending '-ons'); similarly, the **present participle** may generally be formed by substituting -ant for -ons (eg buvant). The **future** may usually be formed by adding -ai, -as, -a, -ons, -ez, -ont to the infinitive or to an infinitive without final 'e' where the ending is -re (eg conduire). The **imperative** usually has the same forms as the second persons singular and plural and first person plural of the present tense.

1 = Present	2 = Imperfect	3 = Past historic	4 = Future
5 = Subjunctive	6 = Imperative	7 = Present participle	8 = Past participle
n = nous	v = vous	*verbs conjugated with **être** only	

abattre	*like*	**battre**
absoudre	1 j'absous, n absolvons 2 j'absolvais	
	3 j'absolus *(rarely used)* 5 j'absolve 7 absolvant	
	8 absous, absoute	
s'abstenir	*like*	**tenir**
abstraire	1 j'abstrais, n abstrayons 2 j'abstrayais 3 *none* 5 j'abstraie	
	7 abstrayant 8 abstrait	
accourir	*like*	**courir**
accroître	*like*	**croître** *except* 8 accru
accueillir	*like*	**cueillir**
acquérir	1 j'acquiers, n acquérons 2 j'acquérais 3 j'acquis	
	4 j'acquerrai 5 j'acquière 7 acquérant 8 acquis	
adjoindre	*like*	**joindre**
admettre	*like*	**mettre**
advenir	*like*	**venir** *(third person only)*
***aller**	1 je vais, tu vas, il va, n allons, v allez, ils vont 4 j'irai	
	5 j'aille, n allions, ils aillent 6 va, allons, allez *(but note* vas-y*)*	
apercevoir	*like*	**recevoir**
apparaître	*like*	**connaître**
appartenir	*like*	**tenir**
apprendre	*like*	**prendre**

asseoir		1 j'assieds, il assied, n asseyons, ils asseyent 2 j'asseyais
		3 j'assis 4 j'assiérai 5 j'asseye 7 asseyant 8 assis
astreindre	*like*	**atteindre**
atteindre		1 j'atteins, n atteignons, ils atteignent 2 j'atteignais
		3 j'atteignis 4 j'atteindrai 5 j'atteigne 7 atteignant 8 atteint
avoir		1 j'ai, tu as, il a, n avons, v avez, ils ont 2 j'avais 3 j'eus
		4 j'aurai 5 j'aie, il ait, n ayons, ils aient 6 aie, ayons, ayez
		7 ayant 8 eu
battre		1 je bats, il bat, n battons 5 je batte
boire		1 je bois, n buvons, ils boivent 2 je buvais 3 je bus
		5 je boive, n buvions 7 buvant 8 bu
bouillir		1 je bous, n bouillons, ils bouillent 2 je bouillais
		3 je bouillis 5 je bouille 7 bouillant
braire		(*defective*) 1 il brait, ils braient 4 il braira, ils brairont
circonscrire	*like*	**écrire**
circonvenir	*like*	**tenir**
clore	*like*	**éclore**
combattre	*like*	**battre**
commettre	*like*	**mettre**
comparaître	*like*	**connaître**
complaire	*like*	**plaire**
comprendre	*like*	**prendre**
compromettre	*like*	**mettre**
concevoir	*like*	**recevoir**
conclure		1 je conclus, n concluons, ils concluent 5 je conclue
concourir	*like*	**courir**
conduire		1 je conduis, n conduisons 3 je conduisis 5 je conduise
		8 conduit
confire	*like*	**suffire**
connaître		1 je connais, il connaît, n connaissons 3 je connus
		5 je connaisse 7 connaissant 8 connu
conquérir	*like*	**acquérir**
consentir	*like*	**mentir**
construire	*like*	**conduire**
contenir	*like*	**tenir**
contraindre	*like*	**craindre**
contredire	*like*	**dire** *except* 1 v contredisez
convaincre	*like*	**vaincre**
convenir	*like*	**tenir**
corrompre	*like*	**rompre**
coudre		1 je couds, il coud, n cousons, ils cousent 3 je cousis
		5 je couse 7 cousant 8 cousu
courir		1 je cours, n courons 3 je courus 4 je courrai 5 je coure
		8 couru
couvrir		1 je couvre, n couvrons 2 je couvrais 5 je couvre 8 couvert
craindre		1 je crains, n craignons, ils craignent 2 je craignais
		3 je craignis 4 je craindrai 5 je craigne 7 craignant
		8 craint

croire		1 je crois, n croyons, ils croient 2 je croyais 3 je crus 5 je croie, n croyions 7 croyant 8 cru
croître		1 je crois, il croît, n croissons 2 je croissais 3 je crûs 5 je croisse 7 croissant 8 crû, crue
cueillir		1 je cueille, n cueillons 2 je cueillais 4 je cueillerai 5 je cueille 7 cueillant
cuire		1 je cuis, n cuisons 2 je cuisais 3 je cuisis 5 je cuise 7 cuisant 8 cuit
débattre	*like*	**battre**
décevoir	*like*	**recevoir**
déchoir		(*defective*) 1 je déchois 2 *none* 3 je déchus 4 je déchoirai 6 *none* 7 *none* 8 déchu
découdre	*like*	**coudre**
découvrir	*like*	**couvrir**
décrire	*like*	**écrire**
décroître	*like*	**croître** *except* 8 décru
se dédire	*like*	**dire**
déduire	*like*	**conduire**
défaillir		1 je défaille, n défaillons 2 je défaillais 3 je défaillis 5 je défaille 7 défaillant 8 défailli
défaire	*like*	**faire**
démentir	*like*	**mentir**
démettre	*like*	**mettre**
se départir	*like*	**mentir**
dépeindre	*like*	**atteindre**
déplaire	*like*	**plaire**
déteindre	*like*	**atteindre**
détenir	*like*	**tenir**
détruire	*like*	**conduire**
*devenir	*like*	**tenir**
se dévêtir	*like*	**vêtir**
devoir		1 je dois, n devons, ils doivent 2 je devais 3 je dus 4 je devrai 5 je doive, n devions 6 *not used* 7 devant 8 dû, due, *pl* dus, dues
dire		1 je dis, n disons, v dites 2 je disais 3 je dis 5 je dise 7 disant 8 dit
disconvenir	*like*	**tenir**
disjoindre	*like*	**joindre**
disparaître	*like*	**connaître**
dissoudre	*like*	**absoudre**
distraire	*like*	**abstraire**
dormir	*like*	**mentir**
échoir		(*defective*) 1 il échoit 2 *none* 3 il échut, ils échurent 4 il échoira 6 *none* 7 échéant 8 échu
éclore		1 il éclôt, ils éclosent 8 éclos
éconduire	*like*	**conduire**

écrire		1 j'écris, n écrivons 2 j'écrivais 3 j'écrivis 5 j'écrive
		7 écrivant 8 écrit
élire	*like*	**lire**
émettre	*like*	**mettre**
émouvoir	*like*	**mouvoir** *except* 8 ému
enclore	*like*	**éclore**
encourir	*like*	**courir**
endormir	*like*	**mentir**
enduire	*like*	**conduire**
enfreindre	*like*	**atteindre**
***s'enfuir**	*like*	**fuir**
enjoindre	*like*	**joindre**
s'enquérir	*like*	**acquérir**
s'ensuivre	*like*	**suivre** (*third person only*)
entreprendre	*like*	**prendre**
entretenir	*like*	**tenir**
entrevoir	*like*	**voir**
entrouvrir	*like*	**couvrir**
envoyer		4 j'enverrai
***s'éprendre**	*like*	**prendre**
équivaloir	*like*	**valoir**
éteindre	*like*	**atteindre**
être		1 je suis, tu es, il est, n sommes, v êtes, ils sont 2 j'étais
		3 je fus 4 je serai 5 je sois, n soyons, ils soient
		6 sois, soyons, soyez 7 étant 8 été
étreindre	*like*	**atteindre**
exclure	*like*	**conclure**
extraire	*like*	**abstraire**
faillir		(*defective*) 3 je faillis 4 je faillirai 8 failli
faire		1 je fais, n faisons, v faites, ils font 2 je faisais 3 je fis
		4 je ferai 5 je fasse 7 faisant 8 fait
falloir		(*impersonal*) 1 il faut 2 il fallait 3 il fallut 4 il faudra
		5 il faille 6 *none* 7 *none* 8 fallu
feindre	*like*	**atteindre**
foutre		1 je fous, n foutons 2 je foutais 3 *none* 5 je foute
		7 foutant 8 foutu
frire		(*defective*) 1 je fris, tu fris, il frit 4 je frirai 6 fris
		8 frit (*for other persons and tenses use* faire frire)
fuir		1 je fuis, n fuyons, ils fuient 2 je fuyais 3 je fuis 5 je fuie
		7 fuyant 8 fui
geindre	*like*	**atteindre**
haïr		1 je hais, il hait, n haïssons
inclure	*like*	**conclure**
induire	*like*	**conduire**
inscrire	*like*	**écrire**
instruire	*like*	**conduire**
interdire	*like*	**dire** *except* 1 v interdisez

interrompre	*like*	**rompre**
intervenir	*like*	**tenir**
introduire	*like*	**conduire**
joindre	1 je joins, n joignons, ils joignent 2 je joignais 3 je joignis 4 je joindrai 5 je joigne 7 joignant 8 joint	
lire	1 je lis, n lisons 2 je lisais 3 je lus 5 je lise 7 lisant 8 lu	
luire	*like*	**nuire**
maintenir	*like*	**tenir**
maudire	1 je maudis, n maudissons 2 je maudissais 3 je maudis 4 je maudirai 5 je maudisse 7 maudissant 8 maudit	
méconnaître	*like*	**connaître**
médire	*like*	**dire** *except* 1 v médisez
mentir	1 je mens, n mentons 2 je mentais 5 je mente 7 mentant	
mettre	1 je mets, n mettons 2 je mettais 3 je mis 5 je mette 7 mettant 8 mis	
moudre	1 je mouds, il moud, n moulons 2 je moulais 3 je moulus 5 je moule 7 moulant 8 moulu	
***mourir**	1 je meurs, n mourons, ils meurent 2 je mourais 3 je mourus 4 je mourrai 5 je meure, n mourions 7 mourant 8 mort	
mouvoir	1 je meus, n mouvons, ils meuvent 2 je mouvais 3 je mus 4 je mouvrai 5 je meuve, n mouvions 8 mû, mue, *pl* mus, mues	
***naître**	1 je nais, il naît, n naissons 2 je naissais 3 je naquis 4 je naîtrai 5 je naisse 7 naissant 8 né	
nuire	1 je nuis, n nuisons 2 je nuisais 3 je nuisis 5 je nuise 7 nuisant 8 nui	
obtenir	*like*	**tenir**
offrir	*like*	**couvrir**
omettre	*like*	**mettre**
ouvrir	*like*	**couvrir**
paître	(*defective*) 1 il paît 2 ils paissait 3 *none* 4 il paîtra 5 il paisse 7 paissant 8 *none*	
paraître	*like*	**connaître**
parcourir	*like*	**courir**
parfaire	*like*	**faire** (*present tense, infinitive and past participle only*)
***partir**	*like*	**mentir**
***parvenir**	*like*	**tenir**
peindre	*like*	**atteindre**
percevoir	*like*	**recevoir**
permettre	*like*	**mettre**
plaindre	*like*	**craindre**
plaire	1 je plais, il plaît, n plaisons 2 je plaisais 3 je plus 5 je plaise 7 plaisant 8 plu	
pleuvoir	(*impersonal*) 1 il pleut 2 il pleuvait 3 il plut 4 il pleuvra 5 il pleuve 6 *none* 7 pleuvant 8 plu	
poindre	(*defective*) 1 il point 4 il poindra 8 point	

poursuivre	*like*	suivre
pourvoir	*like*	voir *except* 3 je pourvus *and* 4 je pourvoirai
pouvoir	1 je peux *or* je puis, tu peux, il peut, n pouvons, ils peuvent	
	2 je pouvais 3 je pus 4 je pourrai 5 je puisse 6 *not used*	
	7 pouvant 8 pu	
prédire	*like*	dire *except* v prédisez
prendre	1 je prends, il prend, n prenons, ils prennent 2 je prenais 3 je pris	
	5 je prenne 7 prenant 8 pris	
prescrire	*like*	écrire
pressentir	*like*	mentir
prévaloir	*like*	valoir *except* 5 je prévale
prévenir	*like*	tenir
prévoir	*like*	voir *except* 4 je prévoirai
produire	*like*	conduire
promettre	*like*	mettre
promouvoir	*like*	mouvoir *except* 8 promu
proscrire	*like*	écrire
*provenir	*like*	tenir
rabattre	*like*	battre
rasseoir	*like*	asseoir
réapparaître	*like*	connaître
recevoir	1 je reçois, n recevons, ils reçoivent 2 je recevais 3 je reçus	
	4 je recevrai 5 je reçoive, n recevions, ils reçoivent 7 recevant	
	8 reçu	
reconduire	*like*	conduire
reconnaître	*like*	connaître
reconquérir	*like*	acquérir
reconstruire	*like*	conduire
recoudre	*like*	coudre
recourir	*like*	courir
recouvrir	*like*	couvrir
récrire	*like*	écrire
recueillir	*like*	cueillir
redevenir	*like*	tenir
redire	*like*	dire
réduire	*like*	conduire
réécrire	*like*	écrire
réélire	*like*	lire
refaire	*like*	faire
rejoindre	*like*	joindre
relire	*like*	lire
reluire	*like*	nuire
remettre	*like*	mettre
*renaître	*like*	naître
rendormir	*like*	mentir
renvoyer	*like*	envoyer
se repaître	*like*	paître

reparaître	*like*	**connaître**
*repartir	*like*	**mentir**
repeindre	*like*	**atteindre**
repentir	*like*	**mentir**
reprendre	*like*	**prendre**
reproduire	*like*	**conduire**
résoudre	1 je résous, n résolvons 2 je résolvais 3 je résolus	
	5 je résolve 7 résolvant 8 résolu	
ressentir	*like*	**mentir**
resservir	*like*	**mentir**
ressortir	*like*	**mentir**
restreindre	*like*	**atteindre**
retenir	*like*	**tenir**
retransmettre	*like*	**mettre**
*revenir	*like*	**tenir**
revêtir	*like*	**vêtir**
revivre	*like*	**vivre**
revoir	*like*	**voir**
rire	1 je ris, n rions 2 je riais 3 je ris 5 je rie, n riions 7 riant 8 ri	
rompre	*regular except* 1 il rompt	
rouvrir	*like*	**couvrir**
satisfaire	*like*	**faire**
savoir	1 je sais, n savons, il savent 2 je savais 3 je sus 4 je saurai	
	5 je sache 6 sache, sachons, sachez 7 sachant 8 su	
séduire	*like*	**conduire**
sentir	*like*	**mentir**
servir	*like*	**mentir**
sortir	*like*	**mentir**
souffrir	*like*	**couvrir**
soumettre	*like*	**mettre**
sourire	*like*	**rire**
souscrire	*like*	**écrire**
soustraire	*like*	**abstraire**
soutenir	*like*	**tenir**
*se souvenir	*like*	**tenir**
subvenir	*like*	**tenir**
suffire	1 je suffis, n suffisons 2 je suffisais 3 je suffis 5 je suffise	
	7 suffisant 8 suffi	
suivre	1 je suis, n suivons 2 je suivais 3 je suivis 5 je suive	
	7 suivant 8 suivi	
surprendre	*like*	**prendre**
*survenir	*like*	**tenir**
survivre	*like*	**vivre**
taire	1 je tais, n taisons 2 je taisais 3 je tus 5 je taise 7 taisant	
	8 tu	
teindre	*like*	**atteindre**
tenir	1 je tiens, ne tenons, ils tiennent 2 je tenais	

		3 je tins, tu tins, il tint, n tînmes, v tîntes, ils tinrent
		4 je tiendrai 5 je tienne 7 tenant 8 tenu
traduire	*like*	**conduire**
traire	*like*	**abstraire**
transcrire	*like*	**écrire**
transmettre	*like*	**mettre**
transparaître	*like*	**connaître**
tressaillir	*like*	**défaillir**

vaincre 1 je vaincs, il vainc, n vainquons 2 je vainquais 3 je vainquis
5 je vainque 7 vainquant 8 vaincu

valoir 1 je vaux, il vaut, n valons 2 je valais 3 je valus 4 je vaudrai
5 je vaille 6 *not used* 7 valant 8 valu

***venir** *like* **tenir**

vêtir 1 je vêts, n vêtons 2 je vêtais 5 je vête 7 vêtant 8 vêtu

vivre 1 je vis, n vivons 2 je vivais 3 je vécus 5 je vive 7 vivant
8 vécu

voir 1 je vois, n voyons 2 je voyais 3 je vis 4 je verrai
5 je voie, n voyions 7 voyant 8 vu

vouloir 1 je veux, il veut, n voulons, ils veulent 2 je voulais
3 je voulus 4 je voudrai 5 je veuille
6 veuille, veuillons, veuillez 7 voulant 8 voulu

Numbers

	Cardinal numbers	
nought, zero	0	zéro
one	1	un
two	2	deux
three	3	trois
four	4	quatre
five	5	cinq
six	6	six
seven	7	sept
eight	8	huit
nine	9	neuf
ten	10	dix
eleven	11	onze
twelve	12	douze
thirteen	13	treize
fourteen	14	quatorze
fifteen	15	quinze
sixteen	16	seize
seventeen	17	dix-sept
eighteen	18	dix-huit
nineteen	19	dix-neuf
twenty	20	vingt
twenty-one	21	vingt et un
twenty-two	22	vingt-deux
thirty	30	trente
forty	40	quarante
fifty	50	cinquante
sixty	60	soixante
seventy	70	soixante-dix
eighty	80	quatre-vingts
eighty-one	81	quatre-vingt-un
ninety	90	quatre-vingt-dix
ninety-one	91	quatre-vingt-onze
a *or* one hundred	100	cent
a hundred and one	101	cent un
a hundred and two	102	cent deux
a hundred and fifty	150	cent cinquante
two hundred	200	deux cents

two hundred and one	201	deux cent un
two hundred and two	202	deux cent deux
a *or* one thousand	1,000 (1 000)	mille
a thousand and one	1,001 (1 001)	mille un
a thousand and two	1,002 (1 002)	mille deux
two thousand	2,000 (2 000)	deux mille
a *or* one million	1,000,000 (1 000 000)	un million

Ordinal numbers

first	1st	1er	premier
second	2nd	2e	deuxième
third	3rd	3e	troisième
fourth	4th	4e	quatrième
fifth	5th	5e	cinquième
sixth	6th	6e	sixième
seventh	7th	7e	septième
eighth	8th	8e	huitième
ninth	9th	9e	neuvième
tenth	10th	10e	dixième
eleventh	11th	11e	onzième
twelfth	12th	12e	douzième
thirteenth	13th	13e	treizième
fourteenth	14th	14e	quatorzième
fifteenth	15th	15e	quinzième
twentieth	20th	20e	vingtième
twenty-first	21st	21e	vingt et unième
twenty-second	22nd	22e	vingt deuxième
thirtieth	30th	30e	trentième

Examples of usage

three (times) out of ten	trois (fois) sur dix
ten at a time, in *or* by tens, ten by ten	dix par dix, dix à dix
the ten of us/you, we ten/you ten	nous/vous dix
all ten of them *or* us *or* you	tous les dix, toutes les dix
there are ten of us/them	nous sommes/elles sont dix
(between) the ten of them	à eux dix, à elles dix
ten of them were living together/came	ils vivaient/sont venus à dix
page ten	page dix
Charles the Tenth	Charles Dix
to live at number ten	habiter au (numéro) dix
to be the tenth to arrive/to leave	arriver/partir le dixième
to come tenth, to be tenth (*in a race*)	arriver dixième, être dixième
to be ten (years old)	avoir dix ans
a child of ten, a ten-year-old (child)	un enfant de dix ans

Conversation Guide
I. The Basics

French has two separate sets of words to translate "you", "your", "yours" and "yourself". **Tu, te, t', ton/ta/tes,** and **le tien** etc. all correspond to the **tu** form of the verb, used when speaking to one person you know well (such as a friend or relative) or to someone younger. **Vous, votre/vos,** and **le vôtre** etc. correspond to the **vous** form of the verb and are used when speaking to more than one person, even if you know them well, or when speaking to one person you do not know well. If in doubt as to whether to call someone **tu** or **vous,** it is always safer to use the polite **vous** form. A French person may invite you to use the less formal **tu** form by saying, "Vous pouvez me tutoyer."

good evening bonsoir

good morning/afternoon bonjour

good night bonne nuit

goodbye au revoir

hello bonjour

hi salut

no non

no, thank you non merci

OK d'accord

please s'il vous/te plaît

see you later à toute à l'heure, à plus tard, or (Fam) à plus, à la prochaine

see you on Monday à lundi

see you soon à bientôt

see you tomorrow à demain

thank you merci

yes oui (*when answering an affirmative question*), si (*when contradicting a negative question*)

yes, please oui, s'il vous/te plaît

1) Meeting someone you know

How are you?
Comment allez-vous ?

Very good, thank you. And you?
Très bien, merci. Et vous(-même) ?

Hi, how are you doing?
Salut, ça va ?

Fine, and you?
Ça va, et toi ?

Good evening, how are you?
Bonsoir, vous allez bien ?

Not too bad.
Pas trop mal.

Not very well, I have the flu.
Pas très bien, j'ai la grippe.

How are your parents/children?
Comment vont vos parents/enfants ?

They're doing well, thanks.
Ils vont très bien, merci.

2) Introducing yourself and meeting people you don't know

Name:

What's your name?
Comment vous appelez-vous ?

My name is John.
Je m'appelle John.

Let me introduce you to my brother Steve. And this is my cousin Rachel.
Je vous présente mon frère Steve. Et voici Rachel, ma cousine.

Hi, I'm Peter, Anna's colleague.
Bonjour, je suis Peter, le collègue d'Anna.

I'm sorry, I've forgotten your name.
Excusez-moi, je n'ai pas retenu votre prénom.

Pleased to meet you.
Enchanté./Ravi de faire votre connaissance.

Age:

How old are you?
Quel âge avez-vous ?

I'm 12/24/45 years old.
J'ai douze/vingt-quatre/quarante-cinq ans.

What's your date of birth?
Quelle est votre date de naissance ?

I was born in 1967
Je suis né en mille neuf cent soixante-sept

Nationality:

What country are you from?
De quel pays venez-vous ?

I'm from the United States.
Je viens des États-Unis.

What's your nationality?
De quelle nationalité êtes-vous ?

I'm American.
Je suis américain.

Where do you live?
Où habitez-vous ?

I live in New York.
J'habite à New York.

I come from a little rural town in Montana.
Je viens d'une petite ville de campagne dans le Montana.

Occupation:

What do you do?
Que faites-vous dans la vie ?

I'm still in high school.
Je suis encore au lycée.

I'm a student/a teacher/a doctor.
Je suis étudiant/professeur/médecin.

I'm retired.
Je suis à la retraite.

I work in a bank.
Je travaille dans une banque.

I work in the export department of a computer hardware company.
Je travaille dans le service export d'une entreprise de matériel informatique.

Family:

Do you have any brothers and sisters?
Est-ce que tu as des frères et sœurs ?

I have two brothers and one sister.
J'ai deux frères et une sœur.

I'm an only child.
Je suis fils/fille unique.

I have an older brother.
J'ai un frère aîné.

I have a younger sister.
J'ai une sœur plus jeune que moi.

I have two little sisters.
J'ai deux petites sœurs.

Are you married?
Êtes-vous marié ?

I'm single/separated/divorced.
Je suis célibataire/séparé/divorcé.

Do you have any children?
Vous avez des enfants ?

I have one son/daughter.
J'ai un fils/une fille.

3) Likes and dislikes

I like skiing/swimming/playing basketball.
J'aime le ski/la natation/le basket.

I'm fond of classical music.
J'aime bien la musique classique.

I love movies.
J'adore le cinéma.

I like/love playing chess/pool.
J'aime/j'adore jouer aux échecs/au billard.

What's your favorite band/ movie/actor?
Quel est ton groupe/film/acteur préféré ?

I prefer reading/shopping.
Je préfère lire/faire les magasins.

I prefer coffee to tea.
J'aime mieux le café que le thé.

I prefer football to basketball.
Je préfère le football américain au basket.

Did you enjoy the movie?
Est-ce que le film t'a plu ?

I really liked it/didn't like it.
Il m'a beaucoup plu/ne m'a pas plu.

I liked/didn't like the ending.
J'ai bien aimé/je n'ai pas aimé la fin.

I don't like going to the opera.
Je n'aime pas aller à l'opéra.

I don't like that at all.
Je n'aime pas ça du tout.

I hate cheese.
Je déteste le fromage.

I can't stand this kind of music.
Je ne supporte pas ce genre de musique.

This book is (really) awful.
Ce livre est (vraiment) nul.

4) Expressing surprise and interest

No, you're kidding! Are you sure?
Non ! C'est pas vrai ! Tu en es sûr ?

Really?
Ah bon ?

You're kidding?
Tu plaisantes ?

Are you pulling my leg?
Tu me fais marcher ?

What a coincidence/a surprise!
Quelle coïncidence/surprise !

Really? I'm a doctor too!
C'est vrai ? Moi aussi je suis médecin !

That's strange.
C'est bizarre/étrange/curieux.

It's really interesting/fascinating/amazing.
C'est vraiment intéressant/passionnant/étonnant.

5) Expressing disappointment

What a shame!
Quel dommage !

It's too bad it's raining.
C'est dommage qu'il pleuve. (*subjunctive*)

What a pity he couldn't come!
Quel dommage qu'il n'ait pas pu venir. (*subjunctive*)

The concert has been canceled, how disappointing!
Le concert a été annulé, c'est vraiment dommage !

6) Saying thank you and expressing gratitude

Thank you.
Merci (bien).

Thank you very much.
Merci beaucoup.

Thank you, that's really nice.
Je vous remercie, c'est très gentil.

Thank you, but you shouldn't have!
Merci, mais vous n'auriez pas dû !

It's very kind of you.
C'est très gentil de votre part.

I'd like that very much.
Ça me ferait très plaisir.

Thanks for your help/for helping me.
Merci pour votre aide/de m'avoir aidé.

To which the other person may reply:

De rien./Il n'y a pas de quoi.
You're welcome.

Je vous en prie.
Please, don't mention it.

7) Apologizing

Sorry, it was an accident!
Pardon, je ne l'ai pas fait exprès !

I'm (really) sorry.
Je suis (vraiment) désolé.

I'm sorry I'm late.
Je suis désolé d'être en retard.

I'm sorry to bother you, but ...
Je m'excuse de vous déranger, mais ...

I apologize.
Je suis désolé./Je m'excuse.

Excuse me.
Excusez-moi.

Sorry for interrupting the conversation.
Désolé d'avoir interrompu la conversation.

Sorry, it's my fault.
Désolé, c'est ma faute.

I'm sorry but it's not my fault.
Je suis désolé mais ce n'est pas de ma faute.

I'm afraid I won't be able to come.
Je suis désolé mais je ne pourrai pas venir.

That's very kind of you but unfortunately I'm not free that day.
C'est très gentil mais malheureusement je ne suis pas libre ce jour-là.

To which the other person may reply:

Ce n'est rien./Ce n'est pas grave./Cela n'a pas d'importance.
It doesn't matter.

Ne vous inquiétez pas/tracassez pas pour ça.
Don't worry about it.

8) Congratulations and compliments

Congratulations!
Félicitations !/Toutes mes félicitations !/Je vous félicite !

I'm very happy for you!
Je suis très heureux pour vous !

I wish you lots of happiness.
Je vous souhaite beaucoup de bonheur.

It was very good/delicious.
C'était très bon.

It's great/wonderful/beautiful!
C'est génial/merveilleux/beau !

The party was a big success.
La soirée était très réussie.

I had a great time.
Je me suis bien amusé.

9) Making suggestions and expressing desires

Do you want to go?
Est-ce que tu veux y aller ?

Would you like to go to the restaurant?
Ça te plairait d'aller au restaurant ?

How about going to the museum?
Et si on allait au musée ?

How about a pizza?
Ça te dit une pizza ?

I think we should meet at seven.
Je propose qu'on se retrouve à sept heures.

Let's meet outside the restaurant.
On se retrouve devant le restaurant ?

I want to go back to the apartment.
Je veux rentrer à l'appartement.

I don't want to go to the swimming pool.
Je ne veux pas aller à la piscine.

I feel like going to the movies.
J'ai envie d'aller au cinéma.

I don't feel like watching TV.
Je n'ai pas envie de regarder la télévision.

I wouldn't mind going to the theater.
J'aimerais bien aller/ça me plairait d'aller au théâtre.

I'd rather stay at home/do something else.
Je préfèrerais rester à la maison/faire autre chose.

I'd like to go to Spain next year.
J'aimerais aller en Espagne l'année prochaine.

I wish I was on vacation.
Je voudrais être en vacances.

I don't mind.
Ça m'est égal./Peu importe.

I have no preference.
Je n'ai pas de préférence.

10) Making requests

Can we have more bread, please?
Est-ce qu'on peut avoir plus de pain, s'il vous plaît ?

Could I have a glass of water?
Est-ce que je pourrais avoir un verre d'eau ?

Could you please make a little less noise?
Pourriez-vous faire un peu moins de bruit ?

Can I open the window?
Est-ce que je peux ouvrir la fenêtre ?

Could I make a phone call?
Est-ce que je pourrais téléphoner ?

Can I borrow ...?
Est-ce que je peux emprunter ... ?

Could you lend me ...?
Est-ce que vous pourriez me prêter ... ?

Do you mind if I smoke?
Ça vous dérange si je fume ?

Would it be possible to go?
Est-ce qu'il serait possible d'y aller ?

Would you be able to give me a ride?
Est-ce qu'il vous serait possible de m'emmener ?

11) Expressing an opinion

What do you think?
Qu'en penses-tu ?

What's your opinion?
Quel est ton avis ?

I think/I don't think that's a very good idea.
Je crois que c'est/je ne crois pas que ce soit une très bonne idée.

I think we should go.
Je pense qu'on devrait y aller.

I think she's very pretty.
Je la trouve très jolie.

In my opinion, he shouldn't have said that.
À mon avis, il n'aurait pas dû dire ça.

I've changed my mind.
J'ai changé d'avis.

I totally agree with him.
Je suis tout à fait d'accord avec lui.

You're (absolutely) right.
Vous avez (entièrement) raison

Of course not!
Bien sûr que non !

You're wrong.
Tu as tort.

Nonsense!
N'importe quoi !

I'm sure they'll win.
Je suis sûr qu'ils vont gagner.

I agree/don't agree with you.
Je suis/ne suis pas d'accord avec vous.

I disagree.
Je ne suis pas d'accord.

No, not at all/absolutely not.
Non, pas du tout/absolument pas.

You're mistaken.
Tu te trompes.

That's true/not true.
C'est vrai/ce n'est pas vrai.

12) Having problems understanding French

Could you speak more slowly?
Est-ce que vous pourriez parler plus lentement ?

I don't understand this expression.
Je ne comprends pas cette expression.

I don't understand a word of that.
Je ne comprends rien.

Can you repeat that, please?
Vous pouvez répéter ?

I understand a little.
Je comprends un petit peu.

I didn't understand.
Je n'ai pas compris.

I can understand French but I can't speak it.
J'arrive à comprendre le français mais je ne peux pas le parler.

I speak hardly any French.
Je parle à peine français.

Do you speak English?
Est-ce que vous parlez anglais ?

What's it called?
Comment on appelle ça ?

How do you spell/pronounce it?
Comment ça s'écrit/se prononce ?

What does it mean?
Qu'est-ce que ça veut dire ?

I have trouble understanding/speaking.
J'ai du mal à comprendre/parler.

Pardon?/What?/Eh?
Pardon ?/Quoi ?/Hein ?

How do you say... in French?
Comment est-ce qu'on dit ... en français ?

Could you write it down?
Est-ce que vous pourriez l'écrire ?

What's that?
Qu'est-ce que c'est ?

II. Vacations in France

1) Traveling and using public transportation

Traveling by plane:

Where is the Air France check-in desk?
Où est l'enregistrement des bagages pour Air France ?

What time does boarding start?
À quelle heure embarque-t-on ?

I'd like to confirm my return flight.
Je voudrais confirmer mon vol de retour.

I'd like a window seat/an aisle seat.
Je voudrais une place côté hublot/côté couloir.

One of my suitcases is missing.
Il me manque une valise.

I'd like to report the loss of my luggage/my hand luggage.
Je voudrais faire une déclaration de perte pour mes bagages/mon bagage à main.

The plane was two hours late and I've missed my connection.
L'avion a eu deux heures de retard et j'ai raté ma correspondance.

Traveling by train:

I'd like to reserve a ticket, please.
Je voudrais réserver un billet, s'il vous plaît.

What are the reduced fares?
Quels sont les tarifs réduits ?

How much is a ticket to ...?
Combien coûte un billet pour ... ?

Are there any tickets left for ...?
Est-ce qu'il vous reste des places pour ... ?

No smoking (section), please.
(Voiture) non fumeur, s'il vous plaît.

Do you have a timetable, please?
Auriez-vous un dépliant avec les horaires ?

When is the next train to Nantes?
À quelle heure est le prochain train pour Nantes ?

Is there an earlier/a later one?
Il n'y en a pas plus tôt/tard ?

What platform does the train for ... leave from?
De quel quai part le train pour ... ?

I've missed the last train.
J'ai raté le dernier train.

On the subway or on the RER (= Paris metropolitan and regional rail system):

Where can I buy tickets?
Où est-ce que je peux acheter des billets ?

A book of ten (tickets), please.
Un carnet de dix (tickets), s'il vous plaît.

Can I have a map of the subway?
Est-ce que je peux avoir un plan du métro ?

Does this RER stop at Versailles?
Est-ce que ce RER s'arrête à Versailles ?

Which line do I take to get to ...?
Quelle ligne dois-je prendre pour aller à ... ?

What time is the last subway train?
Vers quelle heure passe le dernier métro ?

Traveling by bus:

Where can I get a bus to ...?
Où est-ce que je peux prendre un bus pour ... ?

Is this the right stop for ...?
C'est bien l'arrêt pour ... ?

Does the bus for Charles de Gaulle airport leave from here?
C'est bien d'ici que part le car pour l'aéroport Charles de Gaulle/Roissy ?

Where is the bus station?
Où se trouve la gare routière ?

Renting a car:

I'd like to rent a car for a week.
Je voudrais louer une voiture pour une semaine.

How much is the deposit?
À combien s'élève la caution ?

I'd like to take out comprehensive insurance.
Je voudrais prendre une assurance tous risques.

I'd like an automatic/a stickshift.
Je voudrais une voiture à boîte de vitesse automatique/à boîte de vitesse classique.

On the road:

Where can I find a gas station/a garage?
Où est-ce que je peux trouver une station-service/un garage ?

I have a flat tire. Where can I park?
J'ai un pneu à plat. Où puis-je me garer ?

I've broken down.
Je suis (tombé) en panne.

It won't start; the battery's dead.
Elle ne veut pas démarrer ; la batterie est morte.

I have a problem with the brakes/the light indicators.
J'ai un problème avec les freins/les clignotants.

Taking a cab:

I'd like to reserve a taxi for 8 o'clock.
Je voudrais un taxi pour huit heures.

Is this cab for hire?
Est-ce que ce taxi est libre ?

How much will it cost to go to the airport?
Combien ça va me coûter pour aller à l'aéroport ?

I'd like to go to the train station.
Je voudrais aller à la gare.

Could you take me to this address, please?
Pouvez-vous me conduire/m'emmener à cette adresse, s'il vous plaît ?

You can drop me off here, thanks.
Vous pouvez m'arrêter/me déposer/me laisser ici, merci.

Asking for directions:

Excuse me, where is ..., please?
Excusez-moi, où est/où se trouve ..., s'il vous plaît ?

I'm looking for ...
Je cherche ...

Could you tell me how to get to ...?
Est-ce que vous pouvez me dire/m'indiquer comment aller à ... ?

Which way is it to ...?
Quelle est la route pour ... ?

Is it far/near?
C'est loin/près ?

How do I get to the station?
Comment fait-on pour se rendre à la gare ?

Can you show me the way?
Pouvez-vous m'indiquer le chemin ?

Could you show me on the map?
Est-ce que vous pourriez me montrer sur le plan ?

I'm lost.
Je suis perdu.

Understanding the person you asked for help:

C'est la deuxième rue à droite/à gauche.
It's the second street on the right/on the left.

Prenez la prochaine sortie.
Take the next exit.

Continuez tout droit jusqu'au feu.
Keep going straight on until you get to the (traffic) lights.

2) Renting accommodations

Staying in a hotel or a B&B:

Do you have any rooms available?
Est-ce qu'il vous reste des chambres de libres ?

It's for a couple and two children.
C'est pour un couple et deux enfants.

I'd like to reserve a room for tomorrow night, please.
Je voudrais réserver une chambre pour demain soir, s'il vous plaît.

I've reserved three single/double rooms over the phone, in the name of ...
J'ai réservé par téléphone trois chambres pour une personne/deux personnes, au nom de ...

Would it be possible to stay another night/to add an extra bed?
Est-ce qu'il serait possible de rester une autre nuit/d'ajouter un lit supplémentaire ?

Can I see the room?
Est-ce que je peux voir la chambre ?

Do you take credit cards?
Vous acceptez les cartes de crédit ?

How much is a room with its own bathroom?
Combien coûte une chambre avec salle de bains ?

Is breakfast included?
Est-ce que le petit déjeuner est inclus ?

The key for room 12, please.
La clé de la 12, s'il vous plaît.

We're planning to stay for two nights.
Nous pensons rester deux nuits.

Could you wake me up at seven o'clock?
Pouvez-vous me réveiller à sept heures ?

The outlet for razors isn't working.
La prise pour rasoir ne marche pas.

We don't have towels/toilet paper.
Nous n'avons pas de serviettes (de toilette)/de papier toilette.

Understanding the receptionist:

Non, je regrette, nous sommes complets.
No, I'm sorry, we're full.

Est-ce que vous pouvez remplir cette fiche ?
Could you fill out this form?

Les chambres doivent être libérées avant midi.
Check-out time is noon.

Le petit déjeuner est servi entre 7h30 et 9h.
Breakfast is served between 7:30 and 9.

Renting an apartment or a gîte:

I'm looking for something to rent close to the center of town.
Je cherche quelque chose en location près du centre.

Is it completely furnished?
Est-ce que c'est entièrement
meublé ?

Is there a washing machine?
Est-ce qu'il y a une machine à laver ?

Where do I pick up/leave the keys?
Où dois-je prendre/laisser les clés ?

Where is the electricity meter?
Où est le compteur électrique ?

Where do I take the garbage out?
Où dois-je sortir les poubelles ?

Are there any spare ...?
Est-ce qu'il y a des ... de rechange ?

I'm sorry, I can't find/I've broken the ...
Je suis désolé, je ne trouve pas/j'ai
cassé le/la ...

There's no hot water.
Il n'y a pas d'eau chaude.

Camping:

Is there a campsite near here?
Y a-t-il un camping près d'ici ?

I'd like a space for one tent for two days.
Je voudrais un emplacement pour une tente pour deux jours.

We want to rent a camper/trailer.
Nous voulons louer une caravane/
un mobil-home.

Where are the showers?
Où sont les douches ?

Is there a swimming pool/a night club/a tennis court on the campsite?
Est-ce qu'il y a une piscine/une boîte de nuit/un court de tennis dans le camping ?

How much is it a day/per person/per tent?
C'est combien par jour/par personne/par tente ?

3) Visiting

I'd like some information on ...
Je voudrais des renseignements/
informations sur ...

What is there to see/visit in the area?
Qu'est-ce qu'il y a à voir/visiter dans
la région ?

Is it open on Sundays?
Est-ce que c'est ouvert le dimanche ?

Is it free?
C'est gratuit ?

How much does it cost to get in?
Combien coûte l'entrée ?

Are there any discounts for young people?
Est-ce qu'il y a des réductions pour
les jeunes ?

Is this ticket valid for the exhibition too?
Le ticket est valable aussi pour
l'exposition ?

When is the next guided tour?
À quelle heure est la prochaine visite
guidée ?

How long does the tour last?
Combien de temps dure la visite ?

Are there many hiking paths/ski slopes here?
Est-ce qu'il y a beaucoup de sentiers de randonnée/de pistes de ski ici ?

4) Inquiring about the weather

Do you know what the weather's going to be like this weekend?
Est-ce que vous savez quel temps il va faire ce week-end ?

What's the weather forecast for tomorrow?
Quelle est le temps prévu/la météo pour demain ?

Understanding the answer:

Ils annoncent de la pluie/des orages.
They've forecast rain/storms.

Il va pleuvoir/neiger.
It's going to rain/to snow.

Il va faire froid/chaud/une chaleur
étouffante.
**It's going to be cold/hot/
stiflingly hot.**

Normalement il doit faire beau demain.
**The weather should be good
tomorrow.**

Malheureusement ils prévoient du
mauvais temps.
**I'm afraid they're forecasting
bad weather.**

Il va y avoir du brouillard/du verglas.
It's going to be foggy/icy.

On va avoir du soleil, comme
aujourd'hui.
It will be sunny, like today.

Il va y avoir du vent/beaucoup de
vent.
It's going to be windy/very windy.

Il va faire 30° C à l'ombre/moins
deux.
**It's going to be 86° F in the
shade/minus 2.**

Ça va se rafraîchir/se réchauffer.
It's going to get colder/warmer.

III. Going Out

1) Going for a drink

Do you want to go for a drink?
On va boire/prendre un verre ?

Let's go for a coffee.
Allons prendre un café.

Excuse me, please! (*to call the waiter*)
S'il vous plaît !

What are you having?
Qu'est-ce que tu prends ?

I'll buy you a drink. What would you like?
Je t'offre un verre. Qu'est-ce que tu veux ?

It's on me!
C'est moi qui invite !

Could I have a beer?
Je pourrais avoir une bière/une pression ?

I'd like a glass of dry white wine.
Je voudrais un verre de vin blanc sec.

I'll have a Coke® with/without ice, please.
Je vais prendre un Coca® avec des glaçons/sans glaçons, s'il vous plaît.

A coffee and a glass of water, please.
Un café et un verre d'eau, s'il vous plaît.

Something non-alcoholic.
Quelque chose de non alcoolisé.

I'll have the same.
La même chose pour moi.

I'll have the same again.
J'en reprendrai un autre./La même chose.

To your health!
À ta santé !/À la tienne !/Tchin-tchin !

Could you bring me an ashtray?
Est-ce que vous pourriez m'apporter un cendrier ?

We can go to a club afterwards.
On peut aller en boîte après.

2) Going to the restaurant

Reserving a table:

Hello, I'd like to reserve a table for two for tomorrow night, around 8 o'clock.
Allô, bonjour, je voudrais réserver une table pour deux pour demain soir, vers huit heures.

I've reserved a table in the name of ...
J'ai réservé une table au nom de ...

A table for four, please.
Une table pour quatre, s'il vous plaît.

You don't have a table available before then?
Vous n'avez pas de table libre plus tôt ?

Understanding the waiter:

Pour quelle heure ?
For what time?

Huit heures trente, ça vous va ?
Would 8:30 suit you?

Bonjour, c'est pour manger ?
Hello, will you be eating?

Vous êtes combien ?
For how many people?

Est-ce que vous avez réservé ? C'est
à quel nom ?
Have you reserved a table?
What's the name?

Fumeurs ou non fumeurs ?
Smoking or non-smoking?

Ordering food:

Could you bring me the menu/the wine list/the dessert menu, please?
Pourriez-vous m'apporter la carte/la carte des vins/la carte des desserts, s'il
vous plaît ?

What do you recommend?
Qu'est-ce que vous nous conseillez ?

Do you have vegetarian dishes?
Est-ce que vous avez des plats
végétariens ?

What's today's special?
Quel est le plat du jour ?

I'll take that, then.
Je vais prendre ça alors.

We'll both have the set menu.
On va prendre deux menus.

Where is the restroom, please?
Où sont les toilettes, s'il vous plaît ?

This isn't what I ordered, I asked for ...
Ce n'est pas ce que j'ai commandé, j'avais demandé ...

Could we have another jug of water/some more bread, please?
Est-ce qu'on peut avoir une autre carafe d'eau/encore du pain ?

Understanding the waiter:

Vous avez choisi ?
Are you ready to order?

Et comme boisson ?
And what would you like to drink?

Désirez-vous un dessert ?
Would you like a dessert?

Bon appétit !
Enjoy your meal!

Commenting on the food:

It's delicious.
C'est délicieux.

It was really good.
C'était très bon.

It's very greasy/too spicy.
C'est très gras/trop épicé.

It doesn't have enough salt.
Ce n'est pas assez salé.

Asking for the check:

Could I have the check, please?
L'addition, s'il vous plaît.

**I think there's a mistake in the
check.**
Je crois qu'il y a une erreur dans
l'addition.

Is the tip included?
Le service est-il compris ?

We're all paying together.
Nous réglons tout ensemble.

3) Arranging to meet someone

What are you doing tonight?
Qu'est-ce que tu fais ce soir ?

Do you have anything planned?
Tu as quelque chose de prévu ?

How about going to the movies?
Ça te dit d'aller au cinéma ?

When do you want to meet? And where?
On se retrouve à quelle heure ? Et où ?

We can meet in front of the movie theater.
On peut se retrouver/se donner rendez-vous devant le cinéma.

I'll meet you later, I need to stop by the hotel first.
Je vous rejoindrai plus tard, il faut que je passe à l'hôtel d'abord.

4) Going to see movies, shows, and concerts

I'd like three tickets for ...
Je voudrais trois places pour ...

Are there any discounts for students?
Il y a des réductions pour les étudiants ?

What time does the program/movie start?
À quelle heure est la séance/le film ?

How long is the movie?
Combien de temps dure le film ?

Is the movie in the original language?
Est-ce que le film est en version originale ?

It's out next week.
Ça sort la semaine prochaine.

I'd like to go to a show.
J'aimerais aller voir un spectacle.

Do we have to reserve in advance?
Est-ce qu'il faut réserver à l'avance ?

Do we have good seats?
Sommes-nous bien placés ?

Will we be able to see the stage?
Est-ce qu'on verra bien la scène ?

Are there any free/open-air concerts?
Est-ce qu'il y a des concerts gratuits/en plein air ?

What kind of music is it?
C'est quel genre de musique ?

Understanding the clerk in the box office:

Il n'y a plus de places pour cette séance.
This showing is sold out.

C'est complet jusqu'au ...
It's sold out until ...

La pièce (de théâtre)/représentation dure une heure et demie, en comptant l'entracte.
The play/performance lasts for an hour and a half, including the intermission.

IV. Stores, Banks, and Post Offices

1) Buying food

Is there a supermarket/market nearby?
Est-ce qu'il y a un supermarché/marché dans le quartier ?

Where can I find a grocery store that stays open late?
Où est-ce que je peux trouver une épicerie qui ouvre tard le soir ?

I'm looking for the frozen foods/dairy products aisle.
Je cherche le rayon des surgelés/produits laitiers.

I'd like five slices of ham/a little piece of that cheese.
Je voudrais/je vais prendre cinq tranches de jambon/un petit morceau de ce fromage.

It's for four people.
C'est pour quatre personnes.

A kilo of potatoes, please.
Un kilo de pommes de terre, s'il vous plaît.

A little more/less, please.
Un peu plus/moins, s'il vous plaît.

Could I taste it?
C'est possible de goûter ?

That's everything, thanks.
Ce sera tout, merci.

Could I have a (plastic) bag?
Est-ce que je peux avoir un sac (plastique) ?

Paying:

Where can I pay?
Où est-ce qu'on paye ?

How much do I owe you?
Combien je vous dois ?

Can I pay by Visa®?
Est-ce que je peux payer par carte Visa® ?

I'll pay cash.
Je vais payer en liquide.

You've made a mistake with my change.
Vous vous êtes trompé en me rendant la monnaie.

Sorry, I don't have any change.
Désolé, je n'ai pas de monnaie.

Could you give me change, please?
Est-ce vous pouvez me faire de la monnaie ?

Could I have a receipt?
Je peux avoir un reçu ?

Understanding the clerk:

Et avec ceci ?
Is there anything else?

Vous réglez comment ?
How would you like to pay?

Vous n'avez pas du tout de monnaie ?
Don't you have any change?

Vous pouvez composer votre code.
You can type in your number.

2) Buying clothes

No thanks, I'm only looking.
Non merci, je regarde, c'est tout.

I'd like a jacket/a pair of pants/a shirt.
Je voudrais une veste/un pantalon/une chemise.

I'm looking for the men's/children's department.
Je cherche le rayon hommes/enfants.

Where are the dressing rooms?
Où sont les cabines d'essayage ?

I'd like to try on the one in the window.
Je voudrais essayer celui/celle qui est en vitrine.

Can I try it on?
Je peux l'essayer ?

I take a size 8 (shoe).
Je chausse du 39.

It's too small/large.
C'est trop petit/grand.

Do you have it in another color/in red?
Vous ne l'avez pas dans une autre couleur/en rouge ?

I need a bigger/smaller size.
Il me faut la taille au-dessus/en-dessous.

The skirt is too short/long.
La jupe est trop courte/longue.

Yes, that's fine, I'll take them.
Oui, ça va, je les prends.

I'll think about it.
Je vais réfléchir.

Understanding the clerk:

Bonjour, je peux vous aider ?
Hello, can I help you?

Vous cherchez quelque chose ?
Are you looking for something?

Vous faites quelle taille ?
What's your size?

Il ne nous en reste que en bleu ou en noir.
We only have it in blue or black.

Il ne nous en reste plus dans cette taille.
We don't have any left in this size.

Ça vous va bien.
It really suits/fits you.

Nous pouvons le/la commander/faire des retouches.
We can order it/do alterations.

3) Buying presents and souvenirs

I'm looking for a present to take back.
Je cherche un cadeau à ramener.

It's for a little four-year-old girl.
C'est pour une petite fille de quatre ans.

I'd like something easy to transport.
Je voudrais quelque chose de facile à transporter.

Does it keep well?
Ça se conserve bien ?

It's a present; can you gift-wrap it for me?
C'est pour offrir ; vous pouvez me faire un paquet-cadeau ?

4) Going to the bank

Are banks open on Saturdays?
Les banques sont-elles ouvertes le samedi ?

I'm looking for an ATM.
Je cherche un distributeur automatique.

Where can I change money?
Où est-ce qu'il y a un bureau de change ?

I'd like to change $80.
Je voudrais changer 80 dollars.

What commission do you charge?
Qu'est-ce que vous prenez comme commission ?

Can I have €300 in cash?
Je peux avoir 300 euros en espèces/en liquide ?

I'd like to transfer some money.
Je voudrais faire un virement.

I'm waiting for a money order.
J'attends un mandat.

The ATM has swallowed my card.
Le distributeur de billets a avalé ma carte.

I'd like to report the loss of my credit cards.
Je voudrais signaler la perte de mes cartes de crédit.

5) Going to the post office

Is there a mailbox near here?
Y a-t-il une boîte aux lettres par ici ?

Where can I find a post office?
Où est-ce que je peux trouver un bureau de poste ?

Is the post office open on Saturdays?
Est-ce que la poste est ouverte le samedi ?

What time does the post office close?
À quelle heure ferme la poste ?

I'd like five stamps for the United States.
Je voudrais cinq timbres pour les États-Unis.

How much is a stamp for Canada?
Combien coûte un timbre pour le Canada ?

I'd like to send it by registered mail.
Je voudrais l'envoyer en recommandé.

I'd like to send this letter/postcard/package to New York.
Je voudrais envoyer cette lettre/cette carte postale/ce colis à New York.

How long will it take to get there?
Ça va prendre/mettre combien de temps ?

Where can I buy envelopes?
Où est-ce que je peux acheter des enveloppes ?

Is there any mail for me?
Y a-t-il du courrier pour moi ?

Did I receive any mail?
Est-ce que j'ai reçu du courrier ?

V. Expressions of Time

1) The date

Monday	lundi
Tuesday	mardi
Wednesday	mercredi
Thursday	jeudi
Friday	vendredi
Saturday	samedi
Sunday	dimanche
January	janvier
February	février
March	mars
April	avril
May	mai
June	juin
July	juillet
August	août
September	septembre
October	octobre
November	novembre
December	décembre

Note that in French, months and days are masculine and do not have a capital letter. Cardinals (e.g. *deux*, *trois*, etc.) are used for the dates of the month except the first. French write either *mil* or *mille* (a **thousand**) in dates from 1001. *Année*, *journée*, *matinée*, *soirée* (the feminine forms of *an*, *jour*, *matin*, and *soir*) are usually found when duration is implied: *toute la journée*, *dans la matinée*, etc.

What's today's date?
On est le combien aujourd'hui ?

What day is it today?
On est quel jour aujourd'hui ?

It's Tuesday, May first.
On est le mardi premier (1er) mai.

It's November second/third, 2004.
On est le deux/trois novembre deux mille quatre.

Today is July fourteenth.
C'est le quatorze juillet aujourd'hui.

Tomorrow is Tuesday.
Demain c'est mardi.

I wrote to you on March twenty-second.
Je vous ai écrit le vingt-deux mars.

He arrives on Monday.
Il arrive lundi.

See you on Monday!
À lundi !

I'm arriving on the tenth/on May tenth.
J'arrive le dix/le dix mai.

I'm going on vacation two weeks from Monday.
Je pars en vacances lundi en quinze.

This store is open on Sunday mornings.
Ce magasin est ouvert le dimanche matin.

I was born in 1962/1975/1985.
Je suis né en mille neuf cent soixante-deux/mille neuf cent soixante-quinze/mille neuf cent quatre-vingt-cinq.

I've been there before, several years ago. I think it was in 1996.
Je suis déjà venu il y a plusieurs années. Je crois que c'était en mille neuf cent quatre-vingt-seize.

I spent a month in France a few years ago.
J'ai passé un mois en France il y a quelques années.

I came last year at the same time/in 2002.
Je suis venu l'année dernière à la même époque/en deux mille deux.

Understanding:

Ça a été construit au milieu du dix-septième (XVIIe)/dix-neuvième (XIXe) siècle.
It was built in the middle of the 17th/19th century.

Ça sort une fois toutes les deux semaines/deux fois par mois.
It comes out once every two weeks/twice a month.

Prenez-le trois fois par jour/heure.
Take it three times a day/an hour.

Les gens sortent surtout le week-end, très peu en semaine.
People go out mainly on the weekend, but very rarely during the week.

Vous restez jusqu'à quand ?
How long are you staying?

Vous repartez dans deux jours ?
Are you leaving in two days?

2) The time

The 24-hour clock is commonly used in French (e.g. 2:35 p.m. = 14h35 = *deux heures trente-cinq* or *quatorze heures trente-cinq*).

I'm on time/early/late.
Je suis à l'heure/en avance/en retard.

It's very early/late.
Il est très tôt/tard.

Excuse me, do you have the time, please?
Excusez-moi, vous auriez l'heure, s'il vous plaît ?

What time is it?
Quelle heure est-il ?

It's three o'clock exactly.
Il est trois/quinze heures pile.

It's almost one o'clock.
Il est presque une heure/treize heures.

It's ten after one/ten to one.
Il est une heure dix/une heure moins dix.

It's a quarter after one/to one.
Il est une heure et quart/une heure moins le quart.

It's one-thirty.
Il est une heure et demie/une heure trente.

It's noon/midnight.
Il est midi/minuit.

It's eleven-forty.
Il est midi/minuit moins vingt/onze heures quarante.

It's twenty after twelve.
Il est midi/minuit vingt.

It was eight (o'clock) in the morning/in the evening.
Il était huit heures du matin/du soir.

It's two (o'clock) in the afternoon.
Il est deux heures de l'après-midi.

I have an appointment at 8 a.m./8 p.m.
J'ai rendez-vous à huit heures/à vingt heures.

I arrived around two o'clock.
Je suis arrivé vers deux/quatorze heures.

Are you free in the morning? Does 10:30 suit you?
Êtes-vous libre le matin ? Est-ce que 10h30 vous conviendrait ?

I've been waiting for two hours/ since 3 p.m.
Ça fait deux heures que j'attends./ J'attends depuis trois heures de l'après-midi.

I waited for twenty minutes.
J'ai attendu vingt minutes.

The train was fifteen minutes late.
Le train a eu quinze minutes de retard.

I got home an hour ago.
Je suis rentré il y a une heure.

Do you want to meet in half an hour?
On se retrouve dans une demi-heure ?

I'll be back in a quarter of an hour.
Je serai de retour d'ici un quart d'heure.

It lasts for around three quarters of an hour/an hour and a half.
Ça dure environ trois quarts d'heure/une heure et demie.

There's a three-hour time difference between ... and ...
Il y a trois heures de décalage entre ... et ...

I don't have time to take a nap in the afternoon.
Je n'ai pas le temps de faire la sieste l'après-midi.

I'm in a hurry, come on, hurry up!
Je suis pressé, allez, dépêche-toi !

VI. Using the Telephone

answering machine un répondeur

area code un indicatif

cell phone un (téléphone) portable

charger un chargeur

collect call un appel en PCV

dial tone une tonalité

handset un combiné

information les renseignements

international/national/local call un appel international/national/local

landline une ligne terrestre/fixe

message un message

network un réseau

operator (*company*) un opérateur, (*person*) un(e) standardiste

payphone un téléphone public/à pièces

phone book un annuaire

phone booth une cabine téléphonique

phone card une carte de téléphone

phone number un numéro de téléphone

receiver un combiné

receptionist un(e) réceptionniste

ringtone une sonnerie

telephone un téléphone

text (message) un (message) SMS

voicemail une messagerie vocale, un répondeur

Yellow Pages® les Pages Jaunes®

to answer the phone répondre au téléphone	**to hang up** raccrocher
to be on the phone être au téléphone	**to phone** téléphoner
to call someone appeler quelqu'un	**to pick up the phone** décrocher
to call someone back rappeler quelqu'un	**to put one's phone on silent/vibrate** mettre son portable en mode silencieux/vibreur
to dial a number composer un numéro	**to put someone on hold** mettre quelqu'un en attente
to dial a wrong number se tromper de numéro	**to text someone** envoyer un SMS/un message à quelqu'un
to give someone a call passer un coup de téléphone/de fil à quelqu'un	**to turn one's cell phone on/off** allumer/éteindre son portable

When giving their telephone numbers, French people say them two by two: 01 45 67 44 32: *zéro un, quarante-cinq, soixante-sept, quarante-quatre, trente-deux*. The first two numbers will be one of the five main regional codes existing in France: 01= Paris area, 02 = North West, 03 = North East, 04 = South East, 05 =South West. A number starting with 06 is a cell phone number.

When calling from abroad, you need to dial the country code and then delete the 0 of the regional code: 0033 1 45 67 44 32.

1) Calling from a pay phone

Where can I buy a phone card?
Où est-ce que je peux acheter une carte de téléphone ?

Do you know if there's a card-/coin-operated pay phone near here?
Est-ce que vous savez s'il y a une cabine téléphonique à pièces/à carte près d'ici ?

Could you give me change of ... to make a phone call?
Pourriez-vous me faire la monnaie de ..., c'est pour téléphoner ?

I'd like to make a collect call.
Je voudrais appeler en PCV.

2) Asking for information from the operator or switchboard

Could you put me through to information, please?
Est-ce que vous pouvez me passer les renseignements, s'il vous plaît ?

I'm trying to get a number in Marseilles.
J'essaie d'obtenir un numéro à Marseille.

Could you give me the number for ..., please?
Vous pouvez me donner le numéro de ..., s'il vous plaît ?

What's the country code for
Morocco?
Quel est l'indicatif pour le Maroc ?

How do I get an outside line?
Comment fait-on pour appeler à
l'extérieur ?

3) Answering the telephone

When the phone is ringing:

I'll get it!
J'y vais !/Je réponds !

Can you get it, please?
Tu peux répondre, s'il te plaît ?

When you pick up the phone:

Hello?
Allô ?

Hello, Helen Smith speaking.
Allô, Helen Smith à l'appareil.

4) Confirming you are the person to whom the caller wishes to speak

Yes, it's me.
Oui, c'est moi.

This is he/she.
C'est lui-même/elle-même.

How can I help you?
En quoi puis-je vous être utile ?

What can I do for you?
Que puis-je faire pour vous ?

5) Asking to speak to someone

Hi Marie. This is Sharon here. Is Pierre there?
Bonjour Marie. C'est Sharon (à l'appareil). Est-ce que Pierre est là ?

Can/could I speak to Stéphane, please? It's David.
Est-ce que je peux/pourrais parler à Stéphane, s'il vous plaît ? C'est de la part
de David.

To which the other person may reply:

Un instant, s'il vous plaît. Je vais le chercher.
Just a moment, please. I'll get him for you.

Ne quittez pas, je vous le passe.
Hold on, I'll just hand you over to him.

Je suis désolé mais il n'est pas là pour le moment.
I'm sorry, but he's not in right now.

Il est sorti. Il sera de retour dans une demi-heure.
He's gone out. He'll be back in half an hour.

6) Asking to speak to someone in a company or institution

Hello, I'd like to speak to Mr. Dupont, this is Tim Clark.
Allô, bonjour, je voudrais parler à Monsieur Dupont, de la part de Tim Clark.

Could you put me through to the sales manager, please?
Pouvez-vous me passer le responsable du service des ventes, s'il vous plaît ?

Could you put me through to extension 321, please?
Pouvez-vous me passer le poste 321, s'il vous plaît ? (*pronounced trois cent vingt-et-un*)

Phrases used by a receptionist or secretary taking a call:

Déménagements Leclerc, bonjour.
Déménagements Leclerc, je vous écoute.
Good morning/afternoon, Déménagements Leclerc.

C'est de la part de qui ?/Qui est à l'appareil ?
Who's calling?

Qui dois-je annoncer ?
Who should I say is calling?

Ça ne répond pas.
There's no answer.

C'est occupé./Ça sonne occupé.
The line's busy.

Ne quittez pas, je vous le passe.
One moment, I'll put you through.

Je regrette, il est en réunion/en vacances.
I'm sorry, he's in a meeting/on vacation.

Il est en communication, voulez-vous patienter ?
He's on another call, would you like to hold?

Je lui dirai que vous avez appelé.
I'll tell him you called.

Voulez-vous que je lui transmette un message ?
Would you like me to give him a message?

Voulez-vous laisser un message ?
Would you like to leave a message?

7) Leaving a message for someone

Just tell him I called, thanks. I'll try again later.
Dites-lui simplement que j'ai appelé, merci. Je réessaierai plus tard.

Could you tell her that I called? Thank you.
Vous pouvez lui dire que j'ai appelé ? Je vous remercie.

Could you tell him I'll call back later? Do you know when I'll be able to reach him/when he'll be back?
Vous pouvez lui dire que je rappellerai plus tard ? Est-ce que vous savez quand je pourrai le joindre/quand il sera de retour ?

Could you ask her to call me back today? She can reach me at ...
Pouvez-vous lui demander de me rappeler dans la journée ? Elle peut me joindre au ...

Do you have a pen and paper? **My name is ... and my phone**
Vous avez de quoi écrire ? **number is ...**
 Mon nom est ... et mon numéro est
 le ...

8) Stating the reason for one's call

Hi Georges, it's James. I just wanted to know if you had any plans for this evening.
Salut, Georges, c'est James. Je voulais juste savoir si tu avais quelque chose de prévu ce soir.

Hello, Lucie? It's me, Peter. Are you free to go to the movies on Saturday?
Allô, Lucie ? C'est moi, Peter. Est-ce que tu es libre pour aller au ciné samedi ?

Hello, is this Mr. Moreau? ... Hi. This is Frank Simpson. I'm calling about the ad in ...
Allô, est-ce que je suis bien chez Monsieur Moreau ? ... Bonjour. Je m'appelle/je suis Frank Simpson. Je vous appelle au sujet de l'annonce qui est parue dans ...

I'm calling to inform you that I still haven't received my itemized phone bill.
J'appelle pour vous signaler que je n'ai toujours pas reçu ma facture (de téléphone) détaillée.

I'm just calling to let you know I'll be a bit late.
J'appelle pour vous dire que je serai un peu en retard.

I'd like to make an appointment for next Monday.
J'aurais voulu prendre un rendez-vous pour lundi prochain.

9) Understanding recorded messages

On someone's answering machine:

Bonjour. Vous êtes bien chez Laurent et Stéphanie. Nous ne sommes pas là pour le moment mais vous pouvez laisser un message et nous vous rappellerons dès notre retour.
Hello, you've reached Laurent and Stéphanie. We're not available right now, but please leave us a message and we'll return your call as soon as we can.

Veuillez laisser un message après le bip.
Please leave a message after the tone.

When you are asked to follow instructions:

Appuyez sur la touche dièse/étoile.
Press the hash/star key.

If you are put through to an answering machine, the usual recorded message
while waiting is:

Nous vous demandons de bien vouloir patienter quelques instants. Nous allons
donner suite à votre appel.
Please hold while we connect your call.

If you have to leave a message, you will hear the following standard set of sentences:

Vous êtes bien en communication avec … Nous ne pouvons répondre à votre
appel. Veuillez nous laisser votre nom et numéro de téléphone après le signal
sonore et nous vous rappellerons dès que possible. Merci.
**You've reached … We're unable to take your call right now. Please
leave your name and number after the beep and we'll get back to
you as soon as we can. Thank you.**

If you have dialed a number that doesn't exist, you will hear:

Le numéro que vous avez demandé n'est pas attribué.
The number you have dialed has not been recognized.

10) Leaving a message on an answering machine

**Hi, it's Kate. I see you're not at home. Oh well … I'll call back later.
Bye!**
Salut, c'est Kate. Je vois que tu n'es pas chez toi Bon, eh bien … je rappellerai
plus tard. Salut !

**Hello, it's me again. It's just to tell you there are some traffic delays,
but I see you've already left. Too bad.**
Bonjour, c'est encore moi. C'est juste pour te dire qu'il y a des embouteillages
sur la route. Mais je vois que tu es déjà parti. Tant pis.

**Hello, it's David McLean here. Can you contact me on my cell phone
whenever you get this message? The number's 07712 745 792. Thank
you.**
Bonjour, c'est David McLean. Est-ce que vous pouvez me contacter sur mon
portable quand vous aurez ce message ? C'est le 07712 745 792. Merci.

**Hello, this is Kim Thomas from Double Page bookstore. I'm calling to
tell you that the book you ordered has arrived.**
Bonjour, Kim Thomas de la librairie Double Page. J'appelle pour vous dire que
le livre que vous avez commandé est arrivé.

11) Ending the conversation

Thank you, goodbye.
Je vous remercie, au revoir.

Thanks a lot. Bye.
Merci bien. Salut.

Thanks for your help, bye.
Merci pour votre aide, au revoir.

Thank you for calling.
Merci d'avoir appelé.

Sorry, but I've got to hang up. My mom needs the phone. Can I call you back later?
Désolé mais je dois raccrocher. Ma mère a besoin du téléphone. Je peux te rappeler plus tard ?

I've got to go.
Il faut que j'y aille.

We'll talk soon, OK?
On s'appelle bientôt ?

We'll talk again, OK?
On se rappelle, ok ?

12) Cell phones

Do you have a cell phone number?
Vous avez un numéro de portable ?

I've run out of minutes.
Je n'ai plus d'argent sur mon portable.

The signal's very bad.
Il y a une très mauvaise réception.

I can't get any reception here.
Je ne capte pas ici.

Do you know where I can get a new phone card for my cell phone?
Vous savez où je peux acheter une carte pour mon téléphone portable ?

Can I plug my cell phone in here to recharge it? The battery's dead.
Est-ce que je peux brancher mon portable ici pour le recharger ? Je n'ai plus de batterie.

Is there an outlet so that I can recharge my cell phone?
Est-ce qu'il y a une prise pour que je recharge mon portable ?

Did you get my text message?
Tu as eu mon message/mon SMS ?

I forgot my charger.
J'ai oublié mon chargeur.

13) Problems

I'm sorry, I must have dialed the wrong number.
Excusez-moi, j'ai dû faire un faux numéro.

Sorry to have bothered you.
Je suis désolé de vous avoir dérangé.

You've dialed the wrong number.
Vous avez fait un faux numéro.

You've got the wrong number.
Vous vous êtes trompé de numéro.

Could you say that again more slowly?
Est-ce que vous pouvez répéter plus lentement ?

I can barely hear you. Could you speak up?
Je vous entends très mal. Est-ce que vous pouvez parler plus fort ?

I'm sorry, I didn't quite understand. Could you spell it?
Je suis désolé, je n'ai pas très bien compris. Est-ce que vous pouvez l'épeler ?

Hello, can you hear me? **We got cut off.**
Allô, vous m'entendez ? On a été coupés.

Hold on, we're going to be cut off, I need to put some more change in.
Attends, ça va couper, il faut que je rajoute de la monnaie.

I can't reach him. **I keep getting a busy signal.**
Je n'arrive pas à le joindre. C'est toujours occupé.

I don't have many minutes left on my card.
Il ne me reste plus beaucoup d'unités sur ma carte.

Vocabulary Builder

The diagrams on the next pages give you all the key French terms for 15 important vocabulary topics. The terms are laid out in this form to make them easier to remember as you can see the connections between different words and groups of words. Try copying this layout when you want to revise the terms for a certain topic.

All the words can be found with their translations in the main part of the dictionary.

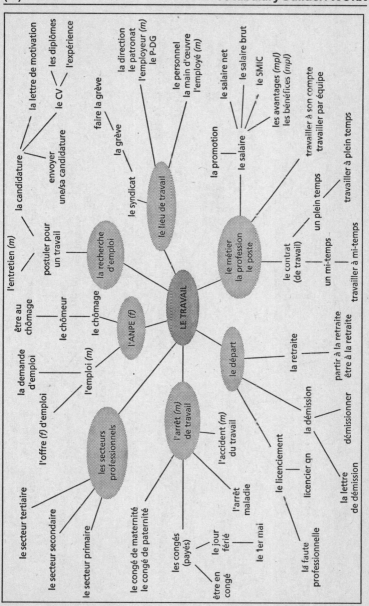

LE TRAVAIL

la recherche d'emploi
- postuler pour un travail
- envoyer une/sa candidature
 - la candidature
 - l'entretien (m)
 - la lettre de motivation
 - le CV
 - les diplômes
 - l'expérience
- faire la grève
 - la grève
- le syndicat

le lieu de travail
- la direction
 - le patronat
 - l'employeur (m)
 - le P-DG
- le personnel
 - la main d'œuvre
 - l'employé (m)
- la promotion
- le salaire
 - le salaire net
 - le salaire brut
 - le SMIC
 - les avantages (mpl)
 - les bénéfices (mpl)

le métier / la profession / le poste
- travailler à son compte
- travailler par équipe
- un plein temps
 - travailler à plein temps
- le contrat (de travail)
- un mi-temps
 - travailler à mi-temps

le chômage
- être au chômage
- le chômeur
- l'ANPE (f)
- l'emploi (m)
 - la demande d'emploi
 - l'offre (f) d'emploi

le départ
- la retraite
 - partir à la retraite
 - être à la retraite
- la démission
 - démissionner
 - la lettre de démission
- le licenciement
 - licencier qn
 - la faute professionnelle

l'arrêt (m) de travail
- l'accident (m) du travail
- l'arrêt maladie
- les congés (payés)
 - être en congé
 - le jour férié
 - le 1er mai
- le congé de maternité
- le congé de paternité

les secteurs professionnels
- le secteur tertiaire
- le secteur secondaire
- le secteur primaire

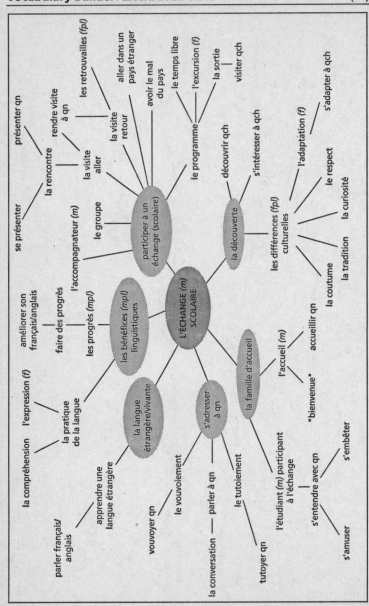

L'ÉCHANGE (m) SCOLAIRE

participer à un échange (scolaire)
- la rencontre
 - présenter qn
 - se présenter
- la visite
 - la visite retour
 - rendre visite à qn
 - aller
- l'accompagnateur (m)
- le groupe
- aller dans un pays étranger
- les retrouvailles (fpl)
- avoir le mal du pays
- le programme
 - le temps libre
 - l'excursion (f)
 - la sortie
 - visiter qch

la découverte
- découvrir qch
- s'intéresser à qch
- les différences (fpl) culturelles
 - l'adaptation (f)
 - s'adapter à qch
 - le respect
 - la curiosité
 - la coutume
 - la tradition

les bénéfices (mpl) linguistiques
- les progrès (mpl)
 - améliorer son français/anglais
 - faire des progrès
- la pratique de la langue
 - la compréhension
 - l'expression (f)
 - parler français/anglais

la langue étrangère/vivante
- apprendre une langue étrangère
- le vouvoiement
 - vouvoyer qn
- la conversation
 - parler à qn
- le tutoiement
 - tutoyer qn

s'adresser à qn

la famille d'accueil
- l'accueil (m)
 - accueillir qn
 - "bienvenue"
- l'étudiant (m) participant à l'échange
- s'entendre avec qn
- s'amuser
- s'embêter

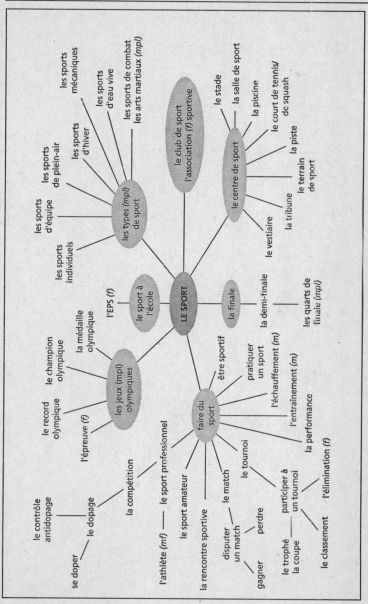

les sports mécaniques
les sports d'eau vive
les sports de combat (mpl)
les arts martiaux (mpl)
les sports d'hiver
les sports de plein-air
les sports d'équipe
les types (mpl) de sport
les sports individuels

le club de sport
l'association (f) sportive

le stade
la salle de sport
la piscine
le court de tennis/ de squash
la piste
le terrain de sport
le centre de sport
la tribune
le vestiaire

l'EPS (f)
le sport à l'école

LE SPORT

la finale
la demi-finale
les quarts de finale (mpl)

la médaille olympique
le champion olympique
le record olympique
les jeux (mpl) olympiques
l'épreuve (f)

être sportif
pratiquer un sport
l'échauffement (m)
l'entraînement (m)
faire du sport
la performance
l'élimination (f)

le dopage
le contrôle antidopage
se doper

la compétition
l'athlète (mf) — le sport professionnel
le sport amateur
la rencontre sportive
disputer un match
le match
le tournoi
participer à un tournoi
perdre
gagner
le trophé
la coupe
le classement

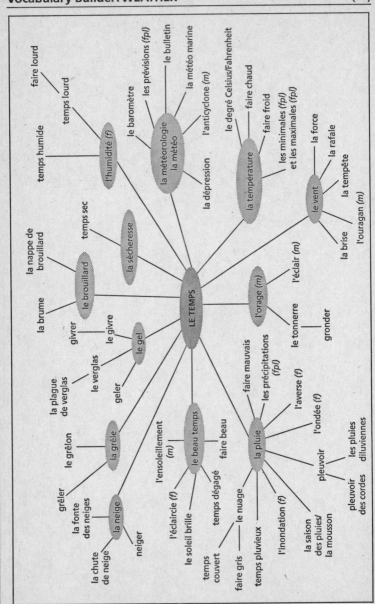

LE TEMPS

la météorologie / la météo
- le baromètre
- les prévisions (fpl)
- le bulletin
- la météo marine
- l'anticyclone (m)
- la dépression

l'humidité (f)
- temps humide
- temps lourd
- faire lourd

la température
- le degré Celsius/Fahrenheit
- faire chaud
- faire froid
- les minimales (fpl) et les maximales (fpl)

le vent
- la force
- la rafale
- la tempête
- l'ouragan (m)
- la brise

le brouillard
- temps sec
- la nappe de brouillard
- la brume
- la sécheresse

le gel
- givrer
- le givre
- geler
- le verglas
- la plaque de verglas

l'orage (m)
- l'éclair (m)
- le tonnerre
- gronder

la grêle
- grêler
- le grêlon

la neige
- la chute de neige
- neiger
- la fonte des neiges

l'ensoleillement (m)
- l'éclaircie (f)
- le soleil brille
- temps dégagé
- le beau temps
- faire beau
- temps couvert
- faire gris
- le nuage
- temps pluvieux

la pluie
- faire mauvais
- les précipitations (fpl)
- l'averse (f)
- l'ondée (f)
- pleuvoir
- les pluies diluviennes
- pleuvoir des cordes
- la saison des pluies/ la mousson
- l'inondation (f)

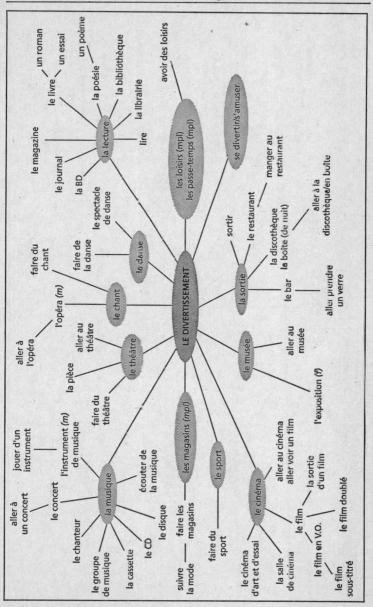

un roman
un essai
un poème

le livre
la poésie
la bibliothèque
la librairie

le magazine
le journal
la BD

lire

la lecture

avoir des loisirs

les loisirs (mpl)
les passe-temps (mpl)

se divertir/s'amuser

manger au restaurant

aller à la discothèque/en boîte

sortir
le restaurant

la discothèque
la boîte (de nuit)

le bar

aller prendre un verre

la sortie

LE DIVERTISSEMENT

le spectacle de danse
faire de la danse
la danse

faire du chant
faire de la danse
le chant

l'opéra (m)
aller à l'opéra

aller au théâtre
le théâtre
la pièce
faire du théâtre

le musée
aller au musée
l'exposition (f)

jouer d'un instrument
l'instrument (m) de musique

écouter de la musique
la musique

les magasins (mpl)
le sport

aller à un concert
le concert
le chanteur
le groupe de musique
la cassette
le CD
le disque

suivre la mode
faire les magasins

faire du sport

le cinéma
aller au cinéma
aller voir un film

le cinéma d'art et d'essai
la salle de cinéma

le film
le film en V.O.
la sortie d'un film
le film doublé

le film sous-titré

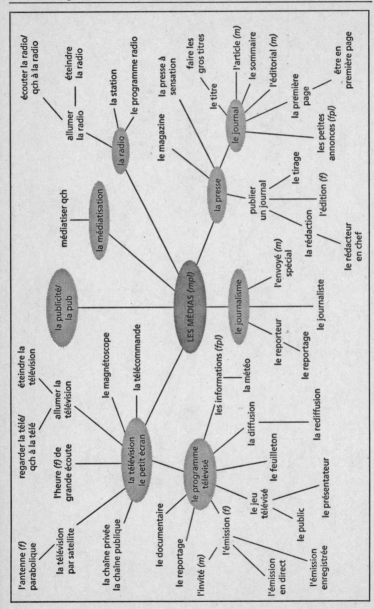

LES MÉDIAS *(mpl)*

la radio
- écouter la radio/qch à la radio
- allumer la radio
- éteindre la radio
- la station
- le programme radio

le magazine

la presse
- la presse à sensation
- le journal
 - faire les gros titres
 - le titre
 - l'article *(m)*
 - le sommaire
 - l'éditorial *(m)*
 - la première page
 - être en première page
 - les petites annonces *(fpl)*
- publier un journal
 - le tirage
 - l'édition *(f)*
- la rédaction
- le rédacteur en chef

la médiatisation
- médiatiser qch

la publicité/la pub

le journalisme
- l'envoyé *(m)* spécial
- le journaliste
- le reporteur
- le reportage

la télévision / le petit écran
- regarder la télé/qch à la télé
- allumer la télévision
- éteindre la télévision
- l'heure *(f)* de grande écoute
- l'antenne *(f)* parabolique
- la télévision par satellite
- la chaîne privée
- la chaîne publique
- le magnétoscope
- la télécommande

le programme télévisé
- les informations *(fpl)*
- la météo
- la diffusion
- la rediffusion
- le feuilleton
- le jeu télévisé
- le public
- le présentateur
- l'émission *(f)*
 - l'émission en direct
 - l'émission enregistrée
- l'invité *(m)*
- le reportage
- le documentaire

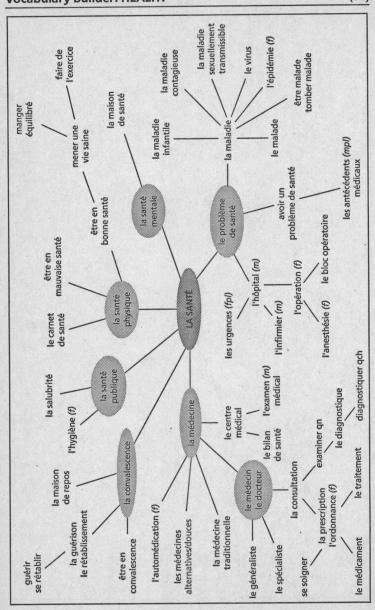

LA SANTÉ

la santé mentale
- être en bonne santé
- mener une vie saine
 - manger équilibré
 - faire de l'exercice
- la maison de santé

le problème de santé
- la maladie
 - la maladie infantile
 - la maladie contagieuse
 - la maladie sexuellement transmissible
 - le virus
 - l'épidémie (f)
 - être malade / tomber malade
 - le malade
- avoir un problème de santé
- les antécédents (mpl) médicaux
- le bloc opératoire
- l'opération (f)
- l'anesthésie (f)
- l'infirmier (m)
- l'hôpital (m)
- les urgences (fpl)

la santé physique
- être en mauvaise santé
- le carnet de santé

la santé publique
- la salubrité
- l'hygiène (f)

la convalescence
- la maison de repos
- la guérison / le rétablissement
 - guérir / se rétablir
- être en convalescence

la médecine
- l'automédication (f)
- les médecines alternatives/douces
- la médecine traditionnelle
- le centre médical
 - l'examen (m) médical
 - le bilan de santé
- le médecin / le docteur
 - le généraliste
 - le spécialiste
 - la consultation
 - examiner qn
 - le diagnostique
 - diagnostiquer qch
 - le traitement
 - le médicament
 - la prescription / l'ordonnance (f)
 - se soigner

Aa

A, a [ɑ] *nm inv* A, a; **A1** (*autoroute*) *Br* ≃ M1, *Am* ≃ I1

a [a] *voir* **avoir**

À [a]

à + le = au [o], à + les = aux [o]

prép (**a**) (*indique la direction*) to; **aller à Paris** to go to Paris; **partir au Venezuela** to leave for Venezuela; **de Paris à Lyon** from Paris to Lyons

(**b**) (*indique la position*) at; **être au bureau/à la ferme/à Paris** to be at *or* in the office/on *or* at the farm/in Paris; **à la maison** at home

(**c**) (*dans l'expression du temps*) **à 8 heures** at 8 o'clock; **du lundi au vendredi** from Monday to Friday, *Am* Monday through Friday; **au vingt-et-unième siècle** in the twenty-first century; **à mon arrivée** on (my) arrival; **à lundi!** see you (on) Monday!

(**d**) (*dans les descriptions*) **l'homme à la barbe** the man with the beard; **verre à vin** wine glass

(**e**) (*introduit le complément d'objet indirect*) **donner qch à qn** to give sth to sb, to give sb sth; **penser à qn/qch** to think about *or* of sb/sth

(**f**) (*devant infinitif*) **apprendre à lire** to learn to read; **avoir du travail à faire** to have work to do; **maison à vendre** house for sale; **prêt à partir** ready to leave

(**g**) (*indique l'appartenance*) **un ami à moi** a friend of mine; **c'est à lui** it's his; **c'est à vous de...** (*il vous incombe de*) it's up to you to...; (*c'est votre tour*) it's your turn to...

(**h**) (*indique le moyen, la manière*) **à bicyclette** by bicycle; **à pied** on foot; **à la main** by hand; **au crayon** in pencil; **deux à deux** two by two

(**i**) (*prix*) **pain à 1 euro** loaf for 1 euro

(**j**) (*poids*) **vendre au kilo** to sell by the kilo

(**k**) (*vitesse*) **100 km à l'heure** 100 km an *or* per hour

(**l**) (*pour appeler*) **au voleur!** (stop) thief!; **au feu!** (there's a) fire!

abaisser [abese] **1** *vt* (*levier, pont-levis*) to lower; (*store*) to pull down **2 s'abaisser** *vpr* (**a**) (*barrière*) to lower (**b**) (*être en pente*) to slope down

abandon [abɑ̃dɔ̃] *nm* (*d'enfant, de projet*) abandonment; (*de lieu*) neglect; (*de sportif*) withdrawal; *Ordinat* abort ■ **abandonner 1** *vt* (*personne, animal, lieu*) to desert, to abandon; (*pouvoir, combat*) to give up; (*projet*) to abandon; **a. ses études** to drop out (of school) **2** *vi* (*renoncer*) to give up; (*sportif*) to withdraw

abasourdi, -e [abazurdi] *adj* stunned

abat-jour [abaʒur] *nm inv* lampshade

abats [aba] *nmpl* offal; (*de volaille*) giblets

abattement [abatmɑ̃] *nm* (*mental*) dejection; (*physique*) exhaustion; **a. fiscal** tax allowance

abattoir [abatwar] *nm* slaughterhouse

abattre* [abatr] **1** *vt* (*arbre*) to cut down; (*personne*) to kill; (*animal de boucherie*) to slaughter; (*animal blessé ou malade*) to destroy; (*avion*) to shoot down; *Fig* (*déprimer*) to demoralize **2 s'abattre** *vpr* (*tomber*) to crash down (**sur** on); (*pluie*) to pour down (**sur** on)

abattu, -e [abaty] *adj* (*mentalement*) dejected; (*physiquement*) exhausted

abbaye [abei] *nf* abbey

abcès [apsɛ] *nm* abscess

abdomen [abdɔmɛn] *nm* abdomen ■ **abdominal, -e, -aux, -ales** *adj* abdominal

abeille [abɛj] *nf* bee

aberrant, -e [aberã, -ãt] *adj* absurd

abîme [abim] *nm* abyss

abîmer [abime] **1** *vt* to spoil, to damage **2 s'abîmer** *vpr (object)* to get spoilt; *(fruit)* to go bad

abject, -e [abʒɛkt] *adj* despicable

abolir [abɔlir] *vt* to abolish ▪ **abolition** *nf* abolition

abominable [abɔminabl] *adj* appalling

abondant, -e [abɔ̃dã, -ãt] *adj* plentiful, abundant ▪ **abondance** *nf* abundance **(de** of) ▪ **abonder** *vi* to be plentiful

abonné, -e [abɔne] *nmf (d'un journal, du téléphone)* subscriber; *(du gaz)* consumer ▪ **abonnement** *nm (de journal)* subscription; *(de téléphone)* line rental ▪ **s'abonner** *vpr (à un journal)* to subscribe **(à** to)

abord [abɔr] *nm* **(a)** *(accès)* **d'un a. facile** easy to approach; **abords** *(d'un bâtiment)* surroundings; *(d'une ville)* outskirts **(b)** *(expressions)* **au premier a., de prime a.** at first sight; **d'a., tout d'a.** *(pour commencer)* at first, to begin with; *(premièrement)* first (and foremost)

abordable [abɔrdabl] *adj (prix, marchandises)* affordable

aborder [abɔrde] **1** *vt (personne, lieu, virage)* to approach; *(problème)* to tackle **2** *vi* to land

aborigène [abɔriʒɛn] *nm (d'un pays)* native; **les Aborigènes d'Australie** the (Australian) Aborigines

aboutir [abutir] *vi (réussir)* to be successful; **a. à qch** *(avoir pour résultat)* to result in sth ▪ **aboutissement** *nm (succès)* success; *(résultat)* outcome

aboyer [abwaje] *vi* to bark

abréger [abreʒe] *vt (texte)* to shorten; *(visite)* to cut short; *(mot)* to abbreviate ▪ **abrégé** *nm (d'un texte)* summary; *(livre)* abstract; **en a.** *(mot)* in abbreviated form

abréviation [abrevjasjɔ̃] *nf* abbreviation

abri [abri] *nm* shelter; **mettre qn/qch à l'a.** to shelter sb/sth; **se mettre à l'a.** to take shelter; **être à l'a. de qch** to be sheltered from sth; **sans a.** homeless ▪ **abriter 1** *vt (protéger)* to shelter **(de** from); *(loger)* to house **2 s'abriter** *vpr* to (take) shelter **(de** from)

abricot [abriko] *nm* apricot

abroger [abrɔʒe] *vt* to repeal

abrupt, -e [abrypt] *adj (pente)* steep

abrutir [abrytir] *vt (hébéter)* to daze ▪ **abrutissant, -e** *adj* mind-numbing

absence [apsɑ̃s] *nf (d'une personne)* absence; *(manque)* lack ▪ **absent, -e 1** *adj (personne)* absent **(de** from); *(chose)* missing **2** *nmf* absentee ▪ **s'absenter** *vpr* to go away

absolu, -e [apsɔly] *adj* absolute ▪ **absolument** *adv* absolutely

absorber [apsɔrbe] *vt (liquid)* to absorb; *(nourriture)* to eat; *(boisson)* to drink; *(médicament)* to take ▪ **absorbant, -e** *adj (papier)* absorbent; *(travail)* absorbing ▪ **absorption** *nf (de liquide)* absorption; *(de nourriture)* eating; *(de boisson)* drinking; *(de médicament)* taking

abstenir* [apstənir] **s'abstenir** *vpr (ne pas voter)* to abstain; **s'a. de qch/ de faire qch** to refrain from sth/from doing sth ▪ **abstention** *nf Pol* abstention

abstrait, -e [apstrɛ, -ɛt] *adj* abstract ▪ **abstraction** *nf* abstraction

absurde [apsyrd] *adj* absurd ▪ **absurdité** *nf* absurdity; **dire des absurdités** to talk nonsense

abus [aby] *nm (excès)* overindulgence **(de** in); *(pratique)* abuse **(de** of); **a. de pouvoir** abuse of power; **a. d'alcool** alcohol abuse; **a. de confiance** breach of trust ▪ **abuser 1** *vi* to go too far; **a. de** *(situation, personne)* to take unfair advantage of; *(autorité)* to abuse; *(nourriture)* to overindulge in **2 s'abuser** *vpr* **si je ne m'abuse** if I am not mistaken

abusif, -ive [abyzif, -iv] *adj* excessive; *(mère)* possessive

académie [akademi] *nf* academy; *(administration scolaire)* ≃ school district; **l'A. française** = learned society responsible for promoting the French language and imposing standards

acajou [akaʒu] *nm* mahogany

accabler [akable] *vt* to overwhelm (**de** with); **accablé de dettes** (over)burdened with debt ■ **accablant, -e** *adj (chaleur)* oppressive; *(témoignage)* damning

accalmie [akalmi] *nf* lull

accaparer [akapare] *vt (personne)* to monopolize

accéder [aksede] *vi* **a. à** *(lieu)* to reach; *(rang)* to gain; *(requête)* to comply with; *Ordinat (programme)* to access; **a. au trône** to accede to the throne

accélérer [akselere] **1** *vt (allure, pas)* to quicken **2** *vi (en voiture)* to accelerate **3 s'accélérer** *vpr* to speed up ■ **accélérateur** *nm (de voiture, d'ordinateur)* accelerator ■ **accélération** *nf* acceleration

accent [aksɑ̃] *nm (prononciation)* accent; *(sur une syllabe)* stress; *Fig* **mettre l'a. sur qch** to stress sth; **a. aigu/ circonflexe/grave** acute/circumflex/ grave (accent) ■ **accentuation** *nf (sur lettre)* accentuation; *(de phénomène)* intensification ■ **accentuer 1** *vt (syllabe)* to stress; *(lettre)* to put an accent on; *Fig (renforcer)* to emphasize **2 s'accentuer** *vpr* to become more pronounced

accepter [aksepte] *vt* to accept; **a. de faire qch** to agree to do sth ■ **acceptable** *adj (recevable)* acceptable ■ **acceptation** *nf* acceptance

acception [aksepsjɔ̃] *nf (de mot)* meaning

accès [aksɛ] *nm* (a) *(approche)* & *Ordinat* access (**à** to); **avoir a. à qch** to have access to sth; **'a. interdit'** 'no entry'; **'a. aux quais'** to the trains (b) *(de folie, de colère)* fit; *(de fièvre)* bout ■ **accessible** *adj (lieu, livre)* accessible

accession [aksesjɔ̃] *nf* accession (**à** to); **a. à la propriété** home ownership

accessoire [akseswar] *adj* minor ■ **accessoires** *nmpl (de théâtre)* props; *(de mode, de voiture)* accessories; **a. de toilette** toilet accessories

accident [aksidɑ̃] *nm* accident; **a. de chemin de fer** train crash; **a. de la route** road accident; **a. du travail** industrial accident; **a. de parcours** hitch; **par a.** by accident; by chance ■ **accidenté, -e 1** *adj (terrain)* uneven; *(voiture)* damaged **2** *nmf* accident victim ■ **accidentel, -elle** *adj* accidental

acclamer [aklame] *vt* to cheer ■ **acclamations** *nfpl* cheers

acclimater [aklimate] **1** *vt Br* to acclimatize, *Am* to acclimate (**à** to) **2 s'acclimater** *vpr* to become *Br* acclimatized or *Am* acclimated (**à** to) ■ **acclimatation** *nf Br* acclimatization, *Am* acclimation (**à** to)

accolade [akɔlad] *nf (embrassade)* embrace; *(signe)* curly bracket

accommoder [akɔmɔde] **1** *vt (nourriture)* to prepare; *(restes)* to use up **2** *vi (œil)* to focus **3 s'accommoder** *vpr* **s'a. de qch** to put up with sth ■ **accommodant, -e** *adj* accommodating

accompagner [akɔ̃paɲe] *vt (personne)* to accompany; **a. qn à la gare** *(en voiture)* to take sb to the station ■ **accompagnateur, -trice** *nmf (musical)* accompanist; *(de touristes)* guide; *(d'enfants)* group leader ■ **accompagnement** *nm (de musique)* accompaniment; *(légumes)* accompaniment

accomplir [akɔ̃plir] *vt (tâche)* to carry out; *(formalités)* to go through ■ **accompli, -e** *adj (parfait)* accomplished

accord [akɔr] *nm (traité, entente)* & *Gram* agreement; *(autorisation)* consent; *(musical)* chord; **être d'a.** to agree (**avec** with); **d'a.!** all right! ■ **accorder 1** *vt (instrument)* to tune; **a. qch à qn** *(faveur)* to grant sb sth; *(prêt)* to authorize sth to sb **2 s'accorder** *vpr (se mettre d'accord)* to agree (**avec/sur** with/on); *Gram (mots)* to agree (**avec** with); **s'a. qch** to allow oneself sth

accordéon [akɔrdeɔ̃] *nm* accordion

accoster [akɔste] **1** *vt (personne)* to approach **2** *vi Naut* to dock

accotement [akɔtmɑ̃] *nm (de route)* verge; *(de voie ferrée)* shoulder

accoucher [akuʃe] *vi* to give birth (**de** to) ■ **accouchement** *nm* delivery

accouder [akude] **s'accouder** *vpr* **s'a. à** *ou* **sur qch** to lean one's elbows on sth ■ **accoudoir** *nm* armrest

accoupler [akuple] **s'accoupler** *vpr (animaux)* to mate

accourir* [akurir] *vi* to run up

accoutrement [akutrəmɑ̃] *nm Péj* rig-out

accoutumer [akutyme] **1** *vt* a. qn à qch to get sb accustomed to sth **2 s'accoutumer** *vpr* to get accustomed (à to) ■ **accoutumance** *nf (adaptation)* familiarization (à with); *Méd (dépendance)* addiction ■ **accoutumé, -e** *adj* usual; **comme à l'accoutumée** as usual

accroc [akro] *nm (déchirure)* tear; *(difficulté)* hitch; **sans a.** without a hitch

accrocher [akrɔʃe] **1** *vt (déchirer)* to catch; *(fixer)* to hook (à onto); *(suspendre)* to hang up (à on)
2 *vi (achopper)* to hit a stumbling block; *(se remarquer)* to grab one's attention
3 s'accrocher *vpr (se fixer)* to fasten; *Fam (persévérer)* to stick at it; **s'a. à qn/qch** *(s'agripper)* to cling to sb/sth ■ **accrochage** *nm (de véhicules)* minor accident ■ **accrocheur, -euse** *adj (personne)* tenacious; *(titre, slogan)* catchy

accroître* [akrwatr] **1** *vt* to increase **2 s'accroître** *vpr* to increase ■ **accroissement** *nm* increase (de in)

accroupir [akrupir] **s'accroupir** *vpr* to squat (down)

accueil [akœj] *nm (bureau)* reception; *(manière)* welcome; **faire un bon a. à qn** to give sb a warm welcome ■ **accueillant, -e** *adj* welcoming ■ **accueillir*** *vt (personne, proposition)* to greet; *(sujet: hôtel)* to accommodate

acculer [akyle] *vt* a. qn à qch to drive sb to sth

accumuler [akymyle] *vt*, **s'accumuler** *vpr* to accumulate ■ **accumulation** *nf* accumulation

accuser [akyze] *vt (dénoncer)* to accuse; *(accentuer)* to bring out; *(baisse)* to show; **a. qn de qch/de faire qch** to accuse sb of sth/of doing sth ■ **accusateur, -trice 1** *adj (regard)* accusing **2** *nmf* accuser ■ **accusation** *nf* accusation ■ **accusé, -e** *nmf* **l'a.** the accused;

(au tribunal) the defendant

achalandé, -e [aʃalɑ̃de] *adj* **bien a.** *(magasin)* well-stocked

acharner [aʃarne] **s'acharner** *vpr* **s'a. sur** *ou* **contre qn** *(persécuter)* to persecute sb; **s'a. à faire qch** to try very hard to do sth ■ **acharné, -e** *adj (effort, travail)* relentless; *(combat)* fierce ■ **acharnement** *nm* relentlessness; *(dans un combat)* fury

achat [aʃa] *nm* purchase; **faire l'a. de qch** to buy sth; **achats** *(paquets)* shopping

acheter [aʃəte] **1** *vt* to buy; **a. qch à qn** *(faire une transaction)* to buy sth from sb; *(faire un cadeau)* to buy sth for sb **2** *vi* to buy **3 s'acheter** *vpr* **je vais m'acheter une glace** I'm going to buy (myself) an ice cream ■ **acheteur, -euse** *nmf* buyer; *(dans un magasin)* shopper

achever [aʃəve] **1** *vt* **(a)** *(finir)* to end; *(travail)* to complete; **a. de faire qch** to finish doing sth **(b)** *(tuer) (animal malade)* to put out of its misery; **a. qn** to finish sb off **2 s'achever** *vpr* to end ■ **achèvement** *nm* completion

acide [asid] **1** *adj* acid(ic); *(au goût)* sour **2** *nm* acid ■ **acidité** *nf* acidity; *(au goût)* sourness

acier [asje] *nm* steel; **a. inoxydable** stainless steel ■ **aciérie** *nf* steelworks

acné [akne] *nf* acne

acompte [akɔ̃t] *nm* down payment; **verser un a.** to make a down payment

à-coup [aku] *(pl* à-coups*) nm* jolt; **sans à-coups** smoothly; **par à-coups** *(avancer)* in fits and starts

acoustique [akustik] *nf (qualité)* acoustics *(pluriel)*

acquérir* [akerir] *vt (acheter)* to purchase; *(obtenir)* to acquire; **a. de la valeur** to increase in value; **tenir qch pour acquis** to take sth for granted ■ **acquéreur** *nm* purchaser ■ **acquis** *nm (expérience)* experience; **les a. sociaux** social benefits ■ **acquisition** *nf (action)* acquisition; *(bien acheté)* purchase

acquitter [akite] **1** *vt (accusé)* to acquit; *(dette)* to pay **2 s'acquitter** *vpr*

s'a. d'un devoir to fulfil a duty ■ **acquittement** *nm (d'un accusé)* acquittal; *(d'une dette)* payment

âcre [akr] *adj (goût)* bitter; *(odeur)* acrid

acrobate [akrɔbat] *nmf* acrobat ■ **acrobatie** *nf* acrobatics *(sing);* **acrobaties aériennes** aerobatics *(sing)*

acrylique [akrilik] *nm* acrylic

acte [akt] *nm (action) & Théât* act; **faire a. de candidature** to apply; **prendre a. de qch** to take note of sth; **a. terroriste** terrorist act; **a. unique européen** Single European Act; **a. de naissance** birth certificate

acteur [aktœr] *nm* actor

actif, -ive [aktif, -iv] **1** *adj* active **2** *nm Gram* active; *Com (d'une entreprise)* assets

action [aksjɔ̃] *nf (acte)* action; *(en Bourse)* share; **bonne a.** good deed; **passer à l'a.** to take action ■ **actionnaire** *nmf* shareholder ■ **actionner** *vt (mettre en marche)* to start up

activer [aktive] **1** *vt (accélérer)* to speed up; *Ordinat (option)* to select **2** **s'activer** *vpr (être actif)* to be busy

activité [aktivite] *nf* activity; **en a.** *(personne)* working; *(volcan)* active

actrice [aktris] *nf* actress

actualisation [aktɥalizasjɔ̃] *nf (de texte)* updating

actualité [aktɥalite] *nf (d'un problème)* topicality; **l'a.** current affairs; **les actualités** *(à la radio, à la télévision)* the news; **d'a.** topical

actuel, -elle [aktɥɛl] *adj (présent)* present; *(d'actualité)* topical ■ **actuellement** *adv* at present

acupuncture [akypɔ̃ktyr] *nf* acupuncture ■ **acupuncteur, -trice** *nmf* acupuncturist

adapter [adapte] **1** *vt* to adapt (à to) **2** **s'adapter** *vpr (s'acclimater)* to adapt (à to); **s'a. à qn/qch** to get used to sb/sth ■ **adaptateur** *nm* adapter ■ **adaptation** *nf* adaptation; **faculté d'a.** adaptability

additif [aditif] *nm (substance)* additive

addition [adisjɔ̃] *nf* addition (à to); *(de restaurant) Br* bill, *Am* check ■ **additionner** *vt* to add (up) (à to)

adepte [adept] *nmf* follower

adéquat, -e [adekwa, -at] *adj* appropriate; *(quantité)* adequate

adhérer [adere] *vi* a. à qch *(coller)* to stick to sth; *(s'inscrire)* to join sth ■ **adhérent, -e** *nmf* member

adhésif, -ive [adezif, -iv] *adj* adhesive ■ **adhésion** *nf (inscription)* joining (à of)

adieu, -x [adjø] **1** *exclam* farewell **2** *nm* farewell; **faire ses adieux** to say one's goodbyes

adjacent, -e [adʒasɑ̃, -ɑ̃t] *adj* adjacent (à to)

adjectif [adʒɛktif] *nm* adjective

adjoint, -e [adʒwɛ̃, -ɛ̃t] *nmf* assistant; **a. au maire** deputy mayor

adjuger [adʒyʒe] **1** *vt* a. qch à qn *(prix, contrat)* to award sth to sb; *(aux enchères)* to knock sth down to sb **2** **s'adjuger** *vpr* s'a. qch to appropriate sth

admettre* [admɛtr] *vt (accueillir, reconnaître)* to admit; *(autoriser)* to allow; **être admis à un examen** to pass an exam

administrer [administre] *vt (gérer)* to administer ■ **administrateur, -trice** *nmf (de société)* director ■ **administration** *nf* administration; **l'A.** *(service public)* ≃ the Civil Service; *(fonctionnaires)* civil servants

admirer [admire] *vt* to admire ■ **admirable** *adj* admirable ■ **admirateur, -trice** *nmf* admirer ■ **admiratif, -ive** *adj* admiring ■ **admiration** *nf* admiration; **être en a. devant qn/qch** to be filled with admiration for sb/sth

admissible [admisibl] *adj (tolérable)* acceptable, admissible; *Scol & Univ* **candidats admissibles** = candidates who have qualified for the oral examination ■ **admission** *nf* admission (à/dans to)

adolescent, -e [adɔlesɑ̃, -ɑ̃t] *nmf* adolescent, teenager ■ **adolescence** *nf* adolescence

adonner [adɔne] **s'adonner** *vpr* s'a. à

qch to devote oneself to sth; **s'a. à la boisson** to be an alcoholic

adopter [adɔpte] vt to adopt ■ **adoptif, -ive** adj (enfant, patrie) adopted; (parents) adoptive ■ **adoption** nf adoption

adorer [adɔre] **1** vt (dieu) to worship; (chose, personne) to adore; **a. faire qch** to adore doing sth **2** **s'adorer** vpr **ils s'adorent** they adore each other ■ **adorable** adj adorable

adosser [adose] **s'adosser** vpr **s'a. à qch** to lean (back) against sth

adoucir [adusir] **1** vt (traits, peau) to soften; (caractère) to take the edge off **2** **s'adoucir** vpr (temps) to turn milder; (voix) to soften; (caractère) to mellow

adresse [adrɛs] nf (a) (domicile) address; **a. électronique** ou **e-mail** e-mail address (b) (habileté) skill ■ **adresser 1** vt (lettre, remarque) to address (à to); **a. qch à qn** (lettre) to send sb sth; **a. la parole à qn** to speak to sb **2** **s'adresser** vpr **s'a. à qn** (parler) to speak to sb; (aller trouver) to go and see sb; (être destiné à) to be aimed at sb

Adriatique [adriatik] nf **l'A.** the Adriatic

adroit, -e [adrwa, -at] adj (habile) skilful

adulte [adylt] **1** adj (personne, animal) adult **2** nmf adult

adultère [adyltɛr] nm adultery

advenir* [advənir] (aux être) v impersonnel to happen; **a. de qn** (devenir) to become of sb

adverbe [advɛrb] nm adverb

adversaire [advɛrsɛr] nmf opponent ■ **adverse** adj opposing

aérer [aere] **1** vt (pièce, lit) to air **2** **s'aérer** vpr to get some fresh air ■ **aération** nf ventilation

aérien, -enne [aerjɛ̃, -ɛn] adj (transport, attaque, défense) air; (photo) aerial; (câble) overhead

aérobic [aerɔbik] nm aerobics (sing) ■ **aérodynamique** adj aerodynamic ■ **aérogare** nf air terminal ■ **aéroglisseur** nm hovercraft ■ **aérogramme** nm airmail letter ■ **aéroport** nm air-

port ■ **aérosol** nm aerosol

affable [afabl] adj affable

affaiblir [afeblir] vt, **s'affaiblir** vpr to weaken ■ **affaiblissement** nm weakening

affaire [afɛr] nf (question) matter, affair; (marché) deal; (firme) business; (scandale) affair; (procès) case; **affaires** (commerce) business (sing); (effets personnels) belongings; **les Affaires étrangères** Br ≃ the Foreign Office, Am ≃ the State Department; **avoir a. à qn/qch** to have to deal with sb/sth; **faire une bonne a.** to get a bargain; **c'est mon a.** that's my business; **ça fera l'a.** that will do nicely; **a. de cœur** love affair

affairer [afere] **s'affairer** vpr to busy oneself ■ **affairé, -e** adj busy

affaisser [afese] **s'affaisser** vpr (personne, bâtiment) to collapse; (sol) to subside

affaler [afale] **s'affaler** vpr to collapse; **affalé dans un fauteuil** slumped in an armchair

affamé, -e [afame] adj starving

affecter [afɛkte] vt (a) (employé) to appoint (à to); (soldat) to post (à to); (fonds) to assign (à to) (b) (feindre, émouvoir) to affect ■ **affectation** nf (d'employé) appointment (à to); (de soldat) posting (à to); (de fonds) assignment (à to); Péj (pose) affectation ■ **affecté, -e** adj Péj (manières, personne) affected

affection [afɛksjɔ̃] nf (attachement) affection; (maladie) ailment; **avoir de l'a. pour qn** to be fond of sb ■ **affectionner** vt to be fond of ■ **affectueux, -euse** adj affectionate

affiche [afiʃ] nf notice; (publicitaire) poster; **être à l'a.** (spectacle) to be on ■ **afficher** vt (avis) to put up; (prix, horaire, résultat) & Ordinat (message) to display; Péj (sentiment) to show; **a. complet** (sujet: spectacle) to be sold out ■ **affichage** nm bill-posting; Ordinat display

affiliation [afiljasjɔ̃] nf affiliation ■ **affilié, -e** adj affiliated

affiner [afine] **1** *vt (métal, goût)* to re-fine **2** *s'affiner vpr (goût)* to become more refined; *(visage)* to get thinner

affinité [afinite] *nf* affinity

affirmatif, -ive [afirmatif, -iv] *adj (réponse)* & *Gram* affirmative

affirmer [afirme] **1** *vt (manifester)* to assert; *(soutenir)* to maintain **2** *s'affir-mer vpr (personne)* to assert oneself; *(tendance)* to be confirmed ▪ **affirma-tion** *nf* assertion

affliger [aflize] *vt (peiner)* to distress; *(atteindre)* to afflict (**de** with)

affluence [aflyãs] *nf (de personnes)* crowd; *(de marchandises)* abundance

affluer [aflye] *vi (sang)* to rush (**à** to); *(gens)* to flock (**vers** to)

afflux [afly] *nm (de sang)* rush; *(de visi-teurs)* flood; *(de capitaux,* influx

affoler [afɔle] **1** *vt* to throw into a pa-nic **2** *s'affoler vpr* to panic ▪ **affolant, -e** *adj* terrifying ▪ **affolement** *nm* pa-nic

affranchir [afrãʃir] *vt (timbrer)* to put a stamp on; *(émanciper)* to free ▪ **af-franchissement** *nm (tarif)* postage

affreux, -euse [afrø, -øz] *adj (laid)* hideous; *(atroce)* dreadful

affront [afrɔ̃] *nm* insult; **faire un a. à qn** to insult sb

affronter [afrɔ̃te] **1** *vt* to confront; *(mauvais temps)* to brave **2** *s'affronter vpr (ennemis, équipes)* to clash ▪ **af-frontement** *nm* confrontation

affût [afy] *nm Fig* **à l'a. de** on the look-out for

affûter [afyte] *vt* to sharpen

Afghanistan [afganistã] *nm* **l'A.** Af-ghanistan ▪ **afghan, -e 1** *adj* Afghan **2** *nmf* **A., Afghane** Afghan

afin [afɛ̃] **1** *prép* **a. de faire qch** in or-der to do sth **2** *conj* **a. que...** *(+ sub-junctive)* so that...

Afrique [afrik] *nf* **l'A.** Africa ▪ **afri-cain, -e 1** *adj* African **2** *nmf* **A., Afri-caine** African

agacer [agase] *vt (personne)* to irritate ▪ **agaçant, -e** *adj* irritating

âge [aʒ] *nm* age; **quel â. as-tu?** how

old are you?; **d'un certain â.** middle-aged ▪ **âgé, -e** *adj* old; **être â. de six ans** to be six years old; **un enfant â. de six ans** a six-year-old child

agence [aʒɑ̃s] *nf* agency; *(de banque)* branch; **a. de voyage** travel agent's; **a. immobilière** *Br* estate agent's, *Am* real estate office

agencer [aʒɑ̃se] *vt* to arrange; **bien agencé** *(maison)* well laid-out

agenda [aʒɛ̃da] *nm Br* diary, *Am* date-book

agenouiller [aʒənuje] *s'agenouiller vpr* to kneel (down); **être agenouillé** to be kneeling (down)

agent [aʒɑ̃] *nm (employé, espion)* agent; **a. de police** police officer; **a. de change** stockbroker; **a. immobilier** *Br* estate agent, *Am* real estate agent; **a. secret** secret agent

agglomération [aglɔmerasjɔ̃] *nf (ville)* built-up area, town; **l'a. pari-sienne** Paris and its suburbs

aggraver [agrave] **1** *vt (situation, ma-ladie)* to make worse; *(difficultés)* to in-crease **2** *s'aggraver vpr (situation, maladie)* to get worse; *(état de santé)* to deteriorate; *(difficultés)* to increase ▪ **aggravation** *nf (de maladie)* aggrava-tion; *(de conflit)* worsening

agile [aʒil] *adj* agile, nimble ▪ **agilité** *nf* agility, nimbleness

agir [aʒir] **1** *vi* to act **2** *s'agir v imper-sonnel* **de quoi s'agit-il?** what is it about?; **il s'agit de se dépêcher** we have to hurry

agitateur, -trice [aʒitatœr, -tris] *nmf* agitator

agitation [aʒitasjɔ̃] *nf (fébrilité)* rest-lessness; *(troubles)* unrest

agiter [aʒite] **1** *vt (remuer)* to stir; *(se-couer)* to shake; *(brandir)* to wave; *(troubler)* to agitate **2** *s'agiter vpr (en-fant)* to fidget ▪ **agité, -e** *adj (mer)* rough; *(personne)* restless; *(enfant)* f.. gety; *(period)* unsettled

agneau, -x [aɲo] *nm* lamb

agonie [agɔni] *nf* death throes; **l'a.** to be at death's door ▪ **ago** to be dying

agrafe [agraf] *nf (pour vêtement)* hook; *(pour papiers)* staple ▪ **agrafer** *vt (vêtement)* to fasten; *(papiers)* to staple ▪ **agrafeuse** *nf* stapler

agrandir [agrɑ̃dir] **1** *vt (rendre plus grand)* to enlarge; *(grossir)* to magnify **2** *s'agrandir vpr (entreprise)* to expand; *(ville)* to grow ▪ **agrandissement** *nm (d'entreprise)* expansion; *(de ville)* growth; *(de maison)* extension; *(de photo)* enlargement

agréable [agreabl] *adj* pleasant

agréer [agree] *vt (fournisseur)* to approve; **veuillez a. l'expression de mes salutations distinguées** *(dans une lettre) (à quelqu'un dont on ne connaît pas le nom)* Br yours faithfully, Am sincerely; *(à quelqu'un dont on connaît le nom)* Br yours sincerely, Am sincerely ▪ **agréé, -e** *adj (fournisseur, centre)* approved

agrégation [agregasjɔ̃] *nf* **(le concours de) l'a.** = competitive examination for posts on the teaching staff of lycées and universities

agrémenter [agremɑ̃te] *vt* to adorn **(de** with)

agrès [agrɛ] *nmpl (de voilier)* tackle; *Gym* Br apparatus, Am equipment

agresser [agrese] *vt* to attack; **se faire a.** to be attacked; *(pour son argent)* to be mugged ▪ **agresseur** *nm* attacker; *(dans un conflit)* aggressor ▪ **agression** *nf* attack; *(pour de l'argent)* mugging; *(d'un État)* aggression; **être victime d'une a.** to be attacked; *(pour son argent)* to be mugged

agressif, -ive [agresif, -iv] *adj* aggressive ▪ **agressivité** *nf* aggressiveness

agricole [agrikɔl] *adj* agricultural; *(ouvrier, machine)* farm; **travaux agricoles** farm work

agriculteur, -trice [agrikyltœr, -tris] *nmf* farmer ▪ **agriculture** *nf* farming, agriculture; **a. biologique** organic farming

agripper [agripe] *s'agripper vpr* **s'a. à qn/qch** to cling on to sb/sth

agrume [agrym] *nm* citrus fruit

aguerri, -e [ageri] *adj* seasoned, hardened

aguets [agɛ] **aux aguets** *adv* on the lookout

aguichant, -e [agiʃɑ̃, -ɑ̃t] *adj* seductive

ahurir [ayrir] *vt (étonner)* to astound

ai [ɛ] *voir* avoir

aide [ɛd] **1** *nf* help, assistance; **à l'a. de qch** with the aid of sth; **appeler à l'a.** to call for help; **a. humanitaire** aid **2** *nmf (personne)* assistant; **a. de camp** aide-de-camp ▪ **aide-mémoire** *nm inv* notes ▪ **aide-soignante** *(pl* **aides-soignantes)** *nf* Br nursing auxiliary, Am nurse's aid

aider [ede] **1** *vt* to help; **a. qn à faire qch** to help sb to do sth **2** *s'aider vpr* **s'a. de qch** to use sth

aïe [aj] *exclam* ouch!

aie(s), aient [ɛ] *voir* avoir

aigle [ɛgl] *nm* eagle

aigre [ɛgr] *adj (acide)* sour; *(parole)* cutting; **d'un ton a.** sharply ▪ **aigreur** *nf (de goût)* sourness; *(de ton)* sharpness; **aigreurs d'estomac** heartburn

aigri, -e [ɛgri] *adj (personne)* embittered

aigu, -ë [egy] *adj (douleur, crise, accent)* acute; *(son)* high-pitched

aiguille [eguij] *nf (à coudre)* needle; *(de montre)* hand; *(de balance)* pointer; **a. (rocheuse)** peak; **a. de pin** pine needle

aiguiller [eguije] *vt (train)* Br to shunt, Am to switch; *Fig (personne)* to steer **(vers** towards) ▪ **aiguillage** *nm (appareil)* Br points, Am switches ▪ **aiguilleur** *nm (de trains)* signalman; **a. du ciel** air-traffic controller

aiguiser [egize] *vt (outil)* to sharpen; *Fig (appétit)* to whet

ail [aj] *nm* garlic

aile [ɛl] *nf* wing; *(de moulin)* sail; *(de voiture)* Br wing, Am fender ▪ **ailé, -e** *adj* winged ▪ **aileron** *nm (de requin)* fin; *(d'avion)* aileron ▪ **ailier** *nm (au football)* winger; *(au rugby)* wing

aille(s), aillent [aj] *voir* aller[1]

ailleurs [ajœr] *adv* somewhere else, elsewhere; **d'a.** *(du reste)* besides, anyway; **par a.** *(en outre)* moreover; *(par d'autres côtés)* in other respects

aimable [ɛmabl] *adj (gentil)* kind

aimant¹ [ɛmɑ̃] *nm* magnet ■ **aimanter** *vt* to magnetize

aimant², -e [ɛmɑ̃, -ɑ̃t] *adj* loving

aimer [eme] **1** *vt* to love; **a. bien qn/ qch** to like sb/sth; **a. faire qch** to like doing sth; **j'aimerais qu'il vienne** I would like him to come; **a. mieux qch** to prefer sth **2** **s'aimer** *vpr* **ils s'aiment** they're in love

aine [ɛn] *nf* groin

aîné, -e [ene] **1** *adj (de deux enfants)* elder; *(de plus de deux)* eldest **2** *nmf (de deux enfants)* elder; *(de plus de deux)* eldest

ainsi [ɛ̃si] *adv (de cette façon)* in this way; *(alors)* so; **a. que...** as well as...; **et a. de suite** and so on; **pour a. dire** so to speak; **a. soit-il!** amen!

air [ɛr] *nm* **(a)** *(gaz)* air; **prendre l'a.** to get some fresh air; **au grand a.** in the fresh air; **en plein a.** outside; **en l'a.** *(jeter)* (up) in the air; *(paroles, menaces)* empty; **regarder en l'a.** to look up
(b) *(expression)* look, appearance; **avoir l'a. content** to look happy; **avoir l'a. de s'ennuyer** to look bored; **a. de famille** family likeness
(c) *(mélodie)* tune

aire [ɛr] *nf (surface)* & *Math* area; *(d'oiseau)* eyrie; **a. de jeux** (children's) play area; **a. de lancement** launch pad; **a. de repos** *(sur autoroute)* rest area; **a. de stationnement** lay-by

aisance [ɛzɑ̃s] *nf (facilité)* ease; *(prospérité)* affluence

aise [ɛz] *nf* **à l'a.** *(dans un vêtement)* comfortable; *(dans une situation)* at ease; *(fortuné)* comfortably off; **mal à l'a.** uncomfortable, ill at ease ■ **aisé, -e** [eze] *adj (fortuné)* comfortably off; *(facile)* easy ■ **aisément** *adv* easily

aisselle [ɛsɛl] *nf* armpit

ait [ɛ] *voir* **avoir**

ajourner [aʒurne] *vt* to postpone; *(après le début de la séance)* to adjourn

ajout [aʒu] *nm* addition (**à** to) ■ **ajouter 1** *vti* to add (**à** to) **2** **s'ajouter** *vpr* **s'a. à qch** to add to sth

ajuster [aʒyste] *vt (appareil, outil)* to adjust; *(vêtement)* to alter

alarme [alarm] *nf* alarm; **donner l'a.** to raise the alarm; **a. antivol/d'incendie** burglar/fire alarm ■ **alarmer 1** *vt* to alarm **2** **s'alarmer** *vpr* **s'a. de qch** to become alarmed at sth

Albanie *nf* **l'A.** Albania ■ **albanais, -e 1** *adj* Albanian **2** *nmf* **A., Albanaise** Albanian

album [albɔm] *nm* album; **a. de photos** photo album

alcool [alkɔl] *nm* *Chim* alcohol; *(spiritueux)* spirits; **a. à 90°** *Br* surgical spirit, *Am* rubbing alcohol; **a. à brûler** *Br* methylated spirits, *Am* wood alcohol ■ **alcoolique** *adj* & *nmf* alcoholic ■ **alcoolisée** *adj f* **boisson a.** alcoholic drink; **boisson non a.** soft drink ■ **alcoolisme** *nm* alcoholism ■ **Alcootest®** *nm (test)* breath test; *(appareil)* Breathalyzer®

alcôve [alkov] *nf* alcove

aléas [alea] *nmpl* hazards ■ **aléatoire** *adj (résultat)* uncertain; *(nombre)* & *Ordinat* random

alentour [alɑ̃tur] *adv* round about; **les villages a.** the surrounding villages ■ **alentours** *nmpl* surroundings; **aux a. de la ville** in the vicinity of the town

alerte [alɛrt] **1** *adj (leste)* sprightly; *(éveillé)* alert **2** *nf* alarm; **en état d'a.** on the alert; **donner l'a.** to give the alarm; **a. à la bombe** bomb scare; **fausse a.** false alarm ■ **alerter** *vt* to alert (**de** to)

alezan, -e [alzɑ̃, -an] *adj* & *nmf (cheval)* chestnut

algèbre [alʒɛbr] *nf* algebra

Algérie [alʒeri] *nf* **l'A.** Algeria ■ **algérien, -enne 1** *adj* Algerian **2** *nmf* **A., Algérienne** Algerian

algues [alg] *nfpl* seaweed

alias [aljɑs] *adv* alias

alibi [alibi] *nm* alibi

aliéner [aljene] **1** *vt* to alienate **2** **s'aliéner** *vpr* **s'a. qn** to alienate sb

aligner [aliɲe] **1** *vt* to line up; *(politique)* to align **(sur** with) **2** **s'aligner** *vpr (personnes)* to line up; *(pays)* to align oneself **(sur** with) **■ alignement** *nm* alignment

aliment [alimɑ̃] *nm* food **■ alimentaire** *adj (ration, industrie)* food; **produits alimentaires** foods **■ alimentation** *nf (action)* feeding; *(en eau, en électricité)* supply(ing); *(régime)* diet; *(nourriture)* food; **avoir une a. saine** to have a healthy diet; **magasin d'a.** grocer's, grocery store **■ alimenter** *vt (nourrir)* to feed; *(fournir)* to supply **(en** with); *(débat, feu)* to fuel

alité, -e [alite] *adj* bedridden

allaiter [alete] *vt (femme)* to breastfeed

allécher [aleʃe] *vt* to tempt

allée [ale] *nf (de parc)* path; *(de ville)* avenue; *(de cinéma, de supermarché)* aisle; *(devant une maison)* driveway; **allées et venues** comings and goings

allégation [alegasjɔ̃] *nf* allegation

alléger [aleʒe] *vt (impôt)* to reduce; *(fardeau)* to lighten **■ allégé, -e** *adj (fromage)* low-fat

allégorie [alegɔri] *nf* allegory

allègre [alɛgr] *adj* lively, cheerful

allégresse [alegrɛs] *nf* joy

Allemagne [almaɲ] *nf* l'A. Germany **■ allemand, -ande 1** *adj* German **2** *nmf* A., **Allemande** German **3** *nm (langue)* German

ALLER¹ [ale] **1** *(aux* être*) vi* to go; **a. à Paris** to go to Paris; **a. à la pêche** to go fishing; **a. faire qch** to go and do sth; **a. à qn** *(convenir à)* to suit sb; **a. avec** *(vêtement)* to go with; **a. bien/mieux** *(personne)* to be well/better; **comment vas-tu?, (comment) ça va?** how are you?; **ça va!** all right!, fine!; **allez-y** go ahead
2 *v aux (futur proche)* **a. faire qch** to be going to do sth; **il va venir** he'll come; **il va partir** he's about to leave
3 **s'en aller** [sɑ̃nale] *vpr (personne)* to go away; *(tache)* to come out

aller² [ale] *nm* outward journey; **a. (simple)** *Br* single (ticket), *Am* one-

way (ticket); **a. (et) retour** *Br* return (ticket), *Am* round-trip (ticket)

allergie [alɛrʒi] *nf* allergy **■ allergique** *adj* allergic **(à** to)

alliage [aljaʒ] *nm* alloy

alliance [aljɑ̃s] *nf (anneau)* wedding ring; *(mariage)* marriage; *(de pays)* alliance

allier [alje] **1** *vt (associer)* to combine **(à** with); *(pays)* to ally **(à** with); *(famille)* to unite by marriage **2** **s'allier** *vpr (couleurs)* to combine; *(pays)* to become allied **(à** with); **s'a. à contre qn/qch** to unite against sb/sth **■ allié, -e** *nmf* ally

allô [alo] *exclam* hello!

allocation [alɔkasjɔ̃] *nf (somme)* allowance; **a. (de) chômage** unemployment benefit; **a. (de) logement** housing benefit; **allocations familiales** child benefit

allocution [alɔkysjɔ̃] *nf* address

allonger [alɔ̃ʒe] **1** *vt (bras)* to stretch out; *(sauce)* to thin; **a. le pas** to quicken one's pace **2** *vi (jours)* to get longer **3** **s'allonger** *vpr (jours)* to get longer; *(personne)* to lie down **■ allongé, -e** *adj (étiré)* elongated; **être a.** *(personne)* to be lying down

allouer [alwe] *vt* **a. qch à qn** *(ration)* to allocate sb sth; *(indemnité)* to grant sb sth

allumer [alyme] **1** *vt (feu, pipe)* to light; *(électricité, radio)* to switch on; *(incendie)* to start **2** **s'allumer** *vpr (lumière, lampe)* to come on **■ allumage** *nm (de feu)* lighting; *(de moteur)* ignition

allumette [alymɛt] *nf* match

allure [alyr] *nf (vitesse)* speed; *(démarche)* gait, walk; *(maintien)* bearing; **à toute a.** at top speed; **avoir de l'a.** to look stylish

allusion [alyzjɔ̃] *nf (référence)* allusion **(à** to); *(voilée)* hint; **faire a. à qch** to allude to sth; *(en termes voilés)* to hint at sth

aloi [alwa] *nm* **de bon a.** *(plaisanterie)* in good taste

alors [alɔr] *adv (donc)* so; *(à ce moment-là)* then; *(dans ce cas)* in that case; **a. que...** *(lorsque)* when...; *(tandis*

que) whereas…; **et a.?** so what?

alouette [alwɛt] *nf* lark

alourdir [alurdir] **1** *vt (chose)* to make heavier **2 s'alourdir** *vpr* to get heavy

alpage [alpaʒ] *nm* mountain pasture ■ **Alpes** *nfpl* **les A.** the Alps ■ **alpestre, alpin, -e** [alpɛ̃, -in] *adj* alpine

alphabet [alfabɛ] *nm* alphabet ■ **alphabétique** *adj* alphabetical

alphanumérique [alfanymerik] *adj* alphanumeric

alpinisme [alpinism] *nm* mountaineering; **faire de l'a.** to go mountaineering ■ **alpiniste** *nmf* mountaineer

altérer [altere] **1** *vt* (a) *(viande, vin)* to spoil (b) *(changer)* to affect **2 s'altérer** *vpr (relations)* to deteriorate

alternatif, -ive [alternatif, -iv] *adj (successif)* alternating; *(de remplacement)* alternative ■ **alternative** *nf* alternative ■ **alternativement** *adv* alternately

alterner [alterne] **1** *vt (crops)* to rotate **2** *vi (se succéder)* to alternate **(avec** with); *(personnes)* to take turns **(avec** with) ■ **alternance** *nf* alternation; **en a.** alternately

Altesse [altɛs] *nf* **son A. royale** His/ Her Royal Highness

altier, -ère [altje, -ɛr] *adj* haughty

altitude [altityd] *nf* altitude; **prendre de l'a.** to climb

aluminium [alyminjom] *nm Br* aluminium, *Am* aluminum; **papier (d')a.** tinfoil

amabilité [amabilite] *nf* kindness

amaigrir [amɛgrir] *vt* to make thin *or* thinner ■ **amaigri, -e** *adj* gaunt

amande [amɑ̃d] *nf* almond

amant [amɑ̃] *nm* lover

amarre [amar] *nf* (mooring) rope; **amarres** moorings

amas [ama] *nm* heap, pile ■ **amasser 1** *vt* to amass **2 s'amasser** *vpr (preuves, foule)* to build up; *(neige)* to pile up

amateur [amatœr] **1** *nm (non professionnel)* amateur; **a. de tennis** tennis enthusiast; **faire de la photo en a.** to be an amateur photographer **2** *adj* **une**

équipe a. an amateur team

amazone [amazon] *nf* horsewoman; **monter en a.** to ride sidesaddle

ambages [ɑ̃baʒ] **sans ambages** *adv* without beating about the bush

ambassade [ɑ̃basad] *nf* embassy ■ **ambassadeur, -drice** *nmf* ambassador

ambiance [ɑ̃bjɑ̃s] *nf* atmosphere ■ **ambiant, -e** *adj* surrounding; **température a.** room temperature

ambidextre [ɑ̃bidɛkstr] *adj* ambidextrous

ambigu, -ë [ɑ̃bigy] *adj* ambiguous ■ **ambiguïté** *nf* ambiguity

ambitieux, -euse [ɑ̃bisjø, -øz] *adj* ambitious ■ **ambition** *nf* ambition ■ **ambitionner** *vt* to aspire to

ambre [ɑ̃br] *nm (résine)* amber

ambulance [ɑ̃bylɑ̃s] *nf* ambulance

ambulant, -e [ɑ̃bylɑ̃, -ɑ̃t] *adj* travelling, itinerant; **marchand a.** (street) hawker

âme [ɑm] *nf* soul; **rendre l'â.** to give up the ghost; **â. sœur** soul mate

améliorer [ameljore] *vt,* **s'améliorer** *vpr* to improve ■ **amélioration** *nf* improvement

amen [amɛn] *adv* amen

aménager *vt (changer)* to adjust, *(maison)* to convert **(en** into) ■ **aménagement** *nm (changement)* adjustment; *(de pièce)* conversion **(en** into); **a. du temps de travail** flexibility of working hours

amende [amɑ̃d] *nf* fine; **infliger une a. à qn** to impose a fine on sb

amender [amɑ̃de] *vt (texte de loi)* to amend

amener [amne] **1** *vt (apporter)* to bring; *(causer)* to bring about; *(tirer à soi)* to pull in; **a. qn à faire qch** *(sujet: personne)* to get sb to do sth; **ce qui nous amène à parler de…** which brings us to the issue of… **2 s'amener** *vpr Fam* to turn up

amenuiser [amənɥize] **s'amenuiser** *vpr* to dwindle; *(écart)* to get smaller

amer, -ère [amɛr] *adj* bitter

Amérique [amerik] *nf* l'A. America; l'A. du Nord/du Sud North/South America; l'A. latine Latin America ▪ **américain, -e 1** *adj* American **2** *nmf* **A., Américaine** American

amertume [amɛrtym] *nf* bitterness

ameublement [amœbləmɑ̃] *nm (meubles)* furniture

ami, -e [ami] **1** *nmf* friend; **petit a.** boyfriend; **petite amie** girlfriend **2** *adj* friendly; **être a. avec qn** to be friends with sb

amiable [amjabl], **à l'amiable 1** *adj* amicable **2** *adv* amicably

amical, -e, -aux, -ales [amikal, -o] *adj* friendly ▪ **amicale** *nf* association

amincir [amɛ̃sir] *vt* to make thin *or* thinner; **cette robe t'amincit** that dress makes you look thinner

amiral, -aux [amiral, -o] *nm* admiral

amitié [amitje] *nf* friendship; **mes amitiés à votre mère** give my best wishes to your mother

amnésie [amnezi] *nf* amnesia

amnistie [amnisti] *nf* amnesty

amoindrir [amwɛ̃drir] *vt*, **s'amoindrir** *vpr* to diminish

amonceler [amɔ̃sle] *vt*, **s'amonceler** *vpr* to pile up ▪ **amoncellement** *nm* heap, pile

amont [amɔ̃] **en amont** *adv* upstream (**de** from)

amoral, -e, -aux, -ales [amɔral, -o] *adj* amoral

amorce [amɔrs] *nf (début)* start; *(de pêcheur)* bait; *(détonateur)* detonator; *(de pistolet d'enfant)* cap ▪ **amorcer 1** *vt (commencer)* to start; *(hameçon)* to bait; *(bombe)* to arm; *Ordinat* to boot up **2** **s'amorcer** *vpr* to start

amortir [amɔrtir] *vt (coup)* to absorb; *(bruit)* to deaden; *(chute)* to break; *(achat)* to recoup the costs of; *Fin (dette)* to pay off ▪ **amortissement** *nm (d'un emprunt)* redemption ▪ **amortisseur** *nm (de véhicule)* shock absorber

amour [amur] *nm (sentiment, liaison)* love; **faire l'a. avec qn** to make love with *or* to sb; **pour l'a. du ciel!** for heaven's sake!; **mon a.** my darling, my love ▪ **amour-propre** *nm* self-respect ▪ **amoureux, -euse 1** *adj* **être a. de qn** to be in love with sb; **tomber a. de qn** to fall in love with sb **2** *nm* boyfriend; **un couple d'a.** a pair of lovers

amovible [amɔvibl] *adj* removable, detachable

amphétamine [ɑ̃fetamin] *nf* amphetamine

amphithéâtre [ɑ̃fiteatr] *nm (romain)* amphitheatre; *(à l'université)* lecture hall

ample [ɑ̃pl] *adj (vêtement)* full; *(geste)* sweeping; **de plus amples renseignements** more detailed information ▪ **amplement** *adv* amply, fully; **c'est a. suffisant** it is more than enough ▪ **ampleur** *nf (de vêtement)* fullness; *(importance)* scale, extent; **prendre de l'a.** to grow in size

amplifier [ɑ̃plifje] **1** *vt (son)* to amplify; *(phénomène)* to intensify **2** **s'amplifier** *vpr (son)* to increase; *(phénomène)* to intensify ▪ **amplificateur** *nm* amplifier ▪ **amplification** *nf (de son)* amplification; *(de phénomène)* intensification

amplitude [ɑ̃plityd] *nf (de désastre)* magnitude; *(variation)* range

ampoule [ɑ̃pul] *nf (électrique)* (light) bulb; *(sur la peau)* blister; *(de médicament)* phial

amputer [ɑ̃pyte] *vt (membre)* to amputate; **a. qn de la jambe** to amputate sb's leg ▪ **amputation** *nf (de membre)* amputation

amuser [amyze] **1** *vt* to amuse **2** **s'amuser** *vpr* to amuse oneself; **s'a. avec qn/qch** to play with sb/sth; **s'a. à faire qch** to amuse oneself doing sth; **bien s'a.** to have a good time ▪ **amusant, -e** *adj* amusing ▪ **amusement** *nm* amusement

amygdales [amidal] *nfpl* tonsils

an [ɑ̃] *nm* year; **il a dix ans** he's ten (years old); **par a.** per year; **en l'an 2005** in the year 2005; **bon a., mal a.** on average over the years

anachronisme [anakrɔnism] *nm* anachronism

anagramme [anagram] *nf* anagram
analogie [analɔʒi] *nf* analogy
analogue [analɔg] *adj* similar (à to)
analphabète [analfabɛt] *adj & nmf* illiterate
analyse [analiz] *nf* analysis; **a. de sang/d'urine** blood/urine test ■ **analyser** *vt* to analyse
ananas [anana(s)] *nm* pineapple
anarchie [anarʃi] *nf* anarchy ■ **anarchiste 1** *adj* anarchistic **2** *nmf* anarchist
anatomie [anatɔmi] *nf* anatomy ■ **anatomique** *adj* anatomical
ancestral, -e, -aux, -ales [ɑ̃sɛstral, -o] *adj* ancestral
ancêtre [ɑ̃sɛtr] *nm* ancestor
anchois [ɑ̃ʃwa] *nm* anchovy
ancien, -enne [ɑ̃sjɛ̃, -ɛn] **1** *adj (vieux)* old; *(meuble)* antique; *(qui n'est plus)* former, old; **dans l'a. temps** in the old days; **a. combattant** *Br* ex-serviceman, *Am* veteran **2** *nmf (par l'âge)* elder ■ **anciennement** *adv* formerly ■ **ancienneté** *nf (âge)* age; *(expérience)* seniority
ancre [ɑ̃kr] *nf* anchor ■ **ancrer** *vt (navire)* to anchor
Andorre [ɑ̃dɔr] *nf* Andorra
andouille [ɑ̃duj] *nf* (a) *(charcuterie)* = sausage made from pigs' intestines (b) *Fam (idiot)* fool
âne [ɑn] *nm (animal)* donkey
anéantir [aneɑ̃tir] *vt (ville)* to destroy; *(armée)* to crush; *(espoirs)* to shatter ■ **anéanti, -e** *adj (épuisé)* exhausted; *(accablé)* overwhelmed ■ **anéantissement** *nm (de ville)* destruction
anecdote [anɛkdɔt] *nf* anecdote ■ **anecdotique** *adj* anecdotal
anémie [anemi] *nf* an(a)emia ■ **anémique** *adj* an(a)emic
anémone [anemɔn] *nf* anemone
ânerie [ɑnri] *nf (parole)* stupid remark; *(action)* stupid act
anesthésie [anɛstezi] *nf* an(a)esthesia; **être sous a.** to be under ana(e)sthetic; **a. générale/locale** general/local an(a)esthetic ■ **anesthésier** *vt* to an(a)esthetize ■ **anesthésiste** *nmf Br*

an(a)esthetist, *Am* anesthesiologist
ange [ɑ̃ʒ] *nm* angel; **être aux anges** to be in seventh heaven; **a. gardien** guardian angel ■ **angélique 1** *adj* angelic **2** *nf Culin* angelica
angine [ɑ̃ʒin] *nf* sore throat; **a. de poitrine** angina (pectoris)
anglais, -e [ɑ̃glɛ, -ɛz] **1** *adj* English **2** *nmf* **A., Anglaise** Englishman, Englishwoman; **les A.** the English **3** *nm (langue)* English **4** *nf Fam* **filer à l'anglaise** to slip away
angle [ɑ̃gl] *nm (point de vue)* & *Math* angle; *(coin de rue)* corner; **la maison qui fait l'a.** the house on the corner; *Aut* **a. mort** blind spot
Angleterre [ɑ̃glətɛr] *nf* **l'A.** England
anglican, -e [ɑ̃glikɑ̃, -an] *adj & nmf* Anglican
anglo-normand, -e [ɑ̃glonɔrmɑ̃, -ɑ̃d] *adj* **les îles anglo-normandes** the Channel Islands
anglophone [ɑ̃glofɔn] **1** *adj* English-speaking **2** *nmf* English speaker
anglo-saxon, -onne [ɑ̃glosaksɔ̃, -ɔn] *(mpl* anglo-saxons, *fpl* anglo-saxonnes) *adj & nmf* Anglo-Saxon
angoisse [ɑ̃gwas] *nf* anguish; **une crise d'a.** an anxiety attack ■ **angoissant, -e** *adj (nouvelle)* distressing; *(attente)* agonizing; *(livre)* frightening ■ **angoissé, -e** *adj (personne)* anxious; *(cri, regard)* anguished ■ **angoisser 1** *vt* **a. qn** to make sb anxious **2 s'angoisser** *vpr* to get anxious
angora [ɑ̃gɔra] *nm (laine)* angora; **pull en a.** angora sweater
anguille [ɑ̃gij] *nf* eel
anguleux, -euse [ɑ̃gylø, -øz] *adj (visage)* angular
anicroche [anikrɔʃ] *nf* hitch, snag
animal, -aux [animal, -o] **1** *nm* animal; **a. domestique** pet **2** *adj (règne, graisse)* animal
animateur, -trice [animatœr, -tris] *nmf (de télévision, de radio)* presenter; *(de club)* leader
animer [anime] **1** *vt (débat)* to lead; *(jeu télévisé)* to present; *(inspirer)* to prompt **2 s'animer** *vpr (rue)* to come

to life; *(visage)* to light up; *(conversation)* to get more lively ▪ **animation** *nf (vie)* life; *(divertissement)* event; *Cin* animation; **mettre de l'a. dans une soirée** to liven up a party ▪ **animé, -e** *adj (personne, conversation)* lively; *(rue, quartier)* busy

animosité [animɔzite] *nf* animosity

anis [ani(s)] *nm* aniseed

ankylosé, -e [ɑ̃kiloze] *adj* stiff

annales [anal] *nfpl* annals

anneau, -x [ano] *nm (bague)* ring; *(de chaîne)* link; *Gym* **les anneaux** the rings

année [ane] *nf* year; **les années 90** the nineties; **a. civile** calendar year; **a. scolaire** school year

annexe [anɛks] **1** *nf (bâtiment)* annexe; *(de lettre)* enclosure; *(de livre)* appendix; **document en a.** enclosed document **2** *adj (pièces)* enclosed; *(revenus)* supplementary; **bâtiment a.** annex(e) ▪ **annexer** *vt (pays)* to annex; *(document)* to append

annihiler [aniile] *vt (ville, armée)* to annihilate

anniversaire [aniverser] **1** *nm (d'événement)* anniversary; *(de naissance)* birthday **2** *adj* **date a.** anniversary

annonce [anɔ̃s] *nf (déclaration)* announcement; *(publicitaire)* advertisement; *(indice)* sign; **passer une a. dans un journal** to put an ad(vertisement) in a newspaper; **petites annonces** classified advertisements, *Br* small ads ▪ **annoncer 1** *vt (déclarer)* to announce; *(dans la presse)* (soldes, exposition) to advertise; *(indiquer)* to herald; **a. qn** *(visiteur)* to show sb in **2 s'annoncer** *vpr* **ça s'annonce bien/mal** things aren't looking too bad/good ▪ **annonceur** *nm (publicitaire)* advertiser

annuaire [anɥer] *nm (d'organisme)* yearbook; *(liste d'adresses)* directory; **être dans l'a** to be in the phone book; **a. téléphonique** telephone directory; **a. électronique** = telephone directory available on Minitel®

annuel, -elle [anɥɛl] *adj* annual, yearly

annuité [anɥite] *nf (d'emprunt)* annual repayment

annulaire [anyler] *nm* ring finger

annuler [anyle] **1** *vt (commande, rendez-vous)* to cancel; *(dette)* to write off; *(mariage)* to annul; *(jugement)* to quash **2 s'annuler** *vpr* to cancel each other out ▪ **annulation** *nf (de commande, de rendez-vous)* cancellation; *(de dette)* writing off; *(de mariage)* annulment; *(de jugement)* quashing; *Ordinat* deletion

anodin, -e [anɔdɛ̃, -in] *adj (remarque)* harmless; *(personne)* insignificant

anomalie [anɔmali] *nf (bizarrerie)* anomaly

anonymat [anɔnima] *nm* anonymity; **garder l'a.** to remain anonymous ▪ **anonyme** *adj & nmf* anonymous

anorak [anɔrak] *nm* anorak

anorexie [anɔrɛksi] *nf Méd* anorexia ▪ **anorexique** *adj & nmf Méd* anorexic

anormal, -e, -aux, -ales [anɔrmal, -o] *adj (non conforme)* abnormal; *(mentalement)* educationally subnormal; *(injuste)* unfair

ANPE [aɛnpeø] *nf (abrév* **Agence nationale pour l'emploi)** = French state employment agency

anse [ɑ̃s] *nf (de tasse, de panier)* handle

antagonisme [ɑ̃tagɔnism] *nm* antagonism

antan [ɑ̃tɑ̃] **d'antan** *adj Littéraire* of yesteryear

antarctique [ɑ̃tarktik] *nm* **l'A.** the Antarctic, Antarctica

antécédent [ɑ̃tesedɑ̃] *nm Gram* antecedent; **antécédents** *(de personne)* past record; **antécédents médicaux** medical history

antenne [ɑ̃ten] *nf (de radio, de satellite)* aerial, antenna; *(d'insecte)* antenna, feeler; *(société)* branch; **être à l'a.** to be on the air; **a. parabolique** satellite dish

antérieur, -e [ɑ̃terjœr] *adj (période)* former; *(année)* previous; *(date)* earlier; *(placé devant)* front; **a. à qch** prior to sth

anthologie [ãtɔlɔʒi] *nf* anthology

anthropologie [ãtrɔpɔlɔʒi] *nf* anthropology

antiaérien, -enne [ãtiaerjɛ̃, -ɛn] *adj* **abri a.** air-raid shelter

antiatomique [ãtiatɔmik] *adj* **abri a.** fallout shelter

antibiotique [ãtibjɔtik] *nm* antibiotic

antibrouillard [ãtibrujar] *adj & nm* **(phare) a.** fog lamp

antichambre [ãtiʃãbr] *nf* antechamber

antichoc [ãtiʃɔk] *adj inv* shock-proof

anticipation [ãtisipasjɔ̃] *nf* anticipation; **d'a.** *(roman, film)* futuristic ■ **anticipé, -e** *adj (retraite, retour)* early; *(paiement)* advance

anticommuniste [ãtikɔmynist] *adj* anti-communist

anticonformiste [ãtikɔ̃fɔrmist] *adj & nmf* nonconformist

anticonstitutionnel, -elle [ãtikɔ̃stitysjɔnɛl] *adj* unconstitutional

anticorps [ãtikɔr] *nm* antibody

anticyclone [ãtisiklon] *nm* anticyclone

antidépresseur [ãtidepresœr] *nm* antidepressant

antidérapant, -e [ãtiderapã, -ãt] *adj (surface, pneu)* non-skid; *(semelle)* non-slip

antidopage [ãtidɔpaʒ] *adj* **contrôle a.** drug detection test

antidote [ãtidɔt] *nm* antidote

antigel [ãtiʒɛl] *nm* antifreeze

antihistaminique [ãtiistaminik] *adj Méd* antihistamine

anti-inflammatoire [ãtiɛ̃flamatwar] *adj Méd* anti-inflammatory

Antilles [ãtij] *nfpl* **les A.** the West Indies ■ **antillais, -e 1** *adj* West Indian **2** *nmf* **A., Antillaise** West Indian

antilope [ãtilɔp] *nf* antelope

antimite [ãtimit] *nm* **de l'a.** mothballs

antinucléaire [ãtinykleɛr] *adj* antinuclear

antipathique [ãtipatik] *adj* unpleasant; **elle m'est a.** I find her unpleasant

antipodes [ãtipɔd] *nmpl* antipodes;

être aux a. de to be on the other side of the world from; *Fig* to be the exact opposite of

antique [ãtik] *adj (de l'Antiquité)* ancient ■ **antiquaire** *nmf* antique dealer ■ **antiquité** *nf (objet ancien)* antique; **l'a. grecque/romaine** ancient Greece/Rome; **antiquités** *(de musée)* antiquities

antirabique [ãtirabik] *adj Méd* anti-rabies

antireflet [ãtirəflɛ] *adj inv* non-reflecting

antiseptique [ãtisɛptik] *adj & nm* antiseptic

antisocial, -e, -aux, -ales [ãtisɔsjal, -o] *adj* antisocial

antitabac [ãtitaba] *adj inv* **lutte a.** anti-smoking campaign

antiterroriste [ãtiterɔrist] *adj* anti-terrorist

antithèse [ãtitɛz] *nf* antithesis

antivol [ãtivɔl] *nm* anti-theft device

Anvers [ãver(s)] *nm ou f* Antwerp

anxiété [ãksjete] *nf* anxiety ■ **anxieux, -euse** *adj* anxious

août [u(t)] *nm* August

apaiser [apeze] **1** *vt (personne)* to calm (down); *(douleur)* to soothe; *(craintes)* to allay **2 s'apaiser** *vpr (personne, colère)* to calm down; *(tempête, douleur)* to subside ■ **apaisant, -e** *adj* soothing

apanage [apanaʒ] *nm* prerogative

aparté [aparte] *nm Théât* aside; *(dans une réunion)* private exchange; **en a.** in private

apathique [apatik] *adj* apathetic

apercevoir* [apersəvwar] **1** *vt* to see; *(brièvement)* to catch a glimpse of **2 s'apercevoir** *vpr* **s'a. de qch** to realize sth; **s'a. que...** to realize that... ■ **aperçu** *nm (idea)* general idea

apéritif [aperitif] *nm* aperitif; **prendre un a.** to have a drink before lunch/dinner

à-peu-près [apøprɛ] *nm inv* vague approximation

apeuré, -e [apœre] *adj* frightened, scared

aphone [afɔn] *adj* voiceless; **je suis complètement a.** I've lost my voice

aphrodisiaque [afrɔdizjak] *nm* aphrodisiac

aphte [aft] *nm* mouth ulcer

aphteuse [aftøz] *adj f* **fièvre a.** foot-and-mouth disease

apiculture [apikyltyr] *nf* beekeeping ■ **apiculteur, -trice** *nmf* beekeeper

apitoyer [apitwaje] **1** *vt* **a. qn** to move sb to pity **2 s'apitoyer** *vpr* **s'a. sur qn** to feel sorry for sb; **s'a. sur son sort** to feel sorry for oneself

aplanir [aplanir] *vt* (*terrain*) to level; (*difficulté*) to iron out

aplatir [aplatir] **1** *vt* to flatten **2 s'aplatir** *vpr* (*être plat*) to be flat; (*devenir plat*) to go flat; **s'a. contre qch** to flatten oneself against sth ■ **aplati, -e** *adj* flat

aplomb [aplɔ̃] *nm* (*assurance*) self-confidence; *Péj* cheek; **mettre qch d'a.** to stand sth up straight

apocalypse [apɔkalips] *nf* apocalypse; **d'a.** (*vision*) apocalyptic

apogée [apɔʒe] *nm* (*d'orbite*) apogee; *Fig* **être à l'a. de sa carrière** to be at the height of one's career

apostrophe [apɔstrɔf] *nf* (*signe*) apostrophe ■ **apostropher** *vt* (*pour attirer l'attention*) to shout at

apothéose [apɔteoz] *nf* (*consécration*) crowning glory

apparaître* [aparɛtr] (*aux* **être**) *vi* (*se montrer, sembler*) to appear; **il m'apparaît comme le seul capable d'y parvenir** he seems to me to be the only person capable of doing it

appareil [aparɛj] *nm* (*instrument, machine*) apparatus; (*téléphone*) telephone; (*avion*) aircraft; **qui est à l'a.?** (*au téléphone*) who's speaking?; **a. (dentaire)** (*correctif*) brace; **a. photo** camera; **appareils ménagers** household appliances

apparence [aparɑ̃s] *nf* appearance; **en a.** outwardly; **sauver les apparences** to keep up appearances ■ **apparemment** *adv* apparently ■ **apparent, -e** *adj* apparent

apparenter [aparɑ̃te] **s'apparenter** *vpr* (*ressembler*) to be akin (**à** to)

apparition [aparisjɔ̃] *nf* (*manifestation*) appearance; (*fantôme*) apparition; **faire son a.** (*personne*) to make one's appearance

appartement [apartəmɑ̃] *nm* *Br* flat, *Am* apartment

appartenance [apartənɑ̃s] *nf* (*de groupe*) belonging (**à** to); (*de parti*) membership (**à** of)

appartenir* [apartənir] **1** *vi* to belong (**à** to) **2** *v impersonnel* **il vous appartient de prendre la décision** it's up to you to decide

appât [apɑ] *nm* (*amorce*) bait; *Fig* (*attrait*) lure ■ **appâter** *vt* (*hameçon*) to bait; (*animal*) to lure; *Fig* (*personne*) to entice

appauvrir [apovrir] **1** *vt* to impoverish **2 s'appauvrir** *vpr* to become impoverished ■ **appauvrissement** *nm* impoverishment

appel [apɛl] *nm* (*cri, attrait*) call; (*invitation*) & *Jur* appeal; *Mil* (*recrutement*) call-up; (*pour sauter*) take-off; **faire l'a.** (*à l'école*) to take the register; *Mil* to have a roll call; **faire a. à qn** to appeal to sb; (*plombier, médecin*) to send for sb; **a. au secours** call for help; **a. gratuit** *Br* freefone call, *Am* toll-free call; **a. téléphonique** telephone call ■ **appeler 1** *vt* (*personne, nom*) to call; (*en criant*) to call out to; *Mil* (*recruter*) to call up; (*nécessiter*) to call for; **a. qn à l'aide** to call to sb for help; **a. qn au téléphone** to call sb **2 s'appeler** *vpr* to be called; **comment vous appelez-vous?** what's your name?; **je m'appelle David** my name is David ■ **appellation** *nf* (*nom*) term; **a. contrôlée** (*de vin*) guaranteed vintage ■ **appelé** *nm* *Mil* conscript

appendice [apɛ̃dis] *nm* (*du corps, de livre*) appendix; (*d'animal*) appendage ■ **appendicite** *nf* appendicitis

appesantir [apəzɑ̃tir] **s'appesantir** *vpr* to become heavier; **s'a. sur** (*sujet*) to dwell upon

appétit [apeti] *nm* appetite (**de** for); **couper l'a. à qn** to spoil sb's appetite; **manger de bon a.** to tuck in; **bon a.!**

enjoy your meal! ▪ **appétissant, -e** *adj*
appetizing

applaudir [aplodir] *vti* to applaud
▪ **applaudissements** *nmpl* applause

applicable [aplikabl] *adj* applicable (**à**
to) ▪ **application** *nf (action, soin)* application; *(de loi)* enforcement; **entrer en
a.** to come into force

applique [aplik] *nf* wall light

appliquer [aplike] **1** *vt* to apply (**à/sur**
to); *(loi, décision)* to enforce **2 s'appliquer** *vpr (se concentrer)* to apply oneself (**à** to); **s'a. à faire qch** to take pains
to do sth; **cette décision s'applique
à...** *(concerne)* this decision applies
to... ▪ **appliqué, -e** *adj (personne)*
hard-working; *(écriture)* careful;
(sciences) applied

appoint [apwɛ̃] *nm* **(a) faire l'a.** to
give the exact money **(b) d'a.** extra

apport [apɔr] *nm* contribution (**à** to);
a. nutritionnel *(d'un aliment)* nutritional value

apporter [apɔrte] *vt* to bring (**à** to);
(preuve) to provide; *(modification)* to
bring about

apposer [apoze] *vt (sceau, signature)*
to affix (**à** to); *(affiche)* to put up

apprécier [apresje] *vt (aimer, percevoir)* to appreciate; *(évaluer)* to estimate ▪ **appréciable** *adj* appreciable
▪ **appréciation** *nf (opinion d'un professeur)* comment (**sur** on); *(évaluation)*
valuation; *(augmentation de valeur)* appreciation

appréhender [apreɑ̃de] *vt (craindre)*
to dread (**de faire qch** doing sth); *(arrêter)* to arrest; *(comprendre)* to grasp
▪ **appréhension** *nf (crainte)* apprehension (**de** about)

apprendre* [aprɑ̃dr] *vti (étudier)* to
learn; *(nouvelle)* to hear; *(mariage,
mort)* to hear of; **a. à faire qch** to learn
to do sth; **a. qch à qn** *(enseigner)* to
teach sb sth; *(informer)* to tell sb sth; **a.
à qn à faire qch** to teach sb to do sth; **a.
que...** to learn that...; *(être informé)* to
hear that...

apprenti, -e [aprɑ̃ti] *nmf* apprentice
▪ **apprentissage** *nm (professionnel)*

training; *(chez un artisan)* apprenticeship; *(d'une langue)* learning (**de** of);
faire l'a. de qch to learn about sth

apprivoiser [aprivwaze] **1** *vt* to tame
2 s'apprivoiser *vpr* to become tame

approbation [aprɔbasjɔ̃] *nf* approval
▪ **approbateur, -trice** *adj* approving

approche [aprɔʃ] *nf* approach; **approches** *(de ville)* outskirts

approcher [aprɔʃe] **1** *vt (objet)* to
bring up; *(personne)* to approach, to
get close to; **a. qch de qn** to bring sth
near to sb **2** *vi* to approach, to get closer; **a. de qn/qch** to approach sb/sth
3 s'approcher *vpr* to approach, to get
closer; **s'a. de qn/qch** to approach sb/
sth; **il s'est approché de moi** he came
up to me

approfondir [aprɔfɔ̃dir] *vt (question,
idée)* to go thoroughly into ▪ **approfondi, -e** *adj (étude, examen)* thorough

approprié, -e [aprɔprije] *adj* appropriate (**à** for)

approprier [aprɔprije] **s'approprier**
vpr **s'a. qch** to appropriate sth

approuver [apruve] *vt (facture, contrat)* to approve; *(décision)* to approve
of

approvisionner [aprɔvizjɔne] **1** *vt
(ville, armée)* to supply (**en** with); *(magasin)* to stock (**en** with); *(compte bancaire)* to pay money into
2 s'approvisionner *vpr* to get supplies (**en** of) ▪ **approvisionnement**
nm (d'une ville, d'une armée) supplying
(**en** with); *(d'un magasin)* stocking (**en**
with)

approximatif, -ive [aprɔksimatif,
-iv] *adj* approximate ▪ **approximation**
nf approximation

appui [apɥi] *nm* support; **prendre a.
sur qch** to lean on sth; **à l'a. de qch** in
support of sth; **a. de fenêtre** window
sill ▪ **appui-tête** *(pl* appuis-tête) *nm*
headrest

appuyer [apɥije] **1** *vt (poser)* to lean,
to rest; *Fig (proposition)* to second; **a.
qch sur qch** *(poser)* to rest sth on sth;
(presser) to press sth on sth **2** *vi (presser)* to press; **a. sur un bouton** to press

a button **3 s'appuyer** *vpr* **s'a. sur qch** to lean on sth, to rest on sth; *Fig (être basé sur)* to be based on sth

âpre [ɑpr] *adj* sour; *Fig (lutte)* fierce

après [aprɛ] **1** *prép (dans le temps)* after; *(dans l'espace)* beyond; **a. tout** after all; **a. avoir mangé** after eating; **a. qu'il t'a vu** after he saw you; **d'a.** *(selon)* according to

2 *adv* after(wards); **l'année d'a.** the following year; **et a.?** *(et ensuite)* and then what?; *(et alors)* so what? ▪ **après-demain** *adv* the day after tomorrow ▪ **après-guerre** *nm* post-war period; **d'a.** post-war ▪ **après-midi** *nm ou f inv* afternoon; **trois heures de l'a.** three o'clock in the afternoon ▪ **après-rasage** *(pl* après-rasages*) nm* aftershave ▪ **après-shampooing** *nm inv* conditioner ▪ **après-ski** *(pl* après-skis*) nm* snowboot ▪ **après-vente** *adj inv Com* **service a.** after-sales service

âpreté [ɑprəte] *nf* sourness; *Fig (lutte)* fierceness

à-propos [apropo] *nm* aptness; **avoir l'esprit d'a.** to have presence of mind

apte [apt] *adj* **a. à qch/à faire qch** fit to sth/for doing sth ▪ **aptitude** *nf* aptitude **(à** *ou* **pour** for); **avoir des aptitudes pour qch** to have an aptitude for sth

aquarelle [akwarɛl] *nf* watercolour

aquarium [akwarjɔm] *nm* aquarium

aquatique [akwatik] *adj* aquatic

arabe 1 *adj (peuple, litterature)* Arab; *(langue)* Arabic **2** *nmf* **A.** Arab **3** *nm (langue)* Arabic ▪ **Arabie** *nf* **l'A.** Arabia; **l'A. Saoudite** Saudi Arabia

arable [arabl] *adj* arable

arachide [araʃid] *nf* peanut

araignée [areɲe] *nf* spider

arbitraire [arbitrɛr] *adj* arbitrary

arbitre [arbitr] *nm (de football)* referee; *(de tennis)* umpire ▪ **arbitrage** *nm (de football)* refereeing; *(de tennis)* umpiring

arborer [arbɔre] *vt (insigne)* to sport

arbre [arbr] *nm (végétal)* tree; *Tech* shaft; **a. fruitier** fruit tree; **a. de transmission** transmission shaft ▪ **arbuste** *nm* shrub

arc [ark] *nm (arme)* bow; *(voûte)* arch; *(de cercle)* arc ▪ **arcade** *nf* archway; **arcades** *(de place)* arcade

arc-boutant [arkbutɑ̃] *(pl* arcs-boutants*) nm* flying buttress

arc-en-ciel [arkɑ̃sjɛl] *(pl* arcs-en-ciel*) nm* rainbow

archaïque [arkaik] *adj* archaic

arche [arʃ] *nf (voûte)* arch; **l'a. de Noé** Noah's ark

archéologie [arkeɔlɔʒi] *nf* archaeology ▪ **archéologique** *adj* archaeological ▪ **archéologue** *nmf* archaeologist

archet [arʃɛ] *nm (de violon)* bow

architecte [arʃitɛkt] *nm* architect ▪ **architecture** *nf* architecture

archives [arʃiv] *nfpl* archives, records

arctique [arktik] **1** *adj* arctic **2** *nm* **l'A.** the Arctic

ardent, -e [ardɑ̃, -ɑ̃t] *adj (désir)* burning; *(soleil)* scorching ▪ **ardeur** *nf (passion)* fervour, ardour; *(du soleil)* intense heat

ardoise [ardwaz] *nf* slate

ardu, -e [ardy] *adj* arduous

arène [arɛn] *nf (pour taureaux)* bullring; *(romaine)* arena; **arènes** bullring; *(romaines)* amphitheatre

arête [arɛt] *nf (de poisson)* bone; *(de cube)* edge; *(de montagne)* ridge

argent [arʒɑ̃] **1** *nm (métal)* silver; *(monnaie)* money; **a. liquide** cash; **a. de poche** pocket money **2** *adj (couleur)* silver ▪ **argenté, -e** *adj (plaqué)* silver-plated; *(couleur)* silvery ▪ **argenterie** *nf* silverware

Argentine [arʒɑ̃tin] *nf* **l'A.** Argentina ▪ **argentin, -e 1** *adj* Argentinian **2** *nmf* **A., Argentine** Argentinian

argile [arʒil] *nf* clay

argot [argo] *nm* slang ▪ **argotique** *adj (terme)* slang

argument [argymɑ̃] *nm* argument

argumenter [argymɑ̃te] *vi* to argue

aride [arid] *adj (terre)* arid, barren; *(sujet)* dry

aristocrate [aristɔkrat] *nmf* aristocrat ▪ **aristocratie** [-asi] *nf* aristocracy ▪ **aristocratique** *adj* aristocratic

arithmétique [aritmetik] *nf* arithmetic

armature [armatyr] *nf (charpente)* framework; *(de lunettes, de tente)* frame

arme [arm] *nf* weapon; **prendre les armes** to take up arms; *Fig* **à armes égales** on equal terms; **a. à feu** firearm; **a. blanche** knife ▪ **armes** *nfpl (blason)* (coat of) arms

armée [arme] *nf* army; **être à l'a.** to be doing one's military service; **a. de l'air** air force; **a. de terre** army; **a. active/ de métier** regular/professional army

armer [arme] **1** *vt (personne)* to arm (**de** with); *(fusil)* to cock; *(appareil photo)* to set **2 s'armer** *vpr* to arm oneself (**de** with); **s'a. de patience** to summon up one's patience ▪ **armements** *nmpl (armes)* armaments

armistice [armistis] *nm* armistice

armoire [armwar] *nf (penderie) Br* wardrobe, *Am* closet; **a. à pharmacie** medicine cabinet

armure [armyr] *nf* armour

aromate [aromat] *nm (herbe)* herb; *(épice)* spice

aromathérapie [aromaterapi] *nf* aromatherapy

aromatique [aromatik] *adj* aromatic

arôme [arom] *nm (goût)* flavour; *(odeur)* aroma

arpenter [arpɑ̃te] *vt (parcourir)* to pace up and down

arqué, -e [arke] *adj (jambes)* bandy

arraché [araʃe] *nm* **gagner à l'a.** to snatch victory

arrache-pied [araʃpje] **d'arrache-pied** *adv* relentlessly

arracher [araʃe] *vt (plante)* to uproot; *(clou, dent, mauvaise herbe)* to pull out; *(page)* to tear out; **a. qch à qn** *(objet)* to snatch sth from sb; *(promesse)* to force sth out of sb; **se faire a. une dent** to have a tooth out

arrangement [arɑ̃ʒmɑ̃] *nm (disposition)* & *Mus* arrangement; *(accord)* agreement

arranger [arɑ̃ʒe] **1** *vt (fleurs)* to arrange; *(col)* to straighten; *(réparer)* to repair; **ça m'arrange** that suits me

(fine) **2 s'arranger** *vpr (se mettre d'accord)* to come to an agreement; *(finir bien)* to turn out fine; *(s'organiser)* to manage

arrestation [arɛstɑsjɔ̃] *nf* arrest

arrêt [arɛ] *nm (halte, endroit)* stop; *(action)* stopping; *Jur* judgment; **temps d'a.** pause; **à l'a.** stationary; **sans a.** continuously; **a. du cœur** cardiac arrest; *Sport* **a. de jeu** stoppage; **a. de mort** death sentence; **a. de travail** *(congé)* sick leave ▪ **arrêt-maladie** sick leave

arrêté¹ [arete] *nm (décret)* order, decree

arrêté², -e [arete] *adj (idées)* fixed

arrêter [arete] **1** *vt (personne, animal, véhicule)* to stop; *(criminel)* to arrest; *(moteur)* to turn off; *(date)* to fix; *(études)* to give up **2** *vi* to stop; **a. de faire qch** to stop doing sth **3 s'arrêter** *vpr* to stop; **s'a. de faire qch** to stop doing sth

arriéré, -e [arjere] **1** *adj (pays, idées, enfant)* backward **2** *nm (dette)* arrears

arrière [arjɛr] **1** *nm (de maison)* back, rear; *(de bateau)* stern; *(au football)* full back; **à l'a.** in/at the back

2 *adj inv (siège)* back, rear; **feu a.** rear light

3 *adv* **en a.** *(marcher, tomber)* backwards; *(rester)* behind; *(regarder)* back, behind; **en a. de qn/qch** behind sb/sth ▪ **arrière-goût** *(pl* **arrière-goûts)** *nm* aftertaste ▪ **arrière-grand-mère** *(pl* **arrière-grands-mères)** *nf* great-grandmother ▪ **arrière-grand-père** *(pl* **arrière-grands-pères)** *nm* great-grandfather ▪ **arrière-grands-parents** *npl* great-grandparents ▪ **arrière-pays** *nm inv* hinterland ▪ **arrière-pensée** *(pl* **arrière-pensées)** *nf* ulterior motive ▪ **arrière-petits-enfants** *npl* great-grandchildren ▪ **arrière-plan** *nm* background; **à l'a.** in the background ▪ **arrière-saison** *(pl* **arrière-saisons)** *nf* late autumn, *Am* late fall

arriver [arive] **1** *(aux* être*)* *vi (venir)* to arrive; **a. à** *(lieu)* to reach; *(résultat)* to achieve; **a. à faire qch** to manage to do sth

2 v impersonnel (survenir) to happen; **a. à qn** to happen to sb; **qu'est-ce qu'il t'arrive?** what's wrong with you? ■ **arrivage** nm consignment ■ **arrivée** nf arrival; (ligne, poteau) winning post ■ **arriviste** nmf Péj social climber

arrogant, -e [arɔgã, -ãt] adj arrogant ■ **arrogance** nf arrogance

arroger [arɔʒe] **s'arroger** vpr (droit) to claim

arrondir [arɔ̃dir] vt (chiffre, angle) to round off; **a. qch** to make sth round; **a. à l'euro supérieur/inférieur** to round up/down to the nearest euro; Fam **a. ses fins de mois** to supplement one's income ■ **arrondi, -e** adj round

arrondissement [arɔ̃dismã] nm = administrative subdivision of Paris, Lyons and Marseilles

arroser [arɔze] vt (plante) to water; (pelouse) to sprinkle; Fam (succès) to drink to ■ **arrosage** nm (de plante) watering; (de pelouse) sprinkling ■ **arrosoir** nm watering can

arsenal, -aux [arsənal, -o] nm Mil arsenal

arsenic [arsənik] nm arsenic

art [ar] nm art; **critique d'a.** art critic; **arts martiaux** martial arts; **arts ménagers** home economics; **arts plastiques** fine arts

artère [arter] nf (veine) artery; (rue) main road

artichaut [artiʃo] nm artichoke; **fond d'a.** artichoke heart

article [artikl] nm (de presse, de contrat) & Gram article; Com item; **articles de toilette** toiletries; **articles de voyage** travel goods

articuler [artikyle] **1** vt (mot) to articulate **2 s'articuler** vpr (membre) to articulate; **s'a. autour de qch** (théorie) to centre on ■ **articulation** nf (de membre) joint; (prononciation) articulation

artifice [artifis] nm trick

artificiel, -elle [artifisjɛl] adj artificial

artillerie [artijri] nf artillery ■ **artilleur** nm artilleryman

artisan [artizã] nm craftsman, artisan ■ **artisanal, -e, -aux, -ales** adj objet a. object made by craftsmen; **bombe artisanale** homemade bomb ■ **artisanat** nm craft industry

artiste [artist] nmf artist; (acteur, musicien) performer, artiste ■ **artistique** adj artistic

as [ɑs] nm (carte, champion) ace

ascendant [asɑ̃dɑ̃] **1** adj ascending; (mouvement) upward **2** nm (influence) influence; **ascendants** ancestors ■ **ascendance** nf (ancêtres) ancestry

ascenseur [asɑ̃sœr] nm Br lift, Am elevator

ascension [asɑ̃sjɔ̃] nf (escalade) ascent; Rel l'A. Ascension Day

Asie [azi] nf l'A. Asia ■ **asiatique 1** adj Asian **2** nmf A. Asian

asile [azil] nm (abri) refuge, shelter; (pour vieillards) home; Péj a. (d'aliénés) (lunatic) asylum; **a. politique** (political) asylum

aspect [aspɛ] nm (air) appearance; (perspective) aspect

asperger [aspɛrʒe] **1** vt (par jeu ou accident) to splash (de with); **se faire a.** to get splashed **2 s'asperger** vpr **s'a. de parfum** to splash oneself with perfume

asperges [aspɛrʒ] nfpl asparagus

asphalte [asfalt] nm asphalt

asphyxie [asfiksi] nf asphyxiation ■ **asphyxier** vt, **s'asphyxier** vpr to suffocate

aspirateur [aspiratœr] nm vacuum cleaner; **passer l'a. dans la maison** to vacuum the house

aspirer [aspire] **1** vt (liquide) to suck up; (air) to breathe in, to inhale **2** vi **a. à qch** (bonheur, gloire) to aspire to sth ■ **aspiration** nf (inhalation) inhalation; (ambition) aspiration (à for)

aspirine [aspirin] nf aspirin

assaillir [asajir] vt to attack ■ **assaillant** nm attacker, assailant

assainir [asenir] vt (purifier) to clean up; (marché, économie) to stabilize

assaisonner [asezɔne] vt to season ■ **assaisonnement** nm seasoning

assassin [asasɛ̃] *nm* murderer; *(de politicien)* assassin ▪ **assassinat** *nm* murder; *(de politicien)* assassination ▪ **assassiner** *vt* to murder; *(politicien)* to assassinate

assaut [aso] *nm* attack, assault; *Mil* charge

assécher [aseʃe] **1** *vt* to drain **2 s'assécher** *vpr* to dry up

assemblée [asɑ̃ble] *nf (personnes réunies)* gathering; *(réunion)* meeting; **a. générale** *(de compagnie)* annual general meeting; **l'A. nationale** *Br* ≃ the House of Commons, *Am* ≃ the House of Representatives

assembler [asɑ̃ble] **1** *vt* to put together, to assemble **2 s'assembler** *vpr* to gather ▪ **assemblage** *nm (montage)* assembly; *(réunion d'objets)* collection

asséner [asene] *vt* **a. un coup à qn** to deliver a blow to sb

asseoir* [aswar] **1** *vt (personne)* to seat **(sur** on); *Fig (autorité)* to establish **2** *vi* **faire a. qn** to ask sb to sit down **3 s'asseoir** *vpr* to sit (down)

assermenté, -e [asɛrmɑ̃te] *adj* sworn; *(témoin)* under oath

asservir [asɛrvir] *vt* to enslave

assez [ase] *adv* **(a)** *(suffisament)* enough; **a. de pain/de gens** enough bread/people; **j'en ai a. (de)** I've had enough (of); **a. grand/intelligent (pour faire qch)** big/clever enough (to do sth) **(b)** *(plutôt)* quite, rather

assidu, -e [asidy] *adj (toujours présent)* regular; *(appliqué)* diligent; **a. auprès de qn** attentive to sb ▪ **assiduité** *nf (d'élève)* regularity

assiéger [asjeʒe] *vt (ville, magasin)* to besiege

assiette [asjɛt] *nf (récipient)* plate; *Culin* **a. anglaise** *Br* (assorted) cold meats, *Am* cold cuts

assigner [asiɲe] *vt (attribuer)* to assign (à to); *(en justice)* to summon ▪ **assignation** *nf Jur* summons

assimiler [asimile] *vt (aliments, savoir, immigrés)* to assimilate

assis, -e¹ [asi, -iz] *(pp de* **asseoir**) *adj* sitting (down), seated; **rester a.** to re-

main seated; **place assise** seat

assise² [asiz] *nf (base)* foundation; **assises** *(d'un parti)* congress; *Jur* **les assises** the assizes

assistance [asistɑ̃s] *nf* **(a)** *(public)* audience **(b)** *(aide)* assistance

assister [asiste] **1** *vt (aider)* to assist **2** *vi* **a. à** *(réunion, cours)* to attend; *(accident)* to witness ▪ **assistant, -e** *nmf* assistant; **assistante maternelle** *Br* child minder, *Am* baby-sitter; **assistante sociale** social worker ▪ **assisté, -e** *adj* **a. par ordinateur** computer-aided

association [asɔsjasjɔ̃] *nf* association; *Com* partnership; **a. de parents d'élèves** parent-teacher association; **a. sportive** sports club

associer [asɔsje] **1** *vt* to associate **(à** with); **a. qn à** *(travaux)* to involve sb in **2 s'associer** *vpr* to join forces **(à** *ou* **avec** with); *Com* **s'a. avec qn** to enter into partnership with sb ▪ **associé, -e** *nmf* partner, associate

assoiffé, -e [aswafe] *adj* thirsty **(de** for)

assombrir [asɔ̃brir] **1** *vt (obscurcir)* to darken; *(attrister)* to cast a shadow over **2 s'assombrir** *vpr (ciel, visage)* to cloud over; *(personne)* to become gloomy

assommer [asɔme] *vt* **a. qn** to knock sb unconscious; *Fig (ennuyer)* to bore sb to death ▪ **assommant, -e** *adj* very boring

Assomption [asɔ̃psjɔ̃] *nf Rel* **l'A.** the Assumption

assortir [asɔrtir] *vt (harmoniser)* to match ▪ **assorti, -e** *adj (objet semblable)* matching; *(bonbons)* assorted; **a. de** accompanied by ▪ **assortiment** *nm* assortment

assoupir [asupir] **s'assoupir** *vpr* to doze off

assouplir [asuplir] **1** *vt (cuir, muscles)* to make supple; *(corps)* to limber up; *Fig (réglementation)* to relax **2 s'assouplir** *vpr (personne, cuir)* to get supple ▪ **assouplissement** *nm* **exercices d'a.** warm-up exercises

assourdissant, -e [asurdisɑ̃, -ɑ̃t] *adj* deafening

assouvir [asuvir] *vt* to satisfy

assujettir [asyʒetir] *vt (soumettre)* to subject (à to); *(peuple)* to subjugate; *(objet)* to fix (à to)

assumer [asyme] **1** *vt (tâche, rôle)* to assume, to take on; *(risque)* to take **2** **s'assumer** *vpr* to come to terms with oneself

assurance [asyrɑ̃s] *nf (confiance)* (self-)assurance; *(promesse)* assurance; *(contrat)* insurance; **prendre une a.** to take out insurance; **a. au tiers/tous risques** third-party/comprehensive insurance; **a. maladie/vie** health/life insurance

assurer [asyre] **1** *vt (garantir) Br* to ensure, *Am* to insure; *(par contrat)* to insure; **a. qn de qch, a. qch à qn** to assure sb of sth; **un service régulier est assuré** there is a regular service **2** **s'assurer** *vpr (par contrat)* to insure oneself; **s'a. de qch/que...** to make sure of sth/that... ■ **assuré, -e 1** *adj (succès)* guaranteed; *(air, personne)* confident **2** *nmf* policyholder ■ **assurément** *adv* certainly

asthme [asm] *nm* asthma ■ **asthmatique** *adj & nmf* asthmatic

asticot [astiko] *nm Br* maggot, *Am* worm

astiquer [astike] *vt* to polish

astre [astr] *nm* star

astreindre* [astrɛ̃dr] **1** *vt* **a. qn à faire qch** to compel sb to do sth **2** **s'astreindre** *vpr* **s'a. à faire qch** to force oneself to do sth ■ **astreignant, -e** *adj* exacting ■ **astreinte** *nf* constraint

astrologie [astrɔlɔʒi] *nf* astrology

astrologue [astrɔlɔg] *nm* astrologer

astronaute [astrɔnot] *nmf* astronaut ■ **astronautique** *nf* space travel

astronomie [astrɔnɔmi] *nf* astronomy ■ **astronome** *nm* astronomer

astuce [astys] *nf (truc)* trick; *(plaisanterie)* witticism ■ **astucieux, -euse** *adj* clever

atelier [atəlje] *nm (d'ouvrier)* workshop; *(de peintre)* studio; *(personnel)* workshop staff; **a. de montage** assembly shop; **a. de réparation** repair shop

athée [ate] **1** *adj* atheistic **2** *nmf* atheist

Athènes [atɛn] *nm ou f* Athens

athlète [atlet] *nmf* athlete ■ **athlétique** *adj* athletic ■ **athlétisme** *nm* athletics *(sing)*

atlantique [atlɑ̃tik] **1** *adj* Atlantic **2** *nm* **l'A.** the Atlantic

atlas [atlɑs] *nm* atlas

atmosphère [atmɔsfɛr] *nf* atmosphere ■ **atmosphérique** *adj* atmospheric

atome [atom] *nm* atom ■ **atomique** *adj* atomic

atomiser [atɔmize] *vt (liquide)* to spray; *(région)* to destroy with nuclear weapons ■ **atomiseur** *nm* spray

atout [atu] *nm* trump; *Fig (avantage)* asset

être [atr] *nm (foyer)* hearth

atroce [atrɔs] *adj* atrocious; *(douleur)* excruciating ■ **atrocité** *nf (cruauté)* atrociousness; **les atrocités de la guerre** the atrocities committed in wartime

attabler [atable] **s'attabler** *vpr* to sit down at a/the table

attache [ataʃ] *nf (lien)* fastener

attaché, -e [ataʃe] **1** *adj (fixé)* fastened; *(chien)* chained up; **être a. à qn** to be attached to sb **2** *nmf* attaché; **a. de presse** press officer

attaché-case [ataʃekɛz] *(pl attachés-cases) nm* attaché case

attacher [ataʃe] **1** *vt* **a. qch à qch** to fasten sth to sth; *(avec de la ficelle)* to tie sth to sth; *(avec une chaîne)* to chain sth to sth; **a. de l'importance à qch** to attach great importance to sth **2** *vi (en cuisant)* to stick (to the pan) **3** **s'attacher** *vpr (se fixer)* to be fastened; **s'a. à qn** to get attached to sb ■ **attachant, -e** *adj* engaging ■ **attachement** *nm (affection)* attachment (à to)

attaque [atak] *nf* attack; **a. aérienne** air raid ■ **attaquer 1** *vt (physiquement, verbalement)* to attack **2** *vi* to attack **3** **s'attaquer** *vpr* **s'a. à** *(adversaire)* to attack; *(problème)* to tackle ■ **attaquant, -e** *nmf* attacker

attarder [atarde] **s'attarder** *vpr* to linger ■ **attardé, -e** *adj (enfant)* mentally retarded

atteindre* [atɛ̃dr] *vt (parvenir à)* to reach; *(cible)* to hit; **être atteint d'une maladie** to be suffering from a disease

atteinte [atɛ̃t] *nf* attack (**à** on); **porter a. à** to undermine; **hors d'a.** *(objet, personne)* out of reach

atteler [atle] **1** *vt (bêtes)* to harness **2 s'atteler** *vpr* **s'a. à une tâche** to apply oneself to a task

attenant, -e [atnã, -ãt] *adj* **a. (à)** adjoining

attendre [atɑ̃dr] **1** *vt (personne, train)* to wait for; **a. son tour** to wait one's turn; **elle attend un bébé** she's expecting a baby; **a. que qn fasse qch** to wait for sb to do sth; **a. qch de qn** to expect sth from sb
2 *vi* to wait; **faire a. qn** to keep sb waiting; **en attendant** meanwhile; **en attendant que... (+ subjunctive)** until...
3 s'attendre *vpr* **s'a. à qch** to expect sth; **s'a. à ce que qn fasse qch** to expect sb to do sth ■ **attendu, -e 1** *adj (prévu)* expected **2** *prép Formel* considering

attendrir [atɑ̃drir] **1** *vt (émouvoir)* to move **2 s'attendrir** *vpr* to be moved (**sur** by) ■ **attendri, -e** *adj* compassionate ■ **attendrissant, -e** *adj* moving

attentat [atɑ̃ta] *nm* attack; **a. à la bombe** bombing; **a. à la pudeur** indecent assault

attente [atɑ̃t] *nf (fait d'attendre)* waiting; *(période)* wait; **en a.** *(au téléphone)* on hold; **contre toute a.** against all expectations

attentif, -ive [atɑ̃tif, -iv] *adj* attentive; **a. à qch** to pay attention to sth

attention [atɑ̃sjɔ̃] *nf (soin, amabilité)* attention; **faire a. à qch** to pay attention to sth; **faire a. (à ce) que... (+ subjunctive)** to be careful that...; **a.!** watch out!; **a. à la voiture!** watch out for the car!; **à l'a. de qn** *(sur lettre)* for the attention of sb ■ **attentionné, -e** *adj* considerate

atténuer [atenɥe] **1** *vt (effet, douleur)* to reduce **2 s'atténuer** *vpr (douleur)* to ease

atterrir [aterir] *vi* to land; **a. en catastrophe** to make an emergency landing ■ **atterrissage** *nm* landing; **a. forcé** forced landing

attester [atɛste] *vt* to testify to; **a. que...** to testify that... ■ **attestation** *nf (document)* certificate

attirail [atiraj] *nm* equipment; *Fam Péj* gear

attirance [atirɑ̃s] *nf* attraction (**pour** for)

attirer [atire] **1** *vt (sujet: aimant, personne)* to attract; *(sujet: matière, pays)* to appeal to; **a. l'attention de qn** to catch sb's attention; **a. qn dans un piège** to lure sb into a trap **2 s'attirer** *vpr (mutuellement)* to be attracted to each other; **s'a. des ennuis** to get oneself into trouble ■ **attirant, -e** *adj* attractive

attitré, -e [atitre] *adj (représentant)* appointed

attitude [atityd] *nf (conduite, position)* attitude

attraction [atraksjɔ̃] *nf (force, centre d'intérêt)* attraction

attrait [atrɛ] *nm* attraction

attraper [atrape] *vt (ballon, maladie, voleur)* to catch; **a. froid** to catch cold

attrayant, -e [atrɛjɑ̃, -ãt] *adj* attractive

attribuer [atribɥe] *vt (allouer)* to assign (**à** to); *(prix, bourse)* to award (**à** to); *(œuvre)* to attribute (**à** to); **a. de l'importance à qch** to attach importance to sth ■ **attribution** *nf (allocation)* assigning (**à** to); *(de prix)* awarding (**à** to); *(d'une œuvre)* attribution (**à** to); **attributions** *(fonctions)* duties

attribut [atriby] *nm (caractéristique)* attribute

attrister [atriste] *vt* to sadden

attrouper [atrupe] **s'attrouper** *vpr* to gather ■ **attroupement** *nm* crowd

au [o] *voir* **à**

aube [ob] *nf* dawn; **dès l'a.** at the crack of dawn

auberge [oberʒ] *nf* inn; **a. de jeu-nesse** youth hostel

aubergine [oberʒin] *nf Br* aubergine, *Am* eggplant

aucun, -e [okœ̃, -yn] **1** *adj* no, not any; **il n'a a. talent** he has no talent; **a. professeur n'est venu** no teacher came **2** *pron* none; **il n'en a a.** he has none (at all); **a. d'entre nous** none of us; **a. des deux** neither of the two

audace [odas] *nf (courage)* daring, boldness; *(impudence)* audacity ■ **audacieux, -euse** *adj (courageux)* daring, bold

au-dehors [odəor] *adv* outside

au-delà [odəla] **1** *adv* beyond; **100 euros mais pas a.** 100 euros but no more **2** *prép* **a. de** beyond **3** *nm* **l'a.** the next world

au-dessous [odəsu] **1** *adv (à l'étage inférieur)* downstairs; *(moins, dessous)* below, under **2** *prép* **a. de** *(dans l'espace)* below, under, beneath; *(âge, prix)* under; *(température)* below

au-dessus [odəsy] **1** *adv* above; *(à l'étage supérieur)* upstairs **2** *prép* **a. de** above; *(âge, température, prix)* over; *(posé sur)* on top of

au-devant [odəvɑ̃] *prép* **aller a. de** *(personne)* to go to meet; *(danger)* to court; *(désirs de qn)* to anticipate

audible [odibl] *adj* audible

audience [odjɑ̃s] *nf (entretien)* audience; *(de tribunal)* hearing; *Jur* **l'a. est suspendue** the case is adjourned

audiovisuel, -elle [odjovizɥɛl] **1** *adj (méthodes)* audiovisual; *(de radio, de télévision)* radio and television **2** *nm* **l'a.** radio and television

auditeur, -trice [oditœr, -tris] *nmf (de radio)* listener ■ **audition** *nf (ouïe)* hearing; *(d'acteurs)* audition; **passer une a.** to have an audition ■ **auditionner** *vti* to audition ■ **auditoire** *nm* audience ■ **auditorium** *nm* concert hall

augmenter [ogmɑ̃te] **1** *vt* to increase (**de** by); **a. qn** to give sb a *Br* rise *or Am* raise **2** *vi* to increase (**de** by); *(prix, population)* to rise ■ **augmentation** *nf* increase (**de** in, of); **a. de salaire** *Br* (pay)

rise, *Am* raise; **être en a.** to be on the increase

augure [ogyr] *nm (présage)* omen; **être de bon/mauvais a.** to be a good/bad omen

aujourd'hui [oʒurdɥi] *adv* today; *(de nos jours)* nowadays, today; **a. en quinze** two weeks from today

auparavant [oparavɑ̃] *adv (avant)* before(-hand); *(d'abord)* first

auprès [oprɛ] **auprès de** *prép (près de)* by, next to; **se renseigner a. de qn** to ask sb

auquel [okɛl] *voir* **lequel**

aura, aurait [ora, orɛ] *voir* **avoir**

auréole [oreol] *nf (de saint)* halo; *(tache)* ring

auriculaire [orikylɛr] *nm* little finger

aurore [oror] *nf* dawn, daybreak; **à l'a.** at dawn

auspices [ospis] *nmpl* **sous les a. de** under the auspices of

aussi [osi] **1** *adv* (a) *(comparaison)* as; **a. lourd que...** as heavy as... (b) *(également)* too, as well; **moi a.** so do/can/am/*etc* I; **a. bien que...** as well as... (c) *(tellement)* so; **un repas a. délicieux** such a delicious meal (d) *(quelque)* **a. bizarre que cela paraisse** however odd this may seem **2** *conj (donc)* therefore

aussitôt [osito] *adv* immediately, straight away; **a. que...** as soon as...; **a. dit, a. fait** no sooner said than done

austère [ostɛr] *adj (vie, style)* austere; *(vêtement)* severe ■ **austérité** *nf (de vie, de style)* austerity; *(de vêtement)* severity; **mesure d'a.** austerity measures

austral, -e, -als, -ales [ostral] *adj* southern

Australie [ostrali] *nf* **l'A.** Australia ■ **australien, -enne 1** *adj* Australian **2** *nmf* **A., Australienne** Australian

AUTANT [otɑ̃] *adv* (a) **a. de... que** *(quantité)* as much... as; *(nombre)* as many... as; **il a a. d'argent/de pommes que vous** he has as much money/as many apples as you (b) **a. de** *(tant de)* so much; *(nombre)*

so many; **je n'ai jamais vu a. d'argent/de pommes** I've never seen so much money/so many apples; **pourquoi manges-tu a.?** why are you eating so much?

(c) **a. que** *(quantité)* as much as; *(nombre)* as many as; **il lit a. que vous/ que possible** he reads as much as you/ as possible; **il n'a jamais souffert a.** he's never suffered as *or* so much

(d) *(expressions)* **d'a. (plus) que...** all the more (so) since...; **en faire a.** to do the same; **j'aimerais a. aller au musée** I'd just as soon go to the museum

autel [otɛl] *nm* altar

auteur [otœr] *nm (de livre)* author, writer; *(de chanson)* composer

authenticité [otɑ̃tisite] *nf* authenticity ▪ **authentique** *adj* genuine, authentic

autiste [otist] *adj* autistic

autobiographie [otobjɔgrafi] *nf* autobiography ▪ **autobiographique** *adj* autobiographical

autobus [otobys] *nm* bus

autocar [otokar] *nm* bus, *Br* coach

autocollant, -e [otokɔlɑ̃, -ɑ̃t] **1** *adj* self-adhesive; *(enveloppe, timbre)* self-seal **2** *nm* sticker

autodéfense [otodefɑ̃s] *nf Br* self-defence, *Am* self-defense

autodidacte [otodidakt] *amf* self-taught person

auto-école [otoekɔl] *(pl* **auto-écoles)** *nf* driving school

autographe [otograf] *nm* autograph

automation [otomasjɔ̃] *nf* automation ▪ **automatiser** *vt* to automate

automatique [otomatik] *adj* automatic ▪ **automatiquement** *adv* automatically

automatisation [otomatizasjɔ̃] *nf* = automation

automédication [otomedikasjɔ̃] *nf* self-medication

automne [otɔn] *nm* autumn, *Am* fall

automobile [otomɔbil] *nf* car *Br* motorcar, *Am* automobile; **l'a.** *(industrie)* the car industry ▪ **automobiliste** *nmf* motorist

autonettoyant, -e [otonetwajɑ̃, -ɑ̃t] *adj* **four a.** self-cleaning oven

autonome [otonom] *adj (région)* autonomous, self-governing; *(personne)* self-sufficient ▪ **autonomie** *nf (de région)* autonomy; *(de personne)* self-sufficiency

autopsie [otopsi] *nf* autopsy, post-mortem

autoradio [otoradjo] *nm* car radio

autoriser [otorize] *vt* **a. qn à faire qch** to authorize *or* permit sb to do sth ▪ **autorisation** *nf (permission)* permission, authorization; *(document)* authorization; **demander à qn l'a. de faire qch** to ask sb permission to do sth; **donner à qn l'a. de faire qch** to give sb permission to do sth ▪ **autorisé, -e** *adj (qualifié)* authoritative; *(permis)* permitted, allowed

autorité [otorite] *nf (fermeté, domination)* authority; **faire qch d'a.** to do sth on one's own authority

autoroute [otorut] *nf Br* motorway, *Am* highway, *Am* freeway; **a. à péage** *Br* toll motorway, *Am* turnpike (road); *Ordinat* **a. de l'information** information superhighway ▪ **autoritaire** *adj* authoritarian

auto-stop [otostop] *nm* hitchhiking; **faire de l'a.** to hitchhike ▪ **auto-stoppeur, -euse** *nmf* hitchhiker

autour [otur] **1** *adv* around; **tout a.** all around **2** *prép* **a. de** around, round; *(environ)* around, round about

AUTRE [otr] *adj & pron* other; **un a. livre** another book; **un a.** another (one); **d'autres** others; **d'autres livres** other books; **quelqu'un d'a.** somebody else; **personne/rien d'a.** no one/ nothing else; **a. chose/part** something/somewhere else; **qui/quoi d'a.?** who/what else?; **l'un ou l'a.** either (of them); **ni l'un ni l'a.** neither (of them)

autrefois [otrəfwa] *adv* in the past, once

autrement [otrəmɑ̃] *adv (différemment)* differently; *(sinon)* otherwise; *(plus)* far more (**que** than)

Autriche [otriʃ] *nf* l'A. Austria ■ **autrichien, -enne 1** *adj* Austrian **2** *nmf* A., **Autrichienne** Austrian

autruche [otryʃ] *nf* ostrich

autrui [otrɥi] *pron* others, other people

auvent [ovɑ̃] *nm (toit)* porch roof; *(de tente, de magasin)* awning, canopy

aux [o] *voir* à

auxiliaire [ɔksiljɛr] **1** *adj (machine, troupes)* auxiliary **2** *nm (verbe)* auxiliary **3** *nmf (aide)* assistant; *(d'hôpital)* auxiliary; *(dans l'administration)* temporary worker

auxquels, -elles [okɛl] *voir* lequel

av. *(abrév* avenue) Ave

avait [avɛ] *voir* avoir

aval [aval] *nm* downstream section; **en a. (de)** downstream (from)

avalanche [avalɑ̃ʃ] *nf* avalanche

avaler [avale] *vti* to swallow

avance [avɑ̃s] *nf (progression, acompte)* advance; *(avantage)* lead; **faire une a. à qn** *(donner de l'argent)* to give sb an advance; **avoir de l'a. sur qn** to be ahead of sb; **à l'a., d'a., par a.** in advance; **en a.** early; **avoir une heure d'a.** to be an hour early

avancé, -e [avɑ̃se] *adj* advanced; **à un âge/stade a.** at an advanced age/stage

avancée [avɑ̃se] *nf (saillie)* projection; *(progression, découverte)* advance

avancement [avɑ̃smɑ̃] *nm (de personne)* promotion; *(de travail)* progress

avancer [avɑ̃se] **1** *vt (dans le temps)* to bring forward; *(dans l'espace)* to move forward; *(pion, thèse)* to advance; *(montre)* to put forward; **a. de l'argent à qn** to lend sb money **2** *vi (aller de l'avant)* to move forward; *(armée)* to advance; *(faire des progrès)* to progress; *(faire saillie)* to jut out (**sur** over); **a. (de cinq minutes)** *(montre)* to be (five minutes) fast **3** **s'avancer** *vpr* to move forward; **s'a. vers qch** to head towards sth

AVANT [avɑ̃] **1** *prép* before; **a. de faire qch** before doing sth; **je vous verrai a. de partir/que vous (ne)**

partiez I'll see you before I/you leave; **a. tout** above all **2** *adv (auparavant)* before; *(d'abord)* beforehand; **a. j'avais les cheveux longs** I used to have long hair; **en a.** *(mouvement)* forward; *(en tête)* ahead; **en a. de** in front of; **la nuit d'a.** the night before **3** *nm (de navire, de voiture)* front; *(joueur de football)* forward; **à l'a.** in (the) front; **aller de l'a.** to get on with it **4** *adj inv (pneu, roue)* front ■ **avant-bras** *nm inv* forearm ■ **avant-centre** *(pl* **avants-centres)** *nm (au football)* centre-forward ■ **avant-dernier, -ère** *(mpl* **avant-derniers,** *fpl* **avant-dernières)** *adj & nmf* second last ■ **avant-hier** *adv* the day before yesterday ■ **avant-première** *(pl* **avant-premières)** *nf* preview ■ **avant-propos** *nm inv* foreword

avantage [avɑ̃taʒ] *nm* advantage; **être/tourner à l'a. de qn** to be/turn to sb's advantage; **avantages sociaux** social security benefits ■ **avantager** *vt* **a. qn** *(favoriser)* to give sb an advantage over; *(faire valoir)* to show sb off to advantage ■ **avantageux, -euse** *adj (offre)* attractive; *(prix)* reasonable

avare [avar] **1** *adj* miserly **2** *nmf* miser ■ **avarice** *nf* miserliness, avarice

avaries [avari] *nf* damage; **subir une a.** to be damaged ■ **avarié, -e** *adj (aliment)* rotten

avec [avɛk] *prép* with; **méchant/aimable a. qn** nasty/kind to sb; **a. enthousiasme** with enthusiasm, enthusiastically; *Fam* **et a. ça?** *(dans un magasin)* anything else?

avenant, -e [avnɑ̃, -ɑ̃t] **1** *adj (personne, manières)* pleasing **2** *nm* **à l'a. (de)** in keeping (with)

avènement [avɛnmɑ̃] *nm (d'une ère)* advent; *(d'un roi)* accession

avenir [avnir] *nm* future; **à l'a.** *(désormais)* in future; **d'a.** *(métier)* with good prospects

aventure [avɑ̃tyr] *nf* adventure; *(en amour)* affair; **dire la bonne a. à qn** to tell sb's fortune ■ **aventurer** *vpr*

s'aventurer to venture (**dans** into) ■ **aventurier, -ère** nmf adventurer

avenue [avny] nf avenue

avérer [avere] **s'avérer** vpr (se révéler) to prove to be; **il s'avère que...** it turns out that... ■ **avéré, -e** adj (fait) established

averse [avɛrs] nf shower

aversion [avɛrsjɔ̃] nf aversion (**pour** to)

avertir [avɛrtir] vt a. qn de qch (informer) to inform sb of sth; (danger) to warn sb of sth ■ **avertissement** nm warning; (de livre) foreword ■ **avertisseur** nm (klaxon®) horn

aveu, -x [avø] nm confession

aveugle [avœgl] **1** adj blind; **devenir a.** to go blind; **avoir une confiance a. en qn** to trust sb implicitly **2** nmf blind man, f blind woman; **les aveugles** the blind ■ **aveuglement** nm (moral, mental) blindness ■ **aveuglément** adv blindly ■ **aveugler** vt (éblouir) & Fig to blind; **aveuglé par la colère** blind with rage

aveuglette [avœglɛt] **à l'aveuglette** adv blindly; **chercher qch à l'a.** to grope for sth

aviateur, -trice [avjatœr, -tris] nmf aviator ■ **aviation** nf (secteur) aviation; (armée de l'air) air force; **l'a.** (activité) flying

avide [avid] adj (cupide) greedy; (passionné) eager (**de** for) ■ **avidité** nf (voracité, cupidité) greed; (passion) eagerness

avilir [avilir] vt to degrade

avion [avjɔ̃] nm plane, Br aeroplane, Am airplane; **par a.** (sur lettre) airmail; **en a., par a.** (voyager) by plane, by air; **a. à réaction** jet; **a. de tourisme** private plane

aviron [avirɔ̃] nm oar; **l'a.** (sport) rowing; **faire de l'a.** to row

avis [avi] nm opinion; (communiqué) notice; (conseil) advice; **à mon a.** in my opinion, to my mind; **être de l'a. de qn** to be of the same opinion as sb; **changer d'a.** to change one's mind; **sauf a. contraire** unless I/you/etc hear to the contrary

aviser [avize] **1** vt a. qn de qch/que... to inform sb of sth/that... **2** s'aviser vpr s'a. de qch to become aware of sth; s'a. que... to notice that... ■ **avisé, -e** adj wise (**de faire** to do); **bien/mal a.** well-/ill-advised

avocat¹, -e [avoka, -at] nmf Jur lawyer; Fig advocate

avocat² [avoka] nm (fruit) avocado

avoine [avwan] nf oats

AVOIR* [avwar] **1** v aux to have; **je l'ai vu** I have or I've seen him

2 vt (posséder) to have; (obtenir) to get; (porter) to wear; Fam (tromper) to take for a ride; **qu'est-ce que tu as?** what's the matter with you?; **j'ai à faire** I have things to do; **il n'a qu'à essayer** he only has to try; **a. faim/chaud** to be or feel hungry/hot; **a. cinq ans** to be five (years old); **a. du diabète** to be diabetic

3 v impersonnel **il y a** there is, pl there are; **il y a six ans** six years ago; **il n'y a pas de quoi!** (en réponse à 'merci') don't mention it!; **qu'est-ce qu'il y a?** what's the matter?

4 nm assets, property; (d'un compte) credit

avoisiner [avwazine] vt (dans l'espace) to border on; (en valeur) to be close to ■ **avoisinant, -e** adj neighbouring, nearby

avorter [avorte] vt (subir une IVG) to have an abortion; Fig (projet) to fall through; **se faire a.** to have an abortion ■ **avortement** nm abortion

avouer [avwe] **1** vt (crime) to confess to; **il faut a. que...** it must be admitted that... **2** s'avouer vpr s'a. vaincu to acknowledge defeat

avril [avril] nm April

axe [aks] nm (géométrique) axis; (essieu) axle; **les grands axes** (routes) the main roads ■ **axer** vt to centre (**sur** on)

ayant [ɛjɑ̃], **ayez** [ɛje], **ayons** [ɛjɔ̃] voir avoir

azote [azot] nm nitrogen

Bb

B, b [be] *nm inv* B, b

babiller [babije] *vi (enfant)* to babble

babines [babin] *nfpl (lèvres)* chops

bâbord [babɔr] *nm* port (side); **à b.** to port

baby-foot [babifut] *nm inv* table football

baby-sitting [babisitiŋ] *nm* baby-sitting **■ baby-sitter** (*pl* **baby-sitters**) *nmf* baby-sitter

bac¹ [bak] *nm (bateau)* ferry(boat); *(cuve)* tank; **b. à glace** ice tray

bac² [bak] *(abrév* **baccalauréat)** *nm Fam* = secondary school examination qualifying for entry to university, *Br* ≃ A-levels, *Am* ≃ high school diploma

baccalauréat [bakalɔrea] *nm* = secondary school examination qualifying for entry to university, *Br* ≃ A-levels, *Am* ≃ high school diploma

bâche [baʃ] *nf (de toile)* tarpaulin; *(de plastique)* plastic sheet **■ bâcher** *vt* to cover *(with a tarpaulin or plastic sheet)*

bachelier, -ère [baʃəlje, -ɛr] *nmf* = student who has passed the "baccalauréat"

bâcler [bɑkle] *vt Fam* to botch (up)

bactérie [bakteri] *nf* bacterium

badaud, -aude [bado, -od] *nmf (promeneur)* stroller; *(curieux)* onlooker

badge [badʒ] *nm Br* badge, *Am* button

badigeonner [badiʒɔne] *vt (surface)* to daub *(de* with); *(mur)* to whitewash; *Culin* to brush *(de* with); *(plaie)* to paint *(de* with)

badinage [badinaʒ] *nm* banter

badine [badin] *nf* switch

badiner [badine] *vi* to jest

baffle [bafl] *nm* speaker

bafouer [bafwe] *vt (person)* to jeer at; *(autorité)* to flout

bafouiller [bafuje] *vti* to stammer

bagages [bagaʒ] *nmpl (valises)* luggage, baggage; **faire ses b.** to pack (one's bags)

bagarre [bagar] *nf* fight, brawl **■ se bagarrer** to fight **■ bagarreur, -euse** *adj (personne, caractère)* aggressive

bague [bag] *nf (anneau)* ring; *(de cigare)* band **■ baguer** *vt (oiseau, arbre)* to ring

baguette [baget] *nf (canne)* stick; *(de chef d'orchestre)* baton; *(pain)* baguette; **baguettes** *(de tambour)* drumsticks; *(pour manger)* chopsticks

bahut [bay] *nm (buffet)* sideboard

baie¹ [bɛ] *nf Géog* bay

baie² [bɛ] *nf (fruit)* berry

baie³ [bɛ] *nf* **b. vitrée** picture window

baignade [bɛɲad] *nf (activité)* swimming; **'b. interdite'** 'no swimming'

baigner [bɛɲe] **1** *vt (pied, blessure)* to bathe; *(enfant) Br* to bath, *Am* to bathe; *(sujet: mer)* to wash **2** *vi (tremper)* to soak **(dans** in) **3 se baigner** *vpr (nager)* to have a swim **■ baigneur, -euse 1** *nmf* swimmer **2** *nm (poupée)* baby doll **■ baignoire** *nf* bath (tub)

bail [baj] *(pl* **baux** [bo]) *nm* lease; *Fam* **ça fait un b. que je ne l'ai pas vu** I haven't seen him for ages **■ bailleur** *nm* **b. de fonds** financial backer

bâiller [bɑje] *vi* to yawn; *(col)* to gape; *(porte)* to be ajar

bâillon [bɑjɔ̃] *nm* gag; **mettre un b. à qn** to gag sb **■ bâillonner** *vt (victime, presse)* to gag

bain [bɛ̃] *nm* bath; **prendre un b.** to have *or* take a bath; **prendre un b. de soleil** to sunbathe; **petit/grand b.** *(de piscine)* small/large pool

baiser [beze] *nm* kiss

baisse [bɛs] *nf* fall, drop (**de** in); **en b.** *(température)* falling; *(popularité)* declining

baisser [bese] **1** *vt (rideau, vitre, prix)* to lower; *(radio, chauffage)* to turn down; **b. la tête** to lower one's head; **b. les yeux** to look down **2** *vi (prix, niveau, température)* to fall; *(vue, mémoire)* to fail; *(popularité, qualité)* to decline **3 se baisser** *vpr* to bend down; *(pour éviter quelque chose)* to duck

baissier [besje] *adj m Fin* **marché b.** bear market

bal [bal] *(pl* **bals)** *nm (élégant)* ball; *(populaire)* dance; **b. costumé, b. masqué** fancy dress ball; **b. populaire** = dance, usually outdoors, open to the public

balade [balad] *nf Fam (à pied)* walk; *(en voiture)* drive; **faire une b.** *(à pied)* to go for a walk; *(en voiture)* to go for a drive **■ balader** *Fam* **1** *vi* **envoyer qn b.** to send sb packing **2 se balader** *vpr (à pied)* to go for a walk; *(en voiture)* to go for a drive **■ baladeur** *nm* personal stereo

balafre [balafr] *nf (cicatrice)* scar; *(coupure)* gash **■ balafrer** *vt* to gash

balai [balɛ] *nm* broom; **donner un coup de b.** to give the floor a sweep

balance [balɑ̃s] *nf* **(a)** *(instrument)* (pair of) scales **(b) la B.** *(signe)* Libra

balancer [balɑ̃se] **1** *vt (bras, jambe)* to swing **2 se balancer** *vpr (arbre, bateau)* to sway; *(sur une balançoire)* to swing **■ balancement** *nm* swaying

balancier [balɑ̃sje] *nm (d'horloge)* pendulum

balançoire [balɑ̃swar] *nf (suspendue)* swing; *(bascule)* see-saw

balayer [baleje] *vt (pièce)* to sweep; *(feuilles, saletés)* to sweep up **■ balayage** *nm (nettoyage)* sweeping; *(coiffure)* highlighting

balayeur, -euse [balɛjœr, -øz] *nmf (personne)* road-sweeper

balbutier [balbysje] *vti* to stammer **■ balbutiement** *nm* **balbutiement(s)** stammering

balcon [balkɔ̃] *nm* balcony; *(de théâtre)*

circle, *Am* mezzanine; **premier/deuxième b.** dress/upper circle

Baléares [balear] *nfpl* **les B.** the Balearic Islands

baleine [balɛn] *nf (animal)* whale; *(de corset)* whalebone; *(de parapluie)* rib

balèze [balɛz] *adj Fam (grand et fort)* hefty; *(intelligent)* brainy

balise [baliz] *nf Naut* beacon; *Aviat* light; *(de piste de ski)* marker; *Ordinat* tag **■ balisage** *nm (signaux) Naut* beacons; *Aviat* lights **■ baliser** *vt (chenal)* to beacon; *(aéroport)* to equip with lights; *(route)* to mark out with beacons; *(piste de ski)* to mark out; *Ordinat* to tag

balivernes [balivern] *nfpl* twaddle

Balkans [balkɑ̃] *nmpl* **les B.** the Balkans

ballant, -e [balɑ̃, -ɑ̃t] *adj (bras, jambes)* dangling

ballast [balast] *nm (de route, de voie ferrée)* ballast

balle [bal] *nf (pour jouer)* ball; *(d'arme)* bullet; **b. de tennis** tennis ball; **b. perdue** stray bullet

ballet [balɛ] *nm* ballet **■ ballerine** *nf (danseuse)* ballerina; *(chaussure)* pump

ballon [balɔ̃] *nm (balle, dirigeable)* balloon; *(verre)* round wine glass; **jouer au b.** to play with a ball; **b. de football** *Br* football, *Am* soccer ball

ballonné [balɔne] *adj m (ventre, personne)* bloated

ballottage [balɔtaʒ] *nm Pol* **il y a b.** there will be a second ballot

ballotter [balɔte] *vt (bateau)* to toss about; *(passagers)* to shake about

balluchon [balyʃɔ̃] *nm* bundle; **faire son b.** to pack one's bags

balnéaire [balneɛr] *adj* **station b.** *Br* seaside resort, *Am* beach resort

balourd, -e [balur, -urd] *adj* oafish

balte [balt] *adj* **les États baltes** the Baltic states

Baltique [baltik] *nf* **la (mer) B.** the Baltic (Sea)

baluchon [balyʃɔ̃] *nm* = **balluchon**

balustrade [balystrad] *nf (de pont)*

railing; *(de balcon)* balustrade

bambou [bãbu] *nm* bamboo

ban [bã] *nm (applaudissements)* round of applause; **bans** *(de mariage)* banns

banal, -e, -als, -ales [banal] *adj (objet, gens)* ordinary; *(idée)* trite, banal; **pas b.** unusual ■ **banalité** *nf (d'objet, de gens)* ordinariness; *(d'idée)* triteness

banaliser [banalize] *vt (rendre commun)* to trivialize

banane [banan] *nf (fruit)* banana; *(coiffure)* quiff ■ **bananier** *nm (arbre)* banana tree

banc [bã] *nm (siège)* bench; *(établi)* (work-)bench; *(de poissons)* shoal; **b. des accusés** dock; **b. d'essai** *Ind* test bed; *Fig* testing ground; **b. de sable** sandbank

bancaire [bãker] *adj (opération)* banking; *(chèque, compte)* bank

bancal, -e, -als, -ales [bãkal] *adj (meuble)* wobbly; *Fig (raisonnement)* unsound

bandage [bãdaʒ] *nm (pansement)* bandage

bande [bãd] *nf* (a) *(de tissu, de papier, de terre)* strip; *(pansement)* bandage; *(pellicule)* film; **b. magnétique** tape; *Aut* **b. d'arrêt d'urgence** *Br* hard shoulder, *Am* shoulder; **b. dessinée** comic strip; **b. sonore** soundtrack (b) *(de personnes)* band, group; *(de voleurs)* gang; *(de loups)* pack; **faire b. à part** *(agir seul)* to do one's own thing ■ **bande-annonce** *(pl* **bandes-annonces)** *nf* trailer (de for) ■ **bande-son** *(pl* **bandes-son)** *nf* soundtrack

bandeau, -x [bãdo] *nm (pour cheveux)* headband; *(sur les yeux)* blindfold

bander [bãde] *vt (blessure, main)* to bandage; *(arc)* to bend; **b. les yeux à qn** to blindfold sb

banderole [bãdrɔl] *nf (de manifestants)* banner; *(publicitaire)* streamer

bandit [bãdi] *nm (escroc)* crook

bandoulière [bãduljer] *nf (de sac)* shoulder strap; **en b.** slung across the shoulder

banlieue [bãljø] *nf* suburbs; **la b. parisienne** the suburbs of Paris; **de b.**

(maison, magasin) suburban; **train de b.** commuter train ■ **banlieusard, -e** *nmf (habitant)* suburbanite; *(voyageur)* commuter

bannière [banjer] *nf* banner; **la b. étoilée** the Star-Spangled Banner

bannir [banir] *vt (personne, idée)* to banish (**de** from)

banque [bãk] *nf (établissement)* bank; **la b.** *(activité)* banking; **employé de b.** bank clerk; *Ordinat* **b. de données** data bank

banqueroute [bãkrut] *nf* bankruptcy; **faire b.** to go bankrupt

banquet [bãke] *nm* banquet

banquette [bãket] *nf (siège)* (bench) seat

banquier, -ère [bãkje, -er] *nmf* banker

banquise [bãkiz] *nf* ice floe

baptême [batem] *nm* christening, baptism ■ **baptiser** *vt* to christen, to baptize

baquet [bake] *nm (cuve)* tub

bar¹ [bar] *nm (café, comptoir)* bar

bar² [bar] *nm (poisson)* bass

baraque [barak] *nf (cabane)* hut, shack; *(de foire)* stall ■ **baraquement** *nm* shacks; *Mil* camp

baratin [baratɛ̃] *nm Fam (verbiage)* waffle; *(de séducteur)* sweet talk; *(de vendeur)* sales talk ■ **baratiner** *vt Fam* to chatter; *(sujet: séducteur) Br* to chat up, *Am* to hit on

barbare [barbar] **1** *adj (cruel, sauvage)* barbaric **2** *nmf* barbarian ■ **barbarie** *nf (cruauté)* barbarity

barbe [barb] *nf* beard; **b. à papa** *Br* candyfloss, *Am* cotton candy

barbecue [barbəkju] *nm* barbecue

barbelés [barbəle] *nmpl* barbed wire

barber [barbe] *Fam* **1** *vt* **b. qn** to bore sb stiff **2 se barber** *vpr* to be bored stiff

barbiche [barbiʃ] *nf* goatee

barbiturique [barbityrik] *nm* barbiturate

barboter [barbɔte] *vi* to splash about ■ **barboteuse** *nf* rompers

barbouiller [barbuje] *vt (salir)* to smear (**de** with)

barbu, -e [barby] **1** *adj* bearded **2** *nm* bearded man

barder¹ [barde] *vt Culin* to bard; *Fig* **bardé de décorations** covered with decorations

barder² [barde] *v impersonnel Fam* **ça va b.!** there's going to be trouble!

barème [barɛm] *nm (de notes, de salaires, de prix)* scale; *(pour calculer)* ready reckoner

baril [baril] *nm (de pétrole, de vin)* barrel; *(de lessive)* drum

bariolé, -e [barjɔle] *adj Br* multicoloured, *Am* multi-colored

barjo(t) [barʒo] *adj inv Fam (fou)* crazy

barman [barman] *(pl* **-men** [-men] *ou* **-mans)** *nm Br* barman, *Am* bartender

baromètre [barɔmɛtr] *nm* barometer

baron [barɔ̃] *nm* baron; *Fig* **b. de la finance** financial tycoon ▪ **baronne** *nf* baroness

baroque [barɔk] **1** *adj (édifice, style, musique)* baroque **2** *nm Archit & Mus* **le b.** the baroque

baroudeur [barudœr] *nm Fam (combattant)* fighter; *(voyageur)* keen traveller

barque [bark] *nf* (small) boat ▪ **barquette** *nf (de fruit)* punnet; *(de plat cuisiné)* container

barrage [baraʒ] *nm (sur l'eau)* dam; **b. de police** police roadblock; **b. routier** roadblock

barre [bar] *nf (de fer, de bois)* bar; *(de danse)* barre; *(trait)* line, stroke; *Naut (volant)* helm; **b. chocolatée** chocolate bar; *Mus* **b. de mesure** bar (line); *Jur* **b. des témoins** *Br* witness box, *Am* witness stand; **b. d'appui** *(de fenêtre)* rail; **b. d'espacement** *(de clavier)* space bar; *Ordinat* **b. d'outils** tool bar; *Ordinat* **b. de sélection** menu bar

barreau, -x [baro] *nm (de fenêtre, de cage)* bar; *(d'échelle)* rung; *Jur* **le b.** the bar; **être derrière les barreaux** *(en prison)* to be behind bars

barrer [bare] **1** *vt (voie)* to block off; *(porte)* to bar; *(chèque)* to cross; *(mot)* to cross out; *Naut (bateau)* to steer; **b. le passage** *ou* **la route à qn** to bar sb's way; **'route barrée'** 'road closed' **2 se barrer** *vpr Fam* to beat it

barrette [barɛt] *nf (pour cheveux) Br* (hair)slide, *Am* barrette

barricade [barikad] *nf* barricade ▪ **barricader 1** *vt (rue, porte)* to barricade **2 se barricader** *vpr* to barricade oneself (**dans** in)

barrière [barjɛr] *nf (obstacle)* barrier; *(de passage à niveau)* gate; *(clôture)* fence

barrique [barik] *nf* (large) barrel

barrir [barir] *vi (éléphant)* to trumpet

baryton [baritɔ̃] *nm Mus* baritone

BAS¹, BASSE¹ [ba, bas] **1** *adj (dans l'espace, en quantité, en intensité) & Mus* low; *(origine)* lowly; *Féj (acte)* mean, low; **à b. prix** cheaply; **enfant en b. âge** young child; **avoir la vue basse** to be short-sighted

2 *adv (dans l'espace)* low (down); *(dans une hiérarchie)* low; *(parler)* quietly; **plus b.** further or lower down; **voir plus b.** *(sur document)* see below; **en b.** at the bottom; **en b. de** at the bottom of; **à b. les dictateurs!** down with dictators!

3 *nm (partie inférieure)* bottom; **l'étagère du b.** the bottom shelf; **au b. de** at the bottom of; **de b. en haut** upwards

bas² [ba] *nm (chaussette)* stocking; *Fig* **b. de laine** *(économies)* nest egg

basané, -e [bazane] *adj (bronzé)* tanned

bas-côté [bakote] *(pl* **bas-côtés)** *nm (de route)* verge; *(d'église)* (side)aisle

bascule [baskyl] *nf (balançoire)* seesaw; *(balance)* weighing machine; **fauteuil à b.** rocking chair ▪ **basculer 1** *vt (chargement)* to tip over; *(benne)* to tip up **2** *vi (tomber)* to topple over; **faire b.** *(personne)* to knock over; *(chargement)* to tip over

base [baz] *nf (partie inférieure) & Chim, Math & Mil* base; *(de parti politique)* rank and file; *(principe)* basis; **avoir de bonnes bases en anglais** to have

a good grounding in English; **de b.** basic; **salaire de b.** basic pay; *Ordinat* **b. de données** database ■ **baser 1** *vt* to base (**sur** on) **2 se baser** *vpr* **se b. sur qch** to base oneself on sth

bas-fond [bafɔ̃] (*pl* **bas-fonds**) *nm* *(de mer, de rivière)* shallow; *Péj* **les bas-fonds** *(de ville)* the rough areas

basic [bazik] *nm Ordinat* BASIC

basilic [bazilik] *nm (plante, aromate)* basil

basilique [bazilik] *nf* basilica

basket-ball [baskɛtbol] *nm* basketball

baskets [baskɛt] *nmpl ou nfpl (chaussures)* baseball boots

basque¹ [bask] **1** *adj* Basque **2** *nmf* **B.** Basque

basque² [bask] *nfpl (de veste)* tail; *Fig* **être toujours pendu aux basques de qn** to be always at sb's heels

basse² [bas] **1** *voir* **bas¹ 2** *nf Mus (contrebasse)* (double) bass; *(guitare)* bass (guitar)

basse-cour [baskur] (*pl* **basses-cours**) *nf Br* farmyard, *Am* barnyard

bassesse [basɛs] *nf (d'action)* lowness; *(action)* low act

bassin [basɛ̃] *nm* (a) *(pièce d'eau)* ornamental lake; *(de fontaine)* basin; *(récipient)* bowl, basin; **petit b.** *(de piscine)* children's pool; **grand b.** *(de piscine)* large pool (b) *(du corps)* pelvis (c) *(région)* basin; **le b. parisien** the Paris Basin ■ **bassine** *nf* bowl

basson [basɔ̃] *nm (instrument)* bassoon; *(musicien)* bassoonist

bastion [bastjɔ̃] *nm aussi Fig* bastion

bas-ventre [bavɑ̃tr] *nm* lower abdomen

bat [ba] *voir* **battre**

bataille [bataj] *nf (lutte)* battle; *(jeu de cartes)* ≃ beggar-my-neighbour ■ **batailleur, -euse** *adj* aggressive

bataillon [batajɔ̃] *nm Mil* batallion

bâtard, -e [batar, -ard] **1** *adj (enfant)* illegitimate; *(solution)* hybrid **2** *nmf (enfant)* illegitimate child; *Péj* bastard; *(chien)* mongrel; *(pain)* = small, thick baguette

bateau, -x [bato] **1** *nm (embarcation)* boat; *(grand)* ship; **faire du b.** to go boating; **b. à moteur** motorboat; **b. à voiles** *Br* sailing boat, *Am* sailboat; **b. de plaisance** pleasure boat **2** *adj inv Fam (sujet)* hackneyed; **col b.** boat neck ■ **bateau-mouche** (*pl* **bateaux-mouches**) *nm* river boat *(on the Seine)*

bâtiment [batimɑ̃] *nm (édifice)* building; *(navire)* vessel; **le b., l'industrie du b.** the building trade

bâtir [batir] *vt (construire)* to build; *Couture* to tack; **terrain à b.** building plot ■ **bâti, -e 1** *adj* **bien b.** *(personne)* well-built **2** *nm (charpente)* frame; *Couture* tacking ■ **bâtisse** *nf Péj* ugly building

bâton [batɔ̃] *nm (canne)* stick; *(de maréchal)* baton; *(d'agent de police) Br* truncheon, *Am* nightstick; *(trait)* vertical line; **donner des coups de b. à qn** to beat sb (with a stick); **b. de rouge** lipstick; **bâtons de ski** ski sticks ■ **bâtonnet** *nm* stick

battant¹ [batɑ̃] *nm* (a) *(de porte, de volet)* leaf; **porte à deux battants** double door (b) *(personne)* fighter

battant², -e [batɑ̃, -ɑ̃t] *adj* **pluie b.** driving rain; **porte b.** *Br* swing door, *Am* swinging door

battement [batmɑ̃] *nm* (a) *(de tambour)* beat(ing); *(de porte)* banging; *(de paupières)* blink(ing); *(d'ailes)* flapping (b) *(délai)* gap

batterie [batri] *nf (d'orchestre)* drums; *(ensemble) & Mil, Él* battery; *(de questions)* series; **être à la b.** *(sujet: musicien)* to be on drums; **élevage en b.** battery farming; **b. de cuisine** kitchen utensils

batteur [batœr] *nm (musicien)* drummer; *(de cuisine)* mixer

battre* [batr] **1** *vt (frapper, vaincre)* to beat; *(œufs)* to whisk; *(beurre)* to churn; *(record)* to break; *(cartes)* to shuffle; *Mus* **b. la mesure** to beat time **2** *vi (cœur)* to beat; *(porte, volet)* to bang; **b. des mains** to clap one's hands; **b. des ailes** to flap its wings **3 se battre** *vpr* to fight (**avec** with); **se b. au couteau** to fight with a knife

battu, -e¹ [baty] *adj (femme, enfant)* battered

battue² [baty] *nf (à la chasse)* beat; *(recherche)* search

baume [bom] *nm aussi Fig* balm

baux [bo] *voir* **bail**

bavard, -e [bavar, -ard] **1** *adj (qui parle beaucoup)* chatty **2** *nmf (qui parle beaucoup)* chatterbox ▪ **bavardage** *nm (action)* chatting; *(commérage)* gossiping; **bavardages** *(paroles)* chats ▪ **bavarder** *vi (parler)* to chat; *(commérer)* to gossip

bave [bav] *nf (de personne)* dribble; *(de chien)* slaver; *(de chien enragé)* froth ▪ **baver** *vi (personne)* to dribble; *(chien)* to slaver; *(chien enragé)* to foam at the mouth; *(stylo)* to leak; *Fam* **en b.** to have a hard time of it

bavette [bavɛt] *nf (de bébé)* bib; *(de bœuf)* skirt (of beef)

baveux, -euse [bavø, -øz] *adj (omelette)* runny

bavoir [bavwar] *nm* bib

bavure [bavyr] *nf (tache)* smudge; *(erreur)* slip-up

bayer [baje] *vi* **b. aux corneilles** to stare into space

bazar [bazar] *nm (marché)* bazaar; *(magasin)* general store; *(désordre)* shambles *(sing)*; *Fam (affaires)* gear; *Fam* **mettre du b. dans qch** to make a shambles of sth

BCG [beseʒe] *nm Méd* BCG

BD [bede] *(abrév* **bande dessinée**) *nf* comic strip

bd *abrév* **boulevard**

béant, -e [beã, -ãt] *adj (gouffre)* yawning

béat, -e [bea, -at] *adj Hum (heureux)* blissful; *Péj (niais)* inane; **être b. d'admiration** to be open-mouthed in admiration ▪ **béatement** *adv (sourire)* inanely

beau, belle [bo, bɛl] *(pl* **beaux, belles**)

> **bel** is used before masculine singular nouns beginning with a vowel or h mute.

1 *adj* (**a**) *(femme, enfant, fleur, histoire)* beautiful; *(homme)* handsome, good-looking; *(spectacle, discours)* fine; *(maison, voyage, temps)* lovely; **une belle somme** a tidy sum; **se faire b.** to smarten oneself up; **c'est trop b. pour être vrai** it's too good to be true; **c'est le plus b. jour de ma vie!** it's the best day of my life!

(**b**) *(expressions)* **au b. milieu de** right in the middle of; **bel et bien** *(complètement)* well and truly

2 *adv* **il fait b.** the weather's nice; **j'ai b. crier...** it's no use (my) shouting...

3 *nm* **le b.** *(la beauté)* beauty

4 *nf* **belle** *(jeu, partie)* decider ▪ **beau-fils** *(pl* **beaux-fils**) *nm (gendre)* son-in-law; *(après remariage)* stepson ▪ **beau-frère** *(pl* **beaux-frères**) *nm* brother-in-law ▪ **beau-père** *(pl* **beaux-pères**) *nm (père du conjoint)* father-in-law; *(après remariage)* stepfather ▪ **beaux-arts** *nmpl* fine arts; **école des b., les B.** art school ▪ **beaux-enfants** *nmpl (conjoint des enfants)* children-in-law; *(après remariage)* stepchildren ▪ **beaux-parents** *nmpl* parents-in-law

beaucoup [boku] *adv (intensément, en grande quantité)* a lot; **aimer b. qch** to like sth very much; **s'intéresser b. à qch** to be very interested in sth; **b. d'entre nous** many of us; **b. de** *(quantité)* a lot of; *(nombre)* many, a lot of; **pas b. d'argent** not much money; **pas b. de gens** not many people; **j'en ai b.** *(quantité)* I have a lot; *(nombre)* I have lots; **b. plus/moins (que)** much more/less (than), a lot more/less (than); *(nombre)* many or a lot more/a lot fewer (than)

beauté [bote] *nf (qualité, femme)* beauty

bébé [bebe] *nm* baby ▪ **bébé-éprouvette** *(pl* **bébés-éprouvette**) *nm* test-tube baby

bec [bɛk] *nm (d'oiseau)* beak, bill; *(de pot)* lip; *(de flûte)* mouthpiece; *Fam (bouche)* mouth; *Fam* **clouer le b. à qn** to shut sb up; **b. verseur** spout ▪ **bec-de-lièvre** *(pl* **becs-de-lièvre**) *nm* harelip

bêche [bɛʃ] *nf* spade ▪ **bêcher** *vt* to dig

bedonnant, -e [bədɔnɑ̃, -ɑ̃t] *adj* pot-bellied, paunchy

bée [be] *adj f* **j'en suis resté bouche b.** I was speechless

beffroi [befrwa] *nm* belfry

bégayer [begeje] *vi* to stutter, to stammer

bègue [bɛg] **1** *adj* **être b.** to stutter, to stammer **2** *nmf* stutterer, stammerer

beige [bɛʒ] *adj & nm* beige

beignet [bɛɲe] *nm* fritter; *(au sucre, à la confiture)* doughnut

Beijing [beidʒiŋ] *nm ou f* Beijing

bel [bɛl] *voir* **beau**

bêler [bɛle] *vi* to bleat

belette [bəlɛt] *nf* weasel

Belgique [bɛlʒik] *nf* **la B.** Belgium ▪ **belge 1** *adj* Belgian **2** *nmf* **B.** Belgian

bélier [belje] *nm (animal, machine)* ram; **le B.** *(signe)* Aries

belle [bɛl] *voir* **beau** ▪ **belle-famille** *(pl* **belles-familles)** *nf* in-laws ▪ **belle-fille** *(pl* **belles-filles)** *nf (épouse du fils)* daughter-in-law; *(après remariage)* stepdaughter ▪ **belle-mère** *(pl* **belles-mères)** *nf (mère du conjoint)* mother-in-law; *(après remariage)* stepmother ▪ **belle-sœur** *(pl* **belles-sœurs)** *nf* sister-in-law

belvédère [belvedɛr] *nm (construction)* gazebo; *(sur site naturel)* viewpoint

bémol [bemɔl] *nm Mus* flat

bénédiction [benediksjɔ̃] *nf Rel & Fig* blessing

bénéfice [benefis] *nm (financier)* profit; *(avantage)* benefit; **accorder le b. du doute à qn** to give sb the benefit of the doubt

bénéficiaire [benefisjɛr] **1** *nmf (de chèque)* payee; *Jur* beneficiary **2** *adj (entreprise)* profit-making; *(compte)* in credit

bénéficier [benefisje] *vi* **b. de qch** *(profiter de)* to benefit from sth; *(avoir)* to have sth

bénéfique [benefik] *adj* beneficial (**à** to)

Bénélux [benelyks] *nm* **le B.** the Benelux

bénévolat [benevɔla] *nm* voluntary work

bénévole [benevɔl] **1** *adj (travail, infirmière)* voluntary **2** *nmf* volunteer, voluntary worker

bénin, -igne [benɛ̃, -iɲ] *adj (accident, opération)* minor; *(tumeur)* benign

bénir [benir] *vt* to bless; **que Dieu te bénisse!** God bless you! ▪ **bénit, -e** *adj* **eau bénite** holy water

benne [bɛn] *nf (de camion)* tipping body; *(de téléphérique)* cable car; **b. à ordures** bin lorry

BEP [beape] *(abrév* **brevet d'études professionnelles)** *nm Scol* = vocational diploma taken at 18

BEPC [beapese] *(abrév* **brevet d'études du premier cycle)** *nm Scol* = former school leaving certificate taken at 15

béquille [bekij] *nf (canne)* crutch; *(de moto)* stand

berceau, -x [bɛrso] *nm (de bébé)* cradle; *Fig (de civilisation)* birthplace

bercer [bɛrse] **1** *vt (bébé)* to rock **2 se bercer** *vpr* **se b. d'illusions** to delude oneself ▪ **berceuse** *nf* lullaby

béret [bere] *nm* beret

berge [bɛrʒ] *nf (rive)* bank

berger [bɛrʒe] *nm* shepherd; **b. allemand** German shepherd, *Br* Alsatian ▪ **bergère** *nf* shepherdess

berline [bɛrlin] *nf (voiture) Br* (four-door) saloon, *Am* sedan

berlingot [bɛrlɛ̃go] *nm (bonbon) Br* boiled sweet, *Am* hard candy; *(de lait)* carton

bermuda [bɛrmyda] *nm* Bermuda shorts

Bermudes [bɛrmyd] *nfpl* **les B.** Bermuda

berner [bɛrne] *vt* to fool

besogne [bəzɔɲ] *nf* job, task; *Fig* **aller vite en b.** to jump the gun

besoin [bəzwɛ̃] *nm* need; **avoir b. de qn/qch** to need sb/sth; **avoir b. de faire qch** to need to do sth; **au b., si**

b. est if necessary, if need be

bestial, -e, -aux, -ales [bɛstjal, -o] *adj* bestial ■ **bestiaux** *nmpl* livestock

bestiole [bɛstjɔl] *nf (insecte) Br* creepy-crawly, *Am* creepy-crawler

bétail [betaj] *nm* livestock

bête¹ [bɛt] *adj* stupid, silly

bête² [bɛt] *nf* animal; *(insecte)* bug; **b. féroce** wild animal; **b. noire** *Br* pet hate, *Am* pet peeve ■ **bêtement** *adv* stupidly; **tout b.** quite simply ■ **bêtise** *nf (manque d'intelligence)* stupidity; *(action, parole)* stupid thing; **faire une b.** to do something stupid; **dire des bêtises** to talk nonsense

béton [betɔ̃] *nm (matériau)* concrete; **mur en b.** concrete wall

bette [bɛt] *nf* Swiss chard

betterave [bɛtrav] *nf (plante) Br* beetroot, *Am* beet; **b. sucrière** sugar beet

beur [bœr] *nmf* = North African born in France of immigrant parents

beurre [bœr] *nm* butter ■ **beurrer** *vt* to butter

bévue [bevy] *nf* slip-up

biais [bjɛ] *nm (de mur)* slant; *(moyen)* way; *(aspect)* angle; **regarder qn de b.** to look sideways at sb; **par le b. de** through

biaiser [bjeze] *vi (ruser)* to dodge the issue

bibelot [biblo] *nm* small ornament

biberon [bibrɔ̃] *nm (feeding)* bottle; **nourrir un bébé au b.** to bottle-feed a baby

bible [bibl] *nf* bible; **la B.** the Bible ■ **biblique** *adj* biblical

bibliographie [biblijɔgrafi] *nf* bibliography

bibliothèque [biblijɔtɛk] *nf (bâtiment, salle)* library; *(meuble)* bookcase; **b. municipale** public library ■ **bibliothécaire** *nmf* librarian

Bic® [bik] *nm* ballpoint, *Br* biro®

bicarbonate [bikarbɔnat] *nm Chim* bicarbonate; **b. de soude** bicarbonate of soda

biceps [bisɛps] *nm* biceps

biche [biʃ] *nf (animal)* doe, hind

bicolore [bikɔlɔr] *adj* two-coloured

bicyclette [bisiklɛt] *nf* bicycle; **faire de la b.** to go cycling

bidet [bidɛ] *nm (cuvette)* bidet

bidon [bidɔ̃] **1** *nm (d'essence, d'huile)* can; *(de lait)* churn; **b. d'essence** petrol can, jerry can **2** *adj inv Fam (simulé)* phoney, fake

bidonville [bidɔ̃vil] *nf* shantytown

bidule [bidyl] *nm Fam (chose)* whatsit; **B.** *(personne)* what's-his-name, *f* what's-her-name

BIEN [bjɛ̃] **1** *adv* (a) *(convenablement)* well; **il joue b.** he plays well; **je vais b.** I'm fine *or* well; **écoutez-moi b.!** listen carefully

(b) *(moralement)* right; **b. se conduire** to behave (well); **vous avez b. fait** you did the right thing; **tu ferais b. de te méfier** you would be wise to behave

(c) *(très)* very

(d) *(beaucoup)* a lot, a great deal; **b. plus/moins** much more/less; **b. des gens** a lot of people; **b. des fois** many times; **tu as b. de la chance** you're really lucky!; **merci b.!** thanks very much!

(e) *(en intensif)* **regarder qn b. en face** to look sb right in the face; **je sais b.** I'm well aware of it; **je vous l'avais b. dit** I told you so!; **nous verrons b.!** we'll see!; **c'est b. fait pour lui** it serves him right; **c'est b. ce que je pensais** that's what I thought

(f) *(locutions)* **b. que...** (+ *subjunctive)* although; **b. entendu, b. sûr** of course; **b. sûr que non!** of course, not!; **b. sûr que je viendrai!** of course, I'll come!

2 *adj inv (satisfaisant)* good; *(à l'aise)* comfortable; *(en forme)* well; *(moral)* decent; *(beau)* attractive; **être b. avec qn** *(en bons termes)* to be on good terms with sb; **on est b. ici** it's nice here; **ce n'est pas b. de mentir** it's not nice to lie; **elle est b. sur cette photo** she looks good on this photo

3 *exclam* fine!, right!; **eh b.!** well!

4 *nm Phil & Rel* good; *(chose, capital)* possession; *Jur* asset; **le b. et le mal** good and evil; *Jur* **biens** property;

faire le b. to do good; **ça te fera du b.** it will do you good; **dire du b. de qn** to speak well of sb; **c'est pour ton b.** it's for your own good; **biens de consommation** consumer goods; **biens immobiliers** real estate or property ■ **bien-aimé, -e** (mpl **bien-aimés**, fpl **bien-aimées**) adj & nmf beloved ■ **bien-être** nm well-being

bienfaisance [bjɛ̃fəzɑ̃s] nf œuvre de b. charity

bienfaisant, -e [bjɛ̃fəzɑ̃, -ɑ̃t] adj (remède) beneficial; (personne) charitable

bienfait [bjɛ̃fɛ] nm (acte) kindness; (avantage) benefit

bienfaiteur, -trice [bjɛ̃fɛtœr, -tris] nmf benefactor, f benefactress

bien-fondé [bjɛ̃fɔ̃de] nm validity

bienheureux, -euse [bjɛ̃nœrø, -øz] adj blissful; Rel blessed

bienséance [bjɛ̃seɑ̃s] nf propriety

bientôt [bjɛ̃to] adv soon; **à b.!** see you soon!

bienveillant, -e [bjɛ̃vɛjɑ̃, -ɑ̃t] adj kind ■ **bienveillance** nf kindness

bienvenu, -e[1] [bjɛ̃vny] **1** adj (repos, explication) welcome **2** nmf **soyez le b.!** welcome!

bienvenue[2] [bjɛ̃vny] nf welcome; **souhaiter la b. à qn** to welcome sb

bière[1] [bjɛr] nf (boisson) beer; **b. blonde** lager; **b. brune** Br brown ale, Am dark beer; **b. pression** Br draught beer, Am draft beer

bière[2] [bjɛr] nf (cercueil) coffin

biffer [bife] vt to cross out

bifteck [biftɛk] nm steak; **b. haché** Br mince, Am mincemeat

bifurquer [bifyrke] vi (route, chemin) to fork; (automobiliste) to turn off ■ **bifurcation** nf fork

bigamie [bigami] nf bigamy

bigarré, -e [bigare] adj (étoffe) multicoloured; (foule) motley

bigorneau, -x [bigorno] nm winkle

bigoudi [bigudi] nm (hair) curler or roller

bijou, -x [biʒu] nm jewel; Fig gem ■ **bijouterie** nf (boutique) Br jeweller's shop, Am jewelry shop; (commerce, fabrication) jeweller's trade ■ **bijoutier, -ère** nmf Br jeweller, Am jeweler

bilan [bilɑ̃] nm (de situation) assessment; (résultats) results; (d'un accident) toll; Com **déposer son b.** to file for bankruptcy; Fin **b. (comptable)** balance sheet; **b. de santé** complete check-up

bilatéral, -e, -aux, -ales [bilateral, -o] adj bilateral

bile [bil] nf bile

bilingue [bilɛ̃g] adj bilingual

billard [bijar] nm (jeu) billiards; (table) billiard table; **b. américain** pool; **b. électrique** pinball

bille [bij] nf (de verre) marble; (de billard) billiard ball

billet [bijɛ] nm ticket; **b. (de banque)** Br (bank)note, Am bill; **b. d'avion/de train** plane/train ticket; **b. de première/seconde** first-class/second-class ticket; **b. simple** single ticket, Am one-way ticket; **b. aller retour** return ticket, Am round trip ticket

billetterie [bijɛtri] nf (lieu) ticket office; **b. automatique** (de billet de transport) ticket machine

billion [biljɔ̃] nm trillion

bimensuel, -elle [bimɑ̃sɥɛl] adj bimonthly, Br fortnightly

bimoteur [bimɔtœr] adj twin-engined

binaire [binɛr] adj Math binary

biner [bine] vt to hoe

binocle [binɔkl] nm pince-nez

biochimie [bjoʃimi] nf biochemistry

biodégradable [bjodegradabl] adj biodegradable

biodiversité [bjodivɛrsite] nf biodiversity

biographie [bjografi] nf biography ■ **biographique** adj biographical

bio-industrie [bjoɛ̃dystri] (pl **bio-industries**) nf biotechnology industry

biologie [bjɔlɔʒi] nf biology ■ **biologique** adj biological; (sans engrais chimiques) organic; **les produits biologiques** organic products ■ **biologiste** nmf biologist

biotechnologie [bjɔtɛknɔlɔʒi] *nf* biotechnology

bip [bip] *nm (son)* beep; *(appareil)* beeper

bipède [biped] *nm* biped

Birmanie [birmani] *nf* la B. Burma ▪ **birman, -e 1** *adj* Burmese **2** *nmf* **B., Birmane** Burmese

bis¹ [bis] *adv (au théâtre)* encore; *(en musique)* repeat; **4 bis** *(adresse)* ≃ 4A

bis², bise¹ [bi, biz] *adj Br* greyish-brown, *Am* grayish-brown

biscornu, -e [biskɔrny] *adj (objet)* oddly shaped; *Fam (idée)* cranky

biscotte [biskɔt] *nf* rusk

biscuit [biskɥi] *nm Br* biscuit, *Am* cookie

bise² [biz] *nf (vent)* north wind

bise³ [biz] *nf Fam (baiser)* kiss; **faire la b. à qn** to kiss sb on both cheeks

bisexuel, -elle [bisɛksɥɛl] *adj* bisexual

bison [bizɔ̃] *nm* bison

bisou [bizu] *nm Fam* kiss

bissextile [bisɛkstil] *adj f* **année b.** leap year

bistro(t) [bistro] *nm Fam* bar

bitume [bitym] *nm (revêtement)* asphalt

bizarre [bizar] *adj* odd

blafard, -e [blafar, -ard] *adj* pallid

blague [blag] *nf (plaisanterie)* joke; **faire une b. à qn** to play a joke on sb

blaguer [blage] *vi Fam* to joke ▪ **blagueur, -euse** *nmf Fam* joker

blaireau, -x [blɛro] *nm (animal)* badger; *(brosse)* shaving brush

blâme [blam] *nm (reproche)* blame; *(sanction)* reprimand ▪ **blâmer** *vt (désapprouver)* to blame; *(sanctionner)* to reprimand

blanc, blanche [blɑ̃, blɑ̃ʃ] **1** *adj* white; *(peau)* pale; *(page)* blank **2** *nm (couleur)* white; *(espace)* blank; *(vin)* white wine; **(article de) b.** *(linge)* linen; **en b.** *(chèque)* blank; **tirer à b.** to fire blanks; **b. d'œuf** egg white; **b. de poulet** chicken breast **3** *nf (note de musique) Br* minim, *Am* half-note

4 *nmf* **B.** *(personne)* White man, *f* White woman; **les B.** the Whites ▪ **blanchâtre** *adj* whitish ▪ **blancheur** *nf* whiteness

blanchiment [blɑ̃ʃimɑ̃] *nm (d'argent)* laundering

blanchir [blɑ̃ʃir] **1** *vt (to whiten; (mur)* to whitewash; *(linge)* to launder; *Culin* to blanch; *Fig (argent)* to launder; **b. qn** *(disculper)* to clear sb **2** *vi* to turn white ▪ **blanchisserie** *nf (lieu)* laundry ▪ **blanchisseur, -euse** *nmf* laundryman, *f* laundrywoman

blanquette [blɑ̃kɛt] *nf* **b. ce veau** = blanquette of veal; **b. de Limoux** = sparkling white wine from Limoux

blasé, -e [blaze] *adj* blasé

blason [blazɔ̃] *nm* coat of arms

blasphème [blasfɛm] *nm* blasphemy ▪ **blasphémer** *vi* to blaspheme

blatte [blat] *nf* cockroach

blazer [blazœr] *nm* blazer

bld *(abrév* **boulevard)** Blvd

blé [ble] *nm* wheat, *Br* corn

blême [blɛm] *adj* sickly pale; **b. de colère** livid ▪ **blêmir** *vi* to turn pale

blesser [blese] **1** *vt (dans un accident)* to injure, to hurt; *(par arme)* to wound; *(offenser)* to hurt **2 se blesser** *vpr (par accident)* to hurt or injure oneself; *(avec une arme)* to wound oneself; **se b. au bras** to hurt one's arm ▪ **blessant, -e** *adj* hurtful ▪ **blessé, -e** *nmf (victime d'accident)* injured person; *(victime d'agression)* wounded person; **les blessés** the injured/wounded ▪ **blessure** *nf (dans un accident)* injury; *(par arme)* wound

blette [blɛt] *nf* = **bette**

bleu, -e [blø] *(mpl* **-s) 1** *adj* blue; *(steak)* very rare **2** *n (couleur)* blue; *(ecchymose)* bruise; *(fromage)* blue cheese; *Fam (novice)* novice; **b de travail** *Br* overalls, *Am* overall; **b. ciel** sky blue; **b. marine** navy blue; **b. roi** royal blue

bleuet [bløɛ] *nm (plante)* cornflower

blinder [blɛ̃de] *vt (véhicule) Br* to armour-plate, *Am* to armor-plate

■ **blindé, -e 1** *adj Mil Br* armoured, armour-plated, *Am* armored, armorplated; *(voiture)* bulletproof **2** *nm Mil Br* armoured *or Am* armored vehicle

bloc [blɔk] *nm (de pierre, de bois)* block; *(de papier)* pad; *(de maison) & Pol* bloc; **en b.** *(démissionner)* all together; **à b.** *(visser, serrer)* as tightly as possible; **b. opératoire** operating theatre ■ **bloc-notes** *(pl blocs-notes) nm* notepad

blocage [blɔkaʒ] *nm (de mécanisme)* jamming; *(de freins, de roues)* locking

blocus [blɔkys] *nm* blockade; **lever le b.** to raise the blockade

blond, -e [blɔ̃, -ɔ̃d] **1** *adj (cheveux, personne)* blond; *(sable)* golden **2** *nm (homme)* fair-haired *or* blond man; *(couleur)* blond; **b. cendré** ash blond; **b. vénitien** strawberry blond **3** *nf (femme)* fair-haired woman, blonde ■ **blondeur** *nf* fairness, blondness

bloquer [blɔke] **1** *vt (route, ballon, compte)* to block; *(porte, mécanisme)* to jam; *(roue)* to lock; *(salaires, prix, crédits)* to freeze; *(grouper)* to group together; **b. le passage à qn** to block sb's way; **bloqué par la neige** snowbound **2 se bloquer** *vpr (machine)* to get stuck

blottir [blɔtir] **se blottir** *vpr* to snuggle up; **se b. contre qn** to snuggle up to sb

blouse [bluz] *nf (tablier)* overall; *(corsage)* blouse; **b. blanche** *(de médecin, de biologiste)* white coat ■ **blouson** *nm* short jacket; **b. en cuir** leather jacket; **b. d'aviateur** bomber jacket

bluff [blœf] *nm* bluff ■ **bluffer** *vi (aux cartes) & Fam* to bluff

boa [bɔa] *nm (serpent, tour de cou)* boa

bobard [bɔbar] *nm Fam* tall story

bobine [bɔbin] *nf (de ruban, de fil)* reel; *(de machine à coudre)* bobbin; *(de film, de papier)* roll; *(de machine à écrire)* spool; *Él* coil

bocal, -aux [bɔkal, -o] *nm* jar; *(aquarium)* bowl

bœuf [bœf] *(pl* **bœufs** [bø]) *nm (animal)* bullock; *(de trait)* ox *(pl* oxen); *(viande)* beef

bogue [bɔg] *nm Ordinat* bug

bohème [bɔɛm] *adj & nmf* bohemian ■ **bohémien, -enne** *adj & nmf* gypsy

boire* [bwar] **1** *vt (sujet: personne)* to drink; *(sujet: plante)* to soak up **2** *vi (sujet: personne)* to drink; *(sujet: plante)* to soak in; *Fam* **b. un coup** to have a drink **3 se boire** *vpr* to be drunk **4** *nm* **le b. et le manger** food and drink

bois [bwa] *nm (matériau, forêt)* wood; *(de raquette)* frame; **en** *ou* **de b.** wooden; **les b.** *(d'un cerf)* the antlers; *(d'un orchestre)* woodwind instruments; **b. de chauffage** firewood; **b. de construction** timber ■ **boisé, -e** *adj* wooded ■ **boiseries** *nfpl Br* panelling, *Am* paneling

boisson [bwasɔ̃] *nf* drink

boit [bwa] *voir* **boire**

boîte [bwat] *nf* (a) *(récipient)* box; **b. d'allumettes** *(pleine)* box of matches; *(vide)* matchbox; **des haricots en b.** canned *or Br* tinned beans; **b. à bijoux** jewel box; **b. à gants** glove compartment; **b. à** *ou* **aux lettres** *Br* postbox, *Am* mailbox; *Ordinat* **b. à lettres électronique** mailbox; **b. de conserve** can, *Br* tin; *Aut* **b. de vitesses** gearbox; **b. postale** Post Office Box; *Ordinat* **b. de réception** inbox; **b. vocale** voice mail **(b)** *Fam (entreprise)* firm; **b. de nuit** nightclub ■ **boîtier** *nm (de montre)* case

boiter [bwate] *vi* to limp ■ **boiteux, -euse** *adj (personne)* lame; *Fig (raisonnement)* shaky

boive [bwav] *subjonctif de* **boire**

bol [bɔl] *nm (récipient, contenu)* bowl

bolide [bɔlid] *nm (voiture)* racing car

Bolivie [bɔlivi] *nf* **la B.** Bolivia ■ **bolivien, -enne 1** *adj* Bolivian **2** *nmf* **B., Bolivienne** Bolivian

bombardement [bɔ̃bardəmɑ̃] *nm (avec des bombes)* bombing; *(avec des obus)* shelling

bombarder [bɔ̃barde] *vt (avec des bombes)* to bomb; *(avec des obus)* to shell; **b. qn de questions** to bombard

sb with questions ■ **bombardier** *nm*
(avion) bomber

bombe [bɔ̃b] *nf* (**a**) *(explosif)* bomb;
Fig **faire l'effet d'une b.** to be a
bombshell (**b**) *(atomiseur)* spray (can)
(**c**) *(chapeau)* riding hat

bomber [bɔ̃be] **1** *vt* **b. le torse** to
throw out one's chest **2** *vi (mur)* to
bulge; *(planche)* to warp

BON¹, BONNE¹ [bɔ̃, bɔn] **1** *adj* (**a**)
(satisfaisant) good; **c'est b.** *(d'accord)*
that's fine

(**b**) *(agréable)* nice, good; **passer une
bonne soirée** to spend a pleasant
evening; **b. anniversaire!** happy
birthday!; **bonne année!** Happy New
Year!

(**c**) *(charitable)* kind, good (**avec qn** to
sb)

(**d**) *(correct)* right

(**e**) *(apte)* fit; **b. à manger** fit to eat;
elle n'est bonne à rien she's useless

(**f**) *(prudent)* wise, good; **juger b. de
partir** to think it wise to leave

(**g**) *(compétent)* good; **b. en français**
good at French

(**h**) *(profitable)* *(investissement, con-
seil, idée)* good; **c'est b. à savoir** it's
worth knowing

(**i**) *(valable)* valid

(**j**) *(en intensif)* **un b. rhume** a bad
cold; **dix bonnes minutes** a good ten
minutes; **j'ai mis un b. moment à
comprendre** it took me a while to un-
derstand

(**k**) *(locutions)* **à quoi b.?** what's the
point?; **quand b. vous semble** when-
ever you like; **pour de b.** *(partir, re-
venir)* for good; **tenir b.** *(personne)* to
hold out; **elle est bien bonne!** that's a
good one!

2 *nm* avoir du b. to have some good
points; **un b. à rien** a good-for-noth-
ing; **les bons et les méchants** the
goodies and the baddies

3 *adv* **sentir b.** to smell good; **il fait b.**
it's nice and warm

4 *exclam* **b.! on y va?** right, shall we
go?; **ah b., je ne le savais pas** really? I
didn't know; **ah b.?** is that so?

bon² [bɔ̃] *nm (papier)* coupon, *Br* vou-

cher; *Fin (titre)* bond; **b. d'achat** gift
voucher; **b. de réduction** money-off
coupon

bonbon [bɔ̃bɔ̃] *nm Br* sweet, *Am* can-
dy

bonbonne [bɔ̃bɔn] *nf (bouteille)*
demijohn; *(de gaz)* cylinder

bond [bɔ̃] *nm* leap, jump; *(de balle)*
bounce; **faire un b.** to leap up; **se lever
d'un b.** *(du lit)* to jump out of bed;
(d'une chaise) to leap up; **faire faux b.
à qn** to leave sb in the lurch

bonde [bɔ̃d] *nf (bouchon)* plug; *(trou)*
plughole

bondé, -e [bɔ̃de] *adj* packed,
crammed

bondir [bɔ̃dir] *vi* to leap, to jump; **b.
sur qn/qch** to pounce on sb/sth

bonheur [bɔnœr] *nm (bien-être)* hap-
piness; *(chance)* good fortune; **porter
b. à qn** to bring sb luck; **par b.** luckily

bonhomie [bɔnɔmi] *nf* good-natu-
redness

bonhomme [bɔnɔm] (*pl* **bons-
hommes** [bɔ̃zɔm]) *nm* fellow, guy; **b.
de neige** snowman

bonjour [bɔ̃ʒur] *nm & exclam (le ma-
tin)* hello, good morning; *(l'après-midi)*
hello, good afternoon

bonne¹ [bɔn] *voir* **bon¹**

bonne² [bɔn] *nf (domestique)* maid; **b.
d'enfants** nanny

bonnement [bɔnmɑ̃] *adv* **tout b.**
simply

bonnet [bɔnɛ] *nm (coiffure)* hat; *(de
soutien-gorge)* cup; *Fam* **gros b.** big-
shot; **b. de bain** bathing cap ■ **bonne-
terie** *nf (bas)* hosiery

bonniche [bɔniʃ] *nf* = **boniche**

bonsoir [bɔ̃swar] *nm & exclam (en ren-
contrant quelqu'un)* hello, good even-
ing; *(en partant)* goodbye; *(au coucher)*
goodnight

bonté [bɔ̃te] *nf* kindness, goodness

bonus [bɔnys] *nm (de salaire)* bonus;
(d'assurance) no-claims bonus

bord [bɔr] *nm (limite)* edge; *(de cha-
peau)* brim; *(de verre)* rim; **le b. du
trottoir** *Br* the kerb, *Am* the curb; **au**

b. de la route at the side of the road; **au b. de la rivière** beside the river; **au b. de la mer** at the seaside; **au b. des larmes** on the verge of tears; **à b. d'un bateau/d'un avion** on board a boat/a plane; **monter à b.** to go on board; **par-dessus b.** overboard

bordeaux [bɔrdo] **1** *nm (vin)* Bordeaux (wine); *(rouge)* claret **2** *adj inv* burgundy

bordée [bɔrde] *nf Naut (salve)* broadside; *Fig (d'injures)* torrent

border [bɔrde] *vt (lit)* to tuck in; *(sujet: arbres)* to line

bordereau, -x [bɔrdəro] *nm Fin & Com* note

bordure [bɔrdyr] *nf (bord)* edge; *(de vêtement)* border; **en b. de route** by the roadside

borgne [bɔrɲ] *adj (personne)* one-eyed

borne [bɔrn] *nf (limite)* boundary marker; *(pierre)* boundary stone; *Él* terminal; *Fam (kilomètre)* kilometer; *Fig* **sans bornes** boundless; *Fig* **dépasser les bornes** to go too far

borné, -e [bɔrne] *adj (personne)* narrow-minded; *(esprit)* narrow

borner [bɔrne] **1** *vt (terrain)* to mark out **2 se borner** *vpr* **se b. à qch/à faire qch** *(personne)* to restrict oneself to sth/to doing sth; **se b. à qch** *(chose)* to be limited to sth

Bosnie [bɔzni] *nf* **la B.** Bosnia

bosquet [bɔskɛ] *nm* grove

bosse [bɔs] *nf (de bossu, de chameau)* hump; *(enflure)* bump, lump; *(de terrain)* bump

bosseler [bɔsle] *vt (déformer)* to dent

bosser [bɔse] *vi Fam* to work

bosseur, -euse [bɔsœr, -øz] *nmf Fam* hard-worker

bossu, -e [bɔsy] **1** *adj (personne)* hunchbacked **2** *nmf* hunchback

botanique [bɔtanik] **1** *adj* botanical **2** *nf* botany

botte [bɔt] *nf (chaussure)* boot; *(de fleurs, de radis)* bunch; **bottes en caoutchouc** rubber boots ▪ **botter** *vt* **botté de cuir** wearing leather boots;

Fam **b. le derrière à qn** to boot sb up the backside ▪ **bottillon** *nm*, **bottine** *nf* ankle boot

Bottin® [bɔtɛ̃] *nm* phone book

bouc [buk] *nm (animal)* billy goat; *(barbe)* goatee; **b. émissaire** scapegoat

boucan [bukɑ̃] *nm Fam* din, row; **faire du b.** to kick up a row

bouche [buʃ] *nf* mouth; **b. à oreille** by word of mouth; **b. d'égout** manhole; **b. d'incendie** *Br* fire hydrant, *Am* fireplug ▪ **bouchée** *nf* mouthful ▪ **bouche-à-bouche** *nm* mouth-to-mouth resuscitation

boucher¹ [buʃe] **1** *vt (fente, trou)* to fill in; *(conduite, fenêtre)* to block up; *(vue, rue, artère)* to block; *(bouteille)* to cork **2 se boucher** *vpr (conduite)* to get blocked up; **se b. le nez** to hold one's nose ▪ **bouché, -e** *adj (conduite)* blocked; *Fam (personne)* dense; **j'ai le nez b.** my nose is stuffed up ▪ **bouche-trou** *(pl* **bouche-trous)** *nm Fam* stopgap

boucher², -ère [buʃe, -ɛr] *nmf* butcher ▪ **boucherie** *nf* butcher's (shop); *Fig (carnage)* slaughter

bouchon [buʃɔ̃] *nm* **(a)** *(à vis)* cap, top; *(de tonneau)* stopper; *(de liège)* cork; *(de canne à pêche)* float **(b)** *(embouteillage)* traffic jam ▪ **bouchonner** *vt Fam* **ça bouchonne** *(sur la route)* there's congestion

boucle [bukl] *nf (de ceinture)* buckle; *(de cheveu)* curl; *(méandre)* loop; **b. d'oreille** earring

boucler [bukle] **1** *vt (ceinture, valise)* to buckle; *(quartier)* to seal off; **b. ses valises** *(se préparer à partir)* to pack one's bags **2** *vi (cheveux)* to be curly ▪ **bouclé, -e** *adj (cheveux)* curly

bouclier [buklije] *nm* shield

bouddhiste [budist] *adj & nmf* Buddhist

bouder [bude] **1** *vi* to sulk **2** *vt (personne)* to refuse to talk to; **b. une élection** to refuse to vote ▪ **boudeur, -euse** *adj* sulky

boudin [budɛ̃] *nm* **b. noir** *Br* black

pudding, *Am* blood sausage; **b. blanc** white pudding

boue [bu] *nf* mud ■ **boueux, -euse** *adj* muddy

bouée [bwe] *nf Naut* buoy; **b. de sauvetage** lifebelt; **b. (gonflable)** *(d'enfant)* (inflatable) rubber ring

bouffe [buf] *nf Fam (nourriture)* grub

bouffée [bufe] *nf (de fumée)* puff; *(de parfum)* whiff; *Fig (de colère)* outburst; *Méd* **b. de chaleur** *Br* hot flush, *Am* hot flash

bouffer[1] [bufe] *vti Fam (manger)* to eat

bouffer[2] [bufe] *vi (manche, jupe)* to puff out ■ **bouffi, -e** *adj (yeux, visage)* puffy

bouffon, -onne [bufɔ̃, -ɔn] **1** *adj* farcical **2** *nm* buffoon ■ **bouffonneries** *nfpl (actes)* antics

bougeoir [buʒwar] *nm* candlestick

bougeotte [buʒɔt] *nf Fam* **avoir la b.** to be fidgety

bouger [buʒe] **1** *vti* to move; **rester sans b.** to keep still **2 se bouger** *vpr Fam (se déplacer)* to move; *(s'activer)* to get a move on

bougie [buʒi] *nf (en cire)* candle; *(de moteur)* spark plug

bougonner [bugɔne] *vi Fam* to grumble

bouillabaisse [bujabɛs] *nf* bouillabaisse, = Provençal fish soup

bouilli, -e[1] [buji] *adj* boiled

bouillie[2] [buji] *nf (pour bébé)* baby food; *(à base de céréales)* baby cereal

bouillir* [bujir] *vi* to boil; **faire b. qch** to boil sth; **b. de colère** to be seething (with anger) ■ **bouillant, -e** *adj (qui bout)* boiling; *(très chaud)* boiling hot

bouilloire [bujwar] *nf* kettle

bouillon [bujɔ̃] *nm (aliment)* stock; *(bulles)* bubbles ■ **bouillonner** *vi* to bubble

bouillotte [bujɔt] *nf* hot-water bottle

boulanger, -ère [bulɑ̃ʒe, -ɛr] *nmf* baker ■ **boulangerie** *nf* baker's (shop)

boule [bul] *nf (sphère)* ball; **boules** *(jeu)* bowls; **b. de neige** snowball; *Fig*

faire b. de neige to snowball; **boules Quiès®** earplugs

bouledogue [buldɔg] *nm* bulldog

boulet [bulɛ] *nm (de forçat)* ball and chain; **b. de canon** cannonball

boulette [bulɛt] *nf (de papier)* ball; *(de viande)* meatball

boulevard [bulvar] *nm* boulevard

bouleverser [bulverse] *vt (émouvoir)* to move deeply; *(perturber)* to distress; *(projets, habitudes)* to disrupt; *(vie)* to turn upside down ■ **bouleversant, -e** *adj (émouvant)* deeply moving, *(perturbant)* distressing

boulimie [bulimi] *nf Méd* bulimia ■ **boulimique** *adj* **être b.** to have bulimia

boulon [bulɔ̃] *nm* bolt

boulot[1] [bulo] *nm Fam (emploi)* job; *(travail)* work

boulot[2]**, -otte** [bulo, -ɔt] *adj Fam* tubby

bouquet [bukɛ] *nm (fleurs)* bunch of flowers; *(d'arbres)* clump; *(de vin)* bouquet; *Fig* **c'est le b.!** that takes the *Br* biscuit *or Am* cake!

bouquin [bukɛ̃] *nm Fam* book ■ **bouquiner** *vti Fam* to read ■ **bouquiniste** *nmf* second-hand bookseller

bourbier [burbje] *nm (lieu, situation)* quagmire

bourde [burd] *nf Fam (gaffe)* blunder; **faire une b.** to put one's foot in it

bourdon [burdɔ̃] *nm (insecte)* bumblebee ■ **bourdonnement** *nm (d'insecte)* buzz(ing) ■ **bourdonner** *vi (insecte, oreilles)* to buzz

bourg [bur] *nm* market town ■ **bourgade** *nf* village

bourgeois, -e [burʒwa, -waz] **1** *adj* middle-class **2** *nmf* middle-class person ■ **bourgeoisie** *nf* middle class

bourgeon [burʒɔ̃] *nm* bud ■ **bourgeonner** *vi* to bud

bourgogne [burgɔɲ] *nm (vin)* Burgundy

bourrage [buraʒ] *nm Fam* **b. de crâne** brainwashing

bourrasque [burask] *nf* squall, gust of wind

bourratif, -ive [buratif, -iv] *adj Fam* stodgy

bourre [bur] *nf (pour rembourrer)* stuffing

bourreau, -x [buro] *nm* executioner; **b. de travail** workaholic

bourrelet [burlɛ] *nm (contre les courants d'air)* weather strip; **b. de graisse** spare *Br* tyre *or Am* tire

bourrer [bure] **1** *vt (coussin)* to stuff (**de** with); *(sac)* to cram (**de** with); *(pipe)* to fill; **b. qn de qch** *(gaver)* to fill sb up with sth **2 se bourrer** *vpr* **se b. de qch** *(se gaver)* to stuff oneself up with ▪ **bourré, -e** *adj* (a) *(plein)* **b. à craquer** full to bursting (b) *Fam (ivre)* plastered

bourrique [burik] *nf* she-ass; *Fam* **faire tourner qn en b.** to drive sb crazy

bourru, -e [bury] *adj* surly

bourse [burs] *nf (sac)* purse; *Scol. & Univ* **b. (d'étude)** grant; **la B.** the Stock Exchange ▪ **boursier, -ère 1** *adj* **opération boursière** Stock Exchange transaction **2** *nmf (élève, étudiant)* grant holder

boursouflé, -e [bursufle] *adj (visage, yeux)* puffy

bous [bu] *voir* **bouillir**

bousculer [buskyle] **1** *vt (pousser)* to jostle; *(presser)* to rush; *Fig (habitudes)* to disrupt **2 se bousculer** *(foule)* to push and shove ▪ **bousculade** *nf (agitation)* pushing and shoving

bousiller [buzije] *vt Fam* to wreck

boussole [busɔl] *nf* compass

bout¹ [bu] *voir* **bouillir**

bout² [bu] *nm (extrémité)* end; *(de langue, de doigt)* tip; *(morceau)* bit; **faire un b. de chemin** to go part of the way; **d'un b. à l'autre** from one end to the other; **au b. de la rue** at the end of the street; **au b. d'un moment** after a while; *Fam* **au b. du fil** *(au téléphone)* on the other end; **jusqu'au b.** *(lire, rester)* (right) to the end; **à b. de forces** exhausted; **à b. de souffle** out of breath; **pousser qn à b.** to push sb too far

boutade [butad] *nf (plaisanterie)* quip

boute-en-train [butɑ̃trɛ̃] *nm inv (personne)* live wire

bouteille [butɛj] *nf* bottle; *(de gaz)* cylinder

boutique [butik] *nf Br* shop, *Am* store; *(de couturier)* boutique; **fermer b.** to shut up shop ▪ **boutiquier, -ère** *nmf Br* shopkeeper, *Am* storekeeper

bouton [butɔ̃] *nm (bourgeon)* bud; *(au visage)* spot; *(de vêtement)* button; *(de porte, de télévision)* knob; **b. de manchette** cufflink ▪ **bouton-d'or** *(pl* **boutons-d'or)** *nm* buttercup ▪ **boutonner** *vt*, **se boutonner** *vpr (vêtement)* to button (up) ▪ **boutonnière** *nf* buttonhole

bouture [butyr] *nf* cutting

bovins [bɔvɛ̃] *nmpl* cattle

bowling [boliŋ] *nm (jeu) Br* tenpin bowling, *Am* tenpins; *(lieu)* bowling alley

box [bɔks] *(pl* **boxes)** *nm (d'écurie)* stall; *(de dortoir)* cubicle; *(garage)* lockup garage; *Jur* **b. des accusés** dock

boxe [bɔks] *nf* boxing ▪ **boxer** *vi* to box ▪ **boxeur** *nm* boxer

boyau, -x [bwajo] *nm (intestin)* gut; *(corde)* catgut; *(de vélo)* tubular *Br* tyre *or Am* tire; *(de mine)* narrow gallery

boycotter [bɔjkɔte] *vt* to boycott ▪ **boycottage** *nm* boycott

BP [bepe] *(abrév* **boîte postale)** *nf* PO Box

bracelet [braslɛ] *nm (bijou)* bracelet; *(rigide)* bangle; *(de montre) Br* strap, *Am* band ▪ **bracelet-montre** *(pl* **bracelets-montres)** *nm* wristwatch

braconner [brakɔne] *vi* to poach ▪ **braconnier** *nm* poacher

brader [brade] *vt* to sell off cheaply ▪ **braderie** *nf* clearance sale

braguette [bragɛt] *nf (de pantalon)* fly, *Br* flies

braille [braj] *nm* Braille; **en b.** in Braille

brailler [braje] *vti* to yell

braire* [brɛr] *vi (âne)* to bray

braises [brɛz] *nfpl* embers ▪ **braiser** *vt Culin* to braise

brancard [brɑ̃kar] *nm (civière)* stretcher; *(de charrette)* shaft

branche [brɑ̃ʃ] *nf (d'arbre, de science)* branch; *(de lunettes)* side piece ■ **branchages** *nmpl (des arbres)* branches; *(coupés)* cut branches

brancher [brɑ̃ʃe] **1** *vt (à une prise)* to plug in; *(à un réseau)* to connect **2 se brancher** *vpr* **se b. sur** *(station de radio)* to tune in to ■ **branchement** *nm (fils)* connection

brandir [brɑ̃dir] *vt* to brandish

branle [brɑ̃l] *nm* **mettre qch en b.** *(mécanisme, procédure)* to set sth in motion ■ **branlant, -e** *adj (chaise, escalier)* rickety ■ **branler** *vi (chaise, escalier)* to be rickety

braquer [brake] **1** *vt (diriger)* to point **(sur** at); *(regard)* to fix **(sur** on); *Fam (banque)* to hold up; **b. qn contre qn/qch** to turn sb against sb/sth **2** *vi Aut* to turn the steering wheel

braquet [brakɛ] *nm* gear ratio

bras [bra] *nm* arm; **b. dessus b. dessous** arm in arm; **les b. croisés** with one's arms folded; *Fig* **b. droit** *(assistant)* right-hand man

brasier [brazje] *nm* blaze, inferno

brassard [brasar] *nm* armband

brasse [bras] *nf (nage)* breaststroke; *(mouvement)* stroke; **b. papillon** butterfly stroke

brassée [brase] *nf* armful

brasser [brase] *vt (mélanger)* to mix; *(bière)* to brew ■ **brassage** *nm (mélange)* mixing; *(de la bière)* brewing

brasserie [brasri] *nf (usine)* brewery; *(café)* brasserie

brassière [brasjɛr] *nf (de bébé) Br* vest, *Am* undershirt

bravade [bravad] *nf* bravado

brave [brav] **1** *adj (courageux)* brave; *(bon)* good **2** *nm (héros)* brave man

braver [brave] *vt (personne)* to defy; *(danger)* to brave

bravo [bravo] *exclam* bravo!

bravoure [bravur] *nf* bravery

break [brek] *nm (voiture) Br* estate car, *Am* station wagon

brebis [brəbi] *nf* ewe; *Fig* **b. galeuse** black sheep

brèche [brɛʃ] *nf* gap; *(dans la coque d'un bateau)* hole

bréchet [breʃɛ] *nm* breastbone

bredouille [brəduj] *adj* empty-handed

bredouiller [brəduje] *vti* to mumble

bref, brève [brɛf, brɛv] **1** *adj* brief, short **2** *adv* in short; **enfin b....** in a word...

Brésil [brezil] *nm* **le B.** Brazil ■ **brésilien, -enne 1** *adj* Brazilian **2** *nmf* **B., Brésilienne** Brazilian

Bretagne [brətaɲ] *nf* **la B.** Brittany ■ **breton, -onne 1** *adj* Breton **2** *nmf* **B., Bretonne** Breton

bretelle [brətɛl] *nf* strap; **bretelles** *(de pantalon) Br* braces, *Am* suspenders; **b. (d'accès)** *(route)* access road

breuvage [brœvaʒ] *nm* potion

brève [brɛv] *voir* **bref**

brevet [brəvɛ] *nm (certificat)* certificate; *(diplôme)* diploma; *Scol* **b. des collèges** = exam taken at 14; **b. de technicien supérieur** = advanced vocational training certificate; **b. (d'invention)** patent ■ **breveter** *vt* to patent

bric-à-brac [brikabrak] *nm inv (vieux objets)* odds and ends

bricole [brikɔl] *nf (objet, futilité)* trifle

bricoler [brikɔle] **1** *vt (construire)* to put together; *(réparer)* to fix **2** *vi* to do-it-yourself ■ **bricolage** *nm (travail)* DIY, do-it-yourself; **faire du b.** to do some DIY ■ **bricoleur, -euse 1** *adj* **être b.** to be good with one's hands **2** *nmf* handyman, *f* handywoman

bride [brid] *nf (de cheval)* bridle ■ **brider** *vt (cheval)* to bridle; *(personne, désir)* to curb; **avoir les yeux bridés** to have slanting eyes

bridge [bridʒ] *nm (jeu, prothèse)* bridge

brièvement [brijɛvmɑ̃] *adv* briefly ■ **brièveté** *nf* brevity

brigade [brigad] *nf (de gendarmerie)* squad; *Mil* brigade ■ **brigadier** *nm (de*

police) police sergeant; *Mil* corporal

brigand [brigɑ̃] *nm (bandit)* brigand

briguer [brige] *vt (honneur, poste)* to sollicit

brillant, -e [brijɑ̃, -ɑ̃t] **1** *adj (luisant)* shining; *(couleur)* bright; *(cheveux, cuir)* shiny; *Fig (remarquable)* brilliant **2** *nm (éclat)* shine; *(diamant)* diamond; **b. à lèvres** lip gloss ▪ **brillamment** [-amɑ̃] *adv* brilliantly

briller [brije] *vi* to shine; **le soleil brille** the sun's shining; **faire b. qch** to polish sth

brimer [brime] *vt* to bully ▪ **brimades** *nfpl (vexations)* bullying

brin [brɛ̃] *nm (d'herbe)* blade; *(de muguet)* spray; *(de fil)* strand; *Fig* **un b. de qch** a bit of sth; **faire un b. de toilette** to have a quick wash

brindille [brɛ̃dij] *nf* twig

bringue¹ [brɛ̃g] *nf Fam* **faire la b.** to go on a binge

bringue² [brɛ̃g] *nf Fam* **grande b.** *(fille)* beanpole

brio [brijo] *nm* brilliance

brioche [brijɔʃ] *nf* brioche ▪ **brioché** *adj* **pain b.** = milk bread

brique [brik] *nf (de construction)* brick; **mur de briques** brick wall

briquer [brike] *vt (nettoyer)* to scrub down

briquet [brikɛ] *nm (cigarette)* lighter

bris [bri] *nm (de verre)* breaking; **b. de glaces** broken windows

brise [briz] *nf* breeze

briser [brize] **1** *vt* to break; *(opposition, résistance)* to crush; *(espoir, carrière)* to wreck; *(fatiguer)* to exhaust **2 se briser** *vpr* to break ▪ **brise-glace** *nm inv (navire)* ice breaker ▪ **brise-lames** *nm inv* breakwater

britannique [britanik] **1** *adj* British **2** *nmf* **B.** Briton; **les Britanniques** the British

broc [bro] *nm* pitcher, jug

brocante [brɔkɑ̃t] *nf (commerce)* second-hand trade ▪ **brocanteur** *nm* second-hand dealer

broche [brɔʃ] *nf (pour rôtir)* spit; *(bi-*

jou) brooch; *(pour fracture)* pin; **faire cuire qch à la b.** to spit-roast sth ▪ **brochette** *nf (tige)* skewer; *(plat)* kebab

broché, -e [brɔʃe] *adj* **livre b.** paperback

brochet [brɔʃɛ] *nm* pike

brochure [brɔʃyr] *nf* brochure, pamphlet

brocolis [brɔkɔli] *nmpl* broccoli

broder [brɔde] *vt* to embroider (**de** with) ▪ **broderie** *nf (activité)* embroidery

broncher [brɔ̃ʃe] *vi* **il n'a pas bronché** he didn't bat an eyelid

bronches [brɔ̃ʃ] *nfpl* bronchial tubes ▪ **bronchite** *nf* bronchitis; **avoir une b.** to have bronchitis

bronze [brɔ̃z] *nm* bronze

bronzer [brɔ̃ze] *vi* to tan ▪ **bronzage** *nm* (sun)tan

brosse [brɔs] *nf* brush; **donner un coup de b. à qch** to give sth a brush; **cheveux en b.** crew cut; **b. à dents** toothbrush ▪ **brosser 1** *vt (tapis, cheveux)* to brush; **b. un tableau de qch** to give an outline of sth **2 se brosser** *vpr* **se b. les dents/les cheveux** to brush one's teeth/one's hair

brouette [bruɛt] *nf* wheelbarrow

brouhaha [bruaa] *nm* hubbub

brouillard [brujar] *nm* fog; **il y a du b.** it's foggy

brouiller [bruje] **1** *vt (idées)* to muddle up; *(vue)* to blur; *(émission)* to jam **2 se brouiller** *vpr (vue)* to get blurred; *(se disputer)* to fall out (**avec** with) ▪ **brouillé, -e** *adj (teint)* blotchy; **être b. avec qn** to have fallen out with sb

brouillon, -onne [brujɔ̃, -ɔn] **1** *adj (mal organisé)* disorganized; *(mal présenté)* untidy **2** *nm* rough draft; **(papier) b.** *Br* scrap paper, *Am* scratch paper

broussailles [brusaj] *nfpl* scrub

brousse [brus] *nf* **la b.** the bush

brouter [brute] *vti* to graze

broyer [brwaje] *vt* to grind; *(doigt, bras)* to crush

bru [bry] *nf* daughter-in-law

brugnon [bryɲɔ̃] *nm* nectarine

bruine [brɥin] *nf* drizzle ■ **bruiner** *v impersonnel* to drizzle; **il bruine** it's drizzling

bruissement [brɥismɑ̃] *nm (de feuilles)* rustle, rustling

bruit [brɥi] *nm* noise, sound; *(nouvelle)* rumour; **faire du b.** to make a noise ■ **bruitage** *nm Cin* sound effects

brûlant, -e [brylɑ̃, -ɑ̃t] *adj (objet, soupe)* burning hot; *(soleil)* scorching; *Fig (sujet)* burning

brûlé, -e [bryle] *nm* odeur de b. burnt smell; **sentir le b.** to smell burnt

brûle-pourpoint [brylpurpwɛ̃] **à brûle-pourpoint** *adv* point-blank

brûler [bryle] **1** *vt (sujet: flamme, acide)* to burn; *(feu rouge)* to go through **2** *vi* to burn **3 se brûler** *vpr* to burn oneself; **se b. la langue** to burn one's tongue

brûlure [brylyr] *nf* burn

brume [brym] *nf* mist, haze ■ **brumeux, -euse** *adj* misty, hazy

brun, -e [brœ̃, bryn] **1** *adj (cheveux)* dark, brown; *(personne)* dark-haired; **être b. de peau** to be dark-skinned **2** *nm (couleur)* brown **3** *nmf* dark-haired man, *f* dark-haired woman ■ **brunette** *nf* brunette ■ **brunir** *vi (personne, peau)* to tan; *(cheveux)* to darken

brushing® [brœʃiŋ] *nm* blow-dry; **faire un b. à qn** to blow-dry sb's hair

brusque [brysk] *adj* abrupt ■ **brusquement** [-əmɑ̃] *adv* abruptly ■ **brusquer** *vt (décision)* to rush ■ **brusquerie** *nf* abruptness

brut, -e [bryt] *adj (pétrole)* crude; *(diamant)* rough; *(poids, salaire)* gross; *(champagne)* extra-dry; **à l'état b.** in its raw state

brutal, -e, -aux, -ales [brytal, -o] *adj (personnes, manières, paroles)* brutal; *(franchise, réponse)* crude, blunt; *(changement)* abrupt; **être b. avec qn** to be rough with sb ■ **brutalement** *adv (violemment)* brutally; *(avec brusquerie)* bluntly; *(soudainement)* abrupt-ly ■ **brutaliser** *vt* to ill-treat ■ **brutalité** *nf (violence, acte)* brutality; *(soudaineté)* abruptness ■ **brute** *nf* brute

Bruxelles [brysɛl] *nm ou f* Brussels

bruyant, -e [brɥijɑ̃, -ɑ̃t] *adj* noisy ■ **bruyamment** [-amɑ̃] *adv* noisily

bruyère [brɥijɛr] *nf (plante)* heather; *(terrain)* heath

BTS [beteɛs] *(abrév* **brevet de technicien supérieur)** *nm* = advanced vocational training certificate

bu, -e [by] *pp de* **boire**

buanderie [bɥɑ̃dri] *nf (lieu)* laundry

bûche [byʃ] *nf* log; **b. de Noël** Yule log ■ **bûcher** *nm (à bois)* woodshed; *(de supplice)* stake

bûcheron [byʃrɔ̃] *nm* woodcutter

bûcheur, -euse [byʃœr, -øz] *nmf Br* swot, *Am* grind

budget [bydʒɛ] *nm* budget ■ **budgétaire** *adj* budgetary; *(année)* financial

buée [bɥe] *nf (sur vitre)* condensation; *(sur miroir)* mist

buffet [byfɛ] *nm (meuble bas)* sideboard; *(meuble haut)* dresser; *(repas)* buffet

buffle [byfl] *nm* buffalo

buisson [bɥisɔ̃] *nm* bush

buissonnière [bɥisɔnjɛr] *adj f* **faire l'école b.** *Br* to play truant, *Am* to play hookey

bulbe [bylb] *nm* bulb

Bulgarie [bylgari] *nf* **la B.** Bulgaria ■ **bulgare 1** *adj* Bulgarian **2** *nmf* **B.** Bulgarian

bulldozer [byldozœr] *nm* bulldozer

bulle [byl] *nf (d'air, de savon)* bubble; *(de bande dessinée)* balloon; **faire des bulles** to blow bubbles

bulletin [byltɛ̃] *nm (communiqué, revue)* bulletin; **b. d'informations** news bulletin; **b. de paie** *ou* **de salaire** *Br* pay slip, *Am* pay stub; **b. de santé** medical bulletin; **b. de vote** ballot paper; **b. météo** weather report; **b. scolaire** *Br* school report, *Am* report card

bureau, -x [byro] *nm (table)* desk; *(lieu)* office; *(comité)* committee; **b. de change** bureau de change; **b. de poste**

post office; **b. de tabac** *Br* tobacconist's (shop), *Am* tobacco store

bureaucratie [byrokrasi] *nf* bureaucracy ▪ **bureaucratique** *adj* bureaucratic

Bureautique® [byrotik] *nf* office automation

burette [byrɛt] *nf (pour huile)* oilcan; *(de chimiste)* burette

burin [byrɛ̃] *nm (de graveur)* burin; *(pour découper)* (cold) chisel

buriné, -e [byrine] *adj (visage)* lined

burlesque [byrlɛsk] *adj (idée)* ludicrous; *(genre)* burlesque

bus¹ [bys] *nm* bus

bus² [by] *pt de* boire

buste [byst] *nm (torse)* chest; *(sculpture)* bust ▪ **bustier** *nm (corsage)* bustier

but¹ [by(t)] *nm (objectif)* aim, goal; *(intention)* purpose; *Sport* goal

but² [by] *pt de* boire

butane [bytan] *nm* butane

buter [byte] **1** *vt* **b. qn** to put sb's back up **2** *vi* **b. contre qch** *(cogner)* to bump into sth; *(trébucher)* to stumble over sth; *Fig (difficulté)* to come up against sth **3 se buter** *vpr (s'entêter)* to dig one's heels in ▪ **buté, -e** *adj* obstinate

butin [bytɛ̃] *nm (de voleur)* loot; *(de pillards)* spoils; *(d'armée)* booty

butoir [bytwar] *nm (pour train)* buffer; *(de porte)* stopper, *Br* stop

buvard [byvar] *nm* blotting paper

buvette [byvɛt] *nf* refreshment bar

buveur, -euse [byvœr, -øz] *nmf* drinker; **un grand b.** a heavy drinker

buviez [byvje] *voir* boire

Cc

C, c [se] *nm inv* C, c

c' [s] *voir* ce[2]

ÇA [sa] (*abrév* cela) *pron démonstratif* (*pour désigner*) that; (*plus près*) this; (*sujet indéfini*) it, that; **où/quand ça?** where?/when?; **ça dépend** it depends; **ça va?** how are things?; **ça va! fine!**, OK!; **c'est ça** that's right

çà [sa] **çà et là** *adv* here and there

cabane [kaban] *nf* (*baraque*) hut; (*en rondin*) cabin; (*de jardin*) shed; **c. à outils** tool shed

cabaret [kabarɛ] *nm* cabaret

cabillaud [kabijo] *nm* (*fresh*) cod

cabine [kabin] *nf* (*de bateau*) cabin; **c. d'essayage** fitting room; **c. de pilotage** cockpit; **c. téléphonique** phone box

cabinet [kabinɛ] *nm* (*de médecin*) *Br* surgery, *Am* office; (*d'avocat*) firm; (*de ministre*) departmental staff; **c. de toilette** (small) bathroom; *Fam* **les cabinets** *Br* the loo, *Am* the john

câble [kabl] *nm* cable; *TV* **le c.** cable ∎ **câbler** *vt TV* (*ville, quartier*) to install cable television

cabrer [kabre] **se cabrer** *vpr* (*cheval*) to rear (up)

cabriole [kabriɔl] *nf* (*saut*) caper; **faire des cabrioles** to caper about

cabriolet [kabriɔlɛ] *nm* (*auto*) convertible

cacah(o)uète [kakawɛt] *nf* peanut

cacao [kakao] *nm* (*poudre*) cocoa

cache [kaʃ] *nf* hiding place ∎ **cache-cache** *nm inv* **jouer à c.** to play hide and seek ∎ **cache-nez** *nm inv* scarf

cachemire [kaʃmir] *nm* (*laine*) cashmere

cacher [kaʃe] **1** *vt* to hide (à from) **2** **se cacher** *vpr* to hide

cachet [kaʃɛ] *nm* (*sceau*) seal; (*de fabrication*) stamp; (*comprimé*) tablet; (*d'acteur*) fee; (*originalité*) character; **c. de la poste** postmark ∎ **cacheter** *vt* to seal

cachette [kaʃɛt] *nf* hiding place; **en c.** in secret

cachot [kaʃo] *nm* dungeon

cachotteries [kaʃɔtri] *nfpl* **faire des cachotteries** to be secretive

cactus [kaktys] *nm* cactus

cadavre [kadavr] *nm* corpse ∎ **cadavérique** *adj* (*teint*) deathly pale

caddie® [kadi] *nm Br* trolley, *Am* cart

cadeau, -x [kado] *nm* present, gift; **faire un c. à qn** to give sb a present

cadenas [kadna] *nm* padlock

cadence [kadɑ̃s] *nf* (*taux, vitesse*) rate; (*de chanson*) rhythm

cadet, -ette [kade, -ɛt] **1** *adj* (*de deux*) younger; (*de plus de deux*) youngest **2** *nmf* (*de deux*) younger (one); (*de plus de deux*) youngest (one); *Sport* junior

cadran [kadrɑ̃] *nm* (*de téléphone*) dial; (*de montre*) face; **c. solaire** sundial

cadre [kadr] *nm* (a) (*de photo, de vélo*) frame; (*décor*) setting; **dans le c. de** within the framework of (b) (*d'entreprise*) executive; **les cadres** the management; *Mil* the officers

cadrer [kadre] **1** *vt* (*photo*) to centre **2** *vi* (*correspondre*) to tally (**avec** with)

caduc, caduque [kadyk] *adj* (*feuille*) deciduous

cafard [kafar] *nm* (*insecte*) cockroach

café [kafe] *nm* (*produit, boisson*) coffee; (*bar*) café; **c. au lait**, **c. crème** *Br* white coffee, *Am* coffee with milk; **c. noir** black coffee; **c. soluble** *ou* **instantané** instant coffee ∎ **caféine** *nf*

caffeine ■ **cafétéria** *nf* cafeteria ■ **cafetier** *nm* café owner ■ **cafetière** *nf* (*récipient*) coffeepot; (*électrique*) coffee machine

cage [kaʒ] *nf* (*d'oiseau, de zoo*) cage; (*d'ascenseur*) shaft; *Sport* goal; **c. d'escalier** stairwell

cageot [kaʒo] *nm* crate

cagneux [kaɲø] *adj* **avoir les genous c.** to have knock-knees

cagnotte [kaɲɔt] *nf* (*caisse commune*) kitty; (*de jeux*) pool

cagoule [kagul] *nf* (*de bandit*) hood; (*d'enfant*) *Br* balaclava, *Am* ski mask

cahier [kaje] *nm* notebook; (*d'écolier*) exercise book; **c. de brouillon** *Br* rough book, *Am* ≃ scratch pad; *Scol* **c. d'appel** register

cahin-caha [kaɛ̃kaa] *adv Fam* **aller c.** (*se déplacer*) to struggle along

caille [kaj] *nf* (*oiseau*) quail

cailler [kaje] *vi* (*lait*) to curdle ■ **caillot** *nm* (*de sang*) clot

caillou, -x [kaju] *nm* stone; (*sur la plage*) pebble

Caire [kɛr] *nm* **le C.** Cairo

caisse [kɛs] *nf* (a) (*boîte*) case; (*d'outils*) box; (*cageot*) crate (b) (*de magasin*) cash desk; (*de supermarché*) checkout; **c. d'épargne** savings bank; **c. enregistreuse** cash register

caissier, -ère [kesje, -ɛr] *nmf* cashier; (*de supermarché*) checkout operator

cajoler [kaʒɔle] *vt* to cuddle

cajou [kaʒu] *nm* **noix de c.** cashew nut

calamité [kalamite] *nf* (*fléau*) calamity; (*malheur*) great misfortune

calcaire [kalkɛr] **1** *adj* (*eau*) hard; (*terrain*) chalky **2** *nm Géol* limestone; (*dépôt*) fur

calciné, -e [kalsine] *adj* burnt to a cinder

calcium [kalsjɔm] *nm* calcium

calcul [kalkyl] *nm* (a) (*opérations, estimation*) calculation; *Scol* **le c.** arithmetic; **faire un c.** to make a calculation (b) *Méd* stone; **c. rénal** kidney stone

calculatrice [kalkylatris] *nf* **c. (de poche)** (pocket) calculator

calculer [kalkyle] *vt* (*prix, superficie*) to calculate; (*chances, conséquences*) to weigh (up)

calculette [kalkylɛt] *nf* (pocket) calculator

cale [kal] *nf* (a) (*de meuble, de porte*) wedge (b) (*de navire*) hold

caleçon [kalsɔ̃] *nm* boxer shorts

calembour [kalɑ̃bur] *nm* pun, play on words

calendrier [kalɑ̃drije] *nm* (*mois et jours*) calendar; (*programme*) timetable

calepin [kalpɛ̃] *nm* notebook

caler [kale] **1** *vt* (*meuble, porte*) to wedge; (*chargement*) to secure **2** *vi* (*moteur*) to stall **3** **se caler** *vpr* (*dans un fauteuil*) to settle oneself comfortably

calfeutrer [kalføtre] *vt* (*brèches*) to block up

calibre [kalibr] *nm* (*diamètre*) *Br* calibre, *Am* caliber; (*d'œuf, de fruit*) grade; (*outil*) gauge

Californie [kalifɔrni] *nf* **la C.** California

califourchon [kalifurʃɔ̃] **à califourchon** *adv* astride; **se mettre à c. sur qch** to sit astride sth

câlin, -e [kalɛ̃, -in] **1** *adj* affectionate **2** *nm* cuddle; **faire un c. à qn** to give sb a cuddle

calmant [kalmɑ̃] *nm* (*pour les nerfs*) sedative

calmar [kalmar] *nm* squid

calme [kalm] **1** *adj* (*flegmatique*) calm, cool; (*tranquille*) quiet; (*mer*) calm **2** *nm* calm(ness); **garder/perdre son c.** to keep/lose one's calm; **du c.!** (*taisez-vous*) keep quiet!; (*pas de panique*) keep calm!

calmer [kalme] **1** *vt* (*douleur*) to soothe; (*inquiétude*) to calm; (*faim*) to appease; **c. qn** to calm sb down **2** **se calmer** *vpr* (*personne*) to calm down; (*vent*) to die down; (*mer*) to become calm; (*douleur*) to subside

calomnie [kalɔmni] *nf* (*en paroles*) slander; (*par écrit*) libel ■ **calomnier** *vt* (*en paroles*) to slander; (*par écrit*) to libel ■ **calomnieux, -euse** *adj* (*paroles*)

slanderous; *(écrits)* libellous

calorie [kalɔri] *nf* calorie

calotte [kalɔt] *nf (chapeau rond)* skull-cap

calque [kalk] *nm (copie)* tracing; **(papier-)c.** tracing paper

calvaire [kalvɛr] *nm Rel* calvary; *Fig* ordeal

calvitie [kalvisi] *nf* baldness

camarade [kamarad] *nmf* friend; **c. de classe** classmate; **c. d'école** school friend; **c. de jeu** playmate ■ **camaraderie** *nf* camaraderie

Cambodge [kɑ̃bɔdʒ] *nm* **le C.** Cambodia

cambouis [kɑ̃bwi] *nm* dirty oil

cambrer [kɑ̃bre] **1** *vt* to arch **2 se cambrer** *vpr* to arch one's back ■ **cambrure** *nf (du pied, du dos)* arch

cambrioler [kɑ̃brijɔle] *vt Br* to burgle, *Am* to burglarize ■ **cambriolage** *nm* burglary. ■ **cambrioleur, -euse** *nmf* burglar

camée [kame] *nm* cameo

caméléon [kameleɔ̃] *nm* chameleon

camelot [kamlo] *nm* street peddler *or Br* hawker, *Am* huckster ■ **camelote** *nf (pacotille)* junk; *(marchandise)* stuff

camembert [kamɑ̃bɛr] *nm (fromage)* Camembert (cheese)

caméra [kamera] *nf* camera ■ **cameraman** *(pl* **-mans** *ou* **-men)** *nm* cameraman

Caméscope® [kameskɔp] *nm* camcorder

camion [kamjɔ̃] *nm Br* lorry, *Am* truck; **c. de déménagement** *Br* removal van, *Am* moving van ■ **camion-citerne** *(pl* **camions-citernes)** *nm Br* tanker, *Am* tank truck ■ **camionnette** *nf* van ■ **camionneur** *nm (conducteur) Br* lorry driver, *Am* truck driver; *(entrepreneur) Br* haulier, *Am* trucker

camomille [kamɔmij] *nf (plante)* camomile; *(tisane)* camomile tea

camoufler [kamufle] *vt Mil* to camouflage ■ **camouflage** *nm Mil* camouflage

camp [kɑ̃] *nm (campement)* camp; *(de parti, de jeu)* side; **c. de concentration** concentration camp; **c. de prisonniers** prison camp

campagne [kɑ̃paɲ] *nf* **(a)** *(par opposition à la ville)* country; *(paysage)* countryside; **à la c.** in the country; **en pleine c.** deep in the countryside **(b)** *Mil, Com & Pol* campaign; **c. de presse/publicité** press/publicity campaign ■ **campagnard, -e** *adj* country

camper [kɑ̃pe] **1** *vi* to camp **2** *vt (chapeau)* to plant **3 se camper** *vpr* to plant oneself **(devant** in front of) ■ **campeur, -euse** *nmf* camper

camping [kɑ̃piŋ] *nm (activité)* camping; *(terrain)* camp(ing) site; **faire du c.** to go camping; **c. sauvage** unauthorized camping ■ **camping-car** *(pl* **camping-cars)** *nm* camper; **partir en c.** to go on a camper holiday

campus [kɑ̃pys] *nm* campus

Canada [kanada] *nm* **le C.** Canada ■ **canadien, -enne 1** *adj* Canadian **2** *nmf* **C., Canadienne** Canadian

canal, -aux [kanal, -o] *nm (cours d'eau)* canal; *(conduite)* conduit; *Fig* channel

canaliser [kanalize] *vt (rivière, fleuve)* to canalize; *Fig (foule, énergie)* to channel ■ **canalisation** *nf (conduite)* pipe

canapé [kanape] *nm* **(a)** *(siège)* sofa, couch **(b)** *(pour l'apéritif)* canapé ■ **canapé-lit** *(pl* **canapés-lits)** *nm* sofa bed

canard [kanar] *nm* duck; *(mâle)* drake; *Fam (journal)* rag

canari [kanari] *nm* canary

cancaner [kɑ̃kane] *vi* to gossip

cancans [kɑ̃kɑ̃] *nmpl* gossip

cancer [kɑ̃sɛr] *nm (maladie)* cancer; **c. de l'estomac** stomach cancer; **avoir un c.** to have cancer; **le C.** *(signe)* Cancer ■ **cancéreux, -euse 1** *adj* cancerous **2** *nmf* cancer patient ■ **cancérigène** *adj* carcinogenic

candeur [kɑ̃dœr] *nf* guilelessness

candidat, -e [kɑ̃dida, -at] *nmf (d'examen, d'élection)* candidate **(à** for); *(de poste)* applicant **(à** for); **être c. aux élections** to stand for election ■ **candidature** *nf (à un poste)* application **(à**

for); *(aux élections)* candidature (à for); **poser** *ou* **envoyer sa c.** to apply (à for); **c. spontanée** unsolicited application

candide [kɑ̃did] *adj* guileless

cane [kan] *nf* (female) duck ■ **caneton** *nm* duckling

canette [kanɛt] *nf (boîte)* can

canevas [kanva] *nm (toile)* canvas

caniche [kaniʃ] *nm* poodle

canicule [kanikyl] *nf* heatwave

canif [kanif] *nm* penknife

canine [kanin] **1** *adj f (espèce, race)* canine **2** *nf (dent)* canine (tooth)

caniveau, -x [kanivo] *nm* gutter

canne [kan] *nf (tige)* cane; *(pour marcher)* (walking) stick; **c. à pêche** fishing rod; **c. à sucre** sugar cane

cannelle [kanɛl] *nf* cinnamon

cannette [kanɛt] *nf* = **canette**

cannibale [kanibal] *nmf* cannibal

canoë-kayak [kanɔekajak] *nm* canoeing

canon¹ [kanɔ̃] *nm* gun; *(ancien, à boulets)* cannon; *(de fusil)* barrel

canon² [kanɔ̃] *nm Rel & Fig (règle)* canon

canot [kano] *nm* boat; **c. de sauvetage** lifeboat; **c. pneumatique** rubber dinghy

cantatrice [kɑ̃tatris] *nf* opera singer

cantine [kɑ̃tin] *nf* **(a)** *(réfectoire)* canteen; *(d'école)* dining hall **(b)** *(coffre)* trunk

canton [kɑ̃tɔ̃] *nm (en France)* canton *(division of a department)*; *(en Suisse)* canton *(semi-autonomous region)*

cantonade [kɑ̃tɔnad] **à la cantonade** *adv* to everyone present

cantonner [kɑ̃tɔne] **1** *vt (troupes)* to quarter; **c. qn dans/à** to confine sb to **2 se cantonner** *vpr* **se c. dans/à** to confine oneself to ■ **cantonnement** *nm (lieu)* quarters

canular [kanylar] *nm Fam* hoax

CAO [seao] *(abrév* **conception assistée par ordinateur)** *nf Ordinat* CAD

caoutchouc [kautʃu] *nm* rubber; *(élastique)* rubber band

CAP [seape] *(abrév* **certificat d'apti-**

tude professionnelle) *nm Scol* = vocational training certificate

cap [kap] *nm Géog* cape, headland; *Naut (direction)* course

capable [kapabl] *adj* capable, able; **c. de qch** capable of sth; **c. de faire qch** able to do sth, capable of doing sth ■ **capacité** *nf* capacity; *(aptitude)* ability

CAPES [kapɛs] *(abrév* **certificat d'aptitude professionnelle à l'enseignement secondaire)** *nm* = postgraduate teaching certificate

capillaire [kapilɛr] *adj* **huile/lotion c.** hair oil/lotion

capitaine [kapitɛn] *nm* captain

capital, -e, -aux, -ales [kapital, -o] **1** *adj (essentiel)* major **2** *adj f* **lettre capitale** capital letter **3** *nm Fin* capital ■ **capitale** *nf (lettre, ville)* capital

capitalisme [kapitalism] *nm* capitalism ■ **capitaliste** *adj & nmf* capitalist

capiteux, -euse [kapitø, -øz] *adj (parfum)* heady

capitonné, -e [kapitɔne] *adj* padded

capituler [kapityle] *vi* to surrender ■ **capitulation** *nf* surrender

caporal, -aux [kapɔral, -o] *nm Mil* corporal

capot [kapo] *nm Aut Br* bonnet, *Am* hood

capote [kapɔt] *nf Aut (de décapotable)* top, *Br* hood

capoter [kapɔte] *vi (véhicule)* to overturn

câpre [kɑpr] *nf* caper

caprice [kapris] *nm* whim; **faire un c.** to throw a tantrum ■ **capricieux, -euse** *adj (personne)* capricious

Capricorne [kaprikɔrn] *nm* **le C.** *(signe)* Capricorn

capsule [kapsyl] *nf (spatiale, de médicament)* capsule; *(de bouteille)* cap

capter [kapte] *vt (signal, radio)* to pick up; *(attention)* to capture

captif, -ive [kaptif, -iv] *adj & nmf* captive ■ **captivité** *nf* captivity; **en c.** in captivity

captiver [kaptive] *vt* to captivate ■ **captivant, -e** *adj* captivating

capture [kaptyr] *nf* capture ■ **capturer** *vt* to capture

capuche [kapyʃ] *nf* hood ■ **capuchon** *nm (de manteau)* hood; *(de stylo, de tube)* cap, top

caqueter [kakte] *vi (poule)* to cackle

car¹ [kar] *conj* because, for

car² [kar] *nm* bus, *Br* coach; **c. de police** police van ■ **car-ferry** *nm* car-ferry

carabine [karabin] *nf* rifle; **c. à air comprimé** air gun

caractère¹ [karaktɛr] *nm (lettre)* character; **en caractères gras** in bold characters; **caractères d'imprimerie** block letters

caractère² [karaktɛr] *nm (tempérament, nature)* character, nature; **avoir bon c.** to be good-natured; **avoir mauvais c.** to be bad-tempered

caractériser [karakterize] **1** *vt* to characterize **2 se caractériser** *vpr* **se c. par** to be characterized by

caractéristique [karakteristik] *adj & nf* characteristic

carafe [karaf] *nf (pour l'eau, le vin)* carafe

carambolage [karãbɔlaʒ] *nm* pile-up

caramel [karamɛl] *nm* caramel ■ **caraméliser** *vti* to caramelize

carapace [karapas] *nf (de tortue) & Fig* shell

carat [kara] *nm* carat; **or à 18 carats** 18-carat gold

caravane [karavan] *nf (pour camper) Br* caravan, *Am* trailer; *(dans le désert)* caravan; **des vacances en c.** a caravanning holiday ■ **caravaning** *nm* caravanning; **faire du c.** to go caravanning

carbone [karbɔn] *nm* carbon; **(papier) c.** carbon (paper) ■ **carbonique** *adj* **gaz c.** carbon dioxide; **neige c.** dry ice

carbonisé, -e [karbɔnize] *adj (nourriture)* burnt to a cinder

carburant [karbyrã] *nm* fuel ■ **carburateur** *nm Aut Br* carburettor, *Am* carburetor

carcasse [karkas] *nf (os)* carcass; *(d'immeuble)* shell

carcéral, -e, -aux, -ales [karseral, -o] *adj* prison

cardiaque [kardjak] **1** *adj (arrêt, massage)* cardiac; **être c.** to have a heart condition **2** *nmf* heart patient

cardigan [kardigã] *nm* cardigan

cardinal, -e, -aux, -ales [kardinal, -o] **1** *adj (nombre, point, vertu)* cardinal **2** *nm Rel* cardinal

cardiologie [kardjɔlɔʒi] *nf* cardiology

carême [karɛm] *nm Rel* **le c.** Lent; **faire c.** to fast

carence [karãs] *nf (manque)* deficiency

caresse [karɛs] *nf* caress; **faire des caresses à qn** to caress sb

caresser [karese] *vt (personne)* to caress; *(animal)* to stroke; *Fig (espoir)* to cherish

cargaison [kargɛzɔ̃] *nf* cargo

caricature [karikatyr] *nf* caricature

carie [kari] *nf* **c. (dentaire)** tooth decay; **avoir une c.** to have a cavity

carillon [karijɔ̃] *nm (sonnerie)* chimes; *(horloge)* chiming clock; *(de porte)* door chime

caritatif, -ive [karitatif, -iv] *adj* charitable

carlingue [karlɛ̃g] *nf (d'avion)* cabin

carnage [karnaʒ] *nm* carnage

carnassier, -ère [karnasje, -ɛr] **1** *adj* flesh-eating **2** *nm* carnivore

carnaval, -als [karnaval] *nm* carnival

carnet [karnɛ] *nm* notebook; *(de tickets)* = book of tickets; **c. d'adresses** address book; **c. de chèques** *Br* cheque book, *Am* check book; **c. de notes** *Br* school report, *Am* report card; **c. de santé** health record

carnivore [karnivɔr] **1** *adj* carnivorous **2** *nm* carnivore

carotte [karɔt] *nf* carrot

carpette [karpɛt] *nf* rug

carré, -e [kare] **1** *adj* square; *(épaules)* square, broad; **mètre c.** square metre **2** *nm* square; **avoir une coupe au c.** to have (one's hair in) a bob; *Culin* **c. d'agneau** rack of lamb

carreau, -x [karo] *nm (motif)* square;

(sur tissu) check; *(de céramique)* tile; *(vitre)* (window) pane; *Cartes (couleur)* diamonds; **tissu à carreaux** check(ed) material

carrefour [karfur] *nm* crossroads *(sing)*

carrelage [karlaʒ] *nm (sol)* tiled floor; *(carreaux)* tiles

carrelet [karlɛ] *nm Br* plaice, *Am* flounder

carrément [karemɑ̃] *adv Fam (franchement)* straight out; *(très)* really

carrière [karjɛr] *nf* (a) *(lieu)* quarry (b) *(métier)* career; **faire c. dans** to make a career in

carrosse [karɔs] *nm Hist* (horse-drawn) carriage ■ **carrosserie** *nf (de véhicule)* bodywork

carrure [karyr] *nf (de personne)* build; *(de vêtement)* width across the shoulders

cartable [kartabl] *nm* school bag

carte [kart] *nf* (a) *(carton, document officiel, informatisé)* & *Ordinat* card; *(géographique)* map; *(marine, météo)* chart; *Fig* **avoir c. blanche** to have a free hand; **c. (à jouer)** (playing) card; **jouer aux cartes** to play cards; **c. à puce** smart card; **c. de crédit** credit card; **c. d'identité** identity card; **c. de séjour** residence permit; **c. de téléphone** phonecard; **c. de visite** *Br* visiting card, *Am* calling card; *(professionnelle)* business card; **c. de vœux** greetings card; **c. postale** postcard; **c. routière** road map (b) *(de restaurant)* menu; **manger à la c.** to eat à la carte; **c. des vins** wine list

cartel [kartɛl] *nm Écon* cartel

cartomancien, -enne [kartɔmɑ̃sjɛ̃, -ɛn] *nmf* fortune-teller *(who uses cards)*

carton [kartɔ̃] *nm (matière)* cardboard; *(boîte)* cardboard box; **c. à dessin** portfolio; **c. jaune/rouge** *(au football)* yellow/red card ■ **cartonné** *adj* **livre c.** hardback

cartouche [kartuʃ] *nf* cartridge; *(de cigarettes)* carton

cas [kɑ] *nm* case; **en tout c.** in any case; **en c. de besoin** if need be; **en c.**

d'accident in the event of an accident; **en c. d'urgence** in an emergency; **au c. où elle tomberait** if she should fall

casanier, -ère [kazanje, -ɛr] *adj* stay-at-home

cascade [kaskad] *nf* (a) *(d'eau)* waterfall; **en c.** in succession (b) *(de cinéma)* stunt ■ **cascadeur, -euse** *nmf* stunt man, *f* stunt woman

case [kɑz] *nf* (a) *(de tiroir)* compartment; *(d'échiquier)* square; *(de formulaire)* box (b) *(hutte)* hut

caser [kaze] *Fam* **1** *vt (placer)* to fit in **2 se caser** *vpr (se marier)* to get married and settle down

caserne [kazɛrn] *nf* barracks; **c. de pompiers** fire station

casier [kazje] *nm* compartment; *(pour courrier)* pigeonhole; *(pour vêtements)* locker; **c. à bouteilles** bottle rack; *Jur* **c. judiciaire** criminal *or* police record

casino [kazino] *nm* casino

casque [kask] *nm* helmet; **c. (à écouteurs)** headphones ■ **casquette** [kaskɛt] *nf* cap

cassation [kasasjɔ̃] *nf Jur* annulment

casse [kɑs] *nf (objets cassés)* breakages; **aller à la c.** to go for scrap

casser [kɑse] **1** *vt* (a) *(briser)* to break; *(noix)* to crack; *(voix)* to strain; *Fam* **c. les pieds à qn** to get on sb's nerves (b) *Jur (verdict)* to quash; *(mariage)* to annul

2 *vi* to break

3 se casser *vpr* to break; **se c. la jambe** to break one's leg; *Fam* **se c. la figure** *(tomber)* to fall flat on one's face ■ **cassant, -e** *adj (fragile)* brittle; *(brusque)* curt, abrupt ■ **casse-cou** *nmf inv (personne)* daredevil ■ **casse-croûte** *nm inv Fam* snack ■ **casse-noisettes, casse-noix** [kasnwa] *nm inv* nutcrackers ■ **casse-pieds** *nmf inv Fam (personne)* pain (in the neck) ■ **casse-tête** *nm inv (problème)* headache; *(jeu)* puzzle ■ **casseur** *nm (manifestant)* rioter

casserole [kasrɔl] *nf* (sauce)pan

cassette [kasɛt] *nf (magnétique)* cassette, tape; **enregistrer qch sur c.** to

tape sth; **c. video** video cassette

cassis [kasis] *nm (fruit)* blackcurrant; *(boisson)* blackcurrant liqueur

cassoulet [kasule] *nm* cassoulet, = stew of beans, pork and goose

cassure [kasyr] *nf* break

castagnettes [kastaɲɛt] *nfpl* castanets

caste [kast] *nf* caste

castor [kastɔr] *nm* beaver

castrer [kastre] *vt* to castrate; *(chat, chien)* to neuter

catalogue [katalɔg] *nm Br* catalogue, *Am* catalog ■ **cataloguer** *vt Br* to catalogue, *Am* to catalog; *Fig & Péj* to label

catalyseur [katalizœr] *nm Chim & Fig* catalyst

catalytique [katalitik] *adj* **pot c.** catalytic converter

catapulte [katapylt] *nf* catapult

catastrophe [katastrɔf] *nf* disaster, catastrophe ■ **catastrophique** *adj* disastrous, catastrophic

catch [katʃ] *nm* wrestling ■ **catcheur, -euse** *nmf* wrestler

catéchisme [kateʃism] *nm Rel* catechism

catégorie [kategɔri] *nf* category; *(d'hôtel)* grade

catégorique [kategɔrik] *adj* categorical; **c'est lui, je suis c.** I'm positive it's him

cathédrale [katedral] *nf* cathedral

catholicisme [katɔlisism] *nm* Catholicism ■ **catholique** *adj & nmf* (Roman) Catholic

catimini [katimini] **en catimini** *adv* on the sly

cauchemar [koʃmar] *nm aussi Fig* nightmare; **faire un c.** to have a nightmare

cause [koz] *nf (origine)* cause; *(procès, parti)* case; **à c. de qn/qch** because of sb/sth

causer¹ [koze] *vt (provoquer)* to cause

causer² [koze] *vi (bavarder)* to chat **(de** about); *(cancaner)* to talk ■ **causerie** *nf* talk

caustique [kostik] *adj (substance, esprit)* caustic

caution [kosjɔ̃] *nf (d'appartement)* deposit; *Jur* bail; *(personne)* guarantor; *Fig (appui)* backing; *Jur* **sous c.** on bail ■ **cautionner** *vt Fig (approuver)* to back

cavalier, -ère [kavalje, -ɛr] **1** *nmf (à cheval)* rider; *Échecs* knight; *(de bal)* partner, escort; *Fig* **faire c. seul** to go it alone **2** *adj (manière, personne)* cavalier

cave [kav] *nf* cellar ■ **caveau, -x** *nm (sépulture)* burial vault

caverne [kavɛrn] *nf* cave, cavern; **homme des cavernes** caveman

caviar [kavjar] *nm* caviar

cavité [kavite] *nf* hollow, cavity

CCP [sesepe] *(abrév* **compte chèque postal)** *nm Br* ≃ PO Giro account, *Am* ≃ Post Office checking account

CD [sede] *(abrév* **disque compact)** *nm* CD

CDI [sedei] *nm inv* **(a)** *(abrév* **contrat à durée indéterminée)** permanent contract **(b)** *(abrév* **centre de documentation et d'information)** school library *(with special resources on how to find information)*

CD-Rom [sederɔm] *nm inv Ordinat* CD-ROM

CE [seə] **1** *(abrév* **cours élémentaire)** *nm Scol* **CE1** = second year of primary school; **CE2** = third year of primary school **2** *(abrév* **Communauté européenne)** *nf* EC

CE¹, CETTE, CES [sə, sɛt, se]

cet is used before a masculine singular adjective beginning with a vowel or mute h.

adj démonstratif this, that, *pl* these, those; **cet homme** this/that man; **cet homme-ci** this man; **cet homme-là** that man

CE² [sə]

ce becomes **c'** before a vowel.

pron démonstratif **(a)** *(pour désigner, pour qualifier)* it, that; **c'est facile** it's easy; **c'est exact** that's right; **c'est mon père** that's my father; *(au téléphone)* it's my father; **ce sont eux**

qui... they are the people who...; **qui est-ce?** *(en général)* who is it?; *(en désignant)* who is that?; **ce faisant** in so doing; **sur ce** thereupon
(b) *(après une proposition)* **ce que...,** **ce qui...** what...; **je sais ce qui est bon/ce que tu veux** I know what is good/what you want; **ce que c'est beau!** it's so beautiful!

ceci [səsi] *pron démonstratif* this; **c. étant dit** having said this

cécité [sesite] *nf* blindness

céder [sede] **1** *vt (donner)* to give up (**à** to); *(par testament)* to leave (**à** to); **'cédez le passage'** *Br* 'give way', *Am* 'yield'; **'à céder'** 'for sale' **2** *vi (personne)* to give in (**à/devant** to); *(branche, chaise)* to give way

cédérom [sederɔm] *nm Ordinat* CD-ROM

cèdre [sɛdr] *nm (arbre, bois)* cedar

CEI [seøi] *(abrév* **Communauté d'États Indépendants)** *nf* CIS

ceinture [sɛ̃tyr] *nf (accessoire)* belt; *(taille)* waist; **c. de sécurité** *(de véhicule)* seatbelt

cela [s(ə)la] *pron démonstratif (pour désigner)* that; *(sujet indéfini)* it, that; **c. m'attriste que...** it saddens me that...; **quand/comment c.?** when?/ how?

célèbre [selɛbr] *adj* famous ▪ **célébrité** *nf* fame; *(personne)* celebrity

célébrer [selebre] *vt* to celebrate ▪ **célébration** *nf* celebration (**de** of)

céleri [sɛlri] *nm* celery

céleste [selɛst] *adj* celestial, heavenly

célibat [seliba] *nm (de prêtre)* celibacy ▪ **célibataire 1** *adj (non marié)* single, unmarried **2** *nmf* bachelor, *f* single woman

celle *voir* **celui**

cellier [selje] *nm* storeroom

Cellophane® [selɔfan] *nf* cellophane®; **sous c.** cellophane®-wrapped

cellule [selyl] *nf (de prison)* & *Biol* cell ▪ **cellulaire** *adj Biol* cell; **téléphone c.** cellular phone

celte [sɛlt] *adj* Celtic

celui, celle, ceux, celles [səlɥi, sɛl, sø, sɛl] *pron démonstratif* the one, *pl* those, the ones; **c. de Jean** Jean's (one); **ceux de Jean** Jean's (ones), those of Jean; **c. qui appartient à Jean** the one that belongs to Jean; **c.-ci** this one; *(le dernier)* the latter; **c.-là** that one; *(le premier)* the former

cendre [sɑ̃dr] *nf* ash

cendrier [sɑ̃drije] *nm* ashtray

censé, -e [sɑ̃se] *adj* **être c. faire qch** to be supposed to do sth

censeur [sɑ̃sœr] *nm (de films, de journaux)* censor; *(de lycée) Br* deputy head, *Am* assistant principal ▪ **censure** *nf (activité)* censorship; *(comité)* board of censors ▪ **censurer** *vt (film)* to censor

cent [sɑ̃] *adj & nm* a hundred; **c. pages** a *or* one hundred pages; **deux cents pages** two hundred pages; **cinq pour c.** five per cent ▪ **centaine** *nf* **une c. (de)** about a hundred; **des centaines de** hundreds of ▪ **centenaire 1** *adj* hundred-year-old; **être c.** to be a hundred **2** *nmf* centenarian **3** *nm (anniversaire)* centenary ▪ **centième** *adj & nmf* hundredth

centigrade [sɑ̃tigrad] *adj* centigrade

centimètre [sɑ̃timɛtr] *nm* centimetre; *(ruban)* tape measure

central, -e, -aux, -ales [sɑ̃tral, -o] **1** *adj* central **2** *nm* **c. téléphonique** telephone exchange ▪ **centrale** *nf* **c. électrique** *Br* power station, *Am* power plant; **c. nucléaire** nuclear *Br* power station *or Am* power plant ▪ **centraliser** *vt* to centralize

centre [sɑ̃tr] *nm* centre; **c. aéré** outdoor activity centre; **c. commercial** *Br* shopping centre, *Am* (shopping) mall; **c. hospitalo-universitaire** ≃ teaching hospital; **c. médicale** clinic; **c. de sport** sports centre; **c. de vacances** holiday centre *or* complex; ▪ **centre-ville** *(pl* **centres-villes)** *nm* town centre; *(de grande ville) Br* city centre, *Am* downtown ▪ **centrer** *vt* to centre

centuple [sɑ̃typl] *nm* **x est le c. de y** x

is a hundred times y; **au c.** a hundred-fold

cependant [səpãdã] *conj* however, yet

céramique [seramik] *nf (matière)* ceramic; *(art)* ceramics *(sing)*; **de** *ou* **en c.** ceramic

cercle [sɛrkl] *nm (forme, groupe)* circle; **le c. polaire arctique** the Arctic Circle; **c. vicieux** vicious circle

cercueil [sɛrkœj] *nm* coffin

céréale [sereal] *nf* cereal

cérébral, -e, -aux, -ales [serebral, -o] *adj* cerebral

cérémonie [seremɔni] *nf* ceremony

cerf [sɛr] *nm* stag ■ **cerf-volant** (*pl* **cerfs-volants**) *nm (jeu)* kite

cerise [səriz] *nf* cherry ■ **cerisier** *nm* cherry tree

cerne [sɛrn] *nm* ring ■ **cerner** *vt* to surround; *(problème)* to define; **avoir les yeux cernés** to have rings under one's eyes

certain, -e [sɛrtɛ̃, -ɛn] **1** *adj (sûr)* certain; **il est c. que tu réussiras** you're certain to succeed; **je suis c. de réussir** I'm certain I'll be successful *or* of being successful; **être c. de qch** to be certain of sth

2 *adj indéfini (avant nom)* certain; **un c. temps** a while

3 *pron indéfini* **certains pensent que...** some people think that...; **certains d'entre nous** some of us ■ **certainement** *adv* most probably

certificat [sɛrtifika] *nm* certificate

certifier [sɛrtifje] *vt* to certify; **je te certifie que...** I assure you that...

certitude [sɛrtityd] *nf* certainty; **avoir la c. que...** to be certain that...

cerveau, -x [sɛrvo] *nm (organe)* brain; *(intelligence)* mind, brain(s); *Fam (de projet)* mastermind

cervelle [sɛrvɛl] *nf (substance)* brain; *(plat)* brains

CES [seøes] *(abrév* **collège d'enseignement secondaire)** *nm Anciennement* = secondary school for pupils aged 12 to 15

ces *voir* **ce¹**

César [sezar] *nm Cin* = French cinema award

césarienne [sezarjɛn] *nf Méd* Caesarean (section)

cesse [sɛs] *nf* **sans c.** constantly

cesser [sese] *vti* to stop; **faire c. qch** to put a stop to sth; **c. de faire qch** to stop doing sth ■ **cessez-le-feu** *nm inv* cease-fire

c'est-à-dire [setadir] *conj* that is (to say)

cet, cette *voir* **ce¹**

ceux *voir* **celui**

chacun, -e [ʃakœ̃, -yn] *pron indéfini* each (one), every one; *(tout le monde)* everyone; **(à) c. son tour!** wait your turn!

chagrin [ʃagrɛ̃] *nm* grief, sorrow; **avoir du c.** to be upset ■ **chagriner** *vt (peiner)* to grieve; *(contrarier)* to bother

chahut [ʃay] *nm Fam* racket ■ **chahuter** *Fam* **1** *vi* to make a racket **2** *vt (professeur)* to bait

chaîne [ʃen] *nf (attache, décoration, série)* chain; *(de montagnes)* chain, range; **réaction en c.** chain reaction; **travailler à la c.** to work on the assembly line; *Aut* **chaînes** (snow) chains; **c. de montage** assembly line; **c. de télévision** television channel; **c. privée** private channel; **c. publique** public *or* state-owned channel; **c. (hi-fi)** hi-fi (system) ■ **chaînette** *nf* (small) chain ■ **chaînon** *nm* link

chair [ʃɛr] *nf* flesh; **(couleur) c.** flesh-coloured; **en c. et en os** in the flesh; **avoir la c. de poule** to have *Br* goose pimples *or Am* goose bumps

chaire [ʃɛr] *nf (d'université)* chair; *(d'église)* pulpit

chaise [ʃez] *nf* chair; **c. longue** deck-chair; **c. roulante** wheelchair

châle [ʃɑl] *nm* shawl

chalet [ʃalɛ] *nm* chalet

chaleur [ʃalœr] *nf* heat; *(de personne, de couleur, de voix)* warmth; **coup de c.** heatstroke ■ **chaleureux, -euse** *adj* warm

challenge [ʃalɑ̃ʒ] *nm Sport* tournament; *(défi)* challenge

chaloupe [ʃalup] *nf* launch

chalumeau, -x [ʃalymo] *nm* blow-torch, *Br* blowlamp

chalutier [ʃalytje] *nm* trawler

chamailler [ʃamɑje] **se chamailler** *vpr* to squabble

chambre [ʃɑ̃br] *nf* bedroom; *(de tribunal)* division; **c. (d'hôtel)** (hotel) room; **c. à coucher** *(pièce)* bedroom; *(mobilier)* bedroom suite; **c. à un lit/deux lits** single/twin room; **c. d'ami** spare room; **c. d'hôte** ≃ guest house; **C. de commerce** Chamber of Commerce; *Pol* **C. des députés** = lower chamber of Parliament ∎ **chambrer** *vt (vin)* to bring to room temperature

chameau, -x [ʃamo] *nm* camel

champ [ʃɑ̃] *nm (étendue)* & *Él, Ordinat* field; *Fig (portée)* scope; *Fig* **laisser le c. libre à qn** to leave the field free for sb; **c. de bataille** battlefield; **c. de courses** *Br* racecourse, *Am* racetrack

champagne [ʃɑ̃paɲ] *nm* champagne

champêtre [ʃɑ̃pɛtr] *adj* rustic

champignon [ʃɑ̃piɲɔ̃] *nm (végétal)* mushroom; *Méd* fungus; **c. de Paris** button mushroom; **c. vénéneux** toadstool, poisonous mushroom

champion, -onne [ʃɑ̃pjɔ̃, -ɔn] **1** *nmf* champion; **le c. olympique** the Olympic champion **2** *adj* **l'équipe championne du monde** the world champions ∎ **championnat** *nm* championship

chance [ʃɑ̃s] *nf (sort favorable)* luck; *(possibilité)* chance; **avoir de la c.** to be lucky; **ne pas avoir de c.** to be unlucky; **par c.** luckily ∎ **chanceux, -euse** *adj* lucky

chanceler [ʃɑ̃sle] *vi* to stagger

chancelier [ʃɑ̃səlje] *nm Pol* chancellor

chandail [ʃɑ̃daj] *nm* sweater

Chandeleur [ʃɑ̃dlœr] *nf* **la C.** Candlemas

chandelier [ʃɑ̃dəlje] *nm (à une branche)* candlestick; *(à plusieurs branches)* candelabra

chandelle [ʃɑ̃dɛl] *nf* candle

change [ʃɑ̃ʒ] *nm Fin* exchange

changer [ʃɑ̃ʒe] **1** *vt (modifier, remplacer, convertir)* to change; **c. qch de place** to move sth
2 *vi* to change; **c. de voiture/d'adresse** to change one's car/address; **c. de vitesse/de couleur** to change gear/colour
3 se changer *vpr* to change (one's clothes); **se c. en qch** to change into sth ∎ **changeant, -e** *adj (temps)* unsettled ∎ **changement** *nm* change; *Aut* **c. de vitesse** *(levier) Br* gear lever, *Am* gear shift

chanson [ʃɑ̃sɔ̃] *nf* song ∎ **chant** *nm (art)* singing; *(chanson)* song; **c. de Noël** Christmas carol

chanter [ʃɑ̃te] **1** *vt (chanson)* to sing; *(exploits)* to sing of **2** *vi (personne, oiseau)* to sing; *(coq)* to crow; **faire c. qn** to blackmail sb ∎ **chantage** *nm* blackmail ∎ **chanteur, -euse** *nmf* singer

chantier [ʃɑ̃tje] *nm* (building) site; *(sur route)* roadworks; **mettre qch en c.** to get sth under way; **c. naval** shipyard

chantilly [ʃɑ̃tiji] *nf* whipped cream

chantonner [ʃɑ̃tɔne] *vti* to hum

chaos [kao] *nm* chaos ∎ **chaotique** *adj* chaotic

chapeau, -x [ʃapo] *nm* hat; **c. de paille** straw hat; **c. melon** bowler hat

chapelle [ʃapɛl] *nf* chapel; **c. ardente** chapel of rest

chapelure [ʃaplyr] *nf* breadcrumbs

chapiteau, -x [ʃapito] *nm (de cirque)* big top; *(pour expositions)* tent, *Br* marquee

chapitre [ʃapitr] *nm* chapter

chaque [ʃak] *adj* each, every

char [ʃar] *nm (romain)* chariot; *(de carnaval)* float; *Mil* **c. (d'assaut)** tank

charabia [ʃarabja] *nm Fam* gibberish

charbon [ʃarbɔ̃] *nm* coal; **c. de bois** charcoal

charcuterie [ʃarkytri] *nf (magasin)* pork butcher's shop; *(aliments)* cooked (pork) meats ∎ **charcutier, -ère** *nmf* pork butcher

chardon [ʃardɔ̃] *nm (plante)* thistle

charge [ʃarʒ] *nf (poids)* load; *(responsabilité)* responsibility; *(d'une arme)* &

Él, Mil charge; *(fonction)* office; **être en c. de qch** to be in charge of sth; **prendre qn/qch en c.** to take charge of sb/ sth; **être à la c. de qn** *(personne)* to be dependent on sb; *(frais)* to be payable by sb; **charges sociales** *Br* national insurance contributions, *Am* Social Security contributions

charger [ʃaʒe] **1** *vt (véhicule, marchandises, arme)* & *Ordinat* to load; *(batterie)* & *Mil* to charge; **c. qn de qch** to entrust sb with; **c. qn de faire qch** to give sb the responsibility of doing sth **2** *vi Ordinat* to load up; *Mil* to charge **3 se charger** *vpr (s'encombrer)* to weigh oneself down; **se c. de qn/qch** to take care of sb/sth; **se c. de faire qch** to undertake to do sth ▪ **chargé, -e 1** *adj (véhicule)* loaded (**de** with); *(arme)* loaded; *(journée, programme)* busy; **être c. de faire qch** to be responsible for doing sth **2** *nmf Univ* **c. de cours** = part-time lecturer ▪ **chargement** *nm (action)* loading; *(marchandises)* load

chariot [ʃarjo] *nm (de supermarché) Br* trolley, *Am* cart; *(de ferme)* waggon; *(de machine à écrire)* carriage; **c. à bagages** luggage trolley

charisme [karism] *nm* charisma

charitable [ʃaritabl] *adj* charitable (**envers** towards)

charité [ʃarite] *nf (vertu)* charity; **faire la c.** to give to charity

charme [ʃarm] *nm (attrait,* charm; *(magie)* spell

charmer [ʃarme] *vt* to charm ▪ **charmant, -e** *adj* charming ▪ **charmeur, -euse 1** *adj (sourire, air)* charming **2** *nmf* charmer

charnel, -elle [ʃarnɛl] *adj* carnal

charnier [ʃarnje] *nm* mass grave

charnière [ʃarnjɛr] *nf* hinge

charnu, -e [ʃarny] *adj* fleshy

charpente [ʃarpɑ̃t] *nf* framework; *(de personne)* build ▪ **charpentier** *nm* carpenter

charpie [ʃarpi] *nf* **mettre qch en c.** to tear sth to shreds

charrette [ʃarɛt] *nf* cart

charrier [ʃarje] *vt (transporter)* to cart; *(rivière)* to carry along

charrue [ʃary] *nf Br* plough, *Am* plow

charter [ʃartɛr] *nm (vol)* charter (flight); *(avion)* charter plane

chasse¹ [ʃas] *nf (activité)* hunting; *(événement)* hunt; *(poursuite)* chase; **aller à la c.** to go hunting; **c. à courre** hunting; **c. au trésor** treasure hunt; **c. gardée** private hunting ground

chasse² [ʃas] *nf* **c. d'eau** flush; **tirer la c.** to flush the toilet

chassé-croisé [ʃasekrwaze] *(pl* **chassés-croisés)** *nm (de personnes)* comings and goings

chasser [ʃase] **1** *vt (animal)* to hunt; *(faisan, perdrix)* to shoot; **c. qn** *(expulser)* to chase sb away; *(employé)* to dismiss sb **2** *vi* to hunt ▪ **chasse-neige** *nm inv Br* snowplough, *Am* snowplow ▪ **chasseur, -euse 1** *nmf* hunter; **c. de têtes** headhunter **2** *nm (d'hôtel) Br* pageboy, *Am* bellboy; *(avion)* fighter

châssis [ʃasi] *nm* frame; *(d'automobile)* chassis

chat [ʃa] *nm* cat; **c. sauvage** wildcat

châtaigne [ʃatɛɲ] *nf* chestnut ▪ **châtaignier** *nm* chestnut tree ▪ **châtain** *adj (cheveux)* (chestnut) brown; *(personne)* brown-haired

château, -x [ʃato] *nm (forteresse)* castle; *(manoir)* mansion

châtiment [ʃatimɑ̃] *nm* punishment; **c. corporel** corporal punishment

chaton [ʃatɔ̃] *nm* **(a)** *(chat)* kitten **(b)** *(de bague)* bezel **(c)** *(d'arbre)* catkin

chatouiller [ʃatuje] *vt* to tickle ▪ **chatouilleux, -euse** *adj* ticklish

chatoyer [ʃatwaje] *vi* to shimmer; *(pierre)* to sparkle

châtrer [ʃatre] *vt* to castrate

chatte [ʃat] *nf* (female) cat

chaud, -e [ʃo, ʃod] **1** *adj* **(a)** *(modérément)* warm; *(intensément)* hot **(b)** *Fig (couleur)* warm; *(voix)* sultry **2** *nm* **avoir c.** to be hot; **il fait c.** it's hot ▪ **chaudement** *adv (s'habiller, féliciter)* warmly

chaudière [ʃodjɛr] *nf* boiler

chauffage [ʃofaʒ] *nm* heating; *(de voiture)* heater

chauffard [ʃofar] *nm* reckless driver

chauffer [ʃofe] **1** *vt* to heat (up); *(moteur)* to warm up
2 *vi* to heat (up); *(s'échauffer) (moteur)* to overheat; **faire c. qch** to heat sth up
3 se chauffer *vpr* to warm oneself ▪ **chauffant, -e** *adj* **couverture chauffante** electric blanket; **plaque chauffante** hot plate ▪ **chauffé, -e** *adj (piscine)* heated ▪ **chauffe-eau** *nm inv* water heater; **c. électrique** immersion heater ▪ **chauffe-plat** *(pl chauffe-plats)* *nm* hotplate ▪ **chaufferie** *nf* boiler room

chauffeur [ʃofœr] *nm (de véhicule)* driver; *(employé)* chauffeur; **c. de taxi** taxi driver

chaume [ʃom] *nm (pour toits)* thatch; **toit de c.** thatched roof ▪ **chaumière** *nf (à toit de chaume)* thatched cottage; *(maison pauvre)* cottage

chaussée [ʃose] *nf* road(way)

chausser [ʃose] **1** *vt (chaussures, lunettes, skis)* to put on; **c. qn** to put shoes on sb; **c. du 40** to take a size 40 shoe **2 se chausser** *vpr* to put one's shoes on

chaussette [ʃosɛt] *nf* sock

chausson [ʃosɔ̃] *nm (pantoufle)* slipper; *(de danse)* ballet shoe; *(de bébé)* bootee; *Culin* **c. aux pommes** apple turnover

chaussure [ʃosyr] *nf* shoe; **chaussures de ski** ski boots

chauve [ʃov] **1** *adj* bald **2** *nm* bald(-headed) man

chauve-souris [ʃovsuri] *(pl* **chauves-souris)** *nf* bat

chauvin, -e [ʃovɛ̃, -in] **1** *adj* chauvinistic **2** *nmf* chauvinist

chaux [ʃo] *nf* lime; **blanchir qch à la c.** to whitewash sth

chavirer [ʃavire] *vti (bateau)* to capsize

chef [ʃɛf] *nm* **(a)** *(de parti, de bande)* leader; *(de tribu)* chief; **rédacteur en c.** editor in chief; **le c. du gouvernement** the head of government; **c. d'entreprise** company head; **c. d'État** head

of state; **c. d'orchestre** conductor **(b)** *(cuisinier)* chef

chef-d'œuvre [ʃedœvr] *(pl* **chefs-d'œuvre)** *nm* masterpiece

chef-lieu [ʃɛfljø] *(pl* **chefs-lieux)** *nm* = administrative centre of a 'département'

chemin [ʃəmɛ̃] *nm (route étroite)* path, track; *(itinéraire)* way (**de** to); **à mi-c.** half-way; **en c., c. faisant** on the way; **c. de grande randonnée** hiking trail; **c. de terre** track ▪ **chemin de fer** *(pl* **chemins de fer)** *nm Br* railway, *Am* railroad

cheminée [ʃəmine] *nf (âtre)* fireplace; *(encadrement)* mantelpiece; *(sur le toit)* chimney

cheminot [ʃəmino] *nm Br* railwayman, *Am* railroader

chemise [ʃəmiz] *nf (vêtement)* shirt; *(classeur)* folder; **c. de nuit** *(de femme)* nightdress ▪ **chemisier** *nm (corsage)* blouse

chenal, -aux [ʃənal, -o] *nm* channel

chêne [ʃɛn] *nm (arbre, bois)* oak

chenil [ʃəni(l)] *nm Br* kennels, *Am* kennel

chenille [ʃənij] *nf (insecte)* caterpillar; *(de char)* caterpillar track

chèque [ʃɛk] *nm Br* cheque, *Am* check; **faire un c. à qn** to write sb a cheque; **payer qch par c.** to pay sth by cheque; **c. de voyage** *Br* traveller's cheque, *Am* traveler's check ▪ **chèque-repas** *(pl* **chèques-repas)**, **chèque-restaurant** *(pl* **chèques-restaurants)** *nm Br* luncheon voucher, *Am* meal ticket ▪ **chéquier** *nm Br* cheque book, *Am* checkbook

cher, chère [ʃɛr] **1** *adj* **(a)** *(aimé)* dear (**à** to); **C. Monsieur** *(dans une lettre)* Dear Mr X; *(officiel)* Dear Sir **(b)** *(coûteux)* expensive, dear **2** *adv* **coûter c.** to be expensive **3** *nmf* **mon c., ma chère** my dear ▪ **chèrement** *adv (à un prix élevé)* dearly

chercher [ʃɛrʃe] **1** *vt* to look for; *(dans ses souvenirs)* to try to think of; *(dans un dictionnaire)* to look up; **aller c. qn/qch** to (go and) fetch sb/sth; **c. à faire**

qch to try to do sth **2 se chercher** *vpr (chercher son identité)* to try to find oneself ■ **chercheur, -euse** *nmf (scientifique)* researcher; **c. d'or** gold digger

chérir [ʃerir] *vt* to cherish ■ **chéri, -e** *adj* dear

cherté [ʃɛrte] *nf* high cost

chétif, -ive [ʃetif, -iv] *adj (personne)* puny

cheval, -aux [ʃəval, -o] *nm* horse; **à c.** on horseback; **faire du c.** *Br* to go horse riding, *Am* to go horseback riding; **c. de course** racehorse; *Aut* **c. (-vapeur)** horsepower

chevalet [ʃəvalɛ] *nm (de peintre)* easel

chevalier [ʃəvalje] *nm* knight

chevalière [ʃəvaljɛr] *nf* signet ring

chevaline [ʃəvalin] *adj f* **boucherie c.** horse butcher's (shop)

chevaucher [ʃəvoʃe] **1** *vt* to straddle **2** *vi* **se chevaucher** *vpr* to overlap

chevelu, -e [ʃəvly] *adj* long-haired ■ **chevelure** *nf* (head of) hair

chevet [ʃəvɛ] *nm* bedhead; **rester au c. de qn** to stay at sb's bedside

cheveu, -x [ʃəvø] *nm* un c. a hair; **cheveux** hair; **avoir les cheveux noirs** to have black hair

cheville [ʃəvij] *nf (partie du corps)* ankle

chèvre [ʃɛvr] **1** *nf* goat **2** *nm* goat's cheese

chevreau, -x [ʃəvro] *nm* kid

chèvrefeuille [ʃɛvrəfœj] *nm* honeysuckle

chevreuil [ʃəvrœj] *nm* roe deer; *(viande)* venison

chevronné, -e [ʃəvrone] *adj* experienced

chez [ʃe] *prép* **c. qn** at sb's house; **il n'est pas c. lui** he isn't at home; **elle est rentrée c. elle** she's gone home; **c. Mme Dupont** *(adresse)* c/o Mme Dupont ■ **chez-soi** *nm inv* **son petit c.** one's own little home

chic [ʃik] **1** *adj inv* smart, stylish; *Fam (gentil)* decent **2** *nm (élégance)* style; **avoir le c. pour faire qch** to have the knack of doing sth

chicaner [ʃikane] *vi* **c. sur qch** to quibble over sth

chicorée [ʃikore] *nf (en poudre)* chicory

chien, chienne [ʃjɛ̃, ʃjɛn] *nmf* dog, *f* bitch; *Fam* **quel temps de c.!** what foul weather!; **c. d'aveugle** guide dog; **c. de berger** sheepdog; **c. de garde** guard dog; **c. policier** police dog

chiendent [ʃjɛ̃dɑ̃] *nm (plante)* couch grass

chiffon [ʃifɔ̃] *nm* rag; **passer un coup de c. sur qch** to give sth a dust; **c. (de poussière)** *Br* duster, *Am* dustcloth

chiffonner [ʃifone] *vt* to crumple; *Fig (ennuyer)* to bother

chiffre [ʃifr] *nm (nombre)* figure, number; *(total)* total; **chiffres romains/ arabes** Roman/Arabic numerals; **c. d'affaires** turnover ■ **chiffrer 1** *vt (montant)* to work out; *(réparations)* to assess **2** **se chiffrer** *vpr* **se c. à** to amount to

chignon [ʃiɲɔ̃] *nm* bun, chignon

Chili [ʃili] *nm* **le C.** Chile ■ **chilien, -enne 1** *adj* Chilean **2** *nmf* **C., Chilienne** Chilean

chimie [ʃimi] *nf* chemistry ■ **chimique** *adj* chemical ■ **chimiste** *nmf (research)* chemist

chimiothérapie [ʃimjoterapi] *nf Méd* chemotherapy

chimpanzé [ʃɛ̃pɑ̃ze] *nm* chimpanzee

Chine [ʃin] *nf* **la C.** China ■ **chinois, -e 1** *adj* Chinese **2** *nmf* **C., Chinoise** Chinese; **les C.** the Chinese **3** *nm (langue)* Chinese

chiot [ʃjo] *nm* puppy, pup

chipoter [ʃipote] *vi (contester)* to quibble (**sur** about)

chips [ʃips] *nf Br (potato)* crisp, *Am (potato)* chip

chiromancien, -enne [kiromɑ̃sjɛ̃, -ɛn] *nmf* palmist

chirurgie [ʃiryrʒi] *nf* surgery; **c. esthétique** plastic surgery ■ **chirurgical, -e, -aux, -ales** *adj* surgical ■ **chirurgien, -enne** *nmf* surgeon ■ **chirurgien-dentiste** *(pl* **chirurgiens-dentistes)** *nm* dental surgeon

chlem [ʃlɛm] *nm Sport* **le grand c.** the grand slam

chlore [klɔr] *nm* chlorine

choc [ʃɔk] **1** *nm (coup)* impact; *(forte émotion)* shock; *Fig (conflit)* clash; **faire un c. à qn** to give sb a shock; **c. pétrolier** oil crisis **2** *adj* **image-c.** shocking image; **'prix-chocs'** 'drastic reductions'

chocolat [ʃɔkɔla] **1** *nm* chocolate; **gâteau au c.** chocolate cake; **c. à croquer** *Br* plain chocolate, *Am* bittersweet chocolate; **c. au lait** milk chocolate **2** *adj inv Br* chocolate(-coloured), *Am* chocolate(-colored) ▪ **chocolaté, -e** *adj* chocolate

chœur [kœr] *nm (chanteurs, nef)* choir; *(d'opéra)* chorus; **en c.** *(chanter)* in chorus; *(répéter)* (all) together

choisir [ʃwazir] *vt* to choose, to pick; **c. de faire qch** to choose to do sth ▪ **choisi, -e** *adj (œuvres)* selected; *(langage)* careful

choix [ʃwa] *nm* choice; *(assortiment)* selection; **avoir le c.** to have a choice

cholestérol [kɔlɛsterɔl] *nm Méd* cholesterol

chômer [ʃome] *vi* **vous n'avez pas chômé!** you've not been idle!; **jour chômé** (public) holiday ▪ **chômage** *nm* unemployment; **être au c.** to be unemployed ▪ **chômeur, -euse** *nmf* unemployed person; **les chômeurs** the unemployed

choquer [ʃɔke] *vt (scandaliser)* to shock ▪ **choquant, -e** *adj* shocking

choral, -e, -aux *ou* **-als, -ales** [kɔral] *adj* choral ▪ **chorale** *nf (club)* choral society; *(chanteurs)* choir ▪ **choriste** *nmf* chorister

chorégraphe [kɔregraf] *nmf* choreographer

chose [ʃoz] *nf* thing; **avant toute c.** first of all

chou, -x [ʃu] *nm* cabbage; **choux de Bruxelles** Brussels sprouts; **c. à la crème** cream puff ▪ **chou-fleur** *(pl* **choux-fleurs)** *nm* cauliflower

choucroute [ʃukrut] *nf* sauerkraut

chouette [ʃwɛt] **1** *nf (oiseau)* owl **2** *adj*

Fam (chic) great **3** *exclam* great!

choyer [ʃwaje] *vt* to pamper

chrétien, -enne [kretjɛ̃, -ɛn] *adj & nmf* Christian ▪ **Christ** [krist] *nm* **le C.** Christ ▪ **christianisme** *nm* Christianity

chrome [krom] *nm* chromium; **chromes** *(de voitures)* chrome

chronique¹ [krɔnik] *adj (malade, chômage)* chronic

chronique² [krɔnik] *nf (de journal)* column; *(annales)* chronicle

chronologie [krɔnɔlɔʒi] *nf* chronology ▪ **chronologique** *adj* chronological

chronomètre [krɔnɔmɛtr] *nm* chronometer; *(pour le sport)* stopwatch ▪ **chronométrer** *vt* to time

chrysanthème [krizɑ̃tɛm] *nm* chrysanthemum

chuchoter [ʃyʃɔte] *vti* to whisper ▪ **chuchotement** *nm* whisper

chuinter [ʃwɛ̃te] *vi (siffler)* to hiss

chut [ʃyt] *exclam* sh!, shush!

chute [ʃyt] *nf* fall; *(d'histoire drôle)* punchline; *(de tissu)* scrap; **c. de neige** snowfall; **c. libre** free fall ▪ **chuter** *vi (diminuer)* to fall, to drop; *Fam (tomber)* to fall

Chypre [ʃipr] *nm ou f* Cyprus ▪ **chypriote 1** *adj* Cypriot **2** *nmf* **C.** Cypriot

ci [si] *pron démonstratif* **comme ci comme ça** so so

-ci [si] *adv* (a) **par-ci, par-là** here and there (b) *voir* **ce¹**, **celui** ▪ **ci-après** *adv* below ▪ **ci-contre** *adv* opposite ▪ **ci-dessous** *adv* below ▪ **ci-dessus** *adv* above ▪ **ci-gît** *adv* here lies... *(on gravestones)* ▪ **ci-joint, -e** *(mpl* **ci-joints, fpl ci-jointes) 1** *adj* **le document c.** the enclosed document **2** *adv* **vous trouverez c. copie de...** please find enclosed a copy of...

cible [sibl] *nf* target

ciboulette [sibulɛt] *nf* chives

cicatrice [sikatris] *nf* scar

cicatriser [sikatrize] *vti*, **se cicatriser** *vpr* to heal ▪ **cicatrisation** *nf* healing

cidre [sidr] *nm* cider

Cie *(abrév* **compagnie)** Co

ciel [sjɛl] *nm* (a) (*pl* ciels) sky; **à c. ouvert** open-air (b) (*pl* cieux [sjø]) *(paradis)* heaven

cierge [sjɛrʒ] *nm Rel* candle

cigale [sigal] *nf* cicada

cigare [sigar] *nm* cigar ▪ **cigarette** *nf* cigarette

cigogne [sigɔɲ] *nf* stork

cil [sil] *nm* eyelash

cime [sim] *nf* *(d'arbre)* top *(de montagne)* peak

ciment [simɑ̃] *nm* cement

cimetière [simtjɛr] *nm* cemetery; *(d'église)* graveyard

cinéaste [sineast] *nm* film maker ▪ **ciné-club** (*pl* ciné-clubs) *nm* film club ▪ **cinéphile** *nmf Br* film *or Am* movie enthusiast

cinéma [sinema] *nm (art, industrie) Br* cinema, *Am* movies; *(salle) Br* cinema, *Am* movie theater; **c. d'art et d'essai** *(art, industrie)* arthouse *(movies); (salle)* arthouse *Br* cinema *or Am* movie theater; **faire du c.** to be a movie actor/actress; **aller au c.** to go to the *Br* cinema *or Am* movies ▪ **cinématographique** *adj* film; **industrie c.** film industry

cinglé, -e [sɛ̃gle] *adj Fam* crazy

cingler [sɛ̃gle] *vt* to lash ▪ **cinglant, -e** *adj (pluie)* lashing; *(remarque)* cutting

cinq [sɛ̃k] **1** *adj inv* five **2** *nm inv* five ▪ **cinquième** *adj & nmf* fifth; **un c.** a fifth

cinquante [sɛ̃kɑ̃t] *adj & nm inv* fifty ▪ **cinquantaine** *nf* **une c. (de)** about fifty; **avoir la c.** to be about fifty ▪ **cinquantenaire** *nm (anniversaire)* fiftieth anniversary ▪ **cinquantième** *adj & nmf* fiftieth

cintre [sɛ̃tr] *nm* coathanger

cirage [siraʒ] *nm* (shoe) polish

circonscription [sirkɔ̃skripsjɔ̃] *nf* division, district; **c. (électorale)** *Br* constituency, *Am* district

circonscrire* [sirkɔ̃skrir] *vt (encercler)* to encircle; *(incendie)* to contain

circonspect, -e [sirkɔ̃spɛ, -ɛkt] *adj* cautious, circumspect

circonstance [sirkɔ̃stɑ̃s] *nf* circumstance; **en pareilles circonstances** under such circumstances

circuit [sirkɥi] *nm Él & Sport* circuit; *(chemin)* way; **c. automobile** racing circuit; **c. touristique** (organized) tour

circulaire [sirkylɛr] **1** *adj* circular **2** *nf (lettre)* circular

circulation [sirkylɑsjɔ̃] *nf (du sang, de l'information, de billets)* circulation; *(d'autos)* traffic; **c. routière/aérienne** road/air traffic ▪ **circuler** *vi (sang, air, information)* to circulate; *(voyageur)* to travel; *(train, bus)* to run

cire [sir] *nf* wax; *(pour meubles)* polish ▪ **ciré** *nm (vêtement)* oilskin(s) ▪ **cirer** *vt* to polish ▪ **cireux, -euse** *adj* waxy

cirque [sirk] *nm (spectacle)* circus

cisailles [sizaj] *nfpl* (garden) shears ▪ **ciseau, -x** *nm (de menuisier)* chisel; **(une paire de) ciseaux** (a pair of) scissors

ciseler [sizle] *vt* to chisel; *(or, argent)* to chase

citadelle [sitadɛl] *nf* citadel ▪ **citadin, -e 1** *adj* city **2** *nmf* city dweller

cité [site] *nf (ville)* city; *(immeubles) Br* housing estate, *Am* housing development; **c. universitaire** *Br* (students') halls of residence, *Am* university dormitory complex

citer [site] *vt (auteur, texte)* to quote; *(énumérer)* to name ▪ **citation** *nf* quotation

citerne [sitɛrn] *nf* tank

citoyen, -enne [sitwajɛ̃, -ɛn] *nmf* citizen ▪ **citoyenneté** *nf* citizenship

citron [sitrɔ̃] *nm* lemon; **c. pressé** = freshly squeezed lemon juice served with water and sugar; **c. vert** lime ▪ **citronnade** *nf Br* lemon squash, *Am* lemonade

citrouille [sitruj] *nf* pumpkin

civet [sivɛ] *nm* stew

civière [sivjɛr] *nf* stretcher

civil, -e [sivil] **1** *adj (guerre, mariage, droits)* civil; *(non militaire)* civilian; *(courtois)* civil; **année civile** calendar year **2** *nm* civilian; **dans le c.** in civilian life; **en c.** *(policier)* in plain clothes ▪ **civilité** *nf* civility

civilisation [sivilizɑsjɔ̃] *nf* civilization ■ **civilisé, -e** *adj* civilized

civique [sivik] *adj* civic; *Scol* **instruction c.** civics

clair, -e [klɛr] **1** *adj (net, limpide, évident)* clear; *(éclairé, pâle)* light; **bleu/vert c.** light blue/green **2** *adv (voir)* clearly; **il fait c.** it's light **3** *nm* **en c.** in plain language; **c. de lune** moonlight

clairière [klɛrjɛr] *nf* clearing

clairon [klɛrɔ̃] *nm* bugle; *(soldat)* bugler

clairsemé, -e [klɛrsəme] *adj (auditoire, population)* sparse

clairvoyant, -e [klɛrvwajɑ̃, -ɑ̃t] *adj* perceptive

clameur [klamœr] *nf* clamour

clan [klɑ̃] *nm (tribu)* clan; *Péj (groupe)* clique

clandestin, -e [klɑ̃dɛstɛ̃, -in] *adj (rencontre)* clandestine; *(mouvement)* underground; *(travailleur)* illegal

clapier [klapje] *nm* (rabbit) hutch

clapoter [klapɔte] *vi (vagues)* to lap

claque [klak] *nf Fam* slap

claquer [klake] **1** *vt (porte)* to slam **2** *vi (porte)* to slam; *(drapeau)* to flap; *(talons)* to click; *(coup de feu)* to ring out; **elle claque des dents** her teeth are chattering **3** **se claquer** *vpr* **se c. un muscle** to pull a muscle ■ **claquement** *nm (de porte)* slam(ming)

claquettes [klakɛt] *nfpl* tap dancing; **faire des c.** to do tap dancing

clarifier [klarifje] *vt* to clarify ■ **clarification** *nf* clarification

clarinette [klarinɛt] *nf* clarinet

clarté [klarte] *nf (lumière)* light; *(transparence)* clearness; *Fig (d'explications)* clarity; **avec c.** clearly

classe [klɑs] *nf (catégorie, leçon, élèves)* class; **en c. de sixième** *Br* in the first year, *Am* in fifth grade; **aller en c.** to go to school; **avoir de la c.** *(personne)* to have class; **(salle de) c.** classroom; **de première c.** *(billet, compartiment)* first-class; **c. ouvrière/moyenne** working/middle class; **c. sociale** social class

classer [klɑse] **1** *vt (objets)* to classify; *(papiers)* to file; **c. une affaire** to consider a matter closed

2 **se classer** *vpr* **se c. parmi les meilleurs** to rank among the best; *Sport* **se c. troisième** to be placed third ■ **classé, -e** *adj (monument)* listed; *(au tennis)* seeded ■ **classement** *nm* classification; *(de papiers)* filing; *(rang)* place; *Sport* table ■ **classeur** *nm (meuble)* filing cabinet; *(portefeuille)* ring binder

classifier [klasifje] *vt* to classify ■ **classification** *nf* classification

classique [klasik] **1** *adj (période)* classical; *(typique, conventionnel)* classic **2** *nm (œuvre)* classic; *(auteur)* classical author

claustrophobe [klostrɔfɔb] *adj* claustrophobic

clavecin [klavsɛ̃] *nm* harpsichord

clavicule [klavikyl] *nf* collarbone

clavier [klavje] *nm* keyboard

clé, clef [kle] **1** *nf (de porte)* key; *(outil)* *Br* spanner, *Am* wrench; **fermer qch à c.** to lock sth; **c. de contact** ignition key; *Mus* **c. de sol** treble clef; *Fig* **c. de voûte** cornerstone **2** *adj* key; **poste c.** key post

clément, -e [klemɑ̃, -ɑ̃t] *adj (juge)* clement; *(temps)* mild ■ **clémence** *nf (de juge)* clemency; *(de temps)* mildness

clémentine [klemɑ̃tin] *nf* clementine

clerc [klɛr] *nm Rel* cleric; **c. de notaire** ≃ solicitor's clerk ■ **clergé** *nm* clergy ■ **clérical, -e, -aux, -ales** *adj* clerical

cliché [kliʃe] *nm (photo)* photo; *(negative)* negative; *(idée)* cliché

client, -e [klijɑ̃, -ɑ̃t] *nmf (de magasin)* customer; *(d'avocat)* client; *(d'hôtel)* guest; *(de taxi)* fare ■ **clientèle** *nf (de magasin)* customers; *(d'avocat)* practice

cligner [kliɲe] *vi* **c. des yeux** to blink; **c. de l'œil** to wink

clignoter [kliɲɔte] *vi (lumière, voyant)* to flash ■ **clignotant** *nm (de voiture)* *Br* indicator, *Am* flasher; **mettre son c.** to indicate

climat [klima] *nm (de région)* & *Fig*

climate ■ **climatique** *adj* climatic

climatisation [klimatizasjɔ̃] *nf* air-conditioning ■ **climatisé, -e** *adj* air-conditioned

clin d'œil [klɛ̃dœj] *(pl* **clins d'œil)** *nm* wink; **faire un c. à qn** to wink at sb; **en un c.** in a flash

clinique [klinik] *nf (hôpital)* clinic

clinquant, -e [klɛ̃kɑ̃, -ɑ̃t] *adj* flashy

clip [klip] *nm (vidéo)* (music) video

cliquer [klike] *vi Ordinat* to click

cliqueter [klikte] *vi (monnaie, clefs)* to jingle ■ **cliquetis** *nm (de monnaie, de clefs)* jingling

clivage [klivaʒ] *nm (de société)* divide; *(de parti)* split

clochard, -e [klɔʃar, -ard] *nmf* tramp

cloche [klɔʃ] *nf (d'église)* bell; **c. à fromage** covered cheese dish ■ **clocher 1** *nm (d'église)* bell tower, steeple **2** *vi Fam* **il y a quelque chose qui cloche** there's something wrong somewhere

cloche-pied [klɔʃpje] **à cloche-pied** *adv* **sauter à c.** to hop

cloison [klwazɔ̃] *nf (entre pièces)* partition

cloître [klwatr] *nm (de monastère)* cloister; *(pour moines)* monastery; *(pour religieuses)* convent

clone [klon] *nm Biol* clone

clopin-clopant [klɔpɛ̃klɔpɑ̃] *adv* **aller c.** to hobble along

cloque [klɔk] *nf (au pied)* blister

clore* [klɔr] *vt (réunion)* to conclude; *(débat)* to close; *Ordinat* **c. une session** to log off

clos, -e [klo, kloz] **1** *adj (porte, volets)* closed; **l'incident est c.** the matter is closed; **espace c.** enclosed space **2** *nm* enclosure

clôture [klotyr] *nf (barrière)* fence; *(de réunion)* conclusion; *(de débat)* closing; *(de Bourse)* close ■ **clôturer** *vt (terrain)* to enclose

clou [klu] *nm (pointe)* nail; *(de spectacle)* main attraction; **les clous** *(passage)* Br the pedestrian crossing, Am the crosswalk; **c. de girofle** clove

■ **clouer** *vt (au mur)* to nail up; *(ensemble)* to nail together; **cloué au lit** confined to (one's) bed

clown [klun] *nm* clown; **faire le c.** to clown around

club [klœb] *nm* club

cm *(abrév* **centimètre)** cm

coalition [kɔalisjɔ̃] *nf* coalition

cobaye [kɔbaj] *nm (animal, & Fig* guinea pig

cocaïne [kɔkain] *nf* cocaine

coccinelle [kɔksinɛl] *nf (insecte)* Br ladybird, Am ladybug; *(voiture)* Beetle

cocher¹ [kɔʃe] *vt Br* to tick, Am to check

cocher² [kɔʃe] *nm* coachman

cochon, -onne [kɔʃɔ̃, -ɔn] **1** *nm (animal)* pig; *(viande)* pork; **c. d'Inde** guinea pig **2** *nmf (personne sale,* pig **3** *adj (histoire, film)* dirty ■ **cochonnerie** *nf (chose sans valeur)* trash, Br rubbish; *(obscénité)* smutty remark; **manger des cochonneries** to eat junk food

cocktail [kɔktɛl] *nm (boisson)* cocktail; *(réunion)* cocktail party; **c. de fruits** fruit cocktail

coco [koko] *nm* **noix de c.** coconut

cocu, -e [kɔky] **1** *adj* **il est c.** his wife's cheating on him **2** *nm* cuckold

code [kɔd] *nm (symboles, lois)* & *Ordinat* code; **passer le c.** *(du permis de conduire)* = to sit the written part of one's driving test; **codes** *Br* dipped headlights, Am low beams; **le C. de la route** Br the Highway Code, Am the traffic regulations; *Jur* **c. civ l/pénal** civil/penal code; **c. confident e** of security code; *(de carte bancaire,* PIN; **c. postal** Br postcode, Am zip code ■ **code-barres** *(pl* **codes-barres)** *nm* bar code ■ **coder** *vt* to code

coéquipier, -ère [kɔekipje, -ɛr] *nmf* team-mate

cœur [kœr] *nm* heart; *Cartes (couleur)* hearts; **avoir mal au c.** to feel sick; **par c.** (off) by heart; **de bon c.** *(volontiers)* willingly; *(rire)* heartily

coexister [kɔɛgziste] *vi* to coexist

coffre [kɔr] *nm (meuble)* chest; *(pour objets de valeur)* safe; *(de voiture)* Br

boot, *Am* trunk; **c. à bagages** *(d'avion)* baggage compartment; **c. à jouets** toy box ▪ **coffre-fort** (*pl* **coffres-forts**) *nm* safe ▪ **coffret** *nm (petit coffre)* box; **c. à bijoux** *Br* jewellery *or Am* jewelry box

cogner [kɔɲe] **1** *vt (heurter)* to knock **2** *vi (buter)* to bang (**sur/contre** on) **3 se cogner** *vpr* to bang oneself; **se c. la tête contre qch** to bang one's head on sth; **se c. à qch** to bang into sth

cohabiter [kɔabite] *vi* to live together; **c. avec qn** to live with sb

cohérent, -e [kɔerã, -ãt] *adj (discours)* coherent; *(attitude)* consistent ▪ **cohérence** *nf (de discours)* coherence; *(d'attitude)* consistency ▪ **cohésion** *nf* cohesion

cohue [kɔy] *nf* crowd

coiffe [kwaf] *nf* headdress

coiffer [kwafe] **1** *vt Fig (surmonter)* to cap; *(service)* to head; **c. qn de qch** to put sth on sb's head; **elle est bien coiffée** her hair is lovely **2 se coiffer** *vpr* to do one's hair; **se c. de qch** to put sth on

coiffeur, -euse¹ [kwafœr, -øz] *nmf* hairdresser ▪ **coiffeuse²** *nf (meuble)* dressing table ▪ **coiffure** *nf (chapeau)* headgear; *(coupe de cheveux)* hairstyle

coin [kwɛ̃] *nm (angle)* corner; *(endroit)* spot; *(cale)* wedge; **faire le c.** to be on the corner; **dans le c.** in the area; *Fam* **le petit c.** *(toilettes)* the smallest room in the house

coincer [kwɛ̃se] **1** *vt (mécanisme, tiroir)* to jam; *(caler)* to wedge **2** *vi (mécanisme, tiroir)* to jam **3 se coincer** *vpr (mécanisme)* to jam; **se c. le doigt dans la porte** to catch one's finger in the door ▪ **coincé, -e** *adj (mécanisme, tiroir)* stuck, jammed

coïncider [kɔɛ̃side] *vi* to coincide (**avec** with) ▪ **coïncidence** *nf* coincidence

col [kɔl] *nm (de chemise)* collar; *Géog* col; **c. en V** V-neck; **c. roulé** *Br* polo neck, *Am* turtleneck

colère [kɔlɛr] *nf* anger; **être en c. (contre qn)** to be angry (with sb); **se**

mettre en c. to get angry (**contre** with) ▪ **coléreux, -euse** *adj (personne)* quick-tempered

colimaçon [kɔlimasɔ̃] **en colimaçon** *adv* **escalier en c.** spiral staircase

colin [kɔlɛ̃] *nm (merlu)* hake; *(lieu noir)* coley

colique [kɔlik] *nf Br* diarrhoea, *Am* diarrhea

colis [kɔli] *nm* parcel

collaborer [kɔlabɔre] *vi* collaborate (**avec** with); **c. à qch** *(projet)* to take part in sth ▪ **collaborateur, -trice** *nmf (aide)* assistant ▪ **collaboration** *nf (aide)* collaboration

collage [kɔlaʒ] *nm (œuvre, jeu)* collage

collant, -e [kɔlã, -ãt] **1** *adj (papier)* sticky; *(vêtement)* skin-tight **2** *nm Br* tights, *Am* pantihose

colle [kɔl] *nf (transparente)* glue; *(blanche)* paste; *Fam (question)* poser; *Fam (retenue)* detention

collecte [kɔlɛkt] *nf* collection ▪ **collecter** *vt* to collect

collectif, -ive [kɔlɛktif, -iv] *adj* collective ▪ **collectivité** *nf (groupe)* community

collection [kɔlɛksjɔ̃] *nf (ensemble)* collection; **faire la c. de qch** to collect sth ▪ **collectionner** *vt* to collect ▪ **collectionneur, -euse** *nmf* collector

collège [kɔlɛʒ] *nm (école)* school ▪ **collégien** *nm* schoolboy ▪ **collégienne** *nf* schoolgirl

collègue [kɔlɛg] *nmf* colleague

coller [kɔle] **1** *vt (timbre)* to stick; *(à la colle transparente)* to glue; *(à la colle blanche)* to paste; *(enveloppe)* to stick (down); *(deux objets)* to stick together; *(affiche)* to stick up; *Fam* **c. un élève** *(en punition)* to keep a pupil in; *Fam* **être collé** *(à un examen)* to fail **2 se coller** *vpr* **se c. contre un mur** to flatten oneself against a wall

collier [kɔlje] *nm (bijou)* necklace; *(de chien)* collar

colline [kɔlin] *nf* hill

collision [kɔlizjɔ̃] *nf (de véhicules)* collision; **entrer en c. avec qch** to collide with sth

colloque [kɔlɔk] *nm (conférence)* seminar

colmater [kɔlmate] *vt* to fill in

colombe [kɔlɔ̃b] *nf* dove

Colombie [kɔlɔ̃bi] *nf* la C. Columbia ■ **colombien, -enne 1** *adj* Columbian **2** *nmf* C., **Colombienne** Columbian

colon [kɔlɔ̃] *nm (pionnier)* settler, colonist

colonel [kɔlɔnɛl] *nm (d'infanterie)* colonel

colonial, -e, -aux, -ales [kɔlɔnjal, -jo] *adj* colonial

colonie [kɔlɔni] *nf* colony; c. de vacances *Br* (children's) holiday camp, *Am* summer camp

coloniser [kɔlɔnize] *vt* to colonize

colonne [kɔlɔn] *nf* column; *Anat* c. vertébrale spine

colorer [kɔlɔre] *vt* to colour; c. qch en vert to colour sth green ■ **colorant, -e** *nm (pour teindre)* colorant; *(alimentaire)* colouring ■ **colorier** *vt (dessin)* to colour (in) ■ **coloris** *nm (nuance)* shade

colosse [kɔlɔs] *nm* giant ■ **colossal, -e, -aux, -ales** *adj* colossal

colporter [kɔlpɔrte] *vt (marchandises)* to hawk; *(rumeur)* to spread

colza [kɔlza] *nm* rape

coma [kɔma] *nm* coma; être dans le c. to be in a coma

combat [kɔ̃ba] *nm (bataille)* & *Fig* fight; c. de boxe boxing match ■ **combatif, -ive** *adj* combative

combattre* [kɔ̃batr] **1** *vt (personne, incendie)* to fight (against); *(maladie)* to fight **2** *vi* to fight ■ **combattant, -e 1** *adj (troupes)* fighting **2** *nmf* combattant; anciens combattants veterans

combien [kɔ̃bjɛ̃] **1** *adv* (a) *(en quantité)* how much; *(en nombre)* how many; c. d'argent how much money; c. de temps how long; c. de gens how many people; c. y a-t-il d'ici à…? how far is it to…? (b) *(comme)* how; tu verras c. il est bête you'll see how silly he is **2** *nm inv Fam* le c. sommes-nous? what's the date?

combinaison [kɔ̃binɛzɔ̃] *nf (assemblage)* combination; *(vêtement de travail)* Br boiler suit, *Am* coveralls; c. de ski ski suit

combiner [kɔ̃bine] **1** *vt (unir)* to combine **2** se combiner *vpr* to combine ■ **combiné** *nm (de téléphone)* receiver

comble [kɔ̃bl] **1** *adj (salle, bus)* packed; *Théât* faire salle c. to have a full house **2** *nm* le c. du bonheur the height of happiness; c'est un *ou* le c.! that's the last straw!

combler [kɔ̃ble] *vt (trou)* to fill in; *(lacune)* to fill; *(désir)* to satisfy

combustible [kɔ̃bystibl] **1** *adj* combustible **2** *nm* fuel ■ **combustion** *nf* combustion

comédie [kɔmedi] *nf* comedy; jouer la c. to act; c. musicale musical ■ **comédien** *nm* actor ■ **comédienne** *nf* actress

comestible [kɔmɛstibl] *adj* edible

comète [kɔmɛt] *nf* comet

comique [kɔmik] **1** *adj (amusant)* funny, comical; *(acteur, rôle)* comedy **2** *nm (genre)* comedy; *(acteur)* comic actor

comité [kɔmite] *nm* committee; c. d'entreprise works council

commandant [kɔmɑ̃dɑ̃] *nm (de navire)* captain; *(grade) (dans l'infanterie)* major; *(dans l'aviation)* squadron leader; *Aviat* c. de bord captain

commande [kɔmɑ̃d] *nf* (a) *(achat)* order; sur c. to order; passer une c. to place an order (b) *Tech (action, manette)* control; *Ordinat* command; c. à distance remote control; à c. vocale voice-activated

commandement [kɔmɑ̃dmɑ̃] *nm (ordre, autorité)* command; *Rel* Commandment

commander [kɔmɑ̃de] **1** *vt (diriger, exiger)* to command; *(marchandises)* to order (à from) **2** *vi* c. à qn de faire qch to command sb to do sth

commando [kɔmɑ̃do] *nm* commando

COMME [kɔm] **1** *adv* (a) *(devant nom, pronom)* like; c. moi/elle like me/her; c. cela like that; qu'as-tu c. diplômes? what do you have in the way of

certificates?; **les femmes c. les hommes** men and women alike; **P c. pomme** p as in 'pomme'
(b) *(devant proposition)* as; **il écrit c. il parle** he writes as he speaks; **c. si** as if; **c. pour faire qch** as if to do sth
2 *adv (exclamatif)* **regarde c. il pleut!** look how it's raining!; **c. c'est petit!** isn't it small!
3 *conj (cause)* as, since; **c. tu es mon ami...** as *or* since you're my friend...; **c. elle entrait** (just) as she was coming in

commémorer [kɔmemɔre] *vt* to commemorate ▪ **commémoration** *nf* commemoration

commencer [kɔmɑ̃se] *vti* to begin, to start (**à faire** to do, doing; **par qch** with sth; **par faire** by doing); **pour c.** to begin with ▪ **commencement** *nm* beginning, start; **au c.** at the beginning *or* start

comment [kɔmɑ̃] *adv* how; **c. le sais-tu?** how do you know?; **c. t'appelles-tu?** what's your name?; **c. est-il?** what is he like?; **c. va-t-il?** how is he?; **c. faire?** what's to be done?; **c.?** *(pour faire répéter)* pardon?

commentaire [kɔmɑ̃tɛr] *nm (remarque)* comment; *(de radio, de télévision)* commentary ▪ **commentateur, -trice** *nmf* commentator ▪ **commenter** *vt* to comment (up)on

commérages [kɔmeraʒ] *nmpl* gossip

commerçant, -e [kɔmɛrsɑ̃, -ɑ̃t] **1** *nmf* trader; *(de magasin)* shopkeeper **2** *adj* **rue commerçante** shopping street

commerce [kɔmɛrs] *nm (activité, secteur)* trade; *(affaires, magasin)* business; **c. de proximité** *Br* local shop, *Am* local store ▪ **commercial, -e, -aux, -ales** *adj* commercial ▪ **commercialisation** *nf* marketing ▪ **commercialiser** *vt* to market

commère [kɔmɛr] *nf* gossip

commettre* [kɔmɛtr] *vt (meurtre)* to commit; *(erreur)* to make

commis [kɔmi] *nm (de magasin)* shop assistant; *(de bureau)* clerk

commissaire [kɔmisɛr] *nm (de*

course) steward; **c. (de police)** *Br* ≃ police superintendent, *Am* ≃ police captain ▪ **commissariat** *nm* **c. (de police)** (central) police station

commission [kɔmisjɔ̃] *nf (course)* errand; *(message)* message; *(comité)* commission, committee; *Com (pourcentage)* commission (**sur** on); **faire les commissions** to go shopping

commode [kɔmɔd] **1** *adj (pratique)* handy; **pas c.** *(pas aimable)* awkward; *(difficile)* tricky **2** *nf Br* chest of drawers, *Am* dresser ▪ **commodité** *nf* convenience

commun, -e [kɔmœ̃, -yn] **1** *adj (non exclusif, répandu, vulgaire)* common; *(cuisine)* shared; *(démarche)* joint; **peu c.** uncommon; **ami c.** mutual friend; **en c.** in common; **mettre qch en c.** to share sth **2** *nm* **hors du c.** out of the ordinary

communauté [kɔmynote] *nf (collectivité)* community; **la C. (économique) européenne** the (European) Economic Community; **la C. d'États indépendants** the Commonwealth of Independent States ▪ **communautaire** *adj (de la CE)* Community; **vie c.** community life

commune [kɔmyn] *nf (municipalité)* commune ▪ **communal, -e, -aux, -ales** *adj Br* ≃ council, *Am* ≃ district; **école communale** ≃ local *Br* primary *or Am* grade school

communicatif, -ive [kɔmynikatif, -iv] *adj (personne)* communicative; *(rire)* infectious

communication [kɔmynikasjɔ̃] *nf* communication; **c. téléphonique** telephone call; **je vous passe la c.** I'll put you through; **la c. est mauvaise** the line is bad

communion [kɔmynjɔ̃] *nf* communion; *Rel* (Holy) Communion

communiquer [kɔmynike] **1** *vt* to communicate (**à** to); *(maladie)* to pass on (**à** to) **2** *vi (personne, pièces)* to communicate (**avec** with) **3** *se communiquer vpr* to spread (**à** to) ▪ **communiqué** *nm (avis)* communiqué; **c. de presse** press release

communisme [kɔmynism] *nm* communism ■ **communiste** *adj & nmf* communist

commutateur [kɔmytatœr] *nm (bouton)* switch

compact, -e [kɔpakt] **1** *adj (foule, amas)* dense; *(appareil)* compact **2** *nm (CD)* compact disc

compagne [kɔpaɲ] *nf (camarade)* companion; *(concubine)* partner

compagnie [kɔpaɲi] *nf (présence, société, soldats)* company; **tenir c. à qn** to keep sb company

compagnon [kɔpaɲɔ̃] *nm* companion; *(concubin)* partner; **c. de jeu** playmate; **c. de route** travelling companion

comparaître* [kɔparɛtr] *vi (devant tribunal)* to appear (in court) (**devant** before)

comparer [kɔpare] *vt* to compare (**à** to, with) ■ **comparable** *adj* comparable (**à** to, with) ■ **comparaison** *nf* comparison (**avec** with); **en c. de...** in comparison with...

compartiment [kɔpartimɑ̃] *nm* compartment; **c. à bagages** *(de car)* luggage compartment; **c. fumeurs** smoking compartment

compas [kɔpa] *nm Math Br* (pair of) compasses, *Am* compass; *Naut* compass

compassion [kɔpasjɔ̃] *nf* compassion

compatible [kɔpatibl] *adj* compatible (**avec** with) ■ **compatibilité** *nf* compatibility

compatir [kɔpatir] *vi* to sympathize ■ **compatissant, -e** *adj* compassionate, sympathetic

compatriote [kɔpatrijɔt] *nmf* compatriot

compenser [kɔpɑ̃se] **1** *vt (perte, défaut)* to make up for, to compensate for **2** *vi* to compensate ■ **compensation** *nf (de perte)* compensation; **en c.** in compensation (**de** for)

compétent, -e [kɔpetɑ̃, -ɑ̃t] *adj* competent ■ **compétence** *nf* competence; **compétences** *(connaissances)* skills, abilities

compétition [kɔpetisjɔ̃] *nf (rivalité)* competition; *(épreuve sportive)* event; **être en c. avec qn** to compete with sb; **sport de c.** competitive sport ■ **compétitif, -ive** *adj* competitive

compiler [kɔpile] *vt* to compile

complaire* [kɔplɛr] **se complaire** *vpr* **se c. dans qch/à faire qch** to delight in sth/in doing sth

complaisant, -e [kɔplezɑ̃, -ɑ̃t] *adj (bienveillant)* kind, obliging; *(satisfait)* complacent ■ **complaisance** *nf (bienveillance)* kindness; *(vanité)* complacency

complément [kɔplemɑ̃] *nm (reste)* rest; *Gram* complement; **un c. d'information** additional information; **c. d'objet direct/indirect** direct/indirect object ■ **complémentaire** *adj* complementary; *(détails)* additional

complet, -ète [kɔplɛ, -ɛt] **1** *adj (entier, absolu)* complete; *(train, hôtel, théâtre)* full; *(pain)* wholemeal **2** *nm (costume)* suit

compléter [kɔplete] **1** *vt (collection, formation)* to complete; *(formulaire)* to fill in; *(somme)* to make up **2** **se compléter** *vpr* to complement each other

complexe [kɔplɛks] **1** *adj* complex **2** *nm (sentiment, construction)* complex; **avoir des complexes** to have a hang-up ■ **complexé, -e** *adj Fam* hung up (**par** about) ■ **complexité** *nf* complexity

complication [kɔplikasjɔ̃] *nf (ennui) & Méd* complication; *(complexité)* complexity

complice [kɔplis] **1** *nm* accomplice **2** *adj (regard)* knowing; *(silence)* conniving; **être c. de qch** to be a party to sth ■ **complicité** *nf* complicity

compliment [kɔplimɑ̃] *nm* compliment; **faire des compliments à qn** to pay sb compliments ■ **complimenter** *vt* to compliment (**sur** on)

compliquer [kɔplike] **1** *vt* to complicate **2** **se compliquer** *vpr (situation)* to get complicated; **se c. la vie** to make life complicated for oneself ■ **compliqué, -e** *adj* complicated

complot [kɔplo] *nm* conspiracy (**contre** against)

comporter [kɔporte] **1** *vt (contenir)* to contain; *(être constitué de)* to consist of **2 se comporter** *vpr (personne)* to behave ▪ **comportement** [-əmɑ̃] *nm Br* behaviour, *Am* behavior

composer [kɔpoze] **1** *vt (faire partie de)* to make up; *(musique, poème)* to compose; *(numéro de téléphone)* to dial; *Typ* to set; **être composé de qch** to be made up *or* composed of sth

2 *vi (étudiant)* to take a test

3 se composer *vpr* **se c. de qch** to be made up *or* composed of sth ▪ **composant** *nm* component ▪ **composante** *nf* component

compositeur, -trice [kɔpozitœr, -tris] *nmf (musicien)* composer; *(typographe)* typesetter

composition [kɔpozisjɔ̃] *nf (de musique, de poème)* composing; *Typ* typesetting; *(éléments)* composition; *(d'aliment)* ingredients; *(examen)* test

composter [kɔposte] *vt (billet)* to cancel

compote [kɔpot] *nf Br* stewed fruit, *Am* sauce; **c. de pommes** *Br* stewed apples, *Am* applesauce

compréhensible [kɔpreɑ̃sibl] *adj (justifié)* understandable; *(clair)* comprehensible ▪ **compréhensif, -ive** *adj* understanding ▪ **compréhension** *nf* understanding

comprendre* [kɔprɑ̃dr] **1** *vt (par l'esprit, par les sentiments)* to understand; *(être composé de)* to consist of; *(comporter)* to include; **mal c. qch** to misunderstand sth; **je n'y comprends rien** I can't make head or tail of it **2 se comprendre** *vpr* **ça se comprend** that's understandable

compresse [kɔpres] *nf* compress

comprimé [kɔprime] *nm (médicament)* tablet

comprimer [kɔprime] *vt (gaz, artère)* to compress

compris, -e [kɔpri, -iz] **1** *pp voir* **comprendre 2** *adj (inclus)* included (**dans** in); **y c.** including

compromettre* [kɔprɔmetr] *vt (personne)* to compromise; *(sécurité)* to jeopardize ▪ **compromis** *nm* compromise

comptabiliser [kɔtabilize] *vt (compter)* to count

comptabilité [kɔtabilite] *nf (comptes)* accounts; *(science)* book-keeping, accounting; *(service)* accounts department ▪ **comptable** *nmf* accountant

comptant [kɔtɑ̃] **1** *adv* **payer c.** to pay (in) cash **2** *nm* **acheter au c.** to buy for cash

COMPTE [kɔt] *nm* (a) *(de banque, de commerçant)* account; *(calcul)* calculation; **avoir un c. en banque** to have a bank account; **faire ses comptes** to do one's accounts; **c. chèque** *Br* current account, *Am* checking account; **c. à rebours** countdown

(b) *(expressions)* **en fin de c.** all things considered; **tenir c. de qch** to take sth into account; **c. tenu de qch** considering sth; **se rendre c. de qch** to realize sth; **rendre c. de qch** *(exposer)* to report on sth; *(justifier)* to account for sth; **travailler à son c.** to be self-employed; *Fig* **être loin du c.** to be wide of the mark ▪ **compte-gouttes** *nm inv* dropper; *Fig* **au c.** in dribs and drabs

compter [kɔte] **1** *vt (calculer)* to count; *(prévoir)* to allow; *(include)* to include; **c. faire qch** *(espérer)* to expect to do sth; *(avoir l'intention de)* to intend to do sth; **c. qch à qn** *(facturer)* to charge sb for sth; **sans c....** *(sans parler de)* not to mention…

2 *vi (calculer, être important)* to count; **c. sur qn/qch** to count *or* rely on sb/ sth; **à c. de demain** as from tomorrow

3 se compter *vpr* **ses membres se comptent par milliers** it has thousands of members ▪ **compteur** *nm* meter; **c. de gaz** gas meter; *Aut* **c. kilométrique** *Br* milometer, *Am* odometer; *Aut* **c. de vitesse** speedometer

compte rendu [kɔtrɑ̃dy] *(pl* **comptes rendus)** *nm* report; *(de livre, de film)* review

comptoir [kɔtwar] *nm (de magasin)* counter; *(de café)* bar

comte [kɔ̃t] *nm (noble)* count; *(en Grande-Bretagne)* earl ■ **comtesse** *nf* countess

concéder [kɔ̃sede] *vt (victoire, but)* to concede; **c. qch à qn** to grant sb sth

concentrer [kɔ̃sɑ̃tre] **1** *vt* to concentrate; *(attention)* to focus **2 se concentrer** *vpr (réfléchir)* to concentrate ■ **concentration** *nf* concentration ■ **concentré, -e 1** *adj (lait)* condensed; *(attentif)* concentrating (hard) **2** *nm* **c. de tomates** tomato purée

concept [kɔ̃sept] *nm* concept ■ **conception** *nf (d'idée)* conception; *(création)* design; **c. assistée par ordinateur** computer-aided design

concerner [kɔ̃serne] *vt* to concern; **en ce qui me concerne** as far as I'm concerned ■ **concernant** *prép* concerning

concert [kɔ̃ser] *nm (de musique)* concert

concerter [kɔ̃serte] **se concerter** *vpr* to consult together ■ **concertation** *nf* consultation

concession [kɔ̃sesjɔ̃] *nf (compromis)* concession (à to); *(terrain)* plot ■ **concessionnaire** *nmf* dealer

concevoir* [kɔ̃səvwar] **1** *vt (enfant, plan, idée)* to conceive; *(produit)* to design; *(comprendre)* to understand **2 se concevoir** *vpr* **ça se conçoit** that's understandable ■ **concevable** *adj* conceivable

concierge [kɔ̃sjerʒ] *nmf* caretaker, *Am* janitor

concilier [kɔ̃silje] *vt (choses)* to reconcile

concis, -e [kɔ̃si, -is] *adj* concise

conclure* [kɔ̃klyr] *vt (terminer)* to conclude; *(accord)* to finalize; *(marché)* to clinch ■ **concluant, -e** *adj* conclusive ■ **conclusion** *nf* conclusion; **tirer une c. de qch** to draw a conclusion from sth

concombre [kɔ̃kɔ̃br] *nm* cucumber

concorder [kɔ̃kɔrde] *vi (preuves, dates, témoignages)* to tally (**avec** with)

concourir* [kɔ̃kurir] *vi Sport* to compete (**pour** for); *(converger)* to converge; **c. à qch/faire qch** to contribute to sth/to do sth

concours [kɔ̃kur] *nm (examen)* competitive examination; *(jeu)* competition; *(aide)* assistance; **c. de beauté** beauty contest

concret, -ète [kɔ̃kre, -et] *adj* concrete ■ **concrétiser 1** *vt (rêve)* to realize; *(projet)* to carry out **2 se concrétiser** *vpr* to materialize

conçu, -e [kɔ̃sy] **1** *pp de* **concevoir 2** *adj* **c. pour faire qch** designed to do sth

concubine [kɔ̃kybin] *nf Jur* cohabitant ■ **concubinage** *nm* cohabitation; **vivre en c.** to cohabit

concurrent, -e [kɔ̃kyrɑ̃, -ɑ̃t] *nmf* competitor ■ **concurrence** *nf* competition; **faire c. à** to compete with; **jusqu'à c. de 100 euros** up to the amount of 100 euros ■ **concurrencer** *vt* to compete with

condamnation [kɔ̃danasjɔ̃] *nf Jur (jugement)* conviction (**pour** for); *(peine)* sentence (**à** to); *(critique)* condemnation; **c. à mort** death sentence

condamner [kɔ̃dane] *vt (blâmer)* to condemn; *Jur* to sentence (**à** to); *(porte)* to block up; **c. qn à une amende** to fine sb; **c. qn à qch** *(forcer à)* to force sb into sth ■ **condamné, -e 1** *adj (malade)* terminally ill **2** *nmf (prisonnier)* convicted person

condensation [kɔ̃dɑ̃sasjɔ̃] *nf* condensation

condescendant, -e [kɔ̃desɑ̃dɑ̃, -ɑ̃t] *adj* condescending

condition [kɔ̃disjɔ̃] *nf (état, stipulation, sort)* condition; *(classe sociale)* station; **conditions** *(circonstances)* conditions; *(de contrat)* terms; **à c. de faire qch, à c. que l'on fasse qch** providing *or* provided (that) one does sth ■ **conditionnel, -elle 1** *adj* conditional **2** *nm Gram* conditional

conditionner [kɔ̃disjɔne] *vt (être la condition de)* to govern; *(emballer)* to package; *(personne)* to condition ■ **conditionnement** *nm (emballage)*

packaging; *(de personne)* conditioning

condoléances [kɔ̃dɔleɑ̃s] *nfpl* condolences

conducteur, -trice [kɔ̃dyktœr, -tris] **1** *nmf (de véhicule, de train)* driver **2** *adj* *Él* **fil c.** lead (wire)

conduire* [kɔ̃dɥir] **1** *vt (troupeau)* to lead; *(voiture)* to drive; *(moto)* to ride; *(électricité)* to conduct; **c. qn à** *(accompagner)* to take sb to **2** *vi (en voiture)* to drive; **c. à** *(lieu)* to lead to **3 se conduire** *vpr* to behave

conduit [kɔ̃dɥi] *nm (tuyau)* pipe

conduite [kɔ̃dɥit] *nf (de véhicule)* driving (**de** of); *(d'entreprise)* management; *(tuyau)* pipe; *(comportement)* conduct, behaviour; **c. à gauche/droite** *(volant)* left-hand/right-hand drive; **c. de gaz** gas main

cône [kon] *nm* cone

confection [kɔ̃fɛksjɔ̃] *nf (réalisation)* making (**de** of); *(industrie)* clothing industry; **vêtements de c.** ready-to-wear clothes ■ **confectionner** *vt* to make

confédération [kɔ̃federasjɔ̃] *nf* confederation

conférence [kɔ̃ferɑ̃s] *nf (réunion)* conference; *(exposé)* lecture; **c. de presse** press conference

conférer [kɔ̃fere] *vt (titre)* to confer (**à** on)

confesser [kɔ̃fese] *Rel* **1** *vt* to confess **2 se confesser** *vpr* to confess (**à** to) ■ **confession** *nf* confession

confettis [kɔ̃feti] *nmpl* confetti

confiance [kɔ̃fjɑ̃s] *nf* confidence; **faire c. à qn, avoir c. en qn** to trust sb; **de c.** *(mission)* of trust; *(personne)* trustworthy; **c. en soi** self-confidence; **avoir c. en soi** to be self-confident ■ **confiant, -e** *adj (qui fait confiance)* trusting; *(optimiste)* confident; *(qui a confiance en soi)* self-confident

confidence [kɔ̃fidɑ̃s] *nf* confidence; **faire une c. à qn** to confide in sb ■ **confident, -e** *nmf* confidant, *f* confidante ■ **confidentiel, -elle** *adj* confidential

confier [kɔ̃fje] **1** *vt* **c. qch à qn** *(laisser)* to entrust sb with sth; *(dire)* to confide sth to sb **2 se confier** *vpr* **se c. à qn** to confide in sb

configuration [kɔ̃figyrasjɔ̃] *nf (disposition)* layout; *Ordinat* configuration

confiner [kɔ̃fine] **1** *vt* to confine **2** *vi* **c. à** to border on **3 se confiner** *vpr* **se c. chez soi** to shut oneself up indoors

confins [kɔ̃fɛ̃] *nmpl* confines; **aux c. de** on the edge of

confirmation [kɔ̃firmasjɔ̃] *nf* confirmation

confirmer [kɔ̃firme] **1** *vt* to confirm (**que** that) **2 se confirmer** *vpr (nouvelle)* to be confirmed; *(tendance)* to continue

confiserie [kɔ̃fizri] *nf (magasin) Br* sweetshop, *Am* candy store; **confiseries** *(bonbons) Br* sweets, *Am* candy ■ **confiseur** *nm* confectioner

confisquer [kɔ̃fiske] *vt* to confiscate (**à qn** from sb)

confit, -e [kɔ̃fi] **1** *adj (fruits)* candied **2** *nm* **c. d'oie** potted goose

confiture [kɔ̃fityr] *nf* jam; **c. de fraises** strawberry jam

conflit [kɔ̃fli] *nm* conflict; **conflits sociaux** industrial disputes ■ **conflictuel, -elle** *adj (intérêts)* conflicting

confondre [kɔ̃fɔ̃dr] **1** *vt (choses, personnes)* to mix up, to confuse; *(consterner)* to astound; *(démasquer)* to confound; **c. qn/qch avec qn/qch** to mistake sb/sth for sb/sth
 2 se confondre *vpr (couleurs, intérêts)* to merge; **se c. en excuses** to apologize profusely

conforme [kɔ̃fɔrm] *adj* **c. à** in accordance with; *(modèle)* true to ■ **conformément** *adv* **c. à** in accordance with

conformer [kɔ̃fɔrme] **1** *vt* to model **2 se conformer** *vpr* to conform (**à** to)

conformiste [kɔ̃fɔrmist] *adj & nmf* conformist

conformité [kɔ̃fɔrmite] *nf* conformity (**à** with)

confort [kɔ̃fɔr] *nm* comfort ■ **confortable** *adj* comfortable

confrère [kɔ̃frɛr] *nm (de profession)* colleague

confronter [kɔ̃frɔ̃te] *vt (personnes)* to confront; *(expériences, résultats)* to compare; **confronté à** *(difficulté)* confronted with ▪ **confrontation** *nf (face-à-face)* confrontation; *(comparaison)* comparison

confus, -e [kɔ̃fy, -yz] *adj (esprit, situation, explication)* confused; *(gêné)* embarrassed ▪ **confusion** *nf (désordre, méprise)* confusion; *(gêne)* embarrassment

congé [kɔ̃ʒe] *nm (vacances) Br* holiday, *Am* vacation; *(arrêt de travail)* leave; *(avis de renvoi)* notice; **donner son c. à qn** *(employé, locataire)* to give notice to sb; **être en c.** to be on holiday *or* off work; **c. de maladie** sick leave; **c. de maternité** maternity leave; **c. de paternité** paternity leave; **congés payés** *Br* paid holidays, *Am* paid vacation

congédier [kɔ̃ʒedje] *vt* to dismiss

congeler [kɔ̃ʒle] *vt* to freeze ▪ **congelé, -e** *adj* frozen; **les produits congelés** frozen food ▪ **congélateur** *nm* freezer

congère [kɔ̃ʒɛr] *nf* snowdrift

Congo [kɔ̃go] *nm* **le C.** Congo ▪ **congolais, -e** 1 *adj* Congolese 2 *nmf* **C.,** Congolaise Congolese

congratuler [kɔ̃gratyle] *vt* to congratulate (**sur** on)

congrès [kɔ̃grɛ] *nm* conference; **le C.** *(aux États-Unis)* the Congress

conique [kɔnik] *adj* conical

conjoint, -e [kɔ̃ʒwɛ̃, -wɛ̃t] 1 *adj* joint 2 *nm* spouse; **conjoints** husband and wife

conjonction [kɔ̃ʒɔ̃ksjɔ̃] *nf (union)* union; *Gram* conjunction

conjonctivite [kɔ̃ʒɔ̃ktivit] *nf Méd* conjunctivitis

conjoncture [kɔ̃ʒɔ̃ktyr] *nf* circumstances

conjugal, -e, -aux, -ales [kɔ̃ʒygal, -o] *adj (bonheur)* marital; *(vie)* married; *(devoir)* conjugal

conjuguer [kɔ̃ʒyge] 1 *vt (verbe)* to conjugate; *(efforts)* to combine 2 **se conjuguer** *vpr (verbe)* to be conjuga-

ted ▪ **conjugaison** *nf Gram* conjugation

conjurer [kɔ̃ʒyre] *vt (danger)* to avert; *(mauvais sort)* to ward off; **c. qn de faire qch** to beg sb to do sth ▪ **conjuré, -e** *nmf* conspirator

connaissance [kɔnɛsɑ̃s] *nf (savoir)* knowledge; *(personne)* acquaintance; **à ma c.** to my knowledge; **avoir c. de qch** to be aware of sth; **faire c. avec qn** to get to know sb; **perdre/reprendre c.** to lose/regain consciousness; **sans c.** unconscious ▪ **connaisseur** *nm* connoisseur

connaître* [kɔnɛtr] 1 *vt (personne, endroit, faits)* to know; *(rencontrer)* to meet; *(famine, guerre)* to experience; **faire c. qch** to make sth known; **faire c. qn** *(présenter)* to introduce sb; *(rendre célèbre)* to make sb known

2 **se connaître** *vpr* **nous nous connaissons déjà** we've met before; **s'y c. en qch** to know all about sth

connecter [kɔnɛkte] *vt (appareil électrique)* to connect; *Ordinat* **connecté** on line ▪ **connexion** *nf* connection

connu, -e [kɔny] 1 *pp de* **connaître** 2 *adj (célèbre)* well-known

conquérir* [kɔ̃kerir] *vt (pays, sommet)* to conquer; *(marché)* to capture ▪ **conquérant, -e** *nmf* conqueror ▪ **conquête** *nf* conquest

consacrer [kɔ̃sakre] 1 *vt (temps)* to devote (**à** to); *(église)* to consecrate; *(entériner)* to establish 2 **se consacrer** *vpr* **se c. à** to devote oneself to

consciemment [kɔ̃sjamɑ̃] *adv* consciously

conscience [kɔ̃sjɑ̃s] *nf* **(a)** *(esprit)* consciousness; **avoir/prendre c. de qch** to be/become aware of sth; **perdre c.** to lose consciousness **(b)** *(morale)* conscience; **avoir bonne/mauvaise c.** to have a clear/guilty conscience ▪ **consciencieux, -euse** *adj* conscientious

conscient, -e [kɔ̃sjɑ̃, -ɑ̃t] *adj (lucide)* conscious; **c. de qch** aware *or* conscious of sth

conscrit [kɔ̃skri] *nm* conscript

consécutif, -ive [kɔ̃sekytif, -iv] *adj* consecutive; **c. à** following upon

conseil [kɔ̃sɛj] *nm* (a) **un c.** *(recommandation)* a piece of advice; **des conseils** advice (b) *(assemblée)* council, committee; **c. d'administration** board of directors; *Scol* **c. de classe** = staff meeting with participation of class representatives; *Pol* **c. des ministres** cabinet meeting

conseiller¹ [kɔ̃seje] *vt (guider)* to advise; **c. qch à qn** to recommend sth to sb; **c. à qn de faire qch** to advise sb to do sth

conseiller², -ère [kɔ̃seje, -ɛr] *nmf (expert)* consultant, adviser; **c. d'orientation** careers adviser

consentir* [kɔ̃sɑ̃tir] **1** *vi* **c. à qch/à faire qch** to consent to sth/to do sth **2** *vt (prêt)* to grant (à to) ■ **consentement** *nm* consent

conséquence [kɔ̃sekɑ̃s] *nf* consequence; **en c.** accordingly; **sans c.** *(sans importance)* of no importance

conservateur, -trice [kɔ̃sɛrvatœr, -tris] **1** *adj & nmf Pol* Conservative **2** *nmf (de musée)* curator; *(de bibliothèque)* librarian **3** *nm (alimentaire)* preservative

conservatoire [kɔ̃sɛrvatwar] *nm* school, academy

conserve [kɔ̃sɛrv] *nf* **conserves** canned *or Br* tinned food; **en c.** canned, *Br* tinned

conserver [kɔ̃sɛrve] **1** *vt* to keep; *(fruits, tradition)* to preserve **2 se conserver** *vpr (aliment)* to keep

considérable [kɔ̃siderabl] *adj* considerable

considérer [kɔ̃sidere] *vt* to consider **(que** that); **tout bien considéré** all things considered ■ **considération** *nf (respect)* regard, esteem; **prendre qch en c.** to take sth into consideration

consigne [kɔ̃siɲ] *nf (instructions)* orders; *(de bouteille)* deposit; **c. (à bagages)** *Br* left-luggage office, *Am* checkroom; **c. automatique** lockers ■ **consigner** *vt (bouteille)* to charge a deposit on; *(bagages) Br* to deposit in the left-luggage office, *Am* to check;

(écrire) to record; *(punir) (soldat)* to confine to barracks

consistant, -e [kɔ̃sistɑ̃, -ɑ̃t] *adj (sauce, bouillie)* thick; *(repas)* substantial ■ **consistance** *nf* consistency

consister [kɔ̃siste] *vi* **c. en qch** to consist of sth; **c. à faire qch** to consist in doing sth

consœur [kɔ̃sœr] *nf* female colleague

console [kɔ̃sɔl] *nf (d'ordinateur, de jeux)* console

consoler [kɔ̃sɔle] **1** *vt* to comfort, to console **2 se consoler** *vpr* **se c. de qch** to get over sth ■ **consolation** *nf* comfort, consolation

consolider [kɔ̃sɔlide] *vt (mur, position)* to strengthen ■ **consolidation** *nf* strengthening

consommateur, -trice [kɔ̃sɔmatœr, -tris] *nmf* consumer; *(au café)* customer ■ **consommation** *nf (de nourriture, d'électricité)* consumption; *(de voiture)* fuel consumption; *(boisson)* drink

consommer [kɔ̃sɔme] **1** *vt (aliment, carburant)* to consume; *(mariage)* to consumate **2** *vi (au café)* to drink

consonne [kɔ̃sɔn] *nf* consonant

consortium [kɔ̃sɔrsjɔm] *nm (entreprises)* consortium

conspirer [kɔ̃spire] *vi (comploter)* to conspire **(contre** against); **c. à faire qch** *(concourir)* to conspire to do sth ■ **conspirateur, -trice** *nmf* conspirator ■ **conspiration** *nf* conspiracy

constant, -e [kɔ̃stɑ̃, -ɑ̃t] **1** *adj* constant **2** *nf* **constante** *Math* constant ■ **constamment** [-amɑ̃] *adv* constantly ■ **constance** *nf* constancy

constat [kɔ̃sta] *nm* (official) report

constater [kɔ̃state] *vt (observer)* to note **(que** that); *Jur (enregistrer)* to record; *(décès)* to certify ■ **constatation** *nf (remarque)* observation

constellation [kɔ̃stɛlasjɔ̃] *nf* constellation

consterner [kɔ̃stɛrne] *vt* to dismay

constipation [kɔ̃stipasjɔ̃] *nf* constipation

constituer [kɔ̃stitɥe] **1** *vt (composer)* to make up; *(équivaloir à)* to constitute;

(former) to form; **constitué de** made up of **2 se constituer** *vpr* **se c. prisonnier** to give oneself up

constitution [kɔ̃stitysjɔ̃] *nf (santé, lois)* constitution; *(de gouvernement)* formation ▪ **constitutionnel, -elle** *adj* constitutional

constructeur [kɔ̃stryktœr] *nm (bâtisseur)* builder; *(fabricant)* maker **(de** of); **c. automobile** car manufacturer ▪ **constructif, -ive** *adj* constructive ▪ **construction** *nf (de pont, de route, de maison)* building, construction **(de** of); *(édifice)* building; **en c.** under construction

construire* [kɔ̃strɥir] *vt (maison, route)* to build

consul [kɔ̃syl] *nm* consul ▪ **consulat** *nm* consulate

consulter [kɔ̃sylte] **1** *vt* to consult **2** *vi (médecin)* to see patients, *Br* to take surgery **3 se consulter** *vpr (discuter)* to confer ▪ **consultation** *nf* consultation

consumer [kɔ̃syme] *vt (brûler)* to consume

contact [kɔ̃takt] *nm* contact; **être en c. avec qn** to be in contact with sb; **prendre c.** to get in touch **(avec** with); *Aut* **mettre/couper le c.** to switch on/off ▪ **contacter** *vt* to contact

contagieux, -euse [kɔ̃taʒjø, -øz] *adj (maladie, personne)* contagious

contaminer [kɔ̃tamine] *vt* to contaminate ▪ **contamination** *nf* contamination

conte [kɔ̃t] *nm* tale; **c. de fées** fairy tale

contempler [kɔ̃tɑ̃ple] *vt* to gaze at, to contemplate

contemporain, -e [kɔ̃tɑ̃pɔrɛ̃, -ɛn] *adj & nmf* contemporary

contenance [kɔ̃tnɑ̃s] *nf* **(a)** *(de récipient)* capacity **(b)** *(allure)* bearing

contenir* [kɔ̃tnir] *vt (renfermer)* to contain; *(contrôler)* to hold back, to contain ▪ **conteneur** *nm* container

content, -e [kɔ̃tɑ̃, -ɑ̃t] **1** *adj* pleased, happy **(de** with; **de faire** to do); **être c. de soi** to be pleased with oneself **2** *nm*

avoir son c. to have had one's fill **(de** of)

contenter [kɔ̃tɑ̃te] **1** *vt (satisfaire)* to satisfy; *(faire plaisir à)* to please **2 se contenter** *vpr* **se c. de qch** to content oneself with sth ▪ **contentement** *nm* contentment, satisfaction

contentieux [kɔ̃tɑ̃sjø] *nm (querelles)* dispute; *Jur* litigation; *(service)* legal department

contenu [kɔ̃tny] *nm (de paquet, de bouteille)* contents; *(de lettre, de film)* content

conter [kɔ̃te] *vt* to tell **(à** to) ▪ **conteur, -euse** *nmf* storyteller

contestable [kɔ̃testabl] *adj* debatable

contestation [kɔ̃testasjɔ̃] *nf* protest

conteste [kɔ̃test] **sans conteste** *adv* indisputably

contester [kɔ̃teste] **1** *vt* to dispute **2** *vi* **faire qch sans c.** to do sth without protest ▪ **contesté, -e** *adj (théorie, dirigeant)* controversial

contexte [kɔ̃tɛkst] *nm* context

contigu, -ë [kɔ̃tigy] *adj (maisons)* adjoining; **c. à qch** adjoining sth

continent [kɔ̃tinɑ̃] *nm* continent; *(opposé à une île)* mainland ▪ **continental, -e, -aux, -ales** *adj (climat, plateau)* continental

contingent [kɔ̃tɛ̃ʒɑ̃] *nm Mil* contingent; *(quota)* quota

continu, -e [kɔ̃tiny] *adj* continuous ▪ **continuel, -elle** *adj (ininterrompu)* continuous; *(qui se répète)* continual ▪ **continuellement** *adv (de façon ininterrompue)* continuously; *(de façon répétitive)* continually

continuer [kɔ̃tinɥe] **1** *vt (études, efforts, politique)* to continue, to carry on with; **c. à** *ou* **de faire qch** to continue or carry on doing sth **2** *vi* to continue, to go on ▪ **continuation** *nf* continuation

continuité [kɔ̃tinɥite] *nf* continuity

contour [kɔ̃tur] *nm* outline

contourner [kɔ̃turne] *vt* to go round; *Fig (difficulté, loi)* to get round

contraceptif, -ive [kɔ̃traseptif, -iv] *adj & nm* contraceptive

contracter [kɔ̃trakte] **1** vt (muscle, habitude, dette) to contract **2 se contracter** vpr (muscle) to contract; (personne) to tense up ▪ **contraction** nf contraction

contractuel, -elle [kɔ̃traktɥɛl] **1** adj (politique) contractual **2** nmf Br ≃ traffic warden, Am ≃ traffic policeman, f traffic policewoman

contradiction [kɔ̃tradiksjɔ̃] nf contradiction; **être en c. avec qch** to contradict sth ▪ **contradictoire** adj contradictory

contraindre* [kɔ̃trɛ̃dr] **1** vt to compel, to force (**à faire** to do) **2 se contraindre** vpr to compel or force oneself (**à faire** to do) ▪ **contraignant, -e** adj restricting ▪ **contrainte** nf (obligation, limitation) constraint; **sous la c.** under duress

contraire [kɔ̃trɛr] **1** adj (opposé) conflicting; **c. à qch** contrary to sth; **en sens c.** in the opposite direction **2** nm opposite; **(bien) au c.** on the contrary ▪ **contrairement** adv **c. à** contrary to; **c. à qn** unlike sb

contrarier [kɔ̃trarje] vt (projet, action) to thwart; (personne) to annoy ▪ **contrariant, -e** adj (situation) annoying; (personne) contrary ▪ **contrariété** nf annoyance

contraste [kɔ̃trast] nm contrast ▪ **contraster** vi to contrast (**avec** with)

contrat [kɔ̃tra] nm contract

contravention [kɔ̃travɑ̃sjɔ̃] nf (amende) fine; (pour stationnement interdit) (parking) ticket

contre [kɔ̃tr] **1** prép against; (en échange de) (in exchange) for; **échanger qch c. qch** to exchange sth for sth; **fâché c. qn** angry with sb; **six voix c. deux** six votes to two; **Nîmes c. Arras** (match) Nîmes versus or against Arras; **sirop c. la toux** cough mixture; Fam **par c.** on the other hand **2** nm (au volley, au basket) block ▪ **contre-attaque** nf counter-attack ▪ **contre-attaquer** vt to counter-attack

contrebalancer [kɔ̃trəbalɑ̃se] vt to counterbalance; Fig (compenser) to offset

contrebande [kɔ̃trəbɑ̃d] nf (activité) smuggling; (marchandises) contraband; **tabac de c.** smuggled tobacco; **faire de la c.** to smuggle goods ▪ **contrebandier, -ère** nmf smuggler

contrebas [kɔ̃trəba] **en contrebas** adv & prép (down) below; **en c. de** below

contrebasse [kɔ̃trəbas] nf (instrument) double-bass

contrecarrer [kɔ̃trəkare] vt to thwart

contrecœur [kɔ̃trəkœr] **à contrecœur** adv reluctantly

contrecoup [kɔ̃trəku] nm repercussions

contre-courant [kɔ̃trəkurɑ̃] **à contre-courant** adv (nager) against the current

contredire* [kɔ̃trədir] **1** vt to contradict **2 se contredire** vpr (soi-même) to contradict oneself; (l'un l'autre) to contradict each other

contrée [kɔ̃tre] nf Littéraire (region) region; (pays) land

contre-espionnage [kɔ̃trɛspjɔnaʒ] nm counter-espionage

contrefaçon [kɔ̃trəfasɔ̃] nf (pratique) counterfeiting; (produit) fake ▪ **contrefaire*** vt (écriture) to disguise; (argent) to counterfeit; (signature) to forge

contre-jour [kɔ̃trəʒur] **à contre-jour** adv against the light

contremaître [kɔ̃trəmɛtr] nm foreman

contre-offensive [kɔ̃trɔfɑ̃siv] (pl **contre-offensives**) nf counter-offensive

contrepartie [kɔ̃trəparti] nf compensation; **en c.** in return (**de** for)

contre-pied [kɔ̃trəpje] nm Sport **prendre son adversaire à c.** to wrongfoot one's opponent

contreplaqué [kɔ̃trəplake] nm plywood

contrepoids [kɔ̃trəpwa] nm counterbalance

contrepoison [kɔ̃trəpwazɔ̃] nm antidote

contrer [kɔ̃tre] vt (personne, attaque) to counter

contresens [kɔ̃trəsɑ̃s] *nm* misinterpretation; *(en traduisant)* mistranslation; **prendre une rue à c.** to go down/up a street the wrong way

contresigner [kɔ̃trəsiɲe] *vt* to countersign

contretemps [kɔ̃trətɑ̃] *nm* hitch, mishap

contrevenir* [kɔ̃trəvnir] *vi* **c. à** to contravene

contribuable [kɔ̃tribɥabl] *nmf* taxpayer

contribuer [kɔ̃tribɥe] *vi* to contribute **(à** to); **c. à faire qch** to help (to) do sth

contribution [kɔ̃tribysjɔ̃] *nf* contribution **(à** to); *(impôt)* tax; **contributions** *(administration)* tax office

contrôle [kɔ̃trol] *nm* *(vérification)* checking **(de** of); *(surveillance)* monitoring; *(maîtrise)* control; *Scol* test; **avoir le c. de qch** to have control of sth; **le c. des naissances** birth control; **c. de soi** self-control; **c. fiscal** tax inspection

contrôler [kɔ̃trole] **1** *vt (vérifier)* to check; *(surveiller)* to monitor; *(maîtriser)* to control **2 se contrôler** *vpr* to control oneself ■ **contrôleur, -euse** *nmf (de train, de bus) Br* (ticket) inspector, *Am* conductor; **c. aérien** air-traffic controller

controverse [kɔ̃trɔvɛrs] *nf* controversy ■ **controversé, -e** *adj* controversial

contumace [kɔ̃tymas] **par contumace** *adv Jur* in absentia

contusion [kɔ̃tyzjɔ̃] *nf* bruise

convaincre* [kɔ̃vɛ̃kr] *vt* to convince **(de** of); **c. qn de faire qch** to persuade sb to do sth ■ **convaincant, -e** *adj* convincing ■ **convaincu, -e** *adj* convinced **(de** of; **que** that); *(partisan)* committed

convalescent, -e [kɔ̃valesɑ̃, -ɑ̃t] *adj & nmf* convalescent ■ **convalescence** *nf* convalescence; **être en c.** to be convalescing

convenable [kɔ̃vnabl] *adj (approprié)* suitable; *(acceptable, décent)* decent

convenance [kɔ̃vnɑ̃s] *nf* **faire qch à sa c.** to do sth at one's own convenience

convenir* [kɔ̃vnir] **1** *vi* **c. à** *(être fait pour)* to be suitable for; *(plaire à, aller à)* to suit; **c. de qch** *(lieu, prix)* to agree upon sth; **c. de faire qch** to agree to do sth; **c. que...** to admit that... **2** *v impersonnel* **il convient de...** it is advisable to...; *(selon les usages)* it is proper to...; **il fut convenu que...** *(décidé)* it was agreed that... ■ **convenu, -e** *adj (décidé)* agreed

convention [kɔ̃vɑ̃sjɔ̃] *nf (accord)* agreement; *(règle)* convention; **c. collective** collective agreement

conventionné, -e [kɔ̃vɑ̃sjone] *adj (médecin, clinique)* attached to the health system, *Br* ≃ NHS; **médecin non c.** private doctor

conventionnel, -elle [kɔ̃vɑ̃sjonɛl] *adj* conventional

convergence [kɔ̃vɛrʒɑ̃s] *nf* convergence ■ **converger** *vi* to converge **(vers** on)

conversation [kɔ̃vɛrsɑsjɔ̃] *nf* conversation

conversion [kɔ̃vɛrsjɔ̃] *nf (changement)* conversion **(en** into); *(à une doctrine)* conversion **(à** to) ■ **convertible 1** *adj* convertible **(en** into) **2** *nm* sofa bed ■ **convertir 1** *vt (changer)* to convert **(en** into); *(à une doctrine)* to convert **(à** to) **2 se convertir** *vpr (à une doctrine)* to be converted **(à** to)

conviction [kɔ̃viksjɔ̃] *nf (certitude, croyance)* conviction; **avoir la c. que...** to be convinced that...

convier [kɔ̃vje] *vt Formel* to invite **(à** to; **à faire** to do)

convive [kɔ̃viv] *nmf* guest

convivial, -e, -aux, -ales [kɔ̃vivjal, -jo] *adj* convivial; *Ordinat* user-friendly

convoi [kɔ̃vwa] *nm (véhicules, personnes)* convoy; *(train)* train; **c. funèbre** funeral procession

convoiter [kɔ̃vwate] *vt (poste, richesses)* to covet

convoquer [kɔ̃vɔke] *vt (employé, postulant)* to call in; **c. qn à un examen** to notify sb of an examination ■ **convocation** *nf (lettre)* notice to attend; **c. à un examen** notification of an examination

convoyer [kɔ̃vwaje] *vt (troupes)* to convoy; *(fonds)* to transport under armed guard

convulsion [kɔ̃vylsjɔ̃] *nf* convulsion

coopérer [kɔɔpere] *vi* to cooperate (**à** in, **avec** with) ■ **coopératif, -ive** *adj & nf* cooperative ■ **coopération** *nf* cooperation (**entre** between); *Pol* overseas development

coordonner [kɔɔrdɔne] *vt* to coordinate (**à** *ou* **avec** with) ■ **coordination** *nf* coordination ■ **coordonnées** *nfpl (adresse, téléphone)* address and telephone number

copain [kɔpɛ̃] *nm Fam (camarade)* pal; *(petit ami)* boyfriend

copeau, -x [kɔpo] *nm (de bois)* shaving

copie [kɔpi] *nf (manuscrit, double)* copy; *Scol (devoir, examen)* paper

copier [kɔpje] *vt (texte, musique, document) & Scol (à un examen)* to copy (**sur** from) ■ **copieur, -euse 1** *nmf (élève)* copier **2** *nm (machine)* photocopier

copieux, -euse [kɔpjø, -øz] *adj (repas)* copious; *(portion)* generous

copine [kɔpin] *nf Fam (camarade)* pal; *(petite amie)* girlfriend

copropriété [kɔprɔprijete] *nf* joint ownership

coq [kɔk] *nm* cock, *Am* rooster

coque [kɔk] *nf (de noix)* shell; *(de navire)* hull; *(fruit de mer)* cockle

coquelet [kɔklɛ] *nm* cockerel

coquelicot [kɔkliko] *nm* poppy

coqueluche [kɔklyʃ] *nf (maladie)* whooping cough

coquet, -ette [kɔkɛ, -ɛt] *adj (intérieur)* charming; *Fam (somme)* tidy

coquetier [kɔktje] *nm* egg-cup

coquille [kɔkij] *nf* shell; *(faute d'imprimerie)* misprint; *Culin* c. **Saint-Jacques** scallop ■ **coquillage** *nm (mollusque)* shellfish *inv; (coquille)* shell

coquin, -e [kɔkɛ̃, -in] **1** *adj (sourire, air)* mischievous; *(sous-vêtements)* naughty **2** *nmf* rascal

cor [kɔr] *nm (instrument)* horn; *(durillon)* corn

corail, -aux [kɔraj, -o] *nm* coral

Coran [kɔrɑ̃] *nm* le C. the Koran

corbeau, -x [kɔrbo] *nm (oiseau)* crow

corbeille [kɔrbɛj] *nf (a) (panier)* basket; c. **à pain** breadbasket; c. **à papier** wastepaper basket **(b)** *(à la Bourse)* trading floor **(c)** *Théât* dress circle

corbillard [kɔrbijar] *nm* hearse

corde [kɔrd] *nf (lien)* rope; *(de raquette, de violon)* string; c. **à linge** washing *or* clothes line; c. **à sauter** *Br* skipping rope, *Am* jump-rope; **cordes vocales** vocal cords ■ **cordée** *nf* roped party ■ **corder** *vt (raquette)* to string

cordial, -e, -aux, -ales [kɔrdjal, -o] **1** *adj (accueil, personne)* cordial **2** *nm (remontant)* tonic

cordon [kɔrdɔ̃] *nm (de tablier, de sac)* string; *(de rideau)* cord; *(de policiers)* cordon; *Anat* c. **ombilical** umbilical cord ■ **cordon-bleu** *(pl* **cordons-bleus)** *nm Fam* gourmet cook

cordonnier [kɔrdɔnje] *nm* shoe repairer ■ **cordonnerie** *nf (boutique)* shoe repairer's shop

Corée [kɔre] *nf* la C. Korea ■ **coréen, -enne 1** *adj* Korean **2** *nmf* C., **Coréenne** Korean

coriace [kɔrjas] *adj (viande, personne)* tough

corne [kɔrn] *nf (d'animal, matière, instrument)* horn; *(au pied, à la main)* hard skin; c. **de brume** foghorn

corneille [kɔrnɛj] *nf* crow

cornemuse [kɔrnəmyz] *nf* bagpipes

corner¹ [kɔrne] *vt (page)* to turn down the corner of; *(abîmer)* to make dog-eared

corner² [kɔrner] *nm (au football)* corner; **tirer un** c. to take a corner

cornet [kɔrnɛ] *nm (glace)* cone, *Br* cornet

corniche [kɔrniʃ] *nf (de rocher)* ledge; *(route)* coast road; *(en haut d'un mur)* cornice

cornichon [kɔrniʃɔ̃] *nm* gherkin

cornu, -e [kɔrny] *adj (diable, animal)* horned

corporation [kɔrpɔrasjɔ̃] *nf* corporate body

corporel, -elle [kɔrpɔrɛl] *adj (besoin)* bodily; *(hygiène)* personal

corps [kɔr] *nm (organisme, cadavre)* & *Chim* body; *(partie principale)* main part; **c. et âme** body and soul; **c. d'armée/diplomatique** army/diplomatic corps; **c. enseignant** teaching profession; **c. gras** fat

corpulent, -e [kɔrpylɑ̃, -ɑ̃t] *adj* stout, corpulent

correct, -e [kɔrɛkt] *adj (exact, courtois)* correct; *Fam (acceptable)* reasonable ■ **correctement** *adv (sans faire de fautes, décemment)* correctly; *Fam (de façon acceptable)* reasonably

correcteur, -trice [kɔrɛktœr, -tris] **1** *adj* **verres correcteurs** corrective lenses **2** *nmf (d'examen)* examiner; *(en typographie)* proofreader **3** *nm Ordinat* **c. d'orthographe** spellchecker

correction [kɔrɛksjɔ̃] *nf (rectification)* correction; *(punition)* beating; *(décence, courtoisie)* correctness; *Scol (de devoirs, d'examens)* marking

correctionnel, -elle [kɔrɛksjɔnɛl] **1** *adj* **tribunal c.** criminal court **2** *nf* **correctionnelle** criminal court; **passer en c.** to go before a criminal court

correspondance [kɔrɛspɔ̃dɑ̃s] *nf (relation, lettres)* correspondence; *(de train, d'autocar) Br* connection, *Am* transfer

correspondre [kɔrɛspɔ̃dr] *vi* **c. à qch** to correspond to sth; **c. avec qn** *(par lettres)* to correspond with sb ■ **correspondant, -e 1** *adj* corresponding (**à** to) **2** *nmf (reporter)* correspondent; *(par lettres)* pen friend, pen pal; *(au téléphone)* caller; **c. de guerre** war correspondent

corrida [kɔrida] *nf* bullfight

corridor [kɔridɔr] *nm* corridor

corriger [kɔriʒe] **1** *vt (texte, erreur, myopie, injustice)* to correct; *(exercice, devoir)* to mark; **c. qn** to give sb a beating; **c. qn de qch** to cure sb of sth **2 se corriger** *vpr* to mend one's ways; **se c. de qch** to cure oneself of sth ■ **corrigé** *nm (d'exercice)* correct answers (**de** to)

corrompre* [kɔrɔ̃pr] *vt (personne,* *goût)* to corrupt; *(soudoyer)* to bribe ■ **corrompu, -e** *adj* corrupt ■ **corruption** *nf* corruption

corrosion [kɔrozjɔ̃] *nf* corrosion ■ **corrosif, -ive** *adj* corrosive

corsage [kɔrsaʒ] *nm* blouse

Corse [kɔrs] *nf* la **C.** Corsica ■ **corse 1** *adj* Corsican **2** *nmf* **C.** Corsican

corser [kɔrse] **1** *vt (plat)* to spice up; *Fig (récit)* to liven up **2 se corser** *vpr* **ça se corse** things are getting complicated ■ **corsé, -e** *adj (café) Br* full-flavoured, *Am* full-flavored; *Fig (histoire)* spicy

corset [kɔrse] *nm* corset

cortège [kɔrtɛʒ] *nm (défilé)* procession

corvée [kɔrve] *nf* chore; *Mil* fatigue duty

cosmétique [kɔsmetik] *adj & nm* cosmetic

cosmique [kɔsmik] *adj* cosmic ■ **cosmonaute** *nmf* cosmonaut

cosmopolite [kɔsmɔpɔlit] *adj* cosmopolitan

cossu, -e [kɔsy] *adj (personne,* well-to-do; *(maison, intérieur)* opulent

costaud [kɔsto] *adj* sturdy

costume [kɔstym] *nm (habit)* costume; *(complet)* suit

cotation [kɔtasjɔ̃] *nf* **c. (en Bourse)** quotation (on the Stock Market)

cote [kɔt] *nf (marque de classement)* classification mark; *(valeur)* quotation; *(liste)* share index; *(de cheval)* odds; *(altitude)* altitude

coté, -e [kɔte] *adj* **bien c.** highly rated; **c. en Bourse** quoted on the Stock Market

côte [kɔt] *nf* **(a)** *(os)* rib; **à côtes** *(étoffe)* ribbed; **c. à c.** side by side; **c. d'agneau/de porc** lamb/pork chop; **c. de bœuf** rib of beef **(b)** *(de montagne)* slope **(c)** *(littoral)* coast; **la C. d'Azur** the French Riviera

côté [kote] *nm* side; **de l'autre c.** on the other side (**de** of); *(partir)* the other way; **de ce c.** *(passer)* this way; **du c. de** *(près de)* near; **à c.** close by, nearby; *(pièce)* in the other room; *(maison)* next

door; **la maison d'à c.** the house next door; **à c. de qn/qch** next to sb/sth; *(en comparaison de)* compared to sb/sth; **passer à c.** *(balle)* to fall wide **(de** of**); mettre qch de c.** to put sth aside

coteau, -x [kɔto] *nm* hill; *(versant)* hillside

côtelé, -e [kotle] *adj* **velours c.** corduroy

côtelette [kotlɛt] *nf (d'agneau, de porc)* chop

coter [kɔte] *vt (prix, action)* to quote

côtier, -ère [kotje, -ɛr] *adj* coastal; *(pêche)* inshore

cotiser [kɔtize] **1** *vi (à un cadeau, pour la retraite)* to contribute **(à** to; **pour** towards) **2 se cotiser** *vpr Br* to club together, *Am* to club in ▪ **cotisation** *nf (de club)* dues, subscription; *(de retraite, de chômage)* contribution

coton [kɔtɔ̃] *nm* cotton; **c. hydrophile** *Br* cotton wool, *Am* absorbent cotton

côtoyer [kotwaje] *vt (personnes)* to mix with

cou [ku] *nm* neck

couchage [kuʃaʒ] *nm* **sac de c.** sleeping bag

couchant [kuʃɑ̃, -ɑ̃t] **1** *adj m* **soleil c.** setting sun **2** *nm* **le c.** *(ouest)* the west

couche [kuʃ] *nf* **(a)** *(épaisseur)* layer; *(de peinture)* coat; **la c. d'ozone** the ozone layer **(b)** *(linge de bébé) Br* nappy, *Am* diaper ▪ **couche-culotte** *(pl couches-culottes) nf Br* disposable nappy, *Am* disposable diaper

coucher [kuʃe] **1** *nm (moment)* bedtime; **l'heure du c.** bedtime; **au c.** at bedtime; **c. de soleil** sunset

2 *vt (allonger)* to lay down; **c. qn** to put sb to bed

3 *vi* to sleep **(avec** with)

4 se coucher *vpr (personne)* to go to bed; *(s'allonger)* to lie down; *(soleil)* to set, to go down; **aller se c.** to go to bed ▪ **couché, -e** *adj* **être c.** to be in bed; *(étendu)* to be lying (down)

couchette [kuʃɛt] *nf (de train)* couchette; *(de bateau)* bunk

coude [kud] *nm* elbow; *(tournant)*

bend; **donner un coup de c. à qn** to nudge sb

cou-de-pied [kudpje] *(pl cous-de-pied) nm* instep

coudre* [kudr] *vti* to sew

couette¹ [kwɛt] *nf (édredon)* duvet

couette² [kwɛt] *nf Fam (coiffure)* bunch

couffin [kufɛ̃] *nm (de bébé) Br* Moses basket, *Am* bassinet

coulée [kule] *nf* **c. de lave** lava flow

couler [kule] **1** *vt* **(a)** *(métal, statue)* to cast; *(liquide, ciment)* to pour **(b)** *(navire)* to sink **2** *vi* **(a)** *(eau, rivière)* to flow; *(nez, sueur)* to run; *(robinet)* to leak **(b)** *(bateau, nageur)* to sink

couleur [kulœr] *nf (teinte) Br* colour, *Am* color; *(colorant)* paint; *(pour cheveux)* dye; *Cartes* suit; **de quelle c. est...?** what colour is...?; **télévision c.** *ou* **en couleurs** colour television (set)

couleuvre [kulœvr] *nf* grass snake

coulisse [kulis] *nf (de porte)* runner; **porte à c.** sliding door; *Théât* **les coulisses** the wings ▪ **coulissant, -e** *adj* sliding

couloir [kulwar] *nm (de maison, de train)* corridor; *(en natation, en athlétisme)* lane; **c. de bus** bus lane

COUP [ku] *nm* **(a)** *(choc)* blow; *(essai)* attempt, go; **donner un c. à qn** to hit sb; **se donner un c. contre qch** to knock against sth; **donner un c. de couteau à qn** to knife sb; **c. de pied** kick; **donner un c. de pied à qn** to kick sb; **c. de poing** punch; **donner un c. de poing à qn** to punch sb; **c. de tête** header

(b) *(action soudaine, événement soudain)* **c. de vent** gust of wind; **donner un c. de frein** to brake; **prendre un c. de soleil** to get sunburned; *Fig* **ça a été le c. de foudre** it was love at first sight; **c. d'État** coup; **c. de théâtre** coup de théâtre

(c) *(bruit)* **c. de feu** shot; **c. de fusil** shot; **c. de sifflet** whistle; **c. de tonnerre** clap of thunder; **l'horloge sonna deux coups** the clock struck two

(d) *(expressions)* **après c.** after the event; **sur le c.** *(alors)* at the time; **tué sur le c.** killed outright; **tout à c., tout d'un c.** suddenly; **d'un seul c.** *(avaler)* in one go; *(soudain)* all of a sudden; **du premier c.** at the first attempt; **sous le c. de la colère** in a fit of anger; **tenir le c.** to hold out; **tomber sous le c. de la loi** to be an offence; **c. d'envoi** *(au football, au rugby)* kickoff; **c. de maître** masterstroke; **c. droit** *(au tennis)* forehand; **c. franc** *(au football)* free kick; **c. monté** put-up job

coupable [kupabl] **1** *adj* guilty **(de** of); *(négligence)* culpable; **se sentir c.** to feel guilty **2** *nmf* culprit

coupant, -e [kupã, -ãt] *adj* sharp

coupe¹ [kup] *nf (trophée)* cup; *(récipient)* bowl; **la C. du monde** the World Cup; **c. à champagne** champagne glass

coupe² [kup] *nf (de vêtement)* cut; *(plan)* section; **c. de cheveux** haircut ■ **coupe-papier** *nm inv* paper knife ■ **coupe-vent** *nm inv (blouson) Br* windcheater, *Am* Windbreaker ®

couper [kupe] **1** *vt (trancher, supprimer)* to cut; *(arbre)* to cut down; **c. la parole à qn** to interrupt sb; **nous avons été coupés** *(au téléphone)* we were cut off

2 *vi (être tranchant)* to be sharp; *(aux cartes)* to cut; *(prendre un raccourci)* to take a short cut; **ne coupez pas!** *(au téléphone)* hold the line!

3 se couper *vpr (routes)* to intersect; **se c. au doigt** to cut one's finger; **se c. les cheveux** to cut one's hair ■ **coupé** *nm (voiture)* coupé

couperet [kupre] *nm (de boucher)* cleaver; *(de guillotine)* blade

couple [kupl] *nm* couple

couplet [kuple] *nm* verse

coupole [kupɔl] *nf* dome

coupon [kupɔ̃] *nm (tissu)* remnant; **c. de réduction** money-off coupon; **c.-réponse** reply coupon

coupure [kupyr] *nf (blessure)* cut; **5 000 euros en petites coupures** 5,000 euros in small notes; **c. d'électri-**

cité *ou* **de courant** blackout, *Br* power cut; **c. de presse** newspaper cutting

cour [kur] *nf* **(a)** *(de maison, de ferme)* yard; **c. de récréation** *Br* playground, *Am* schoolyard **(b)** *(de roi, tribunal)* court; **c. d'appel** court of appeal **(c)** **faire la c. à qn** to court sb

courage [kuraʒ] *nm* courage; **bon c.!** good luck! ■ **courageux, -euse** *adj (brave)* courageous; *(énergique)* spirited

couramment [kuramã] *adv (parler)* fluently; *(généralement)* commonly

courant, -e [kurã, -ãt] **1** *adj (commun)* common; *(en cours)* current **2** *nm (de rivière)* current; **être au c. de qch** to know about sth; **mettre qn au c. de qch** to tell sb about sth; **c. d'air** *Br* draught, *Am* draft; **c. électrique** electric current

courbature [kurbatyr] *nf* ache; **avoir des courbatures** to be aching (all over)

courbe [kurb] **1** *adj* curved **2** *nf* curve; **c. de niveau** contour line ■ **courber 1** *vt* to bend **2 se courber** *vpr (personne)* to bend down; **se c. en deux** to bend double

courgette [kurʒet] *nf Br* courgette, *Am* zucchini

courir* [kurir] **1** *vi* to run; *(à une course automobile)* to race; **c. après qn/qch** to run after sb/sth; **descendre une colline en courant** to run down a hill; **le bruit court que...** rumour has it that...

2 *vt* **c. un risque** to run a risk; **c. le 100 mètres** to run the 100 metres ■ **coureur, -euse** *nmf (sportif)* runner; *(cycliste)* cyclist; **c. automobile** racing driver; **c. de jupons** womanizer

couronne [kurɔn] *nf (de roi, de reine)* crown; *(pour enterrement)* wreath; *(de dent)* crown ■ **couronnement** *nm (de roi)* coronation; *Fig (réussite)* crowning achievement ■ **couronner** *vt (roi)* to crown; *(auteur, ouvrage)* to award a prize to; **et pour c. le tout...** and to crown it all...

courrier [kurje] *nm (lettres)* mail, *Br* post; **par retour du c.** *Br* by return of post, *Am* by return mail; **recevoir du**

c. to receive mail *or Br* post; *Journ* **c. du cœur** problem page; **c. électronique** e-mail

courroie [kurwa] *nf (attache)* strap

cours [kur] *nm* **(a)** *(de rivière, d'astre)* course; *(de monnaie)* currency; *Fin (d'action)* price; **suivre son c.** to run its course; **avoir c.** *(monnaie)* to be legal tender; *(pratique)* to be current; **en c.** *(travail)* in progress; *(année)* current; *(affaires)* outstanding; **au c. de qch** in the course of sth; **c. d'eau** river, stream **(b)** *(leçon)* class; *(série de leçons)* course; *(conférence)* lecture; *(établissement)* school; **suivre un c.** to take a course; **c. particulier** private lesson **(c)** *(allée)* avenue

course¹ [kurs] *nf (action de courir)* running; *Sport (épreuve)* race; *(discipline)* racing; *(trajet en taxi)* journey; *(de projectile, de planète)* course; **les courses de chevaux** the races; **faire la c. avec qn** to race sb; **c. automobile** motor race; **c. cycliste** cycle race

course² [kurs] *nf (commission)* errand; **courses** *(achats)* shopping; **faire une c.** to get something from the shops; **faire les courses** to do the shopping

coursier, -ère [kursje, -ɛr] *nmf* messenger

court, -e [kur, kurt] **1** *adj* short **2** *adv* short; **à c. d'argent** short of money **3** *nm* **c.** *(de tennis/de squash)* tennis/squash court ▪ **court-circuit** *(pl* **courts-circuits)** *nm* short-circuit

courtier, -ère [kurtje, -ɛr] *nmf* broker

courtisan [kurtizɑ̃] *nm Hist* courtier ▪ **courtiser** *vt (femme)* to court

courtois, -e [kurtwa, -az] *adj* courteous ▪ **courtoisie** *nf* courtesy

couru, -e [kury] *adj (spectacle, lieu)* popular

cousin, -e [kuzɛ̃, -in] **1** *nmf* cousin; **c. germain** first cousin **2** *nm (insecte)* mosquito

coussin [kusɛ̃] *nm* cushion

cousu, -e [kuzy] *adj* sewn; **c. main** hand-sewn

coût [ku] *nm* cost; **le c. de la vie** the cost of living ▪ **coûter** *vti* to cost; **ça**

coûte combien? how much is it?, how much does it cost?

couteau, -x [kuto] *nm* knife; **c. à pain** breadknife; **c.-scie** serrated knife

coûteux, -euse [kutø, -øz] *adj* costly, expensive

coutume [kutym] *nf (habitude, tradition)* custom; **avoir c. de faire qch** to be accustomed to doing sth; **comme de c.** as usual

couture [kutyr] *nf (activité)* sewing, needlework; *(raccord)* seam; **faire de la c.** to sew ▪ **couturier** *nm* fashion designer ▪ **couturière** *nf* dressmaker

couvent [kuvɑ̃] *nm (de religieuses)* convent; *(de moines)* monastery; *(pensionnat)* convent school

couver [kuve] **1** *vt (œufs)* to sit on; *(maladie)* to be coming down with **2** *vi (poule)* to brood; *(feu) Br* to smoulder, *Am* to smolder ▪ **couveuse** *nf (pour nouveaux-nés)* incubator

couvercle [kuvɛrkl] *nm* lid; *(vissé)* cap

couvert¹ [kuvɛr] *nm* **(a)** **mettre le c.** to set *or Br* lay the table; **table de cinq couverts** table set *or Br* laid for five; **couverts** *(ustensiles)* cutlery **(b)** **sous le c. de** *(sous l'apparence de)* under cover of; **se mettre à c.** to take cover

couvert², -e [kuvɛr, -ɛrt] **1** *pp de* **couvrir 2** *adj* covered (**de** with *or* in); *(ciel)* overcast; **être bien c.** *(habillé chaudement)* to be warmly dressed

couverture [kuvɛrtyr] *nf (de lit)* blanket; *(de livre, de magazine)* cover; *(de bâtiment)* roofing; *Journ* coverage; **c. chauffante** electric blanket; **c. sociale** social security cover

couvrir* [kuvrir] **1** *vt* to cover (**de** with); *(bruit)* to drown **2 se couvrir** *vpr (s'habiller)* to wrap up; *(se coiffer)* to cover one's head; *(ciel)* to cloud over ▪ **couvre-feu** *(pl* **couvre-feux)** *nm* curfew ▪ **couvre-lit** *(pl* **couvre-lits)** *nm* bedspread

cow-boy [kɔbɔj] *(pl* **cow-boys)** *nm* cowboy

CP [sepe] *(abrév* **cours préparatoire)** *nm* = first year of primary school

CPE [sepeə] *(abrév* **conseiller principal**

d'éducation) *nm inv* school administrator

crabe [krab] *nm* crab

crachat [kraʃa] *nm* gob of spit; **crachats** spit

cracher [kraʃe] **1** *vt* to spit out **2** *vi* (*personne*) to spit; (*stylo*) to splutter; (*radio*) to crackle

crachin [kraʃɛ̃] *nm* (fine) drizzle

craie [krɛ] *nf* (*matière*) chalk; (*bâton*) stick of chalk

craindre* [krɛ̃dr] *vt* (*redouter*) to be afraid of, to fear; (*chaleur, froid*) to be sensitive to; **c. de faire qch** to be afraid of doing sth; **je crains qu'elle ne soit partie** I'm afraid she's left; **ne craignez rien** (*n'ayez pas peur*) don't be afraid; (*ne vous inquiétez pas*) don't worry

crainte [krɛ̃t] *nf* fear; **de c. de faire qch** for fear of doing sth

craintif, -ive [krɛ̃tif, -iv] *adj* timid

crampe [krɑ̃p] *nf* cramp

crampon [krɑ̃pɔ̃] *nm* (*de chaussure*) stud; (*pour l'alpinisme*) crampon

cramponner [krɑ̃pɔne] **se cramponner** *vpr* to hold on; **se c. à qn/qch** to hold on to sb/sth

cran [krɑ̃] *nm* **(a)** (*entaille*) notch; (*de ceinture*) hole; **c. d'arrêt** *ou* **de sûreté** safety catch **(b)** (*de cheveux*) wave **(c)** *Fam* (*courage*) guts; **avoir du c.** to have guts **(d)** *Fam* **être à c.** (*excédé*) to be wound up

crâne [krɑn] *nm* skull

crapaud [krapo] *nm* toad

crapule [krapyl] *nf* villain, scoundrel

craquer [krake] **1** *vt* (*allumette*) to strike **2** *vi* (*branche*) to crack; (*escalier*) to creak; (*se casser*) to snap; (*se déchirer*) to rip ▪ **craquements** *nmpl* (*de branches*) cracking; (*d'escalier*) creaking

crasse [kras] *nf* filth ▪ **crasseux, -euse** *adj* filthy

cratère [kratɛr] *nm* crater

cravate [kravat] *nf* tie

crawlé [krole] *adj m* **dos c.** backstroke

crayon [krɛjɔ̃] *nm* (*en bois*) pencil; (*en cire*) crayon

créancier, -ère [kreɑ̃sje, -ɛr] *nmf* debtor

créateur, -trice [kreatœr, -tris] **1** *adj* creative **2** *nmf* creator ▪ **création** *nf* creation; **1000 créations d'emplois** 1,000 new jobs

créature [kreatyr] *nf* (*être vivant*) creature

crèche [krɛʃ] *nf* (*de Noël*) manger, *Br* crib; (*garderie*) (day) nursery, *Br* crèche

crédible [kredibl] *adj* credible

crédit [kredi] *nm* (*prêt, influence*) credit; **crédits** (*somme d'argent*) funds; **à c.** on credit ▪ **créditer** *vt* (*compte*) to credit (**de** with); *Fig* **c. qn de qch** to give sb credit for sth ▪ **créditeur, -trice** *adj* **solde c.** credit balance; **être c.** to be in credit

crédule [kredyl] *adj* credulous ▪ **crédulité** *nf* credulity

créer [kree] *vt* to create

crémaillère [kremajɛr] *nf* **pendre la c.** to have a housewarming (party)

crématorium [krematɔrjɔm] *nm Br* crematorium, *Am* crematory

crème [krɛm] **1** *nf* (*de lait, dessert, cosmétique*) cream; **c. Chantilly** whipped cream; **c. glacée** ice cream; **c. à raser** shaving cream **2** *adj inv* cream(-coloured) **3** *nm Fam* coffee with milk, *Br* white coffee ▪ **crémerie** *nf* (*magasin*) dairy ▪ **crémeux, -euse** *adj* creamy

créneau, -x [kreno] *nm Com* niche; *TV & Radio* slot

créole [kreɔl] **1** *adj* creole **2** *nmf* Creole **3** *nm* (*langue*) Creole

crêpe [krɛp] **1** *nf* pancake, crêpe **2** *nm* (*tissu*) crepe ▪ **crêperie** *nf* pancake restaurant

crépiter [krepite] *vi* (*feu*) to crackle ▪ **crépitement** *nm* (*du feu*) crackling

crépu, -e [krepy] *adj* frizzy

crépuscule [krepyskyl] *nm* twilight

cresson [kresɔ̃] *nm* watercress

Crète [krɛt] *nf* **la C.** Crete

crête [krɛt] *nf* (*de montagne, d'oiseau, de vague*) crest

creuser [krøze] **1** *vt* (*trou, puits*) to dig; (*évider*) to hollow (out); *Fig* (*idée*) to

look into 2 *vi* to dig 3 **se creuser** *vpr*
(joues) to become hollow; *Fam* **se c. la
tête** *ou* **la cervelle** to rack one's brains

creux, -euse [krø, -øz] 1 *adj (tube,
joues, arbre, paroles)* hollow; *(sans acti-
vité)* slack; **assiette creuse** soup plate
2 *nm* hollow; *(moment)* slack period

crevaison [krəvɛzɔ̃] *nf (de pneu)* flat,
Br puncture

crevasse [krəvas] *nf (trou)* crack; *(de
glacier)* crevasse

crever [krəve] 1 *vt (ballon, bulle)* to
burst; *Fam (épuiser)* to wear out 2 *vi
(bulle, ballon, pneu)* to burst ▪ **crevé, -e**
adj (ballon, pneu) burst; *Fam (épuisé)*
worn out

crevette [krəvɛt] *nf (grise)* shrimp;
(rose) prawn

cri [kri] *nm (de personne)* cry, shout;
(perçant) scream; *(d'animal)* cry
▪ **criard, -e** *adj (son)* shrill; *(couleur)*
loud

crier [krije] 1 *vt (injure, ordre)* to shout
(**à** to) 2 *vi (personne)* to shout, to cry
out; *(fort)* to scream; *(parler très fort)*
to shout; **c. au secours** to shout for help

crime [krim] *nm* crime; *(assassinat)*
murder ▪ **criminalité** *nf* crime ▪ **crimi-
nel, -elle** 1 *adj* criminal 2 *nmf* criminal;
(assassin) murderer

crinière [krinjɛr] *nf* mane

crique [krik] *nf* creek

crise [kriz] *nf* crisis; *(de maladie)* at-
tack; **c. de nerfs** fit of hysteria

crisper [krispe] 1 *vt (poing)* to clench;
(muscle) to tense 2 **se crisper** *vpr (vi-
sage)* to tense; *(personne)* to get tense
▪ **crispé, -e** *adj (personne)* tense

crisser [krise] *vi (pneu, roue)* to squeal;
(neige) to crunch

cristal, -aux [kristal, -o] *nm* crystal;
Tech **cristaux liquides** liquid crystal
▪ **cristallin, -e** *adj (eau, son)* crystal-
clear

critère [kritɛr] *nm* criterion

critique [kritik] 1 *adj (situation,
phase)* critical 2 *nf (reproche)* criticism;
(de film, de livre) review; **faire la c. de**
(film) to review 3 *nm* critic ▪ **critiquer**
vt to criticize

croasser [krɔase] *vi* to caw

Croatie [krɔasi] *nf* la **C.** Croatia

croc [kro] *nm (crochet)* hook; *(dent)*
fang

croche [krɔʃ] *nf Mus Br* quaver, *Am*
eighth (note)

croche-pied [krɔʃpje] *nm* trip; **faire
un c. à qn** to trip sb up

crochet [krɔʃɛ] *nm (pour accrocher, en
boxe)* hook; *(aiguille)* crochet hook;
(parenthèse) square bracket; **faire du
c.** to crochet; **faire un c.** *(détour)* to
make a detour; *(route)* to make a sudden
turn ▪ **crocheter** *vt (serrure)* to pick

crochu, -e [krɔʃy] *adj (nez)* hooked;
(doigts) claw-like

crocodile [krɔkɔdil] *nm* crocodile

croire* [krwar] 1 *vt* to believe; *(penser)*
to think (**que** that); **j'ai cru la voir** I
thought I saw her; **je crois que oui** I
think *or* believe so
2 *vi* to believe (**à** *ou* **en** in)
3 **se croire** *vpr* **il se croit malin** he
thinks he's smart

croisé¹ [krwaze] *nm Hist* crusader
▪ **croisade** *nf Hist* crusade

croiser [krwaze] 1 *vt (passer)* to pass;
(ligne) to cross; *(espèce)* to crossbreed;
c. les jambes to cross one's legs; **c. les
bras** to fold one's arms; *Fig* **c. les
doigts** to keep one's fingers crossed
2 *vi (navire)* to cruise
3 **se croiser** *vpr (voitures)* to pass
each other; *(lignes, routes)* to cross, to
intersect; *(lettres)* to cross; *(regards)* to
meet ▪ **croisé², -e** *adj (bras)* folded;
(veston) double-breasted ▪ **croise-
ment** *nm (de routes)* crossroads *(sing)*,
intersection; *(d'animaux)* crossing

croisière [krwazjɛr] *nf* cruise

croître* [krwatr] *vi (plante)* to grow;
(augmenter) to grow, to increase (**de**
by); *(lune)* to wax ▪ **croissance** *nf*
growth ▪ **croissant, -e** 1 *adj (nombre)*
growing 2 *nm* crescent; *(pâtisserie)*
croissant

croix [krwa] *nf* cross; **la C.-Rouge** the
Red Cross

croquer [krɔke] 1 *vt (manger)* to
crunch 2 *vi (fruit)* to be crunchy; **c.**

dans qch to bite into sth ■ **croquant, -e** *adj* crunchy ■ **croque-monsieur** *nm inv* = toasted cheese and ham sandwich

croquis [krɔki] *nm* sketch

crosse [krɔs] *nf (de fusil)* butt; *(de hockey)* stick; *(d'évêque)* crook

crotte [krɔt] *nf (de mouton, de lapin)* droppings; **c. de chien** dog dirt ■ **crottin** *nm* dung

crouler [krule] *vi (édifice)* to crumble; **c. sous le travail** to be snowed under with work ■ **croulant, -e** *adj (mur)* crumbling

croupe [krup] *nf* rump

croupier [krupje] *nm* croupier

croupir [krupir] *vi (eau)* to stagnate

croustiller [krustije] *vi* to be crunchy; *(pain)* to be crusty ■ **croustillant, -e** *adj* crunchy; *(pain)* crusty; *Fig (histoire)* spicy

croûte [krut] *nf (de pain)* crust; *(de fromage)* rind; *(de plaie)* scab; *Fam* **casser la c.** to have a snack ■ **croûton** *nm (de pain)* end; **croûtons** *(pour la soupe)* croûtons

croyable [krwajabl] *adj* credible, believable ■ **croyance** *nf* belief (**en** in) ■ **croyant, -e 1** *adj* **être c.** to be a believer **2** *nmf* believer

CRS [seɛrɛs] *(abrév* **compagnie républicaine de sécurité)** *nm* = French riot policeman

cru¹, -e¹ [kry] *pp de* **croire**

cru², -e² [kry] **1** *adj (aliment)* raw; *(lait)* unpasteurized; *(lumière)* garish; *(propos)* crude; **monter à c.** to ride bareback **2** *nm (vignoble)* vineyard; **un grand c.** *(vin)* a vintage wine; **vin du c.** local wine

cruauté [kryote] *nf* cruelty (**envers** to)

cruche [kryʃ] *nf* pitcher, jug

crucial, -e, -aux, -ales [krysjal, -o] *adj* crucial

crucifier [krysifje] *vt* to crucify ■ **crucifix** *nm* crucifix ■ **crucifixion** *nf* crucifixion

crudités [krydite] *nfpl (légumes)* assorted raw vegetables

crue [kry] *nf (montée)* swelling; *(inon-*

dation) flood; **er c.** *(rivière, fleuve)* in spate

cruel, -elle [kryɛl] *adj* cruel **(envers** *ou* **avec** to) ■ **cruellement** *adv* cruelly

crûment [krymã] *adv (sans détour)* bluntly; *(grossièrement)* crudely

crustacés [krystase] *nmpl Culin* shellfish *inv*

crypte [kript] *nf* crypt

crypté, -e [kripte] *adj (message)* & *TV* coded

Cuba [kyba] *n* Cuba ■ **cubain, -e 1** *adj* Cuban **2** *nmf* **C., Cubaine** Cuban

cube [kyb] **1** *nm* cube; *(de jeu)* building block **2** *adj* **mètre c.** cubic metre ■ **cubique** *adj* cubic

cueillir* [kœjir] *vt* to pick, to gather

cuiller, cuillère [kɥijɛr] *nf* spoon; *(mesure)* spoonful; **c. à café, petite c.** teaspoon; **c. à soupe** tablespoon ■ **cuillerée** *nf* spoonful; **c. à café** teaspoonful; **c. à soupe** tablespoonful

cuir [kɥir] *nm* leather; *(d'éléphant)* hide; **pantalon en c.** leather trousers; **c. chevelu** scalp

cuirassé [kɥirase] *nm Naut* battleship

cuire* [kɥir] **1** *vt (aliment, plat)* to cook; **c. qch à l'eau** to boil sth; **c. qch au four** to bake sth; *(viande)* to roast sth **2** *vi (aliment)* to cook; **faire c. qch** to cook sth

cuisant, -e [kɥizã, -ãt] *adj (douleur)* burning; *(affront)* stinging

cuisine [kɥizin] *nf (pièce)* kitchen; *(art)* cookery, cooking; **faire la c.** to do the cooking ■ **cuisiner** *vti* to cook

cuisinier, -ère¹ [kɥizinje, -ɛr] *nmf* cook

cuisinière² [kɥizinjɛr] *nf (appareil)* stove, *Br* cooker

cuisse [kɥis] *nf* thigh; **c. de poulet** chicken leg; **cuisses de grenouilles** frogs' legs

cuisson [kɥisɔ̃] *nm (d'aliments)* cooking; *(de pain)* baking

cuit, -e [kɥi, kɥit] **1** *pp de* **cuire 2** *adj* cooked; **bien c.** well done

cuivre [kɥivr] *nm (rouge)* copper; *(jaune)* brass; *Mus* **les cuivres** the

brass (section) ■ **cuivré, -e** *adj Br* copper-coloured, *Am* copper-colored

culbuter [kylbyte] *vi (personne)* to take a tumble

cul-de-sac [kydsak] *(pl* **culs-de-sac)** *nm* dead end, *Br* cul-de-sac

culinaire [kylinɛr] *adj* culinary

culminer [kylmine] *vi (tension, crise)* to peak; **la montagne culmine à 3 000 mètres** the mountain is 3,000 metres at its highest point ■ **culminant** *adj* **point c.** *(de montagne)* highest point

culot [kylo] *nm (d'ampoule, de lampe)* base; *Fam (audace)* nerve, *Br* cheek

culotte [kylɔt] *nf (de femme)* knickers, *Am* panties; *(d'enfant)* pants; **culottes courtes** *Br* short trousers, *Am* short pants

culpabiliser [kylpabilize] **1** *vt* **c. qn** to make sb feel guilty **2 se culpabiliser** *vpr* to feel guilty ■ **culpabilité** *nf* guilt

culte [kylt] **1** *nm (de dieu)* worship; *(religion)* religion **2** *adj* **film c.** cult film

cultiver [kyltive] **1** *vt (terre, amitié)* to cultivate; *(plantes)* to grow **2 se cultiver** *vpr* to improve one's mind ■ **cultivateur, -trice** *nmf* farmer ■ **cultivé, -e** *adj (terre)* cultivated; *(esprit, personne)* cultured, cultivated

culture [kyltyr] *nf* **(a)** *(action)* farming, cultivation; *(de plantes)* growing; **cultures** *(terres)* fields under cultivation; *(plantes)* crops **(b)** *(éducation, civilisation)* & *Biol* culture; **c. générale** general knowledge; **c. physique** physical training ■ **culturel, -elle** *adj* cultural

culturisme [kyltyrism] *nm* body-building

cumulatif, -ive *adj* cumulative ■ **cumuler** *vt* **c. deux fonctions** to hold two offices

cupide [kypid] *adj* avaricious

cure [kyr] *nf (traitement)* (course of) treatment

curé [kyre] *nm* parish priest

curer [kyre] **1** *vt* to clean out **2 se curer** *vpr* **se c. les dents** to clean one's teeth ■ **cure-dents** *nm inv* toothpick

curieux, -euse [kyrjø, -øz] **1** *adj (bizarre)* curious; *(indiscret)* inquisitive, curious **(de** about) **2** *nmf* inquisitive person; *(badaud)* onlooker ■ **curiosité** *nf* curiosity; *(chose)* curio

curriculum vitae [kyrikylɔmvite] *nm inv Br* curriculum vitae, *Am* résumé

curseur [kyrsœr] *nm Ordinat* cursor

cutané, -e [kytane] *adj* **maladie cutanée** skin condition

cuti [kyti] *nf* skin test

cuve [kyv] *nf* tank; *(de fermentation)* vat ■ **cuvée** *nf (récolte)* vintage ■ **cuvette** *nf (récipient)* & *Géog* basin; *(des cabinets)* bowl

CV [seve] *(abrév* **curriculum vitae)** *nm Br* CV, *Am* résumé

cyanure [sjanyr] *nm* cyanide

cybercafé [siberkafe] *nm* cybercafé

cycle [sikl] *nm* **(a)** *(série, movement)* cycle **(b) premier/second c.** *Scol* = lower/upper classes in secondary school; *Univ* = first/last two years of a degree course **(c)** *(bicyclette)* cycle ■ **cyclable** *adj* **piste c.** cycle path

cyclisme [siklism] *nm* cycling ■ **cycliste 1** *nmf* cyclist **2** *adj* **course c.** cycle race

cyclomoteur [siklɔmɔtœr] *nm* moped

cyclone [siklon] *nm* cyclone

cygne [siɲ] *nm* swan

cylindre [silɛ̃dr] *nm* cylinder; *(rouleau)* roller ■ **cylindrée** *nf* (cubic) capacity ■ **cylindrique** *adj* cylindrical

cymbale [sɛ̃bal] *nf* cymbal

cynique [sinik] **1** *adj* cynical **2** *nmf* cynic

cyprès [siprɛ] *nm* cypress

cypriote [siprijɔt] **1** *adj* Cypriot **2** *nmf* **C.** Cypriot

Dd

D, d [de] **1** *nm inv* D, d **2** *(abrév* **route départementale)** = designation of a secondary road

dactylo [daktilo] *nf (personne)* typist; *(action)* typing

daigner [deɲe] *vt* **d. faire qch** to deign to do sth

daim [dɛ̃] *nm (animal)* fallow deer; *(mâle)* buck; *(cuir)* suede

dalle [dal] *nf (de pierre)* paving stone; *(de marbre)* slab

daltonien, -enne [daltɔnjɛ̃, -ɛn] *adj* colour-blind

dame [dam] *nf (femme)* lady; *Cartes* queen; *(au jeu de dames)* king; **dames** *(jeu) Br* draughts, *Am* checkers

damner [dane] *vt* to damn

Danemark [danmark] *nm* **le D.** Denmark ■ **danois, -e 1** *adj* Danish **2** *nmf* **D., Danoise** Dane **3** *nm (langue)* Danish

danger [dɑ̃ʒe] *nm* danger; **en d.** in danger ■ **dangereux, -euse** *adj* dangerous **(pour** to)

DANS [dɑ̃] *prép* **(a)** in; *(changement de lieu)* into; *(à l'intérieur de)* inside

(b) *(provenance)* from, out of; **boire d. un verre** to drink out of a glass

(c) *(exprime la temporalité)* in; **d. deux jours** in two days' time

(d) *(exprime une approximation)* **d. les dix euros** about ten euros

danse [dɑ̃s] *nf* dance; **la d.** *(art)* dancing; **d. classique** ballet ■ **danser** *vti* to dance ■ **danseur, -euse** *nmf* dancer

dard [dar] *nm (d'insecte)* sting

date [dat] *nf* date; **d. de naissance** date of birth; **d. limite** deadline; **d. limite de vente** sell-by date ■ **dater 1** *vt (lettre)* to date **2** *vi* **à d. du 15** as from the 15th

datte [dat] *nf* date

daube [dob] *nf* **bœuf en d.** braised beef stew

dauphin [dofɛ̃] *nm (animal)* dolphin

davantage [davɑ̃taʒ] *adv* more; **d. de temps/d'argent** more time/money

DE¹ [də]

> **de** becomes **d'** before vowel and h mute; de + le = **du**, de + les = **des**.

prép **(a)** *(complément de nom)* of; **le livre de Paul** Paul's book; **un livre de Flaubert** a book by Flaubert; **le train de Londres** the London train; **une augmentation de salaire** an increase in salary

(b) *(complément d'adjectif)* **digne de qn** worthy of sb; **content de qn/qch** pleased with sb/sth; **heureux de partir** happy to leave

(c) *(complément de verbe)* **parler de qn/qch** to speak of sb/sth; **se souvenir de qn/qch** to remember sb/sth; **décider de faire qch** to decide to do sth; **empêcher qn de faire qch** to stop sb from doing sth

(d) *(indique la provenance)* from; **venir de...** to come from...; **sortir de qch** to come out of sth; **le train de Londres** the train from London

(e) *(introduit l'agent)* **accompagné de qn** accompanied by sb; **entouré de qch** surrounded by *or* with sth

(f) *(introduit le moyen)* **armé de qch** armed with sth

(g) *(introduit la manière)* **d'une voix douce** in a gentle voice

(h) *(introduit une cause)* **puni de son impatience** punished for his/her impatience; **mourir de faim** to die of hunger

(i) *(introduit le temps)* **travailler de nuit** to work by night; **six heures du**

matin six o'clock in the morning **(j)** *(mesure)* **avoir six mètres de haut, être haut de six mètres** to be six metres high; **homme de trente ans** thirty-year-old man; **gagner cent francs de l'heure** to earn a hundred francs an hour

DE² [də] *article partitif* some; **elle boit du vin** she drinks (some) wine; **il ne boit pas de vin** he doesn't drink (any) wine; **est-ce que vous buvez du vin?** do you drink (any) wine?

DE³ [də] *article indéfini* **de, des** some; **des fleurs** (some) flowers; **de jolies fleurs** (some) pretty flowers; **d'agréables soirées** (some) pleasant evenings

dé [de] *nm (à jouer)* dice; *(à coudre)* thimble

déballer [debale] *vt* to unpack

débarbouiller [debarbuje] **se débarbouiller** *vpr* to wash one's face

débardeur [debardœr] *nm (vêtement)* vest

débarquer [debarke] **1** *vt (passagers)* to land; *(marchandises)* to unload **2** *vi (passagers)* to disembark ■ **débarquement** *nm (de passagers, de troupes)* landing; *(de marchandises)* unloading

débarras [debara] *nm* storeroom ■ **débarrasser 1** *vt (chambre, table)* to clear *(de* of); **d. qn de qch** to relieve sb of sth **2 se débarrasser** *vpr* **se d. de qn/qch** to get rid of sb/sth

débat [deba] *nm* debate

débattre* [debatr] **1** *vt* to discuss, to debate; **d. de qch** to discuss sth **2 se débattre** *vpr* to struggle

débaucher [deboʃe] *vt* **d. qn** *(licencier)* to lay sb off; *(inciter à la débauche)* to corrupt sb

débit [debi] *nm Fin* debit; *(de fleuve)* flow; *(de personne)* delivery; **d. de tabac** *Br* tobacconist's (shop), *Am* tobacco store

débiter [debite] *vt (découper)* to cut up (**en** into); *(compte)* to debit; *Péj (dire)* to spout ■ **débiteur** *adj m* **solde d.** debit balance; **mon compte est d.** my account is in debit

débloquer [debloke] *vt (mécanisme)* to unjam; *(compte, prix)* to unfreeze

déboiser [debwaze] *vt (terrain)* to clear of trees

déboîter [debwate] **1** *vt (tuyau)* to disconnect **2** *vi (véhicule)* to pull out **3 se déboîter** *vpr* **se d. l'épaule** to dislocate one's shoulder

déborder [deborde] **1** *vi (fleuve, liquide)* to overflow; *(en bouillant)* to boil over **2** *vt (dépasser)* to stick out from; **débordé de travail** snowed under with work

débouché [debuʃe] *nm (carrière)* opening; *(de produit)* outlet

déboucher [debuʃe] **1** *vt (bouteille)* to uncork; *(bouchon vissé)* to uncap; *(lavabo, tuyau)* to unblock **2** *vi (surgir)* to emerge (**de** from); **d. sur** *(rue)* to lead out onto/into

debout [dəbu] *adv (personne)* standing; *(objet)* upright; **se mettre d.** to stand up; **rester d.** to stand; **être d.** *(hors du lit)* to be up

déboutonner [debutone] **1** *vt* to unbutton **2 se déboutonner** *vpr (personne)* to undo one's coat/jacket/*etc*

débraillé, -e [debraje] *adj* slovenly

débrancher [debrɑ̃ʃe] *vt* to unplug

débrayer [debreje] *vi* (**a**) *Aut* to release the clutch (**b**) *(se mettre en grève)* to stop work ■ **débrayage** (**a**) *Aut* declutching (**b**) *(grève)* stoppage

débris [debri] *nmpl (de voiture, d'avion)* debris

débrouiller [debruje] **1** *vt (fil, mystère)* to unravel **2 se débrouiller** *vpr Fam* to manage; **se d. pour faire qch** to manage to do sth ■ **débrouillard, -e** *adj Fam* resourceful

début [deby] *nm* beginning, start; **au d. (de)** at the beginning (of); **dès le d.** (right) from the start *or* beginning

débuter [debyte] *vi* to start, to begin (**par** with); *(dans une carrière)* to start out ■ **débutant, -e** *nmf* beginner

deçà [dəsa] **en deçà 1** *adv* (on) this side **2** *prép* **en d. de** (on) this side of

décadent, -e [dekadɑ̃, -ɑ̃t] *adj* decadent

décaféiné, -e [dekafeine] *adj* decaffeinated

décaler [dekale] **1** *vt (dans le temps)* to change the time of; *(dans l'espace)* to shift, to move **2 se décaler** *vpr* to move, to shift ■ **décalage** *nm (écart)* gap (**entre** between); **d. horaire** time difference; **souffrir du d. horaire** to have jet lag

décalquer [dekalke] *vt* to trace

décaper [dekape] *vt (avec un produit)* to strip; *(au papier de verre)* to sand (down); *(four)* to clean

décapiter [dekapite] *vt (personne)* to decapitate

décapotable [dekapɔtabl] *adj & nf* convertible

décapsuleur [dekapsylœr] *nm* bottle opener

décédé, -e [desede] *adj* deceased

déceler [desle] *vt (trouver)* to detect

décembre [desɑ̃br] *nm* December

décence [desɑ̃s] *nf (de comportement)* propriety; *(d'habillement)* decency

décennie [deseni] *nf* decade

décent, -e [desɑ̃, -ɑ̃t] *adj (comportement)* proper; *(vêtements)* decent

décentralisation [desɑ̃tralizasjɔ̃] *nf* decentralization

déception [desɛpsjɔ̃] *nf* disappointment

décerner [deserne] *vt (prix)* to award (à to)

décès [desɛ] *nm* death

décevant, -e [desvɑ̃, -ɑ̃t] *adj* disappointing

décevoir* [desvwar] *vt* to disappoint

déchaîner [deʃene] **1** *vt (colère, violence)* to unleash **2 se déchaîner** *vpr (tempête)* to rage; *(personne)* to fly into a rage (**contre** with)

décharge [deʃarʒ] *nf* **d. (électrique)** (electric) shock; **d. (publique)** *Br* (rubbish) dump, *Am* (garbage) dump

décharger [deʃarʒe] **1** *vt (camion, navire, cargaison)* to unload; **d. qn de qch** *(tâche, responsabilité)* to relieve sb of **2 se décharger** *vpr (batterie)* to go flat

déchausser [deʃose] **1** *vt* **d. qn** to take

sb's shoes off **2 se déchausser** *vpr (personne)* to take one's shoes off

déchéance [deʃeɑ̃s] *nf (déclin)* decline

déchets [deʃɛ] *nmpl* scraps; **d. radioactifs** radioactive waste

déchiffrer [deʃifre] *vt (message, écriture)* to decipher

déchiqueté, -e [deʃikte] *adj (tissu)* torn to shreds

déchirer [deʃire] **1** *vt (accidentellement)* to tear; *(volontairement)* to tear up **2 se déchirer** *vpr (tissu, papier)* to tear

déchirure [deʃiryr] *nf* tear

déchoir* [deʃwar] *vi (personne)* to demean oneself

déchu, -e [deʃy] *adj* **être d. de qch** to be stripped of sth

décidé, -e [deside] *adj (personne, air)* determined; *(fixé)* settled; **être d. à faire qch** to be determined to do sth

décidément [desidemɑ̃] *adv* really

décider [deside] **1** *vt* **d. quand/que...** to decide when/that... **2** *vi* **d. de qch** to decide on sth; **d. de faire qch** to decide to do sth **3 se décider** *vpr* **se d. (à faire qch)** to make up one's mind (to do sth)

décimal, -e, -aux, -ales [desimal, -o] *adj* decimal

décimer [desime] *vt* to decimate

décimètre [desimetr] *nm* decimetre

décisif, -ive [desizif, -iv] *adj (bataille)* decisive; *(moment)* critical ■ **décision** *nf* decision (**de faire** to do); **prendre une d.** to make a decision

déclaration [deklarasjɔ̃] *nf (annonce)* statement; *(de naissance, de décès)* registration; *(à la police)* report; **d. d'impôts** income tax return

déclarer [deklare] **1** *vt (annoncer)* to declare (**que** that); *(naissance, décès)* to register; **d. qn coupable** to find sb guilty (**de** of); **d. la guerre** to declare war (à on); **rien à d.** *(en douane)* nothing to declare **2 se déclarer** *vpr (incendie, maladie)* to break out

déclencher [deklɑ̃ʃe] **1** *vt (appareil)* to start; *(mécanisme)* to activate; *(sonnerie)* to set off; *(révolte)* to trigger off;

(attaque) to launch **2 se déclencher** *vpr (alarme, sonnerie)* to go off; *(incendie)* to start

déclic [deklik] *nm (bruit)* click

déclin [deklɛ̃] *nm* decline; **être en d.** to be in decline

décliner [dekline] **1** *vi (forces)* to decline; *(jour)* to draw to a close **2** *vt (refuser)* to decline

décocher [dekɔʃe] *vt (flèche)* to shoot

décoder [dekɔde] *vt* to decode ▪ **décodeur** *nm TV* decoder

décoiffer [dekwafe] **1** *vt* **d. qn** to mess up sb's hair **2 se décoiffer** *vpr (se dépeigner)* to mess up one's hair; *(ôter son chapeau)* to remove one's hat

décoincer [dekwɛ̃se] *vt*, **se décoincer** *vpr (tiroir, mécanisme)* to loosen

décollage [dekɔlaʒ] *nm (d'avion)* takeoff

décoller [dekɔle] **1** *vt (enlever)* to peel off **2** *vi (avion)* to take off **3 se décoller** *vpr* to peel off

décolleté, -e [dekɔlte] **1** *adj (robe)* low-cut **2** *nm (de robe)* low neckline

décolorer [dekɔlɔre] **1** *vt (cheveux)* to bleach **2 se décolorer** *vpr (tissu)* to fade; **se d. les cheveux** to bleach one's hair

décombres [dekɔ̃br] *nmpl* ruins, debris

décommander [dekɔmɑ̃de] **1** *vt (marchandises, invitation)* to cancel; *(invité)* to put off **2 se décommander** *vpr* to cancel

décomposer [dekɔ̃poze] **1** *vt Chim* to decompose **2 se décomposer** *vpr (pourrir)* to decompose ▪ **décomposition** *nf* decomposition

décompression [dekɔ̃presjɔ̃] *nf* decompression

décompte [dekɔ̃t] *nm (soustraction)* deduction; *(détail)* breakdown ▪ **décompter** *vt* to deduct **(de** from)

déconcentrer [dekɔ̃sɑ̃tre] **se déconcentrer** *vpr* to lose concentration

déconcerter [dekɔ̃serte] *vt* to disconcert

décongeler [dekɔ̃ʒle] *vt* to thaw, to defrost

décongestionner [dekɔ̃ʒestjɔne] *vt (rue, poumons)* to relieve congestion in

déconnecter [dekɔnɛkte] *vt (appareil, fil)* to disconnect

déconseiller [dekɔ̃seje] *vt* **d. qch à qn** to advise sb against sth; **d. à qn de faire qch** to advise sb against doing sth

déconsidérer [dekɔ̃sidere] *vt* to discredit

décontaminer [dekɔ̃tamine] *vt* to decontaminate

décontracter [dekɔ̃trakte] **1** *vt (muscle)* to relax **2 se décontracter** *vpr* to relax ▪ **décontracté, -e** *adj (ambiance, personne)* relaxed; *(vêtement)* casual

décor [dekɔr] *nm (de maison)* decor; *(paysage)* surroundings; *Théât* **décors** scenery, set

décorer [dekɔre] *vt (maison, soldat)* to decorate **(de** with) ▪ **décorateur, -trice** *nmf* (interior) decorator; *Théât* stage designer ▪ **décoratif, -ive** *adj* decorative ▪ **décoration** *nf (action, ornement, médaille)* decoration; *(d'une maison)* decoration; **faire de la d.** to decorate; **d. d'intérieur** interior decorating; **décorations de Noël** Christmas decorations

décortiquer [dekɔrtike] *vt (riz, orge)* to hull; *(crevette, noisette)* to shell

découdre* [dekudr] **1** *vt (ourlet, vêtement)* to unstitch; *(bouton)* to take off **2 se découdre** *vpr (ourlet, vêtement)* to come unstitched; *(bouton)* to come off

découler [dekule] *vi* **d. de qch** to follow from sth

découper [dekupe] *vt (viande)* to carve; *(gâteau, papier)* to cut up ▪ **découpé, -e** *adj (irrégulier)* jagged

décourager [dekuraʒe] **1** *vt (dissuader)* to discourage **(de faire** from doing); *(démoraliser)* to dishearten, to discourage **2 se décourager** *vpr* to get discouraged *or* disheartened ▪ **découragement** *nm* discouragement

décousu, -e [dekuzy] *adj (ourlet, vêtement)* unstitched; *Fig (propos)* disjointed

découvert, -e [dekuvɛr, -ɛrt] **1** *adj*

(terrain) open; *(tête, épaule)* bare 2 *nm (de compte)* overdraft

découverte [dekuvɛrt] *nf* discovery; **faire une d.** to make a discovery

découvrir* [dekuvrir] 1 *vt (trouver, apprendre à connaître)* to discover; *(secret)* to uncover; **faire d. qch à qn** to introduce sb to sth 2 **se découvrir** *vpr (ciel)* to clear

décrire* [dekrir] *vt (représenter)* to describe

décrocher [dekrɔʃe] 1 *vt (détacher)* to unhook; *(tableau, rideau)* to take down; **d. (le téléphone)** *(pour répondre)* to pick up the phone; *(pour ne pas être dérangé)* to take the phone off the hook 2 **se décrocher** *vpr (tableau, rideau)* to come unhooked

décroître* [dekrwatr] *vi (forces, nombre)* to decrease; *(jours)* to get shorter

décrypter [dekripte] *vt* to decipher

déçu, -e [desy] 1 *pp de* décevoir 2 *adj* disappointed

décupler [dekyple] *vti* to increase tenfold

dédaigner [dedeɲe] *vt (offre, richesses)* to scorn; *(conseil)* to disregard ▪ **dédaigneux, -euse** *adj* scornful, disdainful **(de** of)

dédain [dedɛ̃] *nm* scorn, disdain **(pour/de** for)

dedans [dədɑ̃] *adv* inside; **de d.** from (the) inside; **en d.** on the inside; **tomber d.** *(trou)* to fall in (it)

dédicace [dedikas] *nf* dedication ▪ **dédicacer** *vt (signer)* to sign (à for)

dédier [dedje] *vt* to dedicate (à to)

dédommager [dedɔmaʒe] *vt* to compensate **(de** for) ▪ **dédommagement** *nm* compensation

dédouaner [dedwane] *vt (marchandises)* to clear through customs

déduire* [dedyir] *vt (retirer)* to deduct **(de** from); *(conclure)* to deduce **(de** from) ▪ **déductible** *adj* deductible ▪ **déduction** *nf (raisonnement, décompte)* deduction

déesse [dees] *nf* goddess

défaillir* [defajir] *vi (s'évanouir)* to faint; *(faiblir)* to fail ▪ **défaillance** *nf*

(évanouissement) fainting fit; *(faiblesse)* weakness; *(panne)* failure; **avoir une d.** *(s'évanouir)* to faint; *(faiblir)* to feel weak

défaire* [defɛr] 1 *vt (nœud)* to undo; *(valises)* to unpack 2 **se défaire** *vpr (nœud)* to come undone

défait, -e¹ [defɛ, -ɛt] *adj (lit)* unmade; *(visage)* haggard

défaite² [defɛt] *nf* defeat

défaut [defo] *nm (de personne)* fault, shortcoming; *(de machine)* defect; *(de diamant, de raisonnement)* flaw; **à d. de qch** for lack of sth; **ou, à d....** or, failing that...; **d. de fabrication** manufacturing fault; **d. de prononciation** speech impediment

défavorable [defavɔrabl] *adj* unfavourable **(à** to) ▪ **défavorisé, -e** *adj (milieu)* underprivileged ▪ **défavoriser** *vt* to put at a disadvantage

défection [defɛksjɔ̃] *nf (de soldat, d'espion)* defection; **faire d.** *(soldat, espion)* to defect

défectueux, -euse [defɛktɥø, -øz] *adj* faulty, defective

défendre [defɑ̃dr] 1 *vt (protéger, soutenir)* to defend **(contre** against); **d. à qn de faire qch** to forbid sb to do sth; **d. qch à qn** to forbid sb sth 2 **se défendre** *vpr* to defend oneself

défense¹ [defɑ̃s] *nf (protection)* Br defence, Am defense; **sans d.** Br defenceless, Am defenseless; **'d. de fumer'** 'no smoking'

défense² [defɑ̃s] *nf (d'éléphant)* tusk

défenseur [defɑ̃sœr] *nm* defender

défensif, -ive [defɑ̃sif, -iv] 1 *adj* defensive 2 *nf* **sur la défensive** on the defensive

déferler [defɛrle] *vi (vagues)* to break

défi [defi] *nm* challenge **(à** to); **lancer un d. à qn** to challenge sb; **mettre qn au d. de faire qch** to defy sb to do sth

défiance [defjɑ̃s] *nf* mistrust

déficience [defisjɑ̃s] *nf* deficiency

déficit [defisit] *nm* deficit; **être en d.** to be in deficit; **d. commercial** trade deficit ▪ **déficitaire** *adj (budget)* in deficit; *(entreprise)* loss-making; *(compte)* in debit

défier [defje] *vt (provoquer)* to challenge; *(danger, mort)* to defy; **d. qn de faire qch** to defy sb to do sth

défiguré, -e [defigyre] *adj (personne)* disfigured

défilé [defile] *nm (cortège)* procession; *(de manifestants)* march; *Mil* parade; *Géog* pass; **d. de mode** fashion show

définir [definir] *vt* to define ▪ **défini, -e** *adj* definite ▪ **définition** *nf* definition; *(de mots croisés)* clue

définitif, -ive [definitif, -iv] **1** *adj (version)* final; *(fermeture)* permanent **2** *nf* **en définitive** in the final analysis ▪ **définitivement** *adv (partir, exclure)* for good

déflagration [deflagrasjɔ̃] *nf* explosion

défoncer [defɔ̃se] *vt (porte, mur)* to smash in; *(trottoir)* to break up ▪ **défoncé, -e** *adj (route)* bumpy

déformation [defɔrmasjɔ̃] *nf (de membre)* deformation; *(de fait)* distortion

déformer [defɔrme] **1** *vt (membre)* to deform; *(vêtement, chaussures)* to put out of shape; *(image)* to distort; *(propos)* to twist **2 se déformer** *vpr* to lose its shape ▪ **déformé, -e** *adj (objet)* misshapen; *(corps)* deformed

défricher [defriʃe] *vt (terrain)* to clear

défriser [defrize] *vt (cheveux)* to straighten

défroisser [defrwase] *vt* to smooth out

défunt, -e [defœ̃, -œ̃t] **1** *adj (mort)* departed; **mon d. mari** my late husband **2** *nmf* **le d., la défunte** the deceased

dégager [degaʒe] **1** *vt (passage, voie)* to clear (**de** of); *(odeur, chaleur)* to emit; **d. qn de** *(décombres)* to free sb from **2 se dégager** *vpr (odeur)* to be given off; *(ciel)* to clear; **se d. de qch** *(personne)* to free oneself from sth ▪ **dégagé, -e** *adj (ciel)* clear; *(ton)* casual; *(vue)* open ▪ **dégagement** *nm (action)* clearing; *(de chaleur)* emission

dégainer [degene] *vti* to draw

dégarnir [degarnir] **se dégarnir** *vpr (personne)* to go bald

dégâts [dega] *nmpl* damage

dégel [deʒɛl] *nm* thaw ▪ **dégeler 1** *vt* to thaw; *(surgelé)* to defrost; *(crédits)* to unfreeze **2** *vi* to thaw; **faire d. qch** *(surgelé)* to defrost sth **3** *v impersonnel* **il dégèle** it's thawing **4 se dégeler** *vpr Fig (atmosphère)* to become less chilly

dégénérer [deʒenere] *vi* to degenerate (**en** into)

dégonfler [degɔ̃fle] **1** *vt (pneu)* to let the air out of **2 se dégonfler** *vpr (pneu)* to go flat ▪ **dégonflé, -e** *adj (pneu)* flat

dégouliner [deguline] *vi* to trickle

dégourdir [degurdir] **se dégourdir** *vpr* **se d. les jambes** to stretch one's legs ▪ **dégourdi, -e** *adj (malin)* smart

dégoût [degu] *nm* disgust

dégoûter [degute] *vt (moralement)* to disgust; *(physiquement)* to turn sb's stomach; **d. qn de qch** to put sb off sth ▪ **dégoûtant, -e** *adj* disgusting ▪ **dégoûté, -e** *adj* disgusted; **être d. de qch** to be sick of sth

dégradation [degradasjɔ̃] *nf (de matériel)* damage (**de** to)

dégrader [degrade] **1** *vt (matériel)* to damage **2 se dégrader** *vpr (situation)* to deteriorate ▪ **dégradant, -e** *adj* degrading

dégrafer [degrafe] **1** *vt (vêtement)* to undo **2 se dégrader** *vpr (vêtement)* to come undone

degré [dəgre] *nm (d'angle, de température)* degree; *(d'alcool)* proof; *(d'échelle)* rung; **au plus haut d.** in the extreme; **d. Celsius/Fahrenheit** degree Celsius/Fahrenheit

dégrèvement [degrɛvmɑ̃] *nm* **d. fiscal** tax relief

dégrossir [degrosir] *vt (travail)* to rough out

déguiser [degize] **1** *vt (pour tromper)* to disguise; **d. qn en qch** *(costumer)* to dress sb up as sth **2 se déguiser** *vpr (pour s'amuser)* to dress oneself up (**en** as) ▪ **déguisement** *nm* disguise; *(de bal costumé)* fancy dress

déguster [degyste] *vt (savourer)* to savour ▪ **dégustation** *nf* tasting

dehors [dəɔr] **1** adv outside; (pas chez soi) out; (en plein air) out of doors; **en d. de la ville** out of town; Fig **en d. de** (excepté) apart from **2** nm (extérieur) outside; **au d.** on the outside; (se pencher) out

déjà [deʒa] adv already; **est-il d. parti?** has he left yet or already?; **elle l'a d. vu** she's seen it before, she's already seen it

déjeuner [deʒœne] **1** nm lunch; **petit d.** breakfast **2** vi (à midi) to have lunch; (le matin) to have breakfast

déjouer [deʒwe] vt (intrigue) to foil

délabré, -e [delabre] adj (bâtiment) dilapidated

délacer [delase] **1** vt (chaussure) to untie **2 se délacer** vpr (chaussure) to come untied

délai [delɛ] nm (laps de temps) time allowed; (sursis) extension; **dans les plus brefs délais** as soon as possible; **dernier d.** final date

délaisser [delese] vt (négliger) to neglect

délasser [delase] vt, **se délasser** vpr to relax

délavé, -e [delave] adj (tissu, jean) faded; (couleur, ciel) watery

délayer [deleje] vt (poudre) to add water to; (liquide) to water down

délecter [delɛkte] **se délecter** vpr **se d. de qch** to take delight in sth

déléguer [delege] vt to delegate (à to) ▪ **délégation** nf delegation ▪ **délégué, -e** nmf delegate; Scol **d. de classe** = pupil elected to represent his or her class at class meetings

délibération [deliberasjɔ̃] nf deliberation

délibéré, -e [delibere] adj (intentionnel) deliberate

délicat, -e [delika, -at] adj (santé, travail) delicate; (question) tricky, delicate; (peau) sensitive; (geste) tactful ▪ **délicatesse** nf (tact) tact

délice [delis] nm delight ▪ **délicieux, -euse** adj (mets) delicious; (parfum) delightful

délier [delje] vt to untie

délimiter [delimite] vt (terrain) to

mark off; (sujet) to define

délinquant, -e [delɛ̃kã, -ãt] nmf delinquent ▪ **délinquance** nf delinquency

délire [delir] nm Méd delirium; (exaltation) frenzy

délit [deli] nm Br offence, Am offense

délivrer [delivre] vt (a) (captif) to rescue; **d. qn de qch** to rid sb of sth (b) (marchandises) to deliver; (passeport) to issue (à to) ▪ **délivrance** nf (soulagement) relief; (de passeport) issue

déloger [delɔʒe] vt (envahisseur) to drive out (de from)

déloyal, -e, -aux, -ales [delwajal, -o] adj (personne) disloyal; (concurrence) unfair

deltaplane [deltaplan] nm hang-glider; **faire du d.** to go hang-gliding

déluge [delyʒ] nm (de pluie) downpour; (de paroles) flood; (d'insultes) torrent

demain [dəmɛ̃] adv tomorrow; **d. soir** tomorrow evening; **à d.!** see you tomorrow!

demande [dəmãd] nf (requête) request (de for); Écon demand; **faire une d. de qch** (prêt, permis) to apply for sth; **demandes d'emploi** (dans le journal) jobs wanted, Br situations wanted

demander [dəmãde] **1** vt (conseil) to ask for; (prix, raison) to ask; (nécessiter) to require; **d. son chemin/l'heure** to ask the way/the time; **d. qch à qn** to ask sb for sth; **d. à qn de faire qch** to ask sb to do sth; **d. qn en mariage** to propose (marriage) to sb **2 se demander** vpr to wonder, to ask oneself (pourquoi why; si if) ▪ **demandeur, -euse** nmf **d. d'emploi** job seeker

démanger [demãʒe] vti to itch ▪ **démangeaisons** nfpl **avoir des d.** to be itching

démanteler [demãtle] vt to break up

démaquiller [demakije] **se démaquiller** vpr to remove one's make-up ▪ **démaquillant** nm cleanser

démarcation [demarkasjɔ̃] nf demarcation

démarche [demarʃ] *nf (allure)* walk, gait; *(requête)* step; **faire les démarches nécessaires pour...** to take the necessary steps to...

démarcheur, -euse [demarʃœr, -øz] *nmf (vendeur)* door-to-door salesman, *f* saleswoman

démarquer [demarke] *vt (marchandises)* to mark down

démarrer [demare] **1** *vi (moteur)* to start; *(voiture)* to move off; *(ordinateur)* to start (up); *Fig (entreprise)* to get off the ground ■ **démarrage** *nm (de moteur)* starting; **au d.** when moving off; **d. en côte** hill start **2** *vt* to start; *Ordinat* to start up, to boot up ■ **démarreur** *nm Aut* starter

démasquer [demaske] *vt* to unmask

démêler [demele] *vt* to untangle

déménager [demenaʒe] **1** *vi* to move **2** *vt (meubles)* to move ■ **déménagement** *nm* move ■ **déménageur** *nm Br* removal man, *Am* (furniture) mover

démener [demne] **se démener** *vpr (s'agiter)* to thrash about

dément, -e [demã, -ãt] *adj* insane ■ **démentiel, -elle** *adj* insane

démentir [demãtir] *vt (nouvelle, fait)* to deny ■ **démenti** *nm* denial

démesuré, -e [demezyre] *adj* excessive

démettre* [demetr] **1** *vt* **d. qn de ses fonctions** to remove sb from his/her post **2** **se démettre** *vpr* **se d. l'épaule** to dislocate one's shoulder

demeurant [dəmœrã] **au demeurant** *adv (malgré tout)* for all that

demeure [dəmœr] *nf (belle maison)* mansion

demeurer [dəmœre] *vi* (a) *(aux être)* *(rester)* to remain (b) *(aux avoir)* *Formel (habiter)* to reside

demi, -e [dəmi] **1** *adj* half; **une heure et demie** *(90 minutes)* an hour and a half; *(à l'horloge)* half past one, one-thirty

2 *adv* **(à) d. plein** half-full; **à d. nu** half-naked

3 *nmf (moitié)* half

4 *nm (au football)* midfielder; **un d.** *(bière)* a beer, *Br* a half(-pint); **d. de mêlée** *(au rugby)* scrum half

5 *nf* **à la demie** *(à l'horloge)* at half-past ■ **demi-cercle** *(pl* **demi-cercles)** *nm* semicircle ■ **demi-douzaine** *(pl* **demi-douzaines)** *nf* **une d. (de)** half a dozen ■ **demi-écrémé** *adj* semi-skimmed ■ **demi-finale** *(pl* **demi-finales)** *nf Sport* semi-final ■ **demi-frère** *(pl* **demi-frères)** *nm* half brother ■ **demi-heure** *(pl* **demi-heures)** *nf* **une d.** half an hour ■ **demi-journée** *(pl* **demi-journées)** *nf* half-day ■ **demi-pension** *nf Br* half-board, *Am* breakfast and one meal ■ **demi-pensionnaire** *(pl* **demi-pensionnaires)** *nmf Br* = pupil who has school dinners ■ **demi-sœur** *(pl* **demi-sœurs)** *nf* half sister ■ **demi-tarif** *(pl* **demi-tarifs)** *nm* half-price ■ **demi-tour** *(pl* **demi-tours)** *nm Br* about turn, *Am* about face; *(en voiture)* U-turn; **faire d.** *(à pied)* to turn back; *(en voiture)* to do a U-turn

démission [demisjɔ̃] *nf* resignation; **donner sa d.** to hand in one's resignation ■ **démissionner** *vi* to resign

démocrate [demɔkrat] **1** *adj* democratic **2** *nmf* democrat ■ **démocratie** [-asi] *nf* democracy ■ **démocratique** *adj* democratic

démodé, -e [demɔde] *adj* old-fashioned

démographie [demɔɡrafi] *nf* demography

demoiselle [dəmwazɛl] *nf (jeune fille)* young lady; **d. d'honneur** bridesmaid

démolir [demɔlir] *vt (bâtiment)* to pull down, to demolish ■ **démolition** *nf* demolition

démon [demɔ̃] *nm* demon; **le d.** the Devil

démonstratif, -ive [demɔ̃stratif, -iv] *adj* demonstrative

démonstration [demɔ̃strasjɔ̃] *nf* demonstration

démonter [demɔ̃te] **1** *vt (mécanisme, tente)* to dismantle **2** **se démonter** *vpr (mécanisme)* to come apart

démontrer [demɔ̃tre] *vt* to demonstrate

démoraliser [demoralize] **1** *vt* to demoralize **2 se démoraliser** *vpr* to become demoralized

démordre [demordr] *vi* **ne pas d. de qch** to stick to sth

démouler [demule] *vt (gâteau)* to turn out

démuni, -e [demyni] *adj* penniless

démunir [demynir] **se démunir** *vpr* **se d. de qch** to part with sth

démystifier [demistifje] *vt* to demystify

dénier [denje] *vt (responsabilité)* to deny; **d. qch à qn** to deny sb sth

dénigrer [denigre] *vt* to denigrate

dénivellation [denivelasjɔ̃] *nf* difference in level; **dénivellations** *(relief)* bumps

dénombrer [denɔ̃bre] *vt* to count

dénommer [denɔme] *vt* to name

dénoncer [denɔ̃se] **1** *vt (injustice, abus, malfaiteur)* to denounce (à to); *(élève)* to tell on (à to) **2 se dénoncer** *vpr (malfaiteur)* to give oneself up (à to); *(élève)* to own up (à to)

dénoter [denɔte] *vt* to denote

dénouement [denumɑ̃] *nm (de livre)* ending; *(de pièce de théâtre)* dénouement; *(d'affaire)* outcome

dénouer [denwe] **1** *vt (nœud, corde)* to undo, to untie; *(cheveux)* to let down, to undo; *Fig (intrigue)* to unravel **2 se dénouer** *vpr (nœud)* to come undone; *(cheveux)* to come down

denrée [dɑre] *nf* foodstuff; **denrées alimentaires** foodstuffs; **denrées périssables** perishable goods

dense [dɑs] *adj* dense ■ **densité** *nf* density

dent [dɑ̃] *nf* tooth *(pl* teeth); *(de roue)* cog; *(de fourchette)* prong; **d. de lait / sagesse** milk/wisdom tooth; **faire ses dents** *(enfant)* to be teething; **en dents de scie** serrated; *Fig (résultats)* uneven ■ **dentaire** *adj* dental

dentelé, -e [dɑtle] *adj (côte, feuille)* jagged

dentelle [dɑtel] *nf* lace

dentier [dɑtje] *nm* (set of) false teeth, dentures

dentifrice [dɑtifris] *nm* toothpaste

dentiste [dɑtist] *nmf* dentist

dénuder [denyde] *vt* to (lay) bare ■ **dénudé, -e** *adj* bare

dénué, -e [denɥe] *adj* **d. d'intérêt** devoid of interest

dénuement [denymɑ̃] *nm* destitution; **dans le d.** poverty-stricken, destitute

déodorant [deodorɑ̃] *nm* deodorant

dépanner [depane] *vt (machine)* to repair ■ **dépannage** *nm* (emergency) repairs; **voiture / service de d.** breakdown vehicle/service ■ **dépanneur** *nm (de télévision)* repairman; *(de voiture)* breakdown mechanic ■ **dépanneuse** *nf (voiture) Br* breakdown lorry, *Am* wrecker

dépareillé, -e [depareje] *adj (chaussure)* odd

départ [depar] *nm* departure; *(de course)* start; **les grands départs =** the mass exodus of people from major cities at the beginning of the holiday period; **point / ligne de d.** starting point/post; **au d.** at the outset, at the start; **au d. de Paris** *(excursion)* leaving from Paris

départager [departaʒe] *vt* to decide between

département [departəmɑ̃] *nm* department *(division of local government)* ■ **départemental, -e, -aux, -ales** *adj* departmental; **route départementale** secondary road, *Br* ≃ B road

départir* [departir] **se départir** *vpr* **il ne s'est jamais départi de son calme** his calm never deserted him

dépasser [depase] **1** *vt (véhicule) Br* to overtake, *Am* to pass; *(endroit)* to go past; *(vitesse)* to exceed; **d. qn** *(en hauteur)* to be taller than sb **2** *vi (clou)* to stick out ■ **dépassé, -e** *adj (démodé)* outdated; *(incapable)* unable to cope

dépayser [depeize] *vt Br* to disorientate, *Am* to disorient

dépêche [depeʃ] *nf* dispatch ■ **dépêcher 1** *vt* to dispatch **2 se dépêcher**

vpr to hurry (up); **se d. de faire qch** to hurry to do sth

dépendant, -e [depādū, -ūt] dependent (**de** on) ▪ **dépendance** *nf* dependence; **sous la d. de qn** under sb's domination ▪ **dépendances** *nfpl (bâtiments)* outbuildings

dépendre [depūdr] *vi* to depend (**de** on *or* upon); **d. de** *(appartenir à)* to belong to; *(être soumis à)* to be dependent on

dépens [depū] *nmpl* **apprendre qch à ses d.** to learn sth to one's cost

dépense [depūs] *nf (frais)* expense, expenditure; **faire des dépenses** to spend money ▪ **dépenser 1** *vt (argent)* to spend; *(forces)* to exert **2 se dépenser** *vpr* to burn up energy

dépensier, -ère [depūsje, -er] *adj* extravagant

dépérir [deperir] *vi (personne)* to waste away; *(plante)* to wither

dépeupler [depœple] **1** *vt* to depopulate **2 se dépeupler** *vpr* to become depopulated

dépilatoire [depilatwar] *nm* hair-remover

dépister [depiste] *vt (maladie)* to detect ▪ **dépistage** *nm (de maladie)* screening

dépit [depi] *nm* spite; **en d. de qn/qch** in spite of sb/sth

dépité, -e [depite] *adj* annoyed

déplacement [deplasmū] *nm (voyage)* trip; **être en d.** *(homme d'affaires)* to be on a business trip; **frais de d.** *Br* travelling *or Am* traveling expenses

déplacer [deplase] **1** *vt (objet)* to move **2 se déplacer** *vpr (aiguille de montre)* to move; *(personne, animal)* to move (about); *(marcher)* to walk (around); *(voyager)* to travel ▪ **deplacé, -e** *adj (mal à propos)* out of place; **personne déplacée** *(réfugié)* displaced person

déplaire* [depler] **1** *vi* **d. à qn** to displease sb; **ça me déplaît** I don't like it **2 se déplaire** *vpr* **il se déplaît à Paris** he doesn't like it in Paris ▪ **déplaisant, -e** *adj* unpleasant

déplier [deplije] *vt* to open out, to un-

fold ▪ **dépliant** *nm (prospectus)* leaflet

déplorer [deplɔre] *vt (regretter)* to deplore; **d. que...** *(+ subjunctive)* to deplore the fact that...; **d. la mort de qn** to mourn sb's death

déployer [deplwaje] *vt (ailes)* to spread; *(journal, carte)* to unfold; *(troupes)* to deploy ▪ **déploiement** *nm (démonstration)* display; *(d'une armée)* deployment

dépoli, -e [depɔli] *adj* **verre d.** frosted glass

déporter [depɔrte] *vt* **d. qn** to send sb to a concentration camp

déposer [depoze] **1** *vt (poser)* to put down; *(gerbe)* to lay; *(projet de loi)* to introduce; *(souverain)* to depose; **d. qn** *(en voiture)* to drop sb off; **d. de l'argent sur un compte** to deposit money in an account; **d. une plainte contre qn** to lodge a complaint against sb **2** *vi Jur* to testify; *(liquide)* to leave a deposit **3 se déposer** *vpr* to settle

dépositaire [depɔziter] *nmf (vendeur)* agent

déposséder [deposede] *vt* to deprive, to dispossess (**de** of)

dépôt [depo] *nm (de vin)* deposit, sediment; *(entrepôt)* depot; *(prison)* jail; **faire un d.** *(d'argent)* to make a deposit; **d. de munitions** munitions depot

dépouille [depuj] *nf (d'animal)* hide, skin; **d. mortelle** *(de personne)* mortal remains

dépouiller [depuje] **1** *vt (animal)* to skin; *(analyser)* to go through; **d. qn de qch** to deprive sb of sth; **d. un scrutin** to count the votes **2 se dépouiller** *vpr* **se d. de qch** to rid oneself of sth ▪ **dépouillé, -e** *adj (style)* austere ▪ **dépouillement** *nm (de documents)* analysis; *(privation)* deprivation; *(sobriété)* austerity; **d. du scrutin** counting of the votes

dépourvu, -e [depurvy] *adj* **d. de qch** devoid of sth; **prendre qn au d.** to catch sb off guard

dépoussiérer [depusjere] *vt* to dust

dépraver [deprave] *vt* to deprave

déprécier [depresje] **se déprécier** *vpr*

(valeurs, marchandises) to depreciate

dépression [depresjɔ̃] *nf (creux, maladie)* depression; **d. atmosphérique** low, trough; **d. économique** slump; **d. nerveuse** nervous breakdown; **faire de la d.** to be suffering from depression ▪ **dépressif, -ive** *adj* depressive

déprimer [deprime] *vt* to depress ▪ **déprimé, -e** *adj* depressed

DEPUIS [dəpɥi] **1** *prép* since; **d. lundi/2001** since Monday/2001; **j'habite ici d. un mois** I've been living here for a month; **d. quand êtes-vous là?**, **d. combien de temps êtes-vous là?** how long have you been here?; **d. peu/longtemps** for a short/long time
2 *adv* since (then), ever since
3 *conj* **d. que** since

député [depyte] *nm Pol* deputy, *Br* ≃ MP, *Am* ≃ representative; **d. du Parlement européen** Member of the European Parliament

déraciner [derasine] *vt (arbre, personne)* to uproot

dérailler [deraje] *vi (train)* to leave the rails; **faire d. un train** to derail a train

déranger [derɑ̃ʒe] **1** *vt (affaires)* to disturb; **je viendrai si ça ne te dérange pas** I'll come if that's all right with you; **ça vous dérange si je fume?** do you mind if I smoke?
2 se déranger *vpr* to put oneself to a lot of trouble (**pour faire** to do); *(se déplacer)* to move; **ne te dérange pas!** don't bother! ▪ **dérangement** *nm (gêne)* trouble; **en d.** *(téléphone)* out of order

déraper [derape] *vi (véhicule)* to skid; *(personne)* to slip

dérégler [deregle] **1** *vt (mécanisme)* to cause to malfunction **2 se dérégler** *vpr (mécanisme)* to go wrong

dérider [deride] *vt*, **se dérider** *vpr* to cheer up

dérision [derizjɔ̃] *nf* derision; **tourner qch en d.** to deride sth ▪ **dérisoire** *adj (somme)* derisory

dérive [deriv] *nf Naut* drift; **à la d.** adrift

dériver [derive] **1** *vt (cours d'eau)* to divert **2** *vi Naut* to drift

dermatologue [dermatɔlɔg] *nmf* dermatologist

dernier, -ère [dernje, -ɛr] **1** *adj (ultime)* last; *(marquant la fin)* final; *(nouvelles, mode)* latest; *(étage)* top; *(degré)* highest; **le d. rang** the back *or* last row; **ces derniers mois** these past few months; **les dix dernières minutes** the last ten minutes; **en d.** last
2 *nmf* last; **ce d.** *(de deux)* the latter; *(de plusieurs)* the last-mentioned

dérober [derɔbe] **1** *vt (voler)* to steal (**à** from); *(cacher)* to hide (**à** from) **2 se dérober** *vpr (s'esquiver)* to slip away; *(éviter de répondre)* to dodge the issue

dérogation [derɔgasjɔ̃] *nf* exemption (**à** from)

déroger [derɔʒe] *vi* **d. à une règle** to depart from a rule

dérouler [derule] **1** *vt (tapis)* to unroll; *(fil)* to unwind **2 se dérouler** *vpr (tapis)* to unroll; *(fil)* to unwind

déroute [derut] *nf (d'armée)* rout

dérouter [derute] *vt (avion, navire)* to divert, to reroute; *(poursuivant)* to throw off the scent; *Fig (étonner)* to throw

derrière [derjɛr] **1** *prép & adv* behind; **d. moi** behind me; **assis d.** *(dans une voiture)* sitting in the back; **par d.** *(attaquer)* from behind, from the rear **2** *nm (de maison)* back, rear; *(fesses)* behind; **roue de d.** back *or* rear wheel

des [de] *voir* **de, un**

dès [dɛ] *prép* from; **d. le début** (right) from the start; **d. maintenant** from now on; **d. le VIe siècle** as early as *or* as far back as the sixth century; **d. lors** *(dans le temps)* from then on; *(en conséquence)* consequently; **d. leur arrivée** as soon as they arrive/arrived; **d. qu'elle viendra** as soon as she comes

désabusé, -e [dezabyze] *adj* disillusioned

désaccord [dezakɔr] *nm* disagreement; **être en d. avec qn** to disagree with sb

désaffecté, -e [dezafɛkte] *adj* disused

désaffection [dezafɛksjɔ̃] *nf* disaffection (**à l'égard de** with)

désagréable [dezagreabl] *adj* unpleasant

désagrément [dezagremɑ̃] *nm (gêne)* trouble; *(souci, aspect négatif)* problem

désaltérer [dezaltere] **1** *vt* **d. qn** to quench sb's thirst **2 se désaltérer** *vpr* to quench one's thirst

désamorcer [dezamɔrse] *vt (bombe, conflit)* to defuse

désapprouver [dezapruve] **1** *vt* to disapprove of **2** *vi* to disapprove ▪ **désapprobateur, -trice** *adj* disapproving ▪ **désapprobation** *nf* disapproval

désarmer [dezarme] **1** *vt (soldat, nation)* to disarm; *Fig* **d. qn** *(franchise, attitude)* to disarm sb **2** *vi (pays)* to disarm ▪ **désarmement** *nm (de nation)* disarmament

désarroi [dezarwa] *nm* confusion

désastre [dezastr] *nm* disaster ▪ **désastreux, -euse** *adj* disastrous

désavantage [dezavɑ̃taʒ] *nm* disadvantage ▪ **désavantager** *vt* to put at a disadvantage

désavouer [dezavwe] *vt (renier)* to disown

désaxé, -e [dezakse] *nmf* unbalanced person

desceller [desele] **1** *vt (pierre)* to loosen **2 se desceller** *vpr* to come loose

descendant, -e [desɑ̃dɑ̃, -ɑ̃t] *nmf* descendant ▪ **descendance** *nf (enfants)* descendants; *(origine)* descent

descendre [desɑ̃dr] **1** *(aux* **être)** *vi* to come/go down (**de** from); *(d'un train)* to get off (**de** from); *(d'un arbre)* to climb down (**de** from); *(marée)* to go out; **d. à l'hôtel** to put up at a hotel; **d. de** *(être issu de)* to be descended from **2** *(aux* **avoir)** *vt (escalier)* to come/go down; *(objet)* to bring/take down

descente [desɑ̃t] *nf (d'avion)* descent; *(en parachute)* drop; *(pente)* slope; *(de police)* raid (**dans** upon); **d. de lit** bedside rug

descriptif, -ive [deskriptif, -iv] *adj* descriptive ▪ **description** *nf* description

désemparé, -e [dezɑ̃pare] *adj (personne)* at a loss

désemplir [dezɑ̃plir] *vi* **ce magasin ne désemplit pas** this shop is always crowded

désenchanté, -e [dezɑ̃ʃɑ̃te] *adj* disillusioned ▪ **désenchantement** *nm* disenchantment

déséquilibre [dezekilibr] *nm* imbalance; **en d.** unsteady ▪ **déséquilibré, -e 1** *adj* unbalanced **2** *nmf* unbalanced person ▪ **déséquilibrer** *vt* to throw off balance

désert, -e [dezɛr, -ɛrt] **1** *adj (lieu)* deserted; *(région)* uninhabited; **île déserte** desert island **2** *nm* desert ▪ **désertique** *adj* **région d.** desert region

déserter [dezɛrte] *vti* to desert ▪ **désertion** *nf* desertion

désespérer [dezɛspere] **1** *vt* to drive to despair **2** *vi* to despair (**de** of) **3 se désespérer** *vpr* to despair ▪ **désespérant, -e** *adj (situation, personne)* hopeless ▪ **désespéré, -e** *adj (personne)* in dèspair; *(cas, situation, efforts)* desperate ▪ **désespérément** *adv* desperately

désespoir [dezɛspwar] *nm* despair; **en d. de cause** in desperation

déshabiller [dezabije] *vt*, **se déshabiller** *vpr* to undress

désherber [dezɛrbe] *vti* to weed

déshériter [dezerite] *vt* to disinherit

déshonneur [dezɔnœr] *nm* dishonour

déshonorer [dezɔnɔre] *vt* to disgrace ▪ **déshonorant, -e** *adj* dishonourable

déshydrater [dezidrate] **1** *vt* to dehydrate **2 se déshydrater** *vpr* to become dehydrated

désigner [dezine] *vt (montrer)* to point to; *(choisir)* to choose; *(nommer)* to appoint; **d. qn par son nom** to refer to sb by name ▪ **désignation** *nf* designation

désillusion [dezilyzjɔ̃] *nf* disillusion ▪ **désillusionner** *vt* to disillusion

désinfecter [dezɛ̃fɛkte] *vt* to disinfect ▪ **désinfectant** *nm* disinfectant

désinformation [dezɛ̃fɔrmasjɔ̃] *nf* disinformation

désintégrer [dezɛ̃tegre] **se désin-tégrer** *vpr* to disintegrate

désintéresser [dezɛ̃terese] **se désin-téresser** *vpr* **se d. de qch** to lose interest in sth ■ **désintéressé, -e** *adj (altruiste)* disinterested ■ **désintérêt** *nm* lack of interest

désintoxiquer [dezɛ̃tɔksike] *vt (alcoolique, drogué)* to treat for alcoholism/drug abuse

désinvolte [dezɛ̃vɔlt] *adj (dégagé)* casual; *(insolent)* offhand ■ **désinvolture** *nf* casualness; *(insolence)* offhandedness

désir [dezir] *nm* desire ■ **désirable** *adj* desirable ■ **désirer** *vt* to wish; *(convoiter)* to desire

désireux, -euse [dezirø, -øz] *adj* **d. de faire qch** anxious to do sth

désistement [dezistəmɑ̃] *nm* withdrawal

désister [deziste] **se désister** *vpr* to withdraw

désobéir [dezɔbeir] *vi* to disobey; **d. à qn** to disobey sb ■ **désobéissant, -e** *adj* disobedient

désobligeant, -e [dezɔbliʒɑ̃, -ɑ̃t] *adj* disagreeable

désodorisant [dezɔdɔrizɑ̃] *nm* air freshener

désœuvré, -e [dezœvre] *adj* idle

désoler [dezɔle] **1** *vt* to upset **2 se désoler** *vpr* to be upset **(de** at) ■ **désolant, -e** *adj* upsetting ■ **désolé, -e** *adj (région)* desolate; *(affligé)* upset; **être d. que...** *(+ subjunctive)* to be sorry that...; **je suis d. de vous déranger** I'm sorry to disturb you

désolidariser [desɔlidarize] **se désolidariser** *vpr* to dissociate oneself **(de** from)

désordonné, -e [dezɔrdɔne] *adj (personne, chambre)* untidy

désordre [dezɔrdr] *nm (manque d'ordre)* mess; *(manque d'organisation)* disorder; **en d.** untidy, messy; **de graves désordres** *(émeutes)* serious disturbances

désorganiser [dezɔrganize] *vt* to disorganize ■ **désorganisation** *nf* disor-ganization ■ **désorganisé, -e** *adj* disorganized

désorienter [dezɔrjɑ̃te] *vt* **d. qn** to bewilder sb

désormais [dezɔrmɛ] *adv* from now on, in future

despote [despɔt] *nm* despot

desquels, desquelles [dekɛl] *voir* **lequel**

dessaisir [desezir] **se dessaisir** *vpr* **se d. de qch** to relinquish sth

dessaler [desale] *vt (poisson)* to remove the salt from *(by soaking)*

dessécher [deseʃe] **1** *vt (peau)* to dry up; *(végétation)* to wither **2 se dessé-cher** *vpr (peau)* to dry up; *(végétation)* to wither

dessein [desɛ̃] *nm* intention; **à d.** intentionally

desserrer [desere] **1** *vt (ceinture)* to loosen; *(poing)* to unclench; *(frein)* to release **2 se desserrer** *vpr (ceinture)* to come loose

dessert [desɛr] *nm* dessert, *Br* pudding

desserte [desɛrt] *nf* **assurer la d. de** *(village)* to provide a service to

desservir [desɛrvir] *vt (table)* to clear (away); **d. qn** to do sb a disservice; **le car dessert ce village** the bus stops at this village; **ce quartier est bien desservi** this district is well served by public transport

dessin [desɛ̃] *nm* drawing; *(rapide)* sketch; *(motif)* design, pattern; *(contour)* outline; **d. animé** cartoon; **d. humoristique** *(de journal)* cartoon

dessinateur, -trice [desinatœr, -tris] *nmf* drawer; **d. industriel** *Br* draughtsman, *Am* draftsman

dessiner [desine] **1** *vt* to draw; *(rapidement)* to sketch; *(meuble, robe)* to design; *(indiquer)* to outline; **d. (bien) la taille** *(vêtement)* to show off the figure **2 se dessiner** *vpr (colline)* to stand out; *(projet)* to take shape

dessous [dəsu] **1** *adv* underneath; **en d.** underneath; **en d. de** below **2** *nm* underside; **des d.** *(sous-vêtements)* underwear ■ **dessous-de-plat** *nm inv*

table mat ▪ **dessous-de-table** *nm inv* bribe, *Br* backhander

dessus [dəsy] **1** *adv (marcher, écrire)* on it/them; *(monter)* on top (of it/them), on it/them; *(passer)* over it/them; **de d. la table** off *or* from the table

2 *nm* top; *(de chaussure)* upper; **avoir le d.** to have the upper hand; **reprendre le d.** *(se remettre)* to get over it

déstabiliser [destabilize] *vt* to destabilize

destin [dɛstɛ̃] *nm* fate, destiny ▪ **destinée** *nf* destiny

destinataire [dɛstinatɛr] *nmf* addressee

destination [dɛstinasjɔ̃] *nf (lieu)* destination; **trains à d. de…** trains to…; **arriver à d.** to reach one's destination

destiner [dɛstine] **1** *vt* **d. qch à qn** to intend sth for sb; **d. qn à** *(carrière, fonction)* to intend *or* destine sb for **2 se destiner** *vpr* **se d. à** *(carrière)* to intend to take up

destituer [dɛstitɥe] *vt (fonctionnaire)* to remove from office

destructeur, -trice [dɛstryktœr, -tris] *adj* destructive

destruction [dɛstryksjɔ̃] *nf* destruction

désuet, -ète [desɥe, -ɛt] *adj* obsolete ▪ **désuétude** *nf* **tomber en d.** *(expression)* to become obsolete

désunir [dezynir] *vt (famille, personnes)* to divide

détachant [detaʃɑ̃] *nm* stain remover

détachement [detaʃmɑ̃] *nm* (a) *(indifférence)* detachment (b) *(de fonctionnaire)* secondment; *(de troupes)* detachment

détacher¹ [detaʃe] **1** *vt (ceinture, vêtement)* to undo; *(mains)* to untie; *(ôter)* to take off; *(mots)* to pronounce clearly; **d. qn** *(libérer)* to untie sb; *(affecter)* to transfer sb (on assignment) (**à** to)

2 se détacher *vpr (chien, prisonnier)* to break loose; *(se dénouer)* to come undone; **se d.** *(fragment)* to come off (**de qch** sth); **se d. de qn** to break away from sb; **se d. sur qch** *(ressortir)* to

stand out against sth ▪ **détaché, -e** *adj (air, ton)* detached

détacher² [detaʃe] *vt (linge)* to remove the stains from

détail [detaj] *nm* detail; **en d.** in detail; **entrer dans les détails** to go into detail; **prix de d.** retail price

détaillant [detajɑ̃] *nm* retailer

détailler [detaje] *vt (énumérer)* to detail ▪ **détaillé, -e** *adj (récit, description)* detailed; *(facture)* itemized

détaxer [detakse] *vt* to exempt from tax; **produit détaxé** duty-free article

détecter [detɛkte] *vt* to detect ▪ **détecteur** *nm (appareil)* detector

détective [detɛktiv] *nm* **d. (privé)** (private) detective

déteindre* [detɛ̃dr] *vi (couleur, tissu)* to run

détendre [detɑ̃dr] **1** *vt (corde)* to slacken; *(arc)* to unbend; **d. qn** to relax sb **2 se détendre** *vpr (corde)* to slacken; *(arc)* to unbend; *(atmosphère)* to become less tense; *(personne)* to relax ▪ **détendu, -e** *adj (visage, atmosphère)* relaxed; *(ressort, câble)* slack

détenir* [detənir] *vt (record, pouvoir, titre, prisonnier)* to hold; *(secret, objet volé)* to be in possession of ▪ **détenteur, -trice** *nmf (de record)* holder ▪ **détention** *nf (d'armes)* possession; *(captivité)* detention; **d. provisoire** detention pending trial, remand ▪ **détenu, -e** *nmf* prisoner

détente [detɑ̃t] *nf* (a) *(repos)* relaxation; *(entre deux pays)* détente (b) *(saut)* spring (c) *(gâchette)* trigger

détergent [detɛrʒɑ̃] *nm* detergent

détériorer [deterjore] **1** *vt* to damage **2 se détériorer** *vpr* to deteriorate ▪ **détérioration** *nf* damage (**de** to); *(de situation)* deterioration (**de** in)

détermination [determinasjɔ̃] *nf (fermeté)* determination

déterminer [determine] *vt (préciser)* to determine; *(causer)* to bring about ▪ **déterminant, -e** *adj* decisive ▪ **déterminé, -e** *adj (précis)* specific; *(résolu)* determined

déterrer [detere] *vt* to dig up

détester [detɛste] *vt* to hate, to detest; **d. faire qch** to hate doing *or* to do sth ■ **détestable** *adj* foul

détonation [detɔnasjɔ̃] *nf* explosion; *(d'arme)* bang

détonner [detɔne] *vi (contraster)* to clash

détour [detur] *nm (crochet)* detour; *(de route)* bend, curve

détourner [deturne] **1** *vt (dévier)* to divert; *(avion)* to hijack; *(conversation, sens)* to change; *(fonds)* to embezzle; *(coup)* to ward off; **d. la tête** to turn one's head away; **d. les yeux** to look away; **d. qn de** *(son devoir)* to take sb away from; *(sa route)* to lead sb away from
2 se détourner *vpr* to turn away ■ **détourné, -e** *adj (chemin, moyen)* roundabout, indirect ■ **détournement** [-əmɑ̃] *nm (de cours d'eau)* diversion; **d. d'avion** hijack(ing); **d. de fonds** embezzlement

détracteur, -trice [detraktœr, -tris] *nmf* detractor

détraquer [detrake] **1** *vt (mécanisme)* to put out of order **2 se détraquer** *vpr (machine)* to go wrong

détresse [detrɛs] *nf* distress; **en d.** *(navire)* in distress

détriment [detrimɑ̃] **au détriment de** *prép* to the detriment of

détritus [detritys] *nmpl Br* rubbish, *Am* garbage

détroit [detrwa] *nm* strait

détromper [detrɔ̃pe] **1** *vt* **d. qn** to put sb right **2 se détromper** *vpr* **détrompez-vous!** don't you believe it!

détrôner [detrone] *vt (souverain)* to dethrone; *(supplanter)* to supersede

détruire* [detrɥir] *vt (ravager)* to destroy; *(tuer)* to kill

dette [dɛt] *nf* debt; **avoir des dettes** to be in debt; **faire des dettes** to run into debt

DEUG [dœg] *(abrév* **diplôme d'études universitaires générales)** *nm* = degree gained after two years' study at university

deuil [dœj] *nm (affliction, vêtements)* mourning; *(décès)* bereavement; **être en d.** to be in mourning

deux [dø] *adj inv & nm inv* two; **d. fois** twice; **mes d. sœurs** both my sisters, my two sisters; **tous (les) d.** both ■ **deux-pièces** *nm inv (maillot de bain)* bikini; *(appartement)* two-roomed *Br* flat *or Am* apartment ■ **deux-roues** *nm inv* two-wheeled vehicle

deuxième [døzjɛm] *adj & nmf* second

dévaler [devale] *vt (escalier)* to hurtle down

dévaliser [devalize] *vt (personne, banque)* to rob

dévaloriser [devalorize] **1** *vt (monnaie, diplôme)* to devalue **2 se dévaloriser** *vpr (monnaie)* to depreciate ■ **dévalorisation** *nf (de diplôme)* loss of value

dévaluer [devalɥe] *vt (monnaie)* to devalue ■ **dévaluation** *nf* Fin devaluation

devancer [dəvɑ̃se] *vt (concurrent)* to be ahead of; *(arriver avant)* to arrive before

devant [dəvɑ̃] **1** *prép & adv* in front (of); **passer d. une église** to go past a church; **marcher d. qn** to walk in front of sb; **assis d.** *(dans une voiture)* sitting in the front
2 *nm* front; **roue/porte de d.** front wheel/door; **prendre les devants** *(action)* to take the initiative

devanture [dəvɑ̃tyr] *nf (vitrine)* window; *(façade)* front

dévaster [devaste] *vt* to devastate ■ **dévastation** *nf* devastation

développer [devlɔpe] *vt,* **se développer** *vpr* to develop ■ **développement** *nm* development; *(de photo)* developing; **en plein d.** *(entreprise, pays)* growing fast

devenir* [dəvnir] *(aux être) vi* to become; **d. médecin** to become a doctor; **d. vieux** to get *or* grow old; **d. tout rouge** to go all red; **qu'est-elle devenue?** what's become of her?

dévergondé, -e [devergɔ̃de] *adj* shameless

déverser [devɛrse] **1** *vt (liquide)* to

pour out; *(ordures)* to dump **2 se déver-
ser** *vpr (liquide, rivière)* to empty **(dans
into)**

dévêtir [devetir] *vt,* **se dévêtir** *vpr* to
undress

dévier [devje] **1** *vt (circulation)* to di-
vert; *(coup, rayons)* to deflect **2** *vi
(balle)* to deflect; *(véhicule)* to veer; **d.
de sa route** to veer off course ▪ **dévia-
tion** *nf (itinéraire)* Br diversion, *Am* de-
tour

devin [dəvɛ̃] *nm* soothsayer

deviner [dəvine] *vt* to guess **(que** that)
▪ **devinette** *nf* riddle

devis [dəvi] *nm* estimate

dévisager [devizaʒe] *vt* **d. qn** to stare
at sb

devise [dəviz] *nf (légende)* motto;
(monnaie) currency; **devises étran-
gères** foreign currency

dévisser [devise] **1** *vt* to unscrew **2 se
dévisser** *vpr (bouchon)* to unscrew;
(par accident) to come unscrewed

dévoiler [devwale] **1** *vt (statue)* to un-
veil; *Fig (secret)* to disclose **2 se dévoi-
ler** *vpr (mystère)* to come to light

DEVOIR*¹ [dəvwar] *v aux* **(a)** *(in-
dique la nécessité)* **je dois refuser** I
must refuse, I have (got) to refuse; **j'ai
dû refuser** I had to refuse

(b) *(indique une forte probabilité)* **il
doit être tard** it must be late; **elle a dû
oublier** she must have forgotten; **cela
devait arriver** it had to happen

(c) *(indique l'obligation)* **tu dois ap-
prendre tes leçons** you must learn
your lessons; **vous devriez rester** you
should stay, you ought to stay; **il aurait
dû venir** he should have come, he
ought to have come

(d) *(indique l'intention)* **elle doit venir**
she's supposed to be coming, she's due
to come; **le train devait arriver à midi**
the train was due (to arrive) at noon; **je
devais le voir** I was (due) to see him

devoir*² [dəvwar] **1** *vt* to owe; **d. qch
à qn** to owe sb sth, to owe sth to sb
2 se devoir *vpr* **comme il se doit** as
is proper
3 *nm (obligation)* duty; **présenter ses**

devoirs à qn to pay one's respects to
sb; *Scol* **devoirs** homework; **faire ses
devoirs** to do one's homework; **d. sur
table** test

dévorer [devɔre] *vt (manger)* to de-
vour

dévotion [devosjɔ̃] *nf (adoration)* de-
votion

dévouer [devwe] **se dévouer** *vpr (se
sacrifier)* to volunteer; *(se consacrer)* to
devote oneself **(à** to) ▪ **dévoué, -e** *adj
(ami, femme)* devoted **(à** to) ▪ **dévoue-
ment** [-umɑ̃] *nm* devotion; *(de héros)*
devotion to duty

dextérité [dɛksterite] *nf* dexterity, skill

diabète [djabɛt] *nm Méd* diabetes
▪ **diabétique** *adj & nmf* diabetic

diable [djɑbl] *nm* devil; **le d.** the Devil
▪ **diabolique** *adj* diabolical

diadème [djadɛm] *nm* tiara

diagnostic [djagnɔstik] *nm* diagnosis
▪ **diagnostiquer** *vt* to diagnose

diagonal, -e, -aux, -ales [djagɔnal,
-o] *adj* diagonal ▪ **diagonale** *nf* diago-
nal (line); **en d.** diagonally

dialecte [djalɛkt] *nm* dialect

dialogue [djalɔg] *nm Br* dialogue, *Am*
dialog; *(conversation)* conversation
▪ **dialoguer** *vi* to communicate; *Ordi-
nat* to interact

diamant [djamɑ̃] *nm* diamond

diamètre [djamɛtr] *nm* diameter

diapason [djapazɔ̃] *nm Mus (appareil)*
tuning fork

diapositive [djapozitiv] *nf* slide

diarrhée [djare] *nf* diarrhoea

dictateur [diktatœr] *nm* dictator ▪ **dic-
tatorial, -e, -aux, -ales** *adj* dictatorial
▪ **dictature** *nf* dictatorship

dicter [dikte] *vt* to dictate **(à** to) ▪ **dic-
tée** *nf* dictation

diction [diksjɔ̃] *nf* diction

dictionnaire [diksjɔnɛr] *nm* dictiona-
ry

dièse [djez] *adj & nm Mus* sharp

diesel [djezɛl] *adj & nm* **(moteur) d.**
diesel (engine)

diète [djet] *nf (partielle)* diet; *(totale)*

fast; **être à la d.** to be on a diet/to be fasting

diététicien, -enne [djetetisjɛ̃, -ɛn] nmf dietician ■ **diététique 1** adj dietetics (sing) **2** adj **aliment** ou **produit d.** health food; **magasin d.** health-food shop

dieu, -x [djø] nm god; **D.** God; **le bon D.** God

diffamation [difamasjɔ̃] nf (en paroles) slander; (par écrit) libel ■ **diffamatoire** adj (paroles) slanderous; (écrit) libellous

différé [difere] nm **en d.** (émission) prerecorded

différence [diferɑ̃s] nf difference (**de** in); **à la d. de qn/qch** unlike sb/sth; **faire la d. entre** to make a d. distinction between; **différences culturelles** cultural differences

différencier [diferɑ̃sje] **1** vt to differentiate (**de** from) **2 se différencier** vpr to differ (**de** from)

différend [diferɑ̃] nm difference of opinion

différent, -e [diferɑ̃, -ɑ̃t] adj different; **différents** (divers) different, various; **d. de** different from ■ **différemment** [-amɑ̃] adv differently (**de** from)

différer [difere] **1** vt (remettre) to postpone; (paiement) to defer **2** vi to differ (**de** from)

difficile [difisil] adj difficult; (exigeant) fussy; **c'est d. à faire** it's hard or difficult to do ■ **difficilement** adv with difficulty

difficulté [difikylte] nf difficulty (**à faire** in doing); **en d.** in a difficult situation; **avoir de la d. à faire qch** to have difficulty (in) doing sth

difforme [difɔrm] adj deformed, misshapen ■ **difformité** nf deformity

diffus, -e [dify, -yz] adj (lumière) diffuse; (impression) vague

diffuser [difyze] vt (émission) to broadcast; (nouvelle) to spread; (lumière, chaleur) to diffuse ■ **diffusion** nf (d'émission) broadcasting; (de lumière, de chaleur) diffusion

digérer [diʒere] **1** vt to digest **2** vi to digest

digestif, -ive [diʒɛstif, -iv] **1** adj (tube, sucs) digestive **2** nmf after-dinner liqueur

digestion [diʒɛstjɔ̃] nf digestion

Digicode® [diʒikɔd] nm door code (for entrance to building)

digne [diɲ] adj (air, attitude) dignified; **d. de qn/qch** worthy of sb/sth; **d. d'admiration** worthy of or deserving of admiration ■ **dignement** [-amɑ̃] adv with dignity

dignitaire [diɲiter] nm dignitary

dignité [diɲite] nf dignity

digue [dig] nf dike, dyke; (en bord de mer) sea wall

dilapider [dilapide] vt to squander

dilater [dilate] vt, **se dilater** vpr (pupille) to dilate

dilemme [dilɛm] nm dilemma

diluer [dilɥe] vt (liquide, substance) to dilute (**dans** in)

dimanche [dimɑ̃ʃ] nm Sunday

dimension [dimɑ̃sjɔ̃] nf (mesure, aspect) dimension; (taille) size; **à deux dimensions** two-dimensional; **prendre les dimensions de qch** to measure sth up

diminuer [diminɥe] **1** vt (réduire) to reduce, to decrease; (affaiblir) to affect **2** vi (réserves, nombre) to decrease, to diminish; (jours) to get shorter; (prix, profits) to decrease, to drop ■ **diminution** nf reduction, decrease (**ce** in)

diminutif [diminytif] nm (nom) diminutive

dinde [dɛ̃d] nf (volaille, viande) turkey ■ **dindon** nm turkey (cock)

dîner [dine] **1** nm (repas du soir) dinner; (repas de midi) lunch; (soirée) dinner party **2** vi to have dinner; Belg & Can to (have) lunch

dinosaure [dinozɔr] nm dinosaur

diplomate [diplɔmat] **1** adj diplomatic **2** nmf diplomat ■ **diplomatie** [-asi] nf (tact) diplomacy; (carrière, diplomatic service ■ **diplomatique** adj diplomatic

diplôme [diplom] *nm* diploma; *(d'université)* degree ■ **diplômé, -e 1** *adj* qualified; *Univ* **être d. (de)** to be a graduate (of) **2** *nmf* holder of a diploma; *Univ* graduate

DIRE* [dir] **1** *nm* **au d. de** according to; **selon ses dires** according to him/her

2 *vt (mot)* to say; *(vérité, secret)* to tell; **d. des bêtises** to talk nonsense; **d. qch à qn** to tell sb sth, to say sth to sb; **d. à qn que...** to tell sb that..., to say to sb that...; **d. à qn de faire qch** to tell sb to do sth; **d. du mal/du bien de qn** to speak ill/well of sb; **on dirait un château** it looks like a castle; **on dirait du cabillaud** it tastes like cod; **autrement dit** in other words; **à vrai d.** to tell the truth

3 *se dire vpr* **il se dit malade** he says he's ill; **comment ça se dit en anglais?** how do you say that in English?

direct, -e [dirɛkt] **1** *adj* direct **2** *nm* *Radio & TV* live broadcasting; **en d. (de)** live (from) ■ **directement** [-əmɑ̃] *adv (sans intermédiaire)* directly; *(sans détour)* straight

directeur, -trice [dirɛktœr, -tris] **1** *nmf* director; *(de magasin, de service)* manager; *(de journal)* editor; *(d'école) Br* headmaster, *f* headmistress; *Am* principal **2** *adj (principe)* guiding; *(idées)* main; *(équipe)* management

direction [dirɛksjɔ̃] *nf* (a) *(sens)* direction; **train en d. de Lille** train to Lille (b) *(de société, de club)* running, management; *(de parti)* leadership; *Aut* steering; **sous la d. de** under the supervision of; *(orchestre)* conducted by; **un poste de d.** a management post; **d. du personnel** personnel department

dirigeant, -e [diriʒɑ̃, -ɑ̃t] **1** *adj (classe)* ruling **2** *nm (de pays)* leader; *(d'entreprise, de club)* manager

diriger [diriʒe] **1** *vt (entreprise, club)* to run, to manage; *(pays, parti)* to lead; *(orchestre)* to conduct; *(travaux)* to supervise; *(acteur)* to direct; *(orienter)* to turn (**vers** to); *(arme, lumière)* to point

(**sur** at); *(véhicule)* to steer **2** *se diriger vpr* **se d. vers** *(lieu, objet)* to head for; *(personne)* to go up to; *(dans une carrière)* to go into

dis, disant [di, dizɑ̃] *voir* **dire**

discerner [disɛrne] *vt (voir)* to make out; *(différencier)* to distinguish (**de** from) ■ **discernement** [-əmɑ̃] *nm* discernment

disciple [disipl] *nm* disciple

discipline [disiplin] *nf (règle, matière)* discipline

discipliner [disipline] **1** *vt (enfant)* to control **2** *se discipliner vpr* to discipline oneself ■ **discipliné, -e** *adj* well-disciplined

discontinu, -e [diskɔ̃tiny] *adj (ligne)* broken; *(bruit)* intermittent ■ **discontinuer** *vi* **sans d.** without stopping

discorde [diskɔrd] *nf* discord

discothèque [diskɔtɛk] *nf (organisme)* record library; *(club)* disco

discours [diskur] *nm* speech; *(écrit littéraire)* discourse; **faire un d.** to make a speech

discréditer [diskredite] **1** *vt* to discredit **2** *se discréditer vpr (personne)* to discredit oneself

discret, -ète [diskrɛ, -ɛt] *adj (personne, manière)* discreet; *(vêtement)* simple ■ **discrètement** *adv (avec retenue)* discreetly; *(sobrement)* simply

discrétion [diskresjɔ̃] *nf* discretion; **laisser qch à la d. de qn** to leave sth to sb's discretion

discrimination [diskriminasjɔ̃] *nf* discrimination

disculper [diskylpe] *vt* to exonerate (**de** from)

discussion [diskysjɔ̃] *nf* discussion; **avoir une d.** to have a discussion (**sur** about)

discutable [diskytabl] *adj* questionable

discuter [diskyte] **1** *vt* to discuss; *(contester)* to question **2** *vi* to discuss; *(protester)* to argue; **d. de qch avec qn** to discuss sth with sb **3** *se discuter vpr* **ça se discute** that's debatable

dise, disent [diz] *voir* **dire**

disgrace [disgras] *nf* **tomber en d.** to fall into disfavour ■ **disgracier** *vt* to disgrace ■ **disgracieux, -euse** *adj* ungainly

disjoint, -e [disʒwɛ̃, -ɛt] *adj* separated

disjoncter [disʒɔ̃kte] *vi (circuit électrique)* to fuse ■ **disjoncteur** *nm* circuit breaker

dislocation [dislɔkasjɔ̃] *nf (de membre)* dislocation

disloquer [dislɔke] **1** *vt (membre)* to dislocate **2 se disloquer** *vpr* **se d. le bras** to dislocate one's arm

disons [dizɔ̃] *voir* **dire**

disparaître* [disparetr] *vi* to disappear; *(être porté manquant)* to go missing; *(mourir)* to die; *(coutume)* to die out; **faire d. qch** to get rid of sth ■ **disparition** *nf* disappearance; *(mort)* death ■ **disparu, -e 1** *adj (personne)* missing; **être porté d.** to be reported missing **2** *nmf (absent)* missing person; *(mort)* departed

disparité [disparite] *nf* disparity **(entre** *ou* **de** between)

dispensaire [dispãsɛr] *nm* community health centre

dispense [dispãs] *nf (d'obligation)* exemption ■ **dispenser 1** *vt (soins, bienfaits)* to dispense; **d. qn de qch** to exempt sb from sth; **d. qn de faire qch** to exempt sb from doing sth **2** *vpr* **se d. de qch** to get out of sth; **se d. de faire qch** to get out of doing sth

disperser [disperse] **1** *vt (papiers, foule)* to scatter; *(brouillard)* to disperse; *(collection)* to break up **2 se disperser** *vpr (foule)* to scatter, to disperse ■ **dispersion** *nf (d'armée, de manifestants, de brouillard)* dispersal

disponible [dispɔnibl] *adj (article, place, personne)* available ■ **disponibilité** *nf* availability; **disponibilités** *(fonds)* available funds

dispos [dispo] *adj m* **frais et d.** hale and hearty

disposé, -e [dispoze] *adj* **bien/mal d.** in a good/bad mood; **d. à faire qch** disposed to do sth

disposer [dispoze] **1** *vt (objets)* to arrange; **d. qn à (faire) qch** to dispose sb to (do) sth **2** *vi* **d. de qch** to have sth at one's disposal **3 se disposer** *vpr* **se d. à faire qch** to prepare to do sth

dispositif [dispozitif] *nm (mécanisme)* device

disposition [dispozisjɔ̃] *nf* arrangement; *(tendance)* tendency (à to); *(de maison, de page)* layout; **être** *ou* **rester** *ou* **se tenir à la d. de qn** to be or remain at sb's disposal; **dispositions** *(aptitudes)* ability, aptitude **(pour** for)

disproportionné, -e [disprɔpɔrsjɔne] *adj* disproportionate

dispute [dispyt] *nf* quarrel ■ **disputer 1** *vt (match)* to play; *(rallye)* to compete in; *(combat de boxe)* to fight; *(droit)* to contest; **d. qch à qn** *(prix, première place)* to fight with sb for or over sth **2 se disputer** *vpr* to quarrel (**avec** with); *(match)* to take place; **se d. qch** to fight over sth

disqualifier [diskalifje] *vt (équipe, athlète)* to disqualify ■ **disqualification** *nf* disqualification

disque [disk] *nm (de musique)* record; *(cercle) Br* disc, *Am* disk; *Ordinat* disk; *Sport* discus; **d. compact** compact *Br* disc or *Am* disk; **d. dur** hard disk ■ **disquaire** *nmf* record dealer ■ **disquette** *nf Ordinat* floppy (disk), diskette

disséminer [disemine] *vt (graines, mines)* to scatter

disséquer [diseke] *vt* to dissect

dissertation [disɛrtasjɔ̃] *nf* essay

dissident, -e [disidã, -ãt] *nmf* dissident

dissimuler [disimyle] **1** *vt (cacher)* to conceal (à from) **2 se dissimuler** *vpr* to be hidden ■ **dissimulation** *nf* concealment; *(duplicité)* deceit

dissiper [disipe] **1** *vt (nuages)* to disperse; *(brouillard)* to clear; *(malentendu)* to clear up; *(craintes)* to dispel; **d. qn** to lead sb astray **2 se dissiper** *vpr (nuage)* to disperse; *(brume)* to clear; *(craintes)* to vanish; *(élève)* to misbehave ■ **dissipé, -e** *adj (élève)* unruly

dissocier [disɔsje] *vt* to dissociate (**de** from)

dissolu, -e [disɔly] *adj (vie)* dissolute

dissolution [disɔlysjɔ̃] *nf* dissolution

dissolvant [disɔlvɑ̃] *nm* solvent; *(pour vernis à ongles)* nail polish remover

dissoudre* [disudr] *vt*, **se dissoudre** *vpr* to dissolve

dissuader [disɥade] *vt* to dissuade (**de qch** from sth; **de faire** from doing) ▪ **dissuasif, -ive** *adj* deterrent; **avoir un effet d.** to be a deterrent ▪ **dissuasion** *nf* dissuasion; *Mil* **force de d.** deterrent

distance [distɑ̃s] *nf* distance; **à deux mètres de d.** two metres apart; **à d.** at *or* from a distance; **garder ses distances** to keep one's distance (**vis-à-vis de** from); **commandé à d.** remote-controlled

distancer [distɑ̃se] *vt* to outstrip; **se laisser d.** to fall behind

distant, -e [distɑ̃, -ɑ̃t] *adj* distant; *(personne)* aloof, distant; **d. de dix kilomètres** *(éloigné)* ten kilometres away; *(à intervalles)* ten kilometres apart

distendre [distɑ̃dr] *vt*, **se distendre** *vpr* to stretch

distiller [distile] *vt* to distil ▪ **distillerie** *nf (lieu)* distillery

distinct, -e [distɛ̃, -ɛkt] *adj (différent)* distinct, separate (**de** from); *(net)* clear, distinct ▪ **distinctif, -ive** *adj* distinctive ▪ **distinction** *nf (différence, raffinement)* distinction

distinguer [distɛ̃ge] **1** *vt (différencier)* to distinguish; *(voir)* to make out; *(choisir)* to single out; **d. le bien du mal** to tell good from evil **2** **se distinguer** *vpr (s'illustrer)* to distinguish oneself; **se d. de qn/qch (par)** to be distinguishable from sb/sth (by) ▪ **distingué, -e** *adj (bien élevé, éminent)* distinguished

distorsion [distɔrsjɔ̃] *nf* distortion

distraction [distraksjɔ̃] *nf (étourderie)* absent-mindedness ▪ **distraire*** **1** *vt (divertir)* to entertain; **d. qn** to distract sb (**de** from) **2** **se distraire** *vpr* to amuse oneself ▪ **distrait, -e** *adj* absent-minded ▪ **distrayant, -e** *adj* entertaining

distribuer [distribɥe] *vt (donner)* & *Com* to distribute; *(courrier)* to deliver; *(cartes)* to deal; *(tâches)* to allocate; *(eau)* to supply

distributeur [distribytœr] *nm Com* distributor; **d. automatique** vending machine; **d. de billets** *(de train)* ticket machine; *(de billets de banque)* cash machine

distribution [distribysjɔ̃] *nf* distribution; *(du courrier)* delivery; *(de l'eau)* supply; *(acteurs de cinéma)* cast; **d. des prix** prizegiving

district [distrikt] *nm* district

dit¹, dite [di, dit] **1** *pp de* **dire** **2** *adj (convenu)* agreed; *(surnommé)* called

dit², dites [di, dit] *voir* **dire**

divaguer [divage] *vi (dérailler)* to rave

divan [divɑ̃] *nm* divan, couch

divergent, -e [divɛrʒɑ̃, -ɑ̃t] *adj (lignes)* divergent; *(opinions)* differing ▪ **divergence** *nf (de lignes)* divergence; *(d'opinions)* difference ▪ **diverger** *vi* to diverge (**de** from)

divers, -e [divɛr, -ɛrs] *adj (varié)* varied; **divers(es)** *(plusieurs)* various

diversifier [divɛrsifje] *vt*, **se diversifier** *vpr* to diversify

diversion [divɛrsjɔ̃] *nf* diversion; **faire d.** to create a diversion

diversité [divɛrsite] *nf* diversity

divertir [divɛrtir] **1** *vt* to entertain **2** **se divertir** *vpr* to enjoy oneself ▪ **divertissement** *nm* entertainment, amusement

divin, -e [divɛ̃, -in] *adj* divine ▪ **divinité** *nf* divinity

diviser [divize] *vt*, **se diviser** *vpr* to divide (**en** into) ▪ **division** *nf* division

divorce [divɔrs] *nm* divorce ▪ **divorcer** *vi* to get divorced; **d. d'avec qn** to divorce sb ▪ **divorcé, -e** **1** *adj* divorced (**d'avec** from) **2** *nmf* divorcee

divulguer [divylge] *vt* to divulge

dix [dis] ([di] *before consonant*, [diz] *before vowel*) *adj & nm* ten ▪ **dix-huit** *adj & nm* eighteen ▪ **dixième** *adj & nmf*

tenth; **un d.** a tenth ∎ **dix-neuf** *adj* & *nm* nineteen ∎ **dix-sept** *adj* & *nm* seventeen

dizaine [dizen] *nf* **une d. (de)** about ten

do [do] *nm inv (note)* C

docile [dɔsil] *adj* docile

docteur [dɔktœr] *nm (en médecine, d'université)* doctor (**ès/en** of) ∎ **doctorat** *nm* doctorate, ≃ PhD (**ès/en** in)

doctrine [dɔktrin] *nf* doctrine

document [dɔkymã] *nm* document ∎ **documentaire** *adj* & *nm* documentary ∎ **documentaliste** *nmf* archivist; *(à l'école)* (school) librarian

documentation [dɔkymãtasjõ] *nf (documents)* documentation, *(brochures)* literature ∎ **se documenter** *vpr* to gather information *or* material (**sur** on)

dodu, -e [dody] *adj* chubby, plump

doigt [dwa] *nm* finger; **d. de pied** toe; **petit d.** little finger, *Am & Scot* pinkie; **un d. de vin** a drop of wine; **montrer qn du d.** to point at sb

doigté [dwate] *nm Mus* fingering; *(savoir-faire)* tact

dois, doit [dwa] *voir* devoir[1,2]

doléances [dɔleãs] *nfpl (plaintes)* grievances

dollar [dɔlar] *nm* dollar

domaine [dɔmen] *nm (terres)* estate, domain; *(matière)* field, domain; **être du d. public** to be in the public domain

dôme [dom] *nm* dome

domestique [dɔmestik] **1** *adj (vie, marché, produit)* domestic; **travaux domestiques** housework **2** *nmf* servant ∎ **domestiquer** *vt* to domesticate

domicile [dɔmisil] *nm* home; *(demeure légale)* abode; **sans d. fixe** of no fixed abode; *Jur* **d. conjugal** marital home

dominateur, -trice [dɔminatœr, -tris] *adj* domineering ∎ **domination** *nf* domination

dominer [dɔmine] **1** *vt* to dominate; *(situation, sentiment)* to master; *(être supérieur à)* to surpass **2** *vi (être le plus*

fort)* to be dominant; *(être le plus important)* to predominate **3 se dominer** *vpr* to control oneself ∎ **dominant, -e** *adj* dominant

dommage [dɔmaʒ] *nm (tort)* harm; **dommages** *(dégâts)* damage; **quel d.!** what a pity, what a shame!; **c'est (bien) d. qu'elle ne soit pas venue** it's a (great) pity *or* shame she didn't come; **dommages-intérêts** damages

dompter [dɔ̃te] *vt (animal)* to tame

DOM-TOM [dɔmtɔm] *(abrév* **départements et territoires d'outre-mer)** *nmpl* = French overseas departments and territories

don [dɔ̃] *nm (cadeau, aptitude)* gift; *(à un musée, à une œuvre)* donation; **faire d. de qch** to give sth; **d. du sang** blood donation

donateur, -trice [dɔnatœr, -tris] *nmf* donor ∎ **donation** *nf* donation

donc [dɔ̃(k)] *conj* so, then; *(par conséquent)* so, therefore; **asseyez-vous d.!** *(intensif)* do sit down!

donjon [dɔ̃ʒɔ̃] *nm* keep

données [dɔne] *nfpl Ordinat* data

DONNER [dɔne] **1** *vt* to give; *(récolte, résultat)* to produce; *(cartes)* to deal; *(pièce, film)* to put on; **pourriez-vous me d. l'heure?** could you tell me the time?; **d. un coup à qn** to hit sb; **d. à manger à qn** *(animal, enfant)* to feed sb; **elle m'a donné de ses nouvelles** she told me how she was doing; **ça donne soif/faim** it makes you thirsty/hungry; **étant donné...** considering..., in view of...; **étant donné que...** seeing (that), considering (that)...; **à un moment donné** at some stage

2 *vi* **d. sur** *(fenêtre)* to overlook, to look out onto; *(porte)* to open onto

3 se donner *vpr (se consacrer)* to devote oneself (**à** to); **se d. du mal** to go to a lot of trouble (**pour faire** to do)

donneur, -euse [dɔnœr, -øz] *nmf (de sang, d'organe)* donor

dont [dɔ̃] (= **de qui, duquel, de quoi**) *pron relatif (exprime la partie d'un tout)* *(personne)* of whom; *(chose)* of which; *(exprime l'appartenance)* *(personne)*

whose, of whom; *(chose)* of which, whose; **une mère d. le fils est malade** a mother whose son is ill; **la fille d. il est fier** the daughter he is proud of *or* of whom he is proud; **les outils d. j'ai besoin** the tools I need; **la façon d. elle joue** the way (in which) she plays; **cinq enfants d. deux filles** five children two of whom are daughters, five children including two daughters; **voici ce d. il s'agit** here's what it's about

doper [dɔpe] **1** *vt* to dope **2 se doper** *vpr* to take drugs ■ **dopage** *nm (action)* doping; *(de sportif)* drug-taking

dorénavant [dɔrenavɑ̃] *adv* from now on

dorer [dɔre] **1** *vt (objet)* to gild **2** *vi (à la cuisson)* to brown **3 se dorer** *vpr* **se d. au soleil** to sunbathe ■ **doré, -e** *adj (objet)* gilt, gold; *(couleur)* golden

dormir* [dɔrmir] *vi* to sleep; *(être endormi)* to be asleep; *Fig (argent)* to lie idle

dortoir [dɔrtwar] *nm* dormitory

dos [do] *nm (de personne, d'animal)* back; *(de livre)* spine; **'voir au d.'** *(verso)* 'see over'

dose [doz] *nf* dose; *(dans un mélange)* proportion ■ **doser** *vt (médicament, ingrédients)* to measure out

dossard [dosar] *nm (de sportif)* number *(worn by player or competitor)*

dossier [dosje] *nm (de siège)* back; *(documents)* file

dot [dɔt] *nf* dowry

doter [dɔte] *vt (équiper)* to equip **(de** with); **doté d'une grande intelligence** endowed with great intelligence

douane [dwan] *nf* customs; **passer la d.** to go through customs ■ **douanier, -ère** *nmf* customs officer

doublage [dublaʒ] *nm (de film)* dubbing

double [dubl] **1** *adj* double; *(rôle, avantage)* twofold, double; **en d. exemplaire** in duplicate **2** *adv* double **3** *nm (de personne)* double; *(copie)* copy, duplicate; **le d. (de)** *(quantité)* twice as much (as); **je l'ai en d.** I have two of them

doubler [duble] **1** *vt (augmenter)* to double; *(vêtement)* to line; *(film)* to dub; *(acteur)* to dub the voice of; *(classe à l'école)* to repeat **2** *vi (augmenter)* to double **3** *vti (en voiture) Br* to overtake, *Am* to pass **4 se doubler** *vpr* **se d. de** to be coupled with

doublure [dublyr] *nf (étoffe)* lining; *(au théâtre)* understudy; *(au cinéma)* stand-in

douce [dus] *voir* **doux** ■ **doucement** *adv (délicatement)* gently; *(bas)* softly; *(lentement)* slowly; *(sans bruit)* quietly ■ **douceur** *nf (de miel)* sweetness; *(de peau)* softness; *(de temps)* mildness; *(de personne)* gentleness

douche [duʃ] *nf* shower; **prendre une d.** to have *or* take a shower ■ **doucher se doucher** *vpr* to have *or* take a shower

doué, -e [dwe] *adj* gifted, talented **(en** at); **être d. pour qch** to have a gift for sth

douille [duj] *nf (d'ampoule)* socket; *(de cartouche)* case

douillet, -ette [duje, -ɛt] *adj (lit) Br* cosy, *Am* cozy

douleur [dulœr] *nf (mal)* pain; *(chagrin)* sorrow, grief ■ **douloureux, -euse** *adj* painful

doute [dut] *nm* doubt; **sans d.** no doubt, probably; **sans aucun d.** without (any) doubt; **mettre qch en d.** to cast doubt on sth

douter [dute] **1** *vi* to doubt; **d. de qn/qch** to doubt sb/sth **2** *vt* **je doute qu'il soit assez fort** I doubt whether he's strong enough **3 se douter** *vpr* **se d. de quelque chose** to suspect something

douteux, -euse [dutø, -øz] *adj (peu certain)* doubtful; *(louche, médiocre)* dubious

Douvres [duvr] *nm ou f* Dover

doux, douce [du, dus] *adj (miel, son)* sweet; *(peau, lumière)* soft; *(temps, climat)* mild; *(personne, pente)* gentle

douze [duz] *adj & nm* twelve ■ **douzaine** *nf (douze)* dozen; *(environ)* about twelve; **une d. d'œufs** a dozen eggs

dragée [draʒe] *nf* sugared almond

dragon [dragɔ̃] *nm (animal, personne acariâtre)* dragon

drainer [drene] *vt* to drain

drame [dram] *nm (genre littéraire)* drama; *(catastrophe)* tragedy ■ **dramatique 1** *adj* dramatic; **auteur d.** playwright, dramatist **2** *nf* drama

drap [dra] *nm (de lit)* sheet; *(tissu)* cloth; **d.-housse** fitted sheet; **d. de bain** bath towel

drapeau, -x [drapo] *nm* flag

dresser [drese] **1** *vt (échelle, statue)* to put up, to erect; *(liste)* to draw up; *(piège)* to set, to lay; *(animal)* to train; **d. les oreilles** to prick up one's ears **2** **se dresser** *vpr (personne)* to stand up; *(statue, montagne)* to rise up ■ **dressage** *nm* training ■ **dresseur, -euse** *nmf* trainer

drogue [drɔg] *nf (stupéfiant) & Péj (médicament)* drug; **d. dure/douce** hard/soft drug ■ **drogué, -e** *nmf* drug addict ■ **droguer 1** *vt (victime)* to drug; *(malade)* to dose up **2** **se droguer** *vpr* to take drugs

droguerie [drɔgri] *nf* hardware *Br* shop *or Am* store ■ **droguiste** *nmf* hardware dealer

droit¹ [drwa] *nm (privilège)* right; *(d'inscription)* fee(s); **le d.** *(science juridique)* law; **avoir d. à qch** to be entitled to sth; **avoir le d. de faire qch** to be entitled to do sth, to have the right to do sth; **droits de douane** (customs) duty; **droits de l'homme** human rights

droit², droite¹ [drwa, drwat] **1** *adj (route, ligne)* straight; *(angle)* right; *Fig (honnête)* upright **2** *adv* straight; **tout d.** straight *or* right ahead; **aller d. au but** to go straight to the point

droit³, droite² [drwa, drwat] *adj (côté, bras)* right

droite³ [drwat] *nf (ligne)* straight line

droite⁴ [drwat] *nf* **la d.** *(côté)* the right (side); *Pol* the right (wing); **à d.** *(tourner)* (to the) right; *(rouler, se tenir)* on the right, on the right(-hand) side; **de**

d. *(fenêtre)* right-hand; *(candidat)* right-wing; **à d. de** on *or* to the right of

droitier, -ère [drwatje, -ɛr] **1** *adj* right-handed **2** *nmf* right-handed person

droiture [drwatyr] *nf* rectitude

drôle [drol] *adj* funny ■ **drôlement** *adv* funnily; *Fam (extrêmement)* terribly, dreadfully

dru, drue [dry] **1** *adj (herbe)* thick, dense **2** *adv* **tomber d.** *(pluie)* to pour down heavily; **pousser d.** to grow thickly

du [dy] *voir* **de¹,²**

dû, due [dy] **1** *adj* **d. à qch** due to sth; **en bonne et due forme** in due form **2** *nm* due

duc [dyk] *nm* duke ■ **duchesse** *nf* duchess

duel [dɥɛl] *nm* duel

dûment [dymɑ̃] *adv* duly

dune [dyn] *nf* (sand) dune

duo [dɥo] *nm Mus* duet

dupe [dyp] **1** *adj* **être d. de** to be taken in by; **il n'est pas d.** he's well aware of it **2** *nf* dupe ■ **duper** *vt* to fool, to dupe

duplex [dypleks] *nm Br* maisonette, *Am* duplex

duplicata [dyplikata] *nm inv* duplicate

duquel [dykɛl] *voir* **lequel**

dur, dure [dyr] **1** *adj (substance)* hard; *(difficile)* hard, tough; *(viande)* tough; *(hiver, ton)* harsh; *(personne)* hard, harsh; **d. d'oreille** hard of hearing **2** *adv (travailler)* hard ■ **durement** *adv* harshly ■ **dureté** *nf (de substance)* hardness; *(d'hiver, de ton)* harshness; *(de viande)* toughness

durable [dyrabl] *adj* lasting

durant [dyrɑ̃] *prép* during; **d. l'hiver** during the winter; **des heures d.** for hours and hours

durcir [dyrsir] *vti*, **se durcir** *vpr* to harden

durée [dyre] *nf (de film, d'événement)* length; *(période)* duration; **de longue d.** *(bonheur)* lasting; **de courte d.** *(attente)* short; *(bonheur)* short-lived

durer [dyre] *vi* to last

duvet [dyvɛ] *nm (d'oiseau)* down; *(sac)* sleeping bag

dynamique [dinamik] *adj* dynamic

dynamite [dinamit] *nf* dynamite

dynamo [dinamo] *nf* dynamo

dynastie [dinasti] *nf* dynasty

dyslexique [dislɛksik] *adj* dyslexic

Ee

E, e [ə] *nm inv* E, e

EAO [əao] (*abrév* **enseignement assisté par ordinateur**) *nm inv* CAL

eau, -x [o] *nf* water; **sports d'e. vive** whitewater sports; **e. courante** running water; **e. de toilette** eau de toilette; **e. du robinet** tap water; **e. douce** fresh water ▪ **eau-de-vie** (*pl* **eaux-de-vie**) *nf* brandy

ébahir [ebair] *vt* to astound

ébattre [ebatr] **s'ébattre** *vpr* to frolic

ébaucher [eboʃe] *vt* (*tableau, roman*) to rough out

ébéniste [ebenist] *nm* cabinetmaker

éblouir [ebluir] *vt* to dazzle

éboueur [ebwœr] *nm Br* dustman, *Am* garbage collector

ébouillanter [ebujɑ̃te] **1** *vt* to scald **2** **s'ébouillanter** *vpr* to scald oneself

ébouler [ebule] **s'ébouler** *vpr* (*falaise*) to collapse; (*tunnel*) to cave in ▪ **éboulement** *nm* (*écroulement*) collapse; (*de mine*) cave-in

ébouriffé, -e [eburife] *adj* dishevelled

ébranler [ebrɑ̃le] **1** *vt* (*mur, confiance, personne*) to shake **2** **s'ébranler** *vpr* (*train, cortège*) to move off

ébrécher [ebreʃe] *vt* (*assiette*) to chip; (*lame*) to nick

ébriété [ebrijete] *nf* **en état d'é.** under the influence of drink

ébrouer [ebrue] **s'ébrouer** *vpr* (*chien*) to shake itself; (*cheval*) to snort

ébruiter [ebrɥite] *vt* (*nouvelle*) to spread

EBS [øbeɛs] (*abrév* **encéphalite bovine spongiforme**) *nf* BSE

ébullition [ebylisjɔ̃] *nf* boiling; **être en é.** (*eau*) to be boiling; **porter qch à é.** to bring sth to the boil

écaille [ekaj] *nf* (*de poisson*) scale ▪ **écailler 1** *vt* (*poisson*) to scale **2** **s'écailler** *vpr* (*peinture*) to peel (off)

écarquiller [ekarkije] *vt* **é. les yeux** to open one's eyes wide

écart [ekar] *nm* (*intervalle*) gap, distance; (*différence*) difference (**de** in; **entre** between); **faire le grand é.** to do the splits; **à l'é.** out of the way; **à l'é. de qch** away from sth

écartelé, -e [ekartəle] *adj* **é. entre** (*tiraillé*) torn between

écartement [ekartəmɑ̃] *nm* (*espace*) gap, distance (**de** between)

écarter [ekarte] **1** *vt* (*objets, personnes*) to move apart; (*jambes, doigts*) to spread; (*rideaux*) to draw (back); (*idée*) to brush aside; (*proposition*) to turn down; **é. qch de qch** to move sth away from sth

2 **s'écarter** *vpr* (**a**) (*se séparer*) (*personnes*) to move apart (**de** from), (*foule*) to part

(**b**) (*piéton*) to move away (**de** from); **s'é. du sujet** to wander from the subject ▪ **écarté, -e** *adj* **les jambes écartées** with his/her legs (wide) apart

ecclésiastique [eklezjastik] *nm* clergyman

échafaudage [eʃafodaʒ] *nm* scaffolding; **des échafaudages** scaffolding

échalote [eʃalɔt] *nf* shallot

échancré, -e [eʃɑ̃kre] *adj* low-cut ▪ **échancrure** *nf* low neckline

échange [eʃɑ̃ʒ] *nm* exchange; **en é.** in exchange (**de** for); **é. scolaire** (school) exchange; **participer à un é. scolaire** to go on a school exchange ▪ **échanger** *vt* to exchange (**contre** for)

échangeur [eʃɑ̃ʒœr] *nm* interchange

échantillon [eʃɑ̃tijɔ̃] *nm* sample

échapper [eʃape] **1** *vi* **é. à qn** to escape from sb; **son nom m'échappe** his/her name escapes me; **ça lui a échappé des mains** it slipped out of his/her hands
2 *vt* **il l'a échappé belle** he had a narrow escape
3 s'échapper *vpr (personne, gaz, eau)* to escape (**de** from) ■ **échappée** *nf (de cyclistes)* breakaway

écharde [eʃard] *nf* splinter

écharpe [eʃarp] *nf* scarf; *(de maire)* sash; **avoir le bras en é.** to have one's arm in a sling

échasse [eʃas] *nf (bâton)* stilt

échauffer [eʃofe] **1** *vt (moteur)* to overheat **2 s'échauffer** *vpr (sportif)* to warm up ■ **échauffement** *nm (de moteur)* overheating; *(d'athlète)* warm-up

échauffourée [eʃofure] *nf* clash, brawl, skirmish

échéance [eʃeɑ̃s] *nf (de facture, de dette)* date of payment; **à brève/longue é.** *(projet, emprunt)* short-/long-term

échéant [eʃeɑ̃] **le cas échéant** *adv* if need be

échec [eʃɛk] *nm* failure; **faire é. à qch** to hold sth in check; **les échecs** *(jeu)* chess; **é.!** check!; **é. et mat!** checkmate!

échelle [eʃɛl] *nf* **(a)** *(marches)* ladder **(b)** *(de carte)* scale; **à l'é. nationale** on a national scale

échelon [eʃlɔ̃] *nm (d'échelle)* rung; *(d'employé)* grade; *(d'organisation)* echelon; **à l'é. régional** on a regional level

échelonner [eʃlɔne] **1** *vt (paiements)* to spread **2 s'échelonner** *vpr* to be spread out

échevelé, -e [eʃəvle] *adj (ébouriffé)* dishevelled

échiquier [eʃikje] *nm (plateau)* chessboard

écho [eko] *nm (de son)* echo; **échos** *(de presse)* gossip column

échographie [ekografi] *nf* (ultrasound) scan; **passer une é.** to have a scan

échoir* [eʃwar] *vi* **é. à qn** to fall to sb

échouer [eʃwe] **1** *vi* to fail; **é. à** *(examen)* to fail **2** *vi,* **s'échouer** *vpr (navire)* to run aground

éclabousser [eklabuse] *vt* to splash, to spatter (**avec** with) ■ **éclaboussure** *nf* splash

éclair [eklɛr] **1** *nm* **(a)** *(lumière)* flash; *(d'orage)* flash of lightning **(b)** *(gâteau)* éclair **2** *adj inv* **visite é.** lightning visit

éclairage [eklɛraʒ] *nm* lighting

éclaircie [eklɛrsi] *nf* sunny spell

éclaircir [eklɛrsir] **1** *vt (couleur)* to lighten; *(mystère)* to clear up **2 s'éclaircir** *vpr (ciel)* to clear; *(mystère)* to be cleared up; **s'é. la voix** to clear one's throat ■ **éclaircissement** *nm (explication)* explanation

éclairer [eklere] **1** *vt (pièce)* to light (up); **é. qn** *(avec une lampe)* to give sb some light; *(informer)* to enlighten sb (**sur** about)
2 *vi (lampe)* to give light; **é. bien/mal** to give good/poor light
3 s'éclairer *vpr (visage)* to light up; **s'é. à la bougie** to use candlelight; **s'é. à l'électricité** to have electric lighting ■ **éclairé, -e** *adj (averti)* enlightened; **bien/mal é.** *(illuminé)* well-/badly lit

éclaireur, -euse [eklerœr, -øz] **1** *nmf* (boy) scout, (girl) guide **2** *nm (soldat)* scout

éclat [ekla] *nm* **(a)** *(de lumière)* brightness; *(de phare)* glare; *(de diamant)* flash **(b)** *(de verre)* splinter; **é. de rire** burst of laughter

éclatant, -e [eklatɑ̃, -ɑ̃t] *adj (lumière, succès)* brilliant; **être é. de santé** to be glowing with health

éclater [eklate] *vi (pneu)* to burst; *(bombe)* to go off, to explode; *(verre)* to shatter; *(guerre)* to break out; *(orage, scandale)* to break; *(parti)* to break up; **é. de rire** to burst out laughing; **é. en sanglots** to burst into tears ■ **éclatement** *nm (de pneu)* bursting; *(de bombe)* explosion; *(de parti)* break-up

éclectique [eklɛktik] *adj* eclectic

éclipse [eklips] *nf* eclipse ■ **éclipser** *vt* to eclipse

éclore* [eklɔr] *vi (œuf)* to hatch; *(fleur)* to open (out), to blossom

écluse [eklyz] *nf (de canal)* lock

écœurer [ekœre] *vt* **é. qn** *(climent)* to make sb feel sick; *(moralement)* to sicken sb ■ **écœurant, -e** *adj* disgusting, sickening ■ **écœurement** *nm (nausée)* nausea; *(indignation)* disgust

école [ekɔl] *nf* school; **à l'é.** at school; **faire é.** to gain a following; **les grandes écoles** = university-level colleges specializing in professional training; **é. de dessin** art school; **é. privée** private school, *Br* public school; **é. publique** *Br* state school, *Am* public school ■ **écolier, -ère** *nmf* schoolboy, *f* schoolgirl

écologie [ekɔlɔʒi] *nf* ecology ■ **écologique** *adj* ecological ■ **écologiste** *adj & nmf* environmentalist

économe [ekɔnɔm] *adj* thrifty, economical

économie [ekɔnɔmi] *nf (activité, vertu)* economy; **économies** *(argent)* savings; **faire des économies** to save (up) ■ **économique** *adj* (a) *(relatif à l'économie)* economic; **science é** economics *(sing)* (b) *(avantageux)* economical

économiser [ekɔnɔmize] **1** *vt (forces, argent, énergie)* to save **2** *vi* to economize **(sur** on)

écoper [ekɔpe] *vi Fam* **é. de qch** *(punition, amende)* to get sth

écorce [ekɔrs] *nf (d'arbre)* bark; *(de fruit)* peel; **l'é. terrestre** the earth's crust

écorcher [ekɔrʃe] **1** *vt (érafler)* to graze; *Fig (mot)* to mispronounce **2** **s'écorcher** *vpr* to graze oneself; **s'é. le genou** to graze one's knee

Écosse [ekɔs] *nf* **l'É.** Scotland ■ **écossais, -e 1** *adj* Scottish; *(tissu)* tartan **2** *nmf* **É., Écossaise** Scot

écouler [ekule] **1** *vt (se débarrasser de)* to dispose of **2** **s'écouler** *vpr (eau)* to flow out, to run out; *(temps)* to pass ■ **écoulé, -e** *adj (passé)* past ■ **écoule-**ment *nm (de liquide)* flow; *(de marchandises)* sale

écourter [ekurte] *vt (séjour)* to cut short; *(texte, tige)* to shorten

écoute [ekut] *nf* listening; **être à l'é.** to be listening in **(de** tc); **écoutes téléphoniques** phone tapping

écouter [ekute] **1** *vt* to listen to; **faire é. qch à qn** *(disque)* to play sb sth **2** **s'écouter** *vpr* **si je m'écoutais** if I did what I wanted ■ **écouteur** *nm (de téléphone)* earpiece; **écouteurs** *(casque)* headphones

écran [ekrɑ̃] *nm* screen; **à l'é.** on screen; **le petit é.** television; **é. publicitaire** commercial break; **é. total** sun block

écraser [ekraze] **1** *vt (broyer, vaincre)* to crush; *(fruit, insecte)* to squash; *(cigarette)* to put out; *(piéton)* to run over; **se faire é. par une voiture** to get run over by a car **2** **s'écraser** *vpr (avion)* to crash **(contre** into) ■ **écrasant, -e** *adj (victoire, chaleur)* overwhelming

écrémer [ekreme] *vt (lait)* to skim

écrevisse [ekrəvis] *nf* crayfish *inv*

écrier [ekrije] **s'écrier** *vpr* to exclaim, to cry out **(que** that)

écrin [ekrɛ̃] *nm* (jewel) case

écrire* [ekrir] **1** *vt* to write; *(noter)* to write down **2** *vi* to write **3** **s'écrire** *vpr (mot)* to be spelt; **comment ça s'écrit?** how do you spell it? ■ **écrit** *nm (document)* written document; *(examen)* written examination; **par é.** in writing

écriteau, -x [ekrito] *nm* notice, sign

écriture [ekrityr] *nf (système)* writing; *(calligraphie)* (hand)writing; *Com* **écritures** accounts; **les Écritures** *(la Bible)* the Scriptures

écrivain [ekrivɛ̃] *nm* writer

écrou [ekru] *nm (de boulon)* nut

écrouer [ekrue] *vt* to imprison

écrouler [ekrule] **s'écrouler** *vpr (édifice, personne)* to collapse ■ **écroule**ment *nm* collapse

écru, -e [ekry] *adj (beige)* écru; *(naturel)* unbleached

ÉCU [eky] *(abrév* **European Currency Unit)** *nm Anciennement* ECU

écueil [ekœj] *nm (rocher)* reef; *Fig (obstacle)* pitfall

écuelle [ekɥɛl] *nf* bowl

écume [ekym] *nf (de mer)* foam ∎ **écumer 1** *vt (piller)* to plunder **2** *vi* to foam **(de rage** with anger)

écureuil [ekyrœj] *nm* squirrel

écurie [ekyri] *nf* stable

écusson [ekysɔ̃] *nm (en étoffe)* badge

écuyer, -ère [ekɥije, -ɛr] *nmf (cavalier)* rider

édifice [edifis] *nm* edifice ∎ **édifier** *vt (bâtiment)* to erect; *(théorie)* to construct

Édimbourg [edɛ̃bur] *nm ou f* Edinburgh

éditer [edite] *vt (publier)* to publish; *Ordinat* to edit ∎ **éditeur, -trice** *nmf (dans l'édition)* publisher ∎ **édition** *nf (livre, journal)* edition; *(métier, diffusion)* publishing

éditorial, -aux [editɔrjal, -o] *nm (article)* editorial, *Br* leader ∎ **éditorialiste** *nmf* editorial *or Br* leader writer

éducateur, -trice [edykatœr, -tris] *nmf* educator

éducatif, -ive [edykatif, -iv] *adj* educational

éducation [edykasjɔ̃] *nf (enseignement)* education; *(des parents)* upbringing; **avoir de l'é.** to have good manners; **l'É. nationale** ≃ the Department of Education; **é. physique** physical education *or* training ∎ **éduquer** *vt (à l'école)* to educate; *(à la maison)* to bring up

EEE [əəə] *(abrév* **Espace économique européen)** *nm* EEA

effacé, -e [efase] *adj (modeste)* self-effacing

effacer [efase] **1** *vt (avec une gomme)* to rub out, to erase; *(avec un chiffon)* to wipe away; *Fig (souvenir)* to blot out, to erase **2 s'effacer** *vpr (souvenir)* to fade; *(se placer en retrait)* to step aside

effarant, -e [efarɑ̃, -ɑ̃t] *adj* astounding

effaroucher [efaruʃe] **1** *vt* to scare away **2 s'effaroucher** *vpr* to take fright

effectif, -ive [efɛktif, -iv] **1** *adj (réel)* effective **2** *nm (de classe)* size; *(employés)* staff ∎ **effectivement** *adv (en effet)* actually

effectuer [efɛktɥe] *vt (expérience, geste difficile)* to carry out, to perform; *(paiement, trajet)* to make

efféminé, -e [efemine] *adj* effeminate

effervescent, -e [efɛrvesɑ̃, -ɑ̃t] *adj (médicament)* effervescent

effet [efɛ] *nm (résultat)* effect; *(impression)* impression **(sur** on); **en e.** indeed, in fact; **e. de serre** greenhouse effect; **e. secondaire** side effect; *Cin* **effets spéciaux** special effects

efficace [efikas] *adj (mesure)* effective; *(personne)* efficient ∎ **efficacité** *nf (de mesure)* effectiveness; *(de personne)* efficiency

effilocher [efilɔʃe] **s'effilocher** *vpr* to fray

effleurer [eflœre] *vt (frôler)* to touch lightly; **e. qn** *(pensée)* to cross sb's mind

effondrer [efɔ̃dre] **s'effondrer** *vpr (tomber, chuter)* to collapse; *(plan)* to fall through; *Fig (perdre ses forces)* to go to pieces; **s'e. en larmes** to break down and cry ∎ **effondrement** *nm (chute)* collapse; *(sentiment)* dejection

efforcer [efɔrse] **s'efforcer** *vpr* **s'e. de faire qch** to try hard to do sth

effort [efɔr] *nm* effort; **faire des efforts** to make an effort

effraction [efraksjɔ̃] *nf* **entrer par e.** to break in; **vol avec e.** housebreaking

effrayer [efreje] **1** *vt* to frighten, to scare **2 s'effrayer** *vpr* to be frightened *or* scared ∎ **effrayant, -e** *adj* frightening, scary

effriter [efrite] **s'effriter** *vpr* to crumble

effronté, -e [efrɔ̃te] *adj (personne)* impudent

effroyable [efrwajabl] *adj* dreadful

effusion [efyzjɔ̃] *nf* **e. de sang** bloodshed

égal, -e, -aux, -ales [egal, -o] **1** *adj* equal (à to); *(régulier)* even; **ça m'est é.** it's all the same to me **2** *nmf (personne)*

equal ∎ **également** adv (au même degré) equally; (aussi) also, as well ∎ **égaler** vt to equal, to match (en in); **3 plus 4 égale(nt) 7** 3 plus 4 equals 7

égaliser [egalize] vi Sport to equalize

égalité [egalite] nf equality; (régularité) evenness; (au tennis) deuce; Sport **à é.** even, equal (in points) ∎ **égalitaire** adj egalitarian

égard [egar] nm **à l'é. de** (envers) towards; **à cet é.** in this respect; **par é. pour qn** out of consideration for sb

égarer [egare] **1** vt (objet) to mislay; (personne) to mislead **2 s'égarer** vpr (personne, lettre) to get lost; (objet) to go astray

égayer [egeje] **1** vt (pièce) to brighten up; **é. qn** to cheer sb up **2 s'égayer** vpr (s'animer) to cheer up

église [egliz] nf church

égoïste [egoist] **1** adj selfish **2** nmf selfish person

égorger [egɔrʒe] vt to cut or slit the throat of

égout [egu] nm sewer

égoutter [egute] **1** vt to drain **2** vi, **s'égoutter** vpr to drain ∎ **égouttoir** nm (panier) drainer

égratigner [egratiɲe] **1** vt to scratch **2 s'égratigner** vpr to scratch oneself ∎ **égratignure** nf scratch

Égypte [eʒipt] nf l'É. Egypt ∎ **égyptien, -enne** [eʒipsjɛ̃, -ɛn] adj Egyptian **2** nmf É., Égyptienne Egyptian

éjecter [eʒɛkte] vt to eject

élaborer [elabɔre] vt (plan, idée) to develop ∎ **élaboration** nf (de plan, d'idée) development

élan [elɑ̃] nm (vitesse) momentum; (course) run-up; **prendre son é.** to take a run-up

élancé, -e [elɑ̃se] adj (personne) slender

élancer [elɑ̃se] **1** vi (abcès) to give shooting pains **2 s'élancer** vpr (bondir) to rush forward; Sport to take a run-up ∎ **élancement** nm (douleur) shooting pain

élargir [elarʒir] **1** vt (chemin) to widen; (vêtement) to let out **2 s'élargir** vpr

(sentier) to widen out; (vêtement) to stretch

élastique [elastik] **1** adj (tissu) elastic **2** nm (lien) rubber band, Br elastic band; (pour la couture) elastic

élection [elɛksjɔ̃] nf election; **é. partielle** by-election ∎ **électeur, -trice** nmf voter, elector ∎ **électoral, -e, -aux, -ales** adj **campagne électorale** election campaign; **liste électorale** electoral roll ∎ **électorat** nm (électeurs) electorate, voters

électricien, -enne [elɛktrisjɛ̃, -ɛn] nmf electrician ∎ **électricité** nf electricity ∎ **électrifier** vt (voie ferrée) to electrify ∎ **électrique** adj (pendule, décharge) & Fig electric; (courant, fil) electric(al)

électrocuter [elɛktrɔkyte] vt to electrocute

électroménager [elɛktromenaʒe] **1** adj m **appareil é.** household electrical appliance **2** nm household appliances

électronique [elɛktrɔnik] **1** adj electronic **2** nf electronics (sing)

élégant, -e [elegɑ̃, -ɑ̃t] adj (bien habillé) smart, elegant ∎ **élégance** nf elegance

élément [elemɑ̃] nm (composante, personne) & Chim element; (de meuble) unit

élémentaire [elemɑ̃tɛr] adj basic

éléphant [elefɑ̃] nm elephant

élevage [elvaʒ] nm (production) breeding (de of); (ferme) farm

élevé, -e [elve] adj (haut) high; (noble) noble; **bien/mal é.** well-/bad-mannered

élève [elɛv] nmf (à l'école) pupil

élever [elve] **1** vt (objection) to raise; (enfant) to bring up; (animal) to breed **2 s'élever** vpr (montagne) to rise; (monument) to stand; **s'é. à** (prix) to amount to; **s'é. contre** to rise up against

éleveur, -euse [elvœr, -øz] nmf breeder

éliminer [elimine] vt to eliminate ∎ **élimination** nf elimination ∎ **éliminatoire** adj **épreuve é.** Sport qualifying round, heat; Scol qualifying exam;

Scol **note é.** disqualifying mark ▪ **éliminatoires** *nfpl Sport* qualifying rounds

élire* [elir] *vt* to elect (**à** to)

élite [elit] *nf* elite (**de** of)

elle [ɛl] *pron personnel* (**a**) *(sujet)* she; *(chose, animal)* it; **elles** they (**b**) *(complément)* her; *(chose, animal)* it; **elles** them ▪ **elle-même** *pron (personne)* herself; *(chose, animal)* itself; **ellesmêmes** themselves

éloge [elɔʒ] *nm (compliment)* praise ▪ **élogieux, -euse** *adj* laudatory

éloigné, -e [elwaɲe] *adj (lieu)* far away, remote; **é. de** *(village, maison)* far (away) from; *(très différent)* far removed from

éloignement [elwaɲəmã] *nm (distance)* remoteness, distance; *(absence)* separation (**de** from)

éloigner [elwaɲe] **1** *vt (chose, personne)* to move away (**de** from); *(malade)* to keep away; **é. qn de qch** *(sujet, but)* to take sb away from sth **2** **s'éloigner** *vpr (partir)* to move away (**de** from); *(dans le passé)* to become (more) remote; **s'é. de qch** *(sujet, but)* to wander from sth

éloquent, -e [elɔkã, -ãt] *adj* eloquent

élu, -e [ely] **1** *pp de* **élire 2** *nmf Pol* elected member *or* representative

élucider [elyside] *vt* to elucidate

Élysée [elize] *nm* **(le palais de) l'É.** the Élysée palace *(French President's residence)*

e-mail [imɛl] *nm* e-mail; **envoyer un e.** to send an e-mail (**à** to); **recevoir un e.** to receive an e-mail (**de** from); **vérifier son e.** to check one's e-mail

émail, -aux [emaj, -o] *nm* enamel

émanations [emanɑsjɔ̃] *nfpl* **des é.** *(odeurs)* smells; *(vapeurs)* fumes

émanciper [emãsipe] **1** *vt (femmes)* to emancipate **2** **s'émanciper** *vpr* to become emancipated

émaner [emane] *vt* **é. de qch** to emanate from sth

emballer [ãbale] **1** *vt (dans une boîte)* to pack; *(dans du papier)* to wrap (up) **2** **s'emballer** *vpr (cheval)* to bolt; *(mo-*

teur) to race ▪ **emballage** *nm (action)* packing; *(dans du papier)* wrapping; *(boîte)* packaging; **papier d'e.** wrapping paper

embarcadère [ãbarkadɛr] *nm* landing stage

embarcation [ãbarkɑsjɔ̃] *nf* (small) boat

embarquer [ãbarke] **1** *vt (passagers)* to take on board; *(marchandises)* to load **2** *vi,* **s'embarquer** *vpr* to (go on) board ▪ **embarquement** *nm (de passagers)* boarding

embarras [ãbara] *nm (gêne)* embarrassment; **dans l'e.** in an awkward situation; *(financièrement)* in financial difficulties

embarrasser [ãbarase] **1** *vt (encombrer)* to clutter up; *(mettre mal à l'aise)* to embarrass **2** **s'embarrasser** *vpr* **s'e. de qch** to burden oneself with sth ▪ **embarrassant, -e** *adj (paquet)* cumbersome; *(question)* embarrassing

embauche [ãboʃ] *nf (action)* hiring; *(travail)* work ▪ **embaucher** *vt (ouvrier)* to hire, to take on

embaumer [ãbome] **1** *vt (parfumer)* to give a sweet smell to **2** *vi* to smell sweet

embellir [ãbelir] **1** *vt (pièce, personne)* to make more attractive **2** *vi (personne)* to grow more attractive

embêter [ãbete] *Fam* **1** *vt (agacer)* to annoy; *(ennuyer)* to bore **2** **s'embêter** *vpr (s'ennuyer)* to get bored ▪ **embêtant, -e** *adj Fam* annoying

emblée [ãble] **d'emblée** *adv* right away

emblème [ãblɛm] *nm* emblem

emboîter [ãbwate] **1** *vt* to fit together **2** **s'emboîter** *vpr* to fit together

embouchure [ãbuʃyr] *nf (de fleuve)* mouth

embourber [ãburbe] **s'embourber** *vpr (véhicule)* to get bogged down

embouteillage [ãbutejaʒ] *nm* traffic jam

emboutir [ãbutir] *vt (voiture)* to crash into

embranchement [ãbrãʃmã] *nm (de voie)* junction

embraser [ãbraze] **1** *vt* to set ablaze **2** **s'embraser** *vpr (prendre feu)* to flare up

embrasser [ãbrase] **1** *vt* **e. qn** *(donner un baiser à)* to kiss sb; *(serrer contre soi)* to embrace *or* hug sb **2** **s'embrasser** *vpr* to kiss (each other)

embrasure [ãbrazyr] *nf (de fenêtre, de porte)* aperture; **dans l'e. de la porte** in the doorway

embrayer [ãbreje] *vi Aut* to engage the clutch ■ **embrayage** *nm (mécanisme, pédale)* clutch

embrouiller [ãbruje] **1** *vt (fils)* to tangle (up); **e. qn** to confuse sb, to get sb muddled **2** **s'embrouiller** *vpr* to get confused *or* muddled **(dans** in *or* with**)**

embroussaillé, -e [ãbrusaje] *adj (barbe, chemin)* bushy

embûches [ãbyʃ] *nfpl (difficultés)* traps, pitfalls

embuer [ãbɥe] *vt (vitre)* to mist up

embusquer [ãbyske] **s'embusquer** *vpr* to lie in ambush ■ **embuscade** *nf* ambush

émeraude [emrod] *nf & adj inv* emerald

émerger [emɛrʒe] *vi* to emerge **(de** from**)**

émerveiller [emɛrveje] **1** *vt* to amaze, to fill with wonder **2** **s'émerveiller** *vpr* to marvel, to be filled with wonder **(de** at**)**

émettre* [emetr] *vt (lumière, son)* to give out, to emit; *(message radio)* to broadcast; *(monnaie)* to issue; *(vœu)* to express; *(chèque)* to draw; *(emprunt)* to float ■ **émetteur** *nm Radio* transmitter

émeute [emøt] *nf* riot

émietter [emjete] *vt,* **s'émietter** *vpr (pain)* to crumble

émigrer [emigre] *vi (personne)* to emigrate ■ **émigrant, -e** *nmf* emigrant ■ **émigration** *nf* emigration ■ **émigré, -e 1** *adj* **travailleur é.** migrant worker **2** *nmf* exile, émigré

éminent, -e [eminã, -ãt] *adj* eminent ■ **éminence** *nf (colline)* hill; **son É.** *(cardinal)* his Eminence

émissaire [emiser] *nm* emissary

émission [emisjɔ̃] *nf (de radio,* programme; *(diffusion)* transmission; *(de lumière, de son)* emission **(de** of**)**

emmanchure [ãmãʃyr] *nf* armhole

emmêler [ãmele] **1** *vt (fil, cheveux)* to tangle (up) **2** **s'emmêler** *vpr* to get tangled

emménager [ãmenaʒe] *vi* to move in; **e. dans** to move into ■ **emménagement** [-əmã] *nm* moving in

emmener [ãmne] *vt* to take **(à** to**)**; *(prisonnier)* to take away; **e. qn faire une promenade** to take sb for a walk; **e. qn en voiture** to give sb a *Br* lift *or Am* ride

emmitoufler [ãmitufle] **s'emmitoufler** *vpr* to wrap (oneself) up **(dans** in**)**

émotion [emosjɔ̃] *nf (sentiment)* emotion ■ **émotif, -ive** *adj* emotional

émoussé, -e [emuse] *adj (pointe)* blunt

émouvoir* [emuvwar] **1** *vt (affecter)* to move, to touch **2** **s'émouvoir** *vpr* to be moved *or* touched ■ **émouvant, -e** *adj* moving, touching

empailler [ãpaje] *vt (animal)* to stuff

empaqueter [ãpakte] *vt* to pack

emparer [ãpare] **s'emparer** *vpr* **s'e. de** *(lieu, personne, objet)* to seize; *(sujet: émotion)* to take hold of

empêcher [ãpeʃe] *vt* to prevent, to stop; **e. qn de faire qch** to prevent *or* stop sb from doing sth ■ **empêchement** [-ɛʃmã] *nm* hitch; **il a/j'ai eu un e.** something came up

empereur [ãprœr] *nm* emperor

empester [ãpeste] **1** *vt (tabac)* to stink of; *(pièce)* to stink out **2** *vi* to stink

empêtrer [ãpetre] **s'empêtrer** *vpr* to get entangled **(dans** in**)**

empiéter [ãpjete] *vi* **e. sur** to encroach (up)on

empiler [ãpile] **1** *vt* to pile up **(sur** on**)** **2** **s'empiler** *vpr* to pile up **(sur** on**)**; **s'e. dans** *(passagers)* to cram into

empire [ãpir] *nm (territoires)* empire; *(autorité)* hold, influence

empirer [ãpire] *vi* to worsen, to get worse

emplacement [ɑ̃plasmɑ̃] *nm (de construction)* site, location; *(de stationnement)* place

emplettes [ɑ̃plɛt] *nfpl* **faire des e.** to do some shopping

emplir [ɑ̃plir] *vt*, **s'emplir** *vpr* to fill **(de** with)

emploi [ɑ̃plwa] *nm* **(a)** *(usage)* use; **e. du temps** timetable **(b)** *(travail)* job; **sans e.** unemployed

employer [ɑ̃plwaje] **1** *vt (utiliser)* to use; *(personne)* to employ **2 s'employer** *vpr (expression)* to be used ■ **employé, -e** *nmf* employee; **e. de banque** bank clerk; **e. de bureau** office worker ■ **employeur, -euse** *nmf* employer

empocher [ɑ̃pɔʃe] *vt* to pocket

empoigner [ɑ̃pwaɲe] *vt (saisir)* to grab

empoisonner [ɑ̃pwazɔne] **1** *vt (personne, aliment)* to poison **2 s'empoisonner** *vpr (par accident)* to be poisoned; *(volontairement)* to poison oneself ■ **empoisonnement** *nm* poisoning

emporter [ɑ̃pɔrte] **1** *vt (prendre)* to take **(avec soi** with one); *(transporter)* to take away; *(entraîner)* to carry along or away; *(par le vent)* to blow off or away; *(par les vagues)* to sweep away; **pizza à e.** takeaway pizza; **l'e. sur qn** to get the upper hand over sb **2 s'emporter** *vpr* to lose one's temper **(contre** with)

empreinte [ɑ̃prɛ̃t] *nf* mark; **e. digitale** fingerprint

empresser [ɑ̃prese] **s'empresser** *vpr* **s'e. de faire qch** to hasten to do sth

emprise [ɑ̃priz] *nf* hold **(sur** over)

emprisonner [ɑ̃prizɔne] *vt* to imprison ■ **emprisonnement** *nm* imprisonment

emprunt [ɑ̃prœ̃] *nm (argent)* loan; **faire un e.** *(auprès d'une banque)* to take out a loan ■ **emprunter** *vt (argent, objet)* to borrow **(à qn** from sb); *(route)* to take

ému, -e [emy] **1** *pp de* **émouvoir 2** *adj (attendri)* moved; *(attristé)* upset;

(apeuré) nervous; **une voix émue** a voice charged with emotion

EN¹ [ɑ̃] *prép* **(a)** *(indique le lieu)* in; *(indique la direction)* to

(b) *(indique le temps)* in

(c) *(indique le moyen)* by; *(indique l'état)* in; **en avion** by plane; **en fleur** in flower; **en congé** on leave

(d) *(indique la matière)* in; **en bois** made of wood, wooden; **chemise en Nylon®** nylon shirt; **c'est en or** it's (made of) gold

(e) *(domaine)* **étudiant en anglais** English student; **docteur en médecine** doctor of medicine

(f) *(comme)* **en cadeau** as a present; **en ami** as a friend

(g) *(+ participe présent)* **en souriant** smiling, with a smile; **en chantant** while singing; **en apprenant que...** on hearing that...; **sortir en courant** to run out

(h) *(transformation)* into; **traduire en français** to translate into French

EN² [ɑ̃] *pron* **(a)** *(indique la provenance)* from there; **j'en viens** I've just come from there

(b) *(remplace les compléments introduits par 'de')* **en parler** to talk about it; **il en est content** he's pleased with it/him/them; **il s'en souviendra** he'll remember it

(c) *(partitif)* some; **j'en ai** I have some; **en veux-tu?** do you want some? **donne-m'en** give some to me

ENA [ena] *(abrév* **École nationale d'administration)** *nf* = university-level college preparing students for senior positions in law and economics

encadrer [ɑ̃kadre] *vt (tableau)* to frame; *(mot)* to circle; *(personnel)* to manage; *(prisonnier)* to flank ■ **encadrement** *nm (de porte, de photo)* frame

encaisser [ɑ̃kese] *vt (argent)* to collect; *(chèque)* to cash

encart [ɑ̃kar] *nm* **e. publicitaire** insert

encastré, -e [ɑ̃kastre] *adj (cuisinière, lave-linge)* built-in

enceinte¹ [ɑ̃sɛ̃t] *adj f (femme)* pregnant

enceinte² [ɑ̃sɛ̃t] *nf (muraille)* (surrounding) wall; *(espace)* enclosure; **dans l'e. de** within, inside; **e. (acoustique)** speaker

encercler [ɑ̃sɛrkle] *vt (lieu, ennemi)* to surround, to encircle; *(mot)* to circle

enchaîner [ɑ̃ʃene] **1** *vt (animal, prisonnier)* to chain up; *(idées)* to link (up) **2** *vi (continuer à parler)* to continue **3 s'enchaîner** *vpr (idées)* to be linked (up) ▪ **enchaînement** [-ɛnmɑ̃] *nm (succession)* chain, series; *(liaison)* link(ing) (**de** between *or* of)

enchanter [ɑ̃ʃɑ̃te] *vt (ravir)* to delight, to enchant; *(ensorceler)* to bewitch ▪ **enchanté, -e** *adj (ravi)* delighted (**de** with; **que** + *subjunctive* that); *(magique)* enchanted; **e. de faire votre connaissance!** pleased to meet you! ▪ **enchantement** *nm (ravissement)* delight; *(sortilège)* magic spell

enchère [ɑ̃ʃɛr] *nf (offre)* bid; **vente aux enchères** auction; **mettre qch aux enchères** to put sth up for auction, to auction sth

enchérir [ɑ̃ʃerir] *vi* to make a higher bid; **e. sur qn** to outbid sb

enchevêtrer [ɑ̃ʃvetre] **s'enchevêtrer** *vpr* to get entangled (**dans** in)

enclencher [ɑ̃klɑ̃ʃe] *vt* to engage

enclin, -e [ɑ̃klɛ̃, -in] *adj* **e. à** inclined to

enclos [ɑ̃klo] *nm (terrain, clôture)* enclosure

encoche [ɑ̃kɔʃ] *nf* notch (**à** in)

encolure [ɑ̃kɔlyr] *nf (de cheval, de vêtement)* neck; *(tour du cou)* collar (size)

encombre [ɑ̃kɔ̃br] **sans encombre** *adv* without a hitch

encombrer [ɑ̃kɔ̃bre] **1** *vt (pièce, couloir)* to clutter up (**de** with); *(rue, passage)* to block; **e. qn** to hamper sb **2 s'encombrer** *vpr* **s'e. de qch** to load oneself down with sth ▪ **encombrant, -e** *adj (paquet)* bulky, cumbersome ▪ **encombré, -e** *adj (lignes téléphoniques, route)* jammed ▪ **encombrement** [-əmɑ̃] *nm (d'objets)* clutter; *(embouteillage)* traffic jam; *(volume)* bulk(iness)

encontre [ɑ̃kɔ̃trə] **à l'encontre de** *prép* against

ENCORE [ɑ̃kɔr] *adv* (**a**) *(toujours)* still (**b**) *(avec négation)* pas e. not yet; **je ne suis pas e. prêt** I'm not ready yet (**c**) *(de nouveau)* again (**d**) *(de plus, en plus)* **e. un café** another coffee; **e. une fois** (once) again, once more; **e. un** another (one), one more; **e. du pain** (some) more bread; **quoi e.?** what else? (**e**) *(avec comparatif)* even, still; **e. mieux** even better, better still (**f**) *(aussi)* **mais e.** but also (**g**) **et e.** *(à peine)* if that, only just (**h**) **e. que...** (+ *subjunctive*) although...

encourager [ɑ̃kuraʒe] *vt* to encourage (**à faire** to do) ▪ **encourageant, -e** *adj* encouraging ▪ **encouragement** *nm* encouragement

encrasser [ɑ̃krase] **1** *vt* to clog up (with dirt) **2 s'encrasser** *vpr* to get clogged up

encre [ɑ̃kr] *nf* ink

encyclopédie [ɑ̃siklɔpedi] *nf* encyclopedia

endetter [ɑ̃dete] **s'endetter** *vpr* to get into debt ▪ **endettement** *nm* debts

endimanché, -e [ɑ̃dimɑ̃ʃe] *adj* in one's Sunday best

endive [ɑ̃div] *nf* chicory *inv*, endive

endoctriner [ɑ̃dɔktrine] *vt* to indoctrinate

endolori, -e [ɑ̃dɔlɔri] *adj* painful

endommager [ɑ̃dɔmaʒe] *vt* to damage

endormir* [ɑ̃dɔrmir] **1** *vt (enfant)* to put to sleep; *(ennuyer)* to send to sleep **2 s'endormir** *vpr* to fall asleep, to go to sleep ▪ **endormi, -e** *adj* asleep, sleeping

endosser [ɑ̃dose] *vt (vêtement)* to put on; *(chèque)* to endorse

endroit [ɑ̃drwa] *nm* (**a**) *(lieu)* place, spot; **par endroits** in places (**b**) *(de tissu)* right side; **à l'e.** *(vêtement)* the right way round

enduire* [ɑ̃dɥir] *vt* to smear, to coat (**de** with) ▪ **enduit** *nm* coating; *(de mur)* plaster

endurant, -e [ɑ̃dyrɑ̃, -ɑ̃t] *adj* hardy, tough ▪ **endurance** *nf* stamina; **course d'e.** endurance race

endurcir [ãdyrsir] **1** *vt* e. qn à *(douleur)* to harden sb to **2** s'**endurcir** *vpr (moralement)* to become hard; *(physiquement)* to toughen up

endurer [ãdyre] *vt* to endure, to bear

énergie [enɛrʒi] *nf* energy ■ **énergétique** *adj* aliment é. energy food; **ressources énergétiques** energy resources ■ **énergique** *adj (personne)* energetic; *(mesure, ton)* forceful

énerver [enɛrve] **1** *vt* é. qn *(irriter)* to get on sb's nerves; *(rendre nerveux)* to make sb nervous **2** s'**énerver** *vpr* to get worked up ■ **énervé, -e** *adj (agacé)* irritated; *(excité)* on edge, agitated

enfance [ãfãs] *nf* childhood ■ **enfantillages** *nmpl* childish behaviour ■ **enfantin, -e** *adj (voix, joie)* childlike; *(langage)* children's; *(simple)* easy

enfant [ãfã] *nmf* child *(pl* children); **attendre un e.** to be expecting a baby; **e. unique** only child

enfer [ãfɛr] *nm* hell

enfermer [ãfɛrme] **1** *vt (personne, chose)* to shut up; **e. qn/qch à clef** to lock sb/sth up **2** s'**enfermer** *vpr* s'**e. dans** *(chambre)* to shut oneself (up) in; **s'e. à clef** to lock oneself in

enfiler [ãfile] *vt (aiguille)* to thread; *(perles)* to string; *Fam (vêtement)* to slip on

enfin [ãfɛ̃] *adv (à la fin)* finally, at last; *(en dernier lieu)* lastly; *(en somme)* in a word; *(de résignation)* well; *Fam* **e. bref...** *(en somme)* in a word...; **(mais) e.!** for heaven's sake!

enflammer [ãflame] **1** *vt* to set fire to; *(allumette)* to light **2** s'**enflammer** *vpr* to catch fire

enfler [ãfle] *vi (membre)* to swell (up) ■ **enflure** *nf* swelling

enfoncer [ãfɔ̃se] **1** *vt (clou)* to bang in; *(porte)* to smash in; **e. dans qch** *(couteau, mains)* to plunge into sth **2** s'**enfoncer** *vpr (s'enliser)* to sink **(dans** into); *(couteau)* to go in; **s'e. dans** *(pénétrer)* to penetrate into

enfouir [ãfwir] *vt* to bury

enfourner [ãfurne] *vt* to put in the oven

enfreindre* [ãfrɛ̃dr] *vt* to infringe

enfuir* [ãfɥir] s'**enfuir** *vpr* to run away **(de** from)

engager [ãgaʒe] **1** *vt (discussion, combat)* to start; *(bijou)* to pawn; *(clef)* to insert **(dans** into); **e. qn** *(embaucher)* to hire sb
2 s'**engager** *vpr (dans l'armée)* to enlist; *(prendre position)* to commit oneself; *(partie)* to start; **s'e. à faire qch** to undertake to do sth; **s'e. dans** *(voie)* to enter; *(affaire)* to get involved in ■ **engagé, -e** *adj (écrivain)* committed ■ **engageant, -e** *adj* engaging ■ **engagement** *nm (promesse)* commitment; *(de soldats)* enlistment; *(au football)* kick-off; **prendre l'e. de faire qch** to undertake to do sth

engelure [ãʒlyr] *nf* chilblain

engendrer [ãʒãdre] *vt (causer)* to generate, to engender; *(procréer)* to father

engin [ãʒɛ̃] *nm (machine)* machine; *(outil)* device; **e. explosif** explosive device; **e. spatial** spacecraft

englober [ãglɔbe] *vt* to include

engloutir [ãglutir] *vt (nourriture)* to wolf down; *(bateau, village)* to submerge

engorger [ãgɔrʒe] *vt* to block up, to clog

engouement [ãgumã] *nm* craze **(pour** for)

engouffrer [ãgufre] s'**engouffrer** *vpr* s'**e. dans** to rush into

engourdir [ãgurdir] s'**engourdir** *vpr (membre)* to go numb

engrais [ãgrɛ] *nm* fertilizer

engraisser [ãgrese] *vt (animal, personne)* to fatten up

engrenage [ãgrənaʒ] *nm Tech* gears; *Fig* chain; *Fig* **pris dans l'e.** caught in a trap

énigme [enigm] *nf (devinette)* riddle; *(mystère)* enigma ■ **énigmatique** *adj* enigmatic

enjamber [ãʒãbe] *vt* to step over; *(sujet: pont)* *(rivière)* to span ■ **enjambée** *nf* stride

enjeu, -x [ãʒø] *nm (mise)* stake; *Fig (de pari, de guerre)* stakes

enjoliver [ãʒɔlive] *vt* to embellish

enjoué, -e [ãʒwe] *adj* playful

enlacer [ãlase] *vt (mêler)* to entwine; *(embrasser)* to clasp

enlaidir [ãledir] **1** *vt* to make ugly **2** *vi* to grow ugly

enlevé, -e [ãlve] *adj (style, danse)* lively

enlever [ãl(ə)ve] **1** *vt* to remove; *(meubles)* to take away, to remove; *(vêtement, couvercle)* to take off, to remove; *(tapis)* to take up; *(rideau)* to take down; *(enfant)* to kidnap, to abduct; *(ordures)* to collect **2** **s'enlever** *vpr (tache)* to come out; *(vernis)* to come off ■ **enlèvement** [-εvmã] *nm (d'enfant)* kidnapping, abduction; *(d'objet)* removal

enliser [ãlize] **s'enliser** *vpr (véhicule) & Fig* to get bogged down (**dans** in)

enneigé, -e [ãneʒe] *adj* snow-covered

ennemi, -e [enmi] **1** *nmf* enemy **2** *adj (personne)* hostile (**de** to)

ennui [ãnyi] *nm (lassitude)* boredom; *(souci)* problem; **avoir des ennuis** *(soucis)* to be worried; *(problèmes)* to have problems

ennuyer [ãnyije] **1** *vt (agacer)* to annoy; *(préoccuper)* to bother; *(lasser)* to bore **2** **s'ennuyer** *vpr* to get bored ■ **ennuyé, -e** *adj (air)* bored ■ **ennuyeux, -euse** *adj (contrariant)* annoying; *(lassant)* boring

énoncer [enɔse] *vt* to state

énorme [enɔrm] *adj* enormous, huge ■ **énormément** *adv (travailler, pleurer)* an awful lot; **je le regrette é.** I'm awfully sorry about it; **il n'a pas é. d'argent** he hasn't got a huge amount of money ■ **énormité** *nf (de demande, de crime, de somme)* enormity; *(faute)* glaring mistake

enquête [ãket] *nf (de policiers, de journalistes)* investigation; *(judiciaire, administrative)* inquiry; *(sondage)* survey ■ **enquêter** *vi (policier, journaliste)* to investigate; **e. sur qch** to investigate sth

enraciner [ãrasine] **s'enraciner** *vpr* to take root; **enraciné dans** *(personne, souvenir)* rooted in

enrager [ãraʒe] *vi* to be furious **(de faire** about doing); **faire e. qn** to get on sb's nerves ■ **enragé, -e** *adj (chien)* rabid

enrayer [ãreje] **1** *vt (maladie)* to check **2** **s'enrayer** *vpr (fusil)* to jam

enregistrer [ãr(ə)ʒistre] *vt (par écrit, sur bande)* to record; *(afficher)* to register; **faire e. ses bagages** *(à l'aéroport)* to check in, to check one's baggage in ■ **enregistré, -e** *adj* recorded; **émission enregistrée** recorded *Br* programme *or Am* program ■ **enregistrement** [-əmã] *nm (sur bande)* recording; **l'e. des bagages** *(à l'aéroport)* (baggage) check-in; **se présenter à l'e.** to check in

enrhumer [ãryme] **s'enrhumer** *vpr* to catch a cold; **être enrhumé** to have a cold

enrichir [ãriʃir] **1** *vt* to enrich (**de** with) **2** **s'enrichir** *vpr (personne)* to get rich

enrober [ãrɔbe] *vt* to coat (**de** in)

enrouer [ãrwe] **s'enrouer** *vpr* to get hoarse

enrouler [ãrule] **1** *vt (fil)* to wind **2** **s'enrouler** *vpr* **s'e. dans qch** *(couvertures)* to wrap oneself up in sth; **s'e. sur** *ou* **autour de qch** to wind round sth

ensabler [ãsable] **s'ensabler** *vpr (port)* to silt up

ensanglanté, -e [ãsãglãte] *adj* bloodstained

enseignant, -e [ãsεɲã, -ãt] **1** *nmf* teacher **2** *adj* **corps e.** teaching profession

enseigne [ãsεɲ] **1** *nf (de magasin)* sign; **e. lumineuse** neon sign **2** *nm* **e. de vaisseau** *Br* lieutenant, *Am* ensign

enseigner [ãsεɲe] **1** *vt* to teach; **e. qch à qn** to teach sb sth **2** *vi* to teach ■ **enseignement** [-εɲmã] *nm* education; *(action, métier)* teaching; **e. assisté par ordinateur** computer-assisted learning; **e. par correspondance** distance learning; **e. privé** private education; **e. public** *Br* state *or Am* public education

ensemble [āsābl] **1** *adv* together; **aller (bien) e.** *(couleurs)* to go (well) together; *(personnes)* to be well-matched **2** *nm (d'objets)* group, set; *Math* set; *(vêtement)* outfit; *(harmonie)* unity; **l'e. du personnel** *(totalité)* the whole (of the) staff; **l'e. des enseignants** all (of) the teachers; **dans l'e.** on the whole

ensevelir [āsəvlir] *vt* to bury

ensoleillé, -e [āsɔleje] *adj (endroit, journée)* sunny

ensoleillement [āsɔlɛjmā] *nm* sun(shine); **cinq heures d'e. par jour** five hours of sunshine a day

ensommeillé, -e [āsɔmeje] *adj* sleepy

ensorceler [āsɔrsəle] *vt (envoûter, séduire)* to bewitch

ensuite [āsɥit] *adv (puis)* next, then; *(plus tard)* afterwards

ensuivre* [āsɥivr] **s'ensuivre** *v impersonnel* **il s'ensuit que...** it follows that...

entailler [ātaje] *vt (fendre)* to notch; *(blesser)* to gash, to slash

entamer [ātame] *vt (pain)* to cut into; *(bouteille, boîte)* to open; *(négociations)* to enter into

entartrer [ātartre] *vt,* **s'entartrer** *vpr (chaudière)* Br to fur up, Am to scale

entasser [ātase] *vt,* **s'entasser** *vpr (objets)* to pile up, to heap up

entendre [ātādr] **1** *vt* to hear; *(comprendre)* to understand; **e. parler de qn/qch** to hear of sb/sth; **e. dire que...** to hear (it said) that...
2 **s'entendre** *vpr (être entendu)* to be heard; *(être compris)* to be understood; **s'e.** *(être d'accord)* to agree **(sur** on); **(bien) s'e. avec qn** to get along *or* Br on with sb

entendu, -e [ātādy] *adj (convenu)* agreed; *(sourire, air)* knowing; **e.!** all right!; **bien e.** of course

entente [ātāt] *nf (accord)* agreement, understanding; **(bonne) e.** *(amitié)* harmony

entériner [āterine] *vt* to ratify

enterrer [ātere] *vt (défunt)* to bury; Fig *(projet)* to scrap ▪ **enterrement** [-ɛrmā]

nm (ensevelissement) burial; *(funérailles)* funeral

en-tête [ātɛt] *(pl* **en-têtes**) *nm (de papier)* heading; **papier à e.** headed paper, letterhead

entêter [ātete] **s'entêter** *vpr* to persist **(à faire** in doing) ▪ **entêté, -e** *adj* stubborn

enthousiasme [ātuzjasm] *nm* enthusiasm ▪ **enthousiaste** *adj* enthusiastic

enticher [ātiʃe] **s'enticher** *vpr* **s'e. de qn/qch** to become infatuated with sb/sth

entier, -ère [ātje, -ɛr] **1** *adj (total)* whole, entire; *(intact)* intact; *(absolu)* absolute, complete; *(caractère)* uncompromising; **le pays tout e.** the whole *or* entire country **2** *nm* **en e.** in its entirety, completely

entonner [ātone] *vt (air)* to start singing

entonnoir [ātɔnwar] *nm* funnel

entorse [ātɔrs] *nf Méd* sprain; **se faire une e. à la cheville** to sprain one's ankle

entortiller [ātɔrtije] **1** *vt* to wrap **(dans** in) **2** **s'entortiller** *vpr (lierre)* to coil **(autour de** round)

entourage [āturaʒ] *nm (proches)* circle of family and friends

entourer [āture] **1** *vt* to surround **(de** with); *(envelopper)* to wrap **(de** in); **entouré de** surrounded by **2** **s'entourer** *vpr* **s'e. de** to surround oneself with

entracte [ātrakt] *nm* Br interval, *Am* intermission

entraide [ātrɛd] *nf* mutual aid ▪ **s'entraider** *vpr* to help each other

entraînant, -e [ātrɛnā, -āt] *adj (musique)* lively

entraîner [ātrene] **1** *vt* **(a)** *(charrier)* to carry away; *(causer)* to bring about; *(dépenses)* to entail; **e. qn** *(emmener)* to lead sb away; *(de force)* to drag sb away; *(attirer)* to lure sb; **se laisser e.** to allow oneself to be led astray
(b) *(athlète, cheval)* to train **(à** for)
2 **s'entraîner** *vpr* to train oneself **(à faire qch** to do sth); *Sport* to train ▪ **entraînement** [-ɛnmā] *nm Sport* training;

(élan) impulse ▪ **entraîneur** [-ɛnœr] *nm (d'athlète)* coach; *(de cheval)* trainer

entraver [ātrave] *vt* to hinder, to hamper

entre [ātr] *prép* between; *(parmi)* among(st); **l'un d'e. vous** one of you; **se dévorer e. eux** *(réciprocité)* to devour each other

entrebâiller [ātrəbaje] *vt (porte)* to open slightly

entrecôte [ātrəkot] *nf* rib steak

entrecouper [ātrəkupe] *vt (entremêler)* to punctuate (**de** with)

entrée [ātre] *nf (action)* entry, entrance; *(porte)* entrance; *(vestibule)* entrance hall, entry; *(accès)* admission, entry (**de** to); *Ordinat* input; *(plat)* starter; **faire son e.** to make one's entrance; **'e. interdite'** 'no entry', 'no admittance'; **'e. libre'** 'admission free'; **e. de service** service *or Br* tradesmen's entrance; **e. des artistes** stage door

entrelacer [ātrəlase] *vt*, **s'entrelacer** *vpr* to intertwine

entremêler [ātrəmele] *vt*, **s'entremêler** *vpr* to intermingle

entremets [ātrəmɛ] *nm (plat)* dessert, *Br* sweet

entreposer [ātrəpoze] *vt* to store ▪ **entrepôt** *nm* warehouse

entreprendre* [ātrəprādr] *vt (travail, voyage)* to undertake; **e. de faire qch** to undertake to do sth ▪ **entreprenant, -e** [-ənā, -āt] *adj (dynamique)* enterprising; *(galant)* forward

entrepreneur [ātrəprənœr] *nm (en bâtiment)* contractor; *(chef d'entreprise)* entrepreneur

entreprise [ātrəpriz] *nf (firme)* company, firm

entrer [ātre] **1** *vi (aux être) (aller)* to go in, to enter; *(venir)* to come in, to enter; **e. dans** to go into; *(pièce)* to come/go into, to enter; **e. à l'université** to start university; **e. dans les détails** to go into detail; **entrez!** come in!

2 *vt (aux* **avoir***) Ordinat* **e. des données** to enter data (**dans** into)

entresol [ātrəsɔl] *nm* mezzanine floor

entre-temps [ātrətā] *adv* meanwhile

entretenir* [ātrətnir] **1** *vt (voiture, maison, famille)* to maintain; *(relations)* to keep; **e. qn de qch** to talk to sb about sth **2** **s'entretenir** *vpr* **s'e. de qch** to talk about sth (**avec** with) ▪ **entretenu, -e** *adj* **bien/mal e.** *(maison)* well-kept/badly kept

entretien [ātrətjɛ̃] *nm (de route, de maison)* maintenance, upkeep; *(dialogue)* conversation; *(entrevue)* interview

entrevoir* [ātrəvwar] *vt (rapidement)* to catch a glimpse of; *(pressentir)* to foresee

entrevue [ātrəvy] *nf* interview

entrouvrir* [ātruvrir] *vt*, **s'entrouvrir** *vpr* to half-open ▪ **entrouvert, -e** *adj (porte, fenêtre)* half-open

énumérer [enymere] *vt* to list ▪ **énumération** *nf* listing

envahir [āvair] *vt (pays)* to invade; *(marché)* to flood; **e. qn** *(doute, peur)* to overcome sb ▪ **envahissant, -e** *adj (personne)* intrusive ▪ **envahisseur** *nm* invader

enveloppant, -e [āvlɔpā, -āt] *adj (séduisant)* captivating

enveloppe [āvlɔp] *nf (pour lettre)* envelope

envelopper [āvlɔpe] **1** *vt* to wrap (up) (**dans** in) **2** **s'envelopper** *vpr* to wrap oneself (up) (**dans** in)

envenimer [āvnime] **s'envenimer** *vpr (plaie)* to turn septic; *Fig* to become acrimonious

envergure [āvɛrgyr] *nf (d'avion, d'oiseau)* wingspan; *(de personne)* calibre; *(ampleur)* scope

envers [āvɛr] **1** *prép Br* towards, *Am* toward(s), to **2** *nm (de tissu)* wrong side; **à l'e.** *(chaussette)* inside out; *(pantalon)* back to front; *(la tête en bas)* upside down

envie [āvi] *nf (jalousie)* envy; *(désir)* desire; **avoir e. de qch** to want sth; **avoir e. de faire qch** to feel like doing sth ▪ **envier** *vt* to envy (**qch à qn** sb sth) ▪ **envieux, -euse** *adj* envious

environ [āvirɔ̃] *adv (à peu près)* about ▪ **environs** *nmpl* outskirts, surroundings; **aux e. de qch** around sth, in the vicinity of sth

environnant, -e [ãvironã, -ãt] *adj* surrounding

environnement [ãvironmã] *nm* environment

envisager [ãvizaʒe] *vt (considérer)* to consider; *(projeter)* Br to envisage, Am to envision; **e. de faire qch** to consider doing sth

envoi [ãvwa] *nm (action)* sending; *(paquet)* package; *(marchandises)* consignment

envoler [ãvɔle] **s'envoler** *vpr (oiseau)* to fly away; *(avion)* to take off; *(chapeau, papier)* to blow away; *Fig (espoir)* to vanish

envoûter [ãvute] *vt* to bewitch

envoyer* [ãvwaje] *vt* to send; *(lancer)* to throw; **e. chercher qn** to send for sb ■ **envoyé, -e** *nmf* envoy; **e. spécial** *(reporter)* special correspondent ■ **envoyeur** *nm* sender; **retour à l'e.** 'return to sender'

épais, -aisse [epɛ, -ɛs] *adj* thick ■ **épaisseur** *nf* thickness; **avoir 1 mètre d'é.** to be 1 metre thick ■ **épaissir** [epesir] **1** *vt* to thicken **2** *vi*, **s'épaissir** *vpr* to thicken; *(grossir)* to fill out; **le mystère s'épaissit** the mystery is deepening

épanouir [epanwir] **s'épanouir** *vpr (fleur)* to bloom; *Fig (personne)* to blossom; *(visage)* to beam ■ **épanoui, -e** *adj (fleur, personne)* in full bloom; *(visage)* beaming ■ **épanouissement** *nm (de fleur)* full bloom; *(de personne)* blossoming

épargne [eparɲ] *nf (action, vertu)* saving; *(sommes)* savings ■ **épargnant, -e** *nmf* saver ■ **épargner** *vt (argent, provisions)* to save; *(ennemi)* to spare; **e. qch à qn** *(ennuis, chagrin)* to spare sb sth

éparpiller [eparpije] *vt*, **s'éparpiller** *vpr* to scatter; *(efforts)* to dissipate

épaule [epol] *nf* shoulder ■ **épauler 1** *vt (fusil)* to raise (to one's shoulder); **é. qn** *(aider)* to back sb up **2** *vi* to take aim ■ **épaulette** *nf (de veste)* shoulder pad

épave [epav] *nf (bateau, personne)* wreck

épée [epe] *nf* sword

épeler [eple] *vt* to spell

éperon [eprɔ̃] *nm (de cavalier, de coq)* spur

épi [epi] *nm (de blé)* ear; *(de cheveux)* tuft of hair

épice [epis] *nf* spice ■ **épicé, -e** *adj (plat, récit)* spicy ■ **épicer** *vt* to spice

épicier, -ère [episje, -ɛr] *nmf* grocer ■ **épicerie** *nf (magasin)* Br grocer's (shop), Am grocery (store); **é. fine** delicatessen

épidémie [epidemi] *nf* epidemic

épier [epje] *vt (observer)* to watch closely; *(occasion)* to watch out for; **é. qn** to spy on sb

épiler [epile] **s'épiler** *vpr* to remove unwanted hair; **s'é. les jambes à la cire** to wax one's legs

épilogue [epilɔg] *nm* epilogue

épinards [epinar] *nmpl* spinach

épine [epin] *nf (de plante)* thorn; *(d'animal)* spine, prickle ■ **épineux, -euse** *adj (tige, question)* thorny; *(poisson)* spiny

épingle [epɛ̃gl] *nf* pin; **é. à nourrice** safety pin; **é. à linge** Br clothes peg, Am clothes pin ■ **épingler** *vt* to pin

Épiphanie [epifani] *nf* l'É. Epiphany

épique [epik] *adj* epic

épiscopal, -e, -aux, -ales [episkɔpal, -o] *adj* episcopal

épisode [epizɔd] *nm* episode ■ **épisodique** *adj (intermittent)* occasional

épitaphe [epitaf] *nf* epitaph

éplucher [eplyʃe] *vt (carotte, pomme)* to peel ■ **épluchure** *nf* peeling

éponge [epɔ̃ʒ] *nf* sponge; *Fig* **jeter l'é.** to throw in the towel ■ **éponger 1** *vt (liquide)* to mop up; *(dette)* to absorb **2 s'éponger** *vpr* **s'é. le front** to mop one's brow

époque [epɔk] *nf (date)* time, period; *(historique)* age; **meubles d'é.** period furniture; **à l'é.** at the *or* that time

épouse [epuz] *nf* wife

épouser [epuze] *vt* to marry

épousseter [epuste] *vt* to dust

épouvantable [epuvãtabl] *adj* appalling

épouvantail [epuvɑ̃taj] *nm (de jardin)* scarecrow

épouvante [epuvɑ̃t] *nf* terror ■ **épouvanter** *vt* to terrify

époux [epu] *nm* husband; **les é.** the husband and wife

éprendre* [eprɑ̃dr] **s'éprendre** *vpr* **s'é. de qn** to fall in love with sb

épreuve [eprœv] *nf (essai, examen)* test; *(sportive)* event; *(malheur)* ordeal, trial; *(photo)* print; **mettre qn à l'é.** to put sb to the test; **à toute é.** *(patience)* unfailing; *(nerfs)* rock-solid; **à l'é. du feu** fireproof

éprouver [epruve] *vt (méthode, personne)* to test; *(sentiment)* to feel; *(difficultés)* to meet with ■ **éprouvant, -e** *adj (pénible)* trying

éprouvette [epruvɛt] *nf* test tube

EPS [əpeɛs] *(abrév* **éducation physique et sportive)** *nf* PE

épuiser [epɥize] **1** *vt (personne, provisions, sujet)* to exhaust **2 s'épuiser** *vpr (réserves, patience)* to run out; **s'é. à faire qch** to exhaust oneself doing sth ■ **épuisant, -e** *adj* exhausting ■ **épuisé, -e** *adj* exhausted; *(marchandise)* sold out; *(édition)* out of print

épuisette [epɥizɛt] *nf* landing net

épurer [epyre] *vt (eau, gaz)* to purify; *(minerai)* to refine ■ **épuration** *nf* purification; *(de minerai)* refining

équateur [ekwatœr] *nm* equator; **sous l'é.** at the equator

équation [ekwɑsjɔ̃] *nf Math* equation

équerre [ekɛr] *nf* **é. (à dessin)** *Br* set square, *Am* triangle

équestre [ekɛstr] *adj (statue, sports)* equestrian

équilibre [ekilibr] *nm* balance; **garder/perdre l'é.** to keep/lose one's balance

équilibrer [ekilibre] *vt (charge, composition, budget)* to balance

équinoxe [ekinɔks] *nm* equinox

équipage [ekipaʒ] *nm (de navire, d'avion)* crew

équipe [ekip] *nf* team; *(d'ouvriers)* gang; **faire é. avec qn** to team up with sb; **travailler en** *ou* **par é.** to work as a team; **é. de nuit** night shift; **é. de secours** rescue team ■ **équipier, -ère** *nmf* team member

équiper [ekipe] **1** *vt* to equip **(de** with) **2 s'équiper** *vpr* to equip oneself **(de** with) ■ **équipement** *nm* equipment

équitable [ekitabl] *adj* fair, equitable

équitation [ekitɑsjɔ̃] *nf Br* (horse) riding, *Am* (horseback) riding; **faire de l'é.** to go riding

équivalent, -e [ekivalɑ̃, -ɑ̃t] *adj & nm* equivalent ■ **équivalence** *nf* equivalence ■ **équivaloir*** *vi* **é. à qch** to be equivalent to sth

équivoque [ekivɔk] **1** *adj (ambigu)* equivocal; *(douteux)* dubious **2** *nf* ambiguity

érable [erabl] *nm (arbre, bois)* maple

érafler [erafle] *vt* to graze, to scratch ■ **éraflure** *nf* graze, scratch

ère [ɛr] *nf* era; **avant notre è.** BC; **en l'an 800 de notre è.** in the year 800 AD

éreinter [erɛ̃te] **1** *vt (fatiguer)* to exhaust **2 s'éreinter** *vpr* **s'é. à faire qch** to wear oneself out doing sth

ériger [eriʒe] **1** *vt* to erect **2 s'ériger** *vpr* **s'é. en qch** to set oneself up as sth

érosion [erozjɔ̃] *nf* erosion ■ **éroder** *vt* to erode

errer [ere] *vi* to wander ■ **errant** *adj m* **chien/chat e.** stray dog/cat

erreur [erœr] *nf (faute)* mistake, error; **par e.** by mistake; **e. judiciaire** miscarriage of justice

érudit, -e [erydi, -it] **1** *adj* scholarly, erudite **2** *nmf* scholar ■ **érudition** *nf* scholarship, erudition

éruption [erypsjɔ̃] *nf (de volcan)* eruption; *(de boutons)* rash

es [ɛ] *voir* **être**

ès [ɛs] *prép* of; **licencié ès lettres** ≃ BA; **docteur ès lettres** ≃ PhD

escabeau, -x [ɛskabo] *nm (marchepied)* stepladder, *Br* (pair of) steps; *(tabouret)* stool

escadrille [ɛskadrij] *nf Aviat (unité)* flight

escadron [ɛskadrɔ̃] *nm* squadron

escalade [ɛskalad] *nf* climbing; *(de prix, de violence)* escalation ■ **escalader** *vt* to climb, to scale

escale [ɛskal] *nf Aviat* stopover; *Naut (lieu)* port of call; **faire e. à** *(avion)* to stop (over) at; *(navire)* to put in at; **vol sans e.** non-stop flight

escalier [ɛskalje] *nm (marches)* stairs; *(cage)* staircase; **l'é., les escaliers** the stairs; **e. mécanique** *ou* **roulant** escalator; **e. de secours** fire escape

escalope [ɛskalɔp] *nf* escalope

escamoter [ɛskamɔte] *vt (faire disparaître)* to make vanish; *(esquiver)* to dodge

escapade [ɛskapad] *nf* jaunt

escargot [ɛskargo] *nm* snail

escarpé, -e [ɛskarpe] *adj* steep ■ **escarpement** [-əmɑ̃] *nm (côte)* steep slope

escarpin [ɛskarpɛ̃] *nm (soulier)* pump, *Br* court shoe

esclave [ɛsklav] *nmf* slave ■ **esclavage** *nm* slavery

escompte [ɛskɔ̃t] *nm* discount; **taux d'e.** bank discount rate ■ **escompter** *vt (espérer)* to anticipate (**faire** doing), to expect (**faire** to do)

escorte [ɛskɔrt] *nf* escort ■ **escorter** *vt* to escort

escrime [ɛskrim] *nf* fencing; **faire de l'e.** to fence ■ **escrimeur, -euse** *nmf* fencer

escrimer [ɛskrime] **s'escrimer** *vpr* **s'e. à faire qch** to struggle to do sth

escroc [ɛskro] *nm* crook, swindler ■ **escroquer** *vt* **e. qn** to swindle sb; **e. qch à qn** to swindle sb out of sth ■ **escroquerie** *nf (action)* swindling; *(résultat)* swindle

espace [ɛspas] *nm* space; **e. aérien** air space; **e. vert** garden, park

espacer [ɛspase] **1** *vt* to space out; **espacés d'un mètre** one metre apart **2 s'espacer** *vpr (maisons, visites)* to become less frequent

espadrille [ɛspadrij] *nf* espadrille, = rope-soled sandal

Espagne [ɛspaɲ] *nf* **l'E.** Spain ■ **espagnol, -e 1** *adj* Spanish **2** *nmf* **E., Espagnole** Spaniard **3** *nm (langue)* Spanish

espèce [ɛspɛs] *nf (race)* species; *(genre)* kind, sort ■ **espèces** *nfpl (argent)* cash; **en e.** in cash

espérance [ɛsperɑ̃s] *nf* hope; **e. de vie** life expectancy

espérer [ɛspere] **1** *vt* to hope for; **e. que...** to hope that...; **e. faire qch** to hope to do sth **2** *vi* to hope; **j'espère (bien)!** I hope so!

espiègle [ɛspjɛgl] *adj* mischievous

espion, -onne [ɛspjɔ̃, -ɔn] *nmf* spy ■ **espionnage** *nm* spying, espionage ■ **espionner 1** *vt* to spy on **2** *vi* to spy

espoir [ɛspwar] *nm* hope; **avoir l'e. de faire qch** to have hopes of doing sth

esprit [ɛspri] *nm (attitude, fantôme)* spirit; *(intellect)* mind; *(humour)* wit; **venir à l'e. de qn** to cross sb's mind; **avoir de l'e.** to be witty; **avoir l'e. large/étroit** to be broad-/narrow-minded

esquimau, -aude, -aux, -audes [ɛskimo, -od] **1** *adj* Eskimo, *Am* Inuit **2** *nmf* **E., Esquimaude** Eskimo, *Am* Inuit **3** *nm* **Esquimau®** *(glace) Br* ≃ choc-ice *(on a stick)*, *Am* ≃ ice-cream bar

esquisse [ɛskis] *nf (croquis, plan)* sketch ■ **esquisser** *vt* to sketch; **e. un geste** to make a (slight) gesture

esquiver [ɛskive] **1** *vt (coup, problème)* to dodge **2 s'esquiver** *vpr* to slip away

essai [ɛsɛ] *nm (test)* test, trial; *(tentative, au rugby)* try; *(ouvrage)* essay; **à l'e.** *(objet)* on a trial basis

essaim [ɛsɛ̃] *nm* swarm

essayer [eseje] *vt* to try (**de faire** to do); *(vêtement)* to try on; *(méthode)* to try out ■ **essayage** [-ɛjaʒ] *nm (de vêtement)* fitting

essence [ɛsɑ̃s] *nf (carburant) Br* petrol, *Am* gas; *(extrait) & Phil* essence; **e. sans plomb** unleaded; **e. ordinaire** *Br* two-star petrol, *Am* regular gas

essentiel, -elle [ɛsɑ̃sjɛl] **1** *adj* essential (**à/pour** for) **2** *nm* **l'e.** *(le plus important)* the main thing; *(le minimum)* the essentials

essor [esɔr] *nm (d'oiseau)* flight; *(de pays, d'entreprise)* rapid growth; **en plein e.** booming; **prendre son e.** to take off

essorer [esɔre] *vt (dans une essoreuse)* to spin-dry; *(dans une machine à laver)* to spin

essouffler [esufle] **1** *vt* to make out of breath **2 s'essouffler** *vpr* to get out of breath

essuyer [esɥije] **1** *vt (objet, surface)* to wipe; *(liquide)* to wipe up; *(larmes)* to wipe away; *(défaite)* to suffer; *(refus)* to meet with; **e. la vaisselle** to dry the dishes **2 s'essuyer** *vpr* to wipe oneself; **s'e. les yeux** to wipe one's eyes ■ **essuie-glace** *(pl* **essuie-glaces)** *nm Br* windscreen wiper, *Am* windshield wiper

est¹ [ɛ] *voir* **être**

est² [ɛst] **1** *nm* east; **à l'e.** in the east; *(direction)* (to the) east (**ce** of); **d'e.** *(vent)* east(erly); **de l'e.** eastern **2** *adj inv (côte)* east(ern)

estampe [ɛstãp] *nf* print

estampille [ɛstãpij] *nf (de produit)* mark; *(de document)* stamp

esthéticienne [ɛstetisjɛn] *nf* beautician

estime [ɛstim] *nf* esteem, regard

estimer [ɛstime] **1** *vt (tableau)* to value (**à** at); *(prix, distance, poids)* to estimate; *(dommages, besoins)* to assess; *(juger)* to consider (**que** that); **e. qn** to esteem sb
 2 s'estimer *vpr* **s'e. heureux** to consider oneself happy ■ **estimable** *adj* respectable ■ **estimation** *nf (de mobilier)* valuation; *(de prix, de distance, de poids)* estimation; *(de dommages, de besoins)* assessment

estival, -e, -aux, -ales [ɛstival, -o] *adj* **température estivale** summer temperature ■ **estivant, -e** *nmf Br* holidaymaker, *Am* vacationer

estomac [ɛstɔma] *nm* stomach

estomper [ɛstɔpe] **1** *vt (rendre flou)* to blur **2 s'estomper** *vpr* to become blurred

estrade [ɛstrad] *nf* platform

estragon [ɛstragɔ̃] *nm* tarragon

esturgeon [ɛstyrʒɔ̃] *nm* sturgeon

et [e] *conj* and; **vingt et un** twentyone; **et moi?** what about me?

établi [etabli] *nm* workbench

établir [etablir] **1** *vt (paix, relations, principe)* to establish; *(liste)* to draw up; *(record)* to set; *(démontrer)* to establish, to prove **2 s'établir** *vpr (pour habiter)* to settle; *(pour exercer un métier)* to set up in business ■ **établissement** *nm (de paix, de relations, de principe)* establishment; *(entreprise)* business, firm; **é. scolaire** school

étage [etaʒ] *nm (d'immeuble)* floor, *Br* storey, *Am* story; *(de fusée)* stage; **à l'é.** upstairs; **au premier é.** on the *Br* first or *Am* second floor; **maison à deux étages** *Br* two-storeyed or *Am* twostoried house

étagère [etaʒɛr] *nf* shelf; *(meuble)* shelving unit

étain [etɛ̃] *nm (métal)* tin; *(de gobelet)* pewter

étais, était [etɛ] *voir* **être**

étal [etal] *(pl* **étals)** *nm (au marché)* stall

étalage [etalaʒ] *nm* display; *(vitrine)* display window

étaler [etale] **1** *vt (disposer)* to lay out; *(en vitrine)* to display; *(beurre)* to spread; *(vacances, paiements)* to stagger **2 s'étaler** *vpr* **s'é. sur** *(congés, paiements)* to be spread over ■ **étalement** *nm (de vacances, de paiements)* staggering

étanche [etɑ̃ʃ] *adj* watertight; *(montre)* waterproof

étancher [etɑ̃ʃe] *vt (sang)* to stop the flow of; *(soif)* to quench

étang [etɑ̃] *nm* pond

étant [etɑ̃] *p prés de* **être**

étape [etap] *nf (de voyage)* stage; *(lieu)* stop(over); **faire é. à** to stop off or over at; **par étapes** in stages

état [eta] *nm* **(a)** *(condition, manière d'être)* state; **à l'é. neuf** as new; **en bon é.** in good condition; **é. d'esprit** state or frame of mind; **é. des lieux** inventory of fixtures; **é. civil** register office **(b)** *(autorité centrale)* **É.** *(nation)* State

état-major [etamaʒɔr] *(pl* **états-majors)** *nm Mil* (general) staff; *(de parti)* senior staff

États-Unis [etazyni] *nmpl* **les É.** the United States; **les É. d'Amérique** the United States of America

étau, -x [eto] *nm (instrument) Br* vice, *Am* vise

été¹ [ete] *nm* summer

été² [ete] *pp de* **être**

éteindre* [etɛ̃dr] **1** *vt (feu, cigarette)* to put out, to extinguish; *(lampe)* to switch off; *(gaz)* to turn off **2** *vi* to switch off **3 s'éteindre** *vpr (feu)* to go out; *(personne)* to pass away ■ **éteint, -e** *adj (feu, bougie)* out; *(lampe, lumière)* off; *(volcan)* extinct

étendre [etɑ̃dr] **1** *vt (linge)* to hang out; *(agrandir)* to extend; **é. le bras** to stretch out one's arm; **é. qn** to stretch sb out **2 s'étendre** *vpr (personne)* to lie down; *(plaine)* to stretch; *(feu)* to spread; **s'é. sur qch** *(sujet)* to dwell on sth

étendu, -e¹ [etɑ̃dy] *adj (forêt, vocabulaire)* extensive; *(personne)* lying

étendue² [etɑ̃dy] *nf (importance)* extent; *(surface)* area

éternel, -elle [etɛrnɛl] *adj* eternal ■ **s'éterniser** *vpr (débat)* to drag on endlessly; *Fam (visiteur)* to stay for ever ■ **éternité** *nf* eternity

éternuer [etɛrnɥe] *vi* to sneeze

êtes [ɛt] *voir* **être**

Éthiopie [etjɔpi] *nf* **l'É.** Ethiopia ■ **éthiopien, -enne 1** *adj* Ethiopian **2** *nmf* **É., Éthiopienne** Ethiopian

ethnie [ɛtni] *nf* ethnic group ■ **ethnique** *adj* ethnic

étinceler [etɛ̃sle] *vi* to sparkle ■ **étincelle** *nf* spark

étiqueter [etikte] *vt* to label ■ **étiquette** *nf (marque)* label; *(protocole)* (diplomatic *or* court) etiquette

étirer [etire] **1** *vt* to stretch **2 s'étirer** *vpr* to stretch (oneself)

étoffe [etɔf] *nf* material, fabric

étoffer [etɔfe] **1** *vt* to fill out; *(texte)* to make more meaty **2 s'étoffer** *vpr (personne)* to fill out

étoile [etwal] *nf* star; **à la belle é.** in the open; **é. de mer** starfish; **é. filante** shooting star

étonner [etɔne] **1** *vt* to surprise **2 s'étonner** *vpr* to be surprised **(de qch** at sth; **que** + *subjunctive* that) ■ **étonnant, -e** *adj (ahurissant)* surprising; *(remarquable)* amazing ■ **étonnement** *nm* surprise

étouffant, -e [etufɑ̃, -ɑ̃t] *adj (air)* stifling

étouffer [etufe] **1** *vt (tuer)* to suffocate; *Fig (révolte)* to stifle; *Fig (scandale)* to hush up **2** *vi* to suffocate **3 s'étouffer** *vpr (en mangeant)* to choke **(avec** on); *(mourir)* to suffocate

étourdi, -e [eturdi] **1** *adj* scatterbrained **2** *nmf* scatterbrain ■ **étourderie** *nf* absent-mindedness; **une é.** a thoughtless blunder

étourdissant, -e [eturdisɑ̃, -ɑ̃t] *adj (bruit)* deafening; *(beauté)* stunning

étourdissement [eturdismɑ̃] *nm (malaise)* dizzy spell

étrange [etrɑ̃ʒ] *adj* strange, odd ■ **étranger, -ère 1** *adj (d'un autre pays)* foreign; *(non familier)* strange **(à** to) **2** *nmf (d'un autre pays)* foreigner; *(inconnu)* stranger; **à l'é.** abroad; **aller à l'é.** to go abroad

étrangler [etrɑ̃gle] **1** *vt* **é. qn** *(tuer)* to strangle sb **2 s'étrangler** *vpr (de colère, en mangeant)* to choke ■ **étranglé, -e** *adj (voix)* choking

ÊTRE* [ɛtr] **1** *vi* to be; **il est professeur** he's a teacher; **est-ce qu'elle vient?** is she coming?; **il vient, n'est-ce pas?** he's coming, isn't he?; **est-ce qu'il aime le thé?** does he like tea?; **nous sommes dix** there are ten of us; **nous sommes le dix** today is the tenth; **il a été à Paris** *(il y est allé)* he has been to Paris; **elle est de Paris** she's from Paris; **il est cinq heures** it's five (o'clock); **c'est à lire pour demain** this has to be read for tomorrow; **c'est à lui** it's his
2 *v aux (avec 'venir', 'partir' etc)* to have/ to be; **elle est arrivée** she has arrived; **elle est née en 1999** she was born in 1999

3 *nm (personne)* being; **les êtres chers** the loved ones; **ê. humain** human being; **ê. vivant** living being

étreindre* [etrɛ̃dr] *vt* to grip; *(avec amour)* to embrace

étrennes [etrɛn] *nfpl* New Year gift; *(gratification)* ≃ Christmas tip

étrier [etrije] *nm* stirrup

étroit, -e [etrwa, -at] *adj* narrow; *(vêtement)* tight; *(lien, collaboration)* close; **être à l'é.** to be cramped

étude [etyd] *nf (action, ouvrage)* study; *(de notaire)* office; *Scol (pièce)* study room; *(période)* study period; **à l'é.** *(projet)* under consideration; **faire des études de français** to study French; **faire une é. de marché** to do market research

étudiant, -e [etydjɑ̃, -ɑ̃t] **1** *nmf* student; **e. en médecine/en droit** medical/law student; **é participant à un échange** exchange student **2** *adj (vie)* student

étudier [etydje] *vti* to study

étui [etɥi] *nm (à lunettes, à cigarettes)* case; *(de revolver)* holster

eu, eue [y] *pp de* **avoir**

eurent [yr] *voir* **avoir**

euro [øro] *nm (monnaie)* Euro

euro- [øro] *préf* Euro-

eurodéputé [ørodepyte] *nm* Euro MP

Europe [ørɔp] *nf* l'E. Europe; **l'E. verte** European Union agriculture ■ **européen, -enne 1** *adj* European **2** *nmf* E., Européenne European

eut [y] *voir* **avoir**

euthanasie [øtanazi] *nf* euthanasia

eux [ø] *pron personnel (sujet)* they; *(complément)* them; *(réfléchi, emphase)* themselves ■ **eux-mêmes** *pron* themselves

évacuer [evakɥe] *vt (bâtiment)* to evacuate; *(liquide)* to drain off ■ **évacuation** *nf* evacuation

évader [evade] **s'évader** *vpr* to escape (de from) ■ **évadé, -e** *nmf* escaped prisoner

évaluer [evalɥe] *vt (fortune)* to estimate; *(bien)* to value ■ **évaluation** *nf*

estimation; *(de bien)* valuation

évangile [evɑ̃ʒil] *nm* gospel; **l'É.** the Gospel

évanouir [evanwir] **s'évanouir** *vpr (personne)* to faint; *Fig (espoir, crainte)* to vanish ■ **évanoui, -e** *adj* unconscious ■ **évanouissement** *nm (syncope)* fainting fit

évaporer [evapore] **s'évaporer** *vpr* to evaporate; *Fig (disparaître)* to vanish into thin air

évasé, -e [evaze] *adj (jupe)* flared

évasif, -ive [evazif, -iv] *adj* evasive

évasion [evazjɔ̃] *nf* escape (de from); *(de la réalité)* escapism; **é. fiscale** tax evasion

éveil [evɛj] *nm* awakening; **être en é.** to be alert

éveiller [eveje] **1** *vt (susciter)* to arouse **2** **s'éveiller** *vpr* to awaken (à to) ■ **éveillé, -e** *adj* awake; *(vif)* alert

événement [evɛnmɑ̃] *nm* event

éventail [evɑ̃taj] *nm (instrument)* fan; *(choix)* range

éventuel, -elle [evɑ̃tɥɛl] *adj* possible ■ **éventualité** *nf* possibility ■ **éventuellement** *adv* possibly

évêque [evɛk] *nm* bishop

évertuer [evertɥe] **s'évertuer** *vpr* **s'é. à faire qch** to *Br* endeavour *or Am* endeavor to do sth

éviction [eviksjɔ̃] *nf (de concurrent, de président)* ousting; *(de locataire)* eviction

évident, -e [evidɑ̃, -ɑ̃t] *adj* obvious **(que** that) ■ **évidemment** [-amɑ̃] *adv* obviously ■ **évidence** *nf* obviousness; **une é.** an obvious fact; **en é.** in a prominent position

évier [evje] *nm* (kitchen) sink

évincer [evɛ̃se] *vt (concurrent)* to oust (de from)

éviter [evite] *vt* to avoid **(de faire** doing); **é. qch à qn** to spare *or* save sb sth

évoluer [evolɥe] *vi (changer)* to develop; *(société, situation)* to evolve; *(se déplacer)* to move around ■ **évolué, -e** *adj (pays)* advanced; *(personne)* enlightened ■ **évolution** *nf (changement)* development; *Biol* evolution

évoquer [evɔke] *vt* to evoke

exact, -e [ɛgzakt] *adj (quantité, poids, nombre)* exact, precise; *(rapport, description)* exact, accurate; *(mot)* right, correct; *(ponctuel)* punctual ■ **exactement** [-əmã] *adv* exactly ■ **exactitude** *nf (précision, fidélité)* exactness; *(justesse)* correctness; *(ponctualité)* punctuality

ex æquo [ɛgzeko] **1** *adj inv Sport* **être classés e.** to tie, to be equally placed **2** *adv Sport* **être troisième e.** to tie for third place

exagérer [ɛgzaʒere] **1** *vt* to exaggerate **2** *vi (parler)* to exaggerate; *(agir)* to go too far ■ **exagération** *nf* exaggeration ■ **exagéré, -e** *adj* excessive

exalter [ɛgzalte] *vt (passionner)* to stir ■ **exaltant, -e** *adj* stirring ■ **exalté, -e** *adj (sentiment)* impassioned

examen [ɛgzamɛ̃] *nm* examination; **e. blanc** mock exam; **e. médical** medical examination; **e. de la vue** eye test ■ **examinateur, -trice** *nmf* examiner ■ **examiner** *vt (considérer, regarder)* to examine

exaspérer [ɛgzaspere] *vt (personne)* to exasperate

exaucer [ɛgzose] *vt (désir)* to grant

excavation [ɛkskavasjɔ̃] *nf (trou, action)* excavation

excéder [ɛksede] *vt (dépasser)* to exceed; **é. qn** *(énerver)* to exasperate sb ■ **excédent** *nm* surplus, excess ■ **excédentaire** *adj* **poids e.** excess weight

excellent, -e [ɛkselã, -ãt] *adj* excellent ■ **excellence** *nf* excellence ■ **exceller** *vi* to excel **(en** at)

excentrique [ɛksãtrik] *adj & nmf* eccentric

excepté¹ [ɛksɛpte] *prép* except

excepté², -e *adj* except (for)

exception [ɛksɛpsjɔ̃] *nf* exception; **à l'e. de** except (for), with the exception of ■ **exceptionnel, -elle** *adj* exceptional

excès [ɛksɛ] *nm* excess; **e. de vitesse** speeding ■ **excessif, -ive** *adj* excessive

exciter [ɛksite] **1** *vt (faire naître)* to arouse; **e. qn** *(énerver)* to excite sb **2** **s'exciter** *vpr (devenir nerveux)* to get excited ■ **excitant, -e** *nm* stimulant ■ **excitation** *nf (agitation)* excitement ■ **excité, -e** *adj* excited

exclamer [ɛksklame] **s'exclamer** *vpr* to exclaim ■ **exclamation** *nf* exclamation

exclure* [ɛksklyr] *vt (écarter)* to exclude **(de** from); *(chasser)* to expel **(de** from) ■ **exclu, -e** *adj (solution)* out of the question; *(avec une date)* exclusive

exclusif, -ive [ɛksklyzif, -iv] *adj (droit, modèle)* exclusive ■ **exclusivité** *nf Com* exclusive rights; *(dans la presse)* scoop; **en e.** *(film)* having an exclusive showing **(à** at)

exclusion [ɛksklyzjɔ̃] *nf* exclusion; **à l'e. de** with the exception of

excursion [ɛkskyrsjɔ̃] *nf* trip, excursion; *(de plusieurs jours)* tour; **faire une e.** to go on a trip/tour

excuse [ɛkskyz] *nf (prétexte)* excuse; **excuses** *(regrets)* apology; **faire des excuses** to apologize **(à** to) ■ **excuser 1** *vt (justifier, pardonner)* to excuse **(qn d'avoir fait/qn de faire** sb for doing) **2** **s'excuser** *vpr* to apologize **(de** for; **auprès de** to); **excusez-moi!, je m'excuse!** excuse me!

exécrer [ɛgzekre] *vt* to loathe ■ **exécrable** *adj* atrocious

exécuter [ɛgzekyte] **1** *vt (tâche)* to carry out; *(jouer)* to perform; **e. qn** to execute sb **2** **s'exécuter** *vpr* to comply ■ **exécutant, -e** *nmf (ouvrier, employé)* subordinate ■ **exécution** *nf (de tâche)* carrying out; *(de musique)* performance; *(de condamné)* execution

exécutif [ɛgzekytif] **1** *adj m* **pouvoir e.** executive power **2** *nm* **l'e.** the executive

exemplaire [ɛgzãplɛr] **1** *adj* exemplary **2** *nm (livre)* copy

exemple [ɛgzãpl] *nm* example; **par e.** for example, for instance; **donner l'e.** to set an example **(à** to)

exempt, -e [ɛgzã, -ãt] *adj* **e. de** *(dispensé de)* exempt from; *(sans)* free from ■ **exempter** [ɛgzãte] *vt* to exempt **(de** from) ■ **exemption** *nf* exemption

exercer [εgzεrse] **1** vt (voix, droits) to exercise; (autorité, influence) to exert (**sur** on); (profession) Br to practise, Am to practice; **e. qn à qch** to train sb in sth **2** vi (médecin) Br to practise, Am to practice **3 s'exercer** vpr (s'entraîner) to train; **s'e. à qch** to Br practise or Am practice sth; **s'e. à faire qch** to Br practise or Am practice doing sth

exercice [εgzεrsis] nm (physique) & Scol exercise; Mil drill; **en e.** (fonctionnaire) in office; (médecin) in practice; **faire** ou **prendre de l'e.** to exercise, to take exercise

exhiber [εgzibe] vt (documents, passeport) to produce; Péj (savoir, richesses) to show off, to flaunt

exiger [εgziʒe] vt (exiger) to demand (**de** from); (nécessiter) to require ▪ **exigeant, -e** adj demanding, exacting ▪ **exigence** nf (caractère) exacting nature; (condition) demand

exigu, -ë [εgzigy] adj cramped, tiny

exil [εgzil] nm exile ▪ **exilé, -e** nmf (personne) exile ▪ **exiler 1** vt to exile **2 s'exiler** vpr to go into exile

existence [εgzistɑ̃s] nf (fait d'exister) existence; (vie) life; **moyen d'e.** means of existence ▪ **existant, -e** adj existing ▪ **exister 1** vi to exist **2** v impersonnel **il existe...** there is/are...

exode [εgzɔd] nm exodus

exonérer [εgzɔnere] vt to exempt (**de** from) ▪ **exonération** nf exemption

exorbitant, -e [εgzɔrbitɑ̃, -ɑ̃t] adj exorbitant

exotique [εgzɔtik] adj exotic

expansif, -ive [εkspɑ̃sif, -iv] adj expansive

expansion [εkspɑ̃sjɔ̃] nf (de commerce, de pays, de gaz) expansion; **en (pleine) e.** (fast or rapidly) expanding

expatrier [εkspatrije] **s'expatrier** vpr to leave one's country

expédier [εkspedje] vt (envoyer) to send, to dispatch; (affaires, client) to deal promptly with ▪ **expéditeur, -trice** nmf sender ▪ **expéditif, -ive** adj hasty ▪ **expédition** nf (envoi) dispatch; (voyage) expedition

expérience [εksperjɑ̃s] nf (connaissance) experience; (scientifique) experiment; **faire l'e. de qch** to experience sth; **avoir de l'e.** to have experience ▪ **expérimental, -e, -aux, -ales** adj experimental

expérimenter [εksperimɑ̃te] vt (remède, vaccin) to try out (**sur** on) ▪ **expérimenté, -e** adj experienced

expert, -e [εkspεr, -εrt] **1** adj expert, skilled (**en** in) **2** nm expert (**en** on or in); (d'assurances) valuer ▪ **expert-comptable** (pl **experts-comptables**) nm Br ≃ chartered accountant, Am ≃ certified public accountant

expertise [εkspεrtiz] nf (évaluation) valuation; (rapport) expert's report; (compétence) expertise

expier [εkspje] vt (péchés) to expiate, to atone for

expirer [εkspire] **1** vti to breathe out **2** vi (mourir) to pass away; (finir, cesser) to expire ▪ **expiration** nf (respiration) breathing out; (échéance) Br expiry, Am expiration

explication [εksplikasjɔ̃] nf explanation; (mise au point) discussion

explicite [εksplisit] adj explicit

expliquer [εksplike] **1** vt to explain (**à** to; **que** that) **2 s'expliquer** vpr to explain oneself; (discuter) to talk things over (**avec** with); **s'e. qch** (comprendre) to understand sth ▪ **explicatif, -ive** adj explanatory

exploit [εksplwa] nm feat

exploiter [εksplwate] vt (champs) to farm; (ferme) to run; (mine) to work; Fig & Péj (personne, situation) to exploit ▪ **exploitant, -e** nmf e. **agricole** farmer ▪ **exploitation** nf (de champs) farming; (de ferme) running; (de mine) working; Péj exploitation; **e. agricole** farm

explorer [εksplɔre] vt to explore ▪ **explorateur, -trice** nmf explorer

exploser [εksploze] vi (gaz, bombe) to explode; **faire e. qch** to explode sth ▪ **explosif, -ive** adj & nm explosive ▪ **explosion** nf explosion; (de colère) outburst

exporter [ɛkspɔrte] *vt* to export (**vers** to; **de** from) ▪ **exportateur, -trice 1** *nmf* exporter **2** *adj* exporting ▪ **exportation** *nf (produit)* export; *(action)* export(ation)

exposer [ɛkspoze] **1** *vt (tableau)* to exhibit; *(marchandises)* to display; *(théorie)* to set out; *Phot (film)* to expose **2 s'exposer** *vpr* **s'e. au danger** to put oneself in danger; **s'e. à la critique** to lay oneself open to criticism ▪ **exposé, -e 1** *adj* **e. au sud** facing south **2** *nm (compte rendu)* account (**de** of); *(présentation)* talk; *Scol* paper

exposition [ɛkspozisjɔ̃] *nf (d'objets d'art)* exhibition; *(de marchandises)* display; *Phot* exposure (**à** to); *(de maison)* aspect

exprès¹ [ɛksprɛ] *adv* on purpose, intentionally; *(spécialement)* specially

exprès², -esse [ɛksprɛs] *adj (ordre, condition)* express ▪ **expressément** *adv* expressly

exprès³ [ɛksprɛs] *adj inv* **lettre e.** express delivery letter

express [ɛksprɛs] *adj & nm inv (train)* express; *(café)* espresso

expressif, -ive [ɛkspresif, -iv] *adj* expressive ▪ **expression** *nf (phrase, mine)* expression ▪ **exprimer 1** *vt* to express **2 s'exprimer** *vpr* to express oneself

expulser [ɛkspylse] *vt* to expel (**de** from); *(joueur)* to send off ▪ **expulsion** *nf* expulsion; *(de joueur)* sending off

exquis, -e [ɛkski, -iz] *adj (nourriture)* exquisite

extase [ɛkstaz] *nf* ecstasy ▪ **s'extasier** *vpr* to be in raptures (**sur** over *or* about)

extensible [ɛkstãsibl] *adj (métal)* tensile; *(tissu)* stretch ▪ **extension** *nf (de muscle)* stretching; *(de durée, de contrat)* extension

exténué, -e [ɛkstenɥe] *adj* exhausted

extérieur, -e [ɛksterjœr] **1** *adj (monde)* outside; *(surface)* outer, external; *(si-gne)* outward, external; *(politique)* foreign **2** *nm* outside, exterior; **à l'e. (de)** outside; **à l'e.** *(match)* away ▪ **extérieurement** *adv (dehors)* externally; *(en apparence)* outwardly ▪ **extérioriser** *vt* to express

exterminer [ɛkstɛrmine] *vt* to exterminate

externat [ɛkstɛrna] *nm (école)* day school

externe [ɛkstɛrn] **1** *adj* external **2** *nmf (élève)* day pupil; *Méd* = non-resident hospital medical student, *Am* extern

extincteur [ɛkstɛ̃ktœr] *nm* fire extinguisher ▪ **extinction** *nf (de feu)* extinguishing; *(de race)* extinction; **e. de voix** loss of voice

extorquer [ɛkstɔrke] *vt* to extort (**à** from) ▪ **extorsion** *nf* extortion; **e. de fonds** extortion

extradition [ɛkstradisjɔ̃] *nf* extradition ▪ **extrader** *vt* to extradite

extraire* [ɛkstrɛr] *vt* to extract (**de** from); *(charbon)* to mine ▪ **extrait** *nm* extract; **e. de naissance** birth certificate

extralucide [ɛkstralysid] *adj & nmf* clairvoyant

extraordinaire [ɛkstraɔrdinɛr] *adj* extraordinary

extraterrestre [ɛkstraterɛstr] *adj & nmf* extraterrestrial

extravagant, -e [ɛkstravagã, -ãt] *adj (idée, comportement)* extravagant

extraverti, -e [ɛkstraverti] *nmf* extrovert

extrême [ɛkstrɛm] **1** *adj* extreme; *Pol* **l'e. droite/gauche** the far *or* extreme right/left **2** *nm* extreme ▪ **Extrême-Orient** *nm* **l'E.** the Far East ▪ **extrémiste** *adj & nmf* extremist ▪ **extrémité** *nf (bout)* extremity, end; **extrémités** *(pieds et mains)* extremities

exulter [ɛgzylte] *vi* to exult, to rejoice

Ff

F, f [εf] *nm inv* F, f

fa [fa] *nm (note)* F

fabricant, -e [fabrikɑ̃, -ɑ̃t] *nmf* manufacturer ■ **fabrication** *nf* manufacture

fabrique [fabrik] *nf* factory

fabriquer [fabrike] *vt (objet)* to make; *(en usine)* to manufacture

fabuleux, -euse [fabylø, -øz] *adj (légendaire, incroyable)* fabulous

façade [fasad] *nf* façade

face [fas] *nf (visage)* face; *(de cube, de montagne)* side; *(de pièce de monnaie)* head; **en f.** opposite; **en f. de** opposite, facing; *(en présence de)* in front of; **f. à** *(vis-à-vis)* facing; **f. à f.** face to face; **faire f. à qch** to face up to sth; **sauver/perdre la f.** to save/lose face

facette [fasɛt] *nf (de diamant, de problème)* facet

fâcher [faʃe] **se fâcher** *vpr* to get angry *(contre* with*)*; **se f. avec qn** to fall out with sb ■ **fâché, -e** *adj (air)* angry; *(personnes)* on bad terms; **f. contre qn** angry with sb

facile [fasil] *adj* easy; **f. à vivre** easy to get along with ■ **facilité** *nf (simplicité)* easiness; *(aisance)* ease ■ **faciliter** *vt* to make easier, to facilitate

façon [fasɔ̃] *nf (manière)* way; **la f. dont elle parle** the way (in which) she talks; **de quelle f.?** how?; **de toute f.** anyway, anyhow; **de f. à** so as to; **de f. générale** generally speaking; **d'une f. ou d'une autre** one way or another; **à ma f.** my way, (in) my own way

façonner [fasɔne] *vt (former)* to shape; *(fabriquer)* to make

facteur [faktœr] *nm* **(a)** *(employé)* Br postman, *Am* mailman **(b)** *(élément)* factor

facture [faktyr] *nf Com* bill, invoice ■ **facturer** *vt* to bill, to invoice

facultatif, -ive [fakyltatif, -iv] *adj (travail)* optional; *Scol* **matière facultative** optional subject

faculté [fakylte] *nf* **(a)** *(aptitude)* faculty **(b)** *(d'université)* faculty; **à la f.** *Br* at university, *Am* at school

fade [fad] *adj* insipid

faible [fɛbl] **1** *adj* weak, feeble; *(voix)* faint; *(chances)* slight; *(revenus)* small **2** *nm* weakling; **f. d'esprit** feeble-minded person ■ **faiblesse** *nf (physique, morale)* weakness

faiblir [fɛblir] *vi (forces)* to weaken; *(courage, vue)* to fail; *(vent)* to drop

faïence [fajɑ̃s] *nf (matière)* earthenware; **faïences** *(objets)* earthenware

faille[1] [faj] *nf Géol* fault; *Fig* flaw

faille[2] [faj] *voir* **falloir**

faillir* [fajir] *vi* **il a failli tomber** he almost *or* nearly fell

faillite [fajit] *nf Com* bankruptcy; **faire f.** to go bankrupt

faim [fɛ̃] *nf* hunger; **avoir f.** to be hungry

fainéant, -e [feneɑ̃, -ɑ̃t] **1** *adj* idle **2** *nmf* idler

FAIRE* [fɛr] **1** *vt (faute, gâteau, voyage, repas)* to make; *(devoir, ménage)* to do; *(rêve, chute)* to have; *(sourire)* to give; *(promenade, sieste)* to have, to take; *(guerre)* to wage, to make; **ça fait 10 mètres de large** it's 10 metres wide; **ça fait 10 euros** it's *or* that's 10 euros; **2 et 2 font 4** 2 and 2 are 4; **que f.?** what's to be done? **f. du tennis/du piano** to play tennis/the piano; **f. du droit** to study law; **f. du bien à qn** to do sb good; **f. du mal à qn** to hurt *or* harm sb; **ça ne fait rien** that doesn't matter;

comment as-tu fait pour...? how did you manage to...?; **'oui', fit-elle** 'yes', she said

2 *vi (agir)* to do; *(paraître)* to look; **f. comme chez soi** to make oneself at home; **elle ferait bien de partir** she'd do well to leave

3 *v impersonnel* **il fait beau/froid** it's fine/cold; **il fait du vent** it's windy; **quel temps fait-il?** what's the weather like?; **ça fait deux ans que je ne l'ai pas vu** I haven't seen him for two years, it's (been) two years since I saw him

4 *v aux (+ infinitive)* **f. construire une maison** to have a house built (**à qn** for sb; **par qn** by sb); **f. souffrir qn** to make sb suffer

5 se faire *vpr (fabrication)* to be made; *(activité)* to be done; **se f. couper les cheveux** to have one's hair cut; **se f. renverser** to get knocked down; **se f. des amis** to make friends; **il se fait tard** it's getting late; **comment se fait-il que...?** how is it that...?; **ça se fait beaucoup** people do that a lot; **se f. à qch** to get used to sth; **ne t'en fais pas!** don't worry! ■ **faire-part** *nm inv* announcement

fais, fait [fɛ] *voir* **faire**

faisable [fəzabl] *adj* feasible

faisan [fəzɑ̃] *nm* pheasant

faisceau, -x [fɛso] *nm (rayons)* beam

fait, -e [fɛ, fɛt] **1** *pp de* **faire 2** *adj (fromage)* ripe; *(ongles)* polished; **tout f.** ready made **3** *nm (événement)* event; *(donnée, réalité)* fact; **du f. de** on account of; **au f.** *(à propos)* by the way; **en f.** in fact; **prendre qn sur le f.** to catch sb red-handed *or* in the act; *Journ* **faits divers** ≃ news in brief

faîte [fɛt] *nm (haut)* top; *Fig (apogée)* height

faites [fɛt] *voir* **faire**

falaise [falɛz] *nf* cliff

FALLOIR* [falwar] **1** *v impersonnel* **il faut qn/qch** I/you/we/*etc* need sb/sth; **il te faut un stylo** you need a pen; **il faut partir** I/you/we/*etc* have to go; **il faut que je parte** I have to go; **il faudrait qu'elle reste** she ought to stay; **il**

faut un jour it takes a day (**pour faire** to do); **comme il faut** *(adjectif)* proper; *(adverbe)* properly; **s'il le faut** if need be

2 s'en falloir *vpr* **il s'en est fallu de peu qu'il ne pleure** he almost cried; **tant s'en faut** far from it

famé, -e [fame] **mal f.** *adj* disreputable

fameux, -euse [famø, -øz] *adj (célèbre)* famous

familial, -e, -aux, -ales [familjal, -o] *adj (atmosphère, ennuis)* family; *(entreprise)* family-run

familier, -ère [familje, -ɛr] *adj (connu)* familiar (**à** to); *(désinvolte)* informal (**avec** with); *(locution)* colloquial ■ **familiariser 1** *vt* to familiarize (**avec** with) **2 se familiariser** *vpr* to familiarize oneself (**avec** with)

famille [famij] *nf* family; **f. d'accueil** host family; **f. monoparentale** single-parent family; **f. nucléaire** nuclear family

famine [famin] *nf* famine

fanatique [fanatik] **1** *adj* fanatical **2** *nmf* fanatic

faner [fane] **se faner** *vpr (fleur, beauté)* to fade ■ **fané, -e** *adj* faded

fanfare [fɑ̃far] *nf (orchestre)* brass band

fantaisie [fɑ̃tezi] *nf (imagination)* imagination; **bijoux f.** costume jewellery

fantastique [fɑ̃tastik] *adj (imaginaire, excellent)* fantastic

fantôme [fɑ̃tom] **1** *nm* ghost, phantom **2** *adj* **ville/train f.** ghost town/train

faon [fɑ̃] *nm* fawn

farce¹ [fars] *nf (tour)* practical joke, prank; **faire une f. à qn** to play a practical joke *or* a prank on sb ■ **farceur, -euse** *nmf (blagueur)* practical joker

farce² [fars] *nf Culin* stuffing ■ **farcir** *vt (poulet)* to stuff

fardeau, -x [fardo] *nm* burden, load

farder [farde] **1** *vt (maquiller)* to make up **2 se farder** *vpr (se maquiller)* to put

on one's make-up; **se f. les yeux** to put eyeshadow on

farine [farin] *nf (de blé)* flour

farouche [faruʃ] *adj (personne)* shy; *(animal)* timid; *(haine)* fierce

fart [far] *nm* wax

fascicule [fasikyl] *nm (de publication)* instalment; *(brochure)* brochure

fasciner [fasine] *vt* to fascinate ▪ **fascination** *nf* fascination

fascisme [faʃism] *nm* fascism ▪ **fasciste** *adj & nmf* fascist

fasse(s), fassent [fas] *voir* **faire**

faste [fast] **1** *nm* splendour **2** *adj* **jour f.** lucky day

fastidieux, -euse [fastidjø, -øz] *adj* tedious

fatal, -e, -als, -ales [fatal] *adj (mortel)* fatal; *(inévitable)* inevitable; *(moment)* fateful ▪ **fataliste** *adj* fatalistic ▪ **fatalité** *nf (destin)* fate ▪ **fatidique** *adj (jour, date)* fateful

fatigant, -e [fatigã, -ãt] *adj (épuisant)* tiring; *(ennuyeux)* tiresome

fatigue [fatig] *nf* tiredness

fatiguer [fatige] **1** *vt (épuiser)* to tire; *(yeux)* to strain; *(ennuyer)* to bore **2** *vi (personne)* to get tired; *(moteur)* to labour **3 se fatiguer** *vpr (s'épuiser, se lasser)* to get tired (**de** of); **se f. à faire qch** to tire oneself out doing sth; **se f. les yeux** to strain one's eyes ▪ **fatigué, -e** *adj* tired (**de** of)

faucher [foʃe] *vt (herbe)* to mow; *(blé)* to reap

faucon [fokɔ̃] *nm* hawk, falcon

faudra, faudrait [fodra, fodrɛ] *voir* **falloir**

faufiler [fofile] **se faufiler** *vpr* to work one's way (**dans** through *or* into; **entre** between)

faune [fon] *nf* wildlife, fauna

faussaire [fosɛr] *nm* forger

fausse [fos] *voir* **faux¹**

fausser [fose] *vt (réalité)* to distort

fausseté [foste] *nf (hypocrisie)* duplicity

faut [fo] *voir* **falloir**

faute [fot] *nf (erreur)* mistake; *(res-*

ponsabilité) & *(au tennis)* fault; *(au football)* foul; **c'est de ta f.** it's your fault; **f. de mieux** for want of anything better; **faire une f.** to make a mistake; **f. professionnelle** professional misconduct

fauteuil [fotœj] *nm* armchair; *(de président)* chair; **f. roulant** wheelchair

fautif, -ive [fotif, -iv] *adj (personne)* at fault; *(erroné)* faulty

fauve [fov] *nm* big cat

faux, fausse [fo, fos] **1** *adj (pas vrai)* false, untrue; *(inexact)* wrong; *(inauthentique)* false; *(monnaie)* forged; *(tableau)* fake; **faire une fausse couche** to have a miscarriage; **f. départ** false start **2** *adv (chanter)* out of tune **3** *nm (tableau)* fake; *(document)* forgery ▪ **faux-filet** *(pl* **faux-filets**) *nm* sirloin ▪ **faux-monnayeur** *(pl* **faux-monnayeurs**) *nm* counterfeiter

faveur [favœr] *nf Br* favour, *Am* favor; **en f. de** *(au profit de)* in aid of; **être en f. de qch** to be in *Br* favour *or Am* favor of sth ▪ **favorable** *adj Br* favourable (**à** to), *Am* favorable (**à** to) ▪ **favori, -e** *adj & nmf Br* favourite, *Am* favorite ▪ **favoriser** *vt* to *Br* favour *or Am* favor

fax [faks] *nm (appareil, message)* fax; **envoyer un f.** to send a fax (**à** to); **envoyer qch par f.** to send sth by fax; **recevir un f.** to receive a fax; *(de* from) ▪ **faxer** *vt (message)* to fax

fécond, -e [fekɔ̃, -ɔ̃d] *adj (femme, idée)* fertile ▪ **fécondité** *nf* fertility

féculent [fekylã] *nm* starchy food

fédéral, -e, -aux, -ales [federal, -o] *adj* federal ▪ **fédération** *nf* federation

fée [fe] *nf* fairy ▪ **féerique** *adj (personnage, monde)* fairy; *(vision)* enchanting

feindre* [fɛ̃dr] *vt* to feign; **f. de faire qch** to pretend to do sth ▪ **feint, -e** *adj* feigned ▪ **feinte** *nf (ruse)* ruse

fêler [fele] *vt*, **se fêler** *vpr* to crack

féliciter [felisite] *vt* to congratulate (**de** *ou* **sur** on) ▪ **félicitations** *nfpl* congratulations (**pour** on)

félin [felɛ̃] *nm* feline

fêlure [felyr] *nf* crack

femelle [fəmɛl] *adj & nf* female

féminin, -e [feminɛ̃, -in] *adj (prénom, hormone)* female; *(trait, intuition, pronom)* feminine; *(mode)* women's ■ **féministe** *adj & nmf* feminist ■ **féminité** *nf* femininity

femme [fam] *nf* woman (*pl* women); *(épouse)* wife; **f. de ménage** cleaning lady, maid; **f. au foyer** housewife

fendiller [fɑ̃dije] **se fendiller** *vpr* to crack

fendre [fɑ̃dr] **1** *vt (bois, lèvre)* to split; *Fig (cœur)* to break **2 se fendre** *vpr (se fissurer)* to crack

fenêtre [fənɛtr] *nf* window

fenouil [fənuj] *nm* fennel

fente [fɑ̃t] *nf (de tirelire, de palissade)* slit; *(de rocher)* split, crack

féodal, -e, -aux, -ales [feɔdal, -o] *adj* feudal

fer [fɛr] *nm* iron; *(partie métallique)* metal (part); **barre de** *ou* **en f.** iron bar; **f. à cheval** horseshoe; **f. forgé** wrought iron; **f. à repasser** iron

fera, ferait etc [fəra, fərɛ] *voir* **faire**

férié [ferje] *adj m* **jour f.** (public) holiday

ferme¹ [fɛrm] *nf* farm; *(maison)* farm(house)

ferme² [fɛrm] **1** *adj (fruit, beurre, décision)* firm; *(autoritaire)* firm (**avec** with) **2** *adv (travailler)* hard; **s'ennuyer f.** to be bored stiff

fermenter [fɛrmɑ̃te] *vi* to ferment

fermer [fɛrme] **1** *vt* to close, to shut; *(gaz, radio)* to turn *or* switch off; *(passage)* to block; **f. qch à clef** to lock sth; **f. un magasin** *(définitivement)* to close *or* shut (down) a shop **2** *vi*, **se fermer** *vpr* to close, to shut ■ **fermé, -e** *adj (porte, magasin)* closed, shut; *(route, circuit)* closed; *(gaz)* off

fermeté [fɛrməte] *nf* firmness

fermeture [fɛrmətyr] *nf* closing, closure; *(heure)* closing time; *(mécanisme)* catch; **f. annuelle** annual closing; **f. Éclair®** *Br* zip (fastener), *Am* zipper

fermier, -ère [fɛrmje, -ɛr] *nmf* farmer

fermoir [fɛrmwar] *nm* clasp

féroce [ferɔs] *adj* ferocious ■ **férocité** *nf* ferocity

feront [fərɔ̃] *voir* **faire**

ferraille [fɛraj] *nf* scrap iron; **mettre qch à la f.** to scrap sth

ferronnerie [fɛrɔnri] *nf* ironwork

ferroviaire [fɛrɔvjɛr] *adj* **compagnie f.** *Br* railway company, *Am* railroad company

ferry [fɛri] (*pl* **ferrys** *ou* **ferries**) *nm* ferry

fertile [fɛrtil] *adj (terre, imagination)* fertile ■ **fertiliser** *vt* to fertilize ■ **fertilité** *nf* fertility

ferveur [fɛrvœr] *nf* fervour

fesse [fɛs] *nf* buttock; **fesses** *Br* bottom, *Am* butt ■ **fessée** *nf* spanking

festin [fɛstɛ̃] *nm* feast

festival, -als [fɛstival] *nm* festival

festivités [fɛstivite] *nfpl* festivities

fête [fɛt] *nf (civile)* holiday; *(religieuse)* festival, feast; *(entre amis)* party; **jour de f.** (public) holiday; **les fêtes (de Noël et du nouvel an)** the Christmas holidays; **faire la f.** to have a good time; **c'est sa f.** it's his/her saint's day; **la f. des Mères** Mother's Day; **la f. du Travail** Labour Day ■ **fêter** *vt (événement)* to celebrate

feu, -x [fø] *nm* fire; *(de réchaud)* burner; *Aut, Naut & Aviat (lumière)* light; **en f.** on fire, ablaze; **faire du f.** to light *or* make a fire; **mettre le f. à qch** to set fire to sth; **prendre f.** to catch fire; **donner du f. à qn** to give sb a light; **avez-vous du f.?** have you got a light?; **faire cuire qch à f. doux** to cook sth on a low heat; **au f.!** (there's a) fire!; *Aut* **f. rouge** *(lumière)* red light; *(objet)* traffic lights

feuille [fœj] *nf* leaf; *(de papier)* sheet; *(de journal)* newssheet; **f. de garde** *(d'un fax)* cover sheet; **f. de maladie** = form given by doctor to patient for claiming reimbursement from the Social Security; **f. de paie** *Br* pay slip, *Am* pay stub ■ **feuillage** *nm* leaves, foliage

feuilleté [fœjte] *nm* **f. au fromage** cheese pastry

feuilleter [fœjte] *vt (livre)* to flip through

feuilleton [fœjtɔ̃] *nm (roman, film)* serial; **f. télévisé** television serial

feutre [føtr] *nm* felt; **(crayon) f.** felt-tip(ped) pen

fève [fɛv] *nf* (broad) bean

février [fevrije] *nm* February

fiable [fjabl] *adj* reliable

fiancer [fjɑ̃se] **se fiancer** *vpr* to become engaged **(avec** to) ▪ **fiabilité** *nf* reliability ▪ **fiançailles** *nfpl* engagement ▪ **fiancé** *nm* fiancé; **fiancés** engaged couple ▪ **fiancée** *nf* fiancée

fibre [fibr] *nf* fibre; **f. de verre** fibreglass; **fibres optiques** optical fibres

ficelle [fisɛl] *nf (de corde)* string; *(pain)* = long thin loaf ▪ **ficeler** *vt* to tie up

fiche [fiʃ] *nf* (a) *(carte)* index card; *(papier)* form; **f. de paie** *Br* pay slip, *Am* pay stub (b) *Él (broche)* pin; *(prise)* plug ▪ **fichier** *nm* card index, file; *Ordinat* file

ficher [fiʃe] *vt (enfoncer)* to drive in; *(mettre sur fiche)* to put on file

fictif, -ive [fiktif, -iv] *adj* fictitious ▪ **fiction** *nf* fiction

fidèle [fidɛl] **1** *adj* faithful **(à** to) **2** *nmf* faithful supporter; **les fidèles** *(croyants)* the faithful; *(à l'église)* the congregation ▪ **fidélité** *nf* fidelity, faithfulness

fier¹ [fje] **se fier** *vpr* **se f. à qn/qch** to trust sb/sth

fier², fière [fjɛr] *adj* proud **(de** of) ▪ **fierté** *nf* pride

fièvre [fjɛvr] *nf (maladie)* fever; **avoir de la f.** to have a temperature *or* a fever ▪ **fiévreux, -euse** *adj* feverish

figer [fiʒe] **1** *vt (liquide)* to congeal **2 se figer** *vpr (liquide)* to congeal; *Fig (sourire, personne)* to freeze

figue [fig] *nf* fig

figurant, -e [figyrɑ̃, -ɑ̃t] *nmf (de film)* extra

figure [figyr] *nf (visage)* face; *(personnage)* figure

figurer [figyre] **1** *vt* to represent **2** *vi* to appear **3 se figurer** *vpr* to imagine;

figure-toi que...? would you believe that...?

fil [fil] *nm* (a) *(de coton, de pensée)* thread; *(lin)* linen; **f. dentaire** dental floss (b) *(métallique)* wire; **f. de fer** wire (c) *(expressions)* **au f. de l'eau** with the current; **au bout du f.** *(au téléphone)* on the line

file [fil] *nf* line; *Aut (couloir)* lane; **f. d'attente** *Br* queue, *Am* line; **être en double f.** to be double-parked

filer [file] **1** *vt (coton)* to spin; **f. qn** to shadow sb **2** *vi (partir)* to rush off; *(aller vite)* to speed along; *(collant)* to run, *Br* to ladder

filet [filɛ] *nm* (a) *(en maille)* net; **f. à provisions** string bag (b) *(d'eau)* trickle (c) *(de poisson, de viande)* fillet

filial, -e, -aux, -ales [filjal, -o] *adj* filial ▪ **filiale** *nf* subsidiary (company)

filière [filjɛr] *nf (voie obligée)* channels; *(domaine d'études)* field of study; *(organisation clandestine)* network; **suivre la f. normale** to go through the official channels

fille [fij] *nf (enfant)* girl; *(descendante)* daughter; **petite f.** (little *or* young) girl; **jeune f.** girl, young lady ▪ **fillette** *nf* little girl

film [film] *nm (œuvre)* film, movie; *(pour photo)* film; **voir un f.** to see a film *or* movie; **f. muet** silent film *or* movie; **f. policier** thriller ▪ **filmer** *vt (personne, scène)* to film

fils [fis] *nm* son

filtre [filtr] *nm* filter; **bout f.** filter tip ▪ **filtrer 1** *vt (liquide, lumière)* to filter; *(personne, nouvelles)* to screen **2** *vi (liquide)* to filter (through); *(nouvelle)* to leak out

fin¹ [fɛ̃] *nf* (a) *(conclusion)* end; **mettre f. à qch** to put an end to sth; **prendre f.** to come to an end; **à la f.** in the end; **f. mai** at the end of May (b) *(but)* end, aim

fin², fine [fɛ̃, fin] **1** *adj (pointe, tissu)* fine; *(couche)* thin; *(visage, mets)* delicate; *(oreille)* sharp; *(intelligent)* subtle **2** *adv (couper, moudre)* finely

final, -e, -aux *ou* **-als, -ales** [final, -o] *adj* final ▪ **finale** *nf Sport* final

■ **finaliste** *nmf Sport* finalist

finance [finɑ̃s] *nf* finance ■ **finance-ment** *nm* financing ■ **financer** *vt* to finance

financier, -ère [finɑ̃sje, -ɛr] **1** *adj* financial **2** *nm* financier

finesse [finɛs] *nf (de pointe)* fineness; *(de taille)* thinness; *(de visage)* delicacy; *(intelligence)* subtlety

finir [finir] **1** *vt* to finish; *(discours, vie)* to end, to finish **2** *vi* to finish, to end; **f. de faire qch** to finish doing sth; **f. par faire qch** to end up doing sth; **f. par qch** to finish (up) *or* end (up) with sth ■ **fini, -e** *adj (produit)* finished; *(univers) & Math* finite

Finlande [fɛ̃lɑ̃d] *nf* la F. Finland ■ **fin-landais, -e 1** *adj* Finnish **2** *nmf* F., **Fin-landaise** Finn

firme [firm] *nf* firm

fisc [fisk] *nm Br* ≃ Inland Revenue, *Am* ≃ Internal Revenue ■ **fiscal, -e, -aux, -ales** *adj* **charges fiscales** taxes; **fraude fiscale** tax fraud *or* evasion ■ **fiscalité** *nf* tax system

fissure [fisyr] *nf* crack ■ **se fissurer** *vpr* to crack

fixation [fiksasjɔ̃] *nf (action)* fixing; *(dispositif)* fastening, binding; *(idée fixe)* fixation; **faire une f. sur qn/qch** to be fixated on sb/sth

fixe [fiks] *adj* fixed ■ **fixement** [-əmɑ̃] *adv* **regarder qn/qch f.** to stare at sb/sth

fixer [fikse] **1** *vt (attacher)* to fix (à to); *(date, règle)* to decide, to fix; **f. qn/qch du regard** to stare at sb/sth; **être fixé** *(décidé)* to be decided **2 se fixer** *vpr (regard)* to become fixed; *(s'établir)* to settle

flacon [flakɔ̃] *nm* small bottle

flageolet [flaʒɔlɛ] *nm (haricot)* fla-geolet bean

flagrant, -e [flagrɑ̃, -ɑ̃t] *adj (injustice)* flagrant, blatant; **pris en f. délit** caught in the act *or* red-handed

flair [flɛr] *nm (de chien)* (sense of) smell, scent; *(de personne)* intuition, flair ■ **flairer** *vt* to smell, to sniff at

flamand, -e [flamɑ̃, -ɑ̃d] **1** *adj* Fle-mish **2** *nmf* F., **Flamande** Fleming **3** *nm (langue)* Flemish

flamant [flamɑ̃] *nm* **f. rose** flamingo

flambant [flɑ̃bɑ̃] *adv* **f. neuf** brand new

flambeau, -x [flɑ̃bo] *nm* torch

flamber [flɑ̃be] *vi* to blaze

flamboyer [flɑ̃bwaje] *vi* to blaze

flamme [flam] *nf* flame; **en flammes** on fire

flan [flɑ̃] *nm* baked custard

flanc [flɑ̃] *nm* side; *(d'armée, d'animal)* flank

Flandre [flɑ̃dr] *nf* la F., **les Flandres** Flanders

flâner [flɑne] *vi* to stroll

flanquer [flɑ̃ke] *vt* to flank (**de** with)

flaque [flak] *nf (d'eau)* puddle

flash [flaʃ] *(pl* **flashes***) nm Phot* flash-light; *Radio & TV* **f. d'informations** (news)flash

flatter [flate] *vt* to flatter ■ **flatterie** *nf* flattery ■ **flatteur, -euse** *adj* flattering

fléau, -x [fleo] *nm (catastrophe)* scourge

flèche [flɛʃ] *nf (projectile)* arrow; *(d'église)* spire; **monter en f.** *(prix)* to shoot up ■ **fléchette** *nf* dart; **fléchet-tes** *(jeu)* darts

fléchir [fleʃir] **1** *vt (ployer)* to bend **2** *vi (ployer)* to bend; *(faiblir)* to give way; *(baisser)* to fall

flétrir [fletrir] *vt,* **se flétrir** *vpr* to wi-ther

fleur [flœr] *nf* flower; *(d'arbre, d'ar-buste)* blossom; **en fleur(s)** in flower, in bloom; *(arbre)* in blossom

fleurir [flœrir] **1** *vt (table)* to decorate with flowers; *(tombe)* to lay flowers on **2** *vi (plante)* to flower, to bloom; *(arbre)* to blossom; *Fig (prospérer)* to flourish ■ **fleuri, -e** *adj (fleur, jardin)* in bloom; *(tissu)* floral

fleuriste [flœrist] *nmf* florist

fleuve [flœv] *nm* river

flexible [flɛksibl] *adj* flexible ■ **flexi-bilité** *nf* flexibility

flocon [flɔkɔ̃] *nm* flake; **f. de neige** snowflake

floraison [flɔrezɔ̃] *nf* flowering; **en pleine f.** in full bloom ∎ **floral, -e, -aux, -ales** *adj* floral

flore [flɔr] *nf* flora

florissant, -e [flɔrisɑ̃, -ɑ̃t] *adj* flourishing

flot [flo] *nm (de larmes)* flood, stream; **les flots** *(la mer)* the waves; **à f.** *(bateau)* afloat; *Fig* **couler à flots** *(argent, vin)* to flow freely

flotte [flɔt] *nf (de bateaux, d'avions)* fleet

flotter [flɔte] *vi (bateau)* to float; *(drapeau)* to fly ∎ **flotteur** *nm* float

flou, -e [flu] *adj (image)* fuzzy, blurred; *(idée)* vague

fluet, -ette [flye, -et] *adj* thin, slender

fluide [flɥid] *adj & nm (liquide)* fluid

fluorescent, -e [flyɔresɑ̃, -ɑ̃t] *adj* fluorescent

flûte [flyt] *nf (instrument)* flute; *(verre)* champagne glass ∎ **flûtiste** *nmf Br* flautist, *Am* flutist

flux [fly] *nm (abondance)* flow; **f. et reflux** ebb and flow

foi [fwa] *nf* faith; **être de bonne/mauvaise f.** to be sincere/insincere

foie [fwa] *nm* liver; **f. gras** foie gras; **crise de f.** bout of indigestion

foin [fwɛ̃] *nm* hay

foire [fwar] *nf* fair

fois [fwa] *nf* time; **une f.** once; **deux f.** twice; **trois f.** three times; **deux f. trois** two times three; **chaque f. que...** whenever..., each time (that)...; **une f. qu'il sera arrivé** once he has arrived; **à la f.** at the same time, at once; **il était une fois...** once upon a time there was...

foisonner [fwazɔne] *vi* to abound (**de** *ou* **en** in)

fol [fɔl] *voir* **fou**

folie [fɔli] *nf* madness; **aimer qn à la f.** to be madly in love with sb

folklore [fɔlklɔr] *nm* folklore ∎ **folklorique** *adj (costume)* traditional; *(musique, danse)* folk

folle [fɔl] *voir* **fou**

foncé, -e [fɔ̃se] *adj* dark

foncer [fɔ̃se] **1** *vi (aller vite)* to tear *or* charge along; **f. sur qn/qch** to swoop on sb/sth **2** *vti (couleur)* to darken

foncier, -ère [fɔ̃sje, -ɛr] *adj (taxe)* land

fonction [fɔ̃ksjɔ̃] *nf* function; *(emploi)* office; **en f. de** according to; **faire f. de** *(personne)* to act as; *(objet)* to serve *or* act as; **prendre ses fonctions** to take up one's duties; **la f. publique** the civil service ∎ **fonctionnaire** *nmf* civil servant; **haut f.** high-ranking civil servant ∎ **fonctionnel, -elle** *adj* functional

fonctionner [fɔ̃ksjɔne] *vi (machine)* to work, to function; **faire f. qch** to operate sth ∎ **fonctionnement** *nm (de machine)* working; **en état de f.** in working order

fond [fɔ̃] *nm (de boîte, de jardin, de vallée)* bottom; *(de salle, d'armoire)* back; *(arrière-plan)* background; **au f. de** *(boîte, jardin)* at the bottom of; *(salle)* at the back of; *Fig* **au f., dans le f.** basically; **à f.** *(connaître)* thoroughly; **de f. en comble** from top to bottom; **course de f.** long-distance race; **ski de f.** cross-country skiing; **bruits de f.** background noise; **f. sonore** background music

fondamental, -e, -aux, -ales [fɔ̃damɑ̃tal, -o] *adj* fundamental, basic

fonder [fɔ̃de] **1** *vt (ville)* to found; *(commerce)* to set up; *(famille)* to start; **f. qch sur qch** to base sth on sth **2 se fonder** *vpr* **se f. sur qch** *(sujet, théorie)* to be based on sth ∎ **fondateur, -trice** *nmf* founder ∎ **fondation** *nf (création, œuvre)* foundation (**de** of); **fondations** *(de bâtiment)* foundations ∎ **fondement** *nm* foundation

fondre [fɔ̃dr] **1** *vt (métal)* to melt down; *(neige)* to melt; **faites f. le chocolat** melt the chocolate **2** *vi (se liquéfier)* to melt; **f. en larmes** to burst into tears; **f. sur qch** to swoop on sth **3 se fondre** *vpr* **se f. dans qch** *(disparaître)* to merge into sth ∎ **fondant, -e** *adj (aliment)* which melts in the mouth

fonds [fɔ̃] **1** *nm (organisme)* fund; *(de bibliothèque)* collection; **f. de commerce** business; **F. monétaire international** International Monetary Fund

2 *nmpl (argent)* funds; **être en f.** to be in funds

font [fɔ̃] *voir* faire

fontaine [fɔ̃tɛn] *nf (construction)* fountain; *(source)* spring

fonte [fɔ̃t] *nf* (a) *(de neige)* melting; *(d'acier)* smelting (b) *(alliage)* cast iron; **en f.** *(poêle)* cast-iron (c) *Typ* font

football [futbol] *nm Br* football, *Am* soccer ■ **footballeur, -euse** *nmf Br* footballer, *Am* soccer player

forage [fɔraʒ] *nm* drilling, boring

forain [fɔrɛ̃] *nm* fairground stallholder

force [fɔrs] *nf (violence)* & *Phys* force; *(vigueur)* strength; **de toutes ses forces** with all one's strength; **de f.** by force, forcibly; **à f. de faire qch** through doing sth; **les forces armées** the armed forces ■ **forcément** *adv* inevitably; **pas f.** not necessarily

forcer [fɔrse] **1** *vt (obliger)* to force; *(porte)* to force open; *(voix)* to strain; **f. qn à faire qch** to force sb to do sth **2** *vi (appuyer, tirer)* to force it; *(se surmener)* to overdo it **3 se forcer** *vpr* to force oneself (**à faire** to do)

forer [fɔre] *vt* to drill, to bore

forêt [fɔrɛ] *nf* forest

forfait [fɔrfɛ] *nm* (a) *(prix)* all-in price; *(de ski)* pass; **f. week-end** week-end package (b) *(crime)* heinous crime ■ **forfaitaire** *adj (indemnités)* basic; **prix f.** all-in price

forge [fɔrʒ] *nf* forge ■ **forger** *vt (métal, liens)* to forge; *Fig (caractère)* to form ■ **forgeron** [-ərɔ̃] *nm* (black)smith

formaliser [fɔrmalize] **se formaliser** *vpr* to take offence (**de** at)

formalité [fɔrmalite] *nf* formality

format [fɔrma] *nm* format

formater [fɔrmate] *vt Ordinat* to format

formation [fɔrmasjɔ̃] *nf (de roche, de mot)* formation; *(éducation)* education; **f. permanente** continuing education; **f. professionnelle** vocational training ■ **formateur, -trice 1** *adj* formative **2** *nmf* trainer

forme [fɔrm] *nf (contour)* shape, form; *(manière, bonne santé)* form; **en f. de** qch in the shape of sth; **en f. de poire** pear-shaped; **sous f. de qch** in the form of sth; **en (pleine) f.** *(en bonne santé)* on (top) form

formel, -elle [fɔrmɛl] *adj (structure)* formal; *(personne, preuve)* positive; *(interdiction)* strict

former [fɔrme] **1** *vt (groupe, caractère)* to form; *(apprenti)* to train **2 se former** *vpr (apparaître)* to form; *(association, liens)* to be formed; *(apprendre son métier)* to train oneself

formidable [fɔrmidabl] *adj (fantastique)* great; *(gigantesque)* tremendous

formulaire [fɔrmylɛr] *nm* form

formule [fɔrmyl] *nf Math* formula; *(phrase)* expression; *(solution)* method; **nouvelle f.** *(menu)* new-style; **f. magique** magic formula ■ **formulation** *nf* formulation ■ **formuler** *vt* to formulate

fort¹, -e [fɔr, fɔrt] **1** *adj (vigoureux)* strong; *(gros, important)* large; *(pluie, mer, chute de neige)* heavy; *(voix)* loud; *(fièvre)* high; *(pente)* steep; **être f. en qch** *(doué)* to be good at sth

2 *adv (frapper, pleuvoir)* hard; *(parler)* loud(ly); *(serrer)* tight; **sentir f.** to have a strong smell; **respirer f.** to breathe heavily

3 *nm (spécialité)* strong point

fort² [fɔr] *nm Hist* & *Mil* fort ■ **forteresse** *nf* fortress

fortifié, -e [fɔrtifje] *adj (ville, camp)* fortified ■ **fortification** *nf* fortification

fortifier [fɔrtifje] *vt (mur, ville)* to fortify; *(corps)* to strengthen ■ **fortifiant** *nm* tonic

fortune [fɔrtyn] *nf (richesse, hasard)* fortune; **faire f.** to make one's fortune

fosse [fos] *nf (trou)* pit; **f. d'orchestre** orchestra pit

fossé [fose] *nm* ditch; *(de château)* moat; *Fig (désaccord)* gulf

fossette [fosɛt] *nf* dimple

fossoyeur [foswajœr] *nm* gravedigger

fou, folle [fu, fɔl]

> **fol** is used before masculine singular nouns beginning with a vowel or h mute.

1 *adj (personne, projet)* mad, insane;

(succès, temps) tremendous; *(envie)* wild, mad; *(espoir)* foolish; **f. de qch** *(musique, personne)* mad about sth; **f. de joie** beside oneself with joy **2** *nmf* madman, *f* madwoman **3** *nm (bouffon)* jester; *Échecs* bishop

foudre [fudr] *nf* **la f.** lightning ▪ **foudroyant,-e** *adj (succès, vitesse)* staggering ▪ **foudroyer** *vt* to strike; **f. qn du regard** to give sb a withering look

fouet [fwɛ] *nm* whip; *Culin* whisk; **coup de f.** lash (with a whip); **de plein f.** head-on ▪ **fouetter** *vt* to whip; *(sujet: pluie)* to lash (against); **crème fouettée** whipped cream

fougère [fuʒɛr] *nf* fern

fougue [fug] *nf* fire, spirit ▪ **fougueux, -euse** *adj* fiery, ardent

fouille [fuj] **1** *nf (de personne, de bagages)* search **2** *nfpl* **fouilles archéologiques** excavations, dig ▪ **fouiller 1** *vt (personne, maison)* to search **2** *vi* **f. dans qch** *(tiroir)* to search through sth **3** *vti (creuser)* to dig

fouillis [fuji] *nm* jumble

foulard [fular] *nm* (head)scarf

foule [ful] *nf* crowd; **une f. de** *(objets)* a mass of

foulée [fule] *nf (de coureur, de cheval)* stride

fouler [fule] **1** *vt (sol)* to tread; **f. qch aux pieds** to trample sth underfoot **2** **se fouler** *vpr* **se f. la cheville** to sprain one's ankle ▪ **foulure** *nf* sprain

four [fur] *nm (de cuisine)* oven; *(de potier)* kiln; **petit f.** *(gâteau)* (small) fancy cake

fourche [furʃ] *nf (outil, embranchement)* fork; **faire une f.** to fork ▪ **fourcher** *vi (arbre)* to fork ▪ **fourchette** *nf (pour manger)* fork; *(de salaires)* bracket ▪ **fourchu, -e** *adj* forked

fourgon [furgɔ̃] *nm (camion)* van; **f. cellulaire** *Br* prison van, *Am* patrol wagon

fourmi [furmi] *nf (insecte)* ant; **avoir des fourmis dans les jambes** to have pins and needles in one's legs ▪ **fourmiller** *vi* to teem, to swarm (**de** with)

fourneau, -x [furno] *nm (de cuisine)* stove

fournir [furnir] *vt (approvisionner)* to supply (**en** with); *(alibi, preuve, document)* to provide; *(effort)* to make; **f. qch à qn** to provide sb with sth; **pièces à f.** required documents ▪ **fourni, -e** *adj (barbe)* bushy; **bien f.** *(boutique)* well-stocked ▪ **fournisseur** *nm (commerçant)* supplier; *Ordinat* **f. d'accès** access provider ▪ **fournitures** *nfpl* **f. de bureau** office supplies; **f. scolaires** school stationery

fourrage [furaʒ] *nm* fodder

fourré, -e [fure] **1** *adj (vêtement)* fur-lined; *(gâteau)* jam-/cream-filled **2** *nm* *Bot* thicket

fourreau, -x [furo] *nm (gaine)* sheath

fourrer [fure] **1** *vt (vêtement)* to fur-line; *(gâteau)* to fill **2** **se fourrer** *vpr* *Fam* to put oneself (**dans** in); **où est-il allé se f.?** where's he got to? ▪ **fourre-tout** *nm inv (sac)* *Br* holdall, *Am* carry-all

fourrière [furjɛr] *nf (lieu)* pound; **mettre à la f.** *(voiture)* to impound; *(chien)* to put in the pound

fourrure [furyr] *nf* fur

foyer [fwaje] *nm (maison)* home; *(d'étudiants)* residence; *(de travailleurs)* hostel; *(de théâtre)* foyer; *(de lunettes)* focus; *(de chaleur, d'infection)* source; *(d'incendie)* seat; *(âtre)* hearth; *(famille)* family

fracas [fraka] *nm* crash ▪ **fracassant, -e** *adj (nouvelle, révélation)* shattering ▪ **fracasser** *vt*, **se fracasser** *vpr* to smash

fraction [fraksjɔ̃] *nf* fraction; *(partie)* part ▪ **fractionner** *vt*, **se fractionner** *vpr* to split (up)

fracture [fraktyr] *nf* fracture ▪ **fracturer 1** *vt (porte)* to break open; *(os)* to fracture **2** **se fracturer** *vpr* **se f. la jambe** to fracture one's leg

fragile [fraʒil] *adj (objet, matériau)* fragile; *(santé, équilibre)* delicate; *(personne) (physiquement)* frail; *(mentalement)* sensitive ▪ **fragilité** *nf (d'objet, de matériau)* fragility; *(de personne)*

(physique) frailty; *(mentale)* sensitivity

fragment [fragmã] *nm* fragment

fraîcheur [frɛʃœr] *nf (d'aliments)* freshness; *(de température)* coolness

frais¹, fraîche [frɛ, frɛʃ] **1** *adj (aliment, fleurs)* fresh; *(vent, air)* cool, fresh; *(nouvelles)* recent; *(peinture)* wet **2** *adv* **servir f.** *(vin)* to serve chilled **3** *nm* **mettre qch au f.** to put sth in a cool place; *(au réfrigérateur)* to refrigerate sth; **il fait f.** it's cool ■ **fraîchir** *vi (temps)* to freshen

frais² [frɛ] *nmpl* expenses; **à mes f.** at my (own) expense; **faire des f.** to go to great expense; **f. de scolarité** school fees

fraise [frɛz] *nf (fruit)* strawberry; *(de dentiste)* drill ■ **fraisier** *nm (plante)* strawberry plant; *(gâteau)* strawberry cream cake

framboise [frãbwaz] *nf* raspberry ■ **framboisier** *nm* raspberry bush

franc¹, franche [frã, frãʃ] *adj* (a) *(sincère)* frank; *(visage)* open (b) *(net) (couleur)* pure (c) *(zone, ville, port)* free ■ **franchement** *adv (sincèrement)* frankly; *(vraiment)* really; *(sans ambiguïté)* clearly

franc² [frã] *nm Anciennement (monnaie)* franc

France *nf* **la F.** France ■ **français, -e 1** *adj* French **2** *nmf* **F.** Frenchman; **Française** Frenchwoman; **les F.** the French **3** *nm (langue)* French

franchir [frãʃir] *vt (obstacle)* to get over; *(fossé)* to jump over; *(frontière, ligne d'arrivée)* to cross; *(porte)* to go through; *(distance)* to cover

franchise [frãʃiz] *nf (sincérité)* frankness; *(exonération)* exemption; *Com* franchise; **f. postale** ≃ postage paid

franc-maçon [frãmasɔ̃] *(pl* **francs-maçons)** *nm* freemason

francophone [frãkɔfɔn] **1** *adj* French-speaking **2** *nmf* French speaker

franc-parler [frãparle] *nm* **avoir son f.** to speak one's mind

frange [frãʒ] *nf (de cheveux) Br* fringe, *Am* bangs; *(de vêtement)* fringe

frappe [frap] *nf (sur machine à écrire)*

typing; *(sur ordinateur)* keying; **faute de f.** typing error

frapper [frape] **1** *vt (battre)* to strike, to hit; *(monnaie)* to mint; **f. qn** *(impressionner)* to strike sb; *(impôt, mesure)* to hit sb **2** *vi (donner un coup)* to strike, to hit; **f. du pied** to stamp (one's foot); **f. du poing sur la table** to bang (on) the table; **f. à une porte** to knock on a door; **'entrez sans f.'** 'go straight in' ■ **frappant, -e** *adj* striking ■ **frappé, -e** *adj (boisson)* chilled

fraternel, -elle [fratɛrnɛl] *adj* fraternal, brotherly ■ **fraternité** *nf* fraternity, brotherhood

fraude [frod] *nf* fraud; **passer qch en f.** to smuggle sth in; **f. fiscale** tax evasion ■ **frauder 1** *vt* **f. le fisc** to evade tax **2** *vi* to cheat (**sur** on) ■ **fraudeur, -euse** *nmf* defrauder ■ **frauduleux, -euse** *adj* fraudulent

frayer [frɛje] **se frayer** *vpr* **se f. un chemin** to clear a way (**à travers/dans** through)

frayeur [frɛjœr] *nf* fright

fredonner [frədɔne] *vti* to hum

frein [frɛ] *nm* brake; **donner un coup de f.** to put on the brakes; **f. à main** handbrake ■ **freiner 1** *vt (véhicule)* to slow down; *(chute)* to break; *Fig (inflation)* to curb **2** *vi* to brake

frelaté, -e [frəlate] *adj (vin)* & *Fig* adulterated

frêle [frɛl] *adj* frail

frémir [fremir] *vi (personne)* to tremble (**de** with); *(feuilles)* to rustle; *(eau chaude)* to simmer ■ **frémissement** *nm (de peur)* shudder; *(de plaisir)* thrill; *(de colère)* quiver; *(de feuilles)* rustle; *(d'eau chaude)* simmering

frénétique [frenetik] *adj* frenzied

fréquent, -e [frekã, -ãt] *adj* frequent ■ **fréquence** *nf* frequency

fréquenter [frekãte] **1** *vt (lieu)* to frequent; **f. qn** to see sb regularly **2 se fréquenter** *vpr (se voir régulièrement)* to see each other socially ■ **fréquentation** *nf (de lieu)* frequenting; **fréquentations** *(relations)* company ■ **fréquenté, -e** *adj* **mal f.** disreputable, of

ill repute; **bien f.** reputable of good repute

frère [frɛr] *nm* brother

friable [frijabl] *adj* crumbly

friand, -e [frijɑ̃, -ɑ̃d] **1** *adj* **f. de qch** fond of sth **2** *nm (salé)* = small savoury pastry ▪ **friandise** *nf Br* titbit, *Am* tidbit

friction [friksjɔ̃] *nf (massage)* rubdown; *(de cuir chevelu)* scalp massage; *(désaccord)* friction ▪ **frictionner** *vt (partie du corps)* to rub; *(personne)* to rub down

Frigidaire® [friʒidɛr] *nm* fridge

frileux, -euse [frilø, -øz] *adj* **être f.** to feel the cold

friper [fripe] **1** *vt* to crumple **2 se friper** *vpr* to get crumpled ▪ **fripé, -e** *adj* crumpled

frire* [frir] **1** *vt* to fry **2** *vi* to fry; **faire f. qch** to fry sth

friser [frize] **1** *vt (cheveux)* to curl; *(effleurer)* to skim; **f. la catastrophe** to come within an inch of disaster **2** *vi (cheveux)* to curl; *(personne)* to have curly hair ▪ **frisé, -e** *adj (cheveux)* curly; *(personne)* curly-haired

frisson [frisɔ̃] *nm (de froid, de peur)* shiver; *(de plaisir)* thrill ▪ **frissonner** *vi (de froid, de peur)* to shiver

frit, -e [fri, -it] **1** *pp de* **frire 2** *adj* fried ▪ **frites** *nfpl Br* chips, *Am* (French) fries ▪ **friture** *nf (mode de cuisson)* frying; *(aliment)* fried food

frivole [frivɔl] *adj* frivolous

froid, -e [frwa, frwad] **1** *adj* cold **2** *nm* cold; **avoir f.** to be/catch cold; **il fait f.** it's cold

froisser [frwase] **1** *vt (tissu)* to crumple, to crease **2 se froisser** *vpr (tissu)* to crease, to crumple; **se f. un muscle** to strain a muscle

frôler [frole] *vt (effleurer)* to brush against, to touch lightly; *Fig (catastrophe)* to come close to

fromage [frɔmaʒ] *nm* cheese; **f. de chèvre** goat's cheese; **f. blanc** soft cheese; **f. frais** fromage frais ▪ **fromager, -ère** *nmf (fabricant)* cheesemaker; *(commerçant)* cheese seller ▪ **fromagerie** *nf (magasin)* cheese shop

froment [frɔmɑ̃] *nm* wheat

froncer [frɔ̃se] *vt (tissu)* to gather; **f. les sourcils** to frown

front [frɔ̃] *nm (du visage)* forehead; *(avant)*, *Mil & Pol* front; **de f.** *(heurter)* head-on; *(côte à côte)* abreast; *(à la fois)* (all) at once; **faire f. à qn/qch** to face up to sb/sth; **f. de mer** sea front ▪ **frontal, -e, -aux, -ales** *adj (collision)* head-on

frontière [frɔ̃tjɛr] **1** *nf (de pays)* border **2** *adj inv* **ville f.** border town ▪ **frontalier, -ère** *adj* **ville frontalière** border *or* frontier town

frotter [frɔte] **1** *vt* to rub; *(plancher)* to scrub; *(allumette)* to strike **2** *vi* to rub (**contre** against) **3 se frotter** *vpr* to rub oneself; **se f. le dos** to scrub one's back

fructifier [fryktifje] *vi (arbre, capital)* to bear fruit ▪ **fructueux, -euse** *adj* fruitful

frugal, -e, -aux, -ales [frygal, -o] *adj* frugal

fruit [frɥi] *nm* fruit; **des fruits** fruit; **un f.** a piece of fruit; **fruits de mer** seafood; **fruits secs** dried fruit ▪ **fruité, -e** *adj* fruity ▪ **fruitier** *adj m* **arbre f.** fruit tree

frustrer [frystre] *vt* **f. qn** to frustrate sb; **f. qn de qch** to deprive sb of sth ▪ **frustration** *nf* frustration ▪ **frustré, -e** *adj* frustrated

fuel [fjul] *nm* fuel oil

fugitif, -ive [fyʒitif, -iv] **1** *adj (passager)* fleeting **2** *nmf* runaway, fugitive

fugue [fyg] *nf* **faire une f.** *(enfant)* to run away ▪ **fuguer** *vi Fam* to run away

fuir* [fɥir] **1** *vt (pays)* to flee; *(personne)* to run away from; *(guerre)* to escape from **2** *vi (s'échapper)* to run away (**devant** from); *(gaz, robinet, stylo)* to leak ▪ **fuite** *nf (évasion)* flight (**devant** from); *(de gaz)* leak; **en f.** on the run; **prendre la f.** to take flight

fulgurant, -e [fylgyrɑ̃, -ɑ̃t] *adj (progrès)* spectacular; *(douleur)* shooting

fumer [fyme] **1** *vt (cigarette, poisson)* to smoke; **f. la pipe** to smoke a pipe **2** *vi (fumeur, moteur)* to smoke; *(liquide*

brûlant) to steam ■ **fumé, -e** *adj (poisson, verre)* smoked ■ **fumée** *nf* smoke; *(vapeur)* steam ■ **fumeur, -euse** *nmf* smoker

fumeux, -euse [fymø, -øz] *adj Fig (idée)* hazy

fumier [fymje] *nm (engrais)* manure, dung

funambule [fynãbyl] *nmf* tightrope walker

funèbre [fynɛbr] *adj (lugubre)* gloomy; **marche f.** funeral march ■ **funérailles** *nfpl* funeral ■ **funéraire** *adj* funeral

funiculaire [fynikylɛr] *nm* funicular

fur [fyr] **au fur et à mesure** *adv* as one goes along, progressively; **au f. et à mesure que...** as...

furent [fyr] *voir* **être**

furie [fyri] *nf (colère)* fury ■ **furieux, -euse** *adj (en colère)* furious (**contre** with)

fuseau, -x [fyzo] *nm (pantalon)* ski pants; *(bobine)* spindle; **f. horaire** time zone

fusée [fyze] *nf* rocket

fuselage [fyzlaʒ] *nm (d'avion)* fuselage

fusible [fyzibl] *nm Br* fuse, *Am* fuze

fusil [fyzi] *nm* rifle, gun; *(de chasse)* shotgun ■ **fusillade** *nf (tirs)* gunfire ■ **fusiller** *vt (exécuter)* to shoot

fusion [fyzjɔ̃] *nf* (**a**) *(de métal)* melting; *Phys* fusion; **métal en f.** molten metal (**b**) *(de sociétés)* merger ■ **fusionner** *vti (sociétés)* to merge

fut [fy] *voir* **être**

futile [fytil] *adj (personne)* frivolous; *(prétexte)* trivial

futur, -ure [fytyr] **1** *adj* future; **future mère** mother-to-be **2** *nmf* **mon f./ma future** my intended **3** *nm (avenir)* future

fuyant [fɥijã] *p prés de* **fuir** ■ **fuyant, -e** *adj (front)* receding; *(personne)* evasive ■ **fuyard, -e** *nmf* runaway

Gg

G, g [ʒe] *nm inv* G, g

gabarit [gabari] *nm (dimension)* size

gâcher [gɑʃe] *vt (gâter)* to spoil; *(gaspiller)* to waste ■ **gâchis** *nm* waste

gâchette [gɑʃɛt] *nf* trigger

gadget [gadʒɛt] *nm* gadget

gadoue [gadu] *nf* mud

gag [gag] *nm* gag

gage [gaʒ] *nm (garantie)* guarantee; *(au jeu)* forfeit; *(preuve)* token

gagnant, -e [gaɲɑ̃, -ɑ̃t] **1** *adj (billet, cheval)* winning **2** *nmf* winner

gagner [gaɲe] **1** *vt (par le travail)* to earn; *(par le jeu)* to win; *(obtenir)* to gain; *(atteindre)* to reach; *(sujet: feu, épidémie)* to spread to; **g. sa vie** to earn one's living; **g. du temps** *(aller plus vite)* to save time; *(temporiser)* to gain time; **g. du terrain** to gain ground; **g. de la place** to save space **2** *vi (être vainqueur)* to win ■ **gagne-pain** *nm inv* livelihood

gai, -e [gɛ] *adj* cheerful ■ **gaieté** *nf* cheerfulness

gaillard [gajar] *nm (homme)* fellow; **un grand g.** a strapping man

gain [gɛ̃] *nm (profit)* gain, profit; *(succès)* winning; **gains** *(à la Bourse)* profits; *(au jeu)* winnings

gaine [gɛn] *nf (étui)* sheath

gala [gala] *nm* gala

galant, -e [galɑ̃, -ɑ̃t] *adj (homme)* gallant; *(rendez-vous)* romantic ■ **galanterie** *nf* gallantry

galaxie [galaksi] *nf* galaxy

galerie [galri] *nf (passage, salle)* gallery; *(de taupe)* tunnel; **g. d'art** art gallery; **g. marchande** (shopping) mall

galet [galɛ] *nm* pebble; **plage de galets** shingle beach

galette [galɛt] *nf (gâteau)* butter cookie; *(crêpe)* buckwheat pancake; **g. des Rois** = Twelfth Night cake

Galles [gal] *nm* **pays de G.** Wales ■ **gallois, -e 1** *adj* Welsh **2** *nmf* **G.** Welshman; **Galloise** Welshwoman **3** *nm (langue)* Welsh

galon [galɔ̃] *nm (ruban)* braid; *(de soldat)* stripe

galop [galo] *nm* gallop; **aller au g.** to gallop ■ **galoper** *vi (cheval)* to gallop

gambader [gɑ̃bade] *vi* to leap *or* frisk about

Gambie [gɑ̃bi] *nf* **la G.** the Gambia

gamelle [gamɛl] *nf (de chien)* bowl; *(d'ouvrier)* billy(can); *(de soldat)* mess tin

gamin, -e [gamɛ̃, -in] *nmf (enfant)* kid

gamme [gam] *nf* Mus scale; *(éventail)* range; **téléviseur haut/bas de g.** top-of-the-range/bottom-of-the-range television

gang [gɑ̃g] *nm* gang

gant [gɑ̃] *nm* glove; **g. de toilette** ≃ facecloth

garage [garaʒ] *nm (de voitures)* garage ■ **garagiste** *nmf (mécanicien)* garage mechanic; *(propriétaire)* garage owner

garant, -e [garɑ̃, -ɑ̃t] *nmf* Jur *(personne)* guarantor; **se porter g. de qn** to stand guarantor for sb; **se porter g. de qch** to vouch for sth

garantie [garɑ̃ti] *nf* guarantee; *Fig (précaution)* safeguard; **sous g.** under guarantee ■ **garantir** *vt* to guarantee; *(emprunt)* to secure; **g. à qn que...** to guarantee sb that...

garçon [garsɔ̃] *nm* boy; *(jeune homme)* young man; *(serveur)* waiter; **g. de café** waiter; **g. d'honneur** best man; **g. manqué** tomboy

garde [gard] **1** *nm (gardien)* guard; *(soldat)* guardsman; **g. du corps** bodyguard

 2 *nf* (**a**) *(d'enfants, de bagages)* care, custody (**de** of); **avoir la g. de** to be in charge of; **prendre g.** to pay attention (**à qch** to sth); **être de g.** to be on duty; *(soldat)* to be on guard duty; **médecin de g.** duty doctor

 (**b**) *(escorte, soldats)* guard

 3 *nm* **g. de nuit** *(de malade)* night nurse ▪ **garde-à-vous** *nm inv Mil* (position of) attention; **se mettre au g.** to stand to attention ▪ **garde-chasse** (*pl* **gardes-chasses**) *nm* gamekeeper ▪ **garde-côte** (*pl* **garde-côtes**) *nm* *(bateau)* coastguard vessel ▪ **garde-manger** *nm inv (armoire)* food safe; *(pièce)* pantry, *Br* larder ▪ **garde-robe** (*pl* **garde-robes**) *nf* wardrobe

garder [garde] **1** *vt (conserver)* to keep; *(vêtement)* to keep on; *(habitude)* to keep up; *(surveiller)* to look after; *(défendre)* to protect **2 se garder** *vpr (aliment)* to keep; **se g. de qch** to beware of sth; **se g. de faire qch** to take care not to do sth

garderie [gardəri] *nf Br* (day) nursery, *Am* daycare center

gardien, -enne [gardjɛ̃, -ɛn] *nmf (d'immeuble, d'hôtel)* caretaker, *Am* janitor; *(de prison)* (prison) guard, *Br* warder; *(de zoo)* keeper; *(de musée) Br* attendant, *Am* guard; **g. de but** *(au football)* goalkeeper; **gardienne d'enfants** child minder, baby-sitter; **g. de nuit** night watchman; **g. de la paix** policeman

gare [gar] *nf (pour trains)* station; **g. routière** bus *or Br* coach station

garer [gare] **1** *vt (voiture)* to park **2 se garer** *vpr (automobiliste)* to park

gargariser [gargarize] **se gargariser** *vpr* to gargle

gargouiller [garguje] *vi (fontaine, eau)* to gurgle; *(ventre)* to rumble

garnir [garnir] *vt (décorer)* to trim (**de** with); *(équiper)* to fit out (**de** with); *(couvrir)* to cover; *(remplir)* to fill ▪ **garniture** *nf Culin* garnish

garnison [garnizɔ̃] *nf* garrison

gaspiller [gaspije] *vt* to waste ▪ **gaspillage** *nm* waste

gastronomie [gastrɔnɔmi] *nf* gastronomy

gâté, -e [gate] *adj (dent, fruit)* bad; **enfant g.** spoilt child

gâteau, -x [gato] *nm* cake; **g. sec** *Br* biscuit, *Am* cookie

gâter [gate] **1** *vt* to spoil **2 se gâter** *vpr (aliment, dent)* to go bad; *(temps)* to take a turn for the worst

gâteux, -euse [gatø, -øz] *adj* senile

gauche¹ [goʃ] **1** *adj (côté, main)* left **2** *nf* **la g.** *(côté)* the left (side); *Pol* the left (wing); **à g.** *(tourner)* (to the) left; *(marcher)* on the left, on the left(-hand) side; **de g.** *(fenêtre, colonne)* left-hand; *(parti, politique)* left-wing; **à g. de** on or to the left of ▪ **gaucher, -ère 1** *adj* left-handed **2** *nmf* left-hander ▪ **gauchiste** *adj & nmf Pol* (extreme) leftist

gauche² [goʃ] *adj (maladroit)* awkward

gaufre [gofr] *nf* waffle ▪ **gaufrette** *nf* wafer (biscuit)

gaver [gave] **1** *vt (animal)* to force-feed; *Fig (personne)* to stuff (**de** with) **2 se gaver** *vpr* to stuff oneself (**de** with)

gaz [gaz] *nm inv* gas; **masque à g.** gas mask; **g. carbonique** carbon dioxide; **g. d'échappement** exhaust fumes ▪ **gazeux, -euse** *adj (état)* gaseous; *(boisson)* fizzy, carbonated; *(eau)* sparkling

gazole [gazɔl] *nm* diesel oil

gazon [gazɔ̃] *nm (herbe)* grass; *(surface)* lawn

gazouiller [gazuje] *vi (oiseau)* to chirp; *(bébé, ruisseau)* to babble

géant, -e [ʒeɑ̃, -ɑ̃t] *adj & nmf* giant

geindre* [ʒɛ̃dr] *vi (gémir)* to moan

gel [ʒɛl] *nm* (**a**) *(temps, glace)* frost (**b**) *(pour cheveux)* gel ▪ **gelé, -e** *adj* frozen; *Méd* frostbitten ▪ **gelée** *nf* (**a**) frost; **g. blanche** ground frost (**b**) *(de fruits, de viande)* jelly ▪ **geler 1** *vt* to freeze **2** *vi* to freeze; **on gèle ici** it's freezing here **3** *v impersonnel* **il gèle** it's freezing

Gémeaux [ʒemo] *nmpl* **les G.** *(signe)* Gemini

gémir [ʒemir] *vi* to groan, to moan ■ **gémissement** *nm* groan, moan

gênant, -e [ʒɛnɑ̃, -ɑ̃t] *adj (objet)* cumbersome; *(présence, situation)* awkward; *(bruit, personne)* annoying

gencive [ʒɑ̃siv] *nf* gum

gendarme [ʒɑ̃darm] *nm* gendarme, policeman ■ **gendarmerie** *nf (corps)* police force; *(local)* police headquarters

gendre [ʒɑ̃dr] *nm* son-in-law

gène [ʒɛn] *nm Biol* gene

gêne [ʒɛn] *nf (trouble physique)* discomfort; *(confusion)* embarrassment; *(dérangement)* inconvenience

gêné, -e [ʒene] *adj (intimidé)* embarrassed; *(silence, sourire)* awkward

généalogie [ʒenealɔʒi] *nf* genealogy ■ **généalogique** *adj* genealogical; **arbre g.** family tree

gêner [ʒene] **1** *vt (déranger, irriter)* to bother; *(troubler)* to embarrass; *(mouvement)* to hamper; *(circulation)* to hold up; **ça ne me gêne pas** I don't mind **(si** if**) 2 se gêner** *vpr (se déranger)* to put oneself out

général, -e, -aux, -ales [ʒeneral, -o] **1** *adj* general; **en g.** in general **2** *nm Mil* general ■ **généralité** *nf* generality

généralisation [ʒeneralizasjɔ̃] *nf* generalization ■ **généraliser 1** *vti* to generalize **2 se généraliser** *vpr* to become widespread ■ **généraliste** *nmf (médecin) Br* general practitioner, GP, *Am* family doctor

générateur [ʒeneratœr] *nm Él* generator

génération [ʒenerasjɔ̃] *nf* generation

génératrice [ʒeneratris] *nf Él* generator

générer [ʒenere] *vt* to generate

généreux, -euse [ʒenerø, -øz] *adj* generous **(de** with**)**

générique [ʒenerik] **1** *nm (de film)* credits **2** *adj* **produit g.** generic product

générosité [ʒenerozite] *nf* generosity

génétique [ʒenetik] **1** *nf* genetics *(sing)* **2** *adj* genetic; **manipulation g.** genetic engineering ■ **génétiquement**

adv **g. modifié** genetically modified

Genève [ʒənɛv] *nm ou f* Geneva

génial, -e, -aux, -ales [ʒenjal, -jo] *adj (personne, invention)* brilliant

génie [ʒeni] *nm* **(a)** *(aptitude, personne)* genius; **avoir le g. pour faire qch** to have a genius for doing sth **(b)** **g. civil** civil engineering; **g. génétique** genetic engineering **(c)** *(esprit)* genie, spirit

genou, -x [ʒ(ə)nu] *nm* knee; **être à genoux** to be kneeling (down); **se mettre à genoux** to kneel (down)

genre [ʒɑ̃r] *nm (espèce)* kind, sort; *(attitude)* manner; *Beaux-Arts* genre; *Gram* gender; **le g. humain** mankind

gens [ʒɑ̃] *nmpl* people

gentil, -ille [ʒɑ̃ti, -ij] *adj (aimable)* nice **(avec** to**)**; *(sage)* good ■ **gentillesse** *nf* kindness; **avoir la g. de faire qch** to be kind enough to do sth ■ **gentiment** *adv (aimablement)* kindly; *(sagement)* nicely

géographie [ʒeografi] *nf* geography ■ **géographique** *adj* geographical

geôlier, -ère [ʒolje, -jɛr] *nmf* jailer

géologie [ʒeolɔʒi] *nf* geology ■ **géologique** *adj* geological

géomètre [ʒeometr] *nm* surveyor

géométrie [ʒeometri] *nf* geometry ■ **géométrique** *adj* geometric(al)

gérant, -e [ʒerɑ̃, -ɑ̃t] *nmf* manager, *f* manageress

gerbe [ʒɛrb] *nf (de blé)* sheaf; *(de fleurs)* bunch; *(d'eau)* spray

gercer [ʒerse] *vi*, **se gercer** *vpr (peau, lèvres)* to chap ■ **gerçure** *nf* chap, crack

gérer [ʒere] *vt* to manage

germe [ʒɛrm] *nm (microbe)* germ; *(de plante)* shoot ■ **germer** *vi (graine)* to start to grow; *(pomme de terre)* to sprout

geste [ʒɛst] *nm* gesture; **faire un g.** *(bouger, agir)* to make a gesture; **ne pas faire un g.** *(ne pas bouger)* not to make a move

gestion [ʒɛstjɔ̃] *nf (action)* management ■ **gestionnaire** *nmf* administrator

Ghana [gana] *nm* **le G.** Ghana

gibier [ʒibje] *nm* game

giboulée [ʒibule] *nf* sudden shower; **giboulées de mars** ≃ April showers

gicler [ʒikle] *vi (liquide)* to spurt out; *(boue)* to splash up

gifle [ʒifl] *nf* slap in the face ■ **gifler** *vt* **g. qn** to slap sb in the face

gigantesque [ʒigãtɛsk] *adj* gigantic

gigot [ʒigo] *nm* leg of mutton/lamb

gilet [ʒilɛ] *nm (cardigan)* cardigan; *(de costume) Br* waistcoat, *Am* vest; **g. pare-balles** bulletproof vest; **g. de sauvetage** life jacket

gingembre [ʒɛ̃ʒãbr] *nm* ginger

girafe [ʒiraf] *nf* giraffe

giratoire [ʒiratwar] *adj Aut* **sens g.** *Br* roundabout, *Am* traffic circle

girofle [ʒirɔfl] *nm* **clou de g.** clove

gisement [ʒizmã] *nm (de minerai)* deposit; **g. de pétrole** oilfield

gitan, -e [ʒitã, -an] *nmf* gipsy

gîte [ʒit] *nm (abri)* resting place; **g. rural** gîte, = self-catering holiday cottage or apartment

givre [ʒivr] *nm* frost ■ **givré, -e** *adj* frost-covered

glace [glas] *nf* (a) *(eau gelée)* ice; *(crème glacée)* ice cream (b) *(vitre)* window; *(miroir)* mirror

glacer [glase] *vt (durcir)* to freeze; *(gâteau) Br* to ice, *Am* to frost ■ **glaçage** *nm (de gâteau) Br* icing, *Am* frosting ■ **glacé, -e** *adj (eau, pièce)* ice-cold, icy; *(vent)* freezing, icy; *(thé, café)* iced; *(papier)* glazed

glacial, -e, -aux, -ales [glasjal, -o] *adj* icy

glacier [glasje] *nm* (a) *Géol* glacier (b) *(vendeur)* ice-cream seller

glacière [glasjɛr] *nf (boîte)* icebox

glaçon [glasɔ̃] *nm Culin* ice cube; *Géol* block of ice; *(sur toit)* icicle

glande [glãd] *nf* gland

glaner [glane] *vt (blé, renseignement)* to glean

glisse [glis] *nf* **sports de g.** = sports involving sliding and gliding motion, such as skiing, surfing etc

glisser [glise] **1** *vt (introduire)* to slip (**dans** into); *(murmurer)* to whisper **2** *vi (involontairement)* to slip; *(volontairement) (sur glace)* to slide; *(sur l'eau)* to glide; **ça glisse** it's slippery **3 se glisser** *vpr* **se g. dans/sous qch** to slip into/under sth ■ **glissade** *nf (involontaire)* slip; *(volontaire)* slide ■ **glissant, -e** *adj* slippery ■ **glissement** *nm* **g. de terrain** landslide

glissière [glisjɛr] *nf Tech* runner, slide; **porte à g.** sliding door

global, -e, -aux, -ales [glɔbal, -o] *adj* total, global ■ **globalement** *adv* overall

globe [glɔb] *nm* globe; **g. terrestre** *(mappemonde)* globe

globuleux, -euse [glɔbylø, -øz] *adj* **yeux g.** protruding eyes

gloire [glwar] *nf (renom)* glory; *(personne célèbre)* celebrity ■ **glorieux, -euse** *adj* glorious ■ **glorifier 1** *vt* to glorify **2 se glorifier** *vpr* **se g. de qch** to glory in sth

glousser [gluse] *vi (poule)* to cluck; *(personne)* to chuckle

glouton, -onne [glutɔ̃, -ɔn] **1** *adj* greedy, gluttonous **2** *nmf* glutton

gluant, -e [glyã, -ãt] *adj* sticky

glucide [glysid] *nm* carbohydrate

goal [gol] *nm (au football)* goalkeeper

gobelet [gɔblɛ] *nm* tumbler; *(de plastique, de papier)* cup

goéland [gɔelã] *nm* (sea)gull

golf [gɔlf] *nm* golf; *(terrain)* golf course ■ **golfeur, -euse** *nmf* golfer

golfe [gɔlf] *nm* gulf, bay

gomme [gɔm] *nf (pour effacer)* eraser, *Br* rubber ■ **gommer** *vt (effacer)* to rub out, to erase

gond [gɔ̃] *nm (de porte)* hinge

gondoler [gɔ̃dɔle] **1** *vi (planche)* to warp; *(papier)* to crinkle **2 se gondoler** *vpr (planche)* to warp; *(papier)* to crinkle

gonflable [gɔ̃flabl] *adj* inflatable

gonfler [gɔ̃fle] **1** *vt* to swell; *(pneu)* to inflate **2** *vi* to swell ■ **gonflé, -e** *adj* swollen ■ **gonflement** *nm* swelling

gorge [gɔrʒ] *nf* throat; *Géog* gorge; **avoir la g. serrée** to have a lump in one's throat

gorgé, -e [gɔrʒe] *adj* **g. de qch** *(saturé)* gorged with sth

gorgée [gɔrʒe] *nf* mouthful; **petite g.** sip

gorger [gɔrʒe] **1** *vt (remplir)* to stuff (**de** with) **2 se gorger** *vpr* **se g. de qch** to gorge oneself with sth

gorille [gɔrij] *nm (animal)* gorilla

gothique [gɔtik] *adj & nm* Gothic

goudron [gudrɔ̃] *nm* tar

gouffre [gufr] *nm* abyss

goulot [gulo] *nm (de bouteille)* neck; **boire au g.** to drink from the bottle

goulu, -e [guly] *adj* greedy

goupille [gupij] *nf (de grenade)* pin

gourde [gurd] *nf (à eau)* water bottle, flask

gourmand, -e [gurmɑ̃, -ɑ̃d] **1** *adj* fond of eating; **g. de qch** fond of sth **2** *nmf* hearty eater ■ **gourmandise** *nf* fondness for food; **gourmandises** *(mets)* delicacies

gourmet [gurmɛ] *nm* gourmet; **fin g.** gourmet

gousse [gus] *nf* **g. d'ail** clove of garlic

goût [gu] *nm* taste; **de bon g.** in good taste; **par g.** by choice; **avoir du g.** *(personne)* to have (good) taste; **avoir un g. de noisette** to taste of hazelnut

goûter [gute] **1** *vt (aliment)* to taste; *(apprécier)* to enjoy; **g. à qch** to taste (a little of) sth **2** *vi* to have an afternoon snack, *Br* to have tea **3** *nm* afternoon snack, *Br* tea

goutte [gut] *nf (de liquide)* drop; **couler g. à g.** to drip ■ **goutte-à-goutte** *nm inv Méd Br* drip, *Am* IV ■ **gouttelette** *nf* droplet ■ **goutter** *vi* to drip

gouttière [gutjɛr] *nf (le long du toit)* gutter; *(le long du mur)* drainpipe

gouvernail [guvɛrnaj] *nm (pale)* rudder; *(barre)* helm

gouvernante [guvɛrnɑ̃t] *nf* governess

gouvernants [guvɛrnɑ̃] *nmpl* rulers

gouvernement [guvɛrnəmɑ̃] *nm* government ■ **gouvernemental, -e, -aux, -ales** *adj* **politique gouvernementale** government policy

gouverner [guvɛrne] *vti Pol & Fig* to govern, to rule ■ **gouverneur** *nm* governor

grâce [grɑs] **1** *nf (charme) & Rel* grace; *(acquittement)* pardon; **de bonne/ mauvaise g.** with good/bad grace; **délai de g.** period of grace **2** *prép* **g. à** thanks to

gracier [grasje] *vt (condamné)* to pardon

gracieux, -euse [grasjø, -øz] *adj (élégant)* graceful; *(aimable)* gracious; *(gratuit)* gratuitous; **à titre g.** free (of charge) ■ **gracieusement** *adv (avec élégance)* gracefully; *(aimablement)* graciously; *(gratuitement)* free (of charge)

grade [grad] *nm (militaire)* rank; **monter en g.** to be promoted ■ **gradé** *nm Mil* non-commissioned officer

gradins [gradɛ̃] *nmpl (d'amphithéâtre)* rows of seats; *(de stade) Br* terraces, *Am* bleachers

graduel, -elle [gradɥɛl] *adj* gradual

graduer [gradɥe] *vt (règle)* to graduate; *(augmenter)* to increase gradually

graffiti [grafiti] *nmpl* graffiti

grain [grɛ̃] *nm* (a) *(de blé) & Fig* grain; *(de café)* bean; *(de poussière)* speck; **g. de beauté** mole; *(sur le visage)* beauty spot; **g. de raisin** grape (b) *(averse)* shower

graine [grɛn] *nf* seed

graisse [grɛs] *nf* fat; *(lubrifiant)* grease ■ **graisser** *vt* to grease ■ **graisseux, -euse** *adj (vêtement)* greasy, oily; *(tissu)* fatty

grammaire [gramɛr] *nf* grammar ■ **grammatical, -e, -aux, -ales** *adj* grammatical

gramme [gram] *nm* gram(me)

GRAND, -E [grɑ̃, grɑ̃d] **1** *adj* big, large; *(en hauteur)* tall; *(chaleur, découverte, âge, mérite, ami)* great; *(bruit)* loud; *(différence)* big, great; *(adulte)* grown-up, big; *(illustre)* great; **g. frère**

(plus âgé) big brother; **le g. air** the open air; **il est g. temps que je parte** it's high time that I left; **il n'y avait pas g. monde** there were not many people **2** *adv* **g. ouvert** *(yeux, fenêtre)* wide open; **ouvrir g.** to open wide; **en g.** on a grand *or* large scale **3** *nmf (enfant)* senior; *(adulte)* grown-up ▪ **grandement** *adv (beaucoup)* greatly; *(généreusement)* grandly ▪ **grand-mère** *(pl* **grands-mères)** *nf* grandmother ▪ **grand-père** *(pl* **grands-pères)** *nm* grandfather ▪ **grands-parents** *nmpl* grandparents

grand-chose [grɑ̃ʃoz] *pron* **pas g.** not much

Grande-Bretagne [grɑ̃dbrətaɲ] *nf* **la G.** Great Britain

grandeur [grɑ̃dœr] *nf (importance, gloire)* greatness; *(dimension)* size; *(majesté, splendeur)* grandeur; **g. nature** life-size

grandiose [grɑ̃djoz] *adj* imposing

grandir [grɑ̃dir] **1** *vi (en taille)* to grow; *(en âge)* to grow up; **g. de 2 cm** to grow 2 cm **2** *vt* **g. qn** *(faire paraître plus grand)* to make sb look taller

grange [grɑ̃ʒ] *nf* barn

granit(e) [granit] *nm* granite

graphique [grafik] **1** *adj (signe, art)* graphic **2** *nm* graph; *Ordinat* graphic

grappe [grap] *nf (de fruits)* cluster; **g. de raisin** bunch of grapes

gras, grasse [grɑ, grɑs] **1** *adj (personne, ventre)* fat; *(aliment)* fatty; *(graisseux)* greasy, oily; *(toux)* loose; **faire la grasse matinée** to have a lie-in **2** *nm (de viande)* fat ▪ **grassement** *adv* **g. payé** handsomely paid ▪ **grassouillet, -ette** *adj* plump

gratifier [gratifje] *vt* **g. qn de qch** to present sb with sth ▪ **gratification** *nf (prime)* bonus

gratin [gratɛ̃] *nm (plat)* = baked dish with a cheese topping; **chou-fleur au g.** cauliflower cheese

gratis [gratis] *adv* free (of charge)

gratitude [gratityd] *nf* gratitude

gratte-ciel [gratsjɛl] *nm inv* skyscraper

gratter [grate] **1** *vt (avec un outil)* to scrape; *(avec les ongles, les griffes)* to scratch; *(effacer)* to scratch out; *Fam* **ça me gratte** it's itchy **2** *vi (tissu)* to be scratchy **3** **se gratter** *vpr* to scratch oneself

gratuit, -e [gratɥi, -it] *adj (billet, entrée)* free; *(acte)* gratuitous ▪ **gratuité** *nf* **la g. de l'enseignement** free education ▪ **gratuitement** *adv (sans payer)* free (of charge); *(sans motif)* gratuitously

gravats [grava] *nmpl* rubble, debris

grave [grav] *adj (maladie, faute)* serious; *(visage)* grave; *(voix)* deep, low; **ce n'est pas g.!** it's not important! ▪ **gravement** *adv (malade)* seriously; *(dignement)* gravely

graver [grave] *vt (sur métal)* to engrave; *(sur bois)* to carve; *(disque)* to cut ▪ **graveur** *nm* engraver

gravier [gravje] *nm* gravel ▪ **gravillon** *nm* piece of gravel; **gravillons** gravel, *Br* (loose) chippings

gravir [gravir] *vt* to climb

gravité [gravite] *nf (de situation)* seriousness; *(solennité) & Phys* gravity; *Phys* **centre de g.** centre of gravity

graviter [gravite] *vi* to revolve (**autour** around)

gravure [gravyr] *nf (image)* print; *(action, art)* engraving; **g. sur bois** *(action)* woodcarving; *(objet)* woodcut

gré [gre] *nm* **de son plein g.** of one's own free will; **de bon g.** willingly; **contre le g. de qn** against sb's will; **bon g. mal g.** whether we/you/*etc* like it or not; **de g. ou de force** one way or another

Grèce [grɛs] *nf* **la G.** Greece ▪ **grec, grecque 1** *adj* Greek **2** *nmf* **G., Grecque** Greek **3** *nm (langue)* Greek

greffe [grɛf] **1** *nf (de peau, d'arbre)* graft; *(d'organe)* transplant **2** *nm Jur* record office ▪ **greffer** *vt (peau) & Bot* to graft (à on to); *(organe)* to transplant ▪ **greffier** *nm Jur* clerk (of the court)

grêle¹ [grɛl] *nf* hail ▪ **grêler** *v impersonnel* to hail; **il grêle** it's hailing ▪ **grêlon** *nm* hailstone

grêle² [grɛl] *adj (jambes)* skinny; *(voix)* shrill

grelot [grəlo] *nm* (small) bell

grelotter [grəlɔte] *vi* to shiver (**de** with)

grenade [grənad] *nf (fruit)* pomegranate; *(projectile)* grenade

grenier [grənje] *nm (de maison)* attic; *(pour le fourrage)* granary

grenouille [grənuj] *nf* frog

grès [grɛ] *nm (roche)* sandstone; *(poterie)* stoneware

grésiller [grezije] *vi (huile)* to sizzle

grève¹ [grɛv] *nf (arrêt du travail)* strike; **faire g.** to be on strike; **g. de la faim** hunger strike; **g. du zèle** *Br* work-to-rule, *Am* rule-book slowdown ▪ **gréviste** *nmf* striker

grève² [grɛv] *nf (de mer)* shore; *(de rivière)* bank

gribouiller [gribuje] *vti* to scribble

grief [grijɛf] *nm (plainte)* grievance; **faire g. de qch à qn** to hold sth against sb

grièvement [grijɛvmɑ̃] *adv* seriously, badly

griffe [grif] *nf (ongle)* claw; *(de couturier)* (designer) label; *Fig (style)* stamp ▪ **griffer** *vt* to scratch

griffonner [grifɔne] *vt* to scribble, to scrawl

grignoter [griɲɔte] *vti* to nibble; **g. entre les repas** to snack between meals

gril [gril] *nm (ustensile) Br* grill, *Am* broiler ▪ **grillade** *nf (viande) Br* grilled meat, *Am* broiled meat ▪ **grille-pain** *nm inv* toaster ▪ **griller 1** *vt (viande) Br* to grill, *Am* to broil; *(pain)* to toast; *(ampoule électrique)* to blow; *Fam* **g. un feu rouge** to jump the lights; **2** *vi (viande)* to grill; *(pain)* to toast

grille [grij] *nf (clôture)* railings; *(porte)* gate; *(de foyer)* grate; *Fig (de salaires)* scale ▪ **grillage** *nm* wire mesh or netting

grillon [grijɔ̃] *nm* cricket

grimace [grimas] *nf (pour faire rire)* (funny) face; *(de douleur)* grimace;

faire la g. to pull a face ▪ **grimacer** *vi* to make a face; *(de douleur)* to wince (**de** with)

grimer [grime] **se grimer** *vpr* to put one's make-up on

grimper [grɛ̃pe] **1** *vi* to climb (**à qch** up sth) **2** *vt (escalier)* to climb

grincer [grɛ̃se] *vi* to creak; **g. des dents** to grind one's teeth ▪ **grincement** *nm* creaking

grincheux, -euse [grɛ̃ʃø, -øz] *adj* grumpy

grippe [grip] *nf (maladie)* flu, influenza; **prendre qn en g.** to take a strong dislike to sb ▪ **grippé, -e** *adj* **être g.** to have (the) flu

gripper [gripe] **se gripper** *vpr (moteur)* to seize up

gris, -e [gri, griz] **1** *adj Br* grey, *Am* gray; *(temps)* dull; *(ivre)* merry **2** *nm Br* grey, *Am* gray ▪ **grisaille** *nf (caractère morne)* dreariness

grisonner [grizɔne] *vi (cheveux, personne)* to go *Br* grey or *Am* gray

grivois, -e [grivwa, -waz] *adj* bawdy

Groenland [grɔɛnlɑ̃d] *nm* **le G.** Greenland

grog [grɔg] *nm* hot toddy

grogner [grɔɲe] *vi (personne)* to grumble (**contre** at); *(cochon)* to grunt ▪ **grognement** *nm (de personne)* growl; *(de cochon)* grunt ▪ **grognon, -onne** *adj* grumpy

grommeler [grɔm(ə)le] *vti* to mutter

gronder [grɔ̃de] **1** *vt (réprimander)* to scold, to tell off **2** *vi (chien)* to growl; *(tonnerre)* to rumble

GROS, GROSSE [gro, gros] **1** *adj (corpulent, important)* big; *(gras)* fat; *(épais)* thick; *(effort, progrès)* great; *(somme, fortune)* large; *(rhume, mer)* heavy; *(faute)* serious, gross; *(traits, laine)* coarse; **g. mot** swearword

2 *adv* **risquer g.** to take a big risk; **écrire g.** to write big; **en g.** *(globalement)* roughly; *(écrire)* in big letters; *(vendre)* in bulk, wholesale

3 *nmf (personne)* fat man, *f* fat woman

4 *nm* **le g. de** the bulk of; **prix de g.** wholesale prices

groseille [grozɛj] nf redcurrant

grossesse [grosɛs] nf pregnancy

grosseur [grosœr] nf (volume) size; (tumeur) lump

grossier, -ère [grosje, -ɛr] adj (tissu, traits) rough, coarse; (personne, manières) rude, coarse; (erreur) gross; (ruse, instrument) crude ■ **grossièrement** adv (calculer) roughly; (répondre) coarsely, rudely; (se tromper) grossly ■ **grossièreté** nf (incorrection, vulgarité) coarseness; (mot) rude word

grossir [grosir] 1 vt (sujet: verre, loupe) to magnify 2 vi (personne) to put on weight; (fleuve) to swell; (bosse, foule) to get bigger ■ **grossissement** nm (augmentation de taille) increase in size; (de microscope) magnification

grossiste [grosist] nmf Com wholesaler

grosso modo [grosomodo] adv (en gros) roughly

grotesque [grotɛsk] adj ludicrous

grotte [grot] nf cave

grouiller [gruje] vi (se presser) to swarm around; **g. de qch** to swarm with sth

groupe [grup] nm group; **g. sanguin** blood group ■ **groupement** nm (action) grouping; (groupe) group ■ **grouper** 1 vt to group (together) 2 **se grouper** vpr (en association) to form a group

grue [gry] nf (machine, oiseau) crane

grumeau, -x [grymo] nm (dans une sauce) lump

Guadeloupe [gwadlup] nf la G. Guadeloupe

Guatemala [gwatemala] nm le G. Guatemala

gué [ge] nm ford

guenon [gənɔ̃] nf female monkey

guépard [gepar] nm cheetah

guêpe [gɛp] nf wasp

guère [gɛr] adv (ne...) g. (pas beaucoup) not much; (pas longtemps) hardly, scarcely; **il n'a g. d'amis** he hasn't got many friends

guéri, -e [geri] adj cured

guérilla [gerija] nf guerrilla warfare

guérir [gerir] 1 vt (personne, maladie) to cure (**de** of); (blessure) to heal 2 vi (personne) to get better, to recover; (blessure) to heal; (rhume) to get better 3 **se guérir** vpr to get better ■ **guérison** nf (rétablissement) recovery ■ **guérisseur, -euse** nmf faith healer

Guernesey [gɛrnzɛ] nf Guernsey

guerre [gɛr] nf war; (technique) warfare; **en g.** at war (**avec** with); **faire la g.** to wage or make war (**à** on or against); (soldat) to fight; **crime de g.** war crime; **g. d'usure** war of attrition ■ **guerrier, -ère** 1 adj danse guerrière war dance; **chant g.** battle song; 2 nmf warrior

guet [gɛ] nm **faire le g.** to be on the lookout ■ **guetter** vt (occasion) to watch out for; (gibier) to lie in wait for

guet-apens [getapɑ̃] (pl guets-apens) nm ambush

gueule [gœl] nf (d'animal, de canon) mouth

gui [gi] nm mistletoe

guichet [giʃɛ] nm (de gare, de banque) window; **g. automatique** (de banque) cash dispenser ■ **guichetier, -ère** nmf (de banque) Br counter clerk, Am teller; (de gare) ticket clerk

guide [gid] nm (personne, livre) guide; **g. touristique** tourist guide ■ **guider** vt to guide

guidon [gidɔ̃] nm handlebars

guignol [giɲɔl] nm (spectacle) ≃ Punch and Judy show

guillemets [gijmɛ] nmpl Typ inverted commas, quotation marks; **entre g.** in inverted commas, in quotation marks

guillotine [gijotin] nf guillotine ■ **guillotiner** vt to guillotine

guimauve [gimov] nf (confiserie) marshmallow

guindé, -e [gɛ̃de] adj (peu naturel) stiff; (style) stilted

Guinée [gine] nf la G. Guinea

guirlande [girlɑ̃d] nf garland; **g. de Noël** piece of tinsel

guise [giz] nf n'en faire qu'à sa g. to do just as one pleases; **en g. de** by way of

guitare [gitar] *nf* guitar ▪ **guitariste** *nmf* guitarist

Guyane [gɥijan] *nf* la G. Guiana

gymnase [ʒimnɑz] *nm* gymnasium

▪ **gymnaste** *nmf* gymnast ▪ **gymnastique** *nf* gymnastics *(sing)*

gynécologue [ʒinekɔlɔg] *nmf Br* gynaecologist, *Am* gynecologist

Hh

H, h [aʃ] *nm inv* H, h

habile [abil] *adj* skilful, *Am* skillful (**à qch** at sth); **h. de ses mains** good with one's hands ■ **habileté** *nf* skill

habilité, -e [abilite] *adj* (legally) authorized (**à faire** to do)

habillé, -e [abije] *adj* dressed (**de** in; **en** as); *(costume, robe)* smart

habiller [abije] **1** *vt (vêtir)* to dress (**de** in); *(fournir en vêtements)* to clothe **2 s'habiller** *vpr* to dress, to get dressed; *(avec élégance)* to dress up ■ **habillement** *nm (vêtements)* clothes

habit [abi] *nm (tenue de soirée)* evening dress, tails; **habits** *(vêtements)* clothes

habitable [abitabl] *adj* (in)habitable; *(maison)* fit to live in

habitat [abita] *nm (d'animal, de plante)* habitat; *(conditions)* housing conditions

habitation [abitasjɔ̃] *nf (lieu)* dwelling; *(fait de résider)* living

habiter [abite] **1** *vt (maison, région)* to live in **2** *vi* to live (**à/en** in) ■ **habitant, -e** *nmf (de pays)* inhabitant; *(de maison)* occupant; **loger chez l'h.** *(en voyage)* to stay with local people ■ **habité, -e** *adj (région)* inhabited; *(maison)* occupied

habitude [abityd] *nf* habit; **avoir l'h. de qch** to be used to sth; **avoir l'h. de faire qch** to be used to doing sth; **prendre l'h. de faire qch** to get into the habit of doing sth; **d'h.** usually; **comme d'h.** as usual

habituel, -elle [abityɛl] *adj* usual, customary

habituer [abitye] **1** *vt* **h. qn à qch** to accustom sb to sth; **être habitué à qch/à faire qch** to be used to sth/to doing sth **2 s'habituer** *vpr* **s'h. à qn/qch** to get used to sb/sth ■ **habitué, -e** *nmf* regular

hache [aʃ] *nf* axe, *Am* ax

hacher [aʃe] *vt (au couteau)* to chop up; *(avec un appareil) Br* to mince, *Am* to grind ■ **haché, -e** *adj (viande) Br* minced, *Am* ground ■ **hachis** *nm* **h. Parmentier** ≃ cottage pie

hachurer [aʃyre] *vt* to hatch

haie [ɛ] *nf (clôture)* hedge; *(en équitation)* fence; **400 mètres haies** *(épreuve d'athlétisme) Br* 400-metre *or Am* 400-meter hurdles; **h. d'honneur** guard of *Br* honour *or Am* honor

haine [ɛn] *nf* hatred, hate ■ **haineux, -euse** *adj* full of hatred

haïr* [air] *vt* to hate ■ **haïssable** *adj* hateful

hâle [ɑl] *nm* suntan ■ **hâlé, -e** *adj* suntanned

haleine [alɛn] *nf* breath; **reprendre h.** to get one's breath back

haleter [alte] *vi* to pant, to gasp ■ **haletant, -e** *adj* panting, gasping

hall [ol] *nm (de maison)* entrance hall; *(d'hôtel)* lobby; **h. de gare** station concourse

halle [al] *nf* (covered) market; **les halles** the central food market

hallucination [alysinasjɔ̃] *nf* hallucination ■ **hallucinant, -e** *adj* extraordinary

halogène [alɔʒɛn] *nm (lampe)* halogen lamp

halte [alt] *nf (arrêt)* stop; *Mil* halt; *(lieu)* stopping place; *Mil* halting place; **faire h.** to stop

haltère [altɛr] *nm* dumbbell ■ **haltérophile** *nmf* weightlifter ■ **haltérophilie** *nf* weightlifting

hamac [amak] *nm* hammock

hamburger [ʼɑ̃bœrgœr] *nm* (ham)burger

hameau, -x ['amo] *nm* hamlet

hameçon [amsɔ̃] *nm* (fish-)hook

hamster ['amstɛr] *nm* hamster

hanche ['ɑ̃ʃ] *nf* hip

handball ['ɑ̃dbal] *nm* Sport handball

handicap ['ɑ̃dikap] *nm (physique, mental)* disability; *Fig* handicap ▪ **handicapé, -e 1** *adj* disabled **2** *nmf* disabled person; **h. physique/mental** physically/mentally handicapped person

hangar ['ɑ̃gar] *nm (entrepôt)* shed

hanter ['ɑ̃te] *vt (sujet: fantôme, souvenir)* to haunt ▪ **hantise** *nf* **avoir la h. de qch** to really dread sth

harasser ['arase] *vt* to exhaust

harceler ['arsəle] *vt (importuner)* to harass; *(insister auprès de)* to pester ▪ **harcèlement** *nm* harassment

hardi, -e ['ardi] *adj* bold

hardware [ardwɛr] *nm* Ordinat hardware

hargneux, -euse ['arɲø, -øz] *adj* bad-tempered

haricot ['ariko] *nm* bean; *Culin* **h. de mouton** mutton stew; **h. rouge** kidney bean; **h. vert** green bean, *Br* French bean

harmonica [armɔnika] *nm* harmonica, mouthorgan

harmonie [armɔni] *nf* harmony ▪ **harmonieux, -euse** *adj* harmonious ▪ **harmoniser** *vt*, **s'harmoniser** *vpr* to harmonize

harnais ['arnɛ] *nm (de cheval, de bébé)* harness

harpe ['arp] *nf* harp

harpon ['arpɔ̃] *nm* harpoon

hasard ['azar] *nm* **le h.** chance; **un h.** a coincidence; **par h.** by chance; **au h.** *(choisir, répondre)* at random; *(marcher)* aimlessly; **à tout h.** *(par précaution)* just in case; *(pour voir)* on the off chance ▪ **hasarder 1** *vt (remarque)* to venture **2 se hasarder** *vpr* **se h. dans** to venture into; **se h. à faire qch** to risk doing sth ▪ **hasardeux, -euse** *adj* risky, hazardous

hâte ['ɑt] *nf* haste; **à la h.** hastily; **en**

(toute) h. hurriedly; **avoir h. de faire qch** to be eager to do sth ▪ **hâter 1** *vt (pas, départ)* to hasten **2 se hâter** *vpr* to hurry **(de faire** to do) ▪ **hâtif, -ive** *adj (trop rapide)* hasty

hausse ['os] *nf* rise **(de** in); **en h.** rising ▪ **hausser 1** *vt (prix, voix)* to raise; *(épaules)* to shrug **2 se hausser** *vpr* **se h. sur la pointe des pieds** to stand on tiptoe

HAUT, -E ['o, 'ot] **1** *adj* high; *(en taille)* tall; **h. de 5 mètres** 5 metres high *or* tall; **à haute voix, à voix haute** aloud; **en haute mer** out at sea; **la mer est haute** it's high tide; **la haute couture** designer fashion; **un instrument de haute précision** a precision instrument; **un renseignement de la plus haute importance** news of the utmost importance; **haute trahison** high treason

2 *adv (dans l'espace) & Mus* high; *(dans une hiérarchie)* highly; *(parler)* loud, loudly; **tout h.** *(lire, penser)* out loud; **h. placé** *(personne)* in a high position; **plus h.** *(dans un texte)* above

3 *nm (partie haute)* top; **en h. de** at the top of; **en h.** *(loger)* upstairs; *(regarder)* up; *(mettre)* on (the) top; **d'en h.** *(de la partie haute, du ciel)* from high up, from up above; **avoir 5 mètres de h.** to be 5 metres high *or* tall; *Fig* **des hauts et des bas** ups and downs ▪ **haut-parleur** *(pl* **haut-parleurs)** *nm* loudspeaker

hautain, -e ['otɛ̃, -ɛn] *adj* haughty

hautbois ['obwa] *nm* oboe

haut-de-forme ['odfɔrm] *(pl* **hauts-de-forme)** *nm* top hat

hautement ['otmɑ̃] *adv (très)* highly ▪ **hauteur** *nf* height; *(colline)* hill; *Péj (orgueil)* haughtiness; **à la h. de** *(objet)* level with; *(rue)* opposite; **arriver à la h. de qch** *(mesurer)* to reach (the level of) sth; **il n'est pas à la h.** he isn't up to it

Haye ['ɛ] *nf* **La H.** The Hague

hebdomadaire [ɛbdɔmadɛr] *adj & nm* weekly

héberger [ebɛrʒe] *vt* to put up ▪ **hébergement** *nm* putting up

hébreu, -x [ebrø] **1** *adj m* Hebrew **2** *nm (langue)* Hebrew

hectare [ɛktar] *nm* hectare (= 2.47 acres)

hélas ['elɑs] *exclam* unfortunately

héler ['ele] *vt (taxi)* to hail

hélice [elis] *nf (d'avion, de navire)* propeller

hélicoptère [elikɔptɛr] *nm* helicopter

helvétique [ɛlvetik] *adj* Swiss

hémisphère [emisfɛr] *nm* hemisphere

hémophilie [emɔfili] *nf Méd* haemophilia

hémorragie [emɔraʒi] *nf Méd* haemorrhage; *Fig (de capitaux)* drain; **faire une h.** to haemorrhage; **h. cérébrale** stroke

hémorroïdes [emɔrɔid] *nfpl* piles, haemorrhoids

hennir ['enir] *vi (cheval)* to neigh

herbe [ɛrb] *nf* grass; **mauvaise h.** weed; *Culin* **fines herbes** herbs

herbivore [ɛrbivɔr] *adj* herbivorous

hérédité [eredite] *nf* heredity ▪ **héréditaire** *adj* hereditary

hérésie [erezi] *nf* heresy ▪ **hérétique 1** *adj* heretical **2** *nmf* heretic

hérisser ['erise] **1** *vt (poils)* to bristle up; *Fig* **h. qn** *(irriter)* to get sb's back up **2 se hérisser** *vpr (animal, personne)* to bristle; *(poils, cheveux)* to stand on end ▪ **hérissé, -e** *adj (cheveux)* bristly; **h. de** bristling with

hérisson ['erisɔ̃] *nm* hedgehog

hériter [erite] **1** *vt* to inherit **(qch de qn** sth from sb) **2** *vi* **h. de qch** to inherit sth ▪ **héritage** *nm (biens)* inheritance; *Fig (culturel)* heritage; **faire un h.** to come into an inheritance ▪ **héritier** *nm* heir **(de** to) ▪ **héritière** *nf* heiress **(de** to)

hermétique [ɛrmetik] *adj* hermetically sealed; *Fig (obscur)* impenetrable

héros ['ero] *nm* hero ▪ **héroïne** *nf (femme)* heroine; *(drogue)* heroin ▪ **héroïque** *adj* heroic ▪ **héroïsme** *nm* heroism

hésiter [ezite] *vi* to hesitate **(sur** over or about; **entre** between; **à faire** to do) ▪ **hésitant, -e** *adj* hesitant ▪ **hésitation** *nf* hesitation; **avec h.** hesitatingly

hétérogène [eterɔʒɛn] *adj* mixed

hêtre ['ɛtr] *nm (arbre, bois)* beech

HEURE [œr] *nf (mesure)* hour; *(moment)* time; **quelle h. est-il?** what time is it?; **il est six heures** it's six (o'clock); **six heures moins cinq** five to six; **six heures cinq** *Br* five past six, *Am* five after six; **à l'h.** *(arriver)* on time; *(être payé)* by the hour; **100 km à l'h.** 100 km an hour; **de bonne h.** early; **nouvelle de dernière h.** latest or last-minute news; **tout à l'h.** *(futur)* in a few moments, later; *(passé)* a moment ago; **à tout à l'h.!** *(au revoir)* see you soon!; **à toute h.** *(continuellement)* at all hours; **24 heures sur 24** 24 hours a day; **d'h. en h.** hourly, hour by hour; **faire des heures supplémentaires** to work or do overtime; **heures d'affluence, heures de pointe** *(circulation)* rush hour; *(dans les magasins)* peak period; **heures creuses** off-peak or slack periods; **h. d'été** *Br* summer time, *Am* daylight-saving time; **h. de grande écoute** *(à la radio)* prime time

heureux, -euse [œrø, -øz] **1** *adj* happy **(de** with); *(chanceux)* lucky, fortunate; *(issue)* successful **2** *adv (vivre, mourir)* happily ▪ **heureusement** *adv (par chance)* fortunately, luckily **(pour** for); *(avec succès)* successfully

heurter ['œrte] **1** *vt (cogner)* to hit **(contre** against); *(entrer en collision avec)* to collide with; **h. qn** *(choquer)* to offend sb **2 se heurter** *vpr* to collide **(à** ou **contre** against); *Fig* **se h. à qch** to meet with sth

hexagone [ɛgzagɔn] *nm* hexagon; *Fig* **l'H.** France

hiberner [ibɛrne] *vi* to hibernate

hibou, -x ['ibu] *nm* owl

hier [ijɛr] *adv* yesterday; **h. soir** yesterday evening

hiérarchie ['jerarʃi] *nf* hierarchy

hi-fi ['ifi] *adj inv & nf inv* hi-fi

hilare [ilar] *adj* grinning ▪ **hilarant, -e** *adj* hilarious ▪ **hilarité** *nf* hilarity, mirth

hindou, -e [ɛ̃du] *adj & nmf* Hindu

hippie ['ipi] *nmf* hippie, hippy

hippique [ipik] *adj* **concours h.** horse show

hippodrome [ipodrom] *nm Br* racecourse, *Am* racetrack

hippopotame [ipopotam] *nm* hippopotamus

hirondelle [irɔ̃dɛl] *nf* swallow

hisser ['ise] **1** *vt* to hoist up **2 se hisser** *vpr* to heave oneself up

histoire [istwar] *nf (science, événements)* history; *(récit)* story

historien, -enne [istorjɛ̃, -ɛn] *nmf* historian

historique [istorik] **1** *adj (concernant l'histoire)* historical; *(important)* historic **2** *nm* historical account

hiver [ivɛr] *nm* winter ■ **hivernal, -e, -aux, -ales** *adj* winter; *(temps)* wintry

HLM ['aʃɛlɛm] *(abrév* **habitation à loyer modéré)** *nm ou f Br* ≃ council flats, *Am* ≃ low-rent apartment building

hocher ['ɔʃe] *vt* **h. la tête** *(pour dire oui)* to nod; *(pour dire non)* to shake one's head

hockey ['ɔkɛ] *nm* hockey; **h. sur glace** ice hockey; **h. sur gazon** *Br* hockey, *Am* field hockey

hold-up ['ɔldœp] *nm inv* hold-up

Hollande ['ɔlɑ̃d] *nf* **la H.** Holland ■ **hollandais, -e 1** *adj* Dutch **2** *nmf* **H.** Dutchman; **Hollandaise** Dutchwoman; **les H.** the Dutch **3** *nm (langue)* Dutch

homard ['ɔmar] *nm* lobster

homéopathie [ɔmeopati] *nf* homeopathy

homicide [ɔmisid] *nm* homicide; **h. involontaire** *ou* **par imprudence** manslaughter; **h. volontaire** murder

hommage [ɔmaʒ] *nm* homage (**à** to); **rendre h. à qn** to pay homage to sb; **faire qch en h. à qn** to do sth as a tribute to sb *or* in homage to sb

homme [ɔm] *nm* man *(pl* men); **l'h.** *(genre humain)* man(kind); **des vêtements d'h.** men's clothes; **h. d'affaires**

businessman; **h. politique** politician ■ **homme-grenouille** *(pl* **hommes-grenouilles)** *nm* frogman

homogène [ɔmɔʒɛn] *adj* homogeneous

homologue [ɔmɔlɔg] *nmf* counterpart, opposite number

homologuer [ɔmɔlɔge] *vt (décision, accord, record)* to ratify

homonyme [ɔmɔnim] *nm (mot)* homonym

homosexuel, -elle [ɔmɔsɛksɥɛl] *adj & nmf* homosexual

Hongrie ['ɔ̃gri] *nf* **la H.** Hungary ■ **hongrois, -e 1** *adj* Hungarian **2** *nmf* **H., Hongroise** Hungarian **3** *nm (langue)* Hungarian

honnête [ɔnɛt] *adj (intègre)* honest; *(vie, gens)* decent; *(prix)* fair ■ **honnêtement** *adv (avec intégrité)* honestly; *(raisonnablement)* decently ■ **honnêteté** *nf (intégrité)* honesty

honneur [ɔnœr] *nm Br* honour, *Am* honor; **en l'h. de qn** in *Br* honour *or Am* honor of sb; **invité d'h.** guest of *Br* honour *or Am* honor

honorable [ɔnɔrabl] *adj* honourable; *Fig (résultat, salaire)* respectable

honoraires [ɔnɔrɛr] *nmpl* fees

honorer [ɔnɔre] *vt* to honour (**de** with); **h. qn** *(conduite)* to be a credit to sb ■ **honorifique** *adj* honorary

honte ['ɔ̃t] *nf* shame; **avoir h.** to be *or* feel ashamed (**de qch/de faire qch** of sth/to do *or* of doing sth); **faire h. à qn** to put sb to shame ■ **honteux, -euse** *adj (personne)* ashamed (**de** of); *(conduite, acte)* shameful

hôpital, -aux [ɔpital, -o] *nm* hospital; **à l'h.** *Br* in hospital, *Am* in the hospital

hoquet ['ɔkɛ] *nm* hiccup; **avoir le h.** to have the hiccups

horaire [ɔrɛr] **1** *adj (salaire)* hourly; *(vitesse)* per hour **2** *nm* timetable, schedule; **horaires de travail** working hours

horizon [ɔrizɔ̃] *nm* horizon; *(vue, paysage)* view; **à l'h.** on the horizon ■ **horizontal, -e, -aux, -ales** *adj* horizontal

horloge [ɔrlɔʒ] *nf* clock

hormone [ɔrmɔn] *nf* hormone

horoscope [ɔrɔskɔp] *nm* horoscope

horreur [ɔrœr] *nf* horror; **avoir h. de qch** to hate *or* loathe sth; **quelle h.!** how horrible!

horrible [ɔribl] *adj (effrayant)* horrible; *(laid)* hideous ■ **horriblement** [-əmɑ̃] *adv (défiguré)* horribly; *(cher, froid)* terribly

horrifié, -e [ɔrifje] *adj* horrified

hors ['ɔr] *prép* **h. de** *(maison, boîte)* outside; *Fig (danger, haleine)* out of; *(au football)* **être h. jeu** to be offside ■ **hors-bord** *nm inv* speedboat ■ **hors-d'œuvre** *nm inv (plat)* hors-d'oeuvre, starter ■ **hors-jeu** *nm inv (au football)* offside ■ **hors-la-loi** *nm inv* outlaw ■ **hors-piste** *nm inv Ski* off-piste skiing ■ **hors service** *adj inv (appareil)* out of order ■ **hors taxe** *adj inv (magasin, objet)* duty-free

horticulteur, -trice [ɔrtikyltœr, -tris] *nmf* horticulturist ■ **horticulture** *nf* horticulture

hospice [ɔspis] *nm (asile)* home

hospitalier, -ère [ɔspitalje, -ɛr] *adj (accueillant)* hospitable; **centre h.** hospital (complex); **personnel h.** hospital staff ■ **hospitaliser** *vt* to hospitalize ■ **hospitalité** *nf* hospitality

hostile [ɔstil] *adj* hostile (**à** to *or* towards) ■ **hostilité** *nf* hostility (**envers** to *or* towards)

hôte [ot] **1** *nm (qui reçoit)* host **2** *nmf (invité)* guest ■ **hôtesse** *nf* hostess; **h. de l'air** air hostess

hôtel [otɛl] *nm* hotel; **h. particulier** mansion, town house; **h. de ville** *Br* town hall, *Am* city hall ■ **hôtelier, -ère** **1** *nmf* hotel-keeper, hotelier **2** *adj* **industrie hôtelière** hotel industry ■ **hôtellerie** *nf (auberge)* inn; *(métier)* hotel trade

hotte ['ɔt] *nf (panier)* basket *(carried on back); (de cheminée)* hood; **h. aspirante** extractor hood

houille ['uj] *nf* coal; **h. blanche** hydroelectric power ■ **houiller, -ère** *adj* **bassin h.** coalfield

houleux, -euse ['ulø, -øz] *adj (mer)* rough; *Fig (réunion)* stormy

housse ['us] *nf (protective)* cover

houx ['u] *nm* holly

hublot ['yblo] *nm (de navire, d'avion)* porthole

huer ['ɥe] *vt* to boo ■ **huées** *nfpl* boos

huile [ɥil] *nf* oil; **h. d'arachide/d'olive** groundnut/olive oil; **h. essentielle** essential oil; **h. solaire** suntan oil ■ **huiler** *vt* to oil ■ **huileux, -euse** *adj* oily

huis [ɥi] *nm* **à h. clos** behind closed doors; *Jur* in camera ■ **huissier** [ɥisje] *nm (portier)* usher; *Jur* bailiff

huit ['ɥit, 'ɥi *before consonant*] *adj & nm inv* eight; **h. jours** a week ■ **huitième** *adj, nm & nmf* eighth; **un h.** an eighth; *Sport* **h. de finale** last sixteen

huître [ɥitr] *nf* oyster

humain, -e [ymɛ̃, -ɛn] **1** *adj (relatif à l'homme)* human; *(compatissant)* humane **2** *nmpl* **les humains** humans ■ **humainement** *adv (relatif à l'homme)* humanly; *(avec bonté)* humanely ■ **humanitaire** *adj* humanitarian ■ **humanité** *nf (genre humain, sentiment)* humanity

humble [œ̃bl] *adj* humble

humecter [ymɛkte] *vt* to moisten

humer ['yme] *vt (respirer)* to breathe in; *(sentir)* to smell

humeur [ymœr] *nf (disposition)* mood; **être de bonne/mauvaise h.** to be in a good/bad mood

humide [ymid] *adj (linge)* damp, wet; *(climat, temps)* humid ■ **humidifier** *vt* to humidify ■ **humidité** *nf (de maison)* dampness; *(de climat)* humidity

humilier [ymilje] *vt* to humiliate ■ **humiliant, -e** *adj* humiliating ■ **humiliation** *nf* humiliation ■ **humilité** *nf* humility

humour [ymur] *nm Br* humour, *Am* humor; **avoir le sens de l'h.** to have a sense of *Br* humour *or Am* humor ■ **humoriste** *nmf* humorist ■ **humoristique** *adj (récit, ton)* humorous

hurler ['yrle] **1** *vt (slogans, injures)* to yell **2** *vi (loup, vent)* to howl; *(personne)* to scream ■ **hurlement** [-əmɑ̃] *nm (de*

loup, de vent) howl; *(de personne)* scream

hutte ['yt] *nf* hut

hybride [ibrid] *adj & nm* hybrid

hydrater [idrate] *vt (peau)* to moisturize

hydraulique [idrolik] *adj* hydraulic

hydravion [idravjɔ̃] *nm* seaplane

hydrocarbure [idrokarbyr] *nm* hydrocarbon

hydrophile [idrɔfil] *adj* **coton h.** *Br* cotton wool, *Am* (absorbent) cotton

hyène [jɛn] *nf* hyena

hygiène [iʒjɛn] *nf* hygiene ▪ **hygiénique** *adj* hygienic; *(serviette, conditions)* sanitary

hymne [imn] *nm* hymn; **h. national** national anthem

hypermarché [ipɛrmarʃe] *nm* hypermarket

hypermétrope [ipɛrmetrɔp] *adj* longsighted

hypnose [ipnoz] *nf* hypnosis ▪ **hypnotiser** *vt* to hypnotize

hypocrisie [ipɔkrizi] *nf* hypocrisy ▪ **hypocrite 1** *adj* hypocritical **2** *nmf* hypocrite

hypodermique [ipɔdɛrmik] *adj* hypodermic

hypothèque [ipɔtɛk] *nf* mortgage

hypothèse [ipɔtez] *nf* hypothesis; **dans l'h. où...** supposing (that)...

Ii

I, i [i] *nm inv* I, i

iceberg [isbɛrg, ajsbɛrg] *nm* iceberg

ici [isi] *adv* here; **par i.** *(passer)* this way; *(habiter)* around here; **jusqu'i.** *(temps)* up to now; *(lieu)* as far as this or here; **d'i. à mardi** by Tuesday; **d'i. peu** before long

icône [ikon] *nf Rel & Ordinat* icon

idéal, -e, -aux *ou* **-als, -ales** [ideal, -o] **1** *adj* ideal **2** *n* ideal; **l'i. serait de/ que...** the ideal or best solution would be to/if... ■ **idéaliser** *vt* to idealize ■ **idéaliste 1** *adj* idealistic **2** *nmf* idealist

idée [ide] *nf* idea (**de** of; **que** that); **i. fixe** obsession

identifier [idɑ̃tifje] *vt*, **s'identifier** *vpr* to identify (**à** with) ■ **identification** *nf* identification

identique [idɑ̃tik] *adj* identical (**à** to)

identité [idɑ̃tite] *nf* identity

idéologie [ideɔlɔʒi] *nf* ideology

idiot, -e [idjo, -ɔt] **1** *adj* silly, idiotic **2** *nmf* idiot

idole [idɔl] *nf* idol

idyllique [idilik] *adj* idyllic

igloo [iglu] *nm* igloo

ignare [iɲar] **1** *adj* ignorant **2** *nmf* ignoramus

ignoble [iɲɔbl] *adj* vile

ignorant, -e [iɲɔrɑ̃, -ɑ̃t] *adj* ignorant (**de** of) ■ **ignorance** *nf* ignorance

ignorer [iɲɔre] *vt* not to know; **j'ignore si...** I don't know if...; **je n'ignore pas les difficultés** I am not unaware of the difficulties; **i. qn** *(mépriser)* to ignore sb ■ **ignoré, -e** *adj (inconnu)* unknown

il [il] *pron personnel (personne)* he; *(chose, animal, impersonnel)* it; **il est** he/it is; **il pleut** it's raining; **il est vrai que...** it's true that...; **il y a...** there is/ are...; **il y a six ans** six years ago; **il y a une heure qu'il travaille** he has been working for an hour; **qu'est-ce qu'il y a?** what's the matter?, what's wrong?; **il n'y a pas de quoi!** don't mention it!

île [il] *nf* island; **les îles Anglo-Normandes** the Channel Islands; **les îles Britanniques** the British Isles

illégal, -e, -aux, -ales [il(l)egal, -o] *adj* illegal

illégitime [il(l)eʒitim] *adj (enfant, revendication)* illegitimate; *(demande)* unwarranted

illettré, -e [il(l)etre] *adj & nmf* illiterate

illicite [il(l)isit] *adj* unlawful, illicit

illimité, -e [il(l)imite] *adj* unlimited

illisible [il(l)izibl] *adj (écriture)* illegible; *(livre) & Ordinat* unreadable

illogique [il(l)ɔʒik] *adj* illogical

illuminer [il(l)ymine] **1** *vt* to light up, to illuminate **2** **s'illuminer** *vpr (visage, ciel)* to light up ■ **illumination** *nf (action, lumière)* illumination ■ **illuminé, -e** *adj (monument)* floodlit

illusion [il(l)yzjɔ̃] *nf* illusion (**sur** about); **se faire des illusions** to delude oneself (**sur** about); **i. d'optique** optical illusion ■ **illusionniste** *nmf* conjurer ■ **illusoire** *adj* illusory

illustre [il(l)ystr] *adj* illustrious

illustrer [il(l)ystre] **1** *vt (livre, récit)* to illustrate (**de** with) **2** **s'illustrer** *vpr* to distinguish oneself (**par** by) ■ **illustration** *nf* illustration ■ **illustré, -e** *adj (livre, magazine)* illustrated

îlot [ilo] *nm (île)* small island; *(maisons)* block

ils [il] *pron personnel mpl* they; **i. sont ici** they are here

image [imaʒ] *nf* picture; *(ressem-blance, symbole)* image; *(dans une glace)* reflection; *Ordinat* **i. de syn-thèse** computer-generated image ■ **imagé, -e** *adj (style) Br* colourful, *Am* colorful, full of imagery

imaginable [imaʒinabl] *adj* imagi-nable ■ **imaginaire** *adj* imaginary ■ **imaginatif, -ive** *adj* imaginative

imagination [imaʒinɑsjɔ̃] *nf* imagi-nation

imaginer [imaʒine] **1** *vt (se figurer)* to imagine; *(inventer)* to devise **2 s'imagi-ner** *vpr (se figurer)* to imagine **(que** that); *(se voir)* to picture oneself

imbattable [ɛ̃batabl] *adj* unbeatable

imbécile [ɛ̃besil] **1** *adj* idiotic **2** *nmf* idiot, imbecile ■ **imbécillité** *nf (état)* imbecility; **une i.** *(action, parole)* an idiotic thing

imberbe [ɛ̃bɛrb] *adj* beardless

imbiber [ɛ̃bibe] *vt* to soak **(de** with *or* in)

imbriquer [ɛ̃brike] **s'imbriquer** *vpr (s'emboîter)* to overlap

imbu, -e [ɛ̃by] *adj* **i. de soi-même** full of oneself

imbuvable [ɛ̃byvabl] *adj* undrinkable

imiter [imite] *vt* to imitate; *(signature)* to forge; **i. qn** *(pour rire)* to mimic sb; *(faire comme)* to do the same as sb; *(imitateur professionnel)* to imperso-nate sb ■ **imitateur, -trice** *nmf* imita-tor; *(professionnel)* impersonator ■ **imitation** *nf* imitation

immaculé, -e [imakyle] *adj (sans tache, sans péché)* immaculate

immangeable [ɛ̃mɑ̃ʒabl] *adj* inedible

immanquable [ɛ̃mɑ̃kabl] *adj* inevi-table

immatriculer [imatrikyle] *vt* to regis-ter; **se faire i.** to register ■ **immatricu-lation** *nf* registration

immédiat, -e [imedja, -jat] **1** *adj* im-mediate **2** *nm* **dans l'i.** for the time being ■ **immédiatement** *adv* immedi-ately

immense [imɑ̃s] *adj* immense ■ **im-mensément** *adv* immensely ■ **im-mensité** *nf* immensity

immerger [imɛrʒe] *vt* to immerse ■ **immersion** *nf* immersion **(dans** in)

immeuble [imœbl] *nm* building; *(ap-partements) Br* block of flats, *Am* apart-ment block

immigrant, -e [imigrɑ̃, -ɑ̃t] *nmf* im-migrant ■ **immigration** *nf* immigration ■ **immigré, -e** *adj & nmf* immigrant; **travailleur i.** immigrant worker

imminent, -e [iminɑ̃, -ɑ̃t] *adj* immi-nent

immiscer [imise] **s'immiscer** *vpr* to interfere **(dans** in)

immobile [imɔbil] *adj* still, motion-less

immobilier, -ère [imɔbilje, -ɛr] **1** *adj* **marché i.** property market **2** *nm* **l'i.** *Br* property, *Am* real estate

immobiliser [imɔbilize] **1** *vt (blessé)* to immobilize; *(train)* to bring to a stop; *(voiture) (avec un sabot)* to clamp **2 s'immobiliser** *vpr* to come to a stop

immonde [i(m)mɔ̃d] *adj (sale)* foul; *(ignoble, laid)* vile

immoral, -e, -aux, -ales [i(m)mɔral, -o] *adj* immoral ■ **immoralité** *nf* im-morality

immortel, -elle [i(m)mɔrtɛl] *adj* im-mortal ■ **immortaliser** *vt* to immorta-lize ■ **immortalité** *nf* immortality

immuable [i(m)mɥabl] *adj* immu-table, unchanging

immuniser [i(m)mynize] *vt* to immu-nize **(contre** against) ■ **immunitaire** *adj Méd (déficience, système)* immune ■ **immunité** *nf* immunity

impact [ɛ̃pakt] *nm* impact **(sur** on)

impair, -e [ɛ̃pɛr] **1** *adj (nombre)* odd, uneven **2** *nm (maladresse)* blunder

imparable [ɛ̃parabl] *adj (coup)* un-avoidable

impardonnable [ɛ̃pardɔnabl] *adj* unforgivable

imparfait, -e [ɛ̃parfɛ, -ɛt] *adj (con-naissance)* imperfect

impartial, -e, -aux, -ales [ɛ̃parsjal, -o] *adj* impartial, unbiased ■ **impartia-lité** *nf* impartiality

impartir [ɛ̃partir] *vt* **dans le temps**

qui nous est imparti within the allotted time

impasse [ɛ̃pɑs] *nf (rue)* dead end; *Fig (situation)* impasse; **être dans une i.** to be deadlocked

impassible [ɛ̃pasibl] *adj* impassive

impatient, -e [ɛ̃pasjɑ̃, -ɑ̃t] *adj* impatient; **i. de faire qch** impatient to do sth ■ **impatience** *nf* impatience ■ **impatienter 1** *vt* to annoy **2 s'impatienter** *vpr* to get impatient

impayé, -e [ɛ̃peje] *adj* unpaid

impeccable [ɛ̃pekabl] *adj* impeccable

impénétrable [ɛ̃penetrabl] *adj (forêt, mystère)* impenetrable

impensable [ɛ̃pɑ̃sabl] *adj* unthinkable

impératif, -ive [ɛ̃peratif, -iv] *adj (consigne, besoin)* imperative; *(ton)* imperious

impératrice [ɛ̃peratris] *nf* empress

imperceptible [ɛ̃persɛptibl] *adj* imperceptible (**à** to)

imperfection [ɛ̃pɛrfɛksjɔ̃] *nf* imperfection

impérial, -e, -aux, -ales [ɛ̃perjal, -o] *adj* imperial ■ **impérialisme** *nm* imperialism

impérieux, -euse [ɛ̃perjø, -øz] *adj (autoritaire)* imperious; *(besoin)* pressing

impérissable [ɛ̃perisabl] *adj (souvenir)* enduring

imperméable [ɛ̃pɛrmeabl] **1** *adj* impervious (**à** to); *(tissu, manteau)* waterproof **2** *nm* raincoat

impersonnel, -elle [ɛ̃pɛrsɔnɛl] *adj* impersonal

impertinent, -e [ɛ̃pɛrtinɑ̃, -ɑ̃t] *adj* impertinent (**envers** to) ■ **impertinence** *nf* impertinence

imperturbable [ɛ̃pɛrtyrbabl] *adj (personne)* imperturbable

impitoyable [ɛ̃pitwajabl] *adj* merciless

implacable [ɛ̃plakabl] *adj (personne, vengeance)* implacable; *(avancée)* relentless

implanter [ɛ̃plɑ̃te] **1** *vt (installer)* to establish; *(chirurgicalement)* to implant **2 s'implanter** *vpr* to become established ■ **implantation** *nf* establishment

implicite [ɛ̃plisit] *adj* implicit

impliquer [ɛ̃plike] *vt (entraîner)* to imply; **i. que...** to imply that...; **i. qn** to implicate sb (**dans** in) ■ **implication** *nf (conséquence)* implication; *(participation)* involvement

implorer [ɛ̃plɔre] *vt* to implore (**qn de faire** sb to do)

impoli, -e [ɛ̃pɔli] *adj* rude, impolite

impolitesse [ɛ̃pɔlitɛs] *nf* impoliteness, rudeness

impopulaire [ɛ̃pɔpylɛr] *adj* unpopular

import [ɛ̃pɔr] *nm* import

important, -e [ɛ̃pɔrtɑ̃, -ɑ̃t] **1** *adj (personnage, événement)* important; *(quantité, somme, ville)* large; *(dégâts, retard)* considerable **2** *nm* **l'i., c'est de...** the important thing is to... ■ **importance** *nf* importance; *(taille)* size; *(de dégâts)* extent; **ça n'a pas d'i.** it doesn't matter

importer¹ [ɛ̃pɔrte] **1** *vi* to matter (**à** to) **2** *v impersonnel* **il importe de faire qch** it's important to do sth; **il importe que vous y soyez** it is important that you're there; **peu importe, n'importe** it doesn't matter; **n'importe qui/quoi/où/quand/comment** anyone/anything/anywhere/any time/anyhow

importer² [ɛ̃pɔrte] *vt (marchandises)* to import (**de** from) ■ **importateur, -trice 1** *adj* importing **2** *nmf* importer ■ **importation** *nf (objet)* import; *(action)* importing, importation

importun, -e [ɛ̃pɔrtœ̃, -yn] **1** *adj (personne, question)* importunate **2** *nmf* nuisance

imposer [ɛ̃poze] **1** *vt (condition)* to impose; *(taxer)* to tax; **i. qch à qn** to impose sth on sb **2** *vi* **en i. à qn** to impress sb **3 s'imposer** *vpr (faire reconnaître sa valeur)* to assert oneself; *(gagner)* to win; *(être nécessaire)* to be essential; *Péj (chez quelqu'un)* to impose; **s'i. de faire qch** to make it a rule to do sth ■ **imposant, -e** *adj* imposing

impossible [ɛpɔsibl] **1** *adj* impossible (**à faire** to do); **il est i. que...** *(+ subjunctive)* it is impossible that... **2** *nm* **tenter l'i.** to attempt the impossible ▪ **impossibilité** *nf* impossibility

imposteur [ɛpɔstœr] *nm* impostor ▪ **imposture** *nf* deception

impôt [ɛpo] *nm* tax; **(service des) impôts** tax authorities; **impôts locaux** local taxes; **i. sur le revenu** income tax

impraticable [ɛpratikabl] *adj (chemin)* impassable; *(projet)* impracticable

imprécis, -e [ɛpresi, -iz] *adj* imprecise ▪ **imprécision** *nf* imprecision

imprégner [ɛpreɲe] **1** *vt* to impregnate (**de** with); *Fig* **être imprégné de qch** to be full of sth **2 s'imprégner** *vpr* to become impregnated (**de** with)

imprenable [ɛprənabl] *adj (forteresse)* impregnable; *(vue)* unobstructed

impression [ɛpresjɔ̃] *nf* **(a)** *(sensation)* impression; **avoir l'i. que...** to have the impression that...; **faire bonne i. à qn** to make a good impression on sb **(b)** *(de livre)* printing

impressionner [ɛpresjɔne] *vt (bouleverser)* to upset; *(frapper)* to impress ▪ **impressionnable** *adj* easily upset ▪ **impressionnant, -e** *adj* impressive

imprévisible [ɛprevizibl] *adj (temps, réaction, personne)* unpredictable; *(événement)* unforeseeable ▪ **imprévu, -e 1** *adj* unexpected, unforeseen **2** *nm* **en cas d'i.** in case of anything unexpected

imprimer [ɛprime] *vt (livre, tissu)* to print; *Ordinat* to print (out) ▪ **imprimante** *nf* printer ▪ **imprimé** *nm (formulaire)* printed form ▪ **imprimerie** *nf (technique)* printing; *(lieu) Br* printing works, *Am* print shop ▪ **imprimeur** *nm* printer

improbable [ɛprɔbabl] *adj* improbable, unlikely

impropre [ɛprɔpr] *adj* inappropriate; **i. à qch** unfit for sth; **i. à la consommation** unfit for human consumption

improviser [ɛprɔvize] *vti* to improvise ▪ **improvisation** *nf* improvisation

improviste [ɛprɔvist] **à l'improviste** *adv* unexpectedly

imprudent, -e [ɛprydɑ̃, -ɑ̃t] *adj (personne, action)* rash; **il est i. de...** it is unwise to... ▪ **imprudemment** [-amɑ̃] *adv* rashly ▪ **imprudence** *nf* rashness

impudique [ɛpydik] *adj* shameless

impuissant, -e [ɛpɥisɑ̃, -ɑ̃t] *adj* powerless; *Méd* impotent ▪ **impuissance** *nf* powerlessness; *Méd* impotence

impulsif, -ive [ɛpylsif, -iv] *adj* impulsive ▪ **impulsion** *nf* impulse

impunément [ɛpynemɑ̃] *adv* with impunity ▪ **impuni, -e** *adj* unpunished

impur, -e [ɛpyr] *adj* impure ▪ **impureté** *nf* impurity

imputer [ɛpyte] *vt* to attribute (**à** to); *(frais)* to charge (**à** to)

inabordable [inabɔrdabl] *adj (prix)* prohibitive; *(lieu)* inaccessible; *(personne)* unapproachable

inacceptable [inaksɛptabl] *adj* unacceptable

inaccessible [inaksesibl] *adj (lieu)* inaccessible; *(personne)* unapproachable

inachevé, -e [inaʃve] *adj* unfinished

inactif, -ive [inaktif, -iv] *adj (personne)* inactive; *(remède)* ineffective ▪ **inaction** *nf* inaction ▪ **inactivité** *nf* inactivity

inadapté, -e [inadapte] **1** *adj (socialement)* maladjusted; *(physiquement, mentalement)* handicapped; *(matériel)* unsuitable (**à** for) **2** *nmf (socialement)* maladjusted person

inadmissible [inadmisibl] *adj* inadmissible

inadvertance [inadvɛrtɑ̃s] **par inadvertance** *adv* inadvertently

inamical, -e, -aux, -ales [inamikal, -o] *adj* unfriendly

inanimé, -e [inanime] *adj (mort)* lifeless; *(évanoui)* unconscious; *(matière)* inanimate

inaperçu, -e [inapɛrsy] *adj* **passer i.** to go unnoticed

inappréciable [inapresjabl] *adj* invaluable

inapte [inapt] *adj (intellectuellement)* unsuited (**à** for); *(médicalement)* unfit (**à** for) ▪ **inaptitude** *nf (intellectuelle)* inaptitude; *(médicale)* unfitness (**à** for)

inattendu, -e [inatɑ̃dy] *adj* unexpected

inattention [inatɑ̃sjɔ̃] *nf* lack of attention

inaudible [inodibl] *adj* inaudible

inaugurer [inogyre] *vt (édifice)* to inaugurate ■ **inaugural, -e, -aux, -ales** *adj* inaugural

inavouable [inavwabl] *adj* shameful

incalculable [ɛ̃kalkylabl] *adj* incalculable

incapable [ɛ̃kapabl] *adj* incapable; **i. de faire qch** incapable of doing sth ■ **incapacité** *nf (impossibilité)* inability **(de faire** to do); *(invalidité)* disability; **être dans l'i. de faire qch** to be unable to do sth

incarcérer [ɛ̃karsere] *vt* to incarcerate ■ **incarcération** *nf* incarceration

incarnation [ɛ̃karnɑsjɔ̃] *nf* incarnation

incarné, -e [ɛ̃karne] *adj (ongle)* ingrown

incarner [ɛ̃karne] *vt* to embody

incassable [ɛ̃kɑsabl] *adj* unbreakable

incendie [ɛ̃sɑ̃di] *nm* fire; **i. criminel** arson; **i. de forêt** forest fire ■ **incendiaire 1** *adj (bombe)* incendiary **2** *nmf* arsonist ■ **incendier** *vt* to set on fire

incertain, -e [ɛ̃sertɛ̃, -ɛn] *adj (résultat)* uncertain; *(temps)* unsettled; *(personne)* indecisive ■ **incertitude** *nf* uncertainty

incessamment [ɛ̃sesamɑ̃] *adv* very soon

incessant, -e [ɛ̃sesɑ̃, -ɑ̃t] *adj* incessant

inchangé, -e [ɛ̃ʃɑ̃ʒe] *adj* unchanged

incidence [ɛ̃sidɑ̃s] *nf (influence)* impact **(sur** on); *Méd* incidence

incident [ɛ̃sidɑ̃] *nm* incident; *(accroc)* hitch; **i. de parcours** minor setback

incinérer [ɛ̃sinere] *vt (ordures)* to incinerate; *(cadavre)* to cremate ■ **incinération** *nf (d'ordures)* incineration; *(de cadavre)* cremation

inciser [ɛ̃size] *vt (peau)* to make an incision in; *(abcès)* to lance ■ **incision** *nf (entaille)* incision

incisif, -ive¹ [ɛ̃sizif, -iv] *adj* incisive

incisive² [ɛ̃siziv] *nf (dent)* incisor (tooth)

inciter [ɛ̃site] *vt* to encourage **(à faire** to do) ■ **incitation** *nf* incitement **(à** to)

incliner [ɛ̃kline] **1** *vt (pencher)* to tilt; **i. la tête** *(approuver)* to nod; *(saluer)* to bow one's head **2 s'incliner** *vpr (se pencher)* to lean forward; *(pour saluer)* to bow; *Fig (se soumettre)* to give in **(devant** to) ■ **inclinaison** *nf* incline, slope ■ **inclination** *nf (tendance)* inclination

inclure* [ɛ̃klyr] *vt* to include; *(dans un courrier)* to enclose **(dans** with) ■ **inclus, -e** *adj* **du 4 au 10 i.** from the 4th to the 10th inclusive; **jusqu'à lundi i.** *Br* up to and including Monday, *Am* through Monday ■ **inclusion** *nf* inclusion

incognito [ɛ̃kɔɲito] *adv* incognito

incohérent, -e [ɛ̃kɔerɑ̃, -ɑ̃t] *adj (propos)* incoherent; *(histoire)* inconsistent ■ **incohérence** *nf (de propos)* incoherence; *(d'histoire)* inconsistency

incolore [ɛ̃kɔlɔr] *adj* colourless; *(vernis, verre)* clear

incomber [ɛ̃kɔ̃be] *vi* **i. à qn** *(devoir)* to fall to sb; **il lui incombe de faire qch** it falls to him/her to do sth

incommoder [ɛ̃kɔmɔde] *vt* to bother

incomparable [ɛ̃kɔ̃parabl] *adj* matchless

incompatible [ɛ̃kɔ̃patibl] *adj* incompatible **(avec** with)

incompétent, -e [ɛ̃kɔ̃petɑ̃, -ɑ̃t] *adj* incompetent ■ **incompétence** *nf* incompetence

incomplet, -ète [ɛ̃kɔ̃plɛ, -ɛt] *adj* incomplete

incompréhensible [ɛ̃kɔ̃preɑ̃sibl] *adj* incomprehensible ■ **incompréhension** *nf* incomprehension

incompris, -e [ɛ̃kɔ̃pri, -iz] **1** *adj* misunderstood **2** *nmf* **être un i.** to be misunderstood

inconcevable [ɛ̃kɔ̃səvabl] *adj* inconceivable

inconciliable [ɛ̃kɔ̃siljabl] *adj (théorie)* irreconcilable; *(activité)* incompatible

inconditionnel, -elle [ɛkɔ̃disjɔnɛl] *adj* unconditional; *(supporter)* staunch

inconfortable [ɛkɔ̃fɔrtabl] *adj* uncomfortable

inconnu, -e [ɛkɔny] **1** *adj* unknown (**de** to) **2** *nmf (étranger)* stranger; *(auteur)* unknown **3** *nm* **l'i.** the unknown **4** *nf Math* **inconnue** unknown (quantity)

inconscient, -e [ɛkɔ̃sjɑ̃, -ɑ̃t] **1** *adj (sans connaissance)* unconscious; *(imprudent)* reckless; **i. de qch** unaware of sth **2** *nm* **l'i.** the unconscious ▪ **inconsciemment** [-amɑ̃] *adv (dans l'inconscient)* subconsciously ▪ **inconscience** *nf (perte de connaissance)* unconsciousness; *(irréflexion)* recklessness

inconséquence [ɛkɔ̃sekɑ̃s] *nf (manque de prudence)* recklessness; *(manque de cohérence)* inconsistency

inconsidéré, -e [ɛkɔ̃sidere] *adj* thoughtless

inconsistant, -e [ɛkɔ̃sistɑ̃, -ɑ̃t] *adj (personne)* weak; *(film, roman)* flimsy; *(sauce, crème)* thin

inconsolable [ɛkɔ̃sɔlabl] *adj* inconsolable

inconstant, -e [ɛkɔ̃stɑ̃, -ɑ̃t] *adj* fickle

incontestable [ɛkɔ̃tɛstabl] *adj* indisputable ▪ **incontesté, -e** *adj* undisputed

incontournable [ɛkɔ̃turnabl] *adj Fig (film)* unmissable; *(auteur)* who cannot be ignored

incontrôlé, -e [ɛkɔ̃trole] *adj* unchecked ▪ **incontrôlable** *adj (invérifiable)* unverifiable; *(indomptable)* uncontrollable

inconvenant, -e [ɛkɔ̃vnɑ̃, -ɑ̃t] *adj* improper

inconvénient [ɛkɔ̃venjɑ̃] *nm (désavantage)* drawback; **l'i., c'est que...** the annoying thing is that...

incorporer [ɛkɔrpɔre] *vt (insérer)* to insert (**à** in); *(troupes)* to draft; **i. qch à qch** to blend sth into sth ▪ **incorporation** *nf (mélange)* blending (**de qch dans qch** of sth into sth); *Mil* conscription

incorrect, -e [ɛkɔrɛkt] *adj (inexact)* incorrect; *(grossier)* impolite; *(inconvenant)* improper ▪ **incorrection** *nf (impolitesse)* impoliteness; *(propos)* impolite remark; *(faute de grammaire)* mistake

incorrigible [ɛkɔriʒibl] *adj* incorrigible

incorruptible [ɛkɔryptibl] *adj* incorruptible

incrédule [ɛkredyl] *adj* incredulous ▪ **incrédulité** *nf* incredulity

incriminer [ɛkrimine] *vt (personne)* to accuse

incroyable [ɛkrwajabl] *adj* incredible

incrusté, -e [ɛkryste] *adj* **i. de** *(orné)* inlaid with

incubation [ɛkybasjɔ̃] *nf* incubation

inculper [ɛkylpe] *vt (accuser)* to charge (**de** with) ▪ **inculpation** *nf* charge, indictment ▪ **inculpé, -e** *nmf* **l'i.** the accused

inculquer [ɛkylke] *vt* to instil (**à qn** in sb)

inculte [ɛkylt] *adj (terre, personne)* uncultivated

incurable [ɛkyrabl] *adj* incurable

incursion [ɛkyrsjɔ̃] *nf (invasion)* incursion; *Fig (entrée soudaine)* intrusion

Inde [ɛd] *nf* **l'I.** India

indécent, -e [ɛdesɑ̃, -ɑ̃t] *adj* indecent ▪ **indécence** *nf* indecency

indéchiffrable [ɛdeʃifrabl] *adj (illisible)* undecipherable

indécis, -e [ɛdesi, -iz] *adj (personne) (de caractère)* indecisive; *(ponctuellement)* undecided ▪ **indécision** *nf (de caractère)* indecisiveness; *(ponctuelle)* indecision

indéfendable [ɛdefɑ̃dabl] *adj* indefensible

indéfini, -e [ɛdefini] *adj (illimité)* indefinite; *(imprécis)* undefined ▪ **indéfiniment** *adv* indefinitely ▪ **indéfinissable** *adj* indefinable

indélébile [ɛdelebil] *adj* indelible

indélicat, -e [ɛdelika, -at] *adj (grossier)* insensitive; *(malhonnête)* unscrupulous

indemne [ɛ̃dɛmn] *adj* unhurt, unscathed

indemniser [ɛ̃dɛmnize] *vt* to compensate (**de** for) ■ **indemnisation** *nf* compensation ■ **indemnité** *nf (dédommagement)* compensation; *(allocation)* allowance; **i. de licenciement** redundancy payment

indéniable [ɛ̃denjabl] *adj* undeniable

indépendant, -e [ɛ̃depɑ̃dɑ̃, -ɑ̃t] *adj* independent (**de** of); *(chambre)* self-contained; *(travailleur)* self-employed ■ **indépendamment** [-amɑ̃] *adv* independently; **i. de** apart from ■ **indépendance** *nf* independence

indescriptible [ɛ̃dɛskriptibl] *adj* indescribable

indésirable [ɛ̃dezirabl] *adj & nmf* undesirable

indestructible [ɛ̃dɛstryktibl] *adj* indestructible

indéterminé, -e [ɛ̃detɛrmine] *adj (date, heure)* unspecified; *(raison)* unknown

index [ɛ̃dɛks] *nm (doigt)* forefinger, index finger; *(liste) & Ordinat* index

indicateur, -trice [ɛ̃dikatœr, -tris] **1** *nm Tech* indicator, gauge; *Écon* indicator; *(espion)* informer **2** *adj* **panneau i.** road sign

indicatif, -ive [ɛ̃dikatif, -iv] **1** *adj* indicative (**de** of) **2** *nm Radio* theme tune; **i. téléphonique** *Br* dialling code, *Am* area code

indication [ɛ̃dikasjɔ̃] *nf* indication (**de** of); *(renseignement)* (piece of) information; *(directive)* instruction; **indications...** *(de médicament)* suitable for...

indice [ɛ̃dis] *nm (signe)* sign; *(d'enquête)* clue

indien, -enne [ɛ̃djɛ̃, -ɛn] **1** *adj* Indian **2** *nmf* **I., Indienne** Indian

indifférent, -e [ɛ̃diferɑ̃, -ɑ̃t] *adj* indifferent (**à** to) ■ **indifférence** *nf* indifference (**à** to)

indigène [ɛ̃diʒɛn] *adj & nmf* native

indigent, -e [ɛ̃diʒɑ̃, -ɑ̃t] *adj* destitute ■ **indigence** *nf* destitution

indigeste [ɛ̃diʒɛst] *adj* indigestible

■ **indigestion** *nf* **avoir une i.** to have a stomach upset

indignation [ɛ̃diɲasjɔ̃] *nf* indignation

indigne [ɛ̃diɲ] *adj (personne)* unworthy; *(conduite)* shameful; **i. de qn/qch** unworthy of sb/sth ■ **indignité** *nf (de personne)* unworthiness; *(de conduite)* shamefulness; *(action)* shameful act

indigner [ɛ̃diɲe] **1** *vt* **i. qn** to make sb indignant **2 s'indigner** *vpr* to be indignant (**de** at) ■ **indigné, -e** *adj* indignant

indiquer [ɛ̃dike] *vt (sujet: personne)* to point out; *(sujet: panneau)* to show, to indicate; *(sujet: compteur)* to read; *(donner) (date, adresse)* to give; **i. le chemin à qn** to tell sb the way ■ **indiqué, -e** *adj (conseillé)* advisable; **à l'heure indiquée** at the appointed time

indirect, -e [ɛ̃dirɛkt] *adj* indirect

indiscipline [ɛ̃disiplin] *nf* indiscipline ■ **indiscipliné, -e** *adj* unruly

indiscret, -ète [ɛ̃diskrɛ, -ɛt] *adj Péj (curieux)* inquisitive; *(qui parle trop)* indiscreet ■ **indiscrétion** *nf* indiscretion

indiscutable [ɛ̃diskytabl] *adj* indisputable

indispensable [ɛ̃dispɑ̃sabl] *adj* essential, indispensable (**à qch** for sth); **i. à qn** indispensable to sb

indisponible [ɛ̃disponibl] *adj* unavailable

indisposer [ɛ̃dispoze] *vt (contrarier)* to annoy; **i. qn** *(odeur, climat)* to make sb feel ill ■ **indisposé, -e** *adj (malade)* indisposed, unwell ■ **indisposition** *nf* indisposition

indistinct, -e [ɛ̃distɛ̃(kt), -ɛ̃kt] *adj* indistinct ■ **indistinctement** [-ɛ̃ktəmɑ̃] *adv (voir, parler)* indistinctly; *(également)* equally

individu [ɛ̃dividy] *nm* individual; *Péj* individual, character

individualiste [ɛ̃dividɥalist] **1** *adj* individualistic **2** *nmf* individualist

individualité [ɛ̃dividɥalite] *nf* individuality

individuel, -elle [ɛ̃dividɥɛl] *adj* individual; *(maison)* detached

indivisible [ɛ̃divizibl] *adj* indivisible

Indochine [ɛ̃dɔʃin] *nf* l'I. Indo-China

indolent, -e [ɛ̃dɔlɑ̃, -ɑ̃t] *adj* lazy

indolore [ɛ̃dɔlɔr] *adj* painless

indomptable [ɛ̃dɔ̃(p)tabl] *adj (animal)* untamable

Indonésie [ɛ̃dɔnezi] *nf* l'I. Indonesia

indue [ɛ̃dy] *adj f* rentrer à des heures **indues** to come home at all hours of the night

induire* [ɛ̃dɥir] *vt* **i. qn en erreur** to lead sb astray

indulgent, -e [ɛ̃dylʒɑ̃, -ɑ̃t] *adj* indulgent ▪ **indulgence** *nf* indulgence

industrie [ɛ̃dystri] *nf* industry ▪ **industrialisé, -e** *adj* industrialized ▪ **industriel, -elle 1** *adj* industrial **2** *nm* industrialist

inébranlable [inebrɑ̃labl] *adj Fig (certitude, personne)* unshakeable

inédit, -e [inedi, -it] *adj (texte)* unpublished

inefficace [inefikas] *adj (mesure)* ineffective; *(personne)* inefficient ▪ **inefficacité** *nf (de mesure)* ineffectiveness; *(de personne)* inefficiency

inégal, -e, -aux, -ales [inegal, -o] *adj (parts, lutte)* unequal; *(sol, humeur)* uneven; *Fig (travail)* inconsistent ▪ **inégalable** *adj* incomparable ▪ **inégalé, -e** *adj* unequalled ▪ **inégalité** *nf (injustice)* inequality; *(physique)* disparity *(de* in); *(de sol)* unevenness

inéluctable [inelyktabl] *adj* inescapable

inepte [inɛpt] *adj (remarque, histoire)* inane; *(personne)* inept ▪ **ineptie** [inɛpsi] *nf (de comportement, de film)* inanity; *(remarque)* stupid remark

inépuisable [inepɥizabl] *adj* inexhaustible

inespéré, -e [inɛspere] *adj* unhoped-for

inestimable [inɛstimabl] *adj (objet d'art)* priceless

inévitable [inevitabl] *adj* inevitable, unavoidable

inexact, -e [inɛgzakt] *adj (erroné)* inaccurate; *(calcul)* wrong ▪ **inexacti-**

tude *nf (caractère erroné, erreur)* inaccuracy; *(manque de ponctualité)* unpunctuality

inexcusable [inɛkskyzabl] *adj* inexcusable

inexistant, -e [inɛgzistɑ̃, -ɑ̃t] *adj* non-existent

inexpérience [inɛksperjɑ̃s] *nf* inexperience ▪ **inexpérimenté, -e** *adj* inexperienced

inexplicable [inɛksplikabl] *adj* inexplicable ▪ **inexpliqué, -e** *adj* unexplained

inexploré, -e [inɛksplore] *adj* unexplored

inexprimable [inɛksprimabl] *adj* inexpressible

inextricable [inɛkstrikabl] *adj* inextricable

infaillible [ɛ̃fajibl] *adj* infallible

infaisable [ɛ̃fəzabl] *adj (travail)* impossible

infâme [ɛ̃fɑm] *adj (personne)* despicable; *(acte)* unspeakable; *(taudis)* squalid; *(aliment)* revolting

infantile [ɛ̃fɑ̃til] *adj (maladie)* childhood; *Péj (comportement, personne)* infantile

infarctus [ɛ̃farktys] *nm Méd* heart attack

infatigable [ɛ̃fatigabl] *adj* tireless

infect, -e [ɛ̃fɛkt] *adj* foul

infecter [ɛ̃fɛkte] **1** *vt (atmosphère)* to contaminate; *Méd* to infect **2** **s'infecter** *vpr* to become infected ▪ **infection** *nf Méd* infection; *(odeur)* stench

inférieur, -e [ɛ̃ferjœr] **1** *adj (étagère, niveau)* bottom; *(étage, lèvre, membre)* lower; *(qualité, marchandises)* inferior; **i. à la moyenne** below average; **à l'étage i.** on the floor below **2** *nmf* inferior ▪ **infériorité** *nf* inferiority

infernal, -e, -aux, -ales [ɛ̃fɛrnal, -o] *adj (de l'enfer)* & *Fig (chaleur, bruit)* infernal

infidèle [ɛ̃fidɛl] *adj* unfaithful *(à* to) ▪ **infidélité** *nf* unfaithfulness, infidelity

infiltrer [ɛ̃filtre] **1** *vt (party)* to infiltrate **2** **s'infiltrer** *vpr (liquide)* to seep

(**dans** into); *(lumière)* to filter in; *Fig* **s'i. dans** *(groupe, esprit)* to infiltrate ■ **infiltration** *nf (de liquide, d'espions)* infiltration

infime [ɛfim] *adj* tiny

infini, -e [ɛfini] **1** *adj* infinite **2** *nm Math & Phot* infinity; *Phil* infinite; **à l'i.** *(discuter)* ad infinitum; *Math* to infinity ■ **infiniment** *adv* infinitely; **je regrette i.** I'm very sorry ■ **infinité** *nf* **une i. de** an infinite number of

infirme [ɛfirm] **1** *adj* disabled **2** *nmf* disabled person ■ **infirmité** *nf* disability

infirmer [ɛfirme] *vt* to invalidate

infirmerie [ɛfirməri] *nf (d'école, de bateau)* sick room; *(de caserne, de prison)* infirmary ■ **infirmier** *nm* male nurse ■ **infirmière** *nf* nurse

inflammable [ɛflamabl] *adj* (in)flammable

inflammation [ɛflamɑsjɔ̃] *nf Méd* inflammation

inflation [ɛflɑsjɔ̃] *nf Écon* inflation

infléchir [ɛfleʃir] *vt (courber)* to bend; *(politique)* to change the direction of ■ **inflexion** *nf (de courbe, de voix)* inflection

inflexible [ɛflɛksibl] *adj* inflexible

infliger [ɛfliʒe] *vt* to inflict (**à** on); *(amende)* to impose (**à** on)

influence [ɛflyɑ̃s] *nf* influence ■ **influençable** *adj* easily influenced ■ **influencer** *vt* to influence ■ **influent, -e** *adj* influential ■ **influer** *vi* **i. sur qch** to influence sth

informaticien, -enne [ɛfɔrmatisjɛ̃, -ɛn] *nmf* computer scientist

information [ɛfɔrmɑsjɔ̃] *nf* information; *(nouvelle)* piece of news; *Ordinat* data, information; *Radio & TV* **les informations** the news *(sing)*

informatique [ɛfɔrmatik] **1** *nf (science)* computer science; *(technique)* data processing; **un cours d'i.** a computer course; **étudier l'i.** to study computer science; **travailler dans l'i.** to work in computers *or* IT **2** *adj* **programme i.** computer program ■ **informatisation** *nf* computerization ■ **informatiser** *vt* to computerize

informe [ɛfɔrm] *adj* shapeless

informer [ɛfɔrme] **1** *vt* to inform (**de** of *or* about; **que** that) **2** **s'informer** *vpr (se renseigner)* to inquire (**de** about; **si** if *or* whether)

inforoute [ɛfɔrut] *nf* information superhighway

infortune [ɛfɔrtyn] *nf* misfortune ■ **infortuné, -e** *adj* unfortunate

infraction [ɛfraksjɔ̃] *nf (à un règlement)* infringement; *(délit) Br* offence, *Am* offense

infranchissable [ɛfrɑ̃ʃisabl] *adj (mur, fleuve)* impassable; *Fig (difficulté)* insurmountable

infrarouge [ɛfraruʒ] *adj* infrared

infrastructure [ɛfrastryktyr] *nf (de bâtiment)* substructure; *(équipements)* infrastructure

infructueux, -euse [ɛfryktyø, -øz] *adj* fruitless

infuser [ɛfyze] *vi (thé)* to brew; *(tisane)* to infuse ■ **infusion** *nf (tisane)* herb tea

ingénier [ɛʒenje] **s'ingénier** *vpr* to strive (**à faire** to do)

ingénieur [ɛʒenjœr] *nm* engineer ■ **ingénierie** [-iri] *nf* engineering

ingénieux, -euse [ɛʒenjø, -øz] *adj* ingenious ■ **ingéniosité** *nf* ingenuity

ingénu, -e [ɛʒeny] *adj* ingenuous

ingérer [ɛʒere] **s'ingérer** *vpr* to interfere (**dans** in) ■ **ingérence** *nf* interference (**dans** in)

ingrat, -e [ɛgra, -at] *adj (personne)* ungrateful (**envers** to); *(tâche)* thankless; *(sol)* barren; *(visage)* unattractive; **l'âge i.** the awkward age ■ **ingratitude** *nf* ingratitude

ingrédient [ɛgredjɑ̃] *nm* ingredient

inhabitable [inabitabl] *adj* uninhabitable ■ **inhabité, -e** *adj* uninhabited

inhabituel, -elle [inabityɛl] *adj* unusual

inhérent, -e [inerɑ̃, -ɑ̃t] *adj* inherent (**à** in)

inhibé, -e [inibe] *adj* inhibited ■ **inhibition** *nf* inhibition

inhospitalier, -ère [inɔspitalje, -ɛr] *adj* inhospitable

inhumain, -e [inymɛ̃, -ɛn] *adj (cruel, terrible)* inhuman

inhumer [inyme] *vt* to bury

inimaginable [inimaʒinabl] *adj* unimaginable

inimitable [inimitabl] *adj* inimitable

inimitié [inimitje] *nf* enmity

ininflammable [inɛ̃flamabl] *adj* nonflammable

inintelligible [inɛ̃teliʒibl] *adj* unintelligible

ininterrompu, -e [inɛ̃terɔ̃py] *adj* continuous

initial, -e, -aux, -ales [inisjal, -o] *adj* initial ∎ **initiale** *nf* initial

initialiser [inisjalize] *vt Ordinat (disque)* to initialize; *(ordinateur)* to boot

initiation [inisjasjɔ̃] *nf* initiation

initiative [inisjativ] *nf* initiative; **de ma propre i.** on my own initiative

initier [inisje] **1** *vt (former)* to introduce (à to); *(rituellement)* to initiate (à into) **2 s'initier** *vpr* **s'i. à qch** to start learning sth

injecter [ɛ̃ʒɛkte] *vt* to inject (**dans** into) ∎ **injection** *nf* injection

injure [ɛ̃ʒyr] *nf* insult ∎ **injurier** *vt* to insult, to abuse ∎ **injurieux, -euse** *adj* abusive, insulting (**pour** to)

injuste [ɛ̃ʒyst] *adj (contraire à la justice)* unjust; *(non équitable)* unfair ∎ **injustice** *nf* injustice

injustifiable [ɛ̃ʒystifjabl] *adj* unjustifiable ∎ **injustifié, -e** *adj* unjustified

inlassable [ɛ̃lɑsabl] *adj* untiring

inné, -e [ine] *adj* innate, inborn

innocent, -e [inɔsɑ̃, -ɑ̃t] **1** *adj* innocent (**de** of) **2** *nmf (non coupable)* innocent person; *(idiot)* simpleton ∎ **innocence** *nf* innocence ∎ **innocenter** *vt* **i. qn** to clear sb (**de** of)

innombrable [inɔ̃brabl] *adj* countless, innumerable; *(foule)* huge

innommable [inɔmabl] *adj (conduite, actes)* unspeakable; *(nourriture, odeur)* vile

innover [inɔve] *vi* to innovate ∎ **innovateur, -trice 1** *adj* innovative **2** *nmf* innovator ∎ **innovation** *nf* innovation

inoccupé, -e [inɔkype] *adj* unoccupied

inoculer [inɔkyle] *vt* **i. qch à qn** to inoculate sb with sth; **i. qn contre qch** to inoculate sb against sth

inodore [inɔdɔr] *adj* odourless

inoffensif, -ive [inɔfɑ̃sif, -iv] *adj* harmless

inonder [inɔ̃de] *vt (lieu)* to flood; *Fig (marché)* to flood, to inundate (**de** with); **inondé de soleil** bathed in sunlight ∎ **inondation** *nf* flood; *(action)* flooding

inopérable [inɔperabl] *adj* inoperable

inopiné, -e [inɔpine] *adj* unexpected

inopportun, -e [inɔpɔrtœ̃, -yn] *adj* inopportune

inoubliable [inublijabl] *adj* unforgettable

inouï, -e [inwi] *adj* incredible

Inox® [inɔks] *nm* stainless steel; **couteau en I.** stainless-steel knife ∎ **inoxydable** *adj (couteau)* stainless-steel

inqualifiable [ɛ̃kalifjabl] *adj* unspeakable

inquiet, -ète [ɛ̃kjɛ, -ɛt] *adj* worried, anxious (**de** about)

inquiéter [ɛ̃kjete] **1** *vt (préoccuper)* to worry **2 s'inquiéter** *vpr* to worry (**de** about); **s'i. pour qn** to worry about sb ∎ **inquiétant, -e** *adj* worrying

inquiétude [ɛ̃kjetyd] *nf* anxiety, worry

insaisissable [ɛ̃sezisabl] *adj* elusive

insalubre [ɛ̃salybr] *adj (climat, habitation)* insalubrious

insatiable [ɛ̃sasjabl] *adj* insatiable

insatisfait, -e [ɛ̃satisfɛ, -ɛt] *adj (personne)* dissatisfied

inscription [ɛ̃skripsjɔ̃] *nf (action)* entering; *(immatriculation)* registration; *(sur écriteau, mur, tombe)* inscription

inscrire* [ɛ̃skrir] **1** *vt (renseignements, date)* to write down; *(dans un journal, sur un registre)* to enter; *(graver)* to inscribe; **i. qn à un club** to Br enrol or Am enroll sb in a club

2 s'inscrire *vpr* to put one's name down; *(à une activité)* Br to enrol, Am

to enroll (**à** at); *(à l'université)* to register (**à** at); **s'i. à un club** to join a club

insecte [ɛsɛkt] *nm* insect

insécurité [ɛsekyrite] *nf* insecurity

insensé, -e [ɛsɑ̃se] *adj (projet, idée)* crazy; *(espoir)* wild

insensible [ɛsɑ̃sibl] *adj (indifférent)* insensitive (**à** to); *(imperceptible)* imperceptible

inséparable [ɛseparabl] *adj* inseparable (**de** from)

insérer [ɛsere] *vt* to insert (**dans** in) ▪ **insertion** [ɛsɛrsjɔ̃] *nf* insertion

insidieux, -euse [ɛsidjø, -øz] *adj* insidious

insigne [ɛsiɲ] *nm* badge

insignifiant, -e [ɛsiɲifjɑ̃, -ɑ̃t] *adj* insignificant

insinuer [ɛsinɥe] **1** *vt Péj* to insinuate (**que** that) **2 s'insinuer** *vpr (froid)* to creep (**dans** into); *(personne)* to worm one's way (**dans** into)

insipide [ɛsipid] *adj* insipid

insister [ɛsiste] *vi* to insist (**pour faire** on doing); **i. sur qch** to stress sth; **i. pour que...** (+ *subjunctive*) to insist that... ▪ **insistance** *nf* insistence

insolation [ɛsɔlasjɔ̃] *nf Méd* sunstroke

insolent, -e [ɛsɔlɑ̃, -ɑ̃t] *adj (impoli)* insolent; *(luxe)* unashamed ▪ **insolence** *nf* insolence

insolite [ɛsɔlit] *adj* unusual, strange

insoluble [ɛsɔlybl] *adj* insoluble

insomnie [ɛsɔmni] *nf* insomnia ▪ **insomniaque** *nmf* insomniac

insondable [ɛsɔ̃dabl] *adj* unfathomable

insonoriser [ɛsɔnɔrize] *vt* to soundproof

insouciant, -e [ɛsusjɑ̃, -ɑ̃t] *adj* carefree ▪ **insouciance** *nf* carefree attitude

insoumis, -e [ɛsumi, -iz] *adj (personne)* rebellious; *Mil* absentee

insoupçonnable [ɛsupsɔnabl] *adj* beyond suspicion

insoutenable [ɛsutnabl] *adj (spectacle, odeur)* unbearable; *(théorie)* untenable

inspecter [ɛspɛkte] *vt* to inspect ▪ **inspecteur, -trice** *nmf* inspector ▪ **inspection** *nf* inspection

inspirer [ɛspire] **1** *vt* to inspire; **i. qch à qn** to inspire sb with sth **2** *vi* to breathe in **3 s'inspirer** *vpr* **s'i. de qn/qch** to take one's inspiration from sb/sth ▪ **inspiration** *nf (idée)* inspiration; *(respiration)* breathing in ▪ **inspiré, -e** *adj* inspired

instable [ɛstabl] *adj* unstable; *(temps)* changeable ▪ **instabilité** *nf* instability; *(de temps)* changeability

installer [ɛstale] **1** *vt (appareil, meuble)* to install, to put in; *(étagère)* to put up; *(cuisine)* to fit out; **i. qn** *(dans une fonction, dans un logement)* to install sb (**dans** in)
2 s'installer *vpr (s'asseoir)* to settle down; *(dans un bureau)* to install oneself; *(médecin)* to set oneself up; **s'i. à la campagne** to settle in the country ▪ **installation** *nf (de machine)* installation; *(de cuisine)* fitting out; *(emménagement)* move; **installations** *(appareils)* fittings; *(bâtiments)* facilities

instant [ɛstɑ̃] *nm* moment, instant; **à l'i.** a moment ago; **à l'i. où...** just as...; **pour l'i.** for the moment ▪ **instantané, -e 1** *adj* instantaneous; **café i.** instant coffee **2** *nm (photo)* snapshot

instar [ɛstar] *nm* **à l'i. de qn** after the fashion of sb

instaurer [ɛstore] *vt* to establish

instigateur, -trice [ɛstigatœr, -tris] *nmf* instigator

instinct [ɛstɛ̃] *nm* instinct; **d'i.** by instinct ▪ **instinctif, -ive** *adj* instinctive

instituer [ɛstitɥe] *vt* to establish

institut [ɛstity] *nm* institute; **i. de beauté** beauty salon

instituteur, -trice [ɛstitytœr, -tris] *nmf Br* primary *or Am* elementary school teacher

institution [ɛstitysjɔ̃] *nf (création)* establishment; *(coutume)* institution; *(école)* private school ▪ **institutionnel, -elle** *adj* institutional

instructif, -ive [ɛstryktif, -iv] *adj* instructive

instruction [ɛstryksjɔ̃] *nf (éducation)* education; *Mil* training; *Jur* preliminary investigation; instructions *(ordres)* instructions; **i. civique** civics *(sing)* ▪ **instructeur** *nm* instructor

instruire* [ɛstrɥir] **1** *vt* to teach, to educate; *Mil* to train; *Jur* to investigate; **i. qn de qch** to inform sb of sth **2 s'instruire** *vpr* to educate oneself ▪ **instruit, -e** *adj* educated

instrument [ɛstrymɑ̃] *nm* instrument; **i. à vent** wind instrument ▪ **instrumental, -e, -aux, -ales** *adj Mus* instrumental

insu [ɛsy] **à l'insu de** *prép* without the knowledge of; **à mon/son i.** *(sans m'en/s'en apercevoir)* without my/his/her being aware of it

insuffisant, -e [ɛsyfizɑ̃, -ɑ̃t] *adj (en quantité)* insufficient; *(en qualité)* inadequate ▪ **insuffisance** *nf (manque)* insufficiency; *(de moyens)* inadequacy

insulaire [ɛsylɛr] **1** *adj* insular **2** *nmf* islander

insulte [ɛsylt] *nf* insult (**à** to) ▪ **insulter** *vt* to insult

insupportable [ɛsyportabl] *adj* unbearable

insurger [ɛsyrʒe] **s'insurger** *vpr* to rise up (**contre** against)

insurmontable [ɛsyrmɔ̃tabl] *adj* insurmountable

insurrection [ɛsyrɛksjɔ̃] *nf* insurrection, uprising

intact, -e [ɛtakt] *adj* intact

intarissable [ɛtarisabl] *adj* inexhaustible

intégral, -e, -aux, -ales [ɛtegral, -o] *adj (paiement)* full; *(édition)* unabridged; **version intégrale** *(de film)* uncut version ▪ **intégralement** *adv* in full, fully ▪ **intégralité** *nf* whole (**de** of)

intègre [ɛtegr] *adj* upright, honest ▪ **intégrité** *nf* integrity

intégrer [ɛtegre] **1** *vt* to integrate (**dans** in); *(école)* to get into **2 s'intégrer** *vpr* to become integrated ▪ **intégrante** *adj f* **faire partie i. de qch** to be an integral part of sth ▪ **intégra-**

tion *nf (au sein d'un groupe)* integration

intégrisme [ɛtegrism] *nm* fundamentalism

intellectuel, -elle [ɛtelɛktɥel] *adj & nmf* intellectual

intelligent, -e [ɛteliʒɑ̃, -ɑ̃t] *adj* intelligent, clever ▪ **intelligence** *nf (faculté)* intelligence; **avoir l'i. de faire qch** to have the intelligence to do sth; *Ordinat* **i. artificielle** artificial intelligence

intelligible [ɛteliʒibl] *adj* intelligible

intempéries [ɛtɑ̃peri] *nfpl* **les i.** the bad weather

intempestif, -ive [ɛtɑ̃pɛstif, -iv] *adj* untimely

intenable [ɛtnabl] *adj (position)* untenable

intendant, -e [ɛtɑ̃dɑ̃, -ɑ̃t] *nmf Scol* bursar

intense [ɛɑ̃s] *adj* intense; *(circulation)* heavy ▪ **intensif, -ive** *adj* intensive ▪ **intensité** *nf* intensity

intensifier [ɛtɑ̃sifje] *vt*, **s'intensifier** *vpr* to intensify

intenter [ɛ ɑ̃te] *vt Jur* **i. un procès à qn** to institue proceedings against sb

intention [ɛtɑ̃sjɔ̃] *nf* intention; *Jur* intent; **avoir l'i. de faire qch** to intend to do sth ▪ **intentionné, -e** *adj* **bien i.** well-intentioned; **mal i.** ill-intentioned ▪ **intentionnel, -elle** *adj* intentional

interactif, -ive [ɛteraktif, -iv] *adj Ordinat* interactive

interaction [ɛteraksjɔ̃] *nf* interaction

intercaler [ɛterkale] *vt* to insert

intercéder [ɛtersede] *vt* to intercede (**auprès de** with; **en faveur de** on behalf of)

intercepter [ɛtersɛpte] *vt* to intercept

interchangeable [ɛterʃɑ̃ʒabl] *adj* interchangeable

interdire* [ɛterdir] *vt* to forbid (**qch à qn** sb sth); *(film, meeting)* to ban: **i. à qn de faire qch** *(personne)* to forbid sb to do sth ▪ **interdiction** *nf* ban (**de** on); **'i. de fumer'** 'no smoking' ▪ **interdit, -e** *adj (défendu)* forbidden; *(étonné)* disconcerted; **'stationnement i.'** 'no parking'

intéresser [ɛterese] **1** *vt (captiver)* to interest; *(concerner)* to concern **2** **s'intéresser** *vpr* **s'i. à qn/qch** to be interested in sb/sth ▪ **intéressant, -e** *adj (captivant)* interesting; *(prix)* attractive **2** *nmf Péj* **faire l'i.** to show off ▪ **intéressé, -e 1** *adj (avide)* self-interested; *(motif)* selfish; *(concerné)* concerned **2** *nmf* **l'i.** the person concerned

intérêt [ɛterɛ] *nm* interest; *Fin* **intérêts** interest; **tu as i. à le faire** you'd do well to do it; **sans i.** *(personne, film)* uninteresting

intérieur, -eure [ɛterjœr] **1** *adj (escalier, paroi)* interior; *(cour, vie)* inner; *(poche)* inside; *(partie)* internal; *(vol)* internal, domestic; *(mer)* inland **2** *nm (de boîte, de maison)* inside (**de** of); *(de pays)* interior; *(maison)* home; **à l'i. (de)** inside; **d'i.** *(vêtement, jeux)* indoor

intérim [ɛterim] *nm (travail temporaire)* temporary work; **président par i.** acting president ▪ **intérimaire 1** *adj (fonction, employé)* temporary **2** *nmf (travailleur)* temporary worker; *(secrétaire)* temp

interlocuteur, -trice [ɛterlɔkytœr, -tris] *nmf (de conversation)* speaker; *(de négociation)* discussion partner; **mon i.** the person I am/was speaking to

intermède [ɛtermɛd] *nm* interlude

intermédiaire [ɛtermedjɛr] **1** *adj* intermediate **2** *nmf* intermediary; *Com* middleman; **par l'i. de** through; **sans i.** directly

interminable [ɛterminabl] *adj* interminable

intermittent, -e [ɛtermitã, -ãt] *adj* intermittent ▪ **intermittence** *nf* **par i.** intermittently

internat [ɛterna] *nm (école)* boarding school; *(concours de médecine)* = entrance examination for an internship ▪ **interne 1** *adj (douleur)* internal; *(oreille)* inner **2** *nmf (élève)* boarder; **i. des hôpitaux** *Br* house doctor, *Am* intern

international, -e, -aux, -ales [ɛternasjɔnal, -o] **1** *adj* international **2** *nm (footballeur)* international

interner [ɛterne] *vt (prisonnier)* to intern; *(aliéné)* to commit ▪ **internement** [-əmã] *nm (emprisonnement)* internment; *(d'aliéné)* confinement

Internet [ɛternɛt] *nm* Internet; **sur (l')I.** on the Internet; **avoir accès à l'i.** to have access to the Internet, to have Internet access ▪ **internaute** *nmf* Internet surfer

interpeller [ɛterpəle] *vt (appeler)* to call out to; *(dans une réunion)* to question; **i. qn** *(police)* to take sb in for questioning ▪ **interpellation** *nf* sharp address; *(dans une réunion)* question

interposer [ɛterpoze] **s'interposer** *vpr (intervenir)* to intervene (**dans** in)

interprète [ɛterprɛt] *nmf (traducteur)* interpreter; *(chanteur)* singer; *(musicien, acteur)* performer ▪ **interprétariat** *nm* interpreting ▪ **interprétation** *nf (de texte, de rôle, de rêve)* interpretation; *(traduction)* interpreting ▪ **interpréter** *vt (texte, rôle, musique, rêve)* to interpret; *(chanter)* to sing

interroger [ɛterɔʒe] *vt* to question; *(élève)* to test; *Ordinat (banque de données)* to query ▪ **interrogateur, -trice** *adj (air)* questioning ▪ **interrogation** *nf (question)* question; *(de prisonnier)* questioning; *Scol* **i. écrite/orale** written/oral test ▪ **interrogatoire** *nm* interrogation

interrompre* [ɛterɔ̃pr] **1** *vt* to interrupt **2** **s'interrompre** *vpr* to break off ▪ **interrupteur** *nm* switch ▪ **interruption** *nf* interruption; *(de négociations)* breaking off; **sans i.** continuously; **i. volontaire de grossesse** termination

intersection [ɛtersɛksjɔ̃] *nf* intersection

intervalle [ɛterval] *nm (dans l'espace)* gap, space; *(dans le temps)* interval; **dans l'i.** *(entretemps)* in the meantime; **par intervalles** (every) now and then, at intervals

intervenir* [ɛtervənir] *vi (agir, prendre la parole)* to intervene; *(survenir)* to occur; **être intervenu** *(accord)* to be reached ▪ **intervention** *nf* intervention; *(discours)* speech; **i. chirurgicale** operation

intervertir [ɛtervertir] *vt* to invert

interview [ɛ̃tɛrvju] *nm ou f* interview ■ **interviewer** [-vjuve] *vt* to interview

intestin [ɛ̃tɛstɛ̃] *nm* intestine

intime [ɛ̃tim] **1** *adj* intimate; *(ami)* close; *(cérémonie)* quiet **2** *nmf* close friend ■ **intimement** [-əmɑ̃] *adv* intimately; **i. liés** *(problèmes)* closely linked ■ **intimité** *nf (familiarité)* intimacy; *(vie privée)* privacy; **dans l'i.** in private

intimider [ɛ̃timide] *vt* to intimidate

intituler [ɛ̃tityle] **1** *vt* to give a title to **2 s'intituler** *vpr* to be entitled

intolérable [ɛ̃tɔlerabl] *adj* intolerable ■ **intolérance** *nf* intolerance ■ **intolérant, -e** *adj* intolerant

intoxiquer [ɛ̃tɔksike] **1** *vt (empoisonner)* to poison **2 s'intoxiquer** *vpr* to poison oneself ■ **intoxication** *nf (empoisonnement)* poisoning; **i. alimentaire** food poisoning

intraitable [ɛ̃trɛtabl] *adj* uncompromising

intransigeant, -e [ɛ̃trɑ̃ziʒɑ̃, -ɑ̃t] *adj* intransigent

intrépide [ɛ̃trepid] *adj* fearless, intrepid

intrigue [ɛ̃trig] *nf* intrigue; *(de film, roman)* plot ■ **intriguer 1** *vt* **i. qn** to intrigue sb **2** *vi* to scheme

introduire* [ɛ̃trɔdɥir] **1** *vt (insérer)* to insert (**dans** into); *(marchandises)* to bring in; *(réforme, mode)* to introduce; *(visiteur)* to show in **2 s'introduire** *vpr* **s'i. dans une maison** to get into a house ■ **introduction** *nf (texte, action)* introduction

introuvable [ɛ̃truvabl] *adj (produit)* unobtainable; *(personne)* nowhere to be found

introverti, -e [ɛ̃trɔverti] *nmf* introvert

intrus, -e [ɛ̃try, -yz] *nmf* intruder ■ **intrusion** *nf* intrusion (**dans** into)

intuition [ɛ̃tɥisjɔ̃] *nf* intuition ■ **intuitif, -ive** *adj* intuitive

inuit [inɥit] **1** *adj inv* Inuit **2** *nmf inv* **I.** Inuit

inusable [inyzabl] *adj* hard-wearing

inusité, -e [inyzite] *adj (mot, forme)* uncommon

inutile [inytil] *adj (qui ne sert à rien)* useless; *(précaution, bagage)* unnecessary; **c'est i. de crier** it's pointless shouting ■ **inutilement** *adv* needlessly ■ **inutilité** *nf* uselessness

inutilisable [inytilizabl] *adj* unusable ■ **inutilisé, -e** *adj* unused

invaincu, -e [ɛ̃vɛ̃ky] *adj Sport* unbeaten

invalide [ɛ̃valid] **1** *adj* disabled **2** *nmf* disabled person

invalider [ɛ̃valide] *vt* to invalidate

invariable [ɛ̃varjabl] *adj* invariable

invasion [ɛ̃vazjɔ̃] *nf* invasion

invendable [ɛ̃vɑ̃dabl] *adj* unsellable ■ **invendu, -e 1** *adj* unsold **2** *nmpl* **invendus** unsold articles; *(journaux)* unsold copies

inventaire [ɛ̃vɑ̃tɛr] *nm* Com *(liste)* inventory; **faire l'i.** to do the stocktaking (**de** of)

inventer [ɛ̃vɑ̃te] *vt (créer)* to invent; *(concept)* to think up; *(histoire, excuse)* to make up ■ **inventeur, -trice** *nmf* inventor ■ **inventif, -ive** *adj* inventive ■ **invention** *nf* invention

inverse [ɛ̃vers] **1** *adj (sens)* opposite; *(ordre)* reverse; *Math* inverse **2** *nm* **l'i.** the reverse, the opposite ■ **inversement** [-əmɑ̃] *adv* conversely ■ **inverser** *vt (ordre)* to reverse ■ **inversion** *nf* inversion

investigation [ɛ̃vestigasjɔ̃] *nf* investigation

investir [ɛ̃vestir] **1** *vt (capitaux)* to invest (**dans** in); *(édifice, ville)* to besiege **2** *vi* to invest (**dans** in) ■ **investissement** *nm* Fin investment

invincible [ɛ̃vɛ̃sibl] *adj* invincible

invisible [ɛ̃vizibl] *adj* invisible

inviter [ɛ̃vite] *vt* to invite; **i. qn à faire qch** *(prier)* to request sb to do sth; *(inciter)* to urge sb to do sth; **i. qn à dîner** to invite sb to dinner ■ **invitation** *nf* invitation ■ **invité, -e** *nmf* guest

involontaire [ɛ̃vɔlɔ̃tɛr] *adj (geste)* involuntary; *(témoin)* unwilling

invoquer [ɛ̃vɔke] *vt (argument)* to put forward; *(loi, texte)* to refer to; *(divinité)*

to invoke ▪ **invocation** *nf* invocation (à to)

invraisemblable [ɛ̃vrɛsɑ̃blabl] *adj (extraordinaire)* incredible; *(alibi)* implausible ▪ **invraisemblance** *nf (improbabilité)* unlikelihood; *(d'alibi)* implausibility

invulnérable [ɛ̃vylnerabl] *adj* invulnerable

ira, irait etc [ira, irɛ] *voir* **aller¹**

Irak [irak] *nm* l'I. Iraq ▪ **irakien, -enne** 1 *adj* Iraqi 2 *nmf* I., Irakienne Iraqi

Iran [irɑ̃] *nm* l'I. Iran ▪ **iranien, -enne** 1 *adj* Iranian 2 *nmf* I., Iranienne Iranian

iris [iris] *nm (plante)* & *Anat* iris

Irlande [irlɑ̃d] *nf* l'I. Ireland; l'I. du Nord Northern Ireland ▪ **irlandais, -e** 1 *adj* Irish 2 *nmf* I. Irishman; Irlandaise Irishwoman; les I. the Irish 3 *nm (langue)* Irish

ironie [ironi] *nf* irony ▪ **ironique** *adj* ironic(al)

iront [irɔ̃] *voir* **aller¹**

irrationnel, -elle [irasjonɛl] *adj* irrational

irréalisable [irealizabl] *adj (projet)* impracticable

irréaliste [irealist] *adj* unrealistic

irrécusable [irekyzabl] *adj (preuve)* indisputable; *Jur (témoignage)* unimpeachable

irréductible [iredyktibl] 1 *adj (ennemi)* implacable 2 *nm* diehard

irréel, -elle [ireɛl] *adj* unreal

irréfléchi, -e [ireflefi] *adj* rash

irréfutable [irefytabl] *adj* irrefutable

irrégulier, -ère [iregylje, -ɛr] *adj (rythme, verbe, procédure)* irregular; *(sol)* uneven; *(résultats)* inconsistent ▪ **irrégularité** *nf* irregularity; *(de sol)* unevenness

irrémédiable [iremedjabl] *adj* irreparable

irremplaçable [irɑ̃plasabl] *adj* irreplaceable

irréparable [ireparabl] *adj (véhicule)* beyond repair; *(tort, perte)* irreparable

irrépressible [irepresibl] *adj* irrepressible

irréprochable [ireprɔfabl] *adj* irreproachable

irrésistible [irezistibl] *adj (personne, charme)* irresistible

irrésolu, -e [irezɔly] *adj (personne)* indecisive; *(problème)* unresolved

irrespirable [irespirabl] *adj (air)* unbreathable; *Fig (atmosphère)* unbearable

irresponsable [irɛspɔ̃sabl] *adj (personne)* irresponsible

irréversible [ireversibl] *adj* irreversible

irrévocable [irevɔkabl] *adj* irrevocable

irrigation [irigɑsjɔ̃] *nf* irrigation

irriter [irite] 1 *vt* to irritate 2 **s'irriter** *vpr (s'énerver)* to get irritated (**de** with; **contre** at); *(s'enflammer)* to become irritated ▪ **irritable** *adj* irritable ▪ **irritation** *nf (colère)* & *Méd* irritation

irruption [irypsjɔ̃] *nf* faire i. dans to burst into

Islam [islam] *nm* l'I. Islam ▪ **islamique** *adj* Islamic

Islande [islɑ̃d] *nf* l'I. Iceland ▪ **islandais, -e** 1 *adj* Icelandic 2 *nmf* I., Islandaise Icelander

isolant, -e [izɔlɑ̃, -ɑ̃t] 1 *adj* insulating 2 *nm* insulating material

isoler [izɔle] 1 *vt* to isolate (**de** from); *(du froid)* & *Él* to insulate 2 **s'isoler** *vpr* to isolate oneself ▪ **isolation** *nf* insulation ▪ **isolé, -e** *adj (personne, endroit, maison)* isolated; *(du froid)* insulated; i. de cut off *or* isolated from ▪ **isolement** *nm (de personne)* isolation; ▪ **isolément** *adv (agir)* in isolation; *(interroger des gens)* individually

isoloir [izɔlwar] *nm Br* polling *or Am* voting booth

Israël [israɛl] *nm* Israel ▪ **israélien, -enne** 1 *adj* Israeli 2 *nmf* I., Israélienne Israeli ▪ **israélite** 1 *adj* Jewish 2 *nmf* Jew

issu, -e [isy] *adj* être i. de to come from

issue [isy] *nf (sortie)* exit; *Fig (solution)*

way out; *(résultat)* outcome; **à l'i. de** at the end of; **i. de secours** emergency exit

isthme [ism] *nm* isthmus

Italie [itali] *nf* l'**I.** Italy ■ **ital_ien, -enne** **1** *adj* Italian **2** *nmf* **I., Italienne** Italian **3** *nm (langue)* Italian

italique [italik] **1** *adj (lettre)* italic **2** *nm* italics; **en i.** in italics

itinéraire [itinerer] *nm* route, itinerary

IUT [iyte] *(abrév* **institut universitaire de technologie)** *nm* = vocational higher education college

IVG [iveʒe] *(abrév* **interruption volontaire de grossesse)** *nf* abortion, termination

ivoire [ivwar] *nm* ivory; **statuette en i.** *ou* **d'i.** ivory statuette

ivre [ivr] *adj* drunk **(de** with); *Fig* **i. de joie** wild with joy ■ **ivresse** *nf* drunkenness; **en état d'i.** under the influence of drink ■ **ivrogne** *nmf* drunk(ard)

Jj

J, j [ʒi] *nm inv* J, j; **le jour J.** D-day

j' [ʒ] *voir* **je**

jadis [ʒadis] *adv Littéraire* in times past

jaillir [ʒajir] *vi (liquide)* to gush out; *(étincelles)* to shoot out

jalonner [ʒalɔne] *vt (marquer)* to mark out; *(border)* to line

jaloux, -ouse [ʒalu, -uz] *adj* jealous (**de** of) ▪ **jalousie** *nf (sentiment)* jealousy

Jamaïque [ʒamaik] *nf* **la J.** Jamaica

jamais [ʒamɛ] *adv* **(a)** *(négatif)* never; **elle ne sort j.** she never goes out; **sans j. sortir** without ever going out
(b) *(positif)* ever; **à tout j.** for ever; **si j.** if ever; **le film le plus drôle que j'aie j. vu** the funniest film I have ever seen

jambe [ʒɑ̃b] *nf* leg

jambon [ʒɑ̃bɔ̃] *nm* ham

janvier [ʒɑ̃vje] *nm* January

Japon [ʒapɔ̃] *nm* **le J.** Japan ▪ **japonais, -e 1** *adj* Japanese **2** *nmf* **J., Japonaise** Japanese *inv*; **les J.** the Japanese **3** *nm (langue)* Japanese

jardin [ʒardɛ̃] *nm* garden; **j. d'enfants** kindergarten; **j. public** gardens ▪ **jardinage** *nm* gardening ▪ **jardinier** *nm* gardener

jargon [ʒargɔ̃] *nm* jargon

jasmin [ʒasmɛ̃] *nm* jasmine; **thé au j.** jasmine tea

jaune [ʒon] **1** *adj* yellow **2** *nm (couleur)* yellow; **j. d'œuf** (egg) yolk

Javel [ʒavɛl] **eau de Javel** *nf* bleach

javelot [ʒavlo] *nm* javelin

jazz [dʒaz] *nm* jazz

je [ʒə]

> **j'** is used before a word beginning with a vowel or h mute.

pron personnel I; **je suis ici** I'm here

jean [dʒin] *nm* (pair of) jeans; **veste en j.** *Br* denim *or Am* jeans jacket

Jersey [ʒɛrzɛ] *nf* Jersey

jet [ʒɛ] *nm (de pierre)* throwing; *(de vapeur, de liquide)* jet; **j. d'eau** fountain

jetable [ʒətabl] *adj* disposable

jetée [ʒəte] *nf* pier, jetty

jeter [ʒəte] **1** *vt* to throw (**à** to; **dans** into); *(à la poubelle)* to throw away; *(sort)* to cast; **j. un coup d'œil à qn/qch** to have a quick look at sb/sth
2 se jeter *vpr (personne)* to throw oneself; **se j. sur qn** to throw oneself at sb; *Fig* to pounce on sb; **se j. sur qch** *(occasion)* to jump at sth; **se j. contre** *(véhicule)* to crash into; **se j. dans** *(fleuve)* to flow into

jeton [ʒətɔ̃] *nm (pièce)* token; *(au jeu)* chip

jeu, -x [ʒø] *nm* **(a)** *(amusement)* play; *(activité, au tennis)* game; *(d'acteur)* acting; **le j.** *(au casino)* gambling; **en j.** *(en cause)* at stake; *(forces)* at work; **j.-concours** competition; **j. électronique** computer game; **j. de hasard** game of chance; **j. de mots** play on words, pun; **jeux de société** board games; **j. télévisé** television game show; *(avec questions)* television quiz show; **j. vidéo** video game
(b) *(série complète)* set; *(de cartes)* deck, *Br* pack; *(cartes en main)* hand; **j. d'échecs** *(boîte, pièces)* chess set
(c) *Tech (de ressort, de verrou)* play

jeudi [ʒødi] *nm* Thursday

jeun [ʒœ̃] **à jeun 1** *adv* on an empty stomach **2** *adj* **être à j.** to have eaten no food

jeune [ʒœn] **1** *adj* young; *(apparence)* youthful; **jeunes gens** young people **2** *nmf* young person; **les jeunes** young

people ■ **jeunesse** *nf* youth; *(apparence)* youthfulness; **la j.** *(les jeunes)* the young

jeûner [ʒøne] *vi* to fast

joaillier, -ère [ʒɔaje, -ɛr] *nmf Br* jeweller, *Am* jeweler ■ **joaillerie** *nf (bijoux) Br* jewellery, *Am* jewelry; *(magasin) Br* jewellery shop, *Am* jewelry store

jockey [ʒɔkɛ] *nm* jockey

jogging [dʒɔgiŋ] *nm Sport* jogging; *(survêtement)* jogging suit

joie [ʒwa] *nf* joy, delight; **avec j.** with pleasure, gladly

joindre* [ʒwɛdr] **1** *vt (réunir)* to join; *(ajouter)* to add (à to); *(dans une enveloppe)* to enclose (à with); **j. qn** *(contacter)* to get in touch with sb
2 se joindre *vpr* **se j. à qn** to join sb ■ **joint, -e 1** *adj* **à pieds joints** with feet together; **pièces jointes** *(de lettre)* enclosures **2** *nm Tech (articulation)* joint; *(d'étanchéité)* seal; *(de robinet)* washer; **j. de culasse** gasket

joker [ʒɔkɛr] *nm Cartes* joker

joli, -e [ʒɔli] *adj* pretty

jonché [ʒɔ̃ʃe] *adj* **j. de** strewn with

jonction [ʒɔ̃ksjɔ̃] *nf* junction

jongler [ʒɔ̃gle] *vi* to juggle (**avec** with)

jonquille [ʒɔ̃kij] *nf* daffodil

Jordanie [ʒɔrdani] *nf* **la J.** Jordan

joue [ʒu] *nf (du visage)* cheek

jouer [ʒwe] **1** *vt (musique, carte, rôle)* to play; *(pièce de théâtre)* to perform; *(film)* to show; *(parier)* to stake (**sur** on); *(cheval)* to bet on
2 *vi* to play; *(acteur)* to act; *(au tiercé)* to gamble; *(être important)* to count; **j. au tennis/aux cartes** to play tennis/cards; **j. du piano/du violon** to play the piano/violin; **à toi de j.!** it's your turn (to play)!
3 se jouer *vpr (film, pièce)* to be on

jouet [ʒwɛ] *nm* toy

joueur, -euse [ʒwœr, -øz] *nmf* player; *(au tiercé)* gambler

jouir [ʒwir] *vi* **j. de qch** to enjoy sth

jour [ʒur] *nm (journée, date)* day; *(clarté)* daylight; *(éclairage)* light; **il fait j.** it's (day)light; **de j. en j.** day by day;

du j. au lendemain overnight; **en plein j., au grand j.** in broad daylight; **de nos jours** nowadays, these days; *Fig* **sous un j. nouveau** in a different light; **mettre qch à j.** to bring sth up to date; **quel j. sommes-nous?** what day is it?; **il y a dix ans j. pour j.** ten years ago to the day; **le j. de l'an** New Year's Day

journal, -aux [ʒurnal, -o] *nm* (news)-paper; *(spécialisé, intime)* journal; **j. télévisé** (TV) news ■ **journalisme** *nm* journalism ■ **journaliste** *nmf* journalist

journalier, -ère [ʒurnalje, -ɛr] *adj* daily

journée [ʒurne] *nf* day; **pendant la j.** during the day(time); **toute la j.** all day (long)

jovial, -e, -aux, -ales [ʒɔvjal, -o] *adj* jovial, jolly

joyau, -x [ʒwajo] *nm* jewel

joyeux, -euse [ʒwajø, -øz] *adj* joyful; **j. anniversaire!** happy birthday!; **j. Noël!** merry *or Br* happy Christmas!

jubiler [ʒybile] *vi* to be jubilant

jucher [ʒyʃe] *vt, se jucher vpr* to perch (**sur** on)

judicieux, -euse [ʒydisjø, -øz] *adj* judicious

judo [ʒydo] *nm* judo

juge [ʒyʒ] *nm* judge; **j. de touche** *(au football)* linesman, assistant referee

jugé [ʒyʒe] **au jugé** *adv (calculer)* roughly

jugement [ʒyʒmɑ̃] *nm (opinion, discernement)* judgement; *(verdict)* sentence; **porter un j. sur qch** to pass judgement on sth; *Jur* **passer en j.** to stand trial

juger [ʒyʒe] **1** *vt (personne, question)* to judge; *(au tribunal)* to try; *(estimer)* to consider (**que** that) **2** *vi* **j. de** to judge; **jugez de ma surprise!** imagine my surprise!

juif, juive [ʒɥif, ʒɥiv] **1** *adj* Jewish **2** *nmf* **J.** Jew

juillet [ʒɥijɛ] *nm* July

juin [ʒɥɛ̃] *nm* June

jumeau, -elle, -x, -elles [ʒymo, -ɛl]

1 *adj* **frère j.** twin brother; **sœur jumelle** twin sister; **lits jumeaux** twin beds **2** *nmf* twin ■ **jumeler** *vt (villes)* to twin ■ **jumelles** *nfpl (pour regarder)* binoculars

jument [ʒymã] *nf* mare

jungle [ʒœ̃gl] *nf* jungle

junior [ʒynjɔr] *nm & adj inv Sport* junior

jupe [ʒyp] *nf* skirt

jurer [ʒyre] **1** *vt (promettre)* to swear (**que** that; **de faire** to do) **2** *vi (dire un gros mot)* to swear (**contre** at); *(contraster)* to clash (**avec** with); **j. de qch** to swear to sth ■ **juré, -e 1** *adj* **ennemi j.** sworn enemy **2** *nm Jur* juror

juriste [ʒyrist] *nmf* legal expert

juron [ʒyrɔ̃] *nm* swearword

jury [ʒyri] *nm Jur* jury; *(d'examen)* board of examiners

jus [ʒy] *nm (de fruits)* juice; *(de viande)* gravy; **j. d'orange** orange juice

jusque [ʒysk] **1** *prép* **jusqu'à** *(espace)* as far as, (right) up to; *(temps)* until, (up) till, to; *(même)* even; **jusqu'en mai** until May; **jusqu'où?** how far?; **jusqu'ici** as far as this; *(temps)* up till now; **j. chez moi** as far as my place

2 *conj* **jusqu'à ce qu'il vienne** until he comes

juste [ʒyst] **1** *adj (équitable)* fair, just; *(exact)* right, correct; *(étroit)* tight; *(raisonnement)* sound; **un peu j.** *(quantité, qualité)* barely enough

2 *adv (deviner, compter)* correctly, right; *(chanter)* in tune; *(précisément, à peine)* just; **à trois heures j.** on the stroke of three; **un peu j.** *(mesurer, compter)* a bit on the short side ■ **justement** [-əmã] *adv (précisément)* exactly; *(avec justesse, avec justice)* justly; **j. j'allais t'appeler** I was just going to call you

justesse [ʒystɛs] *nf (exactitude)* accuracy; **de j.** *(éviter, gagner)* just

justice [ʒystis] *nf (équité)* justice; **la j.** *(autorité)* the law; **rendre j. à qn** to do justice to sb

justifier [ʒystifje] **1** *vt* to justify **2 se justifier** *vpr* to justify oneself (**de** of) ■ **justification** *nf (explication)* justification; *(preuve)* proof

juteux, -euse [ʒytø, -øz] *adj* juicy

Kk

K, k [ka] *nm inv* K, k
kangourou [kãguru] *nm* kangaroo
karaté [karate] *nm* karate
karting [kartiŋ] *nm* karting
kasher [kaʃɛr] *adj inv Rel* kosher
kayak [kajak] *nm (bateau de sport)* canoe
Kenya [kenja] *nm* **le K.** Kenya
kermesse [kermɛs] *nf* charity fair *or Br* fête; *(en Belgique)* village fair
kérosène [kerozɛn] *nm* kerosene
kidnapper [kidnape] *vt* to kidnap ▪ **kidnappeur, -euse** *nmf* kidnapper
kilo [kilo] *nm* kilo ▪ **kilogramme** *nm* kilogram(me)
kilomètre [kilɔmetr] *nm Br* kilometre, *Am* kilometer ▪ **kilométrage** *nm Aut* ≃ mileage ▪ **kilométrique** *adj* **borne k.** ≃ milestone

kilo-octet [kilɔktɛ] *(pl* **kilo-octets)** *nm Ordinat* kilobyte
kilowatt [kilɔwat] *nm* kilowatt
kinésithérapeute [kineziterapøt] *nmf Br* physiotherapist, *Am* physical therapist
kiosque [kjɔsk] *nm (à fleurs)* kiosk, *Br* stall; **k. à journaux** news-stand
kit [kit] *nm* (self-assembly) kit; **en k.** in kit form
kiwi [kiwi] *nm (oiseau, fruit)* kiwi
Klaxon® [klaksɔn] *nm* horn ▪ **klaxonner** *vi* to sound one's horn
km *(abrév* **kilomètre)** km
km/h *(abrév* **kilomètre-heure)** kph, ≃ mph
Koweït [kɔwɛjt] *nm* **le K.** Kuwait ▪ **koweïtien, -enne 1** *adj* Kuwaiti **2** *nmf* **K., Koweïtienne** Kuwaiti

LI

L, l [εl] *nm inv* L, l

l', la¹ [l, la] *voir* **le**

la² [la] *nm inv (note)* A

là [la] **1** *adv (là-bas)* there; *(ici)* here; **c'est là que…** *(lieu)* that's where…; **à 5 mètres de là** 5 metres away **2** *exclam* **oh là là!** oh dear! **3** *voir* **ce¹, celui**

là-bas [labɑ] *adv* over there

laboratoire [labɔratwar] *nm* laboratory

labourer [labure] *vt (terre) Br* to plough, *Am* to plow

lac [lak] *nm* lake

lacet [lasε] *nm (de chaussure)* lace; **faire ses lacets** to tie one's laces

lâche [lɑʃ] **1** *adj (nœud)* loose, slack; *Péj (personne, acte)* cowardly **2** *nmf* coward ▪ **lâcheté** *nf* cowardice; **une l.** *(action)* a cowardly act

lâcher [lɑʃe] **1** *vt (ne plus tenir)* to let go of; *(bombe)* to drop; *(poursuivant)* to shake off; *(dans une course)* to leave behind; **l. prise** to let go **2** *vi (corde)* to break

là-dedans [ladədɑ̃] *adv (lieu)* in there, inside

là-dessous [ladəsu] *adv* underneath

là-dessus [ladəsy] *adv* on there; *(monter)* on top

là-haut [lao] *adv* up there; *(à l'étage)* upstairs

laid, -e [lε, lεd] *adj (physiquement)* ugly ▪ **laideur** *nf* ugliness

laine [lεn] *nf* wool; **de l., en l.** *Br* woollen, *Am* woolen ▪ **lainage** *nm (vêtement)* sweater, *Br* jumper

laisse [lεs] *nf* lead, leash

laisser [lese] **1** *vt* to leave; **l. qn partir** *(permettre)* to let sb go; **l. qch à qn** *(confier, donner)* to leave sth with sb **2** **se laisser** *vpr* **se l. aller** to let oneself go; **se l. faire** to be pushed around

lait [lε] *nm* milk; **l. entier/demi-écrémé/écrémé** whole/part-skim/skim milk ▪ **laitier** *adj m* **produit l.** dairy product

laitue [lεty] *nf* lettuce

lame [lam] *nf (de couteau, de rasoir)* blade; *(vague)* wave

lamelle [lamεl] *nf* thin strip

lamenter [lamɑ̃te] **se lamenter** *vpr* to moan ▪ **lamentable** *adj (mauvais)* terrible, deplorable; *(voix, cri)* mournful; *(personne)* pathetic

lampadaire [lɑ̃padεr] *nm Br* standard lamp, *Am* floor lamp; *(de rue)* street lamp

lampe [lɑ̃p] *nf* lamp; **l. de poche** *Br* torch, *Am* flashlight

lance [lɑ̃s] *nf* spear

lancer [lɑ̃se] **1** *vt (jeter)* to throw (à to); *(fusée, produit)* to launch; *(appel)* to issue **2** **se lancer** *vpr (se précipiter)* to rush; **se l. dans** *(aventure)* to launch into **3** *nm Sport* **l. du javelot** throwing the javelin; **l. franc** *(au basket)* free throw ▪ **lancement** *nm (de fusée, de produit)* launch(ing)

landau, -s [lɑ̃do] *nm Br* pram, *Am* baby carriage

langage [lɑ̃gaʒ] *nm* language; *Ordinat* **l. machine/naturel** computer/natural language

langer [lɑ̃ʒe] *vt (bébé)* to change

langouste [lɑ̃gust] *nf* crayfish ▪ **langoustine** *nf* langoustine

langue [lɑ̃g] *nf Anat* tongue; *Ling* language; **de l. anglaise/française** English-/French-speaking; **l. étrangère** foreign language; **l. maternelle** mother tongue; **langues vivantes**

modern languages ■ **languette** *nf (patte)* tongue

lanière [lanjɛr] *nf* strap; *(d'étoffe)* strip

lapin [lapɛ̃] *nm* rabbit

laque [lak] *nf (pour cheveux)* hair spray

laquelle [lakɛl] *voir* **lequel**

lard [lar] *nm (viande)* bacon ■ **lardon** *nm Culin* strip of bacon

large [larʒ] **1** *adj (route, porte, chaussure)* wide; *(considérable)* **l. de 6 mètres** 6 metres wide

2 *nm* **avoir 6 mètres de l.** to be 6 *Br* metres *or Am* meters wide; **au l. de Cherbourg** off Cherbourg ■ **largement** [-əmɑ̃] *adv (répandu, critiqué)* widely; *(payer, servir)* generously; *(dépasser)* by a long way; **avoir l. le temps** to have plenty of time ■ **largeur** *nf (dimension)* width, breadth; **en l., dans la l.** widthwise

larguer [large] *vt (bombe)* to drop; *Naut* **l. les amarres** to cast off

larme [larm] *nf* tear; **en larmes** in tears; **rire aux larmes** to laugh till one cries

las, lasse [lɑ, lɑs] *adj* weary **(de** of) ■ **lassant, -e** *adj* tiresome ■ **lasser 1** *vt* to tire **2 se lasser** *vpr* **se l. de qch/de faire qch** to get tired of sth/of doing sth

laser [lazɛr] *nm* laser

latéral, -e, -aux, -ales [lateral, -o] *adj* side

latin, -e [latɛ̃, -in] **1** *adj* Latin **2** *nmf* **L., Latine** Latin **3** *nm (langue)* Latin

lavabo [lavabo] *nm* washbasin; **lavabos** *(toilettes) Br* toilet(s), *Am* washroom

lavande [lavɑ̃d] *nf* lavender

lave [lav] *nf* lava

laver [lave] **1** *vt* to wash; **l. qch à l'eau froide** to wash sth in cold water **2 se laver** *vpr* to wash (oneself), *Am* to wash up; **se l. les mains** to wash one's hands ■ **lavable** *adj* washable ■ **lavage** *nm* washing ■ **lave-auto** *(pl* **lave-autos)** *nm Can* carwash ■ **lave-linge** *nm inv* washing machine ■ **laverie** *nf (automatique) Br* launderette, *Am* Laundromat® ■ **laveur** *nm* **l. de vitres** window *Br* cleaner *or Am* washer ■ **lave-**

vaisselle *nm inv* dishwasher

1 *article défini* **(a)** *(pour définir le nom)* the; **le garçon** the boy; **la fille** the girl; **les petits** the little ones

(b) *(avec les notions)* **la vie** life; **la France** France; **les Français** the French; **les hommes** men; **aimer le café** to like coffee

(c) *(avec les parties du corps)* **il ouvrit la bouche** he opened his mouth; **se blesser au pied** to hurt one's foot; **avoir les cheveux blonds** to have blond hair

(d) *(distributif)* **10 euros le kilo** 10 euros a kilo

(e) *(dans les compléments de temps)* **elle vient le lundi** she comes on Mondays; **l'an prochain** next year

2 *pron (homme)* him; *(femme)* her; *(chose, animal)* it; **les** them; **je la vois** I see her/it; **je le vois** I see him/it; **je les vois** I see them

lécher [leʃe] *vt* to lick

leçon [ləsɔ̃] *nf* lesson

lecteur, -trice [lɛktœr, -tris] *nmf* reader; *Univ* foreign language assistant; **l. de cassettes/de CD** cassette/CD player; *Ordinat* **l. de disques** *ou* **de disquettes** disk drive ■ **lecture** *nf* reading

légal, -e, -aux, -ales [legal, -o] *adj* legal ■ **légaliser** *vt* to legalize ■ **légalité** *nf* legality **(de** of)

légende [leʒɑ̃d] *nf (histoire)* legend; *(de carte)* key; *(de photo)* caption

léger, -ère [leʒe, -ɛr] **1** *adj* light; *(blessure, odeur)* slight; *(café, thé)* weak; *(bière, tabac)* mild; *(frivole)* frivolous; *(irréfléchi)* thoughtless

2 *adv* **manger l.** to have a light meal

3 *nf* **prendre qch à la légère** to make light of sth ■ **légèrement** *adv (inconsidérément)* lightly; *(un peu)* slightly ■ **légèreté** *nf (poids)* lightness; *(de blessure)* slightness; *(d'attitude)* thoughtlessness

légion [leʒjɔ̃] *nf Mil* legion ▪ **légionnaire** *nm (de la Légion étrangère)* legionnaire

législatif, -ive [leʒislatif, -iv] *adj* legislative; *(élections)* parliamentary

légitime [leʒitim] *adj (action, enfant)* legitimate; *(héritier)* rightful; *(colère)* justified; **être en état de l. défense** to be acting in *Br* self-defence *or Am* self-defense

léguer [lege] *vt* to bequeath (**à** to)

légume [legym] *nm* vegetable

lendemain [lɑ̃dmɛ̃] *nm* **le l.** the next day; **le l. de** the day after; **le l. matin** the next morning

lent, -e [lɑ̃, lɑ̃t] *adj* slow

lentille [lɑ̃tij] *nf (plante, graine)* lentil; *(verre)* lens; **lentilles de contact** contact lenses

lequel, laquelle [ləkɛl, lakɛl] *(mpl* **lesquels,** *fpl* **lesquelles** [lekɛl])

> **lequel** and **lesquel(le)s** contract with **à** to form **auquel** and **auxquel(le)s,** and with **de** to form **duquel** and **desquel(le)s.**

1 *pron relatif (chose, animal)* which; *(personne)* who; *(indirect)* whom; **dans l.** in which; **parmi lesquels** *(choses, animaux)* among which; *(personnes)* among whom **2** *pron interrogatif* which (one); **l. préférez-vous?** which (one) do you prefer?

les [le] *voir* **le**

lessive [lesiv] *nf (produit)* washing powder; *(liquide)* liquid detergent; *(linge)* washing; **faire la l.** to do the washing

lettre [lɛtr] *nf (missive, caractère)* letter; **envoyer/recevoir une l.** to send/receive a letter; **l. commerciale** business letter; **l. de démission** letter of resignation; **l. de motivation** covering letter *(sent with job application)* ▪ **lettres** *nfpl (discipline)* arts, humanities

leur [lœr] **1** *adj possessif* their; **l. chat** their cat; **leurs voitures** their cars **2** *pron possessif* **le l., la l., les leurs** theirs **3** *pron personnel (indirect)* to them; **donne-l. ta carte** give them your card

lever [ləve] **1** *vt (objet)* to lift, to raise; *(blocus, immunité)* to lift; *(séance)* to close; *(impôts)* to levy **2** *vi (pâte)* to rise **3 se lever** *vpr* to get up; *(soleil)* to rise; *(jour)* to break; *(brouillard)* to clear, to lift **4** *nm* **le l. du soleil** sunrise; *Théât* **l. de rideau** curtain up ▪ **levé, -e** *adj* **être l.** *(debout)* to be up ▪ **levée** *nf (d'interdiction)* lifting; *(du courrier)* collection

levier [ləvje] *nm* lever; *Aut* **l. de vitesse** *Br* gear lever, *Am* gearshift

lèvre [lɛvr] *nf* lip

lévrier [levrije] *nm* greyhound

levure [ləvyr] *nf* yeast

lézard [lezar] *nm* lizard ▪ **lézarder se lézarder** *vpr* to crack

liaison [ljezɔ̃] *nf (rapport)* connection; *(entre mots)* & *Mil* liaison; **l. aérienne/ferroviaire** air/rail link; **l. amoureuse** love affair

Liban [libɑ̃] *nm* **le L.** (the) Lebanon ▪ **libanais, -e 1** *adj* Lebanese **2** *nmf* **L., Libanaise** Lebanese

libeller [libele] *vt (chèque)* to make out

libéral, -e, -aux, -ales [liberal, -o] *adj* & *nmf* liberal

libérer [libere] **1** *vt (prisonnier)* to free, to release; *(pays)* to liberate (**de** from); *(chambre)* to vacate **2 se libérer** *vpr* to free oneself (**de** from); **je n'ai pas pu me l.** I couldn't get away ▪ **libération** *nf (de prisonnier)* release; *(de pays)* liberation

liberté [liberte] *nf* freedom, liberty; **mettre qn en l.** to set sb free

libraire [librɛr] *nmf* bookseller ▪ **librairie** *nf (magasin)* bookshop

libre [libr] *adj (personne, siège)* free (**de qch** from sth; **de faire** to do); *(voie)* clear; **radio l.** independent radio ▪ **libre-échange** *nm Écon* free trade ▪ **libre-service** *(pl* **libres-services)** *nm (système, magasin)* self-service

Libye [libi] *nf* **la L.** Libya ▪ **libyen, -enne 1** *adj* Libyan **2** *nmf* **L., Libyenne** Libyan

licence [lisɑ̃s] *nf Sport* permit; *Com Br*

licence, *Am* license; *Univ* (bachelor's) degree; **l. ès lettres/sciences** arts/science degree

licencier [lisɑ̃sje] *vt (employé)* to lay off, *Br* to make redundant ▪ **licenciement** *nm* lay-off, *Br* redundancy

lien [ljɛ̃] *nm (rapport)* link, connection; *(attache)* bond; **l. de parenté** family relationship; *Ordinat* **l. hypertexte** hypertext link

lier [lje] **1** *vt (attacher)* to tie up; *(contrat)* to be binding on; *(personnes)* to bind together; *(paragraphes)* to connect, to link; **l. qn** *(unir, engager)* to bind sb; **être très lié avec qn** to be great friends with sb **2 se lier** *vpr* **se l. d'amitié** to become friends

lierre [ljɛr] *nm* ivy

lieu¹, -x [ljø] *nm* place; **les lieux** *(locaux)* the premises; **être sur les lieux** to be on the spot; **avoir l.** to take place; **au l. de qch** instead of sth; **au l. de faire qch** instead of doing sth; **en dernier l.** lastly; **l. de naissance** place of birth; **l. public** public place; **l. de travail** workplace; **l. de vacances** *Br* holiday *or Am* vacation destination

lieu², -s [ljø] *nm (poisson)* **l. noir** coalfish

lieutenant [ljøtnɑ̃] *nm* lieutenant

lièvre [ljɛvr] *nm* hare

ligne [liɲ] *nf (trait)* line; *(silhouette)* figure; *(rangée)* row, line; **les grandes lignes** *(de train)* the main lines; *Fig (idées principales)* the broad outline; **aller à la l.** to begin a new paragraph; *Fig* **sur toute la l.** completely; **l. d'autobus** bus service; *(parcours)* bus route; **l. de chemin de fer** *Br* railway *or Am* railroad line; *Sport* **l. de touche** touchline

ligoter [ligote] *vt* to tie up (**à** to)

liguer [lige] **se liguer** *vpr (États)* to form a league (**contre** against); *(personnes)* to gang up (**contre** against)

lilas [lila] *nm & adj inv* lilac

limace [limas] *nf* slug

limande [limɑ̃d] *nf* dab

lime [lim] *nf (outil)* file; **l. à ongles** nail file

limitation [limitɑsjɔ̃] *nf* limitation; **l. de vitesse** speed limit

limite [limit] **1** *nf* limit (**à** to); *(de propriété)* boundary; **sans l.** unlimited, limitless; **dans la l. des stocks disponibles** while stocks last **2** *adj (vitesse, âge)* maximum

limiter [limite] **1** *vt (restreindre)* to limit, to restrict (**à** to); *(territoire)* to bound **2 se limiter** *vpr* **se l. à qch/à faire qch** to limit or restrict oneself to sth/to doing sth

limoger [limɔʒe] *vt* to dismiss

limonade [limɔnad] *nf (boisson)* lemonade

limpide [lɛ̃pid] *adj (eau, explication)* clear, crystal-clear

lin [lɛ̃] *nm (tissu)* linen

linge [lɛ̃ʒ] *nm (vêtements)* linen; *(à laver)* washing; **l. de corps** underwear ▪ **lingerie** *nf (de femmes)* underwear

lingot [lɛ̃go] *nm* **l. d'or** gold bar

lion [ljɔ̃] *nm* lion; **le L.** *(signe)* Leo

lipide [lipid] *nm (d'aliment)* fat

liqueur [likœr] *nf* liqueur

liquide [likid] **1** *adj* liquid **2** *nm* liquid; *(argent)* cash; **payer en l.** to pay cash

liquider [likide] *vt (stock)* to clear ▪ **liquidation** *nf (de stock)* clearing; *Com* **l. totale** stock clearance

lire¹ * [lir] **1** *vt* to read; **l. qch à qn** to read sth to sb **2** *vi* to read

lire² [lir] *nf (monnaie)* lira

lis, lisant, lise(nt) etc [li, lizɑ̃, liz] *voir* **lire¹**

lisible [lizibl] *adj (écriture)* legible

lisière [lizjɛr] *nf* edge

lisse [lis] *adj* smooth

liste [list] *nf* list; **l. d'attente** waiting list; **l. électorale** electoral roll; **l. noire** blacklist; **être sur la l. rouge** *(du téléphone)* to be *Br* ex-directory *or Am* unlisted

lit¹ [li] *nm* bed; **se mettre au l.** to go to bed; **faire son l.** to make one's bed; **l. de camp** *Br* camp bed, *Am* cot; **l. d'enfant** *Br* cot, *Am* crib; **lits superposés** bunk beds

lit² [li] *voir* **lire¹**

litière [litjɛr] *nf (d'animal)* litter

litige [litiʒ] *nm (conflit)* dispute

litre [litr] *nm Br* litre, *Am* liter

littéraire [literɛr] *adj* .literary ▪ **littérature** *nf* literature

littoral, -e, -aux, -ales [litɔral, -o] **1** *adj* coastal **2** *nm* coast(line)

livraison [livrɛzɔ̃] *nf* delivery

livre [livr] **1** *nm* book; *Naut* **l. de bord** logbook; **l. de poche** paperback (book) **2** *nf (monnaie, poids)* pound

livrer [livre] **1** *vt (marchandises)* to deliver (à to); **l. qn à la police** to hand sb over to the police **2 se livrer** *vpr (se rendre)* to give oneself up (à to) ▪ **livreur, -euse** *nmf* delivery man, *f* delivery woman

livret [livrɛ] *nm (livre)* booklet; **l. d'épargne** bankbook, *Br* passbook; **l. scolaire** school report book

local, -e, -aux, -ales [lɔkal, -o] **1** *adj* local **2** *nm (pièce)* room; **locaux** *(bâtiment)* premises

localité [lɔkalite] *nf* locality

locataire [lɔkatɛr] *nmf* tenant; *(chez le propriétaire)* lodger, *Am* roomer

location [lɔkasjɔ̃] *nf (de maison) (par le locataire)* renting; *(par le propriétaire)* renting out, *Br* letting; *(de voiture)* renting, *Br* hiring; *(logement)* rented *Br* accommodation *or Am* accommodations; *(loyer)* rent; *(pour spectacle)* booking; **bureau de l.** booking office; **en l.** on hire; **voiture de l.** rented *or Br* hired car

locomotion [lɔkɔmosjɔ̃] *nf* **moyen de l.** means of transport

locomotive [lɔkɔmotiv] *nf (de train)* engine

loge [lɔʒ] *nf (de concierge)* lodge; *(d'acteur)* dressing-room; *Théât (de spectateur)* box

loger [lɔʒe] **1** *vt (recevoir, mettre)* to accommodate; *(héberger)* to put up; **être logé et nourri** to have board and lodging

2 *vi (temporairement)* to stay; *(en permanence)* to live

3 se loger *vpr* **trouver à se l.** to find somewhere to live; *(temporairement)* to find somewhere to stay ▪ **logement** *nm (habitation)* lodging, *Br* accommodation, *Am* accommodations; **le l.** housing

logiciel [lɔʒisjɛl] *nm Ordinat* software *inv*

logique [lɔʒik] **1** *adj* logical **2** *nf* logic

loi [lwa] *nf* law; **faire la l.** to lay down the law (à to)

loin [lwɛ̃] *adv* far (away *or* off) (**de** from); **Nice est l. de Paris** Nice is a long way away from Paris; **plus l.** further, farther; **au l.** in the distance, far away; **de l.** from a distance ▪ **lointain, -e** *adj* distant, far-off; *(rapport)* remote

loisirs [lwazir] *nmpl (temps libre)* spare time, leisure (time); *(distractions)* leisure *or* spare-time activities

Londres [lɔ̃dr] *nm ou f* London ▪ **londonien, -enne 1** *adj* London, of London **2** *nmf* **L., Londonienne** Londoner

long, longue [lɔ̃, lɔ̃g] **1** *adj* long; **l. de 2 mètres** 2 metres long

2 *nm* **avoir 2 mètres de l.** to be 2 metres long; **le l. de qch** along sth; **de l. en large** *(marcher)* up and down

3 *adv* **en savoir l. sur qch** to know a lot about sth ▪ **long-courrier** *(pl* **long-courriers)** *nm (avion)* long-haul aircraft

longer [lɔ̃ʒe] *vt (sujet: personne, voiture)* to go along; *(mur, côte)* to hug; *(sujet: sentier, canal)* to run alongside

longtemps [lɔ̃tɑ̃] *adv* (for) a long time; **trop l.** too long; **aussi l. que** as long as

longue [lɔ̃g] *voir* **long** ▪ **longuement** *adv (expliquer)* at length; *(réfléchir)* for a long time ▪ **longueur** *nf* length; *Radio* **l. d'onde** wavelength ▪ **longue-vue** *(pl* **longues-vues)** *nf* telescope

lopin [lɔpɛ̃] *nm* **l. de terre** plot *or* patch of land

loquet [lɔkɛ] *nm* latch

lorgner [lɔrɲe] *vt (regarder)* to eye; *(convoiter)* to have one's eye on

lors [lɔr] *adv* **l. de** at the time of; **dès l.** from then on; **dès l. que** *(puisque)* since

lorsque [lɔrsk(ə)] *conj* when

losange [lɔzɑ̃ʒ] *nm (forme)* diamond

lot [lo] *nm (de marchandises)* batch; *(de loterie)* prize; **gros l.** jackpot

loterie [lɔtri] *nf* lottery

lotion [losjɔ̃] *nf* lotion

lotissement [lɔtismɑ̃] *nm (terrain)* building plot; *(habitations)* housing *Br* estate *or Am* development

loto [lɔto] *nm (jeu)* lotto; *(jeu national)* national lottery

louange [lwɑ̃ʒ] *nf* praise

louche¹ [luʃ] *nf (cuillère)* ladle

louche² [luʃ] *adj (suspect)* dodgy

loucher [luʃe] *vi* to squint

louer¹ [lwe] *vt (prendre en location) (maison, appartement)* to rent; *(voiture)* to rent, *Br* to hire; *(donner en location) (logement)* to rent out, *Br* to let; *(voiture)* to rent out, *Br* to hire out; *(réserver)* to book; **maison/chambre à l.** house/room to rent *or Br* to let

louer² [lwe] **1** *vt (exalter)* to praise **(de** for) **2 se louer** *vpr* **se l. de qch** to be highly satisfied with sth

loup [lu] *nm* wolf

loupe [lup] *nf* magnifying glass

lourd, -e [lur, lurd] **1** *adj* heavy (**de** with); *(temps)* sticky; **il fait l.** *(temps)* it's very sticky **2** *adv* **peser l.** *(personne, objet)* to be heavy ■ **lourdement** [-əmɑ̃] *adv* heavily ■ **lourdeur** *nf* heaviness; **avoir des lourdeurs d'estomac** to feel bloated

loyal, -e, -aux, -ales [lwajal, -o] *adj (honnête)* fair (**envers** to); *(dévoué)* loyal (**envers** to) ■ **loyauté** *nf (honnêteté)* fairness; *(dévouement)* loyalty (**envers** to)

loyer [lwaje] *nm* rent

lu [ly] *pp de* lire¹

lubrifier [lybrifje] *vt* to lubricate

lucarne [lykarn] *nf (fenêtre)* dormer window; *(de toit)* skylight

lucide [lysid] *adj* lucid ■ **lucidité** *nf* lucidity

lucratif, -ive [lykratif, -iv] *adj* lucrative

lueur [lɥœr] *nf (lumière) & Fig* glimmer

luge [lyʒ] *nf Br* sledge, *Am* sled, toboggan

LUI [lɥi] *pron personnel* **(a)** *(objet indirect)* (to) him; *(femme)* (to) her; *(chose, animal)* (to) it; **je le l. ai montré** I showed it to him/her

(b) *(complément direct)* him; **elle n'aime que l.** she only loves him

(c) *(après une préposition)* him; **pour/avec l.** for/with him; **elle pense à l.** she thinks of him; **ce livre est à l.** this book is his

(d) *(dans les comparaisons)* **elle est plus grande que l.** she's taller than he is *or* than him

(e) *(sujet)* **l., il ne viendra pas** *(emphatique)* HE won't come; **c'est l. qui me l'a dit** he is the one who told me ■ **lui-même** *pron* himself; *(chose, animal)* itself

luire* [lɥir] *vi* to shine ■ **luisant, -e** *adj (métal)* shiny

lumière [lymjɛr] *nf* light; **à la l. de** by the light of

lumineux, -euse [lyminø, -øz] *adj (idée, ciel)* bright, brilliant; *(cadran)* luminous

lunaire [lynɛr] *adj* lunar

lundi [lœdi] *nm* Monday

lune [lyn] *nf* moon; **l. de miel** honeymoon

lunette [lynɛt] *nf (astronomique)* telescope; **lunettes** *(de vue)* glasses, spectacles; *(de protection, de plongée)* goggles; **l. arrière** *(de voiture)* rear window; **lunettes de soleil** sunglasses

lustre [lystr] *nm (lampe)* chandelier; *(éclat)* lustre

lutte [lyt] *nf* fight, struggle; *Sport* wrestling ■ **lutter** *vi* to fight, to struggle; *Sport* to wrestle

luxation [lyksasjɔ̃] *nf Méd* dislocation

luxe [lyks] *nm* luxury; **modèle de l. de** luxe model ■ **luxueux, -euse** *adj* luxurious

Luxembourg [lyksɑ̃bur] *nm* **le L.** Luxembourg

lycée [lise] *nm Br* ≃ secondary school, *Am* ≃ high school; **l. technique** *ou* **professionnel** vocational *or* technical school ■ **lycéen, -enne** *nmf* pupil *(at a lycée)*

Mm

M¹, m¹ [ɛm] *nm inv* M, m

m' [m] *voir* me

M² (*abrév* Monsieur) Mr

m² (*abrév* mètre(s)) m

ma [ma] *voir* mon

Mac [mak] *nm Ordinat* Mac

macérer [masere] *vti* to steep

mâcher [mɑʃe] *vt* to chew

machine [maʃin] *nf (appareil)* machine; **m. à calculer** calculator; **m. à coudre** sewing machine; **m. à écrire** typewriter; **m. à laver** washing machine; **m. à laver la vaisselle** dishwasher; **m. à** *ou* **de traitement de texte** word processor ■ **machiniste** *nm (conducteur)* driver

mâchoire [mɑʃwar] *nf* jaw

mâchonner [mɑʃɔne] *vt* to chew

maçon [masɔ̃] *nm (de briques)* bricklayer; *(de pierres)* mason ■ **maçonnerie** *nf (travaux)* building work; *(ouvrage de briques)* brickwork; *(de pierres)* masonry, stonework

Madagascar [madagaskar] *nf* Madagascar

madame [madam] (*pl* **mesdames**) *nf (en apostrophe)* madam; **bonjour mesdames** good morning(, ladies); **M. Legras** Mrs Legras; **M.** *(dans une lettre)* Dear Madam

madeleine *nf* (small) sponge cake

mademoiselle [madmwazɛl] (*pl* **mesdemoiselles**) *nf (avant nom)* Miss; **M. Legras** Miss Legras; **M.** *(dans une lettre)* Dear Madam

magasin [magazɛ̃] *nm Br* shop, *Am* store; *(entrepôt)* warehouse; *(d'arme)* & *Phot* magazine; **grand m.** department store; **en m.** in stock; **faire les magasins** to go shopping

magazine [magazin] *nm (revue)* magazine

magie [maʒi] *nf* magic ■ **magicien, -enne** *nmf* magician ■ **magique** *adj (surnaturel)* magic; *(enchanteur)* magical

magistrat [maʒistra] *nm* magistrate

magnanime [maɲanim] *adj* magnanimous

magnat [magna] *nm* tycoon, magnate

magnésium [maɲezjɔm] *nm* magnesium

magnétique [maɲetik] *adj* magnetic

magnétophone [maɲetɔfɔn] *nm* tape recorder; **m. à cassettes** cassette recorder

magnétoscope [maɲetɔskɔp] *nm Br* video (recorder), *Am* VCR

magnifique [maɲifik] *adj* magnificent

mai [mɛ] *nm* May

maigre [mɛgr] *adj (personne, corps)* thin; *(viande)* lean; *(fromage)* low-fat; *(salaire) Br* meagre, *Am* meager ■ **maigrir** *vi* to get thinner

maillot [majo] *nm (de sportif)* jersey, shirt; **m. de bain** *(de femme)* swimsuit; *(d'homme)* (swimming) trunks; **m. jaune** *(du Tour de France)* yellow jersey

main [mɛ̃] **1** *nf* hand; **à la m.** *(faire, écrire)* by hand; **tenir qch à la m.** to hold sth in one's hand; **en mains propres** in person; **donner la m. à qn** to hold sb's hand; **haut les mains!** hands up! **2** *adj* **fait m.** hand-made ■ **main-d'œuvre** (*pl* **mains-d'œuvre**) *nf Br* labour, *Am* labor

maintenant [mɛ̃tnɑ̃] *adv* now; *(de nos jours)* nowadays; **m. que...** now that...; **dès m.** from now on

maintenir* [mɛ̃tnir] **1** *vt (conserver)*

to keep, to maintain; *(retenir)* to hold in position; *(affirmer)* to maintain **(que that) 2 se maintenir** *vpr (durer)* to remain ■ **maintien** *nm (action)* maintenance *(de* of); *(allure)* bearing

maire [mɛr] *nm* mayor ■ **mairie** *nf Br* town hall, *Am* city hall; *(administration) Br* town council, *Am* city hall

mais [mɛ] *conj* but; **m. oui, m. si** of course; **m. non** definitely not

maïs [mais] *nm Br* maize, *Am* corn

maison [mɛzɔ̃] **1** *nf (bâtiment, famille)* house; *(foyer)* home; *(entreprise)* company; **à la m.** at home; **rentrer à la m.** to go/come (back) home; **m. de la culture** arts centre; **m. d'édition** publishing house; **m. de repos** rest home; **m. de retraite** old people's home; **m. de santé** nursing home; **m. secondaire** second home **2** *adj inv (artisanal)* home-made

maître [mɛtr] *nm* master; **être m. de la situation** to be in control of the situation; **m. d'hôtel** *(de restaurant)* head waiter; **m. de maison** host; **m. chanteur** blackmailer; **m. nageur (sauveteur)** swimming instructor (and lifeguard)

maîtresse [mɛtrɛs] **1** *nf* mistress; **être m. de la situation** to be in control of the situation; **m. d'école** teacher; **m. de maison** hostess **2** *adj f (idée, poutre)* main; *(carte)* master

maîtrise [mɛtriz] *nf (contrôle, connaissance)* mastery **(de** of); *(diplôme)* ≃ master's degree **(de** in); **m. de soi** self-control ■ **maîtriser 1** *vt (incendie, passion)* to control; *(peur)* to overcome; *(sujet)* to master; *(véhicule)* to have under control; **m. qn** to overpower sb **2 se maîtriser** *vpr* to control oneself

majesté [maʒɛste] *nf* majesty; **Votre M.** *(titre)* Your Majesty

majeur, -e [maʒœr] **1** *adj (important)* & *Mus* major; *Jur* **être m.** to be of age; **la majeure partie de** most of **2** *nm (doigt)* middle finger

majorer [maʒɔre] *vt* to increase

majorette [maʒɔrɛt] *nf* (drum) majorette

majoritaire [maʒɔritɛr] *adj* majority; **être m.** to be in the majority

majorité [maʒɔrite] *nf* majority **(de** of); *(gouvernement)* government, party in office; **en m.** *(pour la plupart)* in the main

Majorque [maʒɔrk] *nf* Majorca

majuscule [maʒyskyl] **1** *adj* capital **2** *nf* capital letter

MAL, MAUX [mal, mo] **1** *nm (douleur)* pain; *(préjudice)* harm *(maladie)* illness; *(malheur)* misfortune; *Phil* **le m.** evil; **avoir m. à la tête/à la gorge** to have a headache/sore throat; **ça me fait m., j'ai m.** it hurts (me); **avoir le m. de l'air/de mer** to be airsick/seasick; **avoir le m. des transports** to be travel sick; **faire du m. à qn** to harm sb; **avoir du m. à faire qch** to have trouble doing sth; **avoir le m. du pays** to be homesick; **m. de gorge** sore throat; **m. de tête** headache

2 *adv (avec médiocrité)* badly; *(incorrectement)* wrongly; **aller m.** *(personne)* to be ill; **m. comprendre** to misunderstand; **se trouver m.** to faint; *Fam* **pas m.** *(beaucoup)* quite a lot **(de** of)

malade [malad] **1** *adj* ill, sick; *(arbre, dent)* diseased; **être m. du cœur** to have a bad heart **2** *nmf* sick person; *(de médecin)* patient; **les malades** the sick ■ **maladie** *nf* illness, disease; **m. infantile** childhood illness; **m. sexuellement transmissible** sexually transmitted disease

maladroit, -e [maladrwa, -at] *adj (malhabile)* clumsy, awkward; *(indélicat)* tactless ■ **maladresse** *nf (manque d'habileté)* clumsiness, awkwardness; *(indélicatesse)* tactlessness; *(bévue)* blunder

malaise [malɛz] *nm (angoisse)* uneasiness, malaise; *(indisposition)* feeling of sickness; *(étourdissement)* dizzy spell; **avoir un m.** to feel faint

Malaisie [malɛzi] *nf* **la M.** Malaysia

malbouffe [malbuf] *nf Fam* junk food

malchance [malʃɑ̃s] *nf* bad luck; **jouer de m.** to have no luck at all

■ **malchanceux, -euse** *adj* unlucky

mâle [mal] **1** *adj (du sexe masculin)* male; *(viril)* manly **2** *nm* male

malédiction [malediksjɔ̃] *nf* curse

maléfique [malefik] *adj* evil

malencontreux, -euse [malɑ̃kɔ̃trø, -øz] *adj* unfortunate

malentendant, -e [malɑ̃tɑ̃dɑ̃, -ɑ̃t] *nmf* person who is hard of hearing

malentendu [malɑ̃tɑ̃dy] *nm* misunderstanding

malfaçon [malfasɔ̃] *nf* defect

malfaisant, -e [malfəzɑ̃, -ɑ̃t] *adj* harmful

malfaiteur [malfɛtœr] *nm* criminal

malgré [malgre] *prép* in spite of; **m. tout** for all that, after all

malhabile [malabil] *adj* clumsy

malheur [malœr] *nm (drame)* misfortune; *(malchance)* bad luck; **par m.** unfortunately; **porter m. à qn** to bring sb bad luck ■ **malheureusement** *adv* unfortunately ■ **malheureux, -euse 1** *adj (triste)* unhappy, miserable; *(malchanceux)* unlucky **2** *nmf (infortuné)* poor wretch; *(indigent)* needy person

malhonnête [malɔnɛt] *adj* dishonest ■ **malhonnêteté** *nf* dishonesty

malice [malis] *nf* mischievousness ■ **malicieux, -euse** *adj* mischievous

malin, -igne [malɛ̃, -iɲ] *adj (astucieux)* clever, smart; *Méd (tumeur)* malignant

malintentionné, -e [malɛ̃tɑ̃sjɔne] *adj* ill-intentioned (**à l'égard de** towards)

malle [mal] *nf (coffre)* trunk; *(de véhicule) Br* boot, *Am* trunk

mallette [malɛt] *nf* briefcase

malmener [malməne] *vt* to manhandle, to treat badly

malnutrition [malnytrisjɔ̃] *nf* malnutrition

malpoli, -e [malpɔli] *adj Fam* rude

malsain, -e [malsɛ̃, -ɛn] *adj* unhealthy

Malte [malt] *nf* Malta ■ **maltais, -e 1** *adj* Maltese **2** *nmf* **M., Maltaise** Maltese

maltraiter [maltrɛte] *vt* to ill-treat

malveillant, -e [malvɛjɑ̃, -ɑ̃t] *adj* malevolent

maman [mamɑ̃] *nf Br* mum, *Am* mom

mamie [mami] *nf* grandma, granny

mammifère [mamifɛr] *nm* mammal

Manche [mɑ̃ʃ] *nf* **la M.** the Channel

manche¹ [mɑ̃ʃ] *nf (de vêtement)* sleeve; *Sport & Cartes* round ■ **manchette** *nf (de chemise)* cuff; *(de journal)* headline

manche² [mɑ̃ʃ] *nm (d'outil)* handle; **m. à balai** broomstick; *(d'avion, d'ordinateur)* joystick

manchot, -e [mɑ̃ʃo, -ɔt] **1** *adj* one-armed **2** *nmf* one-armed person

mandarine [mɑ̃darin] *nf (fruit)* mandarin (orange)

mandat [mɑ̃da] *nm (de député)* mandate; *(de président)* term of office; **m. postal** *Br* postal order, *Am* money order

manège [manɛʒ] *nm (de foire)* merry-go-round, *Br* roundabout; *Équitation* riding school

manette [manɛt] *nf* lever

manger [mɑ̃ʒe] **1** *vt* to eat; *(corroder)* to eat into **2** *vi* to eat; **donner à m. à qn** to give sb sth to eat; **faire à m.** to make something to eat; **m. équilibré** to make a balanced diet **3** *nm (nourriture)* food ■ **mangeable** *adj (médiocre)* eatable

mangue [mɑ̃g] *nf* mango

maniaque [manjak] *adj* fussy

manie [mani] *nf (habitude)* odd habit; *(idée fixe)* mania (**de** for)

manier [manje] *vt* to handle ■ **maniable** *adj (outil)* handy; *(véhicule)* easy to handle

manière [manjɛr] *nf* way, manner; **la m. dont elle parle** the way (in which) she talks; **manières** *(politesse)* manners; **de toute m.** anyway, anyhow; **de cette m.** (in) this way; **à la m. de** in the style of; **d'une m. générale** generally speaking ■ **maniéré, -e** *adj* affected

manifeste [manifɛst] **1** *adj* manifest, obvious **2** *nm Pol* manifesto

manifester [manifɛste] **1** *vt (exprimer)* to show **2** *vi (protester)* to demonstrate **3** **se manifester** *vpr*

(maladie) to show or manifest itself; *(personne)* to make oneself known ■ **manifestant, -e** *nmf* demonstrator ■ **manifestation** *nf (défilé)* demonstration; *(réunion, fête)* event

manipuler [manipyle] *vt (appareils, produits)* to handle ■ **manipulation** *nf (d'appareils, de produits)* handling; **manipulations génétiques** genetic engineering

manivelle [manivɛl] *nf* crank

mannequin [mankɛ̃] *nm (personne)* model; *(statue)* dummy

manœuvre [manœvr] **1** *nm (ouvrier)* unskilled worker **2** *nf (opération) & Mil Br* manœuvre, *Am* maneuver ■ **manœuvrer 1** *vt (véhicule, personne) Br* to manoeuvre, *Am* to maneuver; *(machine)* to operate **2** *vi Br* to manœuvre, *Am* to maneuver

manoir [manwar] *nm* manor house

manque [mɑ̃k] *nm (insuffisance)* lack (**de** of); *(lacune)* gap; **par m. de qch** through lack of sth; **être en m.** *(drogué)* to have withdrawal symptoms

manquer [mɑ̃ke] **1** *vt (cible, train, chance)* to miss; *(échouer)* to fail **2** *vi (faire défaut)* to be lacking; *(être absent)* to be missing; *(échouer)* to fail; **m. de** *(pain, argent)* to be short of; *(attention, cohérence)* to lack; **tu me manques** I miss you; **ne m. de rien** to have all one needs **3** *v impersonnel* **il manque/il nous manque dix tasses** there are/we are ten cups short; **il manque quelques pages** there are a few pages missing ■ **manquant, -e** *adj* missing ■ **manqué, -e** *adj (occasion)* missed; *(tentative)* unsuccessful

mansarde [mɑ̃sard] *nf* attic

manteau, -x [mɑ̃to] *nm* coat

manucure [manykyr] *nmf (personne)* manicurist

manuel, -elle [manɥɛl] **1** *adj (travail)* manual **2** *nm (livre)* handbook, manual; **m. scolaire** textbook

manufacture [manyfaktyr] *nf* factory ■ **manufacturé, -e** *adj (produit)* manufactured

manuscrit [manyskri] *nm* manuscript; *(tapé à la machine)* typescript

maquereau, -x [makro] *nm (poisson)* mackerel

maquiller [makije] **1** *vt (personne, visage)* to make up **2 se maquiller** *vpr* to put one's make-up on ■ **maquillage** *nm (fard)* make-up

maraîcher, -ère [mareʃe, -ɛr] **1** *nmf Br* market gardener, *Am* truck farmer **2** *adj* **culture maraîchère** *Br* market gardening, *Am* truck farming

marais [marɛ] *nm* marsh

marathon [maratɔ̃] *nm* marathon

marbre [marbr] *nm* marble ■ **marbré, -e** *adj (surface)* marbled; **gâteau m.** marble cake

marc [mar] *nm* **m. de café** coffee grounds

marchand, -e [marʃɑ̃, -ɑ̃d] **1** *nmf Br* shopkeeper, *Am* storekeeper; *(de vins)* merchant; *(de voitures, de meubles)* dealer; **m. de journaux** *(dans la rue)* newsvendor; *(dans un magasin) Br* newsagent, *Am* newsdealer **2** *adj* **valeur marchande** market value

marchander [marʃɑ̃de] **1** *vt (objet, prix)* to haggle over **2** *vi* to haggle

marchandises [marʃɑ̃diz] *nfpl* goods, merchandise

marche [marʃ] *nf* (**a**) *(d'escalier)* step, stair (**b**) *(action)* walking; *(promenade)* walk; *Mus* march; **un train en m.** a moving train; **la bonne m. de** *(opération)* the smooth running of; **mettre qch en m.** to start sth (up); **faire m. arrière** *(en voiture) Br* to reverse, *Am* to back up; *Fig* to backtrack; **fermer la m.** to bring up the rear; **m. à suivre** procedure

marché [marʃe] **1** *nm (lieu) & Écon* market; *(contrat)* deal; **faire son** *ou* **le m.** to go shopping; **vendre qch au m. noir** to sell sth on the black market; **le m. du travail** the labour market; **le M. commun** the Common Market; **le M. unique européen** the Single European Market; **m. des changes** foreign exchange market **2** *adj inv* **être bon m.** to be cheap;

c'est meilleur m. it's cheaper

marcher [maʃe] *vi (personne)* to walk; *(machine)* to run; *(plans)* to work; **faire m. qch** to operate sth ■ **marcheur, -euse** *nmf* walker

mardi [mardi] *nm* Tuesday; **M. gras** ShroveTuesday

mare [mar] *nf (étang)* pond

marécage [marekaʒ] *nm* marsh

maréchal, -aux [mareʃal, -o] *nm* **m. de France** field marshal ■ **maréchal-ferrant** (*pl* maréchaux-ferrants) *nm* blacksmith

marée [mare] *nf (trace)* tide; *(poissons)* fresh seafood; **m. haute/basse** high/low tide; **m. noire** oil slick

margarine [margarin] *nf* margarine

marge [marʒ] *nf (de page)* margin; **en m. de** *(en dehors de)* on the fringes of; **avoir de la m.** to have some leeway; **m. de manœuvre** room for *Br* manoeuvre *or Am* maneuver ■ **marginal, -e, -aux, -ales 1** *adj (secondaire)* marginal; *(personne)* on the fringes of society **2** *nmf* dropout

marguerite [margərit] *nf (fleur)* daisy

mari [mari] *nm* husband

mariage [marjaʒ] *nm (union)* marriage; *(cérémonie)* wedding; *Fig (de couleurs)* blend

marier [marje] **1** *vt (couleurs)* to blend; **m. qn** *(sujet: prêtre, maire)* to marry sb; *(sujet: père)* to marry sb off **2 se marier** *vpr* to get married; **se m. avec qn** to get married to sb, to marry sb ■ **marié, -e 1** *adj* married **2** *nm* (bride)groom; **les mariés** the bride and groom ■ **mariée** *nf* bride

marin, -e [marɛ̃, -in] **1** *adj (flore)* marine; *(mille)* nautical; **air m.** sea air **2** *nm* sailor, seaman; **m. pêcheur** (deep-sea) fisherman ■ **marine 1** *nf* **m. de guerre** navy; **m. marchande** merchant navy **2** *adj & nm inv* **bleu m.** *(couleur)* navy (blue)

mariner [marine] *vti Culin* to marinate

marionnette [marjɔnɛt] *nf* puppet; *(à fils)* marionette

maritalement [maritalmɑ̃] *adv* **vivre m.** to cohabit

maritime [maritim] *adj (droit, climat)* maritime; **port m.** seaport; **gare m.** *Br* harbour *or Am* harbor station; *Can* **les Provinces maritimes** the Maritime Provinces

marmelade [marmǝlad] *nf Br* stewed fruit, *Am* fruit compote

marmite [marmit] *nf* (cooking) pot

Maroc [marɔk] *nm* **le M.** Morocco ■ **marocain, -e 1** *adj* Moroccan **2** *nmf* **M., Marocaine** Moroccan

maroquinerie [marɔkinri] *nf (magasin)* leather goods shop

marque [mark] *nf (trace, signe)* mark; *(de confiance)* sign; *(de produit)* brand; *(de voiture)* make; *Sport (points)* score; **de m.** *(hôte, visiteur)* distinguished; *(produit)* of quality; **m. déposée** (registered) trademark

marquer [marke] **1** *vt (par une marque)* to mark; *(écrire)* to note down; *(indiquer)* to show; *Sport (point, but)* to score; **m. les points** to keep (the) score **2** *vi (laisser une trace)* to leave a mark; *(date, événement)* to stand out; *Sport* to score ■ **marquant, -e** *adj (remarquable)* outstanding; *(épisode)* significant ■ **marqué, -e** *adj (différence, accent)* marked; *(visage)* lined ■ **marqueur** *nm (stylo)* marker

marquis [marki] *nm* marquis ■ **marquise** *nf* (a) *(personne)* marchioness (b) *(auvent)* canopy

marraine [marɛn] *nf* godmother

marre [mar] *adv Fam* **en avoir m.** to be fed up (**de** with)

marron [marɔ̃] **1** *nm (fruit)* chestnut; *(couleur)* (chestnut) brown **2** *adj inv (couleur)* (chestnut) brown ■ **marronnier** *nm* (horse) chestnut tree

mars [mars] *nm* March

marteau, -x [marto] *nm* hammer; **m. piqueur** pneumatic drill ■ **marteler** *vt* to hammer

martial, -e, -aux, -ales [marsjal, -o] *adj* martial; **cour martiale** court martial

Martinique [martinik] *nf* **la M.** Martinique ■ **martiniquais, -e 1** *adj* Martinican **2** *nmf* **M., Martiniquaise** Martinican

martyriser [martirize] *vt* to torture; *(enfant)* to batter

masculin, -e [maskylɛ̃, -in] **1** *adj (sexe, mode)* male; *(caractère, femme, nom)* masculine **2** *nm (en grammaire)* masculine

masochiste [mazɔʃist] **1** *adj* masochistic **2** *nmf* masochist

masque [mask] *nm* mask; **m. à gaz** gas mask ■ **masquer** *vt (dissimuler)* to mask (à from); *(cacher à la vue)* to block off

massacre [masakr] *nm (tuerie)* massacre ■ **massacrer** *vt* to massacre

massage [masaʒ] *nm* massage

masse [mas] *nf* (a) *(volume)* mass; *(gros morceau, majorité)* bulk (**de** of); **de m.** *(culture, communication)* mass; **en m.** en masse (b) *Él Br* earth, *Am* ground

masser [mase] **1** *vt (rassembler)* to assemble; *(pétrir)* to massage **2 se masser** *vpr (foule)* to form ■ **masseur** *nm* masseur ■ **masseuse** *nf* masseuse

massif, -ive [masif, -iv] **1** *adj* massive; *(or, chêne)* solid **2** *nm (d'arbres, de fleurs)* clump; *Géog* massif

mastic [mastik] *nm (pour vitres)* putty; *(pour bois)* filler ■ **mastiquer** *vt (mâcher)* to chew

mat¹, mate [mat] *adj (papier, couleur)* matt

mat² [mat] *adj m inv & nm Échecs* (check-)mate; **faire m.** to (check)mate

mât [mɑ] *nm (de navire)* mast; *(poteau)* pole

match [matʃ] *nm Sport Br* match, *Am* game; **m. nul** draw; **faire m. nul** to draw; **m. aller** first leg; **m. retour** return leg

matelas [matla] *nm* mattress; **m. pneumatique** air bed

matelot [matlo] *nm* sailor

mater [mate] *vt (dominer)* to bring to heel

matérialiser [materjalize] *vt,* **se matérialiser** *vpr* to materialize

matérialiste [materjalist] **1** *adj* materialistic **2** *nmf* materialist

matériau, -x [materjo] *nm* material; **matériaux** *(de construction)* building material(s)

matériel, -elle [materjɛl] **1** *adj (confort, dégâts, besoins)* material; *(problème)* practical **2** *nm (de camping)* equipment; *Ordinat* **m. informatique** computer hardware ■ **matériellement** *adv* materially; **m. impossible** physically impossible

maternel, -elle [maternɛl] **1** *adj (amour, femme)* maternal; *(langue)* native **2** *adj & nf* **(école) maternelle** *Br* nursery school, *Am* kindergarten ■ **maternité** *nf (hôpital)* maternity hospital

mathématiques [matematik] *nfpl* mathematics *(sing)* ■ **maths** *nfpl Fam Br* maths, *Am* math

matière [matjɛr] *nf (à l'école)* subject; *(de livre)* subject matter; *(substance)* material; *Phys* **la m.** matter; **en m. de** **qch** as regards sth; **m. première** raw material; **matières grasses** fat

Matignon [matiɲɔ̃] *nm* **(l'hôtel) M.** = the French Prime Minister's offices

matin [matɛ̃] *nm* morning; **le m.** *(chaque matin)* in the morning(s); **le mardi matin** every Tuesday morning; **tous les matins** every morning; **le 8 au m.** on the morning of the 8th; **à sept heures du m.** at seven in the morning; **au petit m.** very early (in the morning) ■ **matinal, -e, -aux, -ales** *adj (heure)* early; **être m.** to be an early riser

matinée [matine] *nf* morning; *Théât &* *Cin* matinée; **dans la m.** in the course of the morning

matraque [matrak] *nf* bludgeon; *(de policier) Br* truncheon, *Am* nightstick ■ **matraquage** *nm* **m. publicitaire** hype

matrimonial, -e, -aux, -ales [matrimɔnjal, -o] *adj* matrimonial

maturité [matyrite] *nf* maturity; **arriver à m.** *(fromage, vin)* to mature; *(fruit)* to ripen

maudire* [modir] *vt* to curse ■ **maudit, -e** *adj (damné)* cursed

Maurice [mɔris] *nf* **l'île M.** Mauritius

maussade [mosad] *adj (personne)* sullen; *(temps)* gloomy

mauvais, -e [move, -ɛz] **1** *adj* bad; *(santé, vue)* poor; *(méchant)* nasty; *(mal choisi)* wrong; *(mer)* rough; **plus m. que...** worse than...; **le plus m.** the worst; **être m. en anglais** to be bad at English; **être en mauvaise santé** to be in bad *or* ill *or* poor health
 2 *adv* **il fait m.** the weather's bad; **ça sent m.** it smells bad
 3 *nm* **le bon et le m.** the good and the bad

mauve [mov] *adj & nm (couleur)* mauve

maux [mo] *pl de* **mal**

maximal, -e, -aux, -ales [maksimal, -o] *adj* maximum; **les temperatures maximales** top temperatures

maximum [maksimɔm] *(pl maxima* [-a] *ou* **maximums**) **1** *nm* maximum; **faire le m.** to do one's very best; **au m.** at the most **2** *adj* maximum

mayonnaise [majɔnɛz] *nf* mayonnaise

mazout [mazut] *nm* (fuel) oil

me [mə]

m' is used before a vowel or mute h.

pron personnel (**a**) *(complément direct)* me; **il me voit** he sees me (**b**) *(complément indirect)* (to) me; **elle me parle** she speaks to me; **tu me l'as dit** you told me (**c**) *(réfléchi)* myself; **je me lave** I wash myself (**d**) *(avec les pronominaux)* **je me suis trompé** I made a mistake

mécanicien [mekanisjɛ̃] *nm* mechanic; *(de train)* Br train driver, Am engineer

mécanique [mekanik] **1** *adj* mechanical **2** *nf (science)* mechanics *(sing)*; *(mécanisme)* mechanism ■ **mécanisme** *nm* mechanism

mécène [mesɛn] *nm* patron (of the arts)

méchant, -e [meʃɑ̃, -ɑ̃t] *adj (personne, remarque)* nasty; *(enfant)* naughty; *(chien)* vicious; **'attention! chien m.'** 'beware of the dog' ■ **méchanceté** *nf* nastiness; **une m.** *(parole)* a nasty

remark; *(acte)* a nasty action

mèche [mɛʃ] *nf* (**a**) *(de cheveux)* lock (**b**) *(de bougie)* wick; *(de pétard)* Br fuse, Am fuze; *(de perceuse)* bit

méconnaître* [mekɔnɛtr] *vt (fait)* to fail to take into account; *(talent)* to fail to recognize ■ **méconnaissable** *adj* unrecognizable ■ **méconnu, -e** *adj* unrecognized

mécontent, -e [mekɔ̃tɑ̃, -ɑ̃t] *adj (insatisfait)* displeased (**de** with); *(contrarié)* annoyed ■ **mécontenter** *vt (ne pas satisfaire)* to displease; *(contrarier)* to annoy

Mecque [mɛk] *nf* **La M.** Mecca

médaille [medaj] *nf (décoration, bijou) & Sport* medal; *(portant le nom)* pendant *(with name engraved on it)*; *(de chien)* name tag; *Sport* **m. olympique** Olympic medal; **être m. d'or/d'argent** to be a gold/silver medallist ■ **médaillé, -e** *nmf* medal holder ■ **médaillon** *nm (bijou)* locket; *(de viande)* medallion

médecin [medsɛ̃] *nm* doctor, physician; **m. généraliste** general practitioner; **m. traitant** consulting physician ■ **médecine** *nf* medicine; **médecines douces** alternative medicine; **m. traditionnelle** traditional medicine; **étudiant en m.** medical student ■ **médical, -e, -aux, -ales** *adj* medical ■ **médicament** *nm* medicine ■ **médicinal, -e, -aux, -ales** *adj* medicinal

média [medja] *nm* medium; **les médias** the media ■ **médiatique** *adj* **campagne m.** media campaign ■ **médiatisation** *nf* media coverage ■ **médiatiser** *vt* to give media coverage to

médiateur, -trice [medjatœr, -tris] *nmf* mediator

médiéval, -e, -aux, -ales [medjeval, -o] *adj* medieval

médiocre [medjɔkr] *adj* mediocre ■ **médiocrité** *nf* mediocrity

médire* [medir] *vi* **m. de qn** to speak ill of sb ■ **médisance** *nf (action)* gossiping; **médisances** *(propos)* gossip

méditer [medite] **1** *vt (réfléchir à)* to

contemplate **2** *vi* to meditate (**sur** on) ■ **méditation** *nf* meditation

Méditerranée [mediterane] *nf* la M. the Mediterranean ■ **méditerranéen, -enne** *adj* Mediterranean

médium [medjɔm] *nmf (voyant)* medium

méduse [medyz] *nf* jellyfish

méfiance [mefjɑ̃s] *nf* distrust, mistrust

méfier [mefje] **se méfier** *vpr* to be careful; **se m. de qn** not to trust sb; **se m. de qch** to watch out for sth; **méfie-toi!** watch out!, beware! ■ **méfiant, -e** *adj* suspicious, distrustful

mégaoctet [megaɔkte] *nm Ordinat* megabyte

mégarde [megard] **par mégarde** *adv* inadvertently

mégot [mego] *nm* cigarette butt *or* end

meilleur, -e [mejœr] **1** *adj* better (**que** than); **le m. résultat/moment** the best result/moment **2** *nmf* **le m., la meilleure** the best (one) **3** *adv* **il fait m.** it's warmer

mél [mel] *nm (courrier)* e-mail

mélancolie [melɑ̃kɔli] *nf* melancholy ■ **mélancolique** *adj* melancholy

mélange [melɑ̃ʒ] *nm (résultat)* mixture; *(opération)* mixing ■ **mélanger 1** *vt (mêler)* to mix; *(brouiller)* to mix up **2 se mélanger** *vpr (s'incorporer)* to mix; *(idées)* to get mixed up

mêler [mele] **1** *vt* to mix (**à** with); *(odeurs, thèmes)* to combine; **m. qn à qch** *(affaire, conversation)* to involve sb in sth **2 se mêler** *vpr* to combine (**à** with); **se m. à qch** *(foule)* to mingle with sth; *(conversation)* to join in sth; **se m. de qch** to get involved in sth; **mêle-toi de tes affaires!** mind your own business! ■ **mêlé, -e** *adj* mixed (**de** with) ■ **mêlée** *nf (au rugby)* scrum(mage)

mélodie [melɔdi] *nf* melody

mélodramatique [melɔdramatik] *adj* melodramatic

melon [məlɔ̃] *nm (fruit)* melon; **(chapeau) m.** *Br* bowler (hat), *Am* derby

membre [mɑ̃br] *nm (bras, jambe)* limb; *(de groupe)* member

MÊME [mem] **1** *adj (identique)* same; **en m. temps** at the same time (**que** as); **le m. jour** the same day; **le jour m.** *(exact)* the very day; **lui-m./vous-m.** himself/yourself

2 *pron* **le/la m.** the same (one); **j'ai les mêmes** I have the same (ones); **cela revient au m.** it amounts to the same thing

3 *adv (y compris, aussi)* even; **m. si...** even if...; **ici m.** in this very place; **tout de m.,** *Fam* **quand m.** all the same; **de m.** likewise; **de m. que...** just as...; **être à m. de faire qch** to be in a position to do sth

mémoire [memwar] **1** *nf* memory; **de m.** *(citer)* from memory; **à la m. de** in memory of; *Ordinat* **m. morte/vive** read-only/random access memory **2** *nm (rapport)* report; *Univ* dissertation; **Mémoires** *(chronique)* memoirs ■ **mémorable** *adj* memorable

mémorial, -aux [memɔrjal, -o] *nm (monument)* memorial

menaçant, -e [mənasɑ̃, -ɑ̃t] *adj* threatening

menace [mənas] *nf* threat ■ **menacer** *vt* to threaten (**de faire** to do)

ménage [menaʒ] *nm (entretien)* housekeeping; *(couple)* couple, household; **faire le m.** to do the housework

ménager¹, -ère [menaʒe, -er] **1** *adj (équipement)* household **2** *nf* **ménagère** *(femme)* housewife

ménager² [menaʒe] **1** *vt (argent)* to use sparingly; *(forces)* to save; *(sortie)* to provide; **m. qn** to treat sb carefully; **ne pas m. sa peine** to put in a lot of effort **2 se ménager** *vpr (prendre soin de soi)* to look after oneself; *(se réserver)* to set aside

ménagerie [menaʒri] *nf* menagerie

mendier [mɑ̃dje] **1** *vt* to beg for **2** *vi* to beg ■ **mendiant, -e** *nmf* beggar

mener [məne] **1** *vt (personne)* to take (**à** to); *(course, vie)* to lead; *(enquête)* to carry out; **m. une vie saine** to lead a healthy life; *Fig* **m. qch à bien** to carry sth through **2** *vi Sport* to lead; **m. à un**

lieu to lead to a place ▪ **meneur, -euse** *nmf (de révolte)* ringleader

méningite [menɛʒit] *nf* meningitis

menottes [mənɔt] *nfpl* handcuffs

mensonge [mɑ̃sɔ̃ʒ] *nm (propos)* lie; *(action)* lying ▪ **mensonger, -ère** *adj (propos)* untrue; *(publicité)* misleading

mensuel, -elle [mɑ̃sɥɛl] **1** *adj* monthly **2** *nm (revue)* monthly ▪ **mensualité** *nf* monthly payment

mensurations [mɑ̃syrasjɔ̃] *nfpl* measurements

mental, -e, -aux, -ales [mɑ̃tal, -o] *adj* mental ▪ **mentalité** *nf* mentality

menthe [mɑ̃t] *nf* mint

mention [mɑ̃sjɔ̃] *nf (fait de citer)* mention; *(à un examen)* ≃ distinction; *Scol* **m. passable/assez bien/bien/très bien** ≃ C/B/A; **faire m. de qch** to mention sth; **'rayez les mentions inutiles'** 'delete as appropriate' ▪ **mentionner** *vt* to mention

mentir* [mɑ̃tir] *vi* to lie (**à** to) ▪ **menteur, -euse 1** *adj* lying **2** *nmf* liar

menton [mɑ̃tɔ̃] *nm* chin

menu¹ [məny] *nm (de restaurant)* set menu; *Ordinat* menu; **par le m.** in detail

menu², -e [məny] **1** *adj (petit)* tiny; *(mince)* slim **2** *adv (hacher)* small, finely

menuisier [mənɥizje] *nm* carpenter, joiner ▪ **menuiserie** *nf (atelier)* joiner's workshop; *(boiseries)* woodwork

mépris [mepri] *nm* contempt (**pour** for), scorn (**pour** for); **au m. de qch** without regard to sth ▪ **méprisable** *adj* despicable ▪ **méprisant, -e** *adj* contemptuous, scornful ▪ **mépriser** *vt* to despise

méprise [mepriz] *nf* mistake

mer [mɛr] *nf* sea; *(marée)* tide; **en (haute) m.** at sea; **par m.** by sea; **aller à la m.** to go to the seaside; **prendre la m.** to set sail

mercatique [mɛrkatik] *nf* marketing

mercenaire [mɛrsənɛr] *nm* mercenary

mercerie [mɛrsəri] *nf (magasin) Br* ha-

berdasher's, *Am* notions store

merci [mɛrsi] **1** *exclam* thank you, thanks (**de** *ou* **pour** for); **non m.** no thank you; **m. bien** thanks very much **2** *nf* **à la m. de qn/qch** at the mercy of sb/sth; **sans m.** merciless

mercredi [mɛrkrədi] *nm* Wednesday

mercure [mɛrkyr] *nm* mercury

mère [mɛr] *nf* mother; *Com* **maison m.** parent company; **m. porteuse** surrogate mother

méridional, -e, -aux, -ales [meridjɔnal, -o] **1** *adj* southern **2** *nmf* southerner

mérite [merit] *nm* merit; *(honneur)* credit; **avoir du m. à faire qch** to deserve credit for doing sth ▪ **mériter** *vt (être digne de)* to deserve; *(demander)* to be worth; **m. réflexion** to be worth thinking about; **ce livre mérite d'être lu** this book is worth reading

merle [mɛrl] *nm* blackbird

merlu [mɛrly] *nm* hake

merveille [mɛrvɛj] *nf* wonder, marvel; **à m.** wonderfully (well)

merveilleux, -euse [mɛrvejø, -øz] *adj* wonderful, *Br* marvellous, *Am* marvelous

mes [me] *voir* **mon**

mésaventure [mezavɑ̃tyr] *nf* misadventure

mesdames [medam] *pl de* **madame**

mesdemoiselles [medmwazɛl] *pl de* **mademoiselle**

mésestimer [mezɛstime] *vt* to underestimate

mesquin, -e [mɛskɛ̃, -in] *adj* mean, petty ▪ **mesquinerie** *nf* meanness, pettiness; **une m.** an act of meanness

mess [mɛs] *nm inv Mil (salle)* mess

message [mesaʒ] *nm* message; **laisser un m.** to leave a message; **m. publicitaire** advertisement ▪ **messager, -ère** *nmf* messenger ▪ **messagerie** *nf* courier company; **m. électronique** electronic mail service; **m. vocale** voice mail

messe [mɛs] *nf (office, musique)* mass; **aller à la m.** to go to mass

messeigneurs [mesɛɲœr] *pl de* **monseigneur**

messieurs [mesjø] *pl de* **monsieur**

mesure [məzyr] *nf (dimension)* measurement; *(moyen)* measure; *(retenue)* moderation; *Mus (temps)* time; *Mus (division)* bar; **sur m.** *(vêtement)* made to measure; **être en m. de faire qch** to be in a position to do sth; **prendre des mesures** to take measures; **à m. que…** as…; **dans la m. où…** in so far as…; **dans la m. du possible** as far as possible

mesurer [məzyre] **1** *vt (dimension, taille)* to measure; *(déterminer)* to assess **2** *vi* **m. 1 mètre 83** *(personne)* ≃ to be 6 feet tall; *(objet)* ≃ to measure 6 feet **3 se mesurer** *vpr Fig* **se m. à** *ou* **avec qn** to pit oneself against sb

met [mɛ] *voir* **mettre**

métal, -aux [metal, -o] *nm* metal ▪ **métallique** *adj (éclat, reflet)* metallic ▪ **métallisé, -e** *adj* **bleu m.** metallic blue

métallurgie [metalyrʒi] *nf (industrie)* steel industry; *(science)* metallurgy ▪ **métallurgiste** *nm* metalworker

métamorphoser [metamɔrfoze] *vt,* **se métamorphoser** *vpr* to transform (**en** into)

météo [meteo] *nf Fam (bulletin)* weather forecast; **m. marine** shipping forecast

météorologie [meteɔrɔlɔʒi] *nf (science)* meteorology; *(service)* weather bureau ▪ **météorologique** *adj* meteorological; **bulletin m.** weather report

méthode [metɔd] *nf (manière, soin)* method; *(livre)* course ▪ **méthodique** *adj* methodical

méticuleux, -euse [metikylø, -øz] *adj* meticulous

métier [metje] *nm (manuel, commercial)* trade; *(intellectuel)* profession; *(savoir-faire)* experience; **homme de m.** specialist; **tailleur de son m.** tailor by trade; **être du m.** to be in the business; **m. à tisser** loom

métrage [metraʒ] *nm (action)* measuring; *(tissu)* length; **long m.** feature film; **court m.** short film

mètre [mɛtr] *nm (mesure)* Br metre, Am meter; **m. carré/cube** square/cubic Br metre *or* Am meter ▪ **métrique** *adj (système)* metric

métro [metro] *nm Br* underground, Am subway

métropole [metrɔpɔl] *nf (ville)* metropolis; *(pays)* mother country ▪ **métropolitain, -e** *adj* metropolitan

mets [mɛ] *nm (aliment)* dish

metteur [metœr] *nm* **m. en scène** director

METTRE* [mɛtr] **1** *vt* to put; *(vêtement, lunettes)* to put on; *(chauffage, radio)* to switch on; *(réveil)* to set (à for); **j'ai mis une heure** it took me an hour; **m. qn en colère** to make sb angry; **m. qn à l'aise** to put sb at ease; **m. qch plus fort** to turn sth up; **m. de la musique** to put some music on; **mettons que…** *(+ subjunctive)* let's suppose that…

2 se mettre *vpr (se placer)* to put oneself; *(debout)* to stand; *(assis)* to sit; *(objet)* to go; **se m. en pyjama** to get into one's pyjamas; **se m. à table** to sit (down) at the table; **se m. à l'aise** to make oneself comfortable; **se m. au salon** to go into the dining room; **se m. au travail** to start work; **se m. à faire qch** to start doing sth; **le temps s'est mis au beau** the weather has turned fine

meuble [mœbl] *nm* piece of furniture; **meubles** furniture ▪ **meublé** *nm* furnished *Br* flat *or* Am apartment ▪ **meubler** *vt* to furnish

meule [møl] *nf (d'herbe)* stack; *(de moulin)* millstone; **m. de foin** haystack

meunier, -ère [mønje, -ɛr] *nmf* miller

meurt [mœr] *voir* **mourir**

meurtre [mœrtr] *nm* murder ▪ **meurtrier, -ère 1** *nmf* murderer **2** *adj* murderous; *(épidémie)* deadly

meurtrir [mœrtrir] *vt* to bruise

meute [møt] *nf* pack

Mexique [mɛksik] *nm* **le M.** Mexico

■ **mexicain, -e 1** *adj* Mexican **2** *nmf* **M.**, **Mexicaine** Mexican

mi [mi] *nm inv (note)* E

mi- [mi] *préf* **la mi-mars** mid March; **à mi-distance** midway; **cheveux mi-longs** shoulder-length hair

miauler [mjole] *vi (chat)* to miaow

mi-chemin [miʃmɛ̃] **à mi-chemin** *adv* halfway

mi-clos, -e [miklo, -oz] *(mpl* **mi-clos**, *fpl* **mi-closes)** *adj* half-closed

micro [mikro] *nm (microphone)* mike ■ **microphone** *nm* microphone

microbe [mikrɔb] *nm* germ, microbe

microfilm [mikrɔfilm] *nm* microfilm

micro-informatique [mikroɛ̃for-matik] *nf* microcomputing

micro-ondes [mikrɔɔ̃d] *nm inv* microwave; **four à m.** microwave oven

micro-ordinateur [mikroɔrdinatœr] *(pl* **micro-ordinateurs)** *nm* microcomputer

microprocesseur [mikroprɔsɛsœr] *nm Ordinat* microprocessor

microscope [mikrɔskɔp] *nm* microscope ■ **microscopique** *adj* microscopic

midi [midi] *nm* **(a)** *(heure)* twelve o'clock, midday; *(heure du déjeuner)* lunchtime; **entre m. et deux heures** at lunchtime **(b)** *(sud)* south; **le M.** the South of France

mie [mi] *nf (de pain)* soft part

miel [mjɛl] *nm* honey

mien, mienne [mjɛ̃, mjɛn] **1** *pron possessif* **le m., la mienne** mine, *Br* my one; **les miens, les miennes** mine, *Br* my ones; **les deux miens** my two **2** *nmpl* **les miens** *(ma famille)* my family

miette [mjɛt] *nf (de pain)* crumb

mieux [mjø] **1** *adv* better **(que** than); **aller m.** to be (feeling) better; **de m. en m.** better and better; **le/la/les m.** *(de plusieurs)* the best; *(de deux)* the better; **le m. serait de...** the best thing would be to...; **le plus tôt sera le m.** the sooner the better
2 *adj inv* better; *(plus beau)* better-looking; **si tu n'as rien de m. à faire** if you've got nothing better to do
3 *nm (amélioration)* improvement; **faire de son m.** to do one's best; **faites au m.** do the best you can

mignon, -onne [miɲɔ̃, -ɔn] *adj (charmant)* cute

migraine [migrɛn] *nf* headache; *Méd* migraine

migration [migrasjɔ̃] *nf* migration

mijoter [miʒɔte] **1** *vt (avec soin)* to cook (lovingly); *(lentement)* to simmer **2** *vi* to simmer

mil [mil] *adj inv* **l'an deux m.** the year two thousand

milieu, -x [miljø] *nm (centre)* middle; *(cadre, groupe social)* environment; *(entre extrêmes)* middle course; *Phys* medium; **milieux littéraires** literary circles; **au m. de** in the middle of; **le juste m.** the happy medium; **le m.** *(la pègre)* the underworld

militaire [militɛr] **1** *adj* military **2** *nm* serviceman; *(de l'armée de terre)* soldier

militer [milite] *vi (personne)* to campaign **(pour** for; **contre** against)

mille [mil] **1** *adj inv & nm inv* thousand; **m. hommes** a *or* one thousand men; **deux m.** two thousand; **je vous le donne en m.!** you'll never guess! **2** *nm (de cible)* bull's-eye; **m. (marin)** nautical mile ■ **mille-feuille** *(pl* **mille-feuilles)** *nm Br* ≃ vanilla slice, *Am* ≃ napoleon ■ **millième** *adj, nm & nmf* thousandth; **un m.** a thousandth ■ **millier** *nm* thousand; **un m. (de)** a thousand or so; **par milliers** in their thousands

millénaire [milenɛr] *nm* millennium

milliard [miljar] *nm* billion ■ **milliardaire** *adj & nmf* billionaire

millimètre [milimɛtr] *nm* millimetre

million [miljɔ̃] *nm* million; **un m. de francs** a million francs; **deux millions** two million; **par millions** in millions ■ **millionnaire** *nmf* millionaire

mime [mim] **1** *nm (art)* mime **2** *nmf (artiste)* mime ■ **mimer** *vti (exprimer)* to mime

minable [minabl] *adj (lieu, personne)* shabby

mince [mɛ̃s] *adj* thin; *(élancé,* slim; *(insuffisant)* slight ■ **minceur** *nf* thinness; *(sveltesse)* slimness ■ **mincir** *vi* to get slimmer

mine [min] *nf* (a) *(physionomie)* look; **avoir bonne/mauvaise m.** to look well/ill (b) *(gisement)* & *Fig* mine; **m. de charbon** coalmine (c) *(de crayon)* lead (d) *(engin explosif)* mine

miner [mine] *vt (terrain)* to mine; *Fig (saper)* to undermine; **m. qn** *(chagrin, maladie)* to wear sb down

minerai [minrɛ] *nm* ore

minéral, -e, -aux, -ales [mineral, -o] *adj & nm* mineral

minéralogique [mineralɔʒik] *adj* **plaque m.** *(de véhicule) Br* number or *Am* license plate

mineur, -e [minœr] **1** *nm (ouvrier)* miner; **m. de fond** underground worker **2** *adj (secondaire)* & *Mus* minor; *(de moins de 18 ans)* underage **3** *nmf Jur* minor ■ **minière** *adj f* **industrie minière** mining industry

miniature [minjatyr] **1** *nf* miniature **2** *adj* **train m.** miniature train

minigolf [minigɔlf] *nm* crazy golf

minijupe [miniʒyp] *nf* miniskirt

minimal, -e, -aux, -ales [minimal, -o] *adj* minimal; **les temperatures minimales** lowest temperatures

minimum [minimɔm] *(pl* minima [-a] *ou* minimums) **1** *nm* minimum; **le m. de** *(force)* the minimum (amount of); **faire le m.** to do the bare minimum; **en un m. de temps** in as short a time as possible; **au m.** at the very least; **le m. vital** a minimum to live on; **les minima sociaux** = basic income support **2** *adj* minimum

ministère [minister] *nm (département)* ministry; *(gouvernement)* government, cabinet; **m. des Affaires étrangères** *Br* ≃ Foreign Office, *Am* ≃ State Department; **m. de l'Intérieur** *Br* ≃ Home Office, *Am* ≃ Department of the Interior ■ **ministériel, -elle** *adj* ministerial

ministre [ministr] *nm Pol & Rel* secretary, *Br* minister; **m. des Affaires**

étrangères *Br* ≃ Foreign Secretary, *Am* ≃ Secretary of State; **m. de l'Intérieur** *Br* ≃ Home Secretary, *Am* ≃ Secretary of the Interior

Minitel® [minitɛl] *nm* = consumer information network accessible via home computer terminal

minorité [minorite] *nf* minority ■ **minoritaire** *adj* **être m.** to be in the minority

minuit [minɥi] *nm* midnight, twelve o'clock

minuscule [minyskyl] **1** *adj (petit)* tiny, minute **2** *adj & nf* **(lettre) m.** small letter

minute [minyt] *nf* minute; **à la m.** *(tout de suite)* this (very) minute; **d'une m. à l'autre** any minute (now) ■ **minuterie** *nf (d'éclairage)* time switch

minutie [minysi] *nf* meticulousness ■ **minutieux, -euse** *adj* meticulous

mirabelle [mirabɛl] *nf* mirabelle plum

miracle [mirakl] *nm* miracle; **par m.** miraculously ■ **miraculeux, -euse** *adj* miraculous

mirage [miraʒ] *nm* mirage

mire [mir] *nf* **point de m.** *(cible)* & *Fig* target

miroir [mirwar] *nm* mirror

mis, mise¹ [mi, miz] **1** *pp de* mettre **2** *adj* **bien m.** *(vêtu)* well-dressed

mise² [miz] *nf (a) (placement)* putting; **m. au point** *(de rapport)* finalization; *Phot* focusing; *(de moteur)* tuning; *(de technique)* perfecting; *Fig (clarification)* clarification; **m. en garde** warning; **m. en scène** *Théât* production; *Cin* direction (b) *(argent)* stake (c) **être de m.** to be acceptable

miser [mize] *vt (argent)* to stake **(sur** on); **m. sur qn/qch** *(parier)* to bet on sb/sth; *(compter sur)* to count on sb/sth

misère [mizɛr] *nf* extreme poverty; **être dans la m.** to be poverty-stricken ■ **misérable 1** *(pitoyable)* miserable; *(pauvre)* destitute; *(existence)* wretched; *(logement, quartier)* seedy, slummy **2** *nmf (indigent)* poor wretch; *(scélérat)* scoundrel

missile [misil] *nm* missile

mission [misjɔ̃] *nf (tâche, organisation)* mission; *(d'employé)* task; **partir en m.** *(cadre)* to go away on business; *(diplomate)* to go off on a mission ▪ **missionnaire** *nmf & adj* missionary

mistral [mistral] *nm* **le m.** the mistral

mite [mit] *nf* moth

mi-temps [mitɑ̃] **1** *nf inv* Sport *(pause)* half-time; *(période)* half **2** *nm inv* part-time job; **travailler à m.** to work part-time

mitigé, -e [mitiʒe] *adj (accueil)* lukewarm

mitoyen, -enne [mitwajɛ̃, -ɛn] *adj* common, shared

mitraillette [mitrajɛt] *nf* submachine gun

mitrailleur [mitrajœr] *adj m* **fusil m.** machine gun

mitrailleuse [mitrajøz] *nf* machine gun

mi-voix [mivwa] **à mi-voix** *adv* in a low voice

mixer¹ [mikse] *vt (à la main)* to mix; *(au mixer)* to blend

mixer², mixeur [miksœr] *nm (pour mélanger)* (food) mixer; *(pour rendre liquide)* liquidizer

mixte [mikst] *adj* mixed; *(école)* co-educational, *Br* mixed

mixture [mikstyr] *nf* mixture

MJC [ɛmʒise] *(abrév* **maison des jeunes et de la culture)** *nf* = youth club and arts centre

Mlle *(abrév* **Mademoiselle)** Miss

MM *(abrév* **Messieurs)** Messrs

mm *(abrév* **millimètre(s))** mm

Mme *(abrév* **Madame)** Mrs

mobile [mɔbil] **1** *adj (pièce, cible)* moving; *(panneau)* movable; *(personne)* mobile; *(feuillets)* loose **2** *nm (décoration)* mobile; *(motif)* motive (de for)

mobilier [mɔbilje] *nm* furniture

mobiliser [mɔbilize] *vt,* **se mobiliser** *vpr* to mobilize

Mobylette® [mɔbilɛt] *nf* moped

mode¹ [mɔd] *nf (tendance)* fashion; *(industrie)* fashion industry; **à la m.**
fashionable; **suivre la m.** to follow fashion; **à la m. de** in the manner of

mode² [mɔd] *nm (manière)* mode; **m. d'emploi** instructions; **m. de transport** mode of transport; **m. de vie** way of life

modèle [mɔdɛl] **1** *nm (schéma, exemple, personne)* model; *(au tricot)* pattern; **grand/petit m.** *(de vêtement)* large/small size; **m. déposé** registered design **2** *adj* **élève m.** model pupil ▪ **modeler 1** *vt* to model (**sur** on) **2 se modeler** *vpr* **se m. sur qn** to model oneself on sb

modem [mɔdɛm] *nm* Ordinat modem

modérer [mɔdere] **1** *vt (passions, désirs)* to moderate, to restrain; *(vitesse)* to reduce **2 se modérer** *vpr* to calm down ▪ **modération** *nf (retenue)* moderation; *(réduction)* reduction; **avec m.** in moderation ▪ **modéré, -e** *adj* moderate

moderne [mɔdɛrn] *adj* modern ▪ **moderniser** *vt,* **se moderniser** *vpr* to modernize ▪ **modernité** *nf* modernity

modeste [mɔdɛst] *adj* modest ▪ **modestie** *nf* modesty

modifier [mɔdifje] **1** *vt* to alter, to modify **2 se modifier** *vpr* to alter ▪ **modification** *nf* alteration, modification; **apporter une m. à qch** to make an alteration to sth

modulation [mɔdylɑsjɔ̃] *nf (de son, d'amplitude)* modulation; *Radio* **m. de fréquence** frequency modulation

moelle [mwal] *nf (d'os)* marrow; **m. épinière** spinal cord; **m. osseuse** bone marrow

moelleux, -euse [mwalø, -øz] *adj (lit, tissu)* soft

mœurs [mœr(s)] *nfpl (morale)* morals; *(habitudes)* customs; **entrer dans les m.** to become part of everyday life

moi [mwa] **1** *pron personnel* (a) *(après une préposition)* me; **pour/avec m.** for/with me; *Fam* **un ami à m.** a friend of mine
(b) *(complément direct)* me; **laissez-m.** leave me

(c) *(complément indirect)* (to) me; **montrez-le-m.** show it to me, show me it

(d) *(sujet)* I; **c'est m. qui vous le dis!** I'm telling you!; **il est plus grand que m.** he's taller than I am *or* than me

2 *nm inv* self, ego ∎ **moi-même** *pron* myself

moindre [mwɛ̃dr] *adj (comparatif)* lesser; *(prix)* lower; *(quantité)* smaller; **le/la m.** *(superlatif)* the least; **la m. erreur** the slightest mistake; **dans les moindres détails** in the smallest detail; **c'est la m. des choses** it's the least I/we/*etc* can do

moineau, -x [mwano] *nm* sparrow

MOINS [mwɛ̃] **1** ([mwɛ̃z] *before vowel) adv (comparatif)* less **(que** than); **m. de** *(temps, travail)* less **(que** than); *(gens, livres)* fewer **(que** than); **le/la/les m.** *(superlatif)* the least; **le m. grand, la m. grande, les m. grand(e)s** the smallest; **au m., du m.** at least; **qch de m., qch en m.** *(qui manque)* sth missing; **dix ans de m.** ten years less; **en m.** *(personne, objet)* less; *(personnes, objets)* fewer; **les m. de vingt ans** those under twenty, the under-twenties; **à m. que...** *(+ subjunctive)* unless...

2 *prép Math* minus; **deux heures m. cinq** five to two; **il fait m. 10 (degrés)** it's minus 10 (degrees)

mois [mwa] *nm* month; **au m. de juin** in (the month of) June

moisir [mwazir] *vi* to go *Br* mouldy *or Am* moldy ∎ **moisi, -e 1** *adj Br* mouldy, *Am* moldy **2** *nm Br* mould, *Am* mold; *(sur un mur)* mildew; **sentir le m.** to smell musty ∎ **moisissure** *nf Br* mould, *Am* mold

moisson [mwasɔ̃] *nf* harvest; **faire la m.** to harvest ∎ **moissonner** *vt (céréales)* to harvest; *(champ)* to reap ∎ **moissonneuse-batteuse** *(pl moissonneuses-batteuses) nf* combine harvester

moite [mwat] *adj* sticky

moitié [mwatje] *nf* half; **la m. de la pomme** half (of) the apple; **à m.** *(rem-*

plir) halfway; **à m. plein/vide** half-full/-empty; **à m. prix** (at) half-price

moka [mɔka] *nm (café)* mocha; *(gâteau)* coffee cake

mol [mɔl] *voir* **mou**

molaire [mɔlɛr] *nf* molar

molécule [mɔlekyl] *nf* molecule

molester [mɔlɛste] *vt* to manhandle

molle [mɔl] *voir* **mou**

mollet¹ [mɔlɛ] *nm (de jambe)* calf

mollet² [mɔlɛ] *adj* **œuf m.** soft-boiled egg

mollusque [mɔlysk] *nm Br* mollusc, *Am* mollusk

moment [mɔmɑ̃] *nm (instant, durée)* moment; **un petit m.** a little while; **en ce m.** at the moment; **pour le m.** for the moment, for the time being; **sur le m.** at the time; **à ce m.-là** *(à ce moment précis)* at that (very) moment, at that time; *(dans ce cas)* then; **à un m. donné** at one point; **le m. venu** *(dans le future)* when the time comes; **d'un m. à l'autre** at any moment; **dans ces moments-là** at times like that; **par moments** at times; **au m. de partir** when just about to leave; **au m. où...** just as...; **jusqu'au m. où...** until...; **du m. que...** *(puisque)* seeing that... ∎ **momentané, -e** *adj (temporaire)* momentary; *(bref)* brief ∎ **momentanément** *adv (temporairement)* temporarily; *(brièvement)* briefly

mon, ma, mes [mɔ̃, ma, mɛ]

> **ma** becomes **mon** [mɔ̃n] before a vowel or mute h.

adj possessif my; **m. père** my father; **ma mère** my mother; **m. ami(e)** my friend; **mes parents** my parents

Monaco [mɔnako] *nm* Monaco

monarque [mɔnark] *nm* monarch ∎ **monarchie** *nf* monarchy

monastère [mɔnaster] *nm* monastery

mondain, -e [mɔ̃dɛ̃, -ɛn] *adj* **réunion mondaine** society gathering ∎ **mondanités** *nfpl (événements)* social life; *(conversations)* social chitchat

monde [mɔ̃d] *nm* world; *(gens)* people; **dans le m. entier** worldwide, all over the world; **tout le m.** everybody; **il y a**

du m. there are a lot of people; **venir au m.** to come into the world ▪ **mondial, -e, -aux, -ales** *adj (crise, renommée)* worldwide; **guerre mondiale** world war ▪ **mondialisation** *nf* globalization

monégasque [mɔnegask] **1** *adj* Monegasque **2** *nmf* **M.** Monegasque

monétaire [mɔnetɛr] *adj* monetary

mongolien, -enne [mɔ̃gɔljɛ̃, -ɛn] **1** *adj* **être m.** to have Down's syndrome **2** *nmf* person with Down's syndrome

moniteur, -trice [mɔnitœr, -tris] **1** *nmf* instructor; *(de colonie) Br* assistant, *Am* camp counselor **2** *nm Ordinat (écran)* monitor

monnaie [mɔnɛ] *nf (argent)* money; *(de)* currency; *(pièces)* change; **petite m.** small change; **faire de la m.** to get change; **avoir la m. de 100 euros** to have change for 100 euros; **m. électronique** plastic money; **m. unique** single currency

monoparentale [mɔnoparɑ̃tal] *adj f* **famille m.** one-parent family

monoplace [mɔnɔplas] *adj & nmf* single-seater

monopole [mɔnɔpɔl] *nm* monopoly; **avoir le m. de qch** to have a monopoly on sth ▪ **monopoliser** *vt* to monopolize

monoski [mɔnoski] *nm* mono-ski; **faire du m.** to mono-ski

monotone [mɔnɔtɔn] *adj* monotonous ▪ **monotonie** *nf* monotony

monseigneur [mɔ̃sɛɲœr] *(pl* **messeigneurs)** *nm (évêque)* His/Your Lordship; *(prince)* His/Your Highness

monsieur [məsjø] *(pl* **messieurs)** *nm (homme quelconque)* gentleman; **M. Legras** Mr Legras; **bonsoir, messieursdames!** good evening!; **M.** *(dans une lettre)* Dear Sir

monstre [mɔ̃str] *nm* monster; **m. sacré** giant ▪ **monstrueux, -euse** *adj (mal formé, scandaleux)* monstrous; *(énorme)* huge

mont [mɔ̃] *nm* mount

montage [mɔ̃taʒ] *nm Tech* assembling; *Cin* editing; *(image truquée)* montage

montagne [mɔ̃taɲ] *nf* mountain; **la m.** *(zone)* the mountains; **à la m.** in the mountains; **en haute m.** high in the mountains; **montagnes russes** *(attraction foraine)* rollercoaster ▪ **montagnard, -e** *nmf* mountain dweller ▪ **montagneux, -euse** *adj* mountainous

montant, -e 1 *adj (marée)* rising; *(col)* stand-up **2** *nm (somme)* amount; *(de barrière)* post; **montants compensatoires** subsidies

monte-charge [mɔ̃tʃarʒ] *(pl* **monte-charges)** *nm* service *Br* lift *or Am* elevator

montée [mɔ̃te] *nf (ascension)* climb, ascent; *(chemin)* slope; *(des prix, du fascisme)* rise; **la m. des eaux** the rise in the water level

monter [mɔ̃te] **1** *(aux* **avoir)** *vt (côte)* to climb (up); *(objet)* to bring/take up; *(cheval)* to ride; *(son)* to turn up; *(tente)* to put up; *(machine)* to assemble; *(pièce de théâtre)* to stage; **m. l'escalier** to go/come upstairs *or* up the stairs

2 *(aux* **être)** *vi (personne)* to go/come up; *(prix)* to rise; *(marée)* to come in; *(avion)* to climb; **faire m. qn** to show sb up; **m. dans un véhicule** to get in(to) a vehicle; **m. sur qch** to climb onto sth; **m. sur** *ou* **à une échelle** to climb up a ladder; **m. en courant** to run up; *Sport* **m. à cheval** to ride (a horse)

3 se monter *vpr* **se m. à** *(s'élever à)* to amount to

monteur, -euse [mɔ̃tœr, -øz] *nmf Cin* editor

montre [mɔ̃tr] *nf (instrument)* (wrist)-watch; *Sport & Fig* **course contre la m.** race against the clock

Montréal [mɔ̃real] *nm ou f* Montreal

montrer [mɔ̃tre] **1** *vt* to show (**à** to); **m. qn/qch du doigt** to point at sb/sth; **m. le chemin à qn** to show sb the way **2 se montrer** *vpr* to show oneself; **se m. courageux** to be courageous

monture [mɔ̃tyr] *nf (de lunettes)* frame; *(de bijou)* setting

monument [mɔnymɑ̃] *nm* monument; **m. historique** ancient monument; **m. aux morts** war memorial

■ **monumental, -e, -aux, -ales** *adj*
(imposant, énorme) monumental

moquer [mɔke] **se moquer** *vpr* **se m.
de qn** to make fun of sb; **se m. de qch**
(rire de) to make fun of sth; *(ne pas se
soucier)* not to care about sth ■ **moque-
rie** *nf* mockery ■ **moqueur, -euse** *adj*
mocking

moquette [mɔkɛt] *nf Br* fitted carpet,
Am wall-to-wall carpeting

moral, -e, -aux, -ales [mɔral, -o] **1**
adj moral **2** *nm* **avoir le m.** to be in
good spirits ■ **morale** *nf (d'histoire)*
moral; *(principes)* morals; *(règles)* mo-
rality; **faire la m. à qn** to lecture sb
■ **moralité** *nf (mœurs)* morality; *(de ré-
cit)* moral

morceau, -x [mɔrso] *nm* piece, bit; *(de
sucre)* lump; *(de viande)* cut; **tomber
en morceaux** to fall to pieces ■ **morce-
ler** *vt (terrain)* to divide up

mordiller [mɔrdije] *vt* to nibble

mordre [mɔrdr] **1** *vti* to bite; **m. qn au
bras** to bite sb's arm; **2 se mordre** *vpr
Fig* **se m. les doigts d'avoir fait qch** to
kick oneself for doing sth

mordu, -e [mɔrdy] *pp de* **mordre**

morgue [mɔrg] *nf (d'hôpital)* mortua-
ry; *(pour corps non identifiés)* morgue

moribond, -e [mɔribɔ̃, -ɔ̃d] **1** *adj* dy-
ing **2** *nmf* dying person

morne [mɔrn] *adj (temps)* dismal; *(si-
lence)* gloomy; *(personne)* glum

morose [mɔroz] *adj* morose

mors [mɔr] *nm (de harnais)* bit

morse [mɔrs] *nm (code)* Morse (code)

morsure [mɔrsyr] *nf* bite

mort¹ [mɔr] *nf* death; **se donner la m.**
to take one's own life; **un silence de m.**
a deathly silence ■ **mortalité** *nf* death
rate, mortality ■ **mortel, -elle 1** *adj
(hommes, ennemi, danger)* mortal; *(ac-
cident)* fatal **2** *nmf* mortal ■ **mortelle-
ment** *adv (blessé)* fatally

mort², morte [mɔr, mɔrt] **1** *adj (per-
sonne, plante, ville)* dead; **m. de fati-
gue** dead tired; **m. de froid** numb
with cold; **m. de peur** frightened to
death; **m. ou vif** dead or alive
2 *nmf* dead man, *f* dead woman; **les**

morts the dead; **de nombreux morts**
(victimes) many deaths; **le jour** *ou* **la
fête des Morts** All Souls' Day
■ **morte-saison** *(pl* **mortes-saisons)**
nf off-season ■ **mort-né, -e** *(mpl* **mort-
nés,** *fpl* **mort-nées)** *adj (enfant)* still-
born

morue [mɔry] *nf* cod

mosaïque [mɔzaik] *nf* mosaic

Moscou [mɔsku] *nm ou f* Moscow

mot [mo] *nm* word; **envoyer un m. à
qn** to drop sb a line; **m. à m.** word for
word; **avoir le dernier m.** to have the
last word; **mots croisés** crossword
(puzzle); **m. de passe** password

motel [mɔtɛl] *nm* motel

moteur¹ [mɔtœr] *nm (de véhicule)* en-
gine; *(électrique)* motor; *Ordinat* **m. de
recherche** search engine

moteur², -trice [mɔtœr, -tris] **1** *adj
(nerf, muscle)* motor; **voiture à quatre
roues motrices** four-wheel drive (car)
2 *nf* **motrice** *(de train)* engine

motif [mɔtif] *nm (raison)* reason (**de**
for); *(dessin)* pattern

motiver [mɔtive] *vt (inciter, causer)* to
motivate; *(justifier)* to justify ■ **motiva-
tion** *nf* motivation ■ **motivé, -e** *adj*
motivated

moto [mɔto] *nf* motorbike ■ **motocy-
cliste** *nmf* motorcyclist

motte [mɔt] *nf (de terre)* lump, clod; *(de
beurre)* block

mou, molle [mu, mɔl]

mol is used before masculine singular
nouns beginning with a vowel or h
mute.

adj soft; *(sans énergie)* feeble ■ **mol-
lesse** *nf (de matelas)* softness; *(de per-
sonne)* lethargy

mouche [muʃ] *nf (insecte)* fly; **faire m.**
to hit the bull's-eye ■ **moucheron** *nm*
midge

moucher [muʃe] **1** *vt* **m. qn** to wipe sb
's nose **2 se moucher** *vpr* to blow one's
nose

moucheté, -e [muʃte] *adj* speckled

mouchoir [muʃwar] *nm* handker-
chief; **m. en papier** tissue

moudre* [mudr] *vt* to grind

mouette [mwɛt] *nf* (sea)gull

moufle [mufl] *nf* mitten, mitt

mouiller [muje] **1** *vt* to wet **2** *vi Naut* to anchor **3 se mouiller** *vpr* to get wet ■ **mouillé, -e** *adj* wet (**de** with)

moule¹ [mul] *nm Br* mould, *Am* mold; **m. à gâteaux** cake tin ■ **moulage** *nm (objet)* cast ■ **moulant, -e** *adj (vête-ment)* tight-fitting ■ **mouler** *vt Br* to mould, *Am* to mold; *(statue)* to cast

moule² [mul] *nf (mollusque)* mussel

moulin [mulɛ̃] *nm* mill; **m. à café** coffee grinder; **m. à vent** windmill

moulinet [mulinɛ] *nm (de canne à pêche)* reel

moulu, -e [muly] **1** *pp de* moudre **2** *adj (café)* ground

mourir* [murir] *(aux* être*) vi* to die (**de** of *or* from); **m. de froid** to die of exposure; *Fig* **m. de fatigue** to be dead tired; *Fig* **m. de peur** to be frightened to death; *Fig* **je meurs de faim!** I'm starving! ■ **mourant, -e 1** *adj* dying; *(voix)* faint **2** *nmf* dying person

mousse [mus] **1** *nf (plante)* moss; *(écume)* foam; *(de bière)* head; *(de savon)* lather; **m. à raser** shaving foam; *Culin* **m. au chocolat** chocolate mousse **2** *nm (marin)* ship's boy ■ **mousser** *vi (bière)* to froth; *(savon)* to lather ■ **mousseux, -euse 1** *adj (vin)* sparkling **2** *nm* sparkling wine

mousson [musɔ̃] *nf* monsoon

moustache [mustaʃ] *nf (d'homme) Br* moustache, *Am* mustache; *(de chat)* whiskers ■ **moustachu, -e** *adj* with a *Br* moustache *or Am* mustache

moustique [mustik] *nm* mosquito ■ **moustiquaire** *nf* mosquito net; *(en métal)* screen

moutarde [mutard] *nf* mustard

mouton [mutɔ̃] *nm* sheep *inv; (viande)* mutton; **moutons** *(écume) Br* white horses, *Am* whitecaps; *(poussière)* fluff; **peau de m.** sheepskin

mouvement [muvmɑ̃] *nm (geste, groupe, déplacement)* movement; *(élan)* impulse; *(de gymnastique)* exercise; **en m.** in motion; **m. de colère** fit of anger; **mouvements sociaux** workers' protest movements ■ **mouvementé, -e** *adj (vie, voyage)* eventful

mouvoir* [muvwar] *vi,* **se mouvoir** *vpr* to move; **mû par** *(mécanisme)* driven by

MOYEN¹, -ENNE [mwajɛ̃, -ɛn] **1** *adj* average; *(format, entreprise)* medium(-sized)

2 *nf* **moyenne** average; **en moyenne** on average; **la moyenne d'âge** the average age; **avoir la moyenne** *(à un examen) Br* to get a pass mark, *Am* to get a pass; *(à un devoir) Br* to get 50 percent, *Am* to get half marks; **le M. Âge** the Middle Ages

moyen² [mwajɛ̃] *nm (procédé, façon)* means, way (**de faire** of doing *or* to do); **moyens** *(capacités mentales)* ability; *(argent, ressources)* means; **je n'ai pas les moyens** *(argent)* I can't afford it; **au m. de qch** by means of sth

Mozambique [mɔzɑ̃bik] *nm* **le M.** Mozambique

MST [ɛmɛste] *(abrév* **maladie sexuellement transmissible)** *nf* STD

muer [mɥe] **1** *vi (animal) Br* to moult, *Am* to molt; *(voix)* to break **2 se muer** *vpr* se m. **en qch** to change into sth

muet, muette [mɥe, mɥɛt] **1** *adj (infirme)* dumb; *(de surprise)* speechless; *(film)* silent **2** *nmf* mute

muguet [mygɛ] *nm* lily of the valley

mule [myl] *nf (pantoufle, animal)* mule ■ **mulet** *nm (équidé)* mule; *(poisson)* mullet

multicolore [myltikɔlɔr] *adj Br* multicoloured, *Am* multicolored

multinationale [myltinasjɔnal] *nf* multinational

multiple [myltipl] *adj (nombreux)* numerous; *(varié)* multiple ■ **multiplication** *nf (calcul)* multiplication; *(augmentation)* increase ■ **multiplier 1** *vt* to multiply **2 se multiplier** *vpr* to increase; *(se reproduire)* to multiply

multitude [myltityd] *nf* multitude

municipal, -e, -aux, -ales [mynisipal, -o] *adj* municipal ■ **municipalité** *nf (maires et conseillers)* local council; *(commune)* municipality

munir [mynir] **1** *vt* m. de qch *(personne)* to provide with sth **2 se munir** *vpr* se m. de qch to take sth

munitions [mynisjɔ̃] *nfpl* ammunition

mur [myr] *nm* wall; *Fig* au pied du m. with one's back to the wall; m. du son sound barrier ∎ **muraille** *nf* (high) wall ∎ **mural, -e, -aux, -ales** *adj* carte murale wall map; peinture murale mural (painting) ∎ **murer** *vt (porte)* to wall up

mûr, mûre¹ [myr] *adj (fruit)* ripe; *(personne)* mature; d'âge m. middle-aged ∎ **mûrir** *vti (fruit)* to ripen; *(personne)* to mature

mûre² [myr] *nf (baie)* blackberry

muret [myre] *nm* low wall

murmure [myrmyr] *nm* murmur ∎ **murmurer** *vti* to murmur

muscle [myskl] *nm* muscle ∎ **musclé, -e** *adj (bras)* muscular ∎ **musculaire** *adj (force, douleur)* muscular ∎ **musculature** *nf* muscles

museau, -x [myzo] *nm (de chien, de chat)* muzzle ∎ **museler** *vt (animal, presse)* to muzzle

musée [myze] *nm* museum; m. de peinture art gallery ∎ **muséum** *nm* natural history museum

music-hall [myzikol] *(pl* music-halls) *nm (genre, salle)* music hall

musique [myzik] *nf* music; écouter de la m. to listen to music ∎ **musical, -e, -aux, -ales** *adj* musical ∎ **musicien, -enne 1** *nmf* musician **2** *adj* musical

musulman, -e [myzylmã, -an] *adj & nmf* Muslim, Moslem

muter [myte] *vt* to transfer ∎ **mutant, -e** *adj & nmf* mutant ∎ **mutation** *nf (d'employé)* transfer; *Biol* mutation

mutiler [mytile] *vt* to mutilate, to maim; être mutilé to be disabled

mutin [mytɛ̃] *nm (rebelle)* mutineer ∎ **mutinerie** *nf* mutiny

mutisme [mytism] *nm* silence

mutuel, -elle [mytɥɛl] **1** *adj (réciproque)* mutual **2** *nf* mutuelle mutual insurance company ∎ **mutuellement** *adv* each other

myope [mjɔp] *adj* shortsighted

myrtille [mirtij] *nf (baie)* bilberry

mystère [mister] *nm* mystery ∎ **mystérieux, -euse** *adj* mysterious

mystique [mistik] **1** *adj* mystical **2** *nmf (personne)* mystic

mythe [mit] *nm* myth ∎ **mythique** *adj* mythical ∎ **mythologie** *nf* mythology ∎ **mythologique** *adj* mythological

Nn

N¹, n [ɛn] *nm inv* N, n

N² *(abrév* **route nationale)** M

n' [n] *voir* ne

nacelle [nasɛl] *nf (de ballon)* basket

nacre [nakr] *nf* mother-of-pearl ▪ **nacré, -e** *adj* pearly

nage [naʒ] *nf* (swimming) stroke; **traverser une rivière à la n.** to swim across a river; **n. libre** freestyle

nageoire [naʒwar] *nf (de poisson)* fin; *(de dauphin)* flipper

nager [naʒe] *vti* to swim ▪ **nageur, -euse** *nmf* swimmer

naïf, naïve [naif, naiv] *adj* naïve

nain, naine [nɛ̃, nɛn] *adj & nmf* dwarf

naissance [nɛsɑ̃s] *nf (de personne, d'animal)* birth; **donner n. à** *(enfant)* to give birth to; *(sentiment, difficulté)* to arise **(de** from); *(idée)* to originate

naître* [nɛtr] *vi* to be born; *(sentiment, difficulté)* to arise **(de** from); *(idée)* to originate

naïveté [naivte] *nf* naïvety

nantir [nɑ̃tir] *vt* **n. qn de qch** to provide sb with sth ▪ **nanti, -e 1** *adj* well-to-do **2** *nmpl Péj* **les nantis** the well-to-do

nappe [nap] *nf (de table)* tablecloth; **n. de brouillard** fog patch; **n. d'eau** expanse of water; **n. de pétrole** layer of oil; *(de marée noire)* oil slick

napper [nape] *vt* to coat **(de** with)

narguer [narge] *vt* to taunt

narine [narin] *nf* nostril

narquois, -e [narkwa, -az] *adj* sneering

nasal, -e, -aux, -ales [nazal, -o] *adj* nasal

nasillard, -e [nazijar, -ard] *adj (voix)* nasal

natal, -e, -als, -ales [natal] *adj* native

natalité [natalite] *nf* birth rate

natation [natasjɔ̃] *nf* swimming

natif, -ive [natif, -iv] *adj & nmf* native; **être n. de** to be a native of

nation [nasjɔ̃] *nf* nation; **les Nations unies** the United Nations ▪ **national, -e, -aux, -ales** *adj* national ▪ **nationale** *nf (route)* Br ≃ A road, Am ≃ highway ▪ **nationaliser** *vt* to nationalize ▪ **nationaliste 1** *adj* nationalistic **2** *nmf* nationalist ▪ **nationalité** *nf* nationality

natte [nat] *nf (de cheveux)* Br plait, Am braid

naturaliser [natyralize] *vt* to naturalize ▪ **naturalisation** *nf* naturalization

nature [natyr] **1** *nf (univers, caractère)* nature; *(campagne)* country; **contre n.** unnatural; **en pleine n.** in the middle of the country; **payer en n.** to pay in kind; **n. morte** still life **2** *adj inv (omelette, yaourt)* plain; *(thé)* without milk

naturel, -elle [natyrɛl] **1** *adj* natural; **mort naturelle** death from natural causes **2** *nm (caractère)* nature; *(simplicité)* naturalness ▪ **naturellement** *adv* naturally

naufrage [nofraʒ] *nm* (ship)wreck; **faire n.** *(bateau)* to be wrecked; *(marin)* to be shipwrecked

nausée [noze] *nf* nausea, sickness; **avoir la n.** to feel sick

nautique [notik] *adj* nautical

naval, -e, -als, -ales [naval] *adj* naval

navet [navɛ] *nm (légume)* turnip

navette [navɛt] *nf (véhicule)* shuttle; **faire la n.** *(véhicule, personne)* to shuttle back and forth **(entre** between); **n. spatiale** space shuttle

navigable [navigabl] *adj (fleuve)* navigable

navigant, -e [navigã, -ãt] *adj Aviat*
personnel n. flight crew
navigateur [navigatœr] *nm (marin)*
navigator ■ **navigation** *nf* navigation
naviguer [navige] *vi (bateau)* to sail;
n. sur Internet to surf the Net
navire [navir] *nm* ship
navrer [navre] *vt* to appal ■ **navrant,
-e** *adj* appalling ■ **navré, -e** *adj (air)*
distressed; **je suis n.** I'm terribly sorry
ne [nə] **n'** before vowel or mute h; used
to form negative verb with **pas, jamais,
personne, rien** etc. *adv* **ne... pas** not; **il
ne boit pas** he does not or doesn't
drink; **elle n'ose (pas)** she doesn't
dare; **ne... que** only; **je crains qu'il
ne parte** I'm afraid he'll leave
né, -e [ne] **1** *pp de* **naître** born; **il est
né en 2001** he was born in 2001; **née
Dupont** née Dupont **2** *adj* born; **c'est
un poète-né** he's a born poet
néanmoins [neãmwɛ̃] *adv* neverthe-
less
néant [neã] *nm* nothingness; *'sur for-
mulaire)* ≃ none
nécessaire [neseser] **1** *adj* necessary
2 *nm* **le n.** the necessities; **faire le n.**
to do what's necessary; **n. de toilette**
toilet bag
nécessité [nesesite] *nf* necessity ■ **né-
cessiter** *vt* to require, to necessitate
nectarine [nektarin] *nf* nectarine
néerlandais, -e [neerlãde, -ɛz] **1** *adj*
Dutch **2** *nmf* **N.** Dutchman; **Néerlan-
daise** Dutchwoman **3** *nm (langue)*
Dutch
nef [nef] *nf (d'église)* nave
néfaste [nefast] *adj* harmful (**à** to)
négatif, -ive [negatif, -iv] **1** *adj* nega-
tive **2** *nm (de photo)* negative
négligeable [neglizabl] *adj* negli-
gible; **non n.** *(quantité)* significant
négligent, -e [neglizã, -ãt] *adj* care-
less, negligent ■ **négligence** *nf (défaut)*
carelessness, negligence
négliger [neglize] **1** *vt (personne, tra-
vail, conseil)* to neglect; **n. de faire qch**
to neglect to do sth **2 se négliger** *vpr*
to neglect oneself ■ **négligé, -e** *adj (te-
nue)* untidy; *(travail)* careless

négocier [negosje] *vti* to negotiate
■ **négociable** *adj* negotiable ■ **négo-
ciant, -e** *nmf* merchant, dealer ■ **né-
gociateur, -trice** *nmf* negotiator
■ **négociation** *nf* negotiation
neige [nɛʒ] *nf* snow; **aller à la n.** to go
skiing; **n. fondue** sleet ■ **neiger** *v im-
personnel* to snow; **il neige** it's snowing
néon [neɔ̃] *nm (gaz)* neon; *(enseigne)*
neon sign; **éclairage au n.** neon light-
ing
néo-zélandais, -e [neozelãde, -ɛz]
(mpl néo-zélandais, *fpl* néo-zélan-
daises) **1** *adj* New Zealand **2** *nmf* **N.,
Néo-Zélandaise** New Zealander
nerf [nɛr] *nm* nerve ■ **nerveux, -euse**
adj nervous ■ **nervosité** *nf* nervous-
ness
n'est-ce pas [nɛspɑ] *adv* isn't he?/
don't you?/won't they?/*etc*; **tu vien-
dras, n.?** you'll come, won't you?; **il fait
beau, n.?** the weather's nice, isn't it?
Net [nɛt] *nm* **le N.** the Net
net, nette [nɛt] **1** *adj (propre)* clean;
(image, refus) clear; *(écriture)* neat;
(prix, salaire) net; **n. d'impôt** net of tax
2 *adv (casser, couper)* clean; *(tuer)* out-
right; *(refuser)* flatly; **s'arrêter n.** to
stop dead ■ **nettement** *adv (avec pré-
cision)* clearly; *(incontestablement)* defi-
nitely; **il va n. mieux** he's much
better ■ **netteté** *nf (propreté, précision)*
cleanness; *(de travail)* neatness
netiquette [netiket] *nf Ordinat* neti-
quette
nettoyer [netwaje] **1** *vt* to clean **2 se
nettoyer** *vpr* **se n. les oreilles** to clean
one's ears ■ **nettoyage** *nm* cleaning; **n.
à sec** dry-cleaning
neuf¹, neuve [nœf, nœv] **1** *adj* new;
quoi de n.? what's new? **2** *nm* **remet-
tre qch à n.** to make sth as good as new
neuf² [nœf, nœv *before* **heures, ans**]
adj & nm nine ■ **neuvième** *adj & nmf*
ninth
neutre [nøtr] **1** *adj (pays, personne)*
neutral **2** *nm* *Él* neutral ■ **neutraliser**
vt to neutralize ■ **neutralité** *nf* neutrali-
ty
neveu, -x [nəvø] *nm* nephew

nez [ne] *nm* nose; **n. à n.** face to face (**avec** with); **rire au n. de qn** to laugh in sb's face; **parler du n.** to speak through one's nose

ni [ni] *conj* **ni... ni...** neither... nor...; **ni Pierre ni Paul ne sont venus** neither Pierre nor Paul came; **il n'a ni faim ni soif** he's neither hungry nor thirsty; **sans manger ni boire** without eating or drinking; **ni l'un(e) ni l'autre** neither (of them)

Nicaragua [nikaragwa] *nm* **le N.** Nicaragua

niche [niʃ] *nf (de chien) Br* kennel, *Am* doghouse; *(cavité)* niche, recess

nicher [niʃe] **1** *vi (oiseau)* to nest **2 se nicher** *vpr (oiseau)* to nest ▪ **nichée** *nf (chiens)* litter; *(oiseaux)* brood

nickel [nikɛl] *nm (métal)* nickel

nicotine [nikɔtin] *nf* nicotine

nid [ni] *nm* nest

nièce [njɛs] *nf* niece

nier [nje] **1** *vt* to deny (**que** that) **2** *vi (accusé)* to deny the charge

Niger [niʒɛr] *nm* **le N.** *(pays)* Niger

Nigéria [niʒerja] *nm* **le N.** Nigeria

Nil [nil] *nm* **le N.** the Nile

n'importe [nɛ̃pɔrt] *voir* **importer**[1]

nippon, -one *ou* **-onne** [nipɔ̃, -ɔn] *adj* Japanese

niveau, -x [nivo] *nm (hauteur, étage, degré)* level; *Scol* standard; **au n. de la mer** at sea level; **n. de vie** standard of living ▪ **niveler** *vt (surface)* to level

noble [nɔbl] **1** *adj* noble **2** *nmf* nobleman, *f* noblewoman ▪ **noblesse** *nf (caractère, classe)* nobility

noce [nɔs] *nf* wedding; **noces d'or** golden wedding

nocif, -ive [nɔsif, -iv] *adj* harmful ▪ **nocivité** *nf* harmfulness

nocturne [nɔktyrn] **1** *adj (animal)* nocturnal **2** *nf (de magasin)* late-night opening; *Sport* **(match en) n.** evening match

Noël [nɔɛl] *nm* Christmas; **arbre de N.** Christmas tree; **le père N.** Father Christmas, Santa Claus

nœud [nø] *nm* **(a)** *(entrecroisement)* knot; *(ruban)* bow; **n. papillon** bow tie **(b)** *Naut (vitesse)* knot

noir, -e [nwar] **1** *adj* black; *(sombre)* dark; *(idées)* gloomy; *(misère)* dire; **il fait n.** it's dark; **film n.** film noir **2** *nm (couleur)* black; *(obscurité)* dark; **N.** *(homme)* Black (man) **3** *nf* **noire** *(note) Br* crotchet, *Am* quarter note; **Noire** *(femme)* Black (woman) ▪ **noircir 1** *vt* to blacken **2** *vi* to turn black

noisette [nwazet] *nf* hazelnut

noix [nwa] *nf (du noyer)* walnut; **n. de coco** coconut

nom [nɔ̃] *nm* name; *Gram* noun; **au n. de qn** on sb's behalf; **n. de famille** surname; **n. de jeune fille** maiden name

nomade [nɔmad] **1** *adj* nomadic **2** *nmf* nomad

nombre [nɔ̃br] *nm* number; **être au** *ou* **du n. de** to be among; **ils sont au n. de dix** there are ten of them; **le plus grand n. de** the majority of; **bon n. de** a good many; *Math* **n. premier** prime number

nombreux, -euse [nɔ̃brø, -øz] *adj (amis, livres)* numerous, many; *(famille, collection)* large; **peu n.** few; **venir n.** to come in large numbers

nombril [nɔ̃bri] *nm* navel

nominal, -e, -aux, -ales [nɔminal, -o] *adj* nominal

nomination [nɔminɑsjɔ̃] *nf (à un poste)* appointment; *(pour récompense)* nomination

nommer [nɔme] **1** *vt (appeler)* to name; **n. qn** *(désigner)* to appoint sb (**à un poste** to a post); **n. qn président** to appoint sb chairman **2 se nommer** *vpr (s'appeler)* to be called

non [nɔ̃] *adv* no; **tu viens ou n.?** are you coming or not?; **n. seulement** not only; **n. (pas) que...** (+ *subjunctive*) not that...; **n. loin** not far; **je crois que n.** I don't think so; **(ni) moi n. plus** neither do/am/can/*etc* I

nonante [nɔnɑ̃t] *adj & nm (en Belgique, en Suisse)* ninety

nonchalant, -e [nɔ̃ʃalɑ̃, -ɑ̃t] *adj* nonchalant

non-fumeur, -euse [nɔ̃fymœr, -øz]

1 *adj* non-smoking 2 *nmf* non-smoker

non-retour [nɔ̃rətur] *nm* **point de n.** point of no return

non-violence [nɔ̃vjɔlɑ̃s] *nf* non-violence

non-voyants [nɔ̃vwajɑ̃] *nmpl* **les n.** the unsighted

nord [nɔr] **1** *nm* north; **au n.** in the north; *(direction)* (to the) north (**de** of); **du n.** *(vent, direction)* northerly; *(ville)* northern; *(gens)* from/in the north; **l'Afrique du N.** North Africa; **l'Europe du N.** Northern Europe; **le grand N.** the Frozen North

2 *adj inv (côte)* north; *(régions)* northern ▪ **nord-africain, -e** *(mpl* **nord-africains,** *fpl* **nord-africaines) 1** *adj* North African **2** *nmf* **N., Nord-Africaine** North African ▪ **nord-américain, -e** *(mpl* **nord-américains,** *fpl* **nord-américaines) 1** *adj* North American **2** *nmf* **N., Nord-Américaine** North American ▪ **nord-est** *nm & adj inv* northeast ▪ **nord-ouest** *nm & adj inv* northwest

nordique [nɔrdik] **1** *adj* Scandinavian **2** *nmf* **N.** Scandinavian; *Can* Northern Canadian

normal, -e, -aux, -ales [nɔrmal, -o] *adj* normal ▪ **normale** *nf* norm; **au-dessus/au-dessous de la n.** above/ below average; *Fam* **N. Sup** = university-level college preparing students for senior posts in teaching ▪ **normalement** *adv* normally ▪ **normaliser** *vt (uniformiser)* to standardize; *(relations)* to normalize

normand, -e [nɔrmɑ̃, -ɑ̃d] **1** *adj* Norman **2** *nmf* **N., Normande** Norman ▪ **Normandie** *nf* **la N.** Normandy

norme [nɔrm] *nf* norm; **normes de sécurité** safety standards

Norvège [nɔrvɛʒ] *nf* **la N.** Norway ▪ **norvégien, -enne 1** *adj* Norwegian **2** *nmf* **N., Norvégienne** Norwegian **3** *nm (langue)* Norwegian

nos [no] *voir* **notre**

nostalgie [nɔstalʒi] *nf* nostalgia ▪ **nostalgique** *adj* nostalgic

notable [nɔtabl] *adj & nm* notable

notaire [nɔtɛr] *nm* lawyer, *Br* notary (public)

notamment [nɔtamɑ̃] *adv* notably

note [nɔt] *nf (annotation, communication)* & *Mus* note; *Scol Br* mark, *Am* grade; *(facture) Br* bill, *Am* check; **prendre n. de qch** to make a note of sth; **prendre des notes** to take notes; **n. de frais** expenses

noter [nɔte] *vt (remarquer)* to note; *(écrire)* to note down; *(devoir) Br* to mark, *Am* to grade

notice [nɔtis] *nf (mode d'emploi)* instructions; *(de médicament)* directions

notifier [nɔtifje] *vt* **n. qch à qn** to notify sb of sth

notion [nɔsjɔ̃] *nf* notion; **notions** *(éléments)* rudiments; **avoir des notions de qch** to know the basics of sth

notoriété [nɔtɔrjete] *nf (renom)* fame; **il est de n. publique que...** it's common knowledge that...

notre, nos [nɔtr, no] *adj possessif* our

nôtre [notr] **1** *pron possessif* **le/la n., les nôtres** ours **2** *nmpl* **les nôtres** *(parents)* our family

nouer [nwe] **1** *vt (lacets)* to tie; *(cravate)* to knot; *Fig (relation)* to establish **2 se nouer** *vpr (intrigue)* to take shape

nougat [nuga] *nm* nougat

nouilles [nuj] *nfpl* noodles

nourrice [nuris] *nf (assistante maternelle)* (children's) nurse, *Br* childminder; *(qui allaite)* wet nurse

nourrir [nurir] **1** *vt (alimenter)* to feed; *Fig (espoir)* to cherish **2 se nourrir** *vpr* to eat; **se n. de qch** to feed on sth

nourrisson [nurisɔ̃] *nm* infant

nourriture [nurityr] *nf* food

nous [nu] *pron personnel* **(a)** *(sujet)* we; **n. sommes ici** we are here

(b) *(complément direct)* us; **il n. connaît** he knows us

(c) *(complément indirect)* (to) us; **il n. l'a donné** he gave it to us, he gave us it

(d) *(réfléchi)* ourselves; **n. n. lavons** we wash ourselves; **n. n. habillons** we get dressed

(e) *(réciproque)* each other; **n. n. détestons** we hate each other ▪ **nous-mêmes** *pron* ourselves

nouveau, -elle¹, -x, -elles [nuvo, -ɛl]

> **nouvel** is used before masculine singular nouns beginning with a vowel or mute h.

1 adj new; (mode) latest; **on craint de nouvelles inondations** (d'autres) further flooding is feared

2 nmf (à l'école) new boy, f new girl

3 nm **du n.** something new

4 adv **de n., à n.** again ▪ **nouveau-né, -e** (mpl **nouveau-nés,** fpl **nouveau-nées**) **1** adj newborn **2** nmf newborn baby

nouveauté [nuvote] nf novelty; **nouveautés** (livres) new books; (disques) new releases

nouvelle² [nuvɛl] nf (a) **une n.** (annonce) a piece of news; **la n. de sa mort** the news of his/her death; **les nouvelles** the news (sing); **avoir des nouvelles de qn** (directement) to have heard from sb (b) (récit) short story

Nouvelle-Calédonie [nuvɛlkaledɔni] nf **la N.** New Caledonia

Nouvelle-Zélande [nuvɛlzelãd] nf **la N.** New Zealand

novateur, -trice [nɔvatœr, -tris] adj innovative

novembre [nɔvãbr] nm November

noyade [nwajad] nf drowning

noyau, -x [nwajo] nm (de fruit) stone, Am pit; (d'atome, de cellule) nucleus; (groupe) group; **n. dur** (de groupe) hard core

noyauter [nwajote] vt to infiltrate

noyé, -e [nwaje] nmf drowned person

noyer¹ [nwaje] **1** vt (personne) to drown; (terres) to flood **2 se noyer** vpr to drown; **se n. dans les détails** to get bogged down in details

noyer² [nwaje] nm (arbre) walnut tree

nu, -e [ny] **1** adj (personne, vérité) naked; (mains, chambre) bare; **tout nu** (stark) naked, (in the) nude; **tête nue, nu-tête** bare-headed; **aller pieds nus** to go barefoot **2** nm nude; **mettre qch à nu** to expose sth

nuage [nɥaʒ] nm cloud; Fig **être dans les nuages** to have one's head in the clouds ▪ **nuageux, -euse** adj (ciel) cloudy

nuance [nɥãs] nf (de couleur) shade; (de sens) nuance; (de regret) tinge ▪ **nuancé, -e** adj (jugement) qualified ▪ **nuancer** vt (pensée) to qualify

nucléaire [nykleɛr] **1** adj nuclear **2** nm nuclear energy

nudiste [nydist] nmf nudist ▪ **nudité** nf (de personne) nudity, nakedness

nuée [nɥe] nf **une n. de** (foule) a horde of; (groupe compact) a cloud of

nuire* [nɥir] vi **n. à qn/qch** to harm sb/sth ▪ **nuisible** adj harmful (à to)

nuit [nɥi] nf night; (obscurité) dark, darkness; **la n.** (se promener) at night; **cette n.** (hier) last night; (aujourd'hui) tonight; **avant la n.** before nightfall; **il fait n.** it's dark; **il fait n. noire** it's pitch-black; **bonne n.!** good night! ▪ **nuitée** nf overnight stay

nul, nulle [nyl] **1** adj (médiocre) hopeless, useless; (risque) non-existent, nil; Jur (non valable) null (and void); **être n. en qch** to be hopeless at sth

2 adj indéfini Littéraire (aucun) no; **sans n. doute** without any doubt

3 pron indéfini m Littéraire (aucun) no one ▪ **nulle part** adv nowhere; **n. ailleurs** nowhere else

numérique [nymerik] adj numerical; (montre, clavier, données) digital

numéro [nymero] nm (chiffre) number; (de journal) issue, number; (au cirque) act; Tél **n. vert** Br ≃ Freefone® number, Am ≃ toll-free number; **n. de téléphone/de fax** telephone/fax number ▪ **numéroter** vt (pages, sièges) to number

nuptial, -ale, -aux, -ales [nypsjal, -jo] adj (chambre) bridal; **cérémonie nuptiale** wedding ceremony

nuque [nyk] nf back of the neck

nutrition [nytrisjɔ̃] nf nutrition

Nylon® [nilɔ̃] nm (fibre) nylon; **chemise en N.** nylon shirt

Oo

O, o [o] *nm inv* O, o

obéir [ɔbeir] *vi* to obey; **o. à qn/qch** to obey sb/sth ■ **obéissance** *nf* obedience (à to) ■ **obéissant, -e** *adj* obedient

obèse [ɔbɛz] *adj* obese ■ **obésité** [obesite] *nf* obesity

objecter [ɔbʒɛkte] *vt* **o. que...** to object that... ■ **objecteur** *nm* **o. de conscience** conscientious objector ■ **objection** *nf* objection; **si vous n'y voyez pas d'o.** if you have no objections

objectif, -ive [ɔbʒɛktif, -iv] **1** *adj* objective **2** *nm (but)* objective; *(d'appareil photo)* lens ■ **objectivité** *nf* objectivity

objet [ɔbʒɛ] *nm (chose, sujet, but)* object; **faire l'o. de** *(étude, critiques)* to be the subject of; *(soins, surveillance)* to be given; **o. d'art** objet d'art; **objets trouvés** *(bureau) Br* lost property, *Am* lost and found

obligation [ɔbligasjɔ̃] *nf (contrainte)* obligation; *Fin* bond; **se trouver dans l'o. de faire qch** to be obliged to do sth; **sans o. d'achat** no purchase necessary ■ **obligatoire** *adj* compulsory, obligatory

obliger [ɔbliʒe] **1** *vt (contraindre)* to force (à faire to do); **être obligé de faire qch** to be obliged to do sth **2** **s'obliger** *vpr* **s'o. à faire qch** to force oneself to do sth ■ **obligé, -e** *adj (obligatoire)* necessary

oblique [ɔblik] *adj* oblique

oblitéré, -e [ɔblitere] *adj (timbre)* used

obscène [ɔpsɛn] *adj* obscene ■ **obscénité** *nf* obscenity

obscur, -e [ɔpskyr] *adj (sombre)* dark; *(confus, inconnu)* obscure ■ **obscurcir** **1** *vt (rendre sombre)* to darken; *(rendre confus)* to obscure **2** **s'obscurcir** *vpr* *(ciel)* to darken ■ **obscurité** *nf (noirceur)* darkness; **dans l'o.** in the dark

obséder [ɔpsede] *vt* to obsess ■ **obsédant, -e** *adj* haunting; *(pensée)* obsessive

obsèques [ɔpsɛk] *nfpl* funeral

observateur, -trice [ɔpsɛrvatœr, -tris] **1** *adj* observant **2** *nmf* observer

observation [ɔpsɛrvasjɔ̃] *nf (étude, remarque)* observation; *(reproche)* remark; *(respect)* observance

observatoire [ɔpsɛrvatwar] *nm* observatory

observer [ɔpsɛrve] *vt (regarder, respecter)* to observe; *(remarquer)* to notice; **faire o. qch à qn** to point sth out to sb

obsession [ɔpsesjɔ̃] *nf* obsession ■ **obsessionnel, -elle** *adj* obsessional

obstacle [ɔpstakl] *nm* obstacle; **faire o. à qch** to stand in the way of sth

obstétricien, -enne [ɔpstetrisjɛ̃, -ɛn] *nmf* obstetrician

obstiner [ɔpstine] **s'obstiner** *vpr* to persist (à faire in doing) ■ **obstination** *nf* stubbornness, obstinacy ■ **obstiné, -e** *adj* stubborn, obstinate

obstruction [ɔpstryksjɔ̃] *nf* obstruction ■ **obstruer** *vt* to obstruct

obtempérer [ɔptɑ̃pere] *vi* **o. à qch** to comply with sth

obtenir* [ɔptənir] *vt* to get, to obtain ■ **obtention** *nf* obtaining

obus [ɔby] *nm (projectile)* shell

occasion [ɔkazjɔ̃] *nf* (a) *(chance)* chance, opportunity **(de faire** to do); *(moment)* occasion; **à l'o.** when the occasion arises; **à l'o. de qch** on the occasion of sth; **pour les grandes occasions** for special occasions **(b)** *(affaire)* bargain; *(objet non neuf)*

second-hand item; **d'o.** second-hand

occasionner [ɔkazjɔne] *vt* to cause; **o. qch à qn** to cause sb sth

occident [ɔksidɑ̃] *nm* **l'O.** the West ■ **occidental, -e, -aux, -ales** 1 *adj Géog & Pol* western 2 *nmpl Pol* **les Occidentaux** Westerners

occulte [ɔkylt] *adj* occult

occupant, -e [ɔkypɑ̃, -ɑ̃t] 1 *adj (armée)* occupying 2 *nmf (habitant)* occupant 3 *nm Mil* **l'o.** the occupying forces

occupation [ɔkypasyɔ̃] *nf (activité, travail) & Mil* occupation

occupé, -e [ɔkype] *adj* busy (**à faire** doing); *(place, maison)* occupied; *(ligne téléphonique)* Br engaged, Am busy

occuper [ɔkype] 1 *vt (bâtiment, pays)* to occupy; *(place)* to take up, to occupy; *(poste)* to hold; **o. qn** *(jeu, travail)* to keep sb busy or occupied

2 **s'occuper** *vpr* to keep oneself busy (**à faire** doing); **s'o. de** *(affaire, problème)* to deal with; **s'o. de qn** *(malade)* to take care of sb; *(client)* to see to sb

océan [ɔseɑ̃] *nm* ocean; **l'o. Atlantique/Pacifique** the Atlantic/Pacific Ocean

octante [ɔktɑ̃t] *adj & nm inv (en Belgique, en Suisse)* eighty

octet [ɔkte] *nm Ordinat* byte; **milliard d'octets** gigabyte

octobre [ɔktɔbr] *nm* October

octogonal, -e, -aux, -ales [ɔktɔgɔnal, -o] *adj* octagonal

oculaire [ɔkyler] *adj* **témoin o.** eyewitness ■ **oculiste** *nmf* eye specialist

odeur [ɔdœr] *nf* smell; *(de fleur)* scent ■ **odorat** *nm* sense of smell

odieux, -euse [ɔdjø, -øz] *adj* odious

œil [œj] *(pl* **yeux** [jø]) *nm* eye; **avoir les yeux verts** to have green eyes; **avoir de grands yeux** to have big eyes; **lever/baisser les yeux** to look up/down; **coup d'o.** *(regard)* look, glance; **jeter un coup d'o. sur qch** to have a look at sth; **à vue d'o.** visibly; **regarder qn dans les yeux** to look sb in the eye; *Fig* **o. au beurre noir** black eye

œillères [œjer] *nfpl (de cheval)* Br blinkers, Am blinders

œillet [œje] *nm (fleur)* carnation

œuf [œf] *(pl* **œufs** [ø]) *nm* egg; **œufs** *(de poissons)* (hard) roe; **o. à la coque** boiled egg; **o. sur le plat** fried egg; **o. dur** hard-boiled egg; **œufs brouillés** scrambled eggs; **o. de Pâques** Easter egg

œuvre [œvr] *nf (travail, livre)* work; **o. d'art** work of art; **o. de charité** *(organisation)* charity

offense [ɔfɑ̃s] *nf* insult ■ **offensant, -e** *adj* offensive ■ **offenser** 1 *vt* to offend 2 **s'offenser** *vpr* **s'o. de qch** to take Br offence or Am offense at sth

offensif, -ive [ɔfɑ̃sif, -iv] 1 *adj* offensive 2 *nf* offensive; **passer à l'o.** to go on the offensive

offert, -e [ɔfer, -ɛrt] *pp de* **offrir**

office [ɔfis] *nm* (a) *Rel* service (b) *(pièce)* pantry (c) *(établissement)* office, bureau; **o. du tourisme** tourist information centre (d) *(charge)* office; **d'o.** without having any say; **faire o. de qch** to serve as sth

officiel, -elle [ɔfisjel] *adj & nm* official

officier [ɔfisje] *nm (dans l'armée)* officer

officieux, -euse [ɔfisjø, -øz] *adj* unofficial

offre [ɔfr] *nf* offer; *(aux enchères)* bid; *Écon* **l'o. et la demande** supply and demand; *Fin* **o. publique d'achat** takeover bid; **offres d'emploi** *(de journal)* job vacancies, Br situations vacant ■ **offrande** *nf* offering

offrir* [ɔfrir] 1 *vt (donner)* to give; *(proposer)* to offer; **o. qch à qn** *(donner)* to give sb sth, to give sth to sb; *(proposer)* to offer sb sth, to offer sth to sb; **o. de faire qch** to offer to do sth

2 **s'offrir** *vpr (cadeau)* to treat oneself to; *(se proposer)* to offer oneself (**comme** as) ■ **offrant** *nm* **au plus o.** to the highest bidder

OGM [ɔʒeɛm] *(abrév* **organisme génétiquement modifié)** *nm* GMO

oie [wa] *nf* goose *(pl* geese)

oignon [ɔɲɔ̃] nm (légume) onion

oiseau, -x [wazo] nm bird; **o. de proie** bird of prey

oisif, -ive [wazif, -iv] adj idle ■ **oisiveté** nf idleness

oléoduc [ɔleɔdyk] nm pipeline

olive [ɔliv] 1 nf olive 2 adj inv **vert o.** olive (green) ■ **olivier** nm (arbre) olive tree

olympique [ɔlɛ̃pik] adj Olympic; **les jeux Olympiques** the Olympic games

ombilical, -e, -aux, -ales [ɔ̃bilikal, -o] adj umbilical

ombrage [ɔ̃braʒ] nm (ombre) shade

ombre [ɔ̃br] nf (forme) shadow; (zone sombre) shade; **30° à l'o.** 30° in the shade; **sans l'o. d'un doute** without the shadow of a doubt; **pas l'o. d'un reproche/remords** not a trace of blame/remorse

ombrelle [ɔ̃brɛl] nf sunshade, parasol

omelette [ɔmlɛt] nf omelette; **o. norvégienne** ≃ baked Alaska

omettre* [ɔmɛtr] vt to omit (de faire to do) ■ **omission** nf omission

omnibus [ɔmnibys] adj & nm (train) **o.** slow train (stopping at all stations)

omnipotent, -e [ɔmnipɔtɑ̃, -ɑ̃t] adj omnipotent

omniprésent, -e [ɔmniprezɑ̃, ɑ̃t] adj omnipresent

omnisports [ɔmnispɔr] adj inv **centre o.** sports centre

omnivore [ɔmnivɔr] adj omnivorous

on [ɔ̃] (sometimes **l'on** [lɔ̃]) pron indéfini (les gens) they, people; (nous) we, one; (vous) you, one; **on m'a dit que...** I was told that...; **on me l'a donné** somebody gave it to me

oncle [ɔ̃kl] nm uncle

onctueux, -euse [ɔ̃ktɥø, -øz] adj smooth

onde [ɔ̃d] nf (à la radio) & Phys wave; **grandes ondes** long wave; **ondes courtes/moyennes** short/medium wave; **o. de choc** shock wave

ondée [ɔ̃de] nf sudden downpour

on-dit [ɔ̃di] nm inv rumour, hearsay

ondoyer [ɔ̃dwaje] vi to undulate

ondulé, -e [ɔ̃dyle] adj wavy

onduler [ɔ̃dyle] vi to undulate; (cheveux) to be wavy

onéreux, -euse [ɔnerø, -øz] adj costly

ONG [oɛnʒe] (abrév organisation non gouvernementale) nf NGO

ongle [ɔ̃gl] nm (finger)nail

ont [ɔ̃] voir avoir

ONU [ɔny] (abrév Organisation des Nations unies) nf UN

onze [ɔ̃z] adj & nm eleven ■ **onzième** adj & nmf eleventh

OPA [ɔpea] (abrév offre publique d'achat) nf Fin takeover bid

opaque [ɔpak] adj opaque

opéra [ɔpera] nm (musique) opera; (édifice) opera house

opérateur, -trice [ɔperatœr -tris] nmf (personne) operator; Cin cameraman

opération [ɔperasjɔ̃] nf (action) & Méd, Mil & Math operation ■ **opérationnel, -elle** adj operational

opérer [ɔpere] 1 vt (exécuter) to carry out; (choix) to make; (patient) to operate on (de for); **se faire o.** to have an operation 2 vi (agir) to work; (procéder) to proceed; (chirurgien) to operate

ophtalmologue [ɔftalmɔlɔg] nmf ophthalmologist

opiniâtre [ɔpinjatr] adj stubborn

opinion [ɔpinjɔ̃] nf opinion (sur about or on); **mon o. est faite** my mind is made up; **o. publique** public opinion

opportun, -e [ɔpɔrtœ̃, -yn] adj opportune, timely ■ **opportunité** nf timeliness

opposant, -e [ɔpozɑ̃, -ɑ̃t] nmf opponent (à of)

opposé, -e [ɔpoze] 1 adj (direction) opposite; (intérêts) conflicting; (armées, équipe) opposing; **être o. à qch** to be opposed to sth 2 nm **l'o.** the opposite (de of); **à l'o.** (côté) on the opposite side (de to); **à l'o. de** (contrairement à) contrary to

opposer [ɔpoze] 1 vt (résistance, argument) to put up (à against); **o. qn à qn**

to set sb against sb; **match qui op-pose...** match between... **2 s'opposer** *vpr (équipes)* to confront each other; **s'o. à qch** to be opposed to sth; **je m'y oppose** I'm opposed to it

opposition [ɔpozisjɔ̃] *nf* opposition (à to); **faire o. à** to oppose; *(chèque)* to stop; **par o. à** as opposed to

oppresser [ɔprese] *vt (gêner)* to oppress ■ **oppressant, -e** *adj* oppressive ■ **oppresseur** *nm* oppressor ■ **oppression** *nf* oppression ■ **opprimer** *vt (peuple, nation)* to oppress ■ **opprimés** *nmpl* **les o.** the oppressed

opter [ɔpte] *vi* **o. pour qch** to opt for sth

opticien, -enne [ɔptisjɛ̃, -ɛn] *nmf* optician

optimal, -e, -aux, -ales [ɔptimal, -o] *adj* optimal

optimiser [ɔptimize] *vt* to optimize

optimisme [ɔptimism] *nm* optimism ■ **optimiste 1** *adj* optimistic **2** *nmf* optimist

option [ɔpsjɔ̃] *nf (choix)* option; *(chose)* optional extra; *Scol Br* optional subject, *Am* elective (subject)

optique [ɔptik] **1** *adj (nerf)* optic; *(verre, fibres)* optical **2** *nf* optics *(sing)*; **d'o.** *(instrument, appareil)* optical

opulent, -e [ɔpylɑ̃, -ɑ̃t] *adj* opulent ■ **opulence** *nf* opulence

or¹ [ɔr] *nm* gold; **montre en or** gold watch; **règle/âge d'or** golden rule/age; **cœur d'or** heart of gold; **mine d'or** gold mine; **affaire en or** bargain; **or noir** *(pétrole)* black gold

or² [ɔr] *conj (cependant)* now, well

orage [ɔraʒ] *nm* (thunder)storm ■ **orageux, -euse** *adj* stormy

oral, -e, -aux, -ales [ɔral, -o] **1** *adj* oral **2** *nm Scol & Univ* oral

orange [ɔrɑ̃ʒ] **1** *nf* orange; **o. pressée** (fresh) orange juice **2** *adj & nm inv (couleur)* orange ■ **oranger** *nm* orange tree

orateur [ɔratœr] *nm* speaker, orator

orbite [ɔrbit] *nf (d'astre)* orbit; *(d'œil)* socket; **mettre qch sur o.** *(fusée)* to put sth into orbit

orchestre [ɔrkɛstr] *nm (classique)* orchestra; *(de jazz)* band; *Théât (places)*

Br stalls, *Am* orchestra ■ **orchestrer** *vt (organiser) & Mus* to orchestrate

ordinaire [ɔrdinɛr] *adj (habituel, normal)* ordinary, *Am* regular; *(médiocre)* ordinary, average; **d'o., à l'o.** usually; **comme d'o., comme à l'o.** as usual

ordinateur [ɔrdinatœr] *nm* computer; **o. individuel** personal computer; **o. portable** laptop

ordonnance [ɔrdɔnɑ̃s] *nf (de médecin)* prescription; *(disposition)* arrangement

ordonner [ɔrdɔne] *vt* **(a)** *(commander)* to order **(que + subjunctive** that); **o. à qn de faire qch** to order sb to do sth **(b)** *(ranger)* to organize **(c)** *(prêtre)* to ordain; **il a été ordonné prêtre** he has been ordained (as) a priest ■ **ordonné, -e** *adj (personne, maison)* tidy

ordre [ɔrdr] *nm (organisation, discipline, catégorie, commandement)* order; *(absence de désordre)* tidiness; **en o.** *(chambre)* tidy; **mettre de l'o. dans qch** to tidy sth up; **rentrer dans l'o.** to return to normal; **jusqu'à nouvel o.** until further notice; **de l'o. de** *(environ)* of the order of; **du même o.** of the same order; **de premier o.** first-rate; **par o. d'âge** in order of age; **assurer le maintien de l'o.** to maintain order; *Rel* **entrer dans les ordres** to take holy orders; **o. du jour** agenda; **l'o. public** law and order

ordures [ɔrdyr] *nfpl (déchets) Br* rubbish, *Am* garbage; **mettre qch aux o.** to throw sth out (in the *Br* rubbish *or Am* garbage)

oreille [ɔrɛj] *nf* ear; **faire la sourde o.** to turn a deaf ear

oreiller [ɔreje] *nm* pillow

oreillons [ɔrejɔ̃] *nmpl (maladie)* mumps

ores et déjà [ɔrzedeʒa] **d'ores et déjà** *adv* already

orfèvrerie [ɔrfɛvrəri] *nf (magasin)* goldsmith's/silversmith's shop; *(objets)* gold/silver plate

organe [ɔrgan] *nm Anat & Fig* organ; ■ **organisme** *nm (corps)* body; *Biol* organism; *(bureaux)* organization

organisateur, -trice [ɔrganizatœr, -tris] *nmf* organizer

organisation [ɔrganizasjã] *nf (arrangement, association)* organization

organiser [ɔrganize] 1 *vt* to organize 2 **s'organiser** *vpr* to get organized ■ **organisé, -e** *adj* organized

orge [ɔrʒ] *nf* barley

orgue [ɔrg] 1 *nm* organ 2 *nfpl* **orgues** organ

orgueil [ɔrgœj] *nm* pride ■ **orgueilleux, -euse** *adj* proud

orient [ɔrjã] *nm* **l'O.** the Orient, the East; **en O.** in the East ■ **oriental, -e, -aux, -ales** 1 *adj (côte, région)* eastern; *(langue)* oriental 2 *nmf* **O., Orientale** Oriental

orientation [ɔrjãtasjã] *nf (de position)* orientation; *(d'antenne)* positioning; *(de maison)* aspect; **avoir le sens de l'o.** to have a good sense of direction; **o. professionnelle** careers guidance

orienter [ɔrjãte] 1 *vt (bâtiment)* to orientate; *(canon, télescope)* to point **(vers** at); **o. ses recherches sur** to direct one's research on
2 **s'orienter** *vpr* to get one's bearings; **s'o. vers** *(carrière)* to specialize in ■ **orienté, -e** *adj (peu objectif)* slanted; **o. à l'ouest** *(appartement)* facing west

orifice [ɔrifis] *nm* opening

originaire [ɔriʒinɛr] *adj* **être o. de** *(natif)* to be a native of

original, -e, -aux, -ales [ɔriʒinal, -o] 1 *adj (idée, artiste, version)* original 2 *nm (texte, tableau)* original 3 *nmf (personne)* eccentric ■ **originalité** *nf* originality

origine [ɔriʒin] *nf* origin; **à l'o.** originally; **être à l'o. de qch** to be at the origin of sth; **d'o.** *(pneu)* original; **être d'o. française** to be of French origin ■ **originel, -elle** *adj* original

ornement [ɔrnəmã] *nm* ornament ■ **ornemental, -e, -aux, -ales** *adj* ornamental

orner [ɔrne] *vt* to decorate **(de** with)

orphelin, -e [ɔrfəlɛ̃, -in] *nmf* orphan ■ **orphelinat** *nm* orphanage

orteil [ɔrtɛj] *nm* toe

orthodoxe [ɔrtɔdɔks] *adj* orthodox

orthographe [ɔrtɔgraf] *nf* spelling ■ **orthographier** *vt* to spell; **mal o. qch** to misspell sth

ortie [ɔrti] *nf* nettle

os [ɔs, *pl* o *ou* ɔs] *nm* bone

oscar [ɔskar] *nm (récompense)* Oscar

osciller [ɔsile] *vi Tech* to oscillate; *(pendule)* to swing; *(aiguille, flamme)* to flicker; *Fig (varier)* to fluctuate **(entre** between)

oser [oze] *vt* to dare; **o. faire qch** to dare (to) do sth ■ **osé, -e** *adj* daring

osier [ozje] *nm* wicker; **panier d'o.** wicker basket

ossements [ɔsmã] *nmpl* bones

osseux, -euse [ɔsø, -øz] *adj (maigre)* bony

otage [ɔtaʒ] *nm* hostage; **prendre qn en o.** to take sb hostage

OTAN [ɔtã] *(abrév* **Organisation du traité de l'Atlantique Nord)** *nf* NATO

ôter [ote] *vt* to take away, to remove **(à qn** from sb); *(vêtement)* to take off; *(déduire)* to take (away)

otite [ɔtit] *nf* ear infection

ou [u] *conj* or; **ou elle ou moi** either her or me

où [u] *adv & pron relatif* where; **le jour où...** the day when...; **la table où...** the table on which...; **l'état où...** the condition in which...; **par où?** which way?; **d'où?** where from?; **le pays d'où je viens** the country from which I come

ouate [wat] *nf (pour pansement) Br* cotton wool, *Am* absorbent cotton

oubli [ubli] *nm (trou de mémoire)* oversight; *(lacune)* omission; **tomber dans l'o.** to fall into oblivion

oublier [ublije] *vt* to forget **(de faire** to do); *(omettre)* to leave out

oubliettes [ublijɛt] *nfpl (de château)* dungeons

ouest [west] 1 *nm* west; **à l'o.** in the west; *(direction)* (to the) west **(de** of); **d'o.** *(vent)* west(erly); **de l'o.** western 2 *adj inv (côte)* west; *(région)* western

Ouganda [ugɑ̃da] *nm* l'O. Uganda

oui [wi] **1** *adv* yes; **ah, ça o.!** oh yes (indeed!); **je crois que o.** I think so **2** *nm inv* **pour un o. pour un non** for the slightest thing

ouï-dire [widir] *nm* hearsay; **par o.** by hearsay

ouïe [wi] *nf* hearing

ouïes [wi] *nfpl (de poisson)* gills

ouragan [uragɑ̃] *nm* hurricane

ourlet [urlɛ] *nm* hem

ours [urs] *nm* bear; **o. blanc** polar bear; **o. en peluche** teddy bear ▪ **ourse** *nf* she-bear; **la Grande O.** the Great Bear

oursin [ursɛ̃] *nm* sea urchin

outil [uti] *nm* tool ▪ **outillage** *nm* tools; *(d'usine)* equipment ▪ **outiller** *vt* to equip

outrage [utraʒ] *nm* insult **(à** to)

outrance [utrɑ̃s] *nf (excès)* excess; **à o.** to excess ▪ **outrancier, -ère** *adj* excessive

outre [utr] **1** *prép* besides; **o. mesure** unduly **2** *adv* **en o.** besides; **passer o.** to take no notice (**à** of) ▪ **outre-Manche** *adv* across the Channel ▪ **outre-mer** *adv* overseas; **d'o.** *(marché)* overseas; **territoires d'o.** overseas territories

outré, -e [utre] *adj (révolté)* outraged; *(excessif)* exaggerated

outrepasser [utrəpɑse] *vt* to go beyond, to exceed

ouvert, -e [uvɛr, -ɛrt] **1** *pp de* **ouvrir 2** *adj* open; *(robinet, gaz)* on ▪ **ouverture** *nf* opening; *(trou)* hole

ouvrable [uvrabl] *adj* **jour o.** working or *Am* work day

ouvrage [uvraʒ] *nm (travail, livre, objet)* work; *(couture)* (needle)work; **un o.** *(travail)* a piece of work

ouvreuse [uvrøz] *nf* usherette

ouvrier, -ère [uvrije, -ɛr] **1** *nmf* worker; **o. qualifié/spécialisé** skilled/semi-skilled worker; **o. agricole** farm worker **2** *adj (quartier)* working-class

ouvrir* [uvrir] **1** *vt* to open; *(gaz, radio)* to turn on; *(hostilités)* to begin; *(appétit)* to whet **2** *vi* to open **3 s'ouvrir** *vpr (porte, boîte, fleur)* to open ▪ **ouvre-boîtes** *nm inv Br* tin opener, *Am* can opener ▪ **ouvre-bouteilles** *nm inv* bottle opener

ovale [ɔval] *adj & nm* oval

ovation [ɔvasjɔ̃] *nf* (standing) ovation

ovni [ɔvni] *(abrév* **objet volant non identifié)** *nm* UFO

oxyder [ɔkside] *vt,* **s'oxyder** *vpr* to oxidize

oxygène [ɔksiʒɛn] *nm* oxygen; **masque/tente à o.** oxygen mask/tent ▪ **oxygéné, -e** *adj* **eau oxygénée** (hydrogen) peroxide; **cheveux blonds oxygénés** peroxide blonde hair, bleached hair

ozone [ozon] *nm Chim* ozone

Pp

P, p [pe] *nm inv* P, p

pacifique [pasifik] **1** *adj (manifestation)* peaceful; *(personne, peuple)* peace-loving; *(côte)* Pacific **2** *nm* **le P.** the Pacific

pacifiste [pasifist] *adj & nmf* pacifist

PACS [paks] *(abrév* **Pacte civil de solidarité)** *nm inv* = bill introduced in the French parliament in 1998 allowing unmarried couples to legally formalize their relationship

pacte [pakt] *nm* pact

pagaie [page] *nf* paddle

pagaïe, pagaille [pagaj] *nf Fam (désordre)* mess; **semer la p.** to cause chaos

pagayer [pageje] *vi* to paddle

page [paʒ] *nf (de livre)* page; **la première p.** *(d'un journal)* the front page; **être en première p.** to be on or to make the front page; *Ordinat* **p. d'accueil** home page; **les Pages Jaunes®** *(de l'annuaire)* the Yellow Pages®; *Radio* **p. de publicité** commercial break

paie [pɛ] *nf* pay, wages

paiement [pemɑ̃] *nm* payment

païen, -enne [pajɛ̃, -ɛn] *adj & nmf* pagan, heathen

paillasson [pajasɔ̃] *nm* (door)mat

paille [pɑj] *nf* straw; *(pour boire)* (drinking) straw

paillette [pajɛt] *nf (d'habit)* sequin; **paillettes** *(de savon, lessive)* flakes; *(d'or)* gold dust

pain [pɛ̃] *nm* bread; **un p.** a loaf (of bread); **petit p.** roll; **p. au chocolat** = chocolate-filled pastry; **p. complet** wholemeal bread; **p. d'épices** ≃ gingerbread; **p. grillé** toast; **p. de mie** sandwich loaf

pair, -e [pɛr] **1** *adj (numéro)* even **2** *nm (personne)* peer; **hors p.** unrivalled; **aller de p.** to go hand in hand (**avec** with); **au p.** *(étudiante)* au pair; **travailler au p.** to work as an au pair

paire [pɛr] *nf* pair (**de** of)

paisible [pezibl] *adj (vie, endroit)* peaceful; *(caractère, personne)* quiet

paître* [pɛtr] *vi* to graze

paix [pɛ] *nf* peace; **en p.** *(vivre, laisser)* in peace (**avec** with)

Pakistan [pakistɑ̃] *nm* **le P.** Pakistan ■ **pakistanais, -e 1** *adj* Pakistani **2** *nmf* **P., Pakistanaise** Pakistani

palace [palas] *nm* luxury hotel

palais [palɛ] *nm (château)* palace; *Anat* palate; **P. de justice** law courts; **p. des sports** sports centre

pâle [pɑl] *adj* pale

Palestine [palestin] *nf* **la P.** Palestine ■ **palestinien, -enne 1** *adj* Palestinian **2** *nmf* **P., Palestinienne** Palestinian

palette [palɛt] *nf (de peintre)* palette; *(pour marchandises)* pallet

pâleur [palœr] *nf (de lumière)* paleness; *(de personne)* pallor

palier [palje] *nm (niveau)* level; *(d'escalier)* landing; *(phase)* plateau; **par paliers** in stages

pâlir [palir] *vi* to turn pale (**de** with)

palissade [palisad] *nf* fence

pallier [palje] **1** *vt (difficultés)* to alleviate **2** *vi* **p. à qch** to compensate for sth

palmarès [palmarɛs] *nm* prize list; *(de chansons)* charts

palme [palm] *nf (de palmier)* palm (branch); *(de nageur)* flipper

palmier [palmje] *nm* palm (tree)

palourde [palurd] *nf* clam

palper [palpe] *vt* to feel ■ **palpable** *adj* palpable

palpiter [palpite] *vi (cœur)* to flutter; *(plus fort)* to throb

pamplemousse [pãpləmus] *nm* grapefruit

panaché, -e [panaʃe] **1** *adj Br* multi-coloured, *Am* multicolored; **p. de blanc** streaked with white **2** *nm* shandy

Panama [panama] *nm* **le P.** Panama

pancarte [pãkart] *nf* sign, notice; *(de manifestant)* placard

pané, -e [pane] *adj (poisson)* breaded

panier [panje] *nm (ustensile, contenu)* basket; **p. à linge** *Br* linen basket, *Am* (clothes) hamper

panique [panik] **1** *nf* panic; **pris de p.** panic-stricken **2** *adj* **peur p.** panic

panne [pan] *nf* breakdown; **tomber en p.** to break down; **être en p.** to have broken down; **tomber en p. sèche** to run out of *Br* petrol or *Am* gas; **p. d'électricité** blackout, *Br* power cut

panneau, -x [pano] *nm (écriteau)* sign, notice, board; *(de porte)* panel; **p. d'affichage** *Br* notice board, *Am* bulletin board; **p. de signalisation** road sign ▪ **panonceau, -x** *nm (enseigne)* sign

panoplie [panɔpli] *nf (jouet)* outfit; *(gamme)* set

panorama [panɔrama] *nm* panorama ▪ **panoramique** *adj* panoramic; *Cin* **écran p.** wide screen

panser [pãse] *vt (main)* to bandage; *(plaie)* to dress; **p. qn** to dress sb's wounds ▪ **pansement** *nm* dressing; **faire un p. à qn** to put a dressing on sb; **p. adhésif** *Br* sticking plaster, *Am* Band-aid®

pantalon [pãtalɔ̃] *nm Br* trousers, *Am* pants; **deux pantalons** two pairs of *Br* trousers or *Am* pants

panthère [pãter] *nf* panther

pantoufle [pãtufl] *nf* slipper

paon [pã] *nm* peacock

papa [papa] *nm* dad(dy)

pape [pap] *nm* pope

papeterie [papɛtri] *nf (magasin)* stationer's shop; *(articles)* stationery; *(fabrique)* paper mill

papi [papi] *nm* = **papy**

papier [papje] *nm (matière)* paper; **un p.** *(feuille)* a piece of paper; *(formulaire)* a form; *(de journal)* an article; **p. hygiénique** toilet paper; **papiers d'identité** identity papers; **p. à lettres** writing paper; **p. peint** wallpaper

papillon [papijɔ̃] *nm (insecte)* butterfly; **p. de nuit** moth

papy [papi] *nm* grand(d)ad

Pâque [pɑk] *nf Rel* **la P. juive, P.** Passover

paquebot [pakbo] *nm* liner

pâquerette [pakrɛt] *nf* daisy

Pâques [pɑk] *nm sing & nfpl* Easter

paquet [pakɛ] *nm (sac)* packet; *(de sucre)* bag; *(de cigarettes)* packet, *Am* pack; *Br (postal)* parcel, package

PAR [par] *prép* **(a)** *(indique l'agent, la manière, le moyen)* by; **frappé p. qn** hit by sb; **p. mer** by sea; **p. le train** by train; **p. la force** by or through force; **commencer p. qch** *(récit)* to begin with sth; **p. erreur** by mistake; **p. chance** by a stroke of luck
(b) *(à travers)* through; **p. la porte** through the door; **jeter/regarder p. la fenêtre** to throw/look out (of) the window; **p. ici/là** *(aller)* this/that way; *(habiter)* around here/there; **p. les rues** through the streets
(c) *(à cause de)* out of, from; **p. pitié** out of pity
(d) *(pendant)* **p. ce froid** in this cold; **p. le passé** in the past
(e) *(distributif)* **dix fois p. an/mois** ten times a or per year/month; **50 euros p. personne** 50 euros per person; **deux p. deux** two by two; **p. deux fois** twice
(f) *(avec 'trop')* **p. trop aimable** far too kind

parachute [paraʃyt] *nm* parachute; **p. ascensionnel** parascending ▪ **parachutisme** *nm* parachute jumping ▪ **parachutiste** *nmf* parachutist; *(soldat)* paratrooper

parade [parad] *nf (défilé)* parade; *(étalage)* show

paradis [paradi] *nm* heaven

paradoxe [paradɔks] *nm* paradox

parafer [parafe] *vt* = **parapher**

paraffine [parafin] *nf* paraffin (wax)

parages [paraʒ] *nmpl Naut* waters; **dans les p. de** in the vicinity of

paragraphe [paragraf] *nm* paragraph

Paraguay [paragwe] *nm* **le P.** Paraguay

paraître* [parɛtr] **1** *vi (sembler)* to seem, to appear; *(apparaître)* to appear; *(livre)* to come out, to be published **2** *v impersonnel* **il paraît qu'il va partir** it appears *or* seems (that) he's leaving; **à ce qu'il paraît** apparently

parallèle [paralɛl] **1** *adj* parallel (**à** with *or* to); *(police, marché)* unofficial **2** *nf* parallel (line) **3** *nm (comparaison)* & *Géog* parallel; **mettre qch en p. avec qch** to draw a parallel between sth and sth ▪ **parallèlement** *adv* **p. à** *(simultanément)* at the same time as

paralyser [paralize] *vt Br* to paralyse, *Am* to paralyze ▪ **paralysie** *nf* paralysis ▪ **paralytique** *adj* & *nmf* paralytic

paramédical, -e, -aux, -ales [paramedikal, -o] *adj* paramedical

paramilitaire [paramilitɛr] *adj* paramilitary

parapente [parapɑ̃t] *nm (activité)* paragliding; **faire du p.** to go paragliding

parapet [parapɛ] *nm* parapet

parapher [parafe] *vt* to initial

parapluie [paraplɥi] *nm* umbrella

parasite [parazit] **1** *nm (organisme, personne)* parasite; **parasites** *(à la radio)* interference **2** *adj* parasitic

parasol [parasɔl] *nm* sunshade, parasol; *(de plage)* beach umbrella

paratonnerre [paratɔnɛr] *nm* lightning *Br* conductor *or Am* rod

paravent [paravɑ̃] *nm* screen

parc [park] *nm (jardin)* park; *(de château)* grounds; *(de bébé)* playpen; **p. d'attractions** amusement park; **p. de stationnement** *Br* car park, *Am* parking lot; **p. naturel** nature reserve

parcelle [parsɛl] *nf* small piece; *(terrain)* plot

parce que [parsəkə] *conj* because

parchemin [parʃəmɛ̃] *nm* parchment

par-ci, par-là [parsiparla] *adv* here, there and everywhere

parcmètre [parkmɛtr] *nm* (parking) meter

parcourir* [parkurir] *vt (lieu)* to walk round; *(pays)* to travel through; *(mer)* to sail; *(distance)* to cover *(texte)* to glance through; **p. qch des yeux** *ou* **du regard** to glance at sth; **il reste 2 km à p.** there are 2 km to go ▪ **parcours** *nm (itinéraire)* route; **p. de golf** *(terrain)* golf course

par-delà [pardəla] *prép* & *adv* beyond

par-derrière [parderjɛr] **1** *prép* behind **2** *adv (attaquer)* from behind; *(se boutonner)* at the back; **passer p.** to go in the back door

par-dessous [pardəsu] *prép* & *adv* underneath

pardessus [pardəsy] *nm* overcoat

par-dessus [pardəsy] **1** *prép* over; **p. tout** above all **2** *adv* over

par-devant [pardəvɑ̃] *adv (attaquer)* from the front; *(se boutonner)* at the front

pardon [pardɔ̃] *nm* forgiveness; **p.!** *(excusez-moi)* sorry!; **p.?** *(pour demander)* excuse me?, *Am* pardon me?; **demander p.** to apologize (**à** to) ▪ **pardonner** *vt* to forgive; **p. qch à qn** to forgive sb for sth; **elle m'a pardonné d'avoir oublié** she forgave me for forgetting

pare-balles [parbal] *adj inv* **gilet p.** bulletproof *Br* jacket *or Am* vest

pare-brise [parbriz] *nm inv Br* windscreen, *Am* windshield

pare-chocs [parʃɔk] *nm inv* bumper

pareil, -eille [parɛj] **1** *adj* (a) *(identique)* the same; **p. à** the same as (b) *(tel)* such; **en p. cas** in such cases **2** *adv Fam* the same **3** *nmf (personne)* equal; **sans p.** unparalleled, unique **4** *nf* **rendre la pareille à qn** *(se venger)* to get one's own back on sb ▪ **pareillement** *adv (de la même manière)* in the same way; *(aussi)* likewise

parent, -e [parɑ̃, -ɑ̃t] **1** *nmf (oncle, tante, cousin)* relative, relation **2** *nmpl*

parents *(père et mère)* parents **3** *adj* related (**de** to) ▪ **parental, -e, -aux, -ales** *adj* parental ▪ **parenté** *nf* relationship; **avoir un lien de p.** to be related

parenthèse [parɑ̃tɛz] *nf (signe)* bracket, parenthesis; **entre parenthèses** in brackets

parer¹ [pare] **1** *vt (coup)* to parry **2** *vi* **p. à toute éventualité** to prepare for any contingency

parer² [pare] *vt (orner)* to adorn (**de** with)

paresseux, -euse [parɛsø, -øz] **1** *adj* lazy **2** *nmf* lazy person

parfaire* [parfɛr] *vt* to finish off ▪ **parfait, -e** *adj* perfect ▪ **parfaitement** *adv (sans fautes, complètement)* perfectly; *(certainement)* certainly

parfois [parfwa] *adv* sometimes

parfum [parfœ̃] *nm (essence)* perfume; *(senteur)* fragrance; *(de glace)* flavour ▪ **parfumer 1** *vt (embaumer)* to scent; *(glace)* to flavour (**à** with) **2 se parfumer** *vpr* to put perfume on ▪ **parfumerie** *nf (magasin)* perfumery

pari [pari] *nm* bet; **faire un p.** to make a bet; **p. mutuel** *Br* ≃ tote, *Am* ≃ parimutuel ▪ **parier** *vti* to bet (**sur** on; **que** that); **il y a fort à p. que...** the odds are that...

Paris [pari] *nm ou f* Paris ▪ **parisien, -enne 1** *adj* Parisian **2** *nmf* **P., Parisienne** Parisian

parking [parkiŋ] *nm Br* car park, *Am* parking lot; **'p. payant'** *Br* ≃ 'pay-and-display car park'

parlement [parləmɑ̃] *nm* **le P.** Parliament ▪ **parlementaire 1** *adj* parliamentary **2** *nmf* member of parliament

parlementer [parləmɑ̃te] *vi* to negotiate (**avec** with)

parler [parle] **1** *vi* to talk, to speak (**de** about *or* of; **à** to); **sans p. de...** not to mention...
 2 *vt (langue)* to speak; **p. affaires** to talk business
 3 se parler *vpr (langue)* to be spoken; *(l'un l'autre)* to talk to each other
 4 *nm* speech; *(régional)* dialect

parloir [parlwar] *nm* visiting room

parmi [parmi] *prép* among(st)

paroi [parwa] *nf* wall; *(de rocher)* (rock) face

paroisse [parwas] *nf* parish

parole [parɔl] *nf (mot, promesse)* word; *(faculté, langage)* speech; **paroles** *(de chanson)* words, lyrics; **adresser la p. à qn** to speak to sb; **prendre la p.** to speak; **tenir p.** to keep one's word

parquet [parkɛ] *nm (sol)* wooden floor

parrain [parɛ̃] *nm Rel* godfather; *(de sportif, de club)* sponsor ▪ **parrainer** *vt (sportif, membre)* to sponsor

pars [par] *voir* **partir**

parsemer [parsəme] *vt* to scatter (**de** with)

part¹ [par] *voir* **partir**

part² [par] *nf (portion)* share, part; *(de gâteau)* slice; **prendre p. à** *(activité)* to take part in; **faire p. de qch à qn** to inform sb of sth; **de toutes parts** on all sides; **de p. et d'autre** on both sides; **d'une p.... d'autre p....** on the one hand... on the other hand...; **d'autre p.** *(d'ailleurs)* moreover; **de la p. de qn** from sb; **c'est de la p. de qui?** *(au téléphone)* who's calling?; **pour ma p.** as for me; **à p.** *(mettre)* aside; *(excepté)* apart from; *(personne)* different; **prendre qn à p.** to take sb aside

partage [partaʒ] *nm (action)* dividing up; *(de gâteau, de responsabilités)* sharing out; **faire le p. de qch** to divide sth up

partager [partaʒe] **1** *vt (avoir en commun)* to share (**avec** with); *(répartir)* to divide (up); **p. qch en deux** to divide sth in two; **p. l'avis de qn** to share sb's opinion
 2 se partager *vpr (bénéfices)* to share (between themselves); **se p. entre** to divide one's time between ▪ **partagé, -e** *adj (amour)* mutual; **les avis sont partagés** opinions are divided

partance [partɑ̃s] **en partance** *adv (train)* about to depart; **en p. pour...** for...

partenaire [partənɛr] *nmf* partner ▪ **partenariat** *nm* partnership

parterre [partɛr] *nm (de fleurs)* flower

bed; *Théât Br* stalls, *Am* orchestra; *Fam (sol)* floor

parti [parti] *nm (camp)* side; **tirer p. de qch** to make good use of sth; **p. (politique)** (political) party

partial, -e, -aux, -ales [parsjal, -o] *adj* biased ■ **partialité** *nf* bias

participer [partisipe] *vi* **p. à** *(jeu)* to take part in, to participate in; *(bénéfices, joie)* to share (in); *(financièrement)* to contribute to ■ **participant, -e** *nmf* participant ■ **participation** *nf* participation; *(à élection)* turnout; **p. aux frais** contribution towards costs

particularité [partikylarite] *nf* peculiarity

particule [partikyl] *nf* particle

particulier, -ère [partikylje, -ɛr] **1** *adj (propre)* characteristic (à of); *(remarquable)* unusual; *(soin, intérêt)* particular; *(maison, voiture, leçon)* private; *Péj (bizarre)* peculiar; **en p.** *(surtout)* in particular; *(à part)* in private; **cas p.** special case **2** *nm* private individual; **vente de p. à p.** private sale ■ **particulièrement** *adv* particularly; **tout p.** especially

partie [parti] *nf (morceau)* part; *(jeu)* game; *(domaine)* field; **en p.** partly, in part; **en grande p.** mainly; **faire p. de** to be a part of; *(club)* to belong to; *(comité)* to be on ■ **partiel, -elle** *adj* partial

partir* [partir] *(aux* **être)** *vi (s'en aller)* to go, to leave; *(se mettre en route)* to set off; *(s'éloigner)* to go away; *(coup de feu)* to go off; *(tache)* to come out; *(peinture)* to come off; **p. en voiture** to go by car, to drive; **p. en courant** to run off; **p. de** *(lieu)* to leave from; *(commencer par)* to start (off) with; **à p. de** *(date, prix)* from

partisan [partizã] **1** *nm* supporter; *(combattant)* partisan **2** *adj (esprit)* partisan; **être p. de qch/de faire qch** to be in favour of sth/of doing sth

partition [partisjɔ̃] *nf Mus* score

partout [partu] *adv* everywhere; **p. où je vais** everywhere *or* wherever I go; **un peu p.** all over the place

paru, -e [pary] *pp de* **paraître** ■ **parution** *nf* publication

parure [paryr] *nf (ensemble)* set

parvenir* [parvənir] *(aux* **être)** *vi* **p. à** *(lieu)* to reach; *(objectif)* to achieve; **p. à faire qch** to manage to do sth

PAS¹ [pɑ] *adv (de négation)* **(ne...) p.** not; **je ne sais p.** I do not *or* don't know; **je n'ai p. compris** I didn't understand; **je voudrais ne p. sortir** I would like not to go out; **p. de pain** no bread; **p. du tout** not at all; **elle chantera p. moi!** she'll sing no I won't!

pas² [pɑ] *nm* (a) *(enjambée)* step; *(allure)* pace; *(bruit)* footstep; *(trace)* footprint; **p. à p.** step by step; **à p. de loup** stealthily; **à deux p. (de)** close by; **aller au p.** to go at a walking pace; **rouler au p.** *(véhicule)* to crawl along; **faire un faux p.** *(en marchant)* to trip; **revenir sur ses p.** to retrace one's steps; **marcher à grands p.** to stride along (b) *(de vis)* pitch (c) **le p. de Calais** the Straits of Dover

passable [pɑsabl] *adj* passable, fair

passage [pɑsaʒ] *nm (chemin, extrait)* passage; *(ruelle)* alley(way); *(traversée)* crossing; **être de p. dans une ville** to be passing through a town; **p. clouté** *ou* **pour piétons** *Br* (pedestrian) crossing, *Am* crosswalk; **p. souterrain** *Br* subway, *Am* underpass; **p. à niveau** *Br* level crossing, *Am* grade crossing; **'p. interdit'** 'no through traffic'; **'cédez le p.'** *(au carrefour) Br* 'give way', *Am* 'yield'

passager, -ère [pɑsaʒe, -ɛr] **1** *adj* momentary **2** *nmf* passenger; **p. clandestin** stowaway

passant, -e [pɑsã, -ãt] **1** *adj (rue)* busy **2** *nmf* passer-by **3** *nm (de ceinture)* loop

passe [pɑs] *nf (au football)* pass; *Fig* **une mauvaise p.** a bad patch

passé, -e [pɑse] **1** *adj (temps)* past; *(couleur)* faded; **la semaine passée** last week; **il est dix heures passées** it's after *or Br* gone ten o'clock; **p. de mode** out of fashion **2** *nm (temps, vie passée)* past; **par le p.** in the past **3** *prép* after; **p. huit heures** after eight o'clock

passe-montagne [pɑsmɔ̃taɲ] (*pl* **passe-montagnes**) *nm Br* balaclava, *Am* ski mask

passe-partout [pɑspartu] *nm inv* master key

passeport [pɑspɔr] *nm* passport

PASSER [pɑse] **1** *(aux* avoir*) vt (pont, frontière)* to go over; *(porte, douane)* to go through; *(ballon)* to pass; *(vêtement)* to slip on; *(film)* to show; *(disque)* to play; *(vacances)* to spend; *(examen)* to take; *(commande)* to place; *(visite médicale)* to have; *(omettre)* to leave out; **p. qch à qn** *(prêter)* to pass sth to sb; *Aut* **p. la seconde** to change into second; **p. son temps à faire qch** to spend one's time doing sth; **p. quelques jours quelque part** to spend a few days somewehere

2 *(aux* être*) vi (se déplacer)* to go past; *(disparaître)* to go; *(facteur)* to come; *(temps)* to pass (by), to go by; *(film, programme)* to be on; *(douleur)* to pass; *(courant)* to flow; **laisser p. qn** to let sb through; **p. de qch à qch** to go from sth to sth; **p. dans la classe supérieure** to move up a class; **p. devant qn/qch** to go past sb/sth; **p. par Paris** to pass through Paris; **p. chez le boulanger** to go round to the baker's; **p. à la radio** to be on the radio; **p. pour** *(riche)* to be taken for; **faire p. qn pour** to pass sb off as; **faire p. qch sous/dans qch** to slide/push sth under/into sth; **p. sur** *(détail)* to pass over

3 se passer *vpr (se produire)* to happen; **se p. de qn/qch** to do without sb/sth; **ça s'est bien passé** it went off well

passerelle [pɑsrɛl] *nf (pont)* footbridge; **p. d'embarquement** *(de navire)* gangway; *(d'avion)* steps

passe-temps [pɑstɑ̃] *nm inv* pastime

passeur, -euse [pɑsœr, -øz] *nmf (batelier)* ferryman, *f* ferrywoman; *(contrebandier)* smuggler

passif, -ive [pasif, -iv] *adj* passive

passion [pɑsjɔ̃] *nf* passion; **avoir la p. des voitures** to have a passion for cars

passionner [pɑsjɔne] **1** *vt* to fascinate **2 se passionner** *vpr* **se p. pour qch** to

have a passion for sth ■ **passionnant, -e** *adj* fascinating ■ **passionné, -e** *adj* passionate; **p. de qch** passionately fond of sth

passivité [pasivite] *nf* passiveness, passivity

passoire [pɑswar] *nf (pour liquides)* sieve; *(à thé)* strainer; *(à légumes)* colander

pastel [pastɛl] *adj inv & nm* pastel

pastèque [pastɛk] *nf* watermelon

pasteurisé, -e [pastœrize] *adj* pasteurized

pastille [pastij] *nf* pastille; *(médicament)* lozenge

patauger [patoʒe] *vi (s'embourber)* to squelch; *(barboter)* to splash about

pâte [pɑt] *nf (pour tarte)* pastry; *(pour pain)* dough; *(pour gâteau)* mixture; **p. d'amandes** marzipan; **p. feuilletée** puff pastry; **pâtes (alimentaires)** pasta

pâté [pɑte] *nm (charcuterie)* pâté; *(tache d'encre)* blot; **p. en croûte** ≃ meat pie; **p. de maisons** block of houses

pâtée [pɑte] *nf (pour chien)* dog food; *(pour chat)* cat food

paternel, -elle [patɛrnɛl] *adj* paternal ■ **paternité** *nf (état)* paternity, fatherhood; *(de livre)* authorship

pathétique [patetik] *adj* moving

pathologique [patɔlɔʒik] *adj* pathological

patience [pasjɑ̃s] *nf* patience; **avoir de la p.** to be patient; **perdre p.** to lose patience

patient, -e [pasjɑ̃, -ɑ̃t] **1** *adj* patient **2** *nmf (malade)* patient ■ **patienter** *vi* to wait

patin [patɛ̃] *nm (de patineur)* skate; **p. à glace** ice skate; **p. à roulettes** roller skate

patiner [patine] *vi Sport* to skate; *(véhicule)* to skid ■ **patinage** *nm Sport* skating; **p. artistique** figure skating ■ **patineur, -euse** *nmf* skater ■ **patinoire** *nf* skating rink, ice rink

pâtir [pɑtir] *vi* **p. de** to suffer because of

pâtisserie [pɑtisri] *nf (gâteau)* pastry, cake; *(magasin)* cake shop; *(art)* pastry-making ▪ **pâtissier, -ère** *nmf* pastry cook; *(commerçant)* confectioner **2** *adj* **crème pâtissière** confectioner's custard

patrie [patri] *nf* homeland

patrimoine [patrimwan] *nm* heritage; *(biens)* property

patriote [patrijɔt] **1** *adj* patriotic **2** *nmf* patriot ▪ **patriotique** *adj* patriotic ▪ **patriotisme** *nm* patriotism

patron, -onne [patrɔ̃, -ɔn] **1** *nmf (chef)* boss; *(propriétaire)* owner (**de** of); *(gérant)* manager, *f* manageress; *(de bar)* landlord, *f* landlady **2** *nm Couture* pattern

patronat [patrɔna] *nm* employers ▪ **patronal, -e, -aux, -ales** *adj* employers'

patrouille [patruj] *nf* patrol ▪ **patrouiller** *vi* to patrol

patte [pat] *nf* (a) *(membre)* leg; *(de chat, de chien)* paw (b) *(languette)* tab; *(de poche)* flap ▪ **pattes** *nfpl (favoris)* sideburns

pâturage [pɑtyraʒ] *nm* pasture

paume [pom] *nf* palm

paupière [popjɛr] *nf* eyelid

paupiette [popjɛt] *nf* **p. de veau** veal olive

pause [poz] *nf (arrêt)* break; *(en parlant)* pause

pauvre [povr] **1** *adj (personne, sol, excuse)* poor; *(meubles)* shabby; **p. en** *(calories)* low in; *(ressources)* low on **2** *nmf* poor man, *f* poor woman; **les pauvres** the poor ▪ **pauvreté** [-ǝte] *nf* poverty

pavaner [pavane] **se pavaner** *vpr* to strut about

paver [pave] *vt* to pave ▪ **pavé** *nm* paving stone

pavillon [pavijɔ̃] *nm* (a) *(maison)* detached house; *(d'hôpital)* wing; *(d'exposition)* pavilion (b) *(drapeau)* flag

payable [pejabl] *adj* payable

paye [pɛj] *nf* pay, wages ▪ **payement** *nm* = **paiement**

payer [peje] **1** *vt (personne, somme)* to pay; *(service, objet)* to pay for; *(récompenser)* to repay; **se faire p.** to get paid **2** *vi* to pay ▪ **payant, -e** [pejã, -ãt] *adj (hôte, spectateur)* paying

pays [pei] *nm* country; *(région)* region; **un p. étranger** a foreign country; **aller dans un p. étranger** to go abroad; **du p.** *(vin, gens)* local

paysage [peizaʒ] *nm* landscape, scenery

paysan, -anne [peizã, -an] **1** *nmf* farmer **2** *adj* **coutume paysanne** rural *or* country custom; **le monde p.** the farming community

Pays-Bas [peiba] *nmpl* **les P.** the Netherlands

PC [pece] *(abrév* **personal computer)** *nm Ordinat* PC

P-DG [pedeʒe] *(abrév* **président-directeur général)** *nm Br* chairman and managing director, *Am* chief executive officer

péage [peaʒ] *nm (droit)* toll; *(lieu)* tollbooth; **pont à p.** toll bridge; *TV* **chaîne à p.** pay channel

peau, -x [po] *nf* skin; *(de fruit)* peel, skin; *(cuir)* hide ▪ **Peau-Rouge** *(pl* **Peaux-Rouges)** *nmf* Red Indian

péché [peʃe] *nm* sin ▪ **pécher** *vi* to sin

pêche¹ [pɛʃ] *nf (activité)* fishing; *(poissons)* catch; **p. à la ligne** angling; **aller à la p.** to go fishing ▪ **pêcher** [peʃe] **1** *vt (attraper)* to catch; *(chercher à prendre)* to fish for **2** *vi* to fish ▪ **pêcheur** *nm* fisherman; *(à la ligne)* angler

pêche² [pɛʃ] *nf (fruit)* peach ▪ **pêcher** [peʃe] *nm (arbre)* peach tree

pectoraux [pektɔro] *nmpl* chest muscles

pédagogie [pedagɔʒi] *nf (discipline)* pedagogy ▪ **pédagogique** *adj* educational ▪ **pédagogue** *nmf* teacher

pédale [pedal] *nf (de voiture, de piano)* pedal; **p. de frein** brake pedal

Pédalo® [pedalo] *nm* pedal boat, pedalo

pédestre [pedɛstr] *adj* **randonnée p.** hike

pédiatre [pedjatr] *nmf* paediatrician

pédicure [pedikyr] *nmf Br* chiropodist, *Am* podiatrist

pègre [pɛgr] *nf* **la p.** the underworld

peigne [pɛɲ] *nm* comb; **se donner un coup de p.** to give one's hair a comb ▪ **peigner 1** *vt (cheveux)* to comb; **p. qn** to comb sb's hair **2 se peigner** *vpr* to comb one's hair

peignoir [pɛɲwar] *nm Br* dressing gown, *Am* bathrobe; **p. de bain** bathrobe

peindre* [pɛ̃dr] **1** *vt* to paint **2** *vi* to paint

peine [pɛn] *nf* **(a)** *(châtiment)* punishment; **p. de mort** death penalty; **p. de prison** prison sentence; **'défense d'entrer sous p. d'amende'** 'trespassers will be prosecuted'
(b) *(chagrin)* sorrow; **avoir de la p.** to be upset; **faire de la p. à qn** to upset sb
(c) *(effort)* trouble; *(difficulté)* difficulty; **se donner de la p.** *ou* **beaucoup de p.** to go to a lot of trouble (**pour faire** to do); **avec p.** with difficulty; **ça vaut la p. d'attendre** it's worth waiting; **ce n'est pas** *ou* **ça ne vaut pas la p.** it's not worth it
(d) **à p.** hardly, scarcely; **à p. arrivée, elle...** no sooner had she arrived than she... ▪ **peiner 1** *vt* to upset **2** *vi* to labour

peintre [pɛ̃tr] *nm (artiste)* painter; **p. en bâtiment** painter and decorator ▪ **peinture** *nf (tableau, activité)* painting; *(matière)* paint; **p. à l'huile** oil painting; **'p. fraîche'** 'wet paint'

Pékin [pekɛ̃] *nm ou f* Peking, Beijing

pelage [pəlaʒ] *nm* coat, fur

pelé, -e [pəle] *adj* bare

peler [pəle] **1** *vt* to peel **2** *vi (personne, peau)* to peel

pelle [pɛl] *nf* shovel; *(d'enfant)* spade; **p. à tarte** cake server

pellicule [pelikyl] *nf (pour photos)* film; *(couche)* thin layer; **pellicules** *(de cheveux)* dandruff

pelote [plɔt] *nf (de laine)* ball; *(à épingles)* pincushion; *Sport* **p. basque** pelota

peloton [p(ə)lɔtɔ̃] *nm (de ficelle)* ball; *(de cyclistes)* pack; *Mil* platoon; **p. d'exécution** firing squad

pelotonner [pəlɔtɔne] **se pelotonner** *vpr* to curl up (into a ball)

pelouse [pəluz] *nf* lawn

peluche [pəlyʃ] *nf (tissu)* plush; **(jouet en) p.** soft toy; **peluches** *(de pull)* fluff, lint

pelure [pəlyr] *nf (de légumes)* peelings; *(de fruits)* peel

pénal, -e, -aux, -ales [penal, -o] *adj* penal ▪ **pénaliser** *vt* to penalize ▪ **pénalité** *nf* penalty

penalty [penalti] *nm Sport* penalty

penchant [pɑ̃ʃɑ̃] *nm (préférence)* penchant (**pour** for); *(tendance)* propensity (**pour** for)

penché, -e [pɑ̃ʃe] *adj* leaning

pencher [pɑ̃ʃe] **1** *vt (objet)* to tilt; *(tête)* to lean **2** *vi (arbre)* to lean over **3 se pencher** *vpr* to lean over; **se p. par la fenêtre** to lean out of the window; **se p. sur qch** *(problème)* to examine sth

pendaison [pɑ̃dɛzɔ̃] *nf* hanging

pendant¹ [pɑ̃dɑ̃] *prép (au cours de)* during; **p. deux mois** for two months; **p. tout le trajet** for the whole journey; **p. que...** while...

pendant², -e 1 *adj* hanging; *(langue)* hanging out **2** *nm* **le p. de** the companion piece to

pendentif [pɑ̃dɑ̃tif] *nm (collier)* pendant

penderie [pɑ̃dri] *nf Br* wardrobe, *Am* closet

pendre [pɑ̃dr] **1** *vti* to hang (**à** from); **p. qn** to hang sb **2 se pendre** *vpr (se suicider)* to hang oneself; *(se suspendre)* to hang (**à** from) ▪ **pendu, -e** *adj (objet)* hanging (**à** from)

pendule [pɑ̃dyl] **1** *nf* clock **2** *nm (balancier)* pendulum

pénétrer [penetre] **1** *vi* **p. dans** to enter; *(profondément)* to penetrate (into) **2** *vt (sujet: pluie)* to penetrate **3 se pénétrer** *vpr* **se p. d'une idée** to become convinced of an idea ▪ **pénétration** *nf* penetration

pénible [penibl] *adj (difficile)* difficult;

(douloureux) painful, distressing; *(ennuyeux)* tiresome ∎ **péniblement** [-əmã] *adv* with difficulty

péniche [peniʃ] *nf* barge

pénicilline [penisilin] *nf* penicillin

péninsule [penɛ̃syl] *nf* peninsula

pénitencier [penitãsje] *nm* prison, *Am* penitentiary

pensée [pãse] *nf (idée)* thought; **à la p. de faire qch** at the thought of doing sth

penser [pãse] **1** *vi (réfléchir)* to think (à of *or* about); **p. à qn/qch** to think of *or* about sb/sth; **p. à faire qch** *(ne pas oublier)* to remember to do sth; **penses-tu!** what an idea!
2 *vt (estimer)* to think **(que** that); *(concevoir)* to think out; **je pensais rester** I was thinking of staying; **que pensez-vous de...?** what do you think of *or* about...?; **p. du bien de qn/qch** to think highly of sb/sth ∎ **pensif, -ive** *adj* thoughtful, pensive

pension [pãsjõ] *nf* **(a)** *(école)* boarding school; **mettre un enfant en p.** to send a child to boarding school **(b)** *(hôtel)* **p. de famille** boarding house; **p. complète** *Br* full board, *Am* American plan **(c)** *(allocation)* pension. **p. alimentaire** maintenance, alimony ∎ **pensionnaire** *nmf (élève, résident)* boarder ∎ **pensionnat** *nm* boarding school

pente [pãt] *nf* slope; **être en p.** to be sloping

Pentecôte [pãtkot] *nf Rel Br* Whitsun, *Am* Pentecost

pénurie [penyri] *nf* shortage (**de** of)

pépé [pepe] *nm* grandpa

pépin [pepɛ̃] *nm (de fruit)* seed, *Br* pip, *Am* pit

pépinière [pepinjɛr] *nf (pour plantes)* nursery

pépite [pepit] *nf (d'or)* nugget; **p. de chocolat** chocolate chip

perçant, -e [persã, -ãt] *adj (cri, froid)* piercing; *(vue)* sharp

percée [perse] *nf (ouverture)* opening; *Mil, Sport & Tech* breakthrough

perceptible [perseptibl] *adj* perceptible (**à** to)

perception [persɛpsjõ] *nf* **(a)** *(bureau)* tax office; *(d'impôt)* collection **(b)** *(sensation)* perception

percer [perse] **1** *vt (trouer)* to pierce; *(avec une perceuse)* to drill; *(trou, ouverture)* to make; *(abcès)* to lance; *(mystère)* to solve; **p. une dent** *(bébé)* to cut a tooth; **p. qch à jour** to see through sth **2** *vi (soleil)* to break through; *(abcès)* to burst; *(acteur)* to make a name for oneself ∎ **perceuse** *nf* drill

percevoir* [persəvwar] *vt* **(a)** *(sensation)* to perceive; *(son)* to hear **(b)** *(impôt)* to collect

perche [perʃ] *nf (bâton)* pole

percher [perʃe] **1** *vi (oiseau)* to perch **2 se percher** *vpr (oiseau, personne)* to perch

percuter [perkyte] **1** *vt (véhicule)* to crash into **2** *vi* **p. contre** to crash into **3 se percuter** *vpr* to crash into each other

perdant, -e [perdã, -ãt] **1** *adj* losing **2** *nmf* loser

perdre [perdr] **1** *vt* to lose; *(habitude)* to get out of; **p. qn/qch de vue** to lose sight of sb/sth **2** *vi* to lose **3 se perdre** *vpr (s'égarer)* to get lost; *(disparaître)* to die out; **se p. dans les détails** to get lost in details ∎ **perdu, -e** *adj (égaré)* lost; *(gaspillé)* wasted; *(malade)* finished; *(lieu)* out-of-the-way

père [per] *nm* father; **de p. en fils** from father to son; *Rel* **mon p.** father; **p. de famille** father

péremption [perãpsjõ] *nf* **date de p.** use-by date

perfection [perfeksjõ] *nf* perfection; **à la p.** to perfection

perfectionner [perfeksjone] **1** *vt* to improve, to perfect **2 se perfectionner** *vpr* **se p. en anglais** to improve one's English ∎ **perfectionné, -e** *adj* advanced ∎ **perfectionnement** *nm* improvement (**de** in; **par rapport à** on); **cours de p.** proficiency course

perfectionniste [perfeksjonist] *nmf* perfectionist

perforer [perfore] *vt (pneu, intestin)* to

perforate; *(billet)* to punch; **carte perforée** punch card

performance [pɛrfɔrmɑ̃s] *nf* performance ▪ **performant, -e** *adj* highly efficient

perfusion [pɛrfyzjɔ̃] *nf* drip; **être sous p.** to be on a drip

péril [peril] *nm* danger, peril; **à tes risques et périls** at your own risk; **mettre qch en p.** to endanger sth ▪ **périlleux, -euse** *adj* dangerous, perilous

périmé, -e [perime] *adj (billet)* expired; *(nourriture)* past its sell-by date

période [perjɔd] *nf* period ▪ **périodique 1** *adj* periodic **2** *nm (revue)* periodical

périphérie [periferi] *nf (limite)* periphery; *(banlieue)* outskirts

périphérique [periferik] **1** *adj* peripheral; **radio p.** = radio station broadcasting from outside France **2** *nm & adj* **(boulevard) p.** *Br* ring road, *Am* beltway

périr [perir] *vi* to perish ▪ **périssable** *adj (denrée)* perishable

perle [pɛrl] *nf (bijou)* pearl; *(de bois, de verre)* bead

permanent, -e [pɛrmanɑ̃, -ɑ̃t] **1** *adj* permanent; *Cin (spectacle)* continuous; *(comité)* standing **2** *nf* **permanente** perm ▪ **permanence** *nf* permanence; *(salle d'étude)* study room; *(service, bureau)* duty office; **être de p.** to be on duty; **en p.** permanently

perméable [pɛrmeabl] *adj* permeable (à to)

permettre* [pɛrmɛtr] **1** *vt* to allow, to permit; **p. à qn de faire qch** to allow sb to do sth; **vous permettez?** may I? **2** **se permettre** *vpr* **se p. de faire qch** to take the liberty of doing sth; **je ne peux pas me le p.** I can't afford it

permis, -e [pɛrmi, -iz] **1** *adj* allowed, permitted **2** *nm Br* licence, *Am* license, permit; **p. de conduire** *Br* driving licence, *Am* driver's license; **passer son p. de conduire** to take one's driving test

permission [pɛrmisjɔ̃] *nf* permission; *Mil* leave; *Mil* **en p.** on leave; **demander la p.** to ask permission (**de faire** to do)

permuter [pɛrmyte] **1** *vt (lettres, chiffres)* to transpose **2** *vi* to exchange posts

Pérou [peru] *nm* **le P.** Peru

perpendiculaire [pɛrpɑ̃dikylɛr] *adj & nf* perpendicular (**à** to)

perpétrer [pɛrpetre] *vt* to perpetrate

perpétuel, -elle [pɛrpetɥɛl] *adj* perpetual; *(membre)* permanent ▪ **perpétuer** *vt* to perpetuate ▪ **perpétuité** *adv* **à p.** in perpetuity; **condamnation à p.** life sentence

perplexe [pɛrplɛks] *adj* perplexed, puzzled

perquisition [pɛrkizisjɔ̃] *nf* search ▪ **perquisitionner** *vi* to make a search

perron [pɛrɔ̃] *nm* steps *(leading to a building)*

perroquet [pɛrɔkɛ] *nm* parrot

perruche [peryʃ] *nf Br* budgerigar, *Am* parakeet

perruque [pɛryk] *nf* wig

persan, -e [pɛrsɑ̃, -an] **1** *adj* Persian **2** *nm (langue)* Persian

persécuter [pɛrsekyte] *vt* to persecute ▪ **persécution** *nf* persecution

persévérer [pɛrsevere] *vi* to persevere (**dans** in) ▪ **persévérance** *nf* perseverance ▪ **persévérant, -e** *adj* persevering

persil [pɛrsi] *nm* parsley

Persique [pɛrsik] *adj* **le golfe P.** the Persian Gulf

persister [pɛrsiste] *vi* to persist (**à faire** in doing; **dans qch** in sth) ▪ **persistance** *nf* persistence

personnage [pɛrsɔnaʒ] *nm (de fiction, individu)* character; *(personnalité)* important person; **p. célèbre** celebrity; **p. officiel** VIP

personnaliser [pɛrsɔnalize] *vt* to personalize; *(voiture)* to customize

personnalité [pɛrsɔnalite] *nf (caractère, personnage)* personality; **avoir de la p.** to have lots of personality

personne [pɛrsɔn] **1** *nf* person; **deux**

personnes two people; **p. âgée** elderly person; **en p.** in person **2** *pron indéfini (de négation)* **(ne...) p.** nobody, no one; **je ne vois p.** I don't see anybody *or* anyone; **p. ne saura** nobody *or* no one will know

personnel, -elle [personɛl] **1** *adj* personal; *(joueur, jeu)* individualistic **2** *nm (de firme, d'école)* staff; *(d'usine)* workforce; **manquer de p.** to be understaffed; **p. au sol** ground personnel

personnifier [personifje] *vt* to personify ■ **personnification** *nf* personification

perspective [perspektiv] *nf (de dessin)* perspective; *(idée)* prospect **(de** of); *Fig (point de vue)* viewpoint; **perspectives d'avenir** future prospects

perspicace [perspikas] *adj* shrewd ■ **perspicacité** *nf* shrewdness

persuader [persɥade] *vt* **p. qn (de qch)** to persuade sb (of sth); **p. qn de faire qch** to persuade sb to do sth; **être persuadé de qch/que...** to be convinced of sth/that... ■ **persuasif, -ive** *adj* persuasive ■ **persuasion** *nf* persuasion

perte [pert] *nf* loss; *(destruction)* ruin; **une p. de temps** a waste of time; **à p. de vue** as far as the eye can see; **vendre qch à p.** to sell sth at a loss

pertinent, -e [pertinã, -ãt] *adj* relevant, pertinent ■ **pertinemment** [-amã] *adv* **savoir qch p.** to know sth for a fact ■ **pertinence** *nf* relevance, pertinence

perturber [pertyrbe] *vt (trafic, cérémonie)* to disrupt; *(personne)* to disturb ■ **perturbateur, -trice 1** *adj* disruptive **2** *nmf* troublemaker ■ **perturbation** *nf* disruption

péruvien, -enne [peryvjɛ̃, -jɛn] **1** *adj* Peruvian **2** *nmf* **P., Péruvienne** Peruvian

pervers, -e [perver, -ers] **1** *adj* perverse **2** *nmf* pervert ■ **perversion** *nf* perversion ■ **perversité** *nf* perversity ■ **pervertir** *vt* to pervert

pesant, -e [pəzã, -ãt] **1** *adj* heavy, weighty **2** *nm* **valoir son p. d'or** to be worth one's weight in gold ■ **pesanteur** *nf* heaviness; *Phys* gravity

pesée [pəze] *nf* weighing; *(pression)* force

peser [pəze] **1** *vt* to weigh **2** *vi* to weigh; **p. 2 kilos** to weigh 2 kilos; **p. lourd** to be heavy; *Fig (argument)* to carry weight; **p. sur** *(appuyer)* to press on; *(influer)* to bear upon; **p. sur qn** *(menace)* to hang over sb ■ **pèse-personne** *(pl* **pèse-personnes)** *nm (bathroom)* scales

pessimisme [pesimism] *nm* pessimism ■ **pessimiste 1** *adj* pessimistic **2** *nmf* pessimist

pester [peste] *vi* **p. contre qn/qch** to curse sb/sth

pétale [petal] *nm* petal

pétanque [petãk] *nf (jeu)* ≃ bowls

pétard [petar] *nm (feu d'artifice)* firecracker, *Br* banger

pétiller [petije] *vi (yeux, vin)* to sparkle ■ **pétillant, -e** *adj (gazeux)* sparkling

petit, -e [pəti, -it] **1** *adj* small, little; *(taille, distance)* short; *(bruit, coup)* slight; *(somme)* small; *(accident)* minor; *(mesquin)* petty; **tout p.** tiny; **mon p. frère** my little brother

2 *nmf (little)* boy, *f (little)* girl; *(personne)* small person; *Scol* junior; **petits** *(d'animal)* young; *(de chien)* pups; *(de chat)* kittens

3 *adv* **écrire p.** to write small; **p. à p.** little by little ■ **petite-fille** *(pl* **petites-filles)** *nf* granddaughter ■ **petit-fils** *(pl* **petits-fils)** *nm* grandson ■ **petits-enfants** *nmpl* grandchildren

pétition [petisjɔ̃] *nf* petition

pétrifier [petrifje] *vt* to petrify

pétrir [petrir] *vt* to knead

pétrole [petrɔl] *nm* oil, petroleum ■ **pétrolier, -ère 1** *adj* **industrie pétrolière** oil industry **2** *nm* oil tanker ■ **pétrolifère** *adj* **gisement p.** oilfield

PEU [pø] **1** *adv (avec un verbe)* not much; *(avec un adjectif, un adverbe)* not very; *(un petit nombre)* few; **elle mange p.** she doesn't eat much; **p. intéressant/souvent** not very interesting/often; **p. ont compris** few

understood; **p. de sel/de temps** not much salt/time, little salt/time; **p. de gens/de livres** few people/books; **p. à p.** little by little, gradually; **à p. près** more or less; **p. après/avant** shortly after/before; **sous p.** shortly; **pour p. que...** (+ subjunctive) if by chance...

2 *nm* un **p.** a little, a bit; **un p. grand** a bit big; **un p. de fromage** a little cheese, a bit of cheese; **un (tout) petit p.** a (tiny) little bit; **le p. de fromage que j'ai** the little cheese I have; **reste encore un p.** stay a little longer

peuplade [pœplad] *nf* tribe

peuple [pœpl] *nm (nation, citoyens)* people; **les gens du p.** ordinary people

peupler [pœple] *vt (habiter)* to inhabit ■ **peuplé, -e** *adj (région)* inhabited (**de** by); **très/peu p.** highly/sparsely populated

peuplier [pøplije] *nm (arbre, bois)* poplar

peur [pœr] *nf* fear; **avoir p.** to be afraid *or* frightened (**de qn/qch** of sb/sth); **de faire qch** to do sth *or* of doing sth); **faire p. à qn** to frighten *or* scare sb; **de p. qu'il ne parte** for fear that he would leave; **de p. de faire qch** for fear of doing sth ■ **peureux, -euse** *adj* easily fearful

peut [pø] *voir* **pouvoir 1**

peut-être [pøtetr] *adv* perhaps, maybe; **p. qu'il viendra, p. viendra-t-il** perhaps *or* maybe he'll come; **p. que oui** perhaps; **p. que non** perhaps not

peuvent, peux [pœv, pø] *voir* **pouvoir 1**

phare [far] 1 *nm (pour bateaux)* lighthouse; *(de véhicule)* headlight; **faire un appel de phares** to flash one's lights 2 *adj* **épreuve-p.** star event

pharmacie [farmasi] *nf (magasin)* Br chemist, Am drugstore; *(armoire)* medicine cabinet ■ **pharmaceutique** *adj* pharmaceutical ■ **pharmacien, -enne** *nmf* Br chemist, pharmacist, Am druggist

phase [faz] *nf* phase

phénomène [fenɔmɛn] *nm* phenomenon

philharmonique [filarmɔnik] *adj* philharmonic

Philippines [filipin] *nfpl* **les P.** the Philippines

philosophe [filɔzɔf] 1 *nmf* philosopher 2 *adj* philosophical ■ **philosopher** *vi* to philosophize (**sur** about) ■ **philosophie** *nf* philosophy ■ **philosophique** *adj* philosophical

photo [fɔto] 1 *nf (cliché)* photo; *(art)* photography; **prendre une p. de qn/qch, prendre qn/qch en p.** to take a photo of sb/sth; **p. d'identité** ID photo 2 *adj inv* **appareil p.** camera ■ **photogénique** *adj* photogenic ■ **photographe** *nmf* photographer ■ **photographie** *nf (art)* photography; *(cliché)* photograph ■ **photographier** *vt* to photograph; **se faire p.** to have one's photo taken ■ **photographique** *adj* photographic

photocopie [fɔtɔkɔpi] *nf* photocopy ■ **photocopier** *vt* to photocopy ■ **photocopieur** *nm*, **photocopieuse** [fɔtɔkɔpjøz] *nf* photocopier

Photomaton® [fɔtɔmatɔ̃] *nm* photo booth

phrase [fraz] *nf* sentence

physicien, -enne [fizisjɛ̃, -ɛn] *nmf* physicist

physique [fizik] 1 *adj* physical 2 *nm (de personne)* physique 3 *nf (science)* physics *(sing)*

pianiste [pjanist] *nmf* pianist

piano [pjano] *nm* piano; **p. droit/à queue** upright/grand piano ■ **pianoter** *vi* **p. sur qch** *(table)* to drum one's fingers on sth

pic [pik] *nm (cime)* peak; *(outil)* pick (axe); *(oiseau)* woodpecker; **couler à p.** to sink like a stone; **tomber à p.** *(falaise)* to go straight down; **p. à glace** ice pick

pichet [piʃɛ] *nm* Br jug, Am pitcher

picorer [pikɔre] *vt* to peck

picoter [pikɔte] *vt* **j'ai la gorge qui (me) picote** I've got a tickle in my throat

pièce [pjɛs] *nf (de maison)* room; *(morceau, objet)* piece; *(de pantalon)* patch;

(de dossier) document; **p. (de monnaie)** coin; **p. (de théâtre)** play; **5 euros (la) p.** 5 euros each; **mettre qch en pièces** to tear sth to pieces; **p. d'identité** proof of identity; **pièces détachées** *ou* **de rechange** spare parts

pied [pje] *nm (de personne)* foot *(pl* feet); *(de lit, d'arbre, de colline)* foot; *(de meuble)* leg; *(de verre, de lampe)* base; **à p.** on foot; **aller à p.** to walk, to go on foot; **au p. de** at the foot *or* bottom of; **sur un p. d'égalité** on an equal footing; **avoir p.** to be within one's depth; **mettre qch sur p.** to set sth up

piédestal, -aux [pjedɛstal, -o] *nm* pedestal

piège [pjɛʒ] *nm (pour animal)* & *Fig* trap ■ **piéger** *vt (animal)* to trap; *(voiture)* to booby-trap; **voiture/lettre piégée** car/letter bomb

pierre [pjɛr] *nf* stone; *(de bijou)* gem, stone; **p. précieuse** precious stone, gem ■ **pierreries** *nfpl* gems, precious stones ■ **pierreux, -euse** *adj* stony

piétiner [pjetine] **1** *vt* **p. qch** *(en trépignant)* to stamp on sth; *(en marchant)* to trample on sth **2** *vi (ne pas avancer)* to stand around; **p. d'impatience** to stamp one's feet impatiently

piéton [pjetɔ̃] *nm* pedestrian ■ **piétonne, piétonnière** [pjetɔnjɛr] *adj f* **rue p.** pedestrian(ized) street; **zone p.** pedestrian precinct

pigeon [piʒɔ̃] *nm* pigeon

pile [pil] **1** *nf* (a) **p. (électrique)** battery; **radio à piles** battery radio (b) *(tas)* pile; **en p.** in a pile (c) *(de pièce)* **p. ou face?** heads or tails?; **jouer à p. ou face** to toss for it **2** *adv Fam* **s'arrêter p.** to stop dead; *Fam* **à deux heures p.** at two on the dot

piler [pile] *vt (broyer)* to crush; *(amandes)* to grind

pilier [pilje] *nm* pillar

piller [pije] *vt* to loot, to pillage ■ **pillage** *nm* looting, pillaging

pilon [pilɔ̃] *nm (de poulet)* drumstick

pilonner [pilɔne] *vt (bombarder)* to bombard

pilote [pilɔt] **1** *nm (d'avion, de bateau)* pilot; *(de voiture)* driver; **p. automatique** automatic pilot; **p. de chasse** fighter pilot; **p. d'essai** test pilot; **p. de ligne** airline pilot **2** *adj* **usine(-)p.** pilot factory ■ **pilotage** *nm* piloting ■ **piloter** *vt (avion)* to fly, to pilot; *(bateau)* to pilot; *(voiture)* to drive

pilule [pilyl] *nf* pill; **prendre la p.** to be on the pill

piment [pimɑ̃] *nm* chilli ■ **pimenté, -e** *adj (épicé)* spicy

pin [pɛ̃] *nm (arbre, bois)* pine; **pomme de p.** pine cone; *(de sapin)* fir cone

pince [pɛ̃s] *nf (outil)* pliers; *(sur vêtement)* dart; *(de crustacé)* pincer; **p. à épiler** tweezers; **p. à linge** (clothes) *Br* peg *or Am* pin

pincé, -e [pɛ̃se] *adj (air)* stiff; *(sourire)* tight-lipped

pinceau, -x [pɛ̃so] *nm* (paint)brush

pincer [pɛ̃se] **1** *vt* to pinch **2 se pincer** *vpr* **se p. le doigt** to get one's finger caught **(dans** in); **se p. le nez** to hold one's nose ■ **pincée** *nf* pinch **(de** of)

ping-pong [piŋpɔ̃g] *nm* table tennis, Ping-Pong®

pintade [pɛ̃tad] *nf* guinea fowl

pioche [pjɔʃ] *nf (outil)* pick(axe); *Cartes* stock, pile ■ **piocher** *vt (creuser)* to dig *(with a pick)*; **p. une carte** to draw a card

pion [pjɔ̃] *nm (au jeu de dames)* piece; *Échecs* & *Fig* pawn

pionnier [pjɔnje] *nm* pioneer

pipe [pip] *nf (de fumeur)* pipe

pipeau, -x [pipo] *nm (flûte)* pipe

piquant, -e [pikɑ̃, -ɑ̃t] **1** *adj (au goût)* spicy, hot; *(plante, barbe)* prickly; *(détail)* spicy **2** *nm (de plante)* prickle, thorn; *(d'animal)* spine

pique [pik] **1** *nm Cartes (couleur)* spades **2** *nf (allusion)* cutting remark; *(arme)* pike

pique-nique [piknik] *(pl* pique-niques) *nm* picnic ■ **pique-niquer** *vi* to picnic

piquer [pike] **1** *vt (percer)* to prick; *(langue, yeux)* to sting; *(sujet: moustique)* to bite; **p. qch dans** *(enfoncer)* to stick sth into; **la fumée me pique les**

yeux the smoke is making my eyes sting **2** *vi (moutarde)* to be hot **3 se piquer** *vpr* to prick oneself; **se p. au doigt** to prick one's finger

piquet [pikɛ] *nm (pieu)* stake, post; *(de tente)* peg; **p. de grève** picket

piqûre [pikyr] *nf (d'abeille)* sting; *(de moustique)* bite; *(d'épingle)* prick; *(de tissu)* stitching; *(de rouille)* spot; *Méd* injection; **faire une p. à qn** to give sb an injection

pirate [pirat] **1** *nm (des mers)* pirate; **p. de l'air** hijacker; **p. informatique** hacker **2** *adj* **radio p.** pirate radio; **édition/CD p.** pirated edition/CD ▪ **pirater** *vt (enregistrement)* to pirate; *Ordinat* to hack

pire [pir] **1** *adj* worse **(que** than); **c'est de p. en p.** it's getting worse and worse **2** *nmf* **le/la p.** the worst (one); **le p. de tout** the worst thing of all; **au p.** at (the very) worst; **s'attendre au p.** to expect the (very) worst

pirogue [pirɔg] *nf* canoe, dugout

pis¹ [pi] *nm (de vache)* udder

pis² [pi] *adv* **aller de mal en p.** to go from bad to worse

piscine [pisin] *nf* swimming pool

pistache [pistaʃ] *nf* pistachio

piste [pist] *nf (traces)* track, trail; *(indices)* lead; *(de magnétophone) & Sport* track; *(de cirque)* ring; *(de ski)* run, piste; *(pour chevaux) Br* racecourse, *Am* racetrack; *Sport* **tour de p.** lap; **p. d'atterrissage** runway; **p. cyclable** *Br* cycle path, *Am* bicycle path; **p. de danse** dance floor

pistolet [pistɔlɛ] *nm* gun, pistol; *(de peintre)* spray gun; **p. à eau** water pistol

pitié [pitje] *nf* pity; **avoir de la p. pour qn** to pity sb; **il me fait p.** I feel sorry for him; **être sans p.** to be ruthless ▪ **pitoyable** *adj* pitiful ▪ **piteux, -euse** *adj* pitiful; **en p. état** in a sorry state

piton [pitɔ̃] *nm (d'alpiniste)* piton; **p. (rocheux)** (rocky) peak

pittoresque [pitɔrɛsk] *adj* picturesque

pivoter [pivɔte] *vi* to pivot, to swivel; **faire p. qch** to swivel sth round

pizza [pidza] *nf* pizza ▪ **pizzeria** *nf* pizzeria

placard [plakar] *nm (armoire) Br* cupboard, *Am* closet; **p. publicitaire** large display advertisement

place [plas] *nf (endroit, rang) & Sport* place; *(lieu public)* square; *(espace)* room; *(siège)* seat; *(emploi)* job, post; **à la p. instead (de** of); **à votre p.** in your place; **se mettre à la p. de qn** to put oneself in sb's position; **sur p.** on the spot; **en p.** *(objet)* in place; **mettre qch en p.** to put sth in place; **changer de p.** to change places; **faire de la p.** to make room (**à** for); **faire p. à qn/qch** to give way to sb/sth; **prendre p.** to take a seat; **p. de parking** parking space; **p. de train/bus** train/bus fare; **p. assise** seat

placer [plase] **1** *vt (mettre)* to put, to place; *(faire asseoir)* to seat; *(trouver un emploi à)* to place; *(argent)* to invest **(dans** in) **2 se placer** *vpr (debout)* to stand; *(s'asseoir)* to sit ▪ **placé, -e** *adj (objet) & Sport* placed; **bien/mal p. pour faire qch** well/badly placed to do sth ▪ **placement** *nm (d'argent)* investment

plafond [plafɔ̃] *nm* ceiling ▪ **plafonner** *vi (prix)* to peak; *(salaires)* to have reached a ceiling (**à** of) ▪ **plafonnier** *nm* ceiling light

plage [plaʒ] *nf (grève)* beach; *(surface)* area; *(de disque)* track; **p. de sable** sandy beach; **p. horaire** time slot

plaider [plede] *vti Jur (défendre)* to plead; **p. coupable** to plead guilty ▪ **plaidoyer** *nm Jur* speech for the *Br* defence *or Am* defense

plaie [plɛ] *nf (blessure)* wound

plaindre* [plɛ̃dr] **1** *vt* to feel sorry for, to pity **2 se plaindre** *vpr (protester)* to complain (**de** about; **que** that); **se p. de** *(douleur)* to complain of ▪ **plainte** *nf* complaint; *(gémissement)* moan; **porter p. contre qn** to lodge a complaint against sb

plaine [plɛn] *nf* plain

plaintif, -ive [plɛ̃tif, -iv] *adj* plaintive

plaire* [plɛr] **1** *vi* **elle me plaît** I like

her; **ça me plaît** I like it **2** *v impersonnel* **il me plaît de le faire** I like doing it; **s'il vous/te plaît** please; **comme il vous plaira** as you like it **3 se plaire** *vpr (l'un l'autre)* to like each other; **se p. à Paris** to like it in Paris

plaisance [plɛzɑ̃s] *nf* **navigation de p.** yachting

plaisant, -e [plɛzɑ̃, -ɑ̃t] **1** *adj (drôle)* amusing; *(agréable)* pleasing **2** *nm* **mauvais p.** joker ■ **plaisanter** *vi* to joke **(sur** about) ■ **plaisanterie** *nf* joke; **par p.** for a joke ■ **plaisantin** *nm* joker

plaisir [plɛzir] *nm* pleasure; **faire p. à qn** to please sb; **pour le p.** for the fun of it; **au p. (de vous revoir)** see you again sometime; **faites-moi le p. de...** would you be good enough to...

plan [plɑ̃] *nm (projet, dessin, organisation)* plan; *(de ville)* map; *Math* plane; **au premier p.** in the foreground; *Phot* **au second p.** in the background; **sur le p. politique, au p. politique** from the political viewpoint; **sur le même p.** on the same level; **de premier p.** of importance, major; *Phot & Cin* **gros p.** close-up; **p. d'eau** stretch of water; *Fin* **p. d'épargne** savings plan

planche [plɑ̃ʃ] *nf (en bois)* plank; *(plus large)* board; *(illustration)* plate; **faire la p.** to float on one's back; **p. à dessin** drawing board; **p. à roulettes** skateboard; **p. à voile** sailboard; **faire de la p. à voile** to go windsurfing

plancher [plɑ̃ʃe] *nm* floor

planer [plane] *vi (oiseau, planeur)* to glide

planète [planɛt] *nf* planet

planeur [planœr] *nm (avion)* glider

planifier [planifje] *vt* to plan

plant [plɑ̃] *nm (de plante)* seedling

plantation [plɑ̃tasjɔ̃] *nf (action)* planting; *(exploitation agricole)* plantation

plante [plɑ̃t] *nf Bot* plant; **jardin des plantes** botanical gardens; **p. du pied** sole (of the foot)

planter [plɑ̃te] *vt (fleur, arbre)* to plant; *(clou, couteau)* to drive in; *(tente)* to put up; *(mettre)* to put **(sur** on; **contre** against)

plaque [plak] *nf* plate; *(de verre, de métal)* sheet, plate; *(de verglas)* sheet; *(de marbre)* slab; *(de chocolat)* bar; *(commémorative)* plaque; *(sur la peau)* blotch; **p. chauffante** hotplate; *Aut* **p. minéralogique, p. d'immatriculation** *Br* number or *Am* license plate

plaquer [plake] *vt (métal, bijou)* to plate; *(bois)* to veneer; *(cheveux)* to plaster down; *(au rugby)* to tackle; *(aplatir)* to flatten **(contre** against) **2 se plaquer** *vpr* **se p. contre** to flatten oneself against ■ **plaqué, -e 1** *adj (bijou)* plated; **p. or** gold-plated **2** *nm* **p. or** gold plate

plasma [plasma] *nm Biol* plasma

plastic [plastik] *nm* plastic explosive ■ **plastiquer** *vt* to bomb

plastifier [plastifje] *vt* to laminate

plastique [plastik] *adj & nm* plastic

plat, -e [pla, plat] **1** *adj* flat; *(mer)* calm, smooth; *(ennuyeux)* flat, dull; **à p. ventre** flat on one's face; **à p.** *(pneu, batterie)* flat; **poser qch à p.** to lay sth (down) flat

2 *nm* **(a)** *(de la main)* flat **(b)** *(récipient, nourriture)* dish; *(partie du repas)* course; **p. principal** *ou* **de résistance** main course ■ **plate-bande** *(pl* **plates-bandes)** *nf* flower bed ■ **plate-forme** *(pl* **plates-formes)** *nf* platform; **p. pétrolière** oil rig

plateau, -x [plato] *nm* tray; *(de balance)* pan; *TV & Cin* set; *Géog* plateau; **p. à fromages** cheeseboard

platine¹ [platin] **1** *nm (métal)* platinum **2** *adj inv* platinum; **blond p.** platinum blond

platine² [platin] *nf (d'électrophone, de magnétophone)* deck; **p. laser** CD player

platitude [platityd] *nf (propos)* platitude

plâtre [platr] *nm (matière)* plaster; **un p.** *(de jambe cassée)* a plaster cast; **les plâtres** *(de maison)* the plasterwork ■ **plâtrer** *vt (mur)* to plaster; *(membre)* to put in plaster

plausible [plozibl] *adj* plausible

play-back [plɛbak] *nm inv* **chanter en p.** to mime

plein, -e [plɛ̃, plɛn] **1** *adj (rempli, complet)* full; *(solide)* solid; **p. de** full of; **p. à craquer** full to bursting; **en pleine mer** out at sea, on the open sea; **en pleine figure** right in the face; **en pleine nuit** in the middle of the night; **en p. jour** in broad daylight; **en p. hiver** in the depths of winter; **en p. soleil** in the full heat of the sun; **être en p. travail** to be hard at work; **à la pleine lune** at full moon; **un p. temps** a full-time job; **travailler à p. temps** to work full-time; **p. sud** due south; **p. tarif** full price; *(de transport)* full fare

2 *adv* **de l'argent p. les poches** pockets full of money; **du chocolat p. la figure** chocolate all over one's face

3 *nm Aut* **faire le p. (d'essence)** to fill up (the tank)

pleurer [plœre] **1** *vi* to cry, to weep (**sur** over) **2** *vt (personne)* to mourn (for) ■ **pleurs** *mpl* **en p.** in tears

pleuvoir* [pløvwar] **1** *v impersonnel* to rain; **il pleut** it's raining; *Fig* **il pleut des cordes** it's raining cats and dogs **2** *vi (coups)* to rain down (**sur** on)

Plexiglas® [plɛksiglas] *nm Br* Perspex®, *Am* Plexiglas®

pli [pli] *nm* (a) *(de papier, de rideau, de la peau)* fold; *(de jupe, de robe)* pleat; *(de pantalon, de bouche)* crease; **(faux) p.** crease; **mise en plis** set *(hairstyle)* (b) *(enveloppe)* envelope; *(lettre)* letter (c) *Cartes* trick

plier [plije] **1** *vt (draps, vêtements)* to fold; *(parapluie)* to fold up; *(courber)* to bend; **p. bagages** to pack one's bags (and leave) **2** *vi (branche)* to bend **3 se plier** *vpr (lit, chaise)* to fold up; **se p. à** to submit to ■ **pliable** *adj* foldable ■ **pliage** *nm (manière)* fold; *(action)* folding ■ **pliant, -e 1** *adj (chaise)* folding **2** *nm* folding stool

plisser [plise] *vt (lèvres)* to pucker; *(front)* to wrinkle; *(yeux)* to screw up ■ **plissé, -e** *adj (jupe)* pleated

plomb [plɔ̃] *nm (métal)* lead; *(fusible) Br* fuse, *Am* fuze; *(pour rideau)* lead weight; **plombs** *(de chasse)* lead shot; *Fig* **de p.** *(sommeil)* heavy; *(soleil)* blazing

plomber [plɔ̃be] *vt (dent)* to fill; *(mettre des plombs à)* to weigh with lead ■ **plombage** *nm (de dent)* filling

plombier [plɔ̃bje] *nm* plumber ■ **plomberie** *nf (métier, installations)* plumbing

plonger [plɔ̃ʒe] **1** *vi (personne)* to dive (**dans** into); *(oiseau, avion)* to dive (**sur** onto) **2** *vt (enfoncer)* to plunge (**dans** into) **3 se plonger** *vpr* **se p. dans** *(lecture)* to immerse oneself in; **plongé dans l'obscurité** plunged in darkness ■ **plongée** *nf* diving; *(de sous-marin)* dive; **p. sous-marine** skin *or* scuba diving ■ **plongeoir** *nm* diving board ■ **plongeon** *nm* dive; **faire un p.** to dive ■ **plongeur, -euse** *nmf (nageur)* diver

plu [ply] *pp de* **plaire, pleuvoir**

pluie [plɥi] *nf* rain; **sous la p.** in the rain; **pluies acides** acid rain; **pluies diluviennes** torrential rain; **p. fine** drizzle

plume [plym] *nf (d'oiseau)* feather; *(de stylo)* nib ■ **plumer** *vt (volaille)* to pluck

plupart [plypar] **la plupart** *nf* most; **la p. du temps** most of the time; **la p. d'entre eux** most of them; **pour la p.** mostly

PLUS¹ [ply] ([plyz] *before vowel,* [plys] *in end position) adv* (a) *(comparatif)* more (**que** than); **p. d'un kilo/de dix** more than a kilo/ten; **p. de thé** more tea; **p. beau/rapidement** more beautiful/quickly (**que** than); **p. tard** later; **p. petit** smaller; **de p. en p.** more and more; **de p. en p. vite** quicker and quicker; **p. ou moins** more or less; **en p.** in addition (**de** to); **au p.** at most; **de p.** more (**que** than); *(en outre)* moreover; **les enfants de p. de dix ans** children over ten; **j'ai dix ans de p. qu'elle** I'm ten years older than she is; **il est p. de cinq heures** it's after five (o'clock); **p. il crie, p. il s'enroue** the more he shouts, the more hoarse he gets

(b) *(superlatif)* **le p.** (the) most; **le p.**

beau the most beautiful (**de** in); *(de deux)* the more beautiful; **le p. grand** the biggest *(de deux)* the bigger; **j'ai le p. de livres** I have (the) most books; **j'en ai le p.** I have the most

PLUS² [ply] *adv (négation)* (**ne...**) **p.** no more; **il n'a p. de pain** he has no more bread, he doesn't have any more bread; **il n'y a p. rien** there's nothing left; **elle ne le fait p.** she no longer does it, she doesn't do it any more *or* any longer; **je ne la reverrai p.** I won't see her again; **je ne voyagerai p. jamais** I'll never travel again

plus³ [plys] **1** *conj* plus; **deux p. deux font quatre** two plus two are four; **il fait p. 2 (degrés)** it's 2 degrees above freezing **2** *nm* **le signe p.** the plus sign

plusieurs [plyzjœr] *adj & pron* several

plutôt [plyto] *adv* rather (**que** than)

pluvieux, -euse [plyvjø, -jøz] *adj* rainy, wet

pneu [pnø] *(pl* **pneus)** *nm (de roue)* Br tyre, *Am* tire ■ **pneumatique** *adj (gonflable)* inflatable

poche [pɔʃ] *nf (de vêtement)* pocket; *(de kangourou)* pouch ■ **pochette** *nf (sac)* bag; *(d'allumettes)* book; *(de disque)* sleeve; *(sac à main)* (clutch) bag; *(mouchoir)* pocket handkerchief

pocher [pɔʃe] *vt (œufs)* to poach

poêle [pwal] **1** *nm (chauffage)* stove **2** *nf* **p.** (**à frire**) frying pan

poème [pɔɛm] *nm* poem ■ **poésie** *nf (art)* poetry; *(poème)* poem ■ **poète** *nm* poet

poids [pwa] *nm* weight; *Sport* shot; **au p.** by weight; **prendre/perdre du p.** to gain/lose weight; **p. lourd** *(camion)* Br lorry, *Am* truck; *(en boxe)* heavyweight; **p. plume** *(en boxe)* featherweight

poignant, -e [pwaɲɑ̃, -ɑ̃t] *adj* poignant

poignard [pwaɲar] *nm* dagger; **coup de p.** stab ■ **poignarder** *vt* to stab

poignée [pwaɲe] *nf (quantité)* handful *(de* of); *(de porte, de casserole)* handle; *(d'épée)* hilt; **p. de main** handshake

poignet [pwaɲɛ] *nm* wrist; *(de chemise)* cuff

poil [pwal] *nm* hair; *(pelage)* coat; **poils** *(de brosse)* bristles; *(de tapis)* pile; **p. à gratter** itching powder ■ **poilu, -e** *adj* hairy

poinçonner [pwɛ̃sɔne] *vt (billet)* to punch; *(bijou)* to hallmark

poing [pwɛ̃] *nm* fist

POINT [pwɛ̃] *nm (lieu, score, question)* point; *(sur i, à l'horizon)* dot; *(tache)* spot; *(de notation)* mark; *(de couture)* stitch; **être sur le p. de faire qch** to be about to do sth; **à p.** *(steak)* medium; **déprimé au p. que...** depressed to such an extent that...; **mettre au p.** *(appareil photo)* to focus; *(moteur)* to tune; *(technique)* to perfect; **être au p.** to be up to scratch; **au p. où j'en suis...** at the stage I've reached...; **au plus haut p.** extremely; **p. de côté** stitch; **p. de départ** starting point; **p. de vue** *(opinion)* point of view, viewpoint; *(endroit)* viewing point; **p. faible/fort** weak/strong point

pointe [pwɛ̃t] *nf (extrémité)* tip, point; *(clou)* nail; *Géog* headland; *Fig (maximum)* peak; **une p. d'humour** a touch of humour; **sur la p. des pieds** on tiptoe; **en p.** pointed; **de p.** *(technologie, industrie)* state-of-the-art; **vitesse de p.** top speed; *Fig* **à la p. de** *(progrès)* in *or* at the forefront of; **faire des pointes** *(danseuse)* to dance on points; **p. de vitesse** burst of speed

pointer [pwɛ̃te] **1** *vt (cocher)* Br to tick off, *Am* to check (off); *(braquer)* to point (**sur/vers** at) **2** *vi (employé)* (à l'arrivée) to clock in; *(à la sortie)* to clock out

pointillé [pwɛ̃tije] *nm* dotted line

pointu, -e [pwɛ̃ty] *adj (en pointe)* pointed; *(voix)* shrill; *Fig (spécialisé)* specialized

pointure [pwɛ̃tyr] *nf* size

poire [pwar] *nf (fruit)* pear ■ **poirier** *nm* pear tree

poireau, -x [pwaro] *nm* leek

pois [pwa] *nm (légume)* pea; *(dessin)* (polka) dot; **à p.** *(vêtement)* polka-dot; **petits p.** *Br* (garden) peas, *Am* peas; **p.**

de senteur sweet pea; **p. chiche** *Br* chickpea, *Am* garbanzo (bean)

poison [pwazɔ̃] *nm* poison

poisson [pwasɔ̃] *nm* fish; **les Poissons** *(signe)* Pisces; **p. d'avril** April fool; **p. rouge** goldfish ▪ **poissonnerie** *nf* fish shop ▪ **poissonnier, -ère** *nmf Br* fishmonger, *Am* fish merchant

poitrine [pwatrin] *nf* chest; *(seins)* bust; *Culin (de veau)* breast

poivre [pwavr] *nm* pepper ▪ **poivrer** *vt* to pepper ▪ **poivrière** *nf* pepper pot

poivron [pwavrɔ̃] *nm* pepper

pôle [pol] *nm Géog* pole; **p. Nord/Sud** North/South Pole ▪ **polaire** *adj* polar

polémique [pɔlemik] **1** *adj* polemical **2** *nf* heated debate

poli, -e [pɔli] *adj (courtois)* polite **(avec** ou with); *(lisse)* polished

police [pɔlis] *nf* police; *Typ & Ordinat* **p. de caractères** font; **p. secours** emergency services ▪ **policier, -ère 1** *adj* **enquête policière** police inquiry; **roman p.** detective novel **2** *nm* policeman, detective

polir [pɔlir] *vt* to polish

politesse [pɔlitɛs] *nf* politeness

politique [pɔlitik] **1** *adj* political **2** *nf (activité, science)* politics *(sing)*; *(mesure)* policy; **faire de la p.** to be in politics **3** *nmf* politician ▪ **politicien, -enne** *nmf Péj* politician

pollen [pɔlɛn] *nm* pollen

polluer [pɔlɥe] *vt* to pollute ▪ **polluant** *nm* pollutant ▪ **pollueur, -euse 1** *adj* polluting **2** *nmf* polluter ▪ **pollution** *nf* pollution

Pologne [pɔlɔɲ] *nf* **la P.** Poland ▪ **polonais, -e 1** *adj* Polish **2** *nmf* **P., Polonaise** Pole **3** *nm (langue)* Polish

polycopier [pɔlikɔpje] *vt* to duplicate

polyester [pɔliɛstɛr] *nm* polyester

polygame [pɔligam] *adj* polygamous

Polynésie [pɔlinezi] *nf* **la P.** Polynesia

polyvalent, -e [pɔlivalɑ̃, -ɑ̃t] **1** *adj (salle)* multi-purpose; *(personne)* versatile **2** *adj & nf* **(école) polyvalente** *Br* = secondary school, *Am* = high school

pommade [pɔmad] *nf* ointment

pomme [pɔm] *nf* **(a)** *(fruit)* apple; *Anat* **p. d'Adam** Adam's apple; **p. de terre** potato; **pommes chips** *Br* (potato) crisps, *Am* (potato) chips; **pommes frites** *Br* chips, *Am* (French) fries; **pommes vapeur** steamed potatoes **(b)** *(d'arrosoir)* rose ▪ **pommier** *nm* apple tree

pompe¹ [pɔ̃p] **1** *nf (machine)* pump; **p. à essence** *Br* petrol *or Am* gas station; **p. à vélo** bicycle pump **2** *nfpl* **pompes funèbres** undertaker's; **entrepreneur des pompes funèbres** *Br* undertaker, *Am* mortician

pompe² [pɔ̃p] *nf* **en grande p.** with great ceremony

pomper [pɔ̃pe] **1** *vt (eau, air)* to pump; *(faire monter)* to pump up; *(évacuer)* to pump out **2** *vi* to pump

pompeux, -euse [pɔ̃pø, -øz] *adj* pompous

pompier [pɔ̃pje] *nm* fireman; **voiture des pompiers** fire engine

pompiste [pɔ̃pist] *nmf Br* petrol station *or Am* gas station attendant

ponce [pɔ̃s] *nf* **pierre p.** pumice stone

ponctuel, -elle [pɔ̃ktɥɛl] *adj (à l'heure)* punctual; *(unique) Br* one-off, *Am* one-of-a-kind ▪ **ponctualité** *nf* punctuality

ponctuer [pɔ̃ktɥe] *vt* to punctuate **(de** with)

pondre [pɔ̃dr] *vt (œuf)* to lay

poney [pɔne] *nm* pony

pont [pɔ̃] *nm* bridge; *(de bateau)* deck; *Fig* **faire le p.** to make a long weekend of it ▪ **pont-levis** *(pl* **ponts-levis)** *nm* drawbridge

populaire [pɔpylɛr] *adj (personne, gouvernement)* popular; *(quartier, milieu)* working-class; *(expression)* vernacular ▪ **populariser** *vt* to popularize ▪ **popularité** *nf* popularity **(auprès de** with)

population [pɔpylasjɔ̃] *nf* population

porc [pɔr] *nm (animal)* pig; *(viande)* pork

porcelaine [pɔrsəlɛn] *nf* china, porcelain

porche [pɔrʃ] *nm* porch

pornographie [pɔrnɔgrafi] *nf* pornography

port [pɔr] *nm* (a) *(pour bateaux)* port, harbour; *Ordinat* port (b) *(d'armes)* carrying; *(de barbe)* wearing; *(prix)* carriage, postage; *(attitude)* bearing

portable [pɔrtabl] **1** *adj (ordinateur)* laptop; *(téléphone) Br* mobile, *Am* cellphone **2** *nm (ordinateur)* laptop; *(téléphone) Br* mobile, *Am* cellphone

portail [pɔrtaj] *nm (de jardin)* gate; *(de cathédrale)* portal

portant, -e [pɔrtɑ̃, -ɑ̃t] *adj* **bien p.** in good health

portatif, -ive [pɔrtatif, -iv] *adj* portable

porte [pɔrt] *nf* door, *(de jardin, de ville, de slalom)* gate; **mettre qn à la p.** *(jeter dehors)* to throw sb out; *(renvoyer)* to fire sb; **p. d'embarquement** *(d'aéroport)* (departure) gate; **p. d'entrée** front door ■ **porte-fenêtre** *(pl* **portes-fenêtres)** *nf* French window

portée [pɔrte] *nf* (a) *(de fusil)* range; *Fig* scope; **à la p. de qn** within reach of sb; **à p. de la main** within reach; **hors de p.** out of reach (b) *(animaux)* litter (c) *(impact)* significance (d) *Mus* stave

portefeuille [pɔrtəfœj] *nm Br* wallet, *Am* billfold; *(de ministre, d'actions)* portfolio

portemanteau, -x [pɔrtmɑ̃to] *nm (sur pied)* coat stand; *(crochet)* coat rack

porter [pɔrte] **1** *vt* to carry; *(vêtement, lunettes)* to wear; *(moustache, barbe)* to have; *(trace, responsabilité, fruits)* to bear; *(regard)* to cast; *(inscrire)* to enter; **p. qch à qn** to take/bring sth to sb; **p. bonheur/malheur** to bring good/ bad luck; **p. son attention sur qch** to turn one's attention to sth; **tout (me) porte à croire que...** everything leads me to believe that...; **se faire p. malade** to report sick

2 *vi (voix)* to carry; *(coup)* to strike home; **p. sur** *(concerner)* to be about

3 se porter *vpr (vêtement)* to be worn;

se p. bien to be well; **comment te portes-tu?** how are you?; **se p. candidat** *Br* to stand *or Am* to run as a candidate ■ **porté, -e** *adj* **p. à croire** inclined to believe; **p. sur qch** fond of sth ■ **porte-bonheur** *nm inv* (lucky) charm ■ **porte-clefs** *nm inv* key ring ■ **porte-monnaie** *nm inv* purse ■ **porte-parole** *nmf inv* spokesperson **(de** for) ■ **porte-voix** *nm inv* megaphone

porteur, -euse [pɔrtœr, -øz] **1** *nm (de bagages)* porter **2** *nmf (malade)* carrier; *(de nouvelles, de chèque)* bearer

portier [pɔrtje] *nm* doorkeeper, porter ■ **portière** *nf (de véhicule, de train)* door ■ **portillon** *nm* gate

portion [pɔrsjɔ̃] *nf* portion

Porto Rico [pɔrtoriko] *nm ou f* Puerto Rico

portrait [pɔrtrɛ] *nm (peinture, dessin, photo)* portrait; *(description)* description; **faire le p. de qn** to do sb's portrait ■ **portrait-robot** *(pl* **portraits-robots)** *nm* identikit picture, Photofit®

Portugal [pɔrtygal] *nm* **le P.** Portugal ■ **portugais, -e 1** *adj* Portuguese **2** *nmf* **P., Portugaise** Portuguese *inv*; **les P.** the Portuguese **3** *nm (langue)* Portuguese

pose [poz] *nf* (a) *(de rideau, de papier peint)* putting up; *(de moquette)* laying (b) *(pour photo, portrait)* pose; *Phot* exposure; **prendre la p.** to pose

posé, -e [poze] *adj (calme)* composed, staid

poser [poze] **1** *vt* to put down; *(papier peint, rideaux)* to put up; *(mine, moquette, fondations)* to lay; *(bombe)* to plant; *(conditions, principe)* to lay down; **p. qch sur qch** to put sth on sth; **p. une question à qn** to ask sb a question; **p. sa candidature** *(à une élection)* to put oneself forward as a candidate; *(à un emploi)* to apply (**à** for)

2 *vi (modèle)* to pose (**pour** for)

3 se poser *vpr (oiseau, avion)* to land; *(problème, question)* to arise; **se p. sur** *(sujet; regard)* to rest on; **se p. des questions** to ask oneself questions

positif, -ive [pozitif, -iv] *adj* positive

position [pozisjɔ̃] *nf* position; *Fig* **prendre p.** to take a stand (**contre** against)

posséder [posede] *vt (biens, talent)* to possess; *(sujet)* to have a thorough knowledge of; *(langue)* to have mastered ▪ **possession** *nf* possession; **en p. de qch** in possession of sth; **prendre p. de qch** to take possession of sth

possibilité [posibilite] *nf* possibility; **avoir la p. de faire qch** to have the chance *or* opportunity of doing sth

possible [posibl] **1** *adj* possible (**à faire** to do); **il (nous) est p. de le faire** it is possible (for us) to do it; **il est p. que...** (+ *subjunctive*) it is possible that...; **si p.** if possible; **le plus tôt p.** as soon as possible; **autant que p.** as far as possible; **le plus p.** as much/as many as possible; **le moins de détails p.** as few details as possible **2** *nm* **faire (tout) son p.** to do one's utmost (**pour faire** to do)

postal, -e, -aux, -ales [postal, -o] *adj* postal; *(train)* mail

poste¹ [post] *nf (service)* mail, *Br* post; *(bureau)* post office; **la P.** the postal services; **par la p.** by mail, *Br* by post; **p. aérienne** airmail; **p. restante** *Br* poste restante, *Am* general delivery

poste² [post] *nm* (a) *(lieu, emploi)* post; **être à son p.** to be at one's post; **p. d'essence** *Br* petrol *or Am* gas station; **p. d'incendie** fire point; **p. de police** police station; **p. de secours** first-aid post (b) **p. (de radio/télévision)** radio/television set (c) *(de standard)* extension

poster¹ [poste] *vt (lettre)* to mail, *Br* to post

poster² [poste] **1** *vt (sentinelle, troupes)* to post, to station **2 se poster** *vpr* to take up a position

poster³ [postɛr] *nm* poster

postérieur, -e [posterjœr] *adj (dans le temps)* later; *(de derrière)* back; **p. à** after

postérité [posterite] *nf* posterity

postier, -ère [postje, -ɛr] *nmf* postal worker

postillonner [postijone] *vi* to splutter

postuler [postyle] **1** *vt Math* to postulate **2** *vi* **p. à** *ou* **pour un emploi** to apply for a job ▪ **postulant, -e** *nmf* applicant (**à** for)

posture [postyr] *nf* posture

pot [po] *nm* pot; *(en verre)* jar; *(de bébé)* potty; **p. d'échappement** *Br* exhaust pipe, *Am* tail pipe

potable [potabl] *adj* drinkable; **eau p.** drinking water

potage [potaʒ] *nm* soup

potager, -ère [potaʒe, -ɛr] **1** *adj* **jardin p.** vegetable garden; **plante potagère** vegetable **2** *nm* vegetable garden

pot-au-feu [potofø] *nm inv* = boiled beef with vegetables

pot-de-vin [podvɛ̃] (*pl* **pots-de-vin**) *nm* bribe

poteau, -x [poto] *nm* post; **p. électrique** electricity pylon; **p. indicateur** signpost; **p. télégraphique** telegraph pole

potelé, -e [potle] *adj* plump, chubby

potence [potɑ̃s] *nf (gibet)* gallows *(sing)*

potentiel, -elle [potɑ̃sjɛl] *adj & nm* potential

poterie [potri] *nf (art, objets)* pottery; *(objet)* piece of pottery ▪ **potier, -ère** *nmf* potter

potion [posjɔ̃] *nf* potion

potiron [potirɔ̃] *nm* pumpkin

pot-pourri [popuri] (*pl* **pots-pourris**) *nm (chansons)* medley

pou, -x [pu] *nm* louse (*pl* lice)

poubelle [pubɛl] *nf Br* dustbin, *Am* garbage can; **mettre qch à la p.** to throw sth out

pouce [pus] *nm (doigt)* thumb

poudre [pudr] *nf (poussière, explosif)* powder; **en p.** *(lait)* powdered; *(chocolat)* drinking; **p. à récurer** scouring powder ▪ **poudrer 1** *vt* to powder **2 se poudrer** *vpr* to powder one's face ▪ **poudreux, -euse 1** *adj* powdery **2** *nf* **poudreuse** *(neige)* powder snow

poulain [pulɛ̃] *nm* foal

poule¹ [pul] *nf (animal)* hen; *Culin* fowl

poule² [pul] *nf (groupe)* group

poulet [pulɛ] *nm (animal)* chicken

poulie [puli] *nf* pulley

pouls [pu] *nm Méd* pulse; **prendre le p. de qn** to take sb's pulse

poumon [pumɔ̃] *nm* lung; **à pleins poumons** *(respirer)* deeply

poupée [pupe] *nf* doll

POUR [pur] **1** *prép* for; **p. toi/moi** for you/me; **faites-le p. lui** do it for him, do it for his sake; **partir p. Paris/l'Italie** to leave for Paris/Italy; **elle part p. cinq ans** she's leaving for five years; **elle est p.** she's all for it, she's in favour of it; **p. faire qch** (in order) to do sth; **p. que tu le voies** so (that) you may see it; **p. quoi faire?** what for?; **assez grand p. faire qch** big enough to do sth; **p. affaires** on business; **p. cela** for that reason; **p. ma part** as for me; **jour p. jour/heure p. heure** to the day/hour; **dix p. cent** ten percent

2 *nm* **le p. et le contre** the pros and cons

pourboire [purbwar] *nm* tip

pourcentage [pursɑ̃taʒ] *nm* percentage

pourchasser [purʃase] *vt* to pursue

pourparlers [purparle] *nmpl* negotiations, talks

pourquoi [purkwa] **1** *adv & conj* why; **p. pas?** why not? **2** *nm inv* reason **(de** for); **le p. et le comment** the whys and wherefores

pourra, pourrait [pura, purɛ] *voir* **pouvoir 1**

pourrir [purir] *vti* to rot ■ **pourri, -e** *adj (fruit, temps)* rotten ■ **pourriture** *nf* rot

poursuite [pursɥit] **1** *nf (chasse)* pursuit; *(continuation)* continuation; **se lancer à la p. de qn** to set off in pursuit of sb **2** *nfpl Jur* **poursuites (judiciaires)** legal proceedings **(contre** against); **engager des poursuites contre qn** to start proceedings against sb

poursuivre* [pursɥivr] **1** *vt (chercher à atteindre)* to pursue; *(sujet: idée, crainte)* to haunt; *(sujet: malchance,* to dog; *(harceler)* to pester; *(continuer)* to continue, to go on with; *Jur* **p. qn (en justice)** to bring proceedings against sb; *(au criminel)* to prosecute sb **2 se poursuivre** *vpr* to continue, to go on

pourtant [purtɑ̃] *adv* yet, nevertheless; **et p.** and yet

pourtour [purtur] *nm* perimeter

pourvoir* [purvwar] **1** *vt* to provide **(de** with); **être pourvu de** to be provided with **2** *vi* **p. à** *(besoins)* to provide for **3 se pourvoir** *vpr Jur* **se p. en cassation** to take one's case to the Court of Appeal ■ **pourvoyeur, -euse** *nmf* supplier

pourvu [purvy] **pourvu que** *conj* **(a)** *(condition)* provided (that) **(b)** *(souhait)* **p. qu'elle soit là!** I just hope (that) she's there!

pousse [pus] *nf (croissance)* growth; *(bourgeon)* shoot, sprout

poussée [puse] *nf (pression)* pressure; *(coup)* push; *(d'ennemi)* thrust, push; *(de fièvre)* outbreak

pousser [puse] **1** *vt (presser)* to push; *(moteur)* to drive hard; **p. qn à qch** to drive sb to sth; **p. qn à faire qch** *(sujet: faim)* to drive sb to do sth; *(sujet: personne)* to urge sb to do sth; **p. un cri** to shout; **p. un soupir** to sigh

2 *vi (presser)* to push; *(croître)* to grow; **faire p. qch** *(plante)* to grow sth ■ **se laisser p. les cheveux** to let one's hair grow

3 se pousser *vpr (pour faire de la place)* to move over ■ **poussé, -e** *adj (études)* thorough

poussette [puset] *nf Br* pushchair, *Am* stroller

poussière [pusjɛr] *nf* dust; **une p.** a speck of dust ■ **poussiéreux, -euse** *adj* dusty

poussin [pusɛ̃] *nm (animal)* chick

poutre [putr] *nf (en bois)* beam; *(en acier)* girder

POUVOIR* [puvwar] **1** *v aux (être capable de)* can, to be able to; *(avoir la permission)* can, may, to be allowed; **tu peux entrer** you may *or* can come in

2 *v impersonnel* **il peut neiger** it may snow; **il se peut qu'elle parte** she might leave

3 *nm (puissance, attributions)* power; **au p.** *(parti)* in power; **p. d'achat** purchasing power; **les pouvoirs publics** the authorities

poux [pu] *pl de* **pou**

prairie [preri] *nf* meadow

praline [pralin] *nf* praline

pratique [pratik] **1** *adj (méthode, personne)* practical; *(outil)* handy **2** *nf (application, procédé, coutume)* practice; *(expérience)* practical experience; **la p. de la natation/du golf** swimming/golfing; **la p. d'une langue étrangère** foreign language practice; **mettre qch en p.** to put sth into practice; **dans la p.** *(en réalité)* in practice ▪ **pratiquement** *adv (presque)* practically; *(en réalité)* in practice

pratiquer [pratike] **1** *vt (religion) Br* to practise, *Am* to practice; *(activité)* to take part in; *(langue)* to use; *(sport)* to play; **p. la natation** to go swimming **2** *vi (médecin, avocat) Br* to practise, *Am* to practice ▪ **pratiquant, -e 1** *adj Br* practising, *Am* practicing **2** *nmf Br* practising *or Am* practicing Christian/Jew/Muslim/*etc*

pré [pre] *nm* meadow

préalable [prealabl] **1** *adj* prior, previous; **p. à** prior to **2** *nm* precondition, prerequisite; **au p.** beforehand

préavis [preavi] *nm* (advance) notice **(de** of); **p. de grève** strike notice; **p. de licenciement** notice of dismissal

précaire [preker] *adj* precarious; *(santé)* delicate ▪ **précarité** *nf* precariousness; **p. de l'emploi** lack of job security

précaution [prekosjɔ̃] *nf (mesure)* precaution; *(prudence)* caution; **par p.** as a precaution; **pour plus de p.** to be on the safe side; **prendre des précautions** to take precautions

précédent, -e [presedɑ̃, -ɑ̃t] **1** *adj* previous **2** *nmf* previous one **3** *nm* precedent; **sans p.** unprecedented ▪ **précéder** *vti* to precede

prêcher [preʃe] *vti* to preach

précieux, -euse [presjø, -øz] *adj* precious

précipice [presipis] *nm* chasm, abyss; *(de ravin)* precipice

précipiter [presipite] **1** *vt (hâter)* to hasten; *(jeter)* to hurl down **2 se précipiter** *vpr (se jeter)* to rush **(vers/sur** towards/at); *(se hâter)* to rush; **les événements se sont précipités** things started happening quickly ▪ **précipitamment** [-amɑ̃] *adv* hastily ▪ **précipitation** *nf* haste; **précipitations** *(pluie)* precipitation ▪ **précipité, -e** *adj* hasty

précis, -e [presi, -iz] **1** *adj* precise, exact; *(mécanisme)* accurate, precise; **à deux heures précises** at two o'clock sharp *or* precisely **2** *nm (résumé)* summary; *(manuel)* handbook ▪ **précision** *nf* precision; *(de mécanisme, d'information)* accuracy; *(détail)* detail; **donner des précisions sur qch** to give precise details about sth; **demander des précisions sur qch** to ask for further information about sth

préciser [presize] **1** *vt* to specify **(que** that) **2 se préciser** *vpr* to become clear(er)

précoce [prekɔs] *adj (fruit, été)* early; *(enfant)* precocious

préconiser [prekɔnize] *vt* to advocate **(que** that)

précurseur [prekyrsœr] **1** *nm* forerunner, precursor **2** *adj* **signe p.** forewarning

prédécesseur [predesesœr] *nm* predecessor

prédestiné, -e [predestine] *adj* predestined **(à faire** to do)

prédilection [predileksjɔ̃] *nf* predilection; **de p.** favourite

prédire* [predir] *vt* to predict **(que** that) ▪ **prédiction** *nf* prediction

prédisposer [predispoze] *vt* to predispose **(à qch** to sth; **à faire** to do) ▪ **prédisposition** *nf* predisposition **(à** to)

préfabriqué, -e [prefabrike] *adj* prefabricated

préface [prefas] *nf* preface **(de** to)

préfecture [prefɛktyr] *nf* prefecture; **la P. de police** police headquarters

préférable [preferabl] *adj* preferable (à to)

préférence [preferãs] *nf* preference (**pour** for); **de p.** preferably; **de p. à** in preference to ▪ **préférentiel, -elle** *adj* preferential

préférer [prefere] *vt* to prefer (à to); **p. faire qch** to prefer to do sth; **je préférerais rester** I would rather stay, I would prefer to stay ▪ **préféré, -e** *adj & nmf* favourite

préfet [prefɛ] *nm* prefect *(chief administrator in a 'département')*; **p. de police** = chief commissioner of police

préhistorique [preistɔrik] *adj* prehistoric

préjudice [preʒydis] *nm (à une cause)* prejudice; *(à une personne)* harm; **porter p. à qn** to do sb harm

préjugé [preʒyʒe] *nm* prejudice; **avoir des préjugés** to be prejudiced (**contre** against)

prélasser [prelase] ▪ **se prélasser** *vpr* to lounge

prélever [prel(ə)ve] *vt (échantillon)* to take (**sur** from); *(somme)* to deduct (**sur** from) ▪ **prélèvement** *nm (d'échantillon)* taking; *(de somme)* deduction; **p. automatique** *Br* direct debit, *Am* automatic deduction; **prélèvements obligatoires** = tax and social security contributions

préliminaire [preliminɛr] **1** *adj* preliminary **2** *nmpl* **préliminaires** preliminaries

prélude [prelyd] *nm* prelude (**à** to)

prématuré, -e [prematyre] **1** *adj* premature **2** *nmf* premature baby

préméditer [premedite] *vt* to premeditate ▪ **préméditation** *nf* premeditation; **meurtre avec p.** premeditated murder

premier, -ère [prəmje, -ɛr] **1** *adj* first; *(enfance)* early; *(page de journal)* front; *(qualité)* prime; *(état)* original; *(danseuse, rôle)* leading; *(marche)* bottom; **le p. rang** the front row; **les trois premiers mois** the first three months; **à la première occasion** at the earliest opportunity; **en p.** firstly; **P. ministre** Prime Minister

2 *nm (étage) Br* first or *Am* second floor; **le p. juin** June the first; **le p. de l'an** New Year's Day

3 *nmf* first (one); **arriver le p.** *ou* **en p.** to arrive first

4 *nf* **première** *(wagon, billet)* first class; *(vitesse)* first (gear); *(événement historique)* first; *(de chaussure)* insole; *Théât* opening night; *Cin* première; *Scol Br* ≃ lower sixth, *Am* ≃ eleventh grade

prémonition [premɔnisjɔ̃] *nf* premonition

prénatal, -e, -als, -ales [prenatal] *adj Br* antenatal, *Am* prenatal

PRENDRE* [prãdr] **1** *vt* to take (**à qn** from sb); *(attraper)* to catch; *(repas, boisson, douche)* to have; *(nouvelles)* to get; *(air)* to put on; *(bonne)* to take on; **p. qch dans un tiroir** to take sth out of a drawer; **p. qn pour** to take sb for; **p. feu** to catch fire; **p. du temps/une heure** to take time/an hour; **p. de la place** to take up room; **p. du poids/de la vitesse** to put on weight/gather speed; **p. l'eau** *(bateau, chaussure)* to be leaking

2 *vi (feu)* to catch; *(ciment, gelée)* to set; *(greffe, vaccin, plante)* to take; *(mode)* to catch on; **p. sur soi** to restrain oneself

3 **se prendre** *vpr (médicament)* to be taken; *(s'accrocher)* to get caught; **se p. les pieds dans qch** to get one's feet caught in sth; **s'y p. bien avec qn** to know how to handle sb; **s'en p. à qn** to take it out on sb

prénom [prenɔ̃] *nm* first name ▪ **prénommer** *vt* to name; **il se prénomme Daniel** his first name is Daniel

préoccuper [preɔkype] **1** *vt (inquiéter)* to worry **2** **se préoccuper** *vpr* **se p. de qn/qch** to concern oneself with sb/sth ▪ **préoccupant, -e** *adj* worrying ▪ **préoccupation** *nf* preoccupation, concern ▪ **préoccupé, -e** *adj* worried (**par** about)

préparatifs [preparatif] *nmpl* preparations (**de** for) ▪ **préparation** *nf* preparation ▪ **préparatoire** *adj* preparatory

préparer [prepare] **1** *vt* to prepare (**qch pour** sth for); *(examen)* to study for; **p. qch à qn** to prepare sth for sb; **plats tout préparés** ready-cooked meals

2 se préparer *vpr (être imminent)* to be in the offing; *(s'apprêter)* to prepare oneself (**à** *ou* **pour qch** for sth); **se p. à faire qch** to prepare to do sth; **se p. qch** *(boisson)* to make oneself sth

préposé, -e [prepoze] *nmf* employee; *(facteur)* postman, *f* postwoman

préretraite [prerətrɛt] *nf* early retirement

près [prɛ] *adv* **p. de qn/qch** near sb/sth, close to sb/sth; **p. de deux ans** nearly two years; **p. de partir** about to leave; **tout p.** nearby (**de qn/qch** sb/sth), close by (**de qn/qch** sb/sth); **de p.** *(suivre, examiner)* closely; **à peu de chose p.** more or less; **à cela p.** except for that; **voici le chiffre à un euro p.** here is the figure, give or take a euro; **calculer au euro p.** to calculate to the nearest euro

présage [prezaʒ] *nm* omen, sign ■ **présager** *vt* **ça ne présage rien de bon** it doesn't bode well

presbyte [presbit] *adj* long-sighted

presbytère [presbiter] *nm* presbytery

prescrire* [preskrir] *vt (médicament)* to prescribe ■ **prescription** *nf (ordonnance)* prescription

présence [prezɑ̃s] *nf* presence; *(à l'école)* attendance (**à** at); **en p. de** in the presence of; **faire acte de p.** to put in an appearance; **p. d'esprit** presence of mind

présent, -e [prezɑ̃, -ɑ̃t] **1** *adj (non absent, actuel)* present **2** *nm (temps)* present; **à p.** at present, now; **dès à p.** as from now

présenter [prezɑ̃te] **1** *vt (montrer)* to show, to present; *(facture)* to submit; *(arguments)* to present; **p. qn à qn** to introduce sb to sb

2 se présenter *vpr (dire son nom)* to introduce oneself (**à** to); *(chez qn)* to show up; *(occasion)* to arise; **se p. à** *(examen)* to take, *Br* to sit for; *(élections)* to run in; *(emploi)* to apply for; *(autorités)* to report to; **ça se présente**

bien it looks promising ■ **présentable** *adj* presentable ■ **présentateur, -trice** *nmf* presenter ■ **présentation** *nf* presentation; *(de personnes)* introduction; **faire les présentations** to make the introductions; **p. de mode** fashion show

préserver [prezɛrve] *vt* to protect, to preserve (**de** from) ■ **préservation** *nf* protection, preservation

présidence [prezidɑ̃s] *nf (de nation)* presidency; *(de firme)* chairmanship ■ **président, -e** *nmf (de nation)* president; *(de firme)* chairman, *f* chairwoman; **p.-directeur général** *Br* (chairman and) managing director, *Am* chief executive officer; **p. du jury** *(d'examen)* chief examiner; *(de tribunal)* foreman of the jury ■ **présidentiel, -elle** *adj* presidential

présider [prezide] *vt (réunion)* to chair; *(conseil)* to preside over

presque [prɛsk] *adv* almost, nearly; **p. jamais/rien** hardly ever/anything

presqu'île [prɛskil] *nf* peninsula

pressant, -e [prɛsɑ̃, -ɑ̃t] *adj* urgent, pressing

presse [prɛs] *nf Tech* press; *Typ* (printing) press; **la p.** *(journaux)* the press; **la p. à sensation** the popular press, *Br* the tabloids

pressé, -e [prese] *adj (personne)* in a hurry; *(air)* hurried

pressentir* [presɑ̃tir] *vt (deviner)* to sense (**que** that) ■ **pressentiment** *nm* presentiment; *(de malheur)* foreboding

pressing [presiŋ] *nm* dry cleaner's

pression [presjɔ̃] *nf Tech* pressure; *(bouton)* snap (fastener); **faire p. sur qn** to put pressure on sb, to pressurize sb

pressuriser [presyrize] *vt (avion)* to pressurize

prestataire [prestater] *nmf Ordinat* **p. d'accès** access provider

prestation [prestasjɔ̃] *nf* **(a)** *(allocation)* benefit; **prestations** *(services)* services; **prestations sociales** *Br* social security benefits, *Am* welfare payments **(b)** *(de comédien)* performance

prestidigitateur, -trice [prɛstidiʒi-tatœr, -tris] *nmf* conjurer ▪ **prestidigitation** *nf* tour de p. conjuring trick

prestige [prɛstiʒ] *nm* prestige ▪ **prestigieux, -euse** *adj* prestigious

présumer [prezyme] *vt* to presume (**que** that); **p. de qch** to overestimate sth

prêt¹, -e [prɛ, prɛt] *adj (préparé)* ready (**à faire** to do; **à qch** for sth); **être fin p.** to be all set ▪ **prêt-à-porter** *nm* ready-to-wear clothes

prêt² [prɛ] *nm (somme)* loan; **p. immobilier** home loan, ≃ mortgage

prétendre [pretɑ̃dr] **1** *vt (déclarer)* to claim (**que** that); *(vouloir)* to intend (**faire** to do); **à ce qu'il prétend** according to him **2** *vi* **p. à** *(titre)* to lay claim to **3 se prétendre** *vpr* to claim to be ▪ **prétendu, -e** *adj (progrès)* so-called; *(coupable)* alleged

prétentieux, -euse [pretɑ̃sjø, -øz] *adj* pretentious ▪ **prétention** *nf (vanité)* pretension; *(revendication, ambition)* claim; **sans p.** *(film, robe)* unpretentious

prêter [prete] **1** *vt (argent, objet)* to lend (**à** to); *(aide)* to give (**à** to); *(propos, intention)* to attribute (**à** to); **p. attention** to pay attention (**à** to); **p. serment** to take an oath; **p. main-forte à qn** to lend sb a hand **2** *vi* **p. à confusion** to give rise to confusion **3 se prêter** *vpr* **se p. à** *(consentir)* to agree to; *(convenir)* to lend itself to

prétexte [pretɛkst] *nm* excuse, pretext; **sous p. de/que** on the pretext of/that; **sous aucun p.** under no circumstances ▪ **prétexter** *vt* to plead (**que** that)

prêtre [prɛtr] *nm* priest

preuve [prœv] *nf* piece of evidence; **preuves** evidence; **faire p. de qch** to prove sth; **faire p. de courage** to show courage; **faire ses preuves** *(personne)* to prove oneself; *(méthode)* to be tried and tested

prévaloir* [prevalwar] *vi* to prevail (**sur** over)

prévenant, -e [prevnɑ̃, -ɑ̃t] *adj* considerate

prévenir* [prevnir] *vt* (**a**) *(mettre en garde)* to warn; *(aviser)* to inform (**de** of *or* about) (**b**) *(maladie)* to prevent; *(accident)* to avert ▪ **préventif, -ive** *adj* preventive ▪ **prévention** *nf* prevention; **p. routière** road safety

prévisible [previzibl] *adj* foreseeable

prévision [previzjɔ̃] *nf* forecast; **en p. de** in expectation of; **prévisions météorologiques** weather forecast

prévoir* [prevwar] *vt (météo)* to forecast; *(difficultés, retard, réaction)* to expect; *(organiser)* to plan; **la réunion est prévue pour demain** the meeting is scheduled for tomorrow; **comme prévu** as planned; **plus tôt que prévu** earlier than expected; **prévu pour** *(véhicule, appareil)* designed for

prévoyant, -e [prevwajɑ̃, -ɑ̃t] *adj* far-sighted ▪ **prévoyance** *nf* foresight

prier [prije] **1** *vi Rel* to pray **2** *vt (Dieu)* to pray to; *(supplier)* to beg; **p. qn de faire qch** to ask sb to do sth; **je vous en prie** *(faites-le)* please; *(en réponse à 'merci')* don't mention it

prière [prijer] *nf Rel* prayer; *(demande)* request

primaire [primer] **1** *adj* primary; **école p.** *Br* primary school, *Am* elementary school **2** *nm Scol Br* primary *or Am* elementary education; **entrer en p.** to be at *Br* primary *or Am* elementary school

prime [prim] **1** *nf (sur salaire)* bonus; *(d'État)* subsidy; **en p.** *(cadeau)* as a free gift; **p. (d'assurance)** *(insurance)* premium; **p. de fin d'année** ≃ Christmas bonus; **p. de licenciement** severance allowance; **p. de transport** transport allowance **2** *adj* **de p. abord** at the very first glance

primé, -e [prime] *adj (film, animal)* prizewinning

primer [prime] *vi* to come first; **p. sur qch** to take precedence over sth

primitif, -ive [primitif, -iv] *adj (société, art)* primitive; *(état, sens)* original

primordial, -e, -aux, -ales [primɔrdjal, -jo] *adj* vital (**de faire** to do)

prince [prɛ̃s] *nm* prince ▪ **princesse** *nf* princess ▪ **princier, -ère** *adj* princely ▪ **principauté** *nf* principality

principal, -e, -aux, -ales [prɛ̃sipal, -o] **1** *adj* main, principal; *(rôle)* leading **2** *nm.(de collège)* principal, *Br* headmaster, *f* headmistress; **le p.** *(l'essentiel)* the main thing

principe [prɛ̃sip] *nm* principle; **en p.** theoretically, in principle; **par p.** on principle

printemps [prɛ̃tɑ̃] *nm* spring; **au p.** in the spring

priorité [priorite] *nf* priority (**sur** over); *Aut* right of way; *Aut* **avoir la p.** to have (the) right of way; *Aut* **p. à droite** right of way to traffic coming from the right; **'cédez la p.'** *Br* 'give way', *Am* 'yield'; **en p.** as a matter of priority ▪ **prioritaire** *adj* **secteur p.** priority sector; **être p.** to have priority; *Aut* to have (the) right of way

pris, -e[1] [pri, priz] **1** *pp de* **prendre 2** *adj (place)* taken; **avoir le nez p.** to have a blocked nose; **être p.** *(occupé)* to be busy; *(candidat)* to be accepted; **p. de** *(peur)* seized with; **p. de panique** panic-stricken

prise[2] [priz] *nf (action)* taking; *(objet saisi)* catch; *(manière d'empoigner)* grip; *(de judo)* hold; *(de tabac)* pinch; **lâcher p.** to lose one's grip; **p. de sang** blood test; *Él* **p. (de courant)** *(mâle)* plug; *(femelle)* socket; *Él* **p. multiple** adaptor; **p. d'otages** hostage-taking

prison [prizɔ̃] *nf* prison, jail; *(peine)* imprisonment; **mettre qn en p.** to put sb in prison, to jail sb ▪ **prisonnier, -ère** *nmf* prisoner; **faire qn p.** to take sb prisoner; **p. de guerre** prisoner of war

privation [privasjɔ̃] *nf* deprivation (**de** of); **privations** *(manque)* hardship

privatiser [privatize] *vt* to privatize ▪ **privatisation** *nf* privatization

privé, -e [prive] **1** *adj* private **2** *nm* **le p.** the private sector; *Scol* the private education system; **en p.** in private; **dans le p.** privately; *(travailler)* in the private sector

priver [prive] **1** *vt* to deprive (**de** of) **2** **se priver** *vpr* **se p. de** to do without, to deprive oneself of

privilège [privilɛʒ] *nm* privilege ▪ **privilégié, -e** *adj* privileged

prix [pri] *nm (coût)* price; *(récompense)* prize; **à tout p.** at all costs; **hors de p.** exorbitant; **attacher du p. à qch** to attach importance to sth

probable [prɔbabl] *adj* likely, probable; **peu p.** unlikely ▪ **probabilité** *nf* probability, likelihood; **selon toute p.** in all probability

probant, -e [prɔbɑ̃, -ɑ̃t] *adj* conclusive

probité [prɔbite] *nf* integrity

problème [prɔblɛm] *nm* problem; **p. alimentaire** eating disorder; **p. de santé** health problem ▪ **problématique** *adj* problematic

procédé [prɔsede] *nm (technique)* process; *(méthode)* method

procéder [prɔsede] *vi (agir)* to proceed; **p. à** *(enquête, arrestation)* to carry out; **p. par élimination** to follow a process of elimination ▪ **procédure** *nf (méthode)* procedure; *(règles juridiques)* procedure; *(procès)* proceedings

procès [prɔsɛ] *nm (criminel)* trial; *(civil)* lawsuit; **faire un p. à qn** to take sb to court

procession [prɔsesjɔ̃] *nf* procession

processus [prɔsesys] *nm* process

procès-verbal [prɔsɛverbal] *(pl* **procès-verbaux** [-o]) *nm (amende)* fine

prochain, -e [prɔʃɛ̃, -ɛn] *adj* next; *(mort, arrivée)* impending ▪ **prochainement** *adv* shortly, soon

proche [prɔʃ] *adj (dans l'espace)* near, close; *(dans le temps)* near, imminent; *(parent, ami)* close; **p. de** near (to), close to; **de p. en p.** step by step; **le P.-Orient** the Middle East ▪ **proches** *nmpl* close relations

proclamer [prɔklame] *vt* to proclaim (**que** that) ▪ **proclamation** *nf* proclamation

procréer [prɔkree] *vi* to procreate ▪ **procréation** *nf* procreation; **p. médicalement assistée** assisted conception

procuration [prɔkyrasjɔ̃] *nf* power of attorney; **par p.** by proxy

procurer [prɔkyre] **1** *vt* **p. qch à qn** *(sujet: personne)* to get sth for sb; *(sujet: chose)* to bring sb sth **2 se procurer** *vpr* **se p. qch** to obtain sth

prodige [prɔdiʒ] *nm (miracle)* wonder; *(personne)* prodigy; **tenir du p.** to be extraordinary ■ **prodigieux, -euse** *adj* prodigious

prodiguer [prɔdige] *vt* **p. qch à qn** to lavish sth on sb; **p. des conseils à qn** to pour out advice to sb

production [prɔdyksjɔ̃] *nf* production; *(produit)* product; *(d'usine)* output ■ **producteur, -trice 1** *nmf* producer **2** *adj* producing; **pays p. de pétrole** oil-producing country ■ **productif, -ive** *adj* productive ■ **productivité** *nf* productivity

produire* [prɔdɥir] **1** *vt (marchandise, émission, gaz)* to produce; *(effet, résultat)* to produce, to bring about **2 se produire** *vpr (événement)* to happen, to occur; *(acteur)* to perform ■ **produit** *nm (article)* product; *(de vente, de collecte)* proceeds; **p. de beauté** cosmetic; **p. chimique** chemical; **produits frais** fresh produce; **produits ménagers** cleaning products

profane [prɔfan] **1** *adj* secular **2** *nmf* lay person

profaner [prɔfane] *vt* to desecrate

proférer [prɔfere] *vt* to utter

professer [prɔfese] *vt* to profess (**que** that)

professeur [prɔfesœr] *nm* teacher; *(à l'université)* professor; **p. principal** *Br* class *or* form teacher, *Am* homeroom teacher

profession [prɔfesjɔ̃] *nf* occupation, profession; *(manuelle)* trade; **sans p.** not gainfully employed; **p. libérale** profession ■ **professionnel, -elle 1** *adj* professional; *(enseignement)* vocational **2** *nmf* professional

profil [prɔfil] *nm* profile; **de p.** (viewed) from the side ■ **se profiler** *vpr* to be outlined (**sur** against)

profit [prɔfi] *nm* profit; **tirer p. de qch** to benefit from sth; **mettre qch à p.** to put sth to good use ■ **profitable** *adj* profitable (**à** to) ■ **profiter** *vi* **p. de** to take advantage of; **p. de la vie** to make the most of life; **p. à qn** to benefit sb, to be of benefit to sb

profond, -e [prɔfɔ̃, -ɔ̃d] **1** *adj* deep; *(joie, erreur)* profound; *(cause,* underlying; **p. de 2 mètres** 2 metres deep **2** *adv* deep ■ **profondément** *adv* deeply; *(dormir)* soundly; *(triste, ému)* profoundly; *(creuser)* deep ■ **profondeur** *nf* depth; **faire 6 mètres de p.** to be 6 metres deep; **à 6 mètres de p.** at a depth of 6 metres

profusion [prɔfyzjɔ̃] *nf* profusion; **à p.** in profusion

programmable [prɔgramabl] *adj* programmable ■ **programmation** *nf Radio & TV* programme planning; *Ordinat* programming

programmateur [prɔgramatœr] *nm Tech* automatic control (device)

programme [prɔgram] *nm Br* programme, *Am* program; *(de parti politique)* manifesto; *Scol* curriculum; *(d'un cours)* syllabus; *Ordinat* program ■ **programmer** *vt Ordinat* to program; *Radio, TV & Cin* to schedule ■ **programmeur, -euse** *nmf (computer)* programmer

progrès [prɔgrɛ] *nm & nmpl* progress; **faire des p.** to make (good) progress ■ **progresser** *vi* to progress ■ **progressif, -ive** *adj* progressive ■ **progression** *nf* progression ■ **progressiste** *adj & nmf* progressive ■ **progressivement** *adv* progressively

prohiber [prɔibe] *vt* to prohibit, to forbid ■ **prohibitif, -ive** *adj* prohibitive ■ **prohibition** *nf* prohibition

proie [prwa] *nf* prey; **être la p. des flammes** to be consumed by fire

projecteur [prɔʒektœr] *nm (de monument, de stade)* floodlight; *(de prison, d'armée)* searchlight; *Théât* spotlight; *Cin* projector

projectile [prɔʒektil] *nm* missile

projection [prɔʒeksjɔ̃] *nf (d'objet, de film)* projection; *(séance)* screening

projet [prɔʒɛ] *nm (intention)* plan; *(étude)* project; **faire des projets d'avenir** to make plans for the future; **p. de loi** bill

projeter [prɔʒte] *vt (lancer)* to project; *(liquide, boue)* to splash; *(lumière)* to flash; *(film)* to show; *(ombre)* to cast; *(prévoir)* to plan; **p. de faire qch** to plan to do sth

proliférer [prɔlifere] *vi* to proliferate ▪ **prolifération** *nf* proliferation

prolonger [prɔlɔ̃ʒe] **1** *vt (vie, débat, séjour)* to prolong; *(mur, route)* to extend **2 se prolonger** *vpr (séjour)* to be prolonged; *(réunion)* to go on; *(rue)* to continue ▪ **prolongation** *nf (de séjour)* extension; **prolongations** *(au football)* extra time ▪ **prolongement** *nm (de rue)* continuation; *(de mur)* extension; **prolongements** *(d'affaires)* repercussions

promenade [prɔmənad] *nf (à pied)* walk; *(courte)* stroll; *(avenue)* promenade; **faire une p.** to go for a walk; **faire une p. à cheval** to go for a ride

promener [prɔmne] **1** *vt (personne, chien)* to take for a walk; *(visiteur)* to show around; **p. qch sur qch** *(main, regard)* to run sth over sth **2 se promener** *vpr (à pied)* to go for a walk ▪ **promeneur, -euse** *nmf* stroller, walker

promesse [prɔmɛs] *nf* promise; **tenir sa p.** to keep one's promise

promettre* [prɔmɛtr] **1** *vt* to promise (**qch à qn** sb sth; **que** that); **p. de faire qch** to promise to do sth; **c'est promis** it's a promise **2** *vi Fig* to be promising **3 se promettre** *vpr* **se p. qch** *(à soi-même)* to promise oneself sth; *(l'un l'autre)* to promise each other sth ▪ **prometteur, -euse** *adj* promising

promoteur [prɔmɔtœr] *nm* **p. (immobilier)** property developer

promotion [prɔmosjɔ̃] *nf* **(a)** *(avancement)* & *Com* promotion; **en p.** *(produit)* on (special) offer; **p. sociale** upward mobility **(b)** *(d'une école) Br* year, *Am* class ▪ **promouvoir*** *vt (personne, produit)* to promote; **être promu** *(employé)* to be promoted (**à** to)

prompt, -e [prɔ̃, prɔ̃t] *adj* prompt; **p. à faire qch** quick to do sth

promulguer [prɔmylge] *vt* to promulgate

prononcer [prɔnɔ̃se] **1** *vt (articuler)* to pronounce; *(dire)* to utter; *(discours)* to deliver; *(jugement)* to pronounce **2 se prononcer** *vpr (mot)* to be pronounced; *(personne)* to give one's opinion (**sur** about *or* on); **se p. pour/contre qch** to come out in favour of/against sth ▪ **prononcé, -e** *adj* pronounced, marked ▪ **prononciation** *nf* pronunciation

pronostic [prɔnɔstik] *nm* forecast; *Méd* prognosis ▪ **pronostiquer** *vt* to forecast

propagande [prɔpagɑ̃d] *nf* propaganda

propager [prɔpaʒe] *vt,* **se propager** *vpr* to spread ▪ **propagation** *nf* spreading

prophète [prɔfɛt] *nm* prophet ▪ **prophétie** [-fesi] *nf* prophecy ▪ **prophétique** *adj* prophetic

propice [prɔpis] *adj* favourable (**à** to); **le moment p.** the right moment

proportion [prɔpɔrsjɔ̃] *nf* proportion; **en p. de** in proportion to; **hors de p.** out of proportion (**avec** to) ▪ **proportionné, -e** *adj* proportionate (**à** to); **bien p.** well-proportioned ▪ **proportionnel, -elle 1** *adj* proportional (**à** to) **2** *nf* **proportionnelle** *(scrutin)* proportional representation

propos [prɔpo] *nm (sujet)* subject; *(intention)* purpose; **des p.** *(paroles)* talk, words; **à p. de qn/qch** about sb/sth; **à p.** *(arriver)* at the right time; **à p.** by the way

proposer [prɔpoze] **1** *vt (suggérer)* to suggest, to propose (**qch à qn** sth to sb; **que** + *subjunctive* that); *(offrir)* to offer (**qch à qn** sb sth; **de faire** to do); **je te propose de rester** I suggest (that) you stay **2 se proposer** *vpr* to offer one's services; **se p. pour faire qch** to offer to do sth; **se p. de faire qch** to propose to do sth ▪ **proposition** *nf* suggestion, proposal; *(offre)* offer; **faire une p. à qn** to make a suggestion to sb

propre¹ [prɔpr] **1** *adj* clean; *(soigné)*

neat; **p. comme un sou neuf** spick and span 2 *nm* **mettre qch au p.** to make a fair copy of sth ▪ **proprement** [-əmɑ̃] *adv (avec propreté)* cleanly; *(avec soin)* neatly ▪ **propreté** [-əte] *nf* cleanliness; *(soin)* neatness

propre² [prɔpr] 1 *adj (à soi)* own; **mon p. argent** my own money; **être p. à qn/qch** *(particulier)* to be characteristic of sb/sth; **au sens p.** literally 2 *nm* **le p. de** *(qualité)* the distinctive quality of; **au p.** *(au sens propre)* literally ▪ **proprement** [-əmɑ̃] *adv (strictement)* strictly; **à p. parler** strictly speaking; **le village p. dit** the village proper

propriétaire [prɔprijetɛr] *nmf* owner; *(de location)* landlord, *f* landlady; **p. foncier** landowner

propriété [prɔprijete] *nf (fait de posséder)* ownership; *(chose possédée)* property; *(caractéristique)* property; **p. privée** private property

propulser [prɔpylse] *vt* to propel

proscrire* [prɔskrir] *vt* to proscribe, to ban

prospecter [prɔspɛkte] *vt (sol)* to prospect; *(clients)* to canvass

prospectus [prɔspɛktys] *nm* leaflet

prospère [prɔspɛr] *adj* prosperous; *(santé)* glowing ▪ **prospérer** *vi* to prosper ▪ **prospérité** *nf* prosperity

prosterner [prɔstɛrne] **se prosterner** *vpr* to prostrate oneself **(devant** before)

prostituée [prɔstitɥe] *nf* prostitute ▪ **prostitution** *nf* prostitution

protecteur, -trice [prɔtɛktœr, -tris] 1 *nmf* protector; *(mécène)* patron 2 *adj (geste, crème)* protective ▪ **protection** *nf* protection; **de p.** *(écran)* protective; **assurer la p. de qn** to ensure sb's safety ▪ **protectionnisme** *nm Écon* protectionism

protéger [prɔteʒe] 1 *vt* to protect **(de** from; **contre** against) 2 **se protéger** *vpr* to protect oneself ▪ **protégé** *nm* protégé ▪ **protégée** *nf* protégée

protéine [prɔtein] *nf* protein

protestant, -e [prɔtɛstɑ̃, -ɑ̃t] *adj & nmf* Protestant

protester [prɔtɛste] *vi* to protest **(con-** tre against); **p. de son innocence** to protest one's innocence ▪ **protestataire** *nmf* protester ▪ **protestation** *nf* protest **(contre** against); **en signe de p.** as a protest

prothèse [prɔtɛz] *nf* prosthesis; **p. auditive** hearing aid; **p. dentaire** false teeth

protide [prɔtid] *nm* protein

protocole [prɔtɔkɔl] *nm* protocol

prototype [prɔtɔtip] *nm* prototype

prouesse [prɥɛs] *nf* feat

prouver [prɥve] *vt* to prove **(que** that)

Provence [prɔvɑ̃s] *nf* **la P.** Provence ▪ **provençal, -e, -aux, -ales** 1 *adj* Provençal 2 *nmf* **P., Provençale** Provençal

provenir* [prɔvənir] *vi* **p. de** to come from ▪ **provenance** *nf* origin; **en p. de** from

proverbe [prɔvɛrb] *nm* proverb

providence [prɔvidɑ̃s] *nf* providence ▪ **providentiel, -elle** *adj* providential

province [prɔvɛ̃s] *nf* province; **la p.** the provinces; **en p.** in the provinces; **de p.** *(ville)* provincial ▪ **provincial, -e, -aux, -ales** *adj & nmf* provincial

proviseur [prɔvizœr] *nm Br* headmaster, *f* headmistress, *Am* principal

provision [prɔvizjɔ̃] *nf* (a) *(réserve)* supply, stock; **provisions** *(nourriture)* shopping; **sac à provisions** shopping bag; **faire des provisions de qch** to stock up on sth (b) *(somme)* credit; *(acompte)* deposit

provisoire [prɔvizwar] *adj* temporary; **à titre p.** temporarily

provoquer [prɔvɔke] *vt (incendie, mort)* to cause; *(réaction)* to provoke; *(colère, désir)* to arouse ▪ **provocant, -e** *adj* provocative ▪ **provocateur** *nm* troublemaker ▪ **provocation** *nf* provocation

proximité [prɔksimite] *nf* closeness, proximity; **à p.** close by; **à p. de** close to; **de p.** local

prude [pryd] 1 *adj* prudish 2 *nf* prude

prudent, -e [prydɑ̃, -ɑ̃t] *adj (personne)* cautious, careful; *(décision)* sensible ▪ **prudence** *nf* caution, care; **par p.** as a precaution

prune [pryn] *nf (fruit)* plum ■ **prunier** *nm* plum tree

pruneau, -x [pryno] *nm* prune

pseudonyme [psødɔnim] *nm* pseudonym

psychanalyse [psikanaliz] *nf* psychoanalysis ■ **psychanalyste** *nmf* psychoanalyst

psychiatre [psikjatr] *nmf* psychiatrist ■ **psychiatrie** *nf* psychiatry ■ **psychiatrique** *adj* psychiatric

psychique [psiʃik] *adj* psychic

psychologie [psikɔlɔʒi] *nf* psychology ■ **psychologique** *adj* psychological ■ **psychologue** *nmf* psychologist

psychose [psikoz] *nf* psychosis

pu [py] *pp de* **pouvoir 1**

puant, -e [pɥɑ̃, pɥɑ̃t] *adj* stinking ■ **puanteur** *nf* stink, stench

pub [pyb] *nf Fam (secteur)* advertising; *(annonce)* ad

public, -ique [pyblik] **1** *adj* public; **dette publique** national debt **2** *nm (de spectacle)* audience; **le grand p.** the general public; **film grand p.** film suitable for the general public; **en p.** in public; *(émission)* before a live audience

publication [pyblikɑsjɔ̃] *nf (action, livre)* publication ■ **publier** *vt* to publish

publicité [pyblisite] *nf (secteur)* advertising; *(annonce)* advertisement, advert; *Radio & TV* commercial; **agence de p.** advertising agency; **faire de la p. pour qch** to advertise sth ■ **publicitaire 1** *adj* **film p.** promotional film **2** *nmf* advertising executive

puce [pys] *nf (insecte)* flea; *Ordinat* (micro-)chip; **le marché aux puces, les puces** the flea market

pudeur [pydœr] *nf* modesty; **par p.** out of a sense of decency ■ **pudibond, -e** *adj* prudish ■ **pudique** *adj* modest

puer [pɥe] **1** *vt* to stink of **2** *vi* to stink

puériculture [pɥerikyltyr] *nf* child care ■ **puéricultrice** *nf* nursery nurse

puéril, -e [pɥeril] *adj* puerile ■ **puérilité** *nf* puerility

puis [pɥi] *adv* then; **et p.** *(ensuite)* and then; *(en plus)* and besides

puiser [pɥize] **1** *vt* to draw **(à/dans** from) **2** *vi* **p. dans qch** to dip into sth

puisque [pɥisk(ə)] *conj* since, as

puissant, -e [pɥisɑ̃, -ɑ̃t] *adj* powerful ■ **puissance** *nf (force, nation) & Math* power; **en p.** *(meurtrier)* potential; *Math* **dix p. quatre** ten to the power of four

puisse(s), puissent [pɥis] *voir* **pouvoir 1**

puits [pɥi] *nm* well; *(de mine)* shaft; **p. de pétrole** oil well

pull-over [pylɔver] *(pl* pull-overs), **pull** [pyl] *nm* sweater, *Br* jumper

pulluler [pylyle] *vi (abonder)* to swarm

pulmonaire [pylmɔnɛr] *adj* pulmonary

pulpe [pylp] *nf (de fruits)* pulp

pulvériser [pylverize] *vt (vaporiser)* to spray; *(broyer)* to pulverize ■ **pulvérisateur** *nm* spray

punaise [pynɛz] *nf (insecte)* bug; *(clou) Br* drawing pin, *Am* thumbtack

punir [pynir] *vt* to punish; **p. qn de qch** *(bêtise, crime)* to punish sb for sth ■ **punition** *nf* punishment

pupille [pypij] **1** *nf (de l'œil)* pupil **2** *nmf (enfant)* ward

pupitre [pypitr] *nm (d'écolier)* desk; *(d'orateur)* lectern

pur, -e [pyr] *adj* pure; *(alcool)* neat, straight ■ **pureté** *nf* purity

purée [pyre] *nf* purée; **p. (de pommes de terre)** mashed potatoes, *Br* mash

purge [pyrʒ] *nf (à des fins médicales, politiques)* purge

purger [pyrʒe] *vt (patient)* to purge; *(radiateur)* to bleed; *(peine de prison)* to serve

purifier [pyrifje] *vt* to purify ■ **purification** *nf* purification; **p. ethnique** ethnic cleansing

puriste [pyrist] *nmf* purist

puritain, -e [pyritɛ̃, -ɛn] *adj & nmf* puritan

pur-sang [pyrsɑ̃] *nm inv* thorough-bred

pus¹ [py] *nm (liquide)* pus, matter

pus², **put** [py] *voir* **pouvoir 1**

putréfier [pytrefje] *vt*, **se putréfier** *vpr* to putrefy

puzzle [pœzl] *nm* (jigsaw) puzzle

pyjama [piʒama] *nm Br* pyjamas, *Am* pajamas; **un p.** a pair of *Br* pyjamas *or Am* pajamas

pyramide [piramid] *nf* pyramid

Pyrénées [pirene] *nfpl* **les P.** the Pyrenees

Pyrex® [pireks] *nm* Pyrex®; **plat en P.** Pyrex® dish

pyromane [pirɔman] *nmf* arsonist

Qq

Q, q [ky] *nm inv* Q, q

qu' [k] *voir* que

quadrillage [kadrijaʒ] *nm (de carte)* grid

quadriller [kadrije] *vt (quartier, ville)* to put under tight surveillance; *(papier)* to mark into squares ■ **quadrillé, -e** *adj (papier)* squared

quadrupède [k(w)adrypɛd] *adj & nm* quadruped

quadruple [k(w)adrypl] **1** *adj* fourfold **2** *nm* le q. (de) *(quantité)* four times as much (as); *(nombre)* four times as many (as) ■ **quadrupler** *vti* to quadruple ■ **quadruplés, -es** *nmfpl* quadruplets

quai [kɛ] *nm (de port)* quay; *(de fleuve)* embankment; *(de gare, de métro)* platform

qualification [kalifikasjɔ̃] *nf (action, d'équipe, de sportif)* qualification; *(désignation)* description

qualifier [kalifje] **1** *vt (équipe)* to qualify (**pour qch** for sth); **pour faire** to do); *(décrire)* to describe (**de** as) **2 se qualifier** *vpr (équipe)* to qualify (**pour** for) ■ **qualifié, -e** *adj (équipe)* that has qualified; **q. pour faire qch** qualified to do sth

qualité [kalite] *nf (de personne, de produit)* quality; *(occupation)* occupation; **produit de q.** quality product; **de bonne q.** of good quality; **en q. de** in his/her/*etc* capacity as

quand [kɑ̃] *conj & adv* when; **q. je viendrai** when I come

quant [kɑ̃] **quant à** *prép* as for

quantité [kɑ̃tite] *nf* quantity; **une q., des quantités** *(beaucoup)* a lot (**de** of)

quarante [karɑ̃t] *adj & nm inv* forty; **un q.-cinq tours** *(disque)* a single ■ **quarantaine** *nf* (a) **une q. (de)** *(nombre)* (about) forty; **avoir la q.** *(âge)* to be about forty (**b**) *Méd* quarantine; **mettre qn en q.** to quarantine sb ■ **quarantième** *adj & nmf* fortieth

quart [kar] *nm* (**a**) *(fraction)* quarter; **q. de litre** quarter litre, quarter of a litre; **q. d'heure** quarter of an hour; **une heure et q.** an hour and a quarter; **il est une heure et q.** it's a quarter *Br* past *or Am* after one; **une heure moins le q.** quarter to one; *Sport* **quarts de finale** quarter finals (**b**) *Naut* **être de q.** to be on watch ■ **quart-monde** *nm* **le q.** the least-developed countries

quartier [kartje] *nm* (**a**) *(de ville)* district; **de q.** local; **q. général** headquarters (**b**) *(de lune)* quarter; *(de pomme)* piece; *(d'orange)* segment (**c**) *(expression)* **avoir q. libre** to be free

quartz [kwarts] *nm* quartz; **montre à q.** quartz watch

quasi [kazi] *adv* almost

quasiment [kazimɑ̃] *adv* almost

quatorze [katɔrz] *adj & nm inv* fourteen ■ **quatorzième** *adj & nmf* fourteenth

quatre [katr] *adj & nm inv* four ■ **quatrième** *adj & nmf* fourth

quatre-vingts [katrəvɛ̃] *adj & nm* eighty; **quatre-vingts ans** eighty years; **q.-un** eighty-one; **page q.** page eighty ■ **quatre-vingt-dix** *adj & nm inv* ninety

QUE [kə]

> **que** becomes **qu'** before a vowel or mute h.

1 *conj* (**a**) *(complétif)* that; **je pense qu'elle restera** I think (that) she'll stay; **qu'elle vienne ou non** whether she comes or not; **qu'il s'en aille!** let him leave!; **ça fait un an q. je suis là** I've been here for a year

(b) *(de comparaison)* than; *(avec 'aussi', 'même', 'tel', 'autant')* as; **plus/moins âgé q. lui** older/younger than him; **aussi sage/fatigué q. toi** as wise/ tired as you; **le même q. Pauline** the same as Pauline

(c) (ne...) que only; **tu n'as qu'un stylo** you only have one pen

2 *adv* **(ce) qu'il est bête!** *(comme)* he's really stupid!

3 *pron relatif (chose)* that, which; *(personne)* that, whom; *(temps)* when; **le livre q. j'ai** the book (that *or* which) I have; **l'ami q. j'ai** the friend (that *or* whom) I have

4 *pron interrogatif* what; **q. fait-il?, qu'est-ce qu'il fait?** what is he doing?; **q. préférez-vous?** which do you prefer?

Québec [kebɛk] *nm* **le Q.** Quebec

quel, quelle [kɛl] **1** *adj interrogatif (chose)* what, which; *(personne)* who; **q. livre préférez-vous?** which *or* what book do you prefer?; **q. est cet homme?** who is that man?; **je sais q. est ton but** I know what your aim is; **je ne sais à q. employé m'adresser** I don't know which clerk to ask

2 *pron interrogatif* which (one); **q. est le meilleur?** which (one) is the best?

3 *adj exclamatif* **q. idiot!** what a fool!

4 *adj relatif* **q. qu'il soit** *(chose)* whatever it may be; *(personne)* whoever it *or* he may be

quelconque [kɛlkɔ̃k] **1** *adj indéfini* any; **donne-moi un livre q.** give me any book **2** *adj (insignifiant)* ordinary

quelque [kɛlk] **1** *adj indéfini* some; **quelques** some, a few; **les quelques amies qu'elle a** the few friends she has **2** *adv (environ)* about, some; **q. peu** somewhat; *Fam* **100 euros et q.** 100 euros and a bit

quelque chose [kɛlkəʃoz] *pron indéfini* something; **q. d'autre** something else; **q. de grand** something big; **q. de plus pratique/de moins lourd** something more practical/less heavy

quelquefois [kɛlkəfwa] *adv* sometimes

quelque part [kɛlkəpar] *adv* some-

where; *(dans les questions)* anywhere

quelques-uns, -unes [kɛlkəzœ̃, -yn] *pron* some

quelqu'un [kɛlkœ̃] *pron indéfini* someone, somebody; *(dans les questions)* anyone, anybody; **q. d'intelligent** someone clever

querelle [kərɛl] *nf* quarrel; **chercher q. à qn** to try to pick a fight with sb ■ **se quereller** *vpr* to quarrel

question [kɛstjɔ̃] *nf (interrogation)* question; *(affaire)* matter, question; **il n'en est pas q.** it's out of the question; **en q.** in question ■ **questionnaire** *nm* questionnaire ■ **questionner** *vt* to question (**sur** about)

quête [kɛt] *nf* **(a)** *(collecte)* collection; **faire la q.** to collect money **(b)** *(recherche)* quest (**de** for); **en q. de** in quest *or* search of ■ **quêter** [kete] **1** *vt* to seek **2** *vi* to collect money

queue [kø] *nf* **(a)** *(d'animal)* tail; *(de fleur, de fruit)* stalk; *(de train)* rear; **à la q. leu leu** in single file; **q. de cheval** *(coiffure)* ponytail **(b)** *(file)* Br queue, Am line; **faire la q.** Br to queue up, Am to stand in line

QUI [ki] **1** *pron interrogatif (personne)* who; *(en complément)* whom; **q. (est-ce qui) est là?** who's there?; **q. désirez-vous voir?, q. est-ce que vous désirez voir?** who(m) do you want to see?; **à q. est ce livre?** whose book is this?; **je demande q. a téléphoné** I'm asking who phoned

2 *pron relatif* **(a)** *(sujet) (personne)* who, that; *(chose)* which, that; **l'homme q. est là** the man who's here *or* that's here; **la maison q. se trouve en face** the house which is *or* that's opposite

(b) *(sans antécédent)* **q. que vous soyez** whoever you are

(c) *(après une préposition)* **la femme de q. je parle** the woman I'm talking about

quiconque [kikɔ̃k] *pron (sujet)* whoever; *(complément)* anyone

quille [kij] *nf (de navire)* keel; *(de jeu)* (bowling) pin, Br skittle; **jouer aux quilles** to bowl, Br to play skittles

quincaillerie [kɛkajri] *nf (magasin)* hardware shop; *(objets)* hardware

quinquennal, -e, -aux, -ales [kɛkenal, -o] *adj* plan q. five-year plan ■ **quinquennat** *nm Pol* five-year term (of office)

quintuple [kɛtypl] **1** *adj* q. de fivefold **2** *nm* le q. (de) *(quantité)* five times as much (as); *(nombre)* five times as many (as) ■ **quintupler** *vti* to increase fivefold

quinze [kɛz] *adj & nm inv* fifteen; q. jours two weeks, *Br* a fortnight ■ **quinzaine** *nf* une q. (de) (about) fifteen; une q. (de jours) two weeks, *Br* a fortnight ■ **quinzième** *adj & nmf* fifteenth

quittance [kitɑ̃s] *nf (reçu)* receipt

quitte [kit] *adj* quits (**envers** with); q. à faire qch even if it means doing sth; en être q. pour qch to get off with sth

quitter [kite] **1** *vt (personne, lieu, poste)* to leave; ne pas q. qn des yeux to keep one's eyes on sb **2** *vi* ne quittez pas! *(au téléphone)* hold the line! **3** **se quitter** *vpr* to part; ils ne se quittent plus they are inseparable

QUOI [kwa] *pron* what; *(après une préposition)* which; à q. penses-tu? what are you thinking about?; après q. after which; de q. manger something to eat; *(assez)* enough to eat; de q. écrire something to write with; q. que je dise whatever I say; q. qu'il en soit be that as it may; il n'y a pas de q.! *(en réponse à 'merci')* don't mention it!; q.? what?

quoique [kwak] *conj* (al)though; quoiqu'il soit pauvre (al)though he's poor

quota [kwɔta] *nm* quota

quotidien, -enne [kɔtidjɛ̃, -ɛn] **1** *adj* daily **2** *nm* daily (paper)

Rr

R, r [er] *nm inv* R, r

rabâcher [rabaʃe] **1** *vt* to repeat endlessly **2** *vi* to say the same thing over and over again

rabais [rabɛ] *nm* reduction, discount ▪ **rabaisser 1** *vt (dénigrer)* to belittle **2 se rabaisser** *vpr* to belittle oneself

rabattre* [rabatr] **1** *vt (col)* to turn down; *(couvercle)* to close **2 se rabattre** *vpr (se refermer)* to close; *(véhicule)* to pull back in; *Fig* **se r. sur qch** to fall back on sth

rabbin [rabɛ̃] *nm* rabbi

rabougri, -e [rabugri] *adj (personne, plante)* stunted

raccommoder [rakɔmɔde] *vt (linge)* to mend; *(chaussette)* to darn

raccompagner [rakɔ̃paɲe] *vt* to take back

raccord [rakɔr] *nm (dispositif)* connection; *(de papier peint)* join; *(de peinture)* touch-up ▪ **raccordement** [-əmɑ̃] *nm (action, lien)* connection ▪ **raccorder** *vt*, **se raccorder** *vpr* to link up (à to)

raccourcir [rakursir] **1** *vt* to shorten **2** *vi* to get shorter ▪ **raccourci** *nm* short cut; **en r.** in brief

raccrocher [rakrɔʃe] **1** *vt (objet tombé)* to hang back up; *(téléphone)* to put down **2** *vi (au téléphone)* to hang up **3 se raccrocher** *vpr* **se r. à qch** to catch hold of sth; *Fig* to cling to sth

race [ras] *nf (ethnie)* race; *(animale)* breed; **chien de r.** pedigree dog ▪ **racial, -e, -aux, -ales** *adj* racial ▪ **racisme** *nm* racism ▪ **raciste** *adj & nmf* racist

rachat [raʃa] *nm (de voiture, d'appartement)* repurchase; *(de firme)* buy-out ▪ **racheter 1** *vt (acheter davantage)* to buy some more; *(remplacer)* to buy another; *(firme)* to buy out; *(faute)* to make up for **2 se racheter** *vpr* to make amends, to redeem oneself

racine [rasin] *nf (de plante, de personne)* & *Math* root

racler [rakle] **1** *vt* to scrape; *(peinture, boue)* to scrape off **2 se racler** *vpr* **se r. la gorge** to clear one's throat ▪ **raclette** *nf (outil)* scraper; *(plat)* raclette *(Swiss dish consisting of potatoes and melted cheese)*

raconter [rakɔ̃te] *vt (histoire, mensonge)* to tell; *(événement)* to tell about; **r. qch à qn** *(histoire)* to tell sb sth; *(événement)* to tell sb about sth; **r. à qn que...** to tell sb that... ▪ **racontars** *nmpl* gossip

radar [radar] *nm* radar; **contrôle r.** radar speed check

rade [rad] *nf* harbour

radeau, -x [rado] *nm* raft

radiateur [radjatœr] *nm* radiator; **r. électrique** electric heater

radiation [radjasjɔ̃] *nf Phys* radiation; *(suppression)* removal (**de** from) ▪ **radier** *vt* to strike off (**de** from)

radical, -e, -aux, -ales [radikal, -o] *adj* radical

radieux, -euse [radjø, -øz] *adj (personne, visage, soleil)* radiant; *(temps)* glorious

radio [radjo] **1** *nf* (a) *(poste)* radio; *(station)* radio station; **à la r.** on the radio; **écouter la r./qch à la r.** to listen to the radio/sth on the radio (b) *Méd* X-ray; **passer une r.** to have an X-ray **2** *nm (opérateur)* radio operator ▪ **radio-réveil** *(pl* **radios-réveils)** *nm* radio alarm, clock radio

radioactif, -ive [radjoaktif, -iv] *adj* radioactive ▪ **radioactivité** *nf* radioactivity

radiodiffuser [radjodifyse] *vt* to broadcast ■ **radiodiffusion** *nf* broadcasting

radiographie [radjografi] *nf (photo)* X-ray; *(technique)* radiography ■ **radiographier** *vt* to X-ray ■ **radiologie** *nf Méd* radiology ■ **radiologue** *nmf (technicien)* radiographer; *(médecin)* radiologist

radiophonique [radjofɔnik] *adj* **émission r.** radio broadcast

radis [radi] *nm* radish

radoucir [radusir] **se radoucir** *vpr (personne)* to calm down; *(temps)* to become milder

rafale [rafal] *nf (vent)* gust; *(de mitrailleuse)* burst

raffermir [rafermir] **1** *vt (autorité)* to strengthen; *(muscles)* to tone up **2 se raffermir** *vpr (muscle)* to become stronger

raffiné, -e [rafine] *adj* refined ■ **raffinement** *nm* refinement

raffiner [rafine] *vt* to refine ■ **raffinage** *nm* refining

raffinerie [rafinri] *nf* refinery

rafle [rɑfl] *nf* raid

rafraîchir [rafreʃir] **1** *vt (rendre frais)* to chill; *(pièce)* to air; *(raviver)* to freshen up **2** *vi* to cool down **3 se rafraîchir** *vpr (temps)* to get cooler; *(se laver)* to freshen up ■ **rafraîchissant, -e** *adj* refreshing ■ **rafraîchissement** *nm (boisson)* cold drink

rage [raʒ] *nf (colère)* rage; *(maladie)* rabies; **faire r.** *(incendie, tempête)* to rage

ragoût [ragu] *nm Culin* stew

raid [red] *nm* raid

raide [red] **1** *adj (rigide, guindé)* stiff; *(côte)* steep; *(cheveux)* straight **2** *adv (grimper)* steeply; **tomber r.** to fall to the ground ■ **raideur** *nf (rigidité)* stiffness; *(de côte)* steepness ■ **raidir 1** *vt (bras, jambe)* to brace; *(corde)* to tauten **2 se raidir** *vpr (membres)* to stiffen; *(corde)* to tauten; *(personne)* to tense up

raie [re] *nf (motif)* stripe; *(de cheveux) Br* parting, *Am* part

rail [rɑj] *nm* rail; **le r.** *(chemins de fer)* rail; **r. de sécurité** crash barrier

raisin [rezɛ̃] *nm* **raisin(s)** grapes; **r. sec** raisin

raison [rezɔ̃] *nf* **(a)** *(faculté, motif)* reason; **la r. de mon absence** the reason for my absence; **la r. pour laquelle...** the reason (why)...; **en r. de** *(cause)* on account of; **à r. de** *(proportion)* at the rate of; **à plus forte r.** all the more so **(b) avoir r.** to be right **(de faire** to do *or* in doing); **donner r. à qn** to agree with sb

raisonnable [rezɔnabl] *adj* reasonable

raisonner [rezɔne] *vi (penser)* to reason ■ **raisonnement** *nm (faculté, activité)* reasoning; *(argumentation)* argument

rajeunir [raʒœnir] **1** *vt (moderniser)* to modernize; **r. qn** *(faire paraître plus jeune)* to make sb look younger; *(donner moins que son âge à)* to underestimate how old sb is **2** *vi* to look younger ■ **rajeunissement** *nm (après traitement)* rejuvenation; *(de population)* decrease in age

rajouter [raʒute] *vt* to add **(à** to)

rajuster [raʒyste] *vt (vêtements, lunettes)* to straighten, to adjust

ralentir [ralɑ̃tir] *vti* to slow down ■ **ralenti** *nm Cin & TV* slow motion; **au r.** in slow motion; *(travailler)* at a slower pace; **tourner au r.** *(moteur, usine) Br* to tick over, *Am* to turn over ■ **ralentissement** *nm* slowing down; *(embouteillage)* hold-up

rallier [ralje] **1** *vt (réunir)* to rally; *(regagner)* to return to; **r. qn à qch** *(convertir)* to win sb over to sth **2 se rallier** *vpr* **se r. à** *(avis)* to come round to; *(cause)* to rally to

rallonge [ralɔ̃ʒ] *nf (de table)* extension; *(fil électrique)* extension (lead) ■ **rallonger** *vti* to lengthen

rallumer [ralyme] **1** *vt (feu, pipe)* to light again; *(lampe)* to switch on again **2 se rallumer** *vpr (lumière)* to come back on; *(incendie)* to flare up again

ramasser [ramɑse] **1** *vt (prendre, réunir)* to pick up; *(ordures, copies)* to collect; *(fruits, coquillages)* to gather

2 se ramasser *vpr (se pelotonner)* to curl up; *(se relever)* to pick oneself up ■ **ramassage** *nm (d'ordures)* collection; **r. scolaire** school bus service

rame [ram] *nf (aviron)* oar; *(de métro)* train ■ **ramer** *vi* to row ■ **rameur, -euse** *nmf* rower

ramener [ramne] *vt (amener)* to bring back; *(raccompagner)* to take back; *(ordre, calme)* to restore; **r. qch à qch** to reduce sth to sth; **r. qn à la vie** to bring sb back to life

ramollir [ramɔlir] *vt*, **se ramollir** *vpr* to soften

ramoner [ramɔne] *vt (cheminée)* to sweep

rampe [rɑ̃p] *nf (d'escalier)* banister; *(pente)* slope; **r. d'accès** *(de pont)* access ramp

ramper [rɑ̃pe] *vi* to crawl

rancœur [rɑ̃kœr] *nf* rancour, resentment

rançon [rɑ̃sɔ̃] *nf* ransom ■ **rançonner** *vt* to hold to ransom

rancune [rɑ̃kyn] *nf* spite; **garder r. à qn** to bear sb a grudge ■ **rancunier, -ère** *adj* spiteful

randonnée [rɑ̃dɔne] *nf (à pied)* hike; *(en vélo)* ride

rang [rɑ̃] *nm (rangée)* row; *(classement, grade)* rank; **par r. de taille** in order of size; **de haut r.** high-ranking; **se mettre en r.** to line up *(par trois* in threes) ■ **rangée** *nf* row

ranger [rɑ̃ʒe] **1** *vt (papiers, vaisselle)* to put away; *(chambre)* to tidy (up); *(classer)* to rank *(parmi* among) **2 se ranger** *vpr (se disposer)* to line up; *(s'écarter)* to stand aside ■ **rangé, -e** *adj (chambre)* tidy; *(personne)* steady ■ **rangement** *nm* putting away; *(de chambre)* tidying (up); **rangements** *(placards)* storage space

ranimer [ranime] *vt (personne) (après évanouissement)* to bring round; *(après arrêt cardiaque)* to resuscitate; *(feu)* to rekindle; *(souvenir)* to reawaken; *(débat)* to revive

rapace [rapas] **1** *nm (oiseau)* bird of prey **2** *adj (personne)* grasping

rapatrier [rapatrije] *vt* to repatriate

râpé, -e [rɑpe] *adj (fromage, carottes)* grated ■ **râper** *vt (fromage)* to grate; *(bois)* to rasp

rapetisser [raptise] **1** *vt (rendre plus petit)* to make smaller; *(faire paraître plus petit)* to make look smaller **2** *vi (vêtement, personne)* to shrink

rapide [rapid] **1** *adj* fast; *(progrès)* rapid; *(esprit, lecture)* quick **2** *nm (train)* express (train); *(de fleuve)* rapid ■ **rapidité** *nf* speed

rappel [rapɛl] *nm (de diplomate)* recall; *(d'événement, de promesse)* reminder; *(au théâtre)* curtain call; *(vaccin)* booster; **descendre en r.** *(en alpinisme)* to abseil down

rappeler [raple] **1** *vt (pour faire revenir, au téléphone)* to call back; *(souvenir, diplomate)* to recall; **r. qch à qn** to remind sb of sth **2** *vi (au téléphone)* to call back **3 se rappeler** *vpr* **se r. qn/qch** to remember sb/sth; **se r. que...** to remember that...

rapport [rapɔr] *nm* **(a)** *(lien)* connection, link; **par r. à** compared with; **rapports** *(entre personnes)* relations; **rapports (sexuels)** (sexual) intercourse **(b)** *(profit)* return, yield **(c)** *(compte rendu)* report

rapporter [rapɔrte] **1** *vt (rendre)* to bring back; *(remporter)* to take back; *(raconter)* to report; *(profit)* to be profitable; **r. de l'argent** to bring sb money; *(moralement)* to bring sb sth; **on rapporte que...** it is reported that... **2** *vi (chien)* to retrieve **3 se rapporter** *vpr* **se r. à qch** to relate to sth; **s'en r. à qn/qch** to rely on sb/sth

rapprocher [raprɔʃe] **1** *vt (objet)* to move closer *(de* to); *(réconcilier)* to bring together; *(comparer)* to compare *(de* to *or* with) **2 se rapprocher** *vpr* to get closer *(de* to); *(se réconcilier)* to be reconciled; *(ressembler)* to be similar *(de* to) ■ **rapproché, -e** *adj* close; *(yeux)* close-set ■ **rapprochement** *nm (réconciliation)* reconciliation; *(rapport)* connection

rapt [rapt] *nm* abduction

raquette [rakɛt] *nf (de tennis)* racket; *(de ping-pong)* bat; *(de neige)* snowshoe

rare [rar] *adj* rare; *(argent, main-d'œuvre)* scarce; *(barbe, végétation)* sparse; **c'est r. qu'il pleuve ici** it rarely rains here ■ **rarement** *adv* rarely, seldom ■ **rareté** *nf (objet rare)* rarity; *(de main-d'œuvre)* scarcity; *(de phénomène)* rareness

ras, -e [ra, raz] **1** *adj (cheveux)* close-cropped; *(herbe, barbe)* short; *(mesure)* full; **à r. bord** to the brim; **pull (au) r. du cou** crew-neck sweater **2** *nm* **au r. de, à r. de** level with; **voler au r. du sol** to fly close to the ground **3** *adv (coupé)* short

raser [raze] **1** *vt (menton, personne)* to shave; *(barbe, moustache)* to shave off; *(démolir)* to raze to the ground; *(frôler)* to skim **2 se raser** *vpr* to shave ■ **rasé, -e** *adj* **être bien r.** to be clean-shaven

rasoir [razwar] *nm* razor; *(électrique)* shaver

rassasier [rasazje] *vt (faim, curiosité)* to satisfy

rassembler [rasãble] **1** *vt (gens, objets)* to gather (together) **2 se rassembler** *vpr* to gather, to assemble ■ **rassemblement** [-əmã] *nm (action, groupe)* gathering

rasseoir* [raswar] **se rasseoir** *vpr* to sit down again

rassis, -e [rasi, -iz] *adj (pain)* stale

rassurer [rasyre] **1** *vt* to reassure **2 se rassurer** *vpr* **rassure-toi** don't worry ■ **rassurant, -e** *adj* reassuring

rat [ra] *nm* rat

ratatiner [ratatine] **se ratatiner** *vpr* to shrivel up

ratatouille [ratatuj] *nf* Culin **r. (niçoise)** ratatouille

râteau, -x [rato] *nm* rake

râtelier [ratəlje] *nm (pour outils, pour armes)* rack

rater [rate] *vt (bus, cible, occasion)* to miss; *(travail, gâteau)* to ruin; *(examen)* to fail; *(vie)* to waste ■ **raté, -e** *nmf* loser

ratifier [ratifje] *vt* to ratify

ration [rasjɔ̃] *nf* ration ■ **rationnement** *nm* rationing

rationaliser [rasjɔnalize] *vt* to rationalize

rationnel, -elle [rasjɔnɛl] *adj* rational

ratisser [ratise] *vt (allée)* to rake; *(feuilles)* to rake up

rattacher [ratafe] **1** *vt (lacets)* to tie up again; *(région)* to unite (à with) **2 se rattacher** *vpr* **se r. à** to be linked to

rattraper [ratrape] **1** *vt* to catch; *(prisonnier)* to recapture; **r. qn** *(rejoindre)* to catch up with sb; **r. le temps perdu** to make up for lost time **2 se rattraper** *vpr (se retenir)* to catch oneself in time; *(après une faute)* to make up for it; **se r. à qch** to catch hold of sth ■ **rattrapage** *nm* Scol **cours de r.** remedial class

raturer [ratyre] *vt* to cross out, to delete

rauque [rok] *adj (voix)* hoarse

ravages [ravaʒ] *nmpl* devastation; *(du temps, de maladie)* ravages; **faire des r.** to wreak havoc; *(femme)* to break hearts ■ **ravager** *vt* to devastate

ravaler [ravale] *vt (façade)* to clean

ravi, -e [ravi] *adj* delighted (**de** with; **de faire** to do; **que** that)

ravin [ravɛ̃] *nm* ravine

ravir [ravir] *vt (emporter)* to snatch (**à** from); *(plaire à)* to delight; **chanter à r.** to sing delightfully ■ **ravissement** *nm (extase)* ecstasy ■ **ravisseur, -euse** *nmf* kidnapper

raviser [ravize] **se raviser** *vpr* to change one's mind

ravitailler [ravitaje] **1** *vt (personnes)* to supply; *(avion)* to refuel **2 se ravitailler** *vpr* to get in supplies ■ **ravitaillement** *nm (action)* supplying; *(d'avion)* refuelling; *(denrées)* supplies

raviver [ravive] *vt (feu, sentiment)* to rekindle; *(douleur)* to revive; *(couleur)* to brighten up

rayer [rɛje] *vt (érafler)* to scratch; *(mot)* to cross out ■ **rayé, -e** *adj (verre, disque)* scratched; *(tissu, pantalon)* striped ■ **rayure** *nf (éraflure)* scratch; *(motif)* stripe; **à rayures** striped

rayon [rɛjɔ̃] *nm* **(a)** *(de lumière)* ray; *(de cercle)* radius; *(de roue)* spoke; **dans un r. de** within a radius of; **r. X** X-ray; **r. de**

soleil sunbeam (**b**) *(d'étagère)* shelf; *(de magasin)* department; *(de ruche)* honeycomb ∎ **rayonnage** *nm* shelving, shelves

rayonner [rɛjɔnε] *vi (avenue, douleur)* to radiate; *(dans une région)* to travel around *(from a central base)*; *(soleil)* to beam; *Fig* **r. de joie** to beam with joy ∎ **rayonnant, -e** *adj (soleil)* radiant; *Fig (visage)* beaming (**de** with) ∎ **rayonnement** *nm (du soleil)* radiance; *(influence)* influence

raz de marée [rɑdmare] *nm inv* tidal wave; **r. électoral** landslide

ré [re] *nm inv (note)* D

réacteur [reaktœr] *nm (d'avion)* jet engine; *(nucléaire)* reactor

réaction [reaksjɔ̃] *nf* reaction; **moteur à r.** jet engine

réagir [reaʒir] *vi* to react (**contre** against; **à** to); *Fig (se secouer)* to shake oneself out of it

réaliser [realize] **1** *vt (projet)* to realize; *(rêve, ambition)* Er to fulfil, Am to fulfill; *(bénéfices)* to make; *(film)* to direct; *(comprendre)* to realize (**que** that) **2 se réaliser** *vpr (vœu)* to come true; *(personne)* Br to fulfil *or* Am fulfill oneself ∎ **réalisable** *adj (plan)* workable; *(rêve)* attainable ∎ **réalisateur, -trice** *nmf (de film)* director ∎ **réalisation** *nf (de projet)* realization; *(de rêve)* fulfilment; *(de film)* direction

réalité [realite] *nf* reality; **en r.** in reality

réanimation [reanimasjɔ̃] *nf* resuscitation; **(service de) r.** intensive care unit ∎ **réanimer** *vt* to resuscitate

rebattu, -e [rəbaty] *adj (sujet)* hackneyed

rebelle [rəbɛl] **1** *adj (personne)* rebellious; *(mèche)* unruly **2** *nmf* rebel ∎ **se rebeller** *vpr* to rebel (**contre** against) ∎ **rébellion** *nf* rebellion

rebondir [rəbɔ̃dir] *vi* to bounce; *(par ricochet)* to rebound

rebondissement [rəbɔ̃dismɑ̃] *nm* new development (**de** in)

rebord [rəbɔr] *nm* edge; *(de plat)* rim; *(de vêtement)* hem; **r. de fenêtre** windowsill

reboucher [rəbuʃe] *vt (flacon)* to put the top back on; *(trou)* to fill in again

rebours [rəbur] **à rebours** *adv* the wrong way

rébus [rebys] *nm* rebus

rebut [rəby] *nm* **mettre qch au r.** to throw sth out

rebuter [rəbyte] *vt (décourager)* to put off

récapituler [rekapityle] *vti* to recapitulate

recel [rəsɛl] *nm* receiving stolen goods ∎ **receler, recéler** *vt (mystère, secret)* to conceal; *(objet volé)* to receive; *(criminel)* to harbour

recenser [rəsɑ̃se] *vt (population)* to take a census of ∎ **recensement** *nm (de population)* census

récent, -e [resɑ̃, -ɑ̃t] *adj* recent

récepteur [reseptœr] *nm (téléphone)* receiver ∎ **réceptif, -ive** *adj* receptive (**à** to) ∎ **réception** *nf (accueil, soirée)* & *Radio* reception; *(de lettre)* receipt; *(d'hôtel)* reception (desk); **dès r. de** on receipt of; **avec accusé de r.** with acknowledgement of receipt ∎ **réceptionniste** *nmf* receptionist

récession [resesjɔ̃] *nf* Écon recession

recette [rəsɛt] *nf* Culin & Fig recipe (**de** for); *(argent, bénéfice)* takings; **recettes** *(gains)* takings

recevoir* [rəsəvwar] **1** *vt (amis, lettre, proposition, coup de téléphone)* to receive; *(gifle, coup)* to get; *(client)* to see; *(candidat)* to admit; *(station de radio)* to pick up; **r. la visite de qn** to have a visit from sb; **être reçu à un examen** to pass an exam; **être reçu premier** to come first **2** *vi (faire une fête)* to have guests ∎ **receveur, -euse** *nmf (de bus)* (bus) conductor; **r. des Postes** postmaster, *f* postmistress

rechange [rəʃɑ̃ʒ] **de rechange** *adj (pièce)* spare

recharge [rəʃarʒ] *nf (de stylo)* refill ∎ **rechargeable** *adj (briquet)* refillable; *(pile)* rechargeable ∎ **recharger** *vt (fusil, appareil photo, camion)* to reload; *(briquet, stylo)* to refill; *(pile)* to recharge

réchaud [reʃo] *nm* (portable) stove

réchauffer [reʃofe] **1** *vt (personne, aliment)* to warm up **2 se réchauffer** *vpr (personne)* to get warm ■ **réchauffement** *nm (de température)* rise (**de** in); **le r. de la planète** global warming

rêche [rɛʃ] *adj* rough

recherche [rəʃɛrʃ] *nf* (a) *(quête)* search (**de** for); **à la r. de** in search of; **la r. d'emploi** job-hunting; **r. sur Internet** Internet search; **faire une r. sur Internet** to search the Internet (b) *(scientifique)* research (**sur** into); **faire de la r.** to do research (c) **recherches** *(de police)* search, hunt; **faire des recherches** to make inquiries (d) *(raffinement)* elegance

rechercher [rəʃɛrʃe] *vt (personne, objet)* to search for; *(emploi)* to look for; *(honneurs)* to seek ■ **recherché, -e** *adj* (a) *(très demandé)* in demand; *(rare)* sought-after; **r. pour meurtre** wanted for murder (b) *(élégant)* elegant

rechute [rəʃyt] *nf* relapse ■ **rechuter** *vi* to have a relapse

récidive [residiv] *nf (de malfaiteur)* repeat *Br* offence *or Am* offense; *(de maladie)* recurrence (**de** of) ■ **récidiver** *vi (malfaiteur)* to reoffend ■ **récidiviste** *nmf (malfaiteur)* repeat offender

récif [resif] *nm* reef

récipient [resipjɑ̃] *nm* container

réciproque [resiprɔk] *adj (sentiments)* mutual; *(concessions)* reciprocal

récit [resi] *nm (histoire)* story; *(compte rendu)* account; **faire le r. de qch** to give an account of sth

récital, -als [resital] *nm* recital

réciter [resite] *vt* to recite

réclame [reklam] *nf (publicité)* advertising; *(annonce)* advertisement; **en r.** on special offer

réclamer [reklame] **1** *vt (demander)* to ask for; *(exiger)* to demand; *(nécessiter)* to require **2** *vi* to complain ■ **réclamation** *nf* complaint; **(bureau des) réclamations** complaints department

réclusion [reklyzjɔ̃] *nf* **r. (criminelle) à perpétuité** life imprisonment

recoin [rəkwɛ̃] *nm (de lieu)* nook

recoller [rəkɔle] *vt (objet cassé)* to stick back together

récolte [rekɔlt] *nf (action)* harvesting; *(produits)* harvest; **faire la r.** to harvest the crops ■ **récolter** *vt* to harvest

recommandable [rəkɔmɑ̃dabl] *adj* **peu r.** disreputable

recommandation [rəkɔmɑ̃dasjɔ̃] *nf (appui, conseil)* recommendation

recommander [rəkɔmɑ̃de] *vt (appuyer)* to recommend (**à** to; **pour** for); **r. à qn de faire qch** to advise sb to do sth ■ **recommandé, -e 1** *adj (lettre)* registered **2** *nm* **en r.** registered

recommencer [rəkɔmɑ̃se] *vti* to start or begin again ■ **recommencement** *nm* renewal (**de** of)

récompense [rekɔ̃pɑ̃s] *nf* reward (**pour** *ou* **de** for); *(prix)* award ■ **récompenser** *vt* to reward (**de** *ou* **pour** for)

réconcilier [rekɔ̃silje] **1** *vt* to reconcile (**avec** with) **2 se réconcilier** *vpr* to become reconciled, *Br* to make it up (**avec** with) ■ **réconciliation** *nf* reconciliation

reconduire* [rəkɔ̃dɥir] *vt (contrat)* to renew; **r. qn (à la porte)** to show sb out ■ **reconduction** *nf (de contrat)* renewal

réconfort [rekɔ̃fɔr] *nm* comfort ■ **réconfortant, -e** *adj* comforting ■ **réconforter** *vt* to comfort

reconnaissable [rəkɔnɛsabl] *adj* recognizable (**à qch** by sth)

reconnaissant, -e [rəkɔnɛsɑ̃, -ɑ̃t] *adj* grateful (**à qn de qch** to sb for sth) ■ **reconnaissance** *nf (gratitude)* gratitude (**pour** for); *(de droit, de gouvernement)* recognition; *Mil* reconnaissance; **r. de dette** IOU

reconnaître* [rəkɔnɛtr] **1** *vt (identifier, admettre)* to recognize (**à qch** by sth); *(enfant, erreur)* to acknowledge; *Mil (terrain)* to reconnoitre; **être reconnu coupable** to be found guilty **2 se reconnaître** *vpr (soi-même)* to recognize oneself; *(l'un l'autre)* to recognize each other ■ **reconnu, -e** *adj* recognized

reconquérir* [rəkɔ̃kerir] *vt (territoire)* to reconquer

reconsidérer [rəkɔ̃sidere] *vt* to reconsider

reconstituer [rəkɔ̃stitɥe] *vt (armée, parti)* to reconstitute; *(crime)* to reconstruct ■ **reconstitution** *nf (de crime)* reconstruction; **r. historique** historical reconstruction

reconstruire* [rəkɔ̃strɥir] *vt* to rebuild ■ **reconstruction** *nf* rebuilding

reconvertir [rəkɔ̃vertir] **1** *vt (entreprise)* to convert; *(personne)* to retrain **2 se reconvertir** *vpr (personne)* to retrain ■ **reconversion** *nf (d'usine)* conversion; *(de personne)* retraining

recopier [rəkɔpje] *vt (mettre au propre)* to copy out; *(faire un double de)* to recopy

record [rəkɔr] *nm & adj inv* record; **r. olympique** Olympic record

recoucher [rəkuʃe] **se recoucher** *vpr* to go back to bed

recoudre* [rəkudr] *vt (bouton)* to sew back on; *(vêtement, plaie)* to stitch up

recouper [rəkupe] **1** *vt (couper de nouveau)* to recut; *(confirmer)* to confirm **2 se recouper** *vpr (témoignages)* to tally ■ **recoupement** *nm* crosscheck; **par r.** by crosschecking

recourber [rəkurbe] *vt,* **se recourber** *vpr* to bend ■ **recourbé, -e** *adj (bec)* curved

recours [rəkur] *nm* recourse; **avoir r. à** *(chose)* to resort to; *(personne)* to turn to; **en dernier r.** as a last resort ■ **recourir*** *vi* **r. à** *(moyen, violence)* to resort to; *(personne)* to turn to

recouvrer [rəkuvre] *vt (santé, bien)* to recover; *(vue)* to regain

recouvrir* [rəkuvrir] *vt (revêtir, inclure)* to cover (**de** with); *(couvrir de nouveau)* to re-cover

récréation [rekreasjɔ̃] *nf Scol Br* break, *Am* recess; *(pour les plus jeunes)* playtime

recroqueviller [rəkrɔkvije] **se recroqueviller** *vpr (personne)* to huddle up

recrue [rəkry] *nf* recruit ■ **recrutement** *nm* recruitment ■ **recruter** *vt* to recruit

rectangle [rektãgl] *nm* rectangle

■ **rectangulaire** *adj* rectangular

rectifier [rektifje] *vt (calcul, erreur)* to correct; *(compte)* to adjust ■ **rectification** *nf (de calcul, d'erreur)* correction

recto [rekto] *nm* front; **r. verso** on both sides

rectorat [rektɔra] *nm Br* ≃ local education authority, *Am* ≃ board of education

reçu, -e [rəsy] **1** *pp de* **recevoir 2** *adj (idée)* received; *(candidat)* successful **3** *nm (récépissé)* receipt

recueil [rəkœj] *nm (de poèmes, de chansons)* collection (**de** of)

recueillir* [rəkœjir] **1** *vt (argent, renseignements)* to collect; *(personne, animal)* to take in **2 se recueillir** *vpr* to meditate; *(devant un monument)* to stand in silence ■ **recueillement** *nm* meditation

recul [rəkyl] *nm (d'armée, de négociateur, de maladie)* retreat; *(de canon)* recoil; *(déclin)* decline; **avoir un mouvement de r.** to recoil

reculer [rəkyle] **1** *vi (personne)* to move back; *(automobiliste)* to reverse, *Am* to back up; *(armée)* to retreat; *(épidémie)* to lose ground; *(renoncer)* to back down, to retreat; *(diminuer)* to decline; **faire r. la foule** to move the crowd back

 2 *vt (meuble)* to move back; *(paiement, décision)* to postpone ■ **reculé, -e** *adj (endroit)* remote

reculons [rəkylɔ̃] **à reculons** *adv* backwards

récupérer [rekypere] **1** *vt (objet prêté)* to get back, to recover; *(bagages)* to retrieve; *(forces)* to recover; *(recycler)* to salvage; *Péj (détourner à son profit)* to exploit **2** *vi (reprendre des forces)* to recover ■ **récupération** *nf (d'objet)* recovery; *(de déchets)* salvage

recycler [rəsikle] **1** *vt (matériaux)* to recycle **2 se recycler** *vpr (personne)* to retrain ■ **recyclage** *nm (de matériaux)* recycling; *(de personne)* retraining

rédacteur, -trice [redaktœr, -tris] *nmf* writer; *(de journal)* editor; **r. en chef** editor-in-chief ■ **rédaction** *nf (action)*

writing; *(de contrat)* drawing up; *(journalistes)* editorial staff; *(bureaux)* editorial offices

redemander [rədəmãde] *vt* to ask for more; **il faut que je le lui redemande** *(que je pose la question à nouveau)* I'll have to ask him/her again

redémarrer [rədemare] *vi (voiture)* to start again; *Ordinat* to reboot

redescendre [rədesãdr] **1** *(aux avoir) vt (objet)* to bring/take back down **2** *(aux être) vi* to come/go back down

redevance [rədəvãs] *nf (de télévision)* licence fee

redevenir* [rədəvənir] *(aux être) vi* to become again

rediffusion [rədifyzjõ] *nf (de film)* repeat

rédiger [rediʒe] *vt* to write; *(contrat)* to draw up

redire* [rədir] **1** *vt* to repeat **2** *vi* **avoir** *ou* **trouver à r. à qch** to find fault with sth

redoublant, -e [rədublã, -ãt] *nmf* pupil repeating a year *or Am* a grade

redoubler [rəduble] **1** *vt* to increase; *Scol* **r. une classe** to repeat a year *or Am* a grade **2** *vi Scol* to repeat a year *or Am* a grade ▪ **redoublement** *nm* increase **(de** in)

redouter [rədute] *vt* to dread **(de faire** doing) ▪ **redoutable** *adj (adversaire, arme)* formidable; *(maladie)* dreadful

redresser [rədrese] **1** *vt (objet tordu)* to straighten (out); *(économie, situation)* to put right; **r. la tête** to hold up one's head **2 se redresser** *vpr (personne)* to straighten up; *(pays, économie)* to recover ▪ **redressement** [-ɛsmã] *nm* **r. fiscal** tax adjustment

réduction [redyksjõ] *nf* reduction **(de** in); *(rabais)* discount

réduire* [reduir] **1** *vt* to reduce **(à** to; **de** by); **r. qch en cendres** to reduce sth to ashes; **r. qn à qch** *(misère, désespoir)* to reduce sb to sth **2** *vi (sauce)* to reduce **3 se réduire** *vpr* **se r. à** *(se ramener à)* to come down to ▪ **réduit, -e 1** *adj (prix, vitesse)* reduced **2** *nm (pièce)* small room

réécrire* [reekrir] *vt* to rewrite

rééduquer [reedyke] *vt (personne)* to rehabilitate ▪ **rééducation** *nf (de personne)* rehabilitation; **faire de la r.** to have physiotherapy

réel, -elle [reɛl] *adj* real

réélire* [reelir] *vt* to re-elect

réévaluer [reevalɥe] *vt (monnaie)* to revalue; *(salaires)* to reassess

réexpédier [reɛkspedje] *vt (faire suivre)* to forward; *(à l'envoyeur)* to return

refaire* [rəfɛr] *vt (exercice, travail)* to do again, to redo; *(chambre)* to do up; *(erreur, voyage)* to make again; **r. sa vie** to make a new life for oneself; **r. du riz** to make some more rice

réfectoire [refɛktwar] *nm* dining hall, refectory

référence [referãs] *nf* reference; **faire r. à qch** to refer to sth

référer [refere] **se référer** *vpr* **se r. à** to refer to

refermer [rəfɛrme] *vt,* **se refermer** *vpr* to close *or* shut again

réfléchir [refleʃir] **1** *vt (image, lumière)* to reflect; **r. que...** to realize that... **2** *vi* to think **(à** *ou* **sur** about) **3 se réfléchir** *vpr* to be reflected ▪ **réfléchi, -e** *adj (personne)* thoughtful; *(action, décision)* carefully thought-out; **tout bien r.** all things considered

reflet [rəflɛ] *nm (image)* & *Fig* reflection; *(lumière)* glint; **reflets** *(de cheveux)* highlights ▪ **refléter 1** *vt* to reflect **2 se refléter** *vpr* to be reflected

réflexe [reflɛks] *nm & adj* reflex

réflexion [reflɛksjõ] *nf (d'image, de lumière)* reflection; *(pensée)* thought, reflection; *(remarque)* remark; **faire une r. à qn** to make a remark to sb; **r. faite, à la r.** on second *Br* thoughts *or Am* thought

reflux [rəfly] *nm (de marée)* ebb; *(de foule)* backward surge

réforme [refɔrm] *nf* reform ▪ **réformer** *vt (loi)* to reform; *(soldat)* to discharge as unfit

refouler [rəfule] *vt (personnes)* to

force *or* drive back; *(étrangers)* to turn away; *(sentiment)* to repress; *(larmes)* to hold back

refrain [rəfrɛ̃] *nm (de chanson)* chorus, refrain

réfrigérateur [refriʒeratœr] *nm* refrigerator

refroidir [rəfrwadir] **1** *vt* to cool (down) **2** *vi (devenir froid)* to get cold; *(devenir moins chaud)* to cool down **3 se refroidir** *vpr (temps)* to get colder ▪ **refroidissement** *nm (de température)* drop in temperature; *(de l'eau)* cooling

refuge [rəfyʒ] *nm* refuge; *(de montagne)* (mountain) hut

réfugier [refyʒje] **se réfugier** *vpr* to take refuge ▪ **réfugié, -e** *nmf* refugee

refus [rəfy] *nm* refusal ▪ **refuser 1** *vt* to refuse (**qch à qn** sb sth; **de faire** to do); *(offre, invitation)* to turn down; *(proposition)* to reject; *(candidat)* to fail; *(client)* to turn away **2 se refuser** *vpr (plaisir)* to deny oneself; **se r. à faire qch** to refuse to do sth

regagner [rəgaɲe] *vt (récupérer)* to regain, to get back; *(revenir à)* to get back to

régaler [regale] **se régaler** *vpr* **je me régale** *(en mangeant)* I'm really enjoying it

regard [rəgar] *nm (coup d'œil, expression)* look; **jeter un r. sur** to glance at

regarder [rəgarde] **1** *vt* to look at; *(émission, film)* to watch; *(considérer)* to consider, to regard (**comme** as); *(concerner)* to concern; **r. qn fixement** to stare at sb

2 *vi (observer)* to look; **r. par la fenêtre** *(du dedans)* to look out of the window

3 se regarder *vpr (soi-même)* to look at oneself; *(l'un l'autre)* to look at each other

régénérer [reʒenere] *vt* to regenerate

régie [reʒi] *nf (entreprise)* state-owned company; *TV (organisation)* production management; *(lieu)* control room

régime [reʒim] *nm (politique)* (form of) government; *(de bananes)* bunch; **r.**

(alimentaire) diet; **r. amaigrissant** slimming diet; **être au** *ou* **suivre un r.** to be on a diet

régiment [reʒimɑ̃] *nm (de soldats)* regiment

région [reʒjɔ̃] *nf* region, area ▪ **régional, -e, -aux, -ales** *adj* regional

registre [rəʒistr] *nm* register

réglable [reglabl] *adj* adjustable ▪ **réglage** *nm (de siège, de machine)* adjustment; *(de moteur, de télévision)* tuning

règle [regl] *nf* (a) *(principe)* rule; **en r.** *(papiers d'identité)* in order; **en r. générale** as a (general) rule (b) *(instrument)* ruler

règlement [reglmɑ̃] *nm* (a) *(règles)* regulations (b) *(de conflit)* settling; *(paiement)* payment; *Fig* **r. de comptes** settling of scores ▪ **réglementaire** *adj* in accordance with the regulations; *Mil* **tenue r.** regulation uniform ▪ **réglementation** *nf (règles)* regulations ▪ **réglementer** *vt* to regulate

régler [regle] **1** *vt (problème, conflit)* to settle; *(mécanisme)* to adjust; *(moteur, télévision)* to tune; *(payer)* to pay; **r. qn** to settle up with sb **2** *vi* to pay **3 se régler** *vpr* **se r. sur qn** to model oneself on sb

réglisse [reglis] *nf Br* liquorice, *Am* licorice

règne [rɛɲ] *nm (de souverain)* reign; *(animal, minéral, végétal)* kingdom ▪ **régner** *vi (roi, silence)* to reign (**sur** over); *(prédominer)* to prevail; **faire r. l'ordre** to maintain law and order

regorger [rəgɔrʒe] *vi* **r. de** to be overflowing with

regret [rəgrɛ] *nm* regret; **à r.** with regret; **avoir le r.** *ou* **être au r. de faire qch** to be sorry to do sth ▪ **regrettable** *adj* regrettable ▪ **regretter** [rəgrete] *vt* to regret; **r. qn** to miss sb; **je regrette, je le regrette** I'm sorry; **r. que...** *(+ subjunctive)* to be sorry that...

regrouper [rəgrupe] *vt*, **se regrouper** *vpr* to gather together

régulariser [regylarize] *vt (situation)* to regularize

régulier, -ère [regylje, -ɛr] *adj (intervalles, visage)* regular; *(constant)* steady; *(légal)* legal ■ **régularité** *nf (exactitude)* regularity; *(constance)* steadiness

réhabituer [reabitɥe] **se réhabituer** *vpr* **se r. à qch/à faire qch** to get used to sth/to doing sth again

rein [rɛ̃] *nm* kidney; **les reins** *(dos)* the lower back

reine [rɛn] *nf* queen; **la r. Élisabeth** Queen Elizabeth

réinsertion [reɛ̃sersjɔ̃] *nf* reintegration; **r. sociale** rehabilitation

réintégrer [reɛ̃tegre] *vt (fonctionnaire)* to reinstate; *(lieu)* to return to

rejaillir [rəʒajir] *vi* to spurt out

rejet [rəʒɛ] *nm (refus)* & *Méd* rejection ■ **rejeter** *vt (relancer)* to throw back; *(offre, candidature, greffe, personne)* to reject; *(blâme)* to shift (**on** to)

rejoindre* [rəʒwɛ̃dr] **1** *vt (personne)* to meet; *(rue, rivière)* to join; *(lieu)* to reach; *(concorder avec)* to coincide with **2 se rejoindre** *vpr (personnes)* to meet up; *(rues, rivières)* to join up

réjouir [reʒwir] **1** *vt* to delight **2 se réjouir** *vpr* to be delighted (**de** at; **de faire** to do) ■ **réjoui, -e** *adj* joyful ■ **réjouissance** *nf* rejoicing; **réjouissances** festivities

relâche [rəlɑʃ] *nf* **faire r.** *Théât* & *Cin* to be closed; *Naut* to put in (**dans un port** at a port); **sans r.** without a break

relâcher [rəlɑʃe] **1** *vt (corde, étreinte)* to loosen; *(discipline)* to relax; *(prisonnier)* to release **2** *Naut* to put into port **3 se relâcher** *vpr (corde)* to slacken; *(discipline)* to become lax; *(employé)* to slack off

relais [rəlɛ] *nm (dispositif émetteur)* relay; *Sport* **(course de) r.** relay (race); **passer le r. à qn** to hand over to sb; **prendre le r.** to take over (**de** from); **r. routier** *Br* transport café, *Am* truck stop (café)

relancer [rəlɑ̃se] *vt (lancer à nouveau)* to throw again; *(rendre)* to throw back; *(production)* to boost; *(moteur)* to restart

relatif, -ive [rəlatif, -iv] *adj* relative (**à** to)

relation [rəlasjɔ̃] *nf (rapport)* relationship; *(ami)* acquaintance; **être en r. avec qn** to be in touch with sb; **avoir des relations** *(amis)* to have contacts; **r. (amoureuse)** (love) affair; **relations extérieures** foreign affairs; **relations familiales** family relationships; **relations internationales** international relations

relayer [rəleje] **1** *vt (personne)* to take over from; *(émission)* to relay **2 se relayer** *vpr* to take turns (**pour faire** doing); *Sport* to take over from one another

relevé [rəlve] *nm* list; *(de compteur)* reading; **r. de compte** bank statement; *Scol* **r. de notes** list of *Br* marks *or Am* grades

relève [rəlɛv] *nf* relief; **prendre la r.** to take over (**de** from)

relèvement [rəlɛvmɑ̃] *nm (d'économie, de pays)* recovery; *(de salaires)* raising

relever [rəlve] **1** *vt (ramasser)* to pick up; *(personne)* to help back up; *(pays)* to revive; *(copies)* to collect; *(faute)* to pick out; *(empreinte)* to find; *(défi)* to accept; *(sauce)* to spice up; *(copier)* to note down; *(compteur)* to read; *(relayer)* to relieve; *(augmenter)* to raise; **r. la tête** to look up; **r. qn de ses fonctions** to relieve sb of his/her duties **2** *vi* **r. de** *(dépendre de)* to come under; *(maladie)* to be recovering from **3 se relever** *vpr (après une chute)* to get up

relief [rəljef] *nm (de paysage)* relief; **en r.** in relief; *Fig* **mettre qch en r.** to highlight sth

relier [rəlje] *vt* to connect, to link (**à** to); *(idées, faits)* to link together; *(livre)* to bind

religion [rəliʒjɔ̃] *nf* religion ■ **religieuse** *nf (femme)* nun; *(gâteau)* cream puff ■ **religieux, -euse 1** *adj* religious; **mariage r.** church wedding **2** *nm (moine)* monk

relire* [rəlir] *vt* to reread

reliure [rəljyr] *nf (couverture)* binding; *(art)* bookbinding

reluire* [rəlᴚir] *vi* to shine, to gleam; **faire r. qch** to polish sth up

remanier [rəmanje] *vt (texte)* to revise; *(ministère)* to reshuffle ■ **remaniement** *nm (de texte)* revision; **r. ministériel** cabinet reshuffle

remarier [rəmarje] **se remarier** *vpr* to remarry ■ **remariage** *nm* remarriage

remarquable [rəmarkabl] *adj* remarkable (**par** for)

remarque [rəmark] *nf* remark; **faire une r.** to make a remark

remarquer [rəmarke] *vt (apercevoir)* to notice (**que** that); *(dire)* to remark (**que** that); **faire r. qch** to point sth out (**à** to); **se faire r.** to attract attention

rembobiner [rãbɔbine] *vt*, **se rembobiner** *vpr* to rewind

rembourser [rãburse] *vt (personne)* to pay back; *(billet, frais)* to refund ■ **remboursement** [-ɔmã] *nm* repayment; *(de billet)* refund

remède [rəmed] *nm* cure, remedy (**contre** for) ■ **remédier** *vi* **r. à qch** to remedy sth

remémorer [rəmemɔre] **se remémorer** *vpr* to remember

remercier [rəmɛrsje] *vt (dire merci à)* to thank (**de** *ou* **pour qch** for sth); **je vous remercie d'être venu** thank you for coming ■ **remerciements** *nmpl* thanks

remettre* [rəmɛtr] **1** *vt (replacer)* to put back; *(vêtement)* to put back on; *(disque)* to put on again; *(différer)* to postpone (**à** until); *(ajouter)* to add (**dans** to); **r. qch à qn** *(lettre)* to deliver sth to sb; *(rapport)* to submit sth to sb; *(démission)* to hand sth in to sb; **r. qn en liberté** to set sb free; **r. qch en question** to call sth into question; **r. qch en état** to repair sth; **r. qch à jour** to bring sth up to date

2 se remettre *vpr* **se r. à qch** to start sth again; **se r. à faire qch** to start to do sth again; **se r. de qch** to recover from sth

remise [rəmiz] *nf* **(a)** *(de lettre)* delivery; **r. à neuf** *(de machine)* reconditioning; **r. en question** questioning; **r. en état** *(de maison)* restoration **(b)** *(rabais)* discount **(c)** *Jur* **r. de peine** reduction of sentence **(d)** *(local)* shed

remontée [rəmɔ̃te] *nf* **r. mécanique** ski lift

remonter [rəmɔ̃te] **1** *(aux être)* *vi* to come/go back up; *(niveau, prix,* to rise again, to go back up; *(dans le temps)* to go back (**à** to); **r. dans** *(voiture)* to get back in(to); *(bus, train)* to get back on (to); **r. à dix ans** to go back ten years

2 *(aux avoir)* *vt (escalier, pente)* to come/go back up; *(porter)* to bring/take back up; *(montre)* to wind up; *(relever)* to raise; *(objet démonté)* to put back together, to reassemble; **r. le moral à qn** to cheer sb up ■ **remonte-pente** *(pl* **remonte-pentes)** *nm* ski lift

remords [rəmɔr] *nm* remorse; **avoir des r.** to feel remorse

remorque [rəmɔrk] *nf (de voiture)* trailer ■ **remorquer** *vt (voiture, bateau)* to tow ■ **remorqueur** *nm* tug(boat)

rempart [rãpar] *nm* rampart; **remparts** walls

remplacer [rãplase] *vt* to replace (**par** with); *(professionnellement)* to stand in for ■ **remplaçant, -e** *nmf (personne)* replacement; *(enseignant)* substitute teacher, *Br* supply teacher; *(joueur)* substitute ■ **remplacement** *nm* replacement; **en r. de** in place of

remplir [rãplir] **1** *vt* to fill (up) (**de** with); *(formulaire)* to fill out, *Er* to fill in; *(promesse)* to fulfil **2 se remplir** *vpr* to fill (up) (**de** with)

remporter [rãpɔrte] *vt (objet)* to take back; *(prix, victoire)* to win

remuer [rəmɥe] **1** *vt (bouger)* to move; *(terre)* to turn over **2** *vi* to move; *(gigoter)* to fidget

rémunérer [remynere] *vt (personne)* to pay; *(travail)* to pay for ■ **rémunération** *nf* payment (**de** for)

renaître* [rənɛtr] *vi (personne)* to be born again; *(espoir, industrie)* to revive ■ **renaissance** *nf* rebirth; *(des arts)* renaissance

renard [rənar] *nm* fox

renchérir [rɑ̃ʃerir] *vi (dire plus)* to go one better (**sur** than)

rencontre [rɑ̃kɔ̃tr] *nf (de personnes)* meeting; *(match)* Br match, Am game; **aller à la r. de qn** to go to meet sb ▪ **rencontrer 1** *vt (personne)* to meet; *(difficulté)* to come up against, to encounter; *(trouver)* to come across **2 se rencontrer** *vpr* to meet

rendement [rɑ̃dmɑ̃] *nm (de champ)* yield; *(d'investissement)* return, yield; *(de personne, de machine)* output

rendez-vous [rɑ̃devu] *nm inv (rencontre)* appointment; *(amoureux)* date; *(lieu)* meeting place; **donner r. à qn** to arrange to meet sb; **prendre r. avec qn** to make an appointment with sb; **recevoir sur r.** *(médecin)* to see patients by appointment

rendormir* [rɑ̃dɔrmir] **se rendormir** *vpr* to go back to sleep

rendre [rɑ̃dr] **1** *vt (restituer)* to give back, to return (**à** to); *(jugement)* to deliver; *(armes)* to surrender; *(invitation)* to return; *(santé)* to restore; *(exprimer)* to render; *(vomir)* to bring up; **r. célèbre** to make famous; **r. la monnaie à qn** to give sb his/her change; **r. l'âme** to pass away; **r. les armes** to surrender **2** *vi (vomir)* to vomit **3 se rendre** *vpr (criminel)* to give oneself up (**à** to); *(soldats)* to surrender (**à** to); *(aller)* to go (**à** to); **se r. à l'évidence** *(être lucide)* to face facts; **se r. malade** to make oneself ill

renfermer [rɑ̃fɛrme] *vt* to contain ▪ **renfermé, -e 1** *adj (personne)* withdrawn **2** *nm* **sentir le r.** to smell musty

renforcer [rɑ̃fɔrse] *vt* to strengthen, to reinforce

renfort [rɑ̃fɔr] *nm* **des renforts** *(troupes)* reinforcements; *Fig* **à grand r. de** with (the help of) a great deal of

renfrogner [rɑ̃frɔɲe] **se renfrogner** *vpr* to scowl

renier [rənje] *vt (ami, pays)* to disown; *(foi)* to deny

renifler [rənifle] *vti* to sniff ▪ **reniflement** [-əmɑ̃] *nm (bruit)* sniff

renne [rɛn] *nm* reindeer

renom [rənɔ̃] *nm* renown; **de r.** *(ouvrage, artiste)* famous, renowned ▪ **renommé, -e** *adj* famous, renowned (**pour** for) ▪ **renommée** *nf* fame, renown

renoncer [rənɔ̃se] *vi* **r. à qch** to give sth up, to abandon sth; **r. à faire qch** to give up doing sth

renouer [rənwe] **1** *vt (lacet)* to tie again **2** *vi* **r. avec qch** *(tradition)* to revive sth; **r. avec qn** to take up with sb again

renouveau, -x [rənuvo] *nm* revival

renouveler [rənuvle] **1** *vt* to renew; *(expérience)* to repeat **2 se renouveler** *vpr (incident)* to happen again, to recur; *(cellules, sang)* to be renewed ▪ **renouvelable** *adj* renewable ▪ **renouvellement** [-ɛlmɑ̃] *nm* renewal

rénover [renɔve] *vt (édifice, meuble)* to renovate ▪ **rénovation** *nf (d'édifice, de meuble)* renovation

renseigner [rɑ̃seɲe] **1** *vt* to give some information to (**sur** about) **2 se renseigner** *vpr* to make inquiries (**sur** about) ▪ **renseignement** [-əmɑ̃] *nm* piece of information; **renseignements** information; **les renseignements (téléphoniques)** Br directory inquiries, Am information; **demander des renseignements** to make inquiries

rentable [rɑ̃tabl] *adj* profitable ▪ **rentabilité** *nf* profitability

rente [rɑ̃t] *nf* (private) income; *(pension)* pension

rentrée [rɑ̃tre] *nf* **r. des classes** start of the new school year

rentrer [rɑ̃tre] **1** *(aux* **être***) vi (entrer)* to go/come in; *(entrer de nouveau)* to go/come back in; *(chez soi)* to go/come (back) home; **r. en France** to return to France; **en rentrant de l'école** on my/his/her/*etc* way home from school; **r. dans qch** *(pénétrer)* to get into sth; *(sujet: voiture)* to crash into sth; **r. dans une catégorie** to fall into a category **2** *(aux* **avoir***) vt (linge, troupeau)* to bring/take in; *(chemise)* to tuck in; *(griffes)* to retract

renverse [rãvɛrs] **à la renverse** *adv (tomber)* backwards

renverser [rãverse] *vt (faire tomber)* to knock over; *(liquide)* to spill; *(piéton)* to run over; *(tendance, situation)* to reverse; *(gouvernement)* to overthrow **2 se renverser** *vpr (récipient)* to fall over; *(véhicule)* to overturn

renvoi [rãvwa] *nm (de marchandise, de lettre)* return; *(d'employé)* dismissal; *(d'élève)* expulsion; *(rot)* belch, burp ▪ **renvoyer*** *vt (lettre, cadeau)* to send back, to return; *(employé)* to dismiss; *(élève)* to expel; *(balle)* to throw back; *(lumière, image)* to reflect

réorganiser [reɔrganize] *vt* to reorganize ▪ **réorganisation** *nf* reorganization

repaître* [rəpɛtr] **se repaître** *vpr Fig* **se r. de qch** to revel in sth

répandre [repãdr] **1** *vt (liquide)* to spill; *(odeur)* to give off; *(chargement)* to shed; *(bienfaits)* to lavish **2 se répandre** *vpr (nouvelle, peur)* to spread; *(liquide)* to spill; **se r. dans** *(fumée, odeur)* to spread through ▪ **répandu, -e** *adj (opinion, usage)* widespread

reparaître* [rəparɛtr] *vi* to reappear

réparer [repare] *vt (objet, machine)* to repair, to mend; *(faute)* to make amends for; **faire r. qch** to get sth repaired ▪ **réparable** *adj (machine)* repairable ▪ **réparateur, -trice 1** *nmf* repairer **2** *adj (sommeil)* refreshing ▪ **réparation** *nf (action)* repairing; *(résultat)* repair; *(dédommagement)* reparation; **en r.** under repair

repartir* [rəpartir] *(aux* **être)** *vi (continuer)* to set off again; *(s'en retourner)* to go back; *(machine)* to start again

répartir [repartir] *vt (poids, charge)* to distribute; *(tâches, vivres)* to share (out); *(classer)* to divide (up); *(étaler dans le temps)* to spread (out) **(sur** over) ▪ **répartition** *nf (de poids)* distribution; *(de tâches)* sharing; *(classement)* division

repas [rəpa] *nm* meal

repasser [rəpase] **1** *vi* to come/go back; **r. chez qn** to drop in on sb again

2 *vt (montagne, frontière)* to go across again; *(examen)* to take again, *Br* to resit; *(film)* to show again; *(disque, cassette)* to play again; *(linge)* to iron ▪ **repassage** *nm* ironing

repêcher [rəpeʃe] *vt (objet)* to fish out

repeindre* [rəpɛdr] *vt* to repaint

répercuter [reperkyte] **1** *vt (son)* to reflect; *(augmentation)* to pass **2 se répercuter** *vpr (son, lumière)* to be reflected; *Fig* **se r. sur** to have repercussions on

repère [rəpɛr] *nm* mark; **point de r.** *(espace, temps)* reference point ▪ **repérer 1** *vt (endroit)* to locate **2 se repérer** *vpr* to get one's bearings

répertoire [repɛrtwar] *nm (liste)* index; *(carnet)* (indexed) notebook; *Ordinat* directory; *Théât* repertoire

répéter [repete] **1** *vt* to repeat; *(pièce de théâtre, rôle)* to rehearse; **r. à qn que...** to tell sb again that...

2 *vi (redire)* to repeat; *(acteur)* to rehearse

3 se répéter *vpr (radoter)* to repeat oneself; *(événement)* to happen again ▪ **répétition** *nf (redite)* repetition; *Théât* rehearsal; **r. générale** dress rehearsal

répit [repi] *nm* rest, respite; **sans r.** ceaselessly

replacer [rəplase] *vt* to replace, to put back

replanter [rəplãte] *vt* to replant

repli [rəpli] *nm (de vêtement, de terrain)* fold; *(d'armée)* withdrawal; *(de monnaie)* fall

replier [rəplije] **1** *vt (objet)* to fold up; *(couteau)* to fold away; *(ailes)* to fold; *(jambes)* to tuck up **2 se replier** *vpr (objet)* to fold up; *(armée)* to withdraw

réplique [replik] *nf (réponse)* retort; *(d'acteur)* lines; *(copie)* replica; **sans r.** *(argument)* unanswerable ▪ **répliquer 1** *vt* **r. que...** to reply that... **2** *vi* to reply; *(avec impertinence)* to answer back

répondre [repɔdr] **1** *vi* to answer, to reply; *(avec impertinence)* to answer back; *(réagir)* to respond (à to); **r. à qn**

to answer sb, to reply to sb; *(avec impertinence)* to answer sb back; **r. à** *(lettre, question, objection)* to answer, to reply to; *(besoin)* to meet; **r. au téléphone** to answer the phone; **r. de qn/qch** to answer for sb/sth

2 *vt (remarque)* to answer *or* reply with; **r. que...** to answer *or* reply that... ■ **répondeur** *nm* **r. (téléphonique)** answering machine

réponse [repɔ̃s] *nf* answer, reply; *(réaction)* response (**à** to)

reportage [rəpɔrtaʒ] *nm (article, émission)* report; *(métier)* reporting

reporter¹ [rəpɔrte] **1** *vt (objet)* to take back; *(réunion)* to put off, to postpone (**à** until); *(transcrire)* to transfer (**sur** to) **2 se reporter** *vpr* **se r. à** *(texte)* to refer to

reporter² [rəpɔrtɛr] *nm* reporter

repos [rəpo] *nm (détente)* rest; *(tranquillité)* peace

reposer [rəpoze] **1** *vt (objet)* to put back down; *(problème, question)* to raise again; *(délasser)* to rest, to relax; **r. sa tête sur** *(appuyer)* to lean one's head on

2 *vi (être enterré)* to lie; **r. sur** *(bâtiment)* to be built on; *(théorie)* to be based on; **laisser r.** *(liquide)* to allow to settle

3 se reposer *vpr* to rest; **se r. sur qn** to rely on sb ■ **reposant, -e** *adj* restful, relaxing ■ **reposé, -e** *adj* rested

repousser [rəpuse] **1** *vt (en arrière)* to push back; *(sur le côté)* to push away; *(attaque, ennemi)* to beat off; *(offre)* to reject; *(dégoûter)* to repel **2** *vi (cheveux, feuilles)* to grow again

reprendre* [rəprɑ̃dr] **1** *vt (objet)* to take back; *(évadé, ville)* to recapture; *(activité)* to take up again; *(vêtement)* to alter; *(corriger)* to correct; **r. de la viande** to take some more meat

2 *vi (recommencer)* to start again; *(affaires)* to pick up; *(continuer de parler)* to go on, to continue

3 se reprendre *vpr (se ressaisir)* to get a grip on oneself; *(se corriger)* to correct oneself; **s'y r. à deux fois** to have another go (at it)

représenter [rəprezɑ̃te] **1** *vt* to represent; *(pièce de théâtre)* to perform **2 se représenter** *vpr (s'imaginer)* to imagine ■ **représentant, -e** *nmf* representative ■ **représentatif, -ive** *adj* representative (**de** of) ■ **représentation** *nf* representation; *Théât* performance

répression [represjɔ̃] *nf (d'émeute)* suppression; *(mesures de contrôle)* repression ■ **répressif, -ive** *adj* repressive ■ **réprimer** *vt (sentiment, révolte)* to suppress

réprimander [reprimɑ̃de] *vt* to reprimand

reprise [rəpriz] *nf (recommencement)* resumption; *(de l'économie)* recovery; *(de locataire)* = money for fixtures and fittings *(paid by outgoing tenant)*; *(de marchandise)* taking back; *(pour nouvel achat)* part exchange, trade-in; **faire une r. à qch** to darn sth; **à plusieurs reprises** on several occasions ■ **repriser** *vt (chaussette)* to darn

réprobateur, -trice [reprɔbatœr, -tris] *adj* disapproving

reproche [rəprɔʃ] *nm* reproach; **sans r.** beyond reproach ■ **reprocher** *vt* **r. qch à qn** to blame *or* reproach sb for sth

reproduire* [rəprɔdɥir] **1** *vt (modèle, son)* to reproduce **2 se reproduire** *vpr (animaux)* to reproduce; *(incident)* to happen again ■ **reproduction** *nf (d'animaux, de son)* reproduction; *(copie)* copy

reptile [reptil] *nm* reptile

repu, -e [rəpy] *adj (rassasié)* satiated

république [repyblik] *nf* republic ■ **républicain, -e** *adj & nmf* republican

répugnant, -e [repyɲɑ̃, -ɑ̃t] *adj* repulsive ■ **répugner** *vi* **r. à qn** to be repugnant to sb; **r. à faire qch** to be loath to do sth

réputation [repytasjɔ̃] *nf* reputation; **avoir la r. d'être franc** to have a reputation for being frank *or* for frankness ■ **réputé, -e** *adj (célèbre)* renowned (**pour** for)

requête [rəkɛt] *nf* request

requin [rəkɛ̃] *nm (animal)* shark

réquisitionner [rekizisjɔne] *vt* to requisition, to commandeer

rescapé, -e [rɛskape] **1** *adj* surviving **2** *nmf* survivor

réseau, -x [rezo] *nm* network

réservation [rezɛrvasjɔ̃] *nf* reservation, booking

réserve [rezɛrv] *nf (provision, discrétion)* reserve; *(entrepôt)* storeroom; *(de bibliothèque)* stacks; *(de chasse, de pêche)* preserve; *(restriction)* reservation; *Mil* **la r.** the reserve; **en r.** in reserve; **sans r.** *(admiration)* unqualified; **sous r. de** subject to; **sous toutes réserves** without guarantee; **r. naturelle** nature reserve

réserver [rezɛrve] **1** *vt* to reserve; *(garder)* to save, to keep (**à** for); *(marchandises)* to put aside (**à** for); *(sort, surprise)* to hold in store (**à** for) **2 se réserver** *vpr* **se r. pour qch** to save oneself for sth ▪ **réservé, -e** *adj (personne, place, chambre)* reserved

réservoir [rezɛrvwar] *nm (lac)* reservoir; *(cuve)* tank; **r. d'essence** *Br* petrol *or Am* gas tank

résidence [rezidɑ̃s] *nf* residence; **r. secondaire** second home; **r. universitaire** *Br* hall of residence, *Am* dormitory ▪ **résident, -e** *nmf* resident ▪ **résidentiel, -elle** *adj (quartier)* residential ▪ **résider** *vi* to reside; **r. dans** *(consister en)* to lie in

résidu [rezidy] *nm* residue

résigner [reziɲe] **se résigner** *vpr* to resign oneself (**à qch** to sth; **à faire** to doing) ▪ **résignation** *nf* resignation

résistance [rezistɑ̃s] *nf* resistance (**à** to); *Hist* **la R.** the Resistance

résister [reziste] *vi* **r. à** *(attaque, agresseur, tentation)* to resist; *(chaleur, fatigue, souffrance)* to withstand; *(mauvais traitement)* to stand up to ▪ **résistant, -e 1** *adj* tough; **r. à la chaleur** heat-resistant **2** *nmf Hist* Resistance fighter

résolu, -e [rezɔly] **1** *pp de* **résoudre 2** *adj* determined, resolute; **r. à faire qch** determined to do sth ▪ **résolution** *nf (décision)* resolution; *(fermeté)* determination

résonance [rezɔnɑ̃s] *nf* resonance

résonner [rezɔne] *vi (cri)* to resound; *(salle, voix)* to echo (**de** with)

résoudre* [rezudr] **1** *vt (problème)* to solve; *(difficulté)* to resolve; **r. de faire qch** to resolve to do sth **2 se résoudre** *vpr* **se r. à faire qch** to resolve to do sth

respect [rɛspɛ] *nm* respect (**pour/de** for) ▪ **respectable** *adj (honorable, important)* respectable ▪ **respecter** *vt* to respect; **r. la loi** to abide by the law; **faire r. la loi** to enforce the law ▪ **respectueux, -euse** *adj* respectful (**envers** to; **de** of)

respirer [rɛspire] **1** *vi* to breathe **2** *vt* to breathe (in) ▪ **respiration** *nf* breathing; *(haleine)* breath

responsable [rɛspɔ̃sabl] **1** *adj* responsible (**de qch** for sth; **devant qn** to sb) **2** *nmf (chef)* person in charge; *(d'organisation)* official; *(coupable)* person responsible (**de** for) ▪ **responsabilité** *nf* responsibility; *(légale)* liability

ressaisir [rəsezir] **se ressaisir** *vpr* to pull oneself together

ressemblance [rəsɑ̃blɑ̃s] *nf* likeness, resemblance (**avec** to) ▪ **ressembler 1** *vi* **r. à** to look like, to resemble **2 se ressembler** *vpr* to look alike

ressentir* [rəsɑ̃tir] *vt* to feel

resserrer [rəsere] **1** *vt (nœud, boulon)* to tighten; *Fig (liens)* to strengthen **2 se resserrer** *vpr (nœud)* to tighten

resservir* [rəservir] **1** *vi (outil)* to come in useful (again) **2 se resservir** *vpr* **se r. de** *(plat)* to have another helping of

ressort [rəsɔr] *nm (objet)* spring; **du r. de** within the competence of; **en dernier r.** *(décider)* as a last resort

ressortir* [rəsɔrtir] **1** *(aux être) vi (personne)* to go/come back out; *(film)* to be shown again; *(se voir)* to stand out; **faire r. qch** to bring sth out; **il ressort de...** *(résulte)* it emerges from... **2** *(aux avoir) vi (vêtement)* to get out again

ressortissant, -e [rəsɔrtisɑ̃, -ɑ̃t] *nmf* national

ressource [rəsurs] **1** *nfpl* **ressources**

(moyens, argent) resources; **être sans ressources** to be without means **2** *nf (possibilité)* possibility **(de faire** of doing); **avoir de la r.** to be resourceful; **en dernière r.** as a last resort

ressusciter [resysite] *vi* to rise from the dead

restant, -e [rɛstɑ̃, -ɑ̃t] **1** *adj* remaining **2** *nm* **le r.** the rest, the remainder; **un r. de viande** some leftover meat

restaurant [rɛstɔrɑ̃] *nm* restaurant; **manger au r.** to eat out

restaurateur, -trice [rɛstɔratœr, -tris] *nmf (hôtelier, hôtelière)* restaurant owner; *(de tableaux)* restorer

restaurer [rɛstɔre] **1** *vt (réparer, rétablir)* to restore **2 se restaurer** *vpr* to have something to eat ▪ **restauration** *nf (hôtellerie)* catering; *(de tableau)* restoration

reste [rɛst] *nm* rest, remainder **(de** of); **restes** remains **(de** of); *(de repas)* leftovers; **au r., du r.** moreover, besides

rester [rɛste] *(aux* **être)** *vi* to stay, to remain; *(calme, jeune)* to keep, to stay, to remain; *(subsister)* to be left, to remain; **il reste du pain** there's some bread left (over); **il me reste une pomme** I have one apple left; **l'argent qui lui reste** the money he/she has left; **il me reste deux choses à faire** I still have two things to do

restituer [rɛstitɥe] *vt (rendre)* to return (**à** to); *(argent)* to repay ▪ **restitution** *nf (d'objet)* return

restriction [rɛstriksjɔ̃] *nf* restriction; **sans r.** *(approuver)* unreservedly

résultat [rezylta] *nm* result; **avoir qch pour r.** to result in sth ▪ **résulter 1** *vi* **r. de** to result from **2** *v impersonnel* **il en résulte que...** the result of this is that...

résumer [rezyme] **1** *vt (abréger)* to summarize; *(récapituler)* to sum up **2 se résumer** *vpr (orateur)* to sum up; **se r. à qch** *(se réduire à)* to boil down to sth ▪ **résumé** *nm* summary; **en r.** in short

rétablir [retablir] **1** *vt (communications, ordre)* to restore; *(vérité)* to re-

establish; *(employé)* to reinstate **2 se rétablir** *vpr (malade)* to recover ▪ **rétablissement** *nm (d'ordre, de dynastie)* restoration; *(de vérité)* re-establishment; *(de malade)* recovery

retard [rətar] *nm (de personne)* lateness; *(sur horaire)* delay; **en r.** late; **en r. sur qn/qch** behind sb/sth; **rattraper** *ou* **combler son r.** to catch up; **avoir du r.** to be late; *(sur un programme)* to be behind (schedule); *(montre)* to be slow; **avoir une heure de r.** to be an hour late; **prendre du r.** *(personne)* to fall behind

retarder [rətarde] **1** *vt (faire arriver en retard)* to delay; *(date, montre, départ)* to put back; **r. qn** *(dans une activité)* to put sb behind **2** *vi (montre)* to be slow; **r. de cinq minutes** to be five minutes slow

retenir* [rətnir] **1** *vt (personne)* to keep; *(eau, chaleur)* to retain; *(cotisation)* to deduct (**sur** from); *(suggestion)* to adopt; *(larmes, foule)* to hold back; *Math (chiffre)* to carry; *(se souvenir de)* to remember; *(réserver)* to reserve; **r. qn prisonnier** to keep sb prisoner; **r. l'attention de qn** to catch sb's attention; **r. qn de faire qch** to stop sb (from) doing sth **2 se retenir** *vpr (se contenir)* to restrain oneself; **se r. de faire qch** to stop oneself (from) doing sth; **se r. à qn/qch** to cling to sb/sth

retenue [rətny] *nf (modération)* restraint; *(de salaire)* deduction; *Scol (punition)* detention

retirer [rətire] **1** *vt* to withdraw; *(faire sortir)* to take out; *(ôter)* to take off; *(éloigner)* to take away; *(aller chercher)* to pick up; **r. qch à qn** *(permis)* to take sth away from sb; **r. qch de qch** *(gagner)* to derive sth from sth **2 se retirer** *vpr* to withdraw (**de** from); *(mer)* to ebb

retomber [rətɔ̃be] *vi* to fall again; *(après un saut)* to land; *(intérêt)* to slacken; **r. dans** *(l'oubli)* to sink back into

retouche [rətuʃ] *nf (de vêtement)* alteration ▪ **retoucher** *vt (vêtement, texte)* to alter; *(photo, tableau)* to touch up

retour [rətur] *nm* return; *(trajet)* return journey; **être de r.** to be back (**de** from); **à mon r.** when I get/got back (**de** from); **r. à l'envoyeur** return to sender; **match r.** return *Br* match *or Am* game

retourner [rəturne] **1** *(aux avoir)* vt *(matelas, steak)* to turn over; *(terre)* to turn; *(vêtement, sac)* to turn inside out; *(compliment)* to return; **r. qch contre qn** *(argument)* to turn sth against sb; *(arme)* to turn sth on sb

2 *(aux être)* *vi* to go back, to return

3 se retourner *vpr (pour regarder)* to turn round; *(sur le dos)* to turn over; *(dans son lit)* to toss and turn; *(voiture)* to overturn; *Fig* **se r. contre** to turn against

retrait [rətrɛ] *nm* withdrawal; *(de bagages, de billets)* collection; *(des eaux)* receding; **en r.** *(maison)* set back; **rester en r.** to stay in the background

retraite [rətrɛt] *nf (d'employé)* retirement; *(pension)* (retirement) pension; *(refuge)* retreat, refuge; *(d'armée)* retreat; **prendre sa r.** to retire; **être à la r.** to be retired; **r. anticipée** early retirement ▪ **retraité, -e 1** *adj* retired **2** *nmf* senior citizen, *Br* (old age) pensioner

retraitement [rətrɛtmã] *nm*

retrancher [rətrãʃe] **1** *vt (passage, nom)* to remove (**de** from); *(argent, quantité)* to deduct (**de** from) **2 se retrancher** *vpr (soldats)* to dig in; *Fig* **se r. dans/derrière qch** to hide in/behind sth

retransmettre* [rətrãsmɛtr] *vt* to broadcast ▪ **retransmission** *nf* broadcast

rétrécir [retresir] **1** *vt (vêtement)* to take in **2** *vi (au lavage)* to shrink **3 se rétrécir** *vpr (rue)* to narrow

rétroactif, -ive [retrɔaktif, -iv] *adj* retroactive

rétrograder [retrograde] **1** *vt (fonctionnaire, officier)* to demote **2** *vi (automobiliste)* to change down

rétrospectif, -ive [retrɔspɛktif, -iv] **1** *adj* retrospective **2** *nf* **rétrospective** retrospective

retrouver [rətruve] **1** *vt (objet)* to find again; *(personne)* to meet again; *(forces, santé)* to regain; *(se rappeler)* to recall; *(découvrir)* to rediscover **2 se retrouver** *vpr (être)* to find oneself; *(trouver son chemin)* to find one's way (**dans** round); *(se rencontrer)* to meet; **se r. à la rue** to find oneself homeless

rétroviseur [retrovizœr] *nm* rear-view mirror

Réunion [reynjɔ̃] *nf* **la R.** Réunion

réunion [reynjɔ̃] *nf (séance)* meeting; *(d'objets)* collection, gathering; *(jonction)* joining; **être en r.** to be in a meeting; **r. de famille** family gathering

réunir [reynir] **1** *vt (objets)* to put together; *(documents)* to gather together; *(fonds)* to raise; *(amis, famille)* to get together; *(après une rupture)* to reunite; *(avantages, qualités)* to combine; **r. qch à qch** to join sth to sth **2 se réunir** *vpr (personnes)* to meet; **se r. autour de qn/qch** to gather round sb/sth

réussir [reysir] **1** *vt (bien faire)* to make a success of; *(examen)* to pass **2** *vi* to succeed, to be successful (**à faire** in doing); **r. à un examen** to pass an exam ▪ **réussi, -e** *adj* successful ▪ **réussite** *nf* success; *Cartes* **faire des réussites** to play *Br* patience *or Am* solitaire

revaloriser [rəvalɔrize] *vt (monnaie)* to revalue; *(salaires, profession)* to upgrade

revanche [rəvãʃ] *nf* revenge; *(de match)* return game; **prendre sa r.** to get one's revenge (**sur** on); **en r.** on the other hand

rêve [rɛv] *nm* dream; **faire un r.** to have a dream

réveil [revɛj] *nm (de personnes)* waking; *(pendule)* alarm (clock); **à son r.** on waking

réveiller [reveje] **1** *vt (personne)* to wake (up); *Fig (douleur)* to revive; *Fig (sentiment, souvenir)* to revive **2 se réveiller** *vpr (personne)* to wake (up); *(nature)* to reawaken; *Fig (douleur)* to come back ▪ **réveillé, -e** *adj* awake ▪ **réveille-matin** *nm inv* alarm clock

réveillon [revɛjɔ̃] *nm (repas)* midnight supper; *(soirée)* midnight party *(on Christmas Eve or New Year's Eve)* ■ **réveillonner** *vi* to see in Christmas/the New Year

révéler [revele] **1** *vt* to reveal (**que** that) **2 se révéler** *vpr (personne)* to reveal oneself; *(talent)* to be revealed; **se r. facile** to turn out to be easy ■ **révélateur, -trice** *adj* revealing; **r. de qch** indicative of sth ■ **révélation** *nf (action, découverte)* revelation; *(personne)* discovery; **faire des révélations** to disclose important information

revendiquer [rəvɑ̃dike] *vt* to claim; *(attentat)* to claim responsibility for ■ **revendication** *nf* claim

revendre [rəvɑ̃dr] *vt* to resell

revenir* [rəvənir] *(aux* **être)** *vi (personne)* to come back, to return; *(date)* to come round again; **le dîner nous est revenu à 50 euros** the dinner cost us 50 euros; **r. cher** to work out expensive; **r. à** *(activité, sujet)* to go back to, to return to; *(se résumer à)* to boil down to; **r. à qn** *(forces, mémoire)* to come back to sb; *(honneur)* to fall to sb; **r. de** *(surprise)* to get over; **r. sur** *(décision, promesse)* to go back on; *(passé, question)* to go back over; **r. sur ses pas** to retrace one's steps

revenu [rəvəny] *nm* income (**de** from); *(d'un État)* revenue (**de** from)

rêver [reve] **1** *vt* to dream (**que** that) **2** *vi* to dream (**de** of; **de faire** of doing)

réverbère [reverber] *nm* street lamp

révérence [reverɑ̃s] *nf (respect)* reverence; *(salut)* curtsey

rêverie [revri] *nf* daydream

revers [rəver] *nm (de veste)* lapel; *(de pantalon) Br* turn-up, *Am* cuff; *(d'étoffe)* wrong side; *(de pièce)* reverse; *(coup du sort)* setback; *(au tennis)* backhand; **d'un r. de la main** with the back of one's hand; *Fig* **le r. de la médaille** the other side of the coin

reverser [rəverse] *vt (café, vin)* to pour more; *Fig (argent)* to transfer (**sur un compte** into an account)

réversible [reversibl] *adj* reversible

revêtir* [rəvetir] *vt* to cover (**de** with); *(habit)* to don; *(caractère, forme)* to assume; **r. qn** *(habiller)* to dress sb (**de** in) ■ **revêtement** *nm (surface)* covering; *(de route)* surface

rêveur, -euse [revœr, -øz] **1** *adj* dreamy **2** *nmf* dreamer

revient [rəvjɛ̃] *nm* **prix de r.** *Br* cost price, *Am* wholesale price

revirement [rəvirmɑ̃] *nm (changement) Br* about-turn, *Am* about-face; *(de situation, d'opinion, de politique)* reversal

réviser [revize] *vt (leçon)* to revise; *(machine, voiture)* to service; *(jugement, règlement)* to review ■ **révision** *nf (de leçon)* revision; *(de machine)* service; *(de jugement)* review

revivre* [rəvivr] **1** *vt (incident)* to relive **2** *vi* to live again; **faire r. qch** to revive sth

revoici [rəvwasi] *prép* **me r.** here I am again

revoilà [rəvwala] *prép* **la r.** there she is again

revoir* [rəvwar] *vt* to see (again); *(texte, leçon)* to revise; **au r.** goodbye

révolte [revɔlt] *nf* revolt ■ **révolter 1** *vt* to appal **2 se révolter** *vpr* to rebel, to revolt (**contre** against)

révolu, -e [revɔly] *adj (époque)* past; **avoir trente ans révolus** to be over thirty

révolution [revɔlysjɔ̃] *nf (changement, rotation)* revolution ■ **révolutionner** *vt (transformer)* to revolutionize

revolver [revɔlver] *nm* revolver

revue [rəvy] *nf (magazine)* magazine; *(spécialisée)* journal; *(spectacle)* revue; *Mil* review; **passer qch en r.** to review sth

rez-de-chaussée [redəʃose] *nm inv Br* ground floor, *Am* first floor

Rhin [rɛ̃] *nm* **le R.** the Rhine

rhinocéros [rinɔseros] *nm* rhinoceros

Rhône [ron] *nm* **le R.** the Rhône

rhumatisme [rymatism] *nm* rheumatism; **avoir des rhumatismes** to have rheumatism

rhume [rym] *nm* cold; **r. des foins** hay fever

ri [ri] *pp de* **rire**

ricaner [rikane] *vi (sarcastiquement)* *Br* to snigger, *Am* to snicker; *(bêtement)* to giggle

riche [riʃ] **1** *adj (personne, pays, aliment)* rich; **r. en** *(vitamines, minérai)* rich in **2** *nmf* rich person; **les riches** the rich ■ **richesse** *nf (de personne, de pays)* wealth; *(d'étoffe, de sol)* richness; **richesses** *(trésor)* riches; *(ressources)* wealth

ricocher [rikɔʃe] *vi* to rebound, to ricochet ■ **ricochet** *nm* rebound, ricochet; *Fig* **par r.** indirectly

ride [rid] *nf (de visage)* wrinkle ■ **ridé, -e** *adj* wrinkled ■ **rider 1** *vt (visage, peau)* to wrinkle; *(eau)* to ripple **2 se rider** *vpr (visage, peau)* to wrinkle

rideau, -x [rido] *nm* curtain; *(métallique)* shutter; *Fig (écran)* screen (**de** of)

ridicule [ridikyl] **1** *adj* ridiculous, ludicrous **2** *nm (moquerie)* ridicule; *(absurdité)* ridiculousness; **tourner qn/qch en r.** to ridicule sb/sth ■ **ridiculiser 1** *vt* to ridicule **2 se ridiculiser** *vpr* to make a fool of oneself

RIEN [rjɛ̃] **1** *pron* nothing; **il ne sait r.** he knows nothing, he doesn't know anything; **r. du tout** nothing at all; **r. d'autre/de bon** nothing else/good; **r. de tel** nothing like it; **de r.!** *(je vous en prie)* don't mention it!; **ça ne fait r.** it doesn't matter; **pour r. au monde** never in a thousand years; **comme si de r. n'était** as if nothing had happened

2 *nm* (mere) nothing, trifle; **un r. de** a little; **en un r. de temps** in no time

rieur, -euse [rijœr, -øz] *adj* cheerful

rigide [riʒid] *adj* rigid; *(carton)* stiff; *(éducation)* strict

rigole [rigɔl] *nf (conduit)* channel; *(filet d'eau)* rivulet

rigueur [rigœr] *nf (d'analyse)* rigour; *(de climat)* harshness; *(de personne)* strictness; **être de r.** to be the rule; **à la r.** if need be ■ **rigoureux, -euse** *adj (analyse)* rigorous; *(climat, punition)*

harsh; *(personne, morale, neutralité)* strict

rillettes [rijet] *nfpl* potted minced pork

rimer [rime] *vi* to rhyme (**avec** with)

rincer [rɛ̃se] *vt* to rinse; *(verre)* to rinse (out)

ring [riŋ] *nm* (boxing) ring

riposte [ripɔst] *nf (réponse)* retort; *(attaque)* counterattack ■ **riposter 1** *vt* **r. que...** to retort that... **2** *vi* to counterattack; **r. à** *(attaque)* to counter; *(insulte)* to reply to

rire* [rir] **1** *nm* laugh; **rires** laughter; **le fou r.** the giggles **2** *vi* to laugh (**de** at); *(s'amuser)* to have a good time; *(plaisanter)* to joke; **r. aux éclats** to roar with laughter; **faire qch pour r.** to do sth for a joke *or* laugh

risible [rizibl] *adj* laughable

risque [risk] *nm* risk; **au r. de faire qch** at the risk of doing sth; **à vos risques et périls** at your own risk; **assurance tous risques** comprehensive insurance

risquer [riske] **1** *vt* to risk; *(question)* to venture; **r. de faire qch** to stand a good chance of doing sth **2 se risquer** *vpr* **se r. à faire qch** to dare to do sth ■ **risqué, -e** *adj (dangereux)* risky; *(osé)* risqué

rivage [rivaʒ] *nm* shore

rival, -e, -aux, -ales [rival, -o] *adj & nmf* rival ■ **rivaliser** *vi* to compete (**avec** with; **de** in) ■ **rivalité** *nf* rivalry

rive [riv] *nf (de fleuve)* bank; *(de lac)* shore

riverain, -e [rivərɛ̃, -ɛn] **1** *adj (de rivière)* riverside; *(de lac)* lakeside **2** *nmf (près d'une rivière)* riverside resident; *(près d'un lac)* lakeside resident; *(de rue)* resident

rivière [rivjer] *nf* river

riz [ri] *nm* rice; **r. blanc/complet** white/brown rice; **r. au lait** rice pudding ■ **rizière** *nf* paddy (field), rice-field

RMI [ɛrɛmi] *(abrév* **revenu minimum d'insertion)** *nm Br* ≃ income support, *Am* ≃ welfare

RN *(abrév* **route nationale)** *nf Br* main road, A-road, *Am* (state) highway

robe [rɔb] *nf (de femme)* dress; *(d'ecclésiastique, de juge)* robe; *(pelage)* coat; **r. du soir** evening dress; **r. de chambre** *Br* dressing gown, *Am* bathrobe; **pomme de terre en r. des champs** jacket potato, baked potato

robinet [rɔbinɛ] *nm Br* tap, *Am* faucet

robot [rɔbo] *nm* robot; **r. ménager** food processor

robuste [rɔbyst] *adj* robust

roc [rɔk] *nm* rock

rocaille [rɔkaj] *nf (terrain)* rocky ground; *(de jardin)* rockery ■ **rocailleux, -euse** *adj* rocky, stony; *(voix)* harsh

roche [rɔʃ] *nf* rock ■ **rocher** *nm (bloc, substance)* rock ■ **rocheux, -euse** *adj* rocky

rock [rɔk] **1** *nm (musique)* rock **2** *adj inv* **chanteur/opéra r.** rock singer/opera ■ **rockeur, -euse** *nmf (musicien)* rock musician

roder [rɔde] *vt (moteur, voiture) Br* to run in, *Am* to break in

rôder [rode] *vi* to be on the prowl ■ **rôdeur, -euse** *nmf* prowler

rognon [rɔɲɔ̃] *nm* kidney

roi [rwa] *nm* king; **fête des Rois** Twelfth Night

rôle [rol] *nm* role, part; *(de père)* job; **à tour de r.** in turn

romain, -e [rɔmɛ̃, -ɛn] **1** *adj* Roman **2** *nmf* **R., Romaine** Roman **3** *nf* **romaine** *(laitue) Br* cos (lettuce), *Am* romaine

roman [rɔmɑ̃] *nm* novel; *Fig (histoire)* story ■ **romancier, -ère** *nmf* novelist

romanesque [rɔmanɛsk] *adj* romantic; *(incroyable)* fantastic

romantique [rɔmɑ̃tik] *adj* romantic

romarin [rɔmarɛ̃] *nm* rosemary

rompre* [rɔ̃pr] **1** *vt* to break; *(pourparlers, relations)* to break off **2** *vi (casser)* to break; *(digue)* to burst; *(fiancés)* to break it off **3 se rompre** *vpr (corde)* to break; *(digue)* to burst

ronces [rɔ̃s] *nfpl (branches)* brambles

rond, -e¹ [rɔ̃, -ɔ̃d] **1** *adj* round; *(gras)* plump; **chiffre r.** whole number **2** *adv* **10 euros tout r.** 10 euros exactly **3** *nm*

(cercle) circle; **en r.** *(s'asseoir)* in a circle ■ **rondement** *adv* briskly ■ **rond-point** *(pl* **ronds-points)** *nm Br* roundabout, *Am* traffic circle

ronde² [rɔ̃d] *nf (de soldat)* round; *(de policier)* beat; *(danse)* round (dance); *Mus Br* semibreve, *Am* whole note; **faire sa r.** *(gardien)* to do one's rounds

rondelle [rɔ̃dɛl] *nf (tranche)* slice

ronfler [rɔ̃fle] *vi (personne)* to snore

ronger [rɔ̃ʒe] **1** *vt* to gnaw (at); *(ver, mer, rouille)* to eat into; **r. qn** *(maladie, chagrin)* to consume sb **2 se ronger** *vpr* **se r. les ongles** to bite one's nails ■ **rongeur** *nm* rodent

ronronner [rɔ̃rɔne] *vi* to purr

roquette [rɔkɛt] *nf Mil* rocket

rosace [rozas] *nf* rosette; *(d'église)* rose window

rosbif [rɔzbif] *nm* **du r.** *(rôti)* roast beef; *(à rôtir)* roasting beef; **un r.** a joint of roast/roasting beef

rose [roz] **1** *adj (couleur)* pink; *(situation, teint)* rosy **2** *nm (couleur)* pink **3** *nf (fleur)* rose ■ **rosé, -e 1** *adj* pinkish **2** *adj & nm (vin)* rosé

roseau, -x [rozo] *nm* reed

rosée [roze] *nf* dew

rossignol [rɔsiɲɔl] *nm (oiseau)* nightingale

rôti [roti] *nm* **du r.** roasting meat; *(cuit)* roast meat; **un r.** a joint; **r. de bœuf** (joint of) roast beef

rotin [rɔtɛ̃] *nm* rattan

rôtir [rotir] *vti* to roast; **faire r. qch** to roast sth

roue [ru] *nf* wheel; **r. dentée** cogwheel; **être en r. libre** to freewheel; **les deux roues** two-wheeled vehicles

rouge [ruʒ] **1** *adj* red; *(fer)* red-hot **2** *nm (couleur)* red; **le feu est au r.** the (traffic) lights are at red; **r. à lèvres** lipstick

rougeur [ruʒœr] *nf* redness; *(due à la honte)* blush; *(due à l'émotion)* flush; **rougeurs** *(irritation)* rash, red blotches

rougir [ruʒir] **1** *vt (visage)* to redden **2** *vi (de honte)* to blush **(de** with); *(d'émotion)* to flush **(de** with)

rouille [ruj] **1** *nf* rust **2** *adj inv (couleur)* rust(-coloured) ▪ **rouillé, -e** *adj* rusty ▪ **rouiller 1** *vi* to rust **2 se rouiller** *vpr* to rust

rouleau, -x [rulo] *nm (outil, vague)* roller; *(de papier, de pellicule)* roll; **r. à pâtisserie** rolling pin; **r. compresseur** steamroller

roulement [rulmɑ̃] *nm (bruit)* rumbling, rumble; *(de tambour, de tonnerre)* roll; *(ordre)* rotation; **par r.** in rotation; *Tech* **r. à billes** ball bearing

rouler [rule] **1** *vt* to roll; *(crêpe, ficelle, manches)* to roll up **2** *vi (balle)* to roll; *(train, voiture)* to go, to travel **3 se rouler** *vpr* to roll; **se r. dans** *(couverture)* to roll oneself (up) in ▪ **roulant, -e** *adj (escalier)* moving

roulette [rulɛt] *nf (de meuble)* castor; *(de dentiste)* drill; *(jeu)* roulette

roulotte [rulɔt] *nf (de gitan)* caravan

Roumanie [rumani] *nf* **la R.** Romania ▪ **roumain, -e 1** *adj* Romanian **2** *nmf* **R., Roumaine** Romanian **3** *nm (langue)* Romanian

rousse [rus] *voir* **roux**

rousseur [rusœr] *nf* **tache de r.** freckle ▪ **roussi** *nm* **ça sent le r.** there's a smell of burning ▪ **roussir 1** *vt (brûler)* to scorch, to singe **2** *vi (feuilles)* to turn brown

route [rut] *nf* road **(de** to); *(itinéraire)* way, route; *Fig (chemin)* path; **grand-r., grande r.** main road; **code de la r.** *Br* Highway Code, *Am* traffic regulations; **en r.** on the way, en route; **par la r.** by road; *Fig* **faire fausse r.** to be on the wrong track; **mettre qch en r.** *(voiture)* to start sth (up); **se mettre en r.** to set out **(pour** for); **une heure de r.** *(en voiture)* an hour's drive; **faire r. vers Paris** to head for Paris; **r. départementale** secondary road, *Br* B road; **r. nationale** *Br* main road, A-road, *Am* (state) highway

routier, -ère [rutje, -ɛr] **1** *adj* **carte/sécurité routière** road map/safety; **réseau r.** road network **2** *nm (camionneur)* (long-distance) *Br* lorry *or Am* truck driver; *(restaurant) Br* transport café, *Am* truck stop

routine [rutin] *nf* routine; **contrôle de r.** routine check ▪ **routinier, -ère** *adj* **travail r.** routine work; **être r.** *(personne)* to be set in one's ways

rouvrir* [ruvrir] *vti,* **se rouvrir** *vpr* to reopen

roux, rousse [ru, rus] **1** *adj (cheveux)* red, ginger; *(personne)* red-haired **2** *nmf* redhead

royal, -e, -aux, -ales [rwajal, -jo] *adj (famille, palais)* royal; *(cadeau, festin)* fit for a king; *(salaire)* princely

royaume [rwajom] *nm* kingdom ▪ **Royaume-Uni** *nm* **le R.** the United Kingdom

royauté [rwajote] *nf (monarchie)* monarchy

ruban [rybɑ̃] *nm* ribbon; *(de chapeau)* band; **r. adhésif** sticky *or* adhesive tape

rubis [rybi] *nm (pierre)* ruby; *(de montre)* jewel

rubrique [rybrik] *nf (article de journal)* column; *(catégorie, titre)* heading

ruche [ryʃ] *nf* beehive

rude [ryd] *adj (pénible)* tough; *(hiver, voix)* harsh; *(rêche)* rough

rue [ry] *nf* street; **être à la r.** *(sans domicile)* to be on the streets ▪ **ruelle** *nf* alley(way)

ruer [rɥe] **1** *vi (cheval)* to kick (out) **2 se ruer** *vpr (foncer)* to rush **(sur** at) ▪ **ruée** *nf* rush; **la r. vers l'or** the gold rush

rugby [rygbi] *nm* rugby ▪ **rugbyman** [rygbiman] *(pl* **-men** [-mɛn]) *nm* rugby player

rugir [ryʒir] *vi* to roar ▪ **rugissement** *nm* roar

rugueux, -euse [rygø, -øz] *adj* rough

ruine [rɥin] *nf (décombres, destruction, faillite)* ruin; **en r.** *(bâtiment)* in ruins; **tomber en r.** *(bâtiment)* to become a ruin ▪ **ruiner 1** *vt (personne, santé, pays)* to ruin **2 se ruiner** *vpr (perdre tout son argent)* to ruin oneself; *(dépenser beaucoup d'argent)* to spend a fortune ▪ **ruineux, -euse** *adj (goûts, projet)* ruinously expensive; *(dépense)* ruinous; **ce n'est pas r.** it won't ruin me/you/*etc*

ruisseau, -x [rɥiso] *nm* stream; *(caniveau)* gutter ▪ **ruisseler** *vi* to stream (**de** with)

rumeur [rymœr] *nf (murmure)* murmur; *(nouvelle)* rumour

ruminer [rymine] **1** *vt (herbe)* to chew **2** *vi (vache)* to chew the cud

rupture [ryptyr] *nf* breaking; *(de fiançailles, de relations)* breaking off; *(de pourparlers)* breakdown (**de** in); *(dispute)* break-up; **être en r. de stock** to be out of stock

rural, -e, -aux, -ales [ryral, -o] *adj (population)* rural; **vie rurale** country life

ruse [ryz] *nf (subterfuge)* trick; **la r.** *(habileté)* cunning; *(fourberie)* trickery ▪ **rusé, -e** *adj* cunning, crafty

Russie [rysi] *nf* **la R.** Russia ▪ **russe 1** *adj* Russian **2** *nmf* **R.** Russian **3** *nm (langue)* Russian

rythme [ritm] *nm* rhythm; *(de travail)* rate; *(allure)* pace; **les rythmes scolaires** = the way in which the school year is organized ▪ **rythmé, -e** *adj* rhythmic(al)

Ss

S, s [ɛs] *nm inv* S, s

s' [s] *voir* se, si

sa [sa] *voir* son³

sable [sabl] *nm* sand; **sables mouvants** quicksands

sablé [sable] *nm* shortbread *Br* biscuit *or Am* cookie ▪ **sablée** *adj f* **pâte sablée** shortcrust pastry

sablier [sablije] *nm* hourglass; *Culin* egg timer

saborder [saborde] *vt (navire)* to scuttle

sabot [sabo] *nm (de cheval)* hoof; *(chaussure)* clog; **s. de Denver** wheel clamp

saboter [sabote] *vt (machine, projet)* to sabotage ▪ **sabotage** *nm* sabotage ▪ **saboteur, -euse** *nmf* saboteur

sabre [sɑbr] *nm* sabre

sac [sak] *nm* bag; *(grand, en toile)* sack; **s. à main** handbag; **s. à dos** rucksack; **s. de voyage** travelling bag

saccade [sakad] *nf* jerk, jolt; **par saccades** in fits and starts ▪ **saccadé, -e** *adj* jerky

saccager [sakaʒe] *vt (détruire)* to wreak havoc in

sachant, sache(s), sachent [saʃɑ̃, saʃ] *voir* savoir

sachet [saʃɛ] *nm* (small) bag; **s. de thé** teabag

sacre [sakr] *nm (de roi)* coronation ▪ **sacrer** *vt (roi)* to crown

sacré, -e [sakre] *adj (saint)* sacred ▪ **sacrement** *nm Rel* sacrament

sacrifice [sakrifis] *nm* sacrifice ▪ **sacrifier 1** *vt* to sacrifice (à to) **2** *vi* **s. à la mode** to be a slave to fashion **3 se sacrifier** *vpr* to sacrifice oneself (**pour** for)

sacrilège [sakrilɛʒ] **1** *adj* sacrilegious **2** *nm* sacrilege

sadique [sadik] **1** *adj* sadistic **2** *nmf* sadist

safari [safari] *nm* safari; **faire un s.** to go on safari

safran [safrɑ̃] *nm* saffron

sage [saʒ] **1** *adj (avisé)* wise; *(tranquille)* good **2** *nm* wise man ▪ **sage-femme** *(pl* sages-femmes*) nf* midwife ▪ **sagesse** *nf (philosophie)* wisdom; *(calme)* good behaviour

Sagittaire [saʒiter] *nm* **le S.** *(signe)* Sagittarius

saigner [seɲe] *vti* to bleed; **s. du nez** to have a nosebleed ▪ **saignant, -e** *adj (viande)* rare

saillant, -e [sajɑ̃, -ɑ̃t] *adj* projecting ▪ **saillie** *nf (partie avant)* projection

sain, -e [sɛ̃, sɛn] *adj* healthy; *(nourriture)* wholesome, healthy; **s. et sauf** safe and sound

saint, -e [sɛ̃, sɛ̃t] **1** *adj (lieu)* holy; *(personne)* saintly; **s. Jean** Saint John; **la Sainte Vierge** the Blessed Virgin **2** *nmf* saint ▪ **Saint-Esprit** *nm* **le S.** Holy Spirit ▪ **Saint-Sylvestre** *nf* **la S.** New Year's Eve

sainteté [sɛ̃təte] *nf (de lieu)* holiness; *(de personne)* saintliness

sais [sɛ] *voir* savoir

saisie [sezi] *nf (de biens)* seizure; *Ordinat* **s. de données** data capture, keyboarding

saisir [sezir] **1** *vt* to take hold of; *(brusquement)* to grab; *(occasion)* to seize, to grasp; *(comprendre)* to grasp; *Jur* to seize; *Ordinat (données)* to enter, to key; *(viande)* to seal; **s. un texte** to type a text **2 se saisir** *vpr* **se s. de qn/qch** to take hold of sb/sth; *(brusquement)* to grab sb/sth ▪ **saisissant, -e** *adj (film)* gripping; *(contraste, ressemblance)* striking

saison [sɛzɔ̃] *nf* season; **en/hors s.** in/out of season; **en haute/basse s.** in the high/low season; **la s. des pluies** the rainy season ■ **saisonnier, -ère** *adj* seasonal

sait [sɛ] *voir* **savoir**

salade [salad] *nf (laitue)* lettuce; **s. verte** green salad; **s. de fruits** fruit salad; **s. niçoise** salade niçoise

salaire [salɛr] *nm (mensuel)* salary

salarié, -e [salarje] **1** *adj (payé mensuellement)* salaried **2** *nmf (payé mensuellement)* salaried employee; **salariés** *(de société)* employees

sale [sal] *adj* dirty; *(dégoûtant)* filthy ■ **salement** *adv (se conduire, manger)* disgustingly ■ **saleté** *nf (manque de soin)* dirtiness; *(crasse)* dirt; **saletés** *(détritus) Br* rubbish, *Am* garbage; **faire des saletés** to make a mess

saler [sale] *vt* to salt ■ **salé, -e** *adj (goût, plat)* salty; *(aliment)* salted

salir [salir] **1** *vt* to (make) dirty **2 se salir** *vpr* to get dirty ■ **salissant, -e** *adj (travail)* dirty, messy; *(étoffe)* that shows the dirt

salle [sal] *nf* room; *(très grande, publique)* hall; *(de cinéma) Br* cinema, *Am* movie theater; *(d'hôpital)* ward; **s. à manger** dining room; **s. de bain(s)** bathroom; **s. de classe** classroom; **s. de concert** concert hall; **s. de jeux** *(pour enfants)* games room; *(de casino)* gaming room; **s. de spectacle** auditorium; **s. d'embarquement** *(d'aéroport)* departure lounge; **s. d'opération** *(d'hôpital)* operating *Br* theatre *or Am* room; **s. des professeurs** *Br* staff room, *Am* teachers' lounge; **s. de sport** sports hall

salon [salɔ̃] *nm* living room; *(exposition)* show; **s. de coiffure** hairdressing salon; **s. de thé** tea room

salopette [salɔpɛt] *nf Br* dungarees, *Am* overalls

salubre [salybr] *adj* healthy ■ **salubrité** *nf* healthiness; **s. publique** public health

saluer [salɥe] *vt* to greet; *(en partant)* to take one's leave of; *(de la main)* to

wave to; *(de la tête)* to nod to; *Mil* to salute

salut [saly] **1** *nm* greeting; *(de la main)* wave; *(de la tête)* nod; *Mil* salute; *(sauvegarde)* rescue; *Rel* salvation **2** *exclam Fam* hi!; *(au revoir)* bye!

salutaire [salytɛr] *adj* salutary

samedi [samdi] *nm* Saturday

SAMU [samy] *(abrév* **service d'aide médicale d'urgence)** *nm* emergency medical service

sanctifier [sɑ̃ktifje] *vt* to sanctify

sanction [sɑ̃ksjɔ̃] *nf (approbation, peine)* sanction ■ **sanctionner** *vt (approuver)* to sanction; *(punir)* to punish

sanctuaire [sɑ̃ktɥer] *nm* sanctuary

sandale [sɑ̃dal] *nf* sandal

sandwich [sɑ̃dwitʃ] *nm* sandwich

sang [sɑ̃] *nm* blood ■ **sang-froid** *nm* self-control; **garder son s.** to keep calm; **tuer qn de s.** to kill sb in cold blood ■ **sanglant, -e** *adj* bloody

sangle [sɑ̃gl] *nf* strap

sanglier [sɑ̃glije] *nm* wild boar

sanglot [sɑ̃glo] *nm* sob ■ **sangloter** *vi* to sob

sanguin, -e [sɑ̃gɛ̃, -in] *adj (tempérament)* full-blooded; **vaisseau s.** blood vessel

sanguinaire [sɑ̃giner] *adj* bloodthirsty

sanitaire [saniter] *adj (conditions)* sanitary; *(personnel)* medical; **règlement s.** health regulations

sans [sɑ̃] *(*[sɑ̃z] *before vowel and mute* h) *prép* without; **s. faire qch** without doing sth; **s. qu'il le sache** without him *or* his knowing; **s. cela, s. quoi** otherwise; **s. importance/travail** unimportant/unemployed; **s. argent/manches** penniless/sleeveless ■ **sans-abri** *nmf inv* homeless person; **les s.** the homeless ■ **sans-faute** *nm inv Fig* **faire un s.** not to put a foot wrong ■ **sans-gêne 1** *adj inv* ill-mannered **2** *nm inv* lack of manners ■ **sans-papiers** *nmf inv* illegal immigrant

santé [sɑ̃te] *nf* health; **en bonne/mauvaise s.** in good/bad health; **s. mentale/physique** mental/physical

health; **la s. publique** public health; **(à votre) s.!** *(en trinquant)* cheers!

saoul [su] *adj & nm* = **soûl**

saper [sape] *vt* to undermine; **s. le moral à qn** to sap sb's morale

sapeur-pompier [sapœrpɔ̃pje] *(pl* **sapeurs-pompiers)** *nm* fireman, fire-fighter

saphir [safir] *nm* sapphire

sapin [sapɛ̃] *nm (arbre, bois)* fir; **s. de Noël** Christmas tree

Sardaigne [sardɛɲ] *nf* **la S.** Sardinia ▪ **sarde 1** *adj* Sardinian **2** *nmf* **S.** Sardinian

sardine [sardin] *nf* sardine

sarrasin [sarazɛ̃] *nm (plante)* buckwheat

Satan [satɑ̃] *nm* Satan

satellite [satelit] *nm* satellite; **télévision par s.** satellite television

satiété [sasjete] *nf* **boire/manger à s.** to eat/drink one's fill

satin [satɛ̃] *nm* satin

satire [satir] *nf* satire **(contre** on) ▪ **satirique** *adj* satirical

satisfaction [satisfaksjɔ̃] *nf* satisfaction; **donner s. à qn** to give sb (complete) satisfaction ▪ **satisfaire* 1** *vt* to satisfy **2** *vi* **s. à qch** *(conditions)* to satisfy sth; *(obligation)* to fulfil sth, *Am* to fulfill sth ▪ **satisfaisant, -e** *adj (acceptable)* satisfactory ▪ **satisfait, -e** *adj* satisfied **(de** with)

saturer [satyre] *vt* to saturate **(de** with) ▪ **saturation** *nf* saturation; **arriver à s.** to reach saturation point

sauce [sos] *nf* sauce

saucisse [sosis] *nf* sausage; **s. de Francfort** frankfurter ▪ **saucisson** *nm* (cold) sausage

sauf¹ [sof] *prép* except; **s. erreur** if I'm not mistaken

sauf², sauve [sof, sov] *adj* **avoir la vie sauve** to be unharmed

saumon [somɔ̃] **1** *nm* salmon **2** *adj inv (couleur)* salmon (pink)

sauna [sona] *nm* sauna

saupoudrer [sopudre] *vt* to sprinkle **(de** with)

saur [sɔr] *adj m* **hareng s.** smoked herring

saura, saurait [sora, sorɛ] *voir* **savoir**

saut [so] *nm* jump, leap; **faire un s.** to jump, to leap; **s. à la corde** *Br* skipping, *Am* jumping rope; **s. à l'élastique** bungee jumping; **s. en hauteur** high jump; **s. en longueur** long jump; **s. en parachute** parachute jump; *(activité)* parachute jumping

sauter [sote] **1** *vt (franchir)* to jump (over); *(mot, repas, classe, ligne)* to skip **2** *vi (personne, animal)* to jump, to leap; *(bombe)* to go off, to explode; *(fusible)* to blow; **faire s. qch** *(pont, mine)* to blow sth up; *(serrure)* to force sth; **s. à la corde** *Br* to skip, *Am* to jump rope; **s. en parachute** to do a parachute jump

sauterelle [sotrɛl] *nf* grasshopper

sautes [sot] *nfpl (d'humeur, de température)* sudden changes **(de** in)

sauvage [sovaʒ] *adj (animal, plante)* wild; *(tribu, homme)* primitive; *(cruel)* savage; *(farouche)* unsociable; *(illégal)* unauthorized ▪ **sauvagerie** *nf (insociabilité)* unsociability; *(cruauté)* savagery

sauve [sov] *adj voir* **sauf²**

sauvegarde [sovgard] *nf* safeguard **(contre** against); *Ordinat* backup ▪ **sauvegarder** *vt* to safeguard; *Ordinat* to save

sauver [sove] **1** *vt (personne)* to save, to rescue **(de** from); *(matériel)* to salvage **2** **se sauver** *vpr (s'enfuir)* to run away; *(s'échapper)* to escape ▪ **sauvetage** *nm (de personne)* rescue ▪ **sauveteur** *nm* rescuer

sauvette [sovɛt] **à la sauvette** *adv (pour ne pas être vu)* on the sly; **vendre qch à la s.** to peddle sth illegally on the streets

sauveur [sovœr] *nm* saviour

savant, -e [savɑ̃, -ɑ̃t] **1** *adj (érudit)* learned; *(habile)* clever **2** *nm (scientifique)* scientist

saveur [savœr] *nf (goût)* flavour

Savoie [savwa] *nf* **la S.** Savoy

SAVOIR* [savwar] **1** vt to know; (nouvelle) to have heard; **s. lire/nager** to know how to read/swim; **faire s. à qn que...** to inform sb that...; **à s.** (c'est-à-dire) that is, namely; **pas que je sache** not that I know of; **je n'en sais rien** I have no idea, I don't know; **en s. long sur qn/qch** to know a lot about sb/sth
2 nm (culture) learning, knowledge ■ **savoir-faire** nm inv know-how

savon [savɔ̃] nm soap ■ **savonnette** nf bar of soap ■ **savonneux, -euse** adj soapy

savourer [savure] vt to savour ■ **savoureux, -euse** adj tasty

savoyard, -e [savwajar, -ard] **1** adj Savoyard **2** nmf **S., Savoyarde** Savoyard

saxophone [saksɔfɔn] nm saxophone

scalpel [skalpɛl] nm scalpel

scandale [skɑ̃dal] nm scandal ■ **scandaleux, -euse** adj scandalous ■ **scandaliser 1** vt to scandalize, to shock **2 se scandaliser** vpr to be shocked or scandalized (**de** by)

Scandinavie [skɑ̃dinavi] nf **la S.** Scandinavia ■ **scandinave 1** adj Scandinavian **2** nmf **S.** Scandinavian

scanner 1 [skanɛr] nm scanner **2** [skane] vt to scan

scanneur [skanœr] nm scanner

scaphandrier [skafɑ̃drije] nm diver

sceau, -x [so] nm seal ■ **sceller** vt (document) to seal

scénario [senarjo] nm script, screenplay ■ **scénariste** nmf scriptwriter

scène [sɛn] nf (**a**) (de théâtre) scene; (plateau) stage; (action) action; **mettre qch en s.** (pièce) to stage sth; (film) to direct sth; Fig **sur la s. internationale** on the international scene (**b**) (dispute) scene; **faire une s.** to make a scene; **s. de ménage** domestic quarrel

sceptique [sɛptik] **1** adj Br sceptical, Am skeptical **2** nmf Br sceptic, Am skeptic

schéma [ʃema] nm diagram ■ **schématique** adj schematic

schizophrène [skizɔfrɛn] adj & nmf schizophrenic

scie [si] nf (outil) saw ■ **scier** vt to saw

sciemment [sjamɑ̃] adv knowingly

science [sjɑ̃s] nf science; (savoir) knowledge; **sciences humaines** social sciences; **sciences naturelles** biology ■ **science-fiction** nf science fiction ■ **scientifique 1** adj scientific **2** nmf scientist

scinder [sɛ̃de] **se scinder** vpr to split up (**en** into)

scintiller [sɛ̃tije] vi to sparkle; (étoile) to twinkle ■ **scintillement** nm sparkling; (d'étoile) twinkling

scission [sisjɔ̃] nf (de parti) split (**de** in); **s. de l'atome** splitting of the atom

sclérose [skleroz] nf Méd sclerosis; Fig ossification; **s. en plaques** multiple sclerosis

scolaire [skɔlɛr] adj **année s.** school year; **enfant d'âge s.** child of school age ■ **scolariser** vt (enfant) to send to school ■ **scolarité** nf schooling; **pendant ma s.** during my school years

scooter [skuter] nm (motor) scooter; **s. des mers** jet ski

score [skɔr] nm score

scorpion [skɔrpjɔ̃] nm scorpion; **le S.** (signe) Scorpio

Scotch® [skɔtʃ] (ruban adhésif) Br sellotape®, Am scotch tape® ■ **scotcher** vt Br to sellotape, Am to tape

scout, -e [skut] adj & nm scout

script [skript] nm (écriture) printing; Cin script

scrupule [skrypyl] nm scruple; **sans scrupules** (être) unscrupulous; (agir) unscrupulously ■ **scrupuleux, -euse** adj scrupulous

scruter [skryte] vt to scrutinize

scrutin [skrytɛ̃] nm (vote) ballot; (élection) poll; (système) voting system; **premier tour de s.** first ballot or round; **s. majoritaire** first-past-the-post voting system

sculpter [skylte] vt (statue, pierre) to sculpt; (bois) to carve; **s. qch dans qch** to sculpt/carve sth out of sth ■ **sculpteur** nm sculptor ■ **sculpture**

nf (art, œuvre) sculpture
SDF [ɛsdeef] *(abrév* **sans domicile fixe)** *nm* person of no fixed abode

SE [sə]

se becomes **s'** before vowel or mute h.

pron personnel (**a**) *(complément direct)* himself; *(féminin)* herself; *(non humain)* itself; *(indéfini)* oneself, *pl* themselves; **il se lave** he washes himself; **ils** *ou* **elles se lavent** they wash themselves
(**b**) *(indirect)* to himself/herself/itself/oneself; **il se lave les mains** he washes his hands; **elle se lave les mains** she washes her hands
(**c**) *(réciproque)* each other; *(indirect)* to each other; **ils s'aiment** they love each other; **ils** *ou* **elles se parlent** they speak to each other
(**d**) *(passif)* **ça se fait** that is done; **ça se vend bien** it sells well

séance [seɑ̃s] *nf (de cinéma)* showing, performance; *(d'assemblée, de travail)* session
seau, -x [so] *nm* bucket
sec, sèche [sɛk, sɛʃ] **1** *adj* dry; *(fruits, légumes)* dried; *(ton)* curt; **frapper un coup s.** to knock sharply **2** *adv (boire) Br* neat, *Am* straight; *(frapper, pleuvoir)* hard **3** *nm* **à s.** dry; **au s.** in a dry place
sécession [sesesjɔ̃] *nf* secession; **faire s.** to secede
sèche [sɛʃ] *voir* **sec**
sécher [seʃe] **1** *vti* to dry **2** **se sécher** *vpr* to dry oneself ■ **séchage** *nm* drying ■ **sèche-cheveux** *nm inv* hair dryer ■ **sèche-linge** *nm inv Br* tumble dryer, *Am* (clothes) dryer
sécheresse [seʃrɛs] *nf (d'air, de sol, de peau)* dryness; *(de ton)* curtness; *(manque de pluie)* drought
séchoir [seʃwar] *nm (appareil)* dryer; **s. à linge** clothes horse
second, -e¹ [səgɔ̃, -ɔ̃d] **1** *adj & nmf* second
2 *nm (adjoint)* second in command; *(étage) Br* second floor, *Am* third floor
3 *nf* **seconde** *Rail* second class; *Scol Br* ≃ fifth form, *Am* ≃ tenth grade; *Aut (vitesse)* second (gear) ■ **secon-**

daire *adj* secondary; **école s.** *Br* secondary school, *Am* high school
seconde² [səgɔ̃d] *nf (instant)* second
seconder [səgɔ̃de] *vt* to assist
secouer [səkwe] *vt* to shake; *(poussière)* to shake off; **s. qch de qch** *(enlever)* to shake sth out of sth; **s. la tête** *(réponse affirmative)* to nod (one's head); *(réponse négative)* to shake one's head
secourir [səkurir] *vt* to assist, to help ■ **secourable** *adj* helpful ■ **secourisme** *nm* first aid ■ **secouriste** *nmf* first-aid worker
secours [səkur] *nm* help; *(financier, matériel)* aid; *Mil* **les s.** *(renforts)* relief; **au s.!** help!; **porter s. à qn** to give sb help; **roue de s.** spare wheel
secousse [səkus] *nf* jolt, jerk; *(de tremblement de terre)* tremor
secret, -ète [səkrɛ, -ɛt] **1** *adj* secret; *(cachottier)* secretive **2** *nm* secret; **en s.** in secret, secretly
secrétaire [səkretɛr] *nmf* secretary; **s. d'État** Secretary of State ■ **secrétariat** *nm (bureau)* secretary's office; *(d'organisation internationale)* secretariat; *(métier)* secretarial work
sectaire [sɛktɛr] *adj & nmf Péj* sectarian
secte [sɛkt] *nf* sect
secteur [sɛktœr] *nm (zone)* area; *Écon* sector; *Él* mains; **le s. privé/public** the private/public sector; **s. primaire/secondaire/tertiaire** primary/secondary/tertiary sector
section [sɛksjɔ̃] *nf* section; *(de ligne d'autobus)* stage; *Mil* platoon ■ **sectionner** *vt (couper)* to sever
séculaire [sekylɛr] *adj (tradition)* age-old
sécurité [sekyrite] *nf (absence de danger)* safety; *(tranquillité)* security; **S. sociale** *Br* Social Security, *Am* Welfare; **en s.** *(hors de danger)* safe
séduire* [sedɥir] *vt* to charm; *(plaire à)* to appeal to; *(abuser de)* to seduce ■ **séduisant, -e** *adj* attractive ■ **séducteur, -trice** *nmf* seducer, *f* seductress ■ **séduction** *nf* attraction

ségrégation [segregɑsjɔ̃] *nf* segregation

seigle [sɛgl] *nm* rye; **pain de s.** rye bread

seigneur [sɛɲœr] *nm Hist (noble, maître)* lord; *Rel* **le S.** the Lord

sein [sɛ̃] *nm* breast; **donner le s. à** *(enfant)* to breastfeed; **au s. de** within

Seine [sɛn] *nf* **la S.** the Seine

séisme [seism] *nm* earthquake

seize [sɛz] *adj & nm inv* sixteen ▪ **seizième** *adj & nmf* sixteenth

séjour [seʒur] *nm* stay; **un s. court/long** a short/long stay; **s. linguistique** language-learning trip; **(salle de) s.** living room ▪ **séjourner** *vi* to stay

sel [sɛl] *nm* salt; *Fig (piquant)* spice; **s. de mer** sea salt; **sels de bain** bath salts

sélectif, -ive [selɛktif, -iv] *adj* selective ▪ **sélection** *nf* selection ▪ **sélectionner** *vt* to select ▪ **sélectionneur** *nm* selector

self [sɛlf] *nm* self-service restaurant

selle [sɛl] *nf (de cheval, de vélo)* saddle

selon [səlɔ̃] *prép* according to; **s. que...** depending on whether...

semaine [səmɛn] *nf* week; **en s.** in the week

semblable [sɑ̃blabl] *adj* similar (à to); **de semblables propos** such remarks

semblant [sɑ̃blɑ̃] *nm* **faire s.** to pretend **(de faire** to do)

sembler [sɑ̃ble] **1** *vi* to seem (à to); **il (me) semble vieux** he seems *or* looks old (to me); **s. faire qch** to seem to do sth **2** *v impersonnel* **il semble que...** it seems that...; **il me semble que...** it seems to me that...

semelle [səmɛl] *nf (de chaussure)* sole; *(intérieure)* insole

semer [səme] *vt (graines)* to sow; *Fig (poursuivant)* to shake off; *Fig* **semé de** strewn with ▪ **semence** *nf* seed

semestre [səmɛstr] *nm* half-year; *Univ* semester

séminaire [seminɛr] *nm Univ* seminar; *Rel* seminary

semi-remorque [səmirəmɔrk] *(pl* **semi-remorques)** *nm (camion) Br* articulated lorry, *Am* semi(trailer), trailer truck

semoule [səmul] *nf* semolina

sénat [sena] *nm* senate ▪ **sénateur** *nm* senator

sénile [senil] *adj* senile

SENS [sɑ̃s] *nm* (a) *(faculté, raison, instinct)* sense; **avoir le s. de l'humour** to have a sense of humour; **avoir du bon s.** to be sensible; **bon sens** common sense

(b) *(signification)* meaning, sense; **ça n'a pas de s.** that doesn't make sense

(c) *(direction)* direction; *Aut* **s. giratoire** *Br* roundabout, *Am* traffic circle, *Am* rotary; **s. interdit** *ou* **unique** *(rue)* one-way street; **'s. interdit'** 'no entry'; **à s. unique** *(rue)* one-way; **dans le s. des aiguilles d'une montre** clockwise; **dans le s. inverse des aiguilles d'une montre** *Br* anticlockwise, *Am* counterclockwise

sensation [sɑ̃sɑsjɔ̃] *nf* feeling, sensation; **faire s.** to create a sensation

sensé, -e [sɑ̃se] *adj* sensible

sensible [sɑ̃sibl] *adj* sensitive (à to); *(douloureux)* tender, sore; *(perceptible)* perceptible; *(progrès)* noticeable ▪ **sensibiliser** *vt* **s. qn à qch** *(problème)* to make sb aware of sth ▪ **sensibilité** *nf* sensitivity

sensuel, -elle [sɑ̃sɥɛl] *adj* sensual ▪ **sensualité** *nf* sensuality

sentence [sɑ̃tɑ̃s] *nf Jur (jugement)* sentence

sentier [sɑ̃tje] *nm* path

sentiment [sɑ̃timɑ̃] *nm* feeling; **avoir le s. que...** to have a feeling that... ▪ **sentimental, -e, -aux, -ales** *adj* sentimental; **vie sentimentale** love life

sentinelle [sɑ̃tinɛl] *nf* sentry

sentir* [sɑ̃tir] **1** *vt (douleur)* to feel; *(odeur)* to smell; **s. le moisi** to smell musty; **s. le poisson** to smell of fish **2** *vi* to smell; **s. bon/mauvais** to smell good/bad **3 se sentir** *vpr* **se s. humilié** to feel humiliated

séparation [separɑsjɔ̃] *nf* separation; *(départ)* parting

séparer [separe] **1** vt to separate (**de** from) **2 se séparer** vpr (couple) to separate; (cortège) to disperse, to break up; **se s. de qn/qch** (donner, jeter) to part with sb/sth ∎ **séparé, -e** adj (distinct) separate; (époux) separated (**de** from)

sept [sɛt] adj & nm inv seven

septante [sɛptɑ̃t] adj (en Belgique, en Suisse) seventy

septembre [sɛptɑ̃br] nm September

septième [sɛtjɛm] adj & nmf seventh; **un s.** a seventh

sépulture [sepyltyr] nf burial; (lieu) burial place

séquelles [sekɛl] nfpl (de maladie) after-effects

séquence [sekɑ̃s] nf sequence

séquestrer [sekɛstre] vt **s. qn** to keep sb locked up

sera, serait [səra, sərɛ] voir être

Serbie [sɛrbi] nf la S. Serbia ∎ **serbe 1** adj Serbian **2** nmf S. Serbian

serein, -e [sərɛ̃, -ɛn] adj serene

sérénade [serenad] nf serenade

sérénité [serenite] nf serenity

sergent [sɛrʒɑ̃] nm Mil sergeant

série [seri] nf series; (ensemble) set; **de s.** (article, voiture) standard; **fin de s.** discontinued line; **fabrication en s.** mass production; **numéro hors s.** special issue

sérieux, -euse [serjø, -jøz] **1** adj (personne, doute) serious; (de bonne foi) genuine, serious; (fiable) reliable; **de sérieuses chances de...** a good chance of... **2** nm (application) seriousness; (fiabilité) reliability; **prendre qn/qch au s.** to take sb/sth seriously

seringue [sərɛ̃g] nf syringe

serment [sɛrmɑ̃] nm (affirmation solennelle) oath; (promesse) pledge; **prêter s.** to take an oath; **faire le s. de faire qch** to swear to do sth; Jur **sous s.** on or under oath

sermon [sɛrmɔ̃] nm (de prêtre) sermon ∎ **sermonner** vt (faire la morale à) to lecture

séropositif, -ive [seropozitif, -iv] adj Méd HIV positive ∎ **séronégatif, -ive** adj Méd HIV negative

serpent [sɛrpɑ̃] nm snake

serpenter [sɛrpɑ̃te] vi (sentier) to meander

serpillière [sɛrpijɛr] nf floorcloth; **passer la s. dans la cuisine** to clean the kitchen floor

serre [sɛr] nf greenhouse

serrer [sere] **1** vt (tenir) to grip; (nœud, vis) to tighten; (poing) to clench; **s. la main à qn** to shake hands with sb; **s. qn** (sujet: vêtement) to be too tight for sb **2** vi **s. à droite** to keep (to the) right **3 se serrer** vpr (se rapprocher) to squeeze up; **se s. contre** to squeeze up against ∎ **serré, -e** adj (nœud, vêtement) tight; (gens) packed (together); (lutte) close ∎ **serre-tête** nm inv headband

serrure [seryr] nf lock

serveur, -euse [sɛrvœr, -øz] **1** nmf waiter, f waitress; (de bar) barman, f barmaid **2** nm Ordinat server

serviable [sɛrvjabl] adj helpful, obliging

service [sɛrvis] nm service; (travail) duty; (pourboire) service (charge); (d'entreprise) department; (au tennis) serve, service; **un s.** (aide) a favour; **rendre s.** to be of service (**à qn** to sb); **être de s.** to be on duty; **faire son s. (militaire)** to do one's military service; **s. à café** coffee set; **s. (non) compris** service (not) included; **s. après-vente** aftersales service

serviette [sɛrvjɛt] nf (pour s'essuyer) towel; (sac) briefcase; **s. de bain/de toilette** bath/hand towel; **s. de table** napkin, Br serviette ∎ **serviette-éponge** (pl **serviettes-éponges**) nf terry towel

servir* [sɛrvir] **1** vt to serve (**qch à qn** sb with sth, sth to sb); (convive) to wait on **2** vi to serve; **s. à qch/à faire qch** to be used for sth/to do or for doing sth; **ça ne sert à rien** it's useless, it's no good or use (**de faire** doing); **s. de qch**

to be used for sth, to serve as sth

3 se servir *vpr (à table)* to help oneself (**de** to); **se s. de qch** *(utiliser)* to use sth

serviteur [sɛrvitœr] *nm* servant

ses [se] *voir* **son²**

session [sesjɔ̃] *nf* session

set [sɛt] *nm (au tennis)* set; **s. de table** place mat

seuil [sœj] *nm (entrée)* doorway; *Fig (limite)* threshold; *Fig* **au s. de** on the threshold of

seul, -e [sœl] **1** *adj (sans compagnie)* alone; *(unique)* only; **tout s.** by oneself, on one's own, all alone; **se sentir s.** to feel lonely *or* alone; **la seule femme** the only woman; **un s. chat** only one cat; **une seule fois** only once; **pas un s. livre** not a single book; **seuls les garçons...** only the boys...

2 *adv* **(tout) s.** *(rentrer, vivre)* by oneself, alone, on one's own; *(parler)* to oneself

3 *nmf* **le s., la seule** the only one; **un s., une seule** only one, one only; **pas un s.** not (a single) one

seulement [sœlmɑ̃] *adv* only; **non s.... mais encore...** not only... but (also)...

sève [sɛv] *nf (de plante)* sap

sévère [sevɛr] *adj* severe; *(parents, professeur)* strict ■ **sévérité** *nf* severity; *(de parents)* strictness

sévices [sevis] *nmpl* ill-treatment; **s. à enfant** child abuse

sexe [sɛks] *nm (catégorie, sexualité)* sex; *(organes)* genitals ■ **sexiste** *adj & nmf* sexist ■ **sexualité** *nf* sexuality ■ **sexuel, -elle** *adj* sexual

shampooing [ʃɑ̃pwɛ̃] *nm* shampoo; **s. colorant** rinse; **faire un s. à qn** to shampoo sb's hair

shooter [ʃute] *vti (au football)* to shoot

short [ʃɔrt] *nm* (pair of) shorts

SI¹ [si]

si becomes **s'** [s] before **il, ils**.

1 *conj* if; **si je pouvais** if I could; **s'il vient** if he comes; **si j'étais roi** if I were *or* was king; **je me demande si...** I wonder whether *or* if...; **si on restait?**

(suggestion) what if we stayed?; **si oui** if so; **si non** if not; **si seulement** if only

2 *adv* **(a)** *(tellement)* so; **pas si riche que tu crois** not as rich as you think; **un si bon dîner** such a good dinner; **si bien que...** so much so that...

(b) *(après négative)* yes; **tu ne viens pas? – si!** you're not coming? – yes (I am)!

si² [si] *nm inv (note)* B

siamois, -e [sjamwa, -waz] *adj* Siamese; **frères s., sœurs siamoises** Siamese twins

Sicile [sisil] *nf* la **S.** Sicily

SIDA [sida] *(abrév* **syndrome immunodéficitaire acquis)** *nm* AIDS; **virus du S.** AIDS virus

sidérurgie [sideryrʒi] *nf* iron and steel industry

siècle [sjɛkl] *nm* century

siège [sjɛʒ] *nm* **(a)** *(meuble, centre) & Pol* seat; *(d'autorité, de parti)* headquarters; **s. social** head office **(b)** *Mil* siege; **faire le s. de** to lay siege to

siéger [sjeʒe] *vi (assemblée)* to sit

sien, sienne [sjɛ̃, sjɛn] **1** *pron possessif* **le s., la sienne, les sien(ne)s** *(d'homme)* his; *(de femme)* hers; *(de chose)* its; **les deux siens** his/her two **2** *nmpl* **les siens** *(sa famille)* one's family **3** *nfpl* **faire des siennes** to be up to one's tricks again

sieste [sjɛst] *nf* siesta; **faire la s.** to have a nap

siffler [sifle] **1** *vi* to whistle; *(avec un sifflet)* to blow one's whistle; *(gaz, serpent)* to hiss

2 *vt (chanson)* to whistle; *(chien)* to whistle at; *Sport (faute, fin de match)* to blow one's whistle for; *(acteur, pièce)* to boo; **se faire s.** *(acteur)* to be booed ■ **sifflement** [-əmɑ̃] *nm* whistling; *(de serpent, de gaz)* hissing

sifflet [siflɛ] *nm (instrument)* whistle; **sifflets** *(de spectateurs)* booing ■ **siffloter** *vti* to whistle

sigle [sigl] *nm (initiales)* abbreviation; *(acronyme)* acronym

signal, -aux [siɲal, -o] *nm* signal; **s. d'alarme** alarm signal; **s. lumineux**

warning light; **s. sonore** warning sound

signalement [siɲalmɑ̃] *nm* description, particulars

signaler [siɲale] **1** *vt (faire remarquer)* to point out (**à qn** to sb; **que** that); *(par panneau)* to signpost; *(dire à la police)* to report (**à** to) **2 se signaler** *vpr* se s. **par qch** to distinguish oneself by sth

signalisation [siɲalizasjɔ̃] *nf (sur les routes)* signposting; **s. routière** *(signaux)* road signs

signature [siɲatyr] *nf* signature; *(action)* signing

signe [siɲ] *nm (indice)* sign, indication; **en s. de protestation** as a sign of protest; **faire s. à qn** *(geste)* to motion (to) sb (**de faire** to do); *(contacter)* to get in touch with sb; **faire s. que oui** to nod (one's head); **faire s. que non** to shake one's head; **s. particulier** distinguishing mark; **s. astrologique** astrological sign

signer [siɲe] **1** *vt* to sign **2 se signer** *vpr* to cross oneself

signification [siɲifikasjɔ̃] *nf* meaning ▪ **significatif, -ive** *adj* significant, meaningful

signifier [siɲifje] *vt* to mean (**que** that)

silence [silɑ̃s] *nm* silence; *Mus* rest; **en s.** in silence; **garder le s.** to keep quiet *or* silent (**sur** about) ▪ **silencieux, -euse 1** *adj* silent **2** *nm (de voiture) Br* silencer, *Am* muffler; *(d'arme)* silencer

silhouette [silwɛt] *nf* outline; *(en noir)* silhouette; *(du corps)* figure

sillonner [sijone] *vt (parcourir)* to criss-cross

similaire [similɛr] *adj* similar ▪ **similitude** *nf* similarity

simple [sɛ̃pl] *adj (facile, crédule, sans prétention)* simple; *(fait d'un élément)* single; *(employé, particulier)* ordinary ▪ **simplicité** *nf* simplicity

simplifier [sɛ̃plifje] *vt* to simplify ▪ **simplification** *nf* simplification

simpliste [sɛ̃plist] *adj* simplistic

simuler [simyle] *vt (reproduire)* to simulate; *(feindre)* to feign

simultané, -e [simyltane] *adj* simultaneous

sincère [sɛ̃sɛr] *adj* sincere ▪ **sincérité** *nf* sincerity; **en toute s.** quite sincerely

Singapour [sɛ̃gapur] *nm* Singapore

singe [sɛ̃ʒ] *nm* monkey; **grand s.** ape

singulariser [sɛ̃gylarize] **se singulariser** *vpr* to draw attention to oneself

singulier, -ère [sɛ̃gylje, -ɛr] *adj (peu ordinaire)* peculiar, odd ▪ **singularité** *nf* peculiarity

sinistre [sinistr] **1** *adj (effrayant)* sinister; *(triste)* grim **2** *nm* disaster; *(incendie)* fire; *Jur (dommage)* damage ▪ **sinistré, -e 1** *adj (population, région)* disaster-stricken **2** *nmf* disaster victim

sinon [sinɔ̃] *conj (autrement)* otherwise, or else; *(sauf)* except (**que** that); *(si ce n'est)* if not

sinueux, -euse [sinɥø, -øz] *adj* winding

sinusite [sinyzit] *nf* sinusitis; **avoir une s.** to have sinusitis

siphon [sifɔ̃] *nm* siphon; *(d'évier)* trap, *Br* U-bend

sirène [sirɛn] *nf (d'usine)* siren; *(femme)* mermaid

sirop [siro] *nm* syrup; *(à diluer) (fruit)* cordial; **s. contre la toux** cough mixture

sismique [sismik] *adj* seismic; **secousse s.** earth tremor

site [sit] *nm (endroit)* site; *(pittoresque)* beauty spot; **s. touristique** place of interest; **s. classé** conservation area; *Ordinat* **s. Internet** Internet site; **s. Web** website; **visiter un s. Web** to visit a website

sitôt [sito] *adv* **s. que...** as soon as...; **s. levée, elle partit** as soon as she was up, she left; **pas de s.** not for some time

situation [sitɥasjɔ̃] *nf* situation, position; *(emploi)* position; **s. de famille** marital status ▪ **situé, -e** *adj (maison)* situated (**à** in) ▪ **situer 1** *vt (placer)* to situate; *(trouver)* to locate; *(dans le temps)* to set **2 se situer** *vpr (se trouver)* to be situated

six [sis] ([si] before *consonant*, [siz] before *vowel*) *adj & nm inv* six ▪ **sixième**

[sizjɛm] **1** *adj & nmf* sixth; **un s.** a sixth **2** *nf Scol Br* ≃ first form, *Am* ≃ sixth grade

sketch [skɛtʃ] *(pl* **sketches)** *nm* sketch

ski [ski] *nm (objet)* ski; *(sport)* skiing; **faire du s.** to ski; **s. alpin** downhill skiing; **s. de fond** cross-country skiing; **s. nautique** water skiing ▪ **skiable** *adj (piste)* skiable, fit for skiing ▪ **skier** *vi* to ski ▪ **skieur, -euse** *nmf* skier

slalom [slalɔm] *nm Sport* slalom

slave [slav] **1** *adj* Slav; *(langue)* Slavonic **2** *nmf* **S.** Slav

slip [slip] *nm (d'homme)* briefs, underpants; *(de femme)* panties, *Br* knickers

slogan [slɔgã] *nm* slogan

Slovaquie [slɔvaki] *nf* **la S.** Slovakia

Slovénie [slɔveni] *nf* **la S.** Slovenia

SMIC [smik] *(abrév* **salaire minimum interprofessionnel de croissance)** *nm* guaranteed minimum wage

smoking [smɔkiŋ] *nm (veston, costume)* dinner jacket, *Am* tuxedo

SNCF [ɛsɛnseɛf] *(abrév* **Société nationale des chemins de fer français)** *nf* = French national railway company

snob [snɔb] **1** *adj* snobbish **2** *nmf* snob ▪ **snobisme** *nm* snobbery

sobre [sɔbr] *adj* sober ▪ **sobriété** *nf* sobriety

sociable [sɔsjabl] *adj* sociable ▪ **sociabilité** *nf* sociability

social, -e, -aux, -ales [sɔsjal, -o] *adj* social ▪ **socialisme** *nm* socialism ▪ **socialiste** *adj & nmf* socialist

société [sɔsjete] *nf (communauté)* society; *(compagnie)* company; **s. anonyme** *Br* (public) limited company, *Am* corporation ▪ **sociétaire** *nmf (membre)* member

sociologie [sɔsjɔlɔʒi] *nf* sociology ▪ **sociologique** *adj* sociological ▪ **sociologue** *nmf* sociologist

sœur [sœr] *nf* sister; *(religieuse)* sister, nun

sofa [sɔfa] *nm* sofa, settee

soi [swa] *pron personnel* oneself; **chacun pour s.** every man for himself; **chez s.** at home; **cela va de soi** it's

self-evident **(que** that) ▪ **soi-même** *pron* oneself

soi-disant [swadizã] **1** *adj inv* so-called **2** *adv* supposedly

soie [swa] *nf (tissu)* silk

soient [swa] *voir* être

soif [swaf] *nf* thirst **(de** for); **avoir s.** to be thirsty

soigner [swaɲe] **1** *vt* to look after, to take care of; *(sujet: médecin) (malade, maladie)* to treat; *(présentation, travail)* to take care over; **se faire s.** to have (medical) treatment
 2 se soigner *vpr* to take care of oneself, to look after oneself ▪ **soigné, -e** *adj (personne, vêtement)* neat, tidy; *(travail)* careful

soigneux, -euse [swaɲø, -øz] *adj (attentif)* careful **(de** with); *(propre)* neat, tidy

soin [swɛ̃] *nm (attention)* care; *Méd* **soins** treatment, care; **avoir** *ou* **prendre s. de qch/de faire qch** to take care of sth/to do sth; **avec s.** carefully, with care

soir [swar] *nm* evening; **le s.** *(chaque soir)* in the evening(s); **à neuf heures du s.** at nine in the evening; **repas du s.** evening meal

soirée [sware] *nf* evening; *(réunion)* party

sois, soit¹ [swa] *voir* être

soit² **1** [swa] *conj (à savoir)* that is (to say); **s.... s....** either... or... **2** [swat] *adv (oui)* very well

soixante [swasãt] *adj & nm inv* sixty ▪ **soixantaine** *nf* **une s. (de)** *(nombre)* (about) sixty; **avoir la s.** *(âge)* to be about sixty

soixante-dix [swasãtdis] *adj & nm inv* seventy ▪ **soixante-dixième** *adj & nmf* seventieth

soixantième [swasãtjɛm] *adj & nmf* sixtieth

soja [sɔʒa] *nm (plante)* soya; **germes** *ou* **pousses de s.** beansprouts

sol¹ [sɔl] *nm* ground; *(plancher)* floor; *(territoire, terrain)* soil

sol² [sɔl] *nm inv (note)* G

solaire [sɔlɛr] *adj* solar; **huile s.** sun-tan oil

soldat [sɔlda] *nm* soldier

solde [sɔld] **1** *nm (de compte, à payer)* balance; **en s.** *(acheter)* in the sales, *Am* on sale; **soldes** *(marchandises)* sale goods; *(vente)* clearance sale(s) **2** *nf (de soldat)* pay

solder [sɔlde] **1** *vt (articles)* to clear, to sell off; *(compte)* to pay the balance of **2** **se solder** *vpr* **se s. par un échec** to end in failure ▪ **soldé, -e** *adj (article)* reduced

sole [sɔl] *nf (poisson)* sole

soleil [sɔlɛj] *nm* sun; *(chaleur, lumière)* sunshine; **au s.** in the sun; **il fait s.** it's sunny

solennel, -elle [sɔlanɛl] *adj* solemn

solidaire [sɔlidɛr] *adj* **être s.** *(ouvriers)* to show solidarity **(de** with) ▪ **solidarité** *nf (entre personnes)* solidarity

solide [sɔlid] **1** *adj (objet, état)* solid; *(amitié)* strong; *(nerfs)* sound; *(personne)* sturdy **2** *nm (corps)* solid ▪ **solidité** *nf (d'objet)* solidity

soliste [sɔlist] *nmf Mus* soloist

solitaire [sɔlitɛr] **1** *adj (par choix)* solitary; *(involontairement)* lonely **2** *nmf* loner; **en s.** on one's own ▪ **solitude** *nf* solitude; **aimer la s.** to like being alone

solliciter [sɔlisite] *vt (audience)* to request; *(emploi)* to apply for; **s. qn** *(faire appel à)* to appeal to sb **(de faire** to do) ▪ **sollicitation** *nf* request

sollicitude [sɔlisityd] *nf* solicitude, concern

soluble [sɔlybl] *adj (substance, problème)* soluble

solution [sɔlysjɔ̃] *nf (de problème)* solution **(de** to); *(mélange chimique)* solution

sombre [sɔ̃br] *adj* dark; *(triste)* sombre, gloomy; **il fait s.** it's dark

sombrer [sɔ̃bre] *vi (bateau)* to sink; *Fig* **s. dans** *(folie, sommeil)* to sink into

sommaire [sɔmɛr] **1** *adj* summary; *(repas)* basic **2** *nm (table des matières)* contents

somme [sɔm] **1** *nf* sum; **faire la s. de** to add up; **en s., s. toute** in short **2** *nm (sommeil)* nap; **faire un s.** to have a nap

sommeil [sɔmɛj] *nm* sleep; **avoir s.** to feel sleepy; **être en plein s.** to be fast asleep ▪ **sommeiller** *vi* to doze

sommelier [sɔmalje] *nm* wine waiter

sommer [sɔme] *vt* **s. qn de faire qch** to summon sb to do sth

sommes [sɔm] *voir* **être**

sommet [sɔme] *nm* top; *(de montagne)* summit, top

sommier [sɔmje] *nm (de lit)* base

sommité [sɔmite] *nf* leading light **(de** in)

somnambule [sɔmnɑ̃byl] *nmf* sleepwalker; **être s.** to sleepwalk

somnifère [sɔmnifɛr] *nm* sleeping pill

somnoler [sɔmnɔle] *vi* to doze

somptueux, -euse [sɔ̃ptɥø, -øz] *adj* sumptuous

son¹ [sɔ̃] *nm (bruit)* sound

son² [sɔ̃] *nm (de grains)* bran

son³, sa, ses [sɔ̃, sa, se] sa becomes **son** [sɔn] before a vowel or mute h. *adj possessif (d'homme)* his; *(de femme)* her; *(de chose)* its; *(indéfini)* one's; **s. père/sa mère** his/her/one's father/mother; **s. ami(e)** his/her/one's friend

sondage [sɔ̃daʒ] *nm (de terrain)* drilling; **s. (d'opinion)** opinion poll

sonder [sɔ̃de] *vt (rivière)* to sound; *(terrain)* to drill; *Fig (personne, l'opinion)* to sound out

songe [sɔ̃ʒ] *nm* dream

songer [sɔ̃ʒe] **1** *vi* **s. à qch/à faire qch** to think of sth/of doing sth **2** *vt* **s. que...** to think that... ▪ **songeur, -euse** *adj* thoughtful, pensive

sonner [sɔne] **1** *vi* to ring; *(cor, cloches)* to sound; **on a sonné (à la porte)** there's someone at the door **2** *vt (cloche)* to ring; *(domestique)* to ring for; *(cor)* to sound; *(l'heure)* to strike

sonnerie [sɔnri] *nf (son)* ring(ing); *(de cor)* sound; *(appareil)* bell; *(de téléphone) Br* ringing tone, *Am* ring

sonnette [sɔnɛt] *nf* bell; **coup de s.** ring; **s. d'alarme** alarm (bell)

sonore [sɔnɔr] *adj (rire)* loud; *(voix)*

resonant; **effet s.** sound effect ■ **sonorité** *nf (de salle)* acoustics; *(de violon)* tone

sont [sɔ̃] *voir* être

sophistiqué, -e [sɔfistike] *adj* sophisticated

soporifique [sɔpɔrifik] *adj (médicament, discours)* soporific

sorbet [sɔrbɛ] *nm* sorbet

sorcellerie [sɔrsɛlri] *nf* witchcraft, sorcery ■ **sorcier** *nm* sorcerer ■ **sorcière** *nf* witch

sordide [sɔrdid] *adj (acte, affaire)* sordid; *(maison)* squalid

sort [sɔr] *nm (destin)* fate; *(condition)* lot; *(maléfice)* spell

sortant, -e [sɔrtɑ̃, -ɑ̃t] *adj (numéro)* winning; *(député)* outgoing

sorte [sɔrt] *nf* sort, kind **(de** of); **toutes sortes de** all sorts *or* kinds of; **en quelque s.** in a way, as it were; **de (telle) s. que tu apprennes** so that *or* in such a way that you may learn; **faire en s. que…** (+ *subjunctive)* to see to it that…

sortie [sɔrti] *nf (porte)* exit, way out; *(action de sortir)* leaving, exit, departure; *(promenade)* walk; *(de film, de disque)* release; *(de livre)* appearance; **être de s.** to be out; **s. de bain** bathrobe; **s. de secours** emergency exit

sortir* [sɔrtir] **1** *(aux* être) *vi* to go out, to leave; *(pour s'amuser)* to go out; *(film)* to come out; *(numéro gagnant)* to come up; **s. de** *(endroit)* to leave; *(université)* to be a graduate of; *(famille, milieu)* to come from; *(rails)* to come off; **s. de l'ordinaire** to be out of the ordinary

2 *(aux* avoir) *vt* to take out **(de** of); *(film, livre)* to bring out

3 se sortir *vpr* **s'en s.** *(malade)* to pull through

SOS [ɛsoɛs] *nm* SOS; **lancer un S.** to send (out) an SOS

sosie [sozi] *nm* double

sottise [sɔtiz] *nf* foolishness; *(action, parole)* foolish thing

souche [suʃ] *nf (d'arbre)* stump; *(de carnet)* stub, counterfoil; *(de virus)* strain

souci [susi] *nm (inquiétude)* worry, concern; *(préoccupation)* concern **(de** for); **se faire du s.** to worry, to be worried ■ **se soucier** *vpr* **se s. de** to be worried *or* concerned about ■ **soucieux, -euse** *adj* worried, concerned **(de qch** about sth)

soucoupe [sukup] *nf* saucer

soudain, -e [sudɛ, -ɛn] **1** *adj* sudden **2** *adv* suddenly ■ **soudaineté** *nf* suddenness

Soudan [sudɑ̃] *nm* **le S.** Sudan

souder [sude] **1** *vt (par alliage)* to solder; *(par soudure autogène)* to weld; **lampe à s.** blowlamp **2 se souder** *vpr (os)* to knit (together) ■ **soudure** *nf (par alliage)* soldering; *(autogène)* welding

souffle [sufl] *nm (d'air, de vent)* breath, puff; *(respiration)* breathing; *(de bombe)* blast; **reprendre son s.** to get one's breath back ■ **souffler 1** *vi* to blow; *(haleter)* to puff; **laisser s. qn** *(se reposer)* to give sb time to catch his/her breath **2** *vt (bougie)* to blow out; *(fumée, verre)* to blow; *(faire exploser)* to blast; *(chuchoter)* to whisper

souffrance [sufrɑ̃s] *nf* suffering; **en s.** *(colis)* unclaimed

souffrir* [sufrir] *vi* to suffer; **s. de** to suffer from; **faire s. qn** *(physiquement)* to hurt sb; *(moralement)* to make sb suffer ■ **souffrant, -e** *adj* unwell

souhait [swɛ] *nm* wish; **à vos souhaits!** *(après un éternuement)* bless you! ■ **souhaitable** *adj* desirable ■ **souhaiter** *vt (bonheur)* to wish for; **s. qch à qn** to wish sb sth; **s. faire qch** to hope to do sth; **s. que…** (+ *subjunctive)* to hope that…

soûl, -e [su, sul] **1** *adj* drunk **2** *nm* **tout son s.** *(boire)* to one's heart's content ■ **se soûler** *vpr* to get drunk

soulager [sulaʒe] *vt* to relieve **(de** of) ■ **soulagement** *nm* relief

soulever [suləve] **1** *vt* to lift (up); *(question)* to raise **2 se soulever** *vpr (personne)* to lift oneself (up); *(se révolter)* to rise up ■ **soulèvement** [-ɛvmɑ̃] *nm (révolte)* uprising

soulier [sulje] *nm* shoe

souligner [suliɲe] *vt (d'un trait)* to underline; *(faire remarquer)* to emphasize

soumettre* [sumɛtr] **1** *vt (pays, rebelles)* to subdue; *(rapport, demande)* to submit (à to); **s. qn à** *(assujettir)* to subject sb to
2 se soumettre *vpr* to submit (à to) ■ **soumis, -e** *adj (docile)* submissive; **s. à** subject to ■ **soumission** *nf (à une autorité)* submission; *(docilité)* submissiveness

soupçon [supsɔ̃] *nm* suspicion; **au-dessus de tout s.** above suspicion ■ **soupçonner** *vt* to suspect (**de** of; **d'avoir fait** of doing) ■ **soupçonneux, -euse** *adj* suspicious

soupe [sup] *nf* soup; **s. populaire** soup kitchen ■ **soupière** *nf* (soup) tureen

souper [supe] **1** *nm* supper **2** *vi* to have supper

soupir [supir] *nm* sigh ■ **soupirer** *vi* to sigh

souple [supl] *adj (corps, personne)* supple; *(branche)* flexible ■ **souplesse** *nf (de corps)* suppleness; *(de branche)* flexibility

source [surs] *nf* (a) *(point d'eau)* spring; *(rivière)* **prendre sa s.** to rise (à at) (b) *(origine)* source

sourcil [sursi] *nm* eyebrow ■ **sourciller** *vi Fig* **ne pas s.** not to bat an eyelid

sourd, -e [sur, surd] **1** *adj (personne)* deaf (à to); *(douleur)* dull; **bruit s.** thump **2** *nmf* deaf person ■ **sourd-muet, sourde-muette** *(mpl* **sourds-muets**, *fpl* **sourdes-muettes)* **1** *adj* deaf-and-dumb **2** *nmf* deaf mute

sourire* [surir] **1** *nm* smile; **faire un s. à qn** to give sb a smile **2** *vi* to smile (à at)

souris [suri] *nf (animal)* & *Ordinat* mouse *(pl* mice)

sournois, -e [surnwa, -waz] *adj* sly, underhand

sous [su] *prép (position)* under, underneath, beneath; *(rang)* under; **s. la pluie** in the rain; **nager s. l'eau** to swim underwater; **s. le nom de** under the name of; **s. Charles X** under Charles X; **s. peu** *(bientôt)* shortly

sous-bois [subwa] *nm* undergrowth

sous-chef [suʃɛf] *(pl* **sous-chefs**) *nmf* second-in-command; *(dans un restaurant)* sous-chef

souscrire* [suskrir] *vi* **s. à** *(payer, approuver)* to subscribe to ■ **souscription** *nf* subscription

sous-développé, -e [sudevlɔpe] *(mpl* **sous-développés**, *fpl* **sous-développées)** *adj (pays)* underdeveloped

sous-directeur, -trice [sudirɛktœr, -tris] *(pl* **sous-directeurs**) *nmf* assistant manager

sous-entendre [suzɑ̃tɑ̃dr] *vt* to imply

sous-entendu [suzɑ̃tɑ̃dy] *(pl* **sous-entendus**) *nm* insinuation

sous-estimer [suzɛstime] *vt* to underestimate

sous-jacent, -e [suʒasɑ̃, -ɑ̃t] *(mpl* **sous-jacents**, *fpl* **sous-jacentes**) *adj* underlying

sous-louer [sulwe] *vt (sujet: locataire)* to sublet

sous-marin, -e [sumarɛ̃, -in] *(mpl* **sous-marins**, *fpl* **sous-marines**) **1** *adj* underwater **2** *nm* submarine

sous-préfet [suprefɛ] *(pl* **sous-préfets**) *nm* subprefect ■ **sous-préfecture** *nf* subprefecture

soussigné, -e [susiɲe] *adj & nmf* undersigned; **je s.** I the undersigned

sous-sol [susɔl] *(pl* **sous-sols**) *nm (d'immeuble)* basement; *Géol* subsoil

sous-titre [sutitr] *(pl* **sous-titres**) *nm* subtitle ■ **sous-titré, -e** *adj* subtitled; **un film e. (en anglais)** a film with (English) subtitles

soustraire* [sustrer] **1** *vt* to remove; *Math* to take away, to subtract (**de** from); **s. qn à** *(danger)* to shield or protect sb from **2 se soustraire** *vpr* **se s. à** to escape from; *(devoir, obligation)* to avoid ■ **soustraction** *nf Math* subtraction

soustraitant [sutretɑ̃] *nm* subcontractor

sous-vêtement [suvɛtmɑ̃] *nm* undergarment; **sous-vêtements** underwear

soutenir* [sutənir] *vt* to support, to hold up; *(candidat)* to back; *(thèse)* to defend; *(regard)* to hold; **s. que...** to maintain that... ■ **soutenu, -e** *adj (attention, effort)* sustained

souterrain, -e [suterɛ̃, -ɛn] **1** *adj* underground **2** *nm* underground passage

soutien [sutjɛ̃] *nm* support; *(personne)* supporter ■ **soutien-gorge** *(pl* **soutiens-gorge)** *nm* bra

soutirer [sutire] *vt* **s. qch à qn** to extract sth from sb

souvenir¹ [suvnir] *nm* memory, recollection; *(objet)* memento; *(cadeau)* keepsake; *(pour touristes)* souvenir; **en s. de** in memory of

souvenir²* [suvnir] **se souvenir** *vpr* **se s. de qn/qch** to remember sb/sth; **se s. que...** to remember that...

souvent [suvã] *adv* often; **peu s.** seldom; **le plus s.** usually, more often than not

souverain, -e [suvərɛ̃, -ɛn] *nmf* sovereign ■ **souveraineté** *nf* sovereignty

soviétique [sɔvjetik] *Anciennement* **1** *adj* Soviet; **l'Union s.** the Soviet Union **2** *nmf* Soviet citizen

soyeux, -euse [swajø, -øz] silky

soyons, soyez [swajɔ̃, swaje] *voir* être

spacieux, -euse [spasjø, -øz] *adj* spacious, roomy

spaghettis [spageti] *nmpl* spaghetti

sparadrap [sparadra] *nm (pour pansement) Br* sticking plaster, *Am* adhesive tape

spatial, -e, -aux, -ales [spasjal, -o] *adj* **station spatiale** space station; **engin s.** spaceship, spacecraft

spécial, -e, -aux, -ales [spesjal, -o] *adj* special; *(bizarre)* peculiar ■ **spécialement** *adv (exprès)* specially; *(en particulier)* especially, particularly

spécialiser [spesjalize] **se spécialiser** *vpr* to specialize **(dans** in) ■ **spécialisation** *nf* specialization ■ **spécialiste** *nmf* specialist ■ **spécialité** *nf Br* speciality, *Am* specialty

spécifier [spesifje] *vt* to specify **(que** that)

spécifique [spesifik] *adj* specific

spécimen [spesimɛn] *nm* specimen; *(livre)* specimen copy

spectacle [spɛktakl] *nm* **(a)** *(vue)* sight, spectacle **(b)** *(représentation)* show; **s. de danse** dance show; **s. de variétés** variety show; **le s.** *(industrie)* show business ■ **spectateur, -trice** *nmf* spectator; *(au théâtre, au cinéma)* member of the audience; **spectateurs** *(au théâtre, au cinéma)* audience

spectaculaire [spɛktakylɛr] *adj* spectacular

spéculer [spekyle] *vi* to speculate ■ **spéculateur, -trice** *nmf* speculator ■ **spéculation** *nf* speculation

spéléologie [speleɔlɔʒi] *nf (activité) Br* potholing, caving, *Am* spelunking

sphère [sfɛr] *nf (boule, domaine)* sphere

spirituel, -elle [spiritɥɛl] *adj (amusant)* witty; *(pouvoir, vie)* spiritual

spiritueux [spiritɥø] *nmpl (boissons)* spirits

splendide [splãdid] *adj* splendid ■ **splendeur** *nf* splendour

spontané, -e [spɔ̃tane] *adj* spontaneous ■ **spontanéité** *nf* spontaneity

sport [spɔr] *nm* sport; **faire du s.** to play *Br* sport *or Am* sports; **voiture/terrain de s.** sports car/ground; **sports de combat** combat sports; **sports d'équipe** team sports; **sports d'hiver** winter sports; **aller aux sports d'hiver** to go skiing; **sports individuels** individual sports; **sports mécaniques** motor sports *(on land, in the air, on water)* **sports de plein-air** outdoor sports ■ **sportif, -ive 1** *adj (personne)* fond of *Br* sport *or Am* sports; *(esprit)* sporting; *(association, journal, résultats)* sports, sporting; *(allure)* athletic **2** *nmf* sportsman, *f* sportswoman

spot [spɔt] *nm (lampe)* spotlight; **s. publicitaire** commercial

square [skwar] *nm* public garden

squash [skwaʃ] *nm (jeu)* squash

squatter 1 [skwate] *vi* to squat **2** [skwatœr] *nm* squatter ■ **squatteur, -euse** *nmf* squatter

squelette [skəlɛt] *nm* skeleton

stable [stabl] *adj* stable ■ **stabiliser** *vt*, **se stabiliser** *vpr* to stabilize ■ **stabilité** *nf* stability

stade [stad] *nm Sport* stadium; *(phase)* stage

stage [staʒ] *nm (période)* training period; *(cours)* (training) course; **faire un s.** to undergo training; **être en s.** to be on a training course ■ **stagiaire** *adj & nmf* trainee

stagner [stagne] *vi* to stagnate

stand [stãd] *nm (d'exposition)* stand, stall; **s. de tir** *(de foire)* shooting range

standard [stãdar] **1** *nm (téléphonique)* switchboard **2** *adj inv (modèle)* standard ■ **standardiste** *nmf* (switchboard) operator

standing [stãdiŋ] *nm* standing, status; **immeuble de (grand) s.** *Br* luxury block of flats, *Am* luxury apartment building

station [stasjɔ̃] *nf (de métro, d'observation, de radio)* station; *(de ski)* resort; *(d'autobus)* stop; **s. de taxis** *Br* taxi rank, *Am* taxi stand ■ **station-service** *(pl* **stations-service***) nf* service station, *Br* petrol *or Am* gas station

stationnaire [stasjɔnɛr] *adj* stationary

stationner [stasjɔne] *vi (être garé)* to be parked ■ **stationnement** *nm* parking

statistique [statistik] **1** *adj* statistical **2** *nf (donnée)* statistic; **la s.** *(science)* statistics *(sing)*

statue [staty] *nf* statue

statut [staty] *nm (position)* status; **statuts** *(règles)* statutes

steak [stɛk] *nm* steak

sténographie [stenɔgrafi] *nf* shorthand, stenography

stéréo [stereo] *nf* stereo; **en s.** in stereo ■ **stéréophonique** *adj* stereophonic

stéréotype [stereɔtip] *nm* stereotype ■ **stéréotypé, -e** *adj* stereotyped

stérile [steril] *adj* sterile; *(terre)* barren ■ **stérilisation** *nf* sterilization ■ **stériliser** *vt* to sterilize ■ **stérilité** *nf* sterility; *(de terre)* barrenness

stéthoscope [stetɔskɔp] *nm* stethoscope

steward [stiwart] *nm (d'avion, de bateau)* steward

stigmatiser [stigmatize] *vt (dénoncer)* to stigmatize

stimuler [stimyle] *vt* to stimulate ■ **stimulation** *nf* stimulation

stimulus [stimylys] *(pl* **stimuli** [-li]*) nm (physiologique)* stimulus

stipuler [stipyle] *vt* to stipulate **(que** that)

stock [stɔk] *nm* stock **(de** of**); en s.** in stock ■ **stockage** *nm* stocking ■ **stocker** *vt (provisions)* to stock

stop [stɔp] **1** *exclam* stop **2** *nm Aut (panneau)* stop sign; *(feu arrière)* brake light, *Br* stoplight; *Fam (auto-stop)* hitching, hitch-hiking; **faire du s.** to hitch, to hitch-hike ■ **stopper** *vti* to stop

stratagème [strataʒɛm] *nm* stratagem, ploy

stratège [stratɛʒ] *nm* strategist ■ **stratégie** *nf* strategy ■ **stratégique** *adj* strategic

stress [strɛs] *nm inv* stress ■ **stressant, -e** *adj* stressful ■ **stressé, -e** *adj* under stress

strict, -e [strikt] *adj (principes, professeur)* strict; *(tenue)* plain; **le s. minimum** the bare minimum ■ **strictement** [-əmã] *adv* strictly; *(vêtu)* plainly

strident, -e [stridã, -ãt] *adj* shrill, strident

structure [stryktyr] *nf* structure ■ **structural, -e, -aux, -ales** *adj* structural ■ **structurer** *vt* to structure

studieux, -euse [stydjø, -øz] *adj* studious; *(vacances)* devoted to study

studio [stydjo] *nm (de cinéma, de télévision, de peintre)* studio; *(logement) Br* studio flat, *Am* studio apartment

stupéfait, -e [stypefɛ, -ɛt] *adj* amazed, astounded **(de** at *or* by**)** ■ **stupéfaction** *nf* amazement

stupéfier [stypefje] *vt* to amaze, to astound ■ **stupéfiant, -e 1** *adj* amazing, astounding **2** *nm* drug, narcotic

stupeur [stypœr] *nf (étonnement)* amazement; *(inertie)* stupor

stupide [stypid] *adj* stupid ■ **stupidité** *nf* stupidity; *(action, parole)* stupid thing

style [stil] *nm* style; **meubles de s.** period furniture ■ **stylé, -e** *adj* well-trained ■ **styliste** *nmf (de mode)* designer ■ **stylistique** *adj* stylistic

stylo [stilo] *nm* pen; **s. à bille** ballpoint (pen), *Br* biro®; **s. à encre, s.-plume** fountain pen

su, -e [sy] *pp de* savoir

subdiviser [sybdivize] *vt* to subdivide (en into) ■ **subdivision** *nf* subdivision

subir [sybir] *vt* to undergo; *(conséquences, défaite, perte, tortures)* to suffer; *(influence)* to be under; **faire s. qch à qn** to subject sb to sth

subit, -e [sybi, -it] *adj* sudden

subjectif, -ive [sybʒɛktif, -iv] *adj* subjective ■ **subjectivité** *nf* subjectivity

subjuguer [sybʒyge] *vt* to subjugate, to subdue; *(envoûter)* to captivate

sublime [syblim] *adj & nm* sublime

submerger [sybmɛrʒe] *vt* to submerge; *Fig (envahir)* to overwhelm; *Fig* **submergé de travail** snowed under with work

submersible [sybmɛrsibl] *nm* submarine

subside [sypsid] *nm* grant, subsidy

subsistance [sybzistɑ̃s] *nf* subsistence

subsister [sybziste] **1** *vi (chose)* to remain; *(personne)* to subsist **2** *v impersonnel* to remain; **il subsiste un doute** there remains some doubt

substance [sypstɑ̃s] *nf* substance; *Fig* **en s.** in essence ■ **substantiel, -elle** *adj* substantial

substituer [sypstitɥe] **1** *vt* to substitute (à for) **2 se substituer** *vpr* **se s. à qn** to take the place of sb, to substitute for sb ■ **substitution** *nf* substitution; **produit de s.** substitute (product)

substitut [sypstity] *nm (produit)* substitute (de for); *(magistrat)* deputy public prosecutor

subtil, -e [syptil] *adj* subtle ■ **subtilité** *nf* subtlety

subvenir* [sybvənir] *vi* **s. à** *(besoins, frais)* to meet

subvention [sybvɑ̃sjɔ̃] *nf* subsidy ■ **subventionner** *vt* to subsidize

subversif, -ive [sybvɛrsif, -iv] *adj* subversive ■ **subversion** *nf* subversion

suc [syk] *nm (gastrique, de fruit)* juice; *(de plante)* sap

succéder [syksede] **1** *vi* **s. à qn** to succeed sb; **s. à qch** to follow sth, to come after sth **2 se succéder** *vpr (choses, personnes)* to follow one another

succès [syksɛ] *nm* success; **s. de librairie** *(livre)* best-seller; **avoir du s.** to be successful; **à s.** *(auteur, film)* successful

successeur [syksɛsœr] *nm* successor ■ **successif, -ive** *adj* successive ■ **succession** *nf* succession (de of; à to); *(série)* sequence (de of); *(patrimoine)* inheritance, estate; **prendre la s. de qn** to succeed sb

succinct, -e [syksɛ̃, -ɛ̃t] *adj* succinct, brief

succomber [sykɔ̃be] *vi (mourir)* to die; **s. à** *(céder à)* to succumb to

succulent, -e [sykylɑ̃, -ɑ̃t] *adj* succulent

succursale [sykyrsal] *nf (de magasin)* branch; **magasin à succursales multiples** chain store

sucer [syse] *vt* to suck ■ **sucette** *nf* lollipop; *(tétine) Br* dummy, *Am* pacifier

sucre [sykr] *nm* sugar; *(morceau)* sugar lump; **s. en poudre, s. semoule** *Br* castor *or* caster sugar, *Am* finely ground sugar; **s. d'orge** barley sugar

sucrer [sykre] *vt* to sugar, to sweeten ■ **sucré, -e** *adj* sweet, sugary; *(artificiellement)* sweetened; *Fig (doucereux)* sugary, syrupy

sucrerie [sykrəri] *nf (usine)* sugar refinery; **sucreries** *(bonbons) Br* sweets, *Am* candy

sucrier [sykrije] *nm (récipient)* sugar bowl

sud [syd] **1** *nm* south; **au s.** in the south; *(direction)* (to the) south (**de** of);

du s. *(vent, direction)* southerly; *(ville)* southern; *(gens)* from *or* in the south; **l'Afrique du S.** South Africa

2 *adj inv (côte)* south(ern) ■ **sud-africain, -e** *(mpl* **sud-africains,** *fpl* **sud-africaines) 1** *adj* South African **2** *nmf* **S., S.-Africaine** South African ■ **sud-américain, -e** *(mpl* **sud-américains,** *fpl* **sud-américaines) 1** *adj* South American **2** *nmf* **S., S.-Américaine** South American ■ **sud-est** *nm & adj inv* south-east ■ **sud-ouest** *nm & adj inv* south-west

Suède [sɥɛd] *nf* **la S.** Sweden ■ **suédois, -e 1** *adj* Swedish **2** *nmf* **S., Suédoise** Swede **3** *nm (langue)* Swedish

suer [sɥe] *vi (personne, mur)* to sweat ■ **sueur** *nf* sweat; **(tout) en s.** sweating

suffire* [syfir] **1** *vi* to be enough (**à** for); **ça suffit!** that's enough! **2** *v impersonnel* **il suffit de faire qch** one only has to do sth; **il suffit d'une goutte/ d'une heure pour faire qch** a drop/ an hour is enough to do sth **3 se suffire** *vpr* **se s. à soi-même** to be self-sufficient

suffisance [syfizɑ̃s] *nf (vanité)* conceit

suffisant, -e [syfizɑ̃, -ɑ̃t] *adj (satisfaisant)* sufficient, adequate; *(vaniteux)* conceited ■ **suffisamment** [-amɑ̃] *adv* sufficiently; **s. de** enough, sufficient

suffoquer [syfɔke] *vti* to choke, to suffocate

suffrage [syfraʒ] *nm Pol (voix)* vote; **s. universel** universal suffrage

suggérer [syɡʒere] *vt (proposer)* to suggest (**à** to; **de faire** doing; **que** + *subjunctive* that) ■ **suggestif, -ive** *adj* suggestive ■ **suggestion** *nf* suggestion

suicide [sɥisid] *nm* suicide ■ **se suicider** *vpr* to commit suicide

suie [sɥi] *nf* soot

suinter [sɥɛ̃te] *vi* to ooze ■ **suintement** *nm* oozing

suis [sɥi] *voir* **être, suivre**

Suisse [sɥis] *nf* **la S.** Switzerland; **S. allemande/romande** German-speaking/French-speaking Switzerland ■ **suisse 1** *adj* Swiss **2** *nmf* **S.** Swiss; **les**

Suisses the Swiss ■ **Suissesse** *nf* Swiss *inv*

suite [sɥit] *nf (reste)* rest; *(continuation)* continuation; *(de film, de roman)* sequel; *(série)* series, sequence; *(appartement, escorte)* suite; *(cohérence)* order; **suites** *(séquelles)* effects; *(résultats)* consequences; **faire s. (à)** to follow; **donner s. à** *(demande)* to follow up; **par la s.** afterwards; **par s. de** as a result of; **à la s.** one after another; **à la s. de** *(derrière)* behind; *(événement, maladie)* as a result of; **de s.** *(deux jours)* in a row

suivant, -e [sɥivɑ̃, -ɑ̃t] **1** *adj* next, following; *(ci-après)* following **2** *nmf* next (one); **au s.!** next!, next person! ■ **suivant** *prép (selon)* according to

suivi, -e [sɥivi] *adj (régulier)* regular, steady; *(cohérent)* coherent; **peu/très s.** *(cours)* poorly/well attended

suivre* [sɥivr] **1** *vt* to follow; *(accompagner)* to go with, to accompany; *(cours)* to attend, to go to; **s. qn/qch des yeux** *ou* **du regard** to watch sb/ sth; **s. l'exemple de qn** to follow sb's example; **s. l'actualité** to follow events *or* the news **2** *vi* to follow; **faire s.** *(courrier, lettre)* to forward; **'à s.'** 'to be continued' **3 se suivre** *vpr* to follow each other

sujet¹, -ette [syʒɛ, -ɛt] **1** *adj* **s. à** *(maladie)* subject to; **s. à caution** *(information, nouvelle)* unconfirmed **2** *nmf (personne)* subject

sujet² [syʒɛ] *nm* **(a)** *(question)* subject; *(d'examen)* question; **au s. de** about; **à quel s.?** about what? **(b)** *(raison)* cause; **sujet(s) de dispute** grounds for dispute **(c)** *(individu)* subject; **un brillant s.** a brilliant student

super [sypɛr] *nm (supercarburant) Br* four-star (petrol), *Am* premium *ou* high-test gas

superbe [sypɛrb] *adj* superb

supercherie [sypɛrʃəri] *nf* deception

supérette [sypɛrɛt] *nf* convenience store

superficie [sypɛrfisi] *nf* surface; *(dimensions)* area ■ **superficiel, -elle** *adj* superficial

superflu, -e [syperfly] *adj* superfluous

supérieur, -e [syperjœr] **1** *adj (étages, partie)* upper; *(qualité, air, ton)* superior; **à l'étage s.** on the floor above; **s. à** *(meilleur que)* superior to, better than; *(plus grand que)* above, greater than; **s. à la moyenne** above average; **études supérieures** higher *ou* university studies **2** *nmf* superior ▪ **supériorité** *nf* superiority

supermarché [sypermarʃe] *nm* supermarket

superposer [syperpoze] *vt (objets)* to put on top of each other; *(images)* to superimpose

superproduction [syperprɔdyksjɔ̃] *nf (film)* blockbuster

superpuissance [syperpɥisɑ̃s] *nf Pol* superpower

supersonique [sypersɔnik] *adj* supersonic

superstar [syperstar] *nf* superstar

superstitieux, -euse [syperstisjø, -øz] *adj* superstitious ▪ **superstition** *nf* superstition

superviser [sypervize] *vt* to supervise

supplanter [syplɑ̃te] *vt* to take the place of

suppléer [syplee] *vi* **s. à** *(compenser)* to make up for ▪ **suppléant, -e** *adj & nmf (personne)* substitute, replacement; **(professeur) s.** substitute *or Br* supply teacher

supplément [syplemɑ̃] *nm (argent)* extra charge, supplement; *(de revue, de livre)* supplement; **en s.** extra; **un s. de** *(information, de travail)* extra, additional ▪ **supplémentaire** *adj* extra, additional

supplice [syplis] *nm* torture ▪ **supplier** *vt* **s. qn de faire qch** to beg *or* implore sb to do sth; **je vous en supplie!** I beg *or* implore you!

support [sypɔr] *nm* support; *(d'instrument)* stand

supporter¹ [sypɔrte] *vt (malheur, conséquences)* to bear, to endure; *(chaleur)* to withstand; **je ne peux pas la s.** I can't bear her ▪ **supportable** *adj* bearable; *(excusable, passable)* tolerable

supporter² [sypɔrter] *nm (de football)* supporter

supposer [sypoze] *vt* to suppose, to assume **(que** that); *(impliquer)* to imply **(que** that); **à s.** *ou* **en supposant que...** *(+ subjunctive)* supposing (that)... ▪ **supposition** *nf* assumption, supposition

supprimer [syprime] **1** *vt* to get rid of, to remove; *(mot, passage)* to cut out, to delete; *(train)* to cancel; *(tuer)* to do away with; **s. des emplois** to axe jobs; **s. qch à qn** to take sth away from sb **2 se supprimer** *vpr (se suicider)* to do away with oneself ▪ **suppression** *nf* removal; *(de mot)* deletion; *(de train)* cancellation; *(d'emplois)* axing

suprématie [sypremasi] *nf* supremacy

suprême [syprem] *adj* supreme

sur [syr] *prép* on, upon; *(par-dessus)* over; *(au sujet de)* on, about; **six s. dix** six out of ten; **un jour s. deux** every other day; **six mètres s. dix** six metres by ten; **s. votre gauche** to *or* on your left; **mettre/monter s. qch** to put/climb on (to) sth

sûr, -e [syr] *adj* sure, certain **(de** of; **que** that); *(digne de confiance)* reliable; *(lieu)* safe; *(goût)* discerning; *(main)* steady; **s. de soi** self-assured; **bien s.!** of course!

surcharge [syrʃarʒ] *nf* **(a)** *(poids)* excess weight; **s. de travail** extra work; **en s.** *(passagers)* extra **(b)** *(correction)* alteration; *(à payer)* surcharge ▪ **surcharger** *vt (voiture, personne)* to overload **(de** with)

surchauffer [syrʃofe] *vt* to overheat

surcroît [syrkrwa] *nm* increase **(de** in); **de s., par s.** in addition

surdité [syrdite] *nf* deafness

surdose [syrdoz] *nf (de drogue)* overdose

surélever [syrelve] *vt* to raise

surestimer [syrestime] *vt* to overestimate; *(tableau)* to overvalue

sûreté [syrte] *nf* safety; *(de l'État)* security; *(garantie)* surety; *(de geste)* sureness; **être en s.** to be safe; **mettre**

qn/qch en s. to put sb/sth in a safe place; **pour plus de s.** to be on the safe side

surexcité, -e [syrɛksite] *adj* overexcited

surf [sœrf] *nm Sport* surfing; **faire du s.** to surf, to go surfing ▪ **surfer** *vi* **s. sur le Net** to surf the Net

surface [syrfas] *nf* surface; *(étendue)* (surface) area; **faire s.** *(sous-marin)* to surface; **(magasin à) grande s.** hypermarket; **de s.** *(politesse)* superficial

surfait, -e [syrfɛ, -ɛt] *adj* overrated

surgelé, -e [syrʒəle] *adj* frozen ▪ **surgelés** *nmpl* frozen foods

surgir [syrʒir] *vi* to appear suddenly (**de** from)

surhomme [syrɔm] *nm* superman ▪ **surhumain, -e** *adj* superhuman

sur-le-champ [syrləʃɑ̃] *adv* immediately

surlendemain [syrlɑ̃dəmɛ̃] *nm* **le s.** two days later; **le s. de** two days after

surligner [syrliɲe] *vt* to highlight ▪ **surligneur** *nm* highlighter (pen)

surmener [syrməne] *vt*, **se surmener** *vpr* to overwork ▪ **surmenage** *nm* overwork

surmonter [syrmɔ̃te] *vt (être placé sur)* to surmount; *Fig (obstacle, peur)* to overcome

surnaturel, -elle [syrnatyrɛl] *adj & nm* supernatural

surnom [syrnɔ̃] *nm* nickname

surpasser [syrpase] **1** *vt* to surpass (**en** in) **2 se surpasser** *vpr* to surpass oneself

surpeuplé, -e [syrpœple] *adj* overpopulated

surplomb [syrplɔ̃] *nm* **en s.** overhanging ▪ **surplomber** *vti* to overhang

surplus [syrply] *nm* surplus

surprendre* [syrprɑ̃dr] *vt (étonner)* to surprise; *(prendre sur le fait)* to catch ▪ **surprenant, -e** *adj* surprising ▪ **surpris, -e** *adj* surprised (**de** at; **que** + *subjunctive* that); **je suis s. de te voir** I'm surprised to see you ▪ **surprise** *nf*

surprise; **prendre qn par s.** to catch sb unawares

surréaliste [syrrealist] *adj (poète, peintre)* surrealist

sursaut [syrso] *nm* (sudden) start *ou* jump; **se réveiller en s.** to wake up with a start ▪ **sursauter** *vi* to jump, start

sursis [syrsi] *nm (à l'armée)* deferment; *Fig (répit)* reprieve; **un an (de prison) avec s.** a one-year suspended sentence

surtout [syrtu] *adv* especially; *(avant tout)* above all; **s. pas** certainly not

surveiller [syrvɛje] *vt (garder)* to watch, to keep an eye on; *(contrôler)* to supervise; *(épier)* to watch ▪ **surveillance** *nf* watch (**sur** over); *(de travaux, d'ouvriers)* supervision; *(de police)* surveillance ▪ **surveillant, -e** *nmf (de lycée)* supervisor *(in charge of discipline)*; *(de prison)* (prison) guard, *Br* warder

survenir* [syrvənir] *vi* to occur; *(personne)* to turn up

survêtement [syrvɛtmɑ̃] *nm* tracksuit

survie [syrvi] *nf* survival ▪ **survivre*** *vi* to survive (**à qch** sth); **s. à qn** to outlive sb ▪ **survivant, -e** *nmf* survivor

survoler [syrvɔle] *vt* to fly over; *Fig (question)* to skim over

susceptible [sysɛptibl] *adj (ombrageux)* touchy, sensitive; **s. de** *(interprétations)* open to; **s. de faire qch** likely *ou* liable to do sth; *(capable)* able to do sth ▪ **susceptibilité** *nf* touchiness, sensitivity

susciter [sysite] *vt (sentiment)* to arouse; *(ennuis, obstacles)* to create

suspect, -e [syspɛ, -ɛkt] **1** *adj* suspicious, suspect; **s. de qch** suspected of sth **2** *nmf* suspect ▪ **suspecter** *vt (personne)* to suspect (**de qch** of sth; **de faire** of doing)

suspendre [syspɑ̃dr] **1** *vt (accrocher)* to hang (up) (**à** on); *(destituer, interrompre)* to suspend **2 se suspendre** *vpr* **se s. à** to hang from ▪ **suspendu, -e** *adj* **s. à** hanging from; **pont s.** suspension bridge

suspens [syspɑ̃] **en suspens** *adv (affaire, travail)* in abeyance; *(en l'air)* suspended

suspense [syspɛns] *nm* suspense

suspension [syspɑ̃sjɔ̃] *nf (d'hostilités, d'employé, de véhicule)* suspension

suspicion [syspisjɔ̃] *nf* suspicion

suture [sytyr] *nf Méd* **point de s.** stitch

SVP [ɛsvepe] *(abrév* **s'il vous plaît)** please

symbole [sɛ̃bɔl] *nm* symbol ▪ **symbolique** *adj* symbolic; *(salaire, cotisation, loyer)* nominal; **geste s.** symbolic *ou* token gesture ▪ **symboliser** *vt* to symbolize

sympathie [sɛ̃pati] *nf (affinité)* liking; *(condoléances)* sympathy; **avoir de la s. pour qn** to be fond of sb ▪ **sympathique** *adj* nice; *(accueil)* friendly ▪ **sympathiser** *vi* to get along well, *Br* to get on well (**avec** with)

symphonie [sɛ̃fɔni] *nf* symphony

symptôme [sɛ̃ptom] *nm Méd & Fig* symptom

synagogue [sinagɔg] *nf* synagogue

synchroniser [sɛ̃krɔnize] *vt* to synchronize

syndicat [sɛ̃dika] *nm (d'ouvriers) (Br* trade *or Am* labor) union; *(de patrons)* association; **s. d'initiative** tourist (information) office ▪ **syndicaliste** *nmf Br* trade *or Am* labor unionist

syndiquer [sɛ̃dike] **1** *vt* to unionize **2 se syndiquer** *vpr (adhérer)* to join a (*Br* trade *or Am* labor) union ▪ **syndiqué, -e** *nmf* (*Br* trade *or Am* labor) union member

syndrome [sɛ̃drom] *nm Méd & Fig* syndrome; **s. immunodéficitaire acquis** acquired immune deficiency syndrome

synthèse [sɛ̃tɛz] *nf* synthesis ▪ **synthétique** *adj* synthetic

synthétiseur [sɛ̃tetizœr] *nm* synthesizer

Syrie [siri] *nf* **la S.** Syria ▪ **syrien, -enne 1** *adj* Syrian **2** *nmf* **S., Syrienne** Syrian

système [sistɛm] *nm (structure, réseau) & Anat* system; *Ordinat* **s. d'exploitation** operating system ▪ **systématique** *adj* systematic ▪ **systématiquement** *adv* systematically

Tt

T, t [te] *nm inv* T, t

t' [t] *voir* **te**

ta [ta] *voir* **ton¹**

tabac [taba] *nm* tobacco; *(magasin)* *Br* tobacconist's (shop), *Am* tobacco store

table [tabl] *nf* (a) *(meuble)* table; *(d'école)* desk; **mettre/débarrasser la t.** to set *or Br* lay/clear the table; **être à t.** to be sitting at the table; **à t.!** food's ready!; **t. à repasser** ironing board; **t. de nuit/d'opération** bedside/operating table (b) *(liste)* table; **t. des matières** table of contents

tableau, -x [tablo] *nm* (a) *(peinture)* picture, painting; *(image, description)* picture; **t. de maître** *(peinture)* old master (b) *(panneau)* board; *(liste)* list; *(graphique)* chart; **t. (noir)** (black)-board; **t. d'affichage** *Br* notice board, *Am* bulletin board

tabler [table] *vi* **t. sur qch** to count *or* rely on sth

tablette [tablɛt] *nf (de chocolat)* bar, slab; *(de lavabo)* shelf; *(de cheminée)* mantelpiece

tablier [tablije] *nm (vêtement)* apron; *(d'écolier)* smock

tabouret [taburɛ] *nm* stool

tache [taʃ] *nf* mark; *(salissure)* stain ■ **tacher** *vt*, **se tacher** *vpr (tissu)* to stain

tâche [taʃ] *nf* task, job; **tâches ménagères** housework; **participer aux tâches ménagères** to help with the housework

tâcher [taʃe] *vi* **t. de faire qch** to try *or* endeavour to do sth

tacheté, -e [taʃte] *adj* speckled *(de* with)

tact [takt] *nm* tact; **avoir du t.** to be tactful

tactique [taktik] **1** *adj* tactical **2** *nf* tactics *(sing)*; **une t.** a tactic

Tahiti [taiti] *nm* Tahiti ■ **tahitien, -enne** [taisjɛ̃, -ɛn] **1** *adj* Tahitian **2** *nmf* T., Tahitienne Tahitian

taillader [tajade] *vt* to gash

taille¹ [taj] *nf* (a) *(hauteur)* height; *(dimension, mesure)* size; **de haute t.** *(personne)* tall; **de petite t.** short; **de t. moyenne** medium-sized (b) *(ceinture)* waist; **tour de t.** waist measurement

taille² [taj] *nf* cutting; *(de haie)* trimming; *(d'arbre)* pruning ■ **tailler** *vt* to cut; *(haie, barbe)* to trim; *(arbre)* to prune; *(crayon)* to sharpen

taille-crayon [tajkrɛjɔ̃] *nm inv* pencil sharpener

tailleur [tajœr] *nm (personne)* tailor; *(costume)* suit

taire* [tɛr] **1** *vt* to say nothing about **2** *vi* **faire t. qn** to silence sb **3** **se taire** *vpr (ne rien dire)* to keep quiet *(sur qch* about sth); *(cesser de parler)* to stop talking, to fall silent; **tais-toi!** be quiet!

Taiwan [tajwan] *nm ou f* Taiwan

talc [talk] *nm* talcum powder

talent [talã] *nm* talent; **avoir du t.** to be talented ■ **talentueux, -euse** *adj* talented

talkie-walkie [talkiwalki] *(pl* talkies-walkies) *nm* walkie-talkie

talon [talɔ̃] *nm* (a) *(de chaussure)* heel; **(chaussures) à** talons hauts high heels, high-heeled shoes; **talons aiguilles** stiletto heels (b) *(de chèque)* stub, counterfoil

tambour [tãbur] *nm (de machine, instrument de musique)* drum ■ **tambourin** *nm* tambourine

Tamise [tamiz] *nf* la T. the Thames

tamiser [tamize] *vt (farine)* to sift; *(lumière)* to filter

tampon [tɑ̃pɔ̃] *nm* (a) *(marque, instrument)* stamp; **t. encreur** ink pad (b) *(bouchon)* plug, stopper; *(de coton)* wad, pad; *(pour pansement)* swab; **t. hygiénique** tampon (c) *(de train)* & *Fig* buffer; **état t.** buffer state

tamponner [tɑ̃pɔne] **1** *vt (lettre, document)* to stamp; *(visage)* to dab; *(plaie)* to swab; *(train, voiture)* to crash into **2 se tamponner** *vpr* to crash into each other ■ **tamponneuses** *adj fpl* **autos t.** Dodgems®

tandem [tɑ̃dɛm] *nm (bicyclette)* tandem; *Fig (duo)* duo

tandis [tɑ̃di] **tandis que** *conj (simultanéité)* while; *(contraste)* whereas, while

tanière [tanjɛr] *nf* den, lair

tank [tɑ̃k] *nm* tank

tanker [tɑ̃kɛr] *nm (navire)* tanker

tanner [tane] *vt (cuir)* to tan ■ **tanné, -e** *adj (visage)* weather-beaten

TANT [tɑ̃] *adv (travailler)* so much **(que** that); **t. de** *(pain, temps)* so much **(que** that); *(gens, choses)* so many **(que** that); **t. de fois** so often, so many times; **t. que** *(autant que)* as much as; *(aussi fort que)* as hard as; *(aussi longtemps que)* as long as; **en t. que** *(considéré comme)* as; **t. mieux!** so much the better!; **t. pis!** too bad!, pity!; **t. mieux pour toi!** good for you!; **t. soit peu** (even)·remotely *or* slightly; **un t. soit peu** somewhat; **t. s'en faut** far from it

tante [tɑ̃t] *nf* aunt

tantinet [tɑ̃tinɛ] *nm & adv* **un t.** a tiny bit **(de** of)

tantôt [tɑ̃to] *adv* (a) **t....t....** sometimes… sometimes… (b) *(cet après-midi)* this afternoon

taon [tɑ̃] *nm* horsefly, gadfly

tapage [tapaʒ] *nm* din, uproar ■ **tapageur, -euse** *adj (bruyant)* rowdy; *(criard)* flashy

tape [tap] *nf* slap

taper [tape] **1** *vt (frapper)* to hit; *(marteler)* to bang; **t. qch à la machine** to type sth **2** *vi (soleil)* to beat down; **t. du pied** to stamp one's foot; **t. à la machine** to type; **t. sur qch** to bang on sth ■ **tapant, -e** *adj* **à huit heures tapantes** at eight sharp

tapis [tapi] *nm* carpet; **envoyer qn au t.** *(abattre)* to floor sb; **mettre qch sur le t.** *(sujet)* to bring sth up for discussion; **t. de bain** bath mat; **t. roulant** *(pour marchandises)* conveyor belt; *(pour personnes)* moving walkway

tapisser [tapise] *vt (mur)* to (wall)paper ■ **tapisserie** *nf (papier peint)* wallpaper; *(broderie)* tapestry

tapoter [tapote] **1** *vt* to tap; *(joue)* to pat **2** *vi* **t. sur** to tap (on)

taquin, -e [takɛ̃, -in] *adj* teasing ■ **taquiner** *vt* to tease ■ **taquineries** *nfpl* teasing

tard [tar] *adv* late; **plus t.** later (on); **au plus t.** at the latest; **sur le t.** late in life

tarder [tarde] **1** *vi (lettre, saison)* to be a long time coming; **sans t.** without delay; **t. à faire qch** to take one's time doing sth; **elle ne va pas t.** she won't be long **2** *v impersonnel* **il me tarde de le faire** I long to do it

tardif, -ive [tardif, -iv] *adj* late; *(regrets)* belated ■ **tardivement** *adv* late

tare [tar] *nf (poids)* tare; *Fig (défaut)* defect

targuer [targe] **se targuer** *vpr* **se t. de faire qch** to pride oneself on doing sth

tarif [tarif] *nm (prix)* rate; *(de train)* fare; *(tableau)* price list, *Br* tariff; **plein t.** full price; *(de train, bus)* full fare ■ **tarification** *nf* pricing

tartare [tartar] *adj* **sauce t.** tartar sauce

tarte [tart] *nf* (open) pie, tart ■ **tartelette** [-əlɛt] *nf* (small) tart, tartlet

tartine [tartin] *nf* slice of bread; **t. de confiture** slice of bread and jam ■ **tartiner** *vt (beurre)* to spread; **fromage à t.** cheese spread

tas [tɑ] *nm* pile, heap

tasse [tas] *nf* cup; **t. à café** coffee cup; **t. à thé** teacup

tasser [tɑse] **1** *vt* to pack **(dans** into) **2**

se tasser *vpr (se serrer)* to squeeze up; *(sol)* to sink, to collapse; *(se voûter)* to become bowed

tâter [tɑte] *vt* to feel

tâtonner [tɑtɔne] *vi* to grope about ■ **tâtons** *adv* **avancer à t.** to feel one's way (along); **chercher qch à t.** to grope for sth

tatouer [tatwe] *vt (corps, dessin)* to tattoo; **se faire t.** to get a tattoo ■ **tatouage** *nm (dessin)* tattoo; *(action)* tattooing

taudis [todi] *nm* slum

taupe [top] *nf (animal, espion)* mole

taureau, -x [toro] *nm* bull; **le T.** *(signe)* Taurus ■ **tauromachie** *nf* bull-fighting

taux [to] *nm* rate; **t. de cholestérol** cholesterol rate; **t. d'intérêt** interest rate; **t. de natalité** birth rate

taxe [taks] *nf (impôt)* tax; **t. à la valeur ajoutée** value-added tax ■ **taxation** *nf* taxation

taxer [takse] *vt (produit, personne, firme)* to tax; **t. qn de qch** to accuse sb of sth ■ **taxé, -e** *adj (produit)* taxed

taxi [taksi] *nm* taxi

Tchécoslovaquie [tʃekɔslɔvaki] *nf* *Anciennement* **la T.** Czechoslovakia ■ **tchèque 1** *adj* Czech; **la République t.** the Czech Republic **2** *nmf* **T.** Czech **3** *nm (langue)* Czech

te [tə] **t'** is used before a word beginning with a vowel or h mute. *pron personnel* **(a)** *(complément direct)* you; **je te vois** I see you **(b)** *(indirect)* (to) you; **il te parle** he speaks to you; **elle te l'a dit** she told you **(c)** *(réfléchi)* yourself; **tu te laves** you wash yourself

technicien, -enne [tɛknisjɛ̃, -ɛn] *nmf* technician ■ **technique 1** *adj* technical **2** *nf* technique ■ **technologie** *nf* technology ■ **technologique** *adj* technological

teckel [tekel] *nm* dachshund

tee-shirt [tiʃœrt] *nm* tee-shirt

teindre* [tɛ̃dr] **1** *vt* to dye; **t. qch en rouge** to dye sth red **2 se teindre** *vpr* **se t. (les cheveux)** to dye one's hair

teint [tɛ̃] *nm (de visage)* complexion; **bon** *ou* **grand t.** *(tissu)* colourfast

teinte [tɛ̃t] *nf* shade, tint ■ **teinter** *vt* to tint; *(bois)* to stain

teinture [tɛ̃tyr] *nf* dyeing; *(produit)* dye ■ **teinturerie** [-rri] *nf (boutique)* (dry) cleaner's

TEL, TELLE [tɛl] *adj* such; **un t. livre/ homme** such a book/man; **de tels mots** such words; **t. que** such as, like; **t. que je l'ai laissé** just as I left it; **laissez-le t. quel** leave it just as it is; **en tant que t., comme t.** as such; **t. ou t.** such and such; **rien de t. que...** (there's) nothing like...; **t. père t. fils** like father like son

télé [tele] *nf Fam* TV, *Br* telly; **à la t.** on TV, *Br* on the telly

Télécarte® [telekart] *nf* phone card

télécommande [telekɔmɑ̃d] *nf* remote control ■ **télécommandé, -e** *adj* remote-controlled

télécommunications [telekɔmynikasjɔ̃] *nfpl* telecommunications

télécopie [telekɔpi] *nf* fax ■ **télécopieur** *nm* fax (machine)

téléfilm [telefilm] *nm* TV movie

télégramme [telegram] *nm* telegram

télégraphe [telegraf] *nm* telegraph ■ **télégraphique** *adj* **poteau/fil t.** telegraph pole/wire

téléguider [telegide] *vt* to operate by remote control

télépathie [telepati] *nf* telepathy

téléphérique [teleferik] *nm* cable car

téléphone [telefɔn] *nm* (tele)phone; **coup de t.** (phone) call; **passer un coup de t. à qn** to give sb a ring *or* a call; **au t.** on the (tele)phone; **avoir le t.** to be on the (tele)phone; **t. portable** mobile phone; **t. sans fil** cordless phone ■ **téléphoner 1** *vt (nouvelle)* to (tele)phone (à to) **2** *vi* to (tele)phone; **t. à qn** to (tele)phone sb, to call sb (up) ■ **téléphonique** *adj* **appel t.** telephone call

télescope [teleskɔp] *nm* telescope ■ **télescopique** *adj* telescopic

télescoper [teleskɔpe] **1** *vt (voiture, train)* to smash into **2 se télescoper** *vpr (voiture, train)* to concertina

télésiège [telesjɛʒ] *nm* chair lift

téléski [teleski] *nm* ski tow

téléspectateur, -trice [telespɛktatœr, -tris] *nmf* (television) viewer

télétravail [teletravaj] *nm* teleworking

téléviser [televize] *vt* to televise ▪ **téléviseur** *nm* television (set) ▪ **télévision** *nf* television; **à la t.** on (the) television; **regarder la t./qch à la t.** to watch (the) television/sth on (the) television; **programme de t.** television programme

télex [telɛks] *nm (service, message)* telex

telle [tɛl] *voir* **tel** ▪ **tellement** *adv (si)* so; *(tant)* so much; **t. grand que...** so big that...; **crier t. que...** to shout so much that...; **t. de travail** so much work; **t. de soucis** so many worries; **tu aimes ça? – pas t.!** *(pas beaucoup)* do you like it? – not much *or* a lot!; **personne ne peut le supporter, t. il est bavard** nobody can stand him, he's so talkative

tellurique [telyrik] *adj* **secousse t.** earth tremor

téméraire [temerɛr] *adj* reckless ▪ **témérité** *nf* recklessness

témoigner [temwaɲe] **1** *vt (gratitude)* to show (**à qn** (to) sb); **t. que...** *(attester)* to testify that... **2** *vi* **Jur** to give evidence, to testify (**contre** against); **t. de qch** *(personne, attitude)* to testify to sth ▪ **témoignage** *nm* **Jur** evidence, testimony; *(récit)* account; **faux t.** *(délit)* perjury; **en t. de qch** as a token of sth

témoin [temwɛ̃] **1** *nm* (a) **Jur** witness; **être t. de qch** to witness sth (b) *(de relais)* baton **2** *adj* **appartement t.** *Br* show flat, *Am* model apartment

tempérament [tɑ̃peramɑ̃] *nm (caractère)* temperament; **acheter qch à t.** to buy sth on *Br* hire purchase *or Am* on the installment plan

température [tɑ̃peratyr] *nf* temperature; **avoir de la t.** to have a temperature

tempérer [tɑ̃pere] *vt (ardeurs)* to moderate ▪ **tempéré, -e** *adj (climat, zone)* temperate

tempête [tɑ̃pɛt] *nf* storm

tempêter [tɑ̃pete] *vi (crier)* to storm, to rage (**contre** against)

temple [tɑ̃pl] *nm (romain, grec)* temple; *(protestant)* church

temporaire [tɑ̃pɔrɛr] *adj* temporary

temporel, -elle [tɑ̃pɔrɛl] *adj* temporal; *(terrestre)* wordly

TEMPS¹ [tɑ̃] *nm (durée, période, moment)* time; *(étape)* stage; **en t. de guerre** in wartime, in time of war; **avoir le t.** to have (the) time (**de faire** to do); **il est t.** it is time (**de faire** to do); **il était t.!** it was about time (too)!; **il est (grand) t. que vous partiez** it's (high) time you left; **ces derniers t.** lately; **de t. en t.** [dətɑ̃zɑ̃tɑ̃], **de t. à autre** [dətɑ̃zaotr] from time to time, now and again; **en t. utile** [ɑ̃tɑ̃zytil] in due course; **en t. voulu** in due course; **en même t.** at the same time (**que** as); **à t.** *(arriver)* in time; **à plein t.** *(travailler)* full-time; **à t. partiel** *(travailler)* part-time; **dans le t.** *(autrefois)* in the old days; **avec le t.** *(à la longue)* in time; **tout le t.** all the time; **de mon t.** in my time; **t. d'arrêt** pause, break; **t. libre** free time

temps² [tɑ̃] *nm (climat)* weather; **il fait beau/mauvais t.** the weather's fine/bad; **quel t. fait-il?** what's the weather like?

tenace [tənas] *adj* stubborn, tenacious ▪ **ténacité** *nf* stubbornness, tenacity

tenailles [tənaj] *nfpl (outil)* pincers

tenant, -e [tənɑ̃, -ɑ̃t] **1** *nmf* **le t. du titre** *(champion)* the title holder **2** *nm (partisan)* supporter (**de** of)

tendance [tɑ̃dɑ̃s] *nf (penchant)* tendency; *(évolution)* trend (**à** towards); **avoir t. à faire qch** to tend to do sth, to have a tendency to do sth

tendre¹ [tɑ̃dr] **1** *vt* to stretch; *(main)* to hold out (**à qn** to sb); *(bras, jambe)* to stretch out; *(cou)* to strain, to crane; *(muscle)* to tense; *(arc)* to bend; *(piège)* to set, to lay; *(filet)* to spread; **t. qch à qn** to hold out sth to sb; *Fig* **t. l'oreille** to prick up one's ears

2 *vi* **t. à qch/à faire qch** to tend towards sth/to do sth

3 se tendre *vpr (rapports)* to become strained ■ **tendu, -e** *adj (corde)* tight, taut; *(personne, situation, muscle)* tense; *(rapports)* strained

tendre² [tãdr] *adj (personne)* affectionate (**avec** to); *(parole, regard)* tender, loving; *(viande)* tender; *(bois, couleur)* soft; **depuis ma plus t. enfance** since I was a young child ■ **tendresse** *nf (affection)* affection, tenderness

teneur [tənœr] *nf (de lettre)* content; **t. en alcool** alcohol content (**de** of)

TENIR* [tənir] **1** *vt (à la main)* to hold; *(promesse, comptes, hôtel)* to keep; *(rôle)* to play

2 *vi (nœud)* to hold; *(neige, coiffure)* to last, to hold; *(résister)* to hold out; **t. à qn/qch** to be attached to sb/sth; **t. à faire qch** to be anxious to do sth; **t. dans qch** *(être contenu)* to fit into sth; **t. de qn** to take after sb; **tenez!** *(prenez)* here (you are)!; **tiens!** *(surprise)* well!, hey!

3 *v impersonnel* **il ne tient qu'à vous de le faire** it's up to you to do it

4 se tenir *vpr (avoir lieu)* to be held; *(rester)* to remain; **se t. debout** to stand (up); **se t. droit** to stand up/sit up straight; **se t. par la main** to hold hands; **se t. bien** to behave oneself; **se t. à qch** to hold on to sth

tennis [tenis] **1** *nm* tennis; *(terrain)* (tennis) court; **t. de table** table tennis **2** *nmpl Br (chaussures)* tennis shoes

tension [tãsjõ] *nf* tension; **t. artérielle** blood pressure; **avoir de la t.** to have high blood pressure

tente [tãt] *nf* tent

tenter¹ [tãte] *vt (essayer)* to try; **t. de faire qch** to try *or* attempt to do sth ■ **tentative** *nf* attempt

tenter² [tãte] *vt (faire envie à)* to tempt; **tenté de faire qch** tempted to do sth ■ **tentant, -e** *adj* tempting ■ **tentation** *nf* temptation

tenture [tãtyr] *nf* (wall) hanging; *(de porte)* drape, curtain

tenu, -e [təny] **1** *pp de* **tenir 2** *adj* **t. de faire qch** obliged to do sth; **bien/mal t.** *(maison)* well/badly kept

ténu, -e [teny] *adj (fil)* fine; *(différence)* tenuous; *(voix)* thin

tenue [təny] *nf* **(a)** *(vêtements)* clothes, outfit; **t. de soirée** evening dress **(b)** *(conduite)* (good) behaviour; *(maintien)* posture **(c)** *(de maison, d'hôtel)* running; *(de comptes)* keeping **(d)** **t. de route** *(de véhicule)* road-holding

ter [ter] *adj* **4 t.** ≃ **4B**

terme [term] *nm* **(a)** *(mot)* term **(b)** *(date limite)* time (limit); *(fin)* end; **mettre un t. à qch** to put an end to sth; **à court/long t.** *(conséquences, projet)* short-/long-term **(c)** **moyen t.** *(solution)* middle course **(d)** **en bons/mauvais termes** on good/bad terms *(avec* qn with sb) **(e)** *(loyer)* rent; *(jour)* rent day; *(période)* rental period

terminal, -e, -aux, -ales [terminal, -o] **1** *adj* final; *(phase de maladie)* terminal **2** *adj & nf Scol* **(classe) terminale** *Br* ≃ sixth form, *Am* ≃ twelfth grade **3** *nm (d'ordinateur, pétrolier)* terminal

terminer [termine] **1** *vt* to end; *(achever)* to finish, to complete **2 se terminer** *vpr* to end (**par** with; **en** in) ■ **terminaison** *nf (de mot)* ending

terminologie [terminɔlɔʒi] *nf* terminology

terminus [terminys] *nm* terminus

terne [tern] *adj (couleur, journée)* dull, drab; *(personne)* dull ■ **ternir 1** *vt (métal, réputation)* to tarnish; *(meuble, miroir)* to dull **2 se ternir** *vpr (métal)* to tarnish

terrain [terɛ̃] *nm (sol) & Fig* ground; *(étendue)* land; *(à bâtir)* plot, site; *(pour opérations militaires) & Géol* terrain; **un t.** a piece of land; **gagner/perdre du t.** *(armée) & Fig* to give/gain/lose ground; **t. de camping** campsite; **t. de football/rugby** football/rugby pitch; **t. de golf** golf course; **t. de jeu(x)** *(pour enfants)* playground; *(stade) Br* playing field, *Am* athletic field; **t. de sport** *Br* sports ground, *Am* athletic field

terrasse [teras] *nf (balcon, plateforme)* terrace; *(toit)* terrace (roof); *(de café) Br* pavement *or Am* sidewalk area; **à la t.** outside

terrassement [terasmã] *nm (travail)* excavation

terrasser [terase] *vt (adversaire)* to floor; *Fig (accabler)* to overcome

terre [tɛr] *nf (matière, monde)* earth; *(sol)* ground; *(opposé à mer, étendue)* land; **terres** *(domaine)* land, estate; *El Br* earth, *Am* ground; **la t.** *(le monde)* the earth; **la T.** *(planète)* Earth; **à** ou **par t.** *(tomber)* to the ground; *(poser)* on the ground; **par t.** *(assis, couché)* on the ground; **sous t.** underground; **t. cuite** (baked) clay, earthenware; **t. battue** *(de court de tennis)* clay ■ **terre-à-terre** *adj inv* down-to-earth ■ **terre-plein** *(pl* **terres-pleins)** *nm* (earth) platform; *(de route) Br* central reservation, *Am* median strip

terrer [tere] **se terrer** *vpr (fugitif, animal)* to go to earth

terrestre [terɛstr] *adj (vie, joies)* earthly; **transport t.** land transportation

terreur [terœr] *nf* terror ■ **terrible** *adj* awful, terrible

terrien, -enne [terjɛ̃, -ɛn] **1** *adj* landowning; **propriétaire t.** landowner **2** *nmf (habitant de la terre)* earthling

terrier [terje] *nm (de lapin)* burrow; *(chien)* terrier

terrifier [terifje] *vt* to terrify ■ **terrifiant, -e** *adj* terrifying

terrine [terin] *nf (récipient)* terrine; *(pâté)* pâté

territoire [teritwar] *nm* territory ■ **territorial, -e, -aux, -ales** *adj* territorial

terroir [terwar] *nm (sol)* soil; *(région)* region

terroriser [terɔrize] *vt* to terrorize ■ **terrorisme** *nm* terrorism ■ **terroriste** *adj & nmf* terrorist

tertiaire [tersjer] *adj* tertiary

tes [te] *voir* **ton¹**

test [tɛst] *nm* test ■ **tester** *vt (élève, produit)* to test

testament [tɛstamã] *nm (document)* will; *Rel* **Ancien/Nouveau T.** Old/New Testament

testicule [tɛstikyl] *nm Anat* testicle

tête [tɛt] *nf* head; *(visage)* face; *(cerveau)* brain; *(de lit, de clou, de cortège)* head; *(de page, de liste)* top, head; *(au football)* header; **à la t. de** *(entreprise, parti)* at the head of; *(classe)* at the top of; **de la t. aux pieds** from head or top to toe; **t. nue** bare-headed; **en t.** *(d'une course)* in the lead; *Fig* **perdre la t.** to lose one's head ■ **tête-à-tête** *nm inv* tête-à-tête; **en t.** in private

téter [tete] *vt (lait, biberon)* to suck; **donner à t. à qn** to feed sb ■ **tétée** *nf (de bébé)* feed ■ **tétine** *nf (de biberon) Br* teat, *Am* nipple; *(sucette) Br* dummy, *Am* pacifier

têtu, -e [tety] *adj* stubborn, obstinate

texte [tɛkst] *nm* text; *(de théâtre)* lines ■ **textuellement** *adv* word for word

textile [tɛkstil] *adj & nm* textile

texture [tɛkstyr] *nf* texture

TGV [teʒeve] *(abrév* **train à grande vitesse)** *nm* high-speed train

Thaïlande [tailãd] *nf* **la T.** Thailand ■ **thaïlandais, -e 1** *adj* Thai **2** *nmf* **T., Thaïlandaise** Thai

thé [te] *nm (boisson, réunion)* tea ■ **théière** *nf* teapot

théâtre [teatr] *nm (art, lieu)* theatre; *(œuvres)* drama; **faire du t.** to act ■ **théâtral, -e, -aux, -ales** *adj* theatrical

thème [tɛm] *nm* theme

théologie [teɔlɔʒi] *nf* theology

théorie [teɔri] *nf* theory; **en t.** in theory

théorique [teɔrik] *adj* theoretical

thérapeutique [terapøtik] **1** *adj* therapeutic **2** *nf (traitement)* therapy ■ **thérapie** *nf* therapy

thermal, -e, -aux, -ales [tɛrmal, -o] *adj* **station thermale** spa

thermique [tɛrmik] *adj (énergie, unité)* thermal

thermomètre [tɛrmɔmɛtr] *nm* thermometer

Thermos® [tɛrmɔs] *nm ou f* Thermos® *(Br* flask or *Am* bottle)

thermostat [tɛrmɔsta] *nm* thermostat

thèse [tɛz] *nf (proposition, ouvrage)* thesis

thon [tɔ̃] *nm* tuna (fish)

thym [tɛ̃] *nm (plante, aromate)* thyme

Tibet [tibɛ] *nm* le **T.** Tibet

tic [tik] *nm (contraction)* twitch, tic; *Fig (manie)* mannerism

ticket [tikɛ] *nm* ticket

tiède [tjɛd] *adj* lukewarm, tepid; *(vent, climat)* mild ■ **tiédir** *vti (refroidir)* to cool down; *(réchauffer)* to warm up

tien, tienne [tjɛ̃, tjɛn] **1** *pron possessif* **le t., la tienne, les tien(ne)s** yours; **les deux tiens** your two **2** *nmpl* **les tiens** *(ta famille)* your family

tiens, tient [tjɛ̃] *voir* **tenir**

tiercé [tjɛrse] *nm (pari)* place betting *(on the horses)*; **jouer/gagner au t.** to bet/win on the horses

tiers, tierce [tjɛr, tjɛrs] **1** *adj* third **2** *nm (fraction)* third; *(personne)* third party ■ **Tiers-Monde** *nm* le **T.** the Third World

tige [tiʒ] *nf (de plante)* stem, stalk; *(barre)* rod

tigre [tigr] *nm* tiger ■ **tigresse** *nf* tigress

tilleul [tijœl] *nm (arbre)* lime tree; *(infusion)* lime blossom tea

timbre [tɛ̃br] *nm* (**a**) *(vignette)* stamp; *(pour traitement médicale)* patch (**b**) *(sonnette)* bell (**c**) *(d'instrument, de voix)* tone (quality) ■ **timbrer** *vt (lettre)* to put a stamp on; *(document)* to stamp

timide [timid] *adj (gêné)* shy; *(protestations)* timid ■ **timidité** *nf* shyness

tinter [tɛ̃te] *vi (cloche)* to tinkle; *(clefs, monnaie)* to jingle; *(verres)* to chink

tique [tik] *nf* tick

tir [tir] *nm (sport)* shooting; *(action)* firing, shooting; *(au football)* shot; **t. (forain)** shooting *or* rifle range; **t. à l'arc** archery

tirade [tirad] *nf (au théâtre) & Fig Br* monologue, *Am* monolog

tirage [tiraʒ] *nm* (**a**) *(de journal)* circulation; *(de livre)* print run; *Typ & Phot (impression)* printing (**b**) *(de loterie)* draw; **t. au sort** drawing lots

tirailler [tiraje] **1** *vt* to pull at; *Fig* **tiraillé entre** *(possibilités)* torn between

2 *vi* **j'ai la peau qui tiraille** my skin feels tight

tire [tir] *nf* **vol à la t.** pickpocketing

tirelire [tirlir] *nf Br* money-box, *Am* coin bank

tirer [tire] **1** *vt* to pull; *(langue)* to stick out; *(trait, rideaux, conclusion)* to draw; *(balle)* to fire; *(gibier)* to shoot; *(journal, épreuves de livre, photo)* to print; **t. qch de qch** to pull sth out of sth; *(nom, origine)* to derive sth from sth; *(produit)* to extract sth from sth; **t. qn de qch** *(danger, lit)* to get sb out of sth

2 *vi* to pull (**sur** on/at); *(faire feu)* to shoot, to fire (**sur** at); *(cheminée)* to draw; **t. au sort** to draw lots. **t. à sa fin** to draw to a close

3 **se tirer** *vpr* **se t. de qch** *(travail, problème)* to cope with sth; *(danger, situation)* to get out of sth ■ **tiré, -e** *adj (traits, visage)* drawn ■ **tire-bouchon** *(pl* **tire-bouchons)** *nm* corkscrew

tireur [tirœr] *nm* gunman; **t. d'élite** marksman

tiroir [tirwar] *nm (de commode)* drawer

tisane [tizan] *nf* herbal tea

tisser [tise] *vt* to weave ■ **tissage** *nm (action)* weaving

tissu [tisy] *nm* material, cloth; *Biol* tissue

titre [titr] *nm (nom, qualité)* title; *Fin* security; *(diplôme)* qualification; **(gros) t.** *(de journal)* headline; **faire les gros titres** to hit the headlines; **à t. d'exemple** as an example; **à t. exceptionnel** exceptionally; **à t. indicatif** for general information; **à juste t.** rightly; **t. de transport** ticket

titrer [titre] *vt (film)* to title; *(journal)* to run as a headline ■ **titré, -e** *adj (personne)* titled

tituber [titybe] *vi* to stagger

titulaire [titylɛr] **1** *adj (enseignant)* tenured; **être t. de** *(permis)* to be the holder of; *(poste)* to hold **2** *nmf (de permis, de poste)* holder (**de** of) ■ **titulariser** *vt (fonctionnaire)* to give tenure to

toast [tost] *nm (pain grillé)* piece *or* slice of toast; *(allocution)* toast; **porter un t. à** to drink (a toast) to

toboggan [tɔbɔgã] *nm (d'enfant)* slide; *Can (traîneau)* toboggan; *(voie de circulation)* Br flyover, Am overpass

toc [tɔk] *nm* du t. *(camelote)* trash; **bijou en t.** imitation jewel

toi [twa] *pron personnel* (a) *(après une préposition)* you; **avec t.** with you (b) *(sujet)* you; **t., tu peux** you may; **c'est t. qui...** it's you who... (c) *(réfléchi)* **assieds-t.** sit (yourself) down; **dépêche-t.** hurry up ▪ **toi-même** *pron* yourself

toile [twal] *nf* (a) *(étoffe)* cloth; *(à voile, sac)* canvas; **une t.** a piece of cloth *or* canvas; *Théât & Fig* **t. de fond** backdrop; **t. cirée** oil cloth (b) *(tableau)* painting, canvas (c) **t. d'araignée** (spider's) web, cobweb

toilette [twalɛt] *nf (action)* wash(ing); *(vêtements)* clothes, outfit; **faire sa t.** to wash (and dress); **les toilettes** *(W-C)* Br the toilet(s), Am the men's/ladies' room

toit [twa] *nm* roof ▪ **toiture** *nf* roof(ing)

tôle [tol] *nf* sheet metal; **t. ondulée** corrugated iron

tolérer [tɔlere] *vt (permettre)* to tolerate ▪ **tolérable** *adj* tolerable ▪ **tolérance** *nf* tolerance ▪ **tolérant, -e** *adj* tolerant (**à l'égard de**)

tomate [tɔmat] *nf* tomato

tombe [tɔ̃b] *nf* grave; *(avec monument)* tomb ▪ **tombale** *adj f* **pierre t.** gravestone, tombstone ▪ **tombeau, -x** *nm* tomb

tomber [tɔ̃be] *(aux être)* vi to fall; *(température)* to drop, to fall; *(vent)* to drop (off); **t. malade** to fall ill; **t. par terre** to fall (down); **faire t.** *(personne)* to knock over; *(gouvernement, prix)* to bring down; **laisser t.** *(objet)* to drop; *Fig* **laisser t. qn** to let sb down; **t. un lundi** to fall on a Monday; **t. sur qch** *(trouver)* to come across sth ▪ **tombée** *nf* **la t. de la nuit** nightfall

tome [tɔm] *nm (livre)* volume

ton¹, ta, tes [tɔ̃, ta, te] ta becomes **ton** [tɔ̃n] before a vowel or mute h. *adj possessif* your; **t. père** your father; **ta mère** your mother; **t. ami(e)** your friend

ton² [tɔ̃] *nm (de voix)* tone; *(de couleur)* shade, tone; *Mus (gamme)* key; *(hauteur de son)* pitch ▪ **tonalité** *nf (timbre, impression)* tone; *(de téléphone)* Br dialling tone, Am dial tone

tondre [tɔ̃dr] *vt (mouton)* to shear; *(gazon)* to mow ▪ **tondeuse** *nf* shears; *(à cheveux)* clippers; **t. (à gazon)** (lawn)-mower

tonifier [tɔnifje] *vt (muscles, peau)* to tone up; *(personne)* to invigorate

tonique [tɔnik] **1** *adj (froid, effet)* tonic, invigorating **2** *nm (médicament)* tonic; *(cosmétique)* tonic lotion

tonnage [tɔnaʒ] *nm (de navire)* tonnage

tonne [tɔn] *nf (poids)* metric ton, tonne

tonneau, -x [tɔno] *nm* (a) *(récipient)* barrel, cask (b) *(acrobatie)* roll; **faire un t.** to roll over

tonner [tɔne] **1** *vi (canons)* to thunder; *Fig (crier)* to thunder, to rage (**contre** against) **2** *v impersonnel* **il tonne** it's thundering ▪ **tonnerre** *nm* thunder

tonus [tɔnys] *nm (énergie)* energy, vitality

top [tɔp] *nm (signal sonore)* beep

topographie [tɔpɔgrafi] *nf* topography

toque [tɔk] *nf (de fourrure)* fur hat; *(de jockey)* cap; *(de cuisinier)* hat

torche [tɔrʃ] *nf (flamme)* torch; **t. électrique** Br torch, Am flashlight

torchon [tɔrʃɔ̃] *nm (à vaisselle)* dish towel, Br tea towel

tordre [tɔrdr] **1** *vt* to twist; *(linge, cou)* to wring; *(barre)* to bend **2 se tordre** *vpr* to twist; *(barre)* to bend; **se t. de douleur** to be doubled up with pain; **se t. (de rire)** to split one's sides (laughing); **se t. la cheville** to twist *or* sprain one's ankle ▪ **tordu, -e** *adj* twisted; *(esprit)* warped

tornade [tɔrnad] *nf* tornado

torpille [tɔrpij] *nf* torpedo ▪ **torpiller** *vt (navire, projet)* to torpedo

torrent [tɔrã] *nm* torrent; *Fig* **un t. de larmes** a flood of tears; **il pleut à torrents** it's pouring (down) ▪ **torrentiel, -elle** *adj (pluie)* torrential

torride [tɔrid] *adj (chaleur)* torrid

torse [tɔrs] *nm Anat* chest; **t. nu** stripped to the waist

tort [tɔr] *nm (dommage)* wrong; *(défaut)* fault; **avoir t.** to be wrong *(de faire* to do, in doing); **être dans son t.** *ou* **en t.** to be in the wrong; **faire du t. à qn** to harm sb; **à t.** wrongly; **à t. ou à raison** rightly or wrongly

torticolis [tɔrtikɔli] *nm* **avoir le t.** to have a stiff neck

tortiller [tɔrtije] **1** *vt* to twist; *(moustache)* to twirl **2 se tortiller** *vpr (ver, personne)* to wriggle

tortionnaire [tɔrsjɔnɛr] *nm* torturer

tortue [tɔrty] *nf Br* tortoise, *Am* turtle; *(de mer)* turtle

torture [tɔrtyr] *nf* torture ■ **torturer** *vt* to torture

tôt [to] *adv* early; **au plus t.** at the earliest; **le plus t. possible** as soon as possible; **t. ou tard** sooner or later; **je n'étais pas plus t. sorti que...** no sooner had I gone out than...

total, -e, -aux, -ales [tɔtal, -o] *adj & nm* total; **au t.** all in all, in total; *(somme toute)* all in all ■ **totaliser** *vt* to total ■ **totalité** *nf* entirety; **la t. de** all of; **en t.** *(détruit)* entirely; *(payé)* fully

totalitaire [tɔtalitɛr] *adj (État, régime)* totalitarian

touche [tuʃ] *nf (de clavier)* key; *(de téléphone)* (push-)button; *(au football & au rugby)* throw-in; **téléphone à touches** push-button phone; **une t. de** *(un peu de)* a touch *or* hint of

toucher [tuʃe] **1** *nm (sens)* touch; **au t.** to the touch **2** *vt* to touch; *(paie)* to draw; *(chèque)* to cash; *(émouvoir)* to touch, to move; *(concerner)* to affect **3** *vi* **t. à** to touch; *(sujet)* to touch on; *(but, fin)* to approach **4 se toucher** *vpr (lignes, mains)* to touch ■ **touchant, -e** *adj (émouvant)* moving, touching

touffe [tuf] *nf (de cheveux, d'herbe)* tuft ■ **touffu, -e** *adj (barbe, haie)* thick, bushy

toujours [tuʒur] *adv (exprime la continuité, la répétition)* always; *(encore)* still; **pour t.** for ever

tour¹ [tur] *nf (bâtiment)* & *Ordinat* tower; *(immeuble)* tower block, high-rise; *Échecs* castle, rook

tour² [tur] *nm* **(a)** *(mouvement, ordre, tournure)* turn; *(de magie)* trick; *(excursion)* trip, outing; *(à pied)* stroll, walk; *(en voiture)* drive; **t. (de piste)** *(de course)* lap; **de dix mètres de t.** ten metres round; **faire le t. de** to go round; **faire le t. du monde** to go round the world; **faire un t.** *(à pied)* to go for a stroll *or* walk; *(en voiture)* to go for a drive; **à t. de rôle** in turn; **t. à t.** in turn, by turns **(b)** *Tech* lathe; *(de potier)* wheel

tourbillon [turbijɔ̃] *nm (de vent)* whirlwind; *(d'eau)* whirlpool; *(de sable)* swirl ■ **tourbillonner** *vi* to whirl

tourisme [turism] *nm* tourism; **faire du t.** to do some touring; **agence de t.** tourist agency; **industrie du t.** tourist industry ■ **touriste** *nmf* tourist ■ **touristique** *adj* **guide/menu t.** tourist guide/menu; **route t., circuit t.** scenic route

tourmenter [turmɑ̃te] **1** *vt* to torment **2 se tourmenter** *vpr* to worry

tournage [turnaʒ] *nm (de film)* shooting, filming

tournant [turnɑ̃] *nm (de route)* bend; *Fig (moment)* turning point **(de in)**

tourne-disque [turnədisk] *(pl* tourne-disques) *nm* record player

tournée [turne] *nf (de facteur, de boissons)* round; *(spectacle)* tour; **faire sa t.** to do one's rounds; **faire la t. de** *(magasins, musées)* to go to

tourner [turne] **1** *vt* to turn; *(film)* to shoot, to make; *(difficulté)* to get round; **t. qn/qch en ridicule** to ridicule sb/sth **2** *vi* to turn; *(tête, toupie)* to spin; *(Terre)* to revolve, to turn; *(moteur, usine)* to run; *(lait)* to go off; **t. autour de** *(objet)* to go round; *(maison, personne)* to hang around; *(question)* to centre on; **t. bien/mal** *(évoluer)* to turn out well/badly; **t. au froid** *(temps)* to turn cold

3 se tourner *vpr* to turn **(vers** to, towards)

tournesol [turnəsɔl] *nm* sunflower

tournevis [turnəvis] *nm* screwdriver

tourniquet [turnikɛ] *nm (barrière)* turnstile; *(pour arroser)* sprinkler

tournoi [turnwa] *nm (de tennis) & Hist* tournament; **participer à un t.** to play in a tournament

tournoyer [turnwaje] *vi* to swirl (round)

tournure [turnyr] *nf (expression)* turn of phrase; **t. d'esprit** way of thinking; **t. des événements** turn of events

Toussaint [tusɛ̃] *nf* **la T.** All Saints' Day

tousser [tuse] *vi* to cough

TOUT, TOUTE, TOUS, TOUTES [tu, tut, tu, tut] **1** *adj* all; **tous les livres** all the books; **t. l'argent/le temps/le village** all the money/time/village; **toute la nuit** all night, the whole (of the) night; **tous (les) deux** both; **tous (les) trois** all three

2 *adj indéfini (chaque)* every, each; *(n'importe quel)* any; **tous les ans/jours** every or each year/day; **tous les deux mois** every two months, every second month; **tous les cinq mètres** every five metres; **t. homme** [tutɔm] every *ou* any man

3 *pron pl* **tous** [tus] all; **ils sont tous là, tous sont là** they're all there

4 *pron m sing* **tout** everything; **dépenser t.** to spend everything, to spend it all; **t. ce qui est là** everything that's here; **t. ce que je sais** everything that *or* all that I know; **en t.** *(au total)* in all

5 *adv (tout à fait)* quite; *(très)* very; **t. simplement** quite simply; **t. petit** very small; **t. neuf** brand new; **t. seul** all alone; **t. droit** straight ahead; **t. autour** all around, right round; **t. au début** right at the beginning; **le t. premier** the very first; **t. au plus/moins** at the very most/least; **t. en chantant** while singing; **t. rusé qu'il est** *ou* **soit** however sly he may be; **t. à coup** suddenly, all of a sudden; **t. à fait** completely, quite; **t. de suite** at once

6 *nm* **le t.** everything, the lot; **un t.** a whole; **le t. est que...** *(l'important)* the main thing is that...; **pas du t.** not at all; **rien du t.** nothing at all; **du t. au t.** *(changer)* entirely, completely

toutefois [tutfwa] *adv* nevertheless, however ■ **tout-puissant, toute-puissante** *(mpl* **tout-puissants,** *fpl* **toutes-puissantes)** *adj* all-powerful ■ **tout-terrain 1** *(pl* **tout-terrains)** *adj* **véhicule t.** off-road *or* all terrain vehicle; **vélo t.** mountain bike **2** *nm* **faire du t.** to do off-road racing

toux [tu] *nf* cough

toxicomane [tɔksikɔman] *nmf* drug addict ■ **toxicomanie** *nf* drug addiction

toxique [tɔksik] *adj* poisonous, toxic

TP [tepe] *(abrév* **travaux pratiques)** *nmpl (à l'école)* practical work

trac [trak] *nm* **le t.** *(peur)* the jitters; *(de candidat)* exam nerves; *(d'acteur)* stage fright; **avoir le t.** to be nervous

trace [tras] *nf (quantité, tache, vestige)* trace; *(marque)* mark; *(de fugitif)* trail; **traces** *(de bête, de pneus)* tracks; **traces de pas** footprints; **disparaître sans laisser de traces** to disappear without trace

tracer [trase] *vt (dessiner)* to draw; *(écrire)* to trace; **t. une route** to mark out a route; *(frayer)* to open up a route ■ **tracé** *nm (plan)* layout; *(ligne)* line

tract [trakt] *nm* leaflet

tractations [traktɑsjɔ̃] *nfpl* dealings

tracter [trakte] *vt* to tow

tracteur [traktœr] *nm* tractor

tradition [tradisjɔ̃] *nf* tradition ■ **traditionnel, -elle** *adj* traditional

traduire* [tradɥir] *vt* to translate (**de** from; **en** into) ■ **traducteur, -trice** *nmf* translator ■ **traduction** *nf* translation

trafic [trafik] *nm (automobile, ferroviaire)* traffic; *(de marchandises)* traffic, trade ■ **trafiquant, -e** *nmf* trafficker, dealer

tragédie [traʒedi] *nf (pièce de théâtre, événement)* tragedy ■ **tragique** *adj* tragic; **prendre qch au t.** *(remarque)* to take sth too much to heart

trahir [trair] **1** *vt* to betray; *(secret)* to give away, to betray; *(sujet: forces)* to fail

2 se trahir *vpr* to give oneself away ■ **trahison** *nf* betrayal; *(crime)* treason

train [trɛ̃] *nm* (a) *(de voyageurs, de marchandises)* train; **prendre le t.** to catch *or* take the train; **voyager en t.** to travel by train; **t. à grande vitesse** high-speed train; **t. corail** express train; **t. couchettes** sleeper (b) **en t.** *(en forme)* on form; **être en t. de faire qch** to be (busy) doing sth (c) *(allure)* pace; **t. de vie** life style (d) *(de pneus)* set; *(de péniches, de véhicules)* string (e) **t. d'atterrissage** *(d'avion)* undercarriage

traînard, -e [trɛnar, -ard] *nmf Br* slowcoach, *Am* slowpoke

traîne [trɛn] *nf (de robe)* train

traîneau, -x [trɛno] *nm* sleigh, *Br* sledge, *Am* sled

traînée [trɛne] *nf (de peinture, dans le ciel)* streak

traîner [trɛne] **1** *vt* to drag; *(wagon)* to pull
2 *vi (jouets, papiers)* to lie around; *(s'attarder)* to lag behind, to dawdle; *(errer)* to hang around; *(subsister)* to linger on; **t. par terre** *(robe)* to trail (on the ground); **t. en longueur** to drag on
3 se traîner *vpr (avancer)* to drag oneself (along); *(par terre)* to crawl; *(durer)* to drag on ■ **traînant, -e** *adj (voix)* drawling

traire* [trɛr] *vt (vache)* to milk

trait [trɛ] *nm* line; *(en dessinant)* stroke; *(caractéristique)* feature, trait; **traits** *(du visage)* features; **d'un t.** *(boire)* in one gulp, in one go; **avoir t. à qch** to relate to sth

traite [trɛt] *nf (de vache)* milking; *(lettre de change)* bill, draft; **d'une (seule) t.** *(sans interruption)* in one go; **t. des Noirs** slave trade

traité [trete] *nm (accord)* treaty; *(ouvrage)* treatise *(sur on)*; **t. de paix** peace treaty

traiter [trete] **1** *vt (se comporter envers, soigner)* to treat; *(problème, sujet)* to deal with; *(marché)* to negotiate; *(matériau, produit)* to treat, to process; **t. qn**

de tous le noms to call sb all the names under the sun
2 *vi* to negotiate, to deal **(avec** with); **t. de** *(sujet)* to deal with ■ **traitement** [trɛtmɑ̃] *nm (de personne, de maladie)* treatment; *(de matériau)* processing; *(gains)* salary; **t. de données/de texte** data/word processing; **machine à t. de texte** word processor

traiteur [trɛtœr] *nm (fournisseur)* caterer; **chez le t.** at the delicatessen

traître [trɛtr] **1** *nm* traitor; **en t.** treacherously **2** *adj (dangereux)* treacherous; **être t. à une cause** to be a traitor to a cause ■ **traîtrise** *nf* treachery

trajectoire [traʒɛktwar] *nf* path, trajectory

trajet [traʒɛ] *nm* journey; *(distance)* distance; *(itinéraire)* route

tramer [trame] **se tramer** *vpr* **il se trame quelque chose** something's afoot

trampoline [trɑ̃pɔlin] *nm* trampoline

tramway [tramwɛ] *nm Br* tram, *Am* streetcar

tranche [trɑ̃ʃ] *nf (morceau)* slice; *(bord)* edge; *(partie)* portion; *(de salaire, d'impôts)* bracket; **t. d'âge** age bracket

tranchée [trɑ̃ʃe] *nf* trench

trancher [trɑ̃ʃe] **1** *vt* to cut; *(difficulté, question)* to settle **2** *vi (décider)* to decide; *(contraster)* to contrast **(sur** with) ■ **tranchant, -e 1** *adj (couteau)* sharp; *(ton)* curt **2** *nm* (cutting) edge; *Fig* **à double t.** double-edged ■ **tranché, -e** *adj (couleurs)* distinct; *(opinion)* clearcut

tranquille [trɑ̃kil] *adj* quiet; *(mer)* calm, still; *(esprit)* easy; **avoir la conscience t.** to have a clear conscience; **soyez t.** don't worry; **laisser qn/qch t.** to leave sb/sth alone

tranquilliser [trɑ̃kilize] *vt* to reassure ■ **tranquillisant** *nm* tranquillizer

tranquillité [trɑ̃kilite] *nf (peace and)* quiet; *(d'esprit)* peace of mind

transaction [trɑ̃zaksjɔ̃] *nf (opération)* transaction; *Jur* compromise

transatlantique [trɑ̃zatlɑ̃tik] **1** *adj* transatlantic **2** *nm (paquebot)* transatlantic liner; *(chaise)* deckchair ▪ **transat** *nm (chaise)* deckchair

transcrire* [trɑ̃skrir] *vt* to transcribe ▪ **transcription** *nf* transcription; *(document)* transcript

transe [trɑ̃s] *nf* **en t.** *(mystique)* in a trance; *(excité)* very excited; **entrer en t.** to go into a trance

transférer [trɑ̃sfere] *vt* to transfer (à to) ▪ **transfert** *nm* transfer

transformer [trɑ̃sfɔrme] **1** *vt* to transform; *(maison, au rugby)* to convert; *(matière première)* to process; **t. qch en qch** to turn sth into sth **2 se transformer** *vpr* to change, to be transformed **(en** into) ▪ **transformateur** *nm Él* transformer ▪ **transformation** *nf* change, transformation; *(de maison)* alteration

transfuge [trɑ̃sfyʒ] *nmf* defector

transfusion [trɑ̃sfyzjɔ̃] *nf* **t. (sanguine)** (blood) transfusion

transgresser [trɑ̃sgrese] *vt (ordres)* to disobey; *(loi)* to infringe

transi, -e [trɑ̃zi] *adj (personne)* numb with cold

transiger [trɑ̃ziʒe] *vi* to compromise

transistor [trɑ̃zistɔr] *nm* transistor

transit [trɑ̃zit] *nm* transit; **en t.** in transit

transition [trɑ̃zisjɔ̃] *nf* transition ▪ **transitoire** *adj (qui passe)* transient; *(provisoire)* transitional

transmettre* [trɑ̃smɛtr] **1** *vt (message, héritage)* to pass on **(à** to); *Radio & TV (informations)* to transmit; *(émission)* to broadcast **2 se transmettre** *vpr (maladie, tradition)* to be passed on ▪ **transmetteur** *nm (appareil)* transmitter ▪ **transmission** *nf* transmission

transparaître* [trɑ̃sparetr] *vi* to show (through)

transparent, -e [trɑ̃sparɑ̃, -ɑ̃t] *adj* clear, transparent ▪ **transparence** *nf* transparency; **voir qch par t.** to see sth showing through

transpercer [trɑ̃sperse] *vt* to pierce

transpirer [trɑ̃spire] *vi (suer)* to sweat, to perspire ▪ **transpiration** *nf* perspiration

transplanter [trɑ̃splɑ̃te] *vt (organe, plante)* to transplant

transport [trɑ̃spɔr] *nm (action)* transport, transportation **(de** of); **transports** *(moyens)* transport; **transports en commun** public transport; **moyen de t.** means of transport

transporter [trɑ̃spɔrte] *vt (passagers, troupes, marchandises)* to transport, to carry ▪ **transporteur** *nm* **t. (routier)** *Br* haulier, *Am* trucker

transposer [trɑ̃spoze] *vt* to transpose ▪ **transposition** *nf* transposition

trapèze [trapɛz] *nm (de cirque)* trapeze

trappe [trap] *nf (de plancher)* trap door

trappeur [trapœr] *nm* trapper

trapu, -e [trapy] *adj (personne)* stocky, thickset

traquer [trake] *vt* to hunt (down)

traumatiser [tromatize] *vt* to traumatize ▪ **traumatisant, -e** *adj* traumatic ▪ **traumatisme** *nm (choc)* trauma

travail, -aux [travaj, -o] *nm (activité, lieu)* work; *(à effectuer)* job, task; *(emploi)* job; *(façonnage)* working **(de** of); *(ouvrage, étude)* work, publication; *Écon & Méd* labour; **travaux** work; *(dans la rue) Br* roadworks, *Am* roadwork; *(aménagement)* alterations; *Scol & Univ* **travaux pratiques** practical work; *Scol & Univ* **travaux dirigés** tutorial; *Scol* **travaux manuels** handicrafts; **travaux ménagers** housework

travailler [travaje] **1** *vi (personne)* to work **(à qch** on sth); *(bois)* to warp **2** *vt (discipline, rôle, style)* to work on; *(façonner)* to work ▪ **travailleur, -euse 1** *adj* hard-working **2** *nmf* worker

travailliste [travajist] *Pol* **1** *adj* Labour **2** *nmf* member of the Labour party

travers [traver] **1** *prép & adv* **à t.** through; **en t. (de)** across **2** *adv* **de t.** *(chapeau, nez)* crooked; **j'ai avalé de t.** it went down the wrong way

traverser [traverse] *vt* to cross; *(foule, période, mur)* to go through ▪ **traversée** *nf (voyage)* crossing

travesti [travɛsti] *nm (acteur)* female impersonator; *(homosexuel)* transvestite

travestir [travɛstir] *vt* to disguise

trébucher [trebyʃe] *vi* to stumble (**sur** over); **faire t. qn** to trip sb (up)

trèfle [trɛfl] *nm (plante)* clover; *Cartes (couleur)* clubs

treillis [trɛji] *nm* (**a**) *(treillage)* lattice (work); *(en métal)* wire mesh (**b**) *(tenue militaire)* combat uniform

treize [trɛz] *adj & nm inv* thirteen ■ **treizième** *adj & nmf* thirteenth

tréma [trema] *nm* di(a)eresis

trembler [trɑ̃ble] *vi* to shake, to tremble; *(de froid, peur)* to tremble (**de** with); *(flamme, lumière)* to flicker; *(voix)* to tremble, to quaver; *(avoir peur)* to be afraid (**que** + *subjunctive* that); **t. pour qn** to fear for sb ■ **tremblement** [-əmɑ̃] *nm (action, frisson)* shaking, trembling; **t. de terre** earthquake ■ **trembloter** *vi* to quiver

tremper [trɑ̃pe] **1** *vt* to soak, to drench; *(plonger)* to dip (**dans** in); *(acier)* to temper **2** *vi* to soak; **faire t. qch** to soak sth; *Péj* **t. dans** *(participer)* to be mixed up in

tremplin [trɑ̃plɛ̃] *nm* springboard

trente [trɑ̃t] *adj & nm inv* thirty; **un t.-trois tours** *(disque)* an LP; **se mettre sur son t. et un** to get all dressed up ■ **trentaine** *nf* **une t. (de)** *(nombre)* (about) thirty; **avoir la t.** *(âge)* to be about thirty ■ **trentième** *adj & nmf* thirtieth

très [trɛ] ([trɛz] *before vowel or mute h*) *adv* very; **t. aimé/critiqué** *(with past participle)* much *or* greatly liked/criticized

trésor [trezɔr] *nm* treasure; **le T. (public)** *(service)* public revenue (department); *(finances)* public funds; **des trésors de patience** boundless patience ■ **trésorerie** [-rri] *nf (bureaux d'un club)* accounts department; *(gestion)* accounting; *(capitaux)* funds ■ **trésorier, -ère** *nmf* treasurer

tressaillir* [tresajir] *vi (frémir)* to shake, to quiver; *(de joie, de peur)* to

tremble (**de** with); *(sursauter)* to jump, to start

tresse [trɛs] *nf (cordon)* braid; *(cheveux)* Br plait, Am braid ■ **tresser** [trese] *vt* to braid; Br *(cheveux)* to plait, Am to braid

trêve [trɛv] *nf (de combat)* truce

tri [tri] *nm* sorting (out); **faire le t. de** to sort (out); **(centre de) t.** *(des postes)* sorting office ■ **triage** *nm* sorting (out)

triangle [trijɑ̃gl] *nm* triangle ■ **triangulaire** *adj* triangular

tribord [tribɔr] *nm (de bateau, d'avion)* starboard

tribu [triby] *nf* tribe ■ **tribal, -e, -aux, -ales** *adj* tribal

tribunal, -aux [tribynal, -o] *nm Jur* court; *(militaire)* tribunal

tribune [tribyn] *nf (de salle publique)* gallery; *(de stade)* (grand)stand; *(d'orateur)* rostrum

tribut [triby] *nm* tribute (**à** to)

tricher [triʃe] *vi* to cheat ■ **tricherie** *nf* cheating, trickery ■ **tricheur, -euse** *nmf* cheat, Am cheater

tricolore [trikɔlɔr] *adj (cocarde)* red, white and blue; **le drapeau/l'équipe t.** the French flag/team

tricot [triko] *nm (activité, ouvrage)* knitting; *(chandail)* sweater, Br jumper; *(ouvrage)* piece of knitting; **en t.** knitted; **t. de corps** Br vest, Am undershirt ■ **tricoter** *vti* to knit

trier [trije] *vt (lettres)* to sort; *(vêtements)* to sort through

trilingue [trilɛ̃g] *adj* trilingual

trimestre [trimɛstr] *nm* quarter; Scol term; Scol **premier/second/troisième t.** Br autumn *or* Am fall/winter/summer term ■ **trimestriel, -elle** *adj (revue)* quarterly; **bulletin t.** end-of-term Br report *or* Am report card

Trinité [trinite] *nf* **la T.** *(fête)* Trinity; *(dogme)* the Trinity

trinquer [trɛ̃ke] *vi* to chink glasses; **t. à la santé de qn** to drink to sb's health

trio [trijo] *nm (groupe)* & Mus trio

triomphe [trijɔ̃f] *nm* triumph (**sur** over) ■ **triomphal, -e, -aux, -ales** *adj*

triumphal ∎ **triomphant, -e** *adj* triumphant ∎ **triompher** *vi* to triumph (**de** over); *(jubiler)* to be jubilant

triple [tripl] **1** *adj* treble, triple; *Sport* **t. saut** triple jump **2** *nm* **le t.** three times as much (**de** as) ∎ **tripler** *vti* to treble, to triple ∎ **triplés, -es** *nmfpl* triplets

triste [trist] *adj* sad; *(sinistre)* dreary; *(lamentable)* unfortunate ∎ **tristesse** *nf* sadness; *(du temps)* dreariness

trivial, -e, -aux, -ales [trivjal, -o] *adj* coarse, vulgar

troc [trɔk] *nm* exchange; *(système économique)* barter

trois [trwɑ] *adj & nm inv* three; **les t. quarts (de)** three-quarters (of) ∎ **troisième 1** *adj & nmf* third; **le t. âge** *(vieillesse)* the retirement years; **personne du t. âge** senior citizen **2** *nf Scol* **la t.** *Br* ≃ fourth year, *Am* ≃ eighth grade; *Aut (vitesse)* third gear ∎ **troisièmement** *adv* thirdly

trombe [trɔ̃b] *nf* **trombe(s) d'eau** *(pluie)* rainstorm, downpour

trombone [trɔ̃bɔn] *nm (instrument)* trombone; *(agrafe)* paper clip

trompe [trɔ̃p] *nf (d'éléphant)* trunk; *(d'insecte)* proboscis; *(instrument de musique)* horn

tromper [trɔ̃pe] **1** *vt (abuser)* to fool **(sur** about); *(être infidèle à)* to be unfaithful to; *(échapper à)* to elude **2 se tromper** *vpr* to be mistaken; **se t. de route** to take the wrong road; **se t. de jour** to get the day wrong ∎ **tromperie** [-pri] *nf* deceit, deception ∎ **trompeur, -euse** *adj (apparences)* deceptive, misleading; *(personne)* deceitful

trompette [trɔ̃pɛt] *nf* trumpet ∎ **trompettiste** *nmf* trumpet player

tronc [trɔ̃] *nm (d'arbre) & Anat* trunk; *(boîte)* collection box

tronçon [trɔ̃sɔ̃] *nm* section ∎ **tronçonner** *vt* to cut into sections

trône [tron] *nm* throne ∎ **trôner** *vi Fig (vase, personne)* to occupy the place of *Br* honour *or Am* honor

trop [tro] *adv (avec adjectif, adverbe)* too; *(avec verbe)* too much; **t. dur/loin** too hard/far; **t. fatigué pour jouer** too tired to play; **lire t.** to read too much; **t. de sel** too much salt; **t. de gens** too many people; **du fromage en t.** too much cheese; **un verre en t.** one glass too many; **t. souvent** too often; **t. peu** not enough ∎ **trop-plein** *(pl* **trop-pleins)** *nm (excédent)* overflow; *(dispositif)* overflow pipe

trophée [trɔfe] *nm* trophy

tropique [trɔpik] *nm* tropic; **sous les tropiques** in the tropics ∎ **tropical, -e, -aux, -ales** *adj* tropical

troquer [trɔke] *vt* to exchange **(contre** for)

trot [tro] *nm* trot; **aller au t.** to trot ∎ **trotter** *vi (cheval)* to trot

trottoir [trɔtwar] *nm Br* pavement, *Am* sidewalk

trou [tru] *nm* hole; *(d'aiguille)* eye; *Fig* **t. de mémoire** memory lapse

trouble [trubl] **1** *adj (liquide)* cloudy; *(image)* blurred; *(affaire)* shady **2** *adv* **voir t.** to see things blurred **3** *nm (désarroi)* distress; *(désordre)* confusion; **troubles** *(de santé)* trouble; *(révolte)* disturbances, troubles

troubler [truble] **1** *vt* to disturb; *(vue)* to blur; *(liquide)* to make cloudy; *(esprit)* to unsettle; *(projet)* to upset; *(inquiéter)* to trouble **2 se troubler** *vpr (liquide)* to become cloudy; *(personne)* to become flustered ∎ **troublant, -e** *adj (détail)* disturbing, disquieting

trouer [true] *vt* to make a hole/holes in

troupe [trup] *nf (de soldats)* troop; *(de théâtre)* company, troupe

troupeau, -x [trupo] *nm (de vaches)* herd; *(de moutons)* flock

trousse [trus] *nf (étui)* case, kit; *(d'écolier)* pencil case; **t. à pharmacie** first-aid kit; **t. de toilette** toilet bag

trousseau, -x [truso] *nm (de mariée)* trousseau; **t. de clefs** bunch of keys

trouvaille [truvaj] *nf* (lucky) find

trouver [truve] **1** *vt* to find; **aller t. qn** to go and see sb; **je trouve que...** I think that...; **comment la trouvez-vous?** what do you think of her?

2 se trouver *vpr* to be; *(être situé)* to be situated; **se t. dans une situation difficile** to find oneself in a difficult situation; **se t. mal** *(s'évanouir)* to faint; **se t. petit** to consider oneself small **3** *v impersonnel* **il se trouve que...** it happens that...

trucage [tryka3] *nm* = **truquage**

truffe [tryf] *nf (champignon, confiserie)* truffle; *(de chien)* nose

truffer [tryfe] *vt (remplir)* to stuff (**de** with)

truite [trɥit] *nf* trout

truquer [tryke] *vt (photo)* to fake; *(élections, match)* to rig ▪ **truquage** *nm (de cinéma)* (special) effect; *(action)* faking; *(d'élections)* rigging ▪ **truqué, -e** *adj (élections, match)* rigged; **photo truquée** fake photo

trust [trœst] *nm Com (cartel)* trust

tsar [dzar] *nm* tsar, czar

tsigane [tsigan] **1** *adj* gipsy **2** *nmf* **T.** gipsy

tu¹ [ty] *pron personnel* you *(familiar form of address)*

tu² [ty] *pp de* **taire**

tuba [tyba] *nm (instrument de musique)* tuba; *(de plongée)* snorkel

tube [tyb] *nm* tube; **t. à essai** test tube

tuer [tɥe] **1**.*vt* to kill **2 se tuer** *vpr* to kill oneself; *(dans un accident)* to be killed ▪ **tuerie** *nf* slaughter ▪ **tueur, -euse** *nmf* killer

tulipe [tylip] *nf* tulip

tumeur [tymœr] *nf* tumour

tunique [tynik] *nf* tunic

Tunisie [tynizi] *nf* **la T.** Tunisia ▪ **tunisien, -enne 1** *adj* Tunisian **2** *nmf* **T., Tunisienne** Tunisian

tunnel [tynɛl] *nm* tunnel; **le t. sous la Manche** the Channel Tunnel

turban [tyrbɑ̃] *nm* turban

turbulent, -e [tyrbylɑ̃, -ɑ̃t] *adj (enfant)* boisterous

Turquie [tyrki] *nf* **la T.** Turkey ▪ **turc, turque 1** *adj* Turkish **2** *nmf* **T., Turque** Turk **3** *nm (langue)* Turkish

turquoise [tyrkwaz] *adj inv* turquoise

tuteur, -trice [tytœr, -tris] **1** *nmf (de mineur)* guardian **2** *nm (bâton)* stake, prop

tutoyer [tytwaje] *vt* **t. qn** to address sb using the familiar "tu" form ▪ **tutoiement** *nm* = use of the familiar "tu" instead of the more formal "vous"

tutu [tyty] *nm* tutu

tuyau, -x [tɥijo] *nm* pipe; **t. d'arrosage** hose(pipe); **t. d'échappement** *(de véhicule)* exhaust (pipe)

TVA [tevea] *(abrév* **taxe à la valeur ajoutée)** *nf* VAT

type [tip] **1** *nm (genre)* type; *Fig* **le t. même de** the very model of **2** *adj inv* typical; **lettre t.** standard letter ▪ **typique** *adj* typical (**de** of)

typographie [typografi] *nf* typography, printing

tyran [tirɑ̃] *nm* tyrant ▪ **tyrannie** *nf* tyranny ▪ **tyranniser** *vt* to tyrannize

tzigane [tzigan] *adj & nmf* = **tsigane**

Uu

U, u [y] *nm inv* U, u

UE [yø] (*abrév* **Union européenne**) *nf* EU

Ukraine [ykrɛn] *nf* **l'U.** the Ukraine

ulcère [ylsɛr] *nm* ulcer

ULM [yɛlɛm] (*abrév* **ultraléger motorisé**) *nm inv Aviat* microlight

ultérieur, -e [ylterjœr] *adj* later, subsequent (**à** to) ▪ **ultérieurement** *adv* later (on), subsequently

ultimatum [yltimatɔm] *nm* ultimatum; **lancer un u. à qn** to give sb *or* issue sb with an ultimatum

ultime [yltim] *adj* last; (*préparatifs*) final

ultramoderne [yltramɔdɛrn] *adj* high-tech

ultrason [yltrasɔ̃] *nm* ultrasound

ultraviolet, -ette [yltravjɔlɛ, -ɛt] *adj & nm* ultraviolet

UN, UNE [œ̃, yn] **1** *article indéfini* a; (*devant voyelle*) an; **une page** a page; **un ange** [œ̃nɑ̃ʒ] an angel
2 *adj* one; **la page un** page one; **un kilo** one kilo; **un par un** one by one
3 *pron & nmf* one; **l'un** one by one; **les uns** some; **le numéro un** number one; **j'en ai un** I have one; **l'un d'eux, l'une d'elles** one of them; *Journ* **la une** the front page, page one

unanime [ynanim] *adj* unanimous ▪ **unanimité** *nf* unanimity; **à l'u.** unanimously

uni, -e [yni] *adj* (*famille, couple*) close; (*couleur, étoffe*) plain

unième [ynjɛm] *adj* first; **trente et u.** thirty-first; **cent u.** hundred and first

unifier [ynifje] *vt* to unify ▪ **unification** *nf* unification

uniforme [ynifɔrm] **1** *adj* (*expression*) uniform; (*sol*) even; (*mouvement*) regular **2** *nm* uniform ▪ **uniformément** *adv* uniformly ▪ **uniformiser** *vt* to standardize ▪ **uniformité** *nf* (*de couleurs*) uniformity; (*monotonie*) monotony

unilatéral, -e, -aux, -ales [ynilateral, -o] *adj* (*décision*) unilateral; (*contrat*) one-sided; (*stationnement*) on one side of the road/street only

union [ynjɔ̃] *nf* (*de partis, de consommateurs*) union, association; (*entente*) unity; (*mariage*) marriage; **l'U. européenne** the European Union; **u. monétaire** monetary union; **u. libre** cohabitation

unique [ynik] *adj* (a) (*fille, fils*) only; (*espoir, souci*) only, sole; (*prix, parti, salaire, marché*) single (b) (*exceptionnel*) unique; **u. en son genre** completely unique ▪ **uniquement** *adv* only, just

unir [ynir] **1** *vt* (*personnes, territoires*) to unite; (*marier*) to join in marriage; (*efforts, qualités*) to combine (**à** with) **2** **s'unir** *vpr* (*s'associer*) to unite; (*se marier*) to be joined in marriage; **s'u. à qn** to join forces with sb

unitaire [yniter] *adj* (*prix*) per unit

unité [ynite] *nf* (*de mesure, élément, régiment*) unit; (*cohésion*) unity; **u. de longueur** unit of measurement

univers [yniver] *nm* universe; *Fig* world ▪ **universel, -elle** *adj* universal

université [yniversite] *nf* university; **à l'u.** *Br* at university, *Am* in college ▪ **universitaire 1** *adj* **ville/restaurant u.** university town/refectory **2** *nmf* academic

uranium [yranjɔm] *nm* uranium

urbain, -e [yrbɛ̃, -ɛn] *adj* urban ▪ **urbaniser** *vt* to urbanize ▪ **urbanisme** *nm* *Br* town planning, *Am* city planning

urgent, -e [yrʒɑ̃, -ɑ̃t] *adj* urgent ∎ **urgence** *nf (de décision, de tâche)* urgency; *(cas d'hôpital)* emergency; **d'u.** urgently; *Pol* **état d'u.** state of emergency; **(service des) urgences** *(d'hôpital)* *Br* casualty (department), *Am* emergency room

urne [yrn] *nf (vase)* urn; *(pour voter)* ballot box; **aller aux urnes** to go to the polls

Uruguay [yrygwe] *nm* **l'U.** Uruguay

usage [yzaʒ] *nm (utilisation)* use; *(coutume)* custom; *(de mot)* usage; **faire u. de qch** to make use of sth; **d'u.** *(habituel)* customary; **à l'u. de** for (the use of); **hors d'u.** out of order ∎ **usagé, -e** *adj (vêtement)* worn; *(billet)* used ∎ **usager** *nm* user

user [yze] **1** *vt (vêtement)* to wear out; *(personne)* to wear down; *(consommer)* to use (up) **2** *vi* **u. de qch** to use sth **3** **s'user** *vpr (tissu, machine)* to wear out; *(talons, personne)* to wear down ∎ **usé, -e** *adj (tissu)* worn out; *(sujet)* stale; *(personne)* worn out; **eaux usées** dirty *or* waste water

usine [yzin] *nf* factory; **u. à gaz** gasworks; **u. métallurgique** ironworks

ustensile [ystɑ̃sil] *nm* implement, tool; **u. de cuisine** kitchen utensil

usuel, -elle [yzɥɛl] *adj* everyday

usure [yzyr] *nf (de pneu)* wear

usurper [yzyrpe] *vt* to usurp

utile [ytil] *adj* useful **(à** to)

utiliser [ytilize] *vt* to use ∎ **utilisateur, -trice** *nmf* user ∎ **utilisation** *nf* use ∎ **utilité** *nf* usefulness; **d'une grande u.** very useful

utilitaire [ytiliter] *adj* utilitarian

utopie [ytɔpi] *nf (idéal)* utopia; *(projet, idée)* utopian plan/idea ∎ **utopique** *adj* utopian

UV [yve] *(abrév* **ultraviolet)** *nm inv* UV

Vv

V, v [ve] *nm inv* V, v
va [va] *voir* **aller¹**

vacances [vakɑ̃s] *nfpl Br* holiday(s), *Am* vacation; **être en v** to be on *Br* holiday *or Am* vacation; **partir en v.** to go on *Br* holiday *or Am* vacation; **v. actives/culturelles/reposantes** active/cultural/relaxing *Br* holiday(s) *or Am* vacation; **les v. scolaires** the school *Br* holidays *or Am* vacation; **les grandes v.** the summer *Br* holidays *or Am* vacation ▪ **vacancier, -ère** *nf Br* holidaymaker, *Am* vacationer

vacant, -e [vakɑ̃, -ɑ̃t] *adj* vacant

vacarme [vakarm] *nm* din, uproar

vaccin [vaksɛ̃] *nm* vaccine; **faire un v. à qn** to vaccinate sb ▪ **vaccination** *nf* vaccination ▪ **vacciner** *vt* to vaccinate; **se faire v.** to get vaccinated (**contre** against)

vache [vaʃ] *nf* cow; **maladie de la v. folle** mad cow disease

vaciller [vasije] *vi* to sway; *(flamme, lumière)* to flicker

vagabond, -e [vagabɔ̃, -ɔ̃d] *nmf (clochard)* vagrant, tramp ▪ **vagabonder** *vi* to roam, to wander

vague¹ [vag] *adj* vague; *(regard)* vacant; *(souvenir)* dim, vague

vague² [vag] *nf (de mer) & Fig* wave; **v. de chaleur** heat wave; **v. de froid** cold spell *or* snap

vaille, vailles *voir* **valoir**

vain, -e [vɛ̃, vɛn] *adj (sans résultat)* futile; *(vaniteux)* vain; **en v.** in vain ▪ **vainement** *adv* in vain

vaincre* [vɛ̃kr] *vt (adversaire)* to defeat; *Fig (maladie, difficulté)* to overcome ▪ **vaincu, -e** *nmf* defeated man/woman; *(de match)* loser ▪ **vainqueur** *nm* victor; *(de match)* winner

vais [ve] *voir* **aller¹**

vaisseau, -x [vɛso] *nm Anat* vessel; *(bateau)* ship, vessel; **v. spatial** spaceship

vaisselle [vɛsɛl] *nf* crockery; **faire la v.** to do the washing up, to do the dishes

valable [valabl] *adj (billet, motif)* valid

valet [valɛ] *nm Cartes* jack; **v. de chambre** valet

valeur [valœr] *nf (prix, qualité)* value; *(mérite)* worth; **avoir de la v.** to be valuable; **mettre qch en v.** *(faire ressortir)* to highlight sth; **objets de v.** valuables

valide [valid] *adj (personne)* fit, ablebodied; *(billet)* valid ▪ **valider** *vt* to validate; *(titre de transport)* to stamp; *Ordinat (commande)* to confirm; *(case)* to select ▪ **validité** *nf* validity

valise [valiz] *nf* suitcase; **faire ses valises** to pack (one's bags)

vallée [vale] *nf* valley

valoir* [valwar] **1** *vi (avoir pour valeur)* to be worth; *(s'appliquer)* to apply (**pour** to); **v. mille euros/cher** to be worth a thousand euros/a lot; **il vaut mieux rester** it's better to stay; **il vaut mieux que j'attende** I'd better wait; **faire v. qch** *(faire ressortir)* to highlight sth; *(droit)* to assert sth **2** *vt* **v. qch à qn** *(ennuis)* to bring sb sth **3** **se valoir** *vpr (objets, personnes)* to be as good as each other

valse [vals] *nf* waltz

valve [valv] *nf* valve

vampire [vɑ̃pir] *nm* vampire

vandale [vɑ̃dal] *nmf* vandal ▪ **vandalisme** *nm* vandalism

vanille [vanij] *nf* vanilla

vanité [vanite] *nf (orgueil)* vanity ▪ **vaniteux, -euse** *adj* vain, conceited

vanter [vɑ̃te] **1** *vt* to praise **2 se vanter** *vpr* to boast, to brag (**de** about, of)

vapeur [vapœr] *nf* **v. (d'eau)** steam; **cuire qch à la v.** to steam sth

vaporiser [vapɔrize] *vt* to spray ∎ **vaporisateur** *nm (appareil)* spray

vaquer [vake] *vi* **v. à qch** to attend to sth; **v. à ses occupations** to go about one's business

varappe [varap] *nf* rock-climbing

variable [varjabl] **1** *adj* variable; *(humeur, temps)* changeable **2** *nf* variable ∎ **variation** *nf* variation

varicelle [varisɛl] *nf* chickenpox

varier [varje] *vti* to vary (**de** from) ∎ **varié, -e** *adj (diversifié)* varied

variété [varjete] *nf* variety

variole [varjɔl] *nf* smallpox

vas [va] *voir* **aller**[1]

vase[1] [vaz] *nm (récipient)* vase

vase[2] [vaz] *nf (boue)* mud, silt

vaste [vast] *adj* vast, huge

Vatican [vatikɑ̃] *nm* **le V.** the Vatican

vaut [vo] *voir* **valoir**

veau, -x [vo] *nm (animal)* calf; *(viande)* veal

vécu, -e [veky] **1** *pp de* **vivre 2** *adj (histoire)* real-life **3** *nm* real-life experience

vedette [vədɛt] *nf* (a) *(acteur)* star; **être en v.** *(dans un spectacle)* to top the bill (b) *(bateau)* launch

végétal, -e, -aux, -ales [veʒetal, -o] **1** *adj* **huile végétale** vegetable oil **2** *nm* plant ∎ **végétalien, -enne** *nmf* vegan ∎ **végétarien, -enne** *adj & nmf* vegetarian ∎ **végétation** *nf* vegetation

véhément, -e [veemɑ̃, -ɑ̃t] *adj* vehement ∎ **véhémence** *nf* vehemence

véhicule [veikyl] *nm* vehicle; **v. tout-terrain** off-road *or* all-terrain vehicle

veille [vɛj] *nf* (a) *(jour précédent)* **la v.** the day before (**de qch** sth); **la v. de Noël** Christmas Eve; **à la v. de qch** *(événement)* on the eve of sth (b) *(état)* wakefulness; *Ordinat* standby; **mettre un appareil en v.** to put a machine on standby

veillée [veje] *nf (soirée)* evening

veiller [veje] **1** *vi* to stay up *or* awake; **v. à qch** to see to sth; **v. à ce que...** *(+ subjunctive)* to make sure that ...; **v. sur qn** to watch over sb **2** *vt (malade)* to sit up with

veine [vɛn] *nf Anat, Bot & Géol* vein

véliplanchiste [veliplɑ̃ʃist] *nmf* windsurfer

vélo [velo] *nm* bike, bicycle; *(activité)* cycling; **faire du v.** to cycle, to go cycling; **v. tout-terrain** mountain bike ∎ **vélomoteur** *nm* moped

velours [vəlur] *nm* velvet; **v. côtelé** corduroy ∎ **velouté, -e 1** *adj* velvety **2** *nm* **v. d'asperges** cream of asparagus soup

velu, -e [vəly] *adj* hairy

venaison [vənɛzɔ̃] *nf* venison

vendange [vɑ̃dɑ̃ʒ] *nf (récolte)* grape harvest; *(raisin récolté)* grapes (harvested); **vendanges** *(période)* grape-harvesting time; **faire les vendanges** to harvest *or* pick the grapes ∎ **vendanger** *vi* to pick the grapes ∎ **vendangeur, -euse** *nmf* grape picker

vendre [vɑ̃dr] **1** *vt* to sell; **v. qch à qn** to sell sb sth, to sell sth to sb; **v. qch 10 euros** to sell sth for 10 euros; **'à v.'** 'for sale' **2 se vendre** *vpr* to be sold; **ça se vend bien** it sells well ∎ **vendeur, -euse** *nmf (de magasin) Br* sales *or* shop assistant, *Am* sales clerk; *(non professionnel)* seller

vendredi [vɑ̃drədi] *nm* Friday; **V. saint** Good Friday

vénéneux, -euse [venenø, -øz] *adj* poisonous

vénérable [venerabl] *adj* venerable

venger [vɑ̃ʒe] **1** *vt* to avenge **2 se venger** *vpr* to get one's revenge (**de qn** on sb; **de qch** for sth) ∎ **vengeance** *nf* revenge, vengeance

venin [vənɛ̃] *nm* poison, venom ∎ **venimeux, -euse** *adj* poisonous, venomous

VENIR* [vənir] **1** *(aux être) vi* to come (**de** from); **v. faire qch** to come to do sth; **viens me voir** come and see me; **je viens/venais d'arriver** I've/I'd just arrived; **les jours qui viennent**

the coming days; **faire v. qn** to send for sb

2 *v impersonnel* **s'il venait à pleuvoir** if it happened to rain

vent [vɑ̃] *nm* wind; **il y a** *ou* **il fait du v.** it's windy

vente [vɑ̃t] *nf* sale; **en v.** *(en magasin)* on sale; **mettre qch en v.** to put sth up for sale; **v. aux enchères** auction (sale); **v. par correspondance** mail order

ventilateur [vɑ̃tilatœr] *nm (électrique)* fan ▪ **ventilation** *nf* ventilation ▪ **ventiler** *vt* to ventilate

ventre [vɑ̃tr] *nm* stomach, belly; **à plat v.** flat on one's face; **avoir du v.** to have a paunch; **avoir mal au v.** to have a sore stomach

ventriloque [vɑ̃trilɔk] *nmf* ventriloquist

venu, -e [vəny] **1** *pp de* venir **2** *adj* **bien v.** *(à propos)* timely; **mal v.** untimely **3** *nmf* **nouveau v., nouvelle venue** newcomer; **le premier v.** anyone **4** *nf* **venue** *(de personne, de printemps)* coming

ver [ver] *nm* worm; *(larve)* grub; *(de fruits, de fromage)* maggot; **v. de terre** (earth)worm; **v. à soie** silkworm

véranda [verɑ̃da] *nf* veranda(h); *(en verre)* conservatory

verbe [verb] *nm* verb

verdict [verdikt] *nm* verdict

verdir [verdir] *vti* to turn green ▪ **verdure** *nf (végétation)* greenery

verger [verʒe] *nm* orchard

verglas [vergla] *nm Br* (black) ice, *Am* glaze; **une plaque de v.** a sheet of ice ▪ **verglacé, -e** *adj (route)* icy

véridique [veridik] *adj* truthful

vérifier [verifje] **1** *vt* to check, to verify; *(comptes)* to audit **2 se vérifier** *vpr* to prove correct ▪ **vérifiable** *adj* verifiable ▪ **vérification** *nf* checking, verification; *(de comptes)* audit(ing)

véritable [veritabl] *adj (histoire, ami)* true, real; *(cuir, or, nom)* real, genuine; *(en intensif)* real

vérité [verite] *nf (de déclaration)* truth;

(sincérité) sincerity; **en v.** in fact; **dire la v.** to tell the truth

verni, -e [verni] *adj (meuble, parquet)* varnished

vernir [vernir] *vt (bois)* to varnish; *(céramique)* to glaze ▪ **vernis** *nm* varnish; *(pour céramique)* glaze; **v. à ongles** nail polish *or Br* varnish ▪ **vernissage** *nm (d'exposition)* opening

verra, verrait [vera, vere] *voir* **voir**

verre [ver] *nm (substance, récipient)* glass; **prendre un v.** to have a drink; **v. de bière** glass of beer; **v. à bière/à vin** beer/wine glass; **v. de contact** contact lens ▪ **verrière** *nf (toit)* glass roof

verrou [veru] *nm* bolt; **fermer qch au v.** to bolt sth; **sous les verrous** behind bars

verrouiller [veruje] *vt (porte)* to bolt; *(quartier)* to seal off

verrue [very] *nf* wart; **v. plantaire** verruca

vers[1] [ver] *prép (direction)* toward(s); *(approximation)* around, about

vers[2] [ver] *nm (de poème)* line; **des vers** *(poésie)* verse

versant [versɑ̃] *nm* slope, side

verse [vers] **à verse** *adv* **la pluie tombait à v.** the rain was coming down in torrents

Verseau [verso] *nm (signe)* Aquarius

verser [verse] *vt* to pour (out); *(larmes, sang)* to shed; *(argent)* to pay **(sur un compte** into an account) ▪ **versement** *nm* payment

version [versjɔ̃] *nf (de film, d'incident)* version; *Cin* **en v. originale** in the original language; **en v. française** dubbed *(into French)*

verso [verso] *nm* back (of the page); **'voir au v.'** 'see overleaf'

vert, verte [ver, vert] **1** *adj* green; *(pas mûr)* unripe; **aller en classe verte** to go on a school trip to the countryside **2** *nm* green; *Pol* **les Verts** the Greens

vertical, -e, -aux, -ales [vertikal, -o] *adj & nf* vertical; **à la verticale** vertically

vertige [vɛrtiʒ] *nm (étourdissement)* (feeling of) dizziness *or* giddiness; *(peur du vide)* vertigo; **vertiges** dizzy spells; **avoir le v.** to be *or* feel dizzy *or* giddy ■ **vertigineux, -euse** *adj (hauteur)* giddy, dizzy

vertu [vɛrty] *nf* virtue; **en v. de** in accordance with ■ **vertueux, -euse** *adj* virtuous

verveine [vɛrvɛn] *nf (plante)* verbena; *(tisane)* verbena tea

vessie [vesi] *nf* bladder

veste [vɛst] *nf* jacket, coat

vestiaire [vɛstjɛr] *nm (de théâtre)* cloakroom; *(de piscine, de stade)* changing room, *Am* locker room

vestibule [vɛstibyl] *nm* (entrance) hall

vestiges [vɛstiʒ] *nmpl (ruines)* remains; *(traces)* relics

veston [vɛstɔ̃] *nm* (suit) jacket

vêtement [vɛtmɑ̃] *nm* garment, article of clothing; **vêtements** clothes; **vêtements de sport** sportswear

vétéran [veterɑ̃] *nm* veteran

vétérinaire [veteriner] **1** *adj* veterinary **2** *nmf* vet, *Br* veterinary surgeon, *Am* veterinarian

vêtir* [vetir] *vt*, **se vêtir** *vpr* to dress

veto [veto] *nm inv* veto; **opposer son v. à qch** to veto sth

vêtu, -e [vety] *adj* dressed (**de** in)

vétuste [vetyst] *adj* dilapidated

veuf, veuve [vœf, vœv] **1** *adj* widowed **2** *nm* widower **3** *nf* widow

veuille(s), veuillent [vœj] *voir* **vouloir**

veut, veux [vø] *voir* **vouloir**

vexer [vɛkse] **1** *vt* to upset, to hurt **2 se vexer** *vpr* to get upset (**de** at)

VF [veɛf] *(abrév* **version française**) *nf* **film en VF** film dubbed into French

viable [vjabl] *adj (entreprise, enfant)* viable

viaduc [vjadyk] *nm* viaduct

viande [vjɑ̃d] *nf* meat

vibrer [vibre] *vi* to vibrate; *(être ému)* to be stirred (**de** with); **faire v. qn** to stir sb ■ **vibrant, -e** *adj (hommage)* stirring ■ **vibration** *nf* vibration

vice [vis] *nm (perversité)* vice *(défectuosité)* defect

vice versa [vis(e)vɛrsa] *adv* vice versa

vicié, -e [visje] *adj (air, atmosphère)* polluted

vicieux, -euse [visjø, -øz] *adj (pervers)* depraved; *(perfide)* underhand

victime [viktim] *nf* victim; *(d'accident)* casualty; **être v. de** *(accident, attentat)* to be the victim of

victoire [viktwar] *nf* victory; *(en sport)* win ■ **victorieux, -euse** *adj* victorious; *(équipe)* winning

vidange [vidɑ̃ʒ] *nf* emptying, draining; *(de véhicule)* oil change ■ **vidanger** *vt* to empty, to drain

vide [vid] **1** *adj* empty **2** *nm (espace)* empty space; *(d'emploi du temps)* gap; *Phys* vacuum; **regarder dans le v.** to stare into space; **emballé sous v.** vacuum-packed; **à v.** empty

vidéo [video] *adj inv & nf* video ■ **vidéocassette** *nf* video (cassette) ■ **vidéoclip** *nm* video

vider [vide] *vt*, **se vider** *vpr* to empty ■ **vide-ordures** *nm inv Br* rubbish *or Am* garbage chute ■ **videur** *nm (de boîte de nuit)* bouncer

vie [vi] *nf* life; *(durée)* lifetime; **en v.** living; **à v., pour la v.** for life

vieil, vieille [vjɛj] *voir* **vieux**

vieillard [vjɛjar] *nm* old man; **les vieillards** old people ■ **vieillerie** *nf (objet)* old thing ■ **vieillesse** *nf* old age

vieillir [vjɛjir] **1** *vi* to grow old; *(changer)* to age; *(théorie, mot)* to become old-fashioned **2** *vt* **v. qn** *(vêtement)* to make sb look old(er) ■ **vieilli, -e** *adj (démodé)* old-fashioned ■ **vieillissant, -e** *adj* ageing ■ **vieillissement** *nm* ageing

vieillot, -otte [vjɛjo, -ɔt] *adj* old-fashioned

Vienne [vjɛn] *nm ou f* Vienna

viens, vient [vjɛ̃] *voir* **venir**

vierge [vjɛrʒ] **1** *adj (femme, neige)* virgin; *(feuille de papier, film)* blank; **être v.** *(femme, homme)* to be a virgin **2** *nf* virgin; **la V.** *(signe)* Virgo

Viêt-nam [vjɛtnam] *nm* **le V.** Vietnam

■ **vietnamien, -enne 1** *adj* Vietnamese **2** *nmf* **V., Vietnamienne** Vietnamese

vieux, vieille, vieux, vieilles [vjø, vjɛj]

> **vieil** is used before masculine singular nouns beginning with a vowel or mute h.

1 *adj* old; **être v. jeu** *(adj inv)* to be old-fashioned; **se faire v.** to get old **2** *nm* old man; **les vieux** old people **3** *nf* **vieille** old woman

vif, vive [vif, viv] **1** *adj (personne)* lively; *(imagination)* vivid; *(intelligence, vent, douleur)* sharp; *(intérêt, satisfaction)* great; *(couleur, lumière)* bright; *(froid)* biting; *(pas, mouvement)* quick; **brûler qn v.** to burn sb alive **2** *nm* **entrer dans le v. du sujet** to get to the heart of the matter; **à v.** *(plaie)* open

vigilant, -e [viʒilɑ̃, -ɑ̃t] *adj* vigilant ■ **vigilance** *nf* vigilance

vigile [viʒil] *nm* watchman

vigne [viɲ] *nf (plante)* vine; *(plantation)* vineyard ■ **vigneron, -onne** [-ərɔ̃, -ɔn] *nmf* wine grower ■ **vignoble** *nm* vineyard; *(région)* vineyards

vignette [viɲɛt] *nf (de véhicule)* road tax sticker; *(de médicament)* label *(for reimbursement by Social Security)*

vigueur [vigœr] *nf* vigour; **entrer en v.** *(loi)* to come into force ■ **vigoureux, -euse** *adj (personne)* vigorous

vilain, -e [vilɛ̃, -ɛn] *adj (laid)* ugly; *(peu sage)* naughty

villa [vila] *nf* villa

village [vilaʒ] *nm* village ■ **villageois, -e** *nmf* villager

ville [vil] *nf* town; *(grande)* city; **aller/ être en v.** to go (in)to/be in town; **v. d'eaux** spa (town)

vin [vɛ̃] *nm* wine ■ **vinicole** *adj (région)* wine-growing

vinaigre [vinɛgr] *nm* vinegar ■ **vinaigrette** *nf (sauce)* vinaigrette, *Br* French dressing, *Am* Italian dressing

vingt [vɛ̃] ([vɛ̃t] *before vowel or mute h and in numbers 22–29*) *adj & nm inv* twenty; **v. et un** twenty-one ■ **vingtaine** *nf* **une v. (de)** *(nombre)* about twenty ■ **vingtième** *adj & nmf* twentieth

viol [vjɔl] *nm* rape; *(de lieu)* violation ■ **violation** *nf* violation ■ **violer** *vt (femme)* to rape ■ **violeur** *nm* rapist

violent, -e [vjɔlɑ̃, -ɑ̃t] *adj* violent; *(effort)* strenuous ■ **violence** *nf* violence; **acte de v.** act of violence

violet, -ette [vjɔlɛ, -ɛt] **1** *adj & nm (couleur)* purple **2** *nf* **violette** *(fleur)* violet

violon [vjɔlɔ̃] *nm* violin ■ **violoncelle** *nm* cello ■ **violoncelliste** *nmf* cellist ■ **violoniste** *nmf* violinist

vipère [vipɛr] *nf* adder, viper

virage [viraʒ] *nm (de route)* bend

virer [vire] **1** *vi* to turn; **v. au bleu** to turn blue **2** *vt Fin (somme)* to transfer (à to) ■ **virement** *nm Fin* transfer

virgule [virgyl] *nf (ponctuation)* comma; *Math* (decimal) point; **2 v. 5** 2 point 5

viril, -e [viril] *adj* virile; *(force)* male ■ **virilité** *nf* virility

virtuel, -elle [virtɥɛl] *adj* potential; *(image)* virtual; **réalité virtuelle** virtual reality

virtuose [virtɥoz] *nmf* virtuoso

virulent, -e [virylɑ̃, -ɑ̃t] *adj* virulent

virus [virys] *nm Méd & Ordinat* virus

vis¹ [vi] *voir* **vivre, voir**

vis² [vis] *nf* screw

visa [viza] *nm (de passeport)* visa

visage [vizaʒ] *nm* face

vis-à-vis [vizavi] **1** *prép* **v. de** *(en face de)* opposite; *(envers)* towards **2** *nm inv (personne)* person opposite

viser [vize] **1** *vt (cible)* to aim at; *(concerner)* to be aimed at **2** *vi* to aim (à at); **v. à faire qch** to aim to do sth

visible [vizibl] *adj* visible ■ **visibilité** *nf* visibility

visière [vizjɛr] *nf (de casquette)* peak; *(en plastique)* eyeshade; *(de casque)* visor

vision [vizjɔ̃] *nf (conception, image)* vision; *(sens)* sight ■ **visionnaire** *adj & nmf* visionary ■ **visionner** *vt (film)* to view

visite [vizit] *nf* visit; *(personne)* visitor; *(examen)* inspection; **rendre v. à qn** to visit sb; **avoir de la v.** to have a visitor/visitors; **v. aller** *(d'un échange)* visit; **v. retour** *(d'un échange)* return visit; **v. médicale** medical examination; **v. guidée** guided tour ▪ **visiter** *vt (lieu touristique, patient)* to visit ▪ **visiteur, -euse** *nmf* visitor

vison [vizɔ̃] *nm* mink

visqueux, -euse [viskø, -øz] *adj* viscous; *(surface)* sticky

visser [vise] *vt* to screw on

visuel, -elle [vizɥɛl] *adj* visual ▪ **visualiser** *vt* to visualize

vit [vi] *voir* **vivre, voir**

vital, -e, -aux, -ales [vital, -o] *adj* vital ▪ **vitalité** *nf* vitality

vitamine [vitamin] *nf* vitamin

vite [vit] *adv (rapidement)* quickly, fast; *(sous peu)* soon; **v.!** quick(ly)!

vitesse [vitɛs] *nf* speed; *(de moteur)* gear; **à toute v.** at top full speed

viticole [vitikɔl] *adj (région)* wine-growing ▪ **viticulteur** *nm* wine grower ▪ **viticulture** *nf* wine growing

vitre [vitr] *nf* (window)pane; *(de véhicule, de train)* window ▪ **vitrage** *nm (vitres)* windows ▪ **vitrail, -aux** *nm* stained-glass window ▪ **vitré, -e** *adj* **porte vitrée** glass door ▪ **vitrier** *nm* glazier

vitrine [vitrin] *nf (de magasin)* (shop) window; *(meuble)* display cabinet

vivace [vivas] *adj (plante)* perennial ▪ **vivacité** *nf* liveliness; *(d'imagination)* vividness; *(d'intelligence)* sharpness; *(de couleur)* brightness; *(emportement)* petulance; **v. d'esprit** quick-wittedness

vivant, -e [vivɑ̃, -ɑ̃t] **1** *adj (en vie)* alive, living; *(récit, rue, enfant)* lively; *(être, matière)* living **2** *nm* **de son v.** in one's lifetime; **les vivants** the living

vive¹ [viv] *voir* **vif**

vive² [viv] *exclam* **v. le roi!** long live the king!

vivement [vivmɑ̃] *adv* quickly; *(répliquer)* sharply; *(regretter)* deeply

vivier [vivje] *nm* fish pond

vivifier [vivifje] *vt* to invigorate

vivisection [viviseksjɔ̃] *nf* vivisection

vivre* [vivr] **1** *vi* to live; **elle vit encore** she's still alive *or* living; **faire v. qn** *(famille)* to support sb; **v. vieux** to live to be old; **v. de** *(fruits)* to live on; *(travail)* to live by **2** *vt (vie)* to live; *(aventure, époque)* to live through; *(éprouver)* to experience ▪ **vivres** *nmpl* food, supplies

VO [veo] *(abrév* **version originale**) *nf* **film en VO** film in the original language

vocal, -e, -aux, -ales [vɔkal, -o] *adj* vocal

vocation [vɔkasjɔ̃] *nf* vocation, calling

vociférer [vɔsifere] *vti* to shout angrily

vœu, -x [vø] *nm (souhait)* wish; *(promesse)* vow; **faire un v.** to make a wish; **tous mes vœux!** best wishes!

vogue [vɔg] *nf* fashion, vogue; **en v.** in vogue

voici [vwasi] *prép* here is/are; **me v.** here I am; **v. dix ans** ten years ago; **v. dix ans que...** it's ten years since...

voie [vwa] *nf (route)* road; *(rails)* track, line; *(partie de route)* lane; *(chemin)* way; *(de gare)* platform; *(de communication)* line; *(moyen)* means, way; **pays en v. de développement** developing country; **v. sans issue** dead end

voilà [vwala] *prép* there is/are; **les v.** there they are; **le v. parti** he has left now; **v. dix ans** ten years ago; **v. dix ans que...** it's ten years since...

voile¹ [vwal] *nm (étoffe, coiffure)* veil ▪ **voilé, -e** *adj (femme, allusion)* veiled; *(photo, lumière)* hazy ▪ **voiler** [vwale] **1** *vt (visage, vérité)* to veil **2 se voiler** *vpr (personne)* to wear a veil; *(ciel)* to cloud over

voile² [vwal] *nf (de bateau)* sail; *(sport)* sailing; **faire de la v.** to sail ▪ **voilier** *nm* sailing boat; *(de plaisance)* yacht

voiler [vwale] *vt*, **se voiler** *vpr (roue)* to buckle

VOIR* [vwar] **1** *vt* to see; **faire v. qch** to show sth; **v. qn faire qch** to see sb do/doing sth

2 *vi* to see; **fais v.** let me see, show me; **ça n'a rien à v. avec ça** that's got nothing to do with that

3 se voir *vpr (soi-même)* to see one-self; *(se fréquenter)* to see each other; *(objet, attitude)* to be seen; *(reprise, tache)* to show

voisin, -e [vwazɛ̃, -in] **1** *adj (pays, village) Br* neighbouring, *Am* neighboring; *(maison, pièce)* next (**de** to); *(état)* similar (**de** to) **2** *nmf Br* neighbour, *Am* neighbor ▪ **voisinage** *nm (quartier, voisins) Br* neighbourhood, *Am* neighborhood; *(proximité)* closeness, proximity ▪ **voisiner** *vi* **v. avec** to be side by side with

voiture [vwatyr] *nf* car; *(de train)* carriage, *Br* coach, *Am* car; **en v.!** *(dans le train)* all aboard!; **v. de course** racing/private car

voix [vwa] *nf* voice; *(d'électeur)* vote; **à v. basse** in a whisper; **à haute v.** aloud

vol [vɔl] *nm* (**a**) *(d'avion, d'oiseau)* flight; *(groupe d'oiseaux)* flock, flight; **attraper qch au v.** to catch sth in the air (**b**) *(délit)* theft; **v. à main armée** armed robbery

volaille [vɔlaj] *nf* **la v.** poultry; **une v.** a fowl

volatiliser [vɔlatilize] **se volatiliser** *vpr* to vanish into thin air

volcan [vɔlkɑ̃] *nm* volcano ▪ **volcanique** *adj* volcanic

voler¹ [vɔle] *vi (oiseau, avion)* to fly ▪ **volant** *nm (de véhicule)* (steering) wheel; *(de badminton)* shuttlecock; *(de jupe)* flounce ▪ **volée** *nf (de flèches)* flight; *(de coups)* thrashing

voler² [vɔle] **1** *vt (prendre)* to steal (**à** from); **v. qn** to rob sb **2** *vi (prendre)* to steal

volet [vɔlɛ] *nm (de fenêtre)* shutter; *(de programme)* section, part

voleur, -euse [vɔlœr, -øz] *nmf* thief; **au v.!** stop thief!

volière [vɔljɛr] *nf* aviary

volley-ball [vɔlebol] *nm* volleyball ▪ **volleyeur, -euse** *nmf* volleyball player

volontaire [vɔlɔ̃tɛr] **1** *adj (geste,*

omission) deliberate; *(travail)* voluntary; *(opiniâtre) Br* wilful, *Am* willful **2** *nmf* volunteer ▪ **volontairement** *adv (spontanément)* voluntarily; *(exprès)* deliberately

volontariat [vɔlɔ̃tarja] *nm* voluntary work

volonté [vɔlɔ̃te] *nf (faculté, intention)* will; *(détermination)* willpower; *(souhait)* wish; **bonne v.** willingness; **mauvaise v.** unwillingness; **à v.** *(quantité)* as much as desired

volontiers [vɔlɔ̃tje] *adv* gladly, willingly; **v.!** *(oui)* I'd love to!

volte-face [vɔltəfas] *nf inv* **faire v.** to turn round; *Fig* to do a U-turn

voltiger [vɔltiʒe] *vi (feuilles)* to flutter

volume [vɔlym] *nm (de boîte, de son, livre)* volume ▪ **volumineux, -euse** *adj* bulky, voluminous

volupté [vɔlypte] *nf* sensual pleasure ▪ **voluptueux, -euse** *adj* voluptuous

vomir [vɔmir] **1** *vt* to bring up, to vomit **2** *vi* to vomit, *Br* to be sick ▪ **vomissements** *nmpl* **avoir des v.** to vomit

vont [vɔ̃] *voir* **aller¹**

vorace [vɔras] *adj* voracious

vos [vo] *voir* **votre**

vote [vɔt] *nm (action)* vote, voting; *(suffrage)* vote; *(de loi)* passing; *Br* **bureau de v.** polling station, *Am* polling place ▪ **votant, -e** *nmf* voter ▪ **voter 1** *vt (loi)* to pass; *(crédits)* to vote **2** *vi* to vote

votre, vos [vɔtr, vo] *adj possessif* your ▪ **vôtre 1** *pron possessif* **le** *ou* **la v., les vôtres** yours; **à la v.!** cheers! **2** *nmpl* **les vôtres** *(votre famille)* your family

voudra, voudrait [vudra, vudrɛ] *voir* **vouloir**

vouer [vwe] **1** *vt (promettre)* to vow (**à** to); *(consacrer)* to dedicate (**à** to) **2 se vouer** *vpr* **se v. à** to dedicate oneself to

VOULOIR* [vulwar] *vt* to want (**faire** to do); **je veux qu'il parte** I want him to go; **v. dire** to mean (**que** that); **je voudrais un pain** I'd like a loaf of bread; **je voudrais rester** I'd like to stay; **je veux bien attendre** I don't mind waiting; **voulez-vous me suivre**

will you follow me; **si tu veux** if you like or wish; **en v. à qn d'avoir fait qch** to be angry with sb for doing sth; **v. du bien à qn** to wish sb well; **sans le v.** unintentionally

voulu, -e [vuly] adj (requis) required; (délibéré) deliberate, intentional

vous [vu] pron personnel (a) (sujet, complément direct) you; **v. êtes ici** you are here; **il v. connaît** he knows you (b) (complément indirect) (to) you; **il v. l'a donné** he gave it to you, he gave you it (c) (réfléchi) yourself, pl yourselves; **v. v. lavez** you wash yourself/yourselves (d) (réciproque) each other; **v. v. aimez** you love each other ▪ **vous-même** pron yourself ▪ **vous-mêmes** pron pl yourselves

voûte [vut] nf (arch) vault ▪ **voûté, -e** adj (personne) bent, stooped

vouvoyer [vuvwaje] vt **v. qn** to address sb as "vous" ▪ **vouvoiement** nm = use of the formal "vous" instead of the more familiar "tu"

voyage [vwajaʒ] nm trip, journey; (par mer) voyage; **aimer les voyages** to like Br travelling or Am traveling; **faire un v., partir en v.** to go on a trip; **être en v.** to be (away) Br travelling or Am traveling; **bon v.!** have a pleasant trip!; **v. de noces** honeymoon; **v. organisé** (package) tour ▪ **voyager** vi to travel; **v. à l'étranger** to travel abroad; **v. sac au dos** to go backpacking ▪ **voyageur, -euse** nmf Br traveller, Am traveler; (passager) passenger; **v. de commerce** Br travelling or Am traveling salesman, Br commercial traveller ▪ **voyagiste** nm tour operator

voyant, -e¹ [vwajɑ̃, -ɑ̃t] **1** adj (couleur) gaudy, loud **2** nm (signal) (warning) light; (d'appareil électrique) pilot light

voyant, -e² [vwajɑ̃, -ɑ̃t] nmf clairvoyant

voyou [vwaju] nm hooligan

vrac [vrak] **en vrac** adv (en désordre) in a muddle; (au poids) loose

vrai [vrɛ] adj true; (réel) real; (authentique) genuine ▪ **vraiment** adv really

vraisemblable [vrɛsɑ̃blablə] adj (probable) likely, probable; (crédible) credible ▪ **vraisemblablement** adv probably ▪ **vraisemblance** nf likelihood; (crédibilité) credibility

vrombir [vrɔ̃bir] vi to hum ▪ **vrombissement** nm hum(ming)

VTT [vetete] (abrév **vélo tout terrain**) nm inv mountain bike

vu, -e¹ [vy] **1** pp de **voir 2** adj **bien vu** well thought of; **mal vu** frowned upon **3** prép in view of; **vu que...** seeing that...

vue² [vy] nf (sens) (eye)sight; (panorama, photo) view; **en v.** (proche) in sight; (en évidence) on view; Fig (personne) in the public eye; **avoir qn/qch en v.** to have sb/sth in mind; **à v.** (tirer) on sight; (payable) at sight; **à première v.** at first sight; **à v. d'œil** (grandir) visibly; **de v.** (connaître) by sight; **v. d'ensemble** overall view

vulgaire [vylgɛr] adj (grossier) vulgar; (ordinaire) common ▪ **vulgariser** vt to popularize ▪ **vulgarité** nf vulgarity

vulnérable [vylnerablə] adj vulnerable ▪ **vulnérabilité** nf vulnerability

Ww

W, w [dubləve] *nm inv* W, w

wagon [vagɔ̃] *nm (de voyageurs)* carriage, *Br* coach, *Am* car; *(de marchandises) Br* wagon, *Am* freight car ▪ **wagon-lit** (*pl* **wagons-lits**) *nm* sleeping car, sleeper ▪ **wagon-restaurant** (*pl* **wagons-restaurants**) *nm* dining *or* restaurant car

Walkman® [wɔkman] *nm* Walkman®, personal stereo

wallon, -onne [walɔ̃, -ɔn] **1** *adj* Walloon **2** *nmf* **W., Wallonne** Walloon

watt [wat] *nm Él* watt

w-c [(dublə)vese] *nmpl Br* toilet, *Am* bathroom

week-end [wikɛnd] (*pl* **week-ends**) *nm* weekend; **partir en w.** to go away for the weekend

whisky [wiski] (*pl* -**ies** *ou* -**ys**) *nm Br* whisky, *Am* whiskey

wysiwyg [wiziwig] *adj & nm Ordinat* WYSIWYG

Xx

X, x [iks] *nm inv* (*lettre, personne ou nombre inconnus*) X, x; **Monsieur X** Mr X; **x fois** umpteen times; **dans x années** in x number of years

xénophobe [gsenɔfɔb] *adj* xenophobic ▪ **xénophobie** *nf* xenophobia

xérès [gzeres, kseres] *nm (vin)* sherry

xylophone [gsilɔfɔn] *nm* xylophone

Yy

Y, y¹ [igrɛk] *nm inv* Y, y

y² [i] **1** *adv* there; *(dedans)* in it/them; *(dessus)* on it/them; **elle y vivra** she'll live there; **j'y entrai** I entered (it); **allons-y** let's go **2** *pron* **j'y pense** I'm thinking about it; **je m'y attendais** I was expecting it; **ça y est!** that's it!

yacht [jɔt] *nm* yacht

yaourt [jaurt] *nm* yoghurt

Yémen [jemɛn] *nm* **le Y.** Yemen

yen [jɛn] *nm* yen

yeux [jø] *voir* œil

yoga [jɔga] *nm* yoga; **faire du y.** to do yoga

yog(h)ourt [jɔgurt] *nm* = **yaourt**

Yo-Yo® [jojo] *nm inv* yo-yo

Zz

Z, z [zɛd] *nm inv* Z, z

Zaïre [zair] *nm* **le Z.** Zaïre

zèbre [zɛbr] *nm* zebra

zèle [zɛl] *nm* zeal; **faire du z.** to overdo it ▪ **zélé, -e** *adj* zealous

zéro [zero] *nm (chiffre)* zero, *Br* nought; *(de numéro de téléphone) Br* 0 [əʊ], *Am* zero; *(température)* zero; *Fig (personne)* nonentity; **deux buts à z.** *(au football) Br* two nil, *Am* two zero

zeste [zɛst] *nm* **un z. de citron** a piece of lemon peel

zigzag [zigzag] *nm* zigzag; **en z.** *(route)* zigzag(ging) ▪ **zigzaguer** *vi* to zigzag

Zimbabwe [zimbabwe] *nm* **le Z.** Zimbabwe

zinc [zɛ̃g] *nm (métal)* zinc

zipper [zipe] *vt Ordinat* to zip

zodiaque [zɔdjak] *nm* zodiac; **signe du z.** sign of the zodiac

zone [zon] *nf* zone; **de seconde z.** second-rate; **z. industrielle** industrial *Br* estate *or Am* park; **z. fumeurs/non-fumeurs** smoking/no-smoking area

zoo [zo(o)] *nm* zoo ▪ **zoologie** *nf* zoology ▪ **zoologique** *adj* zoological; **parc z.** zoo

zoom [zum] *nm (objectif)* zoom lens